Eng^d by H.B.Hall's Sons New York.

very sincerely yours

F. Marion Crawford

A LIBRARY OF

AMERICAN LITERATURE

FROM THE EARLIEST SETTLEMENT
TO THE PRESENT TIME

COMPILED AND EDITED BY

EDMUND CLARENCE STEDMAN AND
ELLEN MACKAY HUTCHINSON

NEW EDITION, WITH 303 FULL-PAGE ILLUSTRATIONS

IN ELEVEN VOLUMES

VOL. XI.

NEW-YORK
WILLIAM EVARTS BENJAMIN

PRESS OF
JENKINS & McCOWAN,
NEW YORK.

CONTENTS OF VOLUME XI.

Literature of the Republic. Part IV.—Continued.

Additional Selections. 1834–1889.

NOTED SAYINGS.
    Upon leaving England, in 1629.—A Plantation of Religion, Not of Trade.—" United
    We Stand, Divided We Fall."—To Gov. Hutchinson, Demanding the With-
    drawal of the British Troops from Boston, after the Massacre of 5 March,
    1770.—In the Continental Congress, 5 September, 1774.—At the Signing of the
    Declaration of Independence, 4 July, 1776.—His Last Words, New York, 22 Sep-
    tember, 1776.—"Brother Jonathan."—Si Vis Pacem, Para Bellum.—Noted Appli-
    cation of Mathew Henry's Phrase, 1788.—Of Candidature for Office.—" Few
    Die, and None Resign."—" Declaration of Principles."—From the Same Inau-
    gural Address.—A Word to the New Englanders.—The Discourses of Christ.
    —When Asked to Sit near his " Father."—A Hero's Last Order.—Of Monroe's
    Administration, 1817–25.—The " Monroe Doctrine."—An Advocate's Opinion.
    —The American Chesterfield.— A Border Knight's Motto—War of 1812.—
    From the Bunker Hill Oration—17 June, 1825.—Bunker Hill.—In Denuncia-
    tion of the Administration of Adams and Clay. 1826.—" A Good Enough Mor-
    gan until after the Election."—" Free Trade and Seaman's Rights."—Remark
    to Senator W. C. Preston of South Carolina. 1839.—"No South, no North,
    no East, no West."—Man to Man.—" The Footsteps of my Illustrious Prede-

Portraits and Illustrations in this Volume.

ON STEEL.

MISCELLANEOUS.

LITERATURE
OF THE REPUBLIC

PART IV—Concluded

1861—1888

THERE is a feeling of Eternity in youth which makes us amends for everything. To be young is to be as one of the Immortals.

WILLIAM HAZLITT. A.D. 1821.

America has still a long vista of years stretching before her in which she will enjoy conditions far more auspicious than England can count upon. And that America marks the highest level, not only of material well-being, but of intelligence and happiness, which the race has yet attained, will be the judgment of those who look not at the favored few for whose benefit the world seems hitherto to have framed its institutions, but at the whole body of the people.

JAMES BRYCE. A.D. 1888.

AMERICA.

Nor force nor fraud shall sunder us ! Oh, ye
Who north or south, on east or western land,
Native to noble sounds, say truth for truth,
Freedom for freedom, love for love, and God
For God ; oh ye who in eternal youth
Speak with a living and creative flood
This universal English, and do stand
Its breathing book ; live worthy of that grand
Heroic utterance—parted, yet a whole,
Far yet unsevered,—children brave and free
Of the great Mother-tongue, and ye shall be
Lords of an empire wide as Shakespeare's soul,
Sublime as Milton's immemorial theme,
And rich as Chaucer's speech, and fair as Spenser's dream.

SYDNEY DOBELL. A.D. 185-.

—That in us which more distinctively than anything else we can call Americanism—our faith in humanity, our love of equality. One cannot claim that Americans of English origin are alone the depositaries of this belief, this passion. . . . . The ideal America, which is the only real America, is not in the keeping of any one race ; her destinies are too large for that custody ; the English race is only one of many races with which her future rests.

WILLIAM DEAN HOWELLS. A.D. 1889.

Literature is the fragment of fragments. The smallest part of what has been done and spoken has been recorded ; and the smallest part of what has been recorded has survived.

JOHANN WOLFGANG VON GOETHE. A.D. 182-.

LITERATURE

OF THE REPUBLIC.

PART IV.—Concluded.

1861—1888.

Mary Noailles Murfree.

Born at Grantlands, near Murfreesboro', Tenn.

THE "HARNT" THAT WALKS CHILHOWEE.

[From the Story by that title.—In the Tennessee Mountains. By Charles Egbert Craddock. 1884.]

THE breeze freshened, after the sun went down, and the hop and gourd vines were all astir as they clung about the little porch where Clarsie was sitting now, idle at last. The rain-clouds had disappeared, and there bent over the dark, heavily wooded ridges a pale blue sky, with here and there the crystalline sparkle of a star. A halo was shimmering in the east, where the mists had gathered about the great white moon, hanging high above the mountains. Noiseless wings flitted through the dusk ; now and then the bats swept by so close as to wave Clarsie's hair with the wind of their flight. What an airy, glittering, magical thing was that gigantic spider-web suspended between the silver moon and her shining eyes ! Ever and anon there came from the woods a strange, weird, long-drawn sigh, unlike the stir of the wind in the trees, unlike the fret of the water on the rocks. Was it the voiceless sorrow of the sad earth ? There were stars in the night besides those known to astronomers : the stellular fire-flies gemmed the black shadows with a fluctuating brilliancy; they circled in and out of the porch, and touched the leaves above Clarsie's head with quivering points of light. A steadier and an intenser gleam was advancing along the road, and the sound of languid footsteps came with it ; the aroma of tobacco graced the atmosphere, and a tall figure walked up to the gate.

"Come in, come in," said Peter Giles, rising, and tendering the guest a chair. "Ye air Tom Pratt, ez well ez I kin make out by this light. Waal, Tom, we hain't furgot ye sence ye done been hyar."

As Tom had been there on the previous evening, this might be considered a joke, or an equivocal compliment. The young fellow was restless and awkward under it, but Mrs. Giles chuckled with great merriment.

"An' how air ye a-comin' on, Mrs. Giles ?" he asked propitiatorily.

"Jes' toler'ble, Tom. Air they all well ter yer house ?"

"Yes, they're toler'ble well, too." He glanced at Clarsie, intending to address to her some polite greeting, but the expression of her shy, half-startled eyes, turned upon the far-away moon, warned him. "Thar never war a gal so skittish," he thought. "She'd run a mile, skeered ter death, ef I said a word ter her."

And he was prudently silent.

"Waal," said Peter Giles, "what's the news out yer way, Tom ? Ennything a-goin' on ?"

"Thar war a shower yander on the Backbone ; it rained toler'ble hard fur a while, an' sot up the corn wonderful. Did ye git enny hyar ?"

"Not a drap."

"'Pears ter me ez I kin see the clouds a-circlin' round Chilhowee, an' a-rainin' on everybody's corn-field 'ceptin' ourn," said Mrs. Giles. "Some folks is the favored of the Lord, an' t'others hev ter work fur everything an' git nuthin'. Waal, waal; we-uns will see our reward in the nex' worl'. Thar's a better worl' than this, Tom."

"That 's a fac'," said Tom, in orthodox assent.

"An' when we leaves hyar once, we leaves all trouble an' care behind us, Tom ; fur we don't come back no more." Mrs. Giles was drifting into one of her pious moods.

"I dunno," said Tom. "Thar hev been them ez hev."

"Hev what ?" demanded Peter Giles, startled.

"Hev come back ter this hyar yearth. Thar's a harnt that walks Chilhowee every night o' the worl'. I know them ez hev seen him."

Clarsie's great dilated eyes were fastened on the speaker's face. There was a dead silence for a moment, more eloquent with these looks of amazement than any words could have been.

"I reckons ye remember a puny, shrivelled little man, named Reuben Crabb, ez used ter live yander, eight mile along the ridge ter that thar big sulphur spring," Tom resumed, appealing to Peter Giles. "He war born with only one arm."

"I 'members him," interpolated Mrs. Giles, vivaciously. "He war a mighty porely, sickly little critter, all the days of his life. 'Twar a wonder he war ever raised ter be a man,—an' a pity, too. An' 'twar powerful comical, the way of his takin' off ; a stunted, one-armed little critter a-ondertakin' ter fight folks an' shoot pistols. He hed the use o' his one arm, sure."

" Waal," said Tom, " his house ain't thar now, 'kase Sam Grim's brothers burned it ter the ground fur his a-killin' of Sam. That warn't all that war done ter Reuben fur killin' of Sam. The sheriff run Reuben Crabb down this hyar road 'bout a mile from hyar,—mebbe less,—an' shot him dead in the road, jes' whar it forks. Waal, Reuben war in company with another evil-doer,—*he* war from the Cross-Roads, an' I furgits what he hed done, but he war a-tryin' ter hide in the mountings, too ; an' the sheriff lef' Reuben a-ly-ing thar in the road, while he tries ter ketch up with the t'other ; but his horse got a stone in his hoof, an' he los' time, an' hed ter gin it up. An' when he got back ter the forks o' the road whar he had lef' Reuben a-lyin' dead, thar war nuthin' thar 'ceptin' a pool o' blood. Waal, he went right on ter Reuben's house, an' them Grim boys hed burnt it ter the ground; but he seen Reuben's brother Joel. An' Joel, he tole the sheriff that late that evenin' he hed tuk Reuben's body out 'n the road an' buried it, 'kase it hed been lyin' thar in the road ever sence early in the mornin', an' he couldn't leave it thar all night, an' he hedn't no shelter fur it, sence the Grim boys hed burnt down the house. So he war obleeged ter bury it. An' Joel showed the sheriff a new-made grave, an' Reuben's coat whar the sheriff's bullet hed gone in at the back an' kem out'n the breast. The sheriff 'lowed ez they 'd fine Joel fifty dollars fur a-buryin' of Reuben afore the cor'ner kem ; but they never done it, ez I knows on. The sheriff said that when the cor'ner kem the body would be tuk up fur a 'quest. But thar hed been a powerful big frishet, an' the river 'twixt the cor'ner's house an' Chilhowee couldn't be forded fur three weeks. The cor'ner never kem, an' so thar it all stayed. That war four year ago."

" Waal," said Peter Giles, dryly, "I ain't seen no harnt yit. I knowed all that afore."

Clarsie's wondering eyes upon the young man's moonlit face had elicited these facts, familiar to the elders, but strange, he knew, to her.

" I war jes' a-goin' on ter tell," said Tom, abashed. " Waal, ever sence his brother Joel died, this spring, Reuben's harnt walks Chilhowee. He war seen week afore las', 'bout daybreak, by Ephraim Blenkins, who hed been a-fish-in', an' war a-goin' home. Eph happened ter stop in the laurel ter wind up his line, when all in a minit he seen the harnt go by, his face white, an' his eye-balls like fire, an' puny an' one-armed, jes' like he lived. Eph, he owed me a haffen day's work; I holped him ter plough las' month, an' so he kem ter-day an' hoed along cornsider'ble ter pay fur it. He say he believes the harnt never seen him, 'kase it went right by. He 'lowed ef the harnt hed so much ez cut one o' them blazin' eyes round at him he couldn't but hev drapped dead. Waal, this mornin', 'bout sunrise, my brother Bob's little gal, three year old, strayed off from home while her mother war out milkin' the cow. An' we went a-huntin' of her, mightily worked up, 'kase thar hev been a b'ar prowlin' round our corn-field twict this summer. An' I went to the right, an' Bob went to the lef'. An' he say ez he war a-pushin' 'long through the laurel, he seen the bushes ahead of him a-rustlin'. An' he jes' stood still an' watched 'em. An' fur a while the bushes war still too ; an' then they moved jes' a lit-tle, fust this way an' then that, till all of a suddint the leaves opened, like the mouth of hell mought hev done, an' thar he seen Reuben Crabb's face. He say he never seen sech a face! Its mouth war open, an' its eyes war a-startin' out 'n its head, an' its skin war white till it war blue; an' ef the devil hed hed it a-hangin' over the coals that minit it couldn't hev looked no more skeered. But that war all that Bob seen, 'kase he jes' shet his eyes an' screeched an' screeched like he war *de*stracted. An' when he stopped a second ter ketch his breath he hearn su'thin' a-answerin' him back, sorter weak-like, an' thar war little Peggy a-pullin' through the laurel. Ye know she's too little ter talk good, but the folks down ter our house believes she seen the harnt, too."

"My Lord!" exclaimed Peter Giles. "I 'low I couldn't live a minit ef I war ter see that thar harnt that walks Chilhowee!"

"I know *I* couldn't," said his wife.

"Nor me, nuther," murmured Clarsie.

"Waal," said Tom, resuming the thread of his narrative, "we hev all been a-talkin' down yander ter our house ter make out the reason why Reuben Crabb's harnt hev sot out ter walk *jes' sence his brother Joel died*,—'kase it war never seen afore then. An' ez nigh ez we kin make it out, the reason is 'kase thar's nobody lef' in thish yar worl' what believes he warn't ter blame in that thar killin' o' Sam Grim. Joel always swore ez Reuben never killed him no more'n nuthin'; that Sam's own pistol went off in his own hand, an' shot him through the heart jes' ez he war a-drawing of it ter shoot Reuben Crabb. An' I hev hearn other men ez war a-standin' by say the same thing, though them Grims tells another tale; but ez Reuben never owned no pistol in his life, nor kerried one, it don't 'pear ter me ez what them Grims say air reasonable. Joel always swore ez Sam Grim war a mighty mean man,—a great big feller like him a-rockin' of a deformed little critter, an' a-mockin' of him, an' a-hittin' of him. An' the day of the fight Sam jes' knocked him down fur nuthin' at all; an' afore ye could wink Reuben jumped up suddint, an' flew at him like an eagle, an' struck him in the face. An' then Sam drawed his pistol, an' it went off in his own hand, an' shot him through the heart, an' killed him dead. Joel said that ef he could hev kep' that pore little critter Reuben still, an' let the sheriff arrest him peaceable-like, he war sure the jury would hev let him off; 'kase how war Reuben a-goin' ter shoot ennybody when Sam Grim never left a-holt of the only pistol between 'em, in life, or in death? They tells me they hed ter bury Sam Grim with that thar pistol in his hand; his grip war too tight fur death to unloose it. But Joel said that Reuben war sartain they'd hang him. He hedn't never seen no jestice from enny one man, an' he couldn't look fur it from twelve men. So he jes' sot out ter run through the woods, like a painter or a wolf, ter be hunted by the sheriff, an' he war run down an' kilt in the road. Joel said *he* kep' up arter the sheriff ez well ez he could on foot,—fur the Crabbs never hed no horse,—ter try ter beg fur Reuben, ef he war cotched, an' tell how little an' how weakly he war. I never seen a young man's head turn white like Joel's done; he said he reckoned it war his troubles. But ter the las' he stuck ter his rifle faithful. He war a powerful hunter; he war out rain or shine, hot or cold, in sech weather ez other folks would think thar warn't no use in tryin' ter do nuthin' in. I'm

mightily afeard o' seein' Reuben, now, that's a fac'," concluded Tom, frankly; " 'kase I hev hearn tell, an' I believes it, that ef a harnt speaks ter ye, it
air sartain ye're bound ter die right then."

" 'Pears ter me," said Mrs. Giles, " ez many mountings ez thar air round
hyar, he mought hev tuk ter walkin' some o' them, stiddier Chilhowee."

There was a sudden noise close at hand : a great inverted splint-basket,
from which came a sound of flapping wings, began to move slightly back and
forth. Mrs. Giles gasped out an ejaculation of terror, the two men sprang to
their feet, and the coy Clarsie laughed aloud in an exuberance of delighted
mirth, forgetful of her shyness. "I declar' ter goodness, you-uns air all
skeered fur true! Did ye think it war the harnt that walks Chilhowee?"

"What's under that thar basket?" demanded Peter Giles, rather sheep-
ishly as he sat down again.

"Nuthin' but the duck-legged Dominicky," said Clarsie, "what air bein'
broke up from settin'." The moonlight was full upon the dimpling merriment in her face, upon her shining eyes and parted red lips, and her gurgling
laughter was pleasant to hear. Tom Pratt edged his chair a trifle nearer, as
he, too, sat down.

"Ye oughtn't never ter break up a duck-legged hen, nor a Dominicky,
nuther," he volunteered, " 'kase they air sech a good kind o' hen ter kerry
chickens ; but a hen that is duck-legged an' Dominicky too oughter be let ter
set, whether or no."

Had he been warned in a dream, he could have found no more secure road
to Clarsie's favor and interest than a discussion of the poultry. "I'm a-thinkin'," she said, "that it air too hot fur hens ter set now, an' 'twill be till the
las' of August."

"It don't 'pear ter me ez it air hot much in June up hyar on Chilhowee,—
thar's a differ, I know, down in the valley ; but till July, on Chilhowee, it
don't 'pear ter me ez it air too hot ter set a hen. An' a duck-legged Dominicky air mighty hard ter break up."

"That's a fac'," Clarsie admitted ; "but I'll hev ter do it, somehow, 'kase
I ain't got no eggs fur her. All my hens air kerryin' of chickens."

"Waal !" exclaimed Tom, seizing his opportunity, "I'll bring ye some
ter-morrer night, when I come agin. We-uns hev got eggs ter our house."

"Thanky," said Clarsie, shyly smiling.

This unique method of courtship would have progressed very prosperously
but for the interference of the elders, who are an element always more or less
adverse to love-making. "Ye oughter turn out yer hen now, Clarsie," said
Mrs. Giles, " ez Tom air a-goin' ter bring ye some eggs ter-morrer. I wonder
ye don't think it's mean ter keep her up longer'n ye air obleeged ter. Ye
oughter remember ye war called a merciful critter jes' ter-day."

Clarsie rose precipitately, raised the basket, and out flew the "duck-legged
Dominicky," with a frantic flutter and hysterical cackling. But Mrs. Giles
was not to be diverted from her purpose ; her thoughts had recurred to the
absurd episode of the afternoon, and with her relish of the incongruity of the
joke she opened upon the subject at once.

"Waal, Tom," she said, "we'll be hevin' Clarsie married, afore long, I'm a-thinkin'.'' The young man sat bewildered. He, too, had entertained views concerning Clarsie's speedy marriage, but with a distinctly personal application ; and this frank mention of the matter by Mrs. Giles had a sinister suggestion that perhaps her ideas might be antagonistic. ''An' who d'ye think hev been hyar ter-day, a-speakin' of compli*mints* on Clarsie ?'' He could not answer, but he turned his head with a look of inquiry, and Mrs. Giles continued, '' He is a mighty peart, likely boy,—*he* is.''

There was a growing anger in the dismay on Tom Pratt's face ; he leaned forward to hear the name with a fiery eagerness, altogether incongruous with his usual lack-lustre manner.

'' Old Simon Burney !'' cried Mrs. Giles, with a burst of laughter. '' *Old Simon Burney !* Jes' a-speakin' of compli*mints* on Clarsie !''

The young fellow drew back with a look of disgust. '' Why, he's a old man ; he ain't no fit husband fur Clarsie.''

'' Don't ye be too sure ter count on that. I war jes' a-layin' off ter tell Clarsie that a gal oughter keep mighty clar o' widowers, 'thout she wants ter marry one. Fur I believes,'' said Mrs. Giles, with a wild flight of imagination, '' ez them men hev got some sort'n trade with the Evil One, an' he gives 'em the power ter witch the gals, somehow, so's ter git 'em ter marry ; 'kase I don't think that any gal that's got good sense air a-goin' ter be a man's second ch'ice, an' the mother of a whole pack of step-chil'ren, 'thout she air under some sort'n spell. But them men carries the day with the gals, ginerally, an' I'm a-thinkin' they're banded with the Devil. Ef I war a gal, an' a smart, peart boy like Simon Burney kem around a-speakin' of compli*mints*, an' sayin' I war a merciful critter, I'd jes' give it up, an' marry him fur second ch'ice. Thar's one blessin','' she continued, contemplating the possibility in a cold-blooded fashion positively revolting to Tom Pratt : '' he ain't got no tribe of chil'ren fur Clarsie ter look arter ; nary chick nor child hev old Simon Burney got. He hed two, but they died.''

The young man took leave presently, in great depression of spirit,—the idea that the widower was banded with the powers of evil was rather overwhelming to a man whose dependence was in merely mortal attractions ; and after he had been gone a little while Clarsie ascended the ladder to a nook in the roof, which she called her room.

For the first time in her life her slumber was fitful and restless, long intervals of wakefulness alternating with snatches of fantastic dreams. At last she rose and sat by the rude window, looking out through the chestnut leaves at the great moon, which had begun to dip toward the dark uncertainty of the western ridges, and at the shimmering, translucent, pearly mists that filled the intermediate valleys. All the air was dew and incense ; so subtle and penetrating an odor came from that fir-tree beyond the fence that it seemed as if some invigorating infusion were thrilling along her veins ; there floated upward, too, the warm fragrance of the clover, and every breath of the gentle wind brought from over the stream a thousand blended, undistinguishable perfumes of the deep forests beyond. The moon's idealizing glamour had left no trace of the uncouthness of the place which the daylight revealed ; the little log house, the great overhanging chestnut-oaks, the jagged precipice before the door, the vague outlines of the distant ranges, all suffused with a magic sheen, might have seemed a stupendous alto-rilievo in silver repoussé. Still, there came here and there the sweep of the bat's dusky wings; even they were a part of the night's witchery. A tiny owl perched for a moment or two amid the dew-tipped chestnut-leaves, and gazed with great round eyes at Clarsie as solemnly as she gazed at him.

"I'm thankful enough that ye hed the grace not ter screech while ye war hyar," she said, after the bird had taken his flight. "I ain't ready ter die yit, an' a screech-ow*el* air the sure sign."

She felt now and then a great impatience with her wakeful mood. Once she took herself to task: "Jes' a-sittin' up hyar all night, the same ez ef I war a fox, or that thar harnt that walks Chilhowee!"

And then her mind reverted to Tom Pratt, to old Simon Burney, and to her mother's emphatic and oracular declaration that widowers are in league with Satan, and that the girls upon whom they cast the eye of supernatural fascination have no choice in the matter. "I wish I knowed ef that thar sayin' war true," she murmured, her face still turned to the western spurs, and the moon sinking so slowly toward them.

With a sudden resolution she rose to her feet. She knew a way of telling fortunes which was, according to tradition, infallible, and she determined to try it, and ease her mind as to her future. Now was the propitious moment. "I hev always hearn that it won't come true 'thout ye try it *jes'* before day-break, an' a-kneelin' down at the forks of the road." She hesitated a moment and listened intently. "They'd never git done a-laffin' at me, ef they fund it out," she thought.

There was no sound in the house, and from the dark woods arose only those monotonous voices of the night, so familiar to her ears that she accounted their murmurous iteration as silence too. She leaned far out of the low window, caught the wide-spreading branches of the tree beside it, and swung herself noiselessly to the ground. The road before her was dark with the shadowy foliage and dank with the dew; but now and then, at long intervals, there lay athwart it a bright bar of light, where the moonshine fell through a gap in the trees. Once, as she went rapidly along her way, she saw speeding across the white radiance, lying just before her feet, the ill-omened shadow of a rabbit. She paused, with a superstitious sinking of the heart, and she heard the animal's quick, leaping rush through the bushes near at hand; but she mustered her courage, and kept steadily on. "Tain't no use a-goin' back ter git shet o' bad luck," she argued. "Ef old Simon Burney air my fortune, he'll come whether or no,—ef all they say air true."

The serpentine road curved to the mountain's brink before it forked, and there was again that familiar picture of precipice, and far-away ridges, and shining mist, and sinking moon, which was visibly turning from silver to gold. The changing lustre gilded the feathery ferns that grew in the marshy dip. Just at the angle of the divergent paths there rose into the air a great mass of indistinct white blossoms, which she knew were the exquisite mountain azaleas, and all the dark forest was starred with the blooms of the laurel.

She fixed her eyes upon the mystic sphere dropping down the sky, knelt among the azaleas at the forks of the road, and repeated the time-honored invocation :—

"Ef I'm a-goin' ter marry a young man, whistle, Bird, whistle. Ef I'm a-goin' ter marry an old man, low, Cow, low. Ef I ain't a-goin' ter marry nobody, knock, Death, knock."

There was a prolonged silence in the matutinal freshness and perfume of the woods. She raised her head, and listened attentively. No chirp of half-awakened bird, no tapping of wood-pecker, or the mysterious death-watch; but from far along the dewy aisles of the forest, the ungrateful Spot, that Clarsie had fed more faithfully than herself, lifted up her voice, and set the echoes vibrating. Clarsie, however, had hardly time for a pang of disappointment. While she still knelt among the azaleas her large, deer-like eyes were suddenly dilated with terror. From around the curve of the road came the quick beat of hastening footsteps, the sobbing sound of panting breath, and between her and the sinking moon there passed an attenuated, one-armed figure, with a pallid, sharpened face, outlined for a moment on its brilliant disk, and dreadful starting eyes, and quivering open mouth. It disappeared in an instant among the shadows of the laurel, and Clarsie, with a horrible fear clutching at her heart, sprang to her feet.

Her flight was arrested by other sounds. Before her reeling senses could distinguish them, a party of horsemen plunged down the road. They reined in suddenly as their eyes fell upon her, and their leader, an eager, authoritative man, was asking her a question. Why could she not understand him? With her nerveless hands feebly catching at the shrubs for support, she listened vaguely to his impatient, meaningless words, and saw with helpless deprecation the rising anger in his face. But there was no time to be lost. With a curse upon the stupidity of the mountaineer, who couldn't speak when she was spoken to, the party sped on in a sweeping gallop, and the rocks and the steeps were hilarious with the sound.

When the last faint echo was hushed, Clarsie tremblingly made her way out into the road; not reassured, however, for she had a frightful conviction that there was now and then a strange stir in the laurel, and that she was stealthily watched. Her eyes were fixed upon the dense growth with a morbid fascination, as she moved away; but she was once more rooted to the spot when the leaves parted and in the golden moonlight the ghost stood before her. She could not nerve herself to run past him, and he was directly in her way homeward. His face was white, and lined, and thin; that pitiful quiver was never still in the parted lips; he looked at her with faltering, beseeching eyes. Clarsie's merciful heart was stirred. "What ails ye, ter come back hyar, an' foller me?" she cried out, abruptly. And then a great horror fell upon her. Was not one to whom a ghost should speak doomed to death, sudden and immediate?

The ghost replied in a broken, shivering voice, like a wail of pain, "I war a-starvin',—I war a-starvin'," with despairing iteration.

It was all over, Clarsie thought. The ghost had spoken, and she was a doomed creature. She wondered that she did not fall dead in the road. But while those beseeching eyes were fastened in piteous appeal on hers, she could not leave him. "I never hearn that 'bout ye," she said, reflectively. "I knows ye hed awful troubles while ye war alive, but I never knowed ez ye war starved."

Surely that was a gleam of sharp surprise in the ghost's prominent eyes, succeeded by a sly intelligence.

"Day is nigh ter breakin'," Clarsie admonished him, as the lower rim of the moon touched the silver mists of the west. "What air ye a-wantin' of me?"

There was a short silence. Mind travels far in such intervals. Clarsie's thoughts had overtaken the scenes when she should have died that sudden terrible death: when there would be no one left to feed the chickens; when no one would care if the pigs cried with the pangs of hunger, unless, indeed, it were time for them to be fattened before killing. The mare,—how often would she be taken from the plough, and shut up for the night in her shanty without a drop of water, after her hard day's work! Who would churn, or spin, or weave? Clarsie could not understand how the machinery of the universe could go on without her. And Towse, poor Towse! He was a useless cumberer of the ground, and it was hardly to be supposed that after his protector was gone he would be spared a blow or a bullet, to hasten his lagging death. But Clarsie still stood in the road, and watched the face of the ghost, as he, with his eager, starting eyes, scanned her open, ingenuous countenance.

"Ye do ez ye air bid, or it'll be the worse for ye," said the "harnt," in the same quivering, shrill tone. "Thar's hunger in the nex' worl' ez well ez in this, an' ye bring me some vittles hyar this time ter-morrer, an' don't ye tell nobody ye hev seen me, nuther, or it'll be the worse for ye."

There was a threat in his eyes as he disappeared in the laurel, and left the girl standing in the last rays of moonlight.

A curious doubt was stirring in Clarsie's mind when she reached home, in the early dawn, and heard her father talking about the sheriff and his posse, who had stopped at the house in the night, and roused its inmates, to know if they had seen a man pass that way.

"Clarsie never hearn none o' the noise, I'll be bound, 'kase she always sleeps like a log," said Mrs. Giles, as her daughter came in with the pail, after milking the cow. "Tell her 'bout'n it."

"They kem a-bustin' along hyar a while afore day-break, a-runnin' arter the man," drawled Mr. Giles, dramatically. "An' they knocked me up, ter know ef ennybody hed passed. An' one o' them men—I never seen none of 'em afore; they's all valley folks, I'm a-thinkin'—an' one of 'em bruk his saddle-girt' a good piece down the road, an' he kem back ter borrer mine; an' ez we war a-fixin' of it, he tole me what they war all arter. He said that word war tuk ter the sheriff down yander in the valley—'pears ter me them town-folks don't think nobody in the mountings hev got good sense—word war tuk ter the sheriff 'bout this one-armed harnt that walks Chilhowee; an' he sot it down that Reuben Crabb warn't dead at all, an' Joel jes' purtended ter hev buried him, an' it air Reuben hisself that walks Chilhowee. An' thar air two hunderd dollars blood-money reward fur ennybody ez kin ketch him. These hyar valley folks air powerful cur'ous critters,—two hunderd dollars blood-money reward fur that thar harnt that walks Chilhowee! I jes' sot myself ter laffin' when that thar cuss tole it so solemn. I jes' 'lowed ter him ez he couldn't shoot a harnt nor hang a harnt, an' Reuben Crabb hed about got done with his persecutions in this worl'. An' he said that by the time they hed scoured this mounting, like they hed laid off ter do, they would find that that thar puny little harnt war nuthin' but a mortal man, an' could be kep' in a jail ez handy ez enny other flesh an' blood. He said the sheriff 'lowed ez the reason Reuben hed jes' taken ter walk Chilhowee sence Joel died is 'kase thar air nobody ter feed him, like Joel done, mebbe, in the nights; an' Reuben always war a pore, one-armed, weakly critter, what can't even kerry a gun, an' he air driv by hunger out'n the hole whar he stays, ter prowl round the corn-fields an' hen-coops ter steal suthin',—an' that's how he kem ter be seen frequent. The sheriff 'lowed that Reuben can't find enough roots an' yerbs ter keep him up; but law!—a harnt eatin'! It jes' sot me off ter laffin'. Reuben Crabb hev been too busy in torment fur the las' four year ter be a-studyin' 'bout eatin'; an' it air his harnt that walks Chilhowee."

The next morning, before the moon sank, Clarsie, with a tin pail in her hand, went to meet the ghost at the appointed place. She understood now why the terrible doom that falls upon those to whom a spirit may chance to speak had not descended upon her, and that fear was gone; but the secrecy of her errand weighed heavily. She had been scrupulously careful to put into the pail only such things as had fallen to her share at the table, and which she had saved from the meals of yesterday. "A gal that goes a-robbin' fur a hongry harnt," was her moral reflection, "oughter be throwed bodaciously off'n the bluff."

She found no one at the forks of the road. In the marshy dip were only the myriads of mountain azaleas, only the masses of feathery ferns, only the constellated glories of the laurel blooms. A sea of shining white mist was in the valley, with glinting golden rays striking athwart it from the great cresset of the sinking moon; here and there the long, dark, horizontal line of a distant mountain's summit rose above the vaporous shimmer, like a dreary, sombre island in the midst of enchanted waters. Her large, dreamy eyes, so wild and yet so gentle, gazed out through the laurel leaves upon the floating gilded flakes of light, as in the deep coverts of the mountain, where the fulvous-tinted deer were lying, other eyes, as wild and as gentle, dreamily watched the vanishing moon. Overhead, the filmy, lace-like clouds, fretting the blue heavens, were tinged with a faint rose. Through the trees she caught a glimpse of the red sky of dawn, and the glister of a great lucent, tremulous star. From the ground, misty blue exhalations were rising, alternating with the long lines of golden light yet drifting through the woods. It was all very still, very peaceful, almost holy. One could hardly believe that these consecrated solitudes had once reverberated with the echoes of man's death-dealing ingenuity, and that Reuben Crabb had fallen, shot through and through, amid that wealth of flowers at the forks of the road. She heard suddenly the far-away baying of a hound. Her great eyes dilated, and she lifted her head to listen. Only the solemn silence of the woods, the slow sinking of the noiseless moon, the voiceless splendor of that eloquent day-star.

Morning was close at hand, and she was beginning to wonder that the ghost did not appear, when the leaves fell into abrupt commotion, and he was stand-

Charles Egbert Craddock

ing in the road, beside her. He did not speak, but watched her with an eager, questioning intentness, as she placed the contents of the pail upon the moss at the roadside. "I'm a-comin' agin ter-morrer," she said, gently. He made no reply, quickly gathered the food from the ground, and disappeared in the deep shades of the woods.

She had not expected thanks, for she was accustomed only to the gratitude of dumb beasts; but she was vaguely conscious of something wanting, as she stood motionless for a moment, and watched the burnished rim of the moon slip down behind the western mountains. Then she slowly walked along her misty way in the dim light of the coming dawn. There was a footstep in the road behind her; she thought it was the ghost once more. She turned, and met Simon Burney, face to face. His rod was on his shoulder, and a string of fish was in his hand.

"Ye air a-doin' wrongful, Clarsie," he said, sternly. "It air agin the law fur folks ter feed an' shelter them ez is a-runnin' from jestice. An' ye'll git yerself inter trouble. Other folks will find ye out, besides me, an' then the sheriff'll be up hyar arter ye."

The tears rose to Clarsie's eyes. This prospect was infinitely more terrifying than the awful doom which follows the horror of a ghost's speech.

"I can't holp it," she said, however, doggedly swinging the pail back and forth. "I can't gin my consent ter starvin' of folks, even ef they air a-hidin' an' a-runnin' from jestice."

"They mought put ye in jail, too,—I dunno," suggested Simon Burney.

"I can't holp that, nuther," said Clarsie, the sobs rising, and the tears falling fast. "Ef they comes an' gits me, and puts me in the pen'tiary away down yander, somewhars in the valley, like they done Jane Simpkins, fur a-cuttin' of her step-mother's throat with a butcher-knife, while she war asleep,—though some said Jane war crazy,—I can't gin my consent ter starvin' of folks."

A recollection came over Simon Burney of the simile of "hendering the sun from shining."

"She hev done sot it down in her mind," he thought, as he walked on beside her and looked at her resolute face. Still he did not relinquish his effort.

"Doin' wrong, Clarsie, ter aid folks what air a-doin' wrong, an' mebbe *hev* done wrong, air powerful hurtful ter everybody, an' henders the law an' jestice."

"I can't holp it," said Clarsie.

"It 'pears toler'ble comical ter me," said Simon Burney, with a sudden perception of a curious fact which has proved a marvel to wiser men, "that no matter how good a woman is, she ain't got no respect fur the laws of the country, an' don't sot no store by jestice." After a momentary silence he appealed to her on another basis. "Somebody will ketch him arter a while, ez sure ez ye air born. The sheriff's a-sarchin' now, an' by the time that word gits around, all the mounting boys'll turn out, 'kase thar air two hunderd dollars blood-money fur him. An' then he'll think, when they ketches him,—an' everybody'll say so, too,—ez ye war constant in feedin' him jes' ter 'tice him ter comin' ter one place, so ez ye could tell somebody whar ter go ter ketch him, an' make them gin ye haffen the blood-money, mebbe. That's what the mounting will say, mos' likely."

"I can't holp it," said Clarsie, once more.

He left her walking on toward the rising sun, and retraced his way to the forks of the road. The jubilant morning was filled with the song of birds; the sunlight flashed on the dew; all the delicate enamelled bells of the pink and white azaleas were swinging tremulously in the wind; the aroma of ferns and mint rose on the delicious fresh air. Presently he checked his pace, creeping stealthily on the moss and grass beside the road rather than in the beaten path. He pulled aside the leaves of the laurel with no more stir than the wind might have made, and stole cautiously through its dense growth, till he came suddenly upon the puny little ghost, lying in the sun at the foot of a tree. The frightened creature sprang to his feet with a wild cry of terror, but before he could move a step he was caught and held fast in the strong grip of the stalwart mountaineer beside him. "I hev kem hyar ter tell ye a word, Reuben Crabb," said Simon Burney. "I hev kem hyar ter tell ye that the whole mounting air a-goin' ter turn out ter sarch fur ye; the sheriff air a-ridin' now, an' ef ye don't come along with me they'll hev ye afore night, 'kase thar air two hunderd dollars reward fur ye."

What a piteous wail went up to the smiling blue sky, seen through the dappling leaves above them! What a horror, and despair, and prescient agony were in the hunted creature's face! The ghost struggled no longer; he slipped from his feet down upon the roots of the tree, and turned that woful face, with its starting eyes and drawn muscles and quivering parted lips, up toward the unseeing sky.

"God A'mighty, man!" exclaimed Simon Burney, moved to pity. "Whyn't ye quit this hyar way of livin' in the woods like ye war a wolf? Whyn't ye come back an' stand yer trial? From all I've hearn tell, it 'pears ter me ez the jury air obleeged ter let ye off, an' I'll take keer of ye agin them Grims."

"I hain't got no place ter live in," cried out the ghost, with a keen despair.

Simon Burney hesitated. Reuben Crabb was possibly a murderer,—at the best could but be a burden. The burden, however, had fallen in his way, and he lifted it.

"I tell ye now, Reuben Crabb," he said, "I ain't a-goin' ter holp no man ter break the law an' hender jestice; but ef ye will go an' stand yer trial, I'll take keer of ye agin them Grims ez long ez I kin fire a rifle. An' arter the jury hev done let ye off, ye air welcome ter live along o' me at my house till ye die. Ye air no 'count ter work, I know, but I ain't a-goin' ter grudge ye fur a livin' at my house."

And so it came to pass that the reward set upon the head of the harnt that walked Chilhowee was never claimed.

With his powerful ally, the forlorn little spectre went to stand his trial, and the jury acquitted him without leaving the box. Then he came back to the mountains to live with Simon Burney. The cruel gibes of his burly mockers that had beset his feeble life from his childhood up, the deprivation and loneliness and despair and fear that had filled those days when he walked Chilhowee, had not improved the harnt's temper. He was a helpless creature, not able to carry a gun or hold a plough, and the years that he spent smoking his cob-pipe in Simon Burney's door were idle years and unhappy. But Mrs. Giles said she thought he was "a mighty lucky little critter: fust, he hed Joel ter take keer of him an' feed him, when he tuk ter the woods ter pertend he war a harnt; an' they do say now that Clarsie Pratt, afore she war married, used ter kerry him vittles, too ; an' then old Simon Burney tuk him up an' fed him ez plenty ez ef he war a good workin' hand, an' gin him clothes an' house-room, an' put up with his jawin' jes' like he never hearn a word of it. But law ! some folks dunno when they air well off."

There was only a sluggish current of peasant blood in Simon Burney's veins, but a prince could not have dispensed hospitality with a more royal hand. Ungrudgingly he gave of his best ; valiantly he defended his thankless guest at the risk of his life ; with a moral gallantry he struggled with his sloth, and worked early and late, that there might be enough to divide. There was no possibility of a recompense for him, not even in the encomiums of discriminating friends, nor the satisfaction of tutored feelings and a practised spiritual discernment; for he was an uncouth creature, and densely ignorant.

The grace of culture is, in its way, a fine thing, but the best that art can do —the polish of a gentleman—is hardly equal to the best that Nature can do in her higher moods.

Isaac Henderson.

Born in Brooklyn, N. Y., 1850.

WOMAN AND PRIEST.

[*The Prelate.* 1886.]

DURING the following week Padre Martini visited the villa daily, and had many a chat with the princess and Helen, and many a game with Leo. On Friday afternoon he did not come, and, as Alessandra was not feeling very well, Helen suggested to Leo that they take a stroll together. So they walked smartly for an hour, while Helen told the little fellow, in Italian, the story of "Jack the Giant-Killer," to his immense delight. The road ran through a grove, and before turning back they sat down to rest under the boughs of an old chestnut-tree. Presently the sound of hoofs was heard, and immediately the prince appeared upon his favorite horse. He reined up when he reached them, and told them that his horse was going lame and he had decided to return.

"Take me with you, papa," pleaded Leo.

The prince smiled affectionately upon the boy.

"Can you ride in front and hold on tightly ?"

"Yes, papa. Do take me ; it will be such fun !"

"But would you leave Aunt Elena alone ?"

The child looked distressed. "I hadn't thought of Aunt Elena ; couldn't you take her behind ?"

The prince and Helen laughed heartily.

"Go, dear Leo," said Helen ; "I don't mind walking home alone ; I shall be only half an hour behind you."

"Shall we leave you ?" asked the prince, doubtfully.

"Certainly ; the boy wishes to ride, and I don't mind being left."

So, in a moment, she saw them disappear around a bend in the road, little Leo riding proudly in front of his father.

Helen sat for a few moments, and then started after them. She had not gone far when she noticed a priest, walking toward her slowly. She glanced at his face in passing, and, turning impulsively, exclaimed :

"Giuseppe !"

The young man stopped and regarded her curiously.

"*Dio mio!* Is it you, signorina ?"

"Yes ; I am very glad to meet you."

He looked up and down the road anxiously.

"I must not stop," he said.

"But I wish to speak with you."

"Signorina, it would be very dangerous for me to be seen talking with you ; pray permit me to pass on"; and he made a movement as if to leave her. Helen was in despair, for she felt that an opportunity had come which was not to be lost, and she looked anxiously for a secluded place where they could talk with more privacy. She saw above her an embankment shaded by thick trees.

"Let us go up there," she suggested.

"It will be better for us not to speak together ; have consideration for me, signorina."

"I have had more consideration for you than for myself ; you must hear what I have to say—come !" and she led the way to a sheltered spot under a tree, a dozen yards from the road.

He followed with evident reluctance ; but there was something about the stern young girl which compelled him to obey her.

"You remember me ?" she said, turning to him.

"Perfectly, signorina."

"You know that I delivered your message ?"

"Yes."

"You know that I have been faithful to my promise ?"

"Thank God, yes !"

"Do you know the consequences to me ?"

"No"; and he looked anxiously in her face.

"I dared not take any one with me to the monsignore's, and I was seen to enter his apartment. I was obliged to wait for him until a late hour. I returned home alone, and the next day all Rome talked of me and of him. Good women turned from me. Honest Christians looked askance at him. His usefulness suffered. My reputation perished, and I was forced to leave the friends with whom I was. Your own sister refused to live with such a woman, and to-day I am worse than dead—I am tainted !" She paused a moment, and then added, passionately : "What future have I ? Better none than that which is before me ! I am a vile thing in the eyes of the world. They shrink from me as from a leper, and cry, 'Unclean.'" Her eyes blazed, and, coming close to him, she demanded, "Do I deserve this ?"

"No ; you have suffered a great wrong"; and his heart burned with pity as he noted her changed appearance.

"I have been faithful, then, to my promise,—you believe it ?"

He bowed his head. "But I could not prevent this," he said. "Do you regret having gone to the monsignore ?"

She looked far through the overhanging trees and into the blue sky beyond, and a smile came to her lips, and her face was illumined with a joy which caused him to marvel.

"No," she said ; "no, I don't regret it ; I would do it again to gain the same end. But is my penalty *necessary?* Convince me that it is, and I'll never speak nor think a word of complaint again so long as I live."

He did not reply immediately, but stood looking at her sadly.

"Yes, signorina," he said, at last ; "I fear it is necessary."

She passed her hand over her eyes, as though to see him better.

"Do you mean to tell me there is no escape ; that I must bear this disgrace all my life ?"

He sighed. "You are terribly to be pitied, signorina ; but I see no alternative."

She seemed stunned.

"I had better go now," he said. "I bid you good-by, signorina"; and he moved toward the road. Recalled to the necessity of action she sprang after him, and laid her hand upon his arm.

"Do you realize what you are doing ?" she demanded. "You have made me despised ; I ask you for justice, and you treat me as though it bored you to discuss the matter. I'll not endure it ! You shall listen to me until I dismiss you, which I will do when I'm through with you."

"You misjudge me, signorina. I pity you—God only knows how much ; but I am powerless, and words are useless." He made a motion as if to move on.

"So you would leave me in this terrible position without even telling me why it is necessary ; as though it were some penance you thought fit to put upon me. Indeed, sir, you underrate the circumstances, and you misjudge me."

He turned and looked full into her face, with flashing eyes.

"Well ?" he said.

"Do you wish the truth made known ?"

"You had better strike me dead ! "

"What stands in my way ?"

His voice was low, but trembled with excitement, as he replied slowly :

"*Your sacred promise given in a church of God!*"

She had become so accustomed to believing that, eventually, the priest would vindicate her, that her expectation had grown into a conviction ;

therefore his words and all that they implied struck her with overwhelming force.

She looked at the priest anxiously, clasping her hands together in an effort to control her excitement.

"I know I am in your power," she said ; "but you are human, and you must pity me. Try to realize my position. Think of your own sister placed as I am, disgraced and despised unjustly. What would you say to the only man on earth who could vindicate her ?"

He leaned against a tree, and buried his face in his hands.

The pleading girl came nearer and laid her hand upon his arm.

"Will you not at least tell me what keeps you from admitting the truth ?"

He was silent. She walked away a few paces, and then, turning suddenly, demanded :

"What is it ? Surely, I have a right to know."

He looked away, and was still silent.

"Is it conscience ?"

"I have taken oaths."

"You have taken no oath to connive at wickedness."

"But I have a duty to my Church."

"Have you none to the man who has been so kind to your family and to you? Have you no duty to me, an innocent and helpless woman? Is your Church the guardian of crime ?"

It was a moment before he replied :

"I warned the monsignore ; was that nothing ?"

"A heathen would have done it! You did your duty, nothing more."

"But I have my obligations to my Order."

"And to truth and virtue and your fellow-man." He remained silent. "Sir,"—and she drew herself to her full height,—"you are a coward! This can be no question of conscience, because if your Order compels you to abet wickedness, you are already a perjurer and a traitor in having disclosed what you did to me. No, you are *afraid* to tell the truth ; you fear the consequences, and because of this fear you would sacrifice the man who has lifted you and yours above the brutes, and blight the life of an innocent woman. In some way justice will be done. In the eyes of men you shall yet rank with Judas Iscariot, and the judgment of God will link your lot with his."

The wretched youth shrank before her and sank upon his knees.

"Holy Mother of God, what shall I do!" he exclaimed.

"Stop!" and, thoroughly aroused, she stood above him quivering with excitement. "Never again dare to supplicate the Mother of Jesus while you yourself would crucify virtue!"

He gazed upon her awe-stricken, as she continued :

"Have you no pity? No manhood? No conscience? My promise keeps me silent ; but what forbids your speaking? Are you truly such a coward ?"

"No," he said, proudly ; "I am not a coward."

"I do not believe you, for there can be no other reason."

He covered his face with his hands and rocked backward and forward. "I do not know—I do not know," he cried ; "I loved my Church once," and he groaned with the anguish of his smitten soul. "Now I am not sure that I love her more than myself—God help me!"

"You have to choose between right and wrong. It is clear you have already done a good deed; the question now is, will you turn back, and be the ally of those whose sin you have denounced? You need not stay with those whom you must abhor. The world is large, and God's work is not confined to any people or peculiar order."

He did not repel the suggestion, and, watching him eagerly, she felt that her words had made an impression.

"If you will relieve me of this stigma I will provide you with sufficient money to get beyond the reach of vengeance, and to live independently of your Order. I am rich, and you know I keep my word. I do not propose to bribe you to tell the truth; but I will, so far as I can, protect you in telling it."

He uncovered his face and seemed to be pondering her words.

"Don't weigh chances," she said; "don't measure results; decide to do what is right, and that being your fixed purpose we may consider the material part."

He passed his hand over his forehead as though confused. "No, signorina," he said, "I am not a coward, nor do I wish money. In this you are unjust; but I cannot blame you, for you have suffered greatly. Let me speak frankly. When I left Monsignore Altieri to go to college I judged the whole Church by him, its representative whom I knew best, and I revered it to the utmost depths of my soul. Then I studied its traditions and history under the guidance of men so experienced and gifted that my boyish enthusiasm became man's complete consecration. Then I took my vows and began my practical experience. I was pure and earnest, and my ideal was an exalted one." He shuddered. "You cannot imagine what my experience was: beaten from one stronghold to another, clinging always to the last tenaciously, as a son to his faith in his mother. My associates were human, with selfish, sordid aims; while I, inexperienced in worldly affairs and methods, judged all things by the divine standard. One day, in my anguish, I crept into a cell in an unfrequented part of the convent to commune with myself and pray. Suddenly I heard voices, and, resenting any disturbance, I went to an inner room, perfectly dark and for years unused, and throwing myself upon the damp, stone seat, gave way to my disappointment and sorrow. The voices did not pass away, but grew more distinct, and presently I heard them within the outer cell. I presumed that the intruders were my companions, and that they would soon go out again into the air. They remained, however, and, withdrawing into the darkest part of the room, came near the entrance of the inner cell, where I lay within a few feet of them. I was silent at first, because I wished to hide my emotion; I remained silent afterwards because of the words I heard in connection with the name of Altieri. At last some one said that one who had been a friend of Altieri's must be found who would betray him in the interest of the Church, and my name was suggested. I did not recognize the voices, nor could I identify them. I only know that I was half stunned, and that my heart was well-nigh broken with shame and horror. I made up my mind that, come what might, Altieri should be warned. I was confident that I would be approached soon in reference to the matter, and I thought it better to undertake the work than leave it to an enemy of my old benefactor. I tried to contrive some way to warn him before I should be intrusted with any confidence that would cause them to watch me. In this I failed, for that night the superior sent for me, and, after a few general questions, began to ask me about my early life. I mentioned, casually, that Altieri had been my first instructor, and the superior pretended to be surprised, and asked me many questions about him. In answering, I spoke of the monsignore with some bitterness, half concealed, but apparently heartfelt. The superior's face lit up in response to my seeming emotion, yet he controlled instantly this manifestation of feeling. He spoke with sorrow of Altieri's course, and this gave me an opportunity of deepening the impression I had made. Little by little, under the encouragement of my apparent hatred of this powerful enemy of my Church, the superior became less guarded, until, in a word, he laid before me the part he wished me to play in his accursed plot, the main features of which he intrusted to me, promising me high consideration should I succeed.

"I considered every possible way of communicating secretly and quickly with Altieri, and at last thought of the plan of telling my sister. I knew your habit of going to the festivals at St. Peter's. The rest you know. One of my companions, that afternoon, suspected that I had communicated with you in some way. When the plot was frustrated it was generally believed that I had warned Altieri ; but no one could prove it while you and he were silent, and thus far I've escaped punishment, although I know that they hope eventually to convict me. I heard afterwards that there was a scandal connected with the monsignore, and I wondered if you were the lady ; but I did not think much about you ; I thought always of him and of my Church. You cannot know how I have suffered. I have been nearly frantic with diverse feelings. Should I vindicate my benefactor at the expense of my Church ? A thousand, ten thousand times I have cried, 'What is my duty ? O God, show me my duty !'" He closed his eyes, and his lips moved as if in prayer.

At length he spoke again :

"Signorina, nothing can be worse than what I am now experiencing. I wish sincerely to do what is right ; but I do not feel called upon to sacrifice my liberty and usefulness, even if I can bring myself to state the truth." He was silent for several minutes ; then his face grew stern, and his clasped hands trembled violently, as he said, in a low tone, "It is decided ! I will go to another land, and do what I can for the cause to which my life is consecrated. I will accept enough money to take me where I will go, and I will meet you when you wish, and do whatever you may ask !"

Helen could scarcely credit her senses. She paused to control her excitement ; while her companion, as if to gain strength for the fulfilment of his resolution, prayed silently.

"Come, Sunday, to the villa of the Prince Tolozzi," she said, "and there make a written statement of the truth, before witnesses."

"I will do so"; and then he added, "My statement shall be kept a secret for ten days after I make it ?"

"Certainly; you shall have every opportunity of getting away in safety."

"At what hour shall I come?"

"At eleven, precisely."

"I will be punctual."

The sun was sinking below the horizon, and Helen felt that there was nothing to be gained by further words; so she bade him go, while she would remain where she was for a few moments, lest some of his companions might by chance see them together. The poor fellow came forward, and, kneeling humbly, took her hand and kissed it.

"Signorina," he said, "I am about to make a terrible plunge into a new world; pray for me;" and, rising, he turned from her, and in a moment had disappeared.

David Demarest Lloyd.

BORN in New York, N. Y., 1851. DIED at Weehawken, N. J., 1889.

THE CONVENTION SCENE IN "FOR CONGRESS."

[*For Congress.   A Political Sketch.—This Comedy was first produced at the National Theatre, Washington, D. C., 1883, with John T. Raymond in the part of General Josiah Limber.*]

ACT II.

SCENE.—Ante-room to the Convention Hall. Leaning against scene are political banners, as follows: "Woolley the stern Statesman." "Miggs Forever, Woolley Never." "We want reform in the other party." "The people demand Zephaniah Miggs." "Chunkalunk County solid for Woolley."

[LIMBER *discovered with* JOHN PRICE *and two men.*]

LIMBER. Now, boys, I want Woolley's nomination to be as spontaneous as we can make it. John, I want you to propose Peter Woolley as a compromise candidate, on the ground of his deep interest in politics. Then, Tom, I want you to get up and say you know positively Mr. Woolley will not accept the nomination, and "if any man dare dispute it, meet me outside." If any of them get up to go out, you remain where you are! Then, John, you make another of your grand efforts and say that is the very reason he ought to be nominated; that the office should seek the man, and not the man the office. You're familiar with that tune! Then, Joe, you demand Woolley's nomination in the interests of economy and reform. Throw your whole weight on reform. We're all reformers now! Then cast the vote of your county for Woolley, you ditto, and then holler! Tell all the boys to holler, and we'll start a stampede for old Pete—that will beat Miggs to pieces! But remember, boys, it must be spontaneous!

PRICE. Do you think Woolley will do the right thing by the boys?

LIMBER. John Price, I've been in politics ever since I was thirteen years old. I've been called a rascal a great many times, but nobody has ever taken me for a fool, and it's too late to begin now. Now get in, boys. [*The three men go up.*] Oh, John! [PRICE *comes down.*] You tell Bill Dey I see through his little game.

Chunkalunk County isn't solid for Woolley. He'd have me think it is, and when the critical moment comes, he'll swing his vote over to Miggs. Now, John, you know I never say things I don't know to be true. Woolley's worth a million. And I judge from his appearance that his capacity to shell out for the legitimate expenses of the campaign is simply immense! You tell Bill Dey he is making the biggest mistake of his life. [*Enter* WOOLLEY.]

LIMBER. Peter, here's a special message from his excellency the clerk of the Buzzard Hotel. [*Hands note to* WOOLLEY.]

WOOL. General, I don't understand politics. I can't make this out at all.

LIMBER. Why, I ordered a little refreshment for the boys. They expect it. "Hon. Peter Woolley,"—you're elected, you see, Pete,—"Dr. to the Buzzard Hotel —$100 for six hundred drinks—for one hundred friends of reform."

[*Enter* PELHAM PERRIWINKLE, JULIA FREE, *and* ANNA WOOLLEY.]

ANNA. Have they begun yet?

JULIA. I don't know. How strange the old school-house looks.

[*Enter* MRS. MUFFIN.]

ANNA. I wish it would do for us to go in. I don't see why people think politics are stupid! They're delightful! I was never so excited in my life.

MRS. M. Be still, child. When you're as familiar with politics as I am, you'll understand these things better.

ANNA. But I can't keep still! Julia! Let's go and look in.

MRS. M. Anna, try and behave yourself like a lady.

PELHAM. [*Has gone up stage.*] I say, just look at this.

ANNA and JULIA. Oh, what is it?

MRS. M. [*Pushing in between the girls.*] Girls, don't be so inquisitive. What is it, eh?

PELHAM. [*Reading banners.*] "Woolley the stern Statesman."

ANNA. What funny people these politicians are—the idea of calling papa a stern statesman! [*Shouts. Exit* PELHAM.]

JULIA. But what's this—"The people demand Zephaniah Miggs."

ANNA. The idea of their demanding Miggs or anybody else when they can get my papa!

JULIA. Down with Miggs! Woolley forever! [*Enter* PELHAM.]

PELHAM. I say, they've begun.

JULIA. Oh, do tell us what they are doing.

ANNA. I wish I were in there.

MRS. M. Now, girls, don't be so inquisitive. [*Pulls* ANNA *round to L. H. corner.*] What did you say they were doing?

PELHAM. Well, there's a man making a speech.

ALL the LADIES. Well, well.

PELHAM. He really quite alarmed me, you know. He says the country is going to destruction.

ANNA. Oh, I wonder if that's true?

JULIA. I think they usually change their minds after election. [*Shouts outside.*]

ANNA and JULIA. Oh, hear that! [*They turn up stage.*]

MRS. M. Girls, don't talk about what you don't understand. The country is in a deplorable state. General Limber told me all about it. [*Enter* LIMBER.]

LIMBER. Why, here's an oasis of beauty, blooming right in the desert of politics. How are you, girls?—How are you, Jule?—I had just finished the platform and was about to take it in.

ANNA. Oh, do let us see it.

JULIA. Let us hear it.

PELHAM. Platform ? I don't see any platform.

LIMBER. Our friend from the effete and enervated East doesn't understand. A platform is—the resolutions. It's what we say before election—we'll do after election. We don't always do it, but we always say it.

ANNA and JULIA. Oh, do let us hear it.

LIMBER. Would you like to have me read it just as I am going to read it in there ?

ANNA and JULIA. Oh, do, do!

MRS. M. Girls, be calm. Look at me, I am perfectly calm!

ANNA. Oh, I am so excited!

LIMBER. [*Reading.*] "Your committee, profoundly impressed with the colossal importance of the duty intrusted to them, beg leave to report as follows"—ahem!

"Resolved: That we have met in the midst of a great crisis"—Girls, it is the peculiarity of our party that we always meet in the midst of a great crisis.

PELHAM. There! I told you so!

LIMBER. "Resolved: That our party is a towering monument of public virtue. Resolved: That the other party is a festering slough of political slime."

ANNA. Oh, dear!

MRS. M. It's just like poetry. [*Shouts.   Exit* PELHAM.]

LIMBER. "Resolved: That all the offices should be bestowed upon our party. Resolved: That if the other party should get any of the offices, the stability of our institutions would be eternally imperilled, and the proud figure of Freedom herself would totter on her mountain height."

ANNA. Oh, how splendid!

JULIA. Superb! And so pure, and lofty in tone.

LIMBER. "Resolved"—no, I'll have to fix that. [*Shouts.*]

[JULIA *and* ANNA *run up to C.*]

MRS. M. Girls, girls, don't be so inquisitive.

ANNA. I don't care, I'm going in. [*Exeunt girls C.*]

LIMBER. There! No, no, that won't do. That expresses an idea.

MRS. M. Well, I guess I'll take a little peek myself. [*Exit.*]

LIMBER. There, that heads either way, like a ferry-boat. [*Enter* MISS GRIMM.]

MISS G. Stop! In the name of the down-trodden women of America, I demand the insertion of this woman-suffrage plank in the resolutions of the Convention.

LIMBER. Oh, thanks.

MISS G. I want to know your personal views on woman suffrage. Now, *I* think the exclusion of women from the polls is one of the crying evils of the age.

LIMBER. Well——

MISS G. *I* think our politics will never be pure and picturesque till the refining influence of woman is felt there.

LIMBER. Well——

MISS G. *I* think it is a question our public men must meet at once.

LIMBER. Well——

MISS G. Your views are very satisfactory.

LIMBER. I'm glad she's got my views on woman suffrage. [MISS G. *has taken off her glasses and now turns to* LIMBER.] What, Jemima Grimm!

MISS G. Why, Josiah Limber! Why, I didn't know you at all!

LIMBER. No wonder. You haven't seen me for twenty years, and you're here in Woolleyville. You must have carpet-bagged a good deal.

MISS G. Yes, I have, like all school-teachers.

LIMBER. So have I, like all school-teachers. You're still Jemima Grimm ?

Miss G. Josiah Limber, in a land where women are denied the right to vote, I am proud to say I am an old maid!

Limber. Well, I've had my ups and downs—mostly downs. Yes, I've seen the time when smoked herring was stalled ox to me. But if the scheme I have now succeeds, I shan't have to consider my duster in the light of an ulster next winter. —But Jemima, do you remember when we were boys and girls together in Pennsylvania—at least one boy and one girl? Do you remember how fond I used to be of you?

Miss G. You always were a fool!

Limber. I thought you'd remember that! Do you remember the singing-school, eh—and that night coming home when the candle went out in the lantern—you remember the husking-bees—and the bench under the old apple-tree in the orchard —and the straw rides?—Oh, Jemima! [*Embraces her.*]

Miss G. There's somebody coming. [*Enter* Mrs. Muffin; *exit* Miss G.]

Limber. [*Pretending to be absorbed in the platform.*] "Resolved." [Mrs. M. *angry.*] Jealous! That won't do. She'll withdraw the old man. Did you observe that little episode just now?

Mrs. M. I observed what you call an episode.

Limber. That was political—purely political.

Mrs. M. I didn't see much politics in it.

Limber. Oh, that's politics. That's what we poor politicians have to undergo all the time. You see that's a very dangerous character. She's what we term a woman suffragist, and it won't do for Peter to favor woman suffrage. So I was trying to conciliate her—smooth her down.

Mrs. M. You seemed to be smoothing her down very successfully! [*Shouts.*]

[*Enter* Pelham, Anna, *and* Julia.]

Pelham. I say, Limber, they've begun to vote.

Limber. Well, I'm glad of it.

Pelham. Miggs has got the first ten votes.

Limber. Miggs! [*Rushes off, followed by* Pelham.]

Anna and Julia. Oh, oh!

Mrs. M. Girls, girls! [*Enter* Pelham.]

Pelham. Five for Woolley! [*Exit. Enter* Miss G.]

Anna. Oh, good! but they are only five.

Pelham. [*Enters.*] Five more for Woolley! [*Exit.*]

Anna and Julia. Oh, splendid!

Pelham. [*Enters.*] Fifteen for Miggs. [*Exit.*]

Miss G. Ah, good!

Julia. The hateful thing!

Miss G. I don't hesitate to say that I'm for Miggs. Miggs is in favor of woman suffrage.

Anna. Well, if she's for Miggs, I hope she'll never get the right to vote for him or anybody else. [*Enter* Mike.]

Mike. I'm all tore up! I want to see Mr. Woolley nominated, but I hate to see Moriarty beat. It isn't often an Irishman gets an office. They're too modest! I'll see how things are going anyhow. [*Exit.*]

Pelham. [*Enters.*] Ten more for Miggs! Do you know, I never saw a convention all the time I was abroad. [*Exit.*]

Julia. Oh, Anna, let us keep count. How can we do it?

Pelham. [*Enters.*] What extraordinary names you have here in America! Aristowoobskook County gives ten votes for Woolley. [*Exit.*]

Anna. Oh, hurry! What shall we do?

JULIA. Here's just the thing.

ANNA. One of the school blackboards—just the thing—quick!

[*They place the blackboard on chair, board facing up stage.   Enter* MIKE.]

MIKE. Ould Ireland's been heard from!   Mackerelville gives fifteen votes to Patrick Moriarty!   Aha!   Them Mackerelville boys are the fellows.   Ah, ye divils, ye! [*Exit.*]

PELHAM. [*Enters.*] Five for Woolley.   [*Exit.*]

ANNA. Quick!

JULIA. Where's the chalk ?   Now you keep the tally for Peter Woolley, and I'll put down the votes for Zephaniah Miggs.   Oh, Aunt, I wish you weren't for Miggs! I hate Miggs!   I'd like to count him out!

ANNA. Oh, Julia, if women went into politics wouldn't they cheat though!

MISS G. Pooh!   Pooh!

PELHAM. [*Enters.*] More names! Miggs gets twenty votes from Squashopolis! [*Exit.*]

ANNA. Oh, we haven't put them down.   Hurry before there's another.   5—5—10 —5—.

JULIA. 10—15—10—20—I hate to put it down.   That makes Miggs 30 ahead.

PELHAM. [*Enters.*] Thirty for Woolley!   [*Exit.   Shouts.*]

ANNA. That makes them even——

JULIA. If I have to keep count for Miggs, I'll applaud for Woolley. [*Enter* MIKE.]

MIKE. Ould Ireland's gaining!   Moriarty's got one more vote.   [*Exit.*]

PELHAM. [*Enters.*] Fifteen for Miggs.   [*Exit.*]

MISS G. Good for Miggs !   Miggs will be nominated.   You'll see!

JULIA. I'm opposed to woman suffrage from this hour!

PELHAM. [*Enters.*] Twenty votes for Peter Woolley!   [*Exit.*]

JULIA. What does it make all together ?

ANNA. Oh, I don't know!   They won't add up at all!

PELHAM. [*Enters.*] Twenty more for Woolley!   [*Exit.   Shouts.*]

[*Enter* LIMBER *radiant.*]

ANNA. Will papa be nominated ?

LIMBER. Papa will be nominated unanimously.   You know the old phrase—As old Chunkalunk goes, so goes the Union!   Well, old Chunkalunk, in spite of their banner there, were a little uncertain as to whom they'd give their sixty votes to. But they have agreed, in consideration of—ahem!—of Peter Woolley's many eminent qualities, to give him their sixty votes.   It took me some time, but it's all settled!

MISS G. Has my woman-suffrage resolution been adopted yet ?

LIMBER. Well, not yet.

MISS G. I knew it!

MRS. M. Now, girls, I'm going to find brother Peter, and bring him here.   The candidate ought to be on the spot to be surprised at the nomination.   [*Exit.*]

[*Enter* WOOLLEY.   *Sees portrait on banner.*]

WOOL. Who's that ?

ANNA. Why, here's papa now.

WOOL. Anna!   What's all this about ?   What does it mean ?

ANNA. It's the Convention.   We thought no one would see us, and we were so anxious.

WOOL. What, the Convention ?   Oh, I must go right away!   I haven't done half the work in the garden this morning.

ANNA. Now, wait, papa.   General Limber has told us you will surely be nominated.

WOOL. Dear! dear!

ANNA. Yes, Chunk–a–lunk—yes, that's it, Chunkalunk County is going to give you all its sixty votes!

WOOL. I hope they won't do it now.

ANNA. Now, wait, papa.

PELHAM. [*Enters.*] Twenty for Woolley! [*Exit.*]

WOOL. What a start he gave me. I must go. I had no idea politics were so noisy.

MISS G. What are your views on woman suffrage?

WOOL. I haven't got any. [*Exit. Enter* CHARLES MONTGOMERY.]

CHARLES. Why, Anna, I just heard of this a few moments ago. I had no idea your father thought of running for Congress! I expect every moment to hear whom the other Convention have nominated.

VOICE. [*Outside.*] Sixty votes for Zephaniah Miggs!

MISS G. Sixty votes for Miggs. [*Shouts.*]

JULIA. I wonder what that meant? [*Enter* PELHAM.]

PELHAM. I say, where's Limber? There's something wrong. There's a stampede for Miggs. Miggs is getting all the votes.

OMNES. Limber! Limber! Where's Limber? [*Enter* LIMBER.]

PELHAM. Something's wrong! Chunkalunk County gave sixty votes for Miggs!

LIMBER. What! Grand old Chunkalunk?

PELHAM. Yes, and they're all voting for Miggs. [*Exit.*]

LIMBER. Bill Dey's gone back on my bid! But I'll beat him yet. [*Exit.*]

PELHAM. [*Enters.*] Twenty more for Miggs! [*Shouts.*]

LIMBER. [*Off stage.*] Boys, I appeal to your patriotism and intelligence. [*Shout.*] You've lots of both. [*Shout* "Yes."] Will you hesitate between the Hon. Peter Woolley and the infamous Miggs? ["No."] Remember you are performing a momentous duty. The eyes of the world are on you. This is the hour of your country's peril, and the very crisis of her fate. [*Loud shouts.*]

PELHAM. [*Enters.*] He's making a most eloquent speech. I don't believe there's a fellow in our club ever made such a speech.

JULIA. Too late.

MISS G. I wonder if he will defeat Miggs?

ANNA. Hark!

VOICE. [*Outside.*] Three cheers for Zephaniah Miggs. [*One feeble shout.*]

PELHAM. That wasn't much of a cheer for Miggs.

VOICE. [*Outside.*] Three cheers for Peter Woolley. [*Loud cheers.*]

PELHAM. I say, that meant something. [*Exit. Enter* MIKE.]

MIKE. Oh, Mr. Charles, the other Convention have just up and nominated you for Congress. [*Exit.*]

CHAS. What! me? No, it can't be!

ANNA. Oh, Charles, you and papa running against each other!

CHAS. I don't know what to make of it at all. [*Enter* PELHAM.]

PELHAM. I say, they're changing their votes back to Woolley. Limber is swinging the Convention right around. Chunkalunk County changes sixty votes to Peter Woolley!

[*Enter Brass Band playing " The Star Spangled Banner." Then* LIMBER, *followed by delegate carrying flag on staff, which he waves over* LIMBER *and* WOOLLEY. *Crowd fill in at back, shouting. Enter* WOOLLEY *led by* MRS. MUFFIN.]

CURTAIN.

𝕵𝖚𝖑𝖎𝖆 𝕮𝖔𝖓𝖘𝖙𝖆𝖓𝖈𝖊 𝕱𝖑𝖊𝖙𝖈𝖍𝖊𝖗.

BORN in Rio Janeiro, Brazil.

A SYRIAN ADVENTURE.

[*Mirage. By George Fleming.* 1878.]

OF the two there was one who would have given much to have escaped the necessity of any interview. Naturally enough, this one was the first to speak.

"I am afraid we have been very selfish, Tom and I," she says, with a slight increase of color on her cheeks; "Fanny seems so tired. But these people are interesting. I think this is a delightful place—don't you?"

"I think so—now," says Mr. Stuart.

Some men passing along the road turn again to stare at the strangers, and Mr. Stuart returns their glances with a little of that abounding contempt we instinctively exhibit towards people who, in all probability, will never be in any fashion connected with ourselves.

"It is so seldom Tom can be got to talk. Tom is something like an Englishman in that respect. Did you never notice how an American will invariably endeavor to be interesting at any cost—either to others or to himself? Now an Englishman has the courage to be dull."

"Some of us are dull enough without that," says Jack, moodily.

The Arabs are still standing watching him. They whisper together. As the young man brushes by them there is a hoarse cry of "Backshish!" and then an insolent laugh. It is only a trifling annoyance, but it comes charged with the weight of the morning's exasperation, and sends the hot blood flushing to his forehead. He turns upon Constance with that sudden, irrational resentment of an unpleasant impression which is, perhaps, at the bottom of half the follies of life.

"Don't you think these small travelling-parties are a mistake?" he says, with an air of elaborate impartiality. "One sees the same people so continuously that—in fact, you see the same people so much."

Miss Varley is entirely of his opinion. She says so, and then bends down and busies herself with the folds of her habit to conceal a most unequivocal smile.

"Yes, I am tired of it," says Mr. Stuart.

"Indeed!"

"I am tired of the whole thing. You treat me like a boy. You laugh at me. You—you attempt to—to patronize me, by Jove!" cries the young man, turning very red. "I don't like it. I don't think you are treating me fairly, Constance," he says, with sudden firmness, with an assertion of mastery in his voice that she has never heard before.

Miss Varley draws herself up and turns her face full upon him, and all the light and animation have gone out of that face.

"You are probably not aware of what you are saying. You will excuse me if I fail to understand "—she begins very coldly; and then there comes a sudden look of kindness in her eyes. "What is the use of quarrelling, Jack? You know you are talking nonsense. When have I ever done anything purposely to vex you?" she says very gently.

A group of fair-haired Nablous children are standing in a doorway. At the sight of the strange faces approaching them they dart away like frightened birds, all but one, a little boy of two or three, who stands in the middle of the street and contemplates them meditatively. Such a flower-face as it is! with the beautiful, open look of a peach-blossom overblown. "Come here, you delightful little creature, and get some backshish," says Miss Varley, and holds up a tempting silver coin. There is a moment's hesitation, and then the baby comes forward a few steps, stops, stares about him. "Poor little thing!" says Constance, and stoops to pick him up. To her surprise the child resists her with sudden, shrill cries of alarm.

"Oh, put him down, do!" says Jack, hastily. There is quite a crowd around them by this time.

"Poor little thing! You don't suppose it was afraid I had the evil eye?" begins the girl; and at the same moment a woman, veiled and shapeless in her cotton gown, breaks through the ring, seizes the sobbing child in her arms, and turns and addresses the crowd in high-pitched Arabic.

"Come on!" says Mr. Stuart again, and this time with even stronger emphasis. "Let that little wretch alone; it doesn't want your money. Here, let's get out of this."

But this is not so easily done. It is true the crowd parts before them, but only to close about on every side. "Backshish!" yells a tall, one-eyed lad in a tattered gown, who has followed them persistently since they entered the bazaar. "Backshish!" calls out a man, putting a hand on Miss Varley's shoulder and stooping to look into her face. "Back—" A vigorous push sends him staggering against the wall.

"Take my arm; don't be frightened," says Jack, cheerfully. "If we can only get through this infernal bazaar"— A shove from the yellow fanatic on the outside of the ring sends the nearest beggar upon him. He turns, and a shove from the other side flings Constance against his shoulder. No sound; but the double movement meant mischief.

"Oh, what shall we do?" says Miss Varley, turning pale.

To her dying day she will never forget what takes place within the next few minutes.

He took her hands in his; he looked at her with a sort of despairing tenderness.

"Don't be frightened," he says; "there is going to be a row. Here, stand back under that arch, and don't move, whatever happens. Don't be frightened, and don't cry. Don't cry, my darling, I'll take care of you."

As luck will have it, the arch of which he speaks is the gaudy-painted doorway of the mosque. A savage howl of execration runs through the crowd at sight of this new outrage. They press forward, stop, waver; and then Jack turns and faces them and draws his pistol from his belt.

"Come on, then! Why don't you come on, you blackguards!" he calls out, in English; and, as by the breaking of a spell, the sound of his voice evokes a very storm of frenzy and abuse. With every moment the tumult increases. A piece of mud knocks off his hat; in an instant it is seized and torn to shreds; and the sight of his blond Saxon face is the signal for a new outbreak of impotent rage. Twice already the jeering, hissing mass of infuriated men has pushed and swayed up to the very limit of the steps, and twice the sight of his steady, unblenching face has swept them back again with a sound as of the surf grinding upon the shore. And each time they have lessened the distance between them.

He took three steps forward, paused, then deliberately drew a deep line with the heel of his boot in the dust. " We'll see who crosses *that*, my men !" he says, significantly. A long howl of defiance is the instant answer. And now, with one common impulse, the mob hurls itself forward and stands straining and foaming like a pack of craven, white-toothed pariah dogs on the farther side of the barrier.

"Don't be frightened, my darling," says Jack; his own face is deathly pale, and great beads of moisture are standing on his forehead.

There is a scuffle, a push; one of the foremost assailants, a half-grown lad in a long, blue caftan, is sent staggering across the mark : he falls heavily on his face and is dragged back by his nearest neighbors. And then comes an ominous pause.

From his vantage-ground on the mosque-steps Stuart overlooks the street; and at this moment he is aware of a disturbance in the spirit of the mob— some new object is drawing their attention. There is a cry of " Allah !" the sound of a low, wailing, inarticulate chant, a sudden falling asunder of the close-packed men; in the centre of this space, advancing slowly towards him, is a creature—a man. It has the figure of a man—but whether young or old it is impossible to say. A strip of sheepskin is slung about its waist, a long string of coarse amulets dangles from its neck and down upon the naked breast, covered with hair like the breast of an animal. On his head is a fantastic crown of iron spikes, from under which long and matted locks stream down over his thick arms, his naked, shining shoulders, his fixed and vacant eyes. He comes slowly forward, rolling from side to side in his walk, keeping time to the monotonous, lolling chant. The crowd have fallen respectfully back; he stands alone in the centre of an open space, looking at Stuart with a dull, malignant smile.

"My God! what shall I do ?" thought Stuart, clinching his teeth. He moves, and the dervish catches sight of Constance. A sudden, furious gleam of insanity transfigures the livid face. He turns, with a wild gesture of exhortation—he turns and harangues the mob. He turns again—he walks deliberately forward. Jack raises the revolver slowly to a level.

And then a murderous silence falls upon the crowd. The dervish comes steadily forward; his foot is on the line; he looks up at Stuart with an idiotic laugh, and then, like a mockery from heaven, they hear through the intense silence the innocent, bubbling laughter of a child.

The dervish passes the line. Constance springs forward with a cry. The next sound is the click of the trigger settling back in its lock.

"Jack!" She springs forward and clutches him by the arm. "Don't fire! Hassan!" she says wildly, with white, breathless lips; "Hassan—Hassan"——

And even as she speaks there is a clattering charge of mounted men, a swinging of sabres, a slashing of whips, a cheer. The surging mob sweeps back against the steps. In a moment the dervish is seized, surrounded, forced bodily into the shelter of the mosque. Major Thayer springs from his saddle. The Turkish soldiers clear the piazza of the last terrified stragglers. The dragoman rushes forward flourishing his *koorbash*.

"Thank God!" says Stuart, seizing Constance by the hand. And then, for the first time, Miss Varley breaks down.

"Take me home—take me home, Tom, to Fanny," she says piteously.

"Will you ride?"

"No; I don't know: take me home," she says, and walks on blindly, clinging to his arm, the centre of an excited, questioning, explaining group.

In three or four minutes they have reached the camp. As they enter the tent Miss Varley turns to Stuart:

"I haven't thanked you. But—you know," she says brokenly. She gives him both her hands. Then she sits down on a chair in a corner and begins to cry.

Mr. Stuart, too, sits down. He looks about him with a bewildered air.

"Good heavens! Jack, are you hurt? Will you have some brandy? some water? Your face is as white as a sheet! O Tom, why don't you do something? Don't you see that Jack"——

"I'm not hurt, Fanny. I've been badly frightened. I never knew what it was like before," says Mr. Stuart, simply; "but I had Constance to take care of, you know, and— Look here!"

He threw his revolver down upon the table. Major Thayer picks it up curiously, examines it, starts, and throws it down again with an oath.

"I let Hassan have it for that salute. I had forgotten all about it. You see—it wasn't loaded!" says Jack.

THE FIRING OF THE SHOT.

[*Vestigia. By George Fleming. 1884.*]

THE candle had burnt itself out in its socket. There was no sound in the room but the heavy breathing of the weary sleeper and the ticking of Valdez's watch, which lay before him on the table. He sat there, counting the hours.

And at last the dawn broke, chill and gray; the dim light struggling in at the window made a faint glimmer upon the glasses which stood beside the untouched food. To the old man keeping his faithful watch beside the sleeper, this was perhaps the hardest hour of all—till the darkness wore slowly away; the sky turned to a clear stainless blue; and all the city awoke to the radiance of the April day.

Soon the bells began their joyous clash and clamor. It was hardly eight o'clock when the two men stepped out into the street together, but the rejoicing populace was astir already, and hurrying towards the new quarter of the Macao.

Rome was in festa, heavy and splendid Rome. Bright flags fluttered, and many-colored carpets and rugs were suspended from every available window. All along the Via Nazionale, a double row of gaudily-decked Venetian masts, hung with long wreaths and brilliant flapping banners, marked the course where the royal carriages were to pass. But it was farther on, at the Piazza dell' Indipendenza, that the crowd was already thickest. The cordon of soldiers had been stationed here since early morning. Looking down from any of the neighboring balconies upon that swarming sea of holiday-makers, it seemed impossible that even the great Piazza could contain more ; and yet at every instant the place grew fuller and fuller ; a steady stream of people poured in from every side street ; peasants from the country in gay festa dress ; shepherds from the Campagna in cloaks of matted sheepskin ; and strapping black-haired girls with shrill voices and the step of queens, who had come all the way from Trastevere to look on at the spectacle,—there was no end, no cessation to the thickening and the growing excitement of the crowd.

Dino had taken his place very early. It was exactly at the corner of the Piazza, where a street-lamp made a support for his back, and prevented him from being brushed aside by the gathering force and pressure of the multitude. He had found a safe place for Palmira to stand, on the iron ledge which ran around the lamp-post. The child's little pale face rose high above the crowd ; she was quiet from very excess of excitement, only from time to time she stooped to touch her brother's shoulder in token of mute content.

Valdez stood only a few paces behind them. He had kept the revolver in his own possession to the last moment. It was arranged that he should pass it to Dino at a preconcerted signal, and as the King came riding past for the second time.

Dino had scarcely spoken all that morning, but otherwise there was no sign of unusual excitement about him. He was deadly pale ; at short intervals a faint red flush came and went like a stain upon his colorless cheek. But he answered all little Palmira's questions very patiently. The morning seemed very long to him, that was all. He stood fingering the handkerchief in his pocket with which he was to give Valdez the signal for passing him the weapon.

It was more than twenty-four hours now since he had tasted food, and the long abstinence was beginning to tell upon him ; at times his head felt dizzy, and if he closed his eyes the continuous roar and chatter of the crowd sank— died away far off—like the sound of the surf upon a distant shore. At one moment he let himself go entirely to this curious new sensation of drifting far away ; it was barely an instant of actual time, but he recovered himself with a start which ran like ice from head to foot ; it was a horrible sensation, like a slow return from the very nothingness of death. He shivered and opened his eyes wide and looked about him. He seemed to have been far, far away from it all in that one briefest pause of semi-unconsciousness, yet his eyes opened on the same radiant brightness of the sunshine ; a holiday sun shining bravely down on glancing arms and fretting horses ; on the dark line of the soldiers pressing back the people, and the many-colored dresses, the laughing, talking, good-natured faces of the gesticulating crowd.

One of these mounted troopers was just in front of Dino. As the human mass surged forward, urged by some unexplainable impulse of excitement and curiosity, this man's horse began backing and plunging. The young soldier turned around in his saddle, and his quick glance fell upon Palmira's startled face.

"Take care of your little girl there, my friend," he said to Dino good-humoredly, and forced his horse away from the edge of the pavement.

Dino looked at him without answering. He wondered vaguely if this soldier boy with the friendly blue eyes and the rosy face would be one of the first to fall upon him when he was arrested ? And then his thoughts escaped him again—the dimness came over his eyes.

He roused himself with a desperate effort. He began to count the number of windows in the house opposite ; then the number of policemen stationed at the street corner ; an officer went galloping by ; he fixed his eyes upon the glancing uniform until it became a mere spot of brightness in the distance.

Hark !

The gun at the palace. The King was starting from the Quirinal. All the scattered cries and laughs and voices were welded together into one long quavering roar of satisfaction and excitement.

There—again ! and nearer at hand this second gun.

The cheers rise higher, sink deeper. He is coming, the young soldier King, the master of Italy, the popular hero. See ! hats are waving, men are shouting,—the infection of enthusiasm catches and runs like fire along the line of eager, expectant faces. Here he comes. The roar lifts, swells, grows louder and louder ; the military bands on either side of the piazza break with one accord into the triumphant ringing rhythm of the royal march. They have seen the troops defile before them with scarcely a sign of interest ; but now, at sight of that little isolated group of riders with the plumed and glittering helmets, there comes one mad instant of frantic acclamation, when every man in that crowd feels that he too has some part and possession in all the compelling, alluring splendor and success in life.

And just behind the royal cavalier, among the glittering group of aides-de-camp, rode the young Marchese Balbi. He was so near that Dino could scarcely believe their eyes did not actually meet ; but if Gasparo recognized him he gave no sign, riding on with a smile upon his happy face, his silver-mounted accoutrements shining bravely in the sun.

And so, for the first time, the doomed King passed by.

Dino scarcely heeded him ; at that moment he had forgotten everything unconnected with the sight of that one familiar face. His mother, his old home,—Italia even,—had grown dim and unreal ; he forgot them all in the sensation of that quick rush of renewed affection. All the old pride, the old delight, in Gasparo, which had made so great a part of his boyhood, came back upon him with the irresistible claims of reawakened tenderness. He was there to commit a murder; and out of all that crowd he saw only the one face which he knew—and he loved it.

That curious sense of floating away, far away from everything living, fell upon him again. He lost all count of time. He could never tell how long it was before he heard little Palmira cry out in shrill tones of childish excitement:

"I see him, Dino. There he comes again. The King, the King all in gold!"

Dino started; it seemed to him as if he started wide awake. He drew himself up like a soldier standing at attention; his brain was steady; his senses all alert. He watched eagerly; the white plumes were slowly advancing between the two serried ranks of the soldiery. He waited until he could distinguish the King's face distinctly; he saw him lean a little forward and pat his restive horse——

And then, without turning, he gave Valdez the preconcerted signal.

And even as he raised the handkerchief to his lips he heard, not ten paces off, the sharp ringing report of a shot.

It was all over in an instant—the sound—the plunging of the frightened horses. He saw the white plume of the King pass by unscathed and Gasparo Balbi, who was riding nearest him, throw up his arms and fall backward, quietly, into the rising cloud of dust.

A great cry broke from the people all about him—it rang in his ears—it sounded far away like the beating of a furious tide upon the distant, distant shore. A blackness, a horrible blackness which he could feel, passed over his face like a cloud. And then he knew nothing more.

. . . .

Some quarter of an hour later one of the two *guardie* who were helping to lift his insensible body into a street cab looked compassionately down at Dino's clinched hands and pallid death-like face.

"'Tis no wonder the poor *giovane* fainted," he said sympathetically, addressing the little crowd about him. "'Tis no wonder he fainted, *Perdio!* As it so happens I was looking straight at him,—he was not ten paces away from the villain who fired the shot."

George Parsons Lathrop.

BORN in Oahu, Hawaiian Islands, 1851.

FROM "KEENAN'S CHARGE."

CHANCELLORSVILLE, 2 MAY, 1863.

[*Originally contributed to the Century Magazine, June,* 1881.]

BY the shrouded gleam of the western skies,
Brave Keenan looked in Pleasonton's eyes

For an instant—clear, and cool, and still;
Then, with a smile, he said: "I will."

"Cavalry, charge!" Not a man of them shrank.
Their sharp, full cheer, from rank on rank,
Rose joyously, with a willing breath—
Rose like a greeting hail to death.
Then forward they sprang, and spurred and clashed;
Shouted the officers, crimson-sashed;
Rode well the men, each brave as his fellow,
In their faded coats of the blue and yellow;
And above in the air, with an instinct true,
Like a bird of war their pennon flew.

With clank of scabbards and thunder of steeds,
And blades that shine like sunlit reeds,
And strong brown faces bravely pale
For fear their proud attempt shall fail,
Three hundred Pennsylvanians close
On twice ten thousand gallant foes.

Line after line the troopers came
To the edge of the wood that was ringed with flame;
Rode in and sabred and shot—and fell;
Nor came one back his wounds to tell.
And full in the midst rose Keenan, tall
In the gloom, like a martyr awaiting his fall,
While the circle-stroke of his sabre, swung
'Round his head, like a halo there, luminous hung.
Line after line; ay, whole platoons,
Struck dead in their saddles, of brave dragoons
By the maddened horses were onward borne
And into the vortex flung, trampled and torn;
As Keenan fought with his men, side by side.

So they rode, till there were no more to ride.

But over them, lying there, shattered and mute,
What deep echo rolls ?—'Tis a death-salute
From the cannon in place· for, heroes, you braved
Your fate not in vain: the army was saved!

Over them now—year following year—
Over their graves, the pine-cones fall,
And the whip-poor-will chants his spectre-call;
But they stir not again: they raise no cheer:
They have ceased. But their glory shall never cease,
Nor their light be quenched in the light of peace.
The rush of their charge is resounding still
That saved the army at Chancellorsville.

NIGHT IN NEW YORK.

STILL as death are the places of life;
  The city seems crumbled and gone,
Sunk 'mid invisible deeps—
The city so lately rife
With the stir of brain and brawn.
Haply it only sleeps;
But what if indeed it were dead,
And another earth should arise
To greet the gray of the dawn?
Faint then our epic would wail
To those who should come in our stead.
But what if that earth were ours?
What if, with holier eyes,
We should meet the new hope, and not
    fail?

1884.

Weary, the night grows pale:
With a blush as of opening flowers
Dimly the east shines red.
Can it be that the morn shall fulfil
My dream, and refashion our clay
As the poet may fashion his rhyme?
Hark to that mingled scream
Rising from workshop and mill—
Hailing some marvellous sight;
Mighty breath of the hours,
Poured through the trumpets of steam;
Awful tornado of time,
Blowing us whither it will.
God has breathed in the nostrils of night,
And behold, it is day!

A WIFE'S FORGIVENESS.

[*An Echo of Passion.* 1882.]

FENN rode up and ascertained that they were coming by the usual road;
then Anice and he set off.

Was that transformation of the moonlight something more than a fantasy?
As they flew forward under the moon, with large stars waiting for them in
advance, just above the sweep of the hills, Fenn was imbued with a kind of
illusion that they had been released for the time being from their ordinary
selves, and were gliding into some other phase less sharply defined, and not
hedged around with too many stubborn realities. Yet he thought of how soon
he must cease to see Anice, and this lent a poignancy to the pleasure of the
ride. It recalled him to himself, and quickened into more acute pain the dull
heart-ache into which the wrath that followed Reeves's attack had soon subsided.

When they rode more slowly, they talked of the beauty of the night and of
incidents at the picnic. The memories of both, however, were busy with that
day when they had first ridden over this road; and, through the unseen
agency that was always at work between them, each was aware that the other's
thoughts were taking this direction.

"We are getting very far ahead of the rest," said Anice, as they ascended
one of the many rises they had to traverse. "Let's stop a moment and listen."

They reined in, and gazed back over the lower ground. The road was
empty; the moonlight looked as if it had lain forever on the woods and passive earth, and as if it would never go away. Transient as it is, there is more
of eternity in this calm illumination than in the swift and stimulating light
of the sun. Fenn thought, "What if we two were to be stricken by some last-

ing change, here in this pale light, and kept together forever in it,—dead, or mute and blind,—yet conscious of our companionship!" It was an unearthly fancy, but his heart throbbed warmly and fiercely under it. He felt an insatiable desire for some isolating fate which should separate them from everybody else. Yet there was a something within him that remonstrated against this desire : for an instant, he even felt the despair of a drowning man, and struggled within himself for something to hold by and keep himself from being drawn under. In vain !

Such silence was in the air that they could hear the whistle of a locomotive at some great distance,—so far that it was hardly louder than the coo of a bird. But nearer and slighter sounds from the road they had been travelling, as is sometimes the case, did not reach them.

"It is strange," said Fenn, in a dry tone that gave no hint of what was going on in his mind, "that we don't hear them coming."

"Very," said Anice. "How fresh and sweet it is here !"

Their voices sounded cold in the moonlight.

"Ah, what was that ? Isn't it the carriages ?"

A faint rumbling of the vehicles could be detected. "Yes; that's they at last," assented Fenn, and immediately touched his horse.

They did not wait again, and when they entered the village they were far in advance. As they came up the hill to the junction of roads which formed an irregular common among the houses, some men moving across this space, with their legs very black against the moonlight, presented a queer appearance.

"Up so far above us, they look like insects crawling on the top of the hill," Fenn observed ; and Anice laughed. They tried to put themselves at ease with trifles of this sort.

He accompanied her at a light trot to the farm-house, where Star was housed by the man, and Fenn's gray hitched in the barn. "I shall wait here," Fenn had explained, "until Mr. Evans comes. I don't like to leave you quite alone."

"Let us go around into the garden, then," said Anice. "There are some seats, and it will be pleasanter there." She was nervous at being thus thrown passively alone with him, and fancied that going into the house would increase her constraint.

The garden lay in an angle between the house and the bank formed by the cutting of the hillside. There were trees here and there ; among them one that was dead ; and their shadows fell with soft abundance on the brightly flooded paths and beds.

"This is where you found those flower-pods that you sent me ?" he asked. It was the first allusion he had made to them.

"Yes," she replied, her voice coming much fainter than she wished. She would have offered some remark to divert him, but her wit failed her.

Fenn stopped abruptly. They were under the shadow of the dead tree.

"I cannot be bound by that symbol," he declared, with resistless impetuosity. "I have thrown those skeletons of flowers away, for my honesty is more than a common one ; and before I go I must speak." She drew back, terrified; but he went on, crying, "No, no! Anice—Anice!—don't judge me as you would other men. There is some fate upon me; I don't know what; I cannot resist it. Oh, I have tried! But the passion that was beginning and never had free play, when I knew you so long ago, has come again, and will not be stifled. I love you, Anice! You cannot tell me of faiths and duties. I only know this one thing, and it is truer than all others."

"This is cowardly," she gasped, when she could. "It is unworthy of you."

"No, it is not cowardly," he answered, pale and determined. "It is braver than to keep a lying face. Have you not seen, have we not both known for weeks what was growing up around us? And is it better to part, with that knowledge smouldering in us, than to face it and speak of it faithfully?"

She collected all her force, and said coldly: "If you knew this, you should have gone away long ago, never to see me on earth again. And will you tell me what you think is to be gained by declaring to me now a love that dishonors us all? It is a sin against yourself, and an unpardonable wrong to me."

He looked at her in rigid silence. "You may deceive yourself," he said, "but you cannot me. You know well—very well—the power you have had over me. I fancied it was a thing that could be turned into some new kind of devotion, like that we talked of. But you saw how it was overcoming me, and you forbade me to see you again. Why do you accuse me, when you had it all in your hands, and allowed our acquaintance to continue?"

"Because I trusted you and wished you well," Anice returned, with less firmness. Then, seeing that the only hope was in an immediate parting, she added: "I shall not leave this garden, Mr. Fenn. It is for you to go!" She pointed commandingly towards the entrance by which they had come in.

For an instant all his strength forsook him. Then he burst into a fierce, broken laugh.

"I understand at last," he said, with a bitter intensity she had never even dreamed of. "You have taken a terrific and skilful vengeance. Out of resentment for a clumsy, boyish mistake, you have deliberately ruined a man's heart, and made him put his honor in the dust before you. Yes, I'll go." He turned, so dizzy that he could hardly see the path, and began to move away.

There was a moment of passionate effort on her part to repress the storm within herself; but as she beheld him receding she yielded, and made a detaining gesture. He saw it, and came back rapidly.

"Am I wrong?" he cried, searching her face. "You felt more than that; you—you loved! Tell me it was so."

She tried to steady herself by putting her hands out into the air. Then she gasped, "No—no!"

"You did not?" he repeated.

But she could no longer reply. She was on the point of falling; and with an instinct of protection he stretched out his arms, almost enfolding her in them. As they stood thus for an instant, the shadow of the dead tree lay motionless upon them, and the icy moonlight around gave visible bounds to that isolation for which he had so lately wished.

She had confessed nothing; but at that instant Fenn felt that all had been confessed between them. He saw, with a pity that wrung his heart, what her struggle had been ; and remorse struck through him like a sword, for his own sin against Ethel, and for the attitude into which he had forced this woman who stood with him here. Was this the joy of liberation he had looked forward to ?

Anice recovered herself at once. She drew away from his contact and held on to the bench near at hand. "This will kill me!" she was moaning, like one only half conscious. "All these years—No ; oh, no ! You must leave me instantly. For Ethel's sake go ; go ! Tell her all you have said,—everything."

"Thank God, Anice, you are nobler than I !" Uttering these words with lips that seemed chilled by a frost, he fled.   .   .   .   .

When he came into the hotel, those who saw him wondered at the breathless and exhausted appearance about his face, ordinarily so strong and composed and glowing with healthy color ; but they attributed it to anxiety, for his first words were an inquiry about his wife.   .   .   .   .

He stood still in the street, and noticed all at once that the moonlight had nearly waned,—the weird illumination which, an hour or two before, had seemed so permanent. It gave him a bitter satisfaction to think how his madness had crumbled and slipped away with it. A huge field of cloud was rising, and had swallowed half the stars.

"Oh, my God ! If I should never see Ethel again ! What if some accident has happened, from which she will die?"

This was the cry in his heart.

A horse and rider, springing out of the feeble light a little way off, and dashing by, roused him. It had been but a flash, but the face of Kingsmill seemed to be printed on the night air, and to be lingering behind like a vision, while the rider swept on.

Fenn ran after him towards the hotel, at his greatest speed. The young man was there already, dismounted, quivering with excitement, and talking to a little dusky group of men.

"What is it?" cried Fenn, with an awful fear, as the others fell back before him.

"There has been an accident," said Kingsmill, rapidly.

"Where? Tell me where?"

"The railroad crossing "——

"Is she killed?" The words burst from Fenn like the red drops that spurt from a knife-thrust.

"She was not badly hurt," said Kingsmill. "The cars struck them just as they had got over, and they were thrown out. But some people are taking care of them."

"I must go !" cried Fenn wildly, rushing to get Kingsmill's horse, which was being led away.

"Not that one !" exclaimed the owner. "I have a fresh one in the stable."

There was a sharp scurry to saddle the fresh steed, and just as Fenn put his foot in the stirrup the farmer from Mr. Evans's came up with the tired gray and a message from Anice, who had also become alarmed.

George Parsons Lathrop.

" For God's sake, go and tell her, Kingsmill ! " shouted Fenn, mounting.

The next instant his horse had shot away, under spur, for the tannery road.

. . . .

It was a solemn group that wound up the highway from the railroad crossing, coming back.

By the time the wagon that had been obtained was ready to start, Anice, also, had arrived on horseback ; and the two mounted figures moved at a funereal pace beside the cart. Ethel had fainted at first, but was restored ; and, unless she had suffered internal hurt, was judged to be the worse only for a few bruises. Mr. Evans had not come off so well. He had a broken arm, and was prostrated by the shock he had sustained. His light carriage was left behind, a partial wreck, and the borrowed wagon had to proceed slowly, in order to avoid possible injury to the sufferer.

Fenn and Anice did not exchange a word, but both were lost in wonder at the chance that had thus brought them together again on this same night, under such altered conditions. From time to time Fenn, bringing his horse close to the wheels on Ethel's side, spoke some low word of inquiry or soothing, as indistinguishable to any but her ear as the murmur of the night breeze in the pines. Sometimes, when he fell back and watched the muffled forms reclining in the wagon, a picture presented itself to him in which he saw Ethel as she might have been, motionless and darkly covered and insensible to the jolting of the springs,—a picture of the dead being brought home silently from the place of her death ; and then he would turn away and curse himself, in the midst of a mute thanksgiving.

The chemist sat by his wife all night and watched, while she slept, after many vain attempts. In the morning, the physician who had been telegraphed for from a distance arrived, and pronounced with some confidence that she had no unseen injuries.

It was late in the afternoon that Fenn knelt by his wife's bed, while a soft light from the fading west pervaded the room. Seeing that she was strong and recovered, he spoke : " Ethel, I cannot put off any longer the confession I must make of the wrong that has been in my heart these last few weeks."

" I have been afraid," she answered calmly. " Oh, yes, I knew "; and the tears rose in her eyes. " But I must not hear it. I cannot."

The blood mounted to his face. " How despicable I am ! " he groaned. " But you don't know all, Ethel. You cannot know that I told her "——

She covered her face with her hands, crying, " Oh, why must I believe this ! Why can't I forget it all, pretend that I did not see ? " Then, with a hot beating in her temples, she took away her hands, and said with forced deliberation, " Never tell me any more. I cannot promise to be the same to you or to hold you so ; but I will hear nothing. Only tell me,—did you mean to do me a wrong ? Are you true to me ? "

" The wrong," he replied, " was a madness, an infatuation. That was all. But I am not fit, now, even to say I am true to you." He lifted his eyes to hers.

She looked into them with a calm, just scrutiny; and Fenn thought that he knew what the light in the recording angel's eyes must be like. But it was only the glance of a tender woman possessing deep intuitions. She said at length: "I will believe in you."

Ethel put her hand upon his head, with a touch so simple and gentle that it was the best of benedictions.

He had held, once, that there was a peculiar mystery about Anice, and the belief had made her the more dangerously fascinating. Ethel was transparent enough, exteriorly; but the mystery of her nature lay deeper down, and he was only just beginning to apprehend it. The quality in Anice served merely as a unit of measure for its larger presence in Ethel. Kneeling here before his wife, with too much humility in him even to put his lips to hers, Fenn saw that he was touching the mystery which is profounder than intellectual choice; which diffuses itself through earth and heaven, and solves all but explains nothing,—pure love.

THE PHŒBE-BIRD.

YES, I was wrong about the phœbe-bird:
  Two songs it has, and both of them I've heard.
I did not know those strains of joy and sorrow
Came from one throat, or that each note could borrow
Strength from the other, making one more brave
And one as sad as rain-drops on a grave.

But thus it is. Two songs have men and maidens:
One is for hey-day, one for sorrow's cadence.
Our voices vary with the changing seasons
Of life's long year, for deep and natural reasons.

Therefore despair not. Think not you have altered
If, at some time, the gayer note has faltered.
We are as God has made us. Gladness, pain,
Delight and death, and moods of bliss or bane,
With love and hate or good and evil—all
At separate times in separate accents call;
Yet 'tis the same heart-throb within the breast
That gives an impulse to our worst and best.
I doubt not when our earthly cries are ended,
The Listener finds them in one music blended.

THE SUNSHINE OF THINE EYES.

THE sunshine of thine eyes,
  (O still, celestial beam!)
Whatever it touches it fills
  With the life of its lambent gleam.

The sunshine of thine eyes,
  Oh, let it fall on me!
Though I be but a mote of the air,
  I could turn to gold for thee.

THE FLOWN SOUL.

FRANCIS HAWTHORNE LATHROP, 6 FEBRUARY, 1881.

COME not again! I dwell with you
  Above the realm of frost and dew,
Of pain and fire, and growth to death.
I dwell with you where never breath
Is drawn, but fragrance vital flows
From life to life; even as a rose
Unseen pours sweetness through each
    vein,
And from the air distils again.
You are my rose unseen: we live
Where each to other joy may give
In ways untold, by means unknown
And secret as the magnet-stone.

  For which of us, indeed, is dead ?
No more I lean to kiss your head ;—
The gold-red hair so thick upon it:
Joy feels no more the touch that won it,
When o'er my brow your pearl-cool palm
In tenderness so childish, calm,
Crept softly, once. Yet, see: my arm
Is strong, and still my blood runs warm:
    1883.

I still can work and think, and weep.
But all this show of life I keep
Is but the shadow of your shine;
Flicker of your fire; husk of your vine:
Therefore you are not dead, nor I,
Who hear your laughter's minstrelsy.
Among the stars your feet are set:
Your little feet are dancing yet
Their rhythmic beat, as when on earth.
So swift, so slight, are death and birth!

  Come not again, dear child. If thou
By any chance couldst break that vow
Of silence, at thy last hour made;
If to this grim life, unafraid,
Thou couldst return, and melt the frost
Wherein thy bright limbs' power was
    lost;
Still would I whisper—since so fair
The silent comradeship we share—
Yes, whisper 'mid the unbidden rain
Of tears: "Come not! Come not again!"

Rose Hawthorne Lathrop.

BORN in Lenox, Mass., 1851.

A SONG BEFORE GRIEF.

[*Along the Shore.* 1888.]

SORROW, my friend,
  When shall you come again ?
The wind is slow, and the bent willows send
  Their silvery motions wearily down the plain.
The bird is dead
  That sang this morning through the summer rain!

Sorrow, my friend,
  I owe my soul to you.
And if my life with any glory end
  Of tenderness for others, and the words are true,
Said, honoring, when I'm dead,—
  Sorrow, to you, the mellow praise, the funeral wreath, are due.

And yet, my friend,
  When love and joy are strong,
Your terrible visage from my sight I rend
  With glances to blue heaven.   Hovering along,
By mine your shadow led,
  "Away!" I shriek, "nor dare to work my new-sprung mercies wrong!"

Still, you are near:
  Who can your care withstand ?
When deep eternity shall look most clear,
  Sending bright waves to kiss the trembling land,
My joy shall disappear,—
  A flaming torch thrown to the golden sea by your pale hand.

TWENTY BOLD MARINERS.

TWENTY bold mariners went to the wave,
  Twenty sweet breezes blew over the main;
All were so hearty, so free, and so brave,—
  But they never came back again!

Half the wild ocean rose up to the clouds,
  Half the broad sky scowled in thunder and rain;
Twenty white crests rose around them like shrouds,
  And they stayed in the dancing main!

This is easy to sing, and often to mourn,
  And the breaking of dawn is no newer to-day;
But those who die young or are left forlorn,
  Think grief is no older than they!

THE LOST BATTLE.

TO his heart it struck such terror
  That he laughed a laugh of scorn—
The man in the soldier's doublet,
  With the sword so bravely worn.

It struck his heart like the frost-wind
  To find his comrades fled,
While the battle-field was guarded
  By the heroes who lay dead.

He drew his sword in the sunlight,
  And called with a long halloo:

"Dead men, there is one living
  Shall stay it out with you!"

He raised a ragged standard,
  This lonely soul in war,
And called the foe to onset,
  With shouts they heard afar.

They galloped swiftly toward him.
  The banner floated wide;
It sank; he sank beside it
  Upon his sword, and died.

DOROTHY.

DEAR little Dorothy, she is no more!
   I have wandered world-wide, from shore to shore,
I have seen as great beauties as ever were wed;
But none can console me for Dorothy dead.

Dear little Dorothy! How strange it seems
That her face is less real than the faces of dreams;
That the love which kept true, and the lips which so spoke,
Are more lost than my heart, which died not when it broke!

William Crary Brownell.

BORN in New York, N. Y., 1851.

THE FRENCHWOMAN.

[*French Traits.* 1889.]

THE domesticity aimed at by the Spanish convent and cultivated by the Germanic hearth and chimney-corner is in no sense the object of the Frenchman's ambition for the Frenchwoman. Here as elsewhere his social instinct triumphs over every other, and he regards the family circle as altogether too narrow a sphere for the activities of a being who occupies so much of his mind and heart, and in whose consideration he is as much concerned as she in his. To be the mother of his children and the nurse of his declining years is a destiny which, unrelieved by the gratification of her own instincts of expansion, he would as little wish for her as she would for herself. To be the ornament of a society, to awake perpetual interest, to be perpetually and universally charming, to contribute powerfully to the general aims of her environment, never to lose her character as woman in any of the phases or functions of womanly existence, even in wifehood or maternity—this central motive of the Frenchwoman's existence is cordially approved by the Frenchman. In fact it is because he approves and insists upon it that she is what she is. It is for this reason that she devotes so much attention to dress, which in her thus, spite of those surface indications that mislead the foreigner, is almost never due to the passion for dress in itself to which similar preoccupation infallibly testifies in the women of other societies. A New York belle dresses for her rivals—when she does not, like the aborigines of her species, dress for herself alone. Mr. Henry James acutely represents the Mrs. Westgate of his "International Episode" as "sighing to think the Duchess would never know how well she was dressed." To induce analogous regret in a Frenchwoman a corresponding masculine obtuseness would be absolutely indispensable. And this among her own countrymen she would never encounter. Her dress, then,

is a part of her coquetry—one of the most important weapons in a tolerably
well-stocked arsenal ; but it is nothing more, and it in no degree betokens
frivolity.   Like her figure and her carriage it is a continual ocular demonstration and a strong ally of her instinct, her genius, for *style*.   In these three regards she is unapproachable, and in every other attribute of style she is certainly unsurpassed.   In elegance, in intelligence, in self-possession, in poise,
it would be difficult to find exceptions in other countries to rival the average
Parisienne.   And her coquetry, which endues her style with the element of
charm (of which it is, as I said, the science), is neither more nor less than the
instinct to please highly developed.   It is not, as certainly coquetry elsewhere
may sometimes be called, the instinct to please deeply perverted.   The French
coquette does not flirt.   Her frivolity, her superficiality, may be great in many
directions—in religion, in moral steadfastness, in renunciation, in constancy,
even in sensibility—but in coquetry she is never superficial ; the dimly veiled,
half acknowledged insincerity of what is known as flirtation would seem to
her frivolous to a degree unsuspected by her American contemporary.   To
her as to her countrymen the relations of men and women are too important
and too interesting not to be at bottom entirely serious.

In fine, to estimate the Frenchwoman's moral nature with any approach to
adequacy it is necessary entirely to avoid viewing her from an Anglo-Saxon
standpoint.   Apart from her *milieu* she is not to be understood at all.   The
ideals of woman in general held by this *milieu* are wholly different from our
ideals.   To see how and wherein let us inquire of some frank French friend.
"We shall never agree about women," he will be sure to admit at the outset ;
and he may be imagined to continue very much in this strain : "We Frenchmen have a repugnance, both instinctive and explicit, to your propensity to
make *companionability* the essential quality of the ideal woman.   Consciously
or unconsciously this is precisely what you do.   It is in virtue of their being
more companionable, and in an essentially masculine sense, that the best of
your women, the serious ones, shine superior in your eyes to their frivolous
or pedantic rivals.   You seem to us, in fact, to approach far more nearly than
your English cousins to the ideal in this respect of your common Gothic ancestors.   Your ideal is pretty closely the Alruna woman—an august creature
spiritually endowed with inflexible purity and lofty, respect-compelling virtues, performing the office of a 'guiding-star' amid the perplexities of life,
whose approval or censure is important in a thousand moral exigencies, and
one's feeling for whom is always strongly tinctured—even in the days of courtship—with something akin to filial feeling.   In your daily life this ideal becomes, of course, familiarized—you do not need to be reminded that 'familiarized' is, indeed, an extenuating term to describe the effect upon many of
your ideals when they are brought into the atmosphere of your daily life, that
the contrast between American ideals and American practice frequently strikes
us as grotesque.   In the atmosphere of your daily life the Alruna woman becomes a good fellow.   She despises girls who flirt, as you yourselves despise
our dandies and our *petits jeunes gens*.   She despises with equal vigor the
lackadaisical, the hysterical, the affected in any way.   She plays a good game
of tennis ; it is one of her ambitions to cast a fly adroitly, to handle an oar

Very truly yours.

W. C. Brownell.

well. She is by no means a Di Vernon. She has a thoroughly masculine antipathy to the romantic, and is embarrassed in its presence. She reads the
journals ; she has opinions, which, unlike her inferior sisters, she rarely obtrudes. She is tremendously efficient and never poses. She is saved from
masculinity by great tact, great delicacy in essentials, by her beauty which is
markedly feminine, by her immensely narrower sphere, and by Divine Providence. She is thus thoroughly companionable, and she is after all a woman.
This makes her immensely attractive to you. But nothing could be less seductive to us than this predominance of companionableness over the feminine
element, the element of sex. Of our women, ideal and real (which you know
in France, the country of equality, of homogeneity, of averages, is nearly the
same thing), we could better say that they are thoroughly feminine and that
they are, after all, companionable. Indeed, if what I understand by ' companionable ' be correct, i.e., *rien que s'entendre,* they are quite as much so as
their American sisters, though in a very different way, it is true.

    " Let me explain. The strictness of your social code effectually shuts off
the American woman from interest in, and the American girl from knowledge
of, what is really the essential part of nearly half of life ; I mean from any
mental occupation except in their more superficial aspects with the innumerable phenomena attending one of the two great instincts from which modern
science has taught us to derive all the moral perceptions and habits of human
life. This is explainable no doubt by the unwritten but puissant law which
informs every article of your social constitution that relates to women : name-
ly, the law that insures the precedence of the young girl over the married woman. With you, indeed, the young girl has *le haut du pavé* in what seems to
us a very terrible degree. Your literature, for example, is held by her in a
bondage which to us seems abject, and makes us esteem it superficial. 'Since
the author of " Tom Jones " no one has been permitted to depict a man as he
really is,' complains Thackeray. With you it is even worse, because the young
girl exercises an even greater tyranny than in England. Nothing so forcibly
illustrates her position at the head of your society, however—not even her
overwhelming predominance in all your social reunions within and without
doors, winter and summer, at luncheons, dinners, lawn-parties, balls, receptions, lectures, and church—as the circumstance that you endeavor successfully to keep her a girl after she has become a woman. You desire and contrive that your wives shall be virgins in word, thought, and aspiration. That
this should be the case before marriage every one comprehends. That is the
end of our endeavor equally with yours. In every civilized society men wish
to be themselves the introducers and instructors of their wives in a realm of
such real and vital interest as that of which marriage, everywhere but in your
country, opens the door. But with us the young girl is constantly looking
forward to becoming, and envying the condition of, a woman. That is the
source of our restrictions, of our conventual regulations, which seem to you
so absurd, even so dishonoring. You are saved from having such, however,
by the fact that with you the young girl is the rounded and complete ideal,
the type of womanhood, and that it is her condition, spiritually speaking,
that the wife and even the mother emulate. And you desire ardently that

they should. You do not 'see any necessity,' as you say in your utilitarian phraseology, of a woman's 'losing' anything of the fresh and clear charm which perfumes the existence of the young girl. You have a short way of disposing of our notion that a woman is the flower and fulfilment of that of which the young girl is the bud and the promise. You esteem this notion a piece of sophistry designed to conceal our really immoral desire to rob our women of the innocence and *naïveté* which we insist upon in the young girl, in order that our social life may be more highly spiced. Your view is wholly different from that of your race at the epoch of its most considerable achievements in the 'criticism of life' and antecedent to the Anglo-Saxon invention of prudery as a bulwark of virtue. It is a view which seems to spring directly from the Puritan system of each individual managing independently his own spiritual affairs without any of the reciprocal aids and the division of labor provided for in the more elaborate scheme of Catholicism, in consequence of which each individual left in this way wholly to himself is forced into a timid and distrustful attitude toward temptation. Nothing is more noticeable in your women, thus, than a certain suspicious and timorous exclusion from the field of contemplation of anything unsuited to the attention of the young girl. It is as if they feared contamination for virtue if the attitude and habit of mind belonging to innocence were once abandoned. They probably do fear vaguely that you fear it for them, that your feminine ideal excludes it.

"Now, it is very evident that however admirable in its results this position may be, and however sound in itself, it involves an important limitation of that very companionableness which you so much insist on in your women. In this sense, the average Frenchwoman is an equal, a companion, to a degree almost never witnessed with you. After an hour of feminine society we do not repair to the club for a relaxation of mind and spirit, for a respiration of expansion, and to find in unrestrained freedom an enjoyment that has the additional sense of being a relief. Our clubs are in fact mere excuses for gambling, not refuges for bored husbands and homeless bachelors. Conversation among men is perhaps grosser in quality, the *équivoque* is perhaps not so delicate, so *spirituelle*, but they do not differ in kind from the conversational tissue in mixed company, as with you they do so widely. With you this difference in kind is notoriously an abyss. In virtue of our invention of treating delicate topics with innuendo, our mixed society gains immensely in interest and attractiveness, and our women are more intimately companionable than yours.　.　.　.　.

"Even if your women were intimately companionable they would none the less radically differ from our own; we should still reproach them with a certain masculine quality in the elevated, and a certain prosaic note in the familiar types. By masculine, I certainly do not here intend the signification you give to your derisive epithet 'strong-minded.' In affirming that there is a generous ampleness in the feminine quality of our women unobservable in yours, I do not mean to charge them with inferiority in what you call 'pure mentality'; in intelligence and capacities we believe them unequalled the world over. But they are essentially less masculine in avoiding strictly all competition with men, in conserving all their individuality of sex and following their own bent. Nothing is more common than to hear American women lament their lack of opportunity, envy the opportunity of men. Nothing is rarer with us. It never occurs to a Frenchwoman to regret her sex. It is probable that almost every American woman with any pretensions to 'pure mentality,' feels, on the contrary, that her sex is a limitation, and wishes, with that varying ardor and intermittent energy which characterize her, that she were a man and had a man's opportunity. In a thousand ways she is the man's rival, which with us she never is. Hence the popularity with you of the agitation for woman suffrage, practically unknown in France.   .   .   .

"The difference is nowhere so luminously illustrated as in the respective attitudes of French and American women toward the institution of marriage. With us from the hour when she begins first to think at all of her future—an epoch which arrives probably much earlier than with you—marriage is the end and aim of a woman's existence. And it is so consciously and deliberately. A large part of her conduct is influenced by this particular prospect. It is the conscious and deliberate aim also of her parents or guardians for her. They constantly remind her of it. Failure to attain it is considered by her and by them as the one great failure, to avoid which every effort should tend, every aspiration be directed. In its excess this becomes either ludicrous or repulsive as one looks at it. 'Si tu veux te marier, ne fais jamais ça'—'Cela t'empêchera de te marier'—who has not been fatigued with such maternal admonitions which resound in interiors by no means always of the *basse classe?* But the result is that marriage occupies a share of the young girl's mind and meditation which to your young girls would undoubtedly seem disproportionate, and indeed involve a sense of shame. There is no more provision in the French social constitution than in the order of nature itself for the old maid. Her fate is eternal eccentricity, and is correspondingly dreaded among us who dread nothing more than exclusion from the sympathies of society and a share in its organized activities. Marriage once attained, the young girl, though become by it a woman, is not of course essentially changed, but only more highly organized in her original direction. You may be surprised to hear that sometimes it suffices her—as it suffices English, and used to American women; though it must be admitted that our society does not make of even marriage an excuse for exacting the sum of a woman's activities which it is the Anglo-Saxon tendency to do, and that thus her merit is less conspicuous. If marriage do not suffice her, it is not in 'Sorosis' or Dorcas or Browning societies, or art or books that she seeks distraction, but in the consolation strictly cognate to that of marriage which society offers her. Accordingly, whatever goes to make up the distinctively feminine side of woman's nature tends with us to become highly developed. It acquires a refinement, a subtlety, of organization quite unknown to societies whose ideal women inspire filial feeling. We have as a rule very few Cornelias. Our mothers themselves are far from being Spartan. The Gothic goddess is practically unknown in France. 'Woman's sphere,' as you call it, is totally distinct from man's. The action and reaction of the two which produce the occupation, the amusement, the life of society are far more intimate than with you, but they are the exact reverse of homogeneous.

"It is an inevitable corollary from this that that sentimental side which you seem to us to be endeavoring to subordinate in your more serious women, receives in the Frenchwoman that greatest of all benefits, a harmonious and natural development. Before and after marriage, and however marriage may turn for her, it is her disposition to love and her capacity for loving which are stimulated constantly by her surroundings, and which are really the measure of the esteem in which she is held. To love intensely and passionately is her ideal. It is so much her ideal that if marriage does not enable her to attain it, it is a virtue rather than a demerit in her eyes to seek it elsewhere. Not to die before having attained in its fulness this end of the law of her being is often the source of the Frenchwoman's tragic disasters. But even when indubitable disaster arrives to her it is at least tragic, and a tragedy of this kind is in itself glorious. To remain spiritually an *être incomplet* is to her nearly as dreadful a fate as to become a monstrosity. Both are equally hostile to nature, and we have a national passion for being in harmony with nature. It is probably impossible to make you comprehend how far this is carried by us. Take the life of George Sand as an instance. It was incontestably the inspiration of her works, and to us it is the reverse of reprehensible, 'for she loved much'; it is not her elopement with Musset but her desertion of him that indicates to our mind her weak side. In this way the attitude of the Frenchwoman toward love is one of perfect frankness. So far from dissembling its nature—either transcendentally or pietistically, after the fashion of your maidens, or mystically, after the fashion in the *pays de Gretchen*—she appreciates it directly and simply as a passion, and for her the most potent of the passions, the passion whose praise has been the burden of all the poets since the morning stars first sang together, and whose possession shares equally with the possession of superior intelligence the honor of distinguishing man from the lower animals. This is why to our women, as much as to our men, your literature, your 'criticism of life,' seems pale, as we say—pale and superficial. This is why we had such an *engouement* for your Byron and never heard of your Wordsworth. This is why we occupy ourselves so much with cognate subjects as you will have remarked.

"And the sentimental side, being thus naturally and harmoniously developed, becomes thus naturally and spontaneously the instrument of woman's power and the source of her dignity. Through it she seeks her triumphs and attains her ends. To it is due not her influence over men—as with your inveterate habit of either divorcing the sexes into a friendly rivalry or associating them upon the old-fashioned, English, harem-like basis, you would inevitably express it—but her influence upon society. This results in a great gain to women themselves—increases indefinitely their dignity and power. It is axiomatic that anything inevitable and not in itself an evil it is far better to utilize than to resist. Every one acknowledges the eminence of the sentimental side in woman's nature, the great part which it plays in her conduct, the great influence it has upon her motives. And since it has, therefore, inevitably to be reckoned with, its development accomplishes for women results which could not be hoped for if sentiment were merely treated as an inevitable handicap to be modified and mitigated. Your own logic seems to us exceedingly singular. You argue that men and women should be equal, that the present regrettable inequality with you is due to the greater influence of sentiment on women's minds in viewing purely intellectual matters (you are constantly throwing this up to your woman suffragists), and that therefore the way in which women are to be improved and elevated (as you curiously express it) is clearly by the repression of their sentiment. It is the old story: you are constantly teaching your women to envy the opportunities of men, to regret their 'inferiority' hitherto, and to endeavor to emulate masculine virtues by mastering their emotions and suppressing their sentiment; that is to say, you are constantly doing this by indirection and unconsciously, at least, and by betraying the fact that such is your ideal for them. You never seem to think they can be treated as a fundamentally different order of capacity and disposition. I remember listening for two hours to one of your cleverest women lecturing on Joan of Arc, and the thesis of her lecture was that there was no mystery at all about the Maid and her accomplishments, except the eternal mystery of transcendent military genius, that she was in fact a female Napoleon and that it was the 'accident of sex' simply that had prevented her from being so esteemed by the purblind masculine prejudice which had theretofore dominated people's minds. Thinking of what Jeanne d'Arc stands for to us Frenchmen, of her place in our imaginations, of the way in which she illustrates for us the puissance of the essentially feminine element in humanity, I said to myself, 'No, the Americans and we will never agree about women.'"

Henry Woodfen Grady.

BORN in Athens, Ga., 1851.   DIED in Atlanta, Ga., 1889.

THE SOFTER ASPECTS OF SLAVERY.

[*From a Series of Articles on "The New South."—The New York Ledger.* 1889.]

PERHAPS no period of human history has been more misjudged and less understood than the slave-holding era in the South. Slavery as an institution cannot be defended; but its administration was so nearly perfect among our forefathers as to challenge and hold our loving respect. It is doubtful if the world has seen a peasantry so happy and so well-to-do as the negro slaves in America. The world was amazed at the fidelity with which these slaves guarded, from 1861 to 1865, the homes and families of the masters who were fighting with the army that barred their way to freedom. If "Uncle Tom's Cabin" had portrayed the rule of slavery rather than the rarest exception, not all the armies that went to the field could have stayed the flood of rapine and arson and pillage that would have started with the first gun of the civil war. Instead of that, witness the miracle of the slave in loyalty to his master, closing the fetters upon his own limbs—maintaining and defending the families of those who fought against his freedom—and at night on the far-off battle-field searching among the carnage for his young master, that he might lift the dying head to his breast and bend to catch the last words to the old folks at home, so wrestling the meantime in agony and love that he would lay down his life in his master's stead.

History has no parallel to the faith kept by the negro in the South during the war. Often five hundred negroes to a single white man, and yet through these dusky throngs the women and children walked in safety, and the unprotected homes rested in peace. Unmarshalled, the black battalions moved patiently to the fields in the morning to feed the armies their idleness would have starved, and at night gathered anxiously at the big house to "hear the news from marster," though conscious that his victory made their chains enduring. Everywhere humble and kindly. The body-guard of the helpless. The rough companion of the little ones. The observant friend. The silent sentry in his lowly cabin. The shrewd counsellor. And when the dead came home, a mourner at the open grave. A thousand torches would have disbanded every Southern army, but not one was lighted. When the master, going to a war in which slavery was involved, said to his slave, "I leave my home and loved ones in your charge," the tenderness between man and master stood disclosed.

The Northern man, dealing with casual servants, querulous, sensitive, and lodged for a day in a sphere they resent, can hardly comprehend the friendliness and sympathy that existed between the master and the slave. He cannot understand how the negro stood in slavery days, open-hearted and sympathetic, full of gossip and comradeship, the companion of the hunt, frolic, furrow, and home, contented in the kindly dependence that has been a habit of his blood, and never lifting his eyes beyond the narrow horizon that shut him in with his neighbors and friends. But this relation did exist in the days of slavery. It was the rule of that *régime.* It has survived war, and strife, and political campaigns in which the drum-beat inspired and Federal bayonets fortified. It will never die until the last slave-holder and slave has been gathered to rest. It is the glory of our past in the South. It is the answer to abuse and slander. It is the hope of our future.

The relations of the races in slavery must be clearly understood to understand what has followed, and to judge of what is yet to come. Not less important is it to have some clear idea of the civilization of that period.

That was a peculiar society. Almost feudal in its splendor, it was almost patriarchal in its simplicity. Leisure and wealth gave it exquisite culture. Its wives and mothers, exempt from drudgery, and almost from care, gave to their sons, through patient and constant training, something of their own grace and gentleness and to their homes beauty and light. Its people, homogeneous by necessity, held straight and simple faith, and were religious to a marked degree along the old lines of Christian belief. This same homogeneity bred a hospitality that was as kinsmen to kinsmen, and that wasted at the threshold of every home what the more frugal people of the North conserved and invested in public charities. The code duello furnished the highest appeal in dispute. An affront to a lad was answered at the pistol's mouth. The

H. W. Grady.

sense of quick responsibility tempered the tongues of even the most violent, and the newspapers of South Carolina for eight years, it is said, did not contain one abusive word. The ownership of slaves, even more than of realty, held families steadfast on their estates, and everywhere prevailed the sociability of established neighborhoods. Money counted least in making the social status, and constantly ambitious and brilliant youngsters from no estate married into the families of planter princes. Meanwhile the one character utterly condemned and ostracized was the man who was mean to his slaves. Even the coward was pitied and might have been liked. For the cruel master there was no toleration.

The *ante-bellum* society had immense force. Working under the slavery which brought the suspicion or hostility of the world, and which practically beleaguered it within walls, it yet accomplished good things. For the first sixty-four years of the republic it furnished the president for fifty-two years. Its statesmen demanded the war of 1812, opened it with but five Northern senators supporting it, and its general, Jackson, won the decisive battle of New Orleans. It was a Southern statesman who added the Louisiana territory of more than 1,000,000 square miles to our domain. Under a Southern statesman Florida was acquired from Spain. Against the opposition of the free States, the Southern influence forced the war with Mexico, and annexed the superb empire of Texas, brought in New Mexico, and opened the gates of the republic to the Pacific. Scott and Taylor, the heroes of the Mexican war, were Southern men. In material, as in political affairs, the old South was masterful. The first important railroad operated in America traversed Carolina. The first steamer that crossed the ocean cleared from Savannah. The first college established for girls was opened in Georgia. No naturalist has surpassed Audubon ; no geographer equalled Maury ; and Sims and McDonald led the world of surgery in their respective lines. It was Crawford Long, of Georgia, who gave to the world the priceless blessing of anæsthesia. The wealth accumulated by the people was marvellous. And, though it is held that slavery enriched the poor at the general expense, Georgia and Carolina were the richest States, per capita, in the Union in 1860, saving Rhode Island. Some idea of the desolation of war may be had from the fact that, in spite of their late remarkable recuperation, they are now, excepting Idaho, the poorest States, per capita, in the Union. So rich was the South in 1860, that Mr. Lincoln spoke but common sentiment when he said : "If we let the South go, where shall we get our revenues ?"

In its engaging grace—in the chivalry that tempered even Quixotism with dignity—in the piety that saved master and slave alike—in the charity that boasted not—in the honor held above estate—in the hospitality that neither condescended nor cringed—in frankness and heartiness and wholesome comradeship—in the reverence paid to womanhood and the inviolable respect in which woman's name was held—the civilization of the old slave *régime* in the South has not been surpassed, and perhaps will not be equalled, among men.

And as the fidelity of the slave during the war bespoke the kindness of the master before the war, so the unquestioning reverence with which the young men of the South accepted, in 1865, their heritage of poverty and defeat, proved the strength and excellence of the civilization from which that heritage had come. In cheerfulness they bestirred themselves amid the ashes and the wrecks, and, holding the inspiration of their past to be better than their rich acres and garnered wealth, went out to rebuild their fallen fortunes, with never a word of complaint, nor the thought of criticism!

John Alfred Macon.

BORN in Demopolis, Ala., 1851.

TERPSICHORE IN THE FLAT CREEK QUARTERS.

[Contributed to the Century Magazine. 1880–83.]

LISTEN when I call de figgers! Watch de music es you go!
   Chassay forrard! (Now look at 'em! some too fas' an' some too slow!)
Step out when I gibs de order; keep up eben wid de line;
What's got in dem lazy niggers? Stop dat stringin' out behin'!
All go forrard to de centre! Balance roun' an' den go back!
Keep on in de proper 'rection, right straight up an' down de crack!
Moobe up sides an' mind de music; listen when you hear me speak!
(Jes' look at dem Pea Ridge niggers, how dey's buckin' 'gin de Creek!)
Dat's de proper action, Sambo! den you done de biznis right!
Now show 'em how you knocked de splinters at de shuckin' t'udder night;
Try to do yqur lebbel bes', an' stomp it like you use to do!
Jes' come down on de "Flat Creek step" an' show de Ridge a thing or two!
Now look at dat limber Jonah tryin' to tech de fancy fling!
(Who ebber seed a yaller nigger dat could cut de pidgin-wing?)
Try dat lick agin, dar, Moses; tell you what, dat's hard to beat!
(How kin sich a little nigger handle sich a pile o' feet?)
Swing your corners! Turn your pardners! ('Pears de motion's gittin' slow.)
What's de matter wid de music? Put some rosgum on dat bow!
Moobe up, Tom—don't be so sleepy! Let 'em see what you kin do!
Light off in de "gra'-vine-twis'" an' knock de "double-shuffle," too!
Gosh! dat double-j'inted Steben flings a hifalutin hoof!
He kicks de dus' plum out de planks an' jars de shingles on de roof!
Steady, now, an' check de motion! Let de fiddler stop de chune!
I smell de 'possum froo de crack, an' supper's gwine to call you soon!
De white folks come it mighty handy, waltzin' 'roun' so nice an' fine;
But when you come to reg'lar *dancin'*, *niggers leabes 'em way behin'*!

POLITICS AT THE LOG-ROLLING.

I B'LEBES dat any nigger's in a sorry sort o' way
  Dat swallows all de racket dat de politicians say;
For I's been a grown-up cullud man some forty years or so,
An' I's heard 'em make de same old 'sertions heap o' times befo'.
Dar's lots o' cussed foolishness an' gassin', anyway,
'Bout bustin' up de Consterchusion eb'ry 'lection-day;
'Cause I gib it as de notion ob a plain an' humble man,
Dat de Gub'ment an' de country, too, is tough enough to stan'.
I nebber takes more polertics den one good man kin tote,
An' I don't need any 'visin' when I go to drap my vote;
I talks wid all de canerdates, an' tell 'em what I choose,
But I goes in on de side dat gibs *de biggest bobbykews!*

THE OLD SHIP OF ZION.

OH! eb'rything's ready,—
  De wind is steady,
An' de folks keep a-crowdin' to de gospel
  ship;
'Tis de best time to ride
On de Jordan tide—
Dar's no use o' waitin' for the 'scursion
  trip!

Dey's a-loosenin' de line,
  An' soon she'll be gwine,
For yonder come de deck-hands to push
  her off de bank;
She's a-puffin'! she's a-puffin'!
An' she nebber waits for nuffin'—
Better git abode, sinners, 'fo' dey *pull in
  de plank!*

THE WEDDING ON THE CREEK.

OH! I's got to string de banjer 'g'inst de closin' ob de week,
  For dar's gwine to be a weddin' 'mongst de niggers on de Creek.
Dey's gittin' up a frolic, an' dar's gwine to be a noise
When de Plantation knocks ag'in' de Slab Town boys!
Dar'll be stranger folks a-plenty, an' de gals is comin' too,
All lubly as de day-break, an' fresher dan de jew!
A'nt Dinah's gittin' ready, wid her half a dozen daughters,
An' little Angelina, fum de Chinkypen Quarters;
Anudder gal's a-comin', but I couldn't tell her name;
She's sweet as 'lasses candy an' pretty all de same!
She's nicer dan a rose-bush an' lubly ebrywhar
Fum de bottom ob her slippers to de wroppin's in her ha'r.
Lordy mussy 'pon me, how 'twill flusterate de niggers
To see her slidin' cross de flo' an' steppin' froo de figgers.

Charles Francis Richardson.

BORN in Hallowell, Me., 1851.

NATHANIEL HAWTHORNE.

[*American Literature: 1607-1885. In Two Volumes.* 1887-89.]

HIS GENIUS AS AN ARTIST.

G LADLY we turn toward the singularly beautiful and characteristic list of writings which began with "Fanshawe" in 1828 and closed with the unfinished "Dolliver Romance" in 1864. Throughout nearly all of them we shall find that artlessness which characterizes the true genius, and that art which shows genius to be accompanied by high powers of construction and elaboration. An English painter and poet of Hawthorne's own time wrote, in youth, a story which has for its central thought the idea that "an artist need not seek for intellectualized moral intentions in his work, but will fulfil God's highest purpose by simple truth in manifesting, in a spirit of devout faith, the gift that God has given him." This idea is one which, in some shape, often occurs to Hawthorne's readers, and must more often have been in the romancer's own mind, though he seldom formulated it.

The delight which we take in Hawthorne is, then, the joy of perception of the work of an artist. The several methods of intellectual communication between mind and mind are widely variant in method and result. We derive one impression or pleasure from painting, and another—now stronger, now weaker—from sculpture, architecture, action, music; or from the apprehension of inanimate nature by the sense. It is the privilege and power of literature in the hands of its masters to convey to readers a sort of combination or intense suggestion of almost all other methods of thought-transfer or soul-expression. If printing is the "art preservative of all arts," literature is the art suggestive or inclusive of all arts. The author is an artist, and in direct proportion as he fulfils the highest artistic function in choice and elaboration of his creations does he deserve his craft-name in its highest sense.   .   .   .   .

The precise success which Hawthorne has attained, in his artist-work, is a matter of debate, which it is hopeless to try to settle definitely as yet. The neglect which once surrounded his name has changed to a too silly and reverential laudation. Already this modest writer has fallen into the hands of the zealots who study plays or poems of Shakespeare or Shelley or Browning for "inner meanings" or esoteric doctrine. There can no longer be question, however, that Hawthorne is an artist, to be measured by the canons applicable to the broader and more ambitious creations, and to stand or fall in letters according as his writings endure the large tests which they are brought to face.

Often enough did Hawthorne express his knowledge of the tremendous lesson which life teaches to a great artist like a Dante or a Milton, but cannot teach to a Schopenhauer or an Omar Khayyám. Bunyan never insisted more strongly upon the notion of God, duty, and immortality ; upon the " sinfulness of sin," as the old preachers used to phrase it, and as the liberal romancer in reality accepted it.   The human heart was Hawthorne's highest and most constant theme, and though he never wasted time in orotund sermonizing, and threw away as chaff fit for " Earth's Holocaust " much that creedmakers, from Nice to Plymouth, deem sacred, he was ever, without being less an artist, a force in the world of life and letters.   He watched with keen, deep eyes, but sometimes he wrote with a pen of flame. " The heart, the heart,—there was the little yet boundless sphere wherein existed the original wrong of which the crime and misery of this outward world were merely types. Purify that inward sphere, and the many shapes of evil that haunt the outward, and which now seem almost our only realities, will turn to shadowy phantoms and vanish of their own accord ; but if we go no deeper than the intellect, and strive, with merely that feeble instrument, to discern and rectify what is wrong, our whole accomplishment will be a dream."

This " inward sphere," the human heart, was Hawthorne's field of study and portrayal.   He saw and described its innocence, its purity, its loveliness, its noble hopes, its truest triumphs, its temptations, its sinful tendency, its desperate struggles, its downward motions, its malignity, its " total depravity," at least in appearance, its final petrifaction and self-destruction—the only destruction of which, in the divine plan, it is capable.   Life, in Hawthorne's view, was no Human Comedy, as to Balzac, or tragedy of lost souls, as to the early New England theologians, but the struggle of individual men, women, and children with the powers within and without them, and chiefly the powers within.   Surely a romancer could have no higher theme, and highly did Hawthorne treat it.

ART AND ETHICS.

But did he thereby become the less an artist or the more?

The literature of the two great Anglo-Saxon peoples has always had a tolerably clear idea that there is a necessary connection between art and ethics. It has contained many mischievous or frivolous books ; it has wavered between the austerity of Bunyan and the license of the dramatists of the Restoration ; it has been successively influenced by Norman-French, Italian, Latin, and Greek culture ; but it has never lost sight of certain principles peculiarly its own.   One of these principles is that a book should have a definite purpose, a real reason for being, if it expects a long life.   This principle has not been lost even in the imaginative literature of England and America.

Before the novel, the poem afforded our intellectual ancestors their means of amusement ; and in early English poetry the moral element was seldom lacking.   .   .   .   .

When fiction took the place of poetry, as an intellectual amusement, the same principle held good.   To this day, the best-known work of imagination in English prose is a terribly earnest sermon.   It so happened that the growth of the English novel began when English society and religion were once more in a degraded state, but in the indecency and coarseness of the novel of the eighteenth century there still appears something that is not French, not Italian, not Spanish. Robinson Crusoe is a moral Englishman abroad, who has changed his sky, not his disposition. Moralizing, if not morality, is not absent from the loose sayings of Sterne. Swift, in his malignant, half-insane way, at least had reforms in view. Fielding, like Chaucer and the author of "Piers Plowman," felt that accurate delineation was the precursor of a change for the better. Goldsmith's pictures of virtuous rural life are still beloved because, in Taine's phrase, the chief of them " unites and harmonizes in one character the best features of the manners and morals of the time and country, and creates an admiration and love for pious and orderly, domestic and disciplined, laborious and rural life ; Protestant and English virtue has not a more approved and amiable exemplar." Samuel Richardson, the precursor of the long-regnant school of sentimental novelists, spent his literary lifetime in trying to show that integrity and uprightness, even of the Grandisonian order, are more attractive than the vice of the "town" in the era of the Georges.

Something more than mere amusement, something behind the story, is still more evident in Scott, the Scheherezade of modern literature ; in Dickens, promoting humanity and good fellowship, and attacking abuses in prisons, schools, law courts, and home-life ; in Thackeray, tilting loyally against social shams ; in saddened but brave Charlotte and Emily Brontë, amid the Yorkshire moors ; in George Eliot, describing the Jew as she believed him to be in reality, doing justice to the stern righteousness of a Dinah Morris, or telling how Savonarola was a Protestant in spite of himself. Turning to America, we note, as in England, the almost total disappearance of the outward immorality which defiled British fiction a hundred years ago, and which still disgraces a part of French fiction : and more than this, we find positive qualities, and a belief that story-telling is something more than story-telling. Irving feels with the heart of humanity ; Cooper, like Scott, magnifies the chivalric virtues, under new skies ; and Hawthorne goes to the depth of the soul in his search for the basal principles of human action.

What does all this mean? Is a book great because its moral purpose is sound, or is all literature bad as art and literature if it lacks the righteous purpose? Not at all ; neither has Anglo-Saxon literature monopoly of righteousness and purpose. It means that this literature has insisted more strongly than others upon the necessary connection between art *and* ethics ; that it has never prized a profitless, soulless beauty ; and that, so long as the world can be made better by literature, book-makers can and ought to help. Between two books of equal literary merit, but of unequal purpose, it gives greater and more lasting favor to the more useful book. It believes, with the American poet who is usually considered our chief apostle of the merely beautiful, that "taste holds intimate relations with the intellect and the moral sense." Whether it is right or wrong in this general idea, it is certain that any change in it, whether wrought by believers in "art for art's sake," by pseudo Greek poets, by "cosmic" bards who sometimes confuse right and wrong, or by strictly "realistic" novelists, will change a principle in accord with which the race has acted for ten centuries.

In accord with that principle Nathaniel Hawthorne worked from the be-

Charles F. Richardson.

ginning to the end of his literary life ; but he was too great an artist to confuse for a moment the demands of ethics with those of pure art.   .   .

REALIST AND IDEALIST.

Hawthorne was a pioneer and master of that literary method which, under the name of realism, has so strongly affected the fiction of the latter part of the nineteenth century. He studied minutely, and portrayed with delicate faithfulness, the smallest flower beneath his foot, the faintest bird in the distant sky, the trivial mark or the seemingly unimportant act of the person described. The microscopic artist was not more faithful in noting little characteristics or swiftly-fleeting marks. Such sketches as "A Rill from the Town Pump," "Main Street," "Sights from a Steeple," or "Little Annie's Ramble" are realism in its complete estate. Turguéneff himself, the prototype of so many followers in Russia, France, and America, is not more watchful with the eye or more painstaking with the pen. But between Hawthorne and Turguéneff there is an unlikeness as marked as their external similarity of method. Hawthorne, a realist in portrayal, is a thorough idealist in thought and purpose. The weariness and melancholy of Russian life and literature are nowhere present in his writings. Turguéneff's exquisite "Poems in Prose" virtually end with the query of that weakly pessimistic song the burden of which is : "What is it all when all is done?" In Hawthorne's books, to be sure, are the profoundest sin, the deepest veil of misery and mystery, the "infinite gloom" of which Mrs. Hawthorne wrote ; but always above them the tremendous truth written with characters of fire, and yet with "divine touches of beauty," with many a picture of artlessly lovely nature and life, and with the tender spirit of a child pervading the whole. At the close of Turguéneff's portrayals silently falls the black impenetrable curtain through which we may not peer, behind which there is nothing. But in Hawthorne's pages, beyond the blackness and woe of sin and of slow spiritual suicide, are the glow and the glory of the triumph that follows the struggle ; of the proved virtue that is better than untried innocence, and of the eternity that tells the meaning of time.   .   .   .   .

HAWTHORNE'S BACKGROUND.

Some critics have lamented that Hawthorne, so equipped with the strength and weapons of a genius, lacked the historic background which a great romancer should enjoy. They have actually apologized for the poverty of the materials which he was forced to use. On the contrary, it seems to me that he found at hand scenes possessing remarkable capabilities for literary treatment ; strong and forceful characters never before portrayed ; and (because of the vast changes caused by the Revolution) a sufficient remoteness of time. Castles, draw-bridges, black forests, tournaments, battles, and knights and dames had been used so often that none but a Scott could longer make them interesting. But houses of seven gables ; witch-haunted Puritan villages, fringed by native woods from which the Indians had scarcely fled ; soul-conflicts of stern dogmatists; heart-sorrows of men and women whose lives were forced back into their own selves; lovely little maidens from whom the poetry of nature could not be taken away; children as pure as the field-springs or half-hidden violets amid which they played, were unfamiliar in English fiction before Hawthorne. Irving in his Hudson stories, or Cooper in his Indian tales, was not more fortunate in theme nor more original in treatment; while Poe, the only other American novelist worth mentioning in a chapter devoted to Hawthorne, did not find Ghostland itself a better artistic background than Salem or Concord.

If it be an advantage for a novelist to follow other great workers in the same field, then Hawthorne lacked such advantage. But the great creator, whether he be novelist or poet, does not need prototypes and forerunners. He avails himself freely of the lessons and the work of his predecessors, but he is under no more than minor obligations to them. The man of genius is injured by following others, quite as truly as he is helped. A similar remark may be made concerning the picturesque or imposing historic background of literature. Such a background, in an ancient country, is pretty sure to be an unduly familiar one. A genius, in point of fact, takes his background where he finds it; if at home, and still comparatively unknown, he follows his national bent and local inspiration; if not, he forages all afield, without complaining of the disadvantages of his surroundings. When Hawthorne chose, he made solemn and august Rome his background; for the most part, however, he was glad to employ the singularly rich unused realm close at hand. It is the weaker novelist that is most concerned to find a fit setting for his plot; a mind like Hawthorne's possesses the element of large natural spontaneity which characterizes the world-author as distinct from the provincialist. A Dante is Italian, a Goethe is German, and even a Shakespeare is intensely English; but in their writings the local typifies the general. To the statement, then, that Hawthorne was imprisoned or disadvantaged by his environment, a double reply can be made: first, that he found at hand a rich and virgin field, well suited to the nature of his working genius; and second, that his powers of invention and assimilation were too great to be crushed down by adverse conditions, had such surrounded him. Indeed, Hawthorne was related to his background as closely as flower to root, so naturally did he grow from it and so truly did he represent it to the beholder's eye.   .   .   .   .

CHARACTERISTICS.

Among his faults I have not been able to include morbidness or inartistic incompleteness. That he had faults, however, is unquestionable, and they should be stated definitely and frankly. Pure and fine in mental nature, he was sometimes unexpectedly coarse (I mean coarse, not indecent) in utterance. Descriptions, or at times entire stories, are aggravatingly impassive; he stands without as a spectator, and what should be the broadly dramatic view falls into an apparent indifferentism which we cannot reconcile with his general purpose and attitude in literature. The unconscious strength summoned from a rich personal experience is missed at critical points. At times, as in reading the works of the Laodicean realists themselves, we are ready to cry out against the frigid philosophy of curious external observation. Again, while he was a great delineator of representative elements in the characters of men, women, and children, his colors were sometimes too pale and monotonous,—not the colors of flesh and blood. We seldom recognize a "Hawthorne character" on the streets of our daily walk. We are not always in the presence of vitality, but too often in that of personified ideas. His style is unvaried; half a dozen short stories, or three romances, read in succession, may for some readers emphasize this fact to the extent of weariness. The master seems a mannerist; self-control appears the dead level of a great mountain table-land, as dull as the valley-plains below.

But, after all, these faults are incidental, not inherent. Hawthorne was a great imaginative artist, with a highly ideal purpose and a strong and sure hand; therefore his fame, small at first, has steadily increased in the quarter of a century since his death, and shows no sign of waning as the years go on. He once wrote: "No man who needs a monument ever ought to have one." Hawthorne's monument is not beside the modest grave above which whisper the pines of Concord's Sleepy Hollow; nor is it in the commendations or analyses of his many critics. His monument is in his books, which so combine genius and art, imagination and human nature. Those whose eyes may see the fulness of human existence—its bright gayety and its gloomy grief and sin —perceive in Hawthorne's books the breadth of that mysterious thing in which we are, and which we call life. In "The Marble Faun" we are told that "a picture, however admirable the painter's art and wonderful his power, requires of the spectator a surrender of himself, in due proportion with the miracle which has been wrought. Like all revelations of the better life, the adequate perception of a great work of art demands a gifted simplicity of vision." Hawthorne's students, indeed, need not claim that they must possess high gifts of mind in order to perceive the art of his books; for he but requires in his readers somewhat of his own simplicity and naturalness. They must follow him as a master, for the time being, and learn in his school. He whose knowledge of human nature goes beyond shallow optimism on the one hand, and worldly cynicism on the other, need find no riddles in Hawthorne's pages. Perverse or dull was that French critic who once described Hawthorne as "un romancier pessimiste." It would be difficult to frame a statement less accurate, or one more likely to amuse the romancer himself, if this title has come to his knowledge in the land of shades.

I have said that Hawthorne's readers may follow him as a master, and learn in his school. The same advice is hardly to be given to those who not only read but write, and who would catch the secret of his literary success and apply it to their own novels or romances. Writers as well as readers, to be sure, may follow Hawthorne in his habit of minutely-faithful and ever-delicate observation of things great and small; they may discover that a realism which stoops to note the color of a single petal may be combined with a spiritualism which deems a heart-throb more important than a world of matter. They may study his pellucid English, simple and yet artistic; and may learn not to overcrowd their pages with too numerous figures or irrelevant episodes. He once made answer to a query as to his style : " It is the result of a great deal of practice. It is a desire to tell the simple truth as honestly and vividly as one can." This seems easy enough ; but there is no likelihood that there will be, in America or elsewhere, another Hawthorne. From his name has been derived an adjective, but we always apply the word "Hawthornesque" to a single effect or undeveloped idea, and even then some restriction is usually added to the expression. His field, method, and style were in a large sense his own. . . . . At first unread, then underrated, then called morbid or at best cold and aloof, Hawthorne now stands before us as in some sense "the greatest imaginative writer since Shakespeare," of whose greatness we are "beginning to arrive at some faint sense,"—a greatness "immeasurably vast-er than that of any other American who ever wrote."

In this greatness the spiritual element was of constant importance. Haw-thorne, all in all, was no cold observer and impassive chronicler. As author, he looked into the heart of the world, and wrote. As man, this deathless soul could say in truth : " I have no love of secrecy and darkness. I am glad to think that God sees through my heart, and, if any angel has power to pene-trate into it, he is welcome to know everything that is there."

Mariana Griswold Van Rensselaer.

BORN in New York, N. Y., 1851.

COROT.

[*Corot.—Six Portraits. By Mrs. Schuyler Van Rensselaer.* 1889.]

"TRUTH," said Corot, "is the first thing in art, and the second and the third." But the whole truth cannot be told at once. A selection from the mass of Nature's truths is what the artist shows—a few things at a time, and with sufficient emphasis to make them clearly felt. You cannot paint summer and winter on a single canvas. No two successive hours of a summer's day are just alike, and you cannot paint them both. Nor, as certainly, can you paint everything you see at the chosen moment. Crowd in too much and you spoil the picture, weaken the impression, conceal your meaning, falsify everything in the attempt to be too true.

This was Corot's creed. What now were the truths that he interpreted at the necessary sacrifice of others which were less important in his eyes? They are implied, I think, in the words I have already written.

Corot prized effects rather than what the non-artistic world calls solid facts. But effects are as truly facts as are the individual features and details which make them. Indeed, they are the most essential as well as interesting of all facts. It is effects that we see first when we are in Nature's presence, that impress us most, and dwell the longest in our minds. Outlines, modelling, local colors, minor details—these shift, appear and disappear, or alter vastly as light and shadow change ; and most of them we never really see at all until we take time to analyze. Look at the same scene on a sunny morning or by cloudy sunset light. It is not the same scene. The features are the same, but their effect has changed, and this means a new landscape, a novel picture. The mistake of too many modern painters, especially in England, is that they paint from analysis, not from sight. They paint the things they know are there, not the things they perceive just as they perceive them. This Corot never did. He studied analytically and learned all he could about solid facts ; but he painted synthetically—omitting many things that he knew about, and even many that he saw at the moment, in order to portray more clearly the general result. And this general result he found in the main lines of the scene before him ; in its dominant tone ; in the broad relationships of one mass of color to all others ; in the aspect of the sky, the character of the atmosphere, and the play of light ; and in the palpitating incessant movement of sky and air and leaf.

Look at one of Corot's foregrounds and you will see whether it is soft or hard, wet with dew or dry in the sun ; you will see its color, its mobility. Look at his trees and you will see their mass, their diversities in denseness, their pliability and vital freshness. Look at his sky and you will see its shimmering, pulsating quality : it has the softness of a blue which means vast depths of distance, or of a gray which means layer upon layer of imponderable mist, and the whiteness of clouds which shine as bright as pearls but would dissipate at a touch. And everywhere, over all, behind all, in all, you will see the enveloping air and the light which infiltrates this thing and transfigures that ; the air and the light which make all things what they are, which create the landscape by creating its color, its expression, its effect ; the air and the light which are the movement, the spirit, the very essence of nature. No man had ever perfectly painted the atmosphere till Corot did it, or the diffused, pervading quality of light ; and for this reason no one had painted such delicate, infinite distances, such deep, luminous, palpitating skies.

See now how Corot managed to paint like this—to interpret the life, mood, and meaning of the scene he drew. It was just through that process of omission and suppression which the superficial misread as proof that he did not really "render" nature at all. Even the smallest, simplest, natural fact cannot be "rendered" in the sense of being literally reproduced ; and to attempt the literal imitation of large features is merely to sacrifice the whole in favor of what must remain but a partial rendering of a part. A leaf can be painted, but not a myriad leaves at once ; we are soon forced to generalize, condense, suppress ; and to try to paint too many leaves is to lose the tree, for the tree is not a congregation of countless individual leaves distinctly seen—it is a mass of leaves which are shot through and through with light and air, and always more or less merged together and moving. It is an entity, and a live one ; and which is the more important—that we should see the living thing or the items that compose it ? What we ask the painter is not just how his tree was constructed, but just how it looked as a feature in the beauty and aliveness of the scene. What we want is its general effect and the way it harmonized with the effect of its surroundings.

Does it matter, then, if he omits many things, or even if he alters some things, to get this right result ? Such altering is not falsifying. It is merely emphasis—a stress laid here and a blank left there that (since all facts cannot possibly be given) the accented fact shall at least be plain. The generalized structure of Corot's trees, their blurred contours and flying, feathery spray—these are not untruths. They are merely compromises with the stern necessities of paint, devices he employed, not because he was unable to draw trees with precision, but because, had he done this, his foliage would have been too solid and inert for truth. A twig is never long in one position. It cannot be painted in two positions at once. But a twig that is blurred to the eye because it is passing from one position to another—this can be painted, and this Corot preferred to paint rather than ramifications with exactness or leaf-outlines with a narrow care. So his trees are alive, and, as he loved to say, the light can reach their inmost leaves, and the little birds can fly among their branches.

It is the same thing with color. The color schemes to which Corot kept were never as strong and vivid as those we find with some of his contemporaries and many of his successors. Browns and grays and pale greens predominate on his canvas with rarely an acuter accent, a louder note. But he fitted his themes to his brush, so that we feel no lack ; or, in better words, he chose his color schemes in accordance with the character of the natural effects that he loved most. And within the scale he chose his coloring is perfect. His tone (the harmony, or, as used to be said, the " keeping " of his result) is admirable beyond praise. Yet it is gained at no sacrifice of truth in local color. There are cheap processes for securing tone, which are indeed falsifications of nature,—ways of carrying over into one object the color of another, throwing things out of their right relationships, harmonizing with some universal gauze of brown or gray. But Corot's was not a process like any of these. His power to harmonize and unify his colors sprang from the fact that he studied colors with a more careful and penetrating eye than ever before had been brought to bear, and never forgot their mutual relationships. Look at one of his pictures where the general effect, perhaps, is of soft delicious greens. Everything in it is not greenish. The sky is pure blue and the clouds are purest white. The water is rightly related to the sky, and where things were gray in nature, or brown, or even black, they are so on canvas. Harmony does not mean monotony, tone does not mean untruth ; and this Corot could accomplish because he studied "values" as no painter before him had studied them.

This word—new in our language but indispensable—has been a little hard of comprehension to those who know nothing of the painter's problems and devices. But it means, as simply as I can say it, the difference between given colors as severally compared with the highest note in the scale—white, and the lowest—black ; the difference between them as containing, so to speak, more light or more dark. This does not mean the same thing as the relative degrees of illumination and shadow which may fall upon them. The one quality may be involved in or dependent upon the other, but the two are distinct to the painter's eye.

It is not easy even to perceive differences in value. Given two shades of the same tint, as of a blue-green or a yellow-green, it is easy enough to say which is the darker; but it is more difficult when a yellow-green is compared with a blue-green, and still more when we set a brown beside a green, or a blue beside a yellow. Yet the painter must not only learn to see values in nature but to transpose them correctly on canvas—for color can never be exactly copied on canvas; from the nature of paint, there must always be transposition, adaptation, compromise. Corot mastered the difficulty as no one else had done; and this mastery has made him the guide and teacher of all the landscape painters who have since been born.

Maurice Francis Egan.

Born in Philadelphia, Penn., 1852.

THEOCRITUS.

[*Preludes.—Songs and Sonnets.* 1885.]

DAPHNIS is mute, and hidden nymphs complain,
　And mourning mingles with their fountains' song:
　　Shepherds contend no more, as all day long
They watch their sheep on the wide, cyprus-plain;
The master-voice is silent, songs are vain;
　Blithe Pan is dead, and tales of ancient wrong,
　Done by the gods when gods and men were strong,
Chanted to reeded pipes, no prize can gain:
O sweetest singer of the olden days,
　In dusty books your idyls rare seem dead;
　　The gods are gone, but poets never die;
Though men may turn their ears to newer lays,
　Sicilian nightingales enrapturèd
　　Caught all your songs, and nightly thrill the sky.

MAURICE DE GUÉRIN.

THE old wine filled him, and he saw, with eyes
　Anoint of Nature, fauns and dryads fair
　　Unseen by others; to him maidenhair
And waxen lilacs and those birds that rise
A-sudden from tall reeds at slight surprise
　Brought charmèd thoughts: and in earth everywhere
　He, like sad Jaques, found unheard music rare
As that of Syrinx to old Grecians wise.
A pagan heart, a Christian soul had he,
　He followed Christ, yet for dead Pan he sighed,

Till earth and heaven met within his breast:
As if Theocritus in Sicily
Had come upon the Figure crucified
And lost his gods in deep, Christ-given rest.

BETWEEN THE LIGHTS.

IN the cool, soft, fragrant summer
    grass,
  'Mid trembling stalks of white-tipped
    clover,
I lie and dream, as the shadows pass
  From twilight's gates the cloud-bridge
    over.

On the other side, dim other side,
  Lie starlight, gloom, and the night's
    chill wind,
Calm eve comes forth, like a timid bride,
  And with shaded eyes looks on man-
    kind;—
She looks at me, as I lounge and dream;
  She builds in the sky for my delight
High-towered castles that glow and
    gleam
  Redder than snow-crests in North fires
    bright.

She shows me Ceres, mid corn-flowers
    blue,
  And Pluto's bride on her throne below,
And Helen fair, to her lord untrue,
  Anguished and wailing in deathless
    woe;
Gold arabesques on a jasper ground,
  Gray cameo-faces, cold and grand,
Puck and Peas-blossom hovering round,
  Oberon and his glittering band.

She changes her aspect, opal eve—
  Shows me a plain near the walls of
    Troy,

Where shepherds sheep in low shrubs
    leave
  In haste, to gaze on a bright-haired boy:
The boy is Paris, he cometh out,
  Out of the city, strong-limbed and fair.
Live I in future or past? I doubt
  Am I Greek shepherd or gay trouvère—

Who lieth, dreaming perhaps of her,
  Œnone weeping for him, forlorn?
Who strives with the plaintive lute to stir
  Some love in a Norman heart of scorn?
Out of a balcon of hues that glow,
  There leans a lady against the sky;
Her robe is bordered with pearls, I know,
  Pearls on her neck with her pearl-skin
    vie.

There stands a lover in gay slashed hose,
  With a bright plumed hat and purple
    cloak;
He calls her "lily" and "damask rose";
  Even in cloudland they wear love's
    yoke.
Bold knights ride forward on prancing
    steeds,
  King Arthur's court, with Sir Launce-
    lot—
Presto! 'Tis Syrinx among the reeds:
  Apollo seeks her, but finds her not.

I am so idle in summer grass,
  I cannot think for scent of clover;
No moral I find in clouds that pass,
  I only know that sunset's over.

Maurice Francis Egan.

Edward Page Mitchell.

BORN in Bath, Me., 1852.

THE ABLEST MAN IN THE WORLD.

[*From the Story by that Title.—The New York Sun.* 1879.]

FISHER now had an opportunity to observe the personal characteristics of the Russian Baron. He was a young man of about thirty-five, with exceedingly handsome and clear-cut features, but a peculiar head. The peculiarity of his head was that it seemed to be perfectly round on top—that is, its diameter from ear to ear appeared quite equal to its anterior and posterior diameter. The curious effect of this unusual conformation was rendered more striking by the absence of all hair. There was nothing on the Baron's head but a tightly fitting skull cap of black silk. A very deceptive wig hung upon one of the bedposts.

Being sufficiently recovered to recognize the presence of a stranger, Savitch made a courteous bow.

"How do you find yourself now?" inquired Fisher, in bad French.

"Very much better, thanks to Monsieur," replied the Baron, in excellent English, spoken in a charming voice. "Very much better, though I feel a certain dizziness here." And he pressed his hand to his forehead.

The valet withdrew at a sign from his master, and was followed by the porter. Fisher advanced to the bedside and took the Baron's wrist. Even his unpractised touch told him that the pulse was alarmingly high. He was much puzzled, and not a little uneasy at the turn which the affair had taken. "Have I got myself and the Russian into an infernal scrape?" he thought. "But no—he's well out of his teens, and half a tumbler of such whiskey as that ought not to go to a baby's head."

Nevertheless, the new symptoms developed themselves with a rapidity and poignancy that made Fisher feel uncommonly anxious. Savitch's face became as white as marble—its paleness rendered startling by the sharp contrast of the black skull cap. His form reeled as he sat on the bed, and he clasped his head convulsively with both hands, as if in terror lest it burst.

"I had better call your valet," said Fisher, nervously.

"No, no!" gasped the Baron. "You are a medical man, and I shall have to trust you. There is something—wrong—here." With a spasmodic gesture he vaguely indicated the top of his head.

"But I am not—" stammered Fisher.

"No words!" exclaimed the Russian, imperiously. "Act at once—there must be no delay. Unscrew the top of my head!"

Savitch tore off his skull cap and flung it aside. Fisher had no words to describe the bewilderment with which he beheld the actual fabric of the Baron's cranium. The skull cap had concealed the fact that the entire top of Savitch's head was a dome of polished silver.

"Unscrew it!" said Savitch again.

Fisher reluctantly placed both hands upon the silver skull and exerted a gentle pressure toward the left. The top yielded, turning easily and truly in its threads.

"Faster!" said the Baron, faintly. "I tell you no time must be lost." Then he swooned.

At this instant there was a sound of voices in the outer room, and the door leading into the Baron's bed-chamber was violently flung open and as violently closed. The new-comer was a short, spare man of middle age, with a keen visage and piercing, deep-set little gray eyes. He stood for a few seconds scrutinizing Fisher with a sharp, almost fiercely jealous regard.

The Baron recovered his consciousness and opened his eyes.

"Dr. Rapperschwyll!" he exclaimed.

Dr. Rapperschwyll, with a few rapid strides, approached the bed and confronted Fisher and Fisher's patient. "What is all this?" he angrily demanded.

Without waiting for a reply he laid his hand rudely upon Fisher's arm and pulled him away from the Baron. Fisher, more and more astonished, made no resistance, but suffered himself to be led, or pushed, toward the door. Dr. Rapperschwyll opened the door wide enough to give the American exit, and then closed it with a vicious slam. A quick click informed Fisher that the key had been turned in the lock.

The next morning Fisher met Savitch coming from the Trinkhalle. The Baron bowed with cold politeness and passed on. Later in the day a *valet de place* handed to Fisher a small parcel, with the message : "Dr. Rapperschwyll supposes that this will be sufficient." The parcel contained two gold pieces of twenty marks.

Fisher gritted his teeth. "He shall have back his forty marks," he muttered to himself, "but I will have his confounded secret in return."

The Polish countess abundantly redeemed her promise, throwing in for good measure many choice bits of gossip and scandalous anecdotes about the Russian nobility, which are not relevant to the present narrative. Her story, as summarized by Fisher, was this :

The Baron Savitch was not of an old creation. There was a mystery about his origin that had never been satisfactorily solved in St. Petersburg or in Moscow. It was said by some that he was a foundling from the Vospitatelnoi Dom. Others believed him to be the unacknowledged son of a certain illustrious personage nearly related to the House of Romanoff. The latter theory was the more probable, since it accounted in a measure for the unexampled success of his career from the day that he was graduated at the University of Dorpat.

Rapid and brilliant beyond precedent this career had been. He entered the diplomatic service of the Czar, and for several years was attached to the legations at Vienna, London, and Paris. Created a Baron before his twenty-fifth birthday for the wonderful ability displayed in the conduct of negotiations of supreme importance and delicacy with the House of Hapsburg, he became a pet of Gortchakoff's and was given every opportunity for the exercise of his genius in diplomacy. It was even said in well-informed circles at St. Petersburg that the guiding mind which directed Russia's course throughout the entire Eastern complication, which planned the campaign on the Danube, effected the combinations that gave victory to the Czar's soldiers, and which meanwhile held Austria aloof, neutralized the immense power of Germany, and exasperated England only to the point where wrath expends itself in harmless threats, was the brain of the young Baron Savitch. It was certain that he had been with Ignatieff at Constantinople when the trouble was first fomented, with Shouvaloff in England at the time of the secret conference agreement, with the Grand Duke Nicholas at Adrianople when the protocol of an armistice was signed, and would soon be in Berlin behind the scenes of the Congress, where it was expected that he would outwit the statesmen of all Europe, and play with Bismarck and Disraeli as a strong man plays with two kicking babies.

But the countess had concerned herself very little with this handsome young man's achievements in politics. She had been more particularly interested in his social career. His success in that field had been not less remarkable. Although no one knew with positive certainty his father's name, he had conquered an absolute supremacy in the most exclusive circles surrounding the imperial court. His influence with the Czar himself was supposed to be unbounded. Birth apart, he was considered the best *parti* in Russia. From poverty and by the sheer force of intellect he had won for himself a colossal fortune. Report gave him forty million roubles, and doubtless report did not exceed the fact. Every speculative enterprise which he undertook, and they were many and various, was carried to sure success by the same qualities of cool, unerring judgment, far-reaching sagacity, and apparently superhuman power of organizing, combining, and controlling, which had made him in politics the phenomenon of the age.

About Dr. Rapperschwyll? Yes, the countess knew him by reputation and by sight. He was the medical man in constant attendance upon the Baron Savitch, whose high-strung mental organization rendered him susceptible to sudden and alarming attacks of illness. Dr. Rapperschwyll was a Swiss— had originally been a watchmaker or artisan of some kind, she had heard. For the rest, he was a commonplace little old man, devoted to his profession and to the Baron, and evidently devoid of ambition, since he wholly neglected to turn the opportunities of his position and connections to the advancement of his personal fortunes.

Fortified with this information, Fisher felt better prepared to grapple with Rapperschwyll for the possession of the secret. For five days he lay in wait for the Swiss physician. On the sixth day the desired opportunity unexpectedly presented itself.

Half way up the Mercuriusberg, late in the afternoon, he encountered the custodian of the ruined tower, coming down. "No, the tower was not closed. A gentleman was up there, making observations of the country, and he, the custodian, would be back in an hour or two." So Fisher kept on his way.

The upper part of this tower is in a dilapidated condition. The lack of a stairway to the summit is supplied by a temporary wooden ladder. Fisher's head and shoulders were hardly through the trap that opens to the platform, before he discovered that the man already there was the man whom he sought. Dr. Rapperschwyll was studying the topography of the Black Forest through a pair of field-glasses.

Fisher announced his arrival by an opportune stumble and a noisy effort to recover himself, at the same instant aiming a stealthy kick at the topmost round of the ladder, and scrambling ostentatiously over the edge of the trap. The ladder went down thirty or forty feet with a racket, clattering and banging against the walls of the tower.

Dr. Rapperschwyll at once appreciated the situation. He turned sharply around, and remarked with a sneer, " Monsieur is unaccountably awkward." Then he scowled and showed his teeth, for he recognized Fisher.

"It *is* rather unfortunate," said the New Yorker, with imperturbable coolness. " We shall be imprisoned here a couple of hours at the shortest. Let us congratulate ourselves that we each have intelligent company, besides a charming landscape to contemplate."

The Swiss coldly bowed, and resumed his topographical studies. Fisher lighted a cigar.

" I also desire," continued Fisher, puffing clouds of smoke in the direction of the Teufelmühle, " to avail myself of this opportunity to return forty marks of yours, which reached me, I presume, by a mistake."

" If Monsieur the American physician was not satisfied with his fee," rejoined Rapperschwyll, venomously, " he can without doubt have the affair adjusted by applying to the Baron's valet."

Fisher paid no attention to this thrust, but calmly laid the gold pieces upon the parapet, directly under the nose of the Swiss.

" I could not think of accepting any fee," he said, with deliberate emphasis. " I was abundantly rewarded for my trifling services by the novelty and interest of the case."

The Swiss scanned the American's countenance long and steadily with his sharp little gray eyes. At length he said, carelessly :

" Monsieur is a man of science ? "

" Yes," replied Fisher, with a mental reservation in favor of all sciences save that which illuminates and dignifies our national game.

" Then," continued Dr. Rapperschwyll, " Monsieur will perhaps acknowledge that a more beautiful or more extensive case of trephining has rarely come under his observation."

Fisher slightly raised his eyebrows.

" And Monsieur will also understand, being a physician," continued Dr. Rapperschwyll, " the sensitiveness of the Baron himself, and of his friends upon the subject. He will therefore pardon my seeming rudeness at the time of his discovery."

" He is smarter than I supposed," thought Fisher. " He holds all the cards, while I have nothing—nothing, except a tolerably strong nerve when it comes to a game of bluff."

" I deeply regret that sensitiveness," he continued, aloud, " for it had occurred to me that an accurate account of what I saw, published in one of the scientific journals of England or America, would excite wide attention, and no doubt be received with interest on the Continent."

"What you saw?" cried the Swiss, sharply. "It is false. You saw nothing; when I entered you had not even removed the "——

Here he stopped short and muttered to himself, as if cursing his own impetuosity. Fisher celebrated his advantage by tossing away his half-burned cigar and lighting a fresh one.

"Since you compel me to be frank," Dr. Rapperschwyll went on, with visibly increasing nervousness, "I will inform you that the Baron has assured me that you saw nothing. I interrupted you in the act of removing the silver cap."

"I will be equally frank," replied Fisher, stiffening his face for a final effort. "On that point, the Baron is not a competent witness. He was in a state of unconsciousness for some time before you entered. Perhaps I was removing the silver cap when you interrupted me "——

Dr. Rapperschwyll turned pale.

"And, perhaps," said Fisher, coolly, "I was replacing it."

The suggestion of this possibility seemed to strike Rapperschwyll like a sudden thunderbolt from the clouds. His knees parted, and he almost sank to the floor. He put his hands before his eyes, and wept like a child, or, rather, like a broken old man.

"He will publish it! He will publish it to the court and to the world!" he cried, hysterically. "And at this crisis "——

Then, by a desperate effort, the Swiss appeared to recover to some extent his self-control. He paced the diameter of the platform for several minutes, with his head bent and his arms folded across the breast. Turning again to his companion, he said:

"If any sum you may name will "——

Fisher cut the proposition short with a laugh.

"Then," said Rapperschwyll, "if—if I throw myself on your generosity"——

"Well?" demanded Fisher.

"And ask a promise, on your honor, of absolute silence concerning what you have seen?"

"Silence until such time as the Baron Savitch shall have ceased to exist?"

"That will suffice," said Rapperschwyll. "For when he ceases to exist I die. And your conditions?"

"The whole story, here and now, and without reservation."

"It is a terrible price to ask me," said Rapperschwyll, "but larger interests than my pride are at stake. You shall hear the story.

"I was bred a watchmaker," he continued, after a long pause, "in the Canton of Zurich. It is not a matter of vanity when I say that I achieved a marvellous degree of skill in the craft. I developed a faculty of invention that led me into a series of experiments regarding the capabilities of purely mechanical combinations. I studied and improved upon the best automata ever constructed by human ingenuity. Babbage's calculating machine especially interested me. I saw in Babbage's idea the germ of something infinitely more important to the world.

"Then I threw up my business and went to Paris to study physiology. I spent three years at the Sorbonne and perfected myself in that branch of knowledge. Meanwhile, my pursuits had extended far beyond the purely physical sciences. Psychology engaged me for a time; and then I ascended into the domain of sociology, which, when adequately understood, is the summary and final application of all knowledge.

"It was after years of preparation, and as the outcome of all my studies, that the great idea of my life, which had vaguely haunted me ever since the Zurich days, assumed at last a well-defined and perfect form."

The manner of Dr. Rapperschwyll had changed from distrustful reluctance to frank enthusiasm. The man himself seemed transformed. Fisher listened attentively and without interrupting the relation. He could not help fancying that the necessity of yielding the secret, so long and so jealously guarded by the physician, was not entirely distasteful to the enthusiast.

"Now attend, Monsieur," continued Dr. Rapperschwyll, "to several separate propositions which may seem at first to have no direct bearing on each other.

"My endeavors in mechanism had resulted in a machine which went far beyond Babbage's in its powers of calculation. Given the data, there was no limit to the possibilities in this direction. Babbage's cogwheels and pinions calculated logarithms, calculated an eclipse. It was fed with figures, and produced results in figures. Now, the relations of cause and effect are as fixed and unalterable as the laws of arithmetic. Logic is, or should be, as exact a science as mathematics. My new machine was fed with facts, and produced conclusions. In short, it *reasoned;* and the results of its reasoning were always true, while the results of human reasoning are often, if not always, false. The source of error in human logic is what the philosophers call the 'personal equation.' My machine eliminated the personal equation; it proceeded from cause to effect, from premise to conclusion, with steady precision. The human intellect is fallible; my machine was, and is, infallible in its processes.

"Again, physiology and anatomy had taught me the fallacy of the medical superstition which holds the gray matter of the brain and the vital principle to be inseparable. I had seen men living with pistol balls imbedded in the medulla oblongata. I had seen the hemispheres and the cerebellum removed from the crania of birds and small animals, and yet they did not die. I believed that, though the brain were to be removed from a human skull, the subject would not die, although he would certainly be divested of the intelligence which governed all save the purely involuntary actions of his body.

"Once more: a profound study of history from the sociological point of view, and a not inconsiderable practical experience of human nature, had convinced me that the greatest geniuses that ever existed were on a plane not so very far removed above the level of average intellect. The grandest peaks in my native country, those which all the world knows by name, tower only a few hundred feet above the countless unnamed peaks that surround them.

Napoleon Bonaparte towered only a little over the ablest men around him. Yet that little was everything, and he overran Europe. A man who surpassed Napoleon, as Napoleon surpassed Murat, in the mental qualities which transmute thought into fact, would have made himself master of the whole world.

"Now, to fuse these three propositions into one : suppose that I take a man, and, by removing the brain that enshrines all the errors and failures of his ancestors away back to the origin of the race, remove all sources of weakness in his future career. Suppose, that in place of the fallible intellect which I have removed, I endow him with an artificial intellect that operates with the certainty of universal laws. Suppose that I launch this superior being, who reasons truly, into the hurly-burly of his inferiors, who reason falsely, and await the inevitable result with the tranquillity of a philosopher.

"Monsieur, you have my secret. That is precisely what I have done. In Moscow, where my friend Dr. Duchat had charge of the new institution of St. Vasili for hopeless idiots, I found a boy of eleven whom they called Stépan Borovitch. Since he was born, he had not seen, heard, spoken or thought. Nature had granted him, it was believed, a fraction of the sense of smell, and perhaps a fraction of the sense of taste, but of even this there was no positive ascertainment. Nature had walled in his soul most effectually. Occasional inarticulate murmurings, and an incessant knitting and kneading of the fingers were his only manifestations of energy. On bright days they would place him in a little rocking-chair, in some spot where the sun fell warm, and he would rock to and fro for hours, working his slender fingers and mumbling forth his satisfaction at the warmth in the plaintive and unvarying refrain of idiocy. The boy was thus situated when I first saw him.

"I begged Stépan Borovitch of my good friend Dr. Duchat. If that excellent man had not long since died he should have shared in my triumph. I took Stépan to my home and plied the saw and the knife. I could operate on that poor, worthless, useless, hopeless travesty of humanity as fearlessly and as recklessly as upon a dog bought or caught for vivisection. That was a little more than twenty years ago. To-day Stépan Borovitch wields more power than any other man on the face of the earth. In ten years he will be the autocrat of Europe, the master of the world. He never errs ; for the machine that reasons beneath his silver skull never makes a mistake."

Fisher pointed downward at the old custodian of the tower, who was seen toiling up the hill.

"Dreamers," continued Dr. Rapperschwyll, "have speculated on the possibility of finding among the ruins of the older civilizations some brief inscription which shall change the foundations of human knowledge. Wiser men deride the dream, and laugh at the idea of scientific kabbala. The wiser men are fools. Suppose that Aristotle had discovered on a cuneiform-covered tablet at Nineveh the few words, 'Survival of the Fittest.' Philosophy would have gained twenty-two hundred years. I will give you, in almost as few words, a truth equally pregnant. *The ultimate evolution of the creature is into the creator.* Perhaps it will be twenty-two hundred years before the truth finds general acceptance, yet it is not the less a truth. The Baron Savitch is my creature, and I am his creator—creator of the ablest man in Europe, the ablest man in the world.

"Here is our ladder, Monsieur. I have fulfilled my part of the agreement. Remember yours."

John Bach McMaster.

Born in Brooklyn, N. Y., 1852.

IN THE AMERICA OF 1784.

[A History of the People of the United States.—Vol. I. 1883.]

NOT less important than the school-master, in the opinion of his townsmen, was the doctor. With the exception of the minister and the judge, he was the most important personage in the district. His professional education would now be thought insufficient to admit him to practice ; for there were then but two medical schools in the country, nor were they, by reason of the expense and dangers of travelling, by any means well attended. In general, the medical education of a doctor was such as he could pick up while serving an apprenticeship to some noted practitioner in Boston or New York, during which he combined the duties of a student with many of the menial offices of a servant. He ground the powders, mixed the pills, rode with the doctor on his rounds, held the basin when the patient was bled, helped to adjust plasters, to sew wounds, and ran with vials of medicine from one end of the town to the other. In the moments snatched from duties such as these he swept out the office, cleaned the bottles and jars, wired skeletons, tended the night-bell, and, when a feast was given, stood in the hall to announce the guests.

It was a white day with such a young man when he enjoyed the rare good fortune of dissecting a half-putrid arm, or examining a human heart and lungs. So great, indeed, was the difficulty of procuring anatomical subjects, that even at the medical school which had just been started at Harvard College, a single body was made to do duty for a whole year's course of lectures. It was only by filching from graveyards or begging the dead bodies of criminals from the Governor that subjects could be obtained.

Under such circumstances, the doctor's knowledge was derived from personal experience rather than from books, and the amount so obtained bore a direct relation to the sharpness of his powers of observation and the strength of his memory. If he were gifted with a keen observation, a logical mind, and a retentive memory, such a system of education was of the utmost value. For in medicine, as in mechanics, as in engineering, as in every science, in short, where experience and practical skill are of the highest importance, a practical education is most essential. The surgeon who has studied anatomy from a book without ever having dissected a human body, the physician who learns the names and symptoms of diseases from a work on pathology, and the remedies from the materia medica, without ever having seen the maladies in active operation and the remedies actually applied, is in a fair way to kill far more patients than he will ever cure. But the value of knowledge obtainable from books alone is on that account not the less useful, and by no means to be despised. The student who has read much in his profession is in possession of the results of many centuries of experience derived from the labors of many thousands of men. He is saved from innumerable blunders. He is enabled to begin his career with a knowledge of things which, if left to his own experience to find out, would cost him years of patient waiting and careful observation. The advantages of such a system of study were, however, but sparingly enjoyed by the medical students of the last century, when but few physicians boasted a medical library of fifty volumes.

His apprenticeship ended, the half-educated lad returned to his native town to assume the practice and to follow in the footsteps of his father. There as years went by he grew in popularity and wealth. His genial face, his engaging manners, his hearty laugh, the twinkle with which he inquired of the blacksmith when the next boy was expected, the sincerity with which he asked after the health of the carpenter's daughter, the interest he took in the family of the poorest laborer, the good-nature with which he stopped to chat with the farm-hands about the prospect of the corn crop and the turnip crop, made him the favorite of the county for miles around. When he rode out he knew the names and personal history of the occupants of every house he passed. The farmers' lads pulled off their hats, and the girls dropped courtesies to him. Sunshine and rain, daylight and darkness, were alike to him. He would ride ten miles on the darkest night, over the worst of roads, in a pelting storm, to administer a dose of calomel to an old woman, or to attend a child in a fit. He was present at every birth ; he attended every burial ; he sat with the minister at every death-bed, and put his name with the lawyer to every will.

But a few of the simplest drugs were then to be found stowed away on the shelves of the village store, among heaps of shoes, Rohan hats, balls of twine, packages of seed, and flitches of bacon. The physician was, therefore, compelled to combine the duties both of the doctor and the apothecary. He pounded his own drugs, made his own tinctures, prepared his own infusions, and put up his own prescriptions. His saddle-bag was the only drug-store within forty miles, and there, beside his horn balances and his china mortar, were medicines now gone quite out of fashion, or at most but rarely used. Homœopathy, with its tasteless mixtures and diminutive doses, was unknown, and it is not too much to say that more medicine was then taken every year by the well than is now taken in the same space of time by the sick. Each spring the blood must be purified, the bowels must be purged, the kidneys must be excited, the bile must be moved, and large doses of senna and manna, and loathsome concoctions of rhubarb and molasses, were taken daily. In a thousand ways the practice of medicine has changed since that day, and changed for the better. Remedies now in the medicine-box of every farmer were then utterly unknown. Water was denied the patient tormented with fever, and in its stead he was given small quantities of clam-juice. Mercurial compounds were taken till the lips turned blue and the gums fell away from the teeth. The damsel who fainted was bled profusely. Cupping and leeching were freely prescribed. The alkaloid quinia was unknown till 1820. The only cure for malarial diseases was powdered cinchona bark ; but the amount required to restore the patient was so great, and the supply so small, that the remedy was all but useless. Vaccination was not made known by Jenner till 1798. Inoculation was still held by many to be attended by divine punishment. Small-pox was almost as prevalent as pneumonia now is. The discovery of anæsthesia by the inhalation of ether or chloroform was not given to the world by Morton till 1846. Not one of the many remedies which assuage pain, which destroy disease, which hold in check the most loathsome maladies and the most violent epidemics, was in use. Every few years during the dog-days the yellow fever raged with more violence in the Northern cities than it has ever done in this generation in the cities of the far South. Whole streets were depopulated. Every night the dead-cart shot its scores of corpses into the pits of the Potters' Field. Better surgery is now generously given to every laborer injured by the fall of a scaffold than could then have been purchased at any price.

High as the doctors stood in the good graces of their fellow-men, the ministers formed a yet more respected class of New England society. In no other section of the country had religion so firm a hold on the affections of the people. Nowhere else were men so truly devout, and the minister held in such high esteem. It had, indeed, from the days of the founders of the colony been the fashion among New Englanders to look to the pastor with a profound reverence, not unmingled with awe. He was not to them as other men were. He was the just man made perfect ; the oracle of divine will ; the sure guide to truth. The heedless one who absented himself from the preaching on a Sabbath was hunted up by the tithing-man, was admonished severely, and, if he still persisted in his evil ways, was fined, exposed in the stocks, or imprisoned in the cage. To sit patiently on the rough board seats while the preacher turned the hour-glass for the third time, and, with his voice husky from shouting, and the sweat pouring in streams down his face, went on for an hour more, was a delectable privilege. In such a community the authority of the reverend man was almost supreme. To speak disrespectfully concerning him, to jeer at his sermons, or to laugh at his odd ways, was sure to bring down on the offender a heavy fine. His advice was often sought on matters of state, nor did he hesitate to give, unasked, his opinion on what he considered the arbitrary acts of the high functionaries of the province. In the years immediately preceding the war the power of the minister in matters of government and politics had been greatly impaired by the rise of that class of laymen in the foremost rank of which stood Otis and Hancock and Samuel Adams. Yet his spiritual influence was as great as ever. He was still a member of the most learned and respected class in a community by no means ignorant. He was a divine, and came of a family of divines. Not a few of the preachers who witnessed the Revolution could trace descent through an unbroken line of ministers, stretching back from son to father for three generations, to some canting, psalm-singing Puritan who bore arms with distinc-

John Bach McMaster.

tion on the great day at Naseby, or had prayed at the head of Oliver's troops, and had, at the restoration, when the old soldiers of the Protector were turning their swords into reaping-hooks and their pikes into pruning-knives, come over to New England to seek that liberty of worship not to be found at home. Such a man had usually received a learned education at Harvard or at Yale, and would, in these days, be thought a scholar of high attainments.   . .

In the election sermon which he delivered on the return of every election-day, he taught a very different lesson, exerted his eloquence to set forth the equality of all men and the beauties of a pure democracy, and taxed his learning to defend his politics with passages from scripture and quotations from the writers of Greece.

Hatred of Kings and Princes had, indeed, always been a marked characteristic of his sect, and in the pre-revolutionary days he was among the most eager in the patriot cause. It cannot be denied that this show of patriotism was, in most cases, the result of personal interest rather than of a deeply rooted conviction of the necessity of resisting the oppression of England. If there was one sect of Christians which he detested above another, that sect was the Episcopalian. He firmly believed that the stupid King, who cared as little for the Church of England as for the Church of Scotland, was fully determined to make Episcopacy the established religion of the colonies. He was sure that His Majesty had even matured a plan for the establishment of the Church, and that, before many months had gone by, laws as odious as the Conventicle Act and the Five-Mile Act would be in full operation; that hundreds of dissenting divines would be ejected from their churches, stripped of their livings, and sent to starve among the Indians on the frontier. While, therefore, the rectors of Virginia and the Carolinas were ranging themselves on the Tory side, the ministers of the eastern colonies were all active on the side of the Whigs.   .   .   .

In truth, of the writers who, up to the peace, and for many years after, put forth treatises, arguments, and expositions on metaphysical themes, scarcely one can be named who was not a native of New England, and a pastor of a New England church. Each minister, therefore, felt in duty bound to discuss his text in a philosophical way, and, however crude his attempt, the reasons he advanced, the analogies he drew, the hints and suggestions he threw out, furnished each week many new topics for an evening's talk. And such topics were needed, for of news the dearth was great. Almost every means of collecting and distributing it familiar to this generation was unknown to our great-grandfathers. There were, indeed, newspapers. Forty-three had come safely through the long revolutionary struggle to publish the joyful tidings of peace. But, with a few exceptions, all were printed in the large towns, and news which depended on them for circulation was in much danger of never going fifty miles from the editor's door.

An interchange of papers did go on among the printers; and some copies of the "Spy" and the "Columbian Centinel" found their way to subscribers at New York. But the papers were not received by the post-office, and it was only by rewarding the post-riders that a place was made for a dozen copies in the portmanteaus containing the letters. Even then, on reaching

New York, they were almost a week old, and had they been carried on to Charleston would have entered that city twenty days after the date of publication. Had the time been less it would have mattered little, for the news to be derived from them was usually of small value, and likely to convey only the most general information. Even the Connecticut "Courant," the Boston "Gazette," and the Pennsylvania "Packet," which seem to have been the best among them, were poor and mean-looking, and printed on paper such as would now be thought too bad for hand-bills and ballads. Few came out oftener than thrice in a week, or numbered more than four small pages. The amount of reading-matter which the whole forty-three contained each week would not be sufficient to fill ten pages of ten daily issues of the New York "Herald." Nothing in the nature of an editorial page existed. What is now known as a leading article rarely appeared, and its place was supplied by appeals from the editor, sometimes serious, sometimes humorous, to his delinquent subscribers, begging them to pay their bills, if not in money, in quarters of wheat, in pounds of cheese, or the flesh of hogs. The rest of the paper was filled up with advertisements for runaway slaves or stray horses, with scraps taken from other papers, with letters written from distant places to friends of the editor, a summary of the news brought by the last packet from Lisbon or London, a proclamation by Congress, a note to the editor posting some enemy as a coward in the most abusive and scurrilous language, a long notice setting forth that a new assortment of calamancoes and durants, colored tammies, shalloons, and rattinels were offered for sale at the shop of a leading merchant, and, now and then, a proposal for the reprinting of an old book. When there was a scarcity of intelligence, when no ships had come in from the whale-fisheries, when no strictures were to be passed on the proceedings of Congress, when the mails had been kept back by the rains, when the editor was tired of reviling the Society of the Cincinnati, when nothing further was to be said against the refugees, when no election was to be held, when no distinguished strangers had come to town, when no man of note had been buried, and when, consequently, there was great difficulty in filling the four pages, odes, ballads, and bits of poetry made their appearance in the poet's corner. Now and then a paper of enterprise and spirit undertook to enlighten its readers and to fill its columns by the publication in instalments of works of considerable length and high literary merit. Robertson's "History of America" was reprinted in the "Weekly Advertiser" of Boston, and ran through more than one hundred and fifty numbers. A "History of the American Revolution" came out in the "Spy." "Cook's Voyages" were published in the Pennsylvania "Packet," while other papers of lesser note found room among essays and lampoons, epigrams, anecdotes, coarse "bon-mots," and town resolutions to discourage extravagance, for short treatises on geography and morals. But everything which now gives to the daily paper its peculiar value, and passes under the general name of news, was wanting.

THE AMERICAN WORKMAN IN 1784.

[From the Same.]

THERE can, however, be no doubt that a wonderful amelioration has taken place since that day in the condition of the poor. Their houses were meaner, their food was coarser, their clothing was of commoner stuff; their wages were, despite the depreciation that has gone on in the value of money, lower by one half than at present. A man who performed what would now be called unskilled labor, who sawed wood, who dug ditches, who mended the roads, who mixed mortar, who carried boards to the carpenter and bricks to the mason, or helped to cut hay in the harvest-time, usually received as the fruit of his daily toil two shillings. Sometimes when the laborers were few he was paid more, and became the envy of his fellows if, at the end of a week, he took home to his family fifteen shillings, a sum now greatly exceeded by four dollars. Yet all authorities agree that in 1784 the hire of workmen was twice as great as in 1774.

On such a pittance it was only by the strictest economy that a mechanic kept his children from starvation and himself from jail. In the low and dingy rooms which he called his home were wanting many articles of adornment and of use now to be found in the dwellings of the poorest of his class. Sand sprinkled on the floor did duty as a carpet. There was no glass on his table, there was no china in his cupboard, there were no prints on his wall. What a stove was he did not know, coal he had never seen, matches he had never heard of. Over a fire of fragments of boxes and barrels, which he lit with the sparks struck from a flint, or with live coals brought from a neighbor's hearth, his wife cooked up a rude meal and served it in pewter dishes. He rarely tasted fresh meat as often as once in a week, and paid for it a much higher price than his posterity. Everything, indeed, which ranked as a staple of life was very costly. Corn stood at three shillings the bushel, wheat at eight and sixpence, an assize of bread was fourpence, a pound of salt pork was tenpence. Many other commodities now to be seen on the tables of the poor were either quite unknown or far beyond the reach of his scanty means. Unenviable is the lot of that man who cannot, in the height of the season, when the wharfs and markets are heaped with baskets and crates of fruit, spare three cents for a pound of grapes or five cents for as many peaches, or, when Sunday comes round, indulge his family with watermelons or cantaloupes. One hundred years ago the wretched fox-grape was the only kind that found its way to market, and was the luxury of the rich. Among the fruits and vegetables of which no one had then even heard are cantaloupes, many varieties of peaches and pears, tomatoes and rhubarb, sweet corn, the cauliflower, the egg-plant, head lettuce, and okra. On the window-benches of every tenement-house may be seen growing geraniums and verbenas, flowers not known a century ago. In truth, the best-kept gardens were then rank with hollyhocks and sunflowers, roses and snowballs, lilacs, pinks, tulips, and, above all, the Jerusalem cherry, a plant once much admired, but now scarcely seen.

If the food of an artisan would now be thought coarse, his clothes would be thought abominable. A pair of yellow buckskin or leathern breeches, a checked shirt, a red flannel jacket, a rusty felt hat cocked up at the corners, shoes of neat's-skin set off with huge buckles of brass, and a leathern apron, comprised his scanty wardrobe. The leather he smeared with grease to keep it soft and flexible. His sons followed in his footsteps, or were apprenticed to neighboring tradesmen. His daughter went out to service. She performed, indeed, all the duties at present exacted from women of her class; but with them were coupled many others rendered useless by the great improvement that has since taken place in the conveniences of life. She mended the clothes, she did up the ruffs, she ran on errands from one end of the town to the other, she milked the cows, made the butter, walked ten blocks for a pail of water, spun flax for the family linen, and, when the year was up, received ten pounds for her wages. Yet, small as was her pay, she had, before bestowing herself in marriage on the footman or the gardener, laid away in her stocking enough guineas and joes to buy a few chairs, a table, and a bed.

Willis Brooks Hawkins.

Born in Aurora, Ill., 1852.

LANGUAGE THAT NEEDS A REST.

[*The Washington Post.* 1889.]

I WAS awakened in the middle of the night by a disturbance in the library. It did not seem to be the noise of burglars. It was more like the murmuring sound of many tongues engaged in spirited debate. I listened closely and concluded it must be some sort of a discussion being held by the words in my big unabridged dictionary. Creeping softly to the door, I stood and listened.

"I don't care," said the little word *Of;* "I may not be very big, but that is no reason why everybody should take advantage of me. I am the most mercilessly overworked word in the whole dictionary, and there is no earthly reason for it, either. People say they 'consider of' and 'approve of' and 'accept of' and 'admit of' all sorts of things. Then they say 'all of us,' and 'both of them,' and 'first of all,' and tell about 'looking out of' the window, or cutting a piece of bread 'off of' the loaf, until I am utterly tired out."

"Pshaw!" said the word *Up,* "I am not much bigger than you and I do twice as much work, and a good deal of it needlessly, too. People 'wake up' in the morning and 'get up' and 'shake up' their beds and 'dress up' and 'wash up' and 'draw up' to the table, and 'eat up' and 'drink up' their breakfast. Then they 'jump up' from the table and 'hurry up' to 'go up' to the corner, where the street-car driver 'pulls up' his horses and the passengers 'ascend up' the steps and 'go up' into the front seats and the con-

ductor 'takes up' the tickets. All this is done even before people 'get up'
town and 'take up' their day's work. From that time until they 'put up'
their books and 'shut up' their offices I do more work than any two words in
this book ; and even after business hours I am worked until people 'lock up'
their houses and 'go up' to bed and 'cover themselves up' and 'shut up'
their eyes for the night. It would take a week to tell what I have to 'put up'
with in a day, and I am a good deal 'worked up' over it."

"I agree that both *Up* and *Of* are very much overworked," said the word
Stated, "but I think I, myself, deserve a little sympathy. I am doing not
only my own legitimate work, but also that which ought to be done by my
friend *Said.* Nobody 'says' anything nowadays ; he always 'states' it."

"Yes," chipped in the funny little word *Pun,* "these are very *stately*
times."

Some of the words laughed at this, but *Humor* said : "*Pun* is a simpleton."

"No," answered *Wit ;* "he is a fellow of duplicities."

"He makes me tired," said *Slang.*

Then the discussion was resumed.

"I do a great deal of needless work," said the word *But.* "People say they
have no doubt 'but that' it will rain, and that they shouldn't wonder 'but
what' it would snow, until I don't know 'but' I shall strike."

"What I have most to complain about," said the word *As,* "is that I am
forced to associate so much with the word *Equally.* Only yesterday a man
said he could 'see equally as well as' another man. I don't see what business
Equally had in that sentence."

"Well," retorted *Equally,* "men every day say that something is 'equally
as good' as something else, and I don't see what business *As* has in that sentence."

"I think," said *Propriety,* "you two should be divorced by mutual consent."

There was a fluttering sound and a clamor of voices.

"We, too, ought to be granted divorce," was the substance of what they
said ; and among the voices I recognized those of the following-named
couples : *Cover Over, Enter In, From Thence, Go Fetch, Have Got, Latter
End, Continue On, Converse Together, New Beginner, Old Veteran, Return
Back, Rise Up, Sink Down, They Both, Try And, More Perfect, Seldom
Ever, Almost Never, Feel Badly, United Together, Two First, An One, Over
Again, Repeat Again,* and many others.

When quietude had been restored, the word *Rest* said : "You words all
talk of being overworked as if that were the worst thing that could happen to
a fellow, but I tell you it is much worse to be cut out of your own work. Now,
look at me. Here I am ready and willing to perform my part in the speech of
the day, but almost everybody passes by me and employs my awkward friend
Balance. It is the commonest thing in the world to hear people say they will
pay the 'balance' of a debt or will sleep the 'balance' of the night."

"I suffer considerably from this same kind of neglect," said the word
Deem. "Nobody ever 'deems' a thing beautiful any more ; it is always 'considered' beautiful, when in fact it is not considered at all."

"True," said *Irritate;* "and people talk of being 'aggravated' when they ought instead to give me work."

"And me," said *Purpose;* "look at me. I get hardly anything to do because people are always 'proposing' to do this or that when no idea of a proposition is involved. Why, I read the other day of a man who had 'proposed' to murder another when really he had never said a word about it to a living being. Of course he only purposed to commit the murder."

"If it is my turn," said the word *Among*, "I should like to protest against *Mr. Between* doing my work. The idea of people saying a man divided an orange 'between' his three children! It humiliates me."

"It is no worse," said the word *Fewer*, "than to have people say there were 'less' men in one army than in another."

"No," added *More Than;* "and no worse than to have them say there were 'over' 100,000 men."

"It seems to me," said the word *Likely*, "that nobody has more reason for complaint than I have. My friend *Liable* is doing nearly all my work. They say a man is 'liable' to be sick or 'liable' to be out of town when the question of liability does not enter into the matter at all."

"You're no worse off than I am," said the little word *So;* "that fellow *Such* is doing all my work. People say there never was 'such' a glorious country as this when, of course, they mean there never was 'so' glorious a country elsewhere."

I saw that there was likely to be no end to this discussion, since half the words in the dictionary were making efforts to put in their complaints, so I returned to my couch; and I will leave it to any person who has read this account to say whether I had not already heard enough to make me or anybody else sleepy.

Brander Matthews.

BORN in New Orleans, La., 1852.

PLAYING A PART.

[Playing a Part. A Comedy for Amateur Acting.—In Partnership. 1884.]

SCENE : *A handsomely-furnished parlor, with a general air of home comfort. A curtained window on each side of the central fireplace would light the room if it were not evening, as the lamp on the work-table in the centre of the room informs us. At one side of the work-table is the wife, winding a ball of worsted from a skein which her husband holds in his hands.*

HE, looking at watch, aside. "This wool takes as long to wind up as a bankrupt estate." Fidgets.

SHE. "Do keep still, Jack! Stop fidgeting and jumping around."

HE. "When you pull the string, Jenny, I am always a jumping-jack to dance attendance on you."

SHE, seriously. "Very pretty, indeed! It was true too—once—before we were married; now you lead me a different dance."

HE. "I am your partner still."

SHE, sadly. "But the figure is always the Ladies' Chain."

HE, aside. "If I don't get away soon I sha'n't be able to do any work to-night." Aloud: "What do you mean by that solemn tone?"

SHE. "Oh, nothing—nothing of any consequence."

HE, aside. "We look like two fools acting in private theatricals."

SHE, finishing ball of worsted. "That will do; thank you. Do not let me detain you; I know you are in a hurry."

HE. "I have my work to do."

SHE. "So it seems; and it takes all day and half the night."

HE, rising and going to fireplace. "I am working hard for our future happiness."

SHE, quietly. "I should like a little of the happiness now."

HE, standing with back to fireplace. "Are you unhappy?"

SHE. "Oh no—not very."

HE. "Do you not have everything you wish?"

SHE. "Oh yes—except the one thing I want most."

HE. "Well, my dear, I am at home as much as I can be."

SHE. "So you think I meant you?"

HE, embarrassed. "Well—I did suppose—that——"

SHE. "Yes, I used to want you. The days were long enough while you were away, and I waited for your return. Now I have been alone so much that I am getting accustomed to solitude. And I do not really know what it is I do want. I am listless, nervous, good-for-nothing——"

HE, gallantly. "You are good enough for me."

SHE. "You did think so once; and perhaps you would think so again—if you could spare the time to get acquainted with me."

HE, surprised. "Jenny, are you ill?"

SHE. "Not more so than usual. I was bright enough two years ago, when we were married. But for two years I have not lived; I have vegetated—more like a plant than a human being; and even plants require some sunshine."

HE, aside. "I have never heard her talk like this before. I don't understand it." Aloud: "Why, Jenny, you speak as if I were a cloud over your life."

SHE. "Do I? Well, it does not matter."

HE. "I try to be a good husband, don't I?"

SHE, indifferently. "As well as you know how, I suppose."

HE. "Do I deprive you of anything you want?"

SHE, impatiently. "Of course you do not."

HE. "I work hard, I know, but when I go out in the evening now and then——"

SHE, aside. "Six nights every week." Sighing.

HE. "I really work. There are husbands who say they are at work when they are at the club playing poker. Now, I am really working."

SHE, impatiently. "You have no small vices." Rising. "Is there no work calling you away to-night? Why are you not off?"

HE, looking at watch. "I am a little late, that's a fact; still, I can do what I have to do if I work like a horse."

SHE. "Have you to draw a conveyance? That is the old joke."

HE. "This is no joke. It's a divorce suit."

SHE, quickly. "Is it that Lightfoot person again?"

HE. "It is Mrs. Lightfoot's case. She is a very fine woman, and her husband has treated her shamefully."

SHE. "Better than the creature deserved, I dare say. You will win her case for her?"

HE. "I shall do my best."

SHE, sarcastically. "No doubt." Aside: "I hate that woman!" Crosses the room and sits on sofa on the right of the fireplace.

HE. "But the result of a lawsuit is generally a toss-up; and heads do not always win."

SHE. "I wish you luck this time—for her husband's sake; he'll be glad to be rid of her. But I doubt it; you can't get up any sympathy by exhibiting her to the jury; she isn't good-looking enough."

HE, quickly. "She's a very fine woman indeed."

SHE, aside. "How eagerly he defends her!" Aloud: "She's a great big, tall, giantess creature, with a face like a wax doll and a head of hair like a Circassian girl. No juryman will fall in love with her."

HE. "How often have I told you that Justice does not consider persons! Now, in the eye of the law——"

SHE, interrupting. "Do you acknowledge that the law has but one eye and can see only one side?"

HE. "Are you jealous?" Crossing and standing in front of her.

SHE. "Jealous of this Mrs. Lightfoot?" Laughs. "Ridiculous!"

HE. "I am glad of it, for I think a jealous woman has a very poor opinion of herself."

SHE, forcibly. "And it is her business which takes you out to-night?"

HE, going toward the left-hand door. "I have to go across to the Bar Association to look up some points, and——"

SHE, rising quickly. "And you can just send me a cab. I shall go to Mrs. Playfair's to rehearse again for the private theatricals."

HE, annoyed, coming back. "But I had asked you to give it up."

SHE, with growing excitement. "And I had almost determined to give it up, but I have changed my mind. That's a woman's privilege, isn't it? I am tired of spending my evenings by myself."

HE. "Now be reasonable, Jenny; I must work."

SHE. "And I must play—in the private theatricals."

HE. "But I don't like private theatricals."

SHE. "Don't you? I do."

HE. "And I particularly dislike amateur actors."

SHE. "Do you? I don't. I like some of them very much; and some of them like me, too."

HE. "The deuce they do!"

SHE. "Tom Thursby and Dick Carey and Harry Wylde were all disputing who should make love to me."

HE. "Make love to you?"

SHE. "In the play—in 'Husbands and Wives.'"

HE. "Do you mean to say that you are going to act on the stage with those brainless idiots?"

SHE, interrupting. "Do not call my friends names; it is in bad taste."

HE. "What will people say when they see my wife pawed and clawed by those fellows?"

SHE. "Let them say what they please. Do you think I care for the tittle-tattle of the riffraff of society?"

HE. "But, Jenny—" Brusquely: "Confound it! I have no patience with you!"

SHE "So I have discovered. But you need not lose your temper here, and swear. Go outside and do it, and leave me alone, as I am every evening."

He. "You talk as if I ill-treated you."

She, sarcastically. "Do I? That is very wicked of me, isn't it? You take the best possible care of me, you are ever thinking of me, and you never leave my side for a moment. Oh no, you do not ill-treat me—or abuse me—or neglect me"—breaking down—"or make me miserable. There is nothing the matter with me, of course. But you never will believe I have a heart until you have broken it!" Sinking on chair, C.

He, crossing to her. "You are excited, I see; still, I must say this is a little too much."

She, starting up. "Don't come near me!" Sarcastically: "Don't let me keep you from your work"—going to door—"and don't fail to send me a cab. At last I revolt against your neglect."

He, indignantly protesting. "My neglect? Do you mean to say I neglect you? My conscience does not reproach me."

She, at the door. "That's because you haven't any!" Exit, slamming door.

He, alone. "I never saw her go on that way before. What can be the matter with her? She is not like herself at all; she is low-spirited and nervous. Now, I never could see why women had any nerves. I wonder if she really thinks that I neglect her? I should be sorry, very sorry, if she did. I'll not go out to-night; I'll stay at home and have a quiet evening at my own fireside." Sits in chair in the centre. "I think that will bring her round. I'd like to know what has made her act like this. Has she been reading any sentimental trash, I wonder?" Sees book in work-basket. "Now, here's some yellow-covered literature." Takes it up. "Why, it's that confounded play, 'Husbands and Wives.' Let me see the silly stuff." Reads. "'My darling, one more embrace, one last, long, loving kiss'; and then he hugs her and kisses her." Rising. "And she thinks I'll have her play a part like that? How should I look while that was going on? Can't she find something else?" At work-table. "Here is another." Takes up second pamphlet. "No, it is a 'Guide to the Passions.' I fear I need no guide to get into a passion. I doubt if there's as much hugging and kissing in this as in the other one." Reads. "'It is impossible to describe all the effects of the various passions, but a few hints are here given as to how the more important may be delineated.'" Spoken. "This is interesting. If ever I have to delineate a passion I shall fall back on this guide." Reads. "'Love is a—'" Reads hastily and unintelligibly. "'When successful, love authorizes the fervent embrace of the beloved!' The deuce it does! And I find my wife getting instruction from this Devil's text-book! A little more and I should be jealous." Looks at book. "Ah, here is jealousy; now let's see how I ought to feel." Reads. "'Jealousy is a mixture of passions and—'" Reads hastily and unintelligibly. "Not so bad! I believe I could act up to these instructions." Jumping up. "And I will! My wife wants acting; she shall have it! She complains of monotony; she shall have variety! 'Jealousy is a mixture of passions.' I'll be jealous; I'll give her a mixture of passions. I'll take a leaf out of her book, and I'll find a cure for these nerves of hers. I'll learn my part at once; we'll have some private theatricals to order." Walks up and down studying book.

She reënters, with bonnet on and cloak over her arm, and stands in surprise, watching him.

She. "You here still?"

He. "Yes."

She. "Have you ordered a cab for me?"

He. "No."

She. "And why not?"

He, aside. "Now's my chance. Mixture of passions—I'll try suspicion first." Aloud: "Because I do not approve of the people you are going to meet—these Thursbys and Careys and Wyldes."

SHE, calmly sitting on sofa. "Perhaps you would like to revise my visiting-list, and tell the servant whom I am to receive."

HE. "You may see what ladies you please——"

SHE, interrupting. "Thank you; still, I do not please to see Mrs. Lightfoot."

HE, annoyed. "I say nothing of her."

SHE. "Oh dear, no! I dare say you keep it as secret as you can."

HE, aside. "Simple suspicion is useless. What's next?" Glances in pamphlet. "'Peevish personalities.' I will pass on to peevish personalities." Aloud: "Now, these men, these fellows who strut about the stage for an idle hour, who are they? This Tom Thursby, who wanted to make love to you—who is he?"

SHE. "Are you going to ask many questions? Is this catechism a long one? If it is, I may as well lay aside my shawl."

HE. "Who is he, I say; I insist upon knowing."

SHE. "He's a good enough fellow in his way."

HE, sternly. "He had best beware how he gets in *my* way."

SHE, aside. "There's a great change in his manner. I do not understand it."

HE. "And this Dick Carey—who is he?" Stalking toward her.

SHE, starting up and crossing. "Are you trying to frighten me by this violence?"

HE, aside. "It is producing an effect."

SHE. "But I am not afraid of you, if I am a weak woman and you are a strong man."

HE, aside. "It is going all right." Aloud, fiercely: "Answer me at once! Is this Carey married?"

SHE. "I believe he is."

HE. "You believe! Don't you know? Does his wife act with these strollers? Have you not seen her?"

SHE. "I have never seen her. She and her husband are like the two buckets in a well; they never turn up together. They meet only to clash, and one is always throwing cold water on the other."

HE. "And Harry Wylde! Is he married?"

SHE. "Yes; and his wife is always keeping him in hot water."

HE. "And so he comes to you for consolation?"

SHE, laughing. "He needs no consoling; he has always such a flow of spirits."

HE. "I've heard the fellow drank."

SHE, surprised, aside. "Can Jack be jealous? I wish I could think so, for then I might hope he still loved me."

HE. "And do you suppose I can allow you to associate with these fellows, who all want to make love to you?"

SHE, aside, joyfully. "He *is* jealous! The dear boy!"

HE, fiercely. "Do you think I can permit this, madam?"

SHE, aside. "'Madam!' I could hug him for loving me enough to call me 'madam' like that. But I must not give in too soon."

HE. "Have you nothing to say for yourself? Can you find no words to defend yourself, woman?"

SHE, aside. "'Woman!' He calls me 'woman'! I can forgive him anything now."

HE. "Are you dumb, woman? Have you naught to say?"

SHE, gleefully, aside. "I had no idea I had married an Othello!" She sees the pillow on the sofa, and, crossing to it quietly, hides the pillow behind the sofa.

HE, aside. "What did she mean by that?" Aloud, fiercely: "Do you intend to deny——"

SHE, interrupting. "I have nothing to deny; I have nothing to conceal."

HE. "Do you deny that you confessed these fellows sought to make love to you?"

SHE. "I do not deny that." Mischievously. "But I never thought you would worry about such trifles."

HE. "Trifles! madam? Trifles, indeed!" Glances in book and quoting:

> "'Trifles light as air
> Are to the jealous confirmations strong
> As proofs of holy writ.'"

SHE, surprised, aside. "Where did he get his blank verse?"

HE, aside. "That seemed to tell. I'll give her some more." Glancing in pamphlet, and quoting:

> "'But, alas, to make me
> A fixed figure for the time of scorn
> To point his slow, unmoving finger at!'"

SHE, aside, jumping up with indignation. "Why, it *is* 'Othello' he is quoting! He is acting! He is positively playing a part! It is shameful of him! It's not real jealousy; it's a sham. Oh, the wretch! But I'll pay him back! I'll make him jealous without any make-believe."

HE, aside. "I'm getting on capitally. I'm making a strong impression; I am rousing her out of her nervousness. I doubt if she will want any more private theatricals now. I don't think I shall have to repeat the lesson. This 'Guide to the Passions' is a first-rate book; I'll keep one in the house all the time."

SHE, aside. "If he plays Othello, I can play Iago. I'll give his jealousy something to feed on. I have no blank verse for him, but I'll make him blank enough before I am done with him. Oh, the villain!"

HE, aside. "Now let me try threatening." Glancing in book. "'Pity the sorrows of a poor old man'—I've got the wrong place. That's not threatening—that's senility." Turning over page. "Ah, here it is."

SHE, aside. "And he thinks he can jest with a woman's heart and not be punished? Oh, the wickedness of man!" Forcibly: "Oh, if mamma were only here, now!"

HE, threateningly. "Who are these fellows? This Tom, Dick and Harry are—are they"—hesitates, and glances in pamphlet—"are they 'framed to make women false'?"

SHE, aside. "Why, he's got a book! It's my 'Guide to the Passions.' The wretch has actually been copying his jealousy out of my own book." Aloud, with pretended emotion: "Dear me, Jack, you never before objected to my little flirtations." Aside, watching him: "How will he like that?"

HE, aside, puzzled. "'Little flirtations!' I don't like that—I don't like it at all."

SHE. "They have all been attentive, of course——"

HE, aside. "'Of course!' I don't like that, either."

SHE. "But I did not think you would so take to heart a few innocent endearments."

HE, starting. "'Innocent endearments!' Do you mean to say that they offer you any 'innocent endearments'?"

SHE, quietly. "Don't be so boisterous, Jack; you will crush my book."

HE, looking at pamphlet crushed in his hand, and throwing it from him. Aside: "Confound the book! I do not need any prompting now." Aloud: "Which of these men has dared to offer you any 'innocent endearments'?"

SHE, hesitatingly. "Well—I don't know—that I ought to tell you—since you take things so queerly. But Tom——"

HE, forcibly. "Tom?"

SHE. "Mr. Thursby, I mean. He and I are very old friends, you know—I believe we are third cousins or so—and of course I don't stand on ceremony with him."

HE. "And he does not stand on ceremony with you, I suppose?"

SHE. "Oh, no. In fact, we are first-rate friends. Indeed, when Dick Carey wanted to make love to me, he was quite jealous."

HE. "Oh, *he* was jealous, was he? The fellow's impudence is amazing! When I meet him I'll give him a piece of my mind."

SHE, demurely. "Are you sure you can spare it!"

HE. "Don't irritate me too far, Jenny; I've a temper of my own."

SHE. "You seem to have lost it now."

HE. "Do you not see that I am in a heat about this thing? How can you sit there so calmly? You keep cool like a"—hesitates—"like a——"

SHE, interrupting. "Like a burning-glass, I keep cool myself while setting you on fire? Exactly so, and I suppose you would prefer me to be a looking-glass in which you could see only yourself?"

HE. "A wife should reflect her husband's image, and not that of a pack of fools."

SHE. "Come, come, Jack, you are not jealous?"

HE. "'Jealous!' Of course I am not jealous, but I am very much annoyed."

SHE. "I am glad that you are not jealous, for I have always heard that a jealous man has a very poor opinion of himself." Aside: "There's one for him."

HE. "I am not jealous, but I will probe this thing to the bottom; I must know the truth."

SHE, aside. "He *is* jealous now; and this is real; I am sure it is."

HE. "Go on, tell me more; I must get at the bottom facts. There's nothing like truth."

SHE, aside. "There is nothing like it in what he's learning."

HE, aside. "This Carey is harmless enough, and he can't help talking. He's a—he's a telescope; you have only to draw him out, and anybody can see through him. I'll get hold of him, draw him out, and then shut him up!" Crossing excitedly.

SHE, aside. "How much more his real jealousy moves me than his pretence of it! He seems very much affected. No man could be as jealous as he is unless he was very much in love."

HE, with affected coolness. "You have told me about Tom and Dick; pray, have you nothing to say about Harry?"

SHE. "Mr. Wylde?" Enthusiastically: "He is a man after my own heart!"

HE. "So he is after it?" Savagely: "Just let me get after him!"

SHE, coolly. "Well, if you do not like his attentions, you can take him apart and tell him so."

HE, vindictively. "If I took him apart he'd never get put together again!"

SHE. "Mr. Wylde is very much afraid of his wife, but when she is not there he is more devoted than either of the others."

HE. "'More devoted!' What else shall I hear, I wonder?"

SHE. "It was he who had to kiss me."

HE, startled. "What?"

SHE. "I told him not to do it. I knew I should blush if he kissed me. I always do."

HE, in great agitation. "You always do? Has this man ever—" Breaking down. "Oh, Jenny! Jenny! you do not know what you are doing. I do not blame you—it is not your fault; it is mine. I did not know how much I loved you, and I find it out now, when it is perhaps too late."

SHE, aside. "How I have longed for a few words of love like these! and they have come at last!"

He. "I have been too selfish; I have thought too much of my work and too little of your happiness. I see now what a mistake I have made."

She, aside. "I cannot sit still here and see him waste his love in the air like this."

He. "I shall turn over a new leaf. If you will let me, I shall devote myself to you, taking care of you and making you happy."

She, aside. "If he had only spoken like that before!"

He. "I will try to win you away from these associates. I am sure that in your heart you do not care for them." Crossing to her. "You know that I love you; can I not hope to win you back to me?"

She, aside. "Once before he spoke to me of his love. I can remember every tone of his voice, every word he said."

He. "Jenny, is my task hopeless?"

She, quietly crossing to arm-chair. "The task is easy, Jack." Smiling. "Perhaps you think too much of these associates. Perhaps you think a good deal more of them than I do. In fact, I am sure that to-night you were the one who took to private theatricals first. By the way, where's my 'Guide to the Passions'? Have you seen it lately?"

He, half comprehending. "Your 'Guide to the Passions'? A book with a yellow cover? I think I *have* seen it."

She. "I saw it last in your hand—just after you had been quoting 'Othello.'"

He. "'Othello'? Oh, then you know——"

She, smiling. "Yes, I know. I saw, I understood, and I retaliated on the spot."

He. "You retaliated?"

She. "I paid you off in your own coin—counterfeit, like yours."

He, joyfully. "Then Tom did not make love to you?"

She. "Oh, yes he did—in the play."

He. "And Dick is not devoted?"

She. "Yes, he is—in the play."

He. "And Harry did not try to kiss you?"

She. "Indeed he did—in the play."

He. "Then you have been playing a part?"

She. "Haven't you?"

He. "Haven't I? Certainly not. At least—well, at least I will say nothing more about Tom or Dick or Harry."

She. "And I will say nothing more of Mrs. Lightfoot."

He, dropping in chair to her right. "Mrs. Lightfoot is a fine woman, my dear"—she looks up—"but she is not my style at all. Besides, you know, it was only as a matter of business, for the sake of our future prospects, that I took her part."

She, throwing him a skein of wool. "And it is only for the sake of our future happiness that I have been playing mine."

He holds the wool and she winds the ball, and the curtain falls, leaving them in the same position in which its rising discovered them.

THE NOVEL AND THE DRAMA.

[The Dramatization of Novels.—Longman's Magazine. 1889.]

THIS, I take it, is one of the chief characteristics of the true dramatist—that he sees at once when a form is outworn, and lets the dead past bury its dead; that he utilizes all the latest devices of the stage while recognizing frankly and fully the limitations imposed by the physical conditions of the theatre. As I have already suggested, these limitations forbid not a few of the effects permissible to the novelist. No dramatist may open his story with a solitary horseman, as was once the fashion of fiction; nor can he show the hero casually rescuing the heroine from a prairie on fire, or from a slip into the rapids of Niagara; and he finds it impossible to get rid of the villain by throwing him under the wheels of a locomotive. Not only is the utilization of the forces of nature very difficult on the stage, and extremely doubtful, but the description of nature herself is out of place; and however expert the scene-painter, he cannot hope to vie with Victor Hugo or Hawthorne in calling up before the eye the grandeur or the picturesqueness of the scene where the action of the story comes to its climax.

Time was when the drama was first, and prose-fiction limped a long way after; time was when the novelists, even the greatest of them, began as playwrights. Cervantes, Le Sage, Fielding, all studied the art of character-drawing on the boards of a theatre, although no one of their plays keeps the stage to-day, while we still read with undiminished zest the humorous record of the adventures and misadventures of "Don Quixote," "Gil Blas," and "Tom Jones." Scott was, perhaps, the first great novelist who did not learn his trade behind the scenes. It seemed to Mr. Lowell, that before Fielding "real life formed rather the scenic background than the substance, and that the characters are, after all, merely players who represent certain types rather than the living types themselves." It may be suggested that the earlier novels reflected the easy expedients and artificial manners of the theatre, much as the writers may have employed the processes of the stage. Since Fielding and Scott the novel has been expanding, until it seeks to overshadow its elder brother. The old inter-dependence of the drama and prose-fiction has ceased; nowadays the novel and the play are independent, each with its own aims and with its own methods. The advocates of the one are as boastful as the partisans of the other are intolerant, and each is as self-assertive as the young actress who—so her enterprising advance agent in his advertisement declared—"has appeared in all the countries of the world, and has been pronounced the greatest of them all!"

While on the one hand there are not lacking those who see in the modern novel but a bastard epic in low prose, so there are not wanting others, novelists and critics of literature, chiefly in France, where the principles of dramatic art are better understood than elsewhere, who are so impressed by the number and magnitude of the restrictions which bind the dramatist, that they are inclined to declare the drama itself to be an outworn form. They think that the limitations imposed on the dramatist are so rigid that first-rate literary workmen will not accept them, and that first-rate literary work cannot be hoped for. These critics are on the verge of hinting that nowadays the drama is little more than a polite amusement, just as others might call oratory now little more than the art of making after-dinner speeches. They suggest that the play is sadly primitive when compared with the perfected novel of the nineteenth century. They remark that the drama can show but a corner of life, while prose-fiction may reveal almost the whole of it. They

Brander Matthews

assert boldly that the drama is no longer the form of literature best suited to the treatment of the subjects in which the thinking people of to-day are interested. They declare that the novelist may grapple resolutely with a topic of the times, though the dramatist dare not scorch his fingers with a burning question. The Goncourts, in the preface of their undramatic play, "La Patrie en Danger," announced that "the drama of to-day is not literature."

It is well to mass these criticisms together that they may be met once and for all. It is true that the taste for analysis which dominates the prose-fiction of our time has affected the drama but little ; and it is not easy to say whether or not the formulas of the theatre can be so enlarged, modified, and made more delicate that the dramatist can really rival the novelist in psychologic subtlety. Of course, if the novel continues to develop in one direction in accordance with a general current of literature, and if the drama does not develop along the same lines, then the drama will be left behind, and it will become a mere sport, an empty spectacle, a toy for children, spoonmeat for babes.

A book, however fine or peculiar, delicate or spiritual, goes in time to the hundred or the thousand congenial spirits for whom it was intended ; it may not get to its address at once or even in its author's lifetime ; but sooner or later its message is delivered to all who are ready to receive it. A play can have no such fate ; and for it there is no redemption, if once it is damned. It cannot live by pleasing a few only ; to earn the right to exist, it must please the many. And this is at the bottom of all dislike for the dramatic form— that it appeals to the crowd, to the broad public, to all classes alike, rich and poor, learned and ignorant, rough and refined. And this is to me the great merit of the drama, that it cannot be dilettante, finikin, precious, narrow. It must handle broad themes broadly. It must deal with the common facts of humanity. It is the democrat of literature. Théophile Gautier, who disliked the theatre, said that an idea never found its way on the stage until it was worn threadbare in newspapers and in novels. And he was not far out. As the drama appeals to the public at large, it must consider seriously only those subjects which the public at large can understand and are interested in. There are exceptions, no doubt, now and again, when an adroit dramatist succeeds in captivating the public with a theme still in debate. M. Sardou, for example, wrote "Daniel Rochat" ten years before Mrs. Ward wrote "Robert Elsmere," and the Frenchman's play was acted in New York for more than a hundred nights. M. Alexandre Dumas *fils* has again and again discussed on the stage marriage and divorce and other problems that vex mankind to-day. And in Scandinavia Henrik Ibsen, a dramatist of exceeding technical skill and abundant ethical vigor, has brought out a series of dramas (many of them successful on the stage), of which the most important is the "Genganere," the "Spectres," wherein he considers with awful moral force the doctrine of heredity, proving by example that the sins of the fathers are visited on the children. With instances like these in our memories, we may suggest that the literary deficiencies of the drama are not in the form, but in the inexpertness or inertness of the dramatists of the day. There are few of the corner-stone facts of human life, and there are none of the crucible-tried passions of human character, which the drama cannot discuss quite as well as the novel.

Indeed, the drama is really the noblest form of literature, because it is the most direct. It calls forth the highest of literary faculties in the highest degree—the creation of character, standing firm on its own feet, and speaking for itself. The persons in a play must *be* and *do*, and the spectator must see what he is, and what he does, and why. There is no narrator standing by to act as chorus, and there needs none. If the dramatist knows his trade, if he has the gift of the born playwright, if his play is well made, then there is no call for explanation or analysis, no necessity of dissecting or refining, no demand for comment or sermon, no desire that any one palliate or denounce what all have seen. Actions speak louder than words. That this direct dramatic method is fine enough for the most abstruse intellectual self-questioning when the subject calls for this, and that in the mighty hand of genius it is capable of throwing light in the darkest corners and crannies of the tortured and tortuous human soul, ought not to be denied by any one who may have seen on the stage the "Œdipus" of Sophocles, the "Hamlet" of Shakespeare, the "Misanthrope" of Molière, or the "Faust" of Goethe.

Robert Grant.

BORN in Boston, Mass., 1852.

ONE GIRL OF THE PERIOD.

[*The Knave of Hearts.* 1886.]

"I DON'T know what I shall do without you, Blanche," said the slim young lady.

"You must write to me, Emily, very often."

The porter had placed the bag, which I noticed was marked with the letters B. L., beside the vacant chair across the aisle ; and as the ladies were grouped in very close quarters I delicately left my seat, with the hope that one of them would occupy it until the departure of the train. At this moment I observed Emily, under whose demure air a spice of mischief lurked, whisper something to her friend, who blushed and tittered slightly.

"What nonsense, Emily ! He won't do anything of the kind."

"You just wait and see, dear."

The speaker pressed her face against the window-pane, as if she expected to catch a glimpse of some one outside. Blanche stood at her elbow, and tried, by giggling protestations, to interrupt this action, though I fancied she was far from displeased thereby.

I wandered out to the platform of the car and lighted a cigarette. After a few pensive puffs I drew from my pocket a small note-book, the virgin page of which I inscribed as follows :

No. 1.   Blanche L——.
Residence, New York (probably).
Blonde; superb physique; fine animal spirits; giggles.

Memoranda.

Has been visiting in Boston and has received attentions. Expects admirer at depot. Will be disappointed if he does not bring flowers.
Verb. sap.

Alighting from the car, I began to walk up and down with my hands behind my back. A few minutes must still elapse before the departure of the train. Just then I saw a window open and Emily's delicate face peep out expectantly. I could almost feel the sympathetic squeeze of the hand she doubtless gave Blanche, who leaned upon her shoulder. They plainly were beginning to fear that the tardy admirer was not coming. But I was by no means of their opinion. I felt certain he would arrive. In all probability the florist had disappointed him, and he was ransacking the town for roses.

The gate through which passengers obtained admission to the train was in the rear of the last car, and practically out of range from the Pullman. I sauntered thither. A queue of people filed past me with movements of haste. It lacked but two minutes of the hour. I stepped beyond the wicket into the area of the depot. All was confusion. Passengers were scurrying hither and thither, for there were several other trains in process of arrival and departure. I looked searchingly among the crowd, but there was no sign of the missing youth.

A bell in the office struck warningly. I stood with my watch in hand. Blanche was right. He was not coming. And yet such deliberate desertion struck me as so inartistic as to render me incredulous even at this late moment.

As I replaced my watch in my fob I perceived a figure describing a rapid course through the crowd in the station. By the fashionable cut of his clothes and the green pasteboard box he carried, I recognized the tardy lover. I started toward him with some impetuosity and we came into collision.

"I beg your pardon, sir!" I exclaimed, with the courtesy at my command on all occasions.

The young man, who was almost breathless with hurry, looked as if he could have strangled me on the spot, but with the self-control of good breeding swallowed his wrath, and somewhat fiercely demanded which was the New York train.

"It is there," I cried, pointing to one at the opposite corner of the platform.

He sped like a deer in the direction indicated, and I just had time to pass through the wicket before it closed sharply. I ran forward and caught the railing of my car, which was already in motion. The buxom Blanche stood upon the platform waving her handkerchief to her two friends, who followed the advancing train with similar snowy signals of farewell. There was a rueful expression upon the face of Miss Emily, as if she harbored sympathy for the other's disappointment. The victim looked back smilingly, however.

"Be sure and write soon."

"Yes, dear; and I'm certain there's some mistake," cried Emily, throwing a kiss as a last greeting.

I took my seat, and for nearly an hour interested myself by looking out at the scenery. The fortunate course of events had swathed my soul in a sort of glamour, so that the houses and fields and hills and valleys flying past in swift succession served as a background for the play of my imagination. I found an exquisite pleasure in giving the rein to fancy, and indulging in that adulation of feminality frequent with me even when propinquity furnished no cause ; for I had ever cherished an ideal in regard to the gentler sex. I had a limitless faith in woman, and yearned to encounter the spirit in whose companionship my every aspiration would find content.

Here she was perhaps close at hand. I stole a glance at my neighbor across the aisle, who was sitting twirling the fringe of her sack with a thoughtful air. The memory of her sibilant giggle haunted my ear as the rhythm of a cool mountain brook recalled in the passages of a fever. She was a splendid piece of flesh and blood, whom a pensive brow no more became than a dull sky the laughing stream. A wealth of curling tow-colored hair flowed from under the arch of her bonnet, and dimples nestled in the curves of her fresh-hued cheeks. Instinct told me that the life which even now bubbled upon the margin of those red lips would soon reassert itself and dissipate her disappointment. Take vitality and pique together, and you will have the material for a runaway.

I was in the course of transferring this epigram to my note-book when the news-agent passed through the car with a collection of the literature of the day. I stealthily took note that the two novels he placed upon the lap of my fair companion bore severally the titles of "True to the Last" and "A Lass of Spirit." She examined the first of these with a pensive interest, but, though she sighed once or twice in the course of turning the pages, she ended by selecting the other.

There is an old adage in regard to the danger of letting a hot iron cool, which came to my mind at this juncture. I felt the necessity of bestirring myself instantly. The delicacy of my nature had prompted me to leave Blanche to her own reflections until now, but I must confess I began to fear that in my consideration for her feelings I might have prejudiced my own interests. Her recovery from her discomfiture had been more rapid than my estimate of feminine character gave me reason to expect. The wound not only had time to smart, but to begin to heal.

An opportunity was not long lacking. The volume purchased proved to be one the pages of which were uncut, and as she was wavering between the alternative of employing her index finger and laying the book aside, I hastened to offer her an ivory paper-cutter which belonged to my travelling-bag. It was a plain but tasteful affair, with my monogram blazoned upon the handle.

She expressed her thanks by a smiling but ladylike inclination of the head; and I noticed, as she made use of the instrument, a faint blush suffuse her cheek and creep upward to the roots of her hair.

A quarter of an hour later I aided her to raise a window which resisted her (as I decided) half-hearted pressure, and when the train stopped ten minutes for refreshments, asked her to permit me to get her something to eat. Her refusal was expected, for I felt morally certain that her reticule contained a supply of sandwiches ; but the opportunity was not one to be neglected.

Nor was I mistaken, for when we emerged from the dimness of the way-station she produced a packet of chicken and bread wrapped in a snowy doily. I was not conscious of hinting, by any expression of countenance, a desire to share her repast, but perhaps it was my having no luncheon of my own that led her to ask timidly if I would not take a sandwich. After proper hesitation I accepted her offer, and the opportune removal to the smoking-car of a gentleman who occupied the chair next to hers gave me a chance to establish myself at her side and venture a few remarks.

Our conversation was necessarily very formal for the first few minutes, but the discovery of mutual friends in both New York and Boston broke the ice and established a bond of sympathy between us. The enthusiasm of her manner completely charmed me, and she made use of very extravagant adjectives to express satisfaction regarding trivial matters.

I was altogether happy. She appeared to me the most fascinating person I had ever met. Her fresh beauty filled me with admiration, for under the influence of excitement her eyes seemed lakes of liquid blue. I tried my best to be agreeable, and having come to the conclusion that she preferred to laugh, drew largely on my stock of stories and witticisms. Whenever I essayed any topic of a more serious nature a sort of embarrassment clothed her strict attention, as if implying that my quasipedantry was alarming. In response to queries regarding her opinions on the Irish question and a recent publication, she responded, "Oh, yes," and became unnaturally grave. Clearly she would consider me very uninteresting were I to continue in this fashion.

So, when I had come to the end of the tales and conundrums at my command, I showed her one or two tricks with coins that could be performed without attracting too much attention in the car. She was sure she could imitate them, and her fruitless efforts at success kept us in continuous mirth. I propounded to her that venerable query the answer to which is "the little boy lied," and was amply rewarded for my pains, since it appealed extraordinarily to her risibility, though she declared with a shake of her shoulders, by way of feigned anger, that I was "awfully unkind" to make sport of her. The innocent device of knotting my handkerchief until it bore some resemblance to a rabbit, and causing it to jump spasmodically in imitation of that creature, fairly convulsed my lovely companion, and strengthened our friendship. The strictly impersonal, however, does not long satisfy any woman. So my natural instinct warned me, and I turned by degrees the course of conversation into a more interesting channel. A few direct and simple questions were necessary for the acquirement of one or two facts in regard to herself, but I avoided abandoning more than momentarily the jester's part. Anything in the nature of abstract discussion, which I knew to be an artistic and convenient veil for sentiment, would, in the case of Blanche, be out of place. Badinage was the only available method of paying tribute to her fascinations or interesting her in one's own.

I found that compliments, when couched in a not too serious tone of voice, pleased her greatly. The more delicate ones were not so effective as those easily understood. She pretended to think these laudatory speeches very ridiculous, and accused me of being foolish. Leaning slightly over the back of her chair, I would whisper some still more extravagant bit of flattery as a reply, to be greeted very likely with a declaration that she would have nothing more to do with me. By way of carrying out her threat she would look fixedly in the opposite direction.

"Miss Lombard," said I (I had discovered her name to be Blanche Lombard), "do you dot your eyes?"

My query concealed a society inanity I had heard exploded not long before. Her head was turned the other way, and she seemed deaf to my utterance.

"At least you might answer a civil question," I continued.

There was no response. I thought I could detect a muffled giggle.

"You make a great mistake if you do, for they are *capital* eyes."

"How absurd! What nonsense you do talk!"

She looked still more fixedly away from me, and twisted her shoulders so as to exclude all view of her face.

"But it is true, Miss Lombard. I am only speaking the truth. If you do not believe me, judge for yourself. Here is the opportunity." So saying, I drew from my pocket one of those round, flat pin-cushions carried by men, the back of which contained a mirror.

She turned her head a little in her curiosity to see what this was, but immediately looked the other way again. While in this position she put out her hand suddenly and took the pin-cushion from me.

"Philopena!" I cried.

We had formed an agreement not five minutes before that whoever of us should first receive anything from the hand of the other should pay a forfeit. In the event of my losing, her prize was to be five pounds of bonbons. If I won, she was to make me a tobacco-pouch.

The moment I uttered the fatal word Blanche made an exclamation that would doubtless have been a little shriek had the surroundings permitted.

"Oh!" she cried, with an indignant writhe of her whole figure, "you horrid thing! I never will speak to you again."

The excitement of her manner, which found a partial vent in the intensity of these expressions, caused me a thrill of sweet satisfaction. She seemed to me positively an angel, and I was conscious that the epithet, "you horrid thing," embodied the highest note in her gamut. The quintessence of enraptured vitality was condensed therein, and I was the fortunate being who had evoked it.

From this culmination of the climax the conversation gradually declined in interest, and I shortly had the tact to withdraw and leave my companion to her own meditations. I sought the smoking-car, and, lighting another cigarette, gave myself up to a revery which would have been wholly delicious but for the lurking doubt as to my chances for success. I did not question that I had made an impression on my fellow-traveller; but would she regard me as other than a mere incident of the journey, a transient influence, which would cease to operate upon the morrow? Was she still free, or were there a score of lovers at her feet ? What was the true footing upon which the swain stood whose flowers I had so lately anticipated ? He might, for aught I could tell, be on the eve of conquest, and I the plaything of an hour. I loved—I realized the condition well—deeply and passionately, and all the tortures of a doubting spirit were mine. In the fulness of my infatuation I drew out my note-book once more and wrote as follows:

"*You horrid thing! I never will speak to you again.*"

This shibboleth, still pregnant with the timbre of her voice, floated through the chambers of my brain.

As I completed the last word, I perceived that we had almost reached our destination. I returned to Miss Lombard's side in time to take charge of her wraps, and before consigning her to the care of her father, a florid, full-faced man with mutton-chop whiskers, who was waiting her arrival at the depot, I had obtained her permission to call. In truth, she declared she would never forgive me if I did not.

Esther Bernon Carpenter.

BORN in Wakefield, R. I.

EVENING MEETING AT UNCLE 'SIAS'S.

[*South-County Neighbors.* 1887.]

AT the height of the melody a newly arrived group of women attracted the hospitable attention of Uncle 'Sias.

"This way," he hoarsely whispered, beckoning from the door of the parlor-bedroom to the sisters, who evidently could see but little beyond the range of their imprisoning sunbonnets ; and as they hesitated at noticing the seated occupants of the room, he added, explanatorily, "seats on the edge o' the bed." This somnolent invitation was gratefully accepted, and the log-cabin sunbonnets filed in, and took up their places among the stuffy pillows, just as the singers in the outer room were raising the tune—

> "Shell *I* be kerried toe the skies
> On flowery beds of ease ?"

The bed had not been unoccupied through the evening. For twenty years, or for half her life, it had been the habitat of Uncle 'Sias's unhappy daughter, Luce. Jilted, or, as her people said, "shabbed," by the young man whom she was to have married, she never held up her head again after the shock of this misfortune, and took her bed, which she had never since left,—living there "as if it belonged to her organism," and finally sinking into such a hapless state that for years past her mental obituary might have been read in that line of the thoughtful poet of rustic life—

> "She slowly withered, an imbecile mind."

By one of those coincidences that cease to surprise us by the time that middle age has shown us how often they recur in obedience to some mysterious law, the company of that night happened to include another of the weak-hearted cravens in life's warfare—a man of mature years, who had never been heard to speak since the blow fell that crushed the pride, the hopes, and the affections of his early manhood. No force of entreaties, taunts, or provocations could drag him from the refuge of silence, which he had sought with a sternness of purpose that, like the woman's pitiful cowering away from human eyes, testified to the narrow conditions and imperfect development of lives that went to wreck in the first storm of disaster by which they were overtaken.

The meeting was conducted in the usual way. The customary appeals were made from the leaders to the more timid sisters, and to the young converts, to rise and speak ; and the responses from each class were, in most instances, of an inaudible brevity. The maturer standard-bearers rose and delivered the set speeches with which they always graced these occasions ; their several styles being marked by the repetition of certain texts to which they had acquired a well-defined right—sacred quotations that, as was said of Emerson's prose "'tis," became almost a personal possession. For instance, the trade-mark distinguishing Aunt Rooty, the gatherer and compounder of simples, the Medea of savory and medicinal drinks, was the text, "Oh, taste and see how good the Lord is !" which she dwelt upon with a sort of professional unction, as though she were offering some ptisan of sovereign virtue. And Miss Experience, or 'Speedy Goodspeed, known for her painful and halting utterance, never failed to wind up her remarks with the query, "What shall be done unto thee, O thou false tongue ?" Then there was the usual burst of gratitude from the "skinching" or miserly Deacon Handy, who piously thanked the Lord that he had been saved from dead works, and whose hopes of justification must indeed, according to the testimony of his neighbors, have rested upon faith alone. The usual element of comedy was furnished by the flighty speaker, a sister of infirm wits but pious intentions, much given to raising her voice in a high, cracked tone, and detailing her domestic trials with injudicious frankness, closing with the application of her favorite "varse" to her house-mates, "And five of them were foolish." Her example encouraged "Eelly Dick," the feeble-minded pauper, whose board the town had let out to Uncle 'Sias as the lowest bidder, to make his first appearance on any religious platform—getting slightly astray in his attempted citation, "A woman took a maysure of oil, and hid it in a maysure of wheat, until the whole was leavened," but meeting the Elder's frown with a manly independence, by the declaration, "I may not repeat it as verbatim as some, but it is not for this one, nor that one, nor the other one to say what I shall say in the great congregation!" The Elder urged, warned, and exhorted, addressing the doubters and inquirers, reminding them that Satan desired to have them, and was there among them ; that the spiritual eye might plainly discern him right down there by the stove ; and that all concerned should make haste to leave so dangerous a vicinity for the haven of the anxious-seats. A pause ensued, of appalling length, after which a sister rose, and with the pious intention of rubbing in the Elder's persuasions, quoted her own experience at a similar crisis, when she "felt as if glue couldn't begin to hold her down half so fast as Satan did ; but she broke away from all her bad feelings, and got up and spoke, and felt quite a good deal better for spiting old Satan."

Perhaps these appeals might have met with the desired response if the attention of the young people had not been divided between ghostly warnings and skyey threatenings. The rain, which had been so long gathering in force, was now preluded by keen flashes of lightning and ominous mutterings of thunder. Seeing that no movement was made by the objects of the recent exhortations, Uncle 'Sias rose, just to occupy the time, as he explained. "Alas, alas," he began, with his highest aim at a conventional style, "there was a time of blessed news, when the Lord did marvels amongst us, and we should rej'ice, yea, and did rej'ice. But, alas, the gold is become dim, and the most fine gold is changed. Although I hope the' is some movings on the minds of some few, yit the saints air not so zeelous f'r the Lord's cause an' the good o' souls ez they was in times past. Sin doth greedily abound amongst us, and the love of many waxes cold, for which the Lord is angered with a great anger. Now is plantin' time, in a worldly way o' speakin', but ef we fare ez we desarve, what sorter harvest shell we hev? Brethring, it'll be ez it was in times I knowed when I lived up to Westfield, on Widder Bacon's farm, when the Lord sent his armies o' worms to cut off the fruits o' the airth. Thet season it come 'round so thet they ez expected fifty bushels didn't get sca'cely one. Seth Beebe was one of our gret farmers up thet way. He sowed fo'teen acres o' new ground, an' anticipated on a gret crop. Wal, he ploughed it up, an' planted it with corn. Oh, thet we, ez a people, rememberin' these jedgments o' times past, should beware lest they be let loose in the land agin. Oh, my young frien's, we'm all a lookin' ter you. Oh, think o' the famine in Egypt; think o' the plagues o' the land; think o' the good-will o' the burnin' bush; think"——

But here the worthy man's words were lost in the fierce rush of the gust, the roll of the thunder, and the maddened lashing of the rain. Hysterical women, whose twitching shoulders and quivering chins had for the last quarter of an hour betrayed their nervous agitation, covered their faces before the blue, blinding lights that glared pitilessly in at the great uncurtained windows of the old farmhouse, and sobbed in the abject misery of terror. Stouthearted Aunt Freelove was heard declaring, "Kind of an onseasonable sorter thunder-tempest, but I guess I c'n weather it tell the sullar walls ketches fire." But Brandywine Spears, who had hitherto sat in the seat of the scorners, beside the open house door, now hastily joined the inner circle, a pallid and crestfallen Mephistopheles, as the racking peals shook the giant timbers of the room, and the furious beating of the rain on the roof was like the tramp of a charging host, while a long, lurid dazzle, a roar that seemed to fill the sky, and the sickening sound of a rending, tearing concussion proclaimed that one of the trees of the surrounding forest had fallen. Suddenly, at this crisis of awe, the mood of the people passed at once from the ecstasy of fear to the ecstasy of devotion ; a change effected by the sign and voice of one among them who now assumed the place of a leader. At the signal of this strange, tall hermit figure, known as the solitary dweller in the centre of the haunted Carr's Plain, they rose by one impulse to their feet, and poured out their swelling hearts in a wild burst of sacred song, their voices mounting high in the passionate cry of the triumphant refrain—

> "Oh, Moses smote the waters,
>   And the seas gave way!"

With the singing of the hymn the tempest somewhat abated, as if to the clang of mediæval bells. Angry black clouds still rose fast from the ocean, but the lightning glanced harmlessly through the protecting veil of falling waters, and the house seemed an ark of safety in the midst of the raging floods. All looks now turned upon the new guide of the evening's devotions, as he remained standing in his place, with the abstracted look of a solitary, and yet as if charged with the burden of a word that must make its way to utterance! Unknown and almost nameless as he was to the listening crowd, there was a power in his presence, in the suggestions of his emaciated countenance and the spectral glitter of his eye, which pointed to a reality in the vague background of rumor which had given him, at his coming to live in their community, the repute of a seer of strange visions, and of a fearless host to such ghostly visitants as the inhabitants of the haunted territory which he had chosen to make his dwelling-place. But if a suspicion of something unhallowed had at first clung to his mysterious personality, it disappeared with that fuller knowledge of his brooding enthusiasm, his meditative insight, and his recondite learning which had gained him his common title of "The Preacher," though his voice had never yet been heard in these seasons of worship. A lonely settler in strange places, like the spiritual fathers of Rhode Island—Williams, Blackstone, and Gorton—it was rumored that he, too, claimed to be a witness to a special interpretation of sacred truths, and, like those historic pioneers, had been separated by the stress of conflicting opinions from his earlier associates, or, as it was more darkly hinted, had, at the Divine pleasure, as made known to him in a dream, left home and family and friends to dedicate himself to the contemplative life.

Such were the confused ideas prevailing among the congregation concerning the strange recluse who now spoke to them, wearing a far-away, introverted look, which presently quickened and glowed, as his low and quiet tones grew in intensity with the development of his theme.

"It is written," he said, without preamble or address, "in the Word of God that in the last days He will pour out his spirit upon his servants and handmaidens, and old men shall dream dreams, and young men shall see visions. I had been writing a letter to a friend at a distance, and being weak and feeble, I lay down on my bed, with my face toward the wall, to take repose, and soon fell into a sound sleep. Methought I cast my eyes toward heaven, and saw the blue vault of heaven split asunder, through which, I thought, I saw a stream of light and love proceeding from the throne of God, clear as crystal. As the rays of the sun in the firmament, at its first rising, shine into a door or window, so that the stream through the whole house will be lighter than anywhere else, so the whole stream of light from heaven to where I stood shined with light and love."

The storm was subsiding, and the flashes of lightning were few and distant, faintly illuminating the horizon. The dreaming glances of the speaker wandered out upon the night, and returned kindled with a deeper light, as he offered a newly-suggested image to his rapt listeners.

"Never did I see anything so straight, and on either side the stream was decked with thousands of little rays of light, all pointing one way, even toward heaven. I thought that every drop of light and love that God bestows is to be returned to him again; and while I stood wondering at the sight, I thought I saw the fiery chariot of God's love come through the gap that was in the vault, coming through the midst of the stream, a hundred times swifter than I ever saw an eagle fly. I thought it was all over glorious, and in color like to a rainbow, and was carried on wings of love. In a few moments it was just by where I stood, and turned short about, with the fire part toward heaven, and rested on its wings, keeping its wings in a slow motion to bear it up, and waiting for me to come in. I thought my soul was transported; I thought I stood with my heart and hands extended to heaven, crying, Glory, glory in the highest! and just as I was about to mount into the chariot I turned to a great multitude, crying, Glory, glory, I am going to glory in the fiery chariot of his love! and with these words on my lips I awoke out of sleep. Oh, cried I, in tears, that I had been suffered to take my flight! Oh, thought I, in the bitter disappointment of those waking moments, if one view of glory and love will fill a soul with such joy, even in a dream, what will the open vision and full fruition be in glory?"

The preacher's voice broke and failed, the light died out of his wan face, his Dantean vision was told, his mission was ended. The message that he had delivered was in a tone of fervor and power so far above the usual spiritual ministrations received by the flock that a confused sense of wonder sat upon all the faces. But the Elder, or exhorter of the evening, catching something of the enthusiast's emotion, dismissed them with the genuine dignity of a pastoral guide.

"Brethren," said he, "our brother has spoke to us in the word of power. As we go to our homes, and lay us down to rest, let us meditate well thereupon; and let each one commune with his own heart, and be still." And he gave, and the congregation received, a blessing, with a new sense of reverence.

As the people disappeared on their homeward ways the sky was still obscured by drifting fog, through which glimpses of the clear heavens, set with star-points, promised a further April change to fair weather. But the atmosphere of storm and cloud and mist has ever since hung so heavily over the story of that night that it has finally come to wear the shadowy shape of a legend of the South County.

Charles Howard Shinn.

BORN in Austin, Texas, 1852.

THE BUILDING OF ARACHNE.

[Contributed to The Argonaut. 1889.]

A CITY OF THE FUTURE.

IN the year 2029 the leading Vanderbilt of his time came into his fortune. He had received a remarkable education, and one which the nineteenth century would have considered impossible. Without going into details, young Vanderbilt was evenly developed—physically, mentally and morally. He had been so educated that he found happiness in the full and constant use of his money and his brains for the good of humanity. But he was preëminently practical—a purified and perfected type of one of the industrial kings of the nineteenth century. He lived in a cottage in the hills, and he thought out his plans in long walks under his trees. He was the richest man in America, and yet he had as much freedom as any plain farmer. To sum it all up, he had become, without knowing it, the most unselfish, and at the same time the most patient and persistent of living men.

The friends he had were not numerous, but each one of them was capable of great things. And he and his wife understood each other in that complete way which happens once in a thousand or so. Remember, I am not trying to tell you how it all came about, because that would make a volume. Briefly, Vanderbilt wished to build a city, more pleasant and better to live in than any the world had yet seen. He wanted to see whether such a city could be established under new conditions of social and industrial life, and in such a way that the enormous capital he proposed to invest could be restored unimpaired at the end of a term of years.

The site which was chosen for the city of Arachne was in a sheltered and fertile part of the great valley-plain of California which extends from Shasta to Tehachapi. The floor of the valley at this point was a sloping plain, looking west, with tree-clad foothills east, and hundreds of great oaks scattered here and there, like the ancestral oaks in the heart of England. The region was chiefly occupied by large wheat farms. Vanderbilt was able to purchase, through agents, a tract of land nearly twenty miles square. Then he sent for his engineers.

"What I want," he said, "is a city capable of indefinite extension. The plan is to be based on the web of the geometric spider. Streets, sewerage, water, light, transportation, and the other requirements of this Utopia are to be perfected as far as the science of the day will permit."

The engineers made their report. It was a wonderful situation, they said. There was natural gas underlying the valley ; water could be brought from the Sierras ; railroads from all parts of the continent could centre in the heart of the city ; commerce could occupy miles of wharves—if only people chose to come and live in Arachne.

Then Vanderbilt sent for several great landscape-gardeners to work with the engineers, and he and his wife went with them over the valley, the golden foothills, and the sea-green tule lowlands by the sloughs. As the work went on, so broad and beautiful were the plans developed, so magnificent the scale of operations, that the interest of the country was aroused, and many persons wished to buy and live in the as yet unbuilt city ; but the reply sent out was : " Not yet ; wait until we are ready."

The landscape-gardeners said : " With this soil and climate every home can have its garden and every street can be an avenue of shade and fragrance. All the trees of the temperate zones, and many of the tropics, can thrive here, so we will have no street less than a hundred feet wide, and some of our great avenues shall even be a hundred and fifty feet across, and planted with date-palms and magnolias, for twenty miles into the country. We shall lay out public squares on every street, and two great parks, one on the lowlands by the river, another on the foothills which look down on the city. We shall so arrange our squares as to preserve the best of the oaks, sycamores, and other trees of the valley. And, when the city is built, one of its officers shall be a city forester, educated and efficient, to preserve and develop all this beauty of streets, squares, and parks." And that winter they planted miles of avenues and hundreds of acres of forests. There were four hundred specimens of deciduous trees, forty-eight species of broad-leaved evergreens, and one hundred of conifers chosen to plant on the streets ; some streets had one row of trees down the centre, others had two rows near the sidewalks. The great parks were to be not only pleasure-grounds, but also arboretums. A belt of forest, a mile wide, across the valley, was planted to protect the city from the occasional northers.

The engineers arranged to have all the sewers of the city unite at the edge of a tule marsh, by the river, five miles beyond the city's possible extension, and there their contents were to be heated in vast furnaces, dried, ground to powder, and sold for fertilizers to farmers the world over. They arranged for water and natural gas for cooking and lighting, to be piped into every house, free to the consumer. They arranged for cable-cars up and down every street and avenue, all managed by one system. They laid out the city so that every lot, besides fronting on a street, ran back to a twenty-five-foot alley, and they arranged for a freight cable-system on all these alleyways. They arranged for telegraph, telephone, and phonograph connections throughout the entire system. Railroad men in those days had come to run cars without smoke or noise, by electricity, and it was easy to arrange for the approach of all trains by two broad, sunken avenues, one north, the other south, over which the streets crossed. These avenues led to the centre of the city, where a union depot, the great public buildings, and the offices of all the departments of public works were situated.

It would be too long a story to explain further the physical details of the system of organization, in which beauty and utility were joined in perfect union. When the time came, there appeared one morning in every newspaper in the United States an announcement:

" Lots for sale in Arachne, to actual settlers. Two hundred and fifty million dollars have already been invested here, and sales will be so conducted as merely to restore this capital intact, at the end of twenty years, to the original investor. The object of this experiment is not money-making. Those who cannot read and write had better not come to Arachne, as the charter which it is hoped will be adopted does not allow such to vote at city elections. Copies of the proposed charter mailed to all applicants."

Within a year Arachne was a city. Vanderbilt and his friends succeeded in obtaining their charter, which could not be altered except by a three-fourths vote of the citizens. This charter was the most important part of Arachne, and so I will give a synopsis of some of its provisions. As Vanderbilt stated, at the public meetings of the twenty or thirty thousand voters who finally adopted it, almost as it was written: "It is intended, in this charter, to give intelligence, thrift, and honesty the controlling power in Arachne. Some things the people can do unitedly: some must forever be left to the individual. Arachne will probably contain both rich and poor, weak and strong, wise and foolish, to the end of time, but we hope it will contain less crime, less unhappiness, and fewer failures than any other city in the world. The charter of Arachne will suit neither nationalists nor silurians, but it is worth trying, nevertheless."

The charter provided for the absolute equality of men and women before the law, and for non-sectarian free schools in a chain from the primary grades through the university, with schools of the arts and industries.

Then came the qualifications for voters: "City elections shall be conducted separately from all other elections. Voters at city elections must be able to read and write, and must be freeholders owning one 'unit of real estate.'

"The 'unit of real estate' is a lot of fifty feet frontage and not less than one hundred feet in depth, extending to a rear alley. This unit cannot be subdivided, though it may be held in several undivided interests. If used for residence, only one house can be built on such a lot, and it must have at least five full feet of space left on each side, ten feet in front, and twenty-five feet in the rear. If used for business, the plans of the building must conform to the general ordinances of the board of building commissioners."

The sections relating to "qualifications of officers" were remarkably simple: "All candidates for offices in the gift of the people shall have passed through at least the grammar grade of the public-school system. Heads of departments shall have passed through at least the high-school grade."

The system of voting provided for was unique. Voters were registered by residence. Besides telephonic and phonographic apparatus, and pneumatic tubes for receiving and sending mail, every house contained a "voting-tube," connected with the city hall. At night, between the hours of 6 and 9, every voter sent from his own house or room, to the central voting-office, his vote, recorded on a phonographic piece of metal, which passed at once without any human agency into a mechanical contrivance which counted and recorded the entire vote, and preserved the cylinders and tallies intact for twenty-five years. This gigantic machine was mathematically perfect, and had been tested in every possible way. The entire vote of the city was announced within an hour after the closing of the polls. The introduction of a single unregistered vote, or of a vote from the wrong place, would cause the machine to throw out the entire vote of that house or room. Any voter could give his number at any time within twenty-five years, and hear his own vote read off by the machine. The city had printed on its ballots the names of all persons nominated by fifty or more freeholders. The voter merely read off the names of those he wished to vote for, and his phonograph recorded it. The voting-tubes and the machine were securely closed at all other times of the year except during the three voting-hours. The register of the city was posted, page by page, in many prominent places, for weeks before the election, and the city had a standing offer of a reward for the discovery of any fraudulent entry.

After a few years it became evident that machinery had triumphed and hopelessly broken up all the political machines. Voters staid at home, after dinner, long enough to vote, and then went to the theatres, libraries, or art galleries, returning in time to hear their phonographs report the results of the election.

The organization of the city was said by the charter "to be for the purpose of carrying on, as cheaply and efficiently as possible, the business of the city." The officers were expected to give their entire time to the city's service, and all were salaried.

The head of the government was called "the city president," answering in some respects to the mayor, but with greater powers. He sent all nominations for heads of certain departments to the legislative body, which consisted of twenty-seven members, nine of whom were chosen once in every two years. They were elected not from districts, but at large, and were termed "the city legislature."

The officials nominated by the president, and elected by the legislature, were those belonging to what was termed the "industrial group of the city departments"—the chief forester, the sanitary engineer, the city architect, the chief railroad engineer, and the heads of the water supplies, the gas wells, and the sewage furnaces. These were all trained and educated specialists, for each department worked up to within certain test limits of error, just as the United States mints now do.

The heads of the "governing group" of officers—the city attorney, the school superintendent and directors, the chief librarian, the head of the art schools, the insurance, banking, and fire commissioners, head of the tax department, chief of police, and similar officers—were elected by the people.

The judiciary were twice elected, once by the people and once by the president, legislature, and other elected officers assembled in council on the following day. Usually they ratified the choice of the people, but there were many notable instances where they had reversed that decision. This being a veto power required a two-thirds vote. In that case the people presented new candidates.

Taxes were arranged on the basis of the "unit of real estate." This unit was taxed at a fixed rate, whether improved or unimproved. A fixed amount of water and gas was furnished free to each house, this amount being rated as "sufficient for the use of one family"; everything above this amount was charged at cost of production. The sewage furnaces turned in a large annual revenue to the city. The transportation department, which included all the freight and passenger traffic, had rates of charges fixed from time to time by the city legislature. The income from this source, added to the revenues of the sewage department and the small fixed tax on the unit of real estate, was sufficient to pay all the expenses of the city government. The city had enabled its citizens to escape most of the indirect taxes of the cities of the nineteenth century, and the result was most astonishing in the tax department. It was not necessary to put a dollar of tax on the great buildings, for, as the city grew, the added transportation, at rates that lessened each year, paid all the expenses.

The legislature had the right to raise the tax-rate on the unit of real estate, and even to levy a graduated tax on all buildings which cost more than five thousand dollars, but this was a right which it never exercised. The other sources of income were sufficient.

As Arachne grew from a population of fifty thousand to one of half a million, and, before the close of its first century, to more than two millions, the wisdom of its founders became more and more manifest. It was a city of homes, of health, of happiness. Individuality had its proper play, competition had healthful activity, but the sense of brotherhood was cultivated, and, as the powers and duties of the city grew, the service of the city increased in honor and responsibility, and the organization of public life became more perfect.

The evils of cities like London and New York never existed in Arachne; there were no slums, no tenement-houses, no pestilence-haunted rookeries, no dives and dance-cellars and saloons, for the spirit of the community did not tolerate these things.

Irwin Russell.

BORN in Port Gibson, Miss., 1853. DIED in New Orleans, La., 1879.

THE BANJO.

[*Poems. Collective Edition.* 1888.]

GO 'way, fiddle! folks is tired o' hearin' you a-squawkin'.
 Keep silence fur yo' betters!—don't you heah de banjo talkin'?
About de 'possum's tail she's gwine to lecter—ladies, listen!—
About de ha'r whut isn't dar, an' why de ha'r is missin':

"Dar's gwine to be a' oberflow," said Noah, lookin' solemn—
Fur Noah tuk de "Herald," and he read de ribber column—
An' so he sot his hands to wuk a-cl'arin' timber-patches,
An' 'lowed he's gwine to build a boat to beat de steamah *Natchez.*

Ol' Noah kep' a-nailin' an' a-chippin' an' a-sawin';
An' all de wicked neighbors kep' a-laughin' an' a-pshawin';
But Noah didn't min' 'em, knowin' whut wuz gwine to happen:
An' forty days an' forty nights de rain it kep' a-drappin'.

Now, Noah had done cotched a lot ob ebry sort o' beas'es—
Ob all de shows a-trabbelin', it beat 'em all to pieces!
He had a Morgan colt an' sebral head o' Jarsey cattle—
An' druv 'em 'board de Ark as soon's he heered de thunder rattle.

Den sech anoder fall ob rain!—it come so awful hebby,
De ribber riz immejitly, an' busted troo de lebbee;
De people all wuz drownded out—'cep' Noah an' de critters,
An' men he'd hired to wuk de boat—an' one to mix de bitters.

De Ark she kep' a-sailin' an' a-sailin' *an'* a-sailin';
De lion got his dander up, an' like to bruk de palin';
De sarpints hissed; de painters yelled; tell, whut wid all de fussin',
You c'u'dn't hardly heah de mate a-bossin' 'roun' an' cussin'.

Now, Ham, de only nigger whut wuz runnin' on de packet,
Got lonesome in de barber-shop, an' c'u'dn't stan' de racket;
An' so, fur to amuse he-se'f, he steamed some wood an' bent it,
An' soon he had a banjo made—de fust dat wuz invented.

He wet de ledder, stretched it on; made bridge an' screws an' aprin;
An' fitted in a proper neck—'twuz berry long an' tap'rin';
He tuk some tin, an' twisted him a thimble fur to ring it;
An' den de mighty question riz: how wuz he gwine to string it?

De 'possum had as fine a tail as dis dat I's a-singin';
De ha'r's so long an' thick an' strong,—des fit fur banjo-stringin';
Dat nigger shaved 'em off as short as wash-day-dinner graces;
An' sorted ob 'em by de size, f'm little E's to basses.

He strung her, tuned her, struck a jig,—'twuz "Nebber min' de wedder,
She soun' like forty-lebben bands a-playin' all togedder;
Some went to pattin'; some to dancin': Noah called de figgers;
An' Ham he sot an' knocked de tune, de happiest ob niggers!

Now, sence dat time—it's mighty strange—dere's not de slightes' showin'
Ob any ha'r at all upon de 'possum's tail a-growin';
An' curi's, too, dat nigger's ways: his people nebber los' 'em—
Fur whar you finds de nigger—dar's de banjo an' de 'possum!

NEBUCHADNEZZAR.

YOU, Nebuchadnezzah, whoa, sah!
  Whar is you tryin' to go, sah?
I'd hab you fur to know, sah,
  I's a-holdin' ob de lines.
You better stop dat prancin';
You's pow'ful fond ob dancin',
But I'll bet my yeah's advancin'
  Dat I'll cure you ob yo' shines.

Look heah, mule! Better min' out;
Fus' t'ing you know you'll fin' out
How quick I'll wear dis line out
  On yo' ugly, stubbo'n back.
You needn't try to steal up
An' lif' dat precious heel up;
You's got to plough dis fiel' up,
  You has, sah, fur a fac'.

Dar, *dat's* de way to do it!
He's comin' right down to it;
Jes' watch him ploughin' troo it!
   Dis nigger ain't no fool.
Some folks dey would 'a' beat him;
Now, dat would only heat him—
I know jes' how to treat him:
   You mus' *reason* wid a mule.

He minds me like a nigger.
If he wuz only bigger
He'd fotch a mighty figger,
   He would, I *tell* you! Yes, sah!

See how he keeps a-clickin'!
He's as gentle as a chickin,
An' nebber thinks o' kickin'—
   Whoa dar! Nebuchadnezzah!

Is dis heah me, or not me?
Or is de debbil got me?
Wuz dat a cannon shot me?
   Hab I laid heah more'n a week?
Dat mule do kick amazin'!
De beast wuz sp'iled in raisin'—
But now I 'spect he's grazin'
   On de oder side de creek.

NELLY.

NOT long ago—perhaps—not long—
   My soul heard no discordant tone,
For love and youth's sweet matin song
   It hearkened to, and that alone;

But now the song is hushed,— it hears
   Strange music, in a harsher key,
For every sound a dirge appears
   Since Nelly died, who lived for me.

The summer of my life is past;
   Eternal winter reigns instead;

For how, for me, could summer last,
   When she, my only rose, is dead?

Sweet Nelly! would thou couldst be yet,
   As once, my day, my only light!
But thou art gone—the sun has set—
   And every day, to me, is night.

Yet, be the darkness e'er so deep,
   Let no more suns arise for me:
For night can soothe my heart to sleep,
   And, Nelly, then I'll dream of thee!

Thomas Nelson Page.

BORN at " Oakland," Hanover Co., Va., 1853.

FROM "MARSE CHAN."

[*Marse Chan.—In Ole Virginia.* 1887.]

"ONE night Marse Chan come back from de offis wid a telegram dat say,
'Come at once,' so he wuz to start nex' mawnin'. He uniform wuz all
ready, gray wid yaller trimmin's, an' mine wuz ready too, an' he had ole marster's sword, whar de State gi' 'im in de Mexikin war; an' he trunks wuz all
packed wid ev'rything in 'em, an' my chist wuz packed too, an' Jim Rasher
he druv 'em over to de depo' in de waggin', an' we wuz to start nex' mawnin'
'bout light. Dis wuz 'bout de las' o' spring, yo' know. Dat night ole missis

made Marse Chan dress up in he uniform, an' he sut'n'y did look splendid, wid he long mustache an' he wavin' hyar an' he tall figger.

"Arfter supper he come down an' sez: 'Sam, I wan' you to tek dis note an' kyar it over to Cun'l Chahmb'lin's, an' gi' it to Miss Anne wid yo' own han's, an' bring me wud what she sez. Don' let any one know 'bout it, or know why you've gone.' 'Yes, seh,' sez I.

"Yo' see, I knowed Miss Anne's maid over at ole Cun'l Chahmb'lin's—dat wuz Judy whar is my wife now—an' I knowed I could wuk it. So I tuk de roan an' rid over, an' tied 'im down de hill in de cedars, an' I wen' 'roun' to de back yard. 'Twuz a right blowy sort o' night; de moon wuz jes' risin', but de clouds wuz so big it didn' shine 'cep' th'oo a crack now an' den. I soon foun' my gal, an' arfter tellin' her two or three lies 'bout herse'f, I got her to go in an' ax Miss Anne to come to de do'. When she come, I gi' her de note, an' arfter a little while she bro't me anurr, an' I tole her good-by, an' she gi' me a dollar, an' I come home an' gi' de letter to Marse Chan. He read it, an' tole me to have de hosses ready at twenty minits to twelve at de corner of de garden. An' jes' befo' dat he come out ez ef he wuz gwine to bed, but instid he come, an' we all struck out to'ds Cun'l Chahmb'lin's. When we got mos' to de gate, de hosses got sort o' skeered, an' I see dey wuz some'n or somebody stan'in' jes' inside; an' Marse Chan he jump' off de sorrel an' flung me de bridle and he walked up.

"She spoke fust ('twuz Miss Anne had done come out dyah to meet Marse Chan), an' she sez, jes' ez cold ez a chill, 'Well, seh, I granted your favor. I wished to relieve myse'f of de obligations you placed me under a few months ago, when you made me a present of my father, whom you fust insulted an' then prevented from gittin' satisfaction.'

"Marse Chan he didn' speak fur a minit, an' den he said: 'Who is with you?' (Dat wuz ev'y wud.)

"'No one,' sez she; 'I came alone.'

"'My God!' sez he, 'you didn' come all through those woods by yourse'f at this time o' night?'

"'Yes, I'm not afraid,' sez she. (An' heah dis nigger! I don' b'lieve she wuz.)

"De moon come out, an' I cotch sight o' her stan'in' dyah in her white dress, wid de cloak she had wrapped herse'f up in drapped off on de groun', an' she didn' look like she wuz 'feared o' nuthin'. She wuz mons'us purty ez she stood dyah wid de green bushes behine her, an' she hed jes' a few flowers in her breas'—right hyah—and some leaves in her sorrel hyar; an' de moon come out an' shined down on her hyar an' her frock, an' 'peared like de light wuz jes' stan'in' off it ez she stood dyah lookin' at Marse Chan wid her head tho'd back, jes' like dat mawnin' when she pahss Marse Chan in de road wid-out speakin' to 'im, an' sez to me, 'Good mawnin', Sam.'

"Marse Chan, he den tole her he hed come to say good-by to her, ez he wuz gwine 'way to de war nex' mawnin'. I wuz watchin' on her, an' I tho't, when Marse Chan tole her dat, she sort o' started an' looked up at 'im like she wuz mighty sorry, an' 'peared like she didn' stan' quite so straight arfter dat. Den Marse Chan he went on talkin' right fars' to her; an' he tole her how he had loved her ever sence she wuz a little bit o' baby mos', an' how he nuver 'membered de time when he hedn' 'spected to marry her. He tole her it wuz his love for her dat hed made 'im stan' fust at school an' collige, an' hed kep' 'im good an' pure; an' now he wuz gwine 'way, wouldn' she let it be like 'twuz in ole times, an' ef he come back from de war wouldn' she try to think on him ez she use' to do when she wuz a little guirl ?

"Marse Chan he had done been talkin' so serious, he hed done tuk Miss Anne's han', an' wuz lookin' down in her face like he wuz list'nin' wid his eyes.

"Arfter a minit Miss Anne she said somethin', an' Marse Chan he cotch her urr han' an' sez:

"'But if you love me, Anne ?'

"When he said dat, she tu'ned her head 'way from 'im, an' wait' a minit, an' den she said—right clear:

"'But I don' love yo'.' (Jes' dem th'ee wuds !) De wuds fall right slow— like dirt falls out a spade on a coffin when yo's buryin' anybody, an' sez, 'Uth to uth.' Marse Chan he jes' let her hand drap, an' he stiddy hisse'f 'g'inst de gate-pos', an' he didn' speak torekly. When he did speak, all he sez wuz:

"'I mus' see you home safe.'

"I 'clar, marster, I didn' know 'twuz Marse Chan's voice tell I look at 'im right good. Well, she wouldn' let 'im go wid her. She jes' wrap' her cloak 'roun' her shoulders, an' wen' 'long back by herse'f, widout doin' more'n jes' look up once at Marse Chan leanin' dyah 'g'inst de gate-pos' in he sodger clo's, wid he eyes on de groun'. She said 'Good-by' sort o' sorf, an' Marse Chan, widout lookin' up, shake han's wid her, an' she wuz done gone down de road. Soon ez she got 'mos' 'roun' de curve, Marse Chan he followed her, keepin' under de trees so ez not to be seen, an' I led de hosses on down de road behine 'im. He kep' 'long behine her tell she wuz safe in de house, an' den he come an' got on he hoss, an' we all come home.

"Nex' mawnin' we all come off to j'ine de army. An' dey wuz a-drillin' an' a-drillin' all 'bout for a while an' dey went 'long wid all de res' o' de army, an' I went wid Marse Chan an' clean he boots, an' look arfter de tent, an' tek keer o' him an' de hosses. An' Marse Chan, he wan' a bit like he use' to be. He wuz so solum an' moanful all de time, at leas' 'cep when dyah wuz gwine to be a fight. Den he'd peartin' up, an' he alwuz rode at de head o' de com- pany, 'cause he wuz tall; an' hit wan' on'y in battles whar all his company wuz dat _he_ went, but he use' to volunteer whenever de cun'l wanted anybody to fine out anythin', an' 'twuz so dangersome he didn' like to mek one man go no sooner'n anurr, yo' know, an' ax'd who'd volunteer. _He_ 'peared to like to go prowlin' aroun' 'mong dem Yankees, an' he use' to tek me wid 'im when- ever he could. Yes, seh, he sut'n'y wuz a good sodger ! He didn' mine bul- lets no more'n he did so many draps o' rain. But I use' to be pow'ful skeered sometimes. It jes' use' to 'pear like fun to 'im. In camp he use' to be so sor- rerful he'd hardly open he mouf. You'd 'a' tho't he wuz seekin', he used to look so moanful; but jes' le' 'im git into danger, an' he use' to be like ole times —jolly an' laughin' like when he wuz a boy.

Thos N. Page

"When Cap'n Gordon got he leg shot off, dey mek Marse Chan cap'n on de spot,'cause one o' de lieutenants got kilt de same day, an' turr one (named Mr. Ronny) wan' no 'count, an' all de company said Marse Chan wuz de man.

"An' Marse Chan he wuz jes' de same. He didn' nuver mention Miss Anne's name, but I knowed he wuz thinkin' on her constant. One night he wuz settin' by de fire in camp, an' Mr. Ronny—he wuz de secon' lieutenant —got to talkin' 'bout ladies, an' he say all sorts o' things 'bout 'em, an' I see Marse Chan kinder lookin' mad; an' de lieutenant mention Miss Anne's name. He hed been courtin' Miss Anne 'bout de time Marse Chan fit de duil wid her pa, an' Miss Anne hed kicked 'im, dough he wuz mighty rich, 'cause he warn' nuthin' but a half-strainer, an' 'cause she like Marse Chan, I believe, dough she didn' speak to 'im; an' Mr. Ronny he got drunk, an' 'cause Cun'l Chahmb'lin tole 'im not to come dyah no more, he got mighty mad. An' dat evenin' I'se tellin' yo' 'bout, he wuz talkin', an' he mention' Miss Anne's name. I see Marse Chan tu'n he eye 'roun' on 'im an' keep it on he face, and pres'n'y Mr. Ronny said he wuz gwine hev some fun dyah yit. He didn' mention her name dat time; but he said dey wuz all on 'em a parecel of stuck-up 'risti-crats, an' her pa wan' no gent'man anyway, an'— I don' know what he wuz gwine say (he nuver said it), fur ez he got dat far Marse Chan riz up an' hit 'im a crack, an' he fall like he hed been hit wid a fence-rail. He challenged Marse Chan to fight a duil, an' Marse Chan he excepted de challenge, an' dey wuz gwine fight; but some on 'em tole 'im Marse Chan wan' gwine mek a present o' him to his fam'ly, an' he got somebody to bre'k up de duil; twan' nuthin' dough, but he wuz 'fred to fight Marse Chan. An' purty soon he lef' de comp'ny.

"Well, I got one o' de gent'mens to write Judy a letter for me, an' I tole her all 'bout de fight, an' how Marse Chan knock Mr. Ronny over fur speakin' discontemptuous o' Cun'l Chahmb'lin, an' I tole her how Marse Chan wuz a-dyin' fur love o' Miss Anne. An' Judy she gits Miss Anne to read de letter fur her. Den Miss Anne she tells her pa, an'—you mine, Judy tells me all dis arfterwards, an' she say when Cun'l Chahmb'lin hear 'bout it, he wuz set-tin' on de poach, an' he set still a good while, an' den he sey to hisse'f:

"'Well, he carn' he'p bein' a Whig.'

"An' den he gits up an' walks up to Miss Anne an' looks at her right hard; an' Miss Anne she hed done tu'n away her haid an' wuz makin' out she wuz fixin' a rose-bush 'g'inst de poach; an' when her pa kep' lookin' at her, her face got jes' de color o' de roses on de bush, and pres'n'y her pa sez:

"'Anne!'

"An' she tu'ned roun', an' he sez:

"'Do yo' want 'im?'

"An' she sez, 'Yes,' an' put her head on he shoulder an' begin to cry; an' he sez:

"'Well, I won' stan' between yo' no longer. Write to 'im an' say so.'

"We didn' know nuthin' 'bout dis den. We wuz a-fightin' an' a-fightin' all dat time; an' come one day a letter to Marse Chan, an' I see 'im start to read it in his tent, an' he face hit look so cu'ious, an' he han's trembled so I couldn' mek out what wuz de matter wid 'im. An' he fol' de letter up an' wen' out an' wen' way down 'hine de camp, an' stayed dyah 'bout nigh an hour. Well, seh, I wuz on de lookout for 'im when he come back, an', fo' Gord, ef he face didn' shine like a angel's! I say to myse'f, 'Um'm! ef de glory o' Gord ain' done shine on 'im!' An' what yo' 'spose 'twuz?

"He tuk me wid 'im dat evenin', an' he tell me he hed done git a letter from Miss Anne, an' Marse Chan he eyes look like gre't big stars, an' he face wuz jes' like 'twuz dat mawnin' when de sun riz up over de low groun', an' I see 'im stan'in' dyah wid de pistil in he han', lookin' at it, an' not knowin' but what it mout be de lars' time, an' he done mek up he mine not to shoot ole Cun'l Chahmb'lin fur Miss Anne's sake, what writ 'im de letter.

"He fol' de letter wha' was in his han' up, an' put it in he inside pocket— right dyah on de lef' side; an' den he tole me he tho't mebbe we wuz gwine hev some warm wuk in de nex' two or th'ee days, an' arfter dat ef Gord speared 'im he'd git a leave o' absence fur a few days, an' we'd go home.

"Well, dat night de orders come, an' we all hed to git over to'ds Romney; an' we rid all night till 'bout light; an' we halted right on a little creek, an' we stayed dyah till mos' breakfas' time, an' I see Marse Chan set down on de groun' 'hine a bush an' read dat letter over an' over. I watch 'im, an' de battle wuz a-goin' on, but we had orders to stay 'hine de hill, an' ev'y now an' den de bullets would cut de limbs o' de trees right over us, an' one o' dem big shells what goes '*Awhar—awhar—awhar!*' would fall right 'mong us; but Marse Chan he didn' mine it no mo'n nuthin'! Den it 'peared to git closer an' thicker, and Marse Chan he calls me, an' I crep' up, an' he sez:

"'Sam, we'se goin' to win in dis battle, an' den we'll go home an' git married; an' I'se goin' home wid a star on my collar.' An' den he sez, 'Ef I'm wounded, kyar me home, yo' hear?' An' I sez, 'Yes, Marse Chan.'

"Well, jes' den dey blowed boots an' saddles, an' we mounted; an' de orders come to ride 'roun' de slope, an' Marse Chan's comp'ny wuz de secon', an' when we got 'roun' dyah, we wuz right in it. Hit wuz de wust place ever dis nigger got in. An' dey said, 'Charge 'em!' an' my king! ef ever you see bullets fly, dey did dat day. Hit wuz jes' like hail; an' we wen' down de slope (I long wid de res') an' up de hill right to'ds de cannons, an' de fire wuz so strong dyah (dey hed a whole rigiment o' infintrys layin' down dyah onder de cannons) our lines sort o' broke an' stop; de cun'l was kilt, an' I b'lieve dey wuz jes' 'bout to bre'k all to pieces, when Marse Chan rid up an' cotch hol' de fleg an' hollers, 'Foller me!' an' rid strainin' up de hill 'mong de cannons. I seen 'im when he went, de sorrel four good lengths ahead o' ev'y urr hoss, jes' like he use' to be in a fox-hunt, an' de whole rigiment right arfter 'im. Yo' ain' nuver hear thunder! Fust thing I knowed, de roan roll' head over heels an' flung me up 'g'inst de bank, like yo' chuck a nubbin over 'g'inst de foot o' de corn pile. An' dat's what kep' me from bein' kilt, I 'specks. Judy she say she think 'twuz Providence, but I think 'twuz de bank. O' co'se, Providence put de bank dyah, but how come Providence nuver saved Marse Chan? When I look' 'roun', de roan wuz layin' dyah by me, stone dead, wid a cannon-ball gone 'mos' th'oo him, an' our men hed done swep' dem on t'urr side from de top o' de hill. 'Twan' mo'n a minit, de sorrel come gallupin' back wid his mane flyin', an' de rein hangin' down on one side to his knee. 'Dyah!' sez

I, 'fo' Gord! I 'specks dey done kill Marse Chan, an' I promised to tek care on him.'

"I jumped up an' run over de bank, an' dyah, wid a whole lot o' dead men, an' some not dead yit, onder one o' de guns wid de fleg still in he han', an' a bullet right th'oo he body, lay Marse Chan. I tu'n 'im over an' call 'im, 'Marse Chan!' but 'twan' no use, he wuz done gone home, sho' 'nuff. I pick' 'im up in my arms wid de fleg still in he han's, an' toted 'im back jes' like I did dat day when he wuz a baby, an' ole marster gin 'im to me in my arms, an' sez he could trus' me, an' tell me to tek keer on 'im long ez he lived. I kyar'd 'im 'way off de battlefiel' out de way o' de balls, an' I laid 'im down onder a big tree till I could git somebody to ketch de sorrel for me. He wuz cotched arfter a while, an' I hed some money, so I got some pine plank an' made a coffin dat evenin', an' wrapt Marse Chan's body up in de fleg, an' put 'im in de coffin; but I didn' nail de top on strong, 'cause I knowed ole missis wan' see 'im; an' I got a' ambulance an' set out for home dat night. We reached dyah de nex' evein', arfter travellin' all dat night an' all nex' day.

"Hit 'peared like somethin' hed tole ole missis we wuz comin' so; for when we got home she wuz waitin' for us—done drest up in her best Sunday-clo'es, an' stan'in' at de head o' de big steps, an' ole marster settin' in his big cheer— ez we druv up de hill to'ds de house, I drivin' de ambulance an' de sorrel leadin' 'long behine wid de stirrups crost over de saddle.

"She come down to de gate to meet us. We took de coffin out de ambulance an' kyar'd it right into de big parlor wid de pictures in it, whar dey use' to dance in ole times when Marse Chan wuz a school-boy, an' Miss Anne Chahmb'lin use' to come over, an' go wid ole missis into her chamber an' tek her things off. In dyah we laid de coffin on two o' de cheers, an' ole missis nuver said a wud; she jes' looked so ole an' white.

"When I hed tell 'em all 'bout it, I tu'ned right 'roun' an' rid over to Cun'l Chahmb'lin's, 'cause I knowed dat wuz what Marse Chan he'd 'a' wanted me to do. I didn' tell nobody whar I wuz gwine, 'cause yo' know none on 'em hadn' nuver speak to Miss Anne, not sence de duil, an' dey didn' know 'bout de letter.

"When I rid up in de yard, dyah wuz Miss Anne a-stan'in' on de poach watchin' me ez I rid up. I tied my hoss to de fence, an' walked up de parf. She knowed by de way I walked dyah wuz somethin' de motter, an' she wuz mighty pale. I drapt my cap down on de een' o' de steps an' went up. She nuver opened her mouf; jes' stan' right still an' keep her eyes on my face. Fust, I couldn' speak; den I cotch my voice, an' I say, 'Marse Chan, he done got he furlough.'

"Her face was mighty ashy, an' she sort o' shook, but she didn' fall. She tu'ned roun' an' said, 'Git me de ker'ige!' Dat wuz all.

"When de ker'ige come 'roun', she hed put on her bonnet, an' wuz ready. Ez she got in, she sey to me, 'Hev yo' brought him home?' an' we drove 'long, I ridin' behine.

"When we got home, she got out, an' walked up de big walk—up to de poach by herse'f. Ole missis hed done fin' de letter in Marse Chan's pocket, wid de love in it, while I wuz 'way, an' she wuz a-waitin' on de poach. Dey sey dat wuz de fust time ole missis cry when she find de letter, an' dat she sut'n'y did cry over it, pintedly.

"Well, seh, Miss Anne she walks right up de steps, mos' up to ole missis stan'in' dyah on de poach, an' jes' falls right down mos' to her, on her knees fust, an' den flat on her face right on de flo', ketchin' at ole missis' dress wid her two han's—so.

"Ole missis stood for 'bout a minit lookin' down at her, an' den she drapt down on de flo' by her, an' took her in bofe her arms.

"I couldn' see, I wuz cryin' so myse'f, an' ev'ybody wuz cryin'. But dey went in arfter a while in de parlor, an' shet de do'; an' I heahd 'em say, Miss Anne she tuk de coffin in her arms an' kissed it, an' kissed Marse Chan, an' call' 'im by his name, an' her darlin', an' ole missis lef' her cryin' in dyah tell some on 'em went in, an' found her done faint on de flo'.

"Judy (she's my wife) she tell me she heah Miss Anne when she axed ole missis mout she wear mo'nin' fur 'im. I don' know how dat is; but when we buried 'im nex' day, she wuz de one whar walked arfter de coffin, holdin' ole marster, an' ole missis she walked next to 'em.

"Well, we buried Marse Chan dyah in de ole grabeyard, wid de fleg wrapped roun' 'im, an' he face lookin' like it did dat mawnin' down in de low groun's, wid de new sun shinin' on it so peaceful.

"Miss Anne she nuver went home to stay arfter dat; she stay wid ole marster an' ole missis ez long ez dey lived. Dat warn' so mighty long, 'cause ole marster he died dat fall, when dey wuz fallerin' fur wheat—I had jes' married Judy den—an' ole missis she warn' long behine him. We buried her by him next summer. Miss Anne she went in de hospitals toreckly arfter ole missis died; an' jes' fo' Richmond fell she come home sick wid de fever. Yo' nuver would 'a' knowed her fur de same ole Miss Anne. She wuz light ez a piece o' peth, an' so white, 'cep' her eyes an' her sorrel hyar, an' she kep' on gittin' whiter an' weaker. Judy she sut'n'y did nuss her faithful. But she nuver got no betterment! De fever an' Marse Chan's bein' kilt hed done strain her, an' she died jes' fo' de folks wuz sot free.

"So we buried Miss Anne right by Marse Chan, in a place whar ole missis hed tole us to leave, an' dey's bofe on 'em sleep side by side over in de ole grabe-yard at home.

"An' will yo' please tell me, marster? Dey tells me dat de Bible sey dyar won' be marryin' nor givin' in marriage in heaven, but I don' b'lieve it signi-fies dat—does you?"

I gave him the comfort of my earnest belief in some other interpretation, together with several spare "eighteen-pences," as he called them, for which he seemed humbly grateful. And as I rode away I heard him calling across the fence to his wife, who was standing in the door of a small whitewashed cabin, near which we had been standing for some time:

"Judy, have Marse Chan's dawg got home?"

———————

Katherine Eleanor Conway.

BORN in Rochester, N. Y.

SATURNINUS.

HE might have won the highest guerdon that heaven to earth can give,
  For whoso falleth for justice—dying, he yet shall live.

He might have left us his memory to flame as a beacon light,
When clouds of the false world's raising shut the stars of heaven from sight.

He might have left us his name to ring in our triumph song
When we stand, as we'll stand at to-morrow's dawn, by the grave of a world-old
    wrong.

For he gave thee, O mother of valiant sons—thou fair, and sore oppressed,
The love of his youth and his manhood's choice—first-fruits of his life, and best.

Thine were throb of his heart and thought of his brain and toil of his strong right
    hand;
For thee he braved scorn and reviling and loss of gold and land,

Threat and lure and false-hearted friend, and blight of a broken word—
Terrors of night and delay of light—prison and rack and sword.

For thee he bade death defiance—till the heavens opened wide,
And his face grew bright with reflex of light from the face of the Crucified.

And his crown was in sight and his palm in reach and his glory all but won,
And then—he failed—God help us! with the worst of dying done.

Only to die on the treacherous down by the hands of the tempters spread—
Nay, nay—make way for the strangers! we have no right in the dead.

But oh, for the beacon quenched, that we dreamed would kindle and flame!
And oh, for the standard smirched and shamed, and the name we dare not name!

Over the lonesome grave the shadows gather fast;
Only the mother, like God, forgives, and comforts her heart with the past.

  The Boston Pilot. 1885.

"STAR OF MY DYING-TIME."

"Pray for us—now, and at the hour of our death."

[*On the Sunrise Slope.* 1881.]

MOTHER, the skies are dim,   Weary am I and weak,
  The air is cold,   And sore afraid;—
And forms of terror grim   O Virgin, pure and meek
  The mists unfold.   Sweet Mother—aid!

VOL. XI.—8

If I could see thy face
　'Twere almost Heaven,
A sign of pitying grace
　And sin forgiven.

But O—this awful gloom
　Within, without,
The fiends of wrath and doom,
　Despair and doubt!

O for one bright hour more
　Of strength supreme,
Like those I wasted o'er
　My life's long dream!

But Mother—if thou plead
　With thy dear Son
In this, my woful need,
　My Heaven is won!

William Cranston Lawton.

BORN in New Bedford, Mass., 1853.

THE DELPHIC ORACLE.

[Delphi: the Locality and its Legends.—The Atlantic Monthly. 1889.]

THE priestesses were originally young maidens; but when one of them had proved susceptible to other influences than Apollo's inspiration, a widow over fifty years of age was always selected. In the early time, and again after the power of the oracle decayed, there was one Pythia only. In the height of Delphi's fame, three held the office simultaneously. At first, responses were given only on "Apollo's birthday," in the early spring; the natural time for seeking augury concerning crops, the opening of campaigns, plans for colonizing, etc. Later, the favorable days were more frequent.

Before mounting the tripod, the Pythia chewed leaves of the sacred laurel and drank from the holy spring, to put herself more fully under the divine influence. No doubt she, as well as those seeking the aid of divination, was further excited by the strange, rich odors, perhaps incense, of which we hear, and by music. If her responses were too incoherent or unpoetical, they were reduced to writing and to hexameter verse by the attendant priests, and delivered, either orally or upon a sealed tablet, to the questioner.

Our chief authorities for the period when the oracle's influence was at its height are men who sincerely believed in Apollo, and in his guidance of human affairs through the mouth of the inspired Pythia. The attitude of Herodotos, for instance, whose volume is the best mirror of the age and interpreter of its faith, is that of reverent but intelligent belief. He is aware that the priestess has sometimes been corrupted by bribes or other influences; but such sins were detected and severely punished. Some oracles, he also knows, have been forged after the event; but that again only shows how much assistance the supposed sanction of the god gave to the actions of men. He "does not question, and cannot suffer others to question," the genuineness of Apollo's inspiration on many occasions.

Thoughtful students of the history of mysticism, ancient or modern, will at least agree that the utterances recorded are not to be hastily ascribed to a systematic cool-blooded scheme of deception. In the earlier days, at least, the priestess appears usually to have been in the condition perhaps best described as a trance. Nor have we the slightest right to doubt the sincerity and good faith even of the attendant priests who caught and interpreted her excited, half-articulate words. They were probably informed beforehand, it may be through something resembling a confessional, of the questioner's own hopes and desires. Often they knew that the nature of the response obtained might vitally affect the credit and prosperity of the temple and their corporation. Their human judgment, to use modern terms, doubtless influenced more or less consciously their priestly functions. But all this is not saying that the oracle was a mere machine, shrewdly worked to secure personal advantage from the credulity of mankind. It is essential to the comprehension of any religion to start with the assumption of sincerity on the part of priest no less than of people.

> "Not from a vain or shallow thought
> His awful Jove young Phidias wrought;
> Never from lips of cunning fell
> The thrilling Delphic oracle.
> The litanies of nations came
> Like the volcano's tongue of flame,
> Up from the burning core below."

Even reduced to its crudest form, it is true that successful delusion almost always begins in self-delusion.

I am appealing for the moment merely to those who assume as self-evident that the ancient oracles were in no sense inspired; but we have, of course, always the happier alternative, of believing that man has never in any age or land been wholly cut off from consultation, in the hour of his need, with the Rulers of life. Again Emerson's glowing lines will best utter our thought for us:

> "The word by seers or sibyls told,
> In groves of oak or fanes of gold,
> Still floats upon the morning wind,
> Still whispers to the willing mind.
> One accent of the Holy Ghost
> The heedless world hath never lost."

For those, doubtless the overwhelming majority, who view the question with utterly incredulous eyes, who would deny the Pythia and the priests any claim to inspiration or even to self-deception, it may be added that they will find much amusement and confirmation of their own opinions in Lucian's account of Alexander. This "false prophet" organized a private oracle for revenue only, with all the machinery of deceit. There was no doubt whatever about the fraud in that case. Lucian fully exposed it, at the imminent risk of his own life.   .   .   .   .

Just how far the political movements among the Greeks were controlled from Apollo's mountain sanctuary is indeed still subject of debate. There is no doubt that the great German historian Ernst Curtius, trusting to his sympathetic insight into the spirit of Hellenic institutions and character, has sometimes overstepped the broken and uncertain lines of our classic authorities. It is clear, however, that the Delphians enjoyed for many generations the confidence of all Greeks. Thither every republic and monarch turned for guidance in the great crises of their existence. To the servants of Apollo the secret deeds and plans of each must have been truthfully confessed. The information thus gathered by the chapter was undoubtedly transmitted from generation to generation, and formed the basis of an enlightened and patriotic policy in the treatment of Hellenic affairs generally.

We know that inquiries were often answered at once, without recourse to the god. It may be, indeed, that the decision of the oracle was avowedly only invoked in matters of especial difficulty and doubt: as when the guardians of the temple themselves asked Apollo if they should bury or carry away his treasures, to save them from the advancing forces of Xerxes, and received the lofty reply that the god would defend his own. Perhaps we cannot close this inquiry more instructively than with a quotation from the Memorabilia of Xenophon. We must remember that one of the most devout of the Greek writers is recording words which repeatedly fell from the lips of Socrates, his teacher and friend, who in Delphi, at any rate, fell under no suspicion of heresy, but on the contrary had been declared by the oracle to be the wisest of men.

" But he said they were mad who consulted the oracle as to matters which the gods permit men to decide by the use of reason. . . . . He asserted that it was our duty to discover for ourselves so much as the gods allow us to find out; but whatever is not made plain for men, that we should endeavor to learn from the gods through divination: for he declared the gods made revelation to those men toward whom they were gracious."

Robert Underwood Johnson.

BORN in Washington, D. C., 1853.

NOBLESSE OBLIGE.

[*The Century Magazine.* 1883–89.]

WHAT is diviner than the peace of foes!
　　He conquers not who does not conquer hate,
　Or thinks the shining wheels of heaven wait
On his forgiving. Dimmer the laurel shows
On brows that darken; and war-won repose
　Is but a truce when heroes abdicate
　To Huns—unfabling those of elder date
Whose every corse a fiercer warrior rose.
O ye that saved the land! Ah yes, and ye
　That bless its saving! Neither need forget-
　　The price our destiny did of both demand—
Toil, want, wounds, prison, and the lonely sea
　Of tears at home. Oh, look on these. And yet—
　　Before the human fail you—quick! your hand!

IN THE DARK.

AT dusk, when Slumber's gentle wand
    Beckons to quiet fields my boy,
And day, whose welcome was so fond,
    Is slighted like a rivalled toy,—

When fain to follow, fain to stay,
    Toward night's dim border-line he
        peers,
We say he fears the fading day:
    Is it the inner dark he fears?

His deep eyes, made for wonder, keep
    Their gaze upon some land unknown,
The while the crowding questions leap
    That show his ignorance my own.

For he would go he knows not where,
    And I—I hardly know the more;
Yet what is dark and what is fair
    He would to-night with me explore.

Upon the shoals of my poor creed
    His plummet falls, but cannot rest;
To sound the soundless is his need,
    To find the primal soul, his quest.

In vain these bird-like flutterings,
    As when through cages sighs the wind:
My clearest answer only brings
    New depths of mystery to his mind,—

Vague thoughts, by crude surmise beset,
    And groping doubts that loom and pass
Like April clouds that, shifting, fret
    With tides of shade the sun-wooed
        grass.

O lonely soul within the crowd
    Of souls! O language-seeking cry!
How black were noon without a cloud
    To vision only of the eye!

Sleep, child! while healing Nature breaks
    Her ointment on the wounds of
        Thought;
Joy, that anew with morning wakes,
    Shall bring you sight it ne'er has
        brought.

———

Lord, if there be, as wise men spake,
    No Death, but only Fear of Death,
And when Thy temple seems to shake
    'Tis but the shaking of our breath,—

Whether by day or night we see
    Clouds where Thy winds have driven
        none,
Let unto us as unto Thee
    The darkness and the light be one.

———

ON A GREAT POET'S OBSCURITY.

WHAT means his line? You say none knows?
    Yet one perhaps may learn—in time:
For, sure, could life be told in prose
    There were no need at all for rhyme.

Alike two waters blunt the sight—
    The muddy shallow and the sea;
Here every current leads aright
    To deeps where lucent wonders be.

———

A SEPTEMBER VIOLET.

FOR days the peaks wore hoods of
cloud,
The slopes were veiled in chilly rain;
We said: It is the Summer's shroud,
And with the brooks we moaned aloud,—
Will sunshine never come again ?

At last the west wind brought us one
Serene, warm, cloudless, crystal day,
As though September, having blown
A blast of tempest, now had thrown
A gauntlet to the favored May.

Backward to Spring our fancies flew,
And, careless of the course of Time,
The bloomy days began anew.

Then, as a happy dream comes true,
Or as a poet finds his rhyme—

Half wondered at, half unbelieved—
I found thee, friendliest of the flowers!
Then Summer's joys came back, green-
leaved,
And its doomed dead, awhile reprieved,
First learned how truly they were
ours.

Dear violet! Did the Autumn bring
Thee vernal dreams, till thou, like me,
Didst climb to thy imagining ?
Or was it that the thoughtful Spring
Did come again, in search of thee ?

William Henry Rideing.

BORN in Liverpool, England, 1853.

A PERSON OF "LITERARY TASTES."

[*A Little Upstart.* 1885.]

IF it had been worth looking for, the key to Amelia Bailey's character would
have been found in a reckless ambition frustrated by the lack of any ster-
ling ability. A future of intellectual honors had been predicted for her, and
she had been flattered and spoiled in her girlhood by the people of her native
village. She had always been opinionated and domineering, and at this period
of her life she had not found much resistance in arrogating to herself the
leadership of the young folks in Ashville Centre.

She was fortified in her assumption, moreover, by what her friends called
her "literary tastes." To possess "literary tastes" is, in some parts of New
England, a consecration which compels obeisance in a people who, however
narrow their own education may be, however small their capabilities, revere
intellectuality, and willingly bend the knee before the fetich they make of
literature. Amelia Bailey had "literary tastes," and the endowment increased her authority and influence; for in the eyes of her friends she was a
participant in the sanctification of letters.

She always had a book in her hands or tucked under her arm, and she read
with a rapidity which soon exhausted the contents of the village library.
How superficial and unretentive her reading was, her acquaintances never
suspected. The frequent quotations which she made in her conversation and
in her correspondence were taken as evidence of the opulence of her mind; but

in truth they were, in her case, what they are with many a pretender,—the makeshifts and subterfuges of her mental sterility.

No shyness restrained this young lady; she had no scruples about letting her light shine, but magnified it, and intensified it with catoptric reflectors. When the local newspapers printed her verses, she at once enclosed copies of them, with artful little notes, to every poet of eminence in the land. She described herself as a little girl who had caught the gift of song from the person whom she addressed; she adopted the same method with them all, and now she made the poet of Amesbury her involuntary sponsor, then the author of " Evangeline."

Poets may shut their doors against other bores, but they are always kind with little girls who claim to be learning songs from them; and Amelia insinuated herself into an epistolary intimacy with some very distinguished persons. Long after her frocks had been lengthened above and below in the precautionary manner that denotes the transition from girlhood to womanhood, she still left her correspondents to infer that she was a child. But she did not mean to let the intimacy be simply epistolary; she had a desire to shine, and she was resolved that if her own rays failed to dazzle the world, she would become one of those satellites of fame which in some conditions of the atmosphere appear to be the great star itself.

She visited Boston to make the intimacy personal; and the first call she made was on a poet who had written to say that if she presented herself at one o'clock, he would be glad to have her join him at luncheon. He was a young poet; and he was much embarrassed, in the absence of his wife, when he discovered that he had to entertain a gushing and voluptuous young woman of eighteen instead of the child he had expected. The impropriety of the affair filled him with uneasiness, and he was infinitely relieved when, having occupied a precious afternoon which he had reserved for work, she reluctantly departed.

Her visit led to disaster. She endeavored to take every advantage of it; but her own personality did not prove as attractive to the patrons she sought as the child-poet ambuscaded in a country town had been, and when she returned home the letters with distinguished signatures, which had enriched her autograph album, came to her no more.

The bitterness of defeat was in her cup; bold as her attempts were, she had made no strides. The magazines rejected her contributions, and the local newspaper, which in her heart she despised, was the only medium of publication she could find. All this would have been pitiful if her motives had been worthy, if it had been the failure of honest and modest endeavor; but her incentive was the bubble reputation, and she cultivated literature as a heathen would propitiate his idol,—for the benefits it has to bestow, and not for the love of it.

While she was still smarting from the rebuffs she had received, her mind sought a new diversion.   .   .   .   .

She thought of marriage, of course; but marriage is not ordinarily a sensational proceeding, and the young men who had done conjugal duty in the domestic dramas which she had imagined for herself were not persons with whom anything very startling could be accomplished. One of them was more sentimental than the rest, and she divined that with some tuition he might be led to propose an elopement. She had visions of Gretna Green in her mind, and of runaway couples flying wildly to the Scottish border and reaching it just in time to escape the pursuing fathers. She pined for days less prosaic than our own; but her sense of humor was not so deficient that she could not see that as Gretna Green and post-chaises had gone out of fashion, there would be nothing romantic in having her kind-hearted and indulgent father following her by the Shore Line express from Providence, and gently remonstrating with her in the ladies' parlor of the Astor House. A theatrical life would have suited her; but the stage, viewed from Ashville Centre, was too precarious, too daring a venture even for her. Her desire to excite curiosity and to be discussed was consuming her; and anything, no matter how absurd or scandalous, was preferable in her mind to the privacy and obscurity of a humdrum life at home.

She fully appreciated the value of the unexpected in stirring up the interest of yawning mankind, and an unlooked-for opportunity came to exemplify it. It was abruptly announced that she was going to be married, not six, seven, or eight months later, not to the sentimental youth whom she had been encouraging and prompting for some time past, but to Palmyra Phelps, the elderly widower, her father's friend, who was spending a few weeks at Ashville to console himself for the recent loss of his wife. Palmyra Phelps had been one of the Argonauts of '49, and had, it was said, amassed a very handsome fortune in California. San Francisco, with a house on Rincon Hill, was the new prospect which opened before Amelia; and she breathed freer as she thought of its gayety and the latitudinarian tolerance of its society.

Mr. Phelps was already prepared for the return journey, and calling to say good-by to her parents, he found Amelia alone. While he waited for them she sat with him in the low-studded parlor of their house, which abutted from behind a screen of chestnuts on the main street of Ashville. She picked up a scrap-book, and was rustling the pages, when after a silence of embarrassed duration she exclaimed: "O , Mr. Phelps, what should we be without our poets? Don't you remember what Wordsworth says?—

> 'Blessings be with them, and eternal praise,
> 　Who gave us nobler loves and nobler cares,—
> 　The Poets, who on earth have made us heirs
> 　Of truth and pure delight by heavenly lays!'"

"That's so," he said; "poetry is elegant; I admire it. What have you got? Got some of it there?"

"Oh, nothing,—nothing to speak of; only some nonsensical little songs of my own."

"Go ahead; read some! Your ma told me you were lit'ry. Strange, too, because she ain't, nor your pa. Go ahead!"

She still resisted, but after a little more urging read a sonnet beginning with the line "Ah, Love! with bitter tears bedewed;" and he applauded this with so much vehemence, slapping his knee and crying, "Good!" that she discarded her affected reserve and eagerly read to him every verse she had ever written.

"Why don't you get them out in a book?" he inquired.

"Is it possible that you think that my poor little verses are worthy of being enshrined in a *volume?* Oh, Mr. Phelps, *how* you flatter!" She had been so often and so definitely assured by the publishers to whom she had applied that they were not worthy of perpetuation of any kind, that a contrary opinion from any source was comforting.

"That's what I say: get them out in a volume. I'll pay for it. I guess there'll be no difficulty about that," he said, with the confident emphasis of a man who was not used to having any of his pecuniary obligations called into question.

She glowed with pleasure; she knew that there were publishers who would be quite willing to issue her book if they could be guaranteed against loss.

"Oh, how good of you! It's *too* kind. But if they are published in a book —how absurd it sounds! Me, a little country girl, publishing a book! The idea! If they are published in a book I'll dedicate it to you."

"Well, I don't know as I've got any objection to that," he replied, with some suspicious forethought.

He sat staring at her mutely for some minutes after this. She was comely to his eye; her figure was large and pulpy, her complexion pink and white, her hair yellow and abundant. Her exterior made a favorable impression upon him, and then, too, she was "lit'ry." Though he had travelled and shaken off many of the superstitions of Ashville, Palmyra Phelps still clung to his native faith in the exaltation of literature, and Amelia was enhanced in his estimation by her connection with that sacred calling.

His life had not been ornamental. His late wife had been a plain New England woman to the end of her days, and he had been quite satisfied with her; but now that he had all the money he wanted, it seemed to him that he might venture to "put on some style," and what better start could he make in that direction than by taking a young wife of attractive appearance and "lit'ry" tastes?

She was not silent while he sat observing her cogitatively; her mind was filled with radiant visions of the glory her book was to bring her. When it was published and the world was echoing its praises, those former friends of hers who had dropped her would repent and wish they had been sharp enough to discern the budding genius they once spurned; and the thought of their repentance at too late an hour for their salvation was delicious.

The transitions of her manner, which have been already noticed, were the result of affectation. She was naturally effusive and loquacious, but at times she assumed a pensive languor, which she regarded as a becoming expression of the bruised and lacerated condition of the poetic heart. She had begun the conversation on stilts, but had been brought to her feet by the offer Mr. Phelps had made, and then she babbled with the inconsequential rapidity of which we have had some examples. He paid little heed to her, however, and she had no suspicion of the drift his thoughts were taking.

"Abner Bailey and me were boys together," he said by and by, referring to her father, who had not been mentioned before; "but," he added, with extreme solemnity, "there ain't a man in this village to-day as feels younger than I do."

"I'm sure you *look* young—very young," Amelia affirmed.

She saw that he was constrained, as if feeling his way to some avowal of which he was afraid, and she waited for him to proceed, while she still rustled the pages of her scrap-book. Ordinarily he was brisk and self-assertive, but now he was very sheepish.

"How would you like to go to California?" he said, at last, blurting the words out with visible relief.

"I? Oh, Mr. Phelps, what *do* you mean?" Her uncertainty was unfeigned. "Do you mean for a visit?" she continued, when she had recovered her breath.

"No, not I! I don't mean nothing of the sort," he replied, with restored composure. "You understand, Amelia. As Mrs. Phelps is what I mean."

She was dazed only for an instant by the suddenness of the proposal, and then she expertly sifted it and weighed it in her mind. This was not what she had hoped for, and yet it was not odious nor unfeasible to her. She glanced at him critically; his face was ruddy, and his eyes had a youthful sparkle; his wealth was irresistibly in his favor. But, curiously enough, the most pleasing part of the prospect to her was the gossip there would be when what had happened was transmitted to the neighbors; it would not be ephemeral, but would have something of historic permanence in the annals of Ashville.

"But you don't mean at once?" she inquired.

"I'll give you till the day after to-morrow," he said.

"To decide?"

"No, to start. That's plenty of time. We rush things out in California."

When on their return her father and mother were informed of what had happened, they were bewildered; but they were so accustomed to the state of subjection in which an only child can keep her parents in America that they were easily overborne. Amelia's desire to do something astonishing was thus gratified; in two days she had become the wife of a man as old as her father, and in three days she had started for San Francisco *via* Panama. A month later she was installed as mistress of a resplendently frescoed house on Rincon Hill.

The life she now entered on was a reparation for the past. For a time it seemed to her that she was both shining and making a noise. The newspapers noticed her arrival, and one of them published a whole column about it. "The Hon. Pal. Phelps arrived home yesterday," it said, "bringing with him a young and beautiful wife, who will receive a hearty welcome from the society of this coast. Mrs. Phelps, *née* Bailey, is a stately blonde of the Anglo-Saxon type; and she is not only a lady of great beauty, but a distinguished poetess, who has been prominent in the literary circles of Boston and Concord since her infancy. It may be said of her, as Pope said of himself, she 'lisped in numbers,' and we understand that she now has a volume in press, 'With Bitter Tears Bedewed, and Other Poems,' which will be looked for with deep interest. The Hon. Pal. is to be congratulated, and the East had better recognize the stubborn fact that the Pacific coast is gradually absorbing the culture of America." She read this with hysterical elation, and murmured, melodramatically, "At last! At last! The door is open!" Then she added, musingly, "But I do wish they wouldn't call him Pal."

"With Bitter Tears Bedewed, and Other Poems," made its appearance, and her name became familiar to the readers of newspaper gossip, usually in connection with "personals" concerning the receptions she had given to some peripatetic lecturer or musician. She counted much on her receptions, and watched from afar, with the predatory vigilance of a Bedouin, for approaching travellers. When they arrived she made Palmyra call on them and invite them to the house on Rincon Hill; but if they consulted their friends before accepting they never came, or if they came they never repeated the visit. She repelled them by her insincerities and tactless extravagances. She was too palpably shallow, too restlessly vain.

The guests who filled her parlor—or her *salon,* as she preferred to have it called—were Bohemians of wasted character and debatable talents, and a few friends of her husband, who attended, feeling, as they did when they went to church, that it was not the pleasantest way of spending an hour, but that it was a sign of respectability to mingle with the intellectual society which Mrs. Phelps, according to the "San Francisco Tattler," always had about her. In her anxiety to shine, Amelia even deceived herself as to the character of her guests; she tried to believe that the dingy impostors actually were distinguished, and that their presence in her house was a proof of her elevation to the peerage of art and letters; the illusion satisfied her for a year or two, but after that the truth gradually forced itself upon her, combat it as she would, and the spurious honors yielded her no more pleasure. She shone, but it was with the diamonds her husband had bought; she made a noise, but it was the blare of vulgar ostentation, not the reverberations of Fame. Fame had not heeded her call, nor dropped one chaplet on her brow; and though a door had been opened, it had not admitted her to the place she yearned for.

Charles Henry Phelps.

BORN in Stockton, Cal., 1853.

THE MAID OF ST. HELENA.

[*Californian Verses.* 1882.]

ACROSS the long, vine-covered land
   She gazed, with lifted, shading hand.

Behind were hillsides, purple, brown;
Before were vineyards sloping down;

While northward rose, through golden mist,
St. Helen's mount of amethyst.

But forest, vine, and mountain height
Were less divinely benedight

Than she who so serenely stood
To gaze on mountain, vine, and wood.

Her presence breathed in sweet excess
The fragrance of rare loveliness—

A simple beauty in her face,
And in her form a simple grace.

She was so perfect and so fair,
So like a vision, and so rare,

The air that touched her seemed to me
To thrill with trembling ecstasy.

Spell-bound, for fear she might not stay,
I stood afar in sweet dismay.

At last, she sang some olden song.
I did not know its tale of wrong;

I only knew the oriole's note
Grew garrulous within its throat—

It seemed so shameful birds should sing
To silence so divine a thing.

She faded, singing, from my sight,
A dream of beauty and delight:

And I, with unconsenting will,
Retraced my footsteps down the hill.

RARE MOMENTS.

EACH of us is like Balboa: once in all our lives do we,
Gazing from some tropic summit, look upon an unknown sea;

But upon the dreary morrow, every way our footsteps seek,
Rank and tangled vine and jungle block our pathway to the peak.

HEARING THE NEWS IN IDAHO.

A TRAIL, cut through the banks of
snow,
Winds up and o'er the mountain chain
To where the pines of Idaho
Stand guard upon the Cœur d'Alene;
A thousand feet above the clouds,
A thousand feet below the stars,
The narrow path just rims the shrouds
That wrap the warlike form of Mars.
On Eagle and on Pritchard Creeks,
In Dream Gulch and at Murrayville,
The camp-fires play their ruddy freaks,
Redden the snow with lurid streaks,
And melt, perchance, on every hill,
The nuggets which the miner seeks.

One night in camp the game ran high;
Desperate some and reckless more;
In every cañon revelry;
And boisterous songs went rolling by
With rugged jokes and lusty roar—

When, all at once, a sudden hush
Passed like a whisper through the
pines;
The chorus ceased its noisy rush,
The gamblers broke their eager lines,
And many bared a shaggy head,
And some upon that silent air
Breathed forth a rude, unpractised
prayer;
The sick moaned on his hemlock bed;
For, down the peaks of Idaho,
Across the trail cut through the snow,
Had come this message:
"Grant is dead!"

Then men, who knew each other not,
Gathered, and talked in undertone.
And one said: "I have not forgot
How he led us at Donelson."
And one, who spoke his name to bless,
Said: "I was in the Wilderness."

And one: "I was in Mexico."
  And still another, old and scarred,
  And weather-bronzed and battle-
    marred,
Broke down with this one word:
  "Shiloh."

Then, by the firelight's fitful blaze,
  With broken voice, beneath the
    trees,
One read of those last painful days,
  And of his calm soul's victories,
So like his old heroic ways.

Touched to the heart, they did not seek
  To hide the love of many years,
But down each rough and furrowed cheek
  Crept manly, unaccustomed tears.

Ah! not upon this younger sod
  Shall dew more grateful ever fall;
And never lips to Freedom's God
  In prayer more fervently shall call.
And thou, calm Spirit, in what path
  Thy dauntless footsteps ever tread,
No blessing kindlier meaning hath
  Than brave men speak above their dead.

Maybury Fleming.

BORN in Boston, Mass., 1853.

TO SLEEP.

[*Uncollected Poems.* 1884–88.]

SWEET wooded way in life, forgetful Sleep!
  Dim, drowsy realm where restful shadows fall,
    And where the world's glare enters not at all
Or in soft glimmer making rest more deep;
Where sound comes not, or else like brooks that keep
  The world's noise out, as by a slumberous wall
    Of gentlest murmur; where still whispers call
To smileless gladness those that waking weep;
Beneath the dense veil of thy stirless leaves,
  Where no air is except the calm of space,
    Vexed souls of men have grateful widowhood
Of tedious sense; there thoughts are bound in sheaves
  By viewless hands as silent as the place;
    And man, unsinning, finds all nature good.

UPON A WINTER MORNING.

WHEN hoary frost doth shroud the
    grass,
  And bare death sitteth in the trees,
And life is come to sorry pass,
  And morning lacketh drowsy bees—

Then think I of my lady's mouth,
  And of the violets in her eyes;
So, roses warm the wintry drouth,
  And death, by thinking of her,
    dies.

THE NEW YEAR.

ASHES of oak—Are there no more
    trees?
What if the Yule-log whiten and die—
Blaze and redden and die—what then?
    Are there no more trees?

Fallen from pride and gray with fire,
    Slain by it, never to glow again—
But life is more than ashes and night;
    In it lies new fire.

No trees left? Let the old year go,
    And the old years go, with their bloom
      and blight;
Sated with joy and drunk with pain,
    Let the old year go.

Ended at last—and to come, more trees,
    Leaf and pleasure and—ay, and grief.
Over dead ashes light new fire—
    Are there no more trees?

Howard Pyle.

BORN in Wilmington, Del., 1853.

HOW BARON CONRAD HELD THE BRIDGE.

[*Otto of the Silver Hand.* 1888.]

"HALT," cried the Baron, suddenly, and drew rein.
The others stood bewildered. What did he mean to do? He turned to Hans and his blue eyes shone like steel.

"Hans," said he, in his deep voice, "thou hast served me long and truly; wilt thou for this one last time do my bidding?"

"Ay," said Hans, briefly.

"Swear it," said the Baron.

"I swear it," said Hans, and he drew the sign of the cross upon his heart.

"That is good," said the Baron, grimly. "Then take thou this child, and with the others ride with all the speed that thou canst to St. Michaelsburg. Give the child into the charge of the Abbot Otto. Tell him how that I have sworn fealty to the Emperor, and what I have gained thereby—my castle burnt, my people slain, and this poor, simple child, my only son, mutilated by my enemy."

"And thou, my Lord Baron?" said Hans.

"I will stay here," said the Baron, quietly, "and keep back those who follow as long as God will give me grace so to do."

A murmur of remonstrance rose among the faithful few who were with him, two of whom were near of kin. But Conrad of Drachenhausen turned fiercely upon them. "How now," said he, "have I fallen so low in my troubles that even ye dare to raise your voices against me? By the good Heaven, I will begin my work here by slaying the first man who dares to raise word against my bidding." Then he turned from them. "Here, Hans," said he, "take the boy; and remember, knave, what thou hast sworn."

He pressed Otto close to his breast in one last embrace. "My little child," he murmured, "try not to hate thy father when thou thinkest of him here-after, even though he be hard and bloody as thou knowest."

But with his suffering and weakness, little Otto knew nothing of what was passing; it was only as in a faint flickering dream that he lived in what was done around him.

"Farewell, Otto," said the Baron, but Otto's lips only moved faintly in answer. His father kissed him upon either cheek. "Come, Hans," said he, hastily, "take him hence"; and he loosed Otto's arms from about his neck.

Hans took Otto upon the saddle in front of him.

"Oh! my dear Lord Baron," said he, and then stopped with a gulp, and turned his grotesquely twitching face aside.

"Go," said the Baron, harshly, "there is no time to lose in woman's tears."

"Farewell, Conrad! farewell, Conrad!" said his two kinsmen, and com-ing forward they kissed him upon the cheek; then they turned and rode away after Hans, and Baron Conrad was left alone to face his mortal foe.

As the last of his followers swept around the curving road and was lost to sight, Baron Conrad gave himself a shake, as though to drive away the thoughts that lay upon him. Then he rode slowly forward to the middle of the bridge, where he wheeled his horse so as to face his coming enemies. He lowered the visor of his helmet and bolted it to its place, and then saw that sword and dagger were loose in the scabbard and easy to draw when the need for drawing should arise.

Down the steep path from the hill above swept the pursuing horsemen. Down the steep path to the bridge-head, and there drew rein; for in the mid-dle of the narrow way sat the motionless, steel-clad figure upon the great war-horse, with wide, red, panting nostrils, and body streaked with sweat and flecked with patches of foam.

One side of the roadway of the bridge was guarded by a low stone wall; the other side was naked and open and bare to the deep, slow-moving water be-neath. It was a dangerous place to attack a desperate man clad in armor of proof.

"Forward!" cried Baron Henry, but not a soul stirred in answer, and still the iron-clad figure sat motionless and erect upon the panting horse.

"How," cried the Baron Henry, "are ye afraid of one man? Then follow me!" and he spurred forward to the bridge-head. But still no one moved in answer, and the Lord of Trutz-Drachen reined back his horse again. He wheeled his horse and glared round upon the stolid faces of his followers, until his eyes seemed fairly to blaze with passion beneath the bars of the visor.

Baron Conrad gave a roar of laughter. "How now!" he cried; "are ye all afraid of one man? Is there none among ye that dares come forward and meet me? I know thee, Baron Henry! thou art not afraid to cut off the hand of a little child. Hast thou not now the courage to face the father?"

Baron Henry gnashed his teeth with rage as he glared around upon the faces of his men-at-arms. Suddenly his eye lit upon one of them. "Ha! Carl Spigler," he cried, "thou hast thy cross-bow with thee;—shoot me down yonder dog! Nay," he said, "thou canst do him no harm under his armor; shoot the horse upon which he sits."

Baron Conrad heard the speech. "Oh! thou coward villain!" he cried, "stay; do not shoot the good horse. I will dismount and fight ye upon foot." Thereupon, armed as he was, he leaped clashing from his horse and, turning the animal's head, gave it a slap upon the flank. The good horse first trotted and then walked to the farther end of the bridge, where it stopped and began cropping at the grass that grew beside the road.

"Now then!" cried Baron Henry, fiercely, "now then, ye cannot fear him, villains! Down with him! forward!"

Slowly the troopers spurred their horses forward upon the bridge and toward that one figure that, grasping tightly the great two-handed sword, stood there alone guarding the passage.

Then Baron Conrad whirled the great blade above his head, until it caught the sunlight and flashed again. He did not wait for the attack, but when the first of the advancing horsemen had come within a few feet of him, he leaped with a shout upon them. The fellow thrust at him with his lance, and the Baron went staggering a few feet back, but instantly he recovered himself and again leaped forward. The great sword flashed in the air, whistling; it fell, and the nearest man dropped his lance, clattering, and with a loud, inarticulate cry, grasped the mane of his horse with both hands. Again the blade whistled in the air, and this time it was stained with red. Again it fell, and with another shrill cry the man toppled headlong beneath the horse's feet. The next instant they were upon him, each striving to strike at the one figure, to ride him down, or to thrust him down with their lances. There was no room now to swing the long blade, but, holding the hilt in both hands, Baron Conrad thrust with it as though it were a lance, stabbing at horse or man, it mattered not. Crowded upon the narrow roadway of the bridge, those who attacked had not only to guard themselves against the dreadful strokes of that terrible sword, but to keep their wounded horses (rearing and mad with fright) from toppling bodily over with them into the water beneath.

Presently the cry was raised, "Back! back!" And those nearest the Baron began reining in their horses. "Forward!" roared Baron Henry, from the midst of the crowd; but in spite of his command, and even the blows that he gave, those behind were borne back by those in front, struggling and shouting, and the bridge was cleared again excepting for three figures that lay motionless upon the roadway, and that one who, with the brightness of his armor dimmed and stained, leaned panting against the wall of the bridge.

The Baron Henry raged like a madman. Gnashing his teeth together, he rode back a little way; then turning and couching his lance, he suddenly clapped spurs to his horse, and the next instant came thundering down upon his solitary enemy.

Baron Conrad whirled his sword in the air, as he saw the other coming like a thunderbolt upon him; he leaped aside, and the lance passed close to him. As it passed he struck, and the iron point flew from the shaft of the spear at the blow, and fell clattering upon the stone roadway of the bridge.

Baron Henry drew in his horse until it rested upon its haunches, then slowly reined it backward down the bridge, still facing his foe and still holding the wooden stump of the lance in his hand. At the bridge-head he flung it from him.

"Another lance!" he cried, hoarsely. One was silently reached to him and he took it, his hand trembling with rage. Again he rode to a little distance and wheeled his horse; then, driving his steel spurs into its quivering side, he came again thundering down upon the other. Once more the terrible sword whirled in the air and fell, but this time the lance was snatched to one side and the blow fell harmlessly. The next instant, and with a twitch of the bridle-rein, the horse struck full and fair against the man. Conrad of Drachenhausen was whirled backward and downward, and the cruel iron hoofs crashed over his prostrate body, as horse and man passed with a rush beyond him and to the bridge-head beyond. A shout went up from those who stood watching. The next moment the prostrate figure rose and staggered blindly to the side of the bridge, and stood leaning against the stone wall.

At the farther end of the bridge Baron Henry had wheeled his horse. Once again he couched lance, and again he drove down upon his bruised and wounded enemy. This time the lance struck full and fair, and those who watched saw the steel point pierce the iron breast-plate and then snap short, leaving the barbed point within the wound.

Baron Conrad sunk to his knees, and the Roderburg, looming upon his horse above him, unsheathed his sword to finish the work he had begun.

Then those who stood looking on saw a wondrous thing happen: the wounded man rose suddenly to his feet, and before his enemy could strike he leaped, with a great and bitter cry of agony and despair, upon him as he sat in the saddle above.

Henry of Trutz-Drachen grasped at his horse's mane, but the attack was so fierce, so sudden, and so unexpected that before he could save himself he was dragged to one side and fell crashing in his armor upon the stone roadway of the bridge.

"The dragon! the dragon!" roared Baron Conrad, in a voice of thunder, and with the energy of despair he dragged his prostrate foe toward the open side of the bridge.

"Forward!" cried the chief of the Trutz-Drachen men, and down they rode upon the struggling knights to the rescue of their master in this new danger. But they were too late.

There was a pause at the edge of the bridge, for Baron Henry had gained his feet and, stunned and bewildered as he was by the suddenness of his fall, he was now struggling fiercely, desperately. For a moment they stood swaying backward and forward, clasped in one another's arms, the blood from the wounded man's breast staining the armor of both. The moment passed and then, with a shower of stones and mortar from beneath their iron-shod heels, they toppled and fell; there was a thunderous splash in the water below, and as the men-at-arms came hurrying up and peered with awe-struck faces over the parapet of the bridge, they saw the whirling eddies sweep down with the current of the stream, a few bubbles rise to the surface of the water, and then —nothing; for the smooth river flowed onward as silently as ever.

James Whitcomb Riley.

BORN in Greenfield, Ind., 1853.

WHEN THE FROST IS ON THE PUNKIN.

[*The Old Swimmin'-Hole, and 'Leven More Poems.   By Benj. F. Johnson, of
Boone.* 1883.]

WHEN the frost is on the punkin and the fodder's in the shock,
    And you hear the kyouck and gobble of the struttin' turkey-cock,
And the clackin' of the guineys, and the cluckin' of the hens,
And the rooster's hallylooyer as he tiptoes on the fence;
O it's then's the times a feller is a-feelin' at his best,
With the risin' sun to greet him from a night of peaceful rest,
As he leaves the house, bare-headed, and goes out to feed the stock,
When the frost is on the punkin and the fodder's in the shock.

They's something kind o' harty-like about the atmosphere
When the heat of summer's over and the coolin' fall is here.
Of course we miss the flowers, and the blossoms on the trees,
And the mumble of the hummin'-birds and buzzin' of the bees;
But the air's so appetizin'; and the landscape through the haze
Of a crisp and sunny morning of the airly autumn days
Is a pictur' that no painter has the colorin' to mock—
When the frost is on the punkin and the fodder's in the shock.

The husky, rusty rustle of the tossels of the corn,
And the raspin' of the tangled leaves, as golden as the morn;
The stubble in the furries—kind o' lonesome-like, but still
A-preachin' sermons to us of the barns they growed to fill;
The strawstack in the medder, and the reaper in the shed;
The hosses in theyr stalls below—the clover overhead!—
O, it sets my heart a-clickin' like the tickin' of a clock,
When the frost is on the punkin and the fodder's in the shock!

THE ELF CHILD.

[*The Boss Girl, and Other Sketches.* 1886.]

LITTLE Orphant Allie's come to our house to stay
    An' wash the cups and saucers up, and brush the crumbs away,
An' shoo the chickens off the porch, an' dust the hearth, an' sweep,
An' make the fire, an' bake the bread, an' earn her board-an'-keep;
An' all us other children, when the supper things is done,
We set around the kitchen fire an' has the mostest fun
A-list'nin' to the witch tales 'at Allie tells about,
An' the gobble-uns 'at gits you
                    Ef you
                Don't
            Watch
        Out!

Onc't they was a little boy wouldn't say his pray'rs—
An' when he went to bed at night, away up stairs,
His mammy heerd him holler, an' his daddy heerd him bawl,
An' when they turn't the kivvers down, he wasn't there at all!
An' they seeked him in the rafter-room, an' cubby-hole, an' press,
An' seeked him up the chimbly-flue, an' ever'wheres, I guess,
But all they ever found was thist his pants an' roundabout!
An' the gobble-uns 'll git you
                    Ef you
                        Don't
                            Watch
                                Out!

An' one time a little girl 'ud allus laugh an' grin,
An' make fun of ever' one an' all her blood-an'-kin,
An' onc't when they was " company," an' ole folks was there,
She mocked 'em an' shocked 'em, an' said she didn't care!
An' thist as she kicked her heels, an' turn't to run an' hide,
They was two great big Black Things a-standin' by her side,
An' they snatched her through the ceilin' 'fore she knowed what she's about!
An' the gobble-uns 'll git you
                    Ef you
                        Don't
                            Watch
                                Out!

An' little Orphant Allie says, when the blaze is blue,
An' the lampwick sputters, an' the wind goes woo-oo!
An' you hear the crickets quit, an' the moon is gray,
An' the lightnin'-bugs in dew is all squenched away,—
You better mind yer parents, and yer teachers fond and dear,
An' churish 'em 'at loves you, an' dry the orphant's tear,
An' he'p the pore an' needy ones 'at clusters all about,
Er the gobble-uns 'll git you
                    Ef you
                        Don't
                            Watch
                                Out!

GRIGGSBY'S STATION.

[*Afterwhiles.* 1888.]

PAP'S got his patent-right, and rich as all creation;
    But where's the peace and comfort that we all had before?
Le's go a-visitin' back to Griggsby's Station—
    Back where we ust to be so happy and so pore!

The likes of us a-livin' here!   It's jest a mortal pity
    To see us in this great big house, with cyarpets on the stairs,

And the pump right in the kitchen!   And the city! city! city!
    And nothin' but the city all around us ever'wheres!

Climb clean above the roof and look from the steeple,
    And never see a robin, nor a beech or ellum tree!
And right here in ear-shot of at least a thousan' people,
    And none that neighbors with us, or we want to go and see!

Le's go a-visitin' back to Griggsby's Station—
    Back where the latch-string's a-hangin' from the door,
And ever' neighbor 'round the place is dear as a relation—
    Back where we ust to be so happy and so pore!

I want to see the Wiggenses, the whole kit and bilin',
    A drivin' up from Shallor Ford to stay the Sunday through;
And I want to see 'em hitchin' at their son-in-law's and pilin'
    Out there at 'Lizy Ellen's like they ust to do!

I want to see the piece-quilts the Jones girls is makin';
    And I want to pester Laury 'bout their freckled hired hand,
And joke her 'bout the widower she come purt' nigh a-takin',
    Till her pap got his pension 'lowed in time to save his land.

Le's go a-visitin' back to Griggsby's Station,
    Back where they's nothin' aggervating any more,
Shet away safe in the woods around the old location—
    Back where we ust to be so happy and so pore!

I want to see Marindy and he'p her with her sowin',
    And hear her talk so lovin' of her man that's dead and gone,
And stand up with Emanuel to show me how he's growin',
    And smile as I have saw her 'fore she put her mournin' on.

And I want to see the Samples, on the old lower eighty,
    Where John, our oldest boy, he was tuk and burried—for
His own sake and Katy's,—and I want to cry with Katy
    As she reads all his letters over, writ from The War.

What's in all this grand life and high situation,
    And nary a pink nor hollyhawk bloomin' at the door?
Le's go a-visitin' back to Griggsby's Station—
    Back where we ust to be so happy and so pore!

KNEE-DEEP IN JUNE.

TELL you what I like the best—
    'Long about knee-deep in June,
    'Bout the time strawberries melts
On the vine,—some afternoon
Like to jes' git out and rest,
    And not work at nothin' else!

Orchard's where I'd ruther be—
Needn't fence it in fer me!
    Jes' the whole sky overhead,
    And the whole airth underneath—
    Sorto' so's a man kin breathe
Like he ort, and kind o' has

James Whitcomb Riley

Elbow-room to keerlessly
 Sprawl out len'thways on the grass
  Where the shadders thick and soft
 As the kivvers on the bed
 Mother fixes in the loft
Allus, when they's company!

Jes' a sort o' lazein' there—
 S'lazy, 'at you peek and peer
  Through the wavin' leaves above,
 Like a feller 'at's in love
 And don't know it, ner don't keer!
Ever'thing you hear and see
 Got some sort o' interest—
  Maybe find a bluebird's nest
 Tucked up there conveenently
 Fer the boys 'at's apt to be
Up some other apple-tree!
Watch the swallers skootin' past
 'Bout as peert as you could ast;
 Er the Bobwhite raise and whiz
 Where some other's whistle is.

Ketch a shadder down below,
And look up to find the crow;
Er a hawk away up there,
 'Pearantly froze in the air!
 Hear the old hen squawk, and squat
 Over every chick she's got,
Suddent-like!—And she knows where
 That-air hawk is, well as you!
 You jes' bet yer life she do!
  Eyes a-glitterin' like glass,
  Waitin' till he makes a pass!

Pee-wees' singin', to express
 My opinion, 's second class,
 Yit you'll hear 'em more or less;
 Sapsucks gittin' down to biz,
Weedin' out the lonesomeness;
 Mr. Bluejay, full o' sass,
  In them base-ball clothes o' his,
Sportin' 'round the orchard jes'
Like he owned the premises!
 Sun out in the fields kin sizz,
But flat on yer back, I guess,
 In the shade's where glory is!

That's jes' what I'd like to do
 Stiddy fer a year er two!

Plague! ef they ain't sompin' in
Work 'at kind o' goes ag'in
 My convictions!—'long about
 Here in June especially!
 Under some old apple-tree,
  Jes' a-restin' through and through,
I could git along without
  Nothin' else at all to do
 Only jes' a-wishin' you
Was a-gittin' there like me,
 And June was eternity!

Lay out there and try to see
Jes' how lazy you kin be!—
 Tumble round and souse your head
In the clover-bloom, er pull
 Yer straw hat acrost yer eyes,
 And peek through it at the skies,
Thinkin' of old chums 'at's dead,
 Maybe smilin' back at you
In betwixt the beautiful
 Clouds o' gold and white and blue!
Month a man kin railly love—
June, you know, I'm talkin' of!

March aint never nothin' new!
April's altogether too
 Brash fer me! and May—I jes'
 'Bominate its promises, ·
Little hints o' sunshine and
Green around the timber-land—
A few blossoms, and a few
Chip-birds, and a sprout er two—
Drap asleep, and it turns in
'Fore daylight and snows ag'in!

But when June comes—Clear my throat
 With wild honey! Rench my hair
In the dew! and hold my coat!
 Whoop out loud! and throw my hat!
June wants me, and I'm to spare!
Spread them shadders anywhere,
I'll git down and waller there,
 And obleeged to you at that!

A LIZ-TOWN HUMORIST.

SETTIN' round the stove, last night,
　Down at Wess's store, was me,
And Mart Strimples, Tunk, and White,
　And Doc Bills, and two er three
Fellers of the Mudsock tribe
No use tryin' to describe!
　And says Doc, he says, says he,—
"Talkin' 'bout good things to eat,
Ripe mushmillon's hard to beat!"

I chawed on. And Mart he 'lowed
　Wortermillon beat the mush.
　"Red," he says, "and juicy—Hush!
I'll jes' leave it to the crowd!"
　Then a Mudsock chap, says he,
　"Punkin's good enough fer me—
Punkin pies, I mean," he says,—
"Them beats millons! What say,
　Wess?"

I chawed on. And Wess says,—"Well,
　You jes' fetch that wife of mine
　All yer wortermillon-*rine*,
And she'll bile it down a spell—
　In with sorgum, I suppose,
　And what else, Lord only knows!
But I'm here to tell all hands,
Them p'serves meets my demands!"

I chawed on. And White he says,
　"Well, I'll jes' stand in with Wess—
I'm no hog!" And Tunk says,—"I
Guess I'll pastur' out on pie
With the Mudsock boys!" says he;
"Now what's yourn?" he says to me;
I chawed on—fer—quite a spell—
　Then I speaks up, slow and dry,—
　"Jes' tobacker!" I-says-I.
And you'd orto' heerd 'em yell!

THE OLD MAN AND JIM.

OLD man never had much to say—
　　'Ceptin' to Jim—
And Jim was the wildest boy he had,
　And the old man jes' wrapped up in him!
Never heerd him speak but once
Er twice in my life,—and first time was
When the army broke out, and Jim he went,
The old man backin' him, fer three months.—
And all 'at I heerd the old man say
Was, jes' as we turned to start away,—
　"Well; good-bye, Jim:
　　Take keer of yourse'f!"

'Peared like he was more satisfied
　Jes' lookin' at Jim
And likin' him all to hisse'f-like, see?
　'Cause he was jes' wrapped up in him!
And over and over I mind the day
The old man come and stood round in the way
While we was drillin', a-watchin' Jim;
And down at the deepot a-heerin' him say,—
　"Well; good-bye, Jim:
　　Take keer of yourse'f!"

Never was nothin' about the farm
　Disting'ished Jim;—

Neighbors all ust to wonder why
   The old man 'peared wrapped up in him:
But when Cap. Biggler, he writ back
'At Jim was the bravest boy we had
In the whole dern rigiment, white er black,
And his fightin' good as his farmin' bad—
'At he had led, with a bullet clean
Bored through his thigh, and carried the flag
Through the bloodiest battle you ever seen,—
The old man wound up a letter to him
'At Cap. read to us, 'at said,—" Tell Jim
   Good-bye;
        And take keer of hisse'f!"

Jim come back jes' long enough
   To take the whim
'At he'd like to go back in the calvery—
   And the old man jes' wrapped up in him!
Jim 'lowed 'at he'd had sich luck afore,
Guessed he'd tackle her three years more.
And the old man give him a colt he'd raised
And follered him over to Camp Ben Wade,
And laid around fer a week er so,
Watchin' Jim on dress parade;
Tel finally he rid away,
And last he heerd was the old man say,—
   " Well; good-bye, Jim:
        Take keer of yourse'f! "

Tuk the papers, the old man did,
   A-watchin' fer Jim,
Fully believin' he'd make his mark
   Some way—jes' wrapped up in him!
And many a time the word 'u'd come
'At stirred him up like the tap of a drum:
At Petersburg, fer instance, where
Jim rid right into their cannons there,
And tuk 'em, and p'inted 'em t'other way,
And socked it home to the boys in gray,
As they skooted fer timber, and on and on—
Jim a Lieutenant and one arm gone,
And the old man's words in his mind all day,—
   " Well; good-bye, Jim:
        Take keer of yourse'f! "

Think of a private, now, perhaps,
   We'll say like Jim,
'At's clumb clean up to the shoulder-straps—
   And the old man jes' wrapped up in him!
Think of him—with the war plum' through,
And the glorious old Red-White-and-Blue
A-laughin' the news down over Jim
And the old man, bendin' over him—

The surgeon turnin' away with tears
'At hadn't leaked fer years and years—
As the hand of the dyin' boy clung to
His father's, the old voice in his ears,—
  " Well; good-bye, Jim:
    Take keer of yourse'f! "

The Century Magazine. 1888.

Harry Stillwell Edwards.

BORN in Macon, Ga., 1854.

"MINC"—A PLOT.

[*Two Runaways, and Other Stories.* 1889.]

THE trim little steamboat that plies Lake Harris, the loveliest of all Florida waters, emerged from the picturesque avenue of cypress and trailing moss called Dead River, which leads out of Eustis, and glided as a shadow betwixt sea and sky toward its harbor, fourteen miles away. It had been the perfection of a May day, and the excursionists, wearied at last of sight-seeing, were gathered upon the forward deck. The water-slopes of the highlands on the right, with their dark lines of orange-trees and their nestling cottages, lay restful in the evening shadow fast stretching out toward the boat, for the sun was dipping below the horizon, with the stately pines in silhouette upon his broad red face. "Home, Sweet Home," "Old Kentucky Home," and "Old Folks at Home" had been rendered by the singers of the party with that queer mixture of pathos and bathos so inseparably connected with excursion songs, and a species of nothing-else-to-be-done silence settled over the group, broken only by the soft throb of the engine and the swish of dividing waters. Presently some one began a dissertation upon negro songs, and by easy stages the conversation drifted to negro stories. Among the excursionists sat a gray-haired, tall, soldierly looking gentleman whom every one called "Colonel," and whose kindly eyes beamed out from under his soft felt hat in paternal friendliness upon all.

"It is somewhat singular," he said at length, when there had come a lull in the conversation, "that none of the story-writers have ever dealt with the negro as a resident of two continents. Why could not a good story be written, the scene laid partly in Africa and partly in the South? I am not familiar enough with the literature of this kind and the romances that have been written about our darkies to say positively that it has not been already done, but it seems to me that the opportunity to develop a character from the savage to the civilized state is very fine and would take well. Victor Hugo has a negro in one of his West India romances whose name I forget now—the story used to be familiar——"

"Bug-Jargal," suggested some one.

"So it was. But in this reference is made only to the man's ancestry; and I never thought the character true to life. Hugo did not know the negro."

"But, Colonel, is it not true that these people were the veriest savages, and would it not be too great a strain upon the realistic ideas of the day to venture into Africa for a hero, especially since Rider Haggard has idealized it?"

"I don't think so. We have no way of ascertaining just how much the imported slaves really knew, but it is a fact that a few were remarkable for some kind of skill and intelligence. They were not communicative, and soon drifted into the dialect of their new neighbors, forgetting their own. I had a negro on my plantation who undoubtedly came from Africa. I was present when my father bought him upon the streets of Savannah, becoming interested in his story soon after he was landed. His mother was described as a sort of priestess—or, as we say, a Voodoo—in her native land, which was near the western coast of Africa, some twelve hundred miles north of Cape of Good Hope. Her influence for evil, it seems, was so remarkable that as soon as possible she was separated from the cargo and sent on to one of the Gulf ports. This fellow was then probably about thirty years old—a little jet-black man with small, bright eyes of remarkable brilliancy. He seemed very glad to go with us, and, I may add, never at any time afterward did he ever give trouble, but did readily what was required of him. He seemed to take a fancy to me from the first, and his love—I say love, for I believe it was genuine affection—gradually extended to all white children. For children of his own color—I won't say race, for in many respects he differed from the ordinary negro—he entertained the liveliest disgust. Now, a story-writer could take that slave and with the help I might give him—his life with us, his peculiarities, powers, certain singular coincidences, and the manner of his death—weave a very interesting romance."

"O Colonel, do tell us the story!" The appeal came in the shape of a chorus from the ladies present, and was at once reënforced by the others. A pair of sweethearts who had been leaning over the bow came slowly back on hearing it, and added their solicitations. The genial old gentleman laughed and looked out upon the waters.

"I did not know I was spreading a net for my own feet," he said. "The story of this fellow would require half a night, even were I able to put it in shape, but I can give a rough outline of some features of it. 'Minc,' as he was called, though his name as near as I can imitate his pronunciation was 'Meeng'r,'—Minc was for a long time a sort of elephant on the family's hands. My mother was a little afraid of him, I think, and the negroes themselves never did entirely overcome their respect for him enough to treat him exactly as one of them, although, as I have intimated, he was perfectly harmless.

"Minc, however, one day exhibited a strange power over animals which is even now a mystery to me. He could take a drove of hogs and by a series of queer little sounds, half grunts, half groans, reduce them to submission and drive them where he would. Gradually, as the rules for feeding and taking care of them became known to him, he was given charge of the plantation hogs, of which there were five or six hundred, and no small responsibility it was. I remember he at once fashioned him a little instrument from the horn of a yearling; with this he could go into the swamp and by a few notes thereon call them up on the run. That one horn lasted him all his life, and he was with us thirty-odd years. He used to wear it hung round his neck by a string, and it was the one possession that the children could not get away from him for even a moment. I think that probably some superstition restrained him.

"Another queer power possessed by Minc was in connection with grass-hoppers. I have seen him hundreds of times go into the orchard where the crab-grass was tall, and standing perfectly still give forth from his chest a musical humming sound. If there were any big brown grasshoppers within hearing they would fly up, dart about, and light upon him. Sometimes he would let me stand by him, and then the grasshoppers would come to me also; but Minc could catch them without any trouble, while any movement from my hand drove them off. Minc," continued the speaker, laughing softly, "used to eat the things,"—exclamations from the ladies,—"and I am told that certain tribes in Africa are very fond of them."

"Boiled in a bag and eaten with salt they are not bad," said a young gen-tleman with the reputation of having been everywhere. "I have eaten what was probably the same insect, though under the name of locusts." (More exclamations.) "Why not?" he added in defense. "Can anything be worse to look upon than shrimps?"

"Well," continued the Colonel, "I soon broke Minc of eating them. The grasshoppers were my favorite bait for fish, and Minc developed into a most successful angler, quite abandoning his cane spear—though, by the way, he was as certain of a victim when he struck as was a fish-hawk. I think the plantation rations also had something to do with his change of diet.

"Well, as Minc's queer powers came to be known he was not greatly sought after by the other negroes. They are slow to speak of their superstitions, but it soon developed that they regarded him as being in league with spirits. He lived in a little cabin down on the creek apart from the others, and there was my favorite haunt, for I was more than delighted with Minc's accomplish-ments, and Minc was rapidly learning from me the use of many words, which gave me a sort of proprietary interest in him. In time he came to speak as well as the average negro, but he had a way of running his words together when excited that made him all but unintelligible. I never did get much in-formation from him concerning his former life. He didn't seem to be able to convert terms well enough to express himself. He had lived near great swamps, ate fish, was familiar with the hog—this much I gleaned; and from time to time he would recognize birds and animals and excitedly give me what were evidently their names in his own country. Of course this all came to me at odd times from year to year, and did not make a great impression. I remember, though, that reference to his capture had always a depressing effect upon him, and at such times he would go off about his work. I suppose the memory of his mother was the cause of this; and I soon found that to speak to him of the matter would cost me Minc's company, and so I quit bringing up the subject.

"The things in connection with Minc that puzzled me more were his super-stitions. Doubtless they were taught him by his mother, and the first inti-mation of them I had was when he caught a gopher, and with a bit of wire ground to an exceedingly fine point cut on its shell a number of curious signs, or hieroglyphics, different from anything I had ever seen, except that there was a pretty fair representation of the sun. He then took this gopher back to where he found it and turned him loose at the entrance of his burrow, making gestures indicating that the gopher was going far down into the earth. He did something of this kind for every gopher he caught. One day he suc-ceeded in snaring a green-head duck, and upon its broad bill he carved more hieroglyphics. This done, to my astonishment, and probably to the duck's also, he tossed the bird high in the air and laughed as it sped away. As the years went by I saw him treat many birds after the same fashion. If there was room for only one or two figures, he would put them on, and let the bird go. But as he grew older Minc ate the large majority of his captures, just as any other negro would.'

"Well, many years passed away; I grew up and married. By this time Minc was long since a feature of the plantation. My children in time took my place with him, and many's the ride he gave them in his little two-wheel cart behind the oxen. I should have said before that he used to haul corn to the hogs when in distant fields, and wood for the house-fires on the way back. The negroes no longer feared him, but the negro children would run past his wagon as he plodded along and sing:

> 'Ole Unc' Minc
> Under th' hill,
> His eyes stick out
> Like tater hill.
> Juba dis and Juba dat,
> Juba roun' de kitch'n fat,—
> Juba ketch er—er——'

"Oh, well, I forget how the rhyme ran; but Minc would stop every time and hurl a string of words at them which no one could ever exactly translate; and the little brats, delighted at having provoked the outburst, would kick up their heels and scamper off. But along in the war," continued the Colonel, after yielding a moment to a quiet shake of his sides over the recollections trooping up, "Minc filled another office. It was found that by means of a notched stick, scarcely two feet in length, he could keep books, so to say, as well as anybody. I can't, and never will, I reckon, fathom the fellow's system. He often tried to explain it; but when he had finished, you would know just about what you knew at first and be a little confused as to that. But he never was known to make a mistake. Sent into the fields, he would weigh cotton for forty pickers all day and report at night just what each picked in the morn-ing and evening and the sum of all—and all by means of his notches. I am absolutely sure he brought the system from Africa, for no one ever was able to understand it on the plantation, and Minc never lived a day off it. You will see the relation these incidents bear to my first proposition as to imported negroes being simply savages.

"The death of Minc was tragic and surrounded by some remarkable circumstances, and here again comes the story-writer's field. Two years before his death Minc had caught and tamed a little cooter about twice the size of a silver dollar. He would hum a queer little tune for his pet, and the thing would walk around the floor for all the world as if he was trying to dance. Then he would come when called, and was particularly fond of sleeping in Minc's dark jacket-pocket, where I suspect he found crumbs. Minc would sometimes throw him into the creek just in front of his cabin, but the little thing would scramble out and get back to the hut again if Minc was in sight; if not he staid in an eddy close by. You will understand directly why I speak so particularly of this. As the cooter grew larger, Minc amused himself by cutting hieroglyphics all over its back. Into these lines he rubbed dyes of his own manufacture, and the result was a very variegated cooter. The old man carried him almost continually in his pocket; partly, I think, because the animal's antics always amused the children, and partly because he was the cause of Minc's getting many a biscuit. He would frequently come to the house, and sitting on the back porch make 'Teeta,' as he called the cooter, go through with his tricks. These generally resulted in Minc's getting biscuit or cake for Teeta, and in his lying down and letting the animal crawl into his pocket after it, a feat that closed the performance.

"Well, one day Minc was missing. Everything about his cabin was in order, but he did not return. He never did return. Search was made, of course, and he was finally given up. The negroes dragged the creek, but not with much expectation of finding him, for I am afraid that some of them believed that Old Nick had taken him bodily. But a month afterward my oldest boy was hunting in the big swamp for the hogs, which had become badly scattered since Minc's death, when in crossing a tree that had fallen over one of the many lagoons thereabout, whom should he see sitting there but Teeta, watching him with his keen little black eyes, the patch of sunlight he had chosen bringing out the tattoo marks upon his shell. The next instant Teeta dived off the log and disappeared. Tom came home and told of his adventure. Taking a party of negroes, I returned with him and dragged the lagoon. Just where the cooter had dived we found the body of poor old Minc. He had fallen off the log, and becoming entangled in the sunken branches had drowned. And in the rotting pocket of his old jacket we found the cooter hid away."

The Colonel raised his hand as exclamations broke from the party.

"No; you must let me finish. The finding of the cooter was not the most singular thing connected with the death of Minc. Upon our return home one of the superstitious negroes, greatly to my distress, cut off Teeta's head. He wanted it to place it under his doorstep. This was to protect the place from old Minc, of course; but I had the shell cleaned, and the children kept it as a memento of the faithful old slave whom they had dearly loved.

"Relating this story once to an eminent traveller," continued the Colonel, "he suggested that I should send it to the British Museum with its history written out; and going to New York soon after, I carried it with me. It lay forgotten, however, in my trunk, and I did not notice it again until one day

Harry Stillwell Edwards

I happened to be in New Orleans. There was then in that city an aged negress, claiming to be a Voodoo, and creating considerable stir among the Northern attendants upon Mardi-Gras. I don't know what suggested it, but it occurred to me one day that I would let her look at the shell. It was a mere fancy, or impulse, if you will. I carried it to her. She was, indeed, an old woman, small in stature, and bent nearly double. Without speaking a word, I placed the shell in her hand. She gave one long, fixed look at it, and straightened up as if casting off the weight of half a century. Her lips parted, but she could not speak. Then her form resumed its crook again, and placing her hand against the small of her back, she gasped for breath. With her bright black eyes fixed upon me she said at last, after a violent struggle, 'Meeng'r!' It was a mere whisper. I spent an hour with the poor old creature, and told her the story of her son's life, for it was undoubtedly he. I gleaned from her that the hieroglyphics upon the shell were taught him by her,—what they signified she would not say,—and that he had written them upon the birds of the air, the beasts of the field, and the inhabitants of the water, that they might be borne to her wherever hid. I never got my shell back: it would have been like tearing the miniature of a dead child from its mother's bosom. And the old woman, when I went to see her next day, had disappeared."

Here the old gentleman arose and went forward.

Samuel Minturn Peck.

BORN in Tuskaloosa, Ala., 1854.

BESSIE BROWN, M. D.

[*Cap and Bells.* 1886.]

'TWAS April when she came to town;
  The birds had come, the bees were
      swarming.
Her name, she said, was Doctor Brown:
  I saw at once that she was charming.
She took a cottage tinted green,
  Where dewy roses loved to mingle;
And on the door, next day, was seen
      A dainty little shingle.

Her hair was like an amber wreath;
  Her hat was darker, to enhance it.
The violet eyes that glowed beneath
  Were brighter than her keenest lancet.
The beauties of her glove and gown
  The sweetest rhyme would fail to
      utter.
Ere she had been a day in town
      The town was in a flutter.

The gallants viewed her feet and hands,
  And swore they never saw such wee
      things;
The gossips met in purring bands
  And tore her piecemeal o'er the tea-
      things.
The former drank the Doctor's health
  With clinking cups, the gay carousers;
The latter watched her door by stealth,
      Just like so many mousers.

But Doctor Bessie went her way
  Unmindful of the spiteful cronies,
And drove her buggy every day
  Behind a dashing pair of ponies.
Her flower-like face so bright she bore,
  I hoped that time might never wilt her.
The way she tripped across the floor
      Was better than a philter.

Her patients thronged the village street;
  Her snowy slate was always quite full.
Some said her bitters tasted sweet,
  And some pronounced her pills delight-
    ful.
'Twas strange—I knew not what it
    meant—
  She seemed a nymph from Eldorado;
Where'er she came, where'er she went,
    Grief lost its gloomy shadow.

Like all the rest, I too grew ill;
  My aching heart there was no quelling.
I tremble at my doctor's bill,—
  And lo! the items still are swelling.
The drugs I've drunk you'd weep to
    hear!
  They've quite enriched the fair con-
    cocter,
And I'm a ruined man, I fear,
    Unless—I wed the Doctor!

MY LITTLE GIRL.

MY little girl is nested
  Within her tiny bed,
With amber ringlets crested
  Around her dainty head;
She lies so calm and stilly,
  She breathes so soft and low,
She calls to mind a lily
  Half-hidden in the snow.

A weary little mortal
  Has gone to slumberland;
The Pixies at the portal
  Have caught her by the hand;

She dreams her broken dolly
  Will soon be mended there,
That looks so melancholy
  Upon the rocking-chair.

I kiss your wayward tresses,
  My drowsy little queen;
I know you have caresses
  From floating forms unseen.
O, Angels, let me keep her
  To kiss away my cares,
This darling little sleeper,
  Who has my love and prayers!

THE CAPTAIN'S FEATHER.

THE dew is on the heather,
  The moon is in the sky,
And the captain's waving feather
  Proclaims the hour is nigh
When some upon their horses
  Shall through the battle ride,
And some with bleeding corses
  Must on the heather bide.

The dust is on the heather
  The moon is in the sky,
And about the captain's feather
  The bolts of battle fly;

But hark, what sudden wonder
  Breaks forth upon the gloom?
It is the cannon's thunder—
  It is the voice of doom!

The blood is on the heather,
  The night is in the sky,
And the gallant captain's feather
  Shall wave no more on high;
The grave and holy brother
  To God is saying Mass,
But who shall tell his mother,
  And who shall tell his lass?

francis Marion Crawford.

BORN at the Baths of Lucca, Italy, 1854.

THE TRAGEDY OF GREIFENSTEIN.

[*Greifenstein.* 1889.]

IT is doubtful whether Greifenstein would have recognized his brother, if he had met him under any other circumstances. Forty years had passed since they had met, and both were old men. The difference between their ages was not great, for Greifenstein's father had died within the year of his son's birth, and his mother had married again three years later. In her turn she had died when both were young men, and from that time Greifenstein had seen little of his half-brother, who had been brought up by his own father in a different part of the country. Then young Rieseneck had entered the Prussian service, and a few years later had been ruined by the consequences of his evil deeds.

Greifenstein saw before him a tall man, with abundant white hair and a snowy beard, of bronzed complexion, evidently strong in spite of his years, chiefly remarkable for the heavy black eyebrows that shaded his small gray eyes. The latter were placed too near together, and the eyelids slanted downward at the outer side, which gave the face an expression of intelligence and great cunning. Deep lines furrowed the high forehead, and descended in broad curves from beneath the eyes till they lost themselves in the beard. Kuno von Rieseneck was evidently a man of strong feelings and passions, of energetic temperament, clever, unscrupulous, but liable to go astray after strange ideas, and possibly capable of something very like fanaticism. It was indeed not credible that he should have done the deeds which had wrecked his life out of cold calculation, and yet it was impossible to believe that he could be wholly disinterested in anything he did. The whole effect of his personality was disquieting.

He entered the room with slow steps, keeping his eyes fixed upon his brother. The servant closed the door behind him, and the two men were alone. Rieseneck paused when he reached the middle of the apartment. For a moment his features moved a little uneasily, and then he spoke.

"Hugo, do you know me?"

"Yes," answered Greifenstein, "I know you very well." He kept his hands behind him and did not change his position as he stood before the fire.

"You got my letter?" inquired the fugitive.

"Yes. I will do what you ask of me."

The answers came in a hard, contemptuous voice, for Greifenstein was almost choking with rage at being thus forced to receive and protect a man whom he both despised and hated. But Rieseneck did not expect any very cordial welcome, and his expression did not vary.

"I thank you," he answered. "It is the only favor I ever asked of you, and I give you my word it shall be the last."

Greifenstein's piercing eyes gleamed dangerously, and for an instant the anger that burned in him glowed visibly in his face.

" Your—" He would have said " your word," throwing into the two syllables all the contempt he felt for one whose word had been so broken. But he checked himself gallantly. In spite of all, Rieseneck was his guest and had come to him for protection, and he would not insult him. " You shall be safe to-morrow night," he said, controlling his tongue.

But Rieseneck had heard the first word, and knew what should have followed it. He turned a little pale, bronzed though he was, and he let his hand rest upon the back of a chair beside him.

" I will not trouble you further," he said. " If you will show me a place where I can sleep, I will be ready in the morning."

" No," answered Greifenstein. " That will not do. The servants know that a visitor is in the house. They will expect to see you at dinner. Besides, you are probably hungry."

Perhaps he regretted having shown his brother, even by the suggestion of a phrase, what was really in his heart, and the feeling of the ancient guest-right made him relent a little.

" Sit down, ' he added, as Rieseneck seemed to hesitate. " It will be necessary that you dine with us and meet my wife. We must not excite suspicion."

" You are married then ? " said Rieseneck. It was more like a thoughtful reflection than a question. Though he had written to his brother more than once, the latter's answers, when he vouchsafed any, had been curt and businesslike in the extreme.

" I have been married five and twenty years," Greifenstein replied. It was strange to be informing his brother of the fact.

Rieseneck sat down upon a high chair and rested his elbow upon the table. Neither spoke for a long time, but Greifenstein resumed his seat, relighted his pipe, and placed his feet upon the fender, taking precisely the attitude in which he had been when his brother was announced. The situation was almost intolerable, but his habits helped him to bear it.

" I was also married," said Rieseneck at last, in a low voice, as though speaking to himself. " You never saw my wife ? " he asked rather suddenly.

" No."

" She died," continued the other. " It was very long ago—more than thirty years."

" Indeed," said Greifenstein, as though he cared very little to hear more.

Again there was silence in the room, broken only by the crackling of the fir logs in the fire and by the ticking of the clock in its tall carved case in the corner. A full hour must elapse before the evening meal, and Greifenstein did not know what to do with his unwelcome guest. At last the latter took out a black South American cigar and lit it. For a few moments he smoked thoughtfully, and then, as though the fragrant fumes had the power to unloose his tongue, he again began to talk.

" She died," he said. " She ruined me. Yes; did you never hear how it was ? And yet I loved her. She would not follow me. Then they sent me some of her hair and the boy. But for her, it might never have happened; and yet I forgive her. You never heard how it all happened?"

"I never inquired," answered Greifenstein. "You say she ruined you. How do you mean?"

"She made me do it. She was an enthusiast for liberty and revolution. She filled my mind with ideas of the people's sovereignty. She talked of nothing else. She besought me on her knees to join her party, as she called it. She flattered me with dreams of greatness in a great republic, she illuminated crime in the light of heroism, she pushed me into secret societies, and laughed at me for my want of courage. I loved her, and she made a fool of me, worse than a fool, a traitor, worse than a traitor, a murderer, for she persuaded me to give the arms to the mob; she made me an outlaw, an exile, an object of hatred to my countrymen, a thing loathsome to all who knew me. And yet I loved her, even when it was all over, and I would have given my soul to have her with me."

Greifenstein's face expressed unutterable contempt for this man who in the strength and pride of youth had laid down his honor for a woman's word, not even for her love, since he had possessed that already.

"It seems to me," he said, "that there was one very simple remedy for you."

"A little lead in the right place. I know. And yet I lived, and I live still. Why? I do not know. I believed in the revolution, though she had forced the belief upon me, and I continued to believe in it until long after I went to South America. And when I had ceased to believe in it, no one cared whether I lived or died. Then came this hope, and this blow. I could almost do it now."

Greifenstein looked at him curiously for a moment, and then rose from his place and went deliberately to a huge, dark piece of furniture that stood between the windows. He brought back a polished mahogany case, unlocked it, and set it beside his brother upon the table, under the light of the lamp.

Rieseneck knew what he meant well enough, but he did not wince. On the contrary he opened the case and looked at the beautiful weapon, as it lay all loaded and ready for use in its bed of green baize cloth. Then he laid it on the table again, and pushed it a little away from him.

"Not now," he said quietly. "I am in your house. You would have to declare my identity. It would make a scandal. I will not do it."

"You had better put it into your pocket," answered Greifenstein grimly, but without a trace of unkindness in his voice. "You may like to have it about you, you know."

Rieseneck looked at his brother in silence for a few seconds, and then took the thing once more in his hands.

"Do you mean it as a gift?" he asked. "You might not care to claim it afterwards."

"Yes."

"I thank you." He took the revolver from the case, examined it attentively, and then slipped it into his breast-pocket. "I thank you," he repeated. "I do not possess one."

Greifenstein wondered whether Rieseneck would have the courage to act upon the suggestion. To him there was nothing horrible in the idea. He was merely offering this despicable creature the means of escape from the world's contempt. He himself, in such a case, would have taken his own life long ago, and he could not understand that any man should hesitate when the proper course lay so very clear before him. He went back to his seat as if nothing unusual had happened. Then, as though to turn the conversation, he began to speak of the plans for the morrow. He did not really believe in his brother's intentions, but as an honorable man, according to his lights, he considered that he had done his duty in giving the weapon.

"We can ride a long distance," he said, "and then we can walk. When you are once at the lake, you can find a boat which will take you over. I warn you that it is far."

"It will be enough if you show me the way," answered Rieseneck absently. "You are very kind."

"It is my interest," said Greifenstein, unwilling that his feelings should be misinterpreted. Then he relapsed into silence.   .   .   .   .

When Clara heard that there was to be a guest at dinner, her first sensation was one of extreme terror, but she was reassured by the information her maid gave concerning the general appearance of Herr Brandt. The woman had not seen him, but had of course heard at once a full description of his personality. He was described as a tall old gentleman, exceedingly well dressed, though he had arrived on foot and without luggage. The maid supposed that his effects would follow him, since he had chosen to walk. Beyond that, Clara could ascertain nothing, but it was clear that she did not consider the details she learned as descriptive of the person whose coming she feared. On the contrary, the prospect of a little change from the usual monotony of the evening had the effect of exhilarating her spirits, and she bestowed even more attention than usual upon the adornment of her thin person. The nature of the woman could not die. Her natural vanity was so extraordinary that it might have been expected to survive death itself. She belonged to that strange class of people who foresee even the effect they will produce when they are dead, who leave elaborate directions for the disposal of their bodies in the most becoming manner, and who build for themselves appropriate tombs while they are alive, decorated in a style agreeable to their tastes. Clara arrayed herself in all her glory for the feast; she twisted the ringlets of her abundant faded hair, until each covered at least one obnoxious line of forehead and temples; she laid the delicate color upon her sunken cheeks with amazing precision, and shaded it artistically with the soft hare's foot, till it was blended with the whiteness of the adjacent pearl powder; she touched the colorless eyebrows with the pointed black stick of cosmetic that lay ready to her hand in its small silver case, and made her yellow nails shine with pink paste and doeskin rubbers till they reflected the candle-light like polished horn. With the utmost care she adjusted the rare old lace to hide the sinewy lines of her emaciated throat, and then, observing the effect as her maid held a second mirror beside her face, she hastened to touch the shrivelled lobes of her ears with a delicate rose color that set off the brilliancy of the single diamonds she wore as earrings. She opened and shut her eyelids quickly to make her eyes brighter, and held up her hands so that the blood should leave the raised network of the purple veins less swollen and apparent. The patient tire-woman gave one last scrutinizing glance and adjusted the rich folds of the silk gown with considerable art, although such taste as she possessed was outraged at the effect of the pale straw-color when worn by such an aged beauty. Another look into the tall mirror, and Clara von Greifenstein was satisfied. She had done what she could do to beautify herself, to revive in her own eyes some faint memory of that prettiness she had once seen reflected in her glass, and she believed that she had not altogether failed. She even smiled contentedly at her maid, before she left the chamber to go to the drawing-room. It was a satisfaction to show herself to some one, it was a relief from the thoughts that had tormented her so long, it was a respite from her husband's perpetual effort to amuse her by reading aloud. For a few hours at least she was to hear the sound of an unfamiliar voice, to enjoy the refreshing effect of a slight motion in the stagnant pool of worn-out ideas that surrounded her little island of life.

She drew herself up and walked delicately as she went into the drawing-room. She had judged that her entrance would be effective, and had timed her coming so as to be sure that her husband and Herr Brandt should be there before her. The room looked just as it usually did; it was luxurious, large, warm, and softly lighted. Clara almost forgot her age so far as to wish that there had been more lamps, though the shade was undeniably advantageous to her looks. She came forward, and saw that the two men were standing together before the fire. The door had moved noiselessly on its hinges, but the rustle of the silk gown made Greifenstein and Rieseneck turn their heads simultaneously. Clara's eyes rested on the stranger with some curiosity, and she noticed with satisfaction that his gaze fixed itself upon her own face. He was evidently impressed by her appearance, and her vain old heart fluttered pleasantly.

"Permit me to present Herr Brandt," said Greifenstein, making a step forward.

Clara inclined her head with an expression that was intended to be affable, and Rieseneck bowed gravely. She sank into a chair, and, looking up, saw that he was watching her with evident interest. It struck her that he was a very pale man, and though she had at first been pleased by his stare, she began to feel uncomfortable as it continued.

"You are old friends, I suppose?" she remarked, glancing at her husband with a smile.

Both men bent their heads in assent.

"I had the honor of knowing Herr von Greifenstein when we were both very young," said Rieseneck after a pause that had threatened to be awkward.

"Indeed? And you have not met for a long time! How very strange! But life is full of such things, you know." She laughed nervously.

While she was speaking, the intonations of Rieseneck's voice seemed to be still ringing in her ears, and the vibrations touched a chord of her memory very painfully, so that she forgot what she was saying and hid her confusion in a laugh. Greifenstein was staring at the ceiling and did not see his brother start and steady himself against the chimney-piece.

At that moment dinner was announced. Clara rose with an effort from her seat, and stood still. She supposed that Herr Brandt would offer her his arm, but he did not move from his place. Greifenstein said nothing. A violent conflict arose in his mind and made him hesitate. He could not bear the idea of seeing his wife touch even the sleeve of the man he so despised, and yet he dreaded lest any exhibition of his feelings should make Clara suspicious. The last consideration outweighed everything else.

"Will you give my wife your arm?" he said, addressing Rieseneck very coldly.

There was no choice, and the tall old man went to Clara's side, and led her out of the room, while Greifenstein followed alone. They sat down to the round table, which was laden with heavy plate and curious pieces of old German silver, and was illuminated by a hanging lamp. A hundred persons might have dined in the room, and the shadows made the panelled walls seem even further from the centre than they really were. Vast trophies of skulls and antlers and boars' heads loomed up in the distance, indistinctly visible through the dim shade, but lighted up occasionally by the sudden flare of the logs from the wide hearth. The flashes of flame made the stags' skulls seem to grin horribly and gleamed strangely upon the white tusks that protruded from the black boars' heads, and reflected a deep-red glare from their artificial eyes of colored glass. The servants stepped noiselessly upon the dark carpet, while the three persons who shared the solemn banquet sat silently in their places, pretending to partake of the food that was placed before them.

The meal was a horrible farce. There was something sombrely contemptible to each one in the idea of being forced into the pretence of eating for the sake of the hired attendants who carried the dishes. For the first time in his life Greifenstein's hardy nature was disgusted by the sight of food. Rieseneck sat erect in his chair, from time to time swallowing a glass of strong wine, and looking from Clara's face to the fork he held in his hand. She herself exercised a woman's privilege and refused everything, staring consistently at the monumental silver ornament in the midst of the table. When she looked up, Rieseneck's white face scared her. She had no need to see it now, for she knew who he was better than any one, better than Greifenstein himself. That power whose presence she had once felt, when alone with her husband, was not with her now. A deadly fear overcame every other instinct save that of self-preservation. She struggled to maintain her place at the table, to control the shriek of horror that was on her lips, as she had struggled to produce that feigned laugh ten days ago, with all her might. But the protracted strain was almost more than she could bear, and she felt that her exhausted nerves might leave her helpless at any moment. She had read in books vivid descriptions of the agony of death, but she had never fancied that it could be so horrible as this, so long drawn out, so overwhelmingly bitter.

In truth, a more fearful ordeal could not be imagined than was imposed by a relentless destiny upon this miserable, painted, curled, and jewelled old woman as she sat at the head of her own table. It would have been easier for her had she known that she was to meet him. It would have been far less hard if she had lived her life in the whirl of the world, where we are daily forced to look our misdeeds in the face and to meet with smiling indifference those who know our past and have themselves been a part of it. Even a quarter of an hour for preparation would have been better than this gradual recognition, in which each minute made certainty more positive. There was but one ray of consolation or hope for her, and she tried to make the most of it. He had come because he had failed to obtain his pardon, and his brother was helping him to leave the country quietly. She was as sure of it as though she had been acquainted with all the details. To-morrow he would be gone, and once gone he would never return, and her last years would be free from fear. The fact that he came under a false name showed that she was right. In an hour she could excuse herself and go to her room, never to see his face again. Her hands grasped and crushed the damask of the cloth beneath the table as she tried to steady her nerves by contemplating her near deliverance from torture.

Greifenstein was the bravest of the three, as he had also the least cause for anxiety. He saw that it was impossible to continue the meal in total silence, and he made a tremendous effort to produce a show of conversation.

"There has been much snow this year, Herr Brandt," he said, raising his head and addressing his brother.

Rieseneck did not understand, but he heard Greifenstein's voice, and slowly turned his ghastly face toward him.

"I beg your pardon," he said, "I did not quite hear."

"There has been much snow this year," Greifenstein repeated with forcible distinctness.

"Yes," replied his brother, "it seems so."

"After all, it is nearly Christmas," said Clara, trembling in every limb at the sound of her own voice.

Only an hour more to bear, and she would be safe forever. Only another effort, and Greifenstein would suspect nothing. Rieseneck looked mechanically at his brother, as though he were trying to find something to say. In reality he was almost insensible, and he hardly knew why he did not fall from his chair. A servant brought another dish, and Clara helped herself unconsciously. The man went on to Rieseneck, and waited patiently until the latter should turn his head and see what was offered to him.

Clara saw an opportunity of speaking again. She could call his attention by addressing him. One, two, three seconds passed, and then she spoke. It would be enough to utter his name, so that he should look round and see the attendant at his elbow. "Herr Brandt"—the two syllables were short and simple enough.

"Herr von Rieseneck," she said quietly.

In the extremity of her nervousness, her brain had become suddenly confused, and she was lost.

As the words escaped Clara's lips, Greifenstein started violently and made as though he would rise, laying his hands on the edge of the table and leaning forward toward his wife. The echo of Rieseneck's name had not died away when the unhappy woman realized what she had done. Rieseneck himself turned suddenly toward her and the blood rushed to his pale face. Clara's head fell forward and she covered her eyes with her hands, uttering a short, sharp cry like that of an animal mortally wounded. The servant stood still at Rieseneck's side, staring stupidly from one to the other. Fully ten seconds elapsed before Greifenstein recovered his presence of mind.

"You are ill, Clara," he said in a choking voice. "I will take you to your room."

He did not understand the situation, and he could not guess how his wife had learned that the visitor was not Herr Brandt but Kuno von Rieseneck. But he was horrified by the thought that she should have made the discovery, and his first idea was to get her away as soon as possible. He came to her side, and saw that she was helpless, if not insensible. Then he lifted her from her chair and carried her through the wide door and the small apartment beyond into the drawing-room. Rieseneck followed at a distance.

"You can go," said Greifenstein to the servant. "We shall not want any more dinner to-night."

The man went out and left the three together. Clara lay upon a great divan, her husband standing at her side, and Rieseneck at her feet. Her eyes were open, but they were glassy with terror, though she was quite conscious.

"Clara—are you better?" asked Greifenstein anxiously.

She gasped for breath and seemed unable to speak. Greifenstein looked at his brother.

"I cannot imagine how she knew your name," he said. "Did you know her before?"

Rieseneck had turned white again, and stood twisting his fingers as though in some terrible distress. Greifenstein had not noticed his manner before, and gazed at him now in considerable surprise. He fancied that Rieseneck feared discovery and danger to himself.

"What is the matter?" he asked impatiently. "You are safe enough yet"——

While he spoke Clara endeavored to rise, supporting herself upon one hand, and staring wildly at Rieseneck. The presentiment of a great unknown evil came upon Greifenstein, and he laid his hand heavily upon his brother's arm.

"What is the meaning of this?" he asked sternly. "Do you know each other?"

The words roused Rieseneck. He drew back from his brother's touch and answered in a broken voice:

"Let me go. Let me leave this house"——

"No!" exclaimed the other firmly. "You shall not go yet."

Again he grasped Rieseneck's arm, this time with no intention of relinquishing his hold.

"Let him go, Hugo!" gasped Clara. She struggled to her feet and tried to unloose the iron grip of her husband's fingers, straining her weak hands in the useless attempt. "Let him go!" she repeated frantically. "For God's sake, let him go!"

"What is he to you?" asked Greifenstein. Then, as though he guessed some fearful answer to his question, he repeated it in a fiercer tone: "What is he to you? And what are you to her?" he cried, facing his brother as he shook him by the arm.

"You have cause to be angry," said Rieseneck. "And so have I." He fixed his eyes on Clara's, and something like a smile flitted over his features.

"Speak!" commanded Greifenstein, to whom the suspense was becoming unbearable.

Clara saw that Rieseneck was about to utter the fatal words, and with a last remnant of energy she made a desperate attempt to cover his mouth with her hand. But she was too late.

"This woman is my wife, not yours!" he cried in ringing tones.

In an instant Greifenstein thrust his brother from him, so that he reeled back against the wall.

"Liar!" he almost yelled.

Clara fell upon the floor between the two men, a shapeless heap of finery. Rieseneck looked his brother in the face and answered the insult calmly. From the moment when he had recognized Clara, he had felt that he must see the whole horror of her fall with his own eyes in order to be avenged for his wrongs.

"I told you my wife was dead," he said slowly. "I believed it. She is alive. She has lived to ruin you as she ruined me. Clara von Rieseneck—that is your name—stand upon your feet—lift up your infamous face, and own your lawful husband!"

Even then Clara might have saved herself. One vigorous protest, and Greifenstein would without doubt have slain his brother with his hands. But she had not the strength left to speak the strong lie. She dragged herself to her accuser's feet and threw her arms about his knees.

"Mercy!" She could not utter any other word.

"You see," said Rieseneck. "She is alive; she knows me!"

"Mercy!" groaned the wretched creature, fawning upon him with her wasted hands.

"Down, beast!" answered the tall old man with savage contempt. "There is no mercy for such as you."

Greifenstein had stood still for some seconds, overcome by the horror of his shame. One glance told him that his brother had spoken the truth. He turned away and stood facing the empty room. His face was convulsed, his teeth ground upon each other, his hands were clenched as in the agony of death. From his straining eyes great tears rolled down his gray cheeks, the first and the last that he ever shed. And yet by that strange instinct of his character which abhorred all manifestation of emotion, he stood erect and motionless as a soldier on parade. The death-blow had struck him, but he must die on his feet.

Then after a long pause, broken only by Clara's incoherent groans and sobs, he heard Rieseneck's footstep behind him, and then his brother's voice, calling him by his name.

"Hugo—what has this woman deserved?"

"Death," answered Greifenstein solemnly.

"She helped to ruin me through my faults; she has ruined you through no fault of yours. She must die."

"She must die," repeated Greifenstein.

"She has given you a son who is nameless. She cast off the son she bore to me because through me his name was infamous. She must pay the penalty."

"She must die."

Greifenstein did not turn round even then. He crossed the room to the chimney-piece and laid his two hands upon it. Still he heard his brother's voice, though the words were no longer addressed to him.

"Clara von Rieseneck, your hour is come."

"Mercy, Kuno! For God's sake"——

"There is no mercy. Confess your crime. The time is short."

The wretched old woman tried to rise, but Rieseneck's hand kept her upon her knees.

"You shall do me this justice before you go," he said. "Repeat your misdeeds after me. You, Clara Kurtz, were married to me in the year eighteen hundred and forty-seven."

"Yes—it is true," answered the poor creature in broken tones.

"Say it! You shall say the words!"

Her teeth chattered. Transfixed by fear, her lips moved mechanically.

"I, Clara Kurtz, was married to you in the year eighteen hundred and forty-seven."

The woman's incredible vanity survived everything. Her voice sank to a whisper at the two last words of the date, for Greifenstein had never known her real age.

"You caused me to betray the arsenal," continued Rieseneck inexorably.

"I did."

"You abandoned me when I was in prison. When I escaped you refused to follow me. You sent me false news of your death, with a lock of your hair and the child."

Clara repeated each word, like a person hypnotized and subject to the will of another.

"Then you must have changed your name."

"I changed my name."

"And you induced Hugo von Greifenstein to marry you, knowing that he was my brother and that I was alive. I had often told you of him."

Clara made the statement in the words dictated.

"And now you are to die, and may the Lord have mercy upon your sinful soul."

"And now I am to die. May the Lord have mercy upon my sinful soul."

Released from the stern command of her judge, Clara uttered a low cry and fell upon her face at his feet.

"You have heard," said Rieseneck to his brother. "It is time."

Greifenstein turned. He saw the tall old man's great figure standing flat against the opposite wall, and he saw the ghastly face, half-hidden by the snowy beard. He glanced down, and beheld a mass of straw-colored silk, crumpled and disordered, and just beyond it a coil of faded hair adorned with jewelled pins that reflected the soft light. He crossed the room, and his features were ashy pale, firmly set, and utterly relentless. He had heard her condemnation from her own lips; he thought of his son, nameless through this woman's crime, and his heart was hardened.

"It is time," he said. "Have you anything more to say?"

He waited for an answer, but none came. Clara's hour had struck and she knew it. There was deep silence in the room. Then the stillness was broken by a gasp for breath and by a little rustling of the delicate silk. That was all.

When it was done, the two brothers stooped down again and lifted their burden and bore it silently away, till they reached the room in which they had first met. Then Greifenstein made sign that they should go further, and they entered the chamber beyond, and upon the bed that was there they laid down the dead woman, and covered her poor painted face decently with a sheet and went away, closing the door softly behind them.

For a moment they stood looking at each other earnestly. Then Rieseneck took from his pocket his brother's gift and laid it upon the table.

"It is time for us also," he said.

"Yes. I must write to Greif first."

Half an hour later the short and terrible tragedy was completed, and of the three persons who had sat together at the table, suffering each in his or her own way as much as each could bear, not one was left alive to tell the tale.

Outside the house of death, the silent, spotless snow gleamed in the light of the waning moon. Not a breath of wind sighed amongst the stately black trees. Only, far below, the tumbling torrent roared through its half-frozen bed, and high above, from the summit of the battlement that had sheltered so many generations of Greifensteins from danger in war, and in peace from the bitter north wind, the great horned owls sent forth their melancholy note from time to time, and opened wide their cruel hungry eyes as the dismal sound echoed away among the dark firs.

Edith Matilda Thomas.

BORN in Chatham, Ohio, 1854.

SYRINX.

[*A New Year's Masque, and Other Poems.* 1885.]

COME forth, too timid spirit of the reed!
  Leave thy plashed coverts and elusions shy,
And find delight at large in grove and mead.

No ambushed harm, no wanton peering eye;
The shepherd's uncouth god thou need'st not fear,—
Pan has not passed this way for many a year.

'Tis but the vagrant wind that makes thee start,—
    The pleasure-loving south, the freshening west;
The willow's woven veil they softly part,
    To fan the lily on the stream's warm breast:
No ruder stir, no footstep pressing near,—
Pan has not passed this way for many a year.

Whether he lies in some mossed wood, asleep,
    And heeds not how the acorns drop around,
Or in some shelly cavern near the deep,
    Lulled by its pulses of eternal sound,
He wakes not, answers not our sylvan cheer,—
Pan has been gone this many a silent year.

Else we had seen him, through the mists of morn,
    To upland pasture lead his bleating charge:
There is no shag upon the stunted thorn,
    No hoof-print on the river's silver marge;
Nor broken branch of pine, nor ivied spear,—
Pan has not passed that way for many a year.

O tremulous elf, reach me a hollow pipe,
    The best and smoothest of thy mellow store!
Now I may blow till Time be hoary ripe,
    And listening streams forsake the paths they wore:
Pan loved the sound, but now will never hear,—
Pan has not trimmed a reed this many a year!

And so, come freely forth, and through the sedge
    Lift up a dimpled, warm, Arcadian face,
As on that day when fear thy feet did fledge,
    And thou didst safely win the breathless race. . . . .
I am deceived: nor Pan nor thou art here,—
Pan has been gone this many a silent year!

SNOW.

[*The Round Year.* 1886.]

THE first flakes of the year,—how doubtful, wavering, tentative, as though there were as yet no beaten path for them to follow in their journey from the clouds to earth, or as though they were unwilling to desert the goodly society of their kindred in the sky! The blades of tender autumnal grass look very cold, lifted through the scant coverlet spread by a first snow; one shivers seeing them, and wishes that their retirement might be hastened. The wanderings of the dead leaves are brought to an end by the snow, to which they impart a stain from the coloring-matter not yet leached from their its-

Edith M. Thomas

sues. By this circumstance the age of the season might be gauged, approximately; at least, the snows of the later winter suffer no such discoloration from contact with the leaf-strewn ground.

When the snow is damp and clinging, as it not unfrequently is at the beginning and end of the winter, a wonderful white spring-time comes upon the earth. Behold, the orchards bloom again almost in the similitude of May; the dry stalks in the garden undergo the miracle that befell the bishop's staff in the legend, and deck themselves with beauty. Last summer's nests are again tenanted, brooded by doves of peace descended from heaven. Every cobweb which the wind has spared, under the eaves or in the porch, displays a fluttering increment of snow. What a deal of wool-gathering there has been! The rough bark of the trees, the roofs and clapboards of the houses, are hung with soft shreds and tatters; the "finger of heaven" has put on a white cot. If we walk abroad in this new creation, it shall seem that we have been suddenly let into some magnified frost-picture; nor can we be quite sure that we ourselves are not of the same frail, ethereal texture as the exquisite work around us, and like it destined to glide into naught, under the arrows of the sun. When such damp snow freezes upon the branches, and afterwards falls in crusted fragments, the perforations made in the snow beneath resemble the tracks of many small, cushion-footed animals. One would like to know what Æsopian council, or palaver, was held under the dooryard trees in the sly middle of the night.   .   .   .   .   .

On a stormy evening, when the air is thick with flying snow, I have received charming suggestions from the village lights. Walls, roofs, bounding-lines generally, are lost in the snowy obscurity; but the hospitable windows remain, curtained, mellow-tinted panes, or curtainless pictures of fireside comfort, framed, apparently, by mist and cloud. At a little distance it were easy to imagine that these windows belonged to the ground-floor of heaven, rather than to any houses made with hands.

Though the trumpets of the sky may have been blown in its van, the snow, when it arrives on earth, abhors and annihilates all loud noise. How muffled and remote are the sounds in a village during a great snow-fall—all mutes and subvocals. Stamping of feet in the porch across the way is reported distantly sonorous, as though the noise had been made in a subterranean chamber. Across the high, smooth fields comes the faint pealing of a bell, mysteriously sweet. The bell hangs in the church of a neighboring village; I have often heard it before, but not with the same impression as now. So might have sounded the chimes in the buried church of the legend on a Christmas morning.

The snow has a mediatorial character. Wherever this earth approaches nearest to heaven, on all loftiest summits of the globe, there stands the white altar, perpetually: nor is the religion to which the altar is reared one of pure abstraction, colorless mysticism. Sunrise, sunset, and the winds, with the snow, bring out on the tops of our Western mountains (if current descriptions do not exaggerate) such surprises of form and color, whirling column and waving banner, as were never dreamed of in the pageants beheld by the initiate of the Eleusinian Mysteries.

A FLUTE.

[Lyrics and Sonnets. 1887.]

"HOW shall I liken thee, reed of my choice,
       Spirit-like, fugitive, wavering voice?"

" I am an oread lost to the hills,
Sick for the mountain wind tossing my rills;
Sighing from memory snatches of song
Pine-trees have sung to me all the night long;
Shrouded they sang to me, mingling my dreams;
Down through their tapestries planets shot gleams.
Eagles on cliffs between heaven and me
Looked from their watch-towers, far on the sea."

" How wast thou taken, sweet,—lost to the hills,
Footprints of thine no more seen by the rills?"

" Quickly I answer thee: Sorrow came by,
Made me her foster-child, loving my cry!"

THE QUIET PILGRIM.

Isaiah xxxviii. 15.

WHEN on my soul in nakedness
    His swift, avertless hand did press,
Then I stood still, nor cried aloud,
Nor murmured low in ashes bowed;
And, since my woe is utterless,
To supreme quiet I am vowed;
Afar from me be moan and tears,—
I shall go softly all my years.

Whenso my quick, light-sandalled feet
Bring me where Joys and Pleasures meet,
I mingle with their throng at will;
They know me not an alien still,
Since neither words nor ways unsweet
Of storèd bitterness I spill;
Youth shuns me not, nor gladness fears,—
For I go softly all my years.

Whenso I come where Griefs convene,
And in my ear their voice is keen,
They know me not, as on I glide,
That with Arch Sorrow I abide.
They haggard are, and drooped of mien,
And round their brows have cypress tied:
Such shows I leave to light Grief's peers,—
I shall go softly all my years.

Yea, softly! heart of hearts unknown.
Silence hath speech that passeth moan,
More piercing-keen than breathèd cries
To such as heed, made sorrow-wise.
But save this voice without a tone,
That runs before me to the skies,
And rings above thy ringing spheres,
Lord, I go softly all my years!

MUSIC.

THE god of music dwelleth out of doors.
　　All seasons through his minstrelsy we meet,
Breathing by field and covert haunting-sweet:
From organ-lofts in forests old he pours
A solemn harmony: on leafy floors
To smooth autumnal pipes he moves his feet,
Or with the tingling plectrum of the sleet
In winter keen beats out his thrilling scores.
Leave me the reed unplucked beside the stream,
And he will stoop and fill it with the breeze;
Leave me the viol's frame in secret trees,
Unwrought, and it shall wake a druid theme;
Leave me the whispering shell on nereid shores:
The god of music dwelleth out of doors.

Edgar Watson Howe.

BORN in the present town of Treaty, Wabash Co., Ind., 1854.

A PRAIRIE TOWN.

[*The Story of a Country Town.* 1882.—*Revised Edition.* 1884.]

IN Twin Mounds the citizens spent their idle time in religious discussions, and although I lived there a great many years I do not remember that any of the questions in dispute were ever settled. They never discussed politics with any animation, and read but little, except in the Bible to find points to dispute; but of religion they never tired, and many of them could quote the sacred word by the page. No two of them ever exactly agreed in their ideas, for men who thought alike on baptism violently quarrelled when the resurrection was mentioned, and two of them who engaged a hell-redemptionist one night would in all probability fail to agree themselves the next, on the atonement. The merchants neglected their customers, when they had them, to discuss points in the Bible which I used to think were not of the slightest consequence, and in many instances the men who argued the most were those who chased deer with hounds on Sunday, and ran horse-races, for they did not seem to discuss the subject so much on account of its importance as because of its fitness as a topic to quarrel about.

There was always a number of famous discussions going on, as between the lawyer and the storekeeper, or the blacksmith and the druggist, or the doctor and the carpenter, and whenever I saw a crowd gathering hurriedly in the evening I knew that two of the disputants had got together again to renew their old difficulty, which they kept up until a late hour, in the presence of half the town.

There was a certain man who kept a drug-store, who was always in nervous excitement from something a fat blacksmith had said to him in their discussions, and who had a habit of coming in on him suddenly in the middle of the day; and whenever I went into the place of business of either one of them I heard them telling those present how they had triumphed the night before, or intended to triumph on a future occasion. Some of the greatest oaths I have ever heard were uttered by these men while discussing religion, and frequently the little and nervous drug-store keeper had to be forcibly prevented from jumping at his burly opponent and striking him. The drug-store was not far away from the office where I worked, and whenever loud and boisterous talking was heard in that direction a smile went round, for we knew the blacksmith had suddenly come upon his enemy, and attacked him with something he had thought up while at his work. I never knew exactly what the trouble between them was, though I heard enough of it; but I remember that it had some reference to a literal resurrection and a new body; and I often thought it queer that each one was able to take the Bible and establish his position so clearly. Whenever I heard the blacksmith talk I was sure that the druggist was wrong, but when the druggist called upon the blacksmith to stop right there, and began his argument, I became convinced that, after all, there were two sides to the question.

These two men, as well as most of the others, were members of a church known then as the Campbellite, for I do not remember that there was an infidel or unbeliever in the place. There were a great many backsliders, but none of them ever questioned religion itself, though they could never agree on doctrine. It has occurred to me since that if one of them had thought to dispute the inspiration of the Bible, and argued about that, the people would have been entirely happy, for the old discussions in time became very tiresome.

The people regarded religion as a struggle between the Campbellite church and the Devil, and a sensation was developed one evening when my father remarked to the druggist, in the presence of the usual crowd—he happened to be in the place on an errand, as he never engaged in the amusement of the town—that sprinkling answered every purpose of baptism. The druggist became very much excited immediately and prepared for a discussion, but my father only laughed at him and walked away. The next Sunday, however, he preached a sermon on the subject in the court-house, and attacked the town's religion with so much vigor that the excitement was very intense.

Most of the citizens of Twin Mounds came from the surrounding country, and a favorite way of increasing the population was to elect the county officers from the country, but after their terms expired a new set moved in, for it was thought they became so corrupt by a two years' residence that they could not be trusted to a reëlection. The town increased in size a little in this manner, for none of these men ever went back to their farms again, though they speedily lost standing after they retired from their positions. Many others who left their farms to move to the town said in excuse that the school advantages were better, and seemed very anxious for a time that their children should be educated, but once they were established in Twin Mounds they abused the school a great deal, and said it was not satisfactory, and allowed their children to remain away if they were so inclined.

There was the usual number of merchants, professional men, mechanics, etc., who got along well enough, but I never knew how at least one half the inhabitants lived. Some of them owned teams, and farmed in the immediate vicinity; others " hauled," and others did whatever offered, but they were all poor, and were constantly changing from one house to another. These men usually had great families of boys, who grew up in the same indifferent fashion, and drifted off in time nobody knew where, coming back occasionally, after a long absence, well-dressed, and with money to rattle in their pockets. But none of them ever came back who had business of sufficient importance elsewhere to call them away again, for they usually remained until their good clothes wore out, the delusion of their respectability was broken, and they became town loafers again, or engaged in the hard pursuits of their fathers. The only resident of Twin Mounds who ever distinguished himself ran away with a circus and never came back, for although he was never heard of, it was generally believed that he must have become famous in some way to induce him to forego the pleasure of returning home in good clothes and swaggering up and down the street to allow the people to shake his hand.

This class of men never paid their debts, and to get credit for an amount was equal to earning it, to their way of thinking, and a new merchant who came in did a great business until he found them out. I have said they never paid ; they did sometimes, but if they paid a dollar on account they bought three or four times that amount to go on the books.

They always seemed to me to be boys yet, surprised at being their own masters, and only worked when they had to, as boys do. They engaged in boys' amusements, too, for most of them owned packs of dogs, and short-distance race-horses, and it was one of their greatest accomplishments to drive a quarter-horse to a wood-wagon to some out-of-the-way neighborhood, match it against a farmer's horse threatened with speed, and come back with all the money owned in that direction. I suppose they came West to grow up with the country, like the rest of us, but they were idle where they came from, and did not improve in the West, because work was necessary, whereupon the thought no doubt occurred to them that they could have grown rich in that way anywhere.

A few of them were away most of the time—I never knew where, but so far away that they seldom came home—and their families supported themselves as best they could, but were always expecting the husbands and fathers to return and take them away to homes of luxury. Occasionally news came that they were killed by Indians, and occasionally this was contradicted by the certainty that they were locked up for disreputable transactions, or hanged. Whenever a Twin Mounds man died away from home otherwise than honorably, it was always said that he had been killed by the Indians.   .   .

There was one thing I noticed of Twin Mounds which is probably true of every other country town—it was constantly threatened either with great prosperity or great danger, but whether the event threatening the prosperity

or the danger came to pass, the town progressed about the same. There was
no perceptible effect from any of the events the people were certain would
prove either very disastrous or of great benefit, from which I am led to believe
that no one is familiar with the art of town-building, although I have never
known a man who did not profess to know all there is worth knowing about
the science. Towns seem to be the natural accretion of years, and although
the people in Twin Mounds often related how desperate were their struggles
with adversity, the facts probably are that the place would have been fully as
large as it was three years after Jo's marriage without the great number of
public meetings for public purposes and the endless worry of individuals
with reference to it.

There was a very general impression that manufactories were needed, and
this was talked about so much, and so many inducements were offered, that
the people became discouraged, believing that the average manufacturer had
a wicked heart and a hollow head to thus wrong Twin Mounds in the face of
his own interest; therefore we were very much surprised to learn once, after
all hope had been abandoned, that a quiet man was building a woollen-mill
down the river, which he completed and afterwards operated without the help
of the committees which had been appointed to aid in such matters of public
weal. The trouble was that the man lived in Twin Mounds, whereas we had
been expecting a man and money to come from a distant point for that purpose, and had never thought of looking about home, but spent a great deal of
money in sending committees away to make arrangements for a woollen-mill.
This circumstance, although humiliating, proved a good thing, for it taught
the people that, if the town were to be built up at all, it must be by its own
citizens, which knowledge was afterwards used to good advantage.

The people were always miserable by reason of predictions that, unless impossible amounts of money were given to certain enterprises, the town would
be ruined, and although they always gave, no sooner was one fund exhausted
than it became necessary to raise another. It was said during the collection
of each amount that it would never be necessary again to give to this sort
of charity (as the enterprise then in hand would insure the future of Twin
Mounds), but there was never an end to the ridiculous business, and we were
always in a state of dreariness on this account, as the men demanding the
charity for insignificant enterprises loudly threatened to go to the rival towns
and permit the grass to grow in our streets. In thinking of the matter since,
I have thought that Twin Mounds would have been a much better town but for
the fact that it was always expecting improbable disaster, but which never
came, for the people were thus prevented from exercising their energy, if
they had any.

I never formed a good opinion of a man there that I was not finally told
something to his discredit by another citizen, causing me to regard him with
great suspicion, and if I said a good word for any of them, it was proved beyond question immediately that he was a very unscrupulous, a very ridiculous, a very weak, and a very worthless man. There were no friendships
among them, and they all hated each other in secret, there being much quiet
satisfaction when one of them failed. There seemed to be no regular aristoc-

racy, either, for I heard so frequently how ignorant and awkward the prominent citizens were when they first came, that I finally found them all out. If Dr. Medicine told me what an unpromising lout the present magnificent Honorable Legal was when he first arrived, and how much difficulty he had in getting him introduced into respectable society, I was certain to meet Honorable Legal soon after, and hear him recite a similar experience with reference to Dr. Medicine. One of the stories, and I found afterwards that it was true, was that a man of ordinary worth, who seemed to be prosperous, had collected his money of a railroad company in the country he had moved from, because of an injury to his first wife, and that his second was enabled to go elegantly dressed because of the misfortune of the first. Thus it went on until I was familiar with the poor origin of all of them, and perhaps this was one reason why we did not respect one another more.

It was a popular expression that every one favorably mentioned was the "worst overrated man in America," and the only real ability any of them ever displayed was in looking up the previous history of each other, which they carried on with great vigor, and frequently with alarming results. I began to believe in course of time that it was fortunate that the discreditable part of my history was well known, for it was the sooner forgotten, because it was not necessary to look up old records to find it out, and thus was not made worse than it really was.

Very few of the Twin Mounds men had positive opinions of their own, as they seemed to have got them second-handed from some source, and none of them was original or natural in his methods of conducting business, or in his habits. Two or three times a year most of them visited a city a good many miles away, where they spent a great deal of money they could not afford, to create an impression that they were accustomed to what they supposed was good society, and where they met men who filled their ideas of greatness. These they mimicked, each one choosing a different example; so it happened that the men of Twin Mounds were very ridiculous. There was a lawyer, I remember, who had met somewhere a distinguished member of his profession, who shook hands (Ho! ho!) with everybody, and (Ha! ha!) patronizingly wanted to know how they were getting along. It was not his natural way, and as he only adopted it because he believed it would make him popular, it became him very poorly. Perhaps it was very effective with the man the habit had been copied from, but it was very absurd with our citizen, whose pretence was that every man he shook hands with (and he shook hands cordially with everybody) was not getting along as well as he in his great compassion desired.

Another one, who carried on a business which one busy day would have exhausted, had heard of a man who achieved commercial greatness by finding fault (I am sure the man was mistaken, for no one ever made money in such a ridiculous way), and I never heard of anything that suited him. This he regarded as business shrewdness, and he finally became very sour in disposition because he was generally regarded as a fool instead of a prophet. Still another, naturally full of fool's gab, carried on a bank in awful silence because he had heard that still water runs deep, though I have seen ponds of perfectly still water which were very shallow.

As I grew older, and began to notice more, I thought that every man in Twin Mounds had reason to feel humiliated that he had not accomplished more, but most of them were as conceited as though there was nothing left in the world worthy of their attention. Their small business affairs, their quarrels over the Bible, and an occasional term in the town council, or a mention for the legislature or a county office, satisfied them, and they were as content as men who really amounted to something.

Elisabeth Cavazza.

BORN in Portland, Me.

ALICIA'S BONNET.

[BALLATA ITALIANA.]

LAST night Alicia wore a Tuscan bonnet,
 And many humming-birds were fastened on it.

I sat beside Alicia at the play;
 Her vio'et eyes with tender tears were wet
(The diamonds in her ears less bright than they)
 For pity of the woes of Juliet;
 Alicia's sighs a poet might have set
To delicate music in a dainty sonnet.

Last night Alicia wore a Tuscan bonnet,
And many humming-birds were fastened on it.

And yet to me her graceful ready words
 Sounded like tinkling silver bells that jangled,
For on her golden hair the humming-birds
 Were fixed as if within a sunbeam tangled,
 Their quick life quenched, their tiny bodies mangled,
Poor pretty birds upon Alicia's bonnet.

Last night Alicia wore a Tuscan bonnet,
And many humming-birds were fastened on it.

Caught in a net of delicate creamy crêpe,
 The dainty captives lay there dead together;
No dart of slender bill, no fragile shape
 Fluttering, no stir of any radiant feather;
 Alicia looked so calm, I wondered whether
She cared if birds were killed to trim her bonnet.

Last night Alicia wore a Tuscan bonnet,
And many humming-birds were fastened on it.

If rubies and if sapphires have a spirit,
　Though deep they lie below the weight of earth,
If emeralds can a conscious life inherit
　And beryls rise again to wingèd birth—
　Being changed to birds but not to lesser worth—
Alicia's golden head had such upon it.

Last night Alicia wore a Tuscan bonnet,
And many humming-birds were fastened on it.

Perhaps I dreamed—the house was very still—
　But on a sudden the Academy
Of Music seemed a forest of Brazil,
　Each pillar that supports the balcony
　Took form and stature of a tropic tree
With scarlet odorous flowers blooming on it.

Last night Alicia wore a Tuscan bonnet,
And many humming-birds were fastened on it.

A fragrance of delicious drowsy death
　Was in the air; the lithe lianas clung
About the mighty tree, and birds beneath
　More swift than arrows flashed and flew among
　The perfumed poisonous blossoms as they swung,
The heavy-honeyed flowers that hung upon it.

Last night Alicia wore a Tuscan bonnet,
And many humming-birds were fastened on it.

Like rain-drops when the sun breaks up the shower,
　Or weavers' shuttles carrying golden thread,
Or flying petals of a wind-blown flower,
　Myriads of humming-birds flew overhead—
　Purple and gold and green and blue and red—
Above each scarlet cup, or poised upon it.

Last night Alicia wore a Tuscan bonnet,
And many humming-birds were fastened on it.

What rapid flight! Each one a wingèd flame,
　Burning with brilliant joy of life and all
Delight of motion; to and fro they came,
　An endless dance, a fairy festival;
　Then suddenly I saw them pause and fall,
Slain only to adorn Alicia's bonnet.

Last night Alicia wore a Tuscan bonnet,
And many humming-birds were fastened on it.

My mind came back from the Brazilian land;
　For, as a snowflake falls to earth beneath,
Alicia's hand fell lightly on my hand;

And yet I fancied that a stain of death,
　Like that which doomed the Lady of Macbeth,
Was on her hand: could I perhaps have won it?

　Last night Alicia wore a Tuscan bonnet,
　And many humming-birds were fastened on it.

THE RETURN OF ULYSSES.

[*From "A Calabrian Penelope."—The New Princeton Review.* 1888.]

IT was no less than twelve years after the time that Compare Andrea went to America that a stranger entered on foot the one long street of the village. This man was poorly clothed, a little bent, and walked leaning slightly upon a stick. His conical hat with a wide brim was lowered upon his forehead, and he appeared at the same time weary and in haste. He came to the *piazzetta,* where the women were filling their jars at the fountain, and asked for water to drink. While he was drinking, he looked anxiously at one and another of the women. It seemed as though he wished to ask some question; but in the end he decided not to do so, and contented himself with merely thanking the woman who had offered him her jar. Then he went on his way until he reached the house of Comare Pina. Here he came to a halt before the door. He passed his hand more than once across his brow; for it seemed to him, as to a drowning person, that he saw crowding before his sight all that had happened during so many years. What was it in the odor of the rosemary and the thyme that almost made the tears come to his eyes? Was such a thing ever heard of! *Su animo!* At least, he was again in his own country.

The old dog, which had been the faithful companion of Compare Andrea, lay stretched across the door-stone asleep, rousing himself now and then to snap at the flies that teased him. He heard the step of the stranger, lifted his head, and listened a moment. Then he arose, growled, was silent for an instant, licked the hand of the stranger, and finished with barking joyously.

Comare Pina left the loom, and came to the door to see what ailed Turco that he should bark so loudly. The stranger stretched out his hands to her.

"It is I, Pina *mia,*" he said. "I am come back."

Pina stood motionless, as if she doubted what was said to her. The dog pulled at her skirt. The little daughters came from the field behind the house, and stood staring with great eyes at the stranger. In a few moments there assembled some *comari* of the neighborhood, who had watched the traveller on the road.

"Pina, Pina, I am Andrea," he said. "Will you not recognize me?"

"Look, Pina," interposed Comare Barbara, who always thrust herself into the affairs of others. "Do you not see that it is truly Compare Andrea? He is badly dressed, it is true, so that he appears like a beggar; but that does not prevent one from recognizing the large nose that his mama made him."

"Are you not glad to see me again?" urged Andrea.

"It is so long, so long!" murmured Pina to herself. "Who can say if it be really Andrea? I do not know—and I am Andrea's wife."

"Say, Pina, is not this your man?" asked one of the neighbors.

"What do I know about it?" responded Pina, mournfully.

At this moment her son came down from the forest. Over his shoulder hung some rabbits which he had shot; and his father's large gun, almost too heavy for a youth, was in his hands.

"Who is this that comes to disturb my mama?" he asked, and when he looked angry he was all his father.

"I am your papa," Andrea answered him.

"Is my papa come back again?" said the boy. "We have waited so long, mama, and the little sisters, and I."

Comare Pina snatched the gun from her son's hands. "If you truly are my Andrea," she said, "you can shoot, and so prove it to me."

Andrea's eyes gleamed under the rim of his hat. He held out his hands a little tremulously. "I may have lost my skill," he observed. "I am out of practice."

Nevertheless he took the gun from her hands.

"It may be so," cried Pina, "but you have to shoot."

"Pina, Pina!" entreated the other women, frightened without knowing why.

She drew off her wedding-ring by main force. Andrea, looking on confusedly, saw that her fingers were grown much thinner during the twelve years of his absence. She ran many paces across the road, and, raising her left hand to her head, she held, between thumb and forefinger, the sacramental ring near her throbbing temple.

"Shoot!" she commanded.

"Heavens, no, Pina! For pity's sake!" begged Andrea. "Tell me, rather, to shoot myself."

"Shoot!" repeated his wife.

"Oh! Will you not believe me—I am, I am your Andrea, your husband. I will prove it to you in so many ways, only give me a little time," he prayed her.

"If you are my Andrea," answered Pina, "you can send the bullet through the ring that you gave me. If you are not he—draw the trigger and burn my brain, for I have waited and hoped too long to be disappointed at last. Shoot!"

All the *comari* screamed and hid their faces from fear; the little girls ran into the house and crouched under the bed, not to see what was being done. The boy flung himself across the door-stone, burying his face in the hair of the dog.

Andrea glanced at Pina. She did not look at him. Her wide-open eyes were turned toward the sky and seemed blinded by the rays of the sunset. Andrea threw down his hat, straightened himself, raised the gun to his shoulder, took aim, and fired.

Comare Barbara was the only one who could look at such a horror; it is true that the neighbors said of her that she would have watched the torment of the souls in purgatory, in order to be able to tell the story of it afterward, she was such a chatterbox. In relating this story, she never failed to say it was a pleasure to see the bullet pass straight through the ring, as if it had been the finger of a bride; and Pina's hand that held the ring never moved, though the wind of the bullet ruffled her hair.

And then poor Pina ran, all in tears, fell at her husband's feet, and, clasping his knees, prayed him to put the ring again on her finger, as if they were standing before the priest. He lifted her from the ground, and, with his arm around her, led her into the house.

It was true, the neighbors agreed, that Compare Andrea had brought back little from America; and he said it was like the rest of the world, money was not as the stones of the road, even there. But with what little he had saved from his earnings he was able to buy back his land, and some more with it. He spent much of his time also at the shop of Maso the blacksmith, trying to construct a plow that should be different from those which had satisfied the good souls of his father and grandfather; and in other ways it appeared to the neighbors that his head was no longer up to the mark. It might have been the effect of the yellow fever—who knows?—that gave him the whim of inventing these things. The fact is, too much thinking spoils the brain!

But it was also true that, because of the extraordinary plow or for some other reason, the land of Compare Andrea bore twice as much as the fields of his neighbors; and he had good fortune with his cattle, sheep, and poultry. It became necessary for him, besides himself and his son, to hire men for the herds and the land. The truth is, riches are like ducks; they run to those who know how to call them.

And it was really a consolation to see Comare Pina so contented at the side of her husband that she would not have wished to be the clothes of the queen. The only anxiety which remained to her was lest Andrea should some time desire to cross the ocean again, to revisit America, and seek fortune in the Republica Argentina. Meanwhile, her twelve years of lonely weaving and waiting were ended.

DERELICT.

SHE wanders up and down the main
　　Without a master, nowhere bound;
　The currents turn her round and round,
Her track is like a tangled skein;
And never helmsman by his chart
　　So strange a way as hers may steer
To enter port or to depart
　　For any harbor far or near.

The waters clamor at her sides,
　　The winds cry through her cordage
　　　　torn,
　The last sail hangs, to tatters worn;
Upon the waves the vessel rides

This way or that, as winds may shift,
　　In ghastly dance when airs blow balm,
　　Or held in a lethargic calm,
Or fury-hunted, wild, adrift.

When south winds blow, does she re-
　　　call
　Spices and golden fruits in store?
　Or north winds—nets off Labrador
And icebergs' iridescent wall?
Or east—the isles of Indian seas?
　　Or west—new ports and sails unfurled?
　Her voyages all around the world
To mock her with old memories?

For her no light-house sheds a ray
  Of crimson warning from its tower;
  No watchers wait in hope the hour
To greet her coming up the bay;
No trumpet speaks her, hearty, hoarse—
  Or if a captain hail at first,
  He sees her for a thing accursed,
And turns his own ship from her course.

Alone, in desperate liberty
  She forges on; and how she fares
  No man alive inquires, or cares
Though she were sunk beneath the sea.
Her helm obeys no firm control,
  She drifts—a prey for storms to take,
  For sands to clutch, for rocks to break—
A ship condemned, like a lost soul.

SLUMBER SONG.

COME, sweet Sleep, from afar—
  Not with footsteps that delay,
For thy wool-soft sandals are
  Over-slow upon their way.
On thy floating dusky hair
  Wreaths of poppies thou dost set,
  That we mortals may forget
Waking hours and all their care.
From afar, come, sweet Sleep!

Come, sweet Sleep, on a steed,
  One that weareth golden wings,
That on asphodel doth feed
  And doth drink at heavenly springs.
Ride not through the ivory gate,
  Come to us through gates of horn,
  Bring good dreams made true at
    morn,
Even though the morn be late.
On thy steed, come, sweet Sleep!

Gentle Sleep, weave a wreath
  Of thy drowsiest poppy flowers,
Bind it over and beneath
  The incessant fleeting hours.

Set thy lips against their face,
  Whisper to them, light and low,
  Plead for us before they go
That they stay a little space.
Weave a wreath, gentle Sleep!

Haste thee, Sleep, do not wait,
  For the night is near its noon:
Thou wilt find us over-late
  So thou dost not seek us soon.
For the cock begins to crow
  At the earliest beam of light;
  Then with every other sprite,
Thou, a gentle ghost, must go.
Do not wait, haste thee, Sleep!

Take us, Sleep, on thy horse—
  As a mother, journeying,
Holds her babe and on her course
  Lullaby doth softly sing.
Let thine hair fall round thy face
  Veiling visions in thine eyes,
  Carry us to Paradise
At thy steed's most quiet pace.
On thy horse, take us, Sleep!

Frederic Jesup Stimson.

BORN in Dedham, Mass., 1855.

MRS. KNOLLYS.

[*From "Mrs. Knollys." By J. S. of Dale.—Stories by American Authors. Vol. II.* 1884.]

THEY first saw the great mountains from the summit of the Schafberg.
This is a little height, three-cornered, between three lakes; a natural Bel-

vedere for Central Europe. Mr. and Mrs. Knollys were seated on a couch of Alpine roses behind a rhododendron bush watching the sunset; but as Charles was desirous of kissing Mrs. Knollys, and the rhododendron bush was not thick enough, they were waiting for the sun to go down. He was very slow in doing this, and by way of consolation Knollys was keeping his wife's hand hidden in the folds of her dress. Undoubtedly a modern lady would have been talking of the scenery, giving word-color pictures of the view; but I am afraid Mrs. Knollys had been looking at her husband, and talking with him of the cottage they had bought in a Surrey village, not far from Box Hill, and thinking how the little carvings and embroideries would look there which they had bought abroad. And, indeed, Mrs. Charles secretly thought Box Hill an eminence far preferable to the Venediger, and Charles's face an infinitely more interesting sight than any lake, however expressive. But the sun, looking askance at them through the lower mist, was not jealous; all the same he spread his glory lavishly for them, and the bright little mirror of a lake twinkled cannily upward from below. Finally it grew dark; then there was less talking. It was full night when they went in, she leaning on his arm and looking up; and the moonbeam on the snowy shoulder of the Glockner, twenty leagues away, came over, straightway, from the mountain to her face. Three days later, Charles Knollys, crossing with her the lower portion of the Pasterzen glacier, slipped into a crevasse, and vanished utterly from the earth.

All this you know. And I was also told more of the young girl, bride and widow at eighteen; how she sought to throw herself into the clear blue gulf; how she refused to leave Heiligenblut; how she would sit, tearless, by the rim of the crevasse, day after day, and gaze into its profundity. A guide or man was always with her at these times, for it was still feared she would follow her young husband to the depths of that still sea. Her aunt went over from England to her; the summer waxed; autumn storms set in; but no power could win her from the place whence Charles had gone.

If there was a time worse for her than that first moment, it was when they told her that his body never could be found. They did not dare to tell her this for many days, but busied themselves with idle cranes and ladders, and made futile pretences with ropes. Some of the big, simple-hearted guides even descended into the chasm, absenting themselves for an hour or so, to give her an idea that something was being done. Poor Mrs. Knollys would have followed them had she been allowed, to wander through the purple galleries, calling Charles. It was well she could not; for all Kaspar could do was to lower himself a hundred yards or so, chisel out a niche, and stand in it, smoking his honest pipe to pass the time, and trying to fancy he could hear the murmur of the waters down below. Meantime Mrs. Knollys strained her eyes, peering downward from above, leaning on the rope about her waist, looking over the clear brink of the bergschrund.

It was the Herr Dr. Zimmermann who first told her the truth. Not that the good Doctor meant to do so. The Herr Doctor had had his attention turned to glaciers by some rounded stones in his garden by the Traunsee, and more particularly by the Herr Privatdocent Splüthner. Splüthner, like

Uncle Toby, had his hobby-horse, his pet conjuring words, his gods *ex machinâ*, which he brought upon the field in scientific emergencies; and these gods, as with Thales, were Fire and Water.   Craters and flood were his accustomed scapegoats, upon whose heads were charged all things unaccountable; and the Herr Doctor, who had only one element left to choose from, and that a passive one, but knew, on general principles, that Splüthner must be wrong, got as far off as he could and took Ice.   And Splüthner having poohpoohed this, Zimmermann rode his hypothesis with redoubled zeal.   He became convinced that ice was the embodiment of orthodoxy.   Fixing his professional spectacles on his substantial nose, he went into Carinthia and ascended the great Venice mountains, much as he would have performed any other scientific experiment.   Then he encamped on the shores of the Pasterzen glacier, and proceeded to make a study of it.

So it happened that the Doctor, taking a morning stroll over the subject of his experiment, in search of small things which might verify his theory, met Mrs. Knollys sitting in her accustomed place.   The Doctor had been much puzzled, that morning, on finding in a rock at the foot of the glacier the impression, or sign-manual as it were, of a certain fish, whose acquaintance the Doctor had previously made only in tropical seas.   This fact seeming, superficially, to chime in with Splüthnerian mistakes in a most heterodox way, the Doctor's mind had for a moment been diverted from the ice; and he was wondering what the fish had been going to do in that particular gallery, and secretly doubting whether it had known its own mind, and gone thither with the full knowledge and permission of its maternal relative.   Indeed, the good Doctor would probably have ascribed its presence to the malicious and personal causation of the devil, but that the one point on which he and Splüthner were agreed was the ignoring of unscientific hypotheses.   The Doctor's objections to the devil were none the less strenuous for being purely scientific.

Thus ruminating, the Doctor came to the crevasse where Mrs. Knollys was sitting, and to which a little path had now been worn from the inn.   There was nothing of scientific interest about the fair young English girl, and the Doctor did not notice her; but he took from his waistcoat-pocket a leaden bullet, moulded by himself, and marked "Johannes Carpentarius, Juvavianus, A. U. C. 2590," and dropped it, with much satisfaction, into the crevasse.   Mrs. Knollys gave a little cry; the bullet was heard for some seconds tinkling against the sides of the chasm; the tinkles grew quickly fainter, but they waited in vain for the noise of the final fall.   "May the Splüthner live that he may learn by it," muttered the Doctor; "I can never recover it."

Then he remembered that the experiment had been attended with a sound unaccounted for by the conformity of the bullet to the laws of gravitation; and looking up he saw Mrs. Knollys in front of him, no longer crying, but very pale.   Zimmermann started, and in his confusion dropped his best brass registering thermometer, which also rattled down the abyss.

"You say," whispered Mrs. Knollys, "that it can never be recovered!"

"Madam," spoke the Doctor, doffing his hat, "how would you recofer from a blace when the smallest approximation which I haf yet been able to make puts the depth from the surface to the bed of the gletscher at vrom sixteen hundred to sixteen hundred and sixty *mètres* in distance?" Dr. Zimmermann spoke very good English; and he pushed his hat upon the back of his head, and assumed his professional attitude.

"But they all were trying—" Mrs. Knollys spoke faintly. "They said that they hoped he could be recovered." The stranger was the oldest gentleman she had seen, and Mrs. Knollys felt almost like confiding in him. "Oh, I must have the—the body." She closed in a sob; but the Herr Doctor caught at the last word, and this suggested to him only the language of scientific experiment.

"Recofer it? If, madam," Zimmermann went on with all the satisfaction attendant on the enunciation of a scientific truth, "we take a body and drop it in the schrund of this gletscher; and the ice-stream moves so slower at its base than on the upper part, and the ice will cover it; efen if we could reach the base, which is a mile in depth. Then, see you, it is all caused by the motion of the ice——"

But at this Mrs. Knollys had given a faint cry, and her guide rushed up angrily to the old professor, who stared helplessly forward. "God will help me, sir," said she to the Doctor, and she gave the guide her arm and walked wearily away.

The professor still stared in amazement at her enthusiasm for scientific experiment and the passion with which she greeted his discoveries. Here was a person who utterly refused to be referred to the agency of ice, or even, like Splüthner, of Fire and Water, and went out of the range of allowable hypotheses to call upon a Noumenon. Now both Splüthner and Zimmermann had studied all natural agencies and made allowance for them, but for the Divine they had always hitherto proved an alibi. The Doctor could make nothing of it.

At the inn that evening he saw Mrs. Knollys with swollen eyes; and remembering the scene of the afternoon, he made inquiries about her of the innkeeper. The latter had heard the guide's account of the meeting, and as soon as Zimmermann had made plain what he had told her of the falling body, "Triple blockhead!" said he. *"Es war ihr Mann."* The Herr Professor staggered back into his seat, and the kindly innkeeper ran upstairs to see what had happened to his poor young guest. .   .   .   .

Mrs. Knollys went back to the little cottage in Surrey, and lived there. The chests and cases she brought back lay unopened in the store-room; the little rooms of the cottage that was to be their home remained bare and unadorned, as Charles had seen them last. She could not bring herself to alter them now. What she had looked forward to do with him she had no strength to do alone. She rarely went out. There was no place where she could go to think of him. He was gone; gone from England, gone from the very surface of the earth. If he had only been buried in some quiet English churchyard, she thought,—some green place lying open to the sun, where she could go and scatter flowers on his grave, where she could sit and look forward amid her tears to the time when she should lie side by side with him,—they would then be separated for her short life alone. Now it seemed to her that they were far apart forever.

But late the next summer she had a letter from the place. It was from Dr. Zimmermann. There is no need here to trace the quaint German phrases, the formalism, the cold terms of science in which he made his meaning plain. It spoke of erosion; of the movement of the summer; of the action of the under-waters on the ice. And it told her, with tender sympathy oddly blended with the pride of scientific success, that he had given a year's most careful study to the place; with all his instruments of measurement he had tested the relentless glacier's flow; and it closed by assuring her that her husband might yet be found—in five and forty years. In five and forty years—the poor professor staked his scientific reputation on the fact—in five and forty years she might return, and the glacier would give up its dead.

This letter made Mrs. Knollys happier. It made her willing to live; it made her almost long to live until old age—that her Charles's body might be given back. She took heart to beautify her little home. The trifling articles she had bought with Charles were now brought out,—the little curiosities and pictures he had given her on their wedding journey. She would ask how such and such a thing looked, turning her pretty head to some kind visitor, as she ranged them on the walls; and now and then she would have to lay the picture down and cry a little, silently, as she remembered where Charles had told her it would look best. Still, she sought to furnish the rooms as they had planned them in their mind; she made her surroundings, as nearly as she could, as they had pictured them together. One room she never went into; it was the room Charles had meant to have for the nursery. She had no child.

But she changed, as we all change, with the passing of the years. I first remember her as a woman middle-aged, sweet-faced, hardly like a widow, nor yet like an old maid. She was rather like a young girl in love, with her lover absent on a long journey. She lived more with the memory of her husband, she clung to him more, than if she had had a child. She never married; you would have guessed that; but, after the Professor's letter, she never quite seemed to realize that her husband was dead. Was he not coming back to her?

Never in all my knowledge of dear English women have I known a woman so much loved. In how many houses was she always the most welcome guest! How often we boys would go to her for sympathy! I know she was the confidante of all our love affairs. I cannot speak for girls; but I fancy she was much the same with them. Many of us owed our life's happiness to her. She would chide us gently in our pettiness and folly, and teach us, by her very presence and example, what thing it was that alone could keep life sweet. How well we all remember the little Surrey cottage, the little home fireside where the husband had never been! I think she grew to imagine his presence, even the presence of children: boys, curly-headed, like Charles, and sweet, blue-eyed daughters; and the fact that it was all imagining seemed but to make the place more holy. Charles still lived to her as she had believed him in the month that they were married; he lived through life with her as her young love had fancied he would be. She never thought of evil that might have occurred; of failing affection, of cares. Her happiness was in her mind alone; so all the earthly part was absent.

There were but two events in her life—that which was past and that which was to come. She had lived through his loss; now she lived on for his recovery. But, as I have said, she changed, as all things mortal change; all but the earth and the ice-stream and the stars above it. She read much, and her mind grew deep and broad, none the less gentle with it all; she was wiser in the world; she knew the depths of human hope and sorrow. You remember her only as an old lady whom we loved. Only her heart did not change—I forgot that; her heart, and the memory of that last loving smile upon his face, as he bent down to look into her eyes, before he slipped and fell. She lived on, and waited for his body, as possibly his other self—who knows?—waited for hers. As she grew older she grew taller; her eyes were quieter, her hair a little straighter, darker than of yore; her face changed, only the expression remained the same. Mary Knollys!

Human lives rarely look more than a year, or five, ahead; Mary Knollys looked five and forty. Many of us wait, and grow weary in waiting, for those few years alone, and for some living friend. Mary Knollys waited five and forty years—for the dead. Still, after that first year, she never wore all black; only silvery grays, and white with a black ribbon or two. I have said that she almost seemed to think her husband living. She would fancy his doing this and that with her; how he would joy in this good fortune, or share her sorrows—which were few, mercifully. His memory seemed to be a living thing to her, to go through life with her, hand in hand; it changed as she grew old; it altered itself to suit her changing thought, until the very memory of her memory seemed to make it sure that he had really been alive with her, really shared her happiness or sorrow, in the far-off days of her earliest widowhood. It hardly seemed that he had been gone already then—she remembered him so well. She could not think that he had never been with her in their little cottage. And now, at sixty, I know she thought of him as an old person too; sitting by their fireside, late in life, mature, deep-souled, wise with the wisdom of years, going back with her, fondly, to recall the old, old happiness of their bridal journey, when they set off for the happy honeymoon abroad, and the long life now past stretched brightly out before them both. She never spoke of this, and you children never knew it; but it was always in her mind.

There was a plain stone in the little Surrey churchyard, now gray and moss-grown with the rains of forty years, on which you remember reading: "Charles Knollys—lost in Carinthia." This was all she would have inscribed; he was but lost; no one *knew* that he was dead. Was he not yet to be found? There was no grassy mound beside it; the earth was smooth. Not even the date was there. But Mrs. Knollys never went to read it. She waited until he should come; until that last journey, repeating the travels of their wedding-days, when she should go to Germany to bring him home.

So the woman's life went on in England, and the glacier in the Alps moved on slowly; and the woman waited for it to be gone.

In the summer of 1882, the little Carinthian village of Heiligenblut was haunted by two persons. One was a young German scientist, with long hair and spectacles; the other was a tall English lady, slightly bent, with a face wherein the finger of time had deeply written tender things. Her hair was white as silver, and she wore a long black veil. Their habits were strangely similar. Every morning, when the eastern light shone deepest into the ice-cavern at the base of the great Pasterzen glacier, these two would walk thither; then both would sit for an hour or two and peer into its depths. Neither knew why the other was there. The woman would go back for an hour in the late afternoon; the man, never. He knew that the morning light was necessary for his search.

The man was the famous young Zimmermann, son of his father, the old Doctor, long since dead. But the Herr Doctor had written a famous tract, when late in life, refuting all Splüthners, past, present, and to come; and had charged his son, in his dying moments, as a most sacred trust, that he should repair to the base of the Pasterzen glacier in the year 1882, where he would find a leaden bullet, graven with his father's name, and the date A.U.C. 2590. All this would be vindication of his father's science. Splüthner, too, was a very old man, and Zimmermann the younger (for even he was no longer young) was fearful lest Splüthner should not live to witness his own refutation. The woman and the man never spoke to each other.

Alas, no one could have known Mrs. Knollys for the fair English girl who had been there in the young days of the century; not even the innkeeper, had he been there. But he, too, was long since dead. Mrs. Knollys was now bent and white-haired; she had forgotten, herself, how she had looked in those old days. Her life had been lived. She was now like a woman of another world; it seemed another world in which her fair hair had twined about her husband's fingers, and she and Charles had stood upon the evening mountain, and looked in each other's eyes. That was the world of her wedding-days, but it seemed more like a world she had left when born on earth. And now he was coming back to her in this. Meantime the great Pasterzen glacier had moved on, marking only the centuries; the men upon its borders had seen no change; the same great waves lifted their snowy heads upon its surface; the same crevasse still was where he had fallen. At night, the moonbeams, falling, still shivered off its glassy face; its pale presence filled the night, and immortality lay brooding in its hollows.

Friends were with Mrs. Knollys, but she left them at the inn. One old guide remembered her, and asked to bear her company. He went with her in the morning, and sat a few yards from her, waiting. In the afternoon she went alone. He would not have credited you, had you told him that the glacier moved. He thought it but an Englishwoman's fancy, but he waited with her. Himself had never forgotten that old day. And Mrs. Knollys sat there silently, searching the clear depths of the ice, that she might find her husband.

One night she saw a ghost. The latest beam of the sun, falling on a mountain opposite, had shone back into the ice-cavern; and seemingly deep within, in the grave azure light, she fancied she saw a face turned toward her. She even thought she saw Charles's yellow hair, and the self-same smile his lips had worn when he bent down to her before he fell. It could be but a fancy. She went home, and was silent with her friends about what had happened. In the moonlight she went back, and again the next morning before dawn. She told no one of her going; but the old guide met her at the door, and walked silently behind her. She had slept, the glacier ever present in her dreams.

The sun had not yet risen when she came; and she sat a long time in the cavern, listening to the murmur of the river, flowing under the glacier at her feet. Slowly the dawn began, and again she seemed to see the shimmer of a face—such a face as one sees in the coals of a dying fire. Then the full sun came over the eastern mountain, and the guide heard a woman's cry. There before her was Charles Knollys! The face seemed hardly pale; and there was the same faint smile—a smile like her memory of it, five and forty years gone by. Safe in the clear ice, still, unharmed, there lay—O God! not her Charles; not the Charles of her own thought, who had lived through life with her and shared her sixty years; not the old man she had borne thither in her mind— but a boy, a boy of one and twenty lying asleep, a ghost from another world coming to confront her from the distant past, immortal in the immortality of the glacier. There was his quaint coat, of the fashion of half a century before; his blue eyes open; his young, clear brow; all the form of the past she had forgotten; and she his bride stood there to welcome him, with her wrinkles, her bent figure, and thin white hairs. She was living, he was dead; and she was two and forty years older than he.

Then at last the long-kept tears came to her, and she bent her white head in the snow. The old man came up with his pick, silently, and began working in the ice. The woman lay weeping, and the boy, with his still, faint smile, lay looking at them, through the clear ice-veil, from his open eyes.

I believe that the Professor found his bullet; I know not. I believe that the scientific world rang with his name and the thesis that he published on the glacier's motion, and the changeless temperature his father's lost thermometer had shown. All this you may read. I know no more.

But I know that in the English churchyard there are now two graves, and a single stone, to Charles Knollys and Mary, his wife; and the boy of one and twenty sleeps there with his bride of sixty-three; his young frame with her old one, his yellow hair beside her white. And I do not know that there is not some place, not here, where they are still together, and he is twenty-one and she is still eighteen. I do not know this; but I know that all the pamphlets of the German doctor cannot tell me it is false.

Meantime the great Pasterzen glacier moves on, and the rocks with it; and the mountain flings his shadow of the planets in its face.

Henry Guy Carleton.

Born in Fort Union, New Mexico, 1855.

THE DEATH OF MEMNON.

[*Memnon. A Tragedy in Five Acts.—Printed, not Published. 1884.*]

Act V.—Scene [*at close*]: *The front of the palace of Luxor, at Thebes; the steps approaching which extend across the stage. Entrance to the palace at C. In front of the palace at R, the colossal statue of Amenophis. Time : the hour preceding dawn.*

[*Citizens rush in R and L, to the palace C. Reënter Persians and Egyptians fighting R, and exit L. Clash of swords, R.*]

Sesak. [*Without.*] Down with thee! Now for Memnon! Where is he? [*Enters.*]

[*Reënter Memnon in full armor.*]

Memn. I answer to that name; come, what is thine?

Ses. [*Raising his sword.*] This tongue shall tell it thee.

Memn.   Ha! Thy voice does that.
Well, we have met at last.

Ses.   At last, indeed. [*Unmasks.*]
Well, what's the gossip?

Memn.   Villain of the world,
Hell starves for malice till I send thee there!

Ses. Why, to it, then! [*They fight. After a few passes Memnon strikes Sesak's sword from him. Sesak recoils several paces.*]

[*Enter Phanes with Persian soldiers. Phanes rushes between Memnon and Sesak.*]

Pha.   Stay, Memnon! Memnon, hold!
Seize him! [*Two soldiers seize Sesak.*]

Memn. Why come between me and my prey?
Hold off thy meddling hands, I say! Touch not
The tiger in me—that has tasted blood,
And I am dangerous.

Ses.   Why, let him come.

Pha. Nay, sir, you would not strike a pinioned man!

Memn. Oh, thou hast robbed me! [*Enter Nitetis, attended.*]

Pha.   Is it so? Behold!

Nitet. My father, father! [*Enter Asseth.*]

Memn.   Daughter!

Asseth.   It is dawn.

Memn. Oh, never fairer blossomed in the east!

Nitet. My father!

Memn.   Closer, girl! this is the day
Which pinnacles my calendar. Close, close!

Nitet. How I have hungered for this hour!

Memn.   Behold!
What guide like heaven? Through the grime of war
She comes unblackened.

Asseth. [*To Sesak.*] Well, my dog?

Ses.   Laugh on.

PHA. Sir,——

MEMN.   Thou art hungry, too? [*Looses* NITETIS's *arms from his neck, leads her to* PHANES, *then approaches* SESAK.]
                 Thou art to die.

ASSETH. Hear'st that, my dog?

SES.   I do; I am to die.

[*Enter* MENEPHTAH *with drawn sword, a slave fanning him.*]

MENEPH. A Persian! a Persian, I say! show me a Persian. Great Memnon, where are the Persians? [*Sees Persians, and stops short, hiding his sword and getting behind the slave.*]

PHA. O, if thou giv'st her me—— [*A flourish.*]

MEMN.   What trumpet's that?

[*Enter* PREXASPES, *attended ; after him two pages bearing the Egyptian crown upon a cushion veiled.*]

PHA. Prexaspes!

PREX. [*To* MEMNON.] Mightiest, hail!
         [*To* NITETIS.] Hail, flower of the world; and joy to all!
Thus great Cambyses' greeting. [*Kneels and offers a scroll to* MEMNON.]

MEMN.   What is this?
To Hophra's daughter——

PREX. [*Unveiling the crown.*] Hophra's crown. [ASSETH *directs* SESAK's *attention.*]

SES.   Laugh on!

PREX. Hail, Queen of Egypt!

PHA. [*Aside, turning away.*] Queen? Then never mine. [NITETIS *looks at* PHANES, *then goes to* MEMNON.]

NITET. Father, what would you have me do?

MEMN.   My girl,
Art thou not Hophra's daughter?

NITET. [*Pointing to* PHANES.] But for him?

MEMN. Well, girl? There is thy golden heritage,
Thy father's crown.

NITET.   But he?

MEMN.   Think not of him.
He will surrender thee.

NITET.   Surrender me! [*Turns to* PHANES.]

MEMN. Thou canst not marry with a foreigner,
And sit on Egypt's throne. [PHANES *points to the crown and turns away.*]

NITET.   Alas!

MEMN.   What! Weep?
And in thy grasp the majesty and rule
Of half the world?

NITET.   No, not my world.

MEMN.   Decide.
Still dumb? 'Tis written of thy womankind,
They may love poverty—till wooed by gold.

NITET. Is't so? Then pray correct the lying scroll.
Were this the diadem of fifty worlds,
To sit immortally upon my head,
It could not tempt me.

MEMN.   Why, thou foolish one?

NITET. O, who can analyze a young girl's heart,
Or single out the wherefore of her love?
She only knows she loves, and that one love
Outshines the jewels on an empress' brow.
I love him, sir,—that's my philosophy.
O, my dear love, how proud I am of you! [*To* PHANES.]
Take it away; I am a subject, sir. [*To* PREXASPES.]
Here is my king.—Father, approve my choice. [*Kneels before* MEMNON.]
    MEMN. Approve! [*Raises her and takes her in his arms.*] [*To* PREXASPES.]
              This brow would shame the diadem.
We thank Cambyses.
    PREX.   Then farewell, my lord.

[*Exit* PREXASPES *and pages.* SESAK *steals knife from the girdle of the soldier guarding
him, and secretes it in his bosom.*]

    MEMN. Approve—my girl of noble heart! *approve?*
Why, had'st thou faltered but a moment; touched—
Nay, looked upon the crown—and so forsworn
The love thou'st plighted him—I swear to thee,
Thou never should'st have called me father more.
My Greek, have I not proven her? Link your hands.

[NITETIS *and* PHANES, *joining hands, kneel.*]

I give her to thee wholly. Guard her well:
She will reward thee. She'll not love at morn,
And ere the evening wasteth love thee not;
Nor harbor giddy tales, nor count thy purse
In her decision, nor decry thy gods
That they are different. She'll be wife to thee,
At worst in sunshine, best in doubt and night,
As comforting as is the pilot's star;
Wife to thy spirit, closer than thy body.
My girl, be this thy dower for all life—
Thy husband, unto thee, stands next to God.
    PHA. My own, my own at last! [SESAK *whispers* ASSETH, *who ap-
proaches* MEMNON.]
    ASSETH.   Noble my lord,
He craves a word with you.
    MEMN.   Ha! On what theme?
    ASSETH. Your brother, sir——
    MEMN. [*Starting forward.*]   My brother!
    ASSETH.   Nay, my lord,
He does confess him innocent——
    PHA.   Away! [*Guards lay hold of* SESAK.]
    SES. Great Memnon, hear me!
    NITET.   Hear him, father.
    PHA.   Nay.
    NITET. Upon our wedding day—see it is dawn!
Let us be merciful.
    SES. [*Aside.*] I'll crack this tune!
Rare virgin, thanks.—My lord, I pray you, hear.
    MEMN. What wouldst thou say to me? Devil thou art;
But if thou show'st my brother guiltless, lo!
    VOL. XI.—12

Thou'lt play the angel to me.   Speak, I say.
Thou hast the viper's tooth, but I do swear—
Didst lead him on ?—didst lie to him ?—say that;
Unburden me and wash his memory,
And though thou showest blacker than the fiends,
I'll call thee charitable.   Speak to me!
   Ses. Great sir, am I to utter like a slave ?
These vile ears nearest ?—Stand aside from me! [*To the guards.*]
   Pha. Has he a weapon ?
   Asseth.   No.
   Ses.   Fear ye these hands ?
Why, were these fingers each a knife—but sure—
Aside from me! [*At a signal from* Memnon, *the guard falls back.*]   I hum-
   bly thank you, sir;—
You, lady—you, most gallant general.
Now may I speak, indeed.
   Memn.   Well ? Come to it.
   Ses. Nay, yet a little.—Pray you, general, [*To* Phanes.]
Stand yonder for a moment; 'tis a whim,
A vagary.—I am so soon to die,
And you so happy there—I pray you, sir!
   Pha. Why, this is folly——
   Nitet.   There is reason in 't.
I do beseech you, go.
   Ses.   O, thanks to you.
   Pha. Quickly confess thee——
   Ses.   Ay, so please you, sir.
Stand further from me, knave! Pardon, sweet sirs;
Though I'm your cagèd rat, I must have room,—
A little room to creep and breathe awhile.
Be patient yet.—I do confess me, sir, [*To* Memnon.]
I led your brother on.—Your mercy, sir, [*To* Phanes.]
'Twas I that sent her into Persia.   Then,
I do acknowledge that my dearest aim—
Fulfilled, fulfilled!—was to destroy
And scatter Egypt's glory like a chaff
Before the whirlwind—nay, a moment, sir! [*To* Phanes.]
This much I tell ye freely, with my heart!
Ye were my tools.   Your brawn, your souls, your hands,
Were my good servitors, and I thank ye for it!
Now for my mystery,—catch it who can!
What should I speak—save of the hates I bear ye ?
What do—except complete my sworn revenge ?
I am a viper—look to it—behold,
Ye tread on me! I turn and sting ye—thus!

[*Runs toward* Nitetis *with a knife drawn;* Memnon *throws himself quickly between,
and receives the blow.*]

   Asseth. Disarm him!
   Pha.   Horror!
   Ses. Sister, sister! sleep! [*Stabs himself and falls.*]
   Pha. Justice! where is thy sword! [*Bending over* Sesak.]
   Memn. [*Pointing upward.*]   Nay, peace to death! [*Sinks.*]

NITET. O, father!——
PHA.   Bring a surgeon. Asseth, go!
ASSETH. Nay, it is mortal.
PHA.   Jupiter! 'twas foul.
NITET. O father, speak to me!
MEMN.   Be happy, girl,—
Cherish her, Greek.
PHA.   O Memnon, Memnon, live!
MEMN. Nay, this is better.—Life's an empty dream,
Guessed only by the dead.
NITET.   Father!
MEMN.   My girl,
I loved thee fondly; give thy lips again.
Nay, gentle, mourn me not; my storm-tossed soul
Is at its anchorage, and all is calm. [*Dies.*]

Flora Haines Loughead.

BORN in Milwaukee, Wis., 1855.

THE FORTUNES OF WAR.

[*The Argonaut.* 1887.]

BRIDGET CALLAHAN and Norah O'Grady met at a fish-stall in the
Sixteenth Street Market, and, as luck would have it, each fixed her
fancy upon a particularly large and handsome flounder which lay upon the
slimy marble slab. The two women had come up to the stall at about the
same moment. It was not Bridget Callahan's fault that the dealer, a dark-
skinned Italian with sleepy black eyes, happened to see her first, but the
O'Grady chose to think so and abused her roundly, while the Italian rolled up
the fish in a piece of coarse brown paper, counted out his customer's change,
and bowed his thanks.

The tide of ineffectual wrath which issued from Mrs. O'Grady's lips surprised no one accustomed to the place. It seemed rather to delight its object.
Norah O'Grady was a small woman, stout and firm-set as an ale-bottle, with
a rather long neck and a small head, which was on this occasion crowned with
a sailor-hat belonging to her little daughter, presumably snatched up by mistake in her haste to get out for her daily marketing. Mrs. Callahan, on the
other hand, was of generous proportions, with a large fat face and serene blue
eyes that could be savage enough upon occasion. And she was gorgeously
arrayed, wearing a brilliant Paisley shawl with a fiery red centre, a vaunt of
social superiority which she had waved before Mrs. O'Grady for years.

They met again at the door of the market, and assailed each other with a
storm of invective, for which the fish acted as an excuse.

Both knew that there would be no "making up" or "taking back." The
day for reconciliation was long gone by. Just when this crisis had passed it

would be difficult to say. Whether it occurred on the day, some ten years gone by, that the two families first took up their abode in cottages side by side, and Mrs. Callahan's Tim threw a dead cat at Mrs. O'Grady, and Mrs. O'Grady retaliated by crashing a pane of glass in the Callahan domicile, in her efforts to punish the culprit, and Mrs. Callahan appeared upon the scene, hot, and red, and covered with dust from beating carpets, and essayed to take the carpet-stick to Mrs. O'Grady, to her own discomfiture; whether these small beginnings, which were liable to occur in any families of the Callahan and O'Grady circle, formed the animus and incentive to after-hostilities, who can say? Certain it is that the war had been kept up with unabated vigor ever since. There is a certain convenience in quarrelling over a back fence, which people who have had to nurse their wrath at a distance will readily appreciate. Anger has no chance to cool, as when time and distance intervene. Over the cook-stove, at the wash-tub, ironing, sweeping, scrubbing, rocking their babies, the voice of each could penetrate the other's domicile. It is needless to say that they made free use of their opportunities. If there was an opprobrious epithet in the vocabulary of billingsgate practised in Goats' Hollow—that choice quarter of San Francisco where both had the honor to claim a residence—which they had not at some time flung at each other during their intercourse, both would have thanked you to make it known, that they might at once atone for the deficiency. They had resorted to every expedient to prove their genuine neighborly feeling. When Mrs. Callahan hung her washing over the back fence, Mrs. O'Grady sprinkled it liberally with dish water. The soil in both back yards was generally mulched with broken crockery, old bottles, bustles, corset steels, battered tin cans, and other neighborly courtesies which had been exchanged over this convenient back fence.

In some ways, this feud had been of great benefit to both families. It had served as a sort of safety-valve for the conflicting emotions which often disturb the peace of a household. How much bodily fatigue and parental irritation the two mothers had worked off upon each other will never be positively known. With the youngsters, a proximate estimate of the exact amount of viciousness spared their own flesh and blood might easily be made. When Tim Callahan was spanked by his mother, he immediately cuffed a young O'Grady. When Annie O'Grady was denied a new frock, she made faces at Tim Callahan. The little Callahans and O'Gradys sparred and scratched and bit and stoned each other with promiscuous zeal.

For a time the heads of the two families abstained from any active participation in the general scrimmage, looking with dignified indulgence upon the clashings of the two weaker vessels. Little by little they were drawn into the conflict. Some depredations of more than usual atrocity had fired O'Grady's blood. Callahan had been wrought to a frenzy by the combined effects of an insulting taunt and an unusually generous evening dram, the two men had forthwith indulged in a knock-down fight, and having once aired their grievances within the arena of the police court, regularly contributed to swell its annals.

At the time of which I write, an interesting bit of litigation was pending between the two families. The O'Gradys kept poultry, and a sorry lot of fowls they were, maimed and crippled by the persecution of the Callahans. Nevertheless a feeble tribe of ducks, and geese, and hens wandered about the back yard, or scoured the odorous precincts of Goats' Hollow, contriving to pick up a precarious living. Sometimes they ventured on the premises of neighbors, and were driven away with many a loud "shoo," shower of dirt, or waving of dish-towels. Now, the Callahans had a flower-garden which was at once their glory and their pride, being gorgeous with showy geraniums, prickly with cactus, and redolent with herbs. The O'Grady fowls, sharing the family animosity, spied out this humble paradise, and besieged it with a persistence that was positively ghoulish. By day and by night, through chink and crevice and gates left carelessly ajar, they invaded the Callahan garden and uprooted the choicest plants. When the Callahans walled them out, they burrowed under; when they laid a coping of rocks around the entire lot, they still contrived to make periodical marauds. It was privately whispered that the O'Gradys used to set up a step-ladder in their yard to assist the fowls in their depredations. Be this as it may, the Callahans at length got a dog, a fierce, yellow, whiskered canine, with a stub tail and an evil eye, warranted to be death on fowls. Thereafter, when a chicken, or duck, or goose stole into the Callahan grounds, its mangled body was promptly flung back over the fence. The O'Gradys could not stand this long. One day Mr. O'Grady paid a visit to a neighboring druggist, and the next morning the Callahan dog was stiff and stark. That day at noon Mr. Callahan swore out a warrant for the arrest of Mr. O'Grady, and the trial of the latter was set for a week from the day on which our story begins. Both families were to be out in force, and the suit promised to be the occasion for airing a long list of grievances on both sides.

As the feminine heads of these two warring factions continued their homeward walk, it must not be imagined that they took opposite sides of the street. Had they belonged to a different grade of society they would doubtless have contented themselves with icy stares when they met, and gone their way swelling with horrible things they would have liked to say. Being the women they were, they had the comfort of giving full vent to their feelings, and walked along side by side, in a neighborly fashion, punctuating each step with angry words, tart ejaculations, and venomous sneers. When they had progressed a block or so, a slight distraction, of a not entirely disagreeable nature, occurred. A youthful Callahan was discovered in the act of belaboring a young O'Grady with a five-gallon oil-can, while a bloody nose and a scratch on the assailant's face attested the ability of the O'Grady to give as good as the Callahan sent.

The two mothers watched the battle with pride in the prowess of their offspring. Neither attempted to interfere. This was a consistent result of years of industrious training, a valiant rally to the support of family traditions. It was more than that, it was salve for a secret grievance that each nourished in her heart. For upwards of a year their two eldest had suspended hostilities. Nay, more; Tim and Annie exchanged shy glances of sympathy and affection whenever they met. They had been seen walking together across the Hollow at night. Annie, a pretty, blue-eyed little creature, who was really modest and lady-like, and altogether a very exceptional product of a public-school education working upon raw Hibernian material, had lifted up her voice in defence of the Callahans, in her mother's house. Tim, a sturdy young fellow, who had spent the best days of his youth dodging the police authorities and the Industrial School, but had turned out a very decent machinist after all, had left the paternal mansion the night before, slamming the door behind him, in resentment of some slighting allusion to the O'Gradys. The neighbors were beginning to say that it was a pity such a likely young couple should be kept apart by family differences ; but the parents preserved an uncompromising front.

So absorbed were both women in watching the outcome of the combat that they did not at first observe a crowd that had gathered farther down the street, nor the people running thither from all quarters. Evidently something of interest was occurring ; possibly a fire. The Callahans and the O'Gradys, young and old, never missed a fire if they could help it. With one accord the two women started for the scene of excitement, and as Mrs. O'Grady's short limbs were somewhat more agile than Mrs. Callahan's longer ones, they kept well abreast, and never paused until they had reached the outskirts of the ever-increasing crowd. Then Mrs. Callahan stopped with prophetic instinct, one hand pressed closely to her panting breast.

"It's the sewer. Something's happened in the sewer ; an' my Bill a-goin' to work here the mornin'."

Norah O'Grady gave an exclamation of disgust. The idea of one of the Callahan crowd being singled out for any special disaster was so absurd on the face of it that the very suggestion awoke in her a sense of impatience.

"An' *what's* happened ? " she said, in a debative tone, accenting the second word, addressing a man who stood at her elbow.

"Bank caved in. Men under it."

"No, some men fell into an old cesspool that they uncovered."

Bridget Callahan did not wait to hear more, but pushed her way through the crowd. Norah O'Grady, without waiting to think, or reason that it was none of her concern, followed in her enemy's wake. In spite of oaths, and resistance, and angry words, they threaded their way to the margin of a narrow circle, where banks of loosely heaped earth surrounded a yawning black hole. There they learned the details of what had happened. In extending the system of sewerage along the street, an old cesspool had been uncovered and three men had been sent down to examine it ; two of them had beaten a quick retreat, but the third had succumbed to the foul gases generated there. Two successive attempts had been made by other workmen to rescue him, but neither of the men who went down after him had returned. Three men lay dead or dying at the foot of the ladder, and no workman could be found foolhardy enough to venture down.

"An' who were the men that wint down ? " asked Bridget Callahan.

"Walsh and Williams was the men that went last. Bill Callahan was the first."

"Me husband an' the father of seven children. A man that is honest as the day is long; that niver lost a day's worrk in his life. May the Lord an' all the holy saints have pity on me!" wailed Bridget Callahan.

Even in her first wild cry of grief she managed to sting the woman who stood silently by her side, and Norah O'Grady felt the thrust and winced under it. No one had ever accused Patrick O'Grady of being honest, and as for doing a day's work—since the day, some eight or ten years ago, when O'Grady had abandoned the calling of a hostler and taken up the profession of a ward politician, he had never condescended to soil his hands with a day's manual labor. Yet, strangely enough, Norah O'Grady felt no inclination to triumph over her enemy, but a new and tender feeling crept into her heart.

Meantime Bridget Callahan filled the air with the sound of her lamentation, now sobbing, now pleading, now railing at those about her.

"An' are ye men, an' stand there idle, with three poor fellows perishin' so near, an' not a hand that lifts to save him! Shame on ye for weak-hearted cowards! For the love of heaven, boys! Oh, ye lazy vagabones! Let a woman show ye your duty!" And quick as a flash, before any one could anticipate her movement, in spite of her corpulent and clumsy figure, she had swung herself over upon the ladder, and was preparing to go down.

In the first excitement of their appearance upon the scene, neither of the women had noticed a big, muscular fellow, wearing a flashy checked suit with an air of awkward rakishness, who stood on the bank of fresh earth but a few paces away, smoking a short pipe and gazing speculatively into the black pit below. As the woman's shrill cry of denunciation reached his ears, he might have been seen to remove the pipe from his lips for a moment and smile grimly to himself, like one who hears a compliment intended for him, and hastened to acknowledge it. But Mrs. Callahan had no sooner set foot on the ladder than a heavy hand fell on her shoulder, and a gruff voice sounded in her ears.

"Back!"

She looked up and recognized him, and her face grew red as a lobster with contending emotions.

"Oh, it's you, Patrick O'Grady, is it!" she cried out, in a shrill voice. "Let go of me. Oh, you worthless loafer! You good-for-nothing, do-nothing, dog-poisoning r-rascal! Let me go to save my man. My man, whose little finger is worth more than your whole lazy body. Oh, Bill, Bill!" And she broke out into a fresh storm of sobs; but she suffered herself to be led back without further protest.

Meanwhile, the man whom she had so bitterly denounced, but to whom she had nevertheless yielded an unwilling obedience, felt a light touch upon his shoulder, and turned to face his wife. His eyes asked a question, and her eyes answered.

"All right, if you say so, my girl."

In an instant his attitude had changed. New life seemed infused into him. His huge, brawny frame, but the moment before a torpid, inert mass, became the embodiment of activity and force. The sluggish blood bounded through his veins. Recollections of old times, when he had been a miner on the Comstock and had fought the miner's battle with foul air and fire-damp, came back to him. He flung off his coat and unbuttoned his collar, baring his huge, muscular throat.

"Some rope!" he shouted.

A coil of rope fell at his feet. He caught up a hose, hanging over a bed of mortar close by, and turned a spray of water into the dark pit, at the same time saturating his handkerchief with the water and binding it tightly about his mouth and nostrils. Then, with the rope knotted around him, a direction to the men who were to pay it out, and a parting word to his wife, he stepped upon the ladder and commenced the descent.

Norah O'Grady, her heart wrung with terror, stood on the brink and saw him go—to his death, she thought—and tried to frame some prayer for him, but her white lips refused to move. Standing there, on the threshold of what she felt must be the tragedy of her life, she became suddenly aware of the curious eyes bent upon her, and of the absurd spectacle she presented in her calico wrapper and with the child's hat on her head. She knew that she had sent her husband to his doom, and she must not leave the place where she could see his dead body when the men pulled it up; but she tried to settle the jaunty hat into some expression of propriety, and, fumbling with her belt, strove to arrange the folds of her wrapper.

In the midst of her awkward struggle a mantle seemed to descend upon her from the heavens. Gazing in astonishment over one shoulder, she found herself arrayed in all the glory of the Paisley shawl. Looking up, she saw her enemy awed into silence by the strange turn events had taken, looking down upon her with quite a new expression, and she realized that it was no chance impulse that had prompted her to divest herself of the garment, but tender womanly consideration.

"I don't need it," whispered Mrs. Callahan. Then she quite broke down. "Oh, Norah O'Grady!" Catching the latter's little nervous hand between her large, strong ones, she sobbed over her in penitence and compassion.

There was a cry from those who stood about the ladder.

"Here he comes!"

An instant later, O'Grady's herculean figure appeared, bearing in his arms a slender young fellow who tried to stand, and would have fallen had not strong arms come to his aid.

A shout went up:

"It's Williams!"

A gray-haired woman came forward, and half-led, half-supported her son away.

The next time O'Grady appeared, he stumbled and fell, as he was relieved of his inanimate burden. A whisper ran around:

"It's Walsh."

They laid him on the ground.

A girl stole timidly out from the crowd, and wept over her dead lover. All eyes turned questioningly upon O'Grady, who was leaning up against a box, pale and shaky, making a weak gesture of protest as the swaying of the curious crowd threatened to shut off the air from him. Then he arose, and faltered toward the mortar-box where the hose was playing. He had loosed the handkerchief from his mouth and nose, and now untied it with trembling hands.

" He's going to give it up," some one said.

O'Grady heard the words, and was reminded that he had already done all that could be expected of any man ; that if he stopped now, he would still be a hero in the eyes of those who were looking on ; that neither duty nor reason demanded his return to the poisonous den from which he had escaped, but he looked toward the quarter from which the words had come, and replied with a savage sneer :

" *Not much !* "

He stopped just long enough to take a cool, invigorating draught from the nozzle of the hose and to saturate the handkerchief again, before binding it across his face. He called for another length of rope, and, as he instructed the men to haul up at a given signal, they knew that his strength was giving out. Then he leaped upon the ladder and descended, hand-over-hand, with the swiftness of one who is about to take a desperate risk. No one in the pure, wholesome air above could guess what it was to plunge into this noisome hole, the reeking repository of filth and corruption, from which poisonous gases exhaled, blotting out the light of day that essayed to creep through the narrow opening above, making it impossible for so much as the flame of a candle to survive. Nor did O'Grady find any comfort in the reflection that he was doing a magnanimous and gallant deed, risking his life to save his enemy. To him, Callahan had from the first lost personality and identity. He was simply a fellow-being, suffering, failing, dying.

As O'Grady reached the lower rung of the ladder and stooped to the foul ooze below, the horrible vapors seemed to rise like spectral forms, clutching at him, gripping his throat, crushing his chest in a vise-like embrace. His eyes were blinded, something roared in his ears like the thunder of incoming breakers. Sightless, deafened, choking, he groped about him, and found what he sought.

The men above felt a faint pull on the rope O'Grady had carried in his hands, and hauled it in with a will. A moment later, Callahan, unconscious, but with his chest heaving in slow, convulsive movements, lay stretched upon the ground beside them. Everybody looked to see O'Grady's resolute face and broad shoulders appear at the opening. Cheers were on their lips, praise in their hearts. Somebody pulled gently upon the rope he had tied about his waist when he first went down. Heavy, inanimate weight was the only response. Two of the workmen swung themselves down the ladder until only their heads and shoulders were visible, and, gripping the rope, brought the heavy burden into position to be raised.

" Now, boys! "

Slowly and more carefully than before they pulled upon the rope. When Norah O'Grady saw the lifeless form, she sprang forward with a little cry.

A week later two convalescents sat up in bed and demanded to be dressed. Bridget Callahan hastened to obey her husband's behest with a willing heart and trembling hands. Norah O'Grady scolded and expostulated, but to no effect. O'Grady stormed and swore, and went angrily off without his breakfast, putting in his appearance at the police court a full ten minutes before his antagonist.

He had actually got in a savage plea of "Guilty, an' it plaze your honor!" when the plaintiff appeared on the scene. The two men met for the first time since the day when Callahan had been drawn back from the jaws of a frightful death by his enemy. O'Grady would not look toward him now, but repeated his plea, rather more loudly and decidedly than before:

"Guilty, your honor."

Callahan held a hasty consultation with an official of the court.

"*Nolle prosequi,*" announced the latter, in a careless tone.

"Case dismissed. Call the next," said the Judge.

O'Grady had to be twice informed before he comprehended the turn affairs had taken. Then he left reluctantly, unhappy and dissatisfied. The fact that he had laid his enemy under the heaviest possible obligations to himself had only served to whet his zest in the role of injured innocence, which he had been ready to enact. He had been making ready his powers of oratory all the way down town, rehearsing the pedigree of the game-cocks Callahan's dog had slain, counting his decimated flock of ducks, raking up a score of old injuries which he meant to rehearse if an opportunity was presented. He went out of court crestfallen. Somebody awaited him outside the door.

"O'Grady!" said Callahan, in a voice at once conciliatory, pleading, argumentative, holding out his hand at the same time.

If O'Grady had been the man who had lain at the bottom of the cesspool, and Callahan the man who had saved him, he would have struck aside the proffered hand. But all at once it came to him that one who confers a favor has obligations far more binding than those of the recipient. The man who has once done a noble and unselfish act has a character to maintain. It is the old principle of *noblesse oblige,* among high and low, rich and poor, the world over.

They walked down the stairs together and out into the street. For a long time they did not speak. Then Callahan, timidly:

"They do say as our Tim be coortin' av your Annie."

O'Grady smoked his pipe for some seconds without replying. Then he took it deliberately from his mouth.

"Tim's a loikely lad," he said.

That evening Tim Callahan walked up to the front door of the O'Grady cottage. Annie O'Grady, her face a genuine April of smiles and tears, was there to receive him.

Henry Cuyler Bunner.

BORN in Oswego, N. Y., 1855.

THE WAY TO ARCADY.

[Airs from Arcady and Elsewhere. 1884.]

O*H, what's the way to Arcady,*
    To Arcady, to Arcady;
Oh, what's the way to Arcady,
    Where all the leaves are merry?

Oh, what's the way to Arcady?
The spring is rustling in the tree—
The tree the wind is blowing through—
    It sets the blossoms flickering white.
I knew not skies could burn so blue
    Nor any breezes blow so light.
They blow an old-time way for me,
Across the world to Arcady.

Oh, what's the way to Arcady?
Sir Poet, with the rusty coat,
Quit mocking of the song-bird's note.
How have you heart for any tune,
You with the wayworn russet shoon?
Your scrip, a-swinging by your side,
Gapes with a gaunt mouth hungry-wide.
I'll brim it well with pieces red,
If you will tell the way to tread.

Oh, I am bound for Arcady,
And if you but keep pace with me
You tread the way to Arcady.

And where away lies Arcady,
And how long yet may the journey be?

Ah, that (quoth he) I do not know—
Across the clover and the snow—
Across the frost, across the flowers—
Through summer seconds and winter hours.
I've trod the way my whole life long,
    And know not now where it may be;
My guide is but the stir to song,
That tells me I cannot go wrong,
    Or clear or dark the pathway be
    Upon the road to Arcady.

But how shall I do who cannot sing?
    I was wont to sing, once on a time——

There is never an echo now to ring
    Remembrance back to the trick of
        rhyme.

'Tis strange you cannot sing (quoth he),
The folk all sing in Arcady.

But how may he find Arcady
Who hath nor youth nor melody?

What, know you not, old man (quoth
        he)——
    Your hair is white, your face is wise—
    That Love must kiss that Mortal's eyes
Who hopes to see fair Arcady?
No gold can buy you entrance there;
But beggared Love may go all bare—
No wisdom won with weariness;
But Love goes in with Folly's dress—
No fame that wit could ever win;
But only Love may lead Love in
    To Arcady, to Arcady.

Ah, woe is me, through all my days
    Wisdom and wealth I both have got,
And fame and name, and great men's
        praise;
    But Love, ah, Love! I have it not.
There was a time, when life was new—
    But far away, and half forgot—
I only know her eyes were blue;
    But Love—I fear I knew it not.
We did not wed, for lack of gold,
And she is dead, and I am old.
All things have come since then to me,
Save Love, ah, Love! and Arcady.

Ah, then I fear we part (quoth he),
My way's for Love and Arcady.

But you, you fare alone, like me;
    The gray is likewise in your hair.
    What love have you to lead you there,
To Arcady, to Arcady?

Ah, no, not lonely do I fare ;
 My true companion's Memory.
With love he fills the Spring-time air ;
 With love he clothes the Winter tree.
Oh, past this poor horizon's bound
 My song goes straight to one who stands—
Her face all gladdening at the sound—
 To lead me to the Spring-green lands,
 To wander with enlacing hands.

The songs within my breast that stir
 Are all of her, are all of her.
My maid is dead long years (quoth he),
 She waits for me in Arcady.

Oh, yon's the way to Arcady,
 To Arcady, to Arcady ;
Oh, yon's the way to Arcady,
 Where all the leaves are merry.

SHE WAS A BEAUTY.

SHE was a beauty in the days
 When Madison was President:
And quite coquettish in her ways—
 On conquests of the heart intent.

Grandpapa, on his right knee bent,
Wooed her in stiff, old-fashioned phrase—
She was a beauty in the days
 When Madison was President.

And when your roses where hers went
Shall go, my Rose, who dates from Hayes,
 I hope you'll wear her sweet content
Of whom tradition lightly says:
She was a beauty in the days
 When Madison was President.

A PITCHER OF MIGNONETTE.

A PITCHER of mignonette,
 In a tenement's highest casement:
Queer sort of flower-pot—yet
That pitcher of mignonette
Is a garden in heaven set,
 To the little sick child in the basement—
The pitcher of mignonette,
 In the tenement's highest casement.

LOVE IN OLD CLOATHES.

[*In Partnership.—Stories by Brander Matthews and H. C. Bunner.* 1884.]

NEWE YORK, yᵉ 1ˢᵗ Aprile, 1883.

YE worste of my ailment is this, yᵗ it groweth not Less with much nurs-inge, but is like to those fevres wᶜʰ yᵉ leeches Starve, 'tis saide, for that yᵉ more Bloode there be in yᵉ Sicke man's Bodie, yᵉ more foode is there for yᵉ Distemper to feede upon.—And it is moste fittinge yᵗ I come backe to yᵉ my Journall (wherein I have not writt a Lyne these manye months) on yᵉ 1ˢᵗ of Aprile, beinge in some Sort myne owne foole and yᵉ foole of Love, and a poore Butt on whome his hearte hath play'd a Sorry tricke.—

For it is surelie a strange happenninge, that I, who am ofte accompted a man of yᵉ Worlde, (as yᵉ Phrase goes,) sholde be soe Overtaken and caste downe lyke a Schoole-boy or a countrie Bumpkin, by a meere Mayde, & sholde set to Groaninge and Sighinge, &, for that She will not have me Sighe to Her, to Groaninge and Sighinge on paper, wᶜʰ is yᵉ greter Foolishnesse in Me, yᵗ some one maye reade it Here-after, who hath taken his dose of yᵉ same Phys-icke, and made no Wrye faces over it; in wᶜʰ case I doubte I shall be much laugh'd at.—Yet soe much am I a foole, and soe enamour'd of my Foolish-nesse, yᵗ I have a sorte of Shamefull Joye in tellinge, even to my Journall, yᵗ I am mightie deepe in Love withe yᵉ yonge Daughter of Mistresse Ffrench, and all maye knowe what an Angell is yᵉ Daughter, since I have chose Mʳˢ· Ffrench for my Mother in Lawe.—(Though she will have none of my choos-inge.)—and I likewise take comforte in yᵉ Fancie, yᵗ this poore Sheete, wʰᵒⁿ I write, may be made of yᵉ Raggs of some lucklesse Lover, and maye yᵉ more readilie drinke up my complaininge Inke.—

This muche I have learnt, yᵗ Fraunce distilles not, nor yᵉ Indies growe not, yᵉ Remedie for my Aile.—For when I 1ˢᵗ became sensible of yᵉ folly of my Suite, I tooke to drynkinge & smoakinge, thinkinge to cure my minde, but all I got was a head ache, for fellowe to my Hearte ache.—A sorrie Payre!— I then made Shifte, for a while, withe a Bicycle, but breakinge of Bones mendes no breakinge of Heartes, and 60 myles a Daye bringes me no nearer to a Weddinge.—This being Lowe Sondaye, (wᶜʰ my Hearte telleth me better than yᵉ Allmanack,) I will goe to Churche; wh. I maye chaunce to see her.— Laste weeke, her Eastre bonnett vastlie pleas'd me, beinge most cunninglie devys'd in yᵉ mode of oure Grandmothers, and verie lyke to a coales Scuttle, of white satine.—

2ⁿᵈ Aprile.

I trust I make no more moane, than is just for a man in my case, but there is small comforte in lookinge at yᵉ backe of a white Satine bonnett for two Houres, and I maye saye as much.—Neither any cheere in Her goinge out of yᵉ Churche, & Walkinge downe yᵉ Avenue, with a Puppe by yᵉ name of Wil-liamson.

4ᵗʰ Aprile.

Because a man have a Hatt with a Brimme to it like yᵉ Poope-Decke of a Steam-Shippe, and breeches lyke yᵉ Case of an umbrella, and have loste money on Hindoo, he is not therefore in yᵉ beste Societie.—I made this observation, at yᵉ Clubbe, last nighte, in yᵉ hearinge of W^mson, who made a mightie Pretence to reade yᵉ Sp^t of yᵉ Tymes.—I doubte it was scurvie of me, but it did me muche goode.

7th Aprile.

Yᵉ manner of my meetinge with Her and fallinge in Love with Her (for yᵉ two were of one date) is thus.—I was made acquainte withe Her on a Wednesdaie, at yᵉ House of Mistresse Varick, ('twas a Reception,) but did not hear Her Name, nor She myne, by reason of yᵉ noise, and of M^rsse Varick having but lately a newe sett of Teethe, of wh. she had not yet gott, as it were, yᵉ just Pitche and accordance.—I sayde to Her that yᵉ Weather was warm for that season of yᵉ yeare.—She made answer She thought I was right, for Mr Williamson had saide yᵉ same thinge to Her not a minute past.—I tolde Her She muste not holde it originall or an Invention of W^mson, for yᵉ Speache had beene manie yeares in my Familie.—Answer was made, She wolde be muche bounden to me if I wolde maintaine yᵉ Rightes of my Familie, and lett all others from usinge of my propertie, when perceivinge Her to be of a livelie Witt, I went about to ingage her in converse, if onlie so I mighte looke into Her Eyes, wh. were of a coloure suche as I have never seene before, more like to a Pansie, or some such flower, than anything else I can compair with them. —Shortlie we grew most friendlie, so that She did aske me if I colde keepe a Secrett.—I answering I colde, She saide She was anhungered, having Shopp'd all yᵉ forenoone since Breakfast.—She pray'd me to gett Her some Foode.— What, I ask'd.—She answer'd merrilie, a Beafesteake.—I tolde Her y^t that *Confection* was not on yᵉ Side-Boarde; but I presentlie brought Her such as there was, & She beinge behinde a Screane, I stoode in yᵉ waie, so y^t none mighte see Her, & She did eate and drynke as followeth, to witt—

  iij cupps of Bouillon (wch is a Tea, or Tisane, of Beafe, made verie hott & thinne)
  iv Alberte biscuit
  ij éclairs
  i creame-cake

together with divers small cates and comfeits wh^of I know not yᵉ names.

So y^t I was grievously afeared for Her Digestion, leste it be over-tax'd. Saide this to Her, however addinge it was my Conceite, y^t by some Processe, lyke Alchemie, wh^by yᵉ baser metals are transmuted into golde, so yᵉ grosse mortall foode was on Her lippes chang'd to yᵉ fabled Nectar & Ambrosia of yᵉ Gods.—She tolde me 't was a sillie Speache, yet seam'd not ill-pleas'd withall.—She hath a verie prettie Fashion, or Tricke, of smilinge, when She hath made an end of speakinge, and layinge Her finger upon Her nether Lippe, like as She wolde bid it be stille.—After some more Talke, wh^in She show'd that Her Witt was more deepe, and Her minde more seriouslie inclin'd, than I had Thoughte from our first Jestinge, She beinge call'd to go thence, I did see Her mother, whose face I knewe, & was made sensible, y^t I had given my Hearte to yᵉ daughter of a House wh. with myne owne had longe been at grievous Feud, for yᵉ folly of oure Auncestres.—Havinge come to wh. heavie momente in my Tale, I have no Patience to write more to-nighte.

22ⁿᵈ Aprile.

I was mynded to write no more in yˢ journall, for verie Shame's sake, yᵗ I shoude so complayne, lyke a Childe, whose toie is taken fᵐ him, butt (may-happ for it is nowe yᵉ fulle Moone, & a moste greavous period for them yᵗ are Love-strucke) I am fayne, lyke yᵉ Drunkarde who maye not abstayne fᵐ his cupp, to sett me anewe to recordinge of My Dolorous mishapp.—When I sawe Her agayn, She beinge aware of my name, & of yᵉ division betwixt oure Houses, wolde have none of me, butt I wolde not be putt Off, & made bolde to ques-tion Her, why She sholde showe me suche exceedᵍ Coldness.—She answer'd 't was wel knowne what Wronge my Grandefather had done Her G.father.—I saide, She confounded me with My G.father—we were nott yᵉ same Persone, he beinge muche my Elder, & besydes Dead.—She wᵈ have it, 't was no mat-ter for jestinge.—I tolde Her I wolde be resolv'd, what grete Wronge yⁱˢ was. —Yᵉ more for to make Speache thⁿ for mine owne advertisemᵗ, for I knewe wel yᵉ whole Knaverie, wh. She rehears'd, Howe my G.father had cheated Her G.father of Landes upp yᵉ River, with more, howe my G.father had im-pounded yᵉ Cattle of Hern.—I made answer,'t was foolishnesse, in my mynde, for yᵉ iiiᵈ Generation to so quarrell over a Parsel of rascallie Landes, yᵗ had long ago beene solde for Taxes, yᵗ as to yᵉ Cowes, I wolde make them goode, & thʳ Produce & Offspringe, if it tooke yᵉ whole Washᵗⁿ Markett.—She how-ever tolde me yᵗ yᵉ Ffrenche family had yᵉ where wᵃˡ to buye what they lack'd in Butter, Beafe & Milke, and likewise in *Veale,* wh. laste I tooke muche to Hearte, wh. She seeinge, became more gracious &, on my pleadinge, accorded yᵗ I sholde have yᵉ Privilege to speake with Her when we next met.—Butt neyther then, nor at any other Tyme thᵃᶠᵗᵉʳ wolde She suffer me to visitt Her. So I was harde putt to it to compass waies of gettinge to see Her at such Houses as She mighte be att, for Routs or Feasts, or yᵉ lyke.—

But though I sawe Her manie tymes, oure converse was ever of yⁱˢ Com-plexⁿ, & yᵉ accursed G.father satt downe, and rose upp with us.—Yet colde I see by Her aspecte, yᵗ I had in some sorte Her favoure, & yᵗ I mislyk'd Her not so gretelie as She wᵈ have me thinke.—So yᵗ one daie, ('t was in Januarie, & verie colde,) I, beinge moste distrackt, saide to Her, I had tho't 'twolde pleasure Her more, to be friends w. a man, who had a knave for a G.father, yⁿ with One who had no G.father att alle, lyke Wᵐˢᵒⁿ (yᵉ Puppe).—She made answer, I was exceedinge fresshe, or some such matter. She cloath'd her thoughte in phrase more befittinge a Gentlewoman.—Att this I colde no longer contayne myself, but tolde Her roundlie, I lov'd Her, & 't was my Love made me soe unmannerlie.—And w. yⁱˢ speache I att yᵉ leaste made an End of my Uncertantie, for She bade me speake w. Her no more.—I wolde be de-termin'd, whether I was Naught to Her.—She made Answer She colde not justlie say I was Naught, seeing yᵗ whᵉᵛᵉʳ She mighte bee, I was One too manie. —I saide, 't was some Comforte, I had even a Place in Her thoughtes, were it onlie in Her disfavour.—She saide, my Solace was indeede grete, if it kept pace with yᵉ measure of Her Disfavour, for, in plain Terms, She hated me, & on her intreatinge of me to goe, I went.—Yⁱˢ happ'd att yᵉ house of Mʳˢˢ Varicke, wh. I 1ˢᵗ met Her, who (Mʳˢˢ Varicke) was for staying me, yᵗ I might eate some Ic'd Cream, butt of a Truth I was chill'd to my Taste allreadie.—

Albeit I afterwards tooke to walkinge of yᵉ Streets till near Midnight.—'Twas as I saide before in Januarie & exceedinge colde.

20ᵗʰ Maie.

How wearie is yˡˢ dulle procession of yᵉ Yeare! For it irketh my Soule yᵗ each Monthe shoude come so aptlie after yᵉ Month afore, & Nature looke so Smug, as She had done some grete thinge.—Surelie if she make no Change, she hath work'd no Miracle, for we knowe wel, what we maye look for.—Yᵉ Vine under my Window hath broughte forth Purple Blossoms, as itt hath eache Springe these xii Yeares.—I wolde have had them Redd, or Blue, or I knowe not what Coloure, for I am sicke of likinge of Purple a Dozen Springes in Order.—And wh. moste galls me is yˡˢ, I knowe how yˡˢ sadd Rounde will goe on, & Maie give Place to June, & she to July, & onlie my Hearte blossom not nor my Love growe no greener.

2ⁿᵈ June.

I and my Foolishnesse, we laye Awake last night till yᵉ Sunrise gun, wh. was Shott att 4½ o'ck, & wh. beinge hearde in yᵗ stillnesse fm. an Incredible Distance, seem'd lyke as 't were a Full Stopp, or Period putt to yˡˢ Wakinge-Dreminge, whᵃᵗ I did turne a newe Leafe in my Counsells, and after much Meditation, have commenc't a newe Chapter, wh. I hope maye leade to a better Conclusion, than them yᵗ came afore.—For I am nowe resolv'd, & havinge begunn wil carry to an Ende, yᵗ if I maie not over-come my Passion, I maye at yᵉ least over-com yᵉ Melanchollie, & Spleene, borne yᵒᶠ, & beinge a Lover, be none yᵉ lesse a Man.—To wh. Ende I have come to yˡˢ Resolution, to depart fm. yᵉ Towne, & to goe to yᵉ Countrie-House of my Frend, Will Winthrop, who has often intreated me, & has instantly urg'd, yᵗ I sholde make him a Visitt.—And I take much Shame to myselfe, yᵗ I have not given him yˡˢ Satisfaction since he was married, wh. is nowe ii Yeares.—A goode Fellowe, & I minde me a grete Burden to his Frends when he was in Love, in wh. Plight I mockt him, who am nowe, I much feare me, mockt myselfe.

3ʳᵈ June.

Pack'd my cloathes, beinge Sundaye. Yᵉ better yᵉ Daie, yᵉ better yᵉ Deede.

4ᵗʰ June.

Goe downe to Babylon to-daye.

5ᵗʰ June.

Att Babylon, att yᵉ Cottage of Will Winthrop, wh. is no Cottage, but a grete House, Red, w. Verandahs, & builded in yᵉ Fashⁿ of Her Maiestie Q. Anne.—Found a mighty Housefull of People.—Will, his Wife, a verie proper fayre Ladie, who gave me moste gracious Reception, Mʳˢˢ Smithe, yᵉ ii Gresham girles (knowne as yᵉ Titteringe Twins), Bob White, Virgina Kinge & her Mothʳ, Clarence Winthrop, & yᵉ whole Alexander Family.—A grete Gatheringe for so earlie in yᵉ Summer.—In yᵉ Afternoone play'd Lawne-Tenniss.— Had for Partner one of yᵉ Twinns, agˢᵗ Clarence Winthrop & yᵉ other Twinn, wh. by beinge Confus'd, I loste iii games.—Was voted a Duffer.—Clarence Winthrop moste unmannerlie merrie.—He call'd me yᵉ Sad-Ey'd Romeo, & lykewise cut down yᵉ Hammocke whⁿ I laye, allso tied up my Cloathes wh.

we were att Bath.—He sayde, he Chaw'd them, a moste barbarous worde for a moste barbarous Use.—Wh. we were Boyes, & he did y^{ls} thinge, I was wont to trounce him Soundlie, but nowe had to contente Myselfe w. beatinge of him iii games of Billyardes in ye Evg., & w. daringe of him to putt on ye Gloves w. me, for Funne, wh. he mighte not doe, for I coude knocke him colde.

10th June.

Beinge gon to my Roome somewhatt earlie, for I found myselfe of a peevish humour, Clarence came to me, and pray^d a few minutes' Speache.—Sayde 't was Love made him so Rude & Boysterous, he was privilie betroth'd to his Cozen, Angelica Robertes, she whose Father lives at Islipp, & colde not containe Himselfe for Joye.—I sayinge, there was a Breache in ye Familie, he made Answer, 't was true, her Father & His, beinge Cozens, did hate each other moste heartilie, butt for him he cared not for that, & for Angelica, She gave not a Continentall.—But, sayde I, Your Consideration matters mightie Little, synce ye Governours will not heare to it.—He answered 't was for that he came to me, I must be his allie, for reason of oure olde Friend^{sp}. With that I had no Hearte to heare more, he made so Light of such a Division as parted me & my Happinesse, but tolde him I was his Frend, wolde serve him when he had Neede of me, & presentlie seeing my Humour, he made excuse to goe, & left me to write downe this, sicke in Mynde, and thinkinge ever of ye Woman who wil not oute of my Thoughtes for any change of Place, neither of employe.—For indeede I doe love Her moste heartilie, so y^t my Wordes can not saye it, nor will y^{ls} Booke containe it.—So I wil even goe to Sleepe, y^t in my Dreames perchaunce my Fancie maye do my Hearte better Service.

12th June.

She is here.—What Spyte is y^{ls} of Fate & ye alter'd gods! That I, who mighte nott gett to see Her when to See was to Hope, muste nowe daylie have Her in my Sight, stucke lyke a fayre Apple under olde Tantalus his Nose.—Goinge downe to ye Hotell to-day, for to gett me some Tobackoe, was made aware y^t ye Ffrench familie had hyred one of ye Cottages round-abouts.—'T is a goodlie Dwellinge Without—Would I coude speake with as much Assurance of ye Inn-syde!

13th June.

Goinge downe to ye Hotell againe To-day for more Tobackoe, sawe ye accursed name of W^{mson} on ye Registre.—Went about to a neighboringe Farm & satt me downe behynd ye Barne, for a ½ an Houre.—Frighted ye Horned Cattle w. talkinge to My Selfe.

15th June.

I wil make an Ende to y^{ls} Businesse.—Wil make no longer Staye here.—Sawe Her to-day, driven Home fm. ye Beache, about 4½ of ye After-noone, by W^{mson} in his Dogge-Carte, wh. ye Cadde has broughten here.—Wil betake me to ye Boundlesse Weste—Not y^t I care aught for ye Boundlesse Weste, butt y^t I shal doe wel if haplie I leave my Memourie am^g ye Apaches & bringe Home my Scalpe.

16th June.

To Fyre Islande, in Winthrop's Yacht—ye Twinnes w. us, so Titteringe &

VOL. XI.—13

Choppinge Laughter, y^t 't was worse y^n a Flocke of Sandpipers.—Found a grete Concourse of people there, Her amonge them, in a Suite of blue, y^t became Her bravelie.—She swimms lyke to a Fishe, butt everie Stroke of Her white Arms (of a lovelie Roundnesse) cleft, as 't were my Hearte, rather y^n ye Water.—She bow'd to me, on goinge into ye Water, w. muche Dignitie, & agayn on Cominge out, but y^{ls} Tyme w lesse Dignitie, by reason of ye Water in Her Cloathes, & Her Haire in Her Eyes.—

17th June.

Was for goinge awaie To-morrow, but Clarence cominge againe to my Chamber, & mightilie purswadinge of me, I feare I am comitted to a verie sillie Undertakinge.—For I am promis'd to Help him secretlie to wedd his Cozen. —He wolde take no Deniall, wolde have it, his Brother car'd Naughte, 't was but ye Fighte of theyre Fathers, he was bounde it sholde be done, & 't were best I stoode his Witnesse, who was wel lyked of bothe ye Braunches of ye Family.—So 't was agree'd, y^t I shal staye Home to-morrowe fm. ye Expedition to Fyre Islande, feigning a Head-Ache, (wh. indeede I meante to do, in any Happ, for I cannot see Her againe,) & shall meet him at ye little Churche on ye Southe Roade.—He to drive to Islipp to fetch Angelica, lykewise her Witnesse, who sholde be some One of ye Girles, she hadd not yet made her Choice. —I made y^{ls} Condition, it sholde not be either of ye Twinnes.—No, nor Bothe, for that matter.—Inquiringe as to ye Clergyman, he sayde ye Dominie was allreadie Squar'd.

NEWE YORK, ye BUCKINGHAM HOTELL, 19th June.

I am come to ye laste Entrie I shall ever putt downe in ye Booke, and needes must y^t I putt it downe quicklie, for all hath Happ'd in so short a Space, y^t my Heade whirles w. thynkinge of it. Y^e after-noone of Yesterdaye, I set about Counterfeittinge of a Head-Ache, & so wel did I compasse it, y^t I verilie think one of y^e Twinnes was mynded to Stay Home & nurse me.—All havinge gone off, & Clarence on his waye to Islipp, I sett forth for y^e Churche, where arriv'd I founde it emptie, w. y^e Door open.—Went in & writh'd on y^e hard Benches a $\frac{1}{4}$ of an Houre, when, hearinge a Sounde, I look'd up & saw standinge in y^e Door-waye, Katherine Ffrench.—She seem'd muche astonished, saying You Here! or y^e lyke.—I made Answer & sayde y^t though my Familie were greate Sinners, yet had they never been Excommunicate by y^e Churche. —She sayde, they colde not Putt Out what never was in.—While I was bethynkinge me wh. I mighte answer to y^{ls}, she went on, sayinge I must excuse Her, She wolde goe upp in ye Organ-Lofte.—I enquiring what for? She sayde to practice on ye Organ. She turn'd verie Redd, of a warm Coloure, as She sayde this.—I ask'd Do you come hither often? She replyinge Yes, I enquir'd how ye Organ lyked Her.—She sayde Right well, when I made question more curiously (for She grew more Redd eache moment) how was ye Action? ye Tone? how manie Stopps? Wh^{at} She growinge gretelie Confus'd, I led Her into ye Churche, & show'd Her y^t there was no Organ, ye Choire beinge indeede a Band, of i Tuninge-Forke, i Kitt, & i Horse-Fiddle.—At this She fell to Smilinge & Blushinge att one Tyme.—She perceiv'd our Errandes were ye Same, & crav'd Pardon for Her Fibb.—I tolde Her, If She came Thither to be Witness at her Frend's Weddinge, 'twas no greate Fibb, 'twolde indeede be Practice for Her. —This havinge a rude Sound, I added I thankt y[e] Starrs y[t] had bro't us Together. She sayde if y[e] Starrs appoint'd us to meete no oftener y[n] this Couple shoude be Wedded, She was wel content. This cominge on me lyke a last Buffett of Fate, that She shoude so despitefully intreate me, I was suddenlie Seized with so Sorrie a Humour, & withal so angrie, y[t] I colde scarce Containe myselfe, but went & Sat downe near y[e] Doore, lookinge out till Clarence shd. come w. his Bride. —Looking over my Sholder, I sawe y[t] She wente fm. Windowe to Windowe within, Pluckinge y[e] Blossoms fm. y[e] Vines, & settinge them in her Girdle. —She seem'd most tall and faire, & swete to look uponn, & itt Anger'd me ye More. —Meanwhiles, She discours'd pleasantlie, asking me manie questions, to the wh. I gave but shorte and churlish answers. She ask'd Did I nott Knowe Angelica Roberts was Her best Frend? How longe had I knowne of ye Betrothal? Did I thinke 'twolde knitt ye Housé together, & Was it not Sad to see a Familie thus Divided? —I answer'd Her, I wd. not robb a Man of ye precious Righte to Quarrell with his Relations. —And then, with meditatinge on ye goode Lucke of Clarence, & my owne harde Case, I had suche a sudden Rage of peevishness y[t] I knewe scarcelie what I did. —Soe when she ask'd me merrilie why I turn'd my Backe on Her, I made Reply I had turn'd my Backe on muche Follie. — Wh. was no sooner oute of my Mouthe than I was mightilie Sorrie for it, and turninge aboute, I perceiv'd She was in Teares & weepinge bitterlie. Wh[at] my Hearte wolde holde no More, & I rose upp & tooke Her in my arms & Kiss'd & Comforted Her, She making no Denyal, but seeminge greatlie to Neede such Solace, wh. I was not Loathe to give Her. —Whiles we were at This, onlie She had gott to Smilinge, & to sayinge of Things which even y[is] paper shal not knowe, came in y[e] Dominie, sayinge He judg'd We were the Couple he came to Wed. —With him y[e] Sexton & y[e] Sexton's Wife. —My swete Kate, alle as rosey as Venus's Nape, was for Denyinge of y[is], butt I wolde not have it, & sayde Yes. —She remonstrating w. me, privilie, I tolde Her She must not make me Out a Liar, y[t] to Deceave y[e] Man of God were a greavous Sinn, y[t] I had gott Her nowe, & wd. not lett her Slipp from me, & did soe Talke Her Downe, & w. such Strengthe of joie, y[t] allmost before She knewe it, we Stoode upp, & were Wed, w. a Ringe (tho' She Knewe it nott) wh. belong'd to My G. father. (Him y[t] Cheated Her[n].)—

Wh. was no sooner done, than in came Clarence & Angelica, & were Wedded in theyre Turn. —The Clergyman greatelie surprised, but more att y[e] Largeness of his Fee.

This Businesse being Ended, we fled by y[e] Trayne of $4\frac{1}{2}$ o'cke, to y[is] Place, where we wait till y[e] Bloode of all y[e] Ffrenches have Tyme to coole downe, for y[e] wise Mann who meeteth his Mother in Lawe y[e] 1st tyme, wil meete her when she is Milde. —

And so I close y[is] Journall, wh., tho' for y[e] moste Parte 'tis but a peevish Scrawle, hath one Page of Golde, wh[on] I have writt y[e] laste strange Happ wh[by] I have layd Williamson by y[e] Heeles & found me y[e] sweetest Wife y[t] ever

.　　　.　　　.

stopp'd a man's Mouthe w. kisses for writing of Her Prayses.

LES MORTS VONT VITE.

*L*ES *morts vont vite!* Ay, for a little space
  We miss and mourn them, fallen from their place;
  To take our portion in their rest are fain;
  But by-and-by, having wept, press on again,
Perchance to win their laurels in the race.

What man would find the old in the new love's face?
Seek on the fresher lips the old kisses' trace?
  For withered roses newer blooms disdain?
           Les morts vont vite!

But when disease brings thee in piteous case,
Thou shalt thy dead recall, and thy ill grace
  To them for whom remembrance plead in vain.
  Then, shuddering, think, while thy bed-fellow Pain
Clasps thee with arms that cling like Death's embrace:
           Les morts vont vite!

FOR AN OLD POET.

*W*HEN he is old and past all singing,
  Grant, kindly Time, that he may hear
The rhythm through joyous Nature ringing,
  Uncaught by any duller ear.

Grant that, in memory's deeps still cherished,
  Once more may murmur low to him
The winds that sung in years long perished,
  Lit by the suns of days grown dim.

Grant that the hours when first he listened
  To bird-songs manhood may not know,
In fields whose dew for lovers glistened,
  May come back to him ere he go.

Grant only this, O Time most kindly,
  That he may hear the song you sung
When love was new—and, hearkening blindly,
  Feign his o'er-wearied spirit young.

With sound of rivers singing round him,
  On waves that long since flowed away,
Oh, leave him, Time, where first Love found him,
  Dreaming To-morrow in To-day!

1887.

Poultney Bigelow.

BORN in New York, N. Y., 1855.

EDUCATION OF A YOUNG PRINCE.

[*The German Emperor and his Eastern Neighbors.* 1892.]

IN the topmost story of Frederick the Great's "New Palace," near Potsdam, in what we may vulgarly term the attic, were the quarters occupied by the preceptors of the then Prince William, and his brother the sailor, Prince Henry. To one accustomed to the luxury of American and English houses, the bareness, not to say bleakness, of the upper story of this famous palace was striking, particularly so in contrast to the innumerable gorgeous flunkies who guarded the state saloons below. But it was ample in space and a foretaste of the barrack life that should seem comfort to a Hohenzollern. In wet weather the great attic made a capital play-ground, and many an Imperial pane of glass was smashed by the blundering aim of one of the youngsters. In such romps the Princes entered heart and soul, giving and taking like the manly little fellows that they were. The good Dr. Hinzpeter would repeatedly whisper to me to take care and not hurt the Prince's left arm, a warning I was apt to forget, particularly with one who was so clever with his right.

As to the Emperor's imperfect arm, it is extraordinary that the life which has largely left it should have apparently been utilized in the strengthening of his right. Any one who has shaken it feels as though Goetz von Berlichingen had given him the grip. As a fencer, it was to be expected that he should develop the proficiency that characterized him at Bonn, but it was little thought that he would have the patience and energy requisite to becoming an expert shot, a good swimmer, and a capital oar. In the saddle he manages to hold his reins with his left, in order to have his sword-arm free, and I have many times seen him ride across country taking obstacles which some of his officers have refused. And the moral courage, the persistency, the sense of duty, the pluck, which overcame the impediments to physical development, were constantly at work in other parts of his education.

In the park of Sans Souci, near the Palace, were planted the masts and rigging of a ship, where Prince Henry received practical instruction in sailoring, and which became a favorite romping-place. Netting was stretched over the lower space, and we were occasionally turned loose to scramble about the rigging, some of us playing at pirates making chase after a crew that had taken refuge aloft. Or, what was better still, we sometimes took a cruise about the neighboring lakes on the miniature frigate, a craft that looks very portentous at a distance, with its scowling ports and man-o'-war yards, but in reality, when on board, seems little larger than a good-sized ship's cutter. The cruise on the frigate was always considered the greatest treat of all, and no doubt to the pleasure derived then is due the fact that the Emperor to-day is a devoted patron of yachting, and sails his toy frigate on the Havel whenever opportunity offers.

When the day's romp was over, we had tea before going home, always out-of-doors in fair weather. The late Emperor Frederick and his devoted wife never failed to appear on these occasions, to say a few words to each of us, asking after our families, or about the sports of the day. The Empress in particular, then Crown Princess, always examined our food to see•that it was wholesome, and saw that her little sons and daughters, as well as their guests, had their napkins properly tucked beneath their chins. The food was, it is needless to say, of the plainest and most wholesome,—bread or toast, fresh milk from the Crown Prince's model farm at Bornstedt, and some simple bread-cake, with big raisins in it, perhaps. When the Crown Princess and her husband made their appearance, no face lighted up with more pleasure than that of Prince William, for the relation of parent and child could not be conceived in more happy form than in those days in the park of Sans Souci. I remember once—it was at tea on the steam-yacht, some anniversary, I believe—Prince William whispered to me a fact in which he took enormous pride, that the cake had been made by his mother.

Of course, at these romps, the idea of expecting etiquette to be observed would have been absurd ; Dr. Hinzpeter would have none of it, the Royal parents held it in horror, and no one despised servility more than their eldest son.

Occasionally there came into these hilarious play-ground meetings some youngster, no doubt the son of a highly-placed official, who had been carefully drilled at home to show proper deference in the presence of the blood Royal. Such a poor wretch lived in momentary dread of violating some imaginary rule, and moved about morbidly conscious of his courtly role. Prince William, celebrated as he justly is for tact, could with difficulty conceal his contempt for the little flunkies that now and then were forced upon him.

Not that he ridiculed their shyness ; on the contrary, it was he who invariably set his new arrivals at their ease, discovered their leading tastes and suggested the sport that would please the larger number. And when the sport was once under way it would have been a keen observer indeed who could have said that either Prince relied upon anything beyond his own head and hands to make the day successful. It was my fortune, as an American, to be credited with an intimate acquaintance with the red savages of the Wild West, and this reputation I could in no way shake off, in spite of the fact that at that time I had not even seen one. In consequence of this alleged knowledge, I was frequently called upon to give details as to Indian warfare which I should deeply regret to see reproduced. Prince William knew Cooper from beginning to end, and, for that matter, I was not far behind him, so that our Indian studies usually resolved themselves into impersonating some leather-stocking heroes, arming ourselves as fantastically as possible, and then crawling flat on our stomachs through the underbush, for the purpose of capturing some other party impersonating either a hostile tribe or a party of pale-faces.

But I have said enough to illustrate his character as a plucky, hearty, unaffected lad, affectionate towards his parents, and full of consideration for the youngsters of his own age with whom he was brought into contact. In 1874 Prince William and his brother went to a common public school, with uncommonly hard benches, amidst a lot of the odds and ends of German social life invariably to be found in the national Gymnasium. Let no one imagine this to be like attending Eton, where the expensive life limits the pupils to sons of comparatively rich people, and where an English prince can pass his time in luxury and comparative idleness. The schools of Germany are as inexorable in their requirements as any other branch of its public service, and when Prince William took his seat amidst the German burghers' children at the public school it was with the understanding that he should submit to the same discipline as the rest, and receive his graduating diploma only upon the conscientious fulfilment of the prescribed course.

Dr. Hinzpeter selected his school after having visited the head masters of many others, and found most of them completely unnerved at the idea of having a live prince amongst them. Cassel is about eight hours by rail from Berlin, a distance that meant a great deal to the Princes and their parents. The Court was incensed at the idea of the heir to the throne consorting with ordinary boys ; Dr. Hinzpeter was accused of introducing revolutionary ideas into the educational curriculum of the Hohenzollerns ; the old Emperor William did not disguise his displeasure, and even the parents gave little more encouragement than their bare consent that the experiment should be tried. It was a bold game that Dr. Hinzpeter was playing; no Royal prince had ever been educated in a popular atmosphere, and nobody at Court wished him well in the undertaking. His reputation was at stake, for while in the event of failure every voice would cry out, " I told you so," even successfully carried out there would be little to show for his labor. The tutor held that for once in a lifetime, at least, a prince should feel what his subjects do; that he should share the schoolboy interests of the every-day German and absorb the set of ideas that may enable him to strike the popular keynote when he sits upon the throne. For three years Prince William sat on the Cassel benches, *i.e.*, until he successfully passed his final examination and was declared ripe for matriculation at the University.

These three years were years of torture to the tutor. He lived with them, but could not actively assist their studies, for that would have been unfair to the other boys. Teachers would rush to him in desperation to report this and that of their Royal pupil—what should they do? They dared not reprimand the Lord's anointed ! Hinzpeter had to strengthen them, to encourage the Prince to more complete application. Those were days of tension when any moment might destroy forever the result hoped for. The Princes went to school and returned unattended. What if something happened to them on the way?—a schoolboy quarrel, a blow, an injury?—even so small a thing as that would have called the boys back to Berlin. What if a teacher had lost his head and a prince have raised rebellion in the school-room ? None of these things happened, but nothing seemed more likely to those who did not understand the precocious nature of Prince William's character and the devotion with which he pursued that which he considered his duty. And what this amounted to may be measured by the fact that before entering upon his three years' school course he had to pass an examination far beyond that required for admission to Oxford or Cambridge, and that parallel to his daily tasks on the Gymnasium benches were a series of special labors peculiar to the education of one soon destined to play a conspicuous part at a military Court—possibly to be its leader.

Armistead Churchill Gordon.

BORN in Albemarle Co., Va., 1855.

EBO.

[Befo' de War. Echoes in Negro Dialect. By A. C. Gordon and T. N. Page. 1888.]

ALL o' dese here doin's
　Don't suit me;
Ise an ole-time nigger—
　Don't you see?

Dis here eddication's
　Humbug, sho';
It's done played de devil
　Wid Ebo.

Somewhar 'bout lars' summer,
　Dicey she
Tuk 'n' struck a notion—
　Don't you see?

Says she: "Ise been thinkin'."
　An' I says:
"What *you* done thunk, honey?"
　Says she: "Yes,

"I'se been thinkin' mons'ous
　'Bout Ebo;
He's fo'teen year ole now—
　Don't you know?"

S'I: "Ole 'oman, you is
　Right, I 'spec';
Dar's fo'teen—he kim fus'—
　Dat's kerrec'!"

Says she: "He's a-growin'
　Up a fool;
An' Ise gwine ter sen' him
　Ter de school."

Bein's how it looked like
　She was bent
On de projick, Ebo
　Tuk 'n' went.

An' sence dat lars' summer—
　Don't you see?—

Dat 'ar boy have p'int'ly
　Outdone me!

Whe-ew! de norrations,
　Dem o' his'n!
Umph! I 'busses laughin'
　Jes' ter lissen!

What you think dat Ebo
　Come tell me?
Dat all dis here y'arth here—
　Flat, you see—

Dat it's roun', an' rolls jes'
　Like a ball!
"Ebo, dat's a lie," I
　Says, "dat's all!

"Don't you see yer mammy,
　Evvy night,
Set de water-piggin
　Out o' sight

"Ob you chillun, up dar
　On de shelf?—
Now, Mars' Spellin'-booker,
　'Splain yerself—

"Sunrise, dat 'ar water's
　In dar still;
Ef de y'arth turned over,
　It 'ud spill!"

But he keeps resistin'
　It are so—
Eddication's done gone
　Sp'ilt Ebo.

He's forever tellin'
　Some sich lie;
He's gwi' fine out better
　By-um-by.

Ef Ebo keeps l'arnin'
  At dat school,
Nex' thing, he'll be provin'
  Ise a fool !

I are p'int'ly gwine ter
  Take Ebo
Way f'om dat ar school-'ouse,
  Sartin sho' !

VIRGINIA CREEPERS.

1868.

OLE Mistis offen afo' she died—
  You know how she used ter set
Out dar on de Gre't House porch, o'
  days ;
  I thinks I sees her yet—
Offen she said : " *You's* good enough—
  But Anniky's pizen mean ;
An' dem chillun o' her'n an' yourn's de
  scruff
  O' de y'arth ! " Now, y'all done seen
How what she tole me is done come
  true :
I always knowed it, and said so, too.

What is dat sass you's up ter, now ?
  What does you want ter know?
Ef you says one word 'gin ole Mistis, boy,
  I'll smack you, sartin sho'!
"How come she go call you scruff ?"
  Jes dis :
  Y'all was de lazies' crew
Dat de Lord ever made, in doin' de work
  Dat she wanted you ter do ;
"Ferginyer Creepers ! " she used ter say,
When she seen you a-pokin' along all
  day.

An' now sence de freedom come, it's
  wus'
  Dan ever it was afo';
You stretches out dar in de sun, an'
  sleeps
  An' sleeps foreber mo'.
Ef you's got a rag ter yer back, somehow
  You thinks dat dat's enough.
An', boy, dat's de reason o' how come
  why
  Ole Mistis called you scruff.
You lets me slave fur de grub you eat;
You sleeps while I gethers de bread an'
  meat.

I'm gittin' w'ared out wid dis here thing
  O' t'ilin' fur all o' you;
Sometimes I wishes de ole slave ways
  Was back fur a week or two.
"How come?" Jes dis: ter make you
  work!
De niggers never did lay
Out on a bench in de sunshine den,
  An' sun deyselves all day.
"Ferginyer Creepers" was bad, at fus';
"Ferginyer Sleepers " is p'int'ly wus'!

Maud Howe Elliott.

BORN in Boston, Mass., 1855.

OUT OF THE SEA.

[*The San Rosario Ranch.* 1884.]

THE last day of their visit had come, and the morrow would see them on
  their way back to San Rosario. Millicent and Barbara had prolonged
their sea dip beyond their usual wont. Never before had the water seemed so

bracing and delicious. As there were twenty or thirty bathers to keep her company, Millicent lingered among the breakers, while Barbara regained the shore. She swam leisurely about, displacing the clear water with her white arms and pretty, small feet. She suddenly became aware that a swimmer was gaining on her from behind, and her stroke instinctively quickened. Millicent swam as only the women of Venice can swim; and the race between her and her unseen pursuer bade fair to be hotly contested. With head high lifted from the waves which circled caressingly about the smooth round throat, knotting the tendril curls at the nape of the neck, the girl kept steadily on her course without turning her head to see who might be so audacious as to follow her. Strong as were her strokes, she slowly lost ground; and finally the water about her rippled with the strokes of the man who was gaining. Soon he had caught up with her, and side by side they swam for a space. Then the victor spoke in a voice well known to her, and the girl answered him with a laugh which rang out fresh and crisp as the sound of the wavelets. Then she turned her head and looked full at him as he moved by her side, strong and graceful as a young merman.

"So, my nymph, you are at home in Father Neptune's arms as well as in the embrace of the great tree. Which is your native element, earth, air, or water?"

"I am amphibious."

"And which of your three elemental homes do you like the best?"

"When I am dancing, the air; when I am walking, dear mother earth; and when I swim, the sea."

"When I paint you, it will be as I see you now, triumphing over the waves as our great mother, Aphrodite, triumphed over them before you."

"That compliment would go to my head, were it not mixed with so much water."

Then they both laughed, because the sky was sapphire clear and the sea beryl green; because the golden sun warmed them with its kind rays; because each was fair and good to look upon; because, when they were together, winds blew more softly, and sky and sea took on a more tender hue where they melted at the horizon into one ineffable kiss. A pair of white-winged gulls swept above them, shrieking their love-notes hoarsely, while the white-armed girl and the strong-limbed man breasted the waves together, side by side. Though lapped by the cool water, Graham felt the warm influence which folded about him like a cloak in Millicent's presence. When she grew tired the girl turned upon her side and floated, while Graham swam about her in little circles, first moving like a shark on one side, with long, far-reaching strokes, then swimming upon his back, and finally beneath the waves, looking always at her face seen dimly through the dark-green water.

After a space Millicent looked about to find herself alone, far from the shore with its group of bathers. At first she fancied that her companion must be swimming below the water as he had done before; but, as the slow-passing seconds went by, she realized that some ill must have befallen him. Stretching her arms above her head, she dived straight and swift through the clear water towards the pebbled bottom of the ocean shining through the pellucid waters. In that dim under-current she touched him, stiff and cold, rising toward the surface, but through no effort of his own helpless limbs. In that terrified heart-beat of time she saw his face set and white, with horror-stricken eyes widely strained apart. Into them she looked, her own firing with hope and courage, and giving a mute promise of rescue. She seized his rigid arm with her strong, small hands, and they rose together to the surface. The man was as if paralyzed; and the girl for an instant tried to support him, but, feeling such a strain would soon out-wear her half-spent strength, she cried :

"Put your hand on my shoulder—so, and I will swim below you." Her voice was hoarse and shrill as that of the screaming sea-gulls. He could not speak, but looked toward the shore as if he would have her save herself and abandon him to his fate.

"No, no !" she cried, "I *will* save you"; and placing his hands on her shoulders, struck out bravely toward the shore. To reach it seemed at first an easy thing, but the struggle proved a terrible one, cruelly unequal, between the girl's small strength, with the burden now added to her own weight, and the waves grown hungry for human prey. Their babbling music now was changed to Millicent's ears, and they clamored greedily for her life, for that other life which she was striving to snatch from their cruel embrace. Again and again the man would loosen his hold. She could not save him: why should she die too, she was so young, so fair! This he tried to tell her in gasping accents, but she only gripped his hand more firmly and placed it as before. They should both live or die. Fate, which had been so cruel to her, had cast their lots together for that day at least; and death seemed sweeter by his side than life without him. Her brave spirit fainted not, though her labored strokes grew slower and feebler. Then she gave one great cry for help to those who were so near them, and yet so unconscious of their danger. She heard their voices plainly,—the mothers talking to romping children, whose ringing laughter mocked her agony. Was it their death-knell, this sound of sweet child-voices that drowned her frenzied cry and filled the ears of the strong men and women, keeping out the fainting accents which pleaded for his life and her own? Once again, and this time with a thrilling vibration of despair, the woman's voice rang out across the waves. It was freighted with her last hope; it was the latest sound her gasping lungs could utter. Could love and hope of life outshriek the murmur of the waves, the shrill note of the sca-mews, the noisy prattle of the infants? The man, long since despairing, groaned: it seemed murder to him that his helpless weight should drag down the fair, brave young creature to her grave; his death agony was made more bitter by the thought. The girl's determination never wavered, and her little strength was not wasted in a longer struggle; she managed to keep his face above the waves, but now only held her own, and had ceased to make the slightest progress. She could now no longer see the bathers. Had her cry been heard? O waves! be merciful and still your clamor! White-winged partners, cry no more your mocking love-notes! Sweet mothers, list no longer to your children's laughter, for there is other sound which must reach your fond ears and chill your warm hearts with horror! For a moment there grew a great silence as of listening, and then over the water came answering cries

of women agonized with sympathy, came the hearty voices of strong men saying, "Keep up, keep up! for help is coming, it is close beside you." Ah,
God! it is in time, for the two white faces, lying so close in the green waters,
have but just vanished from sight; they still shine through the waves, but a
little space beneath the surface. Strong helping arms raise the nerveless
bodies from the waves that murmur sullenly, bear them safely to the shore
with its shining white sands, and, last, gently loose the maiden's white hands,
clinging still, though all unconsciously, to the man whose life she has saved.
Weeping women gather about them, lying there so still and fair upon the
white beach; frightened children look curiously at the half-drowned figures
of the man and the woman. Still are they man and woman, and not yet fallen
to that terrible neuter of death, wherein age and sex are not, where serf and
queen are equals.

Elwyn Alfred Barron.

BORN in Nashville, Tenn., 1855.

CLOSING SCENE OF "THE VIKING."

[*The Viking.* 1888.]

ACT IV. SCENE.—*An interior, level with the ground. Arched window above steps,
left, through which* FENJA *views a portion of the battle. Several women up stage,*
GURTH *sits one side disconsolately leaning on his harp.* EYVIND *moves about, up-
braiding himself for the infirmities of age.*

EYSA [*entering hurriedly*]. Oh, my darling lady.   [*Embracing.*]
  FENJA.   Sweet sister! You weep!
What evil fortune do these tears forerun?
  EYSA. We are undone by these most savage Danes,
'Fore whom our vikings disappear as grass
Before the browsing herd. They're all in flight,
And as they run the foe smites them with death.
  FENJA [*aside*]. Horrible! And my accusing terror
Lays the blame upon my wilful soul.
  EYVIND [*at window*].   Gods!
It is a fearful thing to see.
  EYSA [*to* FENJA].   Go look,
If you would have your eyes like mine, weep blood!
  FENJA. Though nature sicken at the sight, I'll look.
  EYVIND [*descending*]. Nay, do not so.
  FENJA.   Deny me not. My will
Is stronger than my fears. Lend me your hand.

[*Takes* EYVIND'S *hand and mounts steps to window.* EYVIND *stands beside her.* FENJA
looks a moment in silence.]

  EYSA. This day fills up the woe of Norway quite.
Would I were underneath their rushing feet,
If so I might find Thord!

EYVIND [*to* FENJA].   You shake with fear.
I pray you be advised; there's danger there.
Descend into the room.
  FENJA [*looking out*]. My veins are chilled
With the cold horror of the bloody scene.
Nor can my startled eyes give shape to men,
Massed like some writhing monster self-destroyed!
I know not which are friends, so close impact
Are slayers and the slain. There is a break!
The moving bulk has stopped. Those in retreat
Have turned to fight as though they do despair
Of safe escape, and mean to sell their lives
At dearest price. They gain some backward way!
But now they're forced again! I see the plume
My brother wears. 'Tis he! he strives to check
The tide of fell disaster. Ne'er till now
Have I beheld him kingly; but he towers
Majestic where he fights. Oh, gods, what now!
One comes against him that I know. Yes, 'tis—
'Tis Hafthor's self encounters him full tide!
Such stroke of swords! I am afraid to look,
But dare not else. So noble both appear,
And yet so deadly fearful, friend and foe
Stand locked from action, wondering to see
Their mighty leaders so engaged! Oh, gods!
Is Hafthor fallen so? He's up again
And lays such rapid blows his shining sword
Is like a halo in the sun. Look now!
My brother yields, his strength declines, his sword
Strikes heavily and slow; he stumbles, falls.
Oh, spare him, Hafthor! put him not to death!
He holds his sword aloft! The gods be thanked,
He lets my brother live! They bind him fast;
And over all there is a sudden hush,—
A deathlike stillness, as the fight were done.
But there's old Swend, who was my purchased lord,
Steps forth and fits an arrow to his bow.
[*Turning.*] Eysa, mount with me; there is no terror now.
Peace has come. [*Cries out and falls.*] 'Twas Swend!

[FENJA *falls into the arms of* EYVIND, *who takes in his hands the shaft of an arrow
snatched from her breast.* FENJA *is borne to couch,* EYSA *and the women gathering
around her.*]
  EYSA.   In holy ruth
Inform me what has chanced! Darling Fenja!
If she be in swoon— What! Look you! She bleeds!
Oh! Came that arrow from her breast? Sweet girl!

     [EYSA *kneels down by* FENJA.]
  EYVIND. Speak to me, Fenja, for I quake to see
The lily wonder of your skin so stained;
You are not but a little hurt? No worse?
  FENJA. I think it touched the core of life! Ah, me!
I did not hope to die; but death were good

Did it withhold till I might speak with him,
And feel his lips—his look—his touch——
 Eyvind.   She faints.
Guard her full tenderly. Stanch close the wound.
I'll look beyond for medicines.   [*Exit, left.*]
 Eysa.   Dear friend,
Most darling lady, look not so composed,
The very counterpart of what we fear.
There is no tremor of her heart. I doubt
If any wistful spark of life remain. [*Bows, weeping.*]

[*The women surround, concealing couch. Enter* Hafthor *with drawn sword, followed by* Eric, *guarding* Harold *bound,* Thord, *and several others.* Hafthor *goes to throne chair, which he mounts, smiting the top with his sword.*]
 Hafthor. In Denmark's name, and for great Denmark's king,
I seize on Norway as the prize of arms.
And, for I know him faithful, capable,
I name, till such good time as Denmark speaks,
Young Thord of Norway to be Norway's jarl.
Kneel you, and you who late were Norway's king.

[*They kneel.* Hafthor *touches sword to the head of* Harold, *then to* Thord's.]
 Hafthor. Thus passes majesty from one to one
As lightly as we breathe a sigh. Arise!
 Fenja. Hafthor!
 Hafthor.   Who calls so faintly on my name?

[*The women move apart, revealing couch and* Eysa *kneeling beside* Fenja.]
 Fenja. Hafthor!
 Hafthor.   Gods! Am I turned to ice within,
That I am struck so cold at heart?
 Fenja.   Hafthor!

[Eysa *rises, and* Hafthor *hastens to take place, kneeling beside* Fenja. Eysa *goes tearfully to* Thord, *and flings herself upon his breast.* Harold *comes quickly and takes place behind couch.*]
 Hafthor. Most precious to my heart, how came this hurt?
What cruel fortune touched you thus? You smile!
Then may my soul drink hope from your wreathed lips.
 Fenja. I did but wait your coming that my life
Might leap into our parting kiss. Your lips.

    [Hafthor *kisses her.* Eyvind *reënters.*]
 Harold. My little sister, speak to me. [Eric *cuts his cords.*]
 Fenja.   That voice—
More tender than it ever spoke. Good-night,—

    [*Giving her hand to* Harold.]
For there is darkness round about me now.
Hafthor, Harold, lead me forth.

[*She dies.* Hafthor *and* Harold *kneel on either side, each holding one of her hands.*]
 Harold [*after a pause*]. She is dead.

[Hafthor *kisses her brow and rises.* Harold *continues kneeling.* Eyvind, *showing grief and as if sorely stricken, comes forward and takes the place vacated by* Hafthor.]
 Hafthor [*aside*]. Shall I, who conquered Norway for her sake,
Now live without her? Yet I may not yield

To self-inflicted death without some shame.
[*Suddenly.*]   Ay! there's a way.   [*To* HAROLD.]   You need not be a slave,
The sport and plaything of a foreign king,—
For we were friends in youth—   Nay, truth to say,
For that I loved your sister,—ah, how well!—
I would not have it so.   Take chance with sword
To gain the liberty you crave.
  HAROLD.   How so ?
  HAFTHOR.   We two will fight in equal combat here;
And if the god of fortune smile on you,
Upon my troth you shall be free to go
Whither your humbled hopes may lead.
  HAROLD.   It is a noble offer.   Let my sword
Speak better than my tongue my thanks.   My sword!

[THORD *hands his sword to* HAROLD. HAFTHOR *and* HAROLD *take position.* THORD *and*
ERIC *stand near.* EYSA *slips around back of couch, kisses* FENJA, *and then watches to
see the combat.* EYVIND *remains bowed, paying no heed.* GURTH *takes place near
front with harp in front of him. After a pass or two,* HAFTHOR *lets fall his guard
just as* HAROLD *makes a thrust, receiving* HAROLD'S *sword in his breast.*]

  THORD [*starting forward*].   That was an unresisted stroke.
  HAFTHOR [*smiling*].   Well struck.
Your arm has strength.
  HAROLD.   I understand you now.
You tricked me to your death.   It was not just.

[THORD *half supports* HAFTHOR, *who wavers, but remains standing.* GURTH *half unconsciously touches his harp, playing.* EYVIND, *dumfounded, arises and goes back of
couch.*]

  HAFTHOR.   You scorned to give her to me when glad life
Was sportive in her dimpled cheeks; but now
Amend the wrong, and I will happier die
Than ever in most joyous hour I lived.

[*Struggles an instant, then clasps his hand to his side and recovers.*]

My tawny ship lies there among the fleet,
A golden dragon at her head.   She came,
My father told me, from the unknown sea,
Full-sailed to court the breeze, and yet unmanned;
Her spacious deck uncumbered, and her hold
Unlined with trace of any former life.
He first beheld her in the summer light
That marked the mid-day calm,—the sea serene
As face of sleeping pool; yet on she moved,
A thing of beauty and of life.   A space,
And from the prow there seemed to rise a flame
That spread its arms and caught the sails and mast,
And wrapped the vessel in a yellow cloak.
Whereat my father sighed that craft so fair
Should burn, thinking it the funeral bed
Of some departed king.   But, as he gazed,
The yellow flame, as though an orb of light,
Rolled from the ship into a ball of fire
That fled along the surface of the sea;
Then, cleft in twain, it rose into the sky,

As 'twere two images, a man and maid,
And vanished where the overhanging blue
Shuts in the fields of Asgard.   All amazed,
My father turned from looking, and behold!
The ship lay moored before him.   Such the tale.
I think I read the omen in my fate;
And if I lie with this fair hapless maid
Upon the mystic deck, my ship again
Will sail into the unknown waiting sea,
Where our two souls entwining will ascend
Into the region of the gods.   Do this;
Let our asundered lives unite in death,
And all will be forgiven.   [*Dies.*]

Bayard Tuckerman.

Born in New York, N. Y., 1855.

LAFAYETTE.

[*Life of General Lafayette.* 1889.]

THE career and character of General Lafayette have been too often judged
by isolated periods of his life. Americans, with thoughts of his services
to them in mind, have been inclined to exaggerate his abilities and pass over
his shortcomings. English Tory writers with difficulty have found terms
sufficiently severe for the commander of the National Guard of 1789. In
France, opinions are even yet colored by party feeling.

The claims of Lafayette to the respect and admiration of posterity do not
rest upon his abilities as a soldier or a statesman, but rather upon his character as a philanthropist. Considering the prominence of the part which he
played during fifty-five years of extraordinary political commotions, he never
gave evidence of more than good abilities. He had been a brave and faithful
officer; but his merits as a soldier lay less in his military talents than in the
affection and confidence which his character inspired among his troops. As
a statesman, his mistakes have been pointed out in these volumes. The undue confidence in human nature which made him give loose rein to the inexperienced aspirations of a people unaccustomed to self-government; the lack
of penetration, which, seeing the misgovernment of the few, could not foresee
the misgovernment of the many ; the imprudent enthusiasm, which, in pursuit of an abstract good, overlooked the circumstances which made its immediate attainment undesirable,—all these were serious failings in a man of such
power and influence.

It is in the force, the nobility, and the unselfishness of his character, in the
elevation, purity, and constancy of his moral nature, that we must look for
the qualities which enabled him to accomplish so much. It was not in the

carefully measured value of his services to America that lay his claim to her gratitude; it was in the spirit of self-sacrifice, in the example set, in the generous adoption of a rightful, though probably unsuccessful, cause. When the States-General met in 1789, it was the well-known unselfishness, patriotism, and honesty of the youthful general that immediately made him the repository of such immense power. It was the constant determination, at any sacrifice, to remain faithful to principles eternally right, however temporarily discredited, that made him the rallying-point of the friends of political liberty through the despotism of the Empire and the grasping tyranny of the Restoration, and in 1830 gave him the opportunity to set his country again on the path to freedom.

The remarkable consistency of Lafayette's political career was an essential result of his character. He remained the man of 1789 to the day of his death. Offers of power from the Jacobins could not attract him to their illegal rule. A return to France from the exile in Belgium was a bribe offered in vain by the Directory. The reaction toward despotism caused by the excesses of the Revolution left Lafayette still cherishing a rational liberty at Lagrange. The nobility and public men of France waited and bowed at Napoleon's court, deserted him for Louis XVIII., returned to their former master in 1815, only to turn against him in the hour of adversity and to seek again the favors of the Bourbon king by servility and self-abasement. Of all this Lafayette made no part. He waited till 1830 and found a reward and a justification.

The faults of Lafayette's character grew out of its virtues. The enthusiasm was too impulsive, the confidence in others too undiscriminating, the desire to do good too little modified by prudence. Yet had he not been enthusiastic, confident, and benevolent he would never have taken up the cause of liberty in the shadow of the old French monarchy. Other weaknesses, prominent in his youth, resulted from that age and passed away with it. The love of popularity, which Jefferson had characterized as a "canine appetite," ceased to influence him when the vicissitudes of the Revolution had taught him the value of popular applause. The "delicious smile of the multitude," seductive to the man of thirty, had lost its charm for the man of forty. The fancy for outward marks of greatness—titles and decorations—had so completely disappeared with experience of life, that Napoleon's offer of the highest dignities of the Legion of Honor did not amount to a temptation.

The fault to be found with Lafayette's political views is that they were too advanced for his country. Liberty had appealed to his ardent imagination as the remedy for the terrible public evils which had grown up under a despotic system. His visit to America had furnished so extraordinary a contrast to the miserable state of France, that he was naturally led to believe that his countrymen would be equally happy under similar political conditions. Some of these conditions have since been attained by the French and have borne the hoped-for fruit. But the mistake made by Lafayette, as by the best of his countrymen, was in the attempt to confer such benefits before they could be understood or enjoyed by the people. Throughout his life, he proclaimed order and respect for the law as the essential accompaniment of liberty. But his countrymen had much to suffer before they could appreciate this doctrine.

Although tenacious of his own views, and looking upon a republic as the ideal form of government, he showed himself in 1791 and in 1830 ready to forget his own preferences before the will of the majority.

Few men have lived more for others than Lafayette. While political liberty was the great object of his philanthropic devotion, the causes of the negroes, of persons persecuted for religious opinions, of the victims of oppressive laws, were ceaselessly in his mind. But a short time before his death he exerted himself for the emancipation of the blacks. A character so unselfish, so humanitarian, could not remain indifferent to the Christian religion, the precepts of which his life illustrated. In his youth he had seen religion either in an aspect of puerile superstition, or as discredited by the vices and unbelief of its courtly ministers. For many years he maintained an attitude of silent indifference; but after the death of his wife his feelings underwent a change. New examination and reflection enabled him to separate the essential good from its accidental accompaniments, and attendance at divine service became a habit.

Lafayette had in an exceptional degree the social qualities and domestic tastes which make the happiness of private life. His manner was extremely gracious, the result of a natural kindliness which embraced all mankind. His long career had furnished a fund of anecdote which enriched his conversation. He had the French sprightliness of mind and liveliness of repartee, with a great deal of Anglo-Saxon solidity. His charities were ceaseless and often involved serious self-sacrifice. In his comments on the conduct of other men, he displayed a remarkable degree of moderation and justice. It would be in vain to look among his voluminous correspondence and papers for a single harsh judgment upon the conduct of any of his political opponents. He took it for granted that they were acting conscientiously, and while criticising their opinions never questioned their motives. While the unsuspecting frankness of his nature sometimes led him into mistakes, it had much to do with the strength of the friendship which he excited and retained. Washington, Jefferson, and Fox loved him. Napoleon and Charles X. were personally attracted to the man whom neither bribes nor threats could affect, who accepted no favors, and was guilty of no disloyalty. The honesty of his public career had been in accord with the delicate sense of honor which belonged to his nature. The grief which was felt by all ranks of society at Lafayette's death was a personal one. His familiar figure and revered character had become an old and precious landmark on the road of progress which all men regretted to see no more.

George Edward Woodberry.

BORN in Beverly, Mass., 1855.

FROM "THE NORTH SHORE WATCH."

[*The North Shore Watch, and Other Poems.* 1890.]

YOUTH AND LOVE.

"ERE yet we knew Love's name," he said to me,
    "He gave the new earth to our boyish hands;
For us morn blossoms, and the azure sea
    Ruffles and smooths his long and gleaming sands
        Upon a hundred strands;
In green and gold the radiant mist exhales,
    When through the willow buds the blue March blows,
    And sowing Persia through the world the rose
        Reddens our western vales:
Clasped with the light, bathed with the glowing air,
Rest we in his embrace who made our paths so fair!"

EXILE.

Heavy is exile wheresoe'er it be!
    Or where his armored ship's strong bows divide
Green, empty hollows of the Afric sea,
    Or where my broad-browed prairies, westering wide,
        A race of men abide;
And life in exile is a thing of fears,
    A song bereaved of music, a delight
    That sorrow's tooth doth feast on, day and night,
        A hope dissolved in tears,
A poem in the dying spirit—aught
Lost to its use and beauty, desolate, idle, naught!

Heavy is exile wheresoe'er it be!
    To miss the sense of love from out the days;
To wake, and work, and tire, nor ever see
    Love's glowing eyes suffused with tender rays—
        Darling of human praise!
To lose Love's ministry from out our life,
    Nor gentle labor know for dear ones wrought,
    When once Love lorded the thronged ways of thought,
        And quelled the harsh world strife;
To feel the hungering spirit slowly stilled,
While hours and months and years the barren seasons build.

Ever to watch, like an unfriended guest,
    The sun rise up and lead the days through heaven,
The silent days, on to the flaming west,
    The unrecorded days, to darkness given,
        Unloved, unwept, unshriven:

With our great mother, Earth, to live alone;
    To clasp in silence Wisdom's moveless knees;
    To fix dumb eyes, that know fate's whelming seas,
        On her eternal throne;
    While better seems it, were the soul sunk deep
In life's death-mantled pool, sealed in oblivious sleep!

"Alas," I cried, beneath the sun-bright sky,
    "What profits it to search what Athens says—
To heap a little learning ere we die,
    Blind pilgrims, walk the world's deserted ways,
    And lose the living days;
To cheat sad memory's self with storied woes;
    To summon up sweet visions out of books
    Wherein old poets have enshrined love's looks;
        To seek in pain repose;
Oh, cup of bitterness he too must taste,
Shut in his homeless ship upon the salt sea-waste!"

What though o'er him the tropic sunset bloom,
    With hyacinthine hues and sanguine dyes,
And down the central deep's profoundest gloom,
    Soft blossoms, fallen from the wreathèd skies,
        The seas imparadise?
With light immingling, colors, dipped in May,
    Through multitudinous changes still endure—
    Orange and unimagined emeralds pure
        Drift through the softened day;
"Alas," he whispers, "and art thou not nigh?
Earth reaches now her height of beauty ere I die."

HOLBEIN'S DANCE OF DEATH.

[*A History of Wood-Engraving.* 1883.]

THE Dance of Death was an old subject. It had possessed for centuries
a powerful and sometimes morbid attraction for the artistic imagination and for popular reflection. It was peculiarly the product of mediæval
Christian life, and survives as a representative of the great mediæval ideas.
That age first surrounded death with terrors, fastened the attention of man
continually upon his doom, and affrighted his spirit with the dread of that
unknown hour of his dissolution which should put him in danger of the
second death of immortal agony. In Greece death had been the breaking of
the chrysalis by the winged butterfly, or, at least, only the extinction of the
torch; here it was the gaunt and grinning skeleton always jostling the flesh
of the living, however beautiful or joyous they might be. In the churches of
the thirteenth century there swung a banner emblazoned upon one side with
the figures of a youth and maiden before a mirror of their loveliness, and, upon the reverse, with Death holding his spade beside the worm-pierced corpse;

G. E. Woodberry

it was the type of mediæval Christian teaching. The fear of death was the recurring burden of the pulpit; it made the heart of every bowed worshipper tremble, and was taught with fearful distinctness by the pestilence that again and again suddenly struck the populations of Europe. The chord of feeling was overstrained; the elastic force of life asserted itself, and, by a strange transformation, men made a jest of their terror, and played with death as they have never since done; they acted the ravages of death in pantomime, made the tragedy comic, put the figure of Death into their carnivals, and changed the object of their alarm into the theme of their sport. In the spirit of that democracy which, in spite of the aristocratic structure of mediæval society, was embedded in the heart of the Christian system, where every soul was of equal value before God, the people turned the universal moral lesson of death into a satire against the great; Death was not only the common executioner, he arrested the prelates and the nobles, stripped them of their robes and their possessions, and tried them whether they were of God or Mammon. In these many-varied forms of terror, sport, and irony Death filled the imagination and reflection of the age; the shrouded figure or the naked skeleton was seen on the stage of the theatre, amid the games of the people, on the walls of the churches and the monasteries, throughout the whole range of art and literature. Holbein had looked on many representations of this idea: where, as in Dürer's work, Death attends knight and beggar; or where, as in the Nuremberg Chronicle, the skeletons dance by the open grave; or where, as in the famous series at Bâsle, Death humbles every rank of life in turn. But Holbein did not look on these scenes as his predecessors had done; he was free from their spirit. He took the mediæval idea and remoulded it, as Shakespeare remoulded the tradition of Denmark and Italy, into a work for all times and generations. He represented Death, but with an artistic power, an imaginative fervor, a perception of the constant element in its interest for mankind, which lifted his work out of mediævalism into universal truth; and in doing this he not only showed the high power of his art, but he unlocked the secrets of his character.

This work is, in the first edition [1538], a series of forty-one small cuts, in each of which is depicted the triumph of Death over some person who is typical of a whole class. Each design represents with intense dramatic power some scene from daily life; Death lays his summons upon all in the midst of their habitual occupations: the trader has escaped shipwreck, and "on the beach undoes his corded bales"—Death plucks him by the cloak; the weary, pack-laden peddler, plodding on in his unfinished journey, turns questioningly to the delaying hand upon his shoulder; the priest goes to the burial of the poor—Death carries the candle in a lantern before him, and rings the warning bell; the drunkard gulps his liquor, the judge takes his bribe, the miser counts his gold—Death interrupts them with a sneer. What poetic feeling, what dramatic force, there is in the picture of the Nun! She kneels with head averted from the altar of her devotions toward the youth who sits upon the bed playing the lute to her sleeping soul, and at the moment Death stands there to put out the light of the taper which shall leave her in darkness forever. What sharp satire there is in the representation of the Preacher dilating, perhaps, in his accustomed, half-mechanical way, upon the terrors of that very Death already at his elbow! What justness of sight, what grimness of reality, there is in the representation of the Ploughman; how directly does Holbein bring us face to face with the human curse—in the sweat of thy brow thou shalt earn death! George Sand, looking out on the spring fields of her remote province and seeing the French peasants ploughing up the soft and smoking soil, remembered this type of peasant life as Holbein saw it, and described this cut in words that vivify the concentrated meaning of the whole series. "The engraving," she says, "represents a farmer guiding the plough in the middle of a field. A vast plain extends into the distance, where there are some poor huts; the sun is setting behind a hill. It is the close of a hard day's work. The peasant is old, thickset, and in tatters; the team which he drives before him is lean, worn out by fatigue and scanty food; the ploughshare is buried in a rugged and stubborn soil. In this scene of sweat and habitual toil there is only one being in good spirits and light of foot, a fantastic character, a skeleton with a whip, that runs in the furrow beside the startled horses and beats them—as it were, a farmer's boy. It is Death." She takes up the story again, after a while. "Is there much consolation," she asks, "in this stoicism, and do devout souls find their account therein? The ambitious, the knave, the tyrant, the sensualist, all the proud sinners who abuse life, and whom Death drags away by the hair, are on their way to a reckoning, no doubt; but the blind, the beggar, the fool, the poor peasant, is there any amends for their long wretchedness in the single reflection that death is not an evil for them? No! an inexorable melancholy, a dismaying fatality, weighs upon the artist's work. It is like a bitter curse launched on the universal human lot."

Certainly the artist's work is a bold and naked statement of man's mortality, of the close of life contrasted with the worth of its career; but the melancholy of his work is not more inexorable, its fatality is not more dismaying, than the reality he saw. He did not choose for his pencil what was unusual, extraordinary, or abnormal in life; he depicted its accustomed course and its fixed conclusion in fear, folly, or dignity. He took almost every character among men, almost every passion or vice of the race, almost every toil or pursuit in which his contemporaries engaged, and confronted them with their fate. The king is at his feast, Death pours the wine; the poor mother is cooking her humble meal at the hearth, Death steals her child; the bridal pair walk on absorbed, while Death beats their wedding-march with glee. Throughout the series there is the same dramatic insight, the same unadorned reality, the same humanity. Here and there the spirit of the Reformer reveals itself: the Pope in the exercise of his utmost worldly power crowns the emperor, but behind is Death; a devil lurks in the shadow, and over the heads of the cardinals are other devils; the monk, abbot, and prioress—how they resist and are panic-stricken! There can be no doubt at what Holbein reckoned these men and their trade. Holbein showed here, too, his sympathy with the humbler classes in those days of peasant wars, of the German Bible, and of books in the vulgar tongue—the days when the people began to be a self-conscious body, with a knowledge of the opportunities of life and the power to make good their claim to share in them; as Holbein saw life, it was only the humble to whom Death was not full of scorn and jesting, they alone stood dignified in his presence. Beneath this sympathy with the Reformers and the people need we look farther, as Ruskin does, to find scepticism hidden in the shadows of Holbein's heart? Holbein saw the Church as Avarice, trading in the sins of its children; as Cruelty, rejoicing in the blood of its enemies; as Ignorance, putting out the light of the mind. There was no faltering in his resolute, indignant denial of that Church. Did he find any refuge elsewhere in such hope and faith as remain to man in the suggestions of his own spirit? He saw Death's triumph, and he made men see it with his eyes; if he saw more than that, he kept silence concerning it. He did not menace the guilty with any peril save the peril of Death's mockery; he spoke no word of consolation for the good; for the inevitable sorrow of the child's loss there is no cure, for the ploughman's faithful labor there is no reward except in final repose by the shadow of the distant spire. He did not open the heavens to let through one gleam of immortal life upon the human lot, unless it be in the Judgment, where only the saved have risen; nevertheless, the purport of that scene, even if it be interpreted with the most Christian realism, cannot destroy the spirit of all others. "Inexorable melancholy, dismaying fatality" —these, truly, are the burden of his work.

The series holds high rank, too, merely as a product of artistic skill. It shows throughout the designer's ease, simplicity, and economy in methods of work, his complete control of his resources, and his unerring correctness in choosing the means proper to fulfil his ends; few lines are employed, as in the Italian manner, and there is little cross-hatching; but, as in all great art, every line has its work to do, its meaning, which it expresses perfectly, with no waste of labor and no ineffectual effort. In sureness of stroke and accuracy of proportion the drawing is unsurpassed; you may magnify any of the designs twelve times, and even the fingers will show no disproportion in whole or in part. It is true that there is no anatomical accuracy; no single skeleton is correctly drawn in detail, but the shape of Death, guessed at as a thing unknown, is so expressed that in the earliest days of the work men said that in it "Death seemed to live, and the living to be truly dead." The correctness, vigor, and economy of line in the drawing of these cuts made them a lesson to later artists like Rubens, merely as an example of powerful and truthful effects perfectly obtained at the least expense of labor. In this respect they were in design a triumph of art, as much as they were in conception a triumph of imagination.

AT GIBRALTAR.

I.

ENGLAND, I stand on thy imperial ground,
    Not all a stranger; as thy bugles blow,
  I feel within my blood old battles flow,—
  The blood whose ancient founts in thee are found.

Still surging dark against the Christian bound
   Wide Islam presses; well its peoples know
   Thy heights that watch them wandering below;
I think how Lucknow heard their gathering sound.

I turn, and meet the cruel, turbaned face.
   England, 'tis sweet to be so much thy son!
I feel the conqueror in my blood and race;
   Last night Trafalgar awed me, and to-day
Gibraltar wakened; hark, thy evening gun
   Startles the desert over Africa!

II.

Thou art the rock of empire, set mid-seas
   Between the East and West, that God has built;
   Advance thy Roman borders where thou wilt,
While run thy armies true with his decrees;
Law, justice, liberty,—great gifts are these.
   Watch that they spread where English blood is spilt,
   Lest, mixed and sullied with his country's guilt,
The soldier's life-stream flow, and Heaven displease!

Two swords there are: one naked, apt to smite,
   Thy blade of war; and, battle-storied, one
Rejoices in the sheath, and hides from light.
   American I am; would wars were done!
Now westward, look, my country bids good-night,—
   Peace to the world from ports without a gun!

OUR FIRST CENTURY.

IT cannot be that men who are the seed
   Of Washington should miss fame's true applause;
   Franklin did plan us; Marshall gave us laws;
And slow the broad scroll grew a people's creed,—
One land and free! then at our dangerous need,
   Time's challenge coming, Lincoln gave it pause,
   Upheld the double pillars of the cause,
And dying left them whole,—the crowning deed.

Such was the fathering race that made all fast,
   Who founded us, and spread from sea to sea
   A thousand leagues the zone of liberty,
And built for man this refuge from his past,
   Unkinged, unchurched, unsoldiered; shamed were we,
   Failing the stature that such sires forecast!

ON THE HUNDREDTH ANNIVERSARY OF THE FRENCH REVOLUTION.

SHE matched the world in arms against man's right,
  And when the Fates would bound her, victor France,
  With her own conquests must they dull her lance
And legions worn with fadeless battles smite.
O laughter at the shocks of time, her might
  Rejoiced in more than arms! the great advance
  Through Europe of her triple ordinance
We owe to her.—O century, born to-night,

Fulfil her glory! Europe still hath slaves,
  Scourged by the Turk, mown by the Scythian car;
  Siberia, more rich in heroes' graves
Than the most famous field of glorious war,
  Yet waits; and by the bloody Cretan waves
  Man suffers hope, and pleads his woe afar.

SONG OF EROS, IN "AGATHON."

WHEN love in the faint heart trembles,
  And the eyes with tears are wet,
Oh, tell me what resembles
  Thee, young Regret ?
Violets with dewdrops drooping,
  Lilies o'erfull of gold,
Roses in June rains stooping,
  That weep for the cold,
Are like thee, young Regret.

Bloom, violets, lilies, and roses!
  But what, young Desire,
Like thee, when love discloses
  Thy heart of fire ?
The wild swan unreturning,
  The eagle alone with the sun,
The long-winged storm-gulls burning
  Seaward when day is done,
Are like thee, young Desire.

Barrett Wendell.

BORN in Boston, Mass., 1855.

A REVELATION OF PREËXISTENCE.

[*The Duchess Emilia. A Romance. 1885.*]

IN the midst of Rome there stands an old church, not large and not so fine as most of those that have famous names. But the low round arches, and the dim mosaics that peer down with big eyes from the tribune·in the midst of which Christ blesses the people, show that it belongs to the oldest of Christian days. Legend says that it was built to keep alive the memory of a Roman virgin who suffered martyrdom on the spot where it stands. Emilia, the legend runs, was the daughter of a great nobleman who hated the Christians as bitterly as did the emperor himself. Her father bade her marry an officer of the court, famous for the cruelty with which he hunted down those of the new faith; and preparations were making for a grand wedding. But a Christian slave who was in attendance on the maiden converted her to the truth. So when the wedding-day came she would be the bride of none but Christ. In a rage her father struck her down; and folding her hands, and muttering a last prayer for him, she died. In later times, when the Christians had risen above persecution and ruled the city, the holy martyr Emilia appeared in a vision to a priest; and showing him the spot where the house had stood in which she had met her death, she bade him build a church there. So the church was built; and then, by another miracle, they found somewhere in the Catacombs the body of Santa Emilia, which they placed with solemn rejoicing upon the high altar of the church. And thither for a thousand years men have come to worship.

In this church the Colonnas were buried, at first simply enough, in tombs that no man could envy save for their quietness. But by and by a rich member of the house, stirred by the magnificence with which some rival families decked their burial-places, built beside the little church a grand chapel blazing with strange marbles that had been dug up among the ruins of pagan Rome. In this chapel the Colonnas lie now, and among them the Duchess Emilia.

Elsewhere than in Rome, this old church—sweet with the incense of centuries, and splendid, too, since the door that leads to the princely chapel has been opened in its gray wall—would be a famous spot. But in Rome, overrich with treasures of art and of tradition, it stands unnoticed. Indeed, when I went to Rome, years after Beverly was dead and forgotten, I had much work to find it. The local guides and the grand porter of my hotel had never heard its name. "It is possible that there is such a place," they would say; "but who cares to go there?" All the same I sought it out, and found there many a quiet thought of past time. Such thoughts have come to me in the dead old towns of New England, whose wooden mansions will have rotted away for centuries before a stone falls from the mosaics of Santa Emilia. The world has passed it by. None but the Colonnas remember it, if indeed there are still Colonnas in Rome. For I put no questions to the snuffy *custode* who unlocked for me the iron gate of their chapel; I only passed within it, and stood among the marbles whose splendor seemed strangely out of keeping with the solemnity of death. We of New England think of the dead in quiet churchyards, where gray stone slabs, half overgrown with moss, stand amid the long grass. There rude rhymes sing their dirges in quaintly simple tones that lose themselves in the low harmonies of the wind which plays through the slow-moving branches of elms and pines. In Rome the spirit of the old pagans is not dead. As they strove to make bright the homes of their departed with dancing sprites and merry colors, so the Romans even in our own time deck their graves with such splendors as they love in life.

In the Colonna chapel there is a monument made by some follower of Canova, and on it is the name of the Duchess Emilia. I stood before it, thinking of the time—not far off in years, yet so far in all things else—when Richard Beverly had found his way there too. For there Beverly came, by mere chance; and there at last was revealed to him what he believed with all his heart to be the secret of his life.

It was not long after the time of which he wrote in the last lines I have copied from his journal. Cut off by what seemed a cruel fate rather than any fault of his from all the friends who were near him,—from the Clevelands, from the old Cardinal Colonna, from the Count Luigi, from Filippa, whom he still calls Filippa in his writing,—he wandered about the city, seeking distraction from himself. His journal contains many notes, such as all travellers make, of sights that have been written of a thousand times and will be written of as long as Rome lasts. At length, he found himself one day before the little church of Santa Emilia, and entered to see what might be within. There he found just such an old *custode* as met me there years afterwards,—perhaps the same, for the man I saw looked old enough to have been there since the days of the blessed Emilia herself. And this old creature told him, in a cracked voice that he noted in his journal, the simple story of the saint; and showed him the shrine that holds her bones. So he stood before the shrine, studded with jewels which look very like bits of polished glass, and thought of what her life had been who lies on earth, as she sits in Heaven, in glory. Nothing could be simpler or slighter. A young girl, faithful to the God whom she had learned to worship, would not swerve from what she thought He bade her do. Pure He had made her; pure she would give herself back to him. So she died, and might have been forgotten, but that the Roman Christians have never suffered simple purity to die. What good has come within their ken they have gathered up and treasured. They have decked it, perhaps, in such feeble poetry as is made only in monkish minds; they have shrined its relics in cases that make sane men smile. But all the same they have treasured it. The church that has bred all the subtleties of Roman priestcraft is the church that has kept alive the memory of the saints and the martyrs who gave themselves with all their hearts to what they deemed was the truth.

Some such thoughts came to Beverly as he stood before the shrine of the Roman girl who has outlived the great world that did her to death. But he was not suffered to think of her long. The old *custode*, hungry for another fee, dragged him off to the chapel,—more beautiful, the *custode* said, than Paradise itself,—which was the glory of this old church, and unlocked the iron gate, which creaked on its hinges, and forced him to enter. What he found there he shall tell in his own words.

From Beverly's Journal.

As I stepped within the chapel there came to me more strongly than ever the feeling that I was moving through a world where I had been before. And this old feeling came in a form which I had not yet known. Before, it had been as if I was come back from afar off to spots full of evil memories too vague and distant for me to know what they were. Here at last it was as if I was come face to face with the evil thing that has chased me through my life.

I half thought that some shadowy form would stalk before me and whisper in my ear words that should bear their meaning to my heart. But nothing came; and I smiled at my folly as I looked about me at the marble splendors which the cracked-voiced verger pointed out.

Where I was I did not know; I had not stopped to ask. Whose tombs I looked at I hardly cared. I would have turned back and left the spot, trusting that the evil thoughts which came to me there were only the delusions of a troubled mind. In truth, it seems to me that I did turn back, bidding my old guide show me no more. But of that I know little; for, as I turned, my eyes fell upon a thing that in my earhtly life I had never seen before. And then, for a long time, I saw and knew nothing of what was done about me. But I saw and knew instead the things for which I had strained my mind so long.

For there before me on a sculptured tomb was the name that had echoed through my brain when Cleveland spoke it, the name that the old Cardinal had bidden me never speak to him,—Emilia Colonna. I saw no other word save the date when she died. It was my birth-year. That I had known. But as I looked upon the letters I read more, which had never been told me. It was on the very day when I was born in far-off New England that Emilia Colonna came to her end in Rome. Her life went out of the world as mine came into it. A simple fact enough, men might say; but to me it had a meaning that unlocked the riddle of my life. Not all at once did the truth come to me, but all at once I knew that it was coming; and I stood leaning against the sculptured marble, my eyes fixed upon the formal words, as the truth that I had sought came shining through the murky clouds of mystery that have writhed about me so long. It shone through at last, as the sun shines through a mountain mist,—first faint and dim, then more and more distinct, at last in all the clearness of heaven. But the truth that came to me had little of heaven in it.

For at first there swept over me memories of her sinful life whose bones lay within the marble tomb. I thought of her loveless marriage, of her unhallowed love. I thought of how Duke Pietro, whose tomb was by hers, had fallen murdered before her tearless eyes; of how, while he lay dead, she had sat in her palace waiting for the lover who had dishonored the dead man's name. I thought of how from that day on no touch of penitence had come to her proud spirit; of how she had sunk deep in all the sins of the flesh, smiling, with the lips I had known for mine in the painted face she left behind her, on every lover who pressed his suit. And then at last she had died in the midst of her sin; and they had brought her hither and laid her beside her honest lord, to sleep in peace.

Here she had been, in her marble bed, since the day when I first drew breath in this world. That was strange,—that I, whose simple life was not begun until her stormy life was ended, should be standing by her tomb, telling over the tale of her sins as a monk might tell the beads of his rosary. Nay, I was telling them as if they had been part of my own life, the life that was not yet in being when those sins were done. For with each thought of what her sins had been there came to me a fresh pang. I shrunk from them, as I would have shrunk if I had done them in my own flesh. Yet from them I could not shrink away, even as I could never shrink away from myself.

What all meant I could not tell; but I saw that the truth was at hand. I fell upon my knees, crying out to Heaven in my own tongue that I might be kept in the dark no longer. Vile as I was, let me see the light, and I would struggle toward it with all the might that was in me.

Then my eyes were cleared once more. It was as if some hand had swept away the veil of mystery which had hidden from me the place in which I stood; for in my misery I had ceased to see, to hear, to feel. And when I knew that my eyes could see once more, I found them fixed upon the words which told me that here before me lay the dead woman who died on the day when I was born.

With that came to me the memory of an old tale that my nurse told me when I was a little child. It was in the midst of a stormy night that I came into the world. When I was born I was still and lifeless, and they said that there was no earthly life for me, that I was dead in the womb. But of a sudden, as the clocks were tolling the hour of midnight, I quivered and uttered a great cry, louder and wilder than the cries of other children. And I drew breath with a struggle, as if I would fain lie still but could not; and cried again with a voice of fear that made the women start. Then I lived; and living I was come back here at last.

For from hence I was come. The mystery was clear to me now. The life that has filled my waking hours with agony was come from hence. The spirit that brought life to the baby form that might have lain at peace among my fathers was no blessed sprite from Heaven. But in the stormy midnight the soul that had been Emilia's was whirled about the rolling earth; and coming to my far-off fatherland it found a wretched home in the madman's body that is mine. Saved for a time, by what blessed power no man can tell, from the fires of Hell, it lingers on in this earth with one more chance to expiate its sin.

All the mystery that I have found in Rome was cleared. All the agony that I have suffered was real and true, a thousand-fold more than I had dreamed. I knelt, and prayed with all my heart for light and for mercy. And as I raised my living hands to God, it seemed to me that the dead hands which had been mine raised themselves too within the tomb. Then presently I knew no more.

When my life came back to me I was lying in the sacristy of the old church, and they were bathing my temples with cool water. Before long I raised myself up, stronger and calmer than I had been in the time gone by. And I gave them money, and came my way hither to my chamber in the old palace.

Here I wait to-night, full of agony deeper than I knew of old, for now the sins for which I suffer are as clear to me as they are to the Heaven by whose justice the suffering has followed them. But I am full of hope, too, that the mercy which has saved me to this time will not forsake me now; that it will lead me on through agonies of expiation as great as souls can bear, until at last the sin is washed away. Then shall come rest, rest such as God alone can grant.

James Berry Bensel.

BORN in New York, N. Y., 1856.   DIED there, 1886.

IN ARABIA.

[In the King's Garden, and Other Poems. 1885.]

"CHOOSE thou between!" and to his enemy
   The Arab chief a brawny hand displayed,
Wherein, like moonlight on a sullen sea,
   Gleamed the gray scimitar's enamelled blade.

"Choose thou between death at my hand and thine!
   Close in my power, my vengeance I may wreak,
Yet hesitate to strike.   A hate like mine
   Is noble still.   Thou hast thy choosing,—speak!"

And Ackbar stood.   About him all the band
   That hailed his captor chieftain, with grave eyes
His answer waited, while that heavy hand
   Stretched like a bar between him and the skies.

Straight in the face before him Ackbar sent
   A sneer of scorn, and raised his noble head;
"Strike!" and the desert monarch, as content,
   Rehung the weapon at his girdle red.

Then Ackbar nearer crept and lifted high
   His arms toward the heaven so far and blue
Wherein the sunset rays began to die,
   While o'er the band a deeper silence grew.

"Strike! I am ready!   Didst thou think to see
   A son of Gheva spill upon the dust
His noble blood?   Didst hope to have my knee
   Bend at thy feet, and with one mighty thrust

"The life thou hatest flee before thee here?
   Shame on thee! on thy race!   Art thou the one
Who hast so long his vengeance counted dear?
   My hate is greater; I did strike thy son,

"Thy one son, Noumid, dead before my face;
   And by the swiftest courser of my stud
Sent to thy door his corpse.   Aye, one might trace
   Their flight across the desert by his blood.

"Strike! for my hate is greater than thy own!"
   But with a frown the Arab moved away,
Walked to a distant palm and stood alone,
   With eyes that looked where purple mountains lay.

This for an instant: then he turned again
　　Towards the place where Ackbar waited still,
Walking as one benumbed with bitter pain,
　　Or with a hateful mission to fulfil.

"Strike, for I hate thee!" Ackbar cried once more.
　"Nay, but my hate I cannot find!" said now
His enemy.　"Thy freedom I restore.
　　Live! life were worse than death to such as thou."

So with his gift of life the Bedouin slept
　　That night untroubled; but when dawn broke through
The purple East, and o'er his eyelids crept
　　The long, thin fingers of the light, he drew

A heavy breath and woke: Above him shone
　　A lifted dagger—"Yea, he gave thee life,
But I give death!" came in fierce undertone.
　　And Ackbar died.　It was dead Noumid's wife.

George Edgar Montgomery.

BORN in New York, N. Y., 1856.

A STOLEN SOUL.

[Harper's New Monthly Magazine.]

DEAD, dead!—the nights glide
　　swiftly on,
The days fly past in swallow-herds,
And if the sun had never shone,
If there were neither night nor day,
Nor life that speaks in thrilling words,
Nor song to carol grief away:
The world could not be darker now,
Darker to me, who sit alone
With my despair.　For she is dead,
Like the last breath of summer flown,
She whom I taught to disavow
The God whose mystery she had read.
'Twas I who robbed her of her wings,
And while her spirit soared and sang,
Dragged her from heaven; 'twas I who
　　sprang
Thief-like upon her, thief-like stole
Her simple faith in holy things,
The glory of her soul.

And yet I loved her, loved her!　She
Gave more than woman's love to me

To me who held as light as dreams
The faith by which her soul could see.
I knew her voice in wind and breeze,
In brawls of woodland brooks and
　　streams,
And in the music of the trees;
There were no deeper, starrier skies
Than the dusk splendor of her eyes;
And when she spoke it seemed I heard
The tremulous rapture of a bird.

Why did she love me?　Cruel fate
That would not turn her love to hate,
That bound us ever heart to heart!

She was fair
As the wild flowers, and innocent
As youth before its charm is spent.
She was the very gentlest part
Of all things that are sweet and rare.
Oh! she was Nature's happy child,
Full of the grace of happy years:
For her the world was undefiled,

For her there were no bitter fears,
No mad regrets, no burning tears:
She looked up at the stars and smiled,
And when she bowed in humble prayer
I felt the spot was hallowed where
Her rose-lips whispered to the air.
I was her teacher: day by day
I strove to tear the veil away
Which, like the dust that hides a seed,
Hid all I worshipped as the truth
From the bright vision of her youth.
I taught her to deny the creed
That God is what the preacher saith—
Ruler of life and King of death,
That love, the perfect love of earth,
Shall find in death immortal birth;
And she, who knew not any sin,
Nor any blind desire to win
What a child's instinct cannot know,
She listened, with a mind distraught,
Because she loved me—till the glow
Of faith had faded from her sight
And she was wholly mine at last:
My truth became her truth, my thought
Her thought, my knowledge the dim
     light
Which showed the world's way from the
     past.

I triumphed...She is dead...They say
I broke her heart and drove her mad,
As if some frost of winter had
Driven death into the heart of May.
And still I loved her...It may be
That such poor wisdom as men know,
Men who are wisest in their age,
Stops short of truth. Which man is he
That tells the mocker from the sage,
The friend he harbors from the foe ?...
God lived for her, yet not for me.
And I the teacher! At the end
God lived for neither: so she died.

And now! Why do I tremble, bend?
Shall a man's heart undo his pride
And teach him that his tongue has
     lied ?...
If I spoke falsely when I spoke
What seemed the truth! Ah, then I
     should
Kneel like a pale priest at his shrine,
Kneel in a ghostly gloom alone,
And pray that she, who was divine,
She whom I robbed of utter good,
Shall be at last God's very own:
Lost to men's sight, as one unknown
To earth, to such a love as mine.

Anne Sheldon Coombs.

BORN in Albany, N. Y.

THE HARRISES.

[*As Common Mortals. A Novel.* 1886.]

MRS. BARRON was a much-regarded member of a family which had, numerically speaking, nothing to complain of, whatever might be the opinion of the outside world on that point. Her three sisters and two brothers had set up their household gods in Goverick locations of more or less eligibility; the Harris family always *had* lived in Goverick and were Goverick born, bred, and buried in turn. They were also Goverick married, it not being considered the thing in the Harris family to marry a dangerously unfamiliar person from another city who might possess lax views on the subjects of religion and housekeeping. There is a tradition to the effect that an otherwise unobjectionable young man had once asked for the fair hand of the second Miss Harris (subsequently Mrs. Elkins), and had been sternly denied that blessing by her father, simply on the ground that the unfortunate suitor had once travelled extensively in Mexico.

Excellent people, collectively and individually, were the Harrises, so eminently respectable that no one thought of applying the word to them, seeking few interests outside of family relations, and living and dying in the faith that to be a born Harris was a career in itself.

No pride of birth or wealth gave rise to this cherished conviction; the Harrises were not conspicuously endowed in these particulars, and they would have scorned to attain the isolated distinction of special achievement. It was a mere consciousness of general worth, a calm certainty that the Harris blood flowed in unexceptionable veins, and temperately found show and shabbiness alike distasteful. Keenly alive to their own interests, they showed honorable deference to those of others, and this form of "worldliness without side-dishes" had its touch of poetry which poor humanity is nowhere poor enough to be entirely without. The cloak of simple egotism which kept them warm in a cold and (probably) unappreciative world had its soft lining of genuine family affection and helpful kinship, and, perhaps, the blindness to all unrelated forms of virtue arose from preoccupation with the real excellence to be found at home.

When the four husbands of the whilom Misses Harris and the two Harris brothers went severally through the failure to which every American man of business is doomed once in the course of his mercantile life, the others were ready with prompt aid, advice, and not more regretful head-shaking and reminding of neglected counsel than the occasion demanded. This amiable community of goods extended to views on all subjects, the four sisters only reserving for themselves, unshared by the two brothers, an unbiassed opinion concerning the merits of Mrs. John and Mrs. Edward Harris, who, though distinguished from the ordinary mass of humanity by marrying into the Harris family, yet left something to be desired (by their sisters-in-law) in "ways" acquired in years wasted outside the pale of that desirable connection.

Mrs. Barron and Mrs. Mercer agreed that, considering John's salary, Gertrude's dresses fitted far too well, and Mrs. Elkins, whose lot chronic biliousness, complicated with the unsatisfactory state of the commission business, had much embittered, often remarked that it would be well if Gertrude Harris would remember that as Miss Lawrence she never had a thing made out of the house.

Mrs. White, the most spiritually minded among the sisters, felt that the lukewarm temperature of Mrs. Edward's zeal for the Presbyterian faith (which she had adopted perforce with the name of Harris) was greatly to be deplored, and with the others decided that if Edward *could* be to blame in any matter, his culpable tendency to indulge his wife with frequent attendance at the services of the Episcopal Church would be that matter.

The husbands of these ladies, who regarded the condescension in discarding the name of Harris for their respective patronymics as equivalent to a future of concessions from themselves, fully shared the views of their wives on these points. Mr. Elkins felt that Mrs. John's many bonnets were not quite compatible with full development of the domestic affections, and Mr. White, a warm-hearted man, with—the usual accompaniment of such a tempera-ment—much warmth of language, characterized Mrs. Edward's leaning to candlesticks as "poppy-cock," to which his wife assented with even more than her usual ready meekness, remarking that Maria was always fond of show.

Milly had early been given to understand the fact that to be lacking in proper appreciation of the uncles and aunts was to demonstrate, to a marked degree, her undue share in the total depravity with which the human race is so fatally dowered. But indeed this parental instruction had been hardly necessary. The child had brought into the world with her a heart so rich in affection that there was enough and to spare for all immediate and collateral relatives, and she found herself much restricted in the expression thereof, even with so wide a field for its display.

Mrs. Barron possessed, to a marked degree, the maternal instinct, and loved her children with a fierce motherliness which made her fairly jealous of other childish charms; but after the days of toddling, lisping babyhood were passed she rarely petted them, feeling herself shrink shyly from their percep-tion of her intense affection, which, as infants, they had accepted with the uncomprehending satisfaction of all small, tame animals under caresses.

The pretty boys had never lived to outgrow the little jackets that had been fashioned by the motherly hands for their first "term" at school. The same hands had taken them off one night and hung them up, only to take them down, alas! to fold away with other useless little garments, with worthless, priceless childish treasures, and small books and slates, laid aside now for the long recess.

That grief was many years old now, and Milly had come, a willing com-forter, whose powers of consolation were much mitigated by her red curls, indifference to dolls, and general lack of Harris characteristics.

In her earliest days Milly accepted the infallibility of the uncles and aunts with loving fervor, and to have dared discriminate in her loyal affection, to have preferred one to the other, would have seemed as sacrilegious as distin-guishing one of the four Gospels for especial regard. She prayed for them all after papa and mamma, and hoped she might grow good enough to please them. The child was no innate rebel; hers was not a soul to which opposition is dear. The pathetic faith of childhood, that "whatever is, is right," was strong within her, and this innocent optimism helped over many of the rough places encountered before her years were numbered by two figures.

But the artistic temperament, eternally young in one respect, matures rap-idly in others. Milly's quick sense of the beautiful soon taught her to single out for special adoration her Aunt Lena, Mrs. Mercer, who was quite remark-ably pretty. Milly thought if she could ever look like Aunt Lena, life's trials would become joyfully endurable. The black-browed, black-lashed blue eyes, the pretty arch with which the fair hair grew on the white forehead, the well-defined roses in the creamy cheeks—all these beauties appealed anew to Milly's ardent little soul on the day following the episode of the defrauded dog, as she watched Aunt Lena sitting at the piano and singing—a little bit out of tune—a song which seemed to the child mysteriously beautiful. The unhappy frequenter of amateur concerts can hardly appreciate the rapture stirred by the threadbare ballad "Waiting." It seemed all one to Milly with the sudden rush of passionate admiration that filled her heart, and music and beauty combined proved as fascinating to her as to older mortals.

With a final chase over the key-board, and a vociferous adjuration to the stars and nightingales to guide and speed the flying feet of the expected lover, the music ceased.

"Aunt Lena, I do love you so!" cried Milly, throwing her slender arms around that lady's neck.

"That is very sweet of you, Milly," said Aunt Lena, with a careless kiss, and a careful hand arranging the lace at the throat which the child's impetuous caress had rumpled. "But you should not seize one in that rude manner."

Milly was wounded, but not in the least offended. It was not easy to chill that warm young heart into permanent alienation. The old fatal persuasion that bodily beauty is the inevitable expression of spiritual loveliness impelled her to utter, with a timid trust in comprehension, a psychic experience that she had hitherto kept shyly hidden in one of the innermost folds of her consciousness.

"Aunt Lena," she said, in a gentle, hesitating voice, "did you ever—when you were sitting all alone, you know—have it come over you, 'This is I!' and be afraid?"

Aunt Lena's blue eyes widened. "For goodness' sake! What on earth do you mean, child?"

"I can't say it in words, aunty, not as it really is, but I know what I mean, and you *must* too!" Milly's voice took on a pleading tone. "You must when you look in the glass, deep down into your own eyes, and look and look until by and by it isn't your own self that is looking at its own self, but something that is you, and isn't you, and is watching both of them."

I am not aware if at that time "Kenelm Chillingly" had found a place in Goverick circulating libraries, but it would have attracted Mrs. Mercer at no time, and in her sublime indifference to psychological studies she had thus no soothing parallel in fiction, such as that of the eight-years-old Kenelm astounding his estimable mother with the query: "Mamma, are you not sometimes overcome by a sense of your own identity?"

"I don't understand you, Milly," she said, with an alarmed sense of defective hearing. "Say it again, and don't chatter so fast."

Milly repeated obediently, word for word, a dawning fear in the brown glory of her eyes. She did not want to have that feeling all alone. No one ever understood what she meant about anything. Any one "so pretty" as Aunt Lena ought to know all about it. Mrs. Mercer seized the hot little hands.

"Have you got a fever?" she asked abruptly.

But the hands were moist as well as hot, and indeed were never cold, so Mrs. Mercer, deprived of this physical basis for Milly's aberrations, found it convenient to dismiss this problematic infant and carry the tale of her wanderings to Mrs. Elkins, who was regarded as an authority on all matters of domestic economy, including the government of children.

But notwithstanding the fact of her peculiar insight with regard to the workings of the infant mind, that lady frankly declared that Milly was "beyond" her. This not at all in the admiring sense that the words might convey to the uninitiated, but with a conviction that a child so ill-regulated as to be beyond her aunt's comprehension had little to hope for the future; for the "beyond" was necessarily in the direction of evil, else the Harris divination would never be outstripped.

"That child is more trouble to her mother than all my five are to me," she said, plaintively. "I don't see where she gets it from. Mary was always a sensible little thing, and Mark's people are reasonable folks—though they might be more genteel. It is not ordinary naughtiness with Milly; it would be easier to manage if it was. She isn't greedy or quarrelsome in the natural way, but she'll scream if you lay a finger on that kitten of hers, and she just can't get along with any one. Yesterday she rushed screaming through the streets because she'd had some fuss with my Helen about a dog, and last week she cried herself sick because she said Helen had murdered some roses. Mrs. Banks gave them each a bunch, just common garden roses, and Helen got tired of carrying hers—they were spoiling her glove—so she threw them on the side-walk and then happened to step on them. Milly declared she did it on purpose, said she trampled them to death, and talked about the flowers' blood, and nonsense enough to drive you wild, and finally rushed home without her supper, though Mary had sent her here to stay. She's a very trying child; there's no denying it."

"Look at the way she is with dolls," said Mrs. Mercer, whose English had suffered from a too exclusive devotion to the fine arts as represented by "spatter-work" and the ballads of Claribel and Millard. But then the demand for elegant English in Goverick by no means exceeded the supply.

"I never saw her with a doll."

"That's just it; look at that doll they gave her Christmas. Mary paid three dollars and seventy-five cents for that doll, undressed, and the things she made for it are too lovely for anything. Well, that child never notices it, but goes into the laundry to wash pebbles in a pail, and when they come out glistening with the water calls them jewels, and says she is a lapidary! And I found her one day sailing chips in the gutter and guiding them with a barrel-hoop, and when I asked her what pleasure she found in such a boy's play as that, she said it wasn't a boy's play, but that each chip was a human soul, and that if she could keep it from going down the sewer at the corner it would be saved, but if not, it was eternally lost. Her mother says she kept one chip for weeks, and took it out to sail after every heavy rain. She absolutely cried when it went down the sewer at last. She thought more of that one chip than all her dolls put together. It's just no use to give them to her."

"Well, there isn't a bit of Harris in her," said Mrs. Elkins sadly. "And I don't see as there's much Barron either."

Harry Thurston Peck.

BORN in Stamford, Conn., 1856.

HELIOTROPE.

[*Acta Columbiana.* 1880.]

AMID the chapel's chequered gloom
　　She laughed with Dora and with
　　　　Flora,
And chattered in the lecture-room,—
　　The saucy little sophomora!
　　　　Yet while (as in her other schools)
　　　　She was a privileged transgressor,
　　She never broke the simple rules
　　　　Of one particular professor.

But when he spoke of varied lore,
　　Paroxytones and modes potential,
She listened with a face that wore
　　A look half fond, half reverential.
　　　　To her that earnest voice was sweet,
　　　　And though her love had no con-
　　　　　　fessor,
　　Her girlish heart lay at the feet
　　　　Of that particular professor.

And he had learned, among his books
　　That held the lore of ages olden,
To watch those ever changing looks,
　　The wistful eyes, the tresses golden,
　　　　That stirred his pulse with passion's
　　　　　　pain
　　　　And thrilled his soul with soft de-
　　　　　　sire,
　　And bade fond youth return again
　　　　Crowned with his coronet of fire.

Her sunny smile, her winsome ways,
　　Were more to him than all his knowl-
　　　　edge,
And she preferred his words of praise
　　To all the honors of the college.
　　　　Yet "What am foolish I to him?"

She whispered to her heart's con-
　　　　fessor.
"She thinks me old, and gray, and
　　grim,"
　　In silence pondered the professor.

Yet once when Christmas bells were rung
　　Above ten thousand solemn churches,
And swelling anthems grandly sung
　　Pealed through the dim cathedral
　　　　arches—
　　　　Ere home returning, filled with hope,
　　　　Softly she stole by gate and gable,
　　And a sweet spray of heliotrope
　　　　Left on his littered study-table.

Nor came she more from day to day,
　　Like sunshine through the shadows
　　　　rifting;
Above her grave, far, far away,
　　The ever silent snows were drifting;
　　　　And those who mourned her win-
　　　　　　some face
　　　　Found in its stead a swift successor
　　And loved another in her place—
　　　　All, save the silent old professor.

But, in the tender twilight gray,
　　Shut from the sight of carping critic,
His lonely thoughts would often stray
　　From Vedic verse and tongues Semitic,
　　　　Bidding the ghost of vanished hope
　　　　Mock with its past the sad pos-
　　　　　　sessor
　　Of the dead spray of heliotrope
　　　　That once she gave the old pro-
　　　　　　fessor.

Harold Frederic.

BORN in Utica, N. Y., 1856.

"YOU THOUGHT I DID IT!"

[*Seth's Brother's Wife.* 1887.]

WHEN Seth awoke next morning, the position of the shadow cast by the thick green-paper curtain which covered the upper half of his window told his practised faculties that it was very late, and impelled him to get out of bed, before he began at all to remember the several momentous events of the previous evening. As he dressed he strove to get these arranged in their proper order in his mind. Curiously enough there were certain inchoate recollections of feminine screams, of bursts of hysterical sobbing, of low but rough and strange male voices, doleful and haunting, which confusedly struggled for place in his sleepy thoughts, and seemed now to be a part of the evening's occurrences, now to belong to this present morning, and to have come to him while he was nearing the end of his sleep.

As he passed his Aunt Sabrina's door on his way to the stairs, he heard from within this same sound of suppressed weeping. This much at least of the unlocated recollections must have belonged to the first stages of his waking. "Another quarrel with Isabel!" he thought, as he descended the stairs. "Why is it that women must always be rowing it with each other!" Then his own dispute with Albert came fresh and overpowering in distinctness of impression across his mind, and the grounds of his grievance against the temper of the other sex faded away.

The living-room was vacant—the breakfast-table still standing in the disorder of a meal just finished, and the shades down as though the day had not yet begun, although the clock showed it to be past ten. One of the folding doors of the parlor was open and he heard Isabel's voice—it struck him as being strangely altered toward harshness of fibre—calling him to enter.

She stood, as he remembered her once before, in front of the piano. In the dusk of the drawn curtains—how gloomy and distrait everything about the house was this morning!—her figure was not very clearly visible, but her face was so pale that it seemed to be independent of any light. Her eyes had the effect of slight distention, and, in the shadow, were singularly dark of tint. They were gazing at him with a strange, intent, troubled look, and the expression of the pallid face went with this to disturb him vaguely. He said to himself, in the moment of waiting for her to speak, that he must keep his troth with Annie resolutely in mind, and, if needs be, not shrink from avowing and standing by it.

Isabel did not offer him her hand, or tender him any greeting whatever; only looked him through and through with that searching, unaccustomed gaze.

"I wouldn't let them call you," she said at last, speaking slowly, as if with an effort to both form these words and repress others. "I knew that you needed the sleep."

"I am sorry if I put anybody out by my laziness. But it is such a relief to be able to sleep like that once in a while, instead of having to get down to the office by eight."

"I heard you go out last night. I heard you come in this morning. But not another soul in the house suspects that you were out; not one!"

The tone was unmistakably solemn, and weighted with deep feeling of some sort. Seth uneasily felt that a scene was impending, though he could not foresee its form. He felt, too, that the part he must play in it would of necessity be an awkward one.

"Yes," he answered, "the night seemed too fine to stay in-doors. Besides, I was nervous, and it did me good to walk it off. You can't imagine how light-hearted I was when I returned, or—for that matter—how heavy-hearted when I went out."

"Seth!"

The word came forth like the red flash from clouds which can no longer retain their pent-up, warring, swelling forces—an interjection of passion, of dread, of infinite troubling, of doubt wreathed in struggle with pain. She swayed slightly toward him, her hands clasped and stretched down and forward with a gesture of excessive perturbation, her great eyes lustrous with the excitement of this battle of emotions. Seth fancied that the dominant meaning of the look was reproach. He could not in the least see his way through the dilemma, or even understand it. He could only say to himself that the enchantment was ended, and that, come what might, he would not forget Annie.

The woman glided a step nearer to him. She put one hand to her brow with a sudden movement, and rested the other upon the piano, as if all at once conscious of needing support. With a painful little laugh, hysterically incongruous, she said:

"I am almost beside myself, am I not? I cannot speak to you, it seems! And yet there is so much to say—or no! isn't silence better still?" Her voice trembled as she went on: "For what *could* we say? How meaningless all our words would be in the face of—of "——

She swept both hands to her eyes, with an impetuous gesture. Her form seemed to totter for a moment, so that Seth instinctively moved toward her. Then with a wild outburst of sobs she threw herself upon his breast, convulsed with incessant paroxysms of passionate weeping.

They stood thus together for some minutes. The young man, moved to great tenderness by her evident suffering, the cause of which he vaguely referred to the previous evening's events, put his arm about her, whispered gently to her to be comforted, and stroked her hair with a soft, caressing touch. His hand touched her cheek, and she shuddered at the contact; then swiftly took the hand in hers, and raised it to her lips, murmuring between the sobs:

"Ungrateful! was it not done for me? Ah, dear, I shall not shudder again."

She kissed the hand repeatedly, and pressed it to her bosom, as she spoke. She was still trembling like a leaf in his arms.

What could it all mean? he asked himself—and found no answer.

"We must be brave, dear," she whispered now. "We must be on our guard every instant! Oh—h! they shall tear my heart out before they learn anything—so much as a syllable! We must keep our nerves." She looked up into his astonished face, with almost a smile in her effort to strengthen his courage. "We *will* be brave, won't we, mine? The test will come soon now. Perhaps in an hour they will bring—*it!*"

The trembling seized her frame, and shook it with cruel force. She buried her face in his breast with a long, low cry of anguish, and sobbed there piteously, clinging to his hand still. Once she bent as if to kiss it again, but stopped, then turned her head aside, groaning "Oh how terrible! how terrible!"

The mystification now demanded light of some sort.

"What is it that is so terrible, my poor girl?" he asked. "What are they going to bring in an hour? Tell me, Isabel—my sweet sister—what does it all mean?"

She looked up into his face, with flickering suggestions of a mechanical smile at the corners of her pale lips, and with soft reproach in her eyes:

"Are you going to pretend to *me*, too, dear one? As if it were not all here in my heart—all, all! Ah, they shan't get it! They shan't get the shadow of a hint. You were home here all the while! You were asleep, sound asleep! If it be necessary, I could swear that I *knew* you were asleep, that—but no, there might be suspicion then. That we mustn't have! Don't fear for me, dear one! I shall be so discreet, so circumspect, watching, weighing every word! But oh—h— shall we dream of *it?* What if we should, and should cry out in our sleep—Oh—h, my God! my God!"

She sank again, convulsively clutching his hand, and quivering with feverish sobs upon his breast.

"Upon my soul, I don't in the least know what you are talking about, Isabel! Do try and be calm, and tell me what it is!"

"*He* asks *me!*" she cried, with the same jarring, painful half-laugh he had heard before.

He held her from him, so that he might look into her face.

"Come, come! You are acting like a tragedy-queen on the stage. Do be sensible, and tell me what the matter is. You make me out of patience with you!"

He spoke in the vexed tone of a man needlessly perplexed with foolish mysteries. To her strained senses the simple expression of impatience was cruel mockery. She drew herself still further back from him, and dropped his hand. She was able to speak collectedly now:

"It is *you* who are the actor. You persist in playing the part—to *me!*"

"Still in riddles! *What* part, Isabel?"

"You *will* have me tell you? You want to hear the thing—in words?"

"Yes, by all means."

She had never once taken her frightened, fascinated gaze from his face. "You insist on hearing from my lips that while you were out last night your brother was murdered"——

"What!"

" Murdered not four miles from here, as he was driving on the road, and his body thrown down into a ravine. Some boys found it. Fortunately, everybody thinks it was an accident. The men who brought the news thought so."

She had spoken the words coldly, as if they were commonplaces and had been learned by rote; but all the passion of her being was flaming in her eyes, which transfixed him with their stare.

" Mur-dered!" the young man stammered, feeling his senses reeling. "Albert murdered! Oh-h this must be nonsense! It is too terrible to think of even! You are out of your mind, Isabel!"

Her lips quivered: " It would be no wonder if I were, after *this!* "

The darkened rooms, the sobbing of his aunt upstairs, the sounds of anguish that he knew now had partially awakened him, the crazed demeanor of Isabel—all these rose around him, like a black fog, to choke and confound his mind. Her fixed gaze burned him.

" Tell me what you know!" he cried, wildly.

" Wouldn't it be easier to tell me what *you* know ? "

The chilling tone of the words startled him, as might a sudden contact of warm flesh with ice, before his bewildered brain had grasped their meaning. Then, like the crimson, all-pervading outburst of a conflagration, the thing dawned upon him, and his thoughts seemed blood-red in its hideous light. He pushed her from him fiercely, returning her piteous look of fright with a glare, and biting his tongue for words that should be great enough to fairly overwhelm her. As she cowered, he strode toward her:

" You thought I did it!" he shouted at her.

Her only answer was to bury her face in her hands and sink weakly at his knees.

He stood relentlessly glowering down upon her. The bitter, brutal words that might be heaped upon her, nay, that ought to be, crowded upon his tongue. It was too great a task to restrain them, to keep silence.

" *You* thought *I* did it," he repeated. " And you didn't object—you didn't shrink from me! Why, I remember—my God!—you kissed my hand! You said ' it was done for me!' Oh-h!"

The woman at his feet, her face hidden, had been sobbing violently. She lifted her eyes now, and strove appealingly to conquer him with their power. She rose, unaided, to her feet, and confronted him. Terror and tenderness visibly struggled for the mastery of her facial expression, as for the mood behind it.

" Don't, Seth, don't! Can't you see how I am suffering? Have you no pity? How *can* you have the heart to speak to me like this?"

" *You* talk about pity—about hearts!"

" How long ago was it that they were on your tongue—that you had your arms stretched open for me?"

" Don't recall it!"

" If I were to die this day, this hour, it would be the one thing I should want to remember, the one thing of my life that I should hug to my heart. What is changed since then? A man dead?—a man dies every minute of the day somewhere in the world! Suppose I was wrong! Suppose it *was* an accident—yes, we'll say it was! *Don't* you see—how little that is, how unimportant, compared with—with "——

She finished the sentence by a faltering step toward him, her arms outstretched, her lips parted, her form offering itself for his embrace with a sinuous seduction of moving outlines.

The old witchery flamed up for a second in his pulses; then it was emberless ashes.

Without a word he turned and left her.

Charles Lotin Hildreth.

BORN in New York, N. Y., 1856.

THE KING.

[*The Masque of Death, and Other Poems.* 1889.]

AN ermined spectre on a shaking throne,
  That sits with stony eyes, unmoved and cold,
While round about the people curse and groan;
  An old, wan, withered shape, brow-bound with gold.
      Long live the king!

Dark relic of the blind, benighted years,
  Last of a race defiled by shame and crime
And stained with centuries of blood and tears,
  Abhorrèd in the searching eye of time.
      Long live the king!

Thine is the bitter heritage of hate;
  Thy fathers' heavy deeds are on thy head;
They load thee down as with a leaden weight,
  They cry upon thee from the nameless dead.
      Long live the king!

They haunt thy fevered couch in haggard dreams,
  They mock thy greatness with a secret fear;
They write upon the wall in fiery gleams—
  "Belshazzar, thou art weighed, thy doom is near!"
      Long live the king!

In thee the long, ancestral sin shall cease;
  What place hast thou among the sons of men?
Pass on and give the warring nations peace;
  The like of thee shall not be seen again.
      Long live the king!

Pass on, thou ancient, immemorial lie!
  Thy power is broken in thy feeble hands;

Behold! the long night lifts along the sky,
　　The new day rises fair in many lands.
　　　　Long live the king!

And lo! with clash of brass and clang of drums,
　　And thunder of the world's advancing tread,
The heir of time, thy strong successor comes
　　To pluck the crown from thy dishonored head.
　　　　Long live the king!

Man! meant of God to be sole king of men,
　　Whose birthright is the broad, unbarriered earth,
Whose chariot is the plough, whose sword the pen,
　　Whose crown the majesty of truth and worth.
　　　　Long live the king!

Ay, man! born thrall to gold and place and pride,
　　Back-bent with burdens, beaten with sharp rods,
Self-sold to vice and fear, creed-crucified,
　　Patient of power and prostrate to false gods.
　　　　Long live the king!

Rerisen from world-old darkness and despair,
　　Fire-purified, baptized in agony;
Behold! this is indeed the king and heir,
　　Wise, great, and good, well worthy to be free!
　　　　Long live the king!

IMPLORA PACE.

IN THE CEMETERY OF CERTOSA.

I STOOD within the cypress gloom
　　Where old Ferrara's dead are laid,
And mused on many a sculptured tomb
　　Moss-grown and mouldering in the
　　　　shade.

And there was one the eye might pass,
　　And careless foot might tread upon.
A crumbling tablet in the grass,
　　With weeds and wild vines overrun.

In the dim light I stooped to trace
　　The lines the time-worn marble bore,
Of reverent praise or prayer for grace—
　　"*Implora pace!*"—nothing more.

Name, fame, and rank, if any were,
　　Had long since vanished from the
　　　　stone,
Leaving the meek, pathetic prayer,
　　"Peace I implore!" and this alone.

EVENING.

I FEEL the cool breath of the coming night,
　　Sweet with the scent of meadows and new hay,
And subtly as a failing of the sight
　　The dusk invisibly dissolves the day.

Still in the west an arc of primrose light
   Crowns like an aureole the mountain's brow,
Flecked with thin sprays of palest red and gold,
   And through its lambent heart is piercing now
The point of one large star, keen, still, and cold.

The east lies in the arms of night; the eye
   No longer marks the lines of hedge and lane,
The russet stacks and squares of husbandry,
   The shaven stubble and the furrowed plain;
But over all a clear obscurity—
   A pearly gloom lit from the lucid skies—
Hangs like a tenuous veil, through which is seen
   A world transformed to unfamiliar guise
Of darkling loveliness, cool, dim, serene.

Harriet Leonora Vose Bates.

BORN in Quincy, Ill., 1856.   DIED in Boston, Mass., 1886.

AN OLD SALEM SHOP.

[Old Salem. By Eleanor Putnam.—Edited by Arlo Bates. 1886.]

I WONDER how many people have memories as vivid as mine of the quaint shops which a score of years ago stood placidly along the quiet streets of Salem. In the Salem of to-day there are few innovations. Not many modern buildings have replaced the time-honored landmarks; yet twenty years ago Salem, in certain aspects, was far more like an old colonial town than it is now. When the proprietor of an old shop died it was seldom that a new master entered. Nobody new ever came to Salem, and everybody then living there had already his legitimate occupation. The old shops, lacking tenants, went to sleep. Their green shutters were closed, and they were laid up in ordinary without comment from any one.

I remember one shop of the variety known in Salem as "button stores." It was kept by two quaint old sisters, whose family name I never knew. We always called them Miss Martha and Miss Sibyl. Miss Martha was the older, and sported a magnificent turban of wonderful construction. Miss Sibyl wore caps and little wintry curls. Both had short-waisted gowns, much shirred toward the belts, and odd little housewives of green leather, which hung from their apron-bindings by green ribbons.

Their wares were few and faded. They had a sparse collection of crewels, old-fashioned laces, little crimped cakes of white wax, and emery balls in futile imitation of strawberries. They sold handkerchiefs, antiquated gauze, and brocaded ribbons, and did embroidery stamping for ladies with much care and deliberation. I remember being once sent to take to these ladies an article which was to be stamped with a single letter. Miss Martha consulted at some length with her sister, and then, with an air of gentle importance, said to me: "Tell your mother, dear, that sister Sibyl will have it ready in one week, certainly."

On another occasion Miss Sibyl had chanced to give me a penny too much in change; discovering which before I was well away, I returned to the shop and told her of the mistake. Miss Sibyl dropped the penny into the little till,—so slender were the means of these old gentlewomen that I believe even a penny was of importance to them,—and in her gentle voice she asked, "What is your name, dear?" and when I told her she replied, approvingly, "Well, you are an honest child, and you may go home and tell your mother that Miss Sibyl said so." To this commendation she added the gift of a bit of pink gauze ribbon, brocaded with little yellow and lavender leaves, and I returned to my family in a condition of such conscious virtue that I am convinced that I must have been quite insufferable for some days following.

The only article in which these ladies dealt which specially concerned us children was a sort of gay-colored beads, such as were used in making bags and reticules—that fine old bead embroidery which some people show nowadays as the work of their great-grandmothers. These beads were highly valued by Salem children, and were sold for a penny a thimbleful. They were measured out in a small mustard-spoon of yellow wood, and it took three ladlefuls to fill the thimble. I cannot forget the air of placid and judicial gravity with which dear Miss Martha measured out a cent's worth of beads.

One winter day Miss Sibyl died. The green shutters of the shop were bowed with black ribbons, and a bit of rusty black crape fluttered from the knob of the half-glass door, inside of which the curtains were drawn as for a Sunday. For a whole week the shop was decorously closed. When it was reopened, only Miss Martha, a little older and grayer and more gently serious, stood behind the scantily filled show-case. My mother went in with me that day and bought some laces. Miss Martha folded each piece about a card and secured the ends with pins, after her usual careful fashion, and made out the quaint little receipted bill with which she always insisted on furnishing customers. As she handed the parcel across the counter she answered a look in my mother's eyes.

"I did not think she would go first," she said, simply. "Sibyl was very young to die."

In the following autumn came Miss Martha's turn to go. Then the shutters were closed forever. Nobody took the store. The winter snows drifted unchecked into the narrow doorway, and the bit of black crape affixed to the latch by friendly hands waved forlornly in the chilly winds and shivered in the air,—a thing to affect a child weirdly, and to be hastened past with a "creepy" sensation in the uncertain grayness of a winter twilight.

COUSIN SUSAN'S CUPBOARD.

[From the Same.]

FOREMOST in the memory of delightful Salem cupboards stands the dining-room closet of a second-cousin of ours, whom we called Cousin Susan. She was a widow of some fifty odd years, and kept house for a bachelor brother, who was a retired sea-captain. She was a round, trim, black-eyed woman, greatly afflicted with rheumatism, for which reason she always walked with a cane. The cane was of some dark, foreign wood, highly polished, and the top was carved to resemble a falcon's head, with shining eyes of yellow glass.

Cousin Susan was a kindly soul, who would, I think, have even been merry, had not the austerity of her youthful training warped her natural instincts and given her a certain rigidly virtuous air. She believed very sincerely in the old-time maxim that "children should be seen, and not heard," and she had rather an alarming way at times of saying "Tut, tut!" But she was really fond of young people, and whenever we went to see her she would say seductively :

"I wonder, now, if we could find anything nice in Cousin Susan's dining-room cupboard."

And truly that person who failed to do so must have been hard to please ; for, in our eyes at least, that cupboard held a little of everything that was rare and delightful.

A most delicious odor came forth when the door was opened—a hint of the spiciness of rich cake, a tingling sense of preserved ginger, and a certain ineffable sweetness which no other closet ever possessed, and which I know not how to describe. It might well have proceeded from the walls and shelves of the cupboard itself, for they were indeed emblems of purity. The paint was varnished to a high degree of glossiness, and was so exquisitely kept as to look like white porcelain.

The china here, as in all genuine Salem cupboards, was chiefly of the honest old blue Canton ware. There were shining piles of those plates which, while they are rather heavy to handle, always surprise one by being so thin at the edges. There were generous teacups like small bowls, squat pitchers with big noses, and a tureen whose cover had the head of a boar for a handle. And in all this the blue was dull and deep in tint, with a certain ill-defined, vaporous quality at the edges of the lines, and the white of the cool greenish tinge of a duck's egg. You can buy blue Canton to-day, but it is not old blue Canton. Such china is matchless now, but in this cupboard there were shelves of it.

Cousin Susan possessed also another set of china, which she valued far above her blue. It was always singularly attractive to us as children, though I have come to believe that it is far less beautiful than the Canton. It was a pure, thin, white ware, delicately fluted at the edges and decorated with little raised lilac sprigs. It was used only upon occasions of solemn company tea-drinkings, and Cousin Susan always washed it herself in her little cedar dish-tub. We children considered this china so choice and desirable that a bit of a broken saucer, which included one of the pale, tiny sprays, was cherished far above our real dolls' dishes. We lent it from one to another, each of us keeping it for one day; but it was always one of those unsatisfactory treasures of childhood for which we could never find any adequate use. We could think of nothing to do with this bit of china which seemed at all worthy of so lovely an object.

At the left hand of Cousin Susan's shelves of china was a little cupboard with a diamond-paned glass door. This was the *sanctum sanctorum*—a cupboard within a cupboard ; and here, as one might have expected, were stored the choicest treasures of all. It was not the domestic preserve-closet. Cousin Susan was thrifty, and had good store of home-made dainties, but they were kept in the cool seclusion of a dark cellar store-room. This little glass cupboard held the stock of foreign sweetmeats: the round-shouldered blue jars, inclosed in a network of split bamboo, which contained the fiery, amber ginger ; the flat boxes of guava jelly, hot curry powders, chilli sauce, and choleric Bengal chutney. Here were two miniature casks of tamarinds, jolly and black, Cousin Susan's favorites. She had a certain air of disapproval toward most of these strange conserves. "They are not good for little people," she averred ; and indeed she always maintained that these ardent sweetmeats were fitter for the delectation of rude men than for the delicate palates of gentlewomen. Of tamarinds, however, Cousin Susan did approve. Properly diluted with cool water, they made what she called a "very pretty drink." She was fond of sending a glass to any neighbor who was ill and feverish, and she was always following our cousin the sea-captain about with a blue china bowl of the mixture, begging him to partake of it.

"Susan, I hate tamarind-water," our cousin would protest.

"It will cool your blood, William," his sister would urge.

"But I don't want my blood cool. I want it warm," the captain would reply.

As a general thing, however, Cousin Susan came off triumphant. The captain grumblingly partook of his dose, and was always most generous in sharing it with us children. The beautiful little brown stones also fell to our lot, and we hoarded the useless things with great care, although it always seemed to us a great oversight on the part of nature that tamarind seeds did not have holes through them, that one might string them as beads.

Cousin Susan's cupboard also contained stronger waters than tamarind, for side by side sat two corpulent cut-glass decanters, of which one was half filled with Madeira wine and the other with honest rum. A variety of sweet cakes was near by, to be served with the wine to any chance visitor. There were black fruit-cake in a japanned box ; "hearts and rounds" of rich yellow pound-cake ; and certain delicate but inane little sponge biscuit, of which our cousin spoke by the older-fashioned name of diet—or, as she chose to pronounce it, "dier"—bread. She always called the sponge cakes "little dier breads." Pound- and fruit-cakes were forbidden to our youth, but we might have our ladylike fill of "dier breads," and also of delightful seed-cakes, which were cut in the shape of an oak-leaf, and were marvels of sugary thinness.

These seed-cakes, by the bye, were kept in a jar which deserves at least a passing mention. It was, I suppose, some two or three feet high, though it looked to me then much higher. It was of blue-and-white china, and was fitted with a cover of dull silver. Tradition stated that some seafaring ancestor had brought it home from Calcutta, filled with rock-candy. What was done with so large a supply of this confection I never knew. In those days choice sugar-plums were not as plenty as they have since become; possibly at the time "Black-jacks" and "Gibraltars" were unknown, and this was Salem's only candy. At all events, it is somewhere recorded that the ship Belisarius brought from Calcutta "ten thousand seven hundred and sixty-seven pounds" of this same rocky and crystalline dainty. The fact of such a quantity of candy had for us children a superb and opulent significance. What an idea, to have a choice confection, not by the stick or beggarly ounce, but by the jarful! To think of going and casually helping one's self at will! To imagine lifting that silver lid, and gazing unreproved into the sugary depths! Perhaps nice, white-haired spinsters used it in glittering lumps to sweeten their tea, or even served it at table by the plateful, as one might serve cake. Fancy exhausted itself in all sorts of delightful speculations. The whole legend had a profuse and mythical sound. It was like a fairy tale, a scene from Arabian Nights. It threw about the jar and the cupboard a mystic charm which time fails to efface. Even now a stick of sparkling rock-candy has power to call up Cousin Susan's dining-room cupboard, its sweet, curious perfume, the quaint old silver and blue china, and the huge turkey-feather fan, with its carved ivory handle and wreath of brilliant painted flowers, which hung on the inside of the door.

Harrison Smith Morris.

BORN in Philadelphia, Penn., 1856.

TO A COMRADE.

J. A. H., OBIIT 14 MARCH, 1889.

I.

THE leaves have come—he comes not—he is dead.
 The bugle winds of April blow their note;
The little buds dance in with dewy head
And curtsy to their lover where they spread;
 The robin fills her throat,
 Making the customed answer to his oat,
But he—alas! his fingered airs are fled!

II.

He knew to gather lyrics from the leaves
 And breathe their sweetness through the quiet closes,
 And knew the rustled converse of the roses
About the edges of the country eaves;

And where the dappled sunlight dozes,
And where the ditties wake the sheaves,
 The silence lulled him into long reposes
And happy world-reprieves.

III.

Born was he for the uplands where the sun
 And morning hill-tops meet,
Where breezes through the yellow barley run
 With dimpling feet;
 His heart went thither, though he trod the street.
He left his toil undone
 To listen to the runnel eddies fleet—
He better loved the reveries won
 In some old tree-retreat,
 The mid-bough twitter and the homeward bleat,
And twilight village fun.

IV.

But tyrant toil is harsh with what it owns,
 Nor lets the prodigal forget
 His penitential debt;
And, late, his merry music ebbed in moans.
 Who loved the noonday minuet
 Of sun and shadow forest-met,
 The freshened herbage bending in the wet
And birds in thicket-wones—
Who touched his pipe to a thousand tender tones—
 He passed us woe-beset!

V.

Song slept within him like the winter buds
 That wait the under whisper of the year,
 Then break the crumbling loam and reappear
And work a beauty in the naked woods.
He waited, oh, how long ! for happier moods,
And walked the city's peopled roods,
 With music at his ear:
 With murmur of the leaves he loved to hear
In day-long solitudes—
 But songs that should have made his presence dear,
And purchased love and long beatitudes,
 Like early blossoms drenched with many a tear
 Lay withered on his bier.

VI.

The memories are full, the years are few,
 That bound us into comradeship complete.
 We came together in the rainy street
At night, nor either knew
How close the current of our being drew,
 How wide the circles rippling from our feet.

It was as if a pair of leaves that grew
Bough-neighbors ere the severing autumn blew
 Had come again to meet,
And, finding solace in each other, knew
 Remembrance of the far-off summer sweet.

VII.

We made a bond of song—we made us nights
Arustle with the buskined forest flights,
 And pipe-réveillés of the Doric days.
 We found our attic full of arching ways—
Or, bound afield, beheld the sights
Embalmed in old poetic rites,
 And saw the slender dances of the fays.

VIII.

For he was learnèd in all leafy books
 And knew the winding region of romance;
His fingers fitted to the olden reeds;
And, when the music eddied, in his looks
 Came vision of the wood, the circled dance,
And all the secret sweetness of the deeds
By forest brooks.
His riches were an idle dreamer's meeds;
But yet he gave his best for others' needs,
And nurtured with his love the seeds
Of worth grown up in sordid city nooks.

IX.

And, last, his music ebbed. He trod the street,
 Pursuing hopes of melancholy made:
 The lights that ever seem to fade
And leave the midnight darker by retreat.
 The quiet counsel of the trees
He heeded not, nor sought the country peace,
 But, like a quarry goaded—like a shade
Swept on in darkness, all his being beat
 In maddened seas
Headlong against the granite of defeat.
 He trusted not, but made
 Foemen of guardian laws that give us aid
 And lost his treasured music in the breeze.

X.

So like a sheaf, wherein young birds have learned
 Their matin music ere the grain be eared
And glancing sickles go abroad the field,
He lay storm-broken. Fame, that would have turned
With but a little wooing, could but yield
 A chaplet of her young leaves seared.
 And he who was to earth endeared

By tendril loves that clasped him like a vine;
Who held her soil as something sweet and fine;
    And loved her still, though severed from her long—
He lies, in union grown divine,
    Within her bosom, whence a flower-flight,
    Sole guerdon of his dreams of day and night,
    Springs from his seeds of song.

The Literary World. 1889.

Margaret Deland.

BORN in Alleghany, Penn., 1857.

A CONFLICT OF OPINIONS.

[*John Ward, Preacher.* 1888.]

THEY rode quite silently to the house of the minister with whom John had exchanged, where they were to dine; after that, the preacher was to go back to the church for the afternoon sermon.

Mrs. Grier, a spare, anxious-looking woman, with a tight friz of hair about her temples, which were thin and shining, met them at the door. She had hurried home to "see to things," and be ready to welcome her guests. John she ushered at once into her husband's study, a poor little room, with even fewer books than Mr. Ward's own, while Helen she took to the spare chamber, where she had thoughtfully provided a cambric dress for her, for the day had grown very warm, and the riding-habit was heavy.

She sat down in a splint rocking-chair, and watched her guest brush out her length of shining bronze hair, and twist it in a firm coil low on her neck.

"It was a good gathering," she said; "people came from a distance to hear Mr. Ward. The folks at Lockhaven are favored to listen to such preaching."

"No doubt they feel favored to have Mr. Grier with them to-day," Helen answered, courteously; but there was an absent look in her eyes, and she did not listen closely.

"Well, people like a change once in a while," Mrs. Grier admitted, rocking hard. "Mr. Grier's discourse was to be on the same subject as your husband's, foreign missions. It is one that moves the preachers, and the people seem to like it, I notice, though I don't know that it makes much difference in the collections. But I think they like to get all harrowed up. You'll find there won't be such an attendance in the afternoon. It is ways and means then, you know. Yes, seems as if sermons on hell made them shiver, and they enjoyed it. I've sometimes thought—I don't know as I'm right—they get the same kind of pleasure out of it that worldly people do out of a play. Not that I know much about such things, I'm sure."

Helen smiled, which rather shocked Mrs. Grier; but though the guest scarcely listened, the little sharp babble of talk was kept up until they went down to dinner.

There had been no chance for the husband and wife to speak to each other. John looked at Helen steadily a moment, but her eyes veiled any thought. In the midst of Mrs. Grier's chatter, she had gone into the solitude of her own heart, and slowly and silently light was beginning to shine into the mysterious darkness of the last few days. John's grief must have had something to do with this terrible sermon. She felt her heart leap up from the past anxiety like a bird from a net, and the brooding sadness began to fade from her face. The preacher had come down from the pulpit with a certain exhilaration, as of duty done. He was inspired to hope, and even certainty, by the greatness of the theme. Helen should see the truth, his silence should no longer mislead her, she should believe in the justice of God. He had forgotten his sin of cowardice in the onward-sweeping wave of his convictions; he seemed to yield himself up to the grasp of truth, and lost even personal remorse in the contemplation of its majesty.

Mrs. Grier had four noisy children, who all spoke at once, and needed their mother's constant care and attention, so John and Helen could at least be silent; yet it was hard to sit through the dinner when their hearts were impatient for each other.

In a little breathing-space at the end of the meal, when two of the children had clambered down from their high chairs and been dismissed, Mrs. Grier began to speak of the sermon.

"It was a wonderful discourse, sir," she said; "seems as if nobody could stand against such doctrine as you gave us. I could have wished, though, you'd have told us your thoughts about infants being lost. There is a difference of opinion between Mr. Grier and two of our elders."

"What does Brother Grier hold?" asked the preacher.

"Well," Mrs. Grier answered, shaking her head, "he does say they are all saved. But the elders, they say that the confession of faith teaches that elect infants are saved, and of course it follows that those not elect are lost. My father, Mr. Ward, was a real old-fashioned Christian, and I must say that was what I was taught to believe, and I hold by it. There now, Ellen, you take your little sister and go out into the garden, like a good girl."

She lifted the baby down from her chair, and put her hand into that of her elder sister.

"Mrs. Grier," Helen said, speaking quickly, "you say you believe it, but if you had ever lost a child I am sure you could not."

"I have, ma'am,"—Mrs. Grier's thin lip quivered, and her eyes reddened a little,—"but that can't make any difference in truth; besides, we have the blessed hope that she was an elect infant."

It would have been cruel to press the reason for this hope, and Helen listened instead with a breath of relief to what John was saying. He, at least, did not hold this horrible doctrine.

"No, I agree with your husband," he said. "True, all children are born in sin, and are despised and abhorred as sinners by God. Jonathan Edwards,

Margaret Deland

you know, calls them 'vipers,' which of course was a crude and cruel way of stating the truth that they are sinners. Yet, through the infinite mercy, they are saved because Christ died—not of themselves; in other words, all infants who die are elect."

Mrs. Grier shook her head. "I'm for holding to the catechism," she said; and then, with a sharp, thin laugh, she added: "But you're sound on the heathen, I must say."

Helen shivered, and it did not escape her hostess, who turned and looked at her with interested curiosity. She, too, had heard the Lockhaven rumors.

"But then," she proceeded, "I don't see how a person can help being sound on that, though it is surprising what people will doubt, even the things that are plainest to other people. I've many a time heard my father say that the proper holding of the doctrine of reprobation was necessary to eternal life. I suppose you believe that, Mr. Ward," she added, with a little toss of her head, "even if you don't go all the way with the confession, about infants?"

"Yes," said John sadly, "I must; because not to believe in reprobation is to say that the sacrifice of the cross was a useless offering."

"And of course," Mrs. Grier went on, an edge of sarcasm cutting into her voice, "Mrs. Ward thinks so, too? Of course she thinks that a belief in hell is necessary to get to heaven?"

The preacher looked at his wife with a growing anxiety in his face.

"No," Helen said, "I do not think so, Mrs. Grier."

Mrs. Grier flung up her little thin hands, which looked like bird-claws. "You *don't!*" she cried shrilly. "Well, now, I do say! And what do you think about the heathen, then? Do you think they'll be damned?"

"No," Helen said again.

Mrs. Grier gave a gurgle of astonishment, and looked at Mr. Ward; but he did not speak.

"Well," she exclaimed, "if I didn't think the heathen would be lost, I wouldn't see the use of the plan of salvation! Why, they've got to be!"

"If they had to be," cried Helen, with sudden passion, "I should want to be a heathen. I should be ashamed to be saved, if there were so many lost." She stopped; the anguish in John's face silenced her.

"Well," Mrs. Grier said again, really enjoying the scene, "*I'm* surprised; I wouldn't a' believed it!"

She folded her hands across her waist, and looked at Mrs. Ward with keen interest. Helen's face flushed under the contemptuous curiosity in the woman's eyes. She turned appealingly to John.

"Mrs. Ward does not think quite as we do, yet," he said gently; "you know she has not been a Presbyterian as long as we have."

He rose as he spoke, and came and stood by Helen's chair, and then walked at her side into the parlor.

Mrs. Grier had followed them, and heard Helen say in a low voice, "I would rather not go to church this afternoon, dearest. May I wait for you here?"

"Well," she broke in, "I shouldn't suppose you would care to go, so long as it's just about the ways and means of sending the gospel to the heathen, and you think they're all going right to heaven, any way."

"I do not know where they are going, Mrs. Grier," Helen said wearily; "for all I know, there is no heaven, either. I only know that God—if there is a God who has any personal care for us—could not be so wicked and cruel as to punish people for what they could not help."

"Good land!" cried Mrs. Grier, really frightened at such words, and looking about as though she expected a judgment as immediate as the bears which devoured the scoffing children.

"If you would rather not go," John answered, "if you are tired, wait for me here. I am sure Mrs. Grier will let you lie down and rest until it is time to start for home."

"Oh, of course," responded Mrs. Grier, foreseeing a chance for further investigation; for she, too, was to be at home.

But Helen did not invite her to come into the spare room when she went to lie down, after John's departure for church. She wanted to be alone. She had much to think of, much to reconcile and explain, to protect herself from the unhappiness which John's sermon might have caused her. She had had an unmistakable shock of pain and distress as she realized her husband's belief, and to feel even that seemed unloving and disloyal. To Helen's mind, if she disapproved of her husband's opinions on what to her was an unimportant subject, her first duty was to banish the thought, and forget that she had ever had it. She sat now by the open window, looking out over the bright garden to the distant peaceful hills, and by degrees the pain of it began to fade from her mind, in thoughts of John himself, his goodness, and their love. Yes, they loved one another,—that was enough.

"What does it matter what his belief is?" she said. "I love him!"

So, by and by, the content of mere existence unfolded in her heart, and John's belief was no more to her than a dress of the mind; his character was unchanged. There was a momentary pang that the characters of others might be hurt by this teaching of the expediency of virtue, but she forced the thought back. John, whose whole life was a lesson in the beauty of holiness — John could not injure any one. The possibility that he might be right in his creed simply never presented itself to her.

Helen's face had relaxed into a happy smile; again the day was fair and the wind sweet. The garden below her was fragrant with growing things and the smell of damp earth; and while she sat, drinking in its sweetness, a sudden burst of children's voices reached her ear, and Ellen and the two little boys came around the corner of the house and settled down under the window. A group of lilacs, with feathery purple blossoms, made a deep, cool shade where the children sat; and near them was an old grindstone, streaked with rust and worn by many summers of sharpening scythes; a tin dipper hung on the wooden frame, nearly full of last night's rain, and with some lilac stars floating in the water.

This was evidently a favorite playground with the children, for under the frame of the grindstone were some corn-cob houses, and a little row of broken bits of china, which their simple imagination transformed into "dishes." But to-day the corn-cob houses and the dishes were untouched.

"Now, children," Ellen said, "you sit right down and I'll hear your catechism."

"Who'll hear yours?" Bobby asked discontentedly. "When we play school you're always teacher, and it's no fun."

"This isn't playing school," Ellen answered, skilfully evading the first question. "Don't you know it's wicked to play on the Sabbath? Now sit right down."

There was a good deal of her mother's sharpness in the way she said this, and plucked Bobby by the strings of his pinafore, until he took an uncomfortable seat upon an inverted flower-pot.

Ellen opened a little yellow-covered book and began:

"Now answer, Jim. How many kinds of sin are there?"

"Two," responded little Jim.

"What are these two kinds, Bob?"

"Original and actual," Bob answered.

"What is original sin?" asked Ellen, raising one little forefinger to keep Bobby quiet. This was too hard a question for Jim, and with some stumbling Bobby succeeded in saying:

"It is that sin in which I was conceived and born."

"Now, Jim," said Ellen, "you can answer this question, 'cause it's only one word, and begins with 'y.'"

"No fair!" cried Bob; "that's telling."

But Ellen proceeded to give the question: "Doth original sin wholly defile you, and is it sufficient to send you to hell, though you had no other sin?"

"Yes!" roared Jim, pleased at being certainly right.

"What are you then by nature?" Ellen went on rather carelessly, for she was growing tired of the lesson.

"I am an enemy to God, a child of Satan, and an heir of hell," answered Bobby promptly.

"What will become of the wicked?" asked the little catechist.

Bobby yawned, and then said contemptuously: "Oh, skip that,—cast into hell, of course."

"You ought to answer right," Ellen said reprovingly; but she was glad to give the last question, "What will the wicked do forever in hell?"

"They will roar, curse, and blaspheme God," said little Jim cheerfully; while Bobby, to show his joy that the lesson was done, leaned over on his flower-pot and tried to stand on his head, making all the time an unearthly noise.

"I'm roarin'!" he cried gayly.

Ellen, freed from the responsibility of teaching, put the little yellow book quickly in her pocket and said mysteriously: "Boys, if you won't ever tell, I'll tell you something."

"I won't," said Jim, while Bobby responded briefly, "G'on."

"Well, you know when the circus came,—you know the pictures on the fences?"

"Yes!" said the little boys together.

"'Member the beautiful lady, ridin' on a horse, and standin' on one foot?"

"Yes!" the others cried, breathlessly.

"Well," said Ellen slowly and solemnly, "when I get to be a big girl, that's what I'm going to be. I'm tired of catechism, and church, and those long blessings father asks, but most of catechism, so I'm going to run away and be a circus."

"Father'll catch you," said Jim; but Bobby, with envious depreciation, added:

"How do you know but what circuses have catechism?"

Ellen did not notice the lack of sympathy. "And I'm going to begin to practice now," she said.

Then, while her brothers watched her, deeply interested, she took off her shoes, and in her well-darned little red stockings climbed deliberately upon the grindstone.

"This is my horse," she said, balancing herself, with outstretched arms, on the stone, and making it revolve in a queer, jerky fashion by pressing her feet on it as though it were a treadmill, "and it is bare-backed!"

The iron handle came down with a thud, and Ellen lurched to keep from falling. The boys unwisely broke into cheers.

It made a pretty picture, the sunbeams sifting through the lilacs on the little fair heads and dancing over Ellen's white apron and rosy face; but Mrs. Grier, who had come to the door at the noise of the cheers, did not stop to notice it.

"Oh, you naughty children!" she cried. "Don't you know it is wicked to play on the Sabbath? 'Ellen's playing circus,' do you say, Bobby? You naughty, naughty girl! Don't you know circus people are all wicked, and don't go to heaven when they die? I should think you'd be ashamed! Go right up-stairs, Ellen, and go to bed; and you boys can each learn a psalm, and you'll have no supper, either,—do you hear?"

The children began to cry, but Mrs. Grier was firm; and when, a little later, Helen came down-stairs, ready for her ride, the house was strangely quiet. Mrs. Grier, really troubled at her children's sinfulness, confided their misdeeds to Helen, and was not soothed by the smile that flashed across her face.

"They were such good children to study their catechism first," she interceded, "and making a horse out of a grindstone shows an imagination which might excuse the playing."

But Mrs. Grier was not comforted, and only felt the more convinced of the lost condition of Mrs. Ward's soul. The conviction of other people's sin is sometimes a very pleasing emotion, so she bade her guest good-by with much cordiality and even pulled the skirt of her habit straight and gave the gray a lump of sugar.

Ramsay Morris.

BORN in New York, N. Y., 1858.

CLEOPATRA.

[IN THE METROPOLITAN MUSEUM OF ART.]

TO-DAY you see me here in stone—
  A pulseless queen,
A sculptor's vain imagining
  Of what I've been.
He gave to me a form of grace,
  A regal air:
He fashioned me with artist's skill
  Beyond compare,

Yet hath he missed me for all that—
  His art is cold;
His chiselled likeness halts at life,
  Does not unfold.
I dream in this one attitude
  Through all my days,
While countless eyes pause, where I rest,
  With lingering gaze.

Could they but see me as I was
  In Egypt's land—
My queenly state, my ebon guards,
  My armies grand,
The robes which draped my perfect form
  With matchless grace,
The gems which flashed on all my limbs—
  And, ah, my face!—

That face which conquered Anthony
  With potent wile,
Which made me famed from end to end
  The golden Nile,—

The eyes which poets sung were stars
  Of glorious light,
Which wielded power greater far
  Than warriors' might!

Oh, sculptor, give me back my life,
  To reign once more,
To lead my retinue along
  Nile's tawny shore.
To find again my Anthony,
  To feel his arms,
To rest secure within their fold
  From earth's alarms.

Oh, change me from this icy thing
  To living queen!
I long to show to all the world
  What I have been.
Breathe soul into this shapely form,
  Return my voice:
The multitude will praise your skill,
  And loud rejoice.

Is it not sad that I, who ruled
  By beauty's right,
Should vanquished be by death, and roam
  Through Stygian night?
I wander, desolate and lone,
  Through midnight lands.—
Oh, give me life, and Anthony,
  And Egypt's sands.

Theodore Roosevelt.

Born in New York, N. Y., 1858.

HUNTING "OLD EPHRAIM."

[*Hunting Trips of a Ranchman.* 1886.]

EARLY next morning we were over at the elk carcass, and, as we expected, found that the bear had eaten his fill at it during the night. His tracks showed him to be an immense fellow, and were so fresh that we doubted if he had left long before we arrived; and we made up our minds to follow him up and try to find his lair. The bears that lived on these mountains had evidently been little disturbed; indeed, the Indians and most of the white hunters are rather chary of meddling with "Old Ephraim," as the mountainmen style the grizzly, unless they get him at a disadvantage; for the sport is fraught with some danger and but small profit. The bears thus seemed to have very little fear of harm, and we thought it likely that the bed of the one who had fed on the elk would not be far away.

My companion was a skilful tracker, and we took up the trail at once. For some distance it led over the soft, yielding carpet of moss and pine needles, and the footprints were quite easily made out, although we could follow them but slowly; for we had, of course, to keep a sharp lookout ahead and around us as we walked noiselessly on in the sombre half-light always prevailing under the great pine trees, through whose thickly interlacing branches stray but few beams of light, no matter how bright the sun may be outside. We made no sound ourselves, and every little sudden noise sent a thrill through me as I peered about with each sense on the alert. Two or three of the ravens that we had scared from the carcass flew overhead, croaking hoarsely; and the pine tops moaned and sighed in the slight breeze—for pine trees seem to be ever in motion, no matter how light the wind.

After going a few hundred yards the tracks turned off on a well-beaten path made by the elk; the woods were in many places cut up by these game-trails, which had often become as distinct as ordinary foot-paths. The beast's footprints were perfectly plain in the dust, and he had lumbered along up the path until near the middle of the hill-side, where the ground broke away and there were hollows and bowlders. Here there had been a windfall, and the dead trees lay among the living, piled across one another in all directions; while between and around them sprouted up a thick growth of young spruces and other evergreens. The trail turned off into the tangled thicket, within which it was almost certain we would find our quarry. We could still follow the tracks, by the slight scrapes of the claws on the bark or by the bent and broken twigs, and we advanced with noiseless caution, slowly climbing over the dead tree trunks and upturned stumps, and not letting a branch rustle or catch on our clothes. When in the middle of the thicket we crossed what was almost a breastwork of fallen logs, and Merrifield, who was leading, passed by the upright stem of a great pine. As soon as he was by it he sank suddenly on one knee, turning half round, his face fairly aflame with excitement; and as I strode past him, with my rifle at the ready, there, not ten steps off, was the great bear, slowly rising from his bed among the young spruces. He had heard us, but apparently hardly knew exactly where or what we were, for he reared up on his haunches sideways to us. Then he saw us and dropped down again on all-fours, the shaggy hair on his neck and shoulders seeming to bristle as he turned toward us. As he sank down on his forefeet I had raised the rifle; his head was bent slightly down, and when I saw the top of the white bead fairly between his small, glittering, evil eyes, I pulled trigger. Half rising up, the huge beast fell over on his side in the death-throes, the ball having gone into his brain, striking as fairly between the eyes as if the distance had been measured by a carpenter's rule.

The whole thing was over in twenty seconds from the time I caught sight of the game; indeed, it was over so quickly that the grizzly did not have time to show fight at all or come a step toward us. It was the first I had ever seen, and I felt not a little proud, as I stood over the great brindled bulk which lay stretched out at length in the cool shade of the evergreens. He was a monstrous fellow, much larger than any I have seen since, whether alive or brought in dead by the hunters. As near as we could estimate (for of course we had nothing with which to weigh more than very small portions), he must have weighed about twelve hundred pounds, and, though this is not as large as some of his kind are said to grow in California, it is yet a very unusual size for a bear. He was a good deal heavier than any of our horses, and it was with the greatest difficulty that we were able to skin him. He must have been very old, his teeth and claws being all worn down and blunted; but nevertheless he had been living in plenty, for he was as fat as a prize-hog, the layers on his back being a finger's length in thickness. He was still in the summer coat, his hair being short, and in color a curious brindled brown, somewhat like that of certain bull-dogs, while all the bears we shot afterward had the long thick winter fur, cinnamon or yellowish brown. By the way, the name of this bear has reference to its character and not to its color, and should, I suppose, be properly spelt grisly—in the sense of horrible, exactly as we speak of a "grisly spectre"—and not grizzly; but perhaps the latter way of spelling it is too well established to be now changed.

In killing dangerous game, steadiness is more needed than good shooting. No game is dangerous unless a man is close up, for nowadays hardly any wild beast will charge from a distance of a hundred yards, but will rather try to run off; and if a man is close it is easy enough for him to shoot straight if he does not lose his head. A bear's brain is about the size of a pint bottle; and any one can hit a pint bottle off-hand at thirty or forty feet. I have had two shots at bears at close quarters, and each time I fired into the brain, the bullet in one case striking fairly between the eyes, as told above, and in the other going in between the eye and ear. A novice at this kind of sport will find it best and safest to keep in mind the old Norse viking's advice in reference to a long sword: "If you go in close enough your sword will be long enough." If a poor shot goes in close enough he will find that he shoots straight enough.

I was very proud over my first bear; but Merrifield's chief feeling seemed to be disappointment that the animal had not had time to show fight. He was rather a reckless fellow, and very confident in his own skill with the rifle; and he really did not seem to have any more fear of the grizzlies than if they had been so many jack-rabbits. I did not at all share his feelings, having a hearty respect for my foes' prowess, and in following and attacking them always took all possible care to get the chances on my side. Merrifield was sincerely sorry that we never had to stand a regular charge; while on this trip we killed five grizzlies with seven bullets, and except in the case of the she and cub, spoken of further on, each was shot about as quickly as it got sight of us.   .   .

A day or two after the death of the big bear, we went out one afternoon on horseback, intending merely to ride down to see a great canyon lying some six miles west of our camp; indeed, we went more to look at the scenery than for any other reason, though, of course, neither of us ever stirred out of camp without his rifle. We rode down the valley in which we had camped, through alternate pine groves and open glades, until we reached the canyon, and then skirted its brink for a mile or so. It was a great chasm, many miles in length, as if the table-land had been rent asunder by some terrible and unknown force; its sides were sheer walls of rock, rising three or four hundred feet straight up in the air, and worn by the weather till they looked like the towers and battlements of some vast fortress. Between them at the bottom was a space, in some places nearly a quarter of a mile wide, in others very narrow, through whose middle foamed a deep, rapid torrent of which the sources lay far back among the snow-topped mountains around Cloud Peak. In this valley, dark-green, sombre pines stood in groups, stiff and erect; and here and there among them were groves of poplar and cotton-wood, with slender branches and trembling leaves, their bright green already changing to yellow in the sharp fall weather. We went down to where the mouth of the canyon opened out, and rode our horses to the end of a great jutting promontory of rock, thrust out into the plain; and in the cold, clear air we looked far over the broad valley of the Big Horn as it lay at our very feet, walled in on the other side by the distant chain of the Rocky Mountains.

Turning our horses, we rode back along the edge of another canyon-like valley, with a brook flowing down its centre, and its rocky sides covered with an uninterrupted pine forest—the place of all others in whose inaccessible wildness and ruggedness a bear would find a safe retreat. After some time we came to where other valleys, with steep, grass-grown sides, covered with sage-brush, branched out from it, and we followed one of these out. There was plenty of elk sign about, and we saw several black-tail deer. These last were very common on the mountains, but we had not hunted them at all, as we were in no need of meat. But this afternoon we came across a buck with remarkably fine antlers, and accordingly I shot it, and we stopped to cut off and skin out the horns, throwing the reins over the heads of the horses and leaving them to graze by themselves. The body lay near the crest of one side of a deep valley, or ravine, which headed up on the plateau a mile to our left. Except for scattered trees and bushes the valley was bare; but there was heavy timber along the crests of the hills on its opposite side. It took some time to fix the head properly, and we were just ending when Merrifield sprang to his feet and exclaimed "Look at the bears!" pointing down into the valley below us. Sure enough there were two bears (which afterwards proved to be an old she and a nearly full-grown cub) travelling up the bottom of the valley, much too far off for us to shoot. Grasping our rifles and throwing off our hats we started off as hard as we could run, diagonally down the hill-side, so as to cut them off. It was some little time before they saw us, when they made off at a lumbering gallop up the valley. It would seem impossible to run into two grizzlies in the open, but they were going up hill, and we down, and moreover the old one kept stopping. The cub would forge ahead and could probably have escaped us, but the mother now and then stopped to sit up on her haunches and look round at us, when the cub would run back to her. The upshot was that we got ahead of them, when they turned and went straight up one hill-side as we ran straight down the other behind them. By this time I was pretty nearly done out, for running along the steep ground through the sage-brush was most exhausting work ; and Merrifield kept gaining on me and was well in front. Just as he disappeared over a bank, almost at the bottom of the valley, I tripped over a bush and fell full-length. When I got up I knew I could never make up the ground I had lost, and besides could hardly run any longer ; Merrifield was out of sight below, and the bears were laboring up the steep hill-side directly opposite and about three hundred yards off, so I sat down and began to shoot over Merrifield's head, aiming at the big bear. She was going very steadily and in a straight line, and each bullet sent up a puff of dust where it struck the dry soil, so that I could keep correcting my aim ; and the fourth ball crashed into the old bear's flank. She lurched heavily forward, but recovered herself and reached the timber. while Merrifield, who had put on a spurt, was not far behind.

I toiled up the hill at a sort of trot, fairly gasping and sobbing for breath ; but before I got to the top I heard a couple of shots and a shout. The old bear had turned as soon as she was in the timber, and came toward Merrifield, but he gave her the death-wound by firing into her chest, and then shot at the young one, knocking it over. When I came up he was just walking toward the latter to finish it with the revolver, but it suddenly jumped up as lively as ever and made off at a great pace—for it was nearly full-grown. It was impossible to fire where the tree trunks were so thick, but there was a small opening across which it would have to pass, and collecting all my energies I made a last run, got into position, and covered the opening with my rifle. The instant the bear appeared I fired, and it turned a dozen somersaults down-hill, rolling over and over ; the ball had struck it near the tail and had ranged forward through the hollow of the body. Each of us had thus given the fatal wound to the bear into which the other had fired the first bullet. The run, though short, had been very sharp, and over such awful country that we were completely fagged out, and could hardly speak for lack of breath. The sun had already set, and it was too late to skin the animals ; so we merely dressed them, caught the ponies—with some trouble, for they were frightened at the smell of the bear's blood on our hands—and rode home through the darkening woods. Next day we brought the teamster and two of the steadiest pack-horses to the carcasses, and took the skins into camp.

CIVIL SERVICE EXAMINATIONS.

[Sixth Report of the U. S. Civil Service Commission. 1889.]

IT is not contended that the system is ideally perfect; no governmental methods are. From time to time there have been shown certain defects in the working of the civil service law and rules, though most of these defects already have been, and it is believed that the majority of the remainder soon will be, remedied. But it is most emphatically contended that the merit system shows to very great advantage when compared with any other, whether actual or proposed; and this is especially the case when the comparison is made with the patronage system, which it is now slowly but surely supplanting. The fundamental proposition of the new system is that every American citizen has a right to serve the public (provided that his services are needed) if on his merits he is able to show that he is the man most capable of filling the position he seeks, and all he is required to do is to show this superior capacity in fair competition with other American citizens. In other words, the system is one of common honesty and of fair play for all, and therefore it is essentially American and essentially democratic. The object of the law is to give to the average American citizen what it takes away from the professional politician. How little this object is understood by some men in public life may be gathered from recent proposals to parcel out all the offices among the different Congressional districts according to the political faith of the Congressmen representing them. This would, of course, simply mean a revival of the patronage system, with an added touch of chaos. It is apparently brought forward in the simple faith that all that is needed is to divide the offices among the politicians of both parties instead of among those of only one, and ignores the very common-sense view, which insists that the offices are not the property of the politicians at all, whether of one party or of the other or of both; but, on the contrary, that they belong to the people, and should be filled only with reference to the needs of the public service.

It seems worth while to answer one or two of the accusations often brought against the merit system by its opponents. These accusations have been so incessantly repeated that many people have finally come to believe them.

One of these accusations is that the examinations are of such a character as to favor "boys fresh from school" at the expense of men of maturer age, experience, and capacity. This is simply incorrect. In the last report of the Commission full tables bearing on the subject are given. By these it is shown that nearly two thirds of the applicants for examination succeeded in passing, and that of those passing about two fifths are appointed, the figures proving, by the way, that those that have had a good common-school education do about as well as those who have graduated from college. A glance at these tables shows that the average age of those passing the examinations for the ordinary governmental positions, such as clerk, copyist, letter-carrier, and the like, is about twenty-eight years. In other words, the examinations for these positions are especially suited, not to school-boys, but to men in the prime of life, with experience of the world, who have left school for at least ten years. The most common accusation, however, is that the examinations are "scholastic," or of an "impractical" character; that, as is often asserted, the Commission does not give practical tests, but asks questions "about the sciences," or, at least, on irrelevant subjects. All such statements as these are without foundation; and if those who make them do so in good faith it is only because they have not taken the trouble to ascertain the facts. As a matter of fact, special care is taken to have the examinations as practical in character as possible, and to test each candidate on precisely those subjects demanded by the character of the work in the branch of the service to which he is seeking admission. The Commission strongly objects to irrelevant questions, and surely there can be no questions more irrelevant to a man's duties as clerk or letter-carrier than are inquiries as to how he voted at the last election and how strong his political backing is; and these are precisely the questions that many of the men who thus object to the examinations as "impractical" are in reality desirous of asking.

Examinations are held for scores of different places, and for each place appropriate tests are provided. Thus, it is necessary for an assistant chemist to know something of chemistry, and for an assistant astronomer to know something of astronomy; and applicants for such positions are questioned accordingly. A would-be stenographer and type-writer is examined in stenography and type-writing. But the great bulk of applicants—probably over 90 per cent.—apply for positions as clerk, copyist, letter-carrier, and the like; and the examinations for these positions are those by which the system can best be tested. For each of these positions there is a plain, practical, common-sense examination, such as would appear to the average intelligence to be best suited to find out the men who possess in the highest degree the qualities needed. A copyist is examined on but four subjects—spelling, penmanship, elementary arithmetic, and copying from dictation, from plain copy, and from a rough draft. His duties as a copyist make it necessary for him to spell well, to write a good legible hand, to solve simple problems in arithmetic, and to make a clear, neat-looking copy of a first draft of a letter which is filled with interlineations and erasures; and accordingly these four points are the very ones on which he is examined. A clerk's examination is a little harder, for besides the above-mentioned subjects he is required to show that he can write an intelligent letter on some given topic, that he can turn ungrammatical sentences into good English, that he knows how to keep accounts, and finally that he knows something of United States geography, government, and history. Every question, except the last, has a direct bearing upon the duties to which the clerk will be put as soon as he has been appointed. The only objection that can possibly be made is to the questions about the geography and history of the United States (and no other questions are asked in history and geography); but these combined never count for more than 5 per cent. in the examination, so that an applicant need not answer them at all, and may yet attain an average of 95 per cent. Moreover, these questions are a test of a man's general intelligence. Every good American citizen ought to possess a rudimentary knowledge of his country's history, geography, and government.

Examinations for all the ordinary minor positions are based upon the two for clerk and copyist, some of the questions being dropped and others substituted in each case, according to the character of the work in the special place applied for. Thus, a letter-carrier has to show good knowledge of the local geography of his vicinity—its railway stations, big commercial buildings, and the like. Or, again, a railway mail-clerk has to show acquaintance with the railway systems of his State and section, and to make it evident that he can read off a large number of addresses with speed and accuracy.

Such are fair samples of the tests applied to the great majority of the candidates who come before the examining boards; and if questions on the points indicated above are not practical and pertinent to the duties of the position sought for, then it would be hard to know what questions are.

James Benjamin Kenyon.

BORN in Frankfort, Herkimer Co., N. Y., 1858.

SONG OF THE NORTH WIND.

[*In Realms of Gold.* 1887.]

HARK to the voice of me!
　Hear thou the singing
Of him who has never
Been paid for his song!
This is the choice of me,
Still to go ringing
The rhymes that forever
Are surly and strong.

Know'st thou the regions cold
Whence I have hasted?
Know'st thou the way I take
Over the earth?
Still stand the legends old—
Ice-kings unwasted—
Fending the frigid lake
Where I had birth.

Frost-banded fountains
Snow-fed from far peaks;
Firths of the polar sea
Rigid as stone;

Shag-bearded mountains;
Deeps that no star seeks;
Strange lights that solar be—
These I have known.

Men fear the breath of me;
Sorrow and anguish,
Famine and fever
Follow my path.
I am the death of thee;
I make thee languish;
Swiftly I sever
Love's ties in my wrath.

Chains cannot hold me,
Gyves cannot bind me,
Bolts cannot lock me,
Floods cannot drown!
Fly—and I fold thee;
Hide—and I find thee;
Cry—and I mock thee;
Howling thee down!

QUATRAIN.

S HE would not stir a single jetty lash
  To hear me praised; but when my life was blamed
Her parian cheeks were kindled like a flash,
  And from her heart a sudden love upflamed.

REQUIESCAT.

S HE sleeps, and may her peaceful rest
    Unbroken be;
The flowers that nod above her breast
    She cannot see;
To warbling bird, to purling brook,
    Deaf are her ears;

Sealed is the volume of the book
    Of her brief years.
So let her rest; she will not heed
    The tales they tell;
She recks not now of word or deed—
    She slumbers well.

Edgar Evertson Saltus.

BORN in New York, N. Y., 1858.

A MAID OF MODERN ATHENS.

[*A Transient Guest, and Other Episodes.* 1889.]

"I T was this way," she said, and as she spoke she stooped and flicked a
   speck of dust from her habit. "It was this way: The existence which I
lead in the minds of other people is absolutely of no importance whatever.
Now wait: I care a great deal whether school keeps or not, but in caring I try
chiefly to be true to myself. I may stumble; I may not. In any event I seek
the best. As for the scandal of which you speak, that is nonsense. There is
no criterion. That which is permissible here is inhibited yonder, and what
is permissible yonder is inhibited here. Scandal, indeed!"

There was something about her that stirred the pulse. She was fair; the
sort of girl whose photograph is an abomination, and yet in whose face and
being a charm resides, a charm intangible and coercive, inciting to better
things. A Joan of Arc in a tailor-made gown.

"You remember how it was when we were younger— You—well, there is
no use in going into that. You had a mother to think for you; I had no one.
I had to solve problems unassisted. The weightiest of all was marriage, and
that, in my quality of heiress, I found perplexing to a degree. But how is it
possible, I asked myself, how can a girl pledge her life to a man of whom she
knows absolutely nothing? For, practically speaking, what does the average
girl know of the man whose name she takes? It may be different in the country; but in town! Listen to me; a girl 'comes out,' as the saying is; she meets
a number of men, the majority of whom are more or less agreeable and well-

bred—when she is present. But what are they when she is not? At dinners and routs, or when she receives them in her own house, they are at their best; if they are not they stay away. It is not so difficult to be agreeable once in awhile, but to be so always is a question not of mask but of nature. It seems to me that when an intelligent woman admires her brother it is because that brother is really an admirable man. Has she not every opportunity of judging? But what opportunity is given to the girl whom a man happens to take in and out at dinner, or whom she sees for an hour or two now and then? You must admit that her facilities are slight. That was the way it was with me, and that was the way I fancied it would continue to be, and I determined that it was better to remain spinster forever than to take a man on trust and find that trust misplaced. Suspicious? No, I am not suspicious. When your husband bought this property did you think him suspicious because he had the title searched? Very good; then perhaps you will tell me that the marriage contract is less important than the conveyance of real estate? Besides, my doubts on the subject of love would have defied a catalogue. When I read of the follies and transports of which it was reported to be the prime factor, I was puzzled. It seemed to me that I had either a fibre more or a fibre less than other girls, I could not comprehend. No man I had ever met—and certainly I had met many—had ever caused me so much as a fleeting emotion. There were men with whom I found speech agreeable and argument a pleasure, but, had they worn frocks instead of trousers, such enjoyment as I experienced would have been unimpaired. You see, it was purely mental. And when—there, I remember one man in particular. As Stella said of Swift, he could talk beautifully about a broomstick. He knew the reason of things; he was up in cuneiform inscriptions and at home with meteorites; he was not prosy, and, what is more to the point, he never treated a subject as though it were a matter of life and death. He was not bad-looking, either, and he was the only man of my acquaintance who both understood Kant and got his coats from Poole. That man I liked very much. He was better than a book. I could ask him questions, a thing you can't do even of an encyclopædia. One fine day the personal pronoun cropped out. We had been discussing Herbert Spencer's theory of conceivability, and abruptly, with an inappositeness which, now I think of it, would have been admirable on the stage, but which in the drawing-room was certainly misplaced, he asked me to take a walk with him down the aisle of the swellest church in the commonwealth. I mourned his loss, as we say. But wasn't it stupid of him? But what does get into men? Why should they think that, because a girl is liberal with odd evenings, she is pining for the marriage covenant?"

With the whip she held she gave the hem of her habit a sudden lash.

"That episode gave me food for thought. H'm. By-and-by the scene was occupied by a young man who was an authority on orchids, and wrote sonnets for the "Interstate." My dear, a more guileful little wretch never breathed. When my previous young man disappeared, I felt that I had been hasty. I desired nothing so much as an increase in my store of knowledge, and I determined that if another opportunity occurred I would not be in such a hurry to shut the door on entertaining developments. Consequently, when my poet turned up I was as demure as you please. He was a fox, that man. He began with the fixed purpose of irritating me into liking him. The tactics he displayed were unique. He never came when I expected him, and when he did come he was careful to go just when he thought he had scored a point. If any other man happened in, he first eclipsed him and then left him to me. I saw through that game at once. He understood perfectly that if I preferred the other man I was all the more obliged to him for going, and if I preferred him to the other man I was the sorrier to see him leave. In addition to this, whatever subject I broached, he led it by tangential flights to Love. That Machiavelli *en herbe* knew that to talk love is to make love. And talk of love he did, but in the most impersonal manner. To hear him descant you would have thought his wings were sprouting. Love, as he expressed it, was a sentiment which ennobled every other; a purifying and exalting light. It was the most gracious of despots. It banished the material; it beckoned to the ideal. It turned satiety into a vagabond that had not where to lay its head. It was the reduction of the world, creation, and all the universe to a single being. It was an enchanted upland, inhibited to the herd. It was a chimera to the vulgar, a crown to the refined. 'A perfect lover,' he said, 'must needs be an aristocrat.' And if you will believe me, I actually thought he meant what he said. In spite of myself, I was becoming interested. There were new horizons before me. I seemed to discern something hitherto unseen. My dear, for the moment I felt myself going. I was at the foot of his enchanted upland. I was almost willing to take him for guide. At first I had been merely amused. Once, even, when he quoted the 'Two souls with but a single thought,' I suggested that that must mean but half a thought apiece. The quiet dignity which he then displayed almost fetched me. He had the air of a prelate in whose presence an oaf has trampled on a crucifix. He kept up that sort of thing for two months. To me his sincerity was beyond peradventure. Not once did he speak in a personal way. I was beginning to wonder when he would stop beating about the bush; and I not only wondered, I believe I even wished that he would be a little more enterprising and a trifle less immaterial. Presently I detected a symptom or two which told me that the end of the beginning was in sight. I suppose my manner was more encouraging. In any event, one evening he took my hand and kissed it. From nine-and-ninety men out of a hundred I should have thought nothing of such a thing. In Europe it is an empty homage, a pantomime expressive of thanks. As I say, then, in any other man I should not have given it a second thought, but he had never done it before.

"The next day I lunched with Mrs. Bunker Hill. I mentioned his name; I suppose it was running in my mind. And then, my dear, Fanny began. Well, the things she told me about that transcendental young man were of such a nature that when he next called I was not at home. He came again, of course. And again. He sent me a note, which I returned unopened. That, I confess, was a foolish thing to do. It showed him that I was annoyed. I might better have left it unanswered. After all, there is nothing so impenetrable as silence. Finally, he got one of his friends to come and reconnoitre. Indeed, he did not desist until I had an opportunity of cutting him dead. I was angry, I admit it. And it was after that little experience that I determined, the next time I felt myself going, I would make sure beforehand where I was going to. H'm. I wonder what his sister thought of him. You see, it was not that I had fallen in love; the word was as unintelligible to me as before, but I had fancied that, through him, I might intercept some inkling of its meaning, and I was put out at having been tricked. *Ach! diese Männer!"*

Beneath descending night the sky was gold-barred and green. In the east the moon glittered like a sickle of tin. The air was warm and freighted with the odors of August. You could hear the crickets hum, and here and there was the spark of a fire-fly gyrating in loops of flame. From across the meadows came the slumbrous tinkle of a bell.

She raised a gloved hand to her brow and looked down at the yellow road. To one who loved her, the Helen for whom the war of the world was fought was not so fair as she. And presently the hand moved about the brow, and, resting a second's space on the coil just above the neck, fell again to her side.

"Well," she continued, "you can see how it was. Even before the illusion, disillusionment had come. That winter I went with the Bunker Hills to Monaco. Were it not for the riff-raff, that place would be a paradise in duodecimo. We had a villa, of course. One evening, shortly after our arrival, we went to the Casino. For the fun of the thing I put some money on the *Trente et Quarante*. I did nothing but win. It was tiresome; I would rather have lost; I had to speak to the dealer, and that, as you can fancy, was not to my liking. There was a great crowd. One little old woman put money wherever I did. She won a lot, too. But one man, whom I could not help noticing, backed red when I was on black, and vice versa. He did it persistently, intentionally, and he lost every time. Finally one of the croupiers told me that my stake was above the maximum, and asked how much I would risk. I was tired of answering his questions, and I turned away. A lackey followed me with a salver covered with gold and notes—the money I had won. I didn't want it; I had not even a pocket to put it in, and the purse which I held in my hand would not have held a fraction of it. It was a nuisance. I turned it over to Bunker, and presently we all went out on the terrace that overhangs the sea. It was a perfect night. In the air was a caress, and from the Mediterranean came a tonic. While I was enjoying it all, a beggar ambled up on a crutch and begged a franc. I took from Bunker the money I had won and gave him thirty thousand. You should have heard Bunker then. I actually believe that if I had been his wife instead of his guest he would have struck me. I suppose it was an absurd thing to do. But the next time you are in search of a new sensation, do something of the same sort. The beggar became transfigured. He looked at the gold and notes, and then at me. I do not think I shall ever forget the expression in his face. Did you ever see a child asleep—a child to whom some wonderful dream has come? It was at once infantile and radiant. And all the while Bunker was abusing me like a pickpocket. The beggar gave me one look, dropped on his knees, caught the hem of my skirt, kissed it, threw away his crutch, and *ran*. I burst out laughing, and Bunker, in spite of his rage, burst out laughing too. Fanny called us a pair of idiots, and said that if I was as lavish as that it would be better and wiser, and far more Christian, to keep my money for indigent and deserving Bostonese than to bestow it as a premium on Monacean vice and effrontery. Just as she was working herself into big words and short sentences, the man whom I had noticed at the tables came along. He had met her before, and now, as he expressed it, he precipitated himself to renew the expression of his homage. Fanny, after introducing him to me, began at once on the tale of my misconduct. He had a complexion of the cream-tint order, and a mustache blacker than hate. He was a Florentine, I discovered, a marquis with a name made up of v's, sonorous o's, and n's. We had found a table, and Bunker ordered some ices. The night was really so perfect, and the ice so good, that, like Mme. de Staël over her sherbet in moonlit Venice, I almost wished it were a sin to sit there. The marquis was in very good form and inclined to do the devoted on the slightest provocation.

"'Is mademoiselle,' he asked me, 'is mademoiselle as disdainful of the heart as she is of gold?'

"'Absolutely,' I answered—a remark which may have sounded snobbish, but still was wholly true.

"'Ah!' he exclaimed, 'there are birds that do not sing untaught.'

"'You are beginning well,' I thought.

"The next day he lunched with us, and came again in the evening. In addition to his marquisate, he had a fluty tenorino voice; what they call a *voix de salon*. He sang all sorts of things for us, and he sang them very well. When the air was lively he looked at Fanny, when it was sentimental he looked at me. Thereafter I saw a great deal of him. One day we would make up a party for Nice, on another we would go to San Remo, or else back in the mountains, or to Grasse. Of course, as you know, customs over there are such that he had no opportunity of being alone with me, even for a second; but he had an art of making love in public which must have been the result of long practice. It was both open and discreet. It was not in words; it was in the inflection of the voice and in the paying of the thousand and one little attentions which foreigners perform so well. Now, to me, a tiara might be becoming, but it is an ornament for which I have never felt the vaguest covetousness. Moreover, I had no intention of marrying an Italian, however fabulous the ancestry of that Italian might be. And, besides, the attentions of which I was the apparent object were, I knew, addressed less to me than to the blue eyes of my check-book. The Florentine nobleman who is disposed to marry a dowerless American is yet to be heard from. This by the way. However, I accepted the attentions with becoming grace, and marked the cunning of his tricks. One evening he did not put in an appearance, but at midnight, I heard, on the road before my window, the tinkle of a guitar. I did not need to peer through the curtains to know from whom it came. First he sang a song of Tosti's, and then the serenade from 'Don Pasquale':

> 'Com' è gentil, la notte in mezz' Aprile.
> *   *   *   *   *   *
> Poi quando sarò morto, tu piangerai,
> Ma ritornarmi in vita, tu non potrai.'

Sentimental? Yes, sentimental to the last degree. But on the Riviera, in spring, and at night, one's fancy turns to that sort of thing with astounding ease. I listened with unalloyed pleasure. It was like a Boccaccian echo. And as I listened I wondered whether I should ever learn what love might be. The idea of taking a course of lessons from a man who strummed on a guitar in front of my window never entered my head. The next day Fanny came to me in a state of great excitement. The guitarist, it appeared, had, with all proper and due formality, asked leave to place his coronet at my feet. *Ce que j'ai ri!*

"You can hear Fanny from here. She accused me of flirting with the man. 'You have no right,' she said, 'to treat him as though he were a college boy at Mt. Desert.' What he had done to make her so vicious I never discovered. It must have been the title; a title always went to her head. Poor Fanny! That evening, when he came, she declined to be present. I had to see him alone. My dear, he was too funny. He had prepared a little speech which he got off very well, only at the end of it he lapsed into English. 'We will loaf,' he said, 'we will be always loafers.' He meant, of course, to assert that we should love and be always lovers, but the intricacies of our pronunciation were too much for him. I could have died, it was so amusing. I managed, however, to keep a straight face. 'Marquis,' I said, 'I am deeply honored, but your invitation is one that I am unable to accept.' A more astounded man you never saw. He really thought that he had but to ask, and it would be given. He declined to take No for an answer. He said he would wait. Actually, he was so pertinacious that I had to drag Fanny up to Paris. He followed us in the next train. There was no getting rid of him at all. If he sent me one note he sent me a hundred, and notes ten pages each, at the very least. Finally, as you heard, he tried the dramatic. One afternoon, while I was out shopping, he bribed a waiter at the hotel where we lodged. When I returned, there he was, waiting for me. 'At last,' he cried, 'at last we are face to face. You think I do not love. Cruel one, behold me! I love as no mortal ever loved before. See, I die at your feet!' And there, before my very eyes, he whipped out a pistol, pulled the trigger, tumbled over and seemed fully disposed to carry out the programme to the end. He had shot himself; there was no doubt about that; but he had shot himself in such an intelligent manner that, though there was blood enough to frighten a sensitive young person out of her wits, yet of danger there was none at all. Talk to me about comedians!   .   .   .   .

"It was after that episode that I returned to Beacon street. It was there that what you are pleased to call the scandal began. Fanny, whose desire to marry me off was simply epic, one day caught an Englishman; young, so she said, and good-looking. And that Englishman, she made up her mind, I should ensnare. Fanny, as you know, was possessed with an ungratified desire to pay annual visits to swell country houses on the other side. Hence, I suppose, her efforts. Having caught the Englishman, the next step was to serve him up in becoming form. To that end she gave a tentative dinner. I got to it late; in fact, I was the last to arrive. Fanny, I could see, was in a state of feverish excitement. She presented to me one or two men, whose names I did not catch, and a moment later one of them gave me his arm. When we were seated at table, and while he was sticking a chrysanthemum in his button-hole, I glanced at the card on his plate. It bore for legend Lord Alfred Harrow. It was then I took my first look at him. My dear, he was the ugliest man I have ever seen; he was so ugly that he was positively attractive. His mouth was large enough to sing a duet, but his teeth were whiter than mine."

As she spoke she curled her lips.

"There was no hair on his face, and his features were those of a middle-aged wizard. But about him was the atmosphere of health, of strength, too, and his hands, though bronzed and sinewy, were perfect. I knew he was a thorough-bred at once. 'And how do you like the States?' I asked. He was squeezing some lemon on an oyster, and I noticed that when some white wine was offered him he turned the glass upside down. 'Very much,' he answered; 'and you?' There was more of that sort of thing, and finally I asked him if, like other Englishmen, he thought that Boston suggested one of his provincial towns. 'There seems to be some mistake,' he said. 'I was going into the Somerset five minutes ago when Hill corralled me. He told me that his wife was giving a dinner, and that at the last moment one of the bidden had wired to the effect that he was prevented from coming. Whereupon Mrs. Hill had packed him off to the club, with instructions to bring back the first man he met. I happened to be that man.' He took up the card. 'Lord Alfred is, I fancy, the delinquent. My name,' he added, 'is Mr. Stitt—Ferris Stitt,' he continued, as though apologizing for its inconsequence.

"After that we got on famously. In a day or two he came to the house. When he left the world was larger. He knew nothing about poetry. He had never so much as heard of Fichte. Herbert Spencer was to him a name and nothing more. The only works of ornamental literature which he seemed to have read were the Arabian Nights, which he had forgotten, and something of Dickens, which had put him to sleep. He did not know one note of music from another. But he had hunted big game in Africa, in Bengal, and he had penetrated Thibet. He had been in Iceland and among the Caribs. No carpet-knight was he.

"My dear, I had not seen him five times before I felt myself going. I think he knew it. But I had been cheated before, and so well that I held on with all my strength. While I was holding on, he disappeared. Not a word, not a line, not even so much as a p. p. c. In the course of time, through the merest accident, I learned that he was in Yucatan. Six months later I caught a glimpse of him in the street. Presently he called.

"At once, without so much as a preamble, he told me he had gone away that in absence he might learn whether I was as dear to him as he thought. He hesitated a moment. 'Will you let me love you?' he asked. 'You have been prudent,' I answered; 'let me be prudent, too.' Then I told him of my disenchantments. I told him how difficult I found it to discover what men really were. I told him, as I have told you, that it seemed to me, if an intelligent girl admired her brother, it was because that brother was assuredly an admirable man. And I added that I would accept no man until I had the same opportunities of judging him as a sister has of judging her brother. Besides, I said, I have yet to know what love may be. It was then that we made the agreement of which you disapprove. After all, it was my own suggestion, and, if unconventional, in what does the criterion consist? I was acting for the best. You do not imagine, do you, that I regret it?"

And to her lips came a smile.

"I took Mary, who, you must admit, is respectability personified, and whom I had long since elevated from nurse to sheep-dog—I took Mary, and, together, all three of us, we went abroad. It is in travelling that you get to know a man. Each evening, when he said good-night, my admiration had increased. From England, as you know, we went straight to India. It was a long trip, I had heard, but to me it seemed needlessly brief. During the entire journey I studied him as one studies a new science. I watched him as a cat watches a mouse. Not once did he do the slightest thing that jarred. During the entire journey he did not so much as attempt to take my hand in his. He knew, I suppose, as I knew, that if the time ever came I would give it unasked.

One evening, on going to my stateroom, I found I had left my vinaigrette on deck. Mary was asleep. I went back for it alone. It was very dark. On the way to where I had sat I heard his voice; he was talking to one of the passengers. In spite of myself I listened to what he was saying. I listened for nearly an hour. Not one word was there in it all that he could not have said to me. When I got back to my cabin I wondered whether it might not be that he knew I was standing there. Yes, I admit, I was suspicious; but circumstances had made me so. Oh, he has forgiven me since."

She smiled again complacently to herself, and, tucking the whip under her arm, she drew off a glove. On one finger was a narrow circle of gold. She looked at it and raised it to her lips.

"When we landed our journey had practically begun. You see, I was still unassured. Yet he was irreproachable and ever the same. Well, the details are unimportant. One day, at Benares, he heard that leopards had been seen in the neighborhood of a lake some fifteen or twenty miles out. At once he was for having a crack at them. I determined to accompany him. He was surprised at first, and objected a little, but I managed, as I usually do, to have my own way. It was night when we got there. We left the horses with the guide, and, noiselessly as ghosts, we stole through a coppice which hid the lake from view. Almost at the water's edge we crouched and waited. The stars were white as lilies and splendid as trembling gems. The silence was as absolute as might. How long we waited I cannot now recall. I think I dreamed a bit with open eyes. Then dimly I became conscious of something moving in the distance. The moon had risen like a balloon of gold, and in the air was the scent of sandal. Slowly, with an indolent grace of its own, that something neared the opposite shore. As it reached the water it stopped, arched its back, and turned. I saw then that it was a leopard. No, my dear, you can form no idea of the beauty of that beast. And then suddenly it threw its head back and called. It lapped the water, and then with its tongue gave its fore paw one long, lustrous lick, and called again; a call that was echoless, yet so resonant I felt it thrill my finger-tips. In a moment its mate sprang from the shadows. If the first comer was beautiful, then this one was the ideal. There they stood, caressing each other with amber, insatiate eyes. It was like a scene in fairyland. And as I watched them I felt a movement at my side. I turned. He had taken aim and was about to fire, but, as I turned, he turned to me. Those beasts, I told myself, are far too fair for death; yet I said not a word. My dear, he read my unuttered wish, he lowered the gun, and then—then, for the first time, I knew what love might be. . . . There's the dog-cart now. Come over and dine to-morrow. If you care to, Ferris will show you the gun."

Charles Henry Lüders.

BORN in Philadelphia, Penn., 1858. DIED there, 1891.

FARM FRUITS.

[*Hallo, My Fancy! By C. H. L. and S. D. S., Jr.* 1887.]

A LITTLE ancient man—who wore
  A tall hat, many seasons o'er
    Its days of shining,
And made to fit his shrunken head
With padding of bandanna, red,
    Within the lining—

Came often down the dusty road
Which passed the door of our abode;
    And sometimes tarried
To sell the sweet farm fruit that lay
Within a basket lined with hay,
  · The which he carried.

I shall not soon forget his face,
Perspiring from the sturdy pace
    He ever travelled;
Nor that primeval waistcoat, which
Seemed wholly formed of patch and
    stitch,
    Much frayed and ravelled.

In spring-time, when the violets peeped
Through tears in which their eyes were
    steeped
    Each dewy morning,

He heard the wood-thrush tune his throat
Up to one high delirious note,
    All rivals scorning.

In autumn, when his worn hat-brim
Caught the gay leaves that fell on him,
    He brought ripe apples,—
Great golden "Bell-flowers"—rubbed so
    bright
They seemed to hold the rich noon-light
    In mellow dapples.

I wonder if he walks to-day
The cross-ties of the iron way
    Through Olney running?
If now, along the "O. & M.,"
On Saturdays he weareth them—
    Those clothes so 'stunning'?

Haply; and yet more likely 'tis
That Life—being done with him and
    his—
    Long since forsook him.
And that, while I a tribute pen,
His neighbors scarce remember when
    Death overtook him.

AN OLD THOUGHT.

FRAMED in the cavernous fire-place sits a boy,
  Watching the embers from his grandsire's knee:
One sees red castles rise, and laughs with joy;
  The other marks them crumble, silently.

THE TRYST.

BLOW! winds, and break the blossoms;
  Part! clouds that hide the sun;
For the timid feet of a maiden sweet
  Adown the valley run.

The thorn of the wild rose wounds her;
  The hem of her skirt is torn
Where the cool gray dew has wet it through
  With the tears of a summer morn.

No foot is heard to follow;
  No eye her path may see;
There is no ear her steps to hear
  As she hastens unto me.

O wild, sweet banks of roses!
  O fragrant fields of dew!
My darling's kiss is more, I wis,
  Than a thousand leagues of you!

THE MOUNTEBANKS.

OVER our heads the branches made
  A canopy of woven shade.

The birds about this beechen tent
Like deft attendants came and went.

A shy wood-robin, fluting low,
Furnished the music for the show.

The cricket and the grasshopper
A portion of the audience were.

Thither did Fancy leap to fling
Light summersaults around the ring.

Wit, the sly jester of the Town,
And rustic Humor played the clown.

Reason was ringmaster, and waved
His whip when these his anger braved.

Wishes were horses that each rode
Unto his heart's desire's abode.

There Laughter and Delight and Glee
Performed their parts that all might see,

Till a sweet wind across the clover
Whispered: "At last, the show is over."

And the broad shadow of a cloud
Moved from us like a moving crowd.

THE RIVER-GOD.

A GIANT docile to obey your will,
  A comrade,—a companion,—a refrain
Threading a dream; yet, laughing like a rill,
  He'll bear your drownèd body to the main.

Chas. G. Lüders

THE DRAUGHT.

WHEN I am thirsty, let me drink
 Prone upon the mossy brink
Of a rocky basin, laid
Within the forest's heart of shade.

There may I know the cool caress
The spring gives to my eagerness;

Feeling its bubbles rise and float
Around my chin, across my throat,
Till the swiftly pulsing blood
Circles calmly as the flood;
Till by every sense I'm told
That never flagon tipped with gold
So divine a draught doth hold.

STAR DUST.

INNUMERABLE ages since—before
 The sun's gold paled to silver on the moon,
Or earth ran round to take on both their hues,
A monstrous bubble, out of chaos blown,
Swelled through the dusk—grew luminous—and lit
All space an instant;—then with ringing shock
Burst!—and from out the jewelled mist there swung
Millions of stars to glow forevermore!

MEMORY.

OUT of my door-yard maple
 A gilded leaflet fell,
Twinkling down on a sunbeam,
 Like music from a bell.

Nor hand nor foot disturbed it,
 And frolicsome gusts of air
Whirling the wayside atoms
 Danced on, and left it there.

Slowly away it wasted
 Till only a film remained—
A skeleton leaf, a shadow,
 Lost wholly when it rained.

Yet lo, on the stained footway,
 Etched where the gold had lain,
A delicate shape—a spirit—
 Tarried in wind and rain.

Mary Greenway McClelland.

BORN Norwood, Nelson Co., Va.

THE FLOOD.

[*Oblivion. An Episode.* 1885.]

"LIKE a thief in the night." The simile is hackneyed, but it will serve,
 for so the water came. The overplus of spring, rivulet, and brook,

with the accumulated wash of the mountain-sides, had swelled the river to a mighty torrent which poured itself through the valley in a perfect flood. From hillside to hillside the water went with a current in the middle like a mill-race. The railroad-bridge was still standing, but the water had swept around both ends, isolating it like a scrap of wire fence in the middle of a prairie. Against it, on the upper side, a huge hammock had formed, and it was only a question of moments, and a few more logs and trees, ere the whole structure must give way; so impotent is iron and cunning handiwork against the power of such agents of destruction as weight and water.

All the villagers, men, women, children, and dogs, were abroad upon the hillside, wondering, gazing, commenting, and questioning. The railway-track was seven feet under water, and the river was still rising.

"Thar goes Rideout's sto'," remarked Knapp the carpenter, "startin' out down country on er v'yage o' diskivery. Look, how well she holds together ; every log an' plank in place as solid as the day I j'ined 'em." The speaker paused to regard his handiwork with pride. "Thar she swings out into the current—bound for Tennessee. I call that a good squar lead."

"Ther depot's 'bout followin' suit," observed Thrasher, fishing in his pocket for a twist of home-made tobacco, and helping himself to a liberal "chaw."

The depot building moved slightly, lifted, turned slowly with a waltzing motion, and drifted off down-stream. Telegraph-posts followed, washed up and falling like trees with a sullen splash. A stack or two of rough food, straw and fodder, came sailing by, bowing and bending with the motion of the water. Then more logs and a great pile of drift. And the river was still rising.

John, Dick, and Ralph Woody went out to the extreme end of a knoll of ground that was now a peninsula, and stood looking down on the flood with vivid interest. A hammock of fence-rails, planks, and débris, carried by the current around the end of the bridge, drifted past the spot where they stood; there was a dead tree lying across it, with three or four chickens perched among its branches; a drowned hog was caught between two of the planks. The men looked at each other, but said nothing. More trash, and the body of a dead horse; then something square and large like a great dark box, that turned over and over as it floated down; then another dead horse. Dick glanced round with a great fear in his eyes. "The stage!" he said hoarsely. "Thet fust horse was Carter's dun mare, an' the other "——

"Was mine," finished John, with a break in his voice,—"I know. And Charlie?"

"They'll be out on the hillside safe enough. Carter ain't one to be took onawar' an' lose his head. He knows the ways of water good es any man upon the mountain. Old man Carter knows what to do in er freshet. Depen' upon it he had all ther folks out on ther hillside long afore the wust come. The stable an' lot is a sight nigher the river than the house." Woody spoke reassuringly, but his heart was small and faint within him.

The sun, clear and bright, rose above the crests of the eastern mountains, and sent long level rays like golden fingers across the tree-tops and the valley, touching the breast of the raging flood and the anxious brows of the pallid groups. And the river rose and rose, inch by inch, foot by foot; and the people waited breathless.

A sound from up by the bridge—a crashing and tearing and rending, high above the steady monotonous roar of the water. The iron-work was giving way, was snapping like glass before the assault of the terrible battering-ram the flood was hurling against it. A house, driven end foremost against the pile of logs and débris already collected; a house with human beings—men, women, little children—on the roof, crouching, clinging in mortal terror to the very shingles, the wild wail of whose agony and fear rose high above the fury of the flood, as the house struck. The bridge parted; the hammock, freed at last, broke and floated down stream in fragments; the house remained for a moment stationary, hung against the masonry of the middle pier. God! for power to save them! for strength to hold back the death-torrent! The house bent with the force of the current, recovered itself, bent again. Dick thrust himself in front of John, and held him forcibly back behind his broad shoulder: he *should not* see it. The flooring of the bridge gave way, the house swung round with a sudden lurch as it was caught by the unobstructed might of the torrent; one end caught against the pier held it still, it careened to one side more and more, the water was too strong, and it capsized slowly.

A wail broke from the helpless spectators. Women cast their aprons over their faces and sobbed aloud, and men wrung their hard hands together and groaned.

Is there no end to tragedy? Something else comes floating down the death-stream, past the ruined bridge, in the wake of the house which had proved a sepulchre. A boat; one of the kind peculiar to the rivers of the South—flat-bottomed, almost square at stem and stern, but raked so as to ride the water like a duck. In it stood a boy, waving his hands to them entreatingly, calling aloud in a voice inaudible to them, lost in the roar of the flood. As it neared they saw something white lying in the bottom of the boat, huddled in a heap at the boy's feet.

"It's Charlie!" muttered John, hoarsely, and began to tear off his coat, forgetful of his fifty years and his eighteen-stone weight.

Dick caught him by the arm. "Hold on, John!" he cried, "you can't do it, man; you'll be drowned afore you've gone fifty yards. Hand along thet rope, Thrasher; and stand by, fellows, to haul in when I give ther sign. I'm goin'."

And in less than a moment he was stripped to the trousers, had a rope fastened securely under his shoulders, and a knife between his teeth to cut it if it should foul, and was up to his neck in the turbid flood.

Woody, with his legs well apart and his back braced against a tree, paid out the rope steadily, while Thrasher and John stood by watchfully, ready to render aid at a second's notice. The rest of the villagers, scenting the new excitement, came hurrying up; and Knapp, at John's suggestion, tore off to the store for more rope.

Dick was a stout swimmer and a wary one. Where the water was backed over the land the work was easy. With great, strong strokes he swam, going with the current, and saving his strength for the dash into the strong water when the boat should drift near enough. On it came, the boy kneeling in the head watching eagerly, the white mass in the bottom motionless. Gathering all his strength, Dick drew hard on the rope to slacken it, and dashed into the current. It was hard work, cruel work, battling with the greedy water for its prey; but he fought on with the dauntless resolution that was part of his nature. The great muscles stood out in the powerful arms ; the broad, bare chest rose and fell with each magnificent stroke as evenly and rhythmically as a piece of machinery; the blue eyes were steady and very watchful. They neared each other, the drifting boat and the struggling man. John fell on his knees and cried aloud, "God help him !" and the crowd took it up, crying too, "God help him !"

Woody paid out steadily, letting the rope slip through his hands swiftly as it was needed. The two objects in the water were approaching still more nearly to each other. The boy leaned far over the side, in his eagerness, and stretched out his hand. Dick caught at it, missed it; caught at it again, and was drawn to the side of the boat. A mighty shout went up from the people, who cried, "Thank God! thank God!" But the end was not yet.

Dick swam by the side of the boat, with one hand on the gunwale; but both were in the current drifting down, and there was danger of the rope fouling and dragging him under. Suddenly the strain on it ceased; it hung limp in Woody's hand, and he pulled it in, a yard at a time. Had it broken? The men groaned in terror and excitement as the boat drifted on.

About a mile below, a great mountain-spur jutted boldly out into the valley, causing the river to make a sharp bend in order to sweep around it. In the elbow formed by this bluff the flood was backed, making a great pond of eddy-water comparatively still. As the current rushed down the centre channel, floating drift was cast aside by the force of the sweep into this eddy, where it circled slowly and lodged against the bluff. Already great logs and piles of débris formed hammocks against the hillside, and Dick noticed the action of the water as he swam. If there had been a paddle, a bit of board, or even a shingle in the boat, he would have scrambled in and endeavored to guide the little vessel into the eddy; but there was nothing. He must try to draw it to the edge of the current by swimming, and let the water throw him out. Hauling up the rope, he made Charlie cut it and fasten one end to the head of the boat, passing it through a hole and doubling it around his shoulders for greater strength. Then swimming obliquely, he drew the boat after him, fighting inch by inch, but gaining slowly. All the long mile the battle continued, until at last victory was achieved. The boat, drawn from the swiftest of the current, was thrown into the eddy-water, where Dick, well-nigh exhausted, laid his hand again on the gunwale to guide her and let her float down towards the bluff.

The men, who had kept pace with them by running and scrambling along the hillside, climbed out over the trash and hammocks, regardless of holes and the danger of rolling logs, intent only on getting at the boat and its occupants. Dick had contrived to wedge it into a tolerably secure place near the shore, and had climbed into it, cutting himself free of the rope. He was bending down close over something in the bottom of the boat, shielding it from sight with his body. "Throw me a coat!" he called; and Woody stripped off his and threw it. Dick rose up presently with something in his arms closely enveloped in the folds of the heavy garment, and leaning over, gently put it into Woody's arms. It was small and very heavy—the body of a little child.

Then Dick stepped onto the hammock himself with the form of a woman in his arms; a woman in a long white night-dress that clung wet and close to her form, defining every splendid line and curve, from the superb bust and shoulders to the slender, rounded ankles. Her face, pallid as marble, rested against Dick's breast, and her long black hair, heavy with water, trailed in a dripping mass over his bare white arm and shoulder. Somebody—John—handed him another coat, and he wrapped it around her.

Milicent Washburn Shinn.

BORN in Washington Township, Alameda Co., Cal., 1858.

SUMMER NIGHT.

[*The Century Magazine, The Overland Monthly, etc.* 1881-84.]

THE vast half-sphere of plain and sky
  Brims full with pallid light;
Moon-whitened all the grain-fields lie,
  Like seas grown still with night;
And scattered houses, far and nigh,
  Among their trees gleam white.
Oh, warmly does the night enfold
The earth, caressed with showers of gold.
    And yet, not so, sweet night,
    Not so I long for thee,
    Not so come thou to me.

1881.

Come, mighty shade, till earth might be
  Alone in primal space,
Till I lie drowned beneath a sea
  That upward from my face
Goes on and on unendingly,
  Nor hints of time or place;
Till I might think that o'er my eyes,
Close-shut, the earth forever lies.
    So longs my soul for thee.
    Oh, so, I pray, sweet night,
    So come thou unto me.

A DREAM.

IF I shall find myself, long after death,
  In some vast darkness walking all alone,
And strain my every sense and hold my breath,
  Because each step before me is unknown;
If, all around, the darkness blank and still
  Hangs heavily and thick with shapeless dread,
And I go ever on without my will,
  Yet dare not stop nor even turn my head,
But tremble, sick with terror, lest I may
  At any instant cower to feel the clutch

Of something that has followed all the way—
    If then thy sudden hand my shoulder touch,
I shall not shudder.   Longed-for touch and dear,
How should I fail to know thee even here ?

TO-DAY.

"O HEART, tired out with pain to-day,
        A thousand years to come
Thy pain will all have passed away,
    Thy crying shall be dumb:
As gayly bird-wings o'er the river
    Shall gleam with life that once was
        thine,
As if this pulse, with pain a-quiver,
    Still leaped, with gladness half-divine:
To thee, to all, it is as one
When once thy restless years are done."

Oh, vain to turn upon your heart,
    And think to still it so!
It cries back unto all your art,
    With pleading, "Ah, no, no!
For gladness dies as well as sorrow;
    Then let me live, since I must die.
Ah, quick, for death will come to-mor-
        row—
    Quick, ere my years in vain go by!
Because to-morrow I am clay,
Give me my happiness to-day!"

1883.

LIFE'S ANSWER.

"O HEART, my heart," he said,
        "How bitter is thine aching!
The happy winds are waking,
The linnets nest o'erhead;
    And thou art like to breaking.

"Ah, friend of years," he said,
    "Heart's dearest, unto thee
I bring my misery,
And thou shalt healing shed,
    And set my spirit free."

Unknowing, unafraid,
    He dared the seas that roll
    Blackly 'twixt soul and soul:
Lost, drowning, sore dismayed,
    All baffled of his goal,

Back-driven to solitude,—
    "Ah, woe is me!" he cried,
"To find no love so wide
That it may clasp my mood,
    Or close as grief abide.

"This pain that stays and stings,
    At love's or friendship's door
    Shall knock in vain no more;

1884.

For I will give it wings
    Far, far from me to soar.

"O wide-winged song," he said,
    "Divinest, unto thee
    I bring my misery,
And thou shalt healing shed;
    Set thou my spirit free."

Fluttered the feeble song.
    Unmeet its wings to bear
    One narrow human care,—
Wings wont to soar so strong
    Under a world's despair.

"Ah, what is this?" he cried,
    "Unto the wide world's smart,
    Answers the wide world's heart;
Unheard the cries abide
    Of each small soul apart.

"Ah, silence, thou," he said,—
    "Most merciful, to thee
    I bring my misery.
Be there no healing shed;
    Clasp but my pain and me.
    Strong silence, like a sea,
Flow deep above my head."

A MARIPOSA LILY.

SHELL-LIKE lily, flushed with faintest color,
　　Hid in long grass up the mountain-side,
Where the loud brown torrent's roar comes duller,
　　And in simple gladness you abide,—

Am I heartless that your whole of living
　　Thus I take to please her for one hour?—
Yet I ask of you no greater giving
　　Than of mine own self, poor wasted flower.

1884.

William Morton Payne.

BORN in Newburyport, Mass., 1858.

BJÖRNSON'S NATIONAL TRILOGY.

[*Sigurd Slembe.. A Dramatic Trilogy. By Björnstjerne Björnson.*—*Translated from the Norwegian by W. M. Payne.* 1888.]

BJÖRNSON is the great national writer of Norway because his finer work deals with national themes. His contemporary, Ibsen, endowed with genius of a high order, has chosen to be cosmopolitan rather than national, and so the claim made for Björnson cannot be disputed on behalf of his most famous fellow-worker in the field of letters. Björnson's tales of peasant life are purely national, his more poetic dramas are no less so, and his best lyrics are true Northland notes. Norway is peculiarly rich in materials for a national literature. It is, more than any other part of Europe, the home of that rich mythology which has so profoundly influenced Teutonic thought, and which, had conditions been more favorable, might have borne in earlier times a fruitage comparable for poetic wealth with that of the mythology of southern Europe which so early became embodied in works of imperishable beauty. In central Europe we find this mythology in a somewhat corrupt and perverted state, modified by classical influences and mixed with elements of indigenous growth. In the north alone did it remain comparatively free from foreign admixture; there alone did it acquire form and consistency, and there did it wait in vain, until too late, for some master mind to so mould it that it should be sure forever of the world's regard. But the Norsemen had more pressing work at hand than the cultivation of the art of poetry. Their life was a hard and unremitting struggle for existence, and the rough poetry in which their inheritance of mythical lore became embodied was fitted to the rugged life they were forced to lead. Then Christianity found its way among them, and the chance was missed. The vitality of the old faith waned. Thor and Odin and Balder were dethroned by the new god from the south. Deities and heroes faded into the mists of the past, lingering, indeed, in the popular consciousness for many centuries, but growing ever more impotent to inspire poet or sage.

Yet such a body of myth and hero-story as this could never be quite lost or become wholly meaningless to the race which gave it birth, and the elementary traits of whose character were bound up within it. So it was natural that when, in modern times, and in common with the other nations of Europe, the people of the north were impelled to the development of a studied literature, they should draw largely upon the varied store of tradition for their material, and seek at a later day to do something of the work so long left undone. Thus Tegnèr in Sweden, Ewald and Oehlenschlæger in Denmark, and Björnson in Norway have found many of their themes in the treasure-house of myth and saga. Of all this modern work, that of Björnson seems the most removed from modern ways of thought and expression, exhibits most clearly the modes of feeling of that quasi-historical past which it reproduces, is the most vigorous and the most elemental.

The "Trilogy" has a definite historical basis. During the first half of the twelfth century Norway was plunged into civil strife by the pretensions to the throne of one Sigurd, surnamed "Slembe" (an adjective meaning ill-disposed or worthless), on account of his lawless youth. This Sigurd was a natural son of the great king Magnus Barfod, and, according to the law of Norway, the succession could not rightfully be withheld from him on the score of his illegitimacy. The trilogy of "Sigurd Slembe" deals with the life of this pretender from the time when, in early manhood, he learns the secret of his birth, to the eve of the final struggle which crowns his life with failure and restores peace to his long-suffering country. It is a tale of indomitable but ever-thwarted will, deeply tragic in its import, but not without that final touch of what the Germans call *Versöhnung,* and we, for want of a better word, call reconciliation, which is the attribute of the noblest tragic productions, and by virtue of which tragedy fulfils its purpose as defined by Aristotle, purging the mind of pity and fear. The consummation of a tragic action is found in that supreme moment when the protagonist surrenders, in Schopenhauer's phrase, not merely life, but the very desire to live. Perhaps the most perfect illustration of this in literature is the cry of Gretchen at the close of the first part of "Faust"—*"Heinrich, mir graut's vor dir!"* In the present work this tragic consummation follows, in the closing act, upon the flight of Sigurd's last remaining hope of victory. Failure, absolute and unrelieved, confronts him as the result of all his toil. He attempts in thought each avenue of escape, but they are all closed upon him. He has raised his last force, and no stratagem can avail him further. As all the events of life crowd upon the memory of a dying man, so all Sigurd's past comes before him now face to face with the ruin of the edifice so nearly reared by him. And the peace of mind which he has sought for so many years comes to him also, and all the tempests of life are stilled. He sees that this was indeed the inevitable end, and, recognizing the fitness with which events have shaped themselves, he sees life in its true aspect. No longer veiled in the mists that have hidden it from his passionate gaze, he takes note of what it really is, and casts it from him. In this hour of passionless contemplation such a renunciation is not a thing torn from the reluctant soul, but the clear solution, so long sought, of the problem so long blindly attempted.

Other scenes of great power and beauty are not lacking in this work.   .   .

Björnson has the power, rare even with the greater dramatists, to condense so much of passion in a single pregnant sentence, by means of a word or single phrase so to illuminate as by a lightning flash some tragic situation, as to put the ordinary rhetorical effusion of feeling to shame. He has the instinct which sees, at the fateful moment of the action, how incomparably greater and truer is a direct, rightly chosen word, than the most elaborate rhetorical amplification.

TOURGUÉNIEFF.

SILENT the lips that quivered as they told
   The tale of deep, time-consecrated wrong;
  Quiet the hand which held the pen so long
And used so well, that men, who bought and sold
Their fellow-men, were startled to behold
   Themselves arraigned for judgment in the strong
   Clear light of truth—a conscience-stricken throng,
Plague-spotted, in the ranks of death enrolled.
What thou hast done, we know, but fain would know
   What thou hast seen; what lesson was in life
For thee! This only? that in grief men go
   Even as they came, hence; this, that woe is rife
And hope illusive; this, that with a foe
   Unconquerable men wage ceaseless strife?

1889.

Danske Dandridge.

BORN in Copenhagen, Denmark.

THE DEAD MOON.

[*Joy, and Other Poems.* 1888.]

WE are ghost-ridden:
   Through the deep night
Wanders a spirit,
   Noiseless and white.
Loiters not, lingers not, knoweth not rest;
Ceaselessly haunting the East and the West.

She, whose undoing the ages have wrought,
Moves on to the time of God's rhythmical thought.

In the dark, swinging sea,
 As she speedeth through space,
She reads her pale image;
 The wounds are agape on her face.
She sees her grim nakedness
 Pierced by the eyes
Of the Spirits of God
 In their flight through the skies.
(Her wounds, they are many and hollow.)
The Earth turns and wheels as she flies,
And this Spectre, this Ancient, must follow.

When, in the æons,
 Had she beginning?
What is her story?
 What was her sinning?
Do the ranks of the Holy Ones
 Know of her crime?
Does it loom in the mists
 Of the birthplace of Time?
The stars, do they speak of her
 Under their breath,
"Will this Wraith be forever
 Thus restless in death?"
On, through immensity,
 Sliding and stealing,
On, through infinity,
 Nothing revealing.

I see the fond lovers;
 They walk in her light;
They charge the "soft maiden"
 To bless their love-plight.
Does she laugh in her place,
 As she glideth through space?
Does she laugh in her orbit with never a sound?
 That to her, a dead body,
With nothing but rents in her round—
 Blighted and marred,
 Wrinkled and scarred,
 Barren and cold,
 Wizened and old—
 That to her should be told,
That to her should be sung
The yearning and burning of them that are young?

Our Earth that is young,
 That is throbbing with life,
Has fiery upheavals,
 Has boisterous strife;
But she that is dead has no stir, breathes no air;
She is calm, she is voiceless, in lonely despair.

We dart through the void;
   We have cries, we have laughter;
The phantom that haunts us
   Comes silently after.
This Ghost-lady follows,
   Though none hear her tread;
On, on, we are flying,
   Still tracked by our Dead—
By this white, awful Mystery,
   Haggard and dead.

Sarah Pratt McLean Greene.

BORN in Simsbury, Conn.

GETTING READY FOR MEETIN'.

[*Cape Cod Folks.* 1881.—*Revised Edition.* 1888.]

WHEN the ancient couple made their appearance, I remarked silently, in regard to Grandma Keeler's hair, what proved afterward to be its usual holiday morning arrangement. It was confined in six infinitesimal braids, which appeared to be sprouting out perpendicularly in all directions from her head. The effect of redundancy and expansiveness thus heightened and increased on Grandma's features was striking in the extreme.

While we were eating breakfast, that good soul observed to Grandpa Keeler: "Wall, pa, I suppose you'll be all ready when the time comes to take teacher and me over to West Wallen to Sunday-school, won't ye?"

Grandpa coughed, and coughed again, and raised his eyes helplessly to the window.

"Looks some like showers," said he. "A-hem! a-hem! Looks mightily to me like showers, over yonder."

"Thar', r'aly, husband! I must say I feel mortified for ye," said Grandma. "Seein' as you're a perfessor, too, and thar' ain't been a single Sunday mornin' since I've lived with ye, pa, summer or winter, but what you've seen showers, and it r'aly seems to me it's dreadful inconsistent when thar' ain't no cloud in the sky, and don't look no more like rain than I do." And Grandma's face, in spite of her reproachful tones, was, above all, blandly sunlike and expressive of anything rather than deluge and watery disaster.

Grandpa was silent a little while, then coughed again. I had never seen Grandpa in worse straits.

"A-hem! a-hem! 'Fanny' seems to be a little lame, this mornin'," said he. "I shouldn't wonder. She's been goin' pretty stiddy this week."

"It does beat all, pa," continued Grandma Keeler, "how 't all the horses you've ever had since I've known ye have always been took lame Sunday mornin'. Thar' was 'Happy Jack,' he could go anywhers through the week, and never limp a step, as nobody could see, and Sunday mornin' he was always took lame! And thar' was ' Tantrum ' "——

" Tantrum " was the horse that had run away with Grandma when she was thrown from the wagon and generally smashed to pieces. And now Grandma branched off into the thrilling reminiscences connected with this incident of her life, which was the third time during the week that the horrible tale had been repeated for my delectation.

When she had finished, Grandpa shook his head with painful earnestness, reverting to the former subject of discussion.

" It's a long jaunt! " said he; " a long jaunt! "

" Thar's a long hill to climb before we reach Zion's mount," said Grandma Keeler, impressively.

" Wall, there's a darned sight harder one on the road to West Wallen! " burst out the old sea-captain desperately; " say nothin' about the devilish stones! "

" Thar' now," said Grandma, with calm though awful reproof; " I think we've gone fur enough for one day; we've broke the Sabbath, and took the name of the Lord in vain, and that ought to be enough for perfessors. "

Grandpa replied at length in a greatly subdued tone: " Wall, if you and the teacher want to go over to Sunday-school to-day, I suppose we can go if we get ready "—a long submissive sigh—" I suppose we can. "

" They have preachin' service in the mornin', I suppose," said Grandma. " But we don't generally git along to that. It makes such an early start. We generally try to get around, when we go, in time for Sunday-school. They have singin' and all. It's just about as interestin', I think, as preachin'. The old man r'aly likes it," she observed aside to me, " when he once gets started; but he kind o' dreads the gittin' started. "

When I beheld the ordeal through which Grandpa Keeler was called to pass at the hands of his faithful consort, before he was considered in a fit condition of mind and body to embark for the sanctuary, I marvelled not at the old man's reluctance, nor that he had indeed seen clouds and tempest fringing the horizon.

Immediately after breakfast he set out for the barn, ostensibly to " see to the chores "; really, I believe, to obtain a few moments' respite, before worse evil should come upon him.

Pretty soon Grandma was at the back door calling in firm though persuasive tones:

" Husband! husband! come in, now, and get ready. "

No answer. Then it was in another key, weighty, yet expressive of no weak irritation, that Grandma called, " Come, pa! pa-a! pa-a-a! " Still no answer.

Then that voice of Grandma's sung out like a trumpet, terrible with meaning—" Bijonah Keeler! "

But Grandpa appeared not. Next, I saw Grandma slowly but surely gravitating in the direction of the barn, and soon she returned, bringing with her that ancient delinquent, who looked like a lost sheep indeed and a truly unreconciled one.

"Now the first thing," said Grandma, looking her forlorn captive over, "is boots. Go and get on yer meetin' gaiters, pa."

The old gentleman, having invested himself with those sacred relics, came pathetically limping into the room.

"I declare, ma," said he, "somehow these things,—phew! Somehow they pinch my feet dreadfully. I don't know what it is,—phew! They're dreadful oncomf'table things somehow."

"Since I've known ye, pa," solemnly ejaculated Grandma Keeler, "you've never had a pair o' meetin' boots that set easy on yer feet. You'd ought to get boots big enough for ye, pa," she continued, looking down disapprovingly on the old gentleman's pedal extremities, which resembled two small scows at anchor, in black cloth encasements, "and not be so proud as to go to pinchin' yer feet into gaiters a number o' sizes too small for ye."

"They're number tens, I tell ye!" roared Grandpa, nettled outrageously by this cutting taunt.

"Wall, thar' now, pa," said Grandma, soothingly; "if I had sech feet as that, I wouldn't go to spreadin' it all over town, if I was you—but it's time we stopped bickerin' now, husband, and got ready for meetin'; so set down and let me wash yer head."

"I've washed once this mornin'. It's clean enough," Grandpa protested; but in vain. He was planted in a chair, and Grandma Keeler, with rag and soap and a basin of water, attacked the old gentleman vigorously, much as I have seen cruel mothers wash the faces of their earth-begrimed infants. He only gave expression to such groans as—

"Thar', ma! don't tear my ears to pieces! Come, ma! you've got my eyes so full o' soap now, ma, that I can't see nothin'. Phew! Lordy! ain't ye most through with this, ma?"

Then came the dyeing process, which Grandma Keeler assured me, aside, made Grandpa "look like a man o' thirty"; but to me, after it he looked neither old nor young, human nor inhuman, nor like anything that I had ever seen before under the sun.

"There's the lotion, the potion, the dye-er, and the setter," said Grandma, pointing to four bottles on the table. "Now whar's the directions, Madeline?"

These having been produced from between the leaves of the family Bible, Madeline read, while Grandma made a vigorous practical application of the various mixtures.

"'This admirable lotion,'"—in soft ecstatic tones Madeline rehearsed the flowery language of the recipe—"'though not so instantaneously startling in its effect as our inestimable dyer and setter, yet forms a most essential part of the whole process, opening, as it does, the dry and lifeless pores of the scalp, imparting to them new life and beauty, and rendering them more easily susceptible to the applications which follow. But we must go deeper than this; a tone must be given to the whole system by means of the cleansing and rejuvenating of the very centre of our beings, and, for this purpose, we have prepared our wonderful potion.'" Here Grandpa, with a wry face, was made to swallow a spoonful of the mixture. "'Our unparalleled dyer,'" Madeline continued, "'restores black hair to a more than original gloss and brilliancy, and gives to the faded golden tress the sunny flashes of youth.'" Grandpa was dyed. "'Our world-renowned setter completes and perfects the whole process by adding tone and permanency to the efficacious qualities of the lotion, potion, and dyer, etc.'"; while on Grandpa's head the unutterable dye was set.

"Now, read teacher some of the testimonials, daughter," said Grandma Keeler, whose face was one broad, generous illustration of that rare and peculiar virtue called faith.

So Madeline continued: "'Mrs. Hiram Briggs, of North Dedham, writes: I was terribly afflicted with baldness, so that, for months, I was little more than an outcast from society, and an object of pity to my most familiar friends. I tried every remedy in vain. At length I heard of your wonderful restorative. After a week's application, my hair had already begun to grow in what seemed the most miraculous manner. At the end of ten months, it had assumed such length and proportions as to be a most luxurious burden, and where I had before been regarded with pity and aversion, I became the envied and admired of all beholders.'"

"Just think!" said Grandma Keeler, with rapturous sympathy and gratitude, "how that poor creetur must 'a' felt!"

"'Orion Spaulding of Weedsville, Vermont,'" Madeline went on—but here I had to beg to be excused, and went to my room to get ready for the Sunday-school.

When I came down again, Grandpa Keeler was seated, completely arrayed in his best clothes, opposite Grandma, who held the big family Bible in her lap, and a Sunday-school question-book in one hand.

"Now, pa," said she, "what tribe was it in sacred writ that wore bunnits?"

I was compelled to infer from the tone of Grandpa Keeler's answer that his temper had not undergone a mollifying process during my absence.

"Come, ma," said he; "how much longer ye goin' to pester me in this way?"

"Why, pa," Grandma rejoined calmly, "until you git a proper understandin' of it. What tribe was it in sacred writ that wore bunnits?"

"Lordy!" exclaimed the old man. "How d'ye suppose I know! They must 'a' been a tarnal old-womanish lookin' set any way."

"The tribe o' Judah, pa," said Grandma, gravely. "Now, how good it is, husband, to have your understandin' all freshened up on the Scripters!"

"Come, come, ma!" said Grandpa, rising nervously, "it's time we was startin'. When I make up my mind to go anywhere I always want to git there in time. If I was goin' to the Old Harry, I should want to git there in time."

"It's my consarn that we shall git thar' before time, some on us," said Grandma, with sad meaning, "unless we larn to use more respec'ful language."

DE SHEEPFOL'.

[*Towhead; the Story of a Girl.* 1883.]

DE massa ob de sheepfol',
　　Dat guards de sheepfol' bin,
Look out in de gloomerin' meadows,
Wha'r de long night rain begin—
So he call to de hirelin' shepa'd,
"Is my sheep, is dey all come in?"

Oh den, says de hirelin' shepa'd:
"Dey's some, dey's black and thin,
And some, dey's po' ol' wedda's;
But de res', dey's all brung in.
But de res', dey's all brung in."

Den de massa ob de sheepfol',
Dat guards de sheepfol' bin,

Goes down in de gloomerin' meadows,
Wha'r de long night rain begin—
So he le' down de ba's ob de sheepfol',
Callin' sof', "Come in. Come in."
Callin' sof', "Come in. Come in."

Den up t'ro' de gloomerin' meadows,
T'ro' de col' night rain and win',
And up t'ro' de gloomerin' rain-paf',
Wha'r de sleet fa' pie'cin' thin,
De po' los' sheep ob de sheepfol',
Dey all comes gadderin' in.
De po' los' sheep ob de sheepfol',
Dey all comes gadderin' in.

William Roscoe Thayer.

BORN in Boston, Mass., 1859.

MANKIND'S HIGHEST.

[*The Confessions of Hermes, and Other Poems.* 1884.]

A DREAM enticed the Spirit of the Earth,
　　And as, in sleep, fantastic shapes he chased,
The Hours slumbered and the Laws delayed.
When he awoke, behold! man's puny race
He found had in the fleeting interval
Expired as silently as bubbles burst.
A smile of pity crossed the Spirit's lips:
"To think the weaklings, if I nodded, died!
But, after all," he said, "the tiny imps
Have startled from me many a hearty laugh.
My time would drag could I no longer see
The shifting scenes of Human Comedy."
　　So men he made anew: and that the new
Might differ nowise from the elder breed,
He hunted, 'mid the ruins of the past,
A book wherein true types of men are drawn,
And from these patterns he refilled the globe.
Upon that book, O Shakespeare, was thy name.

THE HYMN OF FORCE.

I AM 'eternal!
   I throb through the ages;
I am the master
   Of each of Life's stages.

I quicken the blood
   Of the mate-craving lover;
The age-frozen heart
   With daisies I cover.

Down through the ether
   I hurl constellations;
Up from their earth-bed
   I wake the carnations.

I laugh in the flame
   As I kindle and fan it;
I crawl in the worm;
   I leap in the planet.

Forth from its cradle
   I pilot the river;
In lightning and earthquake
   I flash and I quiver.

My breath is the wind;
   My bosom the ocean;

My form's undefined;
   My essence is motion.

The braggarts of science
   Would weigh and divide me;
Their wisdom evading,
   I vanish and hide me.

My glances are rays
   From stars emanating;
My voice through the spheres
   Is sound, undulating.

I am the monarch
   Uniting all matter;
The atoms I gather,
   The atoms I scatter.

I pulse with the tides—
   Now hither, now thither;
I grant the tree sap;
   I bid the bud wither.

I always am present,
   Yet nothing can bind me;
Like thought, evanescent,
   They lose me who find me.

Helen Gray Cone.

BORN in New York, N. Y., 1859.

A NOCTURNE OF RUBINSTEIN.

[*Oberon and Puck: Verses Grave and Gay.* 1885.]

I.

WHAT now remains, what now remains but night?
   Night hopeless, since the moon is in her grave!

Late came a glorious light
In one wide flood on spire and field and wave.
   It found a flowing way
To secret places where the dead leaves lay;
   It won the half-hid stream
To shy remembrance of her morning gleam;

Then on the sky's sharp shore
Rolled back, a fading tide, and was no more.
No more on spire and ivied window bright!
No more on field and wave!

What now remains, what now remains but night?
Night hopeless, since the moon is in her grave!

II.

Dumb waits the dim, broad land,
Like one who hears, yet cannot understand,
Tidings of grief to come.
The woods and waters, with the winds, are dumb.
But now a breeze has found
Sorrowful voice, and sobs along the ground:
" Oh the lost light, the last, the best lost light!
No more on field and wave!"

What now remains, what now remains but night?
Night hopeless, since the moon is in her grave!

III.

Hark, how the wind outswells!
Tempting the wood's dark heart till he rebels,
And, shaking his black hair,
Lifts up a cry of passion and despair!
The groaning branches chafe
Till scarce the small, hushed singing-birds are safe,
Tossed rocking in the nest,
Like gentle memories in a stormy breast.
A shudder, as good angels passed in flight,
Thrills over field and wave!

What now remains, what now remains but night?
Night lawless, while the moon is in her grave!

IV.

There falls a mighty hush:
And forth from far recesses fern-scents rush,
Faint as a waft from years
Long past; they touch in heaven the springs of tears.
In great drops, slow and warm,
Breaks all at once the spirit of the storm.

What now remains, what now remains but night?
Night grieving, while the moon is in her grave!

V.

Behold! the rain is over: on the wave
A new, a flashing light!
Lo, she arises calm,
The pale, the patient moon, and pours like balm

Through the wet wood's wrecked aisle
Her own unutterably tender smile!
There is no calm like that when storm is done;
' There is no pleasure keen as pain's release;
There is no joy that lies so deep as peace,
No peace so deep as that by struggle won.

Naught now remains, naught now remains but night—
Night peaceful, with the moon on field and wave!

ELSINORE.

IT is strange in Elsinore
　　Since the day King Hamlet died.

All the hearty sports of yore,
　Sledge and skate, are laid aside;
Stilled the ancient mirth that rang,
　Boisterous, down the fire-lit halls;
They forgot, at Yule, to hang
　Berried holly on the walls.
Claudius lets the mead still flow
　For the blue-eyed thanes that love it;
　But they bend their brows above it,
And forever, to and fro,
Round the board dull murmurs go:
　"It is strange in Elsinore
　Since the day King Hamlet died."

And a swarm of courtiers flit,
　New in slashed and satined trim,
With their freshly-fashioned wit
　And their littleness of limb,—
Flit about the stairways wide,
　Till the pale Prince Hamlet smiles,
As he walks, at twilight tide,
　Through the galleries and the aisles.

For to him the castle seems—
　This old castle, Elsinore—
Like a thing built up of dreams;
　And the king's a mask, no more;
And the courtiers seem but flights
　Of the painted butterflies;
And the arras, wrought with fights,
　Grows alive before his eyes.
Lo, its giant shapes of Danes,
　As without a wind it waves,
Live more nobly than his thanes,
　Sullen carpers, ale-fed slaves!

In the flickering of the fires,
　Through his sleep at night there pass
Gay conceits and young desires—
　Faces out of memory's glass,
Fragments of the actor's art,
　Student's pleasures, college broils,
Poesies that caught his heart,
　Chances with the fencing-foils;
Then he listens oftentimes
　With his boyhood's simple glee,
To dead Yorick's quips and rhymes,
　Leaning on his father's knee.
To that mighty hand he clings,
　Tender love that stern face charms;
All at once the casement rings
　As with strength of angry arms.
From the couch he lifts his head,
　With a shudder and a start;
All the fires are embers red,
　And a weight is on his heart.

It is strange in Elsinore:
　Sure some marvel cometh soon!
　Underneath the icy moon
Footsteps pat the icy floor;
Voices haunt the midnights bleak,
　When the wind goes singing keen;
And the hound, once kept so sleek,
　Slinks and whimpers and grows lean,
And the shivering sentinels,
　Timorous, on their lonesome round,
Starting count the swinging bells,
　Starting at the hollow sound;
And the pine-trees chafe and roar,
　Though the snow would keep them
　　still.
　In the state there's somewhat ill;
It is strange in Elsinore.

A ROSE.

TOO-PERFECT Rose, thy heavy breath has power
        To wake a dim, an unexplained regret:
Art body to the soul of some deep hour
        That all my seasons have not yielded yet?

But if it be so—Hour, too-perfect Hour,
        Ah, blow not full, though all the yearning days
Should tremble bud-like, since the wind must shower
        Thine unreturning grace along the ways!

"AS THE CROW FLIES."

BUCCANEER with blackest sails,
        Steering home by compass true,
Now that all the rich West pales
        From its ingot-hue!

Would that compass in thy breast
        Thou couldst lend, for guiding me
Where my Hope hath made her nest—
        In how far a tree!

Swerving not, nor stooping low,
        To that dear, that distant mark
Could I undiverted go,
        What were coming dark?

—Careless of the twilight ground,
        O'er the wood and o'er the stream
Still he sails, with hollow sound
        Strange, as in a dream!

Clinton Scollard.

BORN in Clinton, Oneida Co., N. Y., 1860.

AS I CAME DOWN FROM LEBANON.

[*With Reed and Lyre.* 1886.—*Old and New World Lyrics.* 1888.]

AS I came down from Lebanon,
        Came winding, wandering slowly
                down,
Through mountain passes bleak and
                brown,
The cloudless day was wellnigh done.
The city, like an opal set
In emerald, showed each minaret
Afire with radiant beams of sun,
And glistened orange, fig, and lime
Where song-birds made melodious chime,
As I came down from Lebanon.

As I came down from Lebanon,
Like lava in the dying glow

Through olive orchards far below
I saw the murmuring river run;
And 'neath the wall upon the sand
Swart sheiks from distant Samarcand,
With precious spices they had won,
Lay long and languidly in wait
Till they might pass the guarded gate,
As I came down from Lebanon.

As I came down from Lebanon
I saw strange men from lands afar,
In mosque and square and gay bazar,
The Magi that the Moslem shun.
And grave Effendi from Stamboul,
Who sherbet sipped in corners cool;

And, from the balconies o'errun
With roses, gleamed the eyes of those
Who dwell in still seraglios,
As I came down from Lebanon.

As I came down from Lebanon
The flaming flower of daytime died,
And night, arrayed as is a bride

Of some great king in garments
    spun
Of purple and the finest gold,
Outbloomed in glories manifold:
Until the moon, above the dun
And darkening desert, void of shade,
Shone like a keen Damascus blade,
As I came down from Lebanon.

WILD COREOPSIS.

A SEA of blossoms, golden as the glow
    Of morning sunlight on a wind-rocked bay,
  Beneath the breeze of this rare autumn day
Heaves in soft undulation to and fro;
Like incense, floating o'er the marsh below,
    Come fragrant odors of the late-mown hay;
    Beyond, in harmony of green and gray,
The tapering tamaracks tower in stately row.

And wading through the shimmering waves, with song
    Upon his lips, a fair-haired youth I see,
      Who swinges off the saffron blossom-bells:
Back roll the years,—a melancholy throng,—
    And I behold, in sea-girt Sicily,
      Theocritus amid the asphodels!

THE BOOKSTALL.

IT stands in a winding street,
    A quiet and restful nook,
Apart from the endless beat
  Of the noisy heart of Trade;
    There's never a spot more cool
    Of a hot midsummer day
  By the brink of a forest pool,
  Or the bank of a crystal brook
  In the maples' breezy shade,
Than the bookstall old and gray.

Here are precious gems of thought
  That were quarried long ago,
Some in vellum bound, and wrought
  With letters and lines of gold;
    Here are curious rows of " calf,"
    And perchance an Elzevir;

Here are countless " mos " of chaff,
And a parchment folio,
Like leaves that are cracked with
    cold,
All puckered and brown and sear.

In every age and clime
  Live the monarchs of the brain:
And the lords of prose and rhyme,
  Years after the long last sleep
    Has come to the kings of earth
    And their names have passed away,
  Rule on through death and birth;
  And the thrones of their domain
  Are found where the shades are
    deep,
In the bookstall old and gray.

THE ACTOR.

NIGHT after night a mimic death he died,
   While sympathetic thousands wept and sighed;
But when at last he came in truth to die,
No teardrop fell from any mourner's eye.

SIDNEY GODOLPHIN.

THEY rode from the camp at morn
   With clash of sword and spur.
The birds were loud in the thorn,
   The sky was an azure blur.
A gallant show they made
   That warm noon-tide of the year,
Led on by a dashing blade,
   By the poet-cavalier.

They laughed through the leafy lanes,
   The long lanes of Dartmoor;
And they sang their soldier strains,
   Pledged "death" to the Roundhead
     boor;
Then they came at the middle day
   To a hamlet quaint and brown
Where the hated troopers lay,
   And they cheered for the King and
     crown.

They fought in the fervid heat,
   Fought fearlessly and well,
But low at the foeman's feet
   Their valorous leader fell.
Full on his fair young face
   The blinding sun beat down;
In the morn of his manly grace
   He died for the King and crown.

O the pitiless blow,
   The vengeance-thrust of strife,
That blotted the golden glow
   From the sky of his glad, brave life!
The glorious promise gone;—
   Night with its grim black frown!
Never again the dawn,
   And all for the King and crown.

Hidden his sad fate now
   In the sealèd book of the years;
Few are the heads that bow,
   Or the eyes that brim with tears,
Reading 'twixt blots and stains
   From a musty tome that saith
How he rode through the Dartmoor
     lanes
   To his woful, dauntless death.

But I, in the summer's prime,
   From that lovely leafy land
Look back to the olden time
   And the leal and loyal band.
I see them dash along,—
   I hear them charge and cheer,
And my heart goes out in a song
   To the poet-cavalier.

PERPETUITY.

LAST night a mighty poet passed away:
   "Who now will sing our songs?" men cried at morn.
Faint hearts, fear not! Somewhere, though far away,
   At that same hour another bard was born.

Mary Eleanor Wilkins.

BORN in Randolph, Mass.

OLD LADY PINGREE.

[*A Humble Romance, and Other Stories.* 1887.]

IT was almost dark at half-past four. Nancy Pingree stood staring out at one of her front windows. Not a person was passing on the wide country road; not one came up the old brick walk between the dry phlox bushes to the house.

It was the same picture out there which the old woman had looked at hundreds of times before in winter twilights like this. The interest in it had died away with the expectation of new developments in it which she had had in her youth. Nature to Nancy Pingree had never been anything but a background for life.

When she had first gone to the window she had said, "I wish I could see somebody comin' that belonged to me."

Then she simply stood thinking. The tall, graceful, leafless trees arching over the quiet snowy road, and the glimpse of clear yellow western sky through them, the whole landscape before her, with all the old lights of her life shining on it, became a mirror in which she saw herself reflected.

She started finally, and went across the room with a long shamble. She was lame in one hip; but, for all that, there was a certain poor majesty in her carriage. Her rusty black dress hung in straight long folds, and trailed a little. She held her head erect, and wore an odd black lace turban. She had made the turban herself, with no pattern. It was a direct outcome of her own individuality; perched on the top of her long old head it really was—Nancy Pingree.

She took down a plaid shawl which was hanging in a little side entry, pinned it over her head, and opened the outer door into the clear twilight. Straight from the door, on this side of the old house, an avenue of pine-trees led to a hen-coop. Whatever majestic idea had been in the head of Nancy's grandfather, Abraham Pingree, when he had set out these trees, it had come to this.

Nancy went down between the windy pines, over the crusty snow, to the hen-coop. She came back with two eggs in her hand. "They've done pretty well to-day," said she to herself.

When she was in the house again she stood shivering for a little while over her sitting-room air-tight stove. She still held the eggs. A question had come up, the answer to which was costing her a struggle.

"Here's two eggs," said she. "I could have one biled for supper; I kinder feel the need of it too; I ain't had anything hearty to-day. An' I could have the other one fried with a little slice of salt pork for breakfast. Seems to me I should reely relish it. I s'pose Mis' Stevens would admire to have an egg for supper. Jenny ain't had any work this week, an' I know she ain't been out anywhere to buy anything to-day. I should think her mother would actilly go

Mary E. Wilkins

faint sometimes, without meat an' egg an' sech hearty things. She's nothin' but skin an' bone anyway. I've a good mind to kerry her one of these eggs. I would ef I didn't feel as ef I reely needed it myself."

The poor soul stood there looking at the eggs. Finally she put the smaller one in a cupboard beside the chimney, and went out of the sitting-room into the front hall with the larger one. She climbed stiffly up the stairs, which were fine old winding ones. Then she knocked at a door on the landing.

A thin, pretty-faced young woman opened it. Nancy proffered the egg. She had a stately manner of extending her lean arm.

"Here's a new-laid egg I thought your mother might relish for her supper, Jenny," said she.

The young woman's sharp, pretty face grew red. "Oh, thank you, Miss Pingree; but I—don't think mother needs it. I am afraid—you will rob yourself."

Nancy held her wide mouth stiff, only opening it a crack when she spoke. "I've got plenty for myself, plenty. I shouldn't use this one before it spiled, mebbe, ef I kep' it. I thought p'rhaps it would go good for your mother's supper; but you can do just as you like about takin' it."

The young woman accepted the egg with reserved thanks, then, and Nancy went stiffly back down-stairs.

"I guess ef Jenny Stevens hadn't took that egg, it would have been the last thing I'd ever offered her," said she, when she was in her sitting-room. "I don't see how she ever got the idea she seems to have that I'm so awful poor."

She made herself a cup of tea, and ate a slice of bread-and-butter for her supper; she had resolved to save her own egg until morning. Then she sat down for the evening with her knitting. She knitted a good many stockings for a friend's family. That friend came in at the side door presently. Nancy heard her fumbling about in the entry, but she did not rise until the sitting-room door opened.

Then, "Why, how do you do, Mis' Holmes?" said she, rising, in apparent surprise.

"I'm pretty well, thank you, Nancy. How do you do?"

"'Bout as usual. Do take off your things an' set down."

The visitor had a prosperous look; she was richly dressed to country eyes, and had a large, masterly, middle-aged face.

"I just heard some sad news," said she, laying aside her shawl.

"You don't say so!"

"Old Mrs. Powers was found dead in her bed this morning."

Nancy's face took on an anxious look; she asked many questions about the sudden death of Mrs. Powers. She kept recurring to the same topic all the evening. "Strange how sudden folks go nowadays," she often repeated.

At length, just before Mrs. Holmes went, she stood up with an air of resolution. "Mis' Holmes," said she, with a solemn tremor in her voice, "I wish you'd jest step in here a minute."

Mrs. Holmes followed her into her bedroom, which opened out of the sitting-room. Nancy pulled out the bottom drawer in a tall mahogany bureau.

"Look here, Mis' Holmes. I've been thinkin' of it over for some time, an' wantin' to speak about it; an' hearin' old Mis' Powers was took so sudden, makes me think mebbe I'd better not put it off any longer. In case anything happened to me, you'd probably be one to come in an' see to things, an' you'd want to know where everything was, so you could put your hand on it. Well, all the clothes you'd need are right there, folded up in that drawer. An' Mis' Holmes, you'll never speak of this to anybody?"

"No, I won't."

"In this corner, under the clothes, you'll find the money to pay for my buryin'. I've been savin' of it up, a few cents at a time, this twenty year. I calculate there's enough for everythin'. I want to be put in that vacant place at the end of the Pingree lot, an' have a flat stone, like the others, you know. If I leave it with you, you'll see that it's all done right, won't you, Mis' Holmes? I feel pretty perticklar about it. I'm the last of the hull family, you know, an' they were pretty smart folks. It's all run out now. I ain't nothin', but I'd kinder like to have my buryin' done like the others. I don't want it done by the town, an' I don't want nobody to give it to me. I want to pay for it with my own money. You'll see to it, won't you?"

"Of course I will. Everything shall be done just as you say, if I have anything to do about it."

Mrs. Holmes was rarely shocked or painfully touched; but the sight of that poor little hoard of white clothes and burial money called up all the practical kindness in her nature. Every one of Nancy's wishes would be faithfully carried out under her supervision.

"If they put the railroad they're talking about through here, it'll make us rich. The Deacon says it will go through the south part of this land. We'd have enough money for burying and living too," said Mrs. Holmes, as Nancy shut and locked the drawer.

"I ain't no stock in the railroad; all the money would belong to the Deacon ef it was put through this land. I've got all over carin' for riches. All I want is to be buried independent, like the rest of my folks."

"How's the woman up-stairs?" asked Mrs. Holmes when she took leave finally. She had three pairs of Nancy's finished stockings in a bundle.

"She's pretty poorly, I think. She keeps me awake 'most all the time."

Nancy did not go farther than the sitting-room door with her departing visitor. When she had heard the outer door close after her, she went swiftly out into the entry. She held the lamp in her hand, and peered sharply into the corners.

"Yes, she did," said she, and took up a good-sized covered basket from behind the door eagerly.

She carried it into the sitting-room, and opened it; it was packed with eatables. Done up in a little parcel at the bottom was the pay for the three pairs of stockings.

This was the code of etiquette, which had to be strictly adhered to, in the matter of Nancy's receiving presents or remuneration. Gifts or presents openly proffered her were scornfully rejected, and ignominiously carried back by the donor. Nancy Pingree was a proud old woman. People called her "Old Lady Pingree." She had not a dollar of her own in the world, except her little hoard of burial money. This immense old mansion, which had been the outcome of the ancient prosperity of the Pingrees, was owned entirely by Mrs. Holmes's husband, through foreclosed mortgages.

"You'd better foreclose, Deacon," Mrs. Holmes had said, "and make sure you've got the place safe in your own hands; an' then you'd better let the poor old lady stay there just the same as long as she lives. She needn't know any difference."

Nancy did know a difference. Down in the depths of her proud old heart rankled the knowledge that an outsider owned the home of her fathers, and that she was living in it on toleration. She let some rooms up-stairs, and received the money for them herself. Mrs. Holmes's benevolence was wide, although it was carefully and coolly calculated. All Nancy had to live on was the rent of these rooms, besides the small proceeds from her three hens and her knitting, and neighborly donations. Some days she had not much for sustenance except her pride. She was over eighty.

The people up-stairs were a widow and daughter. The mother, after an absence of many years and much trouble, had turned back, of her nature, to the town in which she had been born and brought up. All her friends were gone now, but they had used to be there. So they came and hired rooms of Miss Pingree, and Jenny did sewing to support herself and her mother. She was a good daughter. They had a hard struggle to live. Jenny did not find work very plentiful; a good many of the women here did their own sewing. She could scarcely pay the rent of fifty cents per week and buy enough to eat. Her mother was sick now—in consumption, it was thought. Jenny did not realize it. She was not confined to her bed.

Jenny came down and knocked at Nancy's door the next morning. She had fifty cents in her hand, with which to pay the rent. She always paid it punctually on Saturday morning.

Nancy cast a glance at the money. "How's your mother?" said she. "I heerd her coughin' a good deal last night."

"She had a pretty bad night. I'm going for the doctor. This is the money for the rent."

"Let it go."

"Why, I owe it. I can pay it just as well now as any time."

"I don't want it any time. I don't want any pay for this week. I don't need it. I've got enough."

Jenny's face was crimson. "Thank you, but I'd rather pay what I owe, Miss Pingree."

"I sha'n't take it."

The two poor, proud souls stood confronting each other. Then Jenny laid the fifty cents on the window-seat. "You can do just what you've a mind to do with it," said she. "I certainly sha'n't take it back." Then she went out of the room quickly.

"Strange how she got the idea I was so awful poor!" said Nancy, staring at the money resentfully. "I won't tetch it, anyway. She'll see it layin' there next time she comes in."

The next time poor Jenny came in, it was indeed still lying there on the window-seat, a scanty pile of wealth in five and ten cent pieces and coppers.

But Jenny never noticed it; she had something else to think of then. It was very early the next morning, but Miss Pingree was up, kindling the fire in her sitting-room stove. Jenny ran right in without knocking; she had a shawl over her head. "Oh, Miss Pingree," she cried, "can't you go upstairs to mother while I run for the doctor?"

Nancy dropped the tongs, and stood up. "Is she—" she began. But Jenny was gone. When the doctor came there was no need for him. Jenny's mother was dead. All that was required now was the aid of some of the friendly, capable women neighbors. Nancy went for them, and they came promptly, Mrs. Holmes and two others.

When they had done all that was necessary they went home. Shortly afterwards Jenny came into Nancy's room; she had on her shawl and hood. She had been very calm through it all, but her pretty face had a fierce, strained look.

"Miss Pingree," she said, abruptly, "who are the selectmen?"

"Why, Deacon Holmes is one. What do you want to know for?"

"I've got to go to them. The town will have to bury mother."

"Oh!" cried Nancy, with two sharp notes, one of pity, one of horror.

Suddenly at that Jenny's forced composure gave way; she sank helplessly into a chair, and began to half sob, half shriek. "Oh, mother! mother! mother! poor mother! To think it has come to this! To think you must be buried by the town. What would you have said? It's the worst of all. Poor mother! poor mother! oh, poor mother!"

"Haven't you got any money?"

"No. Oh, mother!"

"An' there ain't any of your folks that could help you?"

"We didn't have any folks."

Then she kept on with her cries and moans. Nancy stood motionless. There is no knowing what a clash of spiritual armies with trumpets and banners there was in her brave old heart; but not a line of her face moved; she hardly breathed.

"Wait a minute, Jenny."

Nancy went into her bedroom and unlocked the lowest drawer in the bureau. She took out all of her little hoard of money except a few cents. She limped majestically across the sitting-room to Jenny.

"Here, child; there ain't any need of your goin' to the town. I've got some money here that I can let you have jest as well as not."

"Miss Pingree!"

"Here."

"Oh, what do you mean? How can I take it? What will you do?"

"I shall do well enough. This ain't all; I've got some more."

When all of Jenny's proud scruples which this terrible emergency had left her had been subdued, and she had gone, Nancy took up the fifty cents on the window-seat.

"Guess she's took this now, an' more too," said she, with an odd tone of satisfaction. Even now, in her splendid self-sacrifice, there was a little leaven of pride. There was no mistaking the fact that it gave her some comfort in this harsh charity, which was almost like giving a piece of her own heart. She inspected the neat appointments of poor Mrs. Stevens's funeral with feelings not wholly of grief at her own deprivation of similar honors, nor yet of honest benevolence. There was a grand though half-smothered consciousness of her own giving in her heart. She felt for herself the respect which she would have felt for an old Pingree in his palmiest days.

As time went on she lost this, however; then the humiliating consciousness of her own condition came uppermost. She dreaded to tell Mrs. Holmes of the change in her resources, and now no vanity over her own benevolence rendered the task easier. She simply felt intense humiliation at having to confess her loss of independence.

However, she never regretted what she had done. She grew very fond of Jenny; indeed, the two had much in common. They generally ate their simple meals together. Jenny had plenty of work to do now; Mrs. Holmes gave her a great deal of sewing. She often told Nancy how she was saving up money to pay her debt ; she never suspected the real state of the case. She had taken to thinking that Miss Pingree must have wider resources than she had known.

Nancy would have died rather than let her know of the meagre sum in that consecrated corner of the bureau drawer. It seemed to her sometimes that she would rather die than have Mrs. Holmes know, but that was necessary. Suppose she should be taken away suddenly, what surprise, and perhaps even distrust, would be occasioned by the scantiness of the burial hoard ! However, she had not told her when spring came.

At length, she set out after tea one night. She had resolved to put it off no longer.

The cemetery was on the way. She lingered and looked in. Finally she entered.

" I'll jest look around a minute," said she. " I dare say Mis' Holmes ain't through supper."

The Pingree lot was almost in sight from the street. Nancy went straight there. The cemetery was itself a spring garden, blue and white with Houstonias and violets. The old graves were green, and many little bushes were flowering around them. The gold-green leaf-buds on the weeping-willows were unfolding.

The Pingree lot, however, partook of none of the general lightness and loveliness. No blessing of spring had fallen on that long rank of dead Pingrees. There they lay, in the order of their deaths, men and women and children, each covered with a flat white stone above the grave mould.

Tall, thickly-set evergreen trees fenced in closely the line of graves. In the midst of the cemetery, where gloom was now rendered tender by the infinite promise of the spring, the whole was a ghastly parallelogram of hopeless death.

Nancy Pingree, looking through the narrow entrance gap in the evergreens on the dark, tomb-like enclosure, had, however, no such impression. She regarded this as the most attractive lot in the cemetery. Its singularity had been in subtle accordance with the Pingree character, and she was a Pingree. At one end of the long row of prostrate stones there was a vacant place: enough for another.

Nancy began with this topic when she was seated, a little later, in Mrs. Holmes's Brussels-carpeted, velvet-upholstered parlor. "I looked in the graveyard a minute on my way here," said she, "an' went over to the Pingree lot. I'd allers calculated to have a stone like the others when I was laid at the end there; but now I don' know. You remember that money I showed you, Mis' Holmes? Well, it ain't there now; I've had to use it. I thought I'd better tell you, in case you wouldn't know what to make of it, if anything happened."

Mrs. Holmes stared at her, with a look first of amazement, then of intelligence. "Nancy Pingree, you gave the money to bury that woman up-stairs."

"Hush! don't you say anything about it, Mis' Holmes. Jenny don't know the hull of it. She took on so, I couldn't help it. It come over me that I hadn't got anybody to feel bad ef I was buried by the town, an' it wouldn't make so much difference."

"How much money was there?"

"Eighty dollars," said Nancy, with the tone in which she would have said a million.

Mrs. Holmes was a woman who was seldom governed by hasty impulse; but she was now. She disregarded the strict regulations attached to giving in Nancy's case, and boldly offered to replace the money out of her own pocket. She could well afford to do it.

Nancy looked majestic with resentment. "No," said she. "If it's got to be done by anybody, I'd enough sight rather 'twould be done by the town. The Pingrees have paid taxes enough in times gone by to make it nothin' more'n fair, after all. Thank you, Mis' Holmes, but I ain't quite come to takin' money out an' out from folks yet."

"Well, I didn't mean to hurt your feelings."

"I know you didn't, Mis' Holmes. You meant it kind enough. We won't say no more about it."

"Don't you believe Jenny will be able to pay you back, some time?"

"I don't know. She says she's goin' to, an' I know she means to—she's awful proud. But she can't save up much, poor child, an' I shouldn't wonder ef I died first. Well, never mind. How's the Deacon?"

"He's well, thank you. He's gone to the railroad meeting. Somebody was telling me the other day that Benny Field was waiting on Jenny."

"Well, I believe he's come home with her from meetin' some lately; but I don't know."

When Nancy reached home that night she wondered if Benny Field were not really "waiting on Jenny." She found him sitting with her on the front door-step.

Before long she knew that he was. Jenny came to her one afternoon and told her she was going to marry Benny Field. Nancy had previously received another piece of intelligence on the same day.

Early that morning Mrs. Holmes had come over with an important look on her face, and announced to Nancy that the new railroad was indeed going to be laid through the Pingree land.

"They are going to build the depot down on the corner too," said she; "and—the Deacon thinks, seeing the property has come up so much in value, that it isn't any more'n fair that—he should make you a little present."

"I don't want any present."

"Well, I didn't mean to put it that way. It isn't a present. It's no more than your just due. I don't think the Deacon would ever feel just right in his conscience if he didn't pay you a little something. You know the property wasn't considered worth so much when he foreclosed."

"How much did he think of payin'?"

"I believe he said—about two hundred dollars."

"Two hundred dollars!"

Nancy had been full of the bliss of it all day, but she had said nothing about it to Jenny.

When the girl told her she was going to be married, Nancy looked at her half in awe.

"Well, I am glad, I'm sure," said she, finally. "I hope you'll be happy ef you reely think it's a wise thing to do to git married." Her tone was almost shamefaced. This old woman, who had never had a lover, regarded this young woman with awe, half as if she had stepped on to another level, where it would be indecorous for her to follow even in thought.

"I suppose I am happy," said Jenny. "I never thought anything of this kind would happen to me. There's one thing, Miss Pingree: I wouldn't think of getting married, I'd never consent to getting married, if I didn't think I could pay up what I owe you, if anything, quicker. Benny says (I've told him about it; I said at first I wouldn't get married anyway till you were paid) that I shall have a sewing-machine, and I can have some help, and set up a little dressmaking shop. I ain't going to buy a single new thing to wear when I get married. I told him I wasn't. I've got a little money for you now, Miss Pingree."

"Oh," said Nancy, looking at her with the ecstatic consciousness of her new wealth in her heart, "I don't want it, child, ever. I'm glad I could do it for your poor mother. I've got plenty of money. I wish you'd keep this an' buy yourself some weddin' things with it."

Even Jenny's pride was softened by her happiness. She looked up at Miss Pingree gratefully; she would have put her arms around her and kissed her had Miss Pingree been a woman to caress and she herself given to caresses. "You are real good to me," said she, "and you were good to mother. I do thank you; but—I should never take a bit of comfort in a new dress until I had paid you every dollar of that money."

There was a beautiful clear sunset that night. Nancy Pingree sat looking over at it from her sitting-room window. All her heart was full of a sweet, almost rapturous peace. She had had a bare, hard life; and now the one earthly ambition, pitiful and melancholy as it seemed, which had kept its living fire was gratified.

And perhaps that independent burial in the vacant corner of the ghastly

Pingree lot meant more than itself to this old woman, whose great unselfishness had exalted her over her almost cowardly pride.

Perhaps she caught through it more strongly at the only real prospect of delight which all existence could hold for one like her. Perhaps she saw through it, by her own homely light, the Innocent City and the Angel-people, and the Sweet Green Pastures and Gentle Flocks and Still Waters, and herself changed somehow into something beautiful. Perhaps the grosser ambition held the finer one with its wings.

As she sat there, Benny Field came to the door for Jenny. They were going to walk.

Nancy watched them as they went down the path. "I wonder," said she, "if they are any happier thinkin' about gettin' married than I am thinkin' about gettin' buried."

Frank Dempster Sherman.

BORN in Peekskill, N. Y., 1860.

BACCHUS.

[Madrigals and Catches. 1887.—Uncollected Poems. 1887-89.]

LISTEN to the tawny thief,
  Hid behind the waxen leaf,
Growling at his fairy host,
Bidding her with angry boast
Fill his cup with wine distilled
From the dew the dawn has spilled:
Stored away in golden casks
Is the precious draught he asks.

Who,—who makes this mimic din
In this mimic meadow inn,
Sings in such a drowsy note,
Wears a golden belted coat;
Loiters in the dainty room
Of this tavern of perfume;
Dares to linger at the cup
Till the yellow sun is up?

Bacchus, 'tis, come back again
To the busy haunts of men;
Garlanded and gayly dressed,
Bands of gold about his breast;
Straying from his paradise,
Having pinions angel-wise,—
'Tis the honey-bee, who goes
Revelling within a rose!

FOR SAYNTE VALENTYNE, HIS DAYE.

GOE, little Rhyme, & greete Her,
  Goe, tel Her y^t I thinke
Things infinitely sweeter
  Y^n I maie putt in Inke:
Ye Musick of ye metre
  Shal linger on ye Aire
Y^e whiles She turns ye Leaves & learns
  Ye Secrett hidden there.

Flye, little Leafe of Paper,
  Flye, merrie-hearted Bird,
& lett your Fancie shape Her
  Some dear & simple Word
Soe sweete it sha'n't escape Her,
  & if a Blushe you see
Steale upp & chase across Her face,
  Return & counsell me.

Very truly yours,

Frank Dempster Sherman.

Haste, little God! I send Her,
  Bye You, yˢ MS.,
Wᶜʰ hopefull Love has penned Her
  Withe quill in Honie dipt;

Haste; bidd Her Heart be tender
  Unto yᵉ lightsome Line
Where I in maske have come to aske
  To be Her Valentyne!

WINTER STARLIGHT.

THE air is keen, the sky is clear,
  The winds have gone in whispers
     down;
And, gleaming in the atmosphere,
  A jewel, lies the lighted town.

The winter's mantle stretches white
  Upon the roofs and streets below;
All hushed, the noises of the night,
  Against the bosom of the snow.

The Moon from her blue dwelling-place
  Smiles over all, so pale, so fair,

It seems the Earth's wan, winter face
  Reflected in a mirror there.

Far off the lonely trees uplift
  Their naked branches, like the spars
Of some deserted ship adrift
  Under a canopy of stars.

It is the darkened world that rides
  The sea of space, forever drawn
By secret winds and mighty tides
  Unto the harbor of the Dawn.

PEPITA.

UP in her balcony where
  Vines through the lattices run
Spilling a scent on the air,
  Setting a screen to the sun,
Fair as the morning is fair,
    Sweet as a blossom is sweet,
    Dwells in her rosy retreat
      Pepita.

Often a glimpse of her face,
  When the wind rustles the vine
Parting the leaves for a space,
  Gladdens this window of mine;
Pink in its leafy embrace,—
    Pink as a roseleaf is pink,
    Sweet as a blossom I think
      Pepita.

I who dwell over the way
  Watch where Pepita is hid
Safe from the glare of the day
  Like an eye under its lid:
Over and over I say—
    Name like the song of a bird,
    Melody shut in a word,—
      "Pepita."

Look where the little leaves stir!
  Look,—the green curtains are drawn!
There in a blossomy blur
  Breaks a diminutive dawn,—
Dawn and the pink face of her,—
    Name like the lisp of the South,
    Fit for a rose's small mouth,—
      Pepita!

OMAR KHAYYÁM.

AT Naishápúr his ashes lie
    O'ershadowed by the mosque's blue
      dome;
There folded in his tent of sky
  The star of Persia sleeps at home.

The Rose her buried Nightingale
  Remembers, faithful all these years;
Around his grave the winds exhale
  The fragrant sorrow of her tears.

Sultans and Slaves in caravans
  Since Malik Shah have gone their way,
And ridges in the Kubberstans
  Are their memorials to-day.

But from the dust in Omar's tomb
  A Fakir has revived a Rose,—
Perchance the old, ancestral bloom
  Of that one by the mosque which blows.

Out of its petals he has caught
  The inspiration Omar knew,
Who from the stars his wisdom brought,
  A Persian Rose that drank the dew.

The Fakir now in dust lies low
  With Omar of the Orient;
Fitzgerald,—shall we call him? No;
  'Twas Omar in the Occident!

THE LIBRARY.

GIVE me the room whose every nook
  Is dedicated to a book.
Two windows will suffice for air
And grant the light admission there;
One looking to the south, and one
To speed the red, departing sun.
The eastern wall from frieze to plinth
Shall be the Poet's labyrinth,
Where one may find the lords of rhyme
From Homer's down to Dobson's time;
And at the northern side a space
Shall show an open chimney-place,
Set round with ancient tiles that tell
Some legend old and weave a spell
About the firedog-guarded seat,
Where one may dream and taste the heat:
Above, the mantel should not lack
For curios and bric-à-brac,—
Not much, but just enough to light
The room up when the fire is bright.
The volumes on this wall should be
All prose and all philosophy,
From Plato down to those who are
The dim reflections of that star;

And these tomes all should serve to show
How much we write—how little know;
For since the problem first was set
No one has ever solved it yet.
Upon the shelves toward the west
The scientific books shall rest;
Beside them, History; above,—
Religion,—hope, and faith, and love:
Lastly, the southern wall should hold
The story-tellers, new and old;
Haroun al Raschid, who was truth
And happiness to all my youth,
Shall have the honored place of all
That dwell upon this sunny wall,
And with him there shall stand a throng
Of those who help mankind along
More by their fascinating lies
Than all the learning of the wise.

Such be the library; and take
This motto of a Latin make
To grace the door through which I
  pass:
Hic habitat Felicitas!

Henry Harland.

BORN in New York, N. Y., 1861.

MR. SONNENSCHEIN'S INHERITANCE.

[A Latin-Quarter Courtship, and Other Stories. By Sidney Luska. 1889.]

I.

SCHLEMIEL.

THE English language very likely possesses an equivalent for the Jüdisch word Schlemiel; but I have tried in vain to find it. Briefly, a Schlemiel is a person who never prospers, with whom everything goes wrong. Born under an evil star, or with a leaden spoon in his mouth, he is constitutionally unsuccessful. Misfortune has marked him for her own ; ill luck accompanies him through life. The witty Jewish author Leopold Kompert says that while other people seize opportunities by the head, the Schlemiel lays hold of them by the foot, and allows them to wriggle and kick themselves loose. Put gold into the hands of your Schlemiel, adds Kompert, it turns to copper. Let him purchase a cask of wine; when he opens the spigot, vinegar gushes forth. Yet, of all mortal men, the Schlemiel is usually the best-natured, the lightest-hearted. A perpetual sunny smile illuminates his face. He seems to regard his sorry destiny as an excellent practical joke, at which, though it be at his own expense, he can laugh as well as another. Calamity is his native element. He is impervious to it. He minds it no more than a salamander minds fire, or a duck water. The Lord shapes the back to the burden. That same careless and irresponsible temperament which is constantly bringing the Schlemiel to grief enables him to accept it with a shrug. Not but that, once in a while, you may meet a melancholy, even a crabbed and misanthropic, Schlemiel; but he will also be a highly exceptional Schlemiel.

By his own admission, as well as by the judgment of his friends, Emmanuel Sonnenschein was a Schlemiel. "I ain't no goot," he used to say, with an hilarious twinkle in his eye. "I ain't got no sense. I'm a raikular Schlemiel." He was a very old man, white, and bent, and wrinkled ; but, though he rather prided himself upon his age, and loved to prate about it, the exact figure of it he would never tell.   .   .   .   .   .

II.

SCHLEMIEL'S EXPECTATIONS.

He lived with his crippled daughter Nettie up several flights of dark and rickety stairs, in a tenement-house overlooking Tompkins Square. Nettie passed her life between her bed and her easy-chair. Mr. Sonnenschein did the house-work,—cooked the meals and washed the dishes, made the beds and kept the quarters clean.   .   .   .   .   .

Mr. Sonnenschein commonly arrived just as we had finished dinner, while we were getting into sympathy with our newly lighted cigars. We would install him at the table,—for in respect of that virtue which ranks second only to godliness he was unimpeachable,—fill his plate and his wineglass, and wait expectantly for the good cheer to loosen his tongue. By and by, face fairly radiant of benevolence, he would lean back in his chair, heave a mighty sigh of satisfaction, wipe the tears of enjoyment from his eyes (with his napkin), and the unruly member would begin to wag. I always enjoyed listening to him, he was so simple-minded and so optimistic.

" Vail, now, dis is a funny vorld, Saimmy; it is, and no mistake. Yais, it's an awful funny vorld, dere ain't no use in talking. Vail, now look at here. I vas a Schlemiel,—hey? Dere ain't no kervestion about dot,—I vas a Schlemiel. Vail, now look at here. Maybe you vouldn't belief me,—you might tink I vas trying to fool you,—but, honor bright, I got a brudder ofer in Chairmany who's vun of de very luckiest shentlemen dot vas aifer born. Now, ain't dot funny? . . . . His name is Shakie, and me and him vas tervins. Vail, I suppose dere vasn't goot luck enough to go around beterveen us; so Shakie he got it all, and I didn't get ainy. All de same, I leaf it to you if it ain't awful funny . . . . Vail, Shakie, he vas so fearful lucky, he vent into de chewelry business, and he got rich. Vail, I don't know shust exaictly how rich he vas; I ain't naifer aisked him. But I don't belief he's vort less as fifty or a hoonert tousand tollars. Vail, of course, he might not be vort more as terventy-fife or tirty tousand. But he's an awful rich shentleman ainyhow; you can bet a hat on dot. Vail, Shakie he ain't naifer got mairried, nor haid no children; so fen he dies I get his money. Vail, he cain't expect to live much longer, for he's a fearful old man by dis time already, and it ain't necheral dot he should live to get much older. Him and me vas tervins; so he's shust exactly as old as me; and you ain't got no *i*dea how old dot is. Vail, I'll feel awful sorry fen Shakie dies; yais, I'll feel simply terrible; but he cain't expect to live much longer,—he's so fearful old,—and I'll be glaid to get dot money on account of Nettie. I don't care two cents about money on my own account; I don't, honor bright. But poor little Nettie, she's haid such a hart time of it all her life, I'll be glaid fen I get money enough to let her live in comfort. . . . . Vail, Saimmy, my brudder Shakie he's an awful *goot*-hearted shentleman, and he's got a lot of faimily feeling about him; and I suppose if I wrote him a letter to-morrer, and aisked him to make me a present of a tousand tollars,—vail, I suppose Shakie he'd saind it to me by returner-mail; he's an old bechelor, you know, and he's got so much faimily feeling. But I ain't naifer aisked him for vun single cent. No, sir; I go to de poor-house sooner as aisk my brudder Shakie for a haif a tollar. Dot's becoase I'm so prout. You ain't got no *i*dea how prout I am. Dere ain't no use in talking, I shouldn't vunder if I vas about de proutest shentleman de Lord aifer mait. And dot's the reason I vouldn't aisk no favors of my brudder Shakie. I vouldn't let him know dot I ain't so rich as himself, not for ten hoonert tousand tollars. I'm so fearful prout. Fy, Saimmy, my brudder Shakie he don't dream dot I vas a Schlemiel. Vail, I guess maybe if he knew dot,—he's got so much faimily feeling about him,—I guess maybe if Shakie knew dot, it vould break his heart."

"Well, Mr. Sonnenschein," my mother would presently inquire, "what has Nettie been doing lately? I hope you have brought some of her things with you to show us,"—thus proving herself to be a consummate hypocrite, though from the kindest motives.

His hands would fly up toward the ceiling; his head would begin to sway from side to side; and, "Ach, Nettie!" he would cry in response. "Nettie! She's a born vunder! Industrious ain't no vord for it. She's de graindest vorker in de United States, she simply is. Vork, vork, vork, from de time she vakes oop in de morning till she goes to sleep again at night! I naifer seen nodings like it in all my life before. It's fearful. And such a tailent! I don't know fere she gets it. Vail, I guess maybe she gets it from her mommer. Yais, my vife vas vun of de very smartest ladies de Lord aifer mait; and I guess maybe dot's how my dowter Nettie gets her tailent. Vail, she's been vorking a new paittern lately, fich she mait oop out of her own hait. It's de most maiknificent ting she aifer done; it's elegant; it's immense. I got it in tidies and piller-shaims and table-maits and bait-kervilts. You'll fall daid in loaf mit it; I bet a hat on dot. Hold on."

Therewith he would open his pack, and display treasures, going into raptures of enthusiasm over them. "Ain't dey splendid? Ain't dey serveet? Ain't my dowter got a chenu-wine tailent?" etc., etc. He was generosity incarnate, was Mr. Sonnenschein; and after we had satisfied our consciences by the purchase of tidies enough to fit out a colony, he would throw in two or three extra ones, as he explained, "for loaf." Our protestations to the effect that he mustn't rob himself he would quickly silence, crying, "Don't mention it. Don't say anudder vord about it. Dere ain't nodings stinchy about me. Goot maisure, small proafits, kervick sales,—dot's my motter. Take 'em and vailcome. You say anudder vord about it, I trow in some more." That threat was effectual. We took them.

III.

SCHLEMIEL'S PRUDENCE.

Yes, his habit was to drop in upon us not seldomer than three or four times a year; but a period of quite six months had elapsed, and he had given us no sign of life, and we were beginning to wonder what had become of him,— when, one blustering evening in November, at his usual hour, he entered our dining-room.

From the instant we laid eyes upon him we knew that something extraordinary was in the wind. His accoutrement proclaimed as much, and so did the profound dejection that was painted upon his face. Instead of the motley assortment of other people's superannuated garments in which we were wont to see him clad, he wore a brand-new suit of broadcloth. A black cravat encircled his gnarled and ancient throat. In his hand he carried a glossy stove-pipe hat, with a crape band about it; and under his arm, an oblong thickish parcel, neatly done up in a paper, and tied with pink twine; while the badge and instrument of his profession, his accustomed pack, was nowhere to be seen. His countenance, as I have said, bespoke a deep and consuming melancholy.

"Why, Mr. Sonnenschein!" exclaimed my mother, starting up in alarm and advancing to meet him. "What has happened? What's the matter? Is—has—is Nettie"——

"No," he interrupted, with a solemn gesture and in a sepulchral voice. "No, it ain't Nettie. No, tank de Lord, it ain't so baid as dot. But it's fearful all de same. It's my brudder,—it's my brudder Shakie."

"What!" we all cried in concert. "He's dead?"

"Yais," replied Mr. Sonnenschein, sinking into a chair, the picture of a man prostrated and undone by grief. "Yais, he's daid, my brudder Shakie's daid." After a brief pause, in a sudden passionate outburst: "Ach Gott, and ve vas tervins!"

He bowed his head, and for a little while his sorrow seemed to deprive him of the power of speech. The rest of us, too, kept silence. We were surprised to see him so painfully affected, but we were also very much impressed.

Presently he raised his head, and slowly, in a shaken voice, went on: "Yais, Shakie's daid. It's about two monts ago already I got de news. Vail, it pretty nearly broke my heart. Him and me vas tervins. . . . . Poor Shakie! He vas an awful *goot*-hearted shentleman, and he hadn't oughter been taken avay. Oh, vail, I suppose his time haid come. He vas fearful old; and I guess maybe his time haid come. He couldn't expect to live foraifer; his time haid come; and so he haid to die. Vail, dis is a hart vorld; an outracheous hart vorld, dere's no two vays about it: but de Lord mait it, and I suppose he haid some reason for it. *Boruch dajir.emes!*" With that pious ejaculation, —Blessed be the Most High Judge,—he again bowed his head and held his peace.

Some minutes passed in unbroken silence. Then, all at once, Mr. Sonnenschein drew a deep, loud sigh and straightened up. He gave his shoulders a prodigious shrug, as if to shake off his spiritual burden; he passed his hands over his face as if to wipe away the shadows that darkened it. . . . . Abruptly, with a sudden change of mien and manner,—eyes lighted by their familiar happy smile,—voice vibrant with its familiar jubilant ring,—"But I got de money," he cried. "I got terventy-nine tousand, seven hoonert and sixty tollars; and I've come ofer to haif you conkratulate me. I only got it de day before yesterday, or I'd haif come around sooner. I hope you von't mind, but I brought a couple bottles champagne along to celebrate mit. You folks, you been awful friendly to me fen I vas poor already, and you vas raikular customers of mine; so, now I vas rich, I tought I like to give you a little treat."

With that he undid the mysterious paper parcel which we had noticed at his entrance, and produced surely enough a couple of bottles of champagne.

"Fill oop your glaisses," he urged. "Fill 'em oop. Don't be afraid of it. It's chenu-wine. Vail, here goes! *Shalom alechem!* Peace to you! Drink hearty. Dere's plenty more fere dot comes from."

The gayety of the company was speedily restored, and we drank to our old friend's prosperity with right good will.

"Yais," he said, smacking his lips upon a bumper of his wine, "I got de money de day before yesterday. I got a draift on de bainking estaiblishment

Yours always sincerely

H. Harland

of Schaumberg, Knaus, Bauer & Co., down in Villiam Street. I ain't haid it
caished yet. Dere it is."

He had unbuttoned his coat and extracted from its inside pocket a dilapidated leather wallet. Out of this he picked his draft and handed it to me for
circulation around the table. The amount was, as he had said, $29,760.

"Well, Mr. Sonnenschein," my father asked, "how do you propose to invest this money? Can I be of any assistance to you in attending to its investment?"

"Vail, no, I guess not, tank you," he returned. "It's awful *goot*-nechered
of you to make de oaffer; but I guess not, tank you all de same. No; to tell
you de honest troot, I don't make no investments of dot money; I keep de
caish. You see, I vas a Schlemiel. Vail, a Schlémiel is a party who's bount
to haif bait luck. Vail, if I put dot money in de baink, de first ting I know,
de baink'll bust. Or else, if I buy stoacks mit it, de stoack company vill fail;
or coverment boants, de coverment vill get into a var. If I put it in a mow-
gage on real estate, de title to dot real estate would be defaicted. Dere's no
two vays about it. I vas a Schlemiel. No, sir, I don't make no investments
of dot money; I be sure to lose it, dere ain't no use in talking. But I tell you
fat I do. I tought it all ofer in my own mind, and now I tell you fat I do.
To-morrer morning I go down-town, and I call at de office of Schaumberg,
Knaus, Bauer & Co., in Villiam Street, and I get dot draift caished,—hey?
Vail, den I take dot caish baick oop-town again mit me; and I go to my friend
Mr. Solomon Levinson, who keeps a second-haint clodings estaiblishment in
de basement of de house I live in; and I aisk Mr. Levinson to put dot caish
in his chenu-wine burglar-proof safe, and keep it for me,—you understand?
Vail, den fen me and Nettie needs some money, den I go to dot safe, and I
take out a hoonert tollars,—you see de point? Tirty tousand tollars! My
kracious, dot's enough to laist me and Nettie longer as ve eider of us lives; it
is, honor bright. Ve ain't extraivagant, and ve ain't got no heirs to feel disappointed if ve don't leaf no fortune. No, sir; I vas a Schlemiel. I don't
make no investments of dot money; I be sure to lose it. I keep de caish."

Unanimously and vehemently we protested against this course. We labored long and hard to convince him of its rash unwisdom. We assured him
that of all the possible dispositions of his money which he could make, this
was the wildest, the most hazardous; and we invoked every argument by
which a reasonable human being could be moved to vindicate our proposition.

He heard us respectfully to the end, while a tolerant smile played about
his lips. Then he rejoined, "Dot's all right. Fat you folks say is shust exaictly so. You got an awful lot of sense about you, and you arkue simply
splendid,—especially Saimmy. My kracious, if Saimmy vas to go to de laich-
islature, he'd make a chenu-wine sensation, he arkues so goot. He vas a necheral debater, dere's no two vays about it. But I tell you how it is. Dere's a
proverb fich goes, 'Circumstainces alter cases.' Vail, dot's an aictual faict;
dey do, and no mistake. Vail, now I tell you how it is. You see, I vas a
Schlemiel. Vail, a Schlemiel is a party who's bount to haif bait luck. Vail,
if I make ainy investments of dot money, I be sure to lose it; I vould, honor

bright. So, I don't make no investments of it. I don't run no risks. I keep de caish." . . . .

And so he went away, leaving us in an exasperated and anxious frame of mind. We tried hard to hope for the best; but how could we help fearing the worst? To invite disaster by keeping so large a sum of ready money lying exposed in another man's safe,—who but a Schlemiel could be guilty of such unmitigated folly?

IV.

SCHLEMIEL'S PEN.

It was rather more than a week later that the post brought me one morning a letter, written in a cramped foreign hand, of which the following is a true and perfect copy:

"DIER SAMMY!

"ime Konfeint to de Haus bei a fieful Kolt an de het and Lonks and, i Kand go autt for fier i gett vurs But i leik, to sie You as i got a Fieful gut schoke to tell you and Den annyhau Ime lonsum and i leik to Sie you for Kumpny to schier Me up vel days ane ole vumin of de nehmer rebekah doz our Haus vork for Us and her and nettie is Die onelie piepul i sie Ole Day so i gett Kein der Lonsum and i leik to sie you to tell You dat Schoke vel ittul mchk you Laff to dei sammy it vil and no mistek vel if a parties a Schlemiel day ant no Yous in toking Hies gott to haf bat luck. vel kum sie Me sammy for i gess Mabie mei time is com i do on a Brite, ime a fieful ole Gentulmin you no and de Doktor sais I Gott a bat kase Braun Kietiz, Kom sie me enyhau de Doktor sed, it ant Kesching. give my Lof papa and mama your

"Gut Frent

"E. SONNENSCHEIN!"

I found this epistle lying in wait for me on the breakfast-table. After I had made what sense of it I could, I passed it over to my mother, saying, "I'll stop in and see him on my way down-town."

"I'll go with you," my mother volunteered, some fifteen minutes later, after the sensation created by the exhibition to the rest of the family of Mr. Sonnenschein's effort had subsided. "Poor old man! Perhaps there's something I can do to make him comfortable."

So, together, my mother and I set out for Tompkins Square.

V.

SCHLEMIEL'S "SCHOKE."

Our greeting over, and our inquiries concerning the exact state of his health satisfactorily answered (he had indeed a bad cold, but was not nearly so ill as we had feared to find him): "Vail, now, Saimmy," began Mr. Sonnenschein, "as I told you a great mainy times already, dis is a vunderful vorld. By and by, fen you get so old as me, you'll say de same ting; dough now, file you're young, you might imachine dot I vas only fooling. My kracious, fen I tink about how vunderful it really is—vail, Saimmy, I'm aictually aistonished— vail, honor bright, I cain't hartly belief it. Vail, now look at here. I vas a Schlemiel, hey? Vail, a Schlemiel is a party who's bount to haif bait luck, ain't he? No maitter fat he does, no maitter fat precowtions he takes, he cain't help it; he got to haif bait luck. Vail, now look at here. It's shust exaictly about two weeks ago already I got dot draift from de *eggs*-hecutor of my brudder Shakie ofer in Chairmany. Vail, I guess maybe I told you I vasn't going to make no investments of dot money, becoase, as I vas a Schlemiel, I be sure to lose it. I guess maybe I told you I vas going to keep de caish. Yais, I tought it all ofer, and I mait oop my mind dot I better stay on de safe side and keep de caish. Vail, now look at here. De very next day aifter I seen you, I vent down-town to de office of Schaumberg, Knaus, Bauer & Co., in Villiam Street, and I got dot draift caished. I got terventy-nine vun-tousand-tollar pills, vun fife-hoonert-tollar pill, two vun-hoonert-tollar pills, and de ott sixty tollars in fifes and tens. Vail, Saimmy, den I done all dot money oop, except dose ott sixty tollars, fich I kep in my poacket, I done it all oop mit paper in a poontle, and I vent to my friend Mr. Solomon Levinson, who keeps a second-haint clodings estaiblishment down-stairs in de basement; and I aisked Mr. Levinson to put dot poontle inside his chenu-wine burglar-proof safe and keep it for me; and Mr. Levin on he done it. He put it inside on de toap shelf, file I stood dere and seen him. Vail, Saimmy, Mr. Levinson he's got a lot of curiosity about him, fich is only necheral; and, so, as I vas leafing, Mr. Levinson he aisked me if I haid any *op*-shections to informing him fat dot poontle contained. Vail, I tought to myself, 'I guess maybe I better not let nobody know how much money dere is in dot poontle'; so I said to Mr. Levinson, 'Fy, certainly, I ain't got no *op*-shections. It contains old loaf-letters.' Dot's fat I said to Mr. Levinson. Vail, dot was pretty goot for an oaff-haindcr, vasn't it, Saimmy? Vail, now look at here. Vail, I suppose you'd tink dere vasn't vun chaince in a hoonert tousand of ainydings haippening to dot money, now it vas loacked oop in Mr. Levinson's burglar-proof safe, vouldn't you, Saimmy? Vail, now look at here. Now you'll see shust exaictly how it is fen a party's a Schlemiel. You'll see fat a vunderful vorld dis is. Vail, de day Mr. Levinson put dot money inside his safe vas Friday. Vail, den it stainds to reason de next day vas Schabbas (Sabbath); don't it, Saimmy? Vail, maybe you vouldn't belief me—you might tink I vas trying to fool you,—but, honor bright,—I hope to die de next minute if it ain't a faict,—dot very same night,—Sotturday night,—aifter ve vas gone to bait,—vail, Saimmy, I bet you a brain-new fife tollar silk hat you cain't guess fat haippened. You take de bet? No? You gif it oop? Hey? Vail, now look at here. Dot very same night,—Sotturday night,—vail, Mr. Levinson he haid a fire in his estaiblishment, and my money got burned oop,—aifery red cent of it got burned to cinters!"   .   .   .   .

It never once entered Mr. Sonnenschein's head to fear that his fortune was in danger, for "I tought of course it vas loacked oop in Mr. Levinson's chenu-wine burglar and fire-proof safe." But the next morning Mr. Levinson came to see him, and explained that, as his safe had been somewhat crowded with matter the day before, he had removed Mr. Sonnenschein's bundle of old letters and placed it in the cupboard of his writing-desk. " And den, of course, as I vas a Schlemiel, dot estaiblishment haid to ketch fire, and dot writing-desk, mit aiferydings inside of it, get burned oop. Raikular Schlemiel's luck ain't it, Saimmy? . . . Vail, aifter all, it don't make much difference. Fen I got dot money I mait oop my mind dot I'd retire from business, and be a shentleman of leisure. Vail, now I simply got to go baick into business again; dot's all dere is about it."

VI.

SCHLEMIEL'S FRIEND.

[This chapter, omitted from these pages, recounts the discovery, by the narrator and his friend the Fire Marshal, that Mr. Solomon Levinson had pocketed Sonnenschein's greenbacks, and then kindled the fire to account for their disappearance. It ends with Levinson's confession and surrender of the spoil, in consideration of which he is allowed to enter a plea of guilty to a minor degree of arson, and gets off with a sentence to the State Prison for a term of ten years.]

VII.

SCHLEMIEL'S GRATITUDE.

Mr. Sparks and I climbed upstairs to Mr. Sonnenschein's tenement.

"Vail, my kracious, Saimmy, fat brings you baick again so soon?" was the old man's greeting.

As briefly and as clearly as I could I explained what had happened since my former visit.

"*Mein Gott!* You don't mean it!" he cried, when I had done. "Go 'vay. You don't really mean it! Mr. Levinson, he set fire to dot estaiblishment, and you got baick de money? Vail, if I aifer? Vail, dot beats de record; it does, and no mistake. Talk about brains! Fy, Saimmy, smartness ain't no vord for it. You got vun of de graindest haits on your shoulders de Lord aifer mait. And Mr. Levinson, he aictually set fire to dot estaiblishment, so as to get my money! Vail, dot *vas* outracheous, dere ain't no use in talking. Vail, Saimmy, I cain't hardly belief it; I cain't, honor bright."

The marshal was busy with pen and ink at a table hard by, drawing up an affidavit and a receipt for Mr. Sonnenschein to sign and swear to. After the old man had laboriously traced his name and vouched for the truth of what was written above it, the marshal handed him the bundle containing his inheritance, and, covered with thanks from both of us, went away.

"Vail, now, Saimmy," said Mr. Sonnenschein, "now I tell you fat you do. You cairry dot poontle down-town mit you, and you go to you popper's office, and you gif it to him, and you tell him to make all de investments of dot money fich he likes. Dere's no two vays about it, Saimmy, I vas a raikular Schlemiel; and I guess maybe de best ting I can do is to let your popper mainage dot money shust exaictly as if it vas his own. No maitter fat investments he makes of it, Saimmy, I tell you vun ting, I bet a hat dot vun vay or anudder dot money gets lost inside six monts. Vail, Saimmy, as I told you a great mainy times before already, dis is a fearful funny vorld; and I guess maybe now, aifter dis fire and aiferydings, I guess maybe you'll belief me."

My father made such investments of "dot money" as would yield Mr. Sonnenschein an annual income of fifteen hundred dollars, which the old gentleman, still hale and hearty, is enjoying to this day. Though a Jew by birth and faith, he is as good a Christian as most of the professing ones; for after he learned of Levinson's imprisonment he insisted upon making a liberal provision for Mrs. Levinson and her children. Nor is ingratitude a vice that could justly be attributed to our Schlemiel. When my parents celebrated the thirtieth anniversary of their wedding, a few months ago, they received by express a large and luminous worsted-work picture, enclosed by a massive gilt frame, which represented in the primary colors the nuptial ceremonies of Jacob and Rachel. A card attached informed them that it came with compliments and best wishes from Mr. Sonnenschein and Nettie, and on the obverse of the card, in Mr. Sonnenschein's chirography, we read, "Nettie dun it Ole herself."

But his continued prosperity has undermined the old man's philosophy and upset all his established views of life. He calls at my father's office to receive his allowance on the first day of every month. "Vail, ainydings haippened yet?" is the inquiry with which he invariably begins. And when my father replies that nothing has happened, and proceeds to count out his money, "Vail, *Gott in Himmel,* fat kind of a vorld is dis, ainyhow!" he cries. "I gif it oop. I cain't make haits or tails of it. Here I been a Schlemiel aifer since I vas born already, and now all of a sutten I change ofer, and I ain't no Schlemiel no more. Vail, dot beats me,—it beats me all holler, and no mistake about it. But de Lord done it, and I guess maybe he's got some reason for it. Blessed be de name of de Lord!"

Louise Imogen Guiney.

Born in Boston, Mass., 1861.

KNIGHT FALSTAFF.

[*Songs at the Start.* 1884.—*The White Sail, and Other Poems.* 1887.]

I SAW the dusty curtain, ages old,
　Its purple tatters twitched aside, and lo!
The fourth King Harry's reign in lusty show
Behind, its deeds in living file outrolled
Of peace and war; some sage, some mad, and bold:
Last, near a tree, a bridled neighing row
With latest spoils encumbered, saints do know,
By Hal and Hal's boon cronies; on the wold
Laughter of prince and commons; there and here
Travellers fleeing; drunken thieves that sang;
Wild bells; a tavern's echoing jolly shout;
Signals along the highway, full of cheer;
A gate that closed with not incautious clang,
When that sweet rogue, bad Jack! came lumbering out.

TARPEIA.

WOE : lightly to part with one's soul as the sea with its foam!
    Woe to Tarpeia, Tarpeia, daughter of Rome!

Lo, now it was night, with the moon looking chill as she went:
It was morn when the innocent stranger strayed into the tent.

The hostile Sabini were pleased, as one meshing a bird;
She sang for them there in the ambush: they smiled as they heard.

Her sombre hair purpled in gleams, as she leaned to the light;
All day she had idled and feasted, and now it was night.

The chief sat apart, heavy-browed, brooding elbow on knee;
The armlets he wore were thrice royal, and wondrous to see:

Exquisite artifice, whorls of barbaric design,
Frost's fixèd mimicry; orbic imaginings fine

In sevenfold coils: and in orient glimmer from them,
The variform voluble swinging of gem upon gem.

And the glory thereof sent fever and fire to her eye.
"I had never such trinkets!" she sighed,—like a lute was her sigh.

"Were they mine at the plea, were they mine for the token, all told,
Now the citadel sleeps, now my father the keeper is old,

"If I go by the way that I know, and thou followest hard,
If yet at the touch of Tarpeia the gates be unbarred ? "

The chief trembled sharply for joy, then drew rein on his soul:
"Of all this arm beareth I swear I will cede thee the whole."

And up from the nooks of the camp, with hoarse plaudit outdealt,
The bearded Sabini glanced hotly, and vowed as they knelt,

Bare-stretching the wrists that bore also the glowing great boon:
"Yea! surely as over us shineth the lurid low moon,

"Not alone of our lord, but of each of us take what he hath!
Too poor is the guerdon, if thou wilt but show us the path."

Her nostril upraised, like a fawn's on the arrowy air,
She sped; in a serpentine gleam to the precipice stair,

They climbed in her traces, they closed on their evil swift star:
She bent to the latches, and swung the huge portal ajar.

Repulsed where they passed her, half-tearful for wounded belief,
"The bracelets!" she pleaded.   Then faced her the leonine chief,

And answered her: "Even as I promised, maid-merchant, I do."
Down from his dark shoulder the baubles he sullenly drew.

Louise Imogen Guiney.

"This left arm shall nothing begrudge thee. Accept. Find it sweet.
Give, too, O my brothers!" The jewels he flung at her feet,

The jewels hard, heavy; she stooped to them, flushing with dread,
But the shield he flung after: it clanged on her beautiful head.

Like the Apennine bells when the villagers' warnings begin,
Athwart the first lull broke the ominous din upon din;

With a "Hail, benefactress!" upon her they heaped in their zeal
Death: agate and iron; death: chrysoprase, beryl and steel.

'Neath the outcry of scorn, 'neath the sinewy tension and hurl,
The moaning died slowly, and still they massed over the girl

A mountain of shields! and the gemmy bright tangle in links,
A torrent-like gush, pouring out on the grass from the chinks,

Pyramidal gold! the sumptuous monument won
By the deed they had loved her for, doing, and loathed her for, done.

Such was the wage that they paid her, such the acclaim:
All Rome was aroused with the thunder that buried her shame.

On surged the Sabini to battle. O you that aspire!
Tarpeia the traitor had fill of her woman's desire.

Woe: lightly to part with one's soul as the sea with its foam!
Woe to Tarpeia, Tarpeia, daughter of Rome!

MOUSTACHE.

A FRIENDLESS pup that heard the fife
Sprang to the column thro' the clearing,
And on to Switzerland and strife
    Went grenadiering.

Much he endured, and much he dared
The long hot doomsday of the nations:
He wore a trooper's scars; he shared
    A trooper's rations;

Warned pickets, seized the Austrian spies,
Bore the despatches; thro' the forces
From fallen riders, prompt and wise,
    Led back the horses;

Served round the tents or in the van,
Quick-witted, tireless as a treadle:
"This private wins," said Marshal Lannes,
    "Ribbon and medal."

("Moustache, a brave French dog," it lay
Graven on silver, like a scholar's;
"Who lost a leg on Jena day,
    But saved the colors!")

At Saragossa he was slain;
They buried him, and fired a volley:
End of Moustache. Nay, that were strain
    Too melancholy.

His immortality was won,
His most of rapture came to bless him,
When, plumed and proud, Napoleon
    Stooped to caress him.

His Emperor's hand upon his head!
How, since, shall lesser honors suit him?
Yet ever, in that army's stead,
    Love will salute him.

And since not every cause enrolls
Such little, fond, sagacious henchmen,
Write this dog's moral on your scrolls,
　　Soldiers and Frenchmen!

As law is law, can be no waste
Of faithfulness, of worth and beauty;

Lord of all time the slave is placed
　　Who doth his duty.

No virtue fades to thin romance
But Heaven to use eternal moulds it:
Mark! Some firm pillar of new France,
　　Moustache upholds it.

THE WILD RIDE.

I HEAR *in my heart, I hear in its ominous pulses,*
*　All day, the commotion of sinewy, mane-tossing horses;*
All night, from their cells, the importunate tramping and neighing.

Cowards and laggards fall back; but alert to the saddle,
Straight, grim, and abreast, vault our weather-worn, galloping legion,
With a stirrup-cup each to the one gracious woman that loves him.

The road is through dolor and dread, over crags and morasses;
There are shapes by the way, there are things that appal or entice us:
What odds?   We are knights, and our souls are but bent on the riding!

I hear in my heart, I hear in its ominous pulses,
All day, the commotion of sinewy, mane-tossing horses;
All night, from their cells, the importunate tramping and neighing.

We spur to a land of no name, out-racing the storm-wind;
We leap to the infinite dark, like the sparks from the anvil.
Thou leadest, O God! All's well with Thy troopers that follow.

PAULA'S EPITAPH.

G O you by with gentle tread.
　　This was Paula, who is dead·
Eyes dark-lustrous to the look
As a leaf-pavilioned brook,
Voice upon the ear to cling
Sweeter than the cithern-string;

Whose shy spirit, unaware
Loosed into refreshful air,
With it took for talisman,
Climbing past the starry van,
Names to which the heavens do ope—
Candor, Chastity, and Hope.

Ernest McGaffey.

BORN in London, Ohio, 1861.

DREAMS.

[*Uncollected Poems.* 1885-89.]

OVER the long, rich, billowy grass, up and down are the footsteps flying,
 Of viewless winds that pass and leave no token of their flight;
With never a tree to mar the stretch of the prairie around me lying,
 A dark-green sea, whose rolling waves the sun has tipped with light.

The iron-weed sways on the wind-swept ridge, the wild rose blooms in the hollow,
 A hawk wheels round in circling sweep through trackless paths on high,
And over the grass the breezes go and the tremulous echoes follow,
 Filling the crannies of eddying winds from earth to sky.

Horizon-ward and far to the west, like the smoke of a distant steamer
 Mounting slowly up the skies, on the steps of a hidden stair,
Vague, so vague, as vague and dim as the dream of an idle dreamer.
 A curling cloud-wraith, spiral formed, is rising through the air.

Sun and wind, and the far-off sky; the sun that shines and the wind that passes;
 The life that is, and beyond the clouds the life that is to be—
Dreams; all dreams; that come and go, as the wind's light foot-prints over the
  grasses,
 What is my life but a drop of rain that falls in a shoreless sea?

GERONIMO.

BESIDE that tent and under guard
 In majesty alone he stands
As some chained eagle, broken-winged,
With eyes that gleam like smouldering
 brands;
A savage face, streaked o'er with paint,
And coal-black hair in unkempt mane,
Thin, cruel lips, set rigidly—
A red Apache Tamerlane.

As restless as the desert winds,
Yet here he stands like carven stone,
His raven locks by breezes moved
And backward o'er his shoulders blown;

Silent, yet watchful as he waits,
Robed in his strange, barbaric guise,
While here and there go searchingly
The cat-like wanderings of his eyes.

The eagle feather on his head
Is dull with many a bloody stain,
While darkly on his lowering brow
Forever rests the mark of Cain;
Have you but seen a tiger caged,
And sullen through his barriers
 glare?
Mark well his human prototype,
The fierce Apache fettered there.

DIXIE.

BLUE as the sea, without a single flaw,
  The azure sky reflected back the day,
And quietly, through drowsy summer air,
Magnolia-blossoms, beautiful and rare,
Came floating down and vanished far away
Upon the bosom of the Chickasaw.

The cotton-fields lay white as driven snow,
And wheat was draped in flowing cloth-of-gold,
While, wet with dew upon its blades of green,
The springing grass lay nestled in between,
O'erlooked by pines that, like the bards of old,
Sang rude, sweet music to the earth below.

And at the pine-tree's feet the shining sand,
By Southern river sparkling in the sun,
Basked in the warm and perfumed tropic breath,
Till, ushered in past twilight's shadowed death,
The glad gray stars came twinkling one by one,
And watched like sentinels o'er Dixie's Land.

Grace Elizabeth King.

BORN in New Orleans, La.

THE DEVOTION OF MARCÉLITE.

[*Monsieur Motte.* 1888.]

THE *Externes* were radiant in toilettes unmarred by accident or omission ; the flattering compliments of their mirrors at home had turned their heads in the direction of perfect self-content. Resignation was the only equivalent the unfortunate *Internes* could offer in extenuation of the unfinished appearance of their heads.

" *Mais, dis donc, chère,* what is the matter with your hair ? "

" Marcélite did not come."

" Why, *doudouce,* how could you allow your hair to be combed that way?"

" Marcélite did not come."

" *Chérie,* I think your hair is curled a little tight this evening."

" I should think so; that *diable* Marcélite did not come."

" *Mon Dieu,* look at Madame Joubert *à la sauvagesse !* "

" And Madame *à la grand maman !* "

" Marcélite did not come, you see."

Not only was the room filled, but an eager audience crowded the yard and peeped in through the windows. The stairways, of course, were filled with the colored servants, an enthusiastic, irrepressible *claque.* When it was all over, and the last *bis* and *encore* had subsided, row after row of girls was gleaned by the parents, proud possessors of such shawlfuls of beauty, talent, and prizes. Marie's class, the last to leave, were picked off one by one. She helped the others to put on their wraps, gather up their prizes, and kissed one after another good-by.

Each man that came up was, by a glance, measured and compared with her imaginary standard. "He is too young." "He is too fat." "I hope he is not that cross-looking one." "Maybe it is he." "What a funny little one that is!" "Ah, he is very nice-looking!" "Is it he?" "No, he is Corinne's father." "I feel sure he is that ugly, disagreeable one." "Ah, here he is at last! at last!" "No; he only came to say good-night to Madame." "He is afraid of the crowd." "He is waiting outside." "He is at the gate in a carriage." "After all, he has only sent Marcélite." "I saw her here on the steps a while ago." She looked at the steps, they were deserted. There was but one person left in the room besides herself; Madame and her suite had gone to partake of their yearly exhibitional refreshments,—lemonade and *masse-pain,* served in the little parlor. Her uncle must be that man. The person walked out after finding a fan he had returned to seek.

She remained standing so by the piano a long while, her gold crown on her head, her prizes in her arms, and a light shawl she had thoughtfully provided to wear home. Home! She looked all around very slowly once more. She heard Jeanne crossing the yard, but before the servant could enter the door the white muslin dress, blue sash, and satin boots had bounded into the darkness of the stairway. The white-veiled beds which the night before had nestled the gay *papillotted* heads were deserted and silent in the darkness. What a shelter the darkness was! She caught hold of the bedpost, not thinking, but feeling. Then Madame Joubert came tripping across the gallery with a candle, on her way to bed. The prizes and shawl dropped to the floor, and Marie crouched down close behind the bar. "Oh, God," she prayed, "keep her from seeing me!" The teacher after a pause of reflection passed on to her room; the child on the floor gave herself up to the full grief of a disappointment which was not childish in its bitterness. The events of the evening kept slipping away from her while the contents of her previous life were poured out with never-ending detail, and as they lay there, before and all around her, she saw for the first time how bare, how denuded, of pleasure and comfort it had been. What had her weak little body not endured in patient ignorance? But the others were not ignorant,—the teachers, Marcélite, her uncle! How had they imposed upon the orphan in their hands! She saw it now, and she felt a woman's indignation and pity over it. The maternal instinct in her bosom was roused by the contemplation of her own infancy. "Marcélite! Marcélite!" she called out, "how could you? for you knew, you knew it all!" The thought of a mother compelled to leave her baby on such an earth, the betrayal of the confidence of her own mother by her uncle, drew the first tears from her eyes. She leaned her head against the side of her bed and wept, not for herself, but for all women and all orphans. Her hand fell on the lace of her dress, and she could not recall at first what it was. She bounded up, and with eager, trembling fingers tearing open the fastenings, she threw the grotesque masquerade, boots and all, far from her on the floor, and stood clasping her naked arms over her panting breast; she had forgotten the gilt wreath on her head. "If she could die then and there! that would hurt her uncle who cared so little for her, Marcélite who had deserted her!" Living she had no one; but dead, she felt she had a mother. Before getting into bed, she mechanically fell on her knees, and her lips repeated the formula of a prayer, an uncorrected, rude tradition of her baby days, belonging to the other side of her memory. It consisted of one simple petition for her own welfare, but the blessings of peace, prosperity, and eternal salvation of her uncle and Marcélite were insisted upon with pious determination.

"I know I shall not sleep; I cannot sleep." Even with the words she sank into the oblivion of tired nature at seventeen years; an oblivion which blotted out everything,—toilette, prizes scattered on the floor, graduation, disappointment, and discomfort from the gilt-paper crown still encircling her black plaits.

"Has Marcélite come?" demanded Madame, before she tasted her coffee.

"Not yet, Madame."

"I wonder what has become of her?"

Jeanne sniffed a volume of unspeakable probabilities.

"Well, then, I will not have that *sotte* Julie; tell her so when she comes. I would rather dress myself."

"Will Madame take her breakfast alone, or with Madame Joubert?"

The pleasure of vacation was tempered by the companionship of Madame Joubert at her daily meals,—a presence imposed by that stern tyrant, common courtesy.

"Not to-day, Jeanne; tell Madame Joubert I have *la migraine*. I shall eat breakfast alone."

"And Mamzelle Marie Modeste?"

"Marie Modeste!"

"Yes, Madame; where must she take her breakfast?"

The Gasconne's eyes flamed suddenly from under her red lashes and her voice ventured on its normal loud tones in these sacred precincts.

"It's a shame of that negress! She ought to be punished well for it, too, ha! Not to come for that poor young lady last night; to leave her in that big dormitory all by herself; and all the other young ladies to go home and have their pleasure, and she all by herself, just because she is an orphan. You think she doesn't feel that, *hein?* If I had known it I would have helped her undress, and stayed with her, too; I would have slept on the floor,—a delicate little nervous thing like that; and a great, big, fat, lazy, good-for-nothing quadroon like Marcélite. *Mais c'est infâme!* It is enough to give her *des crises.* Oh, I would not have done that! *tenez*, not to go back to France would I have done that. And when I got up this morning, and saw her sitting in the arbor, so pale, I was frightened myself—I"——

"What is all this you are telling me? Jeanne, Jeanne, go immediately; run, I tell you—run and fetch that poor child here. *Ah, mon Dieu!* egoist that I am to forget her! *Pauvre petite chatte!* What must she think of me?"

She jumped out of bed, threw on a wrapper, and waited at the door, peeping out.

" *Ma fille;* I did not know—Jeanne has just told me."

The pale little figure made an effort to answer with the old pride and indifference.

"It seems my uncle "——

"*Mais qu'est-ce que c'est donc, mon enfant?* Do not cry so! What is one night more in your old school? It is all my fault; the idea that I should forget you, —leave you all alone while we were enjoying our lemonade and *masse-pain!* But why did you not come to me? Oh! oh! if you cry so, I shall think you are sorry not to leave me; besides, it will spoil your pretty eyes."

"If Marcélite had only come "——

" Ah, my dear! do not speak of her! do not mention her name to me. We are *quittes* from this day; you hear me? We are *quittes.* But Marie, my child, you will make yourself ill if you cry so. Really, you must try and compose yourself. What is it that troubles you so? Come here, come sit by me; let me confess you. I shall play that I am your *maman.* There, there, put your head here, my *bébé,* so. Oh, I know how you feel. I have known what disappointment was; but *enfin,* my child, that will all pass; and one day, when you are old and gray-headed like me, you will laugh well over it."

The tender words, the caresses, the enfolding arms, the tears that she saw standing in the august schoolmistress's eyes, the sympathetic movement of the soft, warm bosom,—her idea of a mother was not a vain imagining. This was it; this was what she had longed for all her life. And she did confess to her,—confessed it all, from the first childish trouble to the last disappointment. Oh, the delicious relief of complete, entire confession to a sympathetic ear!

The noble heart of Madame, which had frittered itself away over puny distributions of prizes and deceiving cosmetics, beat young, fresh, and impulsive as in the days when the gray hairs were *chatains clair* and the cheeks bloomed natural roses. Tears fell from her eyes on the little black head lying so truthful, so confiding on her bosom. *Grand Dieu!* and they had been living thirteen years under the same roof,—the poor, insignificant, abandoned, suffering little Marie, and the gay, beautiful, rich, envied Madame Lareveillère! This was their first moment of confidence. Would God ever forgive her? Could she ever forgive herself? How good it feels to have a child in your arms! so. She went to the stand by her bed and filled a small gilded glass with *eau des carmes* and water.

"There, drink that, my child; it will compose you. I must make my toilette; it is breakfast-time. You see, *ma fille,* this is a lesson. You must not expect too much of the men; they are not like us. Oh, I know them well. They are all *égoïstes.* They take a great deal of trouble for you when you do not want it, if it suits them; and then they refuse to raise their little finger for you, though you get down on your knees to them. Now, there's your uncle. You see he has sent you to the best and most expensive school in the city, and he has dressed you well,—oh, yes, very well; look at your toilette last night! real lace; I remarked it. Yet he would not come for you and take you home, and spare you this disappointment. I wrote him a note myself and sent it by Marcélite."

"He *is* old, Madame," said Marie, loyally.

"Ah, bah! *Plus les hommes sont vieux plus ils sont méchants.* Oh, I have done that so often; I said, 'If you do not do this, I will not do that.' And what was the result? They did not do this, and I had *tout simplement et bonnement* to do that. I write to Monsieur Motte, 'Your niece shall not leave the Pension until you come for her'; he does not come, and I take her to him. *Voilà la politique féminine.*"

After breakfast, when they had dressed, bonneted, and gloved themselves, Madame said:

"*Ma foi!* I do not even know where the old Diogène lives. Do you remember the name of the street, Marie?"

"No, Madame; somewhere in the *Faubourg d'en bas.*"

"Ah, well! I must look for it here."

She went to the table and quickly turned over the leaves of a ledger.

"Marie Modeste Motte, niece of Monsieur Motte. *Mais, tiens,* there is no address!"

Marie looked with interest at her name written in red ink.

"No; it is not there."

"*Ah, que je suis bête.* It is in the other one. This one is only for the last ten years. There, *ma fille,* get on a chair; can you reach that one? No, not that; the other one. How warm it is! You look it out for me!"

"I do not see any address here either, Madame."

"Impossible! There must be an address there. True, nothing but Marie Modeste Motte, niece of Monsieur Motte, just like the other one. Now, you see, that's Marcélite again; that's all her fault. It was her duty to give that address thirteen years ago. In thirteen years she has not had the time to do that!"

They both sat down warm and vexed.

"I shall send Jeanne for her again!"

But Jeanne's zeal had anticipated orders.

"I have already been there, Madame; I beat on her door, I beat on it as hard as I could, and the neighbors opened their windows and said they didn't think she had been there all night."

"Well, then, there is nothing for me to do but send for Monsieur le Notaire! Here, Jeanne; take this note to Monsieur Goupilleau."

All unmarried women, widows or maids, if put to the torture, would reveal some secret, unsuspected sources of advisory assistance,—a subterranean passage for friendship which sometimes offers a retreat into matrimony,—and the last possible wrinkle, the last resisting gray hair is added to other female burdens at the death of this secret counsellor or the closing up of the hidden passage. Therefore, how dreadful it is for women to be condemned to a life of such logical exactions where a reason is demanded for everything, even for a *statu quo* affection of fifteen years or more. Madame Lareveillère did not possess courage enough to defy logic, but her imagination and wit could seriously embarrass its conclusions. The *raison d'être* of a Goupilleau in her life had exercised both into athletic proportions.

"An old friend, *ma mignonne;* I look upon him as a father, and he treats me just as if I were his daughter. I go to him as to a confessor. And a great institute like this requires so much advice,—oh, so much! He is very old,—as old as Monsieur Motte himself. We might just as well take off our things; he will not come before evening. You see, he is so discreet, he would not come in the morning for anything in the world. He is just exactly like a father, I assure you, and very, very old."

The graduate and young lady of a day sat in the rocking-chair, quiet, almost happy. She was not in the home she had looked forward to; but Madame's tenderness, the beautiful room in its soothing twilight, and the patronizing majesty of the *lit de justice* made this a very pleasant abiding place in her journey,—the journey so long and so difficult from school to her real home, from girlhood to real young ladyhood. It was nearly two days now since she had seen Marcélite. How she longed for her, and what a scolding she intended to give her when she arrived at her uncle's, where, of course, Marcélite was waiting for her. How silly she had acted about the address! But after all, procrastination is so natural. As for Madame, Marie smiled as she thought how easily a reconciliation could be effected between them, *quittes* though they were.

It is hard to wean young hearts from hoping and planning; they will do it in the very presence of the angel of death, and with their shrouds in full view.

Monsieur Goupilleau came: a Frenchman of small stature but large head. He had the eyes of a poet and the smile of a woman.

The prelude of compliments, the tentative flourish to determine in which key the ensuing variation on their little romance should be played, was omitted. Madame came brusquely to the *motif*, not personal to either of them.

"Monsieur Goupilleau, I take pleasure in presenting you to Mademoiselle Marie Motte, one of our young lady graduates. *Mon ami,* we are in the greatest trouble imaginable. Just imagine, Monsieur Motte, the uncle of mademoiselle could not come for her last night to take her home. He is so old and infirm," added Madame, considerately; "so you see mademoiselle could not leave last night. I want to take her home myself—a great pleasure it is, and not a trouble, I assure you, Marie—but we do not know where he lives."

"Ah! you have not his address."

"No, it should be in the ledger; but an accident,—in fact, the laziness of her *bonne,* who never brought it, not once in thirteen years."

"Her *bonne?*"

"Yes, her *bonne* Marcélite; you know Marcélite *la coiffeuse;* what, you do not know Marcélite, that great, fat "——

"Does Marcélite know where he lives?"

"But of course, my friend, Marcélite knows; she goes there every day."

"Well, send for Marcélite."

"Send for Marcélite! but I have sent for Marcélite at least a dozen times! she is never at her room. Marcélite! ha! my friend, I am done with Marcélite. What do you think? After combing my hair for fifteen years!—fifteen years, I tell you—she did not come yesterday at all, not once; and the concert at night! You should have seen our heads last night! we were frights—frights, I assure you!"

It was a poetical license, but the eyes of Monsieur Goupilleau disclaimed any such possibility for the head before him.

"Does not mademoiselle know the address of her uncle?"

"*Ah, that,* no. Mademoiselle has been a *pensionnaire* at the Institut St. Denis for thirteen years, and she has never been anywhere except to church; she has seen no one without a chaperon; she has received no letter that has not passed through Madame Joubert's hands. Ah! for that I am particular, and it was Monsieur Motte himself who requested it."

"Then you need a directory."

"A what?"

"A directory."

"But what is that,—a directory?"

"It's a volume, Madame, a book containing the addresses of all the residents of the city."

"*Quelle bonne idée!* If I had only known that! I shall buy one. Jeanne! Jeanne! run quick, *ma bonne,* to Morel's and buy me a directory."

"Pardon, Madame, I think it would be quicker to send to Bâle's, the *pharmacien* at the corner, and borrow one. Here, Jeanne, take my card."

"*A la bonne heure!* now we shall find our affair."

But the M's, which started so many names in the directory, were perfectly innocent of any combination applicable to an old uncle by the name of Motte.

"You see, your directory is no better than my books!"

Monsieur Goupilleau looked mortified, and shrugged his shoulders.

"He must live outside the city limits, Madame."

"Marcélite always said, 'in the *Faubourg d'en bas.*'"

Jeanne interrupted stolidly: "Monsieur Bâle told me to bring the book right back; it is against his rules to lend it out of his store."

"Here, take it! take it! Tell him I am infinitely obliged. It was of no use, anyway. Ah, *les hommes!*"

"Madame," began Monsieur Goupilleau in precautionary deprecation.

A sudden noise outside,—apparently an assault at the front door; a violent struggle in the antechamber!

"*Grand Dieu!* what can that be!" Madame's lips opened for a shrill *Au secours! Voleurs!* but seeing the notary rush to the door, she held him fast with her two little white hands on his arm.

"*Mon ami,* I implore you!"

The first recognition; the first expression of a fifteen years' secret affection! The first thrill (old as he was) of his first passion! But danger called him outside; he unloosed the hands and opened the door.

A heavy body propelled by Jeanne's strong hands fell on the floor of the room, accompanied by a shower of leaves from Monsieur Bâle's directory.

"*Misérable! Infâme! Effrontée!* Ah, I have caught you! *Scélérate!*"

" Marcélite!"

" Marcélite! "

" Marcélite!"

" Sneaking outside the gate! Like an animal! like a thief! like a dog! Ha! I caught you well!"

The powerful arms seemed ready again to crush the unresisting form rising from the floor.

"Jeanne! hush! How dare you speak to Marcélite like that? Oh, *ma bonne*, what is the matter with you?"

Shaking, trembling, she cowered before them silent.

"Ah! she didn't expect me, *la fière négresse!* Just look at her!"

They did, in painful, questioning surprise. Was this their own clean, neat, brave, honest, handsome Marcélite,—this panting, tottering, bedraggled wretch before them, threatening to fall on the floor again, not daring to raise even her eyes?

"Marcélite! Marcélite! who has done this to you! Tell me, tell your *bébé*, Marcélite."

"Is she drunk?" whispered Madame to the notary.

Her *tignon* had been dragged from her head. Her calico dress, torn and defaced, showed her skin in naked streaks. Her black woolly hair, always so carefully packed away under her head-kerchief, stood in grotesque masses around her face, scratched and bleeding like her exposed bosom. She jerked herself violently away from Marie's clasp.

"Send them away! Send them away!" she at last said to Monsieur Goupilleau, in a low, unnatural voice. "I will talk to you, but send them all away."

Madame and Marie immediately obeyed his look; but outside the door Marie stopped firmly.

"Madame, Marcélite can have nothing to say which I should not hear"——

"Hush—" Madame put her finger to her lips; the door was still a little open and the voices came to them.

Marcélite, from the corner of her bleared eyes, watched them retire, and then with a great heave of her naked chest she threw herself on the floor at the notary's feet.

"Master! Oh master! Help me!"

All the suffering and pathos of a woman's heart were in the tones; all the weakness, dependence, and abandonment in the words.

The notary started at the unexpected appeal. His humanity, his manhood, his chivalry, answered it.

"*Ma fille*, speak; what can I do for you?"

He bent over her as she lay before him, and put his thin, white, wrinkled hand on her shoulder where it had burst through her dress. His low voice promised the willing devotion of a saviour.

"But don't tell my *bébé;* don't let her know. My God! it will kill her! She's got no uncle—no Monsieur Motte! It was all a lie. It was me,—me, a nigger, that sent her to school and paid for her"——

"You! Marcélite! You!"

Marcélite jumped up and tried to escape from the room. Monsieur Goupilleau quickly advanced before her to the door.

"You fooled me! It was you fooled me!" she screamed to Madame. "God will never forgive you for that! My *bébé* has heard it all!"

Marie clung to her; Monsieur Goupilleau caught her by the arm.

"Marcélite! It was you,—you who sent me to school, who paid for me! And I have no uncle?"

Marcélite looked at the notary,—a prayer for help. The girl fell in a chair and hid her face in her hands.

"Oh, my God! I knew it would kill her! I knew it would! To be supported by a nigger!" She knelt by the chair. "Speak to me, Mamzelle Marie. Speak to me just once! Pardon me, my little mistress! Pardon me! I did not know what I was doing; I am only a fool nigger, anyhow! I wanted you to go to the finest school with ladies, and—and—oh! my *bébé* won't speak to me; she won't even look at me."

Marie raised her head, put both hands on the nurse's shoulders, and looked her straight in the eyes.

"And that also was all a lie about"—she sank her trembling voice—"about my mother?"

"That a lie! That a lie! 'Fore God in heaven, that was the truth; I swear it. I will kiss the crucifix. What do you take me for, Mamzelle Marie? Tell a lie about"——

Marie fell back in the chair with a despairing cry.

"I cannot believe any of it."

"Monsieur! Madame! I swear to you it's the truth! God in heaven knows it is. I wouldn't lie about that,—about my poor dead young mistress. Monsieur! Madame! tell Miss Marie for me; can't you believe me?" She shrieked in desperation to Monsieur Goupilleau.

He came to her unhesitatingly. "I believe you, Marcélite." He put his hand again on her shoulder; his voice faltered, "Poor Marcélite!"

"God bless you, master! God bless you for that. Let me tell you; you believe me when my *bébé* won't. My young mistress, she died; my young master, he had been killed in the war. My young mistress was all alone by herself, with nobody but me, and I didn't take her poor little baby out of her arms till she was dead, as she told me. *Mon bébé, mon bébé!* don't you know that's the truth? Can't you feel that's the truth? You see that; she will never speak to me again. I knew it; I told you so. I heard her last night, in that big room, all by herself, crying for Marcélite. Marcélite! my God! I was afraid to go to her, and I was just under a bed; you think that didn't most kill me?" She hid her face in her arms, and swayed her body back and forth.

"Marcélite," said Monsieur Goupilleau. The voice of the champion trembled, and his eyes glistened with tears at the distress he had pledged himself to relieve. "Marcélite, I believe you, my poor woman; I believe you. Tell me the name of the lady, the mother of mademoiselle."

"Ha! her name! I am not ashamed to tell her name before anybody. Her name! I will tell you her name." She sprang to her feet. "You ask anybody from the Paroisse St. Jacques if they ever heard the name of Mamzelle

Marie Modeste Viel and Monsieur Alphonse Motte. That was the name of her mother and her father, and I am not ashamed of it that I shouldn't tell, ha! Yes, and I am Marcélite Gaulois, and when my mother was sold out the parish, who took me and brought me up, and made me sleep on the foot of her bed, and fed me like her own baby, *hein?* Mamzelle Marie Viel's mother, and Mamzelle was the other baby; and she nursed us like twins, *hein?* You ask anybody from the Paroisse St. Jacques. They know; they can tell you."

Marie stood up.

"Come, Marcélite, let us go. Madame, Monsieur—" She evidently struggled to say something else, but she only reiterated, "I must go; we must go; come, Marcélite, let us go."

No one would have remarked now that her eyes were too old for her face.

"Go? My Lord! Where have you *got* to go to?"

"I want to go home to Marcélite; I want to go away with her; come, Marcélite, let us go. Oh! don't you all see I can't stay here any longer? Let me go! Let me go!"

"Go with me! Go to my home! A white young lady like you go live with a nigger like me!"

"Come, Marcélite; please come; go with me; I don't want to stay here."

"You stand there! You hear that! Monsieur! Madame! You hear that!"

"Marcélite, I want to go with you; I want to live with you; I am not too good for that."

"What! You don't think you ain't white! Oh, God! Strike me dead!"

She raised her naked arms over her head, imploring destruction.

"Marcélite, *ma fille,* do not forget, I have promised to help you. Marcélite, only listen to me a moment. Mademoiselle, do not fear; mademoiselle shall not leave us. I shall protect her; I shall be a father to her"——

"And I," said Madame, drawing Marie still closer to her,—"I shall be her mother."

"Now, try, Marcélite," continued Monsieur Goupilleau,—"try to remember somebody, anybody who knows you, who knew your mistress; I want their names. Anybody, anybody will do, my poor Marcélite! Indeed, I believe you; we all believe you; we know you are telling the truth; but is there not a person, even a book, a piece of paper, anything, you can remember?"

He stood close to her; his head did not reach above her shoulders, but his eyes plead into her face as if petitioning for his own honor; and then they followed the hands of the woman fumbling, feeling, passing, repassing inside her torn dress-waist. He held his hands out,—the kind tender little hands that had rested so gently on her bruised black skin.

"If I have not lost it, if I have not dropped it out of my gown since last night—I never have dropped it, and I have carried it round inside my body now for seventeen years; but I was 'most crazy last night"——

She put a small package all wrapped up in an old bandanna handkerchief in his hands.

"I was keeping that for my *bébé ;* I was going to give it to her when she graduated, just to remind her of her own mother. She gave it to me when she died."

It was only a little worn-out prayer-book, but all filled with written papers and locks of hair and dates and certificates,—frail fluttering scraps that dropped all over the table, but unanswerable champions for the honor of dead men and the purity of dead women.

"*Par la grâce de Dieu!*" exclaimed the notary, while the tears fell from his eyes on the precious relics, discolored and worn from bodily contact. Marie sank on her knees by the table, holding Marcélite tight by the hand.

"*Par la grâce de Dieu!* Nothing is wanting here,—nothing, nothing except the forgiveness of this good woman, and the assurances of our love and gratitude. And they say"—turning to Madame, he hazarded the bold step of taking both her hands in his—"they say"—recollecting the tender pressure on his arm, he ventured still further—"they say, Eugénie, that the days of heroism are past, and they laugh at our romance!"

Langdon Elwyn Mitchell.

Born in Philadelphia, Penn., 1862.

UPON SEEING A FUNERAL IN THE STREET.

[*Sylvian, and Other Poems. By John Philip Varley.* 1885.]

WHEN I do die, enhearse
    My body not at all;
Nor robe me not in black,
    Nor cut me out a pall.

I would not from this earth
    So perishably go;
But, since I die a man,
    Let me be buried so:

Not like a beast that is
    Shut in a box; nor yet
As one that hath lost all,
    And points it out with jet.

For naught of me ye have
    But soon unformèd earth;
Think ye, ye cast in ground
    My melody, my mirth?

My joy, my love, my wit?
    The virtues that I won?
Ye have the frame of it,
    The house—the host is gone.

Place this that did me hold
    Upon a piny pyre,
And swing the censer sweet,
    And set the oil on fire!

Let myrrh be wrapt around,
    Let me be swathed in sweet,
In aloes and in cassia bound,
    And decked as is most meet

With fateful yokes of flowers
    As in the further east;
Let me be clothed like one that goes
    In glory to a feast!

And when the flames are bright,
    And when the fire is hot,
Be all my virtues white,
    Be all my bad forgot.

And as to naught I come,
    And all in ashes lie,
Recite a song or two
    For better memory!

And though your hearts do moan,
    Yet let your loves rehearse
How that I writ, and writ alone
    The lovèd lyric verse!

So shall I buried be,
    As though I came to birth;
And not as one whose hope did lie
    Bound up in slothful earth.

Amélie Rives Chanler.

BORN in Richmond, Va., 1863.

FOR BONNIBEL.

[*Virginia of Virginia.* 1888.]

VIRGINIA was sitting silent by her bedroom window when the first copper glare began to tinge the dense upward column of black smoke. She knew in a minute what it was, although Aunt Tishy muttered something about "bresh" fires.

She leaped to her feet, her heart once more renewing its old-time measure. "Mammy!" she called—"Mammy! that's th' mill stable! th' mill stable's on fire! O God above! Th' pore horses—an' Bonnibel! O pore Mr. Jack—pore Mr. Jack! Ef Bonnibel's hurt, it'll break his heart." She had forgotten everything in her thought for him. Her own sin, his harsh words—all that had passed between them since first he gave Bonnibel into her glad keeping.

"Here!" she called, tossing on her clothes with nervous, eager fingers, "han' me my shoes—quick!—Lord God!—ef only I ken git thar in time!"

She was down-stairs and out of the house almost before the old negress knew what she was about to undertake. Out at a side gate she dashed, and down a grassy hill at the back of the house. Some catalpa-tree roots caught at her flying feet with their knotty fingers as though, fiend-like, they would hinder her on her errand of mercy. On, on; her breath came quick and laboring. She was on the open road now, straining with all her might up a steep, stone-roughed hill. All the northern heavens were ablaze with an angry orange. As she gained the top of the hill a little fan of lilac flames burst from the stable roof against the night. There was yet time—Bonnibel was in a loose-box near the door. O God, the other horses! Must they roast alive—the beautiful, agile creatures that he so loved?

Below, in the placid breast of the large pond, the lurid mass above was reflected with an effect as incongruous as when some world-tossed soul pours out its hot confession into the calm keeping of a saintly heart.

The shallow stream shoaled into fire among the black stems of the water-reeds, and tossed the flames upon its mimic waves. She gained the rough bridge which spanned it; her feet passed with a swift, hollow sound across it. She was there—at the stable, and her breath had not yet given out. Then all at once she remembered. Oh, joy! joy! If she saved Bonnibel, and was herself hurt to death, would not that be atonement? Might he not forgive her then? Poor little savage child—poor, sweet, uncivilized, true heart! I think indeed he would forgive you if he knew.

There were men running frantically about—omnipresent—useless: they had delayed so long to set about extinguishing the fire that it was now beyond all bounds. The wild, dull trampling of the hoofs of the terrified horses made horror in the air. They whinnied and nickered like children pleading for help. One of the English grooms was dashing into the smoke and heat. Virginia seized him by the arm.

"I'm coming with you," she said ; "let me keep hold of your coat."

Alas! alas! the maddened, silly brutes refused to follow. They reared madly whenever approached, and struck with their fore-feet at the plucky little lad. In no way could he approach them; threats and cajolery were in vain. Virginia snatched a whip from the stable wall and tried to beat them out. Usurper, vicious to the last, rushed furiously at her, and but for the lad's striking him over the head with a pitchfork, would inevitably have dashed her brains out with his wicked hoofs. There was no further time to be lost. One side of the roof was blazing ominously, and the wall on the eastern side began to tremble.

Virginia, in spite of entreaties and hands held out to stop her, turned her skirts about her head and went into Bonnibel's box. "Six of us 'ave tried to get 'er out, miss," said the panting lad, who had followed her. "Don't you venture in, for God's sake, miss; she's that mad she'll kill you—th' poor hussy!"

Bonnibel was in truth like a horse distraught. She was leaping back and forth, and trotting from side to side of her capacious box, nickering from time to time, with head aloft and tail held like a plume above her satin quarters. No sooner did she hear Virginia's voice than she stopped short, quivering in every splendid limb and sinew.

"Bonnibel!" said Virginia, in that soft monotone the frightened creature had not now heard for many a day—"Bonnibel!" There was a second's pause; then stooping her bright head, with a low whinny as of welcome and trust, the gallant mare came to the well-known voice.

Virginia tore off her woollen shawl and blindfolded the bright eyes.

In the mean time the rest of the English lads and the head groom had arrived, with fire-engines and more help. They had already succeeded in getting the horse out. The vicious Usurper they were compelled to leave to his awful fate.

"Boys, Bonnibel's coming!" yelled the lad who had entered the stable with Virginia, dashing out ahead of her; "Miss Herrick's got her, and she's coming kind as a lamb!"

A hearty, roaring cheer went up from without, mingled with exultant warwhoops from the negroes gathered around.

Almost they were safe. Why do things happen with only an inch between safety and destruction? One instant more and horse and woman would have been free. But in that tarrying instant a heavy beam from the front of the stable fell crashing down, bringing with it a great mass of bricks and mortar. Virginia and Bonnibel were half buried under the reeking mass. The flames sent up an exultant roar as of triumph. There was a smothered, horrified groan from the men, and then Bonnibel, freeing herself by one powerful effort of her iron quarters, galloped off into the coolness of the night.

They pulled Virginia out, with such gentleness as they could spare to the encroaching flames, and a bed was instantly made for her on the damp turf by means of the men's hastily torn-off coats. She lay there, still, white, most beautiful, with peace at last upon her tired face. Did she dream, perchance, that he forgave her?   .   .   .   .

The surgeon came at daybreak. He was quiet and serious. Little Hicks was the only one to whom he told anything. To him he said: "She may live two or three days; she may die before night."

At one o'clock next day old Herrick returned. He was wordless and almost majestic in his deep grief. All day long he sat holding her in such positions as would ease her; talking to her; trying to follow her wandering fancies. She knew him always, though she knew no one else. "Father," she said, suddenly, in one of the intervals when reason returned to her, "won't you please sen' fur Mr. Jack? Somethin' in my heart tells me he'll come—now. Write to him 'bout Bonnibel. Tell him I saved her. Tell him I jess want ter say good-by. I don' wan' him ever ter furgive me. I only want to—to look at him once more. Father"—wistfully—"*you* think he'll come?"

"Yes, yes, my little girl, I think he'll come."

"Then write, write, father—quick. Don' let it be too late. I wan' so bad to look at him once more!"

He came—oh yes, he came! mad with regret and remorse, repentant, eager to atone. "Where is she? where is she?" he asked as he threw down his hat upon the hall table, and jerked off his spurs, that their jingling might not disturb her. If he had only known the music that they made to her ears!

"She's in yo' room, sur. They tells me ez how 'twar her fancy to be took thar," said Herrick, simply. "I hope ez you don' min', sur."

Mind! Jack's eyes were hot with the saddest tears of all his life.

He went in softly. There she lay, pathetic, fragile as some long-ill child upon his narrow bed. He went and stooped over her, taking into one of his brown hands her restless, slender fingers. Her gentle look rested unknowingly upon him.

"Ain't they goin' ter sen' fur Mr. Jack?" she said. "I think he'll come—now; father thought ez how he would. Please write it down that I saved Bonnibel—please write that down. 'Twas mighty hot, but I saved her. Oh, don' yo' think he'll come?—don' yo' think he'll come? I don' even arst him to speak to me. Ef he'll only stand in th' door so ez I kin see him when I go."

"Virginia—Virginia," said Roden, brokenly. "My dear little girl, don't you know me? Here I am!—here—at your side. Don't you feel my hands, Virginia? Don't you know me?"

She went rambling on. "I wonder ef he would furgive me ef he knew? I wisht Bonnibel could tell him—I wisht I was Bonnibel!" with a little rippling laugh infinitely pathetic. "Oh, wouldn' I kyar him pretty an' straight at his fences, an' win ev'y race fur him!" Her eyes opened vague and sorrowful again upon Roden's pale face. "Oh," she said, with a long sighing breath, "don't you think he'll come? Write to him 'bout Bonnibel—please write that ter him."

"Virginia, look at me—look at me," said the young man, half lifting her in his arms. "Dear little Virginia, here I am. I forgive you with all my heart and soul, Virginia. Oh, please look at me, please remember me."

"Who says 'furgive'?" she said, with her restless, eager eyes searching the room as if for something long expected—"who says 'furgive'?"

"I do, I do," Roden said, weeping at last like any girl. "I forgive you, Virginia—Virginia. You *shall* know me!"

Her eyes fixed themselves upon his face, first vacantly, then with a wonder-stricken radiance. "Mr. Jack," she said, under her breath, "did they tell yo'? I saved her; that's all. Yo' needn' say nothin'; I jess wanted to look at yo'. I saved her. 'Twas awful hot. I kin hear it roarin' now. She come to me; she wouldn' come to nobody else."

"Virginia," said Roden, "listen to me; stop talking. What do I care about Bonnibel? Child, do you want to break my heart? Listen, Virginia; I forgive you—I *forgive you.*"

"Do—you—really?" she said, with the old timid joy in her soft voice. "I ain't dreamin'? Well, God's so good to me! But I did save her. 'Bonnibel!' I said—'Bonnibel!' an' she come right straight ter me with her pretty head tucked down. Then came all that fire on us. I thought 'twas over. But I saved her—I saved her. Please tell him that—*please* tell him that. I reckon he'll sorter remember me kind fur that; don' you, father?"

After a while her reason came again. She asked to see Bonnibel; they could bring her to the window, she said, and she would like also to give her a handful of grass.

They rolled the bed to the window, and little Hicks led Bonnibel up beside it. Roden went out himself and gathered a handful of fresh grass. I think the lad only respected his master more for the tears that ran down his cheeks. He couldn't see very distinctly himself just then, this good little Hicks.

"Bonnibel," said the girl, in her cooing tones—"Bonnibel."

What was the matter? Had suffering charged some magic in that soft voice? Bonnibel turned indifferently away from the anxious hand, and rubbed her bright head with an impatient movement against one of her fore-legs.

"Oh!" said the girl, while the glad flush died out of her face, and the green blades fell from her hold upon the window-sill, "Bonnibel don' know me any more—she don' care. I gave my life for her, an'—an' she don' care."

"Yes she does—she does," said Roden, frantic for her disappointment; "she's just gorged, the little glutton! She's been out at grass ever since you saved her, Virginia dear; that's all."

"No 'tain't," said the girl, sadly. "I ain't the same, I reckon; I reckon I'm right near gone, Mr. Jack. Well, I saved her, anyhow. The most part fell on me; she kicked herself loose. Please, father, ef Mr. Jack don' come in time—*please*, father, tell him ez how I saved Bonnibel. Oh, father, I mus' tell somebody 'fore I go. I kyarn' bear to think there won't be anybody in all th' world ez knows it when I'm gone. I loved him, father dear—I loved him so! An' I've been mighty wicked; an' God's been mighty good ter me; an' I'm goin' to heaven, mammy says. But I won't have him even there—I won't have him—even there."

The soft voice broke suddenly—stopped. The bright head dropped forward on her breast.

Roden had buried his face in her two pale hands. When he looked up, old

Herrick was closing gently with his toil-roughened hand the sweet wide eyes which never more would look on anything this side the stars.

It was at this moment that Bonnibel, repenting, perhaps, of her former coldness, thrust in her little deer-head at the open window, and drew a long sighing breath as of contentment.

The blades of grass, dropped from the thin hand now so still upon the stirless bosom, were blown along the window-sill by the mare's warm breath.

Elaine Goodale.

BORN in Mount Washington, Berkshire Co., Mass., 1863.

ASHES OF ROSES.

[*Apple-Blossoms : Verses of Two Children.* 1878.—*All Round the Year.* 1881.—*Uncollected Poems.* 1881–88.]

SOFT on the sunset sky
  Bright daylight closes,
Leaving, when light doth die,
Pale hues that mingling lie,—
  Ashes of roses.

When Love's warm sun is set,
  Love's brightness closes ;
Eyes with hot tears are wet,
In hearts there linger yet
  Ashes of roses.

INDIAN PIPE.

DEATH in the wood,—
  Death, and a scent of decay ;
Death, and a horror that creeps with
  the blood,
And stiffens the limbs to clay ;
  For the rains are heavy and slow,
And the leaves are shrunken and wan,
  And the winds are sobbing weary and
    low,
And the life of the year is gone.

Death in the wood,—
Death in its fold over fold,
  Death,—that I shuddered and sank
    where I stood,
At the touch of a hand so cold,—
  At the touch of a hand so cold,
And the sight of a clay-white face.
  For I saw the corse of the friend I loved,
And a hush fell over the place.

Death in the wood,—
Death, and a scent of decay,
  Death, and a horror but half understood,
Where blank as the dead I lay ;
  What curse hung over the earth,
What woe to the tribes of men,
  That we felt as a death what was made
    for a birth,—
And a birth sinking deathward again !

Death in the wood,—
In the death-pale lips apart ;
  Death in a whiteness that curdled the
    blood,
Now black to the very heart :
  The wonder by her was formed
Who stands supreme in power ;
  To show that life by the spirit comes
She gave us a soulless flower !

A COUNTRYWOMAN OF MINE.

HANDSOME? I hardly know. Her profile's fine—
Delightful, intellectual, aquiline.

Her keen eyes light it; keen, yet often kind;
Her fair hair crowns it to an artist's mind.

Fine figure and fine manners, without doubt,
Determine half her charm, and bear me out.

Learned? Well, rather. See them for yourself—
Mill, Spencer, Darwin, on her favorite shelf.

Well educated, certainly well read;
Well born, of course, and (not of course) well bred.

Provincial? Never! Cockney? Not at all.
Her world is small enough, yet not too small.

To prove she knows it, only watch a while
That humorous, tender, half-sarcastic smile.

Accomplished? She says not; but who can tell?
She does some simple things, and does them well.

She walks well, stands well, sits well—things so rare,
To praise as they deserve I hardly dare!

She rows, rides, dances—admirably done!
Delights in each, and yet depends on none.

What to take up she knows, and what to drop;
How to say clever things, and when to stop.

Few dress so well; she does what few can do,
Forgets what she has on; and so do you?

She's not too careless, not conventional quite;
Does what she likes; knows what she does is right.

Takes New World freedom and with Old World ease;
She's but to please herself the world to please.

WHEN DID WE MEET?

WHEN did I know thee and not love
thee?
How could I live and know thee not?
The look of thine that first did move
me
I have forgot.

Canst thou recall thy life's beginning?
Will childhood's conscious wonder
last?
Each glance from thee, so worth the
winning,
Blots all the past.

Lizette Woodworth Reese.

BORN in Waverly, Md.

ANNE.

[*A Branch of May. Poems.* 1887.]

Sudbury Meeting-house, 1653.

HER eyes be like the violets,
　Ablow in Sudbury lane;
When she doth smile, her face is sweet
　As blossoms after rain;
With grief I think of my gray hairs,
　And wish me young again.

In comes she through the dark old door
　Upon this Sabbath day;
And she doth bring the tender wind
　That sings in bush and spray,
And hints of all the apple boughs
　That kissed her by the way.

Our parson stands up straight and tall,
　For our dear souls to pray,
And of the place where sinners go
　Some grewsome things doth say;
Now she is highest Heaven to me;
　So Hell is far away.

Most stiff and still the good folk sit
　To hear the sermon through;
But if our God be such a God,
　And if these things be true,
Why did He make her then so fair,
　And both her eyes so blue?

A flickering light, the sun creeps in,
　And finds her sitting there;
And touches soft her lilac gown,
　And soft her yellow hair;
I look across to that old pew,
　And have both praise and prayer.

Oh, violets in Sudbury lane,
　Amid the grasses green,
This maid who stirs ye with her feet
　Is far more fair, I ween!
I wonder how my forty years
　Look by her sweet sixteen!

IN SORROW'S HOUR.

THE brambles blow without you,—at the door
　They make late April,—and the brier too
Buds its first rose for other folk than you;
In the deep grass the elder bush once more
Heaps its sweet snow; and the marsh-marigold
　With its small fire sets all the sedge aflare;
　Like flakes of flame blown down the gray, still air,
The cardinal-flower is out in thickets old.
Oh, love! oh, love! what road is yours to-day?
　For I would follow after, see your face,
　Put my hand in your hand, feel the dear grace
Of hair, mouth, eyes, hear the brave words you say.
　The dark is void, and all the daylight vain.
　Oh, that you were but here with me again!

THE GARDEN AT BEMERTON.

[FOR A FLY-LEAF OF HERBERT'S POEMS.]

YEAR after year, from dusk to dusk,
 How sweet this English garden
  grows!
Steeped in two centuries' sun and musk,
 Walled from the world in gray repose,
 Harbor of honey-freighted bees,
And wealthy with the rose.

Here pinks with spices in their throats
 Nod by the bitter marigold;
Here nightingales with haunting notes,
 When west and east with stars are bold,
  From out the twisted hawthorn trees
Sing back the weathers old.

All tuneful winds do down it pass;
 The leaves a sudden whiteness show,
And delicate noises fill the grass;
 The only flakes its spaces know
  Are petals blown off briers long,
And heaped on blades below.

Ah! dawn and dusk, year after year,
 'Tis more than these that keeps it
  rare!
We see the saintly Master here
 Pacing along the alleys fair,
  And catch the throbbing of a song
Across the amber air!

Madison Julius Cawein.

BORN in Louisville, Ky., 1865.

DISENCHANTMENT OF DEATH.

[*Accolon of Gaul, with Other Poems.* 1889.]

HUSH! She is dead! Tread gently as the light
 Foots dim the weary room. Thou shalt behold.
Look:—In death's ermine pomp of awful white,
 Pale passion of pulseless slumber virgin cold:
Bold, beautiful youth proud as heroic Might—
 Death! and how death hath made it vastly old.

Old earth she is now: energy of birth
 Glad wings hath fledged and tried them suddenly;
The eyes that held have freed their narrow mirth;
 Their sparks of spirit, which made this to be,
Shine fixed in rarer jewels not of earth,
 Far Fairylands beyond some silent sea.

A sod is this whence what were once those eyes
 Will grow blue wild-flowers in what happy air;
Some weed with flossy blossoms will surprise,
 Haply, what summer with her affluent hair;
Blush-roses bask those cheeks; and the wise skies
 Will know her dryad to what young oak fair.

The chastity of death hath touched her so,
   No dreams of life can reach her in such rest;—
No dreams the mind exhausted here below,
   Sleep built within the romance of her breast.
How she will sleep! like music quickening slow
   Dark the dead germs, to golden life caressed.

Low music, thin as winds that lyre the grass,
   Smiting through red roots harpings; and the sound
Of elfin revels when the wild dews glass
   Globes of concentric beauty on the ground;
For showery clouds o'er tepid nights that pass
   The prayer in harebells and faint foxgloves crowned.

So, if she's dead, thou know'st she is not dead.
   Disturb her not; she lies so lost in sleep:
The too-contracted soul its shell hath fled:
   Her presence drifts about us and the deep
Is yet unvoyaged and she smiles o'erhead:—
   Weep not nor sigh—thou wouldst not have *her* weep?

To principles of passion and of pride,
   To trophied circumstance and specious law,
Stale saws of life, with scorn now flung aside,
   From Mercy's throne and Justice would'st thou draw
Her, Hope in Hope, and Chastity's pale bride,
   In holiest love of holy, without flaw?

The anguish of the living merciless,—
   Mad, bitter cruelty unto the grave,—
Wrings the dear dead with tenfold heart's distress,
   Earth chaining love, bound by the lips that rave.
If thou hast sorrow let thy sorrow bless
   That power of death, of death our selfless slave.

"Unjust?"—He is not! for hast thou not all,
   All that thou ever hadst when this dull clay
So heartless, blasted now, flushed spiritual,
   A restless vassal of Earth's night and day?
This hath been thine and is; the cosmic call
   Hath disenchanted that which might not stay.

Thou unjust!—bar not from its high estate,—
   Won with what toil through devastating cares,
What bootless battling with the violent Fate,
   What mailed endeavor with resistless years,—
That soul:—whole-hearted granted once thy mate,
   Heaven only loaned, return it not with tears!

Dora Read Goodale.

BORN in Mount Washington, Berkshire Co., Mass., 1866.

THE SNOWBIRD.

[*Apple-Blossoms.* 1878.—*All Round the Year.* 1881.—*Uncollected Poems.* 1881–88.]

WHEN the leaves are shed,
  And the branches bare,
When the snows are deep,
And the flowers asleep,
And the autumn dead;
And the skies are o'er us bent,
Gray and gloomy, since she went,
  And the sifting snow is drifting
    Through the air;

Then, 'mid snowdrifts white,
  Though the trees are bare,
  Comes the snowbird, bold
  In the winter's cold;
Quick and round, and bright,
Light he steps across the snow,
Cares he not for winds that blow,
  Though the sifting snow be drifting
    Through the air.

CINDERELLA.

HERE by the kitchen fire I sit
  Until the generous loaves be brown:
The firelight flickers up and down;
I, waiting, ponder over it.

The cat comes purring to my knee,
  And, springing to my lap, she lies,
  The firelight darting in her eyes,
And old traditions come to me.

"The black cat," so the legends say,
  "The witches ride by night," forsooth!
  The fancy-witchery of youth
Has touched the room with mystery!

The clock ticks slow, the fire burns down.
  I see strange faces in the grate—
  A hooded monk, a muse, a fate,
An ancient knight with armor on!

I see a mask: I know it hides
  The smile of one I know by day—

  1877.

The face behind it drops away
And leaves a pair of burning eyes!

I wait—the firelight glimmers red—
  Where is my fairy coach and four
  To take me from the narrow door,
By eager longing fancy-led?

The cat is restless where she lies;
  The soul of one who lived below
  A thousand years and more ago
Looks through me from her narrow eyes!

The clock strikes slowly from the wall—
  I count the heavy strokes to eight;
  The fire burns lower in the grate;
A mouse is stirring in the wall!

I rouse me from my revery—
  I strike a match—I kneel before
  And open wide the oven door—
King Alfred fared as ill as I!

MARIETTE.

TOO rash is she for cold coquette,—
  Love dares not claim her:
I can but say, " 'Tis Mariette,"
  Nor more than name her!

She mocks the world her arrows reach
  With light derision;
Yet who would choose the softer speech,
  The graver vision?

An eager glance, and incomplete,
  Repays you, after;
A voice to make all satire sweet—
  Delicious laughter!

I think no woman's warmth is hers—
  How could she use it?
Another's pain no passion stirs,
  Nor would you choose it.

Can warning tame the maiden gaze
  That dares discover?
Pride, mirth, ambition, thirst for praise—
  They're hers—you love her!

No grief should shake the gay disdain
  That will not fear it,

Or mar by one subduing pain
  So rare a spirit.

Who ever watched that rounded grace,
  Born of the minute,
Nor thought the world a prettier place
  That she was in it?

You ask no larger gift than this,
  No nearer honor,—
It is enough for happiness
  To look upon her.

The oval cheek, the rising tread
  In careless measure,
The wilful, bright, ethereal head,
  Alive with pleasure:

On these the old desire is stayed
  That long has waited,
For soul and body, rightly made,
  Are fitly mated.

But what have I, whom men forget,
  To offer to her?
A woman's passion, Mariette,
  There is no truer.

The Century Magazine, 1883.

EVENTIDE.

LOWER and lower the light is fail-
  ing,—
  Waves of color that come and go;
Yellow and purple slowly paling,—
  Flush of pink in the after-glow;
Booming bees forsake the clover.
  Day is over!

Faster and faster from hazy hollow
  Night is closing on field and wood;
Out of the west the late-bound swallow

Hastens back to the crumpled brood;
Stately-winged, the night-hawks hover.
  Day is over!

Forest and fallow grow dark together,
  A bell in the distance sounding
    slow;
Still the light of the rosy weather
  Welling up in the after-glow;
Now the starry skies discover
  Day is over!

From "A June Day."

Various Poems.

I.

FARRAGUT.

MOBILE BAY, 5 AUGUST, 1864.

FARRAGUT, Farragut,
　　Old Heart of Oak,
Daring Dave Farragut,
　　Thunderbolt stroke,
Watches the hoary mist
　　Lift from the bay,
Till his flag, glory-kissed,
　　Greets the young day.

Far, by gray Morgan's walls,
　　Looms the black fleet.
Hark, deck to rampart calls
　　With the drums' beat!
Buoy your chains overboard,
　　While the steam hums;
Men! to the battlement,
　　Farragut comes.

See, as the hurricane
　　Hurtles in wrath
Squadrons of clouds amain
　　Back from its path!
Back to the parapet,
　　To the guns' lips,
Thunderbolt Farragut
　　Hurls the black ships.

Now through the battle's roar
　　Clear the boy sings,
" By the mark fathoms four,"
　　While his lead swings.

The Century Magazine. 1890.

Steady the wheelmen five
　　" Nor' by East keep her,"
" Steady," but two alive:
　　How the shells sweep her!

Lashed to the mast that sways
　　Over red decks,
Over the flame that plays
　　Round the torn wrecks,
Over the dying lips
　　Framed for a cheer,
Farragut leads his ships,
　　Guides the line clear.

On by heights cannon-browed,
　　While the spars quiver;
Onward still flames the cloud
　　Where the hulks shiver.
See, yon fort's star is set,
　　Storm and fire past.
Cheer him, lads—Farragut,
　　Lashed to the mast!

Oh! while Atlantic's breast
　　Bears a white sail,
While the Gulf's towering crest
　　Tops a green vale;
Men thy bold deeds shall tell,
　　Old Heart of Oak,
Daring Dave Farragut,
　　Thunderbolt stroke!

WILLIAM T. MEREDITH. 1839–.

RÉVEILLE.

THE morning is cheery, my boys, arouse!
　　The dew shines bright on the chestnut boughs,
And the sleepy mist on the river lies,
Though the east is flushing with crimson dyes.
　　　Awake! awake! awake!
　　　O'er field and wood and brake,

With glories newly born,
　　Comes on the blushing morn.
　　　　Awake! awake!

You have dreamed of your homes and friends all night;
You have basked in your sweethearts' smiles so bright;
Come, part with them all for a while again,—
Be lovers in dreams; when awake, be men.
　　　　Turn out! turn out! turn out!
　　　　　You have dreamed full long, I know.
　　　　Turn out! turn out! turn out!
　　　　　The east is all aglow.
　　　　　　Turn out! turn out!

From every valley and hill there come
The clamoring voices of fife and drum;
And out in the fresh, cool morning air
The soldiers are swarming everywhere.
　　　　Fall in! fall in! fall in!
　　　　　Every man in his place,
　　　　Fall in! fall in! fall in!
　　　　　Each with a cheerful face,
　　　　　　Fall in! fall in!

　　　　　　　　MICHAEL O'CONNOR. 1837–62.

AT GETTYSBURG.

[From the Poem read in Dedication of the Pennsylvania Monuments, 12 September, 1889.]

HOW soon the first fierce rain of death,
　In big drops dancing on the trees,
Withers the foliage! At a breath,
Hot as the blasts that dried old seas,
The clover falls like drops of blood
From mortal hurts, and stains the sod;
The wheat is clipped, but the ripe grain
Here long ungarnered shall remain;
And many who at the drum's long roll
Sprang to the charge and swelled the
　　cheer,
And set their flags high on the knoll,
Ne'er knew how went the fight fought
　　here;
For them a knell tumultuous shells
Shook from the consecrated bells,
As here they formed that silent rank,
Whose glorious star at twilight sank.

And night, which lulls all discords—
　　night,
Which stills the folds and vocal wood,
And, with the touch of finger light,

Quiets the pink-lipped brook's wild mood,
Which sends the wind to seek the latch,
And seals young eyes while mothers
　　watch—
Night stays the battle, but with day
Their lives, themselves, foes hurl away.
Where thousands fell, but did not yield,
Shall be to-morrow's battle-field.
E'er dying died or dead were cold,
New hosts pressed on the lines to hold,
And held them—hold them now in sleep,
While stars and sentinels go round,
And war-worn chargers shrink like sheep
Beside their riders on the ground.
All through the night—all through the
　　North
Speed doubtful tidings back and forth;
Through North and South, from dusk
　　till day
A sundered people diverse pray.

So gradual sink the deliberate stars,
The sun doth run the laggards down,

At sleep's still meadows bursts the
    bars,
And floods with light the steepled town.
Blow! bugles of the cavalry, blow!

Gettysburg, and Other Poems. 1890.

Forward the infantry, row on row!
While every battery leaps with life,
And swells with tongueless throats the
    strife!

          Isaac Rusling Pennypacker. 1852–.

INSCRIPTION ON THE SOLDIERS' MONUMENT AT WATERBURY, CONN.

BRAVE men, who, rallying at your country's call
    Went forth to fight,—if Heaven willed, to fall!
  Returned, ye walk with us through sunnier years,
And hear a nation say, God bless you all!

Brave men, who yet a heavier burden bore,
And came not home to hearts by grief made sore!
  They call you dead; but lo! ye grandly live,
Shrined in the nation's love forevermore!

          Joseph Anderson. 1836–.

1886.

CAVALRY SONG.

OUR bugles sound gayly.   To horse and away!
  And over the mountains breaks the day;
Then ho! brothers, ho! for the ride or the fight,
There are deeds to be done ere we slumber to-night!
  And whether we fight or whether we fall
  By sabre-stroke or rifle-ball,
  The hearts of the free will remember us yet,
  And our country, our country will never forget!

Then mount and away! let the coward delight
To be lazy all day and safe all night;
Our joy is a charger, flecked with foam,
And the earth is our bed and the saddle our home;
  And whether we fight, etc.

See yonder the ranks of the traitorous foe,
And bright in the sunshine bayonets glow!
Breathe a prayer, but no sigh; think for what you would fight;
Then charge! with a will, boys, and God for the right!
  And whether we fight, etc.

We have gathered again the red laurels of war;
We have followed the traitors fast and far;
But some who rose gayly this morn with the sun
Lie bleeding and pale on the field they have won!

But whether we fight or whether we fall
By sabre-stroke or rifle-ball,
The hearts of the free will remember us yet,
And our country, our country will never forget!

ROSSITER WORTHINGTON RAYMOND. 1840-.

THE LAND OF DREAMS.

I WANDERED in a pleasant land of dreams,
    Through fragrant fields, where harvests rich were laid
In golden swaths, by reaper's swinging blade;
I lingered on the banks of gurgling streams,
Where, through its leafy gates, the sunlight gleams,
    And glimmers, through interstices of shade;
    There every dewdrop is a gem displayed
Upon the brow of Beauty.   Ah! this seems
Her home.   Oh would that I could understand
    Her speech, for now her voice most sweet I hear,
And now her touch, as from a mother's hand,
    I feel, and wake.   'Tis mother standing near;
    And lo, the land of vision doth appear.
Behold! It is "My own, my native land."

SAMUEL ELEAZER MANN. 1853-.

1888.

II.

THE MEMORY OF THE HEART.

IF stores of dry and learnèd lore we gain
    We keep them in the memory of the brain;
Names, things, and facts—whate'er we knowledge call,
There is the common ledger for them all;
And images on this cold surface traced
Make slight impressions, and are soon effaced.

But we've a page more glowing and more bright
On which our friendship and our love to write;
That these may never from the soul depart,
We trust them to the memory of the heart.
There is no dimming—no effacement here;
Each new pulsation keeps the record clear;
Warm, golden letters all the tablet fill,
Nor lose their lustre till the heart stands still.

DANIEL WEBSTER. 1782-1852.

London, 19 Nov., 1839.
See, also, Vol. IV., page 450.

LIBERTY FOR ALL.

THEY tell me, Liberty! that in thy name
   I may not plead for all the human race,
That some are born to bondage and disgrace,—
So, to a heritage of woe and shame,—
And some to power supreme, and glorious fame:
   With my whole soul I spurn the doctrine base
   And, as an equal brotherhood, embrace
All people, and for all fair freedom claim!
Know this, O man! whate'er thy earthly fate—
   God never made a tyrant nor a slave:
Woe, then, to those who dare to desecrate
   His glorious image—for to all He gave
Eternal rights which none may violate;
   And by a mighty hand the oppressed He yet shall save!

WILLIAM LLOYD GARRISON. 1805-79.

See, also, Vol. VI., page 222.

SAMUEL HOAR.

A YEAR ago how often did I meet
   Under these elms, once more in sober bloom,
Thy tall, sad figure pacing down the street,—
But now the robin sings above thy tomb.
Thy name on other shores may ne'er be known,
Though austere Rome no graver Consul knew;
But Massachusetts her true son doth own,—
Out of her soil thy hardy virtues grew.
She loves the man who chose the conquered cause,
The upright soul that bowed to God alone,
The clean hand that upheld her equal laws,
The old religion, never yet outgrown,
The cold demeanor and warm heart beneath,
The simple grandeur of thy life and death.

FRANKLIN BENJAMIN SANBORN. 1831-.

Concord, 27 April, 1867.
See, also, Vol. VIII., page 538.

REST.

SWEET is the pleasure
   Itself cannot spoil!
Is not true leisure
   One with true toil?

Thou that wouldst taste it,
   Still do thy best;
Use it, not waste it—
   Else 'tis no rest.

Wouldst behold beauty
  Near thee ? all round ?
Only hath duty
  Such a sight found.

Rest is not quitting
  The busy career;
Rest is the fitting
  Of self to its sphere.

'Tis the brook's motion,
  Clear without strife,

Fleeing to ocean
  After its life.

Deeper devotion
  Nowhere hath knelt;
Fuller emotion
  Heart never felt.

'Tis loving and serving
  The highest and best;
'Tis onwards! unswerving—
  And that is true rest.

JOHN SULLIVAN DWIGHT. 1813–.

See, also, Vol. VII., page 233.

THE CENOTAPH.

ON THE FINAL BURIAL OF LINCOLN AT SPRINGFIELD, 14 APRIL, 1887.

AND so they buried Lincoln ?   Strange and vain !
  Has any creature thought of Lincoln hid
In any vault, 'neath any coffin-lid,
In all the years since that wild Spring of pain ?
'Tis false,—he never in the grave hath lain.
  You could not bury him although you slid
  Upon his clay the Cheops pyramid
Or heaped it with the Rocky Mountain chain.
They slew themselves; they but set Lincoln free.
  In all the earth his great heart beats as strong,
  Shall beat while pulses throb to chivalry
And burn with hate of tyranny and wrong.
  Whoever will may find him, anywhere
  Save in the tomb.   Not there,—he is not there!

JAMES THOMSON McKAY. 1843-90.

The Century Magazine. 1890.

III.

IF I SHOULD DIE TO-NIGHT.

IF I should die to-night,
  My friends would look upon my quiet face
Before they laid it in its resting-place,
And deem that death had left it almost fair;
And, laying snow-white flowers against my hair,
Would smooth it down with tearful tenderness,
And fold my hands with lingering caress,—
Poor hands, so empty and so cold to-night!

If I should die to-night,
My friends would call to mind with loving thought
Some kindly deed the icy hands had wrought,
Some gentle word the frozen lips had said,
Errands on which the willing feet had sped;
The memory of my selfishness and pride,
My hasty words, would all be put aside,
And so I should be loved and mourned to-night.

If I should die to-night,
Even hearts estranged would turn once more to me,
Recalling other days remorsefully;
The eyes that chill me with averted glance
Would look upon me as of yore, perchance,
And soften in the old familiar way,
For who could war with dumb, unconscious clay?
So I might rest, forgiven of all to-night.

Oh, friends! I pray to-night,
Keep not your kisses for my dead, cold brow:
The way is lonely, let me feel them now.
Think gently of me; I am travel-worn;
My faltering feet are pierced with many a thorn.
Forgive, oh, hearts estranged, forgive, I plead!
When dreamless rest is mine I shall not need
The tenderness for which I long to-night.

BELLE EUGENIA SMITH. 18–.

The Christian Union, 18 June, 1873.

'TIS BUT A LITTLE FADED FLOWER.

'TIS but a little faded flower,
    But oh, how fondly dear!
'Twill bring me back one golden hour,
    Through many a weary year.
I may not to the world impart
    The secret of its power,
But treasured in my inmost heart,
    I keep my faded flower.

Where is the heart that doth not keep,
    Within its inmost core,
Some fond remembrance, hidden deep,
    Of days that are no more?
Who hath not saved some trifling thing
    More prized than jewels rare—
A faded flower, a broken ring,
    A tress of golden hair?

ELLEN CLEMENTINE HOWARTH. 1827–.

1869.

WHAT MY LOVER SAID.

BY the merest chance, in the twilight gloom,
    In the orchard path he met me;
In the tall, wet grass, with its faint perfume,

And I tried to pass, but he made no room,
  Oh I tried, but he would not let me.
So I stood and blushed till the grass grew red,
  With my face bent down above it,
While he took my hand as he whispering said—
(How the clover lifted each pink, sweet head,
To listen to all that my lover said;
  Oh, the clover in bloom, I love it!)

In the high, wet grass went the path to hide,
  And the low, wet leaves hung over;
But I could not pass upon either side,
For I found myself, when I vainly tried,
  In the arms of my steadfast lover.
And he held me there and he raised my head,
  While he closed the path before me,
And he looked down into my eyes and said—
(How the leaves bent down from the boughs o'erhead,
To listen to all that my lover said,
  Oh, the leaves hanging lowly o'er me!)

Had he moved aside but a little way,
  I could surely then have passed him;
And he knew I never could wish to stay,
And would not have heard what he had to say,
  Could I only aside have cast him.
It was almost dark, and the moments sped,
  And the searching night-wind found us,
But he drew me nearer and softly said—
(How the pure, sweet wind grew still, instead,
To listen to all that my lover said;
  Oh, the whispering wind around us!)

I am sure he knew, when he held me fast,
  That I must be all unwilling;
For I tried to go, and I would have passed,
As the night was come with its dew, at last,
  And the sky with its stars was filling.
But he clasped me close when I would have fled,
  And he made me hear his story,
And his soul came out from his lips and said—
(How the stars crept out where the white moon led,
To listen to all that my lover said;
  Oh, the moon and the stars in glory!)

I know that the grass and the leaves will not tell,
  And I'm sure that the wind, precious rover,
Will carry my secret so safely and well
  That no being shall ever discover
One word of the many that rapidly fell
  From the soul-speaking lips of my lover;
  And the moon and the stars that looked over
Shall never reveal what a fairy-like spell

They wove round about us that night in the dell,
    In the path through the dew-laden clover,
Nor echo the whispers that made my heart swell
    As they fell from the lips of my lover.

                                HOMER GREENE. 1853-.

N. Y. Evening Post, 19 *Nov.*, 1875.

DAISY.

COULD you have seen the violets
    That blossomed in her eyes,
Could you have kissed that golden hair,
    And drunk her baby sighs,—
You would have been her tiring-maid
    As joyfully as I;
Content to deck your little queen,
    And let the world go by.

Could you have seen those violets
    Hide in their graves of snow,
Drawn all that gold along your hand,
    While she lay, smiling so,—
O, you would tread this weary earth
    As heavily as I;
Content to clasp her little grave,
    And let the world go by.

                                EMILY WARREN. 18—.

The Overland Monthly. 1870.

SONG.

DEAR eyes, forbear to weep,
    Seeing where heavy-lidded sleep
Stands at the threshold of the day,
Ready to bear thy woes away.

Sad heart, forbear to break,
Knowing that even the violets wake
And seek the spring with wistful eyes
Under the gray of winter skies.

Ah, Love! ask not to die,
Watching the moon fade down the sky,
A trembling crescent, that anew
Rounds to a bubble 'gainst the blue.

And surely we who wait,
Unquestioning, the gifts of fate,
Waiting, shall find life's hoarded sweet
Flung with the flood-tide at our feet.

                        MARY CATHERINE BISHOP. 18—.

The Overland Monthly. 1883.

COUNSEL.

IF thou shouldst bid thy friend farewell,
    —But for one night though that farewell should be—
Press thou his hand in thine; how canst thou tell
            How far from thee

Fate or Caprice may lead his feet
    Ere that to-morrow come ? Men have been known
Lightly to turn the corner of a street,
            And days have grown

To months, and months to lagging years,
   Before they looked in loving eyes again.
Parting, at best, is underlaid with tears,
      —With tears and pain.

Therefore, lest sudden death should come between,
   Or time, or distance, clasp with pressure true
The palm of him who goeth forth.   Unseen
      Fate goeth too!

Yea, find thou alway time to say
   Some earnest word betwixt the idle talk,
Lest with thee henceforth, night and day,
      Regret should walk.

                  MARY EVELYN MOORE DAVIS. 18—.
The Galaxy. 1872.

"MANY THINGS THOU HAST GIVEN ME, DEAR HEART."

MANY things thou hast given me, dear heart;
   But one thing thou hast taken: that high dream
Of heaven as of a country that should seem
Beyond all glory that divinest art
Has pictured:—with this I have had to part
   Since knowing thee;—how long, love, will the gleam
   Of each day's sunlight on my pathway stream,
Richer than what seemed richest at the start?
   Make my days happy, love; yet I entreat
Make not each happier than the last for me;
   Lest heaven itself should dawn to me, complete
In joy, not the surprise I dreamed 'twould be,
   But simply as the natural and sweet
Continuance of days spent here with thee.

               ALICE WELLINGTON ROLLINS. 1847–.
The Ring of Amethyst. 1878.

DESPONDENCY.

SPRING comes with soft caress,
   And paints thy cheek
And perfumes thy long hair,
That dead thou may'st be fair.

Then summer brings her buds
   And wealth of leaves,
   That in the dusty tomb
Thy grave-clothes lack not bloom.

Autumn gives store of fruit
   And goodly cheer,
   That thy funereal feast
Shall not be scant, at least.

And winter brings a shroud,—
   Last gift to thee;
   Cover the grave-mound high;
Thou wert born, sweet, to die!

               ARLO BATES. 1850–.

See, also, Vol. X., page 573.

THE TWO MOTHERS.

FOR fondling arm, warm breast, and life's sweet tide,
 What dost thou to thy mother make return ?
Some madcap girl can win thee from her side;
 Few tears, at best, hast thou above her urn.

Only to Earth, thy mother, art thou just:
 To her thou givest all within thy power,
Thy life, thy breath, thyself,—a pinch of dust,
 To star her bosom with a summer flower.

       EPIPHANIUS WILSON. 1845–.

The Atlantic Monthly. 1889.

DAN'S WIFE.

UP in early morning light,
 Sweeping, dusting, "setting right,"
Oiling all the household springs,
Sewing buttons, tying strings,
Telling Bridget what to do,
Mending rips in Johnny's shoe,
Running up and down the stair,
Tying baby in his chair,
Cutting meat and spreading bread,
Dishing out so much per head,
Eating as she can, by chance,
Giving husband kindly glance;
Toiling, working, busy life,—
 "Smart woman,
 Dan's wife."

Dan comes home at fall of night,
Home so cheerful, neat and bright;
Children meet him at the door,
Pull him in and look him o'er;
Wife asks "how the work has gone ?"
"Busy times with us at home!"
Supper done—Dan reads at ease;
Happy Dan, but one to please!
Children must be put to bed—
All their little prayers are said;
Little shoes are placed in rows,
Bed-clothes tucked o'er little toes;
Busy, noisy, wearing life,—
 Tired woman,
 Dan's wife.

Dan reads on, and falls asleep,—
See the woman softly creep;
Baby rests at last, poor dear,
Not a word her heart to cheer;
Mending-basket full to top,
Stockings, shirts, and little frock;
Tired eyes and weary brain,
Side with darting, ugly pain—
"Never mind, 'twill pass away";
She must work, but never play;
Closed piano, unused books,
Done the walks to cosey nooks,
Brightness faded out of life,—
 Saddened woman,
 Dan's wife.

Up-stairs, tossing to and fro,
Fever holds the woman low;
Children wander, free to play,
When and where they will to-day;
Bridget loiters—dinner's cold,
Dan looks anxious, cross and old;
Household screws are out of place,
Lacking one dear, patient face;
Steady hands—so weak, but true—
Hands that knew just what to do,
Never knowing rest or play,
Folded nòw—and laid away;
Work of six, in one short life,—
 Shattered woman,
 Dan's wife.

       KATE TANNATT WOODS. 18—.

The Salem Observer. 1872.

THE FIRST STEP.

MY little one begins his feet to try,
 A tottering, feeble, inconsistent way;
Pleased with the effort, he forgets his play,
And leaves his infant baubles where they lie.
Laughing and proud his mother flutters nigh,
 Turning to go, yet joy-compelled to stay,
 And bird-like, singing what her heart would say;
But not so certain of my bliss am I,
For I bethink me of the days in store
 Wherein those feet must traverse realms unknown,
And half forget the pathway to our door.
 And I recall that in the seasons flown
 We were his all—as he was all our own—
But never can be quite so any more.

ANDREW BICE SAXTON. 1856-.

The Century Magazine. 1884.

MY OTHER ME.

CHILDREN, do you ever,
 In walks by land or sea,
Meet a little maiden
 Long time lost to me?

She is gay and gladsome,
 Has a laughing face,
And a heart as sunny;
 And her name is Grace.

Naught she knows of sorrow,
 Naught of doubt or blight;
Heaven is just above her—
 All her thoughts are white.

Long time since I lost her,
 That other Me of mine;
She crossed into Time's shadow
 Out of Youth's sunshine.

Now the darkness keeps her;
 And call her as I will,
The years that lie between us
 Hide her from me still.

I am dull and pain-worn,
 And lonely as can be—
Oh, children, if you meet her,
 Send back my other Me!

GRACE DENIO LITCHFIELD. 1849-.

WHAT HAVE I DONE?

I LAY my finger on Time's wrist to score
 The forward-surging moments as they roll;
Each pulse seems quicker than the one before,
 And lo! my days pile up against my soul
As clouds pile up against the golden sun:
Alas! what have I done? what have I done?

I never steep the rosy hours in sleep,
　　Or hide my soul as in a gloomy crypt;
No idle hands into my bosom creep;
　　And yet, as water-drops from house-eaves drip,
So, viewless, melt my days, and from me run:
Alas! what have I done? what have I done?

I have not missed the fragrance of the flowers,
　　Or scorned the music of the flowing rills
Whose numerous liquid tongues sing to the hours;
　　Yet rise my days behind me like the hills,
Unstarred by light of mighty triumphs won:
Alas! what have I done? what have I done?

Be still, my soul; restrain thy lips from woe;
　　Cease thy lament! for life is but the flower;
The fruit comes after death: how canst thou know
　　The roundness of its form, its grace and power?
Death is Life's morning; when thy work's begun,
Then ask thyself, What yet is to be done?

　　　　　　　　　LILLIEN BLANCHE FEARING. 1864–.
The Sleeping World, and Other Poems. 1887.

TRANSITION.

HER eyes looked out across this world of ours—
　　Seen through her lashes as a silken veil—
Wondering that striving mortals e'er could fail,
Startled to see the earth bear aught but flowers.

And all her senses seemed to watch and wait
For something that would touch and stir them all,
And something, lifeless yet, to being call;
　　She wished it come, yet, timid, feared her fate.

And ere she knew the name of Love, one day
(All flushed her cheek, and tear-bedewed her eyes,)
He kissed her lips.　With tender, sweet surprise
The woman lived—the child had passed away.

　　　　　　　STEPHEN DECATUR SMITH, JR. 1861–.
Hallo, My Fancy! 1887.

IV.

CHARLIE'S STORY.

I WAS sitting in the twilight,
　　With my Charlie on my knee,—
(Little two-year-old, forever
　　Teasing, "Talk a 'tory, pease, to me.")

"Now," I said, " 'talk' *me* a ' 'tory.' "
　　"Well," reflectively, "I'll 'mence.
Mamma, I did see a kitty,
　　Great—big—kitty, on the fence."

Mamma smiles.   Five little fingers
  Cover up her laughing lips.
"Is oo laughing?"   "Yes," I tell him,
  But I kiss the finger-tips,
And I say, "Now tell another."
  "Well," (all smiles) "now I will
    'mence.
Mamma, I did see a doggie,
  Great—big—doggie, on the fence."

    Springfield Republican, 9 Nov., 1877.

"Rather similar,—your stories,
  Aren't they, dear?"   A sober
  look
Swept across the pretty forehead,
  Then he sudden courage took.
"But I know a nice, new 'tory,
  'Plendid, Mamma!   Hear me 'mence.
Mamma, I—did—see—a—*elfunt*,
  Great—big—elfunt, on the fence!"

        Kate Upson Clark. 18—.

'SPÄCIALLY JIM.

I WUS mighty good-lookin' when I wus young,
  Peert an' black-eyed an' slim,
With fellers a-courtin' me Sunday nights,
  'Späcially Jim.

The likeliest one of 'em all wus he,
  Chipper an' han'som' an' trim;
But I tossed up my head an' made fun o' the crowd,
  'Späcially Jim.

I said I hadn't no 'pinion o' men,
  An' I wouldn't take stock in *him!*
But they kep' on a-comin' in spite o' my talk,
  'Späcially Jim.

I got so tired o' havin' 'em roun'
  ('Späcially Jim!)
I made up my mind I'd settle down
  An' take up with him.

So we wus married one Sunday in church,
  'Twas crowded full to the brim;
'Twas the only way to git rid of 'em all,
  'Späcially Jim.

        Bessie Morgan. 18—.

The Century Magazine. 1884.

AFEARED OF A GAL.

OH, darn it all!—afeared of her,
  And such a mite of a gal;
Why, two of her size rolled into one
  Won't ditto sister Sal!
Her voice is sweet as the whippoorwill's,
  And the sunshine's in her hair;

But I'd rather face a redskin's knife,
  Or the grip of a grizzly bear.
Yet Sal says, "Why, she's such a dear,
  She's just the one for you."
Oh, darn it all!—afeared of a gal,
  And me just six feet two!

Though she ain't any size, while I'm
  Considerable tall,
I'm nowhere when she speaks to me,
  She makes me feel so small.
My face grows red, my tongue gets
  hitched,
  The cussed thing won't go;
It riles me, 'cause it makes her think
  I'm most tarnation slow.
And though folks say she's sweet on me,
  I guess it can't be true.
Oh, darn it all!—afeared of a gal,
  And me just six feet two!

My sakes! just s'pose if what the folks
  Is saying should be so!
Go, Cousin Jane, and speak to her,
  Find out and let me know;
Tell her the gals should court the men,
  For isn't this leap-year?
That's why I'm kind of bashful like
  A waiting for her here;
And should she hear I'm scared of
  her,
  You'll swear it can't be true.
Oh, darn it all!—afeared of a gal,
  And me just six feet two!

ANONYMOUS.

A DITTY.

TIME hath some secrets he will ne'er disclose,
  Strive as we will, we may not all discover;
True to herself, sweet-fashioned as a rose,
  Jenny doth live, and yet she hath no lover!

Jenny doth live! ye hearts of slighted worth,
  Grieve not though fame with brightest wing doth hover
O'er spirits portionless! Fair as her birth,
  Jenny doth live, and yet she hath no lover.

GILBERT PETER KNAPP. 1855–.

A LITTLE BROTHER OF THE RICH.

TO put new shingles on old roofs;
  To give old women wadded skirts;
To treat premonitory coughs
  With seasonable flannel shirts;
To soothe the stings of poverty
  And keep the jackal from the door—
These are the works that occupy
  The Little Sister of the Poor.

She carries, everywhere she goes,
  Kind words and chickens, jams and
  coals;
Poultices for corporeal woes,
  And sympathy for downcast souls;
Her currant jelly—her quinine,
  The lips of fever move to bless.
She makes the humble sick-room shine
  With unaccustomed tidiness.

A heart of hers the instant twin
  And vivid counterpart is mine;
I also serve my fellow-men,
  Though in a somewhat different line.
The Poor and their concerns she has
  Monopolized, because of which
It falls to me to labor as
  A Little Brother of the Rich.

For their sake at no sacrifice
  Does my devoted spirit quail;
I give their horses exercise;
  As ballast on their yachts I sail.
Upon their Tally-Ho's I ride
  And brave the chances of a storm;
I even use my own inside
  To keep their wines and victuals
  warm.

Those whom we strive to benefit
  Dear to our hearts soon grow to
    be;
I love my Rich, and I admit
  That they are very good to me.

Succor the Poor, my sisters, I,
  While heaven shall still vouchsafe me
    health,
Will strive to share and mollify
  The trials of abounding wealth.

EDWARD SANFORD MARTIN. 1856–.

A Little Brother of the Rich, and Other Poems. 1888.

V.

LAMENT OF A MOCKING-BIRD.

SILENCE instead of thy sweet song, my bird,
  Which through the darkness of my winter days
Warbling of summer sunshine still was heard;
  Mute is thy song, and vacant is thy place.

The spring comes back again, the fields rejoice,
  Carols of gladness ring from every tree;
But I shall hear thy wild triumphant voice
  No more: my summer song has died with thee.

What didst thou sing of, oh, my summer bird?
  The broad, bright, brimming river, whose swift sweep
And whirling eddies by the home are heard,
  Rushing, resistless, to the calling deep.

What didst thou sing of, thou melodious sprite?
  Pine forests, with smooth russet carpets spread,
Where e'en at noonday dimly falls the light,
  Through gloomy blue-green branches overhead.

What didst thou sing of, oh, thou jubilant soul?
  Ever-fresh flowers and never-leafless trees,
Bending great ivory cups to the control
  Of the soft swaying orange-scented breeze.

What didst thou sing of, thou embodied glee?
  The wide wild marshes with their clashing reeds
And topaz-tinted channels, where the sea
  Daily its tides of briny freshness leads.

What didst thou sing of, oh, thou wingèd voice?
  Dark, bronze-leaved oaks, with silver mosses crowned,
Where thy free kindred live, love, and rejoice,
  With wreaths of golden jasmine curtained round.

These didst thou sing of, spirit of delight!
  From thy own radiant sky, thou quivering spark!
These thy sweet southern dreams of warmth and light,
  Through the grim northern winter drear and dark.

FRANCES ANN KEMBLE. 1809–93.

See, also, Vol. VI., page 500.

WHEN THE COWS COME HOME.

WITH klingle, klangle, klingle,
  'Way down the dusty dingle,
The cows are coming home;
Now sweet and clear, and faint and low,
The airy tinklings come and go,
Like chimings from some far-off tower,
Or patterings of an April shower
    That makes the daisies grow.
  Ko-kling, ko-klang, koklinglelingle,
  'Way down the darkening dingle
  The cows come slowly home;
And old-time friends, and twilight plays,
And starry nights and sunny days
Come trooping up the misty ways
    When the cows come home.

  With jingle, jangle, jingle,
  Soft sounds that sweetly mingle,
  The cows are coming home;
Malvine, and Pearl, and Florimel,
DeKamp, Redrose, and Gretchen Schell,
Queen Bess, and Sylph, and Spangled
    Sue—
Across the fields I hear her loo-oo,
    And clang her silver bell.
  Go-ling, go-lang, golinglelingle,
  With faint far sounds that mingle,
  The cows come slowly home;
And mother-songs of long-gone years,
And baby joys, and childish tears,
And youthful hopes, and youthful fears,
    When the cows come home.

  With ringle, rangle, ringle,
  By twos and threes and single,
  The cows are coming home.
Through the violet air we see the town,
And the summer sun a-slipping down;
The maple in the hazel glade
Throws down the path a longer shade,
    And the hills are growing brown.

  To-ring, to-rang, toringleringle,
  By threes and fours and single,
  The cows come slowly home:
The same sweet sound of wordless psalm,
The same sweet June-day rest and calm,
The same sweet scent of bud and balm,
    When the cows come home.

  With a tinkle, tankle, tinkle,
  Through fern and periwinkle,
  The cows are coming home;
A-loitering in the checkered stream,
Where the sun-rays glance and gleam,
Starine, Peachbloom, and Phœbe Phyllis
Stand knee-deep in the creamy lilies,
    In a drowsy dream.
  To-link, to-link, tolinklelinkle,
  O'er banks with buttercups a-twinkle
  The cows come slowly home;
And up through memory's deep ravine
Come the brook's old song and its old-
    time sheen,
And the crescent of the silver queen,
    When the cows come home.

  With a klingle, klangle, klingle,
  With a loo-oo, and moo-oo, and jingle,
  The cows are coming home;
And over there on Merlin hill,
Hear the plaintive cry of the whippoor-
    will;
The dew-drops lie on the tangled vines,
And over the poplars Venus shines,
    And over the silent mill.
  Ko-ling, ko-lang, kolinglelingle,
  With ting-a-ling and jingle,
  The cows come slowly home.
Let down the bars; let in the train
Of long-gone songs, and flowers, and rain;
For dear old times come back again
    When the cows come home.

        AGNES E. MITCHELL. 18—.

THE O'LINCOLN FAMILY.

A FLOCK of merry singing-birds were sporting in the grove;
  Some were warbling cheerily, and some were making love:
There were Bobolincon, Wadolincon, Winterseeble, Conquedle,—
A livelier set was never led by tabor, pipe, or fiddle,—

Crying, "Phew, shew, Wadolincon, see, see, Bobolincon,
Down among the tickletops, hiding in the buttercups!
I know the saucy chap, I see his shining cap
Bobbing in the clover there—see, see, see!"

Up flies Bobolincon, perching on an apple-tree,
Startled by his rival's song, quickened by his raillery,
Soon he spies the rogue afloat, curveting in the air,
And merrily he turns about, and warns him to beware!
"'Tis you that would a-wooing go, down among the rushes O!
But wait a week, till flowers are cheery,—wait a week, and ere you marry
Be sure of a house wherein to tarry!
Wadolink, Whiskodink, Tom Denny, wait, wait, wait!"

Every one's a funny fellow; every one's a little mellow;
Follow, follow, follow, follow, o'er the hill and in the hollow!
Merrily, merrily, there they hie; now they rise and now they fly;
They cross and turn, and in and out, and down in the middle, and wheel
    about,—
With a "Phew, shew, Wadolincon! listen to me, Bobolincon!—
Happy's the wooing that's speedily doing, that's speedily doing,
That's merry and over with the bloom of the clover!
Bobolincon, Wadolincon, Winterseeble, follow, follow me!"

Wilson Flagg. 1805–84.

See, also, Vol. VI., page 237.

THE LITTLE KNIGHT IN GREEN.

WHAT fragrant-footed comer
    Is stepping o'er my head ?
Behold, my queen ! the Summer!
    Who deems her warriors dead.
Now rise, ye knights of many fights,
    From out your sleep profound!
Make sharp your spears, my gallant
    peers,
    And prick the frozen ground.

Before the White Host harm her,
    We'll hurry to her aid;
We'll don our elfin armor,
    And every tiny blade
Shall bear atop a dewy drop,
    The life-blood of the frost,
Till from their king the order ring:
    "Fall back! the day is lost."

Now shame to knighthood, brothers!
    Must Summer plead in vain ?
And shall I wait till others
    My crown of sunshine gain ?

Alone this day I'll dare the fray,
    Alone the victory win;
In me my queen shall find, I ween,
    A sturdy paladin.

To battle! Ho! King Winter
    Hath rushed on me apace,—
My fragile blade doth splinter
    Beneath his icy mace.
I stagger back. I yield—alack!
    I fall. My senses pass.
Woe worth the chance for doughtiest
    lance
    Of all the House of Grass!

Last hope my heart gives over.
    But hark! a shout of cheer!
Don Daisy and Count Clover,
    Sir Buttercup, are here!
Behold! behold! with shield of gold
    Prince Dandelion comes.
Lord Bumble-Bee beats valiantly
    His rolling battle-drums.

My brothers leave their slumbers
  And lead the van of war;
Before our swelling numbers
  The foes are driven far.

The day's our own; but, overthrown,
  A little Knight in green,
I kiss her feet and deem it sweet
  To perish for my queen.

                KATHARINE LEE BATES. 18—,

The Springfield Republican. 1883.
      (*Author's revision.*)

WHAT SEES THE OWL?

HIS velvet wing sweeps through the night;
  With magic of his wondrous sight
He oversees his vast domain,
And king supreme of night doth reign.

Around him lies a silent world,
The day with all its noise is furled;
When every shadow seems a moon,
And every light a sun at noon.

How welcome from the blinding glare
Is the cool grayness of the air!
How sweet the power to reign, a king,
When day his banishment will bring!

For him the colorless moonlight
Burns brilliant, an aurora bright;
The forest's deepest gloom stands clear
From mystery and helpless fear.

He sees the silver cobwebs spun,
The dewdrops set the flowers have won,
The firefly's gleam offends his sight,
It seems a spark of fierce sunlight.

Clear winter nights when he so bold,
"For all his feathers, is a-cold,"
Sees the Frost-spirit fling his lace,
And fashion icicles apace.

At his weird call afar and faint
A sleepy echo, like the quaint
Last notes of some wild chant, replies
And mocks his solitude—and dies.

                ELIZABETH SEARS BATES. 18—,

The Overland Monthly. 1889.

A COUNTRY ROAD.

YELLOW with dust it sleeps in noonday's glare,
  Yellow with dust it stretches far away;
On the mossed wall the chipmunks frisk and play,
Where golden daisies broider all the air.
Now nature seems to dream 'mid fragrance rare,
  For summer silence holds unbroken sway,
  Till round the bend a creaking wain of hay
Comes lumbering down the drowsy thoroughfare;
Then all is still again.   The orchard trees
  Are motionless as the distant purple hills
    On which the shadows of the white clouds rest,
When suddenly the white-flecked clover seas
  All joyous tremble, while the bobolink trills
    His wildest melodies with sweet unrest.

RICHARD KENDALL MUNKITTRICK. 1853-.

Harper's Weekly. 188-.

THE WOOD-SPRITE.

HOW black, how bleak, how cold, how wild!
  Squirrels and mice don't know what's fun;
They skulk below in fur three-piled,
Nor show their nose till all is done;

How blows the snow, how branches bow,
Cut to and fro, lash high and low!
Till crack! alack, they snap and go.
O night of ruin, night of woe!
To-morrow, to the wood-folks' sorrow,
Many a fine tree, lying low
Will show with top-twigs in the snow.

But naught care I should pines fall, pat
I rise from 'neath them like the air;
Or, 'gainst the trunks blown, like a bat,
I cling and stay suspended there.
Or, should a spruce-bough scurry by,
With cones up-pointed, leaf-tufts trailed,
I board it, and away speed I,
The maddest voyage ever sailed.

I skip and skim, and bang and bump,
And bounce and jump, and thud and thump,
And chase ten devils round a stump;
Till rolled in snow, a frozen lump,
I tumble where some soul must stumble
Upon me—down he flounders plump
Like a lost soul at doomsday trump.

Last night, the deacon, hurrying past,
On good works bent, my form did find.
He picked me up and stood aghast,
But wrapped me from the bitter wind,
Then ran through banks and brakes and drifts,
And plunge he did, and slip, and slide,
And fall off rocks, and stick in rifts,
Before he reached his cold fire-side.

Then, while he plies the fire, and tries,
With puffing cheeks and smarting eyes,
His best to raise a flame—my cries
They drown the tempest, pierce the skies;
Hooting, calling, yelling, squalling,
Like everything that runs or flies,
To the good man's wild surprise.

ROGER RIORDAN. 1847-.

The Century Magazine. 1885.

WINTER WOODS.

ZIGZAG branches darkly traced
  On a chilly and ashen sky;
Puffs of powdery snow displaced
  When the winds go by.
Sudden voices in the air,—
  They are crooning a tale of woe,
And my heart is wooed to share
  The sadness of the snow.

Stillness in the naked woods,
  Save the click of a twig that breaks;
In these dim white solitudes,
  Nothing living wakes;—
Nothing, but a wandering bird,
  Which has never a song to sing,—
To my heart a whispered word
  And a dream of spring!

            GEORGE COOPER. 1840-.

The Atlantic Monthly. 1870.

THE SKATER.

BENEATH her skates the curved steel
  bars
Seemed like two naked scimitars
That gleam about the sandals in
The sword-dance of the Bedouin.
  And all around her flying feet
The ice mist flew unceasingly:

As free she was and full as fleet
As sea-gulls skimming o'er the sea.
  It was the sea in different guise.
Like Mercury she wore her wings,
  And deep within her fearless
    eyes
There lived the soul of flying things.

            ORTH HARPER STEIN.

VI.

WAIKIKI.

THE cocoa, with its crest of spears,
  Stands sentry 'round the crescent
    shore,
And algeroba, bent with years,
  Keeps watch beside the lanai door.
The cool winds fan the mango's cheek,
  The mynah flits from tree to tree,
And zephyrs to the roses speak
  Their sweetest words at Waikiki.

Like truant children of the deep
  Escaped behind a coral wall,
The lisping wavelets laugh and leap,
  Nor heed old ocean's stern recall.
All day they frolic with the sands,
  Kiss pink-lipped shells in wanton glee,
Make windrows with their patting hands,
  And, singing, sleep at Waikiki.

The closing curtain of the night
  Is shading down the gold to gray,
And on the reef the flaring light
  Of brown-armed fisher, far away,
Dyes red the waves that thunder by
  The sturdy bulwarks of the sea,
And breaking into ripplets, die
  Upon the breast of Waikiki.

Now come wild echoes through the air,
  And shadow of a rugged face,
With iron limbs and shoulders bare—
  The chieftain of a dusky race
Whose hostile front, with lifted lance,
  And war-prows flecking all the sea,
Swept through the palms with bold ad-
    vance
  Along the shores of Waikiki.

And all unchecked in martial course
  By menace or the spear of foe,
The misty columns move in force,
  Their chieftain leading as they go,
Up, up Nuuanu's rocky bed
  Till, looking down through clouds,
    they see
The beetling front of Diamond Head
  And silver sands of Waikiki.

On! on! the foe has reached the verge,
  And o'er the Pali's awful side,
With shout and stroke and battle-surge
  Is poured a shrieking human tide.
Then all is still; the work is done;
  And thus the shadows come to me
When twilight clouds, kissed by the sun,
  Have bronzed the shores of Waikiki.

  Tributes of Hawaiian Verse. 1882.

And then, with tropic murmurs blent,
  Come distant voices half divine;
While mingled with the ylangylang's
    scent
  Is breath of sage and mountain pine;
And from Diablo's vine-clad feet,
  From desert bleak and green Maumee,
Are wafted strains to me as sweet
  As e'er were heard at Waikiki.

O Waikiki! O scene of peace!
  O home of beauty and of dreams!
No haven in the isles of Greece
  Can chord the harp to sweeter themes;
For houries haunt the broad lanais,
  While scented zephyrs cool the lea,
And, looking down from sunset skies,
  The angels smile on Waikiki.

  ROLLIN MALLORY DAGGETT. 1831–.

UNDER THE PALMS.

PROUD is his heart, and strong his
    limb,
As his own desert's tiger brood,
And all my soul is lost in him!
What recked he then, my fierce Mahmoud,
Of turbaned Sheik or belted Khan,
When, 'neath the date-palm spreading
    wide,
With beating heart I saw him ride
Along the road to Toorkistan?
      Ah me!
Beside his saddle-girth to be!

Beneath the noonday's breathless heat
The whitening sand-leagues flame and
    glow;
At eve the oasis odors sweet
Across the darkening deserts blow.

But ne'er my hungry eyes may scan,
By garish day or evening-tide,
The war-troops of my hero ride
Along the road from Toorkistan.
      Ah me!
The night-birds haunt the rustling
    tree!

Up to my scarlet-woven tent
The way-worn warriors journey slow;
Why is yon silent rider bent
Upon his horse's saddle-bow?
Each eye is dim, each cheek is wan:
Why pale before your chieftain's bride?
The 'broidered burnos falls aside—
      'Tis he!
They bend their spear-points low to
    me!

  FREDERICK K. CROSBY. 1845–74.

  Into Light, and Other Poems. Privately printed. 1876.

A KING IN EGYPT.

I THINK I lie by the lingering Nile,
 I think I am one that has lain long while,
My lips sealed up in a solemn smile,
In the lazy land of the loitering Nile.

I think I lie in the Pyramid,
And the darkness weighs on the closed eyelid,
And the air is heavy where I am hid,
With the stone on stone of the Pyramid.

I think there are graven godhoods grim,
That look from the walls of my chamber dim,
And the hampered hand and the muffled limb
Lie fixed in the spell of their gazes grim.

I think I lie in a languor vast,
Numb, dumb soul in a body fast,
Waiting long as the world shall last,
Lying cast in a languor vast.

Lying muffled in fold on fold,
With the gum and the gold and the spice enrolled,
And the grain of a year that is old, old, old,
Wound around in the fine-spun fold.

The sunshine of Egypt is on my tomb;
I feel it warming the still, thick gloom,
Warming and waking an old perfume,
Through the carven honors upon my tomb.

The old sunshine of Egypt is on the stone;
And the sands lie red that the wind hath sown,
And the lean, lithe lizard at play alone
Slides like a shadow across the stone.

And I lie with the Pyramid over my head,
I am lying dead, lying long, long dead,
With my days all done, and my words all said,
And the deeds of my days written over my head.

                    HELEN THAYER HUTCHESON. 1860-86.

St. Nicholas. 1890.

RIVALS.

GRAY in the east,
 Gray in the west, and a moon.
Dim gleam the lamps of the ended feast
Through the misty dawn of June;

And I turn to watch her go
Swift as the swallows flee,
Side by side with Joaquin Castro,
Heart by heart with me.

Jasmine star afloat
In her soft hair's dusky strands,
Jasmine white is her swelling throat,
And jasmine white her hands.
Ah, the plea of that clinging hand
Through the whirl of that wild waltz
tune!
Lost—lost for a league of land,
Lying dark 'neath the sinking moon!

Over yon stream,
The casa rests on its hard clay floor,
Its red tiles dim in the misty gleam,
Old Pedro Vidal at the door,
And his small eye ranges keen
Over vistas of goodly land—
Brown hills, with wild-oat sweeps be-
tween,
Bought with his daughter's hand.

Tangled and wreathed,
The wild boughs over the wild streams
meet,
And over the swamp flowers musky-
breathed,
And the cresses at their feet;
And over the dimpled springs,
Where the deep brown shadows flaunt,
And the heron folds his ivory wings
And waits in his ferny haunt.

Side-scarred peaks
Where the gray sage hangs like a smoke,
And the vultures wipe their bloody beaks,
From the feast in the crotched oak:
You are Castro's, hemming his acres in;
And I his vaquero, who o'er you rove,
Hold wealth he would barter you all to
win—
The wealth of her broad sweet love.

Joaquin Castro
Rides up from her home where the
stream-mists hang,
And the cañon sides toss to and fro
The tread of his black mustang—
Half wild, a haughty beast,
Scarce held by the taut-drawn rein;
And a madness leaps into my breast,
And that wild waltz whirls in my brain.

The Overland Monthly. 1886.

By his mountain streams
We meet, and the waves glint through
the shades;
And we light the morn with long thin
gleams,
And wake it with clash of blades.
From some pale crag is borne
The owl's derisive laugh;
And the gray deer flies, like a shadow
of dawn,
From the tide it fain would quaff.

A sudden wheel,
Then away, away, and the far hush
rings
With hoof-beat, and chime of the spurrèd
heel;
And the blue air winds and sings
In the coils from each round gathering
strength,
Ere I rise in my saddle for truer throw,
That the rope may spring its serpent
length,
And drag from his seat my foe.

Was it an owl
Speedily flitting the trail across,
Or a twisted bough in its monk-like cowl
And robe of the long gray moss?
Or the race has frenzied the black's wild
brain?
He rears, to the stout rein gives no
heed,
Then backward, backward—curls and
mane
Intermingled, necks broken, rider and
steed.

Ah, señor,
She is mine. It was all long years ago.
And at eve, when we sit in our vine-hung
door,
She speaks of Joaquin Castro.
How they found him there; and sweet
drops start
From sweeter eyes. And who shall
know
That the brand of Cain burns red on my
heart,
Since the scar was spared my brow?

VIRGINIA PEYTON FAUNTLEROY. 18—.

ENGLAND.

THOU art as a lone watcher on a rock,
  With Saxon hair back-floating in the wind,
   Gazing where stranger ships, to doom consigned,
Upon the sullen ledges grind and knock.
Fair were the barks round which the breakers flock,
  Rich freights had they of treasure for mankind,
   And gallant were the hearts that left behind
The sea's broad buffet for the channel's shock.
Slow, slow the ship that brings thy liberties
  Cuts the white tempest or the bright, blue brine;
   And wanders oft before the whelming storm;
And ever the swift straits and shallows flees.
  But near, more near the haven's sheltering line,
  Up the long sea-curve rides its stately form.

                   RICHARD EDWIN DAY. 1852–.

Poems. 1888.

VII.

PRIVATE DEVOTION.

I LOVE to steal awhile away
  From every cumbering care,
And spend the hours of setting day
  In humble, grateful prayer.

I love, in solitude, to shed
  The penitential tear;
And all His promises to plead,
  Where none but God can hear.

I love to think on mercies past,
  And future good implore;

And all my cares and sorrows cast
  On Him whom I adore.

I love, by faith, to take a view
  Of brighter scenes in heaven;
The prospect doth my strength renew,
  While here by tempests driven.

Thus, when life's toilsome day is o'er,
  May its departing ray
Be calm as this impressive hour,
  And lead to endless day.

          PHŒBE HINSDALE BROWN. 1783–1861.

  Compressed in Nettleton's "Village Hymns" (1824) to these stanzas, from the original poem written at Ellington, Conn., 1818.

FOR DIVINE STRENGTH.

FATHER, in Thy mysterious presence kneeling,
  Fain would our souls feel all Thy kindling love;
For we are weak, and need some deep revealing
  Of trust, and strength, and calmness from above.

Lord, we have wandered forth through doubt and sorrow,
 And Thou hast made each step an onward one;
And we will ever trust each unknown morrow,—
 Thou wilt sustain us till its work is done.

In the heart's depths a peace serene and holy
 Abides, and when pain seems to have its will,
Or we despair,—oh, may that peace rise slowly,
 Stronger than agony, and we be still!

Now, Father, now, in Thy dear presence kneeling,
 Our spirits yearn to feel Thy kindling love;
Now make us strong, we need Thy deep revealing
 Of trust, and strength, and calmness from above.

1864.   SAMUEL JOHNSON. 1822–82.

See, also, Vol. VIII., page 61.

THE HOUR OF PEACEFUL REST.

THERE is an hour of peaceful rest
 To mourning wanderers given;
There is a joy for souls distrest,
A balm for every wounded breast,
 'Tis found alone in heaven.

There is a soft, a downy bed,
 Far from these shades of even—
A couch for weary mortals spread,
Where they may rest the aching head,
 And find repose, in heaven.

There is a home for weary souls
 By sin and sorrow driven;

When tossed on life's tempestuous shoals,
Where storms arise, and ocean rolls,
 And all is drear but heaven.

There faith lifts up her cheerful eye,
 To brighter prospects given;
And views the tempest passing by,
The evening shadows quickly fly,
 And all serene in heaven.

There fragrant flowers immortal bloom,
 And joys supreme are given;
There rays divine disperse the gloom:
Beyond the confines of the tomb
 Appears the dawn of heaven.

WILLIAM BINGHAM TAPPAN. 1794–1849.

Originally contributed to the Franklin Gazette, Philadelphia. 1818.

SONG OF THE SEEDS.

'TIS so dark, so dark here under the ground!
 We reach and we struggle, we know not where;
We long for something we have not found,
 We seek and we find not, but cannot despair.

It is warm and sweet here under the earth,
 And so peaceful too—why cannot we stay?
What is this change that is named a *birth?*
 And what is that wonderful thing called Day?

But a power is on us: we may not wait;
    Within us we feel it struggle and thrill,
While upward we reach to find our fate,
    And this ceaseless, mysterious want to fulfil.

They say that at last we shall reach the Air—
    Will breathing be freedom, and Light be Life ?
What mystic change shall we meet with there
    When the blossom shall crown this mute, strange strife ?

So, ending answerless, the song is done—
    The song so oft upon the earth begun,
Whose closing and triumphant harmonies
    Shall ne'er be sounded but beyond the skies.

                                 FLORENCE SMITH. 1845–71.
From the Memorial Volume, edited by H. W. Bellows. 1872.

A PRAYER.

A LITTLE time for laughter,
    A little space for song—
And tears that hurry after,—
    Ere we too go along.

Like ripples on the river,
    As light on wind-swept grain,

So passes our endeavor:
    We go, nor come again.

Then make me, O Eternal,
    Still, as thy forces are:
We thrive as grasses vernal,
    We fade as fades the star.

                GEORGE MELVILLE UPTON. 1861–.

The Overland Monthly. 1887.

WAITING.

A S little children in a darkened hall
    At Christmas-tide await the opening door,
    Eager to tread the fairy-haunted floor
Around the tree with goodly gifts for all,
Oft in the darkness to each other call—
    Trying to guess their happiness before—
    Or knowing elders eagerly implore
To tell what fortune unto them may fall:
So wait we in Time's dim and narrow room,
    And, with strange fancies or another's thought,
Try to divine before the curtain rise
The wondrous scene; forgetting that the gloom
    Must shortly flee from what the ages sought—
The Father's long-planned gift of Paradise.

                CHARLES HENRY CRANDALL. 1858–.

The New-York Tribune. 1882.

OLD AND YOUNG.

I.

THEY soon grow old who grope for
      gold
In marts where all is bought and sold;
  Who live for self, and on some shelf
  In darkened vaults hoard up their pelf,
Cankered and crusted o'er with mould.
For them their youth itself is old.

> *The Studio.* 1887.
>   *See, also, Vol. VII., page* 221.

II.

They ne'er grow old who gather gold
Where spring awakes and flowers un-
      fold;
  Where suns arise in joyous skies,
  And fill the soul within their eyes.
For them the immortal bards have sung,
For them old age itself is young.

CHRISTOPHER PEARSE CRANCH. 1813–92.

THE UNFINISHED PRAYER.

"NOW I lay,"—repeat it, darling.
    "Lay me," lisped the tiny lips
Of my daughter, kneeling, bending
  O'er her folded finger-tips.

"Down to sleep"—"To sleep," she mur-
    mured,
  And the curly head bent low;
"I pray the Lord," I gently added;
  You can say it all, I know.

"Pray the Lord"—the sound came
    faintly,

Fainter still—"My soul to keep";
Then the tired head fairly nodded,
  And the child was fast asleep.

But the dewy eyes half opened
  When I clasped her to my breast,
And the dear voice softly whispered,
  "Mamma, God knows all the rest."

Oh, the trusting, sweet confiding
  Of the child heart! Would that I
Thus might trust my Heavenly Father,
  He who hears my feeblest cry.

ANONYMOUS.

TO A DOUBTER.

I CANNOT say "Believe" to thee
  Whose lips from thought's clear springs have drunk.
  The questions of the age have sunk
Deep in thy quivering soul, I see.

For I should hear thee rightly say,
  "Whate'er is true, thy well-turned speech
  Doth not the mind's recesses reach
Nor light the spirit's hidden way."

Thy soul for certainty is sick,
  While they who wrangle over forms,
  Untroubled by faith's fiercer storms,
Feed well on sweets of rhetoric.

I see thee like a long-caged bird,
　　Thou beat'st thy bars with broken wing,
　　And flutterest, feebly echoing
The far-off music thou hast heard.

Oblivion tempts thee, yet be wise,
　　Walk on awhile in storm and shade;
　　These ghosts that haunt thy feet may fade;
Thought hath its cock-crow and sunrise.

Perhaps the unseen plan shall prove
　　More than thy noblest longings crave;
　　Thy life may sweep beyond the grave
Into a universe of love,

Where doubt may cease, wrong turn to right,
　　God's diverse ways be reconciled,
　　And thou so long His orphan child
Meet Him upon the hills of light.

　　　　　　　　　ARTHUR WENTWORTH HAMILTON EATON. 1854-.

Acadian Legends and Lyrics. 1889.

THERE IS A LAND IMMORTAL.

THERE is a land immortal,
　　The beautiful of lands;
Beside its ancient portal
　　A sentry grimly stands.
He only can undo it,
　　And open wide the door;
And mortals who pass through it
　　Are mortal nevermore.

That glorious land is Heaven,
　　And Death the sentry grim:
The Lord thereof has given
　　The opening keys to him;
And ransomed spirits, sighing
　　And sorrowful for sin,
Pass through the gate in dying,
　　And freely enter in.

Though dark and drear the passage
　　That leadeth to the gate,
Yet grace attends the message
　　To souls that watch and wait;
And at the time appointed
　　A messenger comes down,
And guides the Lord's anointed
　　From cross to glory's crown.

Their sighs are lost in singing;
　　They're blessèd in their tears;
Their journey heavenward winging,
　　They leave on earth their fears.
Death like an angel seeming,
　　"We welcome thee!" they cry:
Their eyes with glory gleaming,
　　'Tis life for them to die.

　　　　　　　　　THOMAS MACKELLAR. 1812-.

Hymns and Metrical Psalms. 1883.

ADDITIONAL SELECTIONS

1834—1889.

The matter in these supplementary pages was obtained and edited too late for presentation, under the chronological arrangement, in the main body of this Work.

ADDITIONAL SELECTIONS.

1834—1889.

David Crockett.

BORN in Limestone, Greene Co., Tenn., 1786. Fell in defence of the Alamo, Texas, 1836.

A NATIVE AMERICAN.

[*A Narrative of the Life of David Crockett, of the State of Tennessee. Written by Himself. 1834.*]

HIS PROLOGUE.

I DON'T know of any thing in my book to be criticised on by honourable men. Is it on my spelling?—that's not my trade. Is it on my grammar? —I hadn't time to learn it, and make no pretensions to it. Is it on the order and arrangement of my book?—I never wrote one before, and never read very many; and, of course, know mighty little about that. Will it be on the authorship of the book?—this I claim, and I'll hang on to it, like a wax plaster. The whole book is my own, and every sentiment and sentence in it. I would not be such a fool, or knave either, as to deny that I have had it hastily run over by a friend or so, and that some little alterations have been made in the spelling and grammar; and I am not so sure that it is not the worse of even that, for I despise this way of spelling contrary to nature. And as for grammar, it's pretty much a thing of nothing at last, after all the fuss that's made about it. In some places, I wouldn't suffer either the spelling, or grammar, or any thing else to be touch'd; and therefore it will be found in my own way.

But if any body complains that I have had it looked over, I can only say to him, her, or them—as the case may be—that while critics were learning grammar, and learning to spell, I, and " Doctor Jackson, L. L. D." were fighting in the wars; and if our books, and messages, and proclamations, and cabinet writings, and so forth, and so on, should need a little looking over, and a little correcting of the spelling and the grammar to make them fit for use, it's just nobody's business. Big men have more important matters to attend to than crossing their *t*'s—, and dotting their *i*'s—, and such like small things. But the "Government's" name is to the proclamation, and my name's to the book; and if I didn't write the book, the "Government" didn't write the proclamation, which no man *dares to deny!*   .   .   .

LOADED FOR BEAR.

I now was compel'd to move on more slowly; and was frequently falling over logs, and into the cracks made by the earthquakes, so that I was very much afraid I would break my gun. However I went on about three miles, when I came to a good big creek, which I waded. It was very cold, and the creek was about knee-deep; but I felt no great inconvenience from it just then, as I was all over wet with sweat from running, and I felt hot enough. After I got over this creek and out of the cane, which was very thick on all our creeks, I listened for my dogs. I found they had either treed or brought the bear to a stop, as they continued barking in the same place. I pushed on as near in the direction to the noise as I could, till I found the hill was too steep for me to climb, and so I backed and went down the creek some distance till I came to a hollow, and then took up that, till I come to a place where I could climb up the hill. It was mighty dark, and was difficult to see my way or any thing else. When I got up the hill, I found I had passed the dogs; and so I turned and went to them. I found, when I got there, they had treed the bear in a large forked poplar, and it was setting in the fork.

I could see the lump, but not plain enough to shoot with any certainty, as there was no moonlight; and so I set in to hunting for some dry brush to make me a light; but I could find none, though I could find that the ground was torn mightily to pieces by the cracks.

At last I thought I could shoot by guess, and kill him; so I pointed as near the lump as I could, and fired away. But the bear didn't come; he only clomb up higher, and got out on a limb, which helped me to see him better. I now loaded up again and fired, but this time he didn't move at all. I commenced loading for a third fire, but the first thing I knowed, the bear was down among my dogs, and they were fighting all around me. I had my big butcher in my belt, and I had a pair of dressed buckskin breeches on. So I took out my knife, and stood, determined, if he should get hold of me, to defend myself in the best way I could. I stood there for some time, and could now and then see a white dog I had, but the rest of them, and the bear, which were dark coloured, I couldn't see at all, it was so miserable dark. They still fought around me, and sometimes within three feet of me; but, at last, the bear got down into one of the cracks, that the earthquakes had made in the ground, about four feet deep, and I could tell the biting end of him by the hollering of my dogs. So I took my gun and pushed the muzzle of it about, till I thought I had it against the main part of his body, and fired; but it happened to be only the fleshy part of his foreleg. With this, he jumped out of the crack, and he and the dogs had another hard fight around me, as before. At last, however, they forced him back into the crack again, as he was when I had shot.

I had laid down my gun in the dark, and I now began to hunt for it; and, while hunting, I got hold of a pole, and I concluded I would punch him awhile with that. I did so, and when I would punch him, the dogs would jump in on him, when he would bite them badly, and they would jump out again. I concluded, as he would take punching so patiently, it might be that he would lie still enough for me to get down in the crack, and feel slowly along till I could find the right place to give him a dig with my butcher. So I got down, and my dogs got in before him and kept his head towards them, till I got along easily up to him; and placing my hand on his rump, felt for his shoulder, just behind which I intended to stick him. I made a lounge with my long knife, and fortunately stuck him right through the heart; at which he just sank down, and I crawled out in a hurry. In a little time my dogs all come out too, and seemed satisfied, which was the way they always had of telling me that they had finished him.

I suffered very much that night with cold, as my leather breeches, and every thing else I had on, was wet and frozen. But I managed to get my bear out of this crack after several hard trials, and so I butchered him, and laid down to try to sleep. But my fire was very bad, and I couldn't find any thing that would burn well to make it any better; and I concluded I should freeze, if I didn't warm myself in some way by exercise. So I got up, and hollered awhile, and then I would just jump up and down with all my might, and throw myself into all sorts of motions. But all this wouldn't do; for my blood was now getting cold, and the chills coming all over me. I was so tired, too, that I could hardly walk; but I thought I would do the best I could to save my life, and then, if I died, nobody would be to blame. So I went to a tree about two feet through, and not a limb on it for thirty feet, and I would climb up it to the limbs, and then lock my arms together around it, and slide down to the bottom again. This would make the insides of my legs and arms feel mighty warm and good. I continued this till daylight in the morning, and how often I clomb up my tree and slid down I don't know, but I reckon at least a hundred times.

In the morning I got my bear hung up so as to be safe, and then set out to hunt for my camp. I found it after awhile, and McDaniel and my son were very much rejoiced to see me get back, for they were about to give me up for lost. We got our breakfasts, and then secured our meat by building a high scaffold, and covering it over. We had no fear of its spoiling, for the weather was so cold that it couldn't.

We now started after my other bear, which had caused me so much trouble and suffering; and before we got him, we got a start after another, and took him also. We went on to the creek I had crossed the night before and camped, and then went to where my bear was, that I had killed in the crack. When we examined the place, McDaniel said he wouldn't have gone into it, as I did, for all the bears in the woods.

We took the meat down to our camp and salted it, and also the last one we had killed; intending, in the morning, to make a hunt in the harricane again.

We prepared for resting that night, and I can assure the reader I was in need of it. We had laid down by our fire, and about ten o'clock there came a most terrible earthquake, which shook the earth so, that we were rocked about like we had been in a cradle. We were very much alarmed; for though we were accustomed to feel earthquakes, we were now right in the region which had been torn to pieces by them in 1812, and we thought it might take a notion and swallow us up, like the big fish did Jonah.

In the morning we packed up and moved to the harricane, where we made another camp, and turned out that evening and killed a very large bear, which made *eight* we had now killed in this hunt.

The next morning we entered the harricane again, and in little or no time my dogs were in full cry. We pursued them, and soon came to a thick cane-brake, in which they had stop'd their bear. We got up close to him, as the cane was so thick that we couldn't see more than a few feet. Here I made my friend hold the cane a little open with his gun till I shot the bear, which was a mighty large one. I killed him dead in his tracks. We got him out and butchered him, and in a little time started another and killed him, which now made *ten* we had killed; and we know'd we couldn't pack any more home, as we had only five horses along; therefore we returned to the camp and salted up all our meat, to be ready for a start homeward next morning.

The morning came, and we packed our horses with the meat, and had as much as they could possibly carry, and sure enough cut out for home. It was about thirty miles, and we reached home the second day. I had now accommodated my neighbour with meat enough to do him, and had killed in all, up to that time, fifty-eight bears, during the fall and winter.

As soon as the time come for them to quit their houses and come out again in the spring, I took a notion to hunt a little more, and in about one month I killed forty-seven more, which made one hundred and five bears I had killed in less than one year from that time.   .   .   .

ON THE TRAIL FOR CONGRESS.

I found the sign was good, almost everywhere I went. On one occasion, while we were in the eastern counties of the district, it happened that we all had to make a speech, and it fell on me to make the first one. I did so after my manner, and it turned pretty much on the old saying, " A short horse is soon curried," as I spoke not very long. Colonel Alexander followed me, and then General Arnold come on.

The general took much pains to reply to Alexander, but didn't so much as let on that there was any such candidate as myself at all. He had been speaking for a considerable time, when a large flock of guinea-fowls came very near to where he was, and set up the most unmerciful chattering that ever was heard, for they are a noisy little brute any way. They so confused the general, that he made a stop, and requested that they might be driven away. I let him finish his speech, and then walking up to him, said aloud, " Well, general, you are the first man I ever saw that understood the language of fowls." I told him that he had not had the politeness to name me in his speech, and that when my little friends, the guinea-fowls, had come up and began to holler "Crockett, Crockett, Crockett," he had been ungenerous enough to stop, and drive *them* all away. This raised a universal shout among the people for me, and the general seemed mighty bad plagued. But he got more plagued than this at the polls in August, as I have stated before.

This election was in 1827, and I can say, on my conscience, that I was, without disguise, the friend and supporter of General Jackson, upon his principles as he laid them down, and as *"I understood them,"* before his election as president. During my two first sessions in Congress, Mr. Adams was president, and I worked along with what was called the Jackson party pretty well. I was re-elected to Congress, in 1829, by an overwhelming majority; and soon after the commencement of this second term, I saw, or thought I did, that it was expected of me that I was to bow to the name of Andrew Jackson, and follow him in all his motions, and mindings, and turnings, even at the expense of my conscience and judgment. Such a thing was new to me, and a total stranger to my principles. I know'd well enough, though, that if I didn't "hurra" for his name, the hue and cry was to be raised against me, and I was to be sacrificed, if possible. His famous, or rather I should say his in-*famous*, Indian bill was brought forward, and I opposed it from the purest motives in the world. Several of my colleagues got around me, and told me how well they loved me, and that I was ruining myself. They said this was a favorite measure of the president, and I ought to go for it. I told them I believed it was a wicked, unjust measure, and that I should go against it, let the cost to myself be what it might; that I was willing to go with General Jackson in every thing that I believed was honest and right; but, further than this, I wouldn't go for him, or any other man in the whole creation; that I would sooner be honestly and politically d—nd, than hypo-critically immortalized. I had been elected by a majority of three thousand five hundred and eighty-five votes, and I believed they were honest men, and wouldn't want me to vote for any unjust motion, to please Jackson or any one else; at any rate, I was of age, and was determined to trust them. I voted against this Indian bill, and my conscience yet tells me that I gave a good honest vote, and one that I believe will not make me ashamed in the day of judgment. I served out my term, and though many amusing things hap-pened, I am not disposed to swell my narrative by inserting them.

When it closed, and I returned home, I found the storm had raised against me sure enough; and it was echoed from side to side, and from end to end of my district, that I had turned against Jackson. This was considered the un-pardonable sin. I was hunted down like a wild varment, and in this hunt every little newspaper in the district, and every little pin-hook lawyer was engaged. Indeed, they were ready to print any and every thing that the in-genuity of man could invent against me. Each editor was furnished with the journals of Congress from head-quarters; and hunted out every vote I had missed in four sessions, whether from sickness or not, no matter; and each one was charged against me at *eight* dollars. In all I had missed about *seventy* votes, which they made amount to five hundred and sixty dollars; and they contended I had swindled the government out of this sum, as I had received my pay, as other members do. I was now again a candidate in 1830, while all the attempts were making against me; and every one of these little papers kept up a constant war on me, fighting with every scurrilous report they could catch.

Over all I should have been elected, if it hadn't been, that but a few weeks before the election, the little four-pence-ha'penny limbs of the law fell on a plan to defeat me, which had the desired effect. They agreed to spread out over the district, and make appointments for me to speak, almost everywhere, to clear up the Jackson question. They would give me no notice of these appointments, and the people would meet in great crowds to hear what excuse Crockett had to make for quitting Jackson.

But instead of Crockett's being there, this small-fry of lawyers would be there, with their saddle-bags full of the little newspapers and their journals of Congress; and would get up and speak, and read their scurrilous attacks on me, and would then tell the people that I was afraid to attend; and in this way would turn many against me. All this intrigue was kept a profound secret from me, till it was too late to counteract it; and when the election came, I had a majority in seventeen counties, putting all their votes together, but the eighteenth beat me; and so I was left out of Congress during those two years. The people of my district were induced, by these tricks, to take a stay on me for that time; but they have since found out that they were imposed on, and on re-considering my case, have reversed that decision; which, as the Dutchman said, "is as fair a ding as eber was."   .   .   .

NO MAN'S FIDO.

But one good thing was, and I must record it, the papers in the district were now beginning to say "fair play a little," and they would publish on both sides of the question. The contest was a warm one, and the battle well-fought; but I gained the day, and the Jackson horse was left a little behind. When the polls were compared, it turned out I had beat Fitz just two hundred and two votes, having made a mash of all their intrigues. After all this, the reader will perceive that I am now here in Congress, this 28th day of January, in the year of our Lord one thousand eight hundred and thirty-four; and that, what is more agreeable to my feelings as a freeman, I am at liberty to vote as my conscience and judgment dictates to be right, without the yoke of any party on me, or the driver at my heels, with his whip in hand, commanding me to ge-wo-haw, just at his pleasure. Look at my arms, you will find no party hand-cuff on them! Look at my neck, you will not find there any collar, with the engraving

> MY DOG.
>
> ANDREW JACKSON.

But you will find me standing up to my rack, as the people's faithful representative, and the public's most obedient, very humble servant,

DAVID CROCKETT.

Richard Adams Locke.

BORN in New York, N. Y., 1800.   DIED on Staten Island, N. Y., 1871.

FROM "THE MOON HOAX."

[*Great Astronomical Discoveries Lately Made by Sir John Herschel, LL.D., F.R.S., etc., at the Cape of Good Hope.—First Published in the " New York Sun" in August and September*, 1835, *from the " Supplement to the Edinburgh Journal of Science."—Reprint of* 1859.]

THE VALE OF THE TRIADS.

"THE dark expanse of waters to the south of the first great ocean has often been considered a fourth ; but we found it to be merely a sea of the first class, entirely surrounded by land, and much more encumbered with promontories and islands than it has been exhibited in any lunar chart.   One of its promontories runs from the vicinity of Pitatus (No. 19), in a slightly curved and very narrow line, to Bullialdus (No. 22), which is merely a circular head to it, 264 miles from its starting place.   This is another mountainous ring, a marine volcano, nearly burnt out, and slumbering upon its cinders. But Pitatus, standing upon a bold cape of the southern shore, is apparently exulting in the might and majesty of its fires.   The atmosphere being now quite free from vapor, we introduced the magnifiers to examine a large bright circle of hills which sweep close beside the western abutments of this flaming mountain.   The hills were either of snow-white marble or semi-transparent crystal, we could not distinguish which, and they bounded another of those lovely green valleys, which, however monotonous in my descriptions, are of paradisaical beauty and fertility, and like primitive Eden in the bliss of their inhabitants.   Dr. Herschel here again predicated another of his sagacious theories.   He said the proximity of the flaming mountain, Bullialdus, must be so great a local convenience to dwellers in this valley during the long periodical absence of solar light as to render it a place of populous resort for the inhabitants of all the adjacent regions, more especially as its bulwark of hills afforded an infallible security against any volcanic eruption that could occur.   We therefore applied our full power to explore it, and rich indeed was our reward.

" The very first object in this valley that appeared upon our canvas was a magnificent work of art.   It was a temple—a fane of devotion, or of science— which, when consecrated to the Creator, *is* devotion of the loftiest order ; for it exhibits his attributes purely free from the masquerade, attire, and blasphemous caricature of controversial creeds, and has the seal and signature of his own hand to sanction its aspirations.   It was an equitriangular temple, built of polished sapphire, or of some resplendent blue stone, which, like it, displayed a myriad points of golden light twinkling and scintillating in the sunbeams.   Our canvas, though fifty feet in diameter, was too limited to receive more than a sixth part of it at one view, and the first part that appeared was near the centre of one of its sides, being three square columns, six feet in diameter at its base, and gently tapering to a height of seventy feet. The intercolumniations were each twelve feet. We instantly reduced our magnitude, so as to embrace the whole structure in one view, and then indeed it was most beautiful. The roof was composed of some yellow metal, and divided into three compartments, which were not triangular planes inclining to the centre, but subdivided, curbed, and separated, so as to present a mass of violently agitated flames rising from a common source of conflagration and terminating in wildly waving points. This design was too manifest, and too skilfully executed to be mistaken for a single moment. Through a few openings in these metallic flames we perceived a large sphere of a darker kind of metal nearly of a clouded copper color, which they enclosed and seemingly raged around, as if hieroglyphically consuming it. This was the roof ; but upon each of the three corners there was a small sphere of apparently the same metal as the large centre one, and these rested upon a kind of cornice, quite new in any order of architecture with which we are acquainted, but nevertheless exceedingly graceful and impressive. It was like a half-opened scroll, swelling off boldly from the roof, and hanging far over the walls in several convolutions. It was of the same metal as the flames, and on each side of the building it was open at both ends. The columns, six on each side, were simply plain shafts, without capitals or pedestals, or any description of ornament ; nor was any perceived in other parts of the edifice. It was open on each side, and seemed to contain neither seats, altars, nor offerings ; but it was a light and airy structure, nearly a hundred feet high from its white glistening floor to its glowing roof, and it stood upon a round green eminence on the eastern side of the valley. We afterwards, however, discovered two others, which were in every respect fac-similes of this one ; but in neither did we perceive any visitants besides flocks of wild doves which alighted upon its lustrous pinnacles. Had the devotees of these temples gone the way of all living, or were the latter merely historical monuments ? What did the ingenious builders mean by the globe surrounded by flames ? Did they by this record any past calamity of *their* world, or predict any future one of *ours?* I by no means despair of ultimately solving not only these but a thousand other questions which present themselves respecting the objects in this planet ; for not the millionth part of her surface has yet been explored, and we have been more desirous of collecting the greatest possible number of new facts than of indulging in speculative theories, however seductive to the imagination.

"But we had not far to seek for inhabitants of this 'Vale of the Triads.' Immediately on the outer border of the wood which surrounded, at the distance of half a mile, the eminence on which the first of these temples stood, we saw several detached assemblies of beings whom we instantly recognized to be of the same species as our winged friends of the Ruby Colosseum near the lake Langrenus. Having adjusted the instrument for a minute examination, we found that nearly all the individuals in these groups were of a larger stature than the former specimens, less dark in color, and in *every respect* an improved variety of the race. They were chiefly engaged in eating a large yellow fruit like a gourd, sections of which they divided with their fingers, and ate with rather uncouth voracity, throwing away the rind. A smaller red fruit, shaped like a cucumber, which we had often seen pendent from trees having a broad dark leaf, was also lying in heaps in the centre of several of the festive groups; but the only use they appeared to make of it was sucking its juice, after rolling it between the palms of their hands and nibbling off an end. They seemed eminently happy, and even polite, for we saw, in many instances, individuals sitting nearest these piles of fruit, select the largest and brightest specimens, and throw them archwise across the circle to some opposite friend or associate who had extracted the nutriment from those scattered around him, and which were frequently not a few. While thus engaged in their rural banquets, or in social converse, they were always seated with their knees flat upon the turf, and their feet brought evenly together in the form of a triangle. And for some mysterious reason or other this figure seemed to be an especial favorite among them; for we found that every group or social circle arranged itself in this shape before it dispersed, which was generally done at the signal of an individual who stepped into the centre and brought his hands over his head in an acute angle. At this signal each member of the company extended his arms forward so as to form an acute horizontal angle with the extremity of the fingers. But this was not the only proof we had that they were creatures of order and subordination. . . . We had no opportunity of seeing them actually engaged in any work of industry or art; and so far as we could judge, they spent their happy hours in collecting various fruits in the woods, in eating, flying, bathing, and loitering about upon the summits of precipices. . . . But although evidently the highest order of animals in this rich valley, they were not its only occupants. Most of the other animals which we had discovered elsewhere, in very distant regions, were collected here, and also at least eight or nine new species of quadrupeds. The most attractive of these was a tall white stag with lofty spreading antlers, black as ebony. We several times saw this elegant creature trot up to the seated parties of the semi-human beings I have described, and browse the herbage close beside them, without the least manifestation of fear on its part or notice on theirs. The universal state of amity among all classes of lunar creatures, and the apparent absence of every carnivorous or ferocious species, gave us the most refined pleasure, and doubly endeared to us this lovely nocturnal companion of our larger but less favored world. Ever again when I 'eye the blue vault and bless the *useful* light,' shall I recall the scenes of beauty, grandeur, and felicity I have beheld upon her surface, not 'as *through* a glass darkly, but face to face'; and never shall I think of that line of our thrice noble poet,

> ' Meek Diana's crest
> Sails through the azure air, an island of the blest,'

without exulting in my knowledge of its truth."

With the careful inspection of this instructive valley, and a scientific classification of its animal, vegetable, and mineral productions, the astronomers closed their labors for the night; labors rather mental than physical, and oppressive from the extreme excitement which they naturally induced. A singular circumstance occurred the next day, which threw the telescope quite out of use for nearly a week, by which time the moon could be no longer observed that month. The great lens, which was usually lowered during the day, and placed horizontally, had, it is true, been lowered as usual, but had been inconsiderately left in a perpendicular position. Accordingly, shortly after sunrise the next morning, Dr. Herschel and his assistants, Dr. Grant and Messrs. Drummond and Home, who slept in a bungalow erected a short distance from the observatory circle, were awakened by the loud shouts of some Dutch farmers and domesticated Hottentots (who were passing with their oxen to agricultural labor), that the "big house" was on fire! Dr. Herschel leaped out of bed from his brief slumbers, and, sure enough, saw his observatory enveloped in a cloud of smoke.

Luckily it had been thickly covered, within and without, with a coat of Roman plaster, or it would inevitably have been destroyed with all its invaluable contents; but, as it was, a hole fifteen feet in circumference had been burnt completely through the "reflecting chamber," which was attached to the side of the observatory nearest the lens, through the canvas field on which had been exhibited so many wonders that will ever live in the history of mankind, and through the outer wall. So fierce was the concentration of the solar rays through the gigantic lens that a clump of trees standing in a line with them was set on fire, and the plaster of the observatory walls, all round the orifice, was vitrified to blue glass. The lens being almost immediately turned, and a brook of water being within a few hundred yards, the fire was soon extinguished, but the damage already done was not inconsiderable. The microscope lenses had fortunately been removed for the purpose of being cleaned, but several of the metallic reflectors were so fused as to be rendered useless. Masons and carpenters were procured from Cape Town with all possible despatch, and in about a week the whole apparatus was again prepared for operation.

Theodore Dwight Woolsey.

See, also, Volume VI., page 58, of this Work.

PLATO.

[*Eros, and Other Poems. Printed for Private Circulation.* 1880.]

Plato, who alone of all the Greeks touched the porch of truth.
　　　　　　EUSEB., *Præp. Evangel.*, XIII., 14.

I STOOD, methought, fast by heaven's outer gate,
　　When Plato, blindfold, humbly to the door
　Came with weak steps, if he might venture o'er
The threshold doubting, or without must wait.

When he, who in the Master's bosom lay,
  And saw the mysteries nearest to the throne,
  Drew nigh, and led the mild enthusiast on
Up to the Eternal Word, Heaven's fount of day.
"There," said the Apostle to the kindred mind,
  "Dwells truth, whose shadows thou wast fain to trace;
There beauty, which thy dreams wandered to find;
  There love, which swells beyond the soul's embrace."
Then loosed the bandage, and the sage, no more
A sage but saint, beheld and knelt to adore.

THE ECLIPSE OF FAITH.

THE shapes that frowned before the
    eyes
  Of the early world have fled,
And all the life of earth and skies,
  Of streams and seas, is dead.

Forgotten is the Titan's fame,
  The dread Chimæra now
Is but a mild innocuous flame
  Upon a mountain's brow,
Around whose warmth its strawberry
    red
The arbutus hangs and goatherds tread.

And now has Typho spent his rage,
  The Sirens now no more
Entice the song-struck mariner
  To give his voyage o'er.
The sailor past Messina hies,
And scorns the den where Scylla lies.

Leda's twin sons no more are seen
  In battle's hottest press,
Nor shine the wind-tost waves between
  To seamen in distress.

The muse is but the poet's soul,
  That looked towards Helicon,
And for its living thought divine
  Raised up a mountain throne.

But ah! is nought save fable slain
  In this new realm of thought?
Or has the shaft Primeval Truth
  And Truth's great Author sought?

Yes, wisdom now is built on sense;
  We measure and we weigh,
We break and join, make rare and dense,
  And reason God away.

The wise have probed this wondrous
    world,
  And searched the stars, and find
All curious facts and laws revealed,
  But no Almighty mind.

From thinking dust we mould the
    spheres,
  And shape earth's wondrous frame:
If God had slept a million years,
  All things would be the same.

O give me back a world of life,
  Something to love and trust,
Something to quench my inward strife,
  And lift me from the dust.

I cannot live with nature dead,
  Mid laws and causes blind;
Powerless on earth, or overhead,
  To trace the all-guiding mind;

Then boast that I have found the keys
  That time and space unlock,
That snatch from heaven its mysteries,
  Its fear from the earthquake shock.

Better the instinct of the brute
  That feels its God afar,
Than reason, to his praises mute,
  Talking with every star.

Better the thousand deities
  That swarmed in Greece of yore,
Than thought that scorns all mysteries
  And dares all depths to explore.

Better is childhood's thoughtless trust
  Than manhood's daring scorn;
The fear that creeps along the dust
  Than doubt in hearts forlorn.

And knowledge, if it cost so dear,
  If such be reason's day,

I'll lose the pearl without a tear,
  And grope my star-lit way.

And be the toils of wisdom curst
  If such the meed we earn;
If freezing pride and doubt are nurst,
  And faith forbid to burn.

Theodore Parker.

See, also, Volume VI., page 514, of this Work.

TWO SONNETS.

[From his Note-Book in the possession of Mr. Frank B. Sanborn.]

I.

TO me thou cam'st, the earliest lamp of light,
  When youthful day must sadly disappear;
A star prophetic in a world of night,
  Revealing what a heaven of love was near;
And full of rapture at thy joyous sight,
  I journeyed fearless on the starlight way;
A thousand other lights came forth on hight,
  But queenliest of all still shone *thy* ray:
O blessed lamp of Beauty and of Love,
  How long I've felt thy shining far away!
  Now, when the morn has chased the shadows gray,
Still guided by thy memory forth I rove.
I'll journey on, till dark still lighter prove,
  And Star and Pilgrim meet where all is Day.

II.

Thee, loved one, do the rocks and woodlands sing,
  And thee the Pine-tree waves with in the snow;
I see thy face in earliest flowers of spring,
  And feel thy kindness in the summer's glow;
  And, wander where I will, I inly know
That thou art with me still; and thy great heart
  Stands, a green pine-tree in the waste of snow,
Whereto I flee, and hold myself apart
  From all the wintry bitterness of Time;
And in thy presence I again am warm,
  Nor fear the tempest in Life's stormy clime,
But unafraid confront the wildest storm:
  For thee the winter and the tempests sing,
  And through the snow I feel the violets spring.

Composed in the Winter of 1853-4.

John Lothrop Motley.

See, also, Volume VII., page 253, of this Work.

GLIMPSES OF NOTED PEOPLE.

[*The Correspondence of John Lothrop Motley, D.C.L. Edited by George William Curtis.* 1889.]

BISMARCK.

WHEN I called, Bismarck was at dinner; so I left my card and said I would come back in half an hour. As soon as my card had been carried to him (as I learned afterwards) he sent a servant after me to the hotel, but I had gone another way. When I came back I was received with open arms. I can't express to you how cordially he received me. If I had been his brother, instead of an old friend, he could not have shown more warmth and affectionate delight in seeing me. I find I like him even better than I thought I did, and you know how high an opinion I always expressed of his talents and disposition. He is a man of very noble character, and of very great powers of mind. The prominent place which he now occupies as a statesman sought *him.* He did not seek it, or any other office. The stand which he took in the Assembly from conviction, on the occasion of the outbreak of 1848, marked him at once to all parties as one of the leading characters of Prussia. Of course I don't now go into the rights and wrongs of the matter, but I listened with great interest, as you may suppose, to his detailed history of the revolutionary events of that year, and his share in them, which he narrated to me in a long conversation which we had last night. He wanted me to stay entirely in his house, but as he has his wife's father and mother with him, and as I saw that it was necessary to put up a bed in a room where there was none, I decidedly begged off. I breakfasted there this morning, and am to dine there, with a party, to-day. To-morrow, I suppose, I shall dine there *en famille.* I am only afraid that the landlord here will turn me into the streets for being such a poor *consommateur* for him, and all I can do is to order vast quantities of seltzer water.

The principal change in Bismarck is that he has grown stouter, but, being over six feet, this is an improvement. His voice and manner are singularly unchanged. His wife I like very much indeed—very friendly, intelligent, and perfectly unaffected, and treats me like an old friend. In short, I can't better describe the couple than by saying that they are as unlike M. and Mme. de ——— as it is possible to be.

In the summer of 1851, he told me that the Minister, Manteuffel, asked him one day abruptly if he would accept the post of Ambassador at Frankfort, to which (although the proposition was as unexpected a one to him as if I should hear by the next mail that I had been chosen Governor of Massachusetts) he answered, after a moment's deliberation, yes, without another word. The King, the same day, sent for him, and asked him if he would accept the place, to which he made the same brief answer, "Ja." His Majesty expressed a little surprise that he made no inquiries or conditions, when Bismarck replied that anything which the King felt strong enough to propose to him, he felt strong enough to accept. I only write these details that you may have an idea of the man. Strict integrity and courage of character, a high sense of honor, a firm religious belief, united with remarkable talents, make up necessarily a combination which cannot be found any day in any Court; and I have no doubt that he is destined to be Prime Minister, unless his obstinate truthfulness, which is apt to be a stumbling-block for politicians, stands in his way.   .   .   .

Well, he accepted the post and wrote to his wife next day, who was preparing for a summer's residence in a small house they had taken on the seacoast, that he could not come because he was already established in Frankfort as Minister. The result, he said, was three days of tears on her part. He had previously been leading the life of a plain country squire with a moderate income, had never held any position in the Government or in diplomacy, and had hardly ever been to Court. He went into the office with a holy horror of the mysterious nothings of diplomacy, but soon found how little there was in the whole "galimatias." Of course my politics are very different from his, although not so antipodal as you might suppose, but I can talk with him as frankly as I could with you, and I am glad of an opportunity of hearing the other side put by a man whose talents and character I esteem, and who so well knows *le dessous des cartes.*

THACKERAY.

I believe you have never seen Thackeray. He has the appearance of a colossal infant, smooth, white, shiny ringlety hair, flaxen, alas, with advancing years, a roundish face, with a little dab of a nose upon which it is a perpetual wonder how he keeps his spectacles, a sweet but rather piping voice, with something of the childish treble about it, and a very tall, slightly stooping figure—such are the characteristics of the great "snob" of England. His manner is like that of everybody else in England—nothing original, all planed down into perfect uniformity with that of his fellow-creatures. There was not much more distinction in his talk than in his white choker or black coat and waistcoat. As you like detail, however, I shall endeavor to Boswellize him a little, but it is very hard work. Something was said of Carlyle the author. Thackeray said: "Carlyle hates everybody that has arrived; if they are on the road, he may perhaps treat them civilly." Mackintosh praised the description in the "French Revolution" of the flight of the King and Queen (which is certainly one of the most living pictures ever painted with ink), and Thackeray agreed with him, and spoke of the passages very heartily. Of the Cosmopolitan Club, Thackeray said: "Everybody is or is supposed to be a celebrity; nobody ever says anything worth hearing, and every one goes there with his white choker at midnight, to appear as if he had just been dining with the aristocracy. I have no doubt," he added, "that half of us put on the white cravat after a solitary dinner at home or at our club, and so go down among the Cosmopolitans."

I have strung these things together, not with the idea that the observations are worth sending (except for peculiar reasons, the last one), but because in your solitude I think that both you and Lily may be as easily amused as the friends of Mr. Peter Magnus were. This is what mainly occupies me when I go out; the thought that perhaps I may suck out something from the somewhat flat and gravelly soil of London society which may flower into a letter for your gratification is about the only one which gives me much satisfaction. Therefore I beg you to find the bouquets very fragrant and very brilliant, although they are in truth about as rare as dandelions.   .   .   .

In the evening I dined at Thackeray's. There were fifteen or sixteen people. I do not know any of their names. I sat between Thackeray's two daughters. They are both intelligent and agreeable. The youngest told me she liked " Esmond " better than any of her father's books. Thackeray, by the way, evidently considers that kind of thing his forte. He told me that he hated the " Book of Snobs," and could not read a word of it. The " Virginians," he said, was devilish stupid, but at the same time most admirable; but that he intended to write a novel of the time of Henry V., which would be his *capo d'opera,* in which the ancestors of all his present characters, Warringtons, Pendennises, and the rest, should be introduced. It would be a most magnificent performance, he said, and nobody would read it. After the ladies had left the house, we went downstairs and smoked cigars till into the small hours.

MACAULAY.

On Monday I dined with the Mackintoshes. Macaulay, Dean Milman, and Mr. and Mrs. Farrar composed the party. Of course you would like a photograph of Macaulay, as faithfully as I can give it. He impressed me on the whole agreeably. To me, personally, he spoke courteously, respectfully; showed by allusion to the subject in various ways that he was quite aware of my book and its subject, although I doubt whether he had read it. He may have done so, but he manifested no special interest in me. I believe that he is troubled about his health (having a kind of bronchial or asthmatic cough), and that he rarely dines out nowadays, so that it is perhaps a good deal of a compliment that he came on this occasion on purpose to meet me. His general appearance is singularly commonplace. I cannot describe him better than by saying he has exactly that kind of face and figure which by no possibility would be selected, out of even a very small number of persons, as those of a remarkable personage. He is of the middle height, neither above nor below it. The outline of his face in profile is rather good. The nose, very slightly aquiline, is well cut, and the expression of the mouth and chin agreeable. His hair is thin and silvery, and he looks a good deal older than many men of his years; for, if I am not mistaken, he is just as old as his century, like Cromwell, Balzac, Charles V., and other notorious individuals. Now those two impostors, so far as appearances go, Prescott and Mignet, who are sixty-two, look young enough, in comparison, to be Macaulay's sons. The face, to resume my description, seen in front, is blank, and as it were badly lighted. There is nothing luminous in the eye, nothing impressive in the brow. The forehead is spacious, but it is scooped entirely away in the region where benevolence ought to be, while beyond rise reverence, firmness, and self-esteem, like Alps on Alps. The under eyelids are so swollen as almost to close the eyes, and it would be quite impossible to tell the color of those orbs, and equally so, from the neutral tint of his hair and face, to say of what complexion he had originally been. His voice is agreeable, and its intonations delightful, although that is so common a gift with Englishmen as to be almost a national characteristic.

As usual, he took up the ribands of the conversation, and kept them in his own hand, driving wherever it suited him. I believe he is thought by many people a bore, and you remember that Sydney Smith spoke of him as "our Tom, the greatest engine of social oppression in England." I should think he might be to those who wanted to talk also. I can imagine no better fun than to have Carlyle and himself meet accidentally at the same dinner-table with a small company. It would be like two locomotives, each with a long train, coming against each other at express speed. Both, I have no doubt, could be smashed into silence at the first collision. Macaulay, however, is not so dogmatic or so outrageously absurd as Carlyle often is, neither is he half so grotesque or amusing. His whole manner has the smoothness and polished surface of the man of the world, the politician, and the new peer, spread over the man of letters within. I do not know that I can repeat any of his conversation, for there was nothing to excite very particular attention in its even flow. There was not a touch of Holmes's ever-bubbling wit, imagination, enthusiasm, and arabesqueness. It is the perfection of the commonplace, without sparkle or flash, but at the same time always interesting and agreeable. I could listen to him with pleasure for an hour or two every day, and I have no doubt I should thence grow wiser every day, for his brain is full, as hardly any man's ever was, and his way of delivering himself is easy and fluent.

BROUGHAM.

I was introduced to Lord Brougham before dinner. He shook hands cordially, and expressed himself as glad to make my acquaintance, but he did not seem to "pant" so much as might have been expected. We soon went to dinner, and his place was at the opposite end of the table from mine, so that our acquaintance for the present is limited. I have no doubt I shall see more of him, but to tell you the truth I fear he is a mere wreck. Let me give you a photograph, while his grotesque image still lingers in the camera-obscura of my brain. He is exactly like the pictures in "Punch," only "Punch" flatters him. The common pictures of Palmerston and Lord John are not like at all to my mind, but Brougham is always hit exactly. His face, like his tongue and his mind, is shrewd, sharp, humorous. His hair is thick and snow-white and shiny; his head is large and knobby and bumpy, with all kinds of phrenological developments, which I did not have a chance fairly to study. The rugged outlines or headlands of his face are wild and bleak, but not forbidding. Deep furrows of age and thought and toil, perhaps of sorrow, run all over it, while his vast mouth, with a ripple of humor ever playing around it, expands like a placid bay under the huge promontory of his fantastic and incredible nose. His eye is dim and could never have been brilliant, but his voice is rather shrill, with an unmistakable Northern intonation; his manner of speech is fluent, not garrulous, but obviously touched by time; his figure is tall, slender, shambling, awkward, but of course perfectly self-possessed. Such is what remains at eighty of the famous Henry Brougham. . . . .

There certainly never was a great statesman and author who so irresistibly suggested the man who does the comic business at a small theatre as Brougham. You are compelled to laugh when you see him, as much as at Keeley or Warren. Yet there is absolutely nothing comic in his mind. On the contrary, he is always earnest, vigorous, impressive; but there is no resisting his nose. It is not merely the configuration of that wonderful feature which surprises you, but its mobility. It has the litheness and almost the length of the elephant's proboscis, and I have no doubt he can pick up pins or scratch his back with it as easily as he could take a pinch of snuff. He is always twisting it about in quite a fabulous manner.

Robert Traill Spence Lowell.

See, also, Volume VII., page 311, of this Work.

THE SEARCH FOR FATHER DE BRIE.

[*The New Priest in Conception Bay.* 1858.—*Revised Edition of* 1889.]

IT was speedily arranged that they should push over to the other side of the Barrens; and while one went straight on to New Harbor, the rest should take every opening through the woods, and every path into the Barrens, and follow it out. Skipper Edward Ressle and Skipper Abram Marchant, it was said, had gone along the Bay Road, to cross from other points.

The only hasty preparations now made had been to put off every unnecessary weight to go back with the horses. Some extra coats, and several bottles of spirits, the advancing party took with them. Skipper Isaac gave the parting directions to the men who took the beasts back.

"Ef snow doesn't come in an hour's time, an' keep on, then, an hour after that, again come in wi' the horses, an' bide an hour, or thereabouts. Ef we'm not here by that time, we shall stay a' t'other side."

Many had come up during the short delay, and among them came, panting, the Parson's dog, who had not been able to keep up with his master. As they were now all foot-travellers, he had no difficulty, and went before them in the dreary path toward the great waste of snow over which the dreary wind came blowing sharply.

The dog mounted the hillock, a little way within the Barrens, and giving a short, sharp bark, plunged down the other side.

The men all rushed together; and in the gulch at the foot of the opposite rise lay, black upon the snow, fair in the mid-pathway, a still body, with the dog nozzling at it.

It was a drift two or three feet deep, in and upon which the still body lay. The cheek of the right side was next the snow; the head was bare; the left hand holding, or seeming to hold, the hat; while the right arm was curved about the head. The outside coat was partly open, from the top downwards, as if the wearer might have unbuttoned it when heated.

The whole attitude was that of one who had laid himself down to sleep at summer-noon, and the face was lovely as in sleep; the eyelids were not fast closed; there was a delicate color in the cheek, and the lips were red. There was a bright, conscious look, too, as of one that was scarcely asleep even.

"Thank God! he's alive!" said young Mr. Urston, speaking first. "Father Ignatius!" he called, taking him by the hand; then, correcting himself, "Mister De Brie!"

"Ay! he'll never spake to yon name, no more," said the Protestant Jesse.

The Parson, having quickly tried the wrist, was now feeling within the clothing, over the heart, and looking anxiously into the face.

The hair was blown restlessly by the wind; but there was no waking, nor any self-moving of the body.

"N'y," said Skipper George, gravely, "I'm afeared this is n' livun.—Oh! Oh!"

"I saw a house not but a step or two off, 's we come along," said Mr. Bangs, who had been chafing the hands with brandy, and had tenderly rubbed a little, with his finger, inside the nostrils.

Mr. Wellon, rising from the snow, shook his head and turned away. "No, no," he said, as if to the question of life;—"*and he'd got into the right road!*"

"Why, he's warm, sir," urged Urston; "certainly, he's warm!" The Constable felt of the flesh and said nothing.

"Shall us take un to the tilt?" asked Jesse. "It's Will Ressle's Mr. Banks manes. He's close by."

"By all means!" answered the Parson. "Yes!" "Yes!" said Skipper Isaac and the bystanders.

"See, sir!" said Skipper George, "'e didn' fall down. 'E've laid himself down to rest, most like, where the snow was soft, and falled asleep. That's bin the w'y of it. I've bin a'most so far gone, myself, sir, afore now."

"See how the hair is smoothed away from his temples," said young Urston.

"'Twas the dog!" answered the old fisherman, tenderly, "wi' tryun to bring un to. Yes," he added, "'e was out o' the path, when the good n'ybors from t'other side comed along, an 'e got into un agen, after—an' 'e was tired when 'e comed to this heavy walkun, an' so— What'll come o' the poor lady!"

As they lifted the body carefully out of the snow, to bear it away, a new voice spoke:

"Won't ye put more clothing on um, for it's blowing bitter cold?"

Father Terence had made his way from New Harbor and approached the group in silence. He offered, for a wrapper, his own great-coat, which he had taken off.

"We've agot store o' wrappuns, sir; many thanks to you, sir, all the same," answered Jesse Hill, very heartily; and others, too, made their acknowledgments. They wrapped the body, from head to foot, in their blankets, hastily.

Mr. Wellon saluted Father Terence, saying that "he had very little hope—indeed, he feared that there was no hope—of that body being restored to life."

"Oh, dear! I fear not, I fear not!" said Father Terence, wiping gentle tears away. "Why *would* he come? Or why did I hinder um comin' last night?—God have mercy upon um! *Absolve, quesumus Domine, animam ejus,*" he added, privately, or something to that effect.

Skipper Isaac held the body against his own; Jesse and Isaac Maffen and young Mr. Urston helped to bear it; and they went, accompanied by all the others, as fast as they could go, through the snow, toward the tilt. Skipper George bore the hat, upon which the grasp of the owner's cold hand had not been fast. "Eppy," who had done his dumb part before any, now followed meekly behind. Behind all came the cold, hard wind from the Barrens, whirling the snow from time to time. The sky over all was hidden by thick clouds, foreboding storm.

Within the tilt all that they knew how to do was done thoroughly. More than once some one of those engaged exclaimed that the flesh was growing warmer; but life did not come back, and the flesh grew surely colder. The body was dead; and they gave over their useless work upon it, and clothed it as before. There it lay; no priest, no layman, no husband, no father, no man!—but it was sacred, and it was reverently treated, as belonging to Christ, who would give it life again.

Some said,—among themselves,—that Father O'Toole had not stayed long.

"What more could 'e do?" asked Gilpin. "'E did more 'n many would;"—"an' 'e spoke proper feelun, like," said others. "Bless the old gentleman!"

Crowds had been gathering about the place where the melancholy work was going on; these the Constable and Mr. Skilton and William Frank occupied, drawing them a little apart, that there might be no hindrance, from the numbers, to those who were busy about the dead. The sad, short story stilled and saddened all. "Dead!"—"Is 'e dead?"—"so near home, too!"—"It's pity for un!"—"But 'e died happy, however!" said different voices.

Presently snow, from the thick sky, began to be borne upon the wind.

Gilpin, at this, hastened to the door, and others, coming out, met him.

"How'll we carry un?" the Constable asked, in a low voice. "O' horseback?"

"We was just spakun," said Jesse, "'twould look like mockun the dead, to take un ridun, to my seemun."

"Ay, but we've got to be quick about it; the snow's coming!"

"What's to hender we carryun? sure it's more feelun. We wouldn' begredge walkun all the w'y to B'y Harbor, ef 'twas to B'y Harbor, even ef it snowed, itself."

"It would be long waiting for a slide," said the Constable.

" An' we could'n have un bide in the cold, here, while we was w'itun," said Jesse, "in course."

It was arranged that one or two of the young men, on the best horses, should make their way at the utmost speed to James Bishop's, the nearest neighborly house in Castle Bay, and bring his sled or "slide," and, in the mean time, relays of bearers were to carry the body onward with what haste they could.

The crowd making a long procession, both before and behind the bearers, trampled the snow, for the most part in silence. Up the hills and down, many men taking turns at bearing the body, they made their way between the woods; while sometimes the snow fell thickly, and sometimes the thick clouds could be seen before them and overhead.

Three heavy miles they had got over, when the slide met them; and then the burden was transferred to it; a sort of dasher, or fender, of boughs was speedily set up to keep off the snow thrown by the horse's feet; and they went on: the Parson, Skipper George, Skipper Isaac, Skipper Henry, Skipper Edward, the Constable, and others of chief authority and dignity, attended at the sides and behind the sledge; all beside giving place to them. Suddenly there was a commotion, making itself felt from the foremost; and then the whole procession opened to either side, leaving the road bare between.

" Cast off the horse!" cried Skipper George in a quick low tone, seeing who was coming. The order was obeyed, as hastily as possible, and then the slide was left alone, in the middle of the way, while the crowd at each side stood huddled upon itself, and hushed.

" Oh, I knew it! Oh!" said a woman's voice, heard by every one, with such a moan of wretchedness that every man seemed to start, as if it were an appeal to himself. Mrs. Barrè, pale as death, with tears streaming down her cheeks, and with light snow lying upon her dark hair and on many parts of her black dress—bearing in her hand (as she had borne, hours before) a letter—rushed between the sundered crowds, and at the side of the sledge fell down across the muffled load that lay upon it. Every person near drew away.

Great passion appropriates absolutely to itself the time and place, and makes all other things and persons subordinate and accessory.

For this widowed lady's sorrow the earth and sky were already fitted; and so were, not less, the kind hearts of these men and women.

She lay with her face buried in the folds of the cloak which Mr. Wellon had spread over her husband's body, and uttered a fondling murmur against the wall of that desolated chamber, as, not long ago, she had murmured fondly against the strong, warm bosom of her recovered love. Many by-standers sobbed aloud.

Then she lifted her head, and turned down the covering from the face.

" Oh, Walter!" she said, clasping her two hands under the heavy head, and gazing at the stiffening features, "Oh, my noble husband!—My beautiful, noble husband!" then, shaking her head, while the tears dropped from her eyes, said, in a broken voice: "Is this all, Walter? Is this the end?—Yes, and it's a good end!" And again she buried her face on the dead bosom. " Well!—Oh, well! I did not seek you for myself!—It never was for myself! No!—No!"

The effort to subdue the human love to the divine triumphed in the midst of tears.

By-and-by she rose up, and with streaming eyes and clasped hands turned toward the Minister and said:

"I am ready, Mr. Wellon! Let us go! God's will be done!"

She stooped once more; looked with intense love and sorrow at the face, wiped her tears from the cold features, covered them again, carefully, and turned her face toward the rest of the way, homeward.

The Constable made a gesture to Jesse Hill and young Mr. Urston, and the horse was again harnessed to the slide. The Parson, leading his horse (which had been brought so far on the return, by one of the young men), came to Mrs. Barrè's side and took her arm in his. He begged her to allow herself to be lifted to the saddle, and to ride. Skipper George, also, had come forward to suggest the same thing.

"It is'n fittun the lady should walk home, sir," said he to the Pastor, apart.

Mrs. Barrè heard and understood, and answered:

"Would it make the load too heavy—?—" she finished with a longing look the sentence which was not finished with words.

The fishermen at first hesitated at the thought of her going upon the sledge that bore her husband's corpse.

"It wouldn't be too *heavy*," one of them said; and as if no objection could be made, she went, and, putting her arm tenderly underneath, lifted the body, seated herself upon the bier, taking the muffled head in her lap, and bent over it, lost to all things else.

All other arrangements for riding and walking having been quietly made, the procession again set forward towards home faster than before. The snow at times fell fast; but in about an hour more they were descending the high hill into Castle Bay; and before them lay the great black sea, with its cold bordering of white.

They passed along the chilly beach. At one point, whether consciously or unconsciously, Mrs. Barrè lifted her head and looked toward both sea and land. On the landward side stretched a little valley, with a knoll and rock and tree at its northern edge; a sweet spot in summer, but now lonely and desolate. She gave a sort of cry, and turned from the sight.

"O my God, thou knowest!" she could be heard to say, sobbing over her husband's body; and she looked up no more until, in another hour, with the cold stars and drifting clouds overhead, they had reached her desolate house.

"My dear brethren," said our priest, "we have not lost our Sunday; let us close this day with prayer!"

He and all the men stood, heedless of the wintry wind, uncovered before God, and he said:

"We thank Thee, O Merciful Father, that Thou hast given to us this, our brother's body, to lay in our hallowed ground; but, above all, for the hope that his soul, washed in the blood of the immaculate Lamb who was slain to take away the sins of the world, has been presented without spot before Thee. Give our sister, we beseech Thee, strength and peace; have her and us in Thy safe-keeping, and bring us to Thy heavenly house, through Jesus Christ, our Lord."

The congregation having been dismissed with the blessing, our priest and the chief men reverently carried the body into the parlor, and disposed it there, amid the memorials of happy former years, and arranged a watch.

George Copway.

BORN in Ontario Co., Canada, N. W., 1818. DIED at Pontiac, Mich., 1869.

THE EDUCATION OF A YOUNG CHIEF.

[Recollections of a Forest Life: or, the Life and Travels of Kah-ge-ga-gah-bowk, or George Copway, Chief of the Ojibway Nation. 1847.—Second Edition. 1851.]

I WAS born in Nature's wide domain! The trees were all that sheltered my infant limbs—the blue heavens all that covered me. I am one of Nature's children; I have always admired her; she shall be my glory; her features—her robes, and the wreath about her brow—the seasons—her stately oaks, and the evergreens—her hair, ringlets over the earth—all contribute to my enduring love of her; and wherever I see her, emotions of pleasure roll in my breast, and swell and burst like waves on the shores of the ocean, in prayer and praise to Him who has placed me in her hand. It is thought great to be born in palaces, surrounded with wealth; but to be born in Nature's wide domain is greater still!   .   .   .   .

I remember the tall trees, and the dark woods—the swamp just by, where the little wren sang so melodiously after the going down of the sun in the west—the current of the broad river Trent—the skipping of the fish, and the noise of the rapids a little above. It was here I first saw the light; a little fallen-down shelter, made of evergreens, and a few dead embers, the remains of the last fire that shed its genial warmth around, were all that marked the spot. When I last visited it, nothing but fir-poles stuck in the ground, and they were leaning on account of decay. Is this dear spot, made green by the tears of memory, any less enticing and hallowed than the palaces where princes are born? I would much more glory in this birthplace, with the broad canopy of heaven above me, and the giant arms of the forest trees for my shelter, than to be born in palaces of marble studded with pillars of gold! Nature will be Nature still, while palaces shall decay and fall in ruins. Yes, Niagara will be Niagara a thousand years hence! The rainbow, a wreath over her brow, shall continue as long as the sun, and the flowing of the river—while the work of art, however impregnable, shall in atoms fall!

Our wigwam we always carried with us wherever we went. It was made in the following manner: Poles were cut about fifteen feet long; three with crotches at the end, which were stuck in the ground some distance apart, the upper ends meeting, and fastened with bark; and then other poles were cut in circular form and bound round the first, and then covered with plaited reeds, or sewed birch-bark, leaving an opening on the top for the smoke to escape. The skins of animals formed a covering for a gap, which answered for a door. The family all sat, tailor-fashion, on mats. In the fall and winter they were generally made more secure, for the purpose of keeping out the rain and cold. The covering of our wigwam was always carried by my mother, whenever we went through the woods. In the summer it was easier and pleasanter to move about from place to place than in the winter. In the summer we had birch-bark canoes, and with these we travelled very rapidly and easily. In the winter everything was carried upon the back. I have known some Indians carry a whole deer—not a small one, but a buck. If an Indian could lift up his pack off the ground by means of his arms, it was a good load, not too light nor too heavy. I once carried 196 pounds weight of flour, twelve pounds of shot, five pounds of coffee, and some sugar, about a quarter of a mile, without resting—the flour was in two bags. It felt very heavy. This was since I travelled with the missionaries, in going over one of the portages in the west.

Our summer houses were made like those in gardens among the whites, except that the skeleton was covered with bark.   .   .   .   .

My father generally took one or two families with him when he went to hunt; all were to hunt, and place their gains into one common stock till spring (for they were often out all winter), when a division took place.

The change of seasons changed also our mode of living, as well as the places where we had our wigwams. In the fall we gathered the wild rice, and in the winter we were in the interior. Some winters we suffered most severely, on account of the depth of snow, and the cold; our wigwams were often buried in snow. We not only suffered from the snow and the cold, but from hunger. Our party would be unable to hunt, and being far from the white settlements, we were often in want of food.   .   .   .   .

My father and another Indian, by the name of Big John, and myself, went out hunting; my father left his family near the mission station, living in the wigwam. While we were out on the hunting-grounds, we found out that some Indians had gone before us on the route up the river, and every day we gained upon them; their tracks were fresh. The river and the lakes were frozen, and we had to walk on the ice. For some days together we did not fire a gun, for fear they would hear it and go from us, where we could not find them. At length we found them by the banks of the river—they were Nah-doo-ways, or Mohawks, from Bay Quinty; there were seven of them, tall fellows. We shook hands with them; they received us kindly. My father had determined to take all they had, if we should overtake them. After they gave us a good dinner of boiled beaver, my father stepped across the fire and ripped open two packs of beaver furs, that were just by him. He said to them: "We have only one custom among us, and that is well known to all; this river and all that is in it are mine. I have come up the river behind you, and you appear to have killed all before you. This is mine, and this is mine," he said, as he touched with the handle of his tomahawk each of the packs of beaver, otter, and muskrat skins. I expected every moment to see my father knocked down with a tomahawk, but none dared touch him; he counted the skins, and then threw them across the fire-place to us. After this was done, the same thing took place with the guns; only one was left them to use on their way home. He talked to them by signs, and bade them, as the sailors say, "weigh anchor, and soon be under way"; they left, and we took possession of the temporary wigwam they had built. We never saw them afterwards on our hunting-grounds, though some of them have been there since.

My father was ever kind and affectionate to me, particularly after the death of my brother, which was occasioned by the going off of a gun, the load passing through the arm, and so fractured it that it soon mortified and caused his death. He believed in persuasion; I know not that he ever used harsh means, but would talk to me for hours together. As soon as it was dark he would call me to his side and begin to talk, and tell me that the Great Spirit would bless me with a long life if I should love my friends, and particularly the aged. He would always take me with him when going anywhere near, and I learned his movements, for I watched him going through the woods. Often would he tell me that when I should be a man that I must do so and so, and do as he did, while fording the rivers, shooting the deer, trapping the beaver, etc. I always imitated him while I was a hunter.

My mother was also kind and affectionate; she seemed to be happy when she saw us enjoying ourselves by her; often she would not eat much for days together; she would leave all for us! She was an industrious woman; in the spring she made more sugar than any one else; she was never idle while the season for gathering wild rice lasted.

I was taught early to hunt the deer. It was a part of our father's duty to teach us how to handle the gun as well as the bow and arrow. I was early reminded to hunt for myself; a thirst to excel in hunting began to increase; no pains were spared, no fatigue was too great, and at all seasons I found something to stimulate me to exertion, that I might become a good hunter. For years I followed my father, observed how he approached the deer, the manner of getting it upon his shoulders to carry it home, etc. The appearance of the sky, the sound of the distant waterfalls in the morning, the appearance of the clouds and the winds, were to be noticed. The step, and the gesture, in travelling in search of the deer, were to be observed.

Many a lecture I received when the deer lay bleeding at the feet of my father; he would give me an account of the nobleness of the hunter's deeds, and said that I should never be in want whenever there was any game, and that many a poor aged man could be assisted by me. "If you reverence the aged, many will be glad to hear of your name," were the words of my father. "The poor man will say to his children, 'my children, let us go to him, for he is a great hunter, and is kind to the poor; he will not turn us away empty.' The Great Spirit, who has given the aged a long life, will bless you. You must never laugh at any suffering object, for you know not how soon you may be in the same condition; never kill any game needlessly." Such was his language when we were alone in the woods. Ah! they were lessons directed from heaven.

In the spring but few deer are killed, because they were not in good order, the venison being poor, and the skin so thin, that it was no object to kill them. To hunt deer in the summer was my great delight, which I did in the following manner: During the day I looked for their tracks, as they came on the shore of the lake or river during the night to feed. If they came on the bank of the river, I lighted pitch-pine, and the current of the river took the canoe along the shore. My lantern was so constructed that the light could not fall on one spot, but sweep along the shore. The deer could see the light, but were not alarmed by it, and continued feeding on the weeds. In this way I have approached so close that I could have reached them with my paddle. In this manner our forefathers shot them, not with a gun, as I did, but with the bow and arrow. Bows were made strong enough, so that the arrows might pierce through them.

Another mode of hunting on the lakes, preferred by some, is shooting without a light. Many were so expert, and possessed such accuracy in hearing, that they could shoot successfully in the dark, with no other guide than the noise of the deer in the water; the position of the deer being well known in this way on the darkest night. I will here relate an occurrence which took place in 1834. My father and I were hunting on the river Trent, in the night; after we had shot two deer, and while returning homewards, we heard the noise of a deer's footsteps. The night was dark as pitch. We approached the deer. I asked my father at what part of the animal I should aim. He replied, "at the head or neck." I poised my gun and fired; hearing no noise I concluded that my game was sure. I lighted some pitch-pine and walked towards the spot from which the noise had come. The deer lay dead and bleeding. On examination, I found that I had shot it just below the ear. In the fall of the year, also, I was accustomed to hunt; the meat was very fine, and the skins (from which our moccasons were made) were much thicker at this season. Those that could track the deer on fallen leaves, and shoot one each day, were considered first-rate hunters. The fall is the best time to determine the skill of the huntsman.

Of all animals the bear is the most dangerous to hunt. I had heard so many stories about its cunning that I dreaded to meet one. One day a party of us were going out to hunt the bear, just below Crooke's Rapids. After we had made a temporary place to stay for several days, we marched in file; after a while we halted, each took a different direction. My father said: "My son, you had better loiter behind the rest. Do not go far, for you may lose yourself." We parted—I took my course, and the rest theirs. I trembled for fear I should see what I was hunting for! I went only where I least expected to see a bear, and every noise I heard in the woods I thought must be one. As I stood on an old mossy log, there was such a crack on the side of the hill that my heart leaped within me. As I turned and looked, there was a large bear running towards me! I hid myself behind a tree—but on he came; I watched him; he came like a hogshead rolling down hill; there were no signs of stopping; when a few feet from me, I jumped aside, and cried *Yah!* (an exclamation of fear). I fired my gun without taking sight; in turning suddenly to avoid me, he threw up the earth and leaves; for an instant I was led to believe that the bear was upon me. I dropped my gun and fell backwards.

while the bear lay sprawling just by me. Having recovered, I took up my gun, and went a few feet from where I fell, and loaded my gun in a hurry. I then sought for a long pole, and with it I poked it on its side, to see if it was really dead. It did not move—it was dead; but even then I had not courage to go and touch it with my hands. When all was over, and I had told my father I had killed a bear, I felt as though my little leggings could hardly contain me. In examining it, I found the ball had gone through its heart. . . . .

When about five years old, I commenced shooting birds, with a small bow and arrow. I have shot many a bird, but am no more a marksman. I used to feel proud when I carried home my own game. The first thing that any of the hunters shot was cooked by the grandfather and grandmother, and there was great rejoicing, to inspire the youthful hunter with fresh ardor. Day after day I searched for the gray squirrel, the woodpecker, the snipe, and the snow-bird, for this was all my employment.

The gun was another instrument put into my hands, which I was taught to use both carefully and skilfully. Seldom do accidents occur from the use of fire-arms among our people. I delighted in running after the deer, in order to head and shoot them. It was a well known fact that I ranked high among the hunters. I remember the first deer I ever shot,—it was about one mile north of the village of Keene. The Indians, as has just been said, once had a custom, which is now done away, of making a great feast of the first deer that a young hunter caught; the young hunter, however, was not to partake of any of it, but wait upon the others. All the satisfaction he could realize was to thump his heels on the ground, while he and others were singing the following hunter's song:

> "Ah yah ba wah, ne gah me koo nah vah!
> Ah yah wa seeh, ne gah me koo nah nah."

> The fattest of the bucks I'll take,
> The choicest of all animals I'll take.

In the days of our ignorance we used to dance around the fire. I shudder when I think of those days of our darkness. I thought the Spirit would be kind to me if I danced before the old men; and day after day, or night after night, I have been employed with others in this way. I thank God that those days will never return.

𝕽𝖎𝖈𝖍𝖆𝖗𝖉 𝕾𝖆𝖑𝖙𝖊𝖗 𝕾𝖙𝖔𝖗𝖗𝖘.

See, also, Volume VII., page 564, of this Work.

ON THE STUDY OF HISTORY.

[*The Broader Range and Outlook of the Modern College Training.—Address before the A. Δ. Φ. of Amherst, 28 June, 1887.*]

IT seems to me plain, that the intuitive moral reason to which the most conspicuous action must give its account, and by which its character is interpreted and adjudged, which puts a candid estimate upon motives, and sets whatever historic achievement presents itself for review in fair connection with special environments of time or of place, must here find as fruitful activity, as systematic and quickening a nurture, as in any department of human research; and that the historical imagination—which of course does not rank with the creative imagination of the poet, but which is surely akin to that, and perhaps not less capable of giving incitement and beautiful pleasure in common experience—that this has such impulse and sustenance in the study of the past as cannot be furnished anywhere else. So it is that many of the aspiring and superior minds which have wrought in letters have taken this study for their own, and have by their successes in it made the world of readers their grateful debtors. The "personal equation" has continually appeared among them, in their judgment of motives, of movements, and of men; but in order to form any judgment at all, which the discerning would respect, they have had to cultivate moral insight, as well as a discursive and commanding intelligence. Records of the centuries, buried in the crypts of archives and libraries, have had to yield up to the survey of their genius living forms; vanished times have had to be reconstructed by their thought, in their outward phenomena, and their constitutive moral and social forces; the manifold sensibilities, desires, passions, which belong to our nature, have had to be recognized, and their operation in public affairs to be patiently exhibited, while the impressions of peoples on each other have filled to the edge the crowded canvas.

No teachers, therefore, have done more than these to educate broadly the ethical and the mental faculty in those whom they addressed, and before whom they unrolled the immense panorama of action, passion, collision, catastrophe, in the story of nations, with the energies exerted at critical points by particular persons, the deeper and more controlling power belonging to tendencies. It is strictly true, what Macaulay said: "He [who reads history] learns to distinguish what is local from what is universal; what is transitory from what is eternal; to discriminate between exceptions and rules; to trace the operation of disturbing causes; to separate the general principles, which are always true and everywhere applicable, from the accidental circumstances with which in every community they are blended, and with which, in an isolated community, they are confounded by the most philosophical mind. Hence it is that in generalization the writers of modern times have far surpassed those of antiquity. The historians of our own country," he adds, "are unequalled in depth and precision of reason; and even in the works of our mere compilers we often meet with speculations beyond the reach of Thucydides or Tacitus." This is the testimony of one who delighted to tear the vigor and flower of his life from the Bar and the Senate, from official distinction and the rarest social opportunities, that he might survey with ampler scope, while investigating with microscopic minuteness, the records of the past; reading a week to fashion a sentence; finding reward for laborious journeys in the more precise outline of a character, or the more exact picture of a scene, in even the more lively turn of a phrase or the more lucid completeness of a paragraph. If one needs to see, in near example, the fitness of historical studies to quicken and maintain high mental enthusiasm, and to discipline and enrich as well as to enlist rare and various mental powers, he may certainly find the immediate demonstration in the instance of Lord Macaulay.

A college like this, too, and an audience like the present, can never fail gratefully to recognize the large and beautiful moral impulse delivered upon spirits prepared to receive it through their contact in history with great, serene and masterful personalities, as these present themselves in the crowded passages which study explores, daring or suffering in the conflicts of their time. In common life we can, at best, but rarely meet such. The saintly and superior souls are not mustered in regiments. Multitudinous companies of elect spirits do not yet surround us on earth. It seems, sometimes, as if the enormous secular advances of which our times are so full and so proud were lowering the height and dimming the lustre of the moral ideal, as represented in the actual of life. Sending messages by lightning, travelling at forty miles to the hour, crossing in a week the ocean which the Mayflower perilously breasted, in our sumptuous vessels, framed of iron, luxurious in appointment, propelled from within, and gay with color as so many swimming summer-gardens—these applauded achievements do not tend of necessity to the upbuilding of nobler courage, to the development of a luminous moral wisdom, to the culture of even philosophical refinement, or the nurture of the temper of devout aspiration. On the other hand, do we not sometimes feel that virtue among us is coming to be too much a matter of manners; that the intense subjective processes from which august character is derived are in a measure being superseded by the mechanical contrivances and the physical successes with which our noisy years resound; and that the grand and lovely spirits, which are present still, and in which, whensoever we touch them, we find strange charm and inspiration, are fewer and lonelier than they were? Surely we do not meet them often, and cannot command their presence at our need.

But in history they abound, and are always at our service. Marcus Aurelius, saddest of men, yet imperturbable in a falling empire, and amid the mad whirl of an unexplained universe; Bernard, with the flaming intensity of his spirit, commander of kings and counsellor of pontiffs while the friend and protector of the lowliest of the poor, crushing before him the insolent noble, and facing the fierce fury of the mob on behalf of the Jew; Melanch-

thon, with his beautiful enthusiasm for letters, writing Greek more easily
than German, modest, peace-loving, yet firm in conviction, devoted to the
Master in almost passionate love, the very St. John of the stormy Reformation; William of Orange, fronting with majestic endurance the apparently
irresistible power which swept the Netherlands with flame and blade, and
recovering for freedom the land which his ancestors might literally be said
to have plucked from the sea—these will come to us when we want them ;
and with them all, orators, statesmen, theologians, artists, leaders of cru-
sades like Godfrey of Bouillon, who would not wear a crown where his Master had borne the cross, rulers of kingdoms like St. Louis, poets, philanthro-
pists, heroes, martyrs, the women with the men, of whom the world of their
time was not worthy, by whom the world is made worthier to-day. We may
wait years, or we may journey thousands of miles, to meet in the present the
special spirit whose office it is, and whose charming prerogative, to kindle
and ennoble ours. It is but to step to the library shelf to come face to face
with such in the past, if we know where to find them; nay, it is but to let the
thought go backward, over what has become distinct to our minds, and the
silent company is around us; the communion of rejoicing and consecrated
souls, the illustrious fellowship, in the presence of whom our meanness is
rebuked, our cowardice is shamed, and we become the freer children of God
and of the Truth.

Not only the romance of the world is in history, but influences so high in
source and in force as to be even sacred descend through it. Benedictive,
sacramental, is its touch upon responsive souls. We become comparatively
careless of circumstances; aware of kinship, in whatever heroic element may
be in us, with the choice, transcendent spirits; regardless of the criticism, or
the snarling scoffs, which here may surround us, if only conscious of a deeper
and more complete correspondence with those whose elate and unsubduable
temper remains among the treasures of mankind. I think that to our times,
especially, the careful and large study of history is among the most essential
sources of moral inspiration. The cultivation of it, in ever larger and richer
measure, is one of the finest and noblest exercises proposed to young minds.
Any college which introduces to the society of the spirits which have made
centuries illustrious takes splendor and majesty from the office.

The importance of individual life and effort is also magnified by it, instead
of being diminished or disguised, as men sometimes fancy; since one is continually reminded afresh of the power which belongs to those spiritual forces
which all may assist in animating and moulding civilizations. Of course an
imperfect study of history, however rapid and rudimental, shows how often
the individual decision and the restraining or inspiring action of great personalities have furnished the pivots on which multitudinous consequences
have turned; how, even after long intervals of time, the effects of such have
made themselves evident, in changed conditions and tendencies of peoples ;
and so it reminds us, with incessant iteration, of the vital interlocking of
every energetic personal life with the series of lives which are unconsciously
dependent upon it, of the reach of its influence upon the great complex of
historical progress, and of the service which each capable or eminent spirit

may render to the cause of universal culture and peace. But those to whom our thoughts are thus turned have been for the most part signal men in their time, remarkable in power, distinguished in opportunity, intuitively discerning the needs of the age, and with peculiar competence to meet them. With such we by no means may mate ourselves; and, so far, the lesson which history teaches may easily seem to be one of discouragement rather than of impulse, inclining us to rely upon occasional great men as the true pioneers and champions of progress, and to feel that for ourselves we have no place and no responsibility in the assistance of large and permanent public advancement.

Roswell Sabine Ripley.

BORN in Worthington, Franklin Co., Ohio, 1823. DIED in New York, N. Y., 1887.

THE STORMING OF CHAPULTEPEC.

[*The War with Mexico.* 1849.]

IN order that the victory might not be left to any uncertainty while these dispositions were being made, Pillow sent a request to General Scott that Worth's division, which was to support his assault, should be posted nearer the scene of action than Tacubaya. General Scott so ordered it; but Worth was already in motion for the purpose. Before he arrived at Molino del Rey, the time for preparation had expired, and Quitman had sent word to Pillow that he was ready for the assault. Pillow had not quite finished his preparations, and during the few minutes which intervened before the arrival of General Scott's staff officer, the heavy guns of battery No. 3 poured successive discharges of heavy grape and shell into the grove. The orders for the cessation of fire were soon received; the American batteries, heavy and light, ceased at once, and the attack commenced.

Lieutenant-Colonel Johnstone led his voltigeurs rapidly down from Molino del Rey to the level ground about the redan which he was to assault, keeping close under the southern wall of the enclosure, to protect his men from the artillery fire of the castle. The stormers under Captain McKenzie, Second Artillery, followed close after. When the advance of the voltigeurs came within musket-range of the redan, the Mexican infantry behind its parapet arose and commenced a lively fire. Johnstone immediately ordered his companies to deploy and reply advancing, which they did with so much effect that the enemy was driven from the work before the rearmost company was in line. The whole battalion, rushing through two ditches across the path and over the parapet, entered the redan, and through the cut into the grove, joining with the main force which had advanced through the gateway of Molino del Rey.

The Mexican batteries on the west of the castle had obtained the range of the gateway during the morning, and kept up a heavy fire of shells for half an hour before the advance. The effect was but to annoy the troops in position, and to render them somewhat restless, for they were protected from the splinters by the walls of the buildings. Under the circumstances, Cadwalader, who was the senior officer immediately at the point, was anxious to commence the assault, and sent to advise Pillow of the existing state of things. The mountain-howitzers, meanwhile, were served through the gateway, under the fire from the castle and from the intrenchments; for, notwithstanding the distance, the enemy kept up heavy discharges of musketry. They had somewhat shaken his line along the point of the grove, when, as the heavy guns ceased firing, Pillow arrived, and ordered Colonel Andrews to advance the first battalion of voltigeurs. The corps, issuing through the gateways, deployed forward at a run, and with a shout, which told the determination for victory, rushed straight at the intrenchments. The Mexicans delivered a scattering fire, and gave way, for Johnstone's soldiers were at the moment breaking into the grove through the redan. Both battalions of voltigeurs took the cover of the trees, and, engaging the enemy, beat him back through the woods in the direction of the castle.

Seeing the first point gained, Pillow ordered the howitzer battery and the Ninth and Fifteenth Regiments to move forward in support. These troops passed the gateway and deployed in the field, and Pillow mounted and took the advance.

Meanwhile the attention of the garrison in the western portions of the castle was given to the assault in this direction. The guns in the priest-cap and on the flanks were depressed, and sent heavy discharges of grape over the heads of the retreating Mexicans. The four-pounder in the round bastion at the angle of the roadway kept up a raking fire on the road by the southern wall, which was sustained by a continued stream of musketry from the intrenchments in its front.

The American advance was continued, though slowly, under the heavy fire, as well as that of the retreating Mexican infantry. It was difficult, for the ground was wet and boggy, and the moral and physical effect of the Mexican shot, crashing and tearing as it did through the foliage, was such as in some cases to render the men averse to leave the shelter of the trees. Pillow placed himself in the front, and by his well-seconded efforts a continued movement was established, although the nature of the ground caused the corps to be thrown into some disarray. Advancing in this manner, the troops drove back the enemy and reached the short open space at the foot of the hill. There they were halted to allow the stormers to take the front, and to form in support. But McKenzie, having his party in close formation, had not been able to keep up with the advance over the boggy ground. He had not arrived at the base of the hill before the enemy rallied in the redan half way up the acclivity, and opened fire thence, as well as from the round bastion and the intrenchments in its front. The galling fire rendered immediate movement necessary, and Pillow, who had just previously been wounded, ordered the assault.

The mountain-howitzers sent a few canisters, and the voltigeur regiment threw a volley up the hill from the base south of the redan. That regiment immediately followed, led by Lieutenant-Colonel Johnstone and Major Caldwell. At the same time, Captain Hooker, who was on the left, repeated the order, and brought up the nearest body of infantry, for the voltigeurs were without bayonets. Captain Chase, of the Fifteenth Infantry, led his company up to the redan from the north. The Americans pressed forward so rapidly that the enemy made short resistance, and fell back to the main work. The voltigeurs, Ninth and Fifteenth, followed close after, passed the redan, and gained the crest of the hill. A Mexican engineer officer was at the time in the act of firing the saucisson of the mines, but the fire of the American advance disabled him. The saucissons were immediately cut, and that element of danger was effectually destroyed.

As the Americans rose over the crest, the Mexican artillery in the priest-cap opened heavily with canister, and the troops on the azoteas and at the windows commenced a rapid rolling discharge of musketry, and many of the assailants fell killed or wounded. Of the former was Colonel Ransom, of the Ninth, who died gallantly at the head of his regiment. As the troops were at the time without ladders with which to scale the walls, further immediate advance was impracticable. They therefore kept in the rocks, and opened fire upon the Mexican artillerymen who were not more than fifty yards distant.

A mountain-howitzer was brought up and opened upon the round bastion, which was commanded by points of the hill already gained. Its fire, and that of a party of voltigeurs closely delivered, soon drove out the enemy, and the point was at once occupied. The effect of the rifles and muskets directed upon the main work was soon apparent from the cessation of the artillery fire, although the infantry, from roofs and windows, still kept up a stream of musketry upon the assailants. These, however, kept close behind the rocks of the height, awaiting the arrival of the storming party and the ladders, and in the while using their weapons with deadly effect upon all of the garrison who presented themselves in sight and within range.

Meantime Captain McKenzie arrived at the base of the hill, and, finding that the other troops had preceded him in the ascent, in obedience to Pillow's order he led his party rapidly up. It climbed over the rocks and made its way to the advance, but the troops around the crest were so closely posted that it was difficult for the stormers to get through. The ladders were not yet up, for the men of the carrying party had thrown them down in the grove, and for the most part engaged in the combat.

Being disabled from active advance, Pillow had sent Cadwalader up the ascent to give immediate attention to the movements of the assault. Seeing the state of affairs, that officer at once sent parties to collect and bring up the ladders. While this work was being accomplished, other troops came up in support.

While advancing through the grove, Pillow had received a message from Worth that his division was outside Molino del Rey, in readiness to support the attack. In answer, Pillow requested that a brigade should be advanced through the buildings to take post in the woods, as, in case of a check, time would be lost in bringing reënforcements forward by the flank through the narrow gateway. Worth ordered Colonel Clarke's brigade to advance, and that corps came rapidly forward. To shelter the troops from the shot which was falling in the grove, Pillow ordered them to be posted on the slope of the hill. The Eighth and Fifth, and a party of the Sixth Regiment, went up the ascent.

The Sixth was, however, ordered around the northern base of the rock, to cut up the fugitives from the castle; for the Mexican garrison was already shaken by the near approach, and many were attempting to make good their escape.

The New York and Second Pennsylvania Regiments of Quitman's command soon after came through the bastion and cut, which had been carried by Johnstone's command, and, passing through the grove, commenced ascending the hill. By the time they had joined the rear of the forces already in position, a number of ladders had been gathered and taken up, and the final assault commenced.

The Mexican artillery fire having been silenced, the troops most in advance had only been awaiting the ladders to make the last attack. When they were brought up, parties from different corps, running quickly forward over the rugged though short space between the crest of the hill and the ditch, leaped in, and at once planted their ladders. Lieutenant Armistead, of the storming party, led the way, and, as the ladders were raised, Lieutenant Selden first mounted to scale the walls. From azoteas and windows the Mexicans redoubled their musketry fire, which killed Lieutenants Rogers and Smith, of the stormers, who were urging on their men, struck down Selden, and with him several soldiers who had been the first to follow his example; but the assailants in the ditch clustered thick around the ladders already planted and constantly being raised. Many fell wounded or dead, yet their places were immediately taken; and, finally, Captain Howard, of the voltigeurs, gained the parapet unhurt. Captain McKenzie and many of his party, Captain Barnard, of the voltigeurs, with the colors of his regiment (the first in the work), Lieutenant Bennet, of the Fifteenth, and a crowd of gallant officers and men, followed after. Long ladders were brought up and laid across the ditch, and, with a shout of victory, the great body of the troops rushed over, under fire from the buildings inside of the castle, and the priest-cap was gained.

Further down the hill, Lieutenant-Colonel Johnstone led a party of voltigeurs and soldiers of other regiments over the round bastion and up the roadway, directly upon the gate of the castle. From the south front of the college, and from the eastern terrace, the enemy fired heavily upon these assailants. Lieutenant Reno's mountain-howitzers, which were with the advance, were opened upon the terrace in reply, while the soldiers used their rifles and muskets against the enemy in the windows and about the parapets so effectually that his fire soon slackened. Running up the roadway, the party entered at the gate, and joined the advance of those assailants which had entered over the priest-cap. The advance was pursued, and the enemy was rapidly pushed from the eastern terrace and the whole southern front of the castle. Many Mexicans, in their flight, jumped down the steep eastern side of the rock, regardless of the height, while the Americans pelted them from the parapets.

This part of the castle being won, and finding the enemy still strong in the lower batteries, and contesting the assault along the Tacubaya road with vigor, Johnstone posted a party of voltigeurs and other troops on the southeastern angle of the castle. These opened a heavy fire upon the enemy's rear, which soon told, and insured his retreat.

Meanwhile the whole castle had been occupied. Different parties entered at different doors of the college, and although the Mexicans kept up a resistance for a time, it was soon overcome; but while it lasted the American soldiers showed more ferocity than had been exhibited by them during the whole course of the war. The remembrance of the murder of their wounded comrades on the field of Molino del Rey was still fresh, and, where resistance was made, quarter was rarely given. General Perez was killed fighting; Colonel Caño, engineer of the castle, and a host of inferior officers and soldiers, fell in the tumult; and although the struggle lasted but a few minutes, it was not until the soldiers were satiated with revenge, and the first fury consequent upon the successful assault had passed away, that the bloodshed was put a stop to. But in the midst of the melée, Generals Bravo, Monterde, Noriega, Dosamantes, and Saldana were taken prisoners and protected from injury.

While the struggle continued on the terre-plein and inside the college, parties of American officers and soldiers made their way through the different rooms of the building to the azotea. Major Seymour, of the Ninth Infantry, tore down the Mexican flag, and, soon after, the standards of the Eighth and Fifteenth Regiments of Infantry, and the New York Volunteers, were thrown out from the highest points of the castle. The shouts of the victors announced to Mexico that Chapultepec, the strong defence on the west of her capital, was in possession of her enemy.

Joseph Jefferson.

BORN in Philadelphia, Penn., 1829.

HOW JEFFERSON CAME TO PLAY RIP VAN WINKLE.

[*The Autobiography of Joseph Jefferson.* 1890.]

ART has always been my sweetheart, and I have loved her for herself alone. I had fancied that our affection was mutual, so that when I failed as a star, which I certainly did, I thought she had jilted me. Not so. I wronged her. She only reminded me that I had taken too great a liberty, and that if I expected to win her I must press my suit with more patience. Checked, but undaunted in the resolve, my mind dwelt upon my vision, and I still indulged in day-dreams of the future.

During these delightful reveries it came up before me that in acting *Asa Trenchard* I had, for the first time in my life on the stage, spoken a pathetic speech; and though I did not look at the audience during the time I was acting,—for that is dreadful,—I felt that they both laughed and cried. I had before this often made my audience smile, but never until now had I moved them to tears. This to me novel accomplishment was delightful, and in casting about for a new character my mind was ever dwelling on reproducing an effect where humor would be so closely allied to pathos that smiles and tears should mingle with each other. Where could I get one? There had been many written, and as I looked back into the dramatic history of the past a long line of lovely ghosts loomed up before me, passing as in a procession : *Job Thornberry, Bob Tyke, Frank Oatland, Zekiel Homespun,* and a host of departed heroes "with martial stalk went by my watch." Charming fellows all, but not for me. I felt I could not do them justice. Besides, they were too human. I was looking for a myth—something intangible and impossible. But he would not come. Time went on, and still with no result.

During the summer of 1859 I arranged to board with my family at a queer old Dutch farmhouse in Paradise Valley, at the foot of Pocono Mountain, in Pennsylvania. A ridge of hills covered with tall hemlocks surrounds the vale, and numerous trout-streams wind through the meadows and tumble over the rocks. Stray farms are scattered through the valley, and the few old Dutchmen and their families who till the soil were born upon it ; there and only there they have ever lived. The valley harmonized with me and our resources. The scene was wild, the air was fresh, and the board was cheap. What could the light heart and purse of a poor actor ask for more than this?

On one of those long rainy days that always render the country so dull I had climbed to the loft of the barn, and lying upon the hay was reading that delightful book "The Life and Letters of Washington Irving." I had gotten well into the volume, and was much interested in it, when to my surprise I came upon a passage which said that he had seen me at Laura Keene's theatre as *Goldfinch* in Holcroft's comedy of "The Road to Ruin," and that I reminded him of my father "in look, gesture, size, and make." Till then I was not aware that he had ever seen me. I was comparatively obscure, and to find myself remembered and written of by such a man gave me a thrill of pleasure I can never forget. I put down the book, and lay there thinking how proud I was, and ought to be, at the revelation of this compliment. What an incentive to a youngster like me to go on !

And so I thought to myself, "Washington Irving, the author of 'The Sketch-Book,' in which is the quaint story of Rip Van Winkle." Rip Van Winkle! There was to me magic in the sound of the name as I repeated it. Why, was not this the very character I wanted? An American story by an American author was surely just the theme suited to an American actor.

In ten minutes I had gone to the house and returned to the barn with "The Sketch-Book." I had not read the story since I was a boy. I was disappointed with it ; not as a story, of course, but the tale was purely a narrative. The theme was interesting, but not dramatic. The silver Hudson stretches out before you as you read, the quaint red roofs and queer gables of the old Dutch cottages stand out against the mist upon the mountains ; but all this is descriptive. The character of *Rip* does not speak ten lines. What could be done dramatically with so simple a sketch? How could it be turned into an effective play?

Three or four bad dramatizations of the story had already been acted, but without marked success. Yates of London had given one in which the hero dies, one had been acted by my father, one by Hackett, and another by Burke. Some of these versions I had remembered when I was a boy, and I should say that Burke's play and performance were the best, but nothing that I remembered gave me the slightest encouragement that I could get a good play out of any of the existing materials. Still I was so bent upon acting the part that I started for the city, and in less than a week, by industriously ransacking the theatrical wardrobe establishments for old leather and mildewed cloth, and by personally superintending the making of the wigs, each article of my costume was completed; and all this too before I had written a line of the play or studied a word of the part.

This is working in an opposite direction from all the conventional methods in the study and elaboration of a dramatic character, and certainly not following the course I would advise any one to pursue. I merely mention the out-of-the-way, upside-down manner of going to work as an illustration of the impatience and enthusiasm with which I entered upon the task. I can only account for my getting the dress ready before I studied the part to the vain desire I had of witnessing myself in the glass, decked out and equipped as the hero of the Catskills.

I got together the three old printed versions of the drama and the story itself. The plays were all in two acts. I thought it would be an improvement in the drama to arrange it in three, making the scene with the spectre crew an act by itself. This would separate the poetical from the domestic side of the story. But by far the most important alteration was in the interview with the spirits. In the old versions they spoke and sang. I remembered that the effect of this ghostly dialogue was dreadfully human, so I arranged that no voice but *Rip's* should be heard. This is the only act on the stage in which but one person speaks while all the others merely gesticulate, and I was quite sure that the silence of the crew would give a lonely and desolate character to the scene and add to its supernatural weirdness. By this means, too, a strong contrast with the single voice of *Rip* was obtained by the death-like stillness of the demons as they glided about the stage in solemn silence. It required some thought to hit upon just the best questions that could be answered by a nod and shake of the head, and to arrange that at times even *Rip* should propound a query to himself and answer it; but I had availed myself of so much of the old material that in a few days after I had begun my work it was finished.

In the seclusion of the barn I studied and rehearsed the part, and by the end of summer I was prepared to transplant it from the rustic realms of an old farmhouse to a cosmopolitan audience in the city of Washington, where I opened at Carusi's Hall under the management of John T. Raymond. I had gone over the play so thoroughly that each situation was fairly engraved on my mind. The rehearsals were therefore not tedious to the actors; no one was delayed that I might consider how he or she should be disposed in the scene. I had by repeated experiments so saturated myself with the action of the play that a few days seemed to perfect the rehearsals. I acted on these occasions with all the point and feeling that I could muster. This answered the double purpose of giving me freedom and of observing the effect of what I was doing on the actors. They seemed to be watching me closely, and I could tell by little nods of approval where and when the points hit.

I became each day more and more interested in the work ; there was in the subject and the part much scope for novel and fanciful treatment. If the sleep of twenty years was merely incongruous, there would be room for argument pro and con ; but as it is an impossibility, I felt that the audience would accept it at once, not because it was an impossibility, but from a desire to know in what condition a man's mind would be if such an event could happen. Would he be thus changed ? His identity being denied both by strangers, friends, and family, would he at last almost accept the verdict and exclaim, "Then I am dead, and that is a fact"? This was the strange and original attitude of the character that attracted me.

In acting such a part what to do was simple enough, but what not to do was the important and difficult point to determine. As the earlier scenes of the play were of a natural and domestic character, I had only to draw upon my experience for their effect, or employ such conventional methods as myself and others had used before in characters of the same ilk. But from the moment *Rip* meets the spirits of Hendrik Hudson and his crew I felt that all colloquial dialogue and commonplace pantomime should cease. It is at this point in the story that the supernatural element begins, and henceforth the character must be raised from the domestic plane and lifted into the realms of the ideal.

To be brief, the play was acted with a result that was to me both satisfactory and disappointing. I was quite sure that the character was what I had been seeking, and I was equally satisfied that the play was not. The action had neither the body nor the strength to carry the hero ; the spiritual quality was there, but the human interest was wanting. The final alterations and additions were made five years later by Dion Boucicault, and will be referred to in their place.

DRAMATIC ACTION.

[From the Same.]

PERHAPS it is well to define, to the non-professional reader, what is meant by dramatic action, as sometimes this term is mistaken for pantomime. Pantomime is action, certainly ; but not necessarily dramatic action, which is the most essential element in the construction of a play. A drama will often give one no idea of its strength in the reading of it; even in rehearsal it will sometimes fail to reveal its power. I have on several occasions seen even the author of a play surprised at the exhibition of it on its first representation before an audience, he himself not being aware that his work contained the hidden treasure, until the sympathy of the public revealed it. Sometimes the point of unexpected interest consists in the relationship between two characters, or the peculiar emphasis laid upon a single word that has been spoken in a previous act. But to illustrate more fully what I desire to explain, I will take two dramatic actions, one from comedy and the other from tragedy, to set forth the subject clearly.

In one of Victorien Sardou's plays—and this gentleman is perhaps the most ingenious playwright of our time—the following incident occurs: The audience are first made fully aware that a lady in the play uses a certain kind of perfume. This is done casually, so that they do not suspect that the matter will again be brought to their notice. She abstracts some valuable papers from a cabinet, and when they are missed no one can tell who has taken them. The mystery is inexplicable. Suspicion falls upon an innocent person. The audience, who well know how the matter stands, are on tenter-hooks of anxiety, fearing that the real culprit will not be detected. When this feeling is at white heat one of the characters finds a piece of paper in the desk and is attracted to it by the perfume. He puts it to his nose, sniffs it, and as a smile of triumph steals over his face the audience, without a word being spoken, realize that the thief is detected: Observe here, too, the ingenuity of the dramatist : the audience are in the secret with him; they have seen the papers stolen; it is no news to them; but when the characters in whom they are interested become as much enlightened as they are the climax is complete.

For an illustration of this point, as applied to tragedy : After the murder of *Duncan, Macbeth,* standing with his wife in a dark and gloomy hall, looks at his bloody hands and apostrophizes them in these terrible words :

> " Will all great Neptune's ocean wash this blood
>   Clean from my hand ?   No, this my hand will rather
>   The multitudinous seas incarnadine,
>   Making the green one red."

Now there is a silence, and when he is alone there echoes through the castle a knocking at the gate. The friends of the murdered guest have come for him ; and they thunder at the portals, while the blood-stained host stands as if stricken down with terror and remorse. It is not the dialogue, as powerful as it is, which strikes the audience with awe; it is simply a stage direction of the great dramatic master—a " knocking at the gate." It will, I think, be seen by these two illustrations that a fluent and imaginative writer may construct plots, create characters, and compose exquisite verse, and yet not succeed as a playwright unless he possesses the art or gift of creating dramatic action.

John George Nicolay and John Hay.

THE DEATH OF LINCOLN.

[*Abraham Lincoln: A History. By John G. Nicolay and John Hay, Private Secretaries to the President. 1888–90.*]

THE subject of the discussion which took place in the Cabinet on that last day of Lincoln's firm and tolerant rule has been preserved for us in the notes of Mr. Welles. They were written out, it is true, seven years afterwards, at a time when Grant was President, seeking reëlection, and when Mr. Welles had followed Andrew Johnson into full fellowship with the Democratic party. Making whatever allowance is due for the changed environment of the writer, we still find his account of the day's conversation candid and trustworthy. The subject of trade between the States was the first that engaged the attention of the Cabinet. Mr. Stanton wished it to be carried on under somewhat strict military supervision; Mr. Welles was in favor of a more liberal system; Mr. McCulloch, new to the Treasury, and embarrassed by his grave responsibilities, favored the abolition of the Treasury agencies, and above all desired a definite understanding of the purpose of the Government. The President, seeing that in this divergence of views among men equally able and honest there lay the best chance of a judicious arrangement, appointed the three Secretaries as a commission with plenary power to examine the whole subject, announcing himself as content in advance with their conclusions.

The great subject of the reëstablishment of civil government in the Southern States was then taken up. Mr. Stanton had, a few days before, drawn up a project for an executive ordinance for the preservation of order and the rehabilitation of legal processes in the States lately in rebellion. The President, using this sketch as his text, not adopting it as a whole, but saying that it was substantially the result of frequent discussions in the Cabinet, spoke at some length on the question of reconstruction, than which none more important could ever engage the attention of the Government. It was providential, he thought, that this matter should have arisen at a time when it could be considered, so far as the Executive was concerned, without interference by Congress. If they were wise and discreet, they should reanimate the States and get their governments in successful operation, with order prevailing and the Union reëstablished, before Congress came together in December. The President felt so kindly towards the South, he was so sure of the Cabinet under his guidance, that he was anxious to close the period of strife without overmuch discussion. He was particularly desirous to avoid the shedding of blood, or any vindictiveness of punishment. He gave plain notice that morning that he would have none of it. "No one need expect he would take any part in hanging or killing these men, even the worst of them. Frighten them out of the country, open the gates, let down the bars, scare them off," said he, throwing up his hands as if scaring sheep. "Enough lives have been sacrificed ; we must extinguish our resentments if we expect harmony and union." He deprecated the disposition he had seen in some quarters to hector and dictate to the people of the South, who were trying to right themselves. He regretted that suffrage, under proper arrangement, had not been given to negroes in Louisiana, but he held that their constitution was in the main a good one. He was averse to the exercise of arbitrary powers by the Executive or by Congress. Congress had the undoubted right to receive or reject members; the Executive had no control in this; but the Executive could do very much to restore order in the States, and their practical relations with the Government, before Congress came together.

Mr. Stanton then read his plan for the temporary military government of the States of Virginia and North Carolina, which for this purpose were combined in one department. This gave rise at once to extended discussion, Mr. Welles and Mr. Dennison opposing the scheme of uniting two States under one government. The President closed the session by saying the same objection had occurred to him, and by directing Mr. Stanton to revise the document and report separate plans for the government of the two States. He did not wish the autonomy nor the individuality of the States destroyed. He commended the whole subject to the most earnest and careful consideration of the Cabinet; it was to be resumed on the following Tuesday; it was, he said, the great question pending—they must now begin to act in the interest of peace.

These were the last words that Lincoln spoke to his Cabinet. They dispersed with these words of clemency and good-will in their ears, never again to meet under his wise and benignant chairmanship. He had told them that morning a strange story, which made some demand upon their faith, but the circumstances under which they were next to come together were beyond the scope of the wildest fancy. The day was one of unusual enjoyment to Mr. Lincoln. His son Robert had returned from the field with General Grant, and the President spent an hour with the young soldier in delighted conversation over the campaign. He denied himself generally to the throng of visitors, admitting only a few friends.

Schuyler Colfax, who was contemplating a visit overland to the Pacific, came to ask whether the President would probably call an extra session of Congress during the summer. Mr. Lincoln assured him that he had no such intention, and gave him a verbal message to the mining population of Colorado and the western slope of the mountains concerning the part they were to take in the great conquests of peace which were coming. In the afternoon he went for a long drive with Mrs. Lincoln. His mood, as it had been all day, was singularly happy and tender. He talked much of the past and the future; after four years of trouble and tumult he looked forward to four years of comparative quiet and normal work; after that he expected to go back to Illinois and practise law again. He was never simpler or gentler than on this day of unprecedented triumph; his heart overflowed with sentiments of gratitude to Heaven, which took the shape usual to generous natures, of love and kindness to all men.

From the very beginning of his Presidency Mr. Lincoln had been constantly subject to the threats of his enemies and the warnings of his friends. The threats came in every form ; his mail was infested with brutal and vulgar menace, mostly anonymous, the proper expression of vile and cowardly minds. The warnings were not less numerous; the vaporings of village bullies, the extravagances of excited secessionist politicians, even the drolling of practical jokers, were faithfully reported to him by zealous or nervous friends. Most of these communications received no notice.   In cases where there seemed a ground for inquiry it was made, as carefully as possible, by the President's private secretary and by the War Department, but always without substantial result.   Warnings that appeared to be most definite, when they came to be examined proved too vague and confused for further attention.   The President was too intelligent not to know he was in some danger.   Madmen frequently made their way to the very door of the Executive offices and sometimes into Mr. Lincoln's presence.   He had himself so sane a mind, and a heart so kindly even to his enemies, that it was hard for him to believe in a political hatred so deadly as to lead to murder.   He would sometimes laughingly say, " Our friends on the other side would make nothing by exchanging me for Hamlin," the Vice-President having the reputation of more radical views than his chief.

He knew indeed that incitements to murder him were not uncommon in the South.   An advertisement had appeared in a paper of Selma, Alabama, in December, 1864, opening a subscription for funds to effect the assassination of Lincoln, Seward, and Johnson before the inauguration.   There was more of this murderous spirit abroad than was suspected.   A letter was found in the Confederate Archives from one Lieutenant Alston, who wrote to Jefferson Davis immediately after Lincoln's reëlection offering to "rid his country of some of her deadliest enemies by striking at the very heart's blood of those who seek to enchain her in slavery."   This shameless proposal was referred, by Mr. Davis's direction, to the Secretary of War ; and by Judge Campbell, Assistant Secretary of War, was sent to the Confederate Adjutant-General indorsed " for attention. "   We can readily imagine what reception an officer would have met with who should have laid before Mr. Lincoln a scheme to assassinate Jefferson Davis.   It was the uprightness and the kindliness of his own heart that made him slow to believe that any such ignoble fury could find a place in the hearts of men in their right minds.   Although he freely discussed with the officials about him the possibilities of danger, he always considered them remote, as is the habit of men constitutionally brave, and positively refused to torment himself with precautions for his own safety. He would sum the matter up by saying that both friends and strangers must have daily access to him in all manner of ways and places; his life was therefore in reach of any one, sane or mad, who was ready to murder and be hanged for it; that he could not possibly guard against all danger unless he were to shut himself up in an iron box, in which condition he could scarcely perform the duties of a President; by the hand of a murderer he could die only once; to go continually in fear would be to die over and over.   He therefore went in and out before the people, always unarmed, generally unattended.   He would receive hundreds of visitors in a day, his breast bare to pistol or knife. He would walk at midnight, with a single secretary or alone, from the Executive Mansion to the War Department, and back. He would ride through the lonely roads of an uninhabited suburb from the White House to the Soldiers' Home in the dusk of evening, and return to his work in the morning before the town was astir. He was greatly annoyed when, late in the war, it was decided that there must be a guard stationed at the Executive Mansion, and that a squad of cavalry must accompany him on his daily ride; but he was always reasonable and yielded to the best judgment of others.

Four years of threats and boastings, of alarms that were not founded, and of plots that came to nothing, thus passed away; but precisely at the time when the triumph of the nation over the long insurrection seemed assured, and a feeling of peace and security was diffused over the country, one of the conspiracies, not seemingly more important than the many abortive ones, ripened in the sudden heat of hatred and despair. A little band of malignant secessionists, consisting of John Wilkes Booth, an actor, of a famous family of players, Lewis Powell, alias Payne, a disbanded rebel soldier from Florida, George Atzerodt, formerly a coachmaker, but more recently a spy and blockade runner of the Potomac, David E. Herold, a young druggist's clerk, Samuel Arnold and Michael O'Laughlin, Maryland secessionists and Confederate soldiers, and John H. Surratt, had their ordinary rendezvous at the house of Mrs. Mary E. Surratt, the widowed mother of the last named, formerly a woman of some property in Maryland, but reduced by reverses to keeping a small boarding-house in Washington. Booth was the leader of the little coterie. He was a young man of twenty-six, strikingly handsome, with a pale olive face, dark eyes, and that ease and grace of manner which came to him of right from his theatrical ancestors. He had played for several seasons with only indifferent success; his value as an actor lay rather in his romantic beauty of person than in any talent or industry he possessed. He was a fanatical secessionist; had assisted at the capture and execution of John Brown, and had imbibed, at Richmond and other Southern cities where he had played, a furious spirit of partisanship against Lincoln and the Union party. After the reëlection of Mr. Lincoln, which rang the knell of the insurrection, Booth, like many of the secessionists North and South, was stung to the quick by disappointment. He visited Canada, consorted with the rebel emissaries there, and at last—whether or not at their instigation cannot certainly be said—conceived a scheme to capture the President and take him to Richmond. He spent a great part of the autumn and winter inducing a small number of loose fish of secession sympathies to join him in this fantastic enterprise. He seemed always well supplied with money, and talked largely of his speculations in oil as a source of income; but his agent afterwards testified that he never realized a dollar from that source; that his investments, which were inconsiderable, were a total loss. The winter passed away and nothing was accomplished. On the 4th of March, Booth was at the Capitol and created a disturbance by trying to force his way through the line of policemen who guarded the passage through which the President walked to the east front of the building. His intentions at this time are not known; he afterwards said he lost an excellent chance of killing the President that day. There are indications in the evidence given on the trial of the conspirators that they suffered some great disappointment in their schemes in the latter part of March, and a letter from Arnold to Booth, dated March 27, showed that some of them had grown timid of the consequences of their contemplated enterprise and were ready to give it up. He advised Booth, before going further, "to go and see how it will be taken in R——d." But timid as they might be by nature, the whole group was so completely under the ascendency of Booth that they did not dare disobey him when in his presence; and after the surrender of Lee, in an access of malice and rage which was akin to madness, he called them together and assigned each his part in the new crime, the purpose of which had arisen suddenly in his mind out of the ruins of the abandoned abduction scheme. This plan was as brief and simple as it was horrible. Powell, alias Payne, the stalwart, brutal, simple-minded boy from Florida, was to murder Seward ; Atzerodt, the comic villain of the drama, was assigned to remove Andrew Johnson; Booth reserved for himself the most difficult and most conspicuous role of the tragedy; it was Herold's duty to attend him as a page and aid in his escape. Minor parts were assigned to stage-carpenters and other hangers-on, who probably did not understand what it all meant. Herold, Atzerodt, and Surratt had previously deposited at a tavern at Surrattsville, Maryland, owned by Mrs. Surratt, but kept by a man named Lloyd, a quantity of ropes, carbines, ammunition, and whiskey, which were to be used in the abduction scheme. On the 11th of April Mrs. Surratt, being at the tavern, told Lloyd to have the shooting-irons in readiness, and on Friday, the 14th, again visited the place and told him they would probably be called for that night.

The preparations for the final blow were made with feverish haste; it was only about noon of the 14th that Booth learned the President was to go to Ford's Theatre that night. It has always been a matter of surprise in Europe that he should have been at a place of amusement on Good Friday; but the day was not kept sacred in America, except by the members of certain churches. It was not, throughout the country, a day of religious observance. The President was fond of the theatre; it was one of his few means of recreation. It was natural enough that, on this day of profound national thanksgiving, he should take advantage of a few hours' relaxation to see a comedy. Besides, the town was thronged with soldiers and officers, all eager to see him; it was represented to him that appearing occasionally in public would gratify many people whom he could not otherwise meet. Mrs. Lincoln had asked General and Mrs. Grant to accompany her; they had accepted, and the announcement that they would be present was made as an advertisement in the evening papers; but they changed their minds and went north by an afternoon train. Mrs. Lincoln then invited in their stead Miss Harris and Major Rathbone, the daughter and the stepson of Senator Harris. The President's carriage called for these young people, and the four went together to the theatre. The President had been detained by visitors, and the play had made some progress when he arrived. When he appeared in his box the band struck up "Hail to the Chief," the actors ceased playing, and the audience rose, cheering tumultuously; the President bowed in acknowledgment of this greeting and the play went on.

From the moment Booth ascertained the President's intention to attend the theatre in the evening his every action was alert and energetic. He and his confederates, Herold, Surratt, and Atzerodt, were seen on horseback in every part of the city. He had a hurried conference with Mrs. Surratt before she started for Lloyd's tavern. He intrusted to an actor named Matthews a carefully prepared statement of his reasons for committing the murder, which he charged him to give to the publisher of the "National Intelligencer," but which Matthews, in the terror and dismay of the night, burned without showing to any one. Booth was perfectly at home in Ford's Theatre, where he was greatly liked by all the employees, without other reason than the sufficient one of his youth and good looks. Either by himself or with the aid of his friends he arranged his whole plan of attack and escape during the afternoon. He counted upon address and audacity to gain access to the small passage behind the President's box; once there, he guarded against interference by an arrangement of a wooden bar to be fastened by a simple mortise in the angle of the wall and the door by which he entered, so that the door could not be opened from without. He even provided for the contingency of not gaining entrance to the box by boring a hole in its door, through which he might either observe the occupants or take aim and shoot. He hired at a livery stable a small, fleet horse, which he showed with pride during the day to barkeepers and loafers among his friends.

The moon rose that night at ten o'clock. A few minutes before that hour he called one of the underlings of the theatre to the back door and left him there holding his horse. He then went to a saloon near by, took a drink of brandy, and, entering the theatre, passed rapidly through the crowd in rear of the dress-circle and made his way to the passage leading to the President's box. He showed a card to a servant in attendance and was allowed to pass in. He entered noiselessly, and, turning, fastened the door with the bar he had previously made ready, without disturbing any of the occupants of the box, between whom and himself there yet remained the slight partition and the door through which he had bored the hole. Their eyes were fixed upon the stage; the play was "Our American Cousin," the original version by Tom Taylor, before Sothern had made a new work of it by his elaboration of the part of *Dundreary.* No one, not even the comedian on the stage, could ever remember the last words of the piece that were uttered that night—the last Abraham Lincoln heard upon earth. The whole performance remains in the memory of those who heard it a vague phantasmagoria, the actors the thinnest of spectres. The awful tragedy in the box makes everything else seem pale and unreal. Here were five human beings in a narrow space—the greatest man of his time, in the glory of the most stupendous success in our history, the idolized chief of a nation already mighty, with illimitable vistas of grandeur to come; his beloved wife, proud and happy; a pair of betrothed lovers, with all the promise of felicity that youth, social position, and wealth could give them; and this young actor, handsome as Endymion upon Latmos, the pet of his little world. The glitter of fame, happiness, and ease was upon the entire group, but in an instant everything was to be changed with the blinding swiftness of enchantment. Quick death was to come on the central figure of that company—the central figure, we believe, of the great and good men of the century. Over all the rest the blackest fates hovered menacingly—fates from which a mother might pray that kindly death would save her children in their infancy. One was to wander with the stain of murder on his soul, with the curses of a world upon his name, with a price set upon his head, in frightful physical pain, till he died a dog's death in a burning barn; the stricken wife was to pass the rest of her days in melancholy and madness; of those two young lovers, one was to slay the other, and then end his life a raving maniac.

The murderer seemed to himself to be taking part in a play. The fumes of brandy and partisan hate had for weeks kept his brain in a morbid state. He felt as if he were playing Brutus off the boards; he posed, expecting applause. Holding a pistol in one hand and a knife in the other, he opened the box door, put the pistol to the President's head, and fired; dropping the weapon, he took the knife in his right hand, and when Major Rathbone sprang to seize him he struck savagely at him. Major Rathbone received the blow on his left arm, suffering a wide and deep wound. Booth, rushing forward, then placed his left hand on the railing of the box and vaulted lightly over to the stage. It was a high leap, but nothing to such a trained athlete. He was in the habit of introducing what actors call sensational leaps in his plays. In "Macbeth," where he met the weird sisters, he leaped from a rock twelve feet high. He would have got safely away but for his spur catching in the folds of the Union flag with which the front of the box was draped. He fell on the stage, the torn flag trailing on his spur, but instantly rose as if he had received no hurt, though in fact the fall had broken his leg, turned to the audience, brandishing his dripping knife and shouting the State motto of Virginia, "*Sic Semper Tyrannis,*" and fled rapidly across the stage and out of sight. Major Rathbone had shouted, "Stop him!" The cry went out, "He has shot the President." From the audience, at first stupid with surprise and afterwards wild with excitement and horror, two or three men jumped upon the stage in pursuit of the flying assassin; but he ran through the familiar passages, leaped upon his horse, which was in waiting in the alley behind, rewarded with a kick and a curse the call-boy who had held him, and rode rapidly away in the light of the just risen moon.

The President scarcely moved; his head drooped forward slightly, his eyes closed. Major Rathbone, at first not regarding his own grievous hurt, rushed to the door of the box to summon aid. He found it barred, and on the outside some one was beating and clamoring for entrance. He opened the door; a young officer named Crawford entered; one or two army surgeons soon followed, who hastily examined the wound. It was at once seen to be mortal. It was afterwards ascertained that a large derringer bullet had entered the back of the head on the left side, and, passing through the brain, had lodged just behind the left eye. By direction of Rathbone and Crawford, the President was carried to a house across the street and laid upon a bed in a small room at the rear of the hall, on the ground floor. Mrs. Lincoln followed, half distracted, tenderly cared for by Miss Harris. Rathbone, exhausted by loss of blood, fainted, and was carried home. Messengers were sent for the members of the Cabinet, for the Surgeon-General, for Dr. Stone, the President's family physician; a crowd of people rushed instinctively to the White House and, bursting through the doors, shouted the dreadful news to Robert Lincoln and Major Hay, who sat gossiping in an upper room. They ran downstairs. Finding a carriage at the door, they entered it to go to Tenth street. As they were driving away, a friend came up and told them that Mr. Seward and most of the Cabinet had been murdered. The news was all so improbable that they could not help hoping it was all untrue. But when they got to Tenth street and found every thoroughfare blocked by the swiftly gathering thousands, agitated by tumultuous excitement, they were prepared for the worst. In a few minutes all who had been sent for, and many others, were gathered in the little chamber where the Chief of the State lay in his agony. His son was met at the door by Dr. Stone, who with grave tenderness informed him that there was no hope. After a natural outburst of grief young Lincoln devoted himself the rest of the night to soothing and comforting his mother.

The President had been shot a few minutes past ten. The wound would have brought instant death to most men, but his vital tenacity was extraordinary. He was, of course, unconscious from the first moment; but he breathed with slow and regular respiration throughout the night. As the dawn came, and the lamplight grew pale in the fresher beams, his pulse began to fail; but his face even then was scarcely more haggard than those of the sorrowing group of statesmen and generals around him. His automatic moaning, which had continued through the night, ceased; a look of unspeakable peace came upon his worn features. At twenty-two minutes after seven he died. Stanton broke the silence by saying, "Now he belongs to the ages." Dr. Gurley kneeled by the bedside and prayed fervently. The widow came in from the adjoining room supported by her son and cast herself with loud outcry on the dead body.

Theodore Bacon.

BORN in New Haven, Conn., 1834.

MISS BACON'S THEORY OF THE SHAKESPEARIAN PLAYS.

[Delia Bacon : a Biographical Sketch. 1888.]

STUDYING and teaching for many years not merely the history of events, but the history and criticism of literature, it is not strange that the strongly English mind of this New England woman became gradually fixed upon the greatest work of English letters, the drama of the Elizabethan and Jacobean age. So complete, indeed, was the spell of fascination under which she fell in the study especially of the plays which bear the name of Shakespeare, that after the beginning of 1853 she could no longer endure the burden of her historical lessons, in which she seemed to have achieved a permanent success, sure to bring her, if only she should continue them, prosperity and credit.

To whom it first occurred to doubt the title of William Shakespeare to the authorship of the plays commonly bearing his name is a question which will not be much discussed in this sketch. . . . .

Many readers, indeed, from the time when criticism began a century and a half ago, found themselves confronted with difficulties elsewhere unknown. The personality of this dramatist glowed through his work with a force and brightness found nowhere else in literature. It seemed, indeed, a multiplied personality. There was in it not only marvellous insight, but exquisite cultivation and refinement, profound learning, and a practical knowledge of men, of the world, and of affairs such as all men were apt to say had never before been joined in any one man. When Coleridge called him the "myriad-minded," he simply put into a felicitous phrase what all men had long been thinking. Many, indeed, had declared their wonder that any one mind could produce creations so diverse in character as "Julius Cæsar" and "The Merry Wives of Windsor," as "The Comedy of Errors" and "Macbeth." In general, however, a single student would content himself with a demonstration which, alone, might have served to solve the difficulty found by every one, but which, when involved with like demonstrations by others, only multiplied perplexity. To prove from the plays that their author must have been a lawyer, as Lord Campbell did, was far from difficult, and would have been very helpful if the demonstration had stood alone. True, there was no historical record of Shakespeare's ever having seen a law-book, a court-room, or a lawyer's chambers; and there was some trouble in imagining how the play-actor and theatre-manager, who was writing immortal dramas before he was thirty, and died, after voluminous authorship, at fifty-two, could have acquired what Lord Campbell calls "the familiar, profound, and accurate knowledge he displayed of juridical principles and practice." It was only making a wonder more wonderful, however; and the new wonder was established by demonstration, and by the authority of a great lawyer's name. But when the eminent Dr. Bucknill, not controverting the argument of Lord Campbell, proved as clearly that Shakespeare "had paid an amount of attention to subjects of medical interest scarcely if at all inferior to that which has served as the basis" of the proposition that he "had devoted seven good years of his life to the practice of law," he hindered rather than helped to understand the real life of the dramatist. So when another proves that in the few years before the playwriting began the poet, so well versed was he in warfare, must have served a campaign or two in the Low Countries; another, that he must have been a Roman Catholic in religion, while another shows him to have been necessarily a Puritan; another, that his prodigious wealth of allusions to and phrases from the then untranslated Greek and Latin authors proves his broad and deep erudition; the understanding consents to one demonstration after another, but may possibly be staggered if called to accept them all together. It might well be that weak souls, invited to believe so much of one man, sought refuge and repose in refusing to believe even what would not otherwise have overtaxed credulity.

There were other things, besides, that had seemed strange in the relations of this man to these plays. No word or hint seems ever to have escaped him to show that he cared for, or even owned, the miraculous offspring which had fallen from him. There is no word or syllable in all the world to indicate that the man whose multifarious learning is the wonder of the third century after him ever owned a book, or ever saw one, although he brought together and left behind him a fair estate. Nor is there to be found in all the world of this profuse and voluminous author, of this bosom-friend of poets and printers and actors, so much as the scratch of a pen on paper, except the three signatures upon his Will, wherein, by an interlineation which shows that he had at first overlooked the wife of his boyhood, he leaves her his "second-best bed." Yet of his less famous contemporaries there are autograph manuscripts in abundance. Even of his forerunners by centuries there are extant writings infinitely more plenty than the scanty subscriptions to a legal instrument. Petrarch died two centuries and a half, Dante three centuries, before him; yet the manuscripts of both abound, while of him who was greater than either, and was almost of our own time, there is nothing but the mean and sordid Will to show that he ever put pen to paper.

But while the difficulty of fixing the canon of the Shakespeare text had long been such as to involve the authorship of every part of the text in more or less doubt; while all men had wondered that so little should be known of the actual man Shakespeare, and that what little was known should be so far remote from any ideal one could form of the author bearing the name: so that Coleridge should exclaim: "Are we to have miracles in sport? Does God choose idiots by whom to convey divine truths to men?" and Emerson: "I cannot marry this fact to his verse. Other admirable men have led lives in some sort of keeping with their thought; but this man, in wide contrast"; yet avowed disbelief went commonly no further. Once, it is true, there was a public assertion that Shakespeare's alleged authorship was impossible. In 1848 there was published by the Harpers, in New York, a light and chatty account of a voyage to Spain, entitled "The Romance of Yachting," by Joseph C. Hart. The incidents of the voyage are interspersed with discussions altogether foreign to it; and upon a trivial pretext the authorship of the plays is considered, with no small acuteness and vigor, upon the pages from 208 to 243. It is summarized, however, in a few of the earlier sentences: "He was not the mate of the literary characters of the day, and none knew it better than himself. It is a fraud upon the world to thrust his surreptitious fame upon us. He had none that was worthy of being transmitted. The inquiry will be, *who were the able literary men who wrote the dramas imputed to him?* The plays themselves, or rather a small portion of them, will live as long as English literature is regarded worth pursuit. The *authorship* of the plays is no otherwise material to us than as a matter of curiosity, and to enable us to render exact justice; but they should not be assigned to Shakespeare alone, if at all."

If there be any merit, therefore, in having been the first to doubt this authorship, it cannot be awarded to Delia Bacon. There is no reason, however, to believe that the speculations which have just been quoted ever came to her knowledge. The ideas, or fancies, which soon after this possessed her, were, as she profoundly believed, her own discovery—indeed, she would rather have said, a revelation direct to her.

Revelation, discovery, or fancy, however,—whatever it was, an utterly subordinate part of it all, though an essential part, was that which concerned merely the authorship of the plays. If they were indeed, as they had been commonly received, a casual collection of stage-plays, knocked together by a money-making play-actor, playwright, and theatre-manager for the money there was in them and to be got out of them, it was a trivial question by what name the playwright should be called; it should not tax credulity to "marry this fact to his verse," however fine the verse might be, if they were nothing more than verse. But to her, studying the plays with a keenness of natural insight and a burning intensity which have not often been applied to them, much more than splendid poesy began to gleam within them. Finding in them a higher philosophy, even, than in the "Advancement of Learning," a broader statesmanship, a profounder jurisprudence, and, above all, a bolder courage than in all the avowed writings of the great Chancellor, she only obeyed the teachings of that Inductive System which he had expounded, in seeking an adequate authorship for so magnificent a creation. But that all these things were in the plays—this was the main fact that concerned her; . this was what she cared to discover first for herself, and then to communicate to the world. If indeed she found them there, it could not but follow, as the night the day, that some better paternity must be admitted for the plays than that of Lord Leicester's groom.

Nor was it enough for her to discover bits and gleams of philosophy and political science in the plays, however frequent or brilliant. To her eager inquiry they came to be revealed at last, not as fortuitously collected though mutually unrelated plays, but as an entire dramatic system, in which the New Philosophy was to be inculcated in unsuspicious minds, under the vehement despotism of the last Tudor and the dull pedantic oppression of the first Stuart. If the plays were really such a system of philosophic teaching, not only was it difficult to accept the competency for it of the Stratford poacher and London horse-boy; it was hardly less trying to credulity to impute so vast an enterprise, added to all the gigantic intellectual labors which he avowed, even to the greatest Englishman of his age. She judged, therefore, that as there had been collaboration before and since in literary work, so here the most brilliant and philosophic minds of the Elizabethan Court coöperated in the work which was too great for one, and consented together, for their common safety, to the imputation of their united work to the theatre-manager who brought out the plays, and whose property they were because they had been given to him.

Reasons why these courtiers and politicians—Bacon, Raleigh, Spenser, and whatever others made up the illustrious coterie—should not have wished to acknowledge the work of which they might well have boasted, were not far to seek. It comported ill with dignity of rank and place to be known as a writer of plays: but to be known to such a queen as Elizabeth, or to such a king as James, as author of such plays as "Coriolanus" or "Julius Cæsar"

—the eager ambition of Bacon would have been quenched by it long before the day when his office was wanted for Williams; upon Raleigh, living for fifteen years under his unexecuted death sentence, the headsman's axe would have fallen earlier than it did.

But while Delia Bacon thoroughly believed that such a worthy coterie, and not the unworthy player, produced the Elizabethan drama, and hid in it the philosophy which it would have been fatal to publish openly; and while she was no less sure that in some cryptic form there was truth involved in these works which was yet to be surrendered to faithful and intelligent study, it is scant justice to her memory to say, that, as the mere authorship of the plays was to her but a small part of the truth concerning them, so she never devoted herself to whims or fancies about capital letters, or irregular pagination, or acrostics, or anagrams, as concealing yet expressing the great philosophy which the plays enclosed. Her mind, it now appears, was already overwrought; before many months it gave way completely; but its unsoundness, whenever it may have begun, never assumed that form.

Lyman Abbott.

See, also, Volume IX., page 317, of this Work.

THE LIBERAL ORTHODOXY OF TO-DAY.

[From his Statement of Belief, before the Council of Clergymen and Laymen assembled to install him as Pastor of Plymouth Church, Brooklyn, N. Y., 16 January, 1890.]

MY faith in God rests on my faith in Christ as God manifest in the flesh —not as God and man, but as God in man. It is true that the argument for a Creator from the creation is by modern sciences modified only to be strengthened. The doctrine of a great first cause gives place to the doctrine of an eternal and perpetual cause; the carpenter conception of creation to the doctrine of the divine immanence ; the Latin notion of an anthropomorphic Jupiter, renamed Jehovah, made to dwell in some bright particular star and holding telephonic communication with the spheres by means of invisible wires which sometimes fail to work, dies, and the old Hebrew conception of a Divinity which inhabiteth eternity, and yet dwells in the heart of the contrite and the humble, takes its place. But the theological argument is strengthened, not weakened, by the doctrine of evolution ; creation is more, not less, creation because it is the thought, not the mere handiwork, of God. It is not possible even to state the doctrine of an atheist creation without using the language of theism in the statement. But the heart finds no refuge in an Infinite or an Eternal Energy from which all things proceed. That refuge is found only in the faith that God has entered a human life, taken the helm, ruled heart and hand and tongue, written in terms of human experience the biography of God in history, revealed in the teaching of

Christ the truth of God, in the life of Christ the righteousness of God, in the Passion of Christ the suffering of God.   .   .   .   .

My eschatology is all summed up in one faith : Christ shall come to judge the world. The dogma of the decisive nature of this world's probation for every man I repudiate as unscriptural. The hypothesis that Christ will be presented in another life to all who have not known Him here I do not accept, for lack of evidence to support it. I cannot offer to any man a hope of future repentance, whether this side or the other of the grave. But I refuse to believe that the accident of death transmutes God's mercy into wrath and makes repentance impossible and so closes the door of hope upon the soul forever. What may be the resources of God's mercy in the future I do not know, and shrink from the dogmatism which attempts to define them. The most awful fact of human life is the power of the human soul to accept God or reject Him as it will. What God may do in the future to overcome the choice of evil I do not know; but I am sure that He will never violate the sacred freedom of the soul and so destroy man in seeming to save him, and never attach other than darkness and death to persistent sin. But I am not less sure that " His mercy endureth forever," and that no soul will be left in the outer darkness which that mercy can call into light; that the end of Christ's redeeming work comes not until He delivers up the kingdom to God and the Father, has all things put under His feet, and is Himself subject unto Him that put all things under Him that God may be all in all; and that when that glad day comes, the song of rejoicing will rise from every creature in heaven, and on the earth, and under the earth, and such as are in the sea. If there are then any voices not joining in that choral of redeeming love, I believe it will be because they are silent in that second death from which there is no resurrection. Endless conscious sin I do not believe in. I could endure the thought of endless suffering, but not of sin growing ever deeper, darker, more awful. It has grown to me unthinkable; I believe it is unscriptural. For my conception of sin depends also upon and has grown out of my faith in and love for Christ. That conviction of sin which I in vain endeavored artificially to evoke in my childhood's days has grown unsummoned in my heart. When I joined the church a good elder asked me what I thought of sin in connection with the Lord Jesus Christ. I did not know that it had any connection with the Lord Jesus Christ, and I did not understand his question, and told him so. I understand it now. When I think how sin deranges and destroys such a nature as Christ has made illustrious, that it is sin against such a love as He has manifested, that it estranges and separates from such a God as He reveals, sin seems to me a more awful penalty than any which can be inflicted because of it, and to save from sin an infinitely diviner work than to save from any consequences which it may involve, natural or inflicted, here or hereafter. The motive of my personal life, the inspiration of my Christian activity, is not fear of pain and penalties, but horror for sin and love for Christ.

On my faith in Christ rests also my faith in the Bible. The Bible is the casket which contains the image of my Lord—that is enough; whether it be lead or silver or gold is matter of minor concern. There are modern writers on law that may be as valuable as Moses; there are poems of Browning and Tennyson and our own Whittier which are far more pervaded with the Christlike spirit than some in the Hebrew Psalmody. But there is no life like the life of Christ ; and the law and the prophets are sacred because they point to and prepare for Him ; and the gospels sacred because they tell the story of His incomparable life; and the epistles sacred because they interpret that life as continuous in the experience of His church. The Bible is unique and incomparable in literature, because it is the history of the revelation of God in human experience, beginning with the declaration that God made man in His own image, bringing out in law, history, drama, poetry, prophecy, that divine image more and more clearly, until it reaches its consummation in the portrait of Him who was the express image of God's person and the brightness of His glory.

So my faith in the miracles rests also on my faith in Christ—He himself a greater miracle by far than any attributed to Him. That beneficent power should have flashed from such a Christ, that death should be powerless to hold such a Christ in the grave, that angels should have announced His coming and proclaimed His resurrection—all this seems to me natural and easy to believe; as easy to believe in these scintillations of divinity from the Person of Christ as to believe in scintillations of genius from a Shakespeare or a Dante. I accept the Christian miracles as adequately attested by competent witnesses. I count the resurrection of Jesus Christ as the best attested fact of ancient history, itself attesting His divinity and inaugurating that life of His in His church which carries on to its consummation the kingdom of God. But my faith in Christ rests not on the miracles, but on Christ Himself. Even as He wrought them He declared them to be but inferior evidences of His divinity. Their subordinate importance is clearer than ever, now that they are no longer wonders which we witness, but the histories of wonders witnessed by others. To believe in Christ—that the Father is in Him and He is in the Father—this is Christian faith. The spirit which in the modern church has sometimes sought to found Christian faith on signs and wonders appears to me to be almost as much one of unbelief as the spirit which outside the church denies the miraculous altogether. Miracles are witnesses to divinity, revelation is the unveiling of divinity, but Christ is Himself Divinity, and he who accepts Christ—who loves Him, reverences Him, obeys Him, follows Him, lives to be like Him—is Christ's disciple, however illogical may seem to me to be his philosophy about natural and revealed religion, about nature and the supernatural. My faith in immortality also rests upon Christ—upon His word, His resurrection. I am coming to distrust all mere philosophical arguments for personal immortality and to rely upon one who professed to be a witness, to testify to the things which He had seen and heard, to have come from God and to be going to God. When He tenderly appeals to me, "Ye believe in God, believe also in me," my heart responds, "I do believe," and what He says I accept, because He is a faithful and true witness.

On this and on every other spiritual theme I more and more distrust the vaunted "scientific method" and more and more rest upon personal faith in the Christ of God, bearing a witness confirmed by the experience of God in my own soul. And I more and more incline to believe that immortality is not the universal attribute of humanity—that God alone hath immortality; and we have it only as here or hereafter we are made partakers of the divine nature. It can hardly be necessary to add that my hope for myself and for the world rests on Christ; that is, on the helpfulness of God as manifested in Christ. The two theories of life which seem to me to be contending in our age are essentially the same which have been contending ever since the days of Paul—the Pagan and the Christian. Pagan philosophy allows man no higher faculty than the senses and the reason ; Christian philosophy endows him with a mystic sense which perceives the invisible. Pagan philosophy casts him on his own resources, if it does not deny him even free will and make him the creature of the forces which environ him. Christianity believes in the power of Infinite Love above, which is drawing humanity to itself. In the Pagan philosophy there is no room for revelation, miracles, atonement, regeneration, divinity of Christ, presence of the Holy Spirit, prayer. Granted the Christian postulate—a God in Christ drawing the world to Himself—and revelation or the unveiling of God, miracles or witnesses to God, atonement or reconciliation to God, regeneration or the beginning of the life of God in the soul of man, the Holy Spirit or the presence of God with men, prayer or the communion of men with God—all follow. The Christian faith is my faith; and because I believe that there is in it a hope for every form of human despair, I have given my life to its proclamation. Redemption is not, to my thought, a mere recovery of man from a fall and his restoration to a primal state of innocence. It is the development of the individual soul, and so of the race, from childhood's innocence, through fall, temptation, sin, and grace, to a divine and manly virtue. Forgiveness is not a remission of penalty, which may be remitted or may remain, but a remission of sin, a personal cleansing and purification, often through punishment, often without it. Sacrifice is not necessary to induce God to remit penalty—it is not an expiation; nor is it necessary to enable God to remit penalty—it is not a substitution. . . . .

I might, brethren, have presented to you a theological statement which would have been both more comprehensive and more compact; but it would have been less my own. My theology has changed in the past and will change in the future ; but if the past be an augury of the future, it will change only to make Christ more central. It is imperfect and always will be ; for we know in part and we prophesy in part, and the truth of God is known in its entirety by none of us. But as the years go by and creeds are less, faith and hope and love are more to me; the faith that looks with ever clearer vision upon the invisible and eternal, while all things earthly and temporal grow more shadowy; the hope that amid all the wreckage of life hears ever, like a bird-song in the tempest, "All things work together for good to those that love God," and the love which counts all humanity one great brotherhood, because children of that Father of whom every family in heaven and on earth is named.

Henry Adams.

BORN in Boston, Mass., 1838.

JEFFERSON.

[*History of the United States.—Vols. I and II. The First Administration of Thomas Jefferson.* 1889.]

ACCORDING to the admitted standards of greatness, Jefferson was a great man. After all deductions on which his enemies might choose to insist, his character could not be denied elevation, versatility, breadth, insight, and delicacy; but neither as a politician nor as a political philosopher did he seem at ease in the atmosphere which surrounded him. As a leader of democracy he appeared singularly out of place. As reserved as President Washington in the face of popular familiarities, he never showed himself in crowds. During the last thirty years of his life he was not seen in a Northern city, even during his Presidency; nor indeed was he seen at all except on horseback, or by his friends and visitors in his own house. With manners apparently popular and informal, he led a life of his own, and allowed few persons to share it. His tastes were for that day excessively refined. His instincts were those of a liberal European nobleman, like the Duc de Liancourt, and he built for himself at Monticello a château above contact with man. The rawness of political life was an incessant torture to him, and personal attacks made him keenly unhappy. His true delight was in an intellectual life of science and art. To read, write, speculate in new lines of thought, to keep abreast of the intellect of Europe, and to feed upon Homer and Horace, were pleasures more to his mind than any to be found in a public assembly. He had some knowledge of mathematics, and a little acquaintance with classical art; but he fairly revelled in what he believed to be beautiful, and his writings often betrayed subtile feeling for artistic form,—a sure mark of intellectual sensuousness. He shrank from whatever was rough or coarse, and his yearning for sympathy was almost feminine. That such a man should have ventured upon the stormy ocean of politics was surprising, the more because he was no orator, and owed nothing to any magnetic influence of voice or person. Never effective in debate, for seventeen years before his Presidency he had not appeared in a legislative body except in the chair of the Senate. He felt a nervous horror for the contentiousness of such assemblies, and even among his own friends he sometimes abandoned for the moment his strongest convictions rather than support them by an effort of authority.

If Jefferson appeared ill at ease in the position of a popular leader, he seemed equally awkward in the intellectual restraints of his own political principles. His mind shared little in common with the provincialism on which the Virginia and Kentucky Resolutions were founded. His instincts led him to widen rather than to narrow the bounds of every intellectual exercise; and if vested with political authority, he could no more resist the temptation to stretch his powers than he could abstain from using his mind on any subject merely because he might be drawn upon ground supposed to be dangerous. He was a deist, believing that men could manage their own salvation without the help of a state church. Prone to innovation, he sometimes generalized without careful analysis. He was a theorist, prepared to risk the fate of mankind on the chance of reasoning far from certain in its details. His temperament was sunny and sanguine, and the atrabilious philosophy of New England was intolerable to him. He was curiously vulnerable, for he seldom wrote a page without exposing himself to attack. He was superficial in his knowledge, and a martyr to the disease of omniscience. Ridicule of his opinions and of himself was an easy task, in which his Federalist opponents delighted, for his English was often confused, his assertions inaccurate, and at times of excitement he was apt to talk with indiscretion; while with all his extraordinary versatility of character and opinions, he seemed during his entire life to breathe with perfect satisfaction nowhere except in the liberal, literary, and scientific air of Paris in 1789.

Jefferson aspired beyond the ambition of a nationality, and embraced in his view the whole future of man. That the United States should become a nation like France, England, or Russia, should conquer the world like Rome, or develop a typical race like the Chinese, was no part of his scheme. He wished to begin a new era. Hoping for a time when the world's ruling interests should cease to be local and should become universal; when questions of boundary and nationality should become insignificant; when armies and navies should be reduced to the work of police, and politics should consist only in non-intervention,—he set himself to the task of governing, with this golden age in view. Few men have dared to legislate as though eternal peace were at hand, in a world torn by wars and convulsions and drowned in blood; but this was what Jefferson aspired to do. Even in such dangers, he believed that Americans might safely set an example which the Christian world should be led by interest to respect and at length to imitate. As he conceived a true American policy, war was a blunder, an unnecessary risk; and even in case of robbery and aggression the United States, he believed, had only to stand on the defensive in order to obtain justice in the end. He would not consent to build up a new nationality merely to create more navies and armies, to perpetuate the crimes and follies of Europe; the central government at Washington should not be permitted to indulge in the miserable ambitions that had made the Old World a hell and frustrated the hopes of humanity.

With these humanitarian ideas which passed beyond the bounds of nationality, Jefferson held other views which seemed narrower than ordinary provincialism. Cities, manufactures, mines, shipping, and accumulation of capital led, in his opinion, to corruption and tyranny.

"Generally speaking," said he, in his only elaborate work, the Notes on Virginia, "the proportion which the aggregate of the other classes of citizens bears in any State to that of its husbandmen is the proportion of its unsound to its healthy parts, and is a good enough barometer whereby to measure its degree of corruption. . . . Those who labor in the earth are the chosen people of God if ever he had a chosen people, whose breasts he has made his peculiar deposit for substantial and genuine virtue."

This doctrine was not original with Jefferson, but its application to national affairs on a great scale was something new in the world, and the theory itself clashed with his intellectual instincts of liberality and innovation.

THE AMERICAN OF 1800.

[*From the Same.*]

WORDSWORTH, although then at his prime, indulging in what sounded like a boast that he alone had felt the sense sublime of something interfused, whose dwelling is the light of setting suns, and the round ocean, and the living air, and the blue sky, and in the mind of man,—even he, to whose moods the heavy and the weary weight of all this unintelligible world was lightened by his deeper sympathies with nature and the soul, could do no better, when he stood in the face of American democracy, than "keep the secret of a poignant scorn."

Possibly the view of Wordsworth and Moore, of Weld, Dennie, and Dickens was right. The American democrat possessed little art of expression, and did not watch his own emotions with a view of uttering them either in prose or verse; he never told more of himself than the world might have assumed without listening to him. Only with diffidence could history attribute to such a class of men a wider range of thought or feeling than they themselves cared to proclaim. Yet the difficulty of denying or even ignoring the wider range was still greater, for no one questioned the force or the scope of an emotion which caused the poorest peasant in Europe to see what was invisible to poet and philosopher,—the dim outline of a mountain-summit across the ocean, rising high above the mist and mud of American democracy. As though to call attention to some such difficulty, European and American critics, while affirming that Americans were a race without illusions or enlarged ideas, declared in the same breath that Jefferson was a visionary whose theories would cause the heavens to fall upon them. Year after year, with endless iteration, in every accent of contempt, rage, and despair, they repeated this charge against Jefferson. Every foreigner and Federalist agreed that he was a man of illusions, dangerous to society and unbounded in power of evil; but if this view of his character was right, the same visionary qualities seemed also to be a national trait, for every one admitted that Jefferson's opinions, in one form or another, were shared by a majority of the American people.

Illustrations might be carried much further, and might be drawn from every social class and from every period in national history. Of all Presidents, Abraham Lincoln has been considered the most typical representative of American society, chiefly because his mind, with all its practical qualities, also inclined, in certain directions, to idealism. Lincoln was born in 1809, the moment when American character stood in lowest esteem. Ralph Waldo Emerson, a more distinct idealist, was born in 1803. William Ellery Channing, another idealist, was born in 1780. Men like John Fitch, Oliver Evans, Robert Fulton, Joel Barlow, John Stevens, and Eli Whitney were all classed among visionaries. The whole society of Quakers belonged in the same category. The records of the popular religious sects abounded in examples of idealism and illusion to such an extent that the masses seemed hardly to find comfort or hope in any authority, however old or well-established. In religion as in politics, Americans seemed to require a system which gave play to their imagination and their hopes.

Some misunderstanding must always take place when the observer is at cross-purposes with the society he describes. Wordsworth might have convinced himself by a moment's thought that no country could act on the imagination as America acted upon the instincts of the ignorant and poor, without some quality that deserved better treatment than poignant scorn; but perhaps this was only one among innumerable cases in which the unconscious poet breathed an atmosphere which the self-conscious poet could not penetrate. With equal reason he might have taken the opposite view,—that the hard, practical, money-getting American democrat, who had neither generosity nor honor nor imagination, and who inhabited cold shades where fancy sickened and where genius died, was in truth living in a world of dream, and acting a drama more instinct with poetry than all the avatars of the East, walking in gardens of emeralds and rubies, in ambition already ruling the world and guiding Nature with a kinder and wiser hand than had ever yet been felt in human history. From this point his critics never approached him,—they stopped at a stone's throw; and at the moment when they declared that the man's mind had no illusions, they added that he was a knave or a lunatic. Even on his practical and sordid side, the American might easily have been represented as a victim to illusion. If the Englishman had lived as the American speculator did—in the future—the hyperbole of enthusiasm would have seemed less monstrous. "Look at my wealth!" cried the American to his foreign visitor. "See these solid mountains of salt and iron, of lead, copper, silver, and gold! See these magnificent cities scattered broadcast to the Pacific! See my cornfields rustling and waving in the summer breeze from ocean to ocean, so far that the sun itself is not high enough to mark where the distant mountains bound my golden seas! Look at this continent of mine, fairest of created worlds, as she lies turning up to the sun's never-failing caress her broad and exuberant breasts, overflowing with milk for her hundred million children! See how she glows with youth, health, and love!" Perhaps it was not altogether unnatural that the foreigner, on being asked to see what needed centuries to produce, should have looked about him with bewilderment and indignation. "Gold! cities! cornfields! continents! Nothing of the sort! I see nothing but tremendous wastes, where sickly men and women are dying of homesickness or are scalped by savages! mountain ranges a thousand miles long, with no means of getting to them, and nothing in them when you get there! swamps and forests choked with their own rotten ruins! nor hope of better for a thousand years! Your story is a fraud, and you are a liar and swindler!"

Met in this spirit, the American, half perplexed and half defiant, retaliated by calling his antagonist a fool, and by mimicking his heavy tricks of manner. For himself he cared little, but his dream was his whole existence. The men who denounced him admitted that they left him in his forest-swamp quaking with fever, but clinging in the delirium of death to the illusions of his dazzled brain. No class of men could be required to support their convictions with a steadier faith, or pay more devotedly with their persons for the mistakes of their judgment. Whether imagination or greed led them to describe more than actually existed, they still saw no more than any inventor or discoverer must have seen in order to give him the energy of success. They said to the rich as to the poor, "Come and share our limitless riches! Come and help us bring to light these unimaginable stores of wealth and power!" The poor came, and from them were seldom heard complaints of deception or delusion. Within a moment, by the mere contact of a moral atmosphere, they saw the gold and jewels, the summer cornfields, and the glowing continent. The rich for a long time stood aloof,—they were timid and narrow-minded; but this was not all,—between them and the American democrat was a gulf.

The charge that Americans were too fond of money to win the confidence of Europeans was a curious inconsistency; yet this was a common belief. If the American deluded himself and led others to their death by baseless speculations; if he buried those he loved in a gloomy forest where they quaked and died while he persisted in seeing there a splendid, healthy, and well-built city, —no one could deny that he sacrificed wife and child to his greed for gain, that the dollar was his god, and a sordid avarice his demon. Yet had this been the whole truth, no European capitalist would have hesitated to make money out of his grave; for, avarice against avarice, no more sordid or meaner type existed in America than could be shown on every 'Change in Europe. With much more reason Americans might have suspected that in America Englishmen found everywhere a silent influence, which they found nowhere in Europe, and which had nothing to do with avarice or with the dollar, but, on the contrary, seemed likely at any moment to sacrifice the dollar in a cause and for an object so illusory that most Englishmen could not endure to hear it discussed. European travellers who passed through America noticed that everywhere, in the White House at Washington and in log cabins beyond the Alleghanies, except for a few Federalists, every American, from Jefferson and Gallatin down to the poorest squatter, seemed to nourish an idea that he was doing what he could to overthrow the tyranny which the past had fastened on the human mind. Nothing was easier than to laugh at the ludicrous expressions of this simple-minded conviction, or to cry out against its coarseness, or grow angry with its prejudices; to see its nobler side, to feel the beatings of a heart underneath the sordid surface of a gross humanity, was not so easy. Europeans seemed seldom or never conscious that the sentiment could possess a noble side, but found only matter for complaint in the remark that every American democrat believed himself to be working for the overthrow of tyranny, aristocracy, hereditary privilege, and priesthood, wherever they existed. Even where the American did not openly proclaim this conviction in words, he carried so dense an atmosphere of the sentiment with him in his daily life as to give respectable Europeans an uneasy sense of remoteness.

Of all historical problems, the nature of a national character is the most difficult and the most important. Readers will be troubled, at almost every chapter of the coming narrative, by the want of some formula to explain what share the popular imagination bore in the system pursued by government. The acts of the American people during the administrations of Jefferson and Madison were judged at the time by no other test. According as bystanders believed American character to be hard, sordid, and free from illusion, they were severe and even harsh in judgment. This rule guided the governments of England and France. Federalists in the United States, knowing more of the circumstances, often attributed to the democratic instinct a visionary quality which they regarded as sentimentality, and charged with many bad consequences. If their view was correct, history could occupy itself to no better purpose than in ascertaining the nature and force of the quality which was charged with results so serious: but nothing was more elusive than the spirit of American democracy. Jefferson, the literary representative of the class, spoke chiefly for Virginians, and dreaded so greatly his own reputation as a visionary that he seldom or never uttered his whole thought. Gallatin and Madison were still more cautious. The press in no country could give shape to a mental condition so shadowy. The people themselves, although millions in number, could not have expressed their finer instincts had they tried, and might not have recognized them if expressed by others.

In the early days of colonization, every new settlement represented an idea and proclaimed a mission. Virginia was founded by a great, liberal movement aiming at the spread of English liberty and empire. The Pilgrims of Plymouth, the Puritans of Boston, the Quakers of Pennsylvania, all avowed a moral purpose, and began by making institutions that consciously reflected a moral idea. No such character belonged to the colonization of 1800. From Lake Erie to Florida, in long, unbroken line, pioneers were at work, cutting into the forests with the energy of so many beavers, and with no more express moral purpose than the beavers they drove away. The civilization they carried with them was rarely illumined by an idea; they sought room for no new truth, and aimed neither at creating, like the Puritans, a government of saints, nor, like the Quakers, one of love and peace; they left such experiments behind them, and wrestled only with the hardest problems of frontier life. No wonder that foreign observers, and even the educated, well-to-do Americans of the sea-coast, could seldom see anything to admire in the ignorance and brutality of frontiersmen, and should declare that virtue and wisdom no longer guided the United States! What they saw was not encouraging. To a new society, ignorant and semi-barbarous, a mass of demagogues insisted on applying every stimulant that could inflame its worst appetites, while at the same instant taking away every influence that had hitherto helped to restrain its passions. Greed for wealth, lust for power, yearning for the blank void of savage freedom such as Indians and wolves delighted in—these were the fires that flamed under the cauldron of American society, in which, as conservatives believed, the old, well-proven, conservative crust of religion, government, family, and even common respect for age, education, and experience was rapidly melting away, and was indeed already broken into fragments, swept about by the seething mass of scum ever rising in greater quantities to the surface.

James Schouler.

BORN in West Cambridge, now Arlington, Mass., 1839.

ANDREW JACKSON.

[*History of the United States of America under the Constitution. Vols. I.–IV.*—
1880–89.]

HE has left a landmark in our annals for all time. Much is said of the influence of ideas in producing history, but the really controlling influence of this epoch was that of personal example. And never did popular parties opposed to one another respond to personal guidance so heartily as those which now grew up under the leadership of those fierce combatants, always at variance with one another, Clay and Jackson; the one combining popular elements too intelligent and opinionated not to show signs of jealous dissension, the other having a blind democracy for a nucleus so dense, so devoted, and withal so carefully disciplined, that rivalry was kept low and political mutiny punishable as though by martial law. Strong in all his traits of character, his vices as well as his virtues, Jackson's public example was one for positive good and positive evil,—a mixture of brass and clay. There could be nothing negative about him. What he purposed, that he put his hand to and bore it safely through. His mind moved rapidly, and with an almost lightning-like perception he had resolved the point while others were deliberating; and right or wrong, he was tenacious of his conclusion, and fought to have his way like one who felt it shame not to win. There was no twilight of dubiety about him; he knew, and knew earnestly; and within the steel horizon which bounded his vision he could pierce to the circumference in all directions. As his intellect admitted of no half-truth, so did his nature revolt at bargains and compromises, such as Clay, his mortal enemy, was an adept in arranging; but with him it was to conquer or die on every occasion, win a clean victory or endure a clean defeat. This temper, as those who knew him best have admitted, gave him a load to carry all his life; every step he took was a contest, and yet, if ever mortal may be said to have triumphed in what he undertook, every contest was a victory. Jackson could not live without a quarrel; and, though capable of strong and lasting attachment, friends and enemies often changed places as his ambition developed, and no one could remain long in his confidence who did not humor his foibles and bend to his purpose. Conscientious difference of opinion he knew not how to tolerate, and friendship that was not all in all was not at all. Gratitude implied a self-abasement, and he felt it for no one; even coequal companionship was something of a yoke to him ; it was admiring devotion that won his heart, and the better angel of his nature was compassion. But though knightly towards women, tender to children, the young, the gentle, the fallen, to all who nestled up confidingly, his contempt for weakness disposed him to snatch whatever he wanted, regardless of others' rights. He could bully a sister republic to get her territory, and drive the half-tamed Indian from his homestead and the white man's neighborhood at the point of the bayonet, and all this with hardly the pretence of compunction. Frank and sincere in the main, and wishing to be thought so whatever ill might be imputed to him, of manners cordial and graceful, he was a generous host at home, and after his own ideal a Southern gentleman. Yet for all this he had something of the borderer's fierce disposition ; with the men among whom he had been born and bred might made right, and honor was vindicated by a brace of pistols at ten paces. Such a citizen could never have been exalted to national distinction in the courtlier age of the republic, and his fame waited long for civil recognition, even after his military success. Springing up out-of-doors and in the free sunshine, rough contact with mankind in a pioneer society gave him an education ; and as a slave-holder, long used to an easy independence and to being waited upon, he acquired that self-confidence in later life without which consciousness of merit must fail of renown. As chief magistrate he was an innovation upon American life, a novelty,—in some sense a protest against the past. He was the first great product of the West, humanly speaking, Clay only excepted, whose genius partook more of Eastern example. He was the first President of this Union chosen from the west of the Alleghanies and a pioneer State; the first ever borne into the chair with a general hurrah and no real sense of civil superiority for the office. He was the first President from what we call the masses; the first whose following vulgarized, so to speak, the national administration and social life at the capital. Old age and debility had much to do with the venerating applause which constantly followed him, and forced even his whims to be respected ; the people seemed anxious to make amends for so long neglecting to advance him.

Jackson ruled by his indomitable force of will, his tenacity of purpose, courage, and energy. He did not investigate nor lean upon advice, but made up his mind by whatever strange and crooked channels came his information, and then took the responsibility. Experience made him rapid rather than rash, though he was always impulsive; and he would despatch the business which engaged his thoughts, and that most thoroughly. Though stretched on the bed of sickness, he held the thread of his purpose where none could take it from him ; his will rallied and beat under the body. He decided affairs quickly, and upon impulse more than reflection ; but his intuitions were keen, often profound, in politics as well as war. His vigor as an Executive at his time of life was truly wonderful. He left nothing in affairs for others to finish, betrayed no sign of fear or timidity, shrank from no burden however momentous, but marched to the muzzle of his purpose, and, like an old soldier, gained half the advantage in a fight by his bold despatch and vigor.

The night march and surprise were points he had learned in Indian warfare; and were it war or politics, he carried out what he had fixed upon with constant intrepidity. This intrepidity went with a conscious sense of duty; for, though a Cromwell in spirit, Jackson's ambition was honestly to serve his country. Loyalty to the Union, sympathy with the American common people, were the chief impulses of his being, for all he loved power; and hence a majority was almost sure to sustain him. Courage and directness the people admire in any man, and a sordid or usurping nature they are apt to discover. Jackson had the Midas touch, which could transmute whatever he handled, if not into solid gold, at least into a substance of popularity. And yet no servant of the ballot-box felt less the need of courting popularity, or of waiting for public opinion to bear his plans forward. Lesser statesmen might be exponents, but he led on, leaving the public to comment as it might.

We have intimated more than once in our narrative that Jackson was neither so frank nor so chivalrous as he passed for, nor yet so little of a politician. Was there ever a great general who did not employ strategy? Jackson could dissimulate, and in his very maladies he gained some crafty advantage. One of his warmest admirers has pronounced him a consummate actor, whose art often imposed the policy of rashness. Van Buren found him a man guarded and self-controlled where he had seemed impetuous. He could put off an inconvenient friendship so as to make his friend appear the wrongdoer. Of darker duplicity signs, though inconclusive, are not wanting. But his blunt perceptions of right and wrong, his brutal obstinacy and the tailwagging subservience which he exacted from those about him did the country he meant to honor an irreparable mischief. While President his irascibility forced those who would influence him to take to tortuous methods. Cabinet officers, men far better versed in affairs than himself, had to fall in with his opinions and seem to yield; overreaching, if they might, when executing his orders, or bringing the subject up again. This, and his preference for the kitchen advisers, had something to do with his frequent cabinet changes. All had to pay court to get on. Van Buren earned most from his intimacy, playing the faithful hound, and it cost him dearly in the end. The circle surrounding the old man fed him with gross flattery. All this gave soon the smirch to decent self-respect. Personalism came to tincture all politics, all policies, all politicians, under his arbitrary and exacting administration; and the painted Jezebel of party patronage seized upon the public trusts for her favorites. Such a state of things was sure to breed corruption sooner or later. Prætorian bands showed the first symptom of Rome's decay; bands of officeholders, united by the necessity of keeping the spoils and salaries from other bands equally ravenous, may prove an early symptom of our own, if the people submit to it. Personally honest and unstained by bribery, Jackson played nevertheless into the hands of others who traded upon his violence; greedy followers milked the offices they had gained by partisan service. Even the battery of the National Bank, in which he led off, had its pugilistic aspect: money put up against money, and monopoly fighting monopoly.

Jackson's illiteracy is admitted by his admirers; but opponents of his day made too much of it, as though administrations were a matter of mere scholarship. Longer experience in popular self-government has dispelled that illusion. It was of greater note that his strong personal feelings mingled in all he said or did, and that opponents were colored by his temperament. In conversation he interested, whether he convinced or not, being clear, earnest, and straight to the point both in thought and expression ; and while no question admitted of two sides to his mind, his own was fearlessly grasped. As his speech was sagacious and incisive, in spite of slips in grammar or mispronunciation, so he could write with powerful effect, though no scholar in the true sense, and in personal controversy he was one to be feared. His state papers engaged able minds in and out of his cabinet, yet the direction of thought, the statement of policy, the temper of the document, were his own. Others might elaborate the argument for him or polish and arrange the composition, but, after all, his was the central thought ; and he would flourish over the paper with a rapid pen, and a huge one, until sheet after sheet lay before him glistening with ink and glowing with expression as though it were written in his heart's blood. That there were misspelt words to be corrected, or awkward sentences to be trussed up afterwards by his secretary, is not to be denied. In short, Andrew Jackson fed little upon books and much upon experience with unconventional life and human nature; but he had what is essential to eminence in either case, a vigorous intellect and a strong will. In the conduct of affairs he took advice wherever he saw fit, and like a commander secretive of his own plans, tested the views of his council and then made up his own mind.

Such was the remarkable man whose shaping influence in national affairs made him the transcendent figure of these times; in him of all Americans the Union, for thirty years prior to the eventful 1860, was personified. In faults and merits alike he was so great, and he produced so much that was good and so much that was vicious, that the historian may well be perplexed to trace the blending line. This warrior first entered office with an easier task before him than any of his predecessors, and twice when he took the official oath he might have shaped his course peacefully to the popular predisposition which was to reward a veteran soldier with the highest mark of honor. Twice, however, as we have seen, did he surprise expectation, both by the vitality of his rule and his peculiar aptitude for fighting out some new political policy. He fought well, as he had always done, and was as pertinacious in returning to the attack and mortifying the foes who had wounded his friends. Quarrels and bad blood made the large component of these eight years' policy; the fight of factions made the spoils of office, for the first time, a national principle; the fight with the Bank, originating, most likely, in personal offence, was a personal one to the close; and but for his personal rupture with Calhoun one may well doubt whether nullification would ever have raised its reptile head. Jackson's best act was to trample down that heresy, though the snake was only scotched, and his worst was to debauch the public service. In the one, as in the other, his example long outlived him. But most pernicious of all, in quick results, he initiated the treacherous policy of Mexican dismemberment and annexation for the sake of slavery; from a motive pseudo-patriotic, however, to preserve the equilibrium of the Union, and with a responsibility quite indirect for the worst that followed after he had set the ball in motion. As for the rest, his foreign policy was brilliant and sagacious; his stand on the tariff and internal improvements judicious for the times; his course to the Indians, though harsh, not without justifying reasons. He paid off the national debt, like the punctilious planter he was, who abhorred all debt, public and private, and with real opportunity might have left to his country some plan for disposing of a national surplus instead of leaving himself on record as a censurer of all plans. Upon his financial policy our narrative has dwelt already, and the full effect of that glorious folly, the transfer of the deposits, will soon be shown. With all his fervent zeal, there were limitations to his theory of public banking, limitations to his theory of a fraternal Union.

No President ever ruled these United States in times of peace with a personal supremacy so absolute as the two great chieftains of our democracy, Jackson and Jefferson, though in methods and character they were so little alike. The one was a born manager of men, the other a stern dictator; the one philanthropic to the socially oppressed, the other a hater rather of the social oppressor; each, however, influenced by a love of country which was a ruling passion, by constitutional restraints somewhat independently interpreted, and, in later life at least, by an unconscious bias to the side of the South whenever slavery was threatened with violence by Northern agitators. This last in Jefferson weakened his practical efforts in the anti-slavery cause, though he was anti-slavery in sentiment to the end; in Jackson, who thought himself no worse for being a master, if a kind one, it stimulated the determination to make his section strong enough to hold out against the abolitionists, for abolitionists and nullifiers were all hell-hounds of disunion. Jefferson had gently manipulated Congress; Jackson ruled in defiance of it, and by arraying the people, or rather a party majority on his side, against it, until the tone of his messages, if not really insolent, was that of conscious infallibility. Congress is elastic, however, and easily rallies, being naturally the encroaching power under our coördinate system. But as for the people, the danger grew that their will in elections would be fettered by machinery and machine managers. In these years the democracy made rapid strides, and the nation, too, advanced in power. Self-confidence increased, and a domineering disposition. There was a vigorous vulgarity about this administration at every point, resolution and a passionate love of danger. And yet at home, factions and mob violence were always on the increase; and though the principles of national institutions and of fundamental authority were discussed as never before nor since, there never was a time short of civil war when lawlessness gained so nearly the upper hand in the community. The most dangerous infractions of the constitution are those not violent enough to provoke the governed to open resistance, and of such there were many. Jackson's school of philosophy was not tolerant and reconciling. There were too many friends to reward, too many foes to punish. Class was inflamed against class, the poor showed their teeth at the rich; and while the Union was constantly held up for reverence, and even idolatry, the joints were strained, the fraternal bonds parted, and men of both sections began to feel themselves less unionists at heart than before. And thus, though decked out with glory, did Jackson's iron rule plough long furrows in the back of the republic whose scars are still visible.

Annie Trumbull Slosson.

BORN in Stonington, Conn.

HE FORSOOK HIS NETS, AND FOLLOWED HIM.

[*Fishin' Jimmy.* 1889.]

BUT one thing troubled Fishin' Jimmy. He wanted to be a "fisher of men." That was what the Great Teacher had promised he would make the fishermen who left their boats to follow him. What strange, literal meaning he attached to the terms, we could not tell. In vain we—especially the boys, whose young hearts had gone out in warm affection to the old man —tried to show him that he was, by his efforts to do good and make others better and happier, fulfilling the Lord's directions. He could not understand it so. "I allers try to think," he said, "that 'twas me in that boat when he come along. I make b'l'eve that it was out on Streeter's Pond, an' I was settin' in the boat, fixin' my lan'in' net, when I see him on the shore. I think mebbe I'm that James—for that's my given name, ye know, though they allers call me Jimmy—an' then I hear him callin' me 'James, James.' I can hear him jest 's plain sometimes, when the wind 's blowin' in the trees, an' I jest ache to up an' foller him. But says he, 'I 'll make ye a fisher o' men,' an' he aint done it. I'm waitin'; mebbe he'll larn me some day."

He was fond of all living creatures, merciful to all. But his love for our dog Dash became a passion, for Dash was an angler. Who that ever saw him sitting in the boat beside his master, watching with eager eye and whole body trembling with excitement the line as it was cast, the flies as they touched the surface—who can forget old Dash? His fierce excitement at rise of trout, the efforts at self-restraint, the disappointment if the prey escaped, the wild exultation if it was captured, how plainly—he who runs might read—were shown these emotions in eye, in ear, in tail, in whole quivering body! What wonder that it all went straight to the fisher's heart of Jimmy! "I never knowed afore they could be Christians," he said, looking, with tears in his soft, keen eyes, at the every-day scene, and with no faintest thought of irreverence. "I never knowed it, but I'd give a stiffikit o' membership in the orthodoxest church goin' to that dog there."

It is almost needless to say that as years went on Jimmy came to know many "fishin' min'sters"; for there are many of that ilk who love our mountain country, and seek it yearly. All these knew and loved the old man. And there were others who had wandered by that sea of Galilee, and fished in the waters of the Holy Land, and with them Fishin' Jimmy dearly loved to talk. But his wonder was never-ending that, in the scheme of evan-

gelizing the world, more use was not made of the "fishin' side" of the story.
"Haint they ever tried it on them poor heathen?" he would ask earnestly of
some clerical angler casting a fly upon the clear water of pond or brook. "I
should think 'twould 'a' ben the fust thing they'd done. Fishin' fust, an'
r'liging 's sure to foller. An' it's so easy; fur heath'n mostly r'sides on
islands, don't they? So ther's plenty o' water, an' o' course ther's fishin';
an' oncet gin 'em poles an' git 'em to work, an' they're out o' mischief fur
that day. They'd like it better 'n cannib'ling, or cuttin' out idles, or scratch-
in' picters all over theirselves, an' bimeby—not too suddent, ye know, to
scare 'em—yo could begin on that story, an' they couldn't stan' that, not a
heath'n on 'em. Won't ye speak to the 'Merican Board about it, an' sen' out
a few fishin' mishneries, with poles an' lines an' tackle gen'ally? I 've tried
it on dreffle bad folks, an' it allers done 'em good. But "—so almost all his
simple talk ended—"I wish I could begin to be a fisher o' men. I 'm gettin'
on now, I 'm nigh seventy, an' I aint got much time, ye see."

One afternoon in July there came over Franconia Notch one of those
strangely sudden tempests which sometimes visit that mountain country. It
had been warm that day, unusually warm for that refreshingly cool spot;
but suddenly the sky grew dark and darker, almost to blackness, there was
roll of thunder and flash of lightning, and then poured down the rain—rain
at first, but soon hail in large frozen bullets, which fiercely pelted any who
ventured out-doors, rattled against the windows of the Profile House with
sharp cracks like sounds of musketry, and lay upon the piazza in heaps like
snow. And in the midst of the wild storm it was remembered that two boys,
guests at our hotel, had gone up Mount Lafayette alone that day. They
were young boys, unused to mountain climbing, and their friends were anxious. It was found that Dash had followed them; and just as some one was
to be sent in search of them, a boy from the stables brought the information
that Fishin' Jimmy had started up the mountain after them as the storm
broke. "Said if he couldn't be a fisher o' men, mebbe he knowed nuff to
ketch boys," went on our informant, seeing nothing more in the speech, full
of pathetic meaning to us who knew him, than the idle talk of one whom
many considered "lackin'." Jimmy was old now, and had of late grown
very feeble, and we did not like to think of him out in that wild storm. And
now suddenly the lost boys themselves appeared through the opening in the
woods opposite the house, and ran in through the hail, now falling more
quietly. They were wet, but no worse apparently for their adventure, though
full of contrition and distress at having lost sight of the dog. He had rushed
off into the woods some hours before, after a rabbit or hedgehog, and had
never returned. Nor had they seen Fishin' Jimmy.

As hours went by and the old man did not return, a search party was sent
out, and guides familiar with all the mountain paths went up Lafayette to
seek for him. It was nearly night when they at last found him, and the
grand old mountains had put on those robes of royal purple which they sometimes assume at eventide. At the foot of a mass of rock, which looked like
amethyst or wine-red agate in that marvellous evening light, the old man
was lying, and Dash was with him. From the few faint words Jimmy could

then gasp out, the truth was gathered. He had missed the boys, leaving the path by which they had returned, and while stumbling along in search of them, feeble and weary, he had heard far below a sound of distress. Looking down over a steep, rocky ledge, he had seen his friend and fishing-comrade, old Dash, in sore trouble. Poor Dash! He never dreamed of harming his old friend, for he had a kind heart. But he was a sad coward in some matters, and a very baby when frightened and away from master and friends. So I fear he may have assumed the role of wounded sufferer when in reality he was but scared and lonesome. He never owned this afterward, and you may be sure we never let him know by word or look the evil he had done. Jimmy saw him holding up one paw helplessly and looking at him with wistful, imploring brown eyes, heard his pitiful, whimpering cry for aid, and never doubted his great distress and peril. Was Dash not a fisherman? And fishermen, in Fishin' Jimmy's category, were always true and trusty. So the old man without a second's hesitation started down the steep, smooth decline to the rescue of his friend.

We do not know just how or where in that terrible descent he fell. To us who afterward saw the spot, and thought of the weak old man, chilled by the storm, exhausted by his exertions, and yet clambering down that precipitous cliff, made more slippery and treacherous by the sleet and hail still falling, it seemed impossible that he could have kept a foothold for an instant. Nor am I sure that he expected to save himself and Dash too. But he tried. He was sadly hurt. I will not tell you of that.

Looking out from the hotel windows through the gathering darkness, we who loved him—it was not a small group—saw a sorrowful sight. Flickering lights thrown by the lanterns of the guides came through the woods. Across the road, slowly, carefully, came strong men, bearing on a rough hastily made litter of boughs the dear old man. All that could have been done for the most distinguished guest, for the dearest, best-beloved friend, was done for the gentle fisherman. We, his friends, and proud to style ourselves thus, were of different, widely separated lands, greatly varying creeds. Some were nearly as old as the dying man, some in the prime of manhood. There were youths and maidens and little children. But through the night we watched together. The old Roman bishop, whose calm, benign face we all know and love; the Churchman, ascetic in faith, but with the kindest, most indulgent heart when one finds it; the gentle old Quakeress with placid, unwrinkled brow and silvery hair; Presbyterian, Methodist, and Baptist,— we were all one that night. The old angler did not suffer—we were so glad of that! But he did not appear to know us, and his talk seemed strange. It rambled on quietly, softly, like one of his own mountain brooks, babbling of green fields, of sunny summer days, of his favorite sport, and ah! of other things. But he was not speaking to us. A sudden, awed hush and thrill came over us as, bending to catch the low words, we all at once understood what only the bishop put into words as he said, half to himself, in a sudden, quick, broken whisper, "God bless the man, he's talking to his Master!"

"Yes, sir, that's so," went on the quiet voice; "'twas on'y a dog, sure nuff; 'twa'n't even a boy, as ye say, an' ye ast me to be a fisher o' men. But

I haint had no chance for that, somehow; mebbe I wa'n't fit for 't. I'm on'y jest a poor old fisherman, Fishin' Jimmy, ye know, sir. Ye useter call me James—no one else ever done it. On'y a dog? But he wa'n't jest a common dog, sir; he was a fishin' dog. I never seed a man love fishin' mor 'n Dash." The dog was in the room, and heard his name. Stealing to the bedside, he put a cold nose into the cold hand of his old friend, and no one had the heart to take him away. The touch turned the current of the old man's talk for a moment, and he was fishing again with his dog friend. "See 'em break, Dashy! See 'em break! Lots on 'em to-day, aint they? Keep still, there's a good dog, while I put on a diffunt fly. Don't ye see they're jumpin' at them gnats? Aint the water jest 'live with 'em? Aint it shinin' an' clear an'—" The voice faltered an instant, then went on : "Yes, sir, I'm comin'—I'm glad, dreffle glad to come. Don't mind 'bout my leavin' my fishin'; do ye think I care 'bout that? I'll jest lay down my pole ahin' the alders here, an' put my lan'in' net on the stuns, with my flies an' tackle—the boys 'll like 'em, ye know—an' I'll be right along.

"I mos' knowed ye was on'y a-tryin' me when ye said that 'bout how I hadn't been a fisher o' men, nor even boys, on'y a dog. 'Twas a—fishin' dog—ye know—an' ye was allers dreffle good to fishermen,—dreffle good to —everybody; died—for 'em, didn't ye?—

"Please wait—on—the bank there, a minnit; I'm comin' 'crost. Water's pretty—cold this—spring—an' the stream 's risin'—but—I—can—do it ;— don't ye mind—'bout me, sir. I'll get acrost." Once more the voice ceased, and we thought we should not hear it again this side that stream.

But suddenly a strange light came over the thin face, the soft gray eyes opened wide, and he cried out, with the strong voice we had so often heard come ringing out to us across the mountain streams above the sound of their rushing: "Here I be, sir! It's Fishin' Jimmy, ye know, from Francony way; him ye useter call James when ye come 'long the shore o' the pond an' I was a-fishin'. I heern ye agin, jest now—an' I—straightway—f'sook—my —nets—an'—follered—"

Had the voice ceased utterly? No, we could catch faint, low murmurs and the lips still moved. But the words were not for us ; and we did not know when he reached the other bank.

Patrick Francis Mullany.

(BROTHER AZARIAS.)

BORN in County Tipperary, Ireland, 1847.

EMERSON AND NEWMAN.

[*On Thinking : An Address Delivered at Rock Hill College, 1878.*—1881.]

THE PHILOSOPHER—THE CHURCHMAN.

THAT you may all the better understand the nature and scope of sound thinking, I will mention for your consideration two living thinkers in different hemispheres of our globe and standing at opposite poles of human thoughts—men at the same time acknowledged masters of our own language. They both have this in common, that each is retiring, sensitive, shrinking from mere notoriety, not over-anxious to speak and speaking only when each has something to say. They are loved by all who know them, admired by thousands and misunderstood by thousands more. One of these is Ralph Waldo Emerson. He is possessed of a mind like the Eolian harp. It is awake to the most delicate impressions, and at every breath of thought gives out a music all its own. His sympathies with Nature are so strong—so intense, so real—that they seem to take root with the plant, to infuse themselves into the brute creation, and to think and act with his fellow-man. A thing, be it an institution, or a custom, or a habit, exists; that suffices for Emerson; it must therefore be good, and useful, and beautiful in its own way. He is a passionate lover of the beautiful; he would reduce all morality to a code of æsthetics. Beauty of thought, beauty of expression, beauty of action, beauty of manners —these are the outcome of his philosophy. Supreme culture is for him supreme human perfection. But withal, he is a thinker who has learned how to assimilate the best thoughts of the best writers and make them fructify in his own mind. His lines of thought are narrow, but he thinks on them intensely. Not unfrequently his language only half expresses that which his mind labors to give utterance to. Some of his assertions are riddles. He speaks with the mysteriousness of the Sphinx. He disdains argument. He will not reason with you. He is content to throw out the hint or the suggestion; you may take it or leave it. He never obtrudes himself upon you.

Unfortunately for Emerson and the value of his utterances, he ignores the supernatural in man. His view of religion is that of a merely human institution. He is tolerant only in certain directions. He has never acquired the large-sightedness that is expected from a man of his culture. Let him expatiate on the Nature he loves, on society, on manners, on experience, on letters and social aims, and he is admirable, suggestive, original; but once he descends to concrete living issues, we find only the lifeless bones of intolerance dressed up with the time-worn garments of New England puritanical prejudices. I hold this man up to you that you may learn both from his strength and his weakness. You can no more make a model of his mind than you can of his style. He is in some respects a law to himself. The secret of his success lies in this: that he does not isolate a thought; he studies its relations so far as his intellectual vision ranges. Could you imbibe his sympathy for Nature without becoming imbued with his pantheism; could you acquire his culture without the dilettanteism that accompanies it; could you make his love for the beautiful in all shapes and under all conditions your own— looking above all beyond the mere surface into the deeper and more spiritual beauty of things—you would be learning the whole lesson I wish you to draw from his intellectual life.

And now that I have led you into the inner chambers of Emerson's mind, and shown you the points of excellence and deficiency in his thinking, let me with less reserve place before you a still greater living example of this power of thinking, that you may in admiration, and at a distance, and each in his own sphere, follow in his footsteps. His word carries weight wherever the English language is known. His name is revered by all classes and creeds; and it is so because he is thoroughly honest in the expression of his convictions. He does not understand the art of special pleading; he has never learned the trick of covering up disagreeable truths or removing out of sight a fact calculated to tell against him. Endowed with one of the most acute intellects ever bestowed upon man, and well disciplined by severe study and profound meditation, it was his delight to grapple with difficulties. That mind, so ingenious and searching, never rested till it found the basis of an opinion or struck the central idea of a system. It is often to me a source of wonder how much patient, earnest thought its eminent possessor must have brought to bear upon an idea before he could see it in so many lights, view it in such different relations, and place it before the mind in all the nakedness of truth. But this is one of the characteristics of great thinkers, and such preëminently is Cardinal John Henry Newman. It is now about three years since I met him in the bare, modest parlor of the Birmingham Oratory, and I need scarcely add that that meeting is one of the most precious incidents in my life. I thought the very simplicity of that parlor was in keeping with the greatness of the man. Tinsel, or decoration, or an air of worldliness would have jarred with the simple, unassuming ways of the noble soul I met there. He had then lately returned from his beloved Oxford, where his old *alma mater*, Trinity College, did itself an honor and him an act of tardy justice in inducting him as Honorary Fellow. This veteran knight of natural and revealed truth looked old and worn ; his hair was blanched ; his features were furrowed with the traces of age. His manners were gentle and condescending. His voice was soft and beautiful in its varied modulations—now serious, now playful, according to the subject he spoke upon. With the most exquisite tact he listened or placed his remark as the case required. There was a charm in his conversation. As it flowed along placid and pleasant, his countenance glowed with a nameless expression; his eyes sparkled, and he spoke with all the strength and clearness of a man whose intellectual vigor is still unimpaired. I was not half an hour in his presence when I felt the spell of that irresistible personal influence which he has swayed through life, whether within the

Brother Azarias

walls of Oriel, or from the Protestant pulpit of St. Mary's or in the retirement of the Oratory. I then understood the power that shook the Anglican Church to its very basis six and thirty years ago. Though endowed with the delicate sensibility of the poet, Cardinal Newman never permits sentiment or feeling or inclination or confirmed habit to control or divert the severe logic of his noble reason. See for instance the caution with which he took the most important step in his long career. For years inclination and grace and the logic of his mind had been leading him into the Catholic Church, but he makes no move that is not first sanctioned by reason and conscience. His sympathies have gone forth to her long before proof or argument point the way; but he holds aloof till reason becomes convinced. He even keeps others for years from entering her Communion. And whilst writing a book in favor of that Church he does not yet make up his mind to become a member; he reserves to himself the chance of changing his views after the whole argumentative process influencing him has been placed before him in writing. And in all this he is acting sincerely and in good faith. Protestants question his honesty; Catholics fear he may be trifling with grace ; but all the same he waits and prays and the truth grows upon him from the gray of dawn to the full light of day. Never for a single moment did he falter through the whole course of the long and painful struggle; from first to last he acted according to his lights; God respected the earnest endeavor and blessed it and crowned it with the grace of conversion. I repeat it, it is this strict and chivalric adherence to truth at all times and under all circumstances that has won him the profound respect and admiration of Christendom. He disciplined his mind into the habit of seeing things as they are and of expressing them as he sees them, till it has become an impossibility for him to do otherwise.

His is a mind well worth your study. Its logical acuteness is something marvellous. Its analyzing power is searching and exhaustive. Its introspection seems to be all-seeing. He understands so well the checks and limitations of the human intellect that he is never satisfied to accept an idea for the reasons on its face. He goes back of the formal demonstration to what he considers the far more powerful motives of credibility. The syllogism says not all. The real convincing and abiding reasons on which a proposition is accepted as true are beyond either premises or conclusion. "As to logic," he remarks, "its chain of conclusions hangs loose at both ends; both the point from which the proof should start, and the points at which it should arrive, are beyond its reach; it comes short both of first principles and of concrete issues." Besides all this there are undercurrents of sentiment and inclination, associations of ideas, obscure memories, half confessed motives, probabilities, popular impressions that determine the frame of mind and the tone of thought, and they all of them enter his calculations. "And such mainly is the way," he tells us, "in which all men, gifted or not gifted, commonly reason,—not by rule, but by an inward faculty." A mind recognizing all these elements of thought and coördinating them, and giving each its value and position, is the highest ideal of a well-thinking mind that I can place before you. But I have not yet said all.

Cardinal Newman's mind is above all a religious mind. Religion is for him a reality—an intense reality; it is a sacred tunic clothing all his thoughts and making them holy and earnest; it is an essential part of his existence; it is the life of his life. And this is not simply the religion of sentiment or of the mere viewiness of doctrine and dogma, but religion based upon clear-cut doctrines and well-defined principles. " From the age of fifteen "—he tells us in one of those revelations of himself that light up his soul and show the man—"dogma has been the fundamental principle of my religion; I know of no other religion; I cannot enter into the idea of any other sort of religion; religion as a sentiment is to me a mere dream and a mockery. As well can there be filial love without the fact of a father, as devotion without the fact of the Supreme Being." Here is the central thought of Cardinal Newman's intellect. All thoughts, all issues group around that one idea. To him who reads between lines, every sermon, every essay, every treatise of the six and thirty volumes penned by his hand, reveals a soul ever questioning, ever struggling with difficulties, ever solving to itself the problems and issues of the day, ever arranging and rearranging in clear, well-defined order its own views and opinions—and all for one object and with one result, that of harmonizing them with the teachings of religion. The thoughts and questionings and theories against which other strong and well-equipped intellects struggled only to be made captives of irreligion and agnosticism, he also wrestled with and became their master, each new effort giving him additional strength; and now, his laurels won, he looks upon the intellectual struggles of the day with the repose of a warrior who has been in the fight and has come out of it a victor.

Mary Hartwell Catherwood.

BORN in Luray, Ohio, 1847.

SIEUR DE LA SALLE AND SAINTE JEANNE.

[*The Story of Tonty.* 1890.]

JEANNE LE BER sat down upon a high-backed bench before the fire in the upper room. This apartment was furnished and decorated only by abundant firelight, which danced on stone walls and hard dark rafters, on rough floor and high enclosure of the stairway. At opposite sides of the room were doors which Jeanne did not know opened into chambers scarcely larger than the sleepers who might lodge therein.

She sat in strained thought, without unwrapping herself, though shudders were sent through her by damp raiment. When her father came up with the sergeant who carried their supper, he took off her cloak, smoothed her hair, and tenderly reproved her. He set the dishes on the bench between them, and persuaded Jeanne to eat what he carved for her,—a swarthy nurse whose solicitude astounded the soldier.

Another man came up and opened the door nearest the chimney, on that side which overlooked the fortress enclosure. He paused in descending, loaded with the commandant's possessions, to say that this bedroom was designed for mademoiselle, and was now ready.

"And thou must get to it as soon as the river's chill is warmed out of thy bones," said Le Ber. "I will sit and hear the worthy friar downstairs tell his strange adventures. The sound of your voice can reach me with no effort whatever. My bedroom will be next yours, or near by, and no harm can befall you in Fort Frontenac."

Jeanne kissed his cheek before he returned to the lower room, and when the supper was removed she sat drying herself by the fire.

The eager piety of her early girlhood, which was almost fantastic in its expression, had yet worked out a nobly spiritual face. She was a beautiful saint.

For several years Jeanne le Ber had refused the ordinary clothing of women. Her visible garment was made of a soft fine blanket of white wool, with long sleeves falling nearly to her feet. It was girded to her waist by a cord from which hung her rosary. Her neck stood slim and white above the top of this robe, without ornament except the peaked monk's hood which hung behind it.

This creature like a flame of living white fire stood up and turned her back to the ruddier logs, and clasped her hands across the top of her head. Her eyes wasted scintillations on rafters while she waited for heavenly peace to calm the strong excitement driving her.

The door of Jeanne's chamber stood open as the soldier had left it. At the opposite side of the room a similar door opened, and La Salle came out. He moved a step toward the hearth, but stopped, and the pallor of a swoon filled his face.

"Sieur de la Salle," said Jeanne in a whisper. She let her arms slip down by her sides. The eccentric robe with its background of firelight cast her up tall and white before his eyes.

In the explorer's most successful moments he had never appeared so majestic. Though his dress was tarnished by the wilderness, he had it carefully arranged ; for he liked to feel it fitting him with an exactness which would not annoy his thoughts.

No formal greeting preluded the crash of this encounter between La Salle and Jeanne le Ber. What had lain repressed by prayer and penance, or had been trodden down league by league in the wilds, leaped out with strength made mighty by such repression.

Voices in loud and merry conversation below and occasional laughter came up the open stairway and made accompaniment to this half-hushed duet.

"Jeanne," stammered La Salle.

"Sieur de la Salle, I was just going to my room."

She moved away from him to the side of the hearth, as he advanced and sat down upon the bench. Unconscious that she stood while he was sitting, as if overcome by sudden blindness he reached toward her with a groping gesture.

" Take hold of my hand, Sainte Jeanne."

" And if I take hold of your hand, Sieur de la Salle," murmured the girl, bending toward him, though she held her arms at her sides, "what profit will it be to either of us?"

" I beg that you will take hold of my hand."

Her hand, quivering to each finger-tip, moved out and met and was clasped in his. La Salle's head dropped on his breast.

Jeanne turned away her face. Voices and laughter jangled in the room below. In this silent room pulse answered pulse, and with slow encounter eyes answered the adoration of eyes. In terror of herself Jeanne uttered the whispered cry :

" I am afraid ! "

She veiled herself with the long sleeve of her robe.

" And of what should you be afraid when we are thus near together?" said La Salle. " The thing to be afraid of is losing this. Such gladness has been long coming ; for I was a man when you were born, Sainte Jeanne."

" Let go my hand, Sieur de la Salle."

" Do you want me to let it go, Sainte Jeanne? "

" No, Sieur de la Salle."

Dropping her sleeve, Jeanne faced heaven through the rafters. Tears stormed down her face, and her white throat swelled with strong repressed sobs. Like some angel caught in a snare, she whispered her up-directed wail :

" All my enormity must now be confessed ! Whenever Sieur de la Salle has been assailed my soul rose up in arms for him. Oh, my poor father ! So dear has Sieur de la Salle been to me that I hated the hatred of my father. What shall I do to tear out this awful love? I have fought it through midnights and solitary days of ceaseless prayer. Oh, Sieur de la Salle, why art thou such a man? Pray to God and invoke the saints for me, and help me to go free from this love!"

" Jeanne," said La Salle, " you are so holy I dare touch no more than this sweet hand. It fills me with life. Ask me not to pray to God that he will take the life from me. Oh, Jeanne, if you could reach out of your eternity of devotion and hold me always by the hand, what a man I might be !"

She dropped her eyes to his face, saying like a soothing mother :

" Thou greatest and dearest, there is a gulf between us which we cannot pass. I am vowed to Heaven. Thou art vowed to great enterprises. The life of the family is not for us. If God showed me my way by thy side I would go through any wilderness. But Jeanne was made to listen in prayer and silence and secrecy and anguish for the word of Heaven. The worst is,"— her stormy sob again shook her from head to foot,—" you will be at court, and beautiful women will love the great explorer. And one will shine; she will be set like a star as high as the height of being your wife. And Jeanne, —oh, Jeanne ! here in this rough, new world,—she must eternally learn to be nothing !"

" My wife !" said La Salle, turning her hand in his clasp, and laying his cheek in her palm. " You are my wife. There is no court. There is no world to discover. There is only the sweet, the rose-tender palm of my wife where I can lay my tired cheek and rest."

Jeanne's fingers moved with involuntary caressing along the lowest curve of his face.

An ember fell on the hearth beside them, and Father Hennepin emphasized some point in his relation with a stamp of his foot.

"You left a glove at my father's house, Sieur de la Salle, and I hid it ; I put my face to it. And when I burned it, my own blood seemed to ooze out of that crisping glove."

La Salle trembled. The dumb and solitary man was dumb and solitary in his love.

"Now we must part," breathed Jeanne. "Heaven is strangely merciful to sinners. I never could name you to my confessor or show him this formless anguish; but now that it has been owned and cast out, my heart is glad."

La Salle rose up and stood by the hearth. As she drew her hand from his continued hold he opened his arms. Jeanne stepped backward, her eyes swarming with motes of light. She turned and reached her chamber-door ; but as the saint receded from temptation the woman rose in strength. She ran to La Salle, and with a tremor and a sob in his arms, met his mouth with the one kiss of her life. As suddenly she ran from him and left him.

La Salle had had his sublime moment of standing at the centre of the universe and seeing all things swing around him, which comes to every one successful in embodying a vast idea. But from this height he looked down at that experience.

He stood still after Jeanne's door closed until he felt his own intrusion. This drove him downstairs and out of the house, regardless of Jacques le Ber, Father Hennepin, and the officers of the fortress, who turned to gaze at his transit.

Proud satisfaction, strange in a ruined man, appeared on the explorer's face. He felt his reverses as cobwebs to be brushed away. He was loved. The king had been turned against him. His enemies had procured Count Frontenac's removal, and La Barre the new governor, conspiring to seize his estate, had ruined his credit. But he was loved. Even on this homeward journey an officer had passed him with authority to take possession of his new post on the Illinois River. His discoveries were doubted and sneered at, as well as half claimed by boasting subordinates, who knew nothing about his greater views. Yet the only softener of this man of noble granite was a spirit-like girl, who regarded the love of her womanhood as sin.

La Salle stood in the midst of enemies. He stood considering merely how his will should break down the religious walls Jeanne built around herself, and how Jacques le Ber might be conciliated by shares in the profits of the West. Behind stretched his shadowed life, full of misfortune ; good was held out to him to be withdrawn at the touch of his fingers. But this good he determined to have ; and thinking of her, La Salle walked the stiffened frost-crisp ground of the fortress half the night.

Nicholas Paine Gilman.

BORN in Quincy, Ill., 1849.

THE WAGES SYSTEM.

[*Profit Sharing between Employer and Employee.* 1889.]

THE declaration is frequently made that the wages system is fundamentally wrong in its partition of benefits. It is said to be, like slavery and serfdom, but one stage in the secular development of industry, out of which we must advance into a new "fourth form of contract," for which "coöperation" is the best name. Chateaubriand even affirmed that the wage-earner is under a system of "prolonged slavery." Declamation to the same effect is frequently heard to-day from labor-reformers. It is hardly necessary to point out that these assertions do not proceed from men who have had practical experience of the lot of the slave. A very brief period of servitude would probably suffice to prove to them the emptiness of such rhetoric. Because slavery and serfdom, under which the laborer was not a free contracting agent, have practically disappeared from the civilized world, it does not, by any means, necessarily follow that the wages system, under which the employee is free from all legal coercion, must also pass away. On general grounds, it is more probable that, having succeeded to slavery and serfdom on its intrinsic merits as a system of free contract, it will endure very long, and will undergo evolution rather than perish in revolution. The advantages it secures to the laboring man, as we see them in observing the simple facts of industrial life, are so great, in comparison with its disadvantages, that we might naturally expect the first complaints against it to proceed from the employer rather than from the employee.

Let us look for a moment at the natural history of a modern manufactory. An enterprising man perceives, as he thinks, an opening to make money by establishing and operating a woollen-manufactory in a certain place. Using capital, his own or borrowed, he erects a building and stocks it with machinery at an expense of tens of thousands of dollars. After he has bought the wool and other material, he must have persons to run his engines and tend his looms. They will not work for nothing, as they must have at least the means of subsistence. What shall he offer them? Suppose that he has been so unwise as to exhaust all his capital, and his credit as well, at the very outset, before a yard of cloth is made. Suppose that he then endeavors to engage workpeople by promising them simply a fixed share in the profits. What would the sensible workman have to say to such a proposition of coöperation, where he himself would invest no money capital and would receive no regular wages? Would he not answer: "How shall I live, and support my family, while the woollens are making and are not yet sold? Other workmen object to the delay of a month in getting their wages. They wish to be paid every fortnight, or every week; and such frequent payment is very advantageous to them. I should have to wait an indefinite number of weeks or months, until you effect a sale of the goods I have helped to make. I might indeed manage to get along on credit, paying more, in the end, than if I bought for cash. But will the grocer, and the butcher, and the tailor, and the house-owner give me credit if I am to receive no wages, and must depend entirely for my deferred recompense upon your skilful conduct of the business? For here comes the pinch. While my associates and myself may do our best in making woollens, you, with all your efforts, may reap but a small profit in selling them. Nay, who knows if there will turn out to be any profit at all? No! I cannot take such a risk. Pay me the average wages, even if they are a less return for my labor than what you would give me out of the profits. Then I shall have some regularity and some certainty about my income, and can adjust my expenses to it. Then I can buy in the cheapest market. Take yourself all the risks of business, reap yourself the profits, and bear yourself the losses as they may come, and give me the certainty of regular wages."

Such would be the probable answer of a prudent workingman to the imprudent manufacturer. If he were then engaged elsewhere on wages, he might afterward have a conflict with his employer as to the fairness of his pay, but he could not ask that the system itself, of a regular fixed payment for so many hours' work, should be abolished in favor of a distant share in precarious profits. How doubtful such a prospect would be, appears from the usual estimates of the proportion of men who fail to make a profit in conducting business of their own. The fact has been already noted that business men often say that only 5 per cent. succeed while 95 per cent. fail. These latter figures may be exaggerated. In France, said a witness before a parliamentary committee previously quoted, "out of 100 business men, 10 make money, 50 vegetate, and 40 fail entirely." Taking this more favorable estimate, we see that the workman's chances of getting a pay out of profits equal to the average wages would be, at the outside, only three out of five; while those employers of labor who "vegetate," in the French phrase, usually pay the lowest wages. Hardly would the laborer, then, have more than one chance in ten of getting good wages under such a coöperative contract as we have supposed. It is not to such risks as these that we should invite the worker who has no capital to fall back upon in case of loss. It is evidently inexpedient if not unjust to make the entire compensation of the operative depend upon the chances of the market, or the commercial skill of the manager. The workingman cannot afford to take these risks; he can support himself on lower wages than are his just due, but he cannot give up the frequency and certainty of recompense which the wages system assures him. M. Paul Leroy-Beaulieu well says: "Wages render the employee responsible for his own work, and do not leave him dependent on the doings of others, on their intelligence, administrative ability, and understanding of affairs, and on the general prosperity. Wages are a kind of insurance against the possible incapacity or the eventual *maladresse* of the commander and director of labor."

The imperative necessity, to modern laborers, of the stability and regularity of wages is practically confessed by those who are working out coöperation in practice. There are very few establishments for coöperative production in which there is not a body of auxiliary workmen, not admitted to a share in the profits but paid by the day, the same as if they were employed in an ordinary establishment. These coöperative associations, again, usually make advances on account to their members, to enable them to meet their running expenses. These advances, large or small, are simply wages under another name. One fact sufficiently proves this. In case these advances are not wages, they must be loans which are capable of recovery by the lender. But when coöperative associations fail, as most of them have done thus far, no creditor takes steps to recover from the members the sums they have received on account. These advances on account are no more repaid in fact than are ordinary wages when the wage-paying firm fails.

Taken as a whole, then, and in its most general operation, the wages system might seem to be more favorable to the employee than to the employer. Granting that the proportion of men who succeed as employers of labor on any considerable scale is larger than any of the estimates usually made, and supposing that it actually amounts to one third instead of one tenth of all who make the attempt, then the advantage of regular wages is two to one in favor of the workman, and against the employer. Only in one case out of three, under this supposition, would the employee receive less than a division of profits in lieu of wages would give him; and it might often be only a little less. In two cases out of three he receives more in wages than a division of the product as sold would entitle him to. It should be obvious, then, that the wages system, so far from being a slightly modified form of slavery, is in fact a kind of coöperative association, in which the larger part of the risks and uncertainties falls to the manager, and the larger portion of the certain and regular return to the men. As M. Émile Chevallier has excellently stated the case, the wages system is "an association *sui generis,* which one of the partners has entered only on condition of being in advance freed from the risks inherent in the enterprise, the part to fall to him being fixed and the time of its payment." Such is the actual character of the ordinary method of remunerating labor in civilized countries at the present day. The workman cannot afford to take more risk than he actually does in contracting with a manager whose business ability is an uncertain quantity. If the employer is so inefficient or unfortunate as to lose money, he fails, and the employee must seek work elsewhere. Against such a loss of employment the workman can have no safeguard, other than his own shrewdness in choosing his employer, when a choice is open to him. This one risk he must take. Nearly every other risk of loss is thrown upon the master, so that practically the workman has many of the advantages of association without most of its inconveniences.

The naturalness of the wages system, as compared with equal coöperation, appears when we consider the truth, which so many injudicious "friends of labor" fail to perceive, that hand-work is but one factor in production. Capital and skill are the two other factors, each as indispensable in the joint work as labor itself. Coöperative producers find it impossible, of course, to do without capital, whether this be borrowed or consist only of their own modest savings. They have not made the attempt, though some political economists of the first rank have committed the mistake of attributing it to them, to do without the capitalist. As President F. A. Walker, in company with leading

French economists, has shown, the actual effort of coöperative producers is "to get rid of the *entrepreneur*, or manager," whose skill brings capital and labor together under his own direction, in a partnership the result of which is proportional to his business ability. We may simply note, in passing, the very meagre results yet achieved in coöperative production, despite great expenditure of effort: the fact indicates a fundamental weakness in the method.

The democratic element in modern society is undoubtedly gaining in strength with every year, and there is no good reason for lamenting its advance. But it will never do away with the natural aristocracy which has made skill in the conduct of business the endowment or the acquisition of a few. The many must continue to follow, as they have always done, when they did not rush to disaster; and the select minority of Nature's choosing must continue to lead, if the many are to prosper. Natural selection makes stern havoc with headless coöperative associations in competition with firms directed by captains of industry. The weakness of coöperative production, thus far, has been its gross undervaluation of the manager. The dream of an equality contradicted by the plain facts of human nature has led coöperators to offer petty salaries and restricted powers to their superintendents. But modern industry takes on more and more the character of a civilized warfare in which regiments composed of brigadier-generals are quite out of place. While, then, attempts at coöperation have been numerous the world over, the percentage of failures is very large in consequence of this fundamental mistake of underrating the part that brains have to play in successful production, under the keen competition which is the rule in the last half of the nineteenth century. The wages system, on the contrary, is continually making inroads into the ranks of the small dealers, who are forced to take service with the large firms. Joint-stock companies multiply in every direction, and the number of persons on wages or salaries increases absolutely and proportionally every year.

It would be difficult, if not impossible, to imagine a feasible system of conducting business, under the actual conditions of the industrial world, more generally applicable, and more in harmony with all the elements involved, than the method which is to-day assailed by many crude thinkers as a relic of feudalism, or even of barbarism. Its general prevalence is a sufficient proof of its logical strength.

PROFIT-SHARING.

[*From the Same.*]

THE ECONOMIC GAIN.

PROFIT-SHARING, the division of realized profits between the capitalist, the employer, and the employee, in addition to regular interest, salary, and wages, is the most equitable and generally satisfactory method of remunerating the three industrial agents.   .   .   .   .

The indirect sharing of profits has a large number of examples in all civilized countries; the kindly interest of the employer in his workers increases, and it remains to be proved that such humaneness is unprofitable in even the lowest sense. As a simple fact, such employers think "it pays," and are usually those most occupied with the thought of dividing the profits of their business with their men in a more direct way.

The great majority of the employers enumerated in this volume as practisers of profit-sharing have probably a touch of philanthropy in them; this, it is needless to say, has not spoiled them for business. But if profit-sharing were purely philanthropy, these employers, sagacious and successful men as most of them are, would not have prospered as they have. On the contrary, they generally agree that the division of a bonus among the workmen is good business policy, and that they have lost nothing by it; in most cases they claim that their own share is greater than the whole profits were under the simple wages system. No fallacy, indeed, could be worse in this connection than the common one, through which the logic of M. Leclaire had to make its way at the outset, that the system of participation does not increase the product, and must therefore diminish the employer's profit. In fact, the tendency of profit-sharing is to enlarge the disposable profits to such a degree that the employer is better off financially than before. He may be more prosperous simply because of freedom from difficulties with his employees: industrial peace has a high money value, as none know better than manufacturers who have suffered from repeated strikes. But, looked at both positively and negatively, profit-sharing advances the prosperity of an establishment by increasing the quantity of the product, by improving its quality, by promoting care of implements and economy of materials, and by diminishing labor difficulties and the cost of superintendence. It thus accumulates an extra fund of profits under the same general conditions, any increased outlay being mainly for the larger amount of raw material demanded for the greater product. Out of this extra profit comes the share of the men, whose diligence and care have created it. By its ability to create such an extra fund, in one or more of the ways mentioned, profit-sharing must stand or fall with the great majority of employers, who are unable, however willing they might be, to conduct their business on philanthropic principles. But if the verdict given by nine employers out of ten who have tried profit-sharing be true, then it must be pronounced poor business policy to neglect such a means of prosperity.   .   .   .   .

PRACTICAL CHRISTIANITY.

Bishop Fraser declared that the duty of this generation is not so much "to christianize Socialism as to socialize Christianity." I have purposely avoided thus far, as irrelevant, the consideration of profit-sharing in the light of moral and religious duty; but I cannot conclude without declaring my conviction that the Christianity which Bishop Fraser desired to see, the religion that its founder had in mind, is profoundly opposed to the class-selfishness which the existing wages system tends to increase, and which profit-sharing, generally diffused, would greatly diminish. The fraternity which participation promotes is thoroughly moral, thoroughly Christian. Profit-sharing recognizes the advancing democratic element which has made itself felt so forcibly in the industrial world of late in wars and rumors of war. It meets that advance with a hearty recognition of human brotherhood and the duties of prosperity. Economic science is good, but "economic science enlightened by the spirit of the Gospel," the spirit of enthusiasm for humanity, is better. Nay, it is, in the last result, the only solution of the problems which beset, with Fate's persistence, the too complacent commercial spirit of our day. A plutocratic development, which has far outrun the slow evolution of conscience among modern men, has at length received sullen challenge from the great majority who live by the labor of their hands. Peace between master and man will come as both begin to entertain a new spirit toward each other, and readjust thereby the relations of the labor contract. In this industrial reformation the voice of the men whose duty it is always to remind us that man does not live by bread alone should be potent on the side of a finer justice and a more philanthropic spirit. The Christian gospel has had a re-birth in more than one perplexed age. The labor difficulties of the troubled nineteenth century will find no more effectual solvent. Economics must be aided by ethics ; the commercial spirit should be tempered by the Christian feeling of the brotherhood of man. The pure Christianity to which Leclaire gave expression in his last will and testament is still the strongest force making for industrial and social progress.

Charles Edwin Markham.

BORN in Oregon, 1852.

THE LAST FURROW.

[*Uncollected Poems.* 188-.]

THE Spirit of Earth with still, restoring hands,
   Mid ruin moves, in glimmering chasm gropes,
   And mosses mantle and the bright flower opes;
But Death the Ploughman wanders in all lands,
And to the last of earth his furrow stands:
   The grave is never hidden: fearful hopes
   Follow the dead upon the fading slopes,
   And there wild memories meet upon the sands.

When willows fling their banners to the plain,
   When rumor of wind and sound of sudden showers
   Disturb the dream of winter—all in vain
The grasses hurry to the graves, the flowers
   Toss their wild torches on their windy towers:
   Yet are the bleak graves lonely in the rain.

POETRY.

SHE comes like the hush and beauty of the night,
But sees too deep for laughter;
Her touch is a vibration and a light
From worlds before and after.

THE VALLEY.

I KNOW a valley in the summer hills,
Haunted by little winds and daffodils;
Faint footfalls and soft shadows pass at noon;
Noiseless, at night, the clouds assemble there;
And ghostly summits hang below the moon—
Dim visions lightly swung in silent air.

Noted Sayings.

[*Continued from Vol. VII., pages* 190–194.]

I can tell thee where that saying was born.
TWELFTH NIGHT, I., 5.

Many other sayings, of equal or greater note, are scattered through our former selections from the works of their authors, and therefore are not reprinted here. A few of those which follow are of trans-atlantic origin, but have gained a new vogue through their American application.

UPON LEAVING ENGLAND, IN 1629.

Farewell, dear England! farewell, the Church of God in England, and all the Christian friends there!—We go to practise the positive part of church reformation, and propagate the gospel in America.

FRANCIS HIGGINSON. 1587–1630.

A PLANTATION OF RELIGION, NOT OF TRADE.

My Fathers and Brethren, this is never to be forgotten, that New-England is originally a plantation of Religion, not a plantation of Trade. Let Merchants and such as are increasing *Cent per Cent* remember this. Let others that have come over since at several times understand this, that worldly gain was not the end and design of the people of New-England, but Religion. And if any amongst us make Religion as twelve, and the world as thirteen, let such an one know he hath neither the spirit of a true New-England man, nor yet of a sincere Christian.—*From an Election Sermon, " The Cause of God and his People in New-England." Cambridge, Mass.,* 27 *May,* 1663.

JOHN HIGGINSON. 1616–1708.

"UNITED WE STAND, DIVIDED WE FALL."

From "The Liberty Song" : first published in the Boston "Gazette," 18 July, 1768.

Then join hand in hand, brave Americans all,—
By uniting we stand, by dividing we fall!

JOHN DICKINSON. 1732–1808.
ARTHUR LEE. 1740–92.

TO GOV. HUTCHINSON, DEMANDING THE WITHDRAWAL OF THE BRITISH
TROOPS FROM BOSTON, AFTER THE MASSACRE OF 5 MARCH, 1770.

Both Regiments, or None!

SAMUEL ADAMS [for the Boston Town Meeting]. 1722–1803.

IN THE CONTINENTAL CONGRESS, 5 SEPTEMBER, 1774.

I am not a Virginian, but an American.

PATRICK HENRY. 1736–99.

AT THE SIGNING OF THE DECLARATION OF INDEPENDENCE, 4 JULY, 1776.

We must all hang together, or assuredly we shall all hang separately.

BENJAMIN FRANKLIN. 1706–90.

HIS LAST WORDS, NEW YORK, 22 SEPTEMBER, 1776.

I only regret that I have but one life to lose for my Country.

NATHAN HALE. 1755–76.

"BROTHER JONATHAN."

We must consult Brother Jonathan.—*Meaning his secretary and aide, Colonel Jonathan Trumbull of Connecticut.*

SI VIS PACEM, PARA BELLUM.

To be prepared for war is one of the most effectual means of preserving peace.—*From a Speech to Congress, 8 January,* 1790.

GEORGE WASHINGTON. 1732–99.

NOTED APPLICATION OF MATHEW HENRY'S PHRASE, 1788.

I consider biennial elections as a security that the sober, second thought of the people shall be law.

FISHER AMES. 1758–1808.

OF CANDIDATURE FOR OFFICE.

That honor ought neither to be solicited nor refused.

"FEW DIE, AND NONE RESIGN."

If a due participation of office is a matter of right, how are vacancies to be obtained? Those by Death are few: by resignation, none.—*To a Committee of the Merchants of New Haven, Conn.,* 1801.

"DECLARATION OF PRINCIPLES."

Equal and exact justice to all men, of whatever state or persuasion, religious or political; peace, commerce, and honest friendship with all nations, entangling alliances with none.—*First Inaugural Address,* 4 *March,* 1801.

FROM THE SAME INAUGURAL ADDRESS.

Error of opinion may be tolerated where reason is left free to combat it.

A WORD TO THE NEW ENGLANDERS.

But I am in hopes of the Eastern people; . . . that they will find their interest in acquiescing in the liberty and science of their country, and that the Christian religion, when divested of the rags in which they have enveloped it, and brought to the original purity and simplicity of its benevolent institutor, is a religion of all others most friendly to liberty, science, and the freest expansion of the human mind.—*Written in* 1801.

THE DISCOURSES OF CHRIST.

Such are the fragments remaining to us to show a master-workman, and that his system of morality was the most benevolent and sublime probably that has ever been taught, and consequently more perfect than those of any of the ancient philosophy.—*Written in* 1804.

THOMAS JEFFERSON. 1743–1826.

WHEN ASKED TO SIT NEAR HIS "FATHER."

The sun is my father, and the earth is my mother; and on her bosom I will repose.—*At the conference with General W. H. Harrison, Vincennes, Ind., August,* 1810.

TECUMSEH. 1768–1813.

A HERO'S LAST ORDER.

Don't give up the Ship!—*Engagement between the Shannon and the Chesapeake,* 1 *June,* 1813.

CAPT. JAMES LAWRENCE. 1781–1813.

OF MONROE'S ADMINISTRATION, 1817–25.

The Era of Good Feeling.—*Title of an Article in the Boston "Centinel," 12 July,* 1817.

THE "MONROE DOCTRINE."

In the wars of the European Powers, in matters relating to themselves, we have never taken any part, nor does it comport with our policy so to do. It is only when our rights are invaded or seriously menaced that we resent injuries or make preparations for our defence. With the movements in this hemisphere we are, of necessity, more immediately connected, and by causes which must be obvious to all enlightened and impartial observers. The political system of the Allied Powers is essentially different in this respect from that of America. This difference proceeds from that which exists in their respective Governments; and to the defence of our own, which has been achieved by the loss of so much blood and treasure, and matured by the wisdom of their most enlightened citizens, and under which we have enjoyed unexampled felicity, this whole nation is devoted.

We owe it, therefore, to candor, and to the amicable relations existing between the United States and those powers, to declare that we should consider any attempt on their part to extend their system to any portion of this hemisphere, as dangerous to our peace and safety.

With the existing Colonies or dependencies of any European power we have not interfered, and shall not interfere. But with the governments who have declared their independence and maintained it, and whose independence we have, on great consideration and on just principles, acknowledged, we could not view any interposition for the purpose of oppressing them, or controlling, in any other manner their destiny, by any European power, in any other light than as the manifestation of an unfriendly disposition toward the United States.—*From the President's Message, 2 December,* 1823.

JAMES MONROE. 1758–1831.

AN ADVOCATE'S OPINION.

Law is whatever is boldly asserted and plausibly maintained.

THE AMERICAN CHESTERFIELD.

The rule of my life is to make business a pleasure, and pleasure my business.

AARON BURR. 1756–1836.

A BORDER KNIGHT'S MOTTO—WAR OF 1812.

Be sure you are right—then go ahead.

DAVID CROCKETT. 1786–1836.

FROM THE BUNKER HILL ORATION—17 JUNE, 1825.

Let our object be, our country, our whole country, and nothing but our country.

DANIEL WEBSTER. 1782–1852.

VOL. XL—29

BUNKER HILL.

Now deeper roll the maddening drums,
　The mingling host like Ocean heaves,
While from the midst a horrid wailing comes,
　And high above the fight the lonely bugle grieves.

GRENVILLE MELLEN. 1799-1841.

IN DENUNCIATION OF THE ADMINISTRATION OF ADAMS AND CLAY.　1826.

I was defeated—by the coalition of Blifil and Black George,—by the combination, unheard of till then, of the Puritan with the blackleg.

JOHN RANDOLPH OF ROANOKE. 1773-1833.

"A GOOD ENOUGH MORGAN UNTIL AFTER THE ELECTION."

That is a good enough Morgan for us until you bring back the one you carried off.— *Reply to the Counsel for the Kidnappers of Morgan, with reference to the body of one Timothy Monroe.* 1827.

THURLOW WEED. 1797-1882.

"FREE TRADE AND SEAMAN'S RIGHTS."

If we fail, let us fail like men, lash ourselves to our gallant tars, and expire together in one common struggle, fighting for Free Trade and Seaman's Rights.—*Speech in the U. S. H. of R.*, 19 *January*, 1813.

REMARK TO SENATOR W. C. PRESTON OF SOUTH CAROLINA.　1839.

Sir, I had rather be right than be President!

"NO SOUTH, NO NORTH, NO EAST, NO WEST."

I have heard something said about allegiance to the South. I know no South, no North, no East, no West, to which I owe any allegiance.—*In the U. S. Senate*, 1848.

HENRY CLAY. 1777-1852.

MAN TO MAN.

I am a man, and you are another.—*To President Jackson, at their first interview, April*, 1833.

BLACK HAWK. 1767-1838.

"THE FOOTSTEPS OF MY ILLUSTRIOUS PREDECESSOR."

I shall, if honored with the choice of the American people, endeavor to tread generally in the footsteps of President Jackson.—*Letter accepting the Nomination for the Presidency*, 29 *May*, 1835.

I tread in the footsteps of illustrious men.　.　.　.　.　In receiving from the people the sacred trust twice confided to my illustrious predecessor, and which he has discharged so faithfully and well, I know that I cannot expect to perform the arduous task with equal ability and success.—*Inaugural Address, 4 March*, 1837.

MARTIN VAN BUREN. 1782–1862.

"THE COHESIVE POWER OF PUBLIC PLUNDER."

A power has risen up in the government greater than the people themselves, consisting of many and various and powerful interests, combined in one mass, and held together by the cohesive power of the vast surplus in the banks.—*Speech in the U. S. Senate, 27 May,* 1836.

JOHN CALDWELL CALHOUN. 1782–1850.

"CONTEMPORANEOUS POSTERITY."

Byron's European fame is the best earnest of his immortality, for a foreign nation is a kind of contemporaneous posterity.—*From the Novel " Stanley; or, The Recollections of a Man of the World."* Phila., 1838.

HORACE BINNEY WALLACE. 1817–52.

"THIS NEW DEPARTURE."

This new page opened in the book of our public expenditures, and this new departure taken, which leads into the bottomless gulf of civil pensions and family gratuities.—*In the U. S. Senate, against the grant of* $25,000 *to President Harrison's widow, April,* 1841.

THOMAS HART BENTON. 1782–1858.

ON THE OLD CONSTITUTION OF THE UNITED STATES.

RESOLVED: That the compact which exists between the North and the South is a Covenant with death and an agreement with hell, involving both parties in atrocious criminality, and should be immediately annulled.—*Adopted by the Mass. Anti-Slavery Society, Faneuil Hall, 27 January,* 1843.

WILLIAM LLOYD GARRISON. 1805–79.

THE BALLOT.

A weapon that comes down as still
As snowflakes fall upon the sod;
But executes a freeman's will,
As lightning does the will of God.

JOHN PIERPONT. 1785–1866.

OREGON BOUNDARY QUESTION.   U. S. SENATE, 1844.

Fifty-four forty, or fight! (54° 40′ N.).

WILLIAM ALLEN. 1806–79.

AT BUENA VISTA, 23 FEBRUARY, 1847.

A little more grape, Captain Bragg!

ZACHARY TAYLOR. 1784–1850.

A WATCHWORD IN THE PRESIDENTIAL CAMPAIGN OF 1848.

General Taylor never surrenders.—*Reply to General Santa Anna, Buena Vista,* 22 *February,* 1847.

THOMAS LEONIDAS CRITTENDEN. 1815–.

PARTY CRY, FROM THE PLATFORM OF THE FREE-SOIL NATIONAL CONVENTION. 1848.

No *more* slave States : *no* slave Territories.

SALMON PORTLAND CHASE. 1808–73.

THE STURDY GODFATHER OF THE C. S. A.

I never use the word "Nation" in speaking of the United States; I always use the word "Union," or Confederacy. We are not a nation, but a *Union*, a confederacy of equal and sovereign States. England is a nation, Austria is a nation, Russia is a nation, but the United States are not a nation.—*Remark to Oliver Dyer,* 1 *January,* 1849.

JOHN CALDWELL CALHOUN. 1782–1850.

"THE CRADLE OF AMERICAN LIBERTY."

I shall defer my visit to Faneuil Hall, the cradle of American Liberty, until its doors shall fly open on golden hinges to lovers of Union as well as of Liberty.—*Upon being refused the use of Faneuil Hall, March,* 1850.

DANIEL WEBSTER. 1782–1852.

WE SELL "OUR GOODS, AND NOT OUR PRINCIPLES."

A Card, when attacked for refusing to sign the call for a " Union Saving " Meeting held in Castle Garden, October, 1850.

A CARD.—The public, including the New York "Journal of Commerce," are informed that we are silk merchants, and keep an extensive and well assorted stock of goods, which we offer to responsible buyers on reasonable terms. As individuals we entertain our own views on the various religious, moral and political questions of the day, which we are neither afraid nor ashamed to declare on all proper occasions. But we wish it distinctly understood that our goods, and not our principles are on the market. The attempt to punish us as merchants for the exercise of our liberty as citizens we leave to the judgment of the community.—BOWEN & MCNAMEE.—[*From the " Journal of Commerce,"* 28 *October,* 1850.]

HENRY CHANDLER BOWEN. 1813–.
THEODORE MCNAMEE. 1813–71.

REPUBLICAN WAR-CRY IN THE PRESIDENTIAL CAMPAIGN OF 1856.

" Give 'em Jessie! "

FRÉMONT'S SUPPORTERS.

THE FIRST REPUBLICAN LEGEND.

Free soil, free men, free speech, Frémont!

PARTY RALLYING CRY. 1856.

FROM THE OPINION IN THE DRED SCOTT CASE, U. S. SUPREME COURT, 1857.

—So far inferior, that they had no rights which the white man was bound to respect.

ROGER BROOKE TANEY. 1777–1864.

AN OLD PROVERB, MEMORABLY USED.

Blood is thicker than water!—*Justifying assistance to the British fleet in the Pei-ho. Despatch to the U. S. Secretary of the Navy, June,* 1859.

JOSIAH TATTNALL. 1795–1871.

"THE TWIN RELICS OF BARBARISM."

With you I hate, deplore, and denounce the Barbarism of Slavery. . . . But I do not agree that the National Government has power under the Constitution to touch Slavery in the States, any more than it has power to touch the twin Barbarism of Polygamy in the States, while fully endowed to arrest and suppress both in all the Territories.—*Letter to A. P. Brooks,* 9 *September,* 1860.—*See also his speech on the Barbarism of Slavery, U. S. Senate,* 4 *June,* 1860.

CHARLES SUMNER. 1811–74.

WHEN ASKED FOR GUIDANCE TO THE CHARLESTON, S. C., INSANE ASYLUM, 1860.

My dear Sir, take any road; you can't go amiss; the whole State is one vast insane asylum!

JAMES LEWIS PETIGRU. 1789–1863.

"LET US ALONE."

All we ask is to be let alone.—*First Message to the Confederate Congress, March,* 1861. [*See Brownell's Poem, Vol. VII., page* 556.]

JEFFERSON DAVIS. 1808–89.

FROM A LETTER TO THE HON. WILLIAM H. SEWARD, 3 MARCH, 1861.

Say to the seceded States—Wayward sisters, depart in peace!

WINFIELD SCOTT. 1786–1866.

A NOTABLE HEAD-LINE IN THE "NEW-YORK TRIBUNE," JUNE–JULY, 1861.

ON TO RICHMOND!—

Adopted by Mr. Dana before the McDowell campaign, as a "standing head," the phrase having been used by a special contributor.

FITZ-HENRY WARREN. 1816–78.

"TREASON AGAINST MANKIND."

Whether right or wrong in its domestic or its foreign policy, judged by whatever standard, whether of expediency or of principle, the American citizen can recognize no social duty intervening between himself and his country. He may urge reform; but he has no right to destroy. Intrusted with the precious inheritance of Liberty, endowed with the gift of participation in a Popular Government, the Constitution makes him at once the beneficiary and the defender of interests and institutions he cannot innocently endanger; and when he becomes a traitor to his country, he commits equal treason against mankind.—*Address to the Mass. Legislature,* 3 *January,* 1862.

JOHN ALBION ANDREW. 1818–67.

A REMARK TO GEN. AVERELL, NOVEMBER, 1862.

Well, General, we have not had many dead cavalrymen lying about lately! [Often misquoted in the phrase "Who ever saw a dead cavalryman?"]

JOSEPH HOOKER. 1814–79.

AN EFFECTUAL REMINDER.

Despatch to Earl Russell, against permitting the Confederate Ironclads, then building at Laird's Shipyards, at Birkenhead, to depart from Liverpool, 5 *September,*1863.

It would be superfluous in me to point out to your Lordship that this is war.

CHARLES FRANCIS ADAMS. 1807–86.

SIGNALLED TO GEN. CORSE IN ALTOONA, FROM THE TOP OF KENESAW, 5 OCTOBER, 1864.

Hold the fort. I am coming.

WILLIAM TECUMSEH SHERMAN. 1820–.

TITLE OF AN ESSAY IN THE "ATLANTIC MONTHLY," SEPTEMBER, 1864.

The Total Depravity of Inanimate Things.

KATHARINE KENT CHILD WALKER. 1841–.

A NATIONAL DEBT A NATIONAL BLESSING.

From a Letter to Robert Morris, 30 April, 1781.

A National debt, if it is not excessive, will be to us a national blessing.—*See Vol. IV., Page* 112, *of this Work.*

ALEXANDER HAMILTON. 1757–1804.

"OUR NATIONAL DEBT A NATIONAL BLESSING."

Title of a Broadside issued by Jay Cooke, June, 1865, to promote the sale of Government Bonds. It was qualified, at the suggestion of Harris Charles Fahnestock (upon the cover of a pamphlet containing the banker's argument), in this wise: "How our National Debt may be a National Blessing." The originator of the title was

SAMUEL WILKESON. 1817–89.

OF THE PRESIDENTIAL "RECONSTRUCTION" TOUR, AUGUST, 1866.

We are swinging around the Circle.

ANDREW JOHNSON. 1808–75.

TELEGRAM TO SECRETARY STANTON, THEN HOLDING THE WAR DEPARTMENT IN DEFIANCE OF HIS ILLEGAL SUSPENSION BY PRESIDENT JOHNSON—SENATE CHAMBER, 21 FEBRUARY, 1868.

Stick.

Ever sincerely yours,

CHARLES SUMNER. 1811–74.

IN THE PRESIDENTIAL CANVASS OF 1868.

Repudiate the Repudiators.

WILLIAM PITT FESSENDEN. 1806–69.

RULE OF THE "HARRY WADSWORTH CLUB"—FROM "TEN TIMES ONE IS TEN." 1870.

To look up and not down,
To look forward and not back,
To look out and not in,—
and
To lend a hand.

EDWARD EVERETT HALE. 1822–.

THE BALLOT IN 1871.

As long as I count the votes, what are you going to do about it? Say!

WILLIAM MARCY TWEED. 1823–78.

"LET NO GUILTY MAN ESCAPE."

Let no guilty man escape, if it can be avoided. No personal consideration should stand in the way of performing a public duty.—*Indorsement of a Letter Relating to the Prosecution of the Western "Whiskey Ring," 29 July*, 1875.

ULYSSES S. GRANT. 1822–85.

POLITICAL INTRODUCTION OF THE "MUGWUMP."

Listen! John A. Logan is the Head Centre, the Hub, the King Pin, the Main Spring, Mogul, and Mugwump of the final plot by which partisanship was installed in the Commission.—*Editorial entitled " Impeach Logan," in the N, Y. " Tribune," 16 February*, 1877.

ISAAC HILL BROMLEY. 1833–.

HEAD-LINE IN THE "NEW YORK SUN," 23 MARCH, 1884.

"Mugwump D. O. Bradley."

The word was applied by the same newspaper, 15 June, 1884, to the "Independents" of the Blaine-Cleveland campaign.

THE NEW YORK SUN.

A BON-MOT IN THE CLEVELAND-BLAINE CAMPAIGN OF 1884.

A Mugwump is a person educated beyond his intellect.

HORACE PORTER. 1837–.

FROM THE PRESIDENT'S INAUGURAL ADDRESS, 5 MARCH, 1877.

The President . . . should strive to be always mindful of the fact that he serves his party best who serves the country best.

RUTHERFORD BIRCHARD HAYES. 1822–93.

ASKED AT THE REPUBLICAN NATIONAL CONVENTION, CHICAGO, 1880.

What are we here for?

WEBSTER FLANAGHAN. 1832–.

FROM THE PRESIDENT'S INAUGURAL SPEECH, 4 MARCH, 1881.

It has been said that unsettled questions have no pity for the repose of nations. It should be said that this question of the suffrage will never give repose to the States or to the Nation until each, within its own jurisdiction, makes and keeps the ballot free and pure by the strong sanction of the law.

WRITTEN WHEN ASKED FOR AN AUTOGRAPH, JULY, 1881.

" James A. Garfield. Strangulatus pro republica."

JAMES ABRAM GARFIELD. 1831-81.

" LIMITED COSMOPOLITANISM."

The truth is, that Mr. James's cosmopolitanism is, after all, limited : to be really cosmopolitan, a man must be at home even in his own country.—*Short Studies of American Authors.* 1879.

THOMAS WENTWORTH HIGGINSON. 1823-.

" WORSE THAN PROVINCIAL,—PAROCHIAL."

Whatever question there may be of his talent, there can be none, I think, of his genius. It was a slim and crooked one, but it was eminently personal. He was imperfect, unfinished, inartistic; he was worse than provincial—he was parochial; it is only at his best that he is readable.— *Of Thoreau, in a Critical Life of Hawthorne.* 1879.

HENRY JAMES, JR. 1843-.

" A FINER ART IN OUR DAY."

The art of fiction has, in fact, become a finer art in our day than it was with Dickens and Thackeray. We could not suffer the confidential attitude of the latter now, nor the mannerism of the former, any more than we could endure the prolixity of Richardson or the coarseness of Fielding.—*Sketch of Henry James, Jr., in the "Century Magazine," November,* 1882.

WILLIAM DEAN HOWELLS. 1837-.

FAITH AND REASON.

Reason is the triumph of the intellect, faith of the heart; and whether the one or the other shall best illumine the dark mysteries of our being, they only are to be despaired of who care not to explore.—*History of the United States under the Constitution, Vol. II.* 1882.

JAMES SCHOULER. 1839-.

" PUBLIC OFFICE IS A PUBLIC TRUST."

From a Speech at Ashland, Ky., March, 1829.

Government is a trust, and the officers of the government are trustees; and both the trust and the trustees are created for the benefit of the people.

HENRY CLAY. 1777-1852.

From a Speech in the U. S. Senate, 31 May, 1872.

The appointing power of the pope is treated as a public trust and not as a personal perquisite.

CHARLES SUMNER. 1811-74.

From the Opening Address of the President of the Mass. Republican State Convention, 1881.

The public offices are a public trust, to be held and administered with the same exact justice and the same conscientious regard for the responsibilities involved as are required in the execution of private trusts.

WILLIAM WALLACE CRAPO. 1830.

From an Article on Civil Service Reform, in Lalor's Cyclopædia of Political Science, 1881.

Public office is a public trust, created only for the common benefit.

DORMAN BRIDGMAN EATON. 1823-.

From a Letter Accepting the Nomination for Mayor, Buffalo, 1881.

Public officials are the trustees of the people.

From a Letter of Acceptance as Candidate for Governor, 7 October, 1882.

Public officers are the servants and agents of the people to execute laws which the people have made, and within the limits of a constitution which they have established.

GROVER CLEVELAND. 1837-.

From the Address upon the Opening of the New York and Brooklyn Bridge, 24 May, 1883.

But what man is fit to hold office? Only he who regards political office as a public trust, and not as a private perquisite to be used for the pecuniary advantage of himself or his family, or even his party.

ABRAM STEVENS HEWITT. 1822-.

Motto of a widely circulated Campaign Pamphlet. 1884.

Public office is a public trust.

DANIEL SCOTT LAMONT. 1851-.

From the President's Inaugural Address, 4 March, 1885.

Your every voter, as surely as your Chief Magistrate, under the same high sanction, though in a different sphere, exercises a public trust.

GROVER CLEVELAND. 1837-.

OTHER SAYINGS BY THE SAME PRESIDENT.

"HONOR LIES IN HONEST TOIL."

A true American sentiment recognizes the dignity of labor and the fact that honor lies in honest toil.--*Letter accepting the nomination for President, 18 August, 1884.*

"OFFENSIVE PARTISANS."

They have proved themselves offensive partisans, and unscrupulous manipulators of local party management.—*Letter to George William Curtis, 25 December,* 1884.

"LABOR IS THE CAPITAL OF OUR WORKINGMEN."

We should also deal with the subject in such manner as to protect the interests of American labor, which is the capital of our workingmen.—*First Annual Message, December,* 1885.

"INNOCUOUS DESUETUDE."

After an existence of nearly twenty years of almost innocuous desuetude these laws are brought forth.—*Message, 1 March,* 1886.

"THE GOVERNMENT SHOULD NOT SUPPORT THE PEOPLE."

Though the people support the Government, the Government should not support the people.—*Veto of Texas Seed-Bill, 16 February,* 1887.

"A CONDITION—NOT A THEORY."

It is a *condition* which confronts us—not a theory.—*Annual Message,* 1887.

"A ROLL OF HONOR."

I cannot believe that the vast peaceful army of Union soldiers who, having contentedly resumed their places in the ordinary avocations of life, cherish as sacred the memory of patriotic service, or who, having been disabled by the casualties of war, justly regard the present pension roll, on which appear their names as a roll of honor, desire at this time and in the present exigency to be confounded with those who, through such a bill as this, are willing to be objects of charity and to gain a place upon the pension roll through alleged dependence.—*Veto of Dependent Pension Bill,* 11 *February,* 1887.

I have considered the pension list of the Republic a roll of honor.—*Veto of Mary Ann Dougherty's Pension, 5 July,* 1888.

"THE COMMUNISM OF CAPITAL."

Communism is a hateful thing and a menace to peace and organized government. But the communism of combined wealth and capital, the outgrowth of overweening cupidity and selfishness which assiduously undermines the justice and integrity of free institutions, is not less dangerous than the communism of oppressed poverty and toil, which, exasperated by injustice and discontent, attacks with wild disorder the citadel of misrule.—*Annual Message,* 1888.

PARTY HONESTY.

Party honesty is party expediency.—*Interview in the N. Y. "Commercial Advertiser,"* 19 *September,* 1889.

GROVER CLEVELAND. 1837-.

"WE LOVE HIM FOR THE ENEMIES HE HAS MADE."

They love him, gentlemen, and they respect him, not only for himself, for his character, for his integrity and judgment and iron will, but they love him most for the enemies he has made. — *Of Mr. Cleveland, by the Chairman of the National Convention, Chicago,* 1884.

EDWARD STUYVESANT BRAGG. 1827-.

FROM THE DEMOCRATIC PLATFORM OF 1884.

Unnecessary taxation is unjust taxation.

ABRAM STEVENS HEWITT. 1822-.

BY ONE OF THE DEPUTATION OF CLERGY VISITING MR. BLAINE, AT THE FIFTH AVENUE HOTEL, NEW YORK CITY, 29 OCTOBER, 1884.

We are Republicans, and don't propose to leave our party and identify ourselves with the party whose antecedents have been Rum, Romanism, and Rebellion!

SAMUEL DICKINSON BURCHARD. 1812-91.

MOTTO OF THE AMERICAN COPYRIGHT LEAGUE. WRITTEN 20 NOVEMBER, 1885.

In vain we call old notions fudge,
  And bend our conscience to our dealing;
The Ten Commandments will not budge,
  And stealing *will* continue stealing.

BEFORE THE U. S. SENATE COMMITTEE ON PATENTS, 29 JANUARY, 1886.

If I were asked what book is better than a cheap book, I should answer that there is one book better than a cheap book, and that is a book honestly come by.

JAMES RUSSELL LOWELL. 1819-.

NAME CONFERRED UPON THE REPUBLICAN STUMP-SPEAKERS, FOR HOLDING THEIR AUDIENCES "SPELL-BOUND." PRESIDENTIAL CAMPAIGN OF 1888.

Here comes another of the Spell-binders!

WILLIAM CASSIUS GOODLOE. 1841-89.

EXPERTO CREDE.

To be seventy years young is sometimes far more cheerful and hopeful than to be forty years old. — *On the seventieth Birthday of Julia Ward Howe,* 27 *May,* 1889.

OLIVER WENDELL HOLMES. 1809-.

"PRACTICAL POLITICS."

*From the Bishop's Address at the Washington Centennial Service in St. Paul's Chapel,
New York City, 30 April, 1889.*

The conception of the National Government as a huge machine, existing mainly for
the purpose of rewarding partisan service—this was a conception so alien to the character and conduct of Washington and his associates that it seems grotesque even to
speak of it. It would be interesting to imagine the first President of the United States
confronted with some one who had ventured to approach him upon the basis of what
is now commonly called "practical politics."

"JACKSONIAN VULGARITY."

We have exchanged the Washingtonian dignity for the Jeffersonian simplicity,
which was, in truth, only another name for the Jacksonian vulgarity.—*Same Address.*

THE ROYALTY OF VIRTUE.

If there be no nobility of descent, all the more indispensable is it that there should
be nobility of ascent—a character in them that bear rule, so fine and high and pure,
that as men come within the circle of its influence they involuntarily pay homage to
that which is the one preëminent distinction, the Royalty of Virtue.—*From the Same.*

HENRY CODMAN POTTER. 1835–.

FROM A SPEECH AT THE WASHINGTON CENTENNIAL CELEBRATION: SUB-TREASURY, WALL ST., NEW YORK CITY, 30 APRIL, 1889.

Self-seeking has no public observance or anniversary. The captain who gives to
the sea his cargo of rags, that he may give safety and deliverance to his imperilled
fellow-men, has fame; he who lands the cargo has only wages.

AT THE WOODSTOCK, CONN., CELEBRATION, 4 JULY, 1889.

It is not in the power of any people upon earth much to harm us, except our own
people.

BENJAMIN HARRISON. 1833–.

BY A JUSTICE OF THE U. S. SUPREME COURT, WHEN ADVISED TO ARM HIMSELF. CALIFORNIA, 1889.

When the Judges shall be obliged to go armed, it will be time for the Courts to be
closed.

STEPHEN JOHNSON FIELD. 1816–.

"MEASURES, NOT MEN, HAVE ALWAYS BEEN MY MARK."—*Goldsmith.*

It used to be an applauded political maxim, which was expressed in the words,
"Measures, not men." I venture to deny the soundness of this maxim, and to propose

in its place its converse, "Men, not measures." I think the first need of good government, like the first need of a large business corporation, is the right men to administer it. Right in character, in ability, in patriotism, in disinterestedness. . . . Better a hundred times an honest and capable administration of an erroneous policy than a corrupt and incapable administration of a good one.—*At the Dinner of the N. Y. Chamber of Commerce*, 19 *November*, 1889.

EDWARD JOHN PHELPS. 1822-.

POPULAR EPITHETS GIVEN TO CERTAIN AMERICANS.

ADAMS, JOHN—"Colossus of Independence." ADAMS, JOHN QUINCY—"Old Man Eloquent." ADAMS, SAMUEL—"American Cato." ARNOLD, BENEDICT—"The Traitor." BENTON, THOMAS—"Old Bullion." BLAINE, JAMES GILLESPIE—"Plumed Knight." BRADSTREET, ANNE—"The Tenth Muse." BROWN, JOHN—"Osawatomie Brown." BUCHANAN, JAMES—"Bachelor President," "Old Public Functionary," "Sage of Wheatland." BURRITT, ELIHU—"The Learned Blacksmith." CLAY, HENRY—"Harry of the West," "Mill-Boy of the Slashes." CORWIN, THOMAS —"Wagoner-Boy." COX, SAMUEL SULLIVAN—"Sunset Cox." DANA, CHARLES ANDERSON—"Nestor of the Press." DOUGLAS, STEPHEN ARNOLD—"Little Giant." EARLY, JUBAL—"Bad Old Man." ELIOT, JOHN—"Apostle of the Indians." EWING, THOMAS—"The Salt-Boiler." FRÉMONT, JOHN CHARLES—"Pathfinder." GARFIELD, JAMES ABRAM—"Canal-Boy." GRANT, ULYSSES S.—"The Tanner," "Uncle Sam," "Unconditional Surrender." HALLECK, HENRY WAGER—"Old Brains." HALSTEAD, MURAT—"Field-Marshal." HANCOCK, WINFIELD SCOTT—"The Superb." HARRISON, BENJAMIN—"Little Ben." HARRISON, WILLIAM HENRY—"Cincinnatus of the West," "Tippecanoe." HOLMES, OLIVER WENDELL—"The Autocrat." HOOKER, JOSEPH—"Fighting Joe." JACKSON, ANDREW—"Old Hickory." JACKSON, THOMAS JONATHAN—"Stonewall." JEFFERSON, THOMAS—"Sage of Monticello." KELLEY, WILLIAM DARRAH—"Father of the House," "Pig-Iron Kelley." LEE, HENRY (1756) —"Light-Horse Harry." LINCOLN, ABRAHAM—"Father Abraham," "Honest Old Abe," "The Railsplitter," "The Martyr President." LOGAN, JOHN ALEXANDER— "Black Eagle," "Blackjack." LORING, WILLIAM WING—"Old Blizzard." MARION, FRANCIS—"Swamp-Fox." MARSHALL, JOHN—"Expounder of the Constitution." McCLELLAN, GEORGE BRINTON—"Little Mac." MEDARY, SAMUEL—"War-Horse of Democracy." MITCHEL, ORMSBY MACKNIGHT—"Old Stars." POLK, JAMES KNOX—"Young Hickory." PHILLIPS, WENDELL—"Silver-tongued." PUTNAM, ISRAEL—"Old Put." RILEY, JAMES WHITCOMB—"Hoosier Poet." SCOTT, WINFIELD—"Hero of Chapultepec," "Old Fuss and Feathers." SEWARD, WILLIAM HENRY—"Sage of Auburn." SHERIDAN, PHILIP—"Little Phil." SHERMAN, WILLIAM TECUMSEH—"Old Tecumseh." SMITH, WILLIAM FARRAR—"Baldy Smith." SPINNER, FRANCIS ELIAS—"Watch-Dog of the Treasury." STEEDMAN, JAMES BARRETT—"Old Chickamauga." STEVENS, THADDEUS—"Great Commoner." TAYLOR, ZACHARY—"Old Rough and Ready," "Old Zach." THOMAS, CHARLES— "Old Reliable," "Pop Thomas." THOREAU, HENRY DAVID—"Poet Naturalist." THURMAN, ALLEN GRANBERY—"Old Bandanna," "Old Roman." TILDEN, SAMUEL JONES—"Sage of Greystone." VAN BUREN, MARTIN—"Little Magician," "Little Van," "Northern Man with Southern Principles." WASHINGTON, GEORGE—"American Fabius," "Father of his Country." WAYNE, ANTHONY—"Mad Anthony." WEBSTER, DANIEL—"Black Dan," "Expounder of the Constitution." WEBSTER, NOAH —"Schoolmaster of the Republic." WHITMAN, WALT—"The Good Grey Poet." WHITTIER, JOHN GREENLEAF—"Bard of Amesbury," "Quaker Poet." WILSON, HENRY—"Natick Cobbler."

NOTE.

Since the completion of this work the attention of the editors has been called to the following memoranda with respect to the Noted Saying (see pages 457, 458) "A public Office is a public Trust." It is believed that Judge Cooley was the American writer who first made use of the exact phrase, and that it became familiar to the legal profession some time before its currency in recent political discussion.

From an Article entitled " The Liability of Public Officers to Private Actions for Neglect of Duty."
Contributed to the Southern Law Review, 1877.

A public office is a public trust. The incumbent has a property right in it, but the office is conferred, not for his benefit, but for the benefit of the political society.

From The Law of Torts. 1878.

Offices are public trusts. Although the incumbent of a public office has a property right in it, yet the office itself is a public trust and is conferred, not for his benefit, but for the benefit of the political society.

THOMAS McINTYRE COOLEY. 1824–

COOLEY, THOMAS McINTYRE, jurist, *b. Attica, N. Y.*, 6 Jan., 1824. Entered the bar at Adrian, Mich., 1846. Was a justice of the supreme court of Michigan from 1864 to 1885, and was chief-justice during 1868-9. Successively professor of law and of American history at the University of Michigan. In 1887 was appointed to the newly-formed Interstate Commerce Commission by President Cleveland, and was elected chairman of the Commission, resigning in 1891. Author of numerous legal works, including " The Law of Torts " (1878), and of " Michigan : a History of Governments " (1885).

INDEX OF AUTHORS, ETC., IN VOL. XI.

INDEX OF AUTHORS, ETC., IN VOL. XI.

The General Index of Authors and Selections, covering the whole Work, is at the end of this Volume.

BUILDING FOR LIBRARY OF CONGRESS.

VIEW FROM SENATE WING OF CAPITOL.

SHORT BIOGRAPHIES

OF ALL AUTHORS REPRESENTED IN THIS WORK

By ARTHUR STEDMAN

ADDENDA.

BANCROFT, GEORGE. *Died, Washington, D. C.*, 17 Jan., 1891.
BOTTA, ANNE CHARLOTTE LYNCH. *Died, New York, N. Y.*, 23 Mar., 1891.
CARPENTER, HENRY BERNARD. *Died, Sorrento, Me.*, 17 July, 1890.
CHEEVER, GEORGE BARRELL. *Died, Englewood, N. J.*, 1 Oct., 1890.
COLES, ABRAHAM. *Died, Monterey, Cal.*, 3 May, 1891.
CONGDON, CHARLES TABER. *Died, New York, N. Y.*, 18 Jan., 1891.
COOMBS, ANNE SHELDON. *Died, Brooklyn, N. Y.*, 22 Nov., 1890.
FRÉMONT, JOHN CHARLES. *Died, New York, N. Y.*, 13 July, 1890.
HEDGE, FREDERIC HENRY. *Died, Cambridge, Mass.*, 21 Aug., 1890.
HOUGHTON, GEORGE WASHINGTON WRIGHT. *Died, Yonkers, N. Y.*, 1 April, 1891.
LOSSING, BENSON JOHN. *Died, Poughkeepsie, N. Y.*, 3 June, 1891.
LOWELL, JAMES RUSSELL. *Died, Cambridge, Mass.*, 12 Aug., 1891.
LÜDERS, CHARLES HENRY. *Died, Philadelphia, Penn.*, 21 Jan., 1891.
O'REILLY, JOHN BOYLE. *Died Hull, Mass.*, 10 Aug., 1890.
PIKE, ALBERT. *Died, Washington, D. C.*, 2 April, 1891.
POWERS, HORATIO NELSON. *Died, Piermont, N. Y.*, 6 Sept., 1890.
SCHUYLER, EUGENE. *Died, Venice, Italy*, 16 July, 1890.
SHERMAN, WILLIAM TECUMSEH. *Died, New York, N. Y.*, 14 Feb., 1891.
SHILLABER, BENJAMIN PENHALLOW. *Died, Chelsea, Mass.*, 25 Nov., 1890.
WILLIAMS, GEORGE WASHINGTON. *Died, Blackpool, Lancashire, England*, 4 Aug., 1891.
WINCHELL, ALEXANDER. *Died, Ann Arbor, Mich.*, 19 Feb., 1891.

NOTE.

Since the completion of this work the attention of the editors has been called to the following memoranda with respect to the Noted Saying (see pages 457, 458) "A public Office is a public Trust." It is believed that Judge Cooley was the American writer who first made use of the exact phrase, and that it became familiar to the legal profession some time before its currency in recent political discussion.

From an Article entitled " The Liability of Public Officers to Private Actions for Neglect of Duty."
Contributed to the Southern Law Review, 1877.

A public office is a public trust. The incumbent has a property right in it, but the office is conferred, not for his benefit, but for the benefit of the political society.

From The Law of Torts. 1878.

Offices are public trusts. Although the incumbent of a public office has a property right in it, yet the office itself is a public trust and is conferred, not for his benefit, but for the benefit of the political society.

THOMAS McINTYRE COOLEY. 1824–

COOLEY, THOMAS McINTYRE, jurist, *b. Attica, N. Y.*, 6 Jan., 1824. Entered the bar at Adrian, Mich., 1846. Was a justice of the supreme court of Michigan from 1864 to 1885, and was chief-justice during 1868–9. Successively professor of law and of American history at the University of Michigan. In 1887 was appointed to the newly-formed Interstate Commerce Commission by President Cleveland, and was elected chairman of the Commission, resigning in 1891. Author of numerous legal works, including "The Law of Torts" (1878), and of "Michigan : a History of Governments" (1885).

SHORT BIOGRAPHIES

OF ALL AUTHORS REPRESENTED IN THIS WORK.

By ARTHUR STEDMAN.

Names of Authors represented by Selections are given in capitals. Authors of Noted Sayings, etc., in "lower-case." Where errors have been detected, by later research, in the data of births and deaths prefixed to selections throughout the LIBRARY, they are corrected in the biographical notices which follow.

ABBEY, Henry, merchant, b. Rondout, N. Y., 11 July, 1842. Fitted for college, but did not enter. Was occupied with journalism in New York city and vicinity until 1864, when he returned to Rondout and engaged in mercantile pursuits. His first volume of poems, "May Dreams," appeared in 1862. Other collections are "Ballads of Good Deeds" (1872), "The City of Success" (1883), and "Poems," complete (1886).

ABBOTT, John Stevens Cabot, clergyman, b. Brunswick, Me., 18 Sept., 1805. Graduated at Bowdoin college. Preached in various cities of Massachusetts and Connecticut until 1844, when he adopted literature as a profession. Author of "The History of Napoleon Bonaparte" (1852–5), "A History of the Civil War in America" (1863–6), and "History of Frederick the Great" (1871). Died, Fair Haven, Conn., 17 June, 1877.

ABBOTT, Lyman, clergyman, b. Roxbury, Mass., 18 Dec., 1835. Graduated at the university of New York. Entered the ministry in 1860 as pastor of a Congregational church at Terre Haute, Ind. In 1869 he turned his entire attention to literature and journalism. Succeeded Henry Ward Beecher as editor of "The Christian Union," and subsequently as pastor of Plymouth church in Brooklyn, N. Y. Some of his works are, "Jesus of Nazareth: His Life and Teachings" (1869), a "Life of H. W. Beecher" (1883), and "In Aid of Faith" (1886).

ADAMS, Abigail [Smith], b. Weymouth, Mass., 23 Nov., 1744. Daughter of Rev. William Smith, Congregational minister of that place, and Elizabeth Quincy. Was married to John Adams, second president of the United States, 25 Oct., 1764. Joined her husband at Paris in 1784, and accompanied him to London on his appointment to the English mission, remaining there until 1788. Resided with him at Philadelphia during his vice-presidency and presidency from 1789 until 1800. The rest of her life was passed at Braintree, Mass. Mrs. Adams received a slender education in her youth, but during her married life became familiar with the best literature of her time. A collection of her letters from 1761 to the last years of her life was published by her grandson, Charles Francis Adams, under the title, "Letters of Mrs. Adams" (1840). They abound with pictures of life in America and Europe during the Revolutionary period. Died, Quincy, Mass., 28 Oct., 1818.

ADAMS, Charles Follen, merchant, b. Dorchester, Mass., 21 April, 1842. With the exception of two years' service during the civil war, has always been occupied with his business at Boston. Has contributed humorous dialect poetry to the periodicals since 1872. Author of "Leedle Yawcob Strauss, and Other Poems" (1878).

ADAMS, Charles Francis, diplomatist, b. Boston, Mass., 18 Aug., 1807. Son of John Quincy Adams. Received his early education in Europe, and graduated at Harvard. Served in the Massachusetts legislature for several years, and in 1848 was the unsuccessful Free-soil candidate for vice-president. Was U. S. minister to England, 1861–8, where he performed valuable services for the Union during the civil war. Edited "The Works of John Adams" (1850–6), and "The Memoirs of John Quincy Adams" (1874–7). Author of numerous orations and addresses. Died, Boston, Mass., 21 Nov., 1886.

ADAMS, Charles Francis, Jr., lawyer and financier, b. Boston, Mass., 27 May, 1835. Graduated at Harvard. Served through the civil war in the Union army.

Subsequently became noted as a railroad commissioner and arbitrator, and in 1884 was made president of the Union Pacific railroad. In 1882 he was elected a member of the Harvard board of overseers. Has published "Chapters of Erie" (1871) and "A College Fetich" (1883), the former in conjunction with Henry Adams.

ADAMS, Hannah, b. Medfield, Mass., 1755. She was the daughter of an intelligent shop-keeper, from the books in whose store she gained most of her early education. Her father's failure compelled her to work at lace-making. This source of income failing, she devoted herself to writing. Her chief works were "View of Religions" (1784), "A Summary History of New England" (1799), "Evidences of Christianity" (1801), and "History of the Jews" (1812). Died, Brookline, Mass., 15 Nov., 1832.

ADAMS, Henry, b. Boston, Mass., 16 Feb., 1838. Son of Charles Francis Adams. Graduated at Harvard. Acted as his father's secretary in London, 1861–8. Was assistant-professor of history at Harvard from 1870 to 1877. After a subsequent residence in London, removed to Washington, D. C. Has written "Essays in Anglo-Saxon Law" (1876), "Life of Albert Gallatin" (1879), "John Randolph" (1882), and "History of the United States"—The First and Second Administrations of Thomas Jefferson—(1889–90).

ADAMS, John, clergyman, b. Nova Scotia, 1704. Graduated at Harvard. Was minister at Newport, R. I., for two years and afterward settled at Philadelphia, Penn. His volume of "Poems on Several Occasions" (1745) appeared after his death. One sermon had been published during his lifetime. Died, Cambridge, Mass., 23 Jan., 1740.

ADAMS, John, second president of the United States, b. Quincy, then a part of Braintree, Mass., 31 Oct., 1735. Son of John Adams, a selectman of Braintree. Graduated at Harvard. Began to practise law in 1758. Draughted resolutions against the stamp-act at a town meeting in Braintree in 1765, which were adopted by more than forty towns in Massachusetts. Removed his residence to Boston in 1768. Defended Captain Preston and his soldiers in 1770 for their action in the so-called "Boston massacre," although at that time Adams was a leader in the American party. Was elected a delegate to the first Continental congress in 1774. In this body, and in its successor, he drew up and advocated many of the most important measures passed, and to conciliate the Southern colonies proposed Washington for the chief commander. Was one of the committee for preparing the Declaration of Independence, and led the three-days debate upon it. First appointed commissioner to France in 1777. Obtained the recognition

of the United States by Holland in April, 1782. With Jay and Franklin completed the treaty of 1783 with Great Britain. Was first U. S. minister to the English court from 1785 to 1788, and first vice-president of the United States from 1788 to 1797. Was president 1797–1801, and failing of a reëlection, passed the remainder of his life in retirement at Quincy. "The Life and Works of John Adams," edited by C. F. Adams. appeared in 1850–6. Died, Quincy, Mass., 4 July, 1826.

ADAMS, John Quincy, sixth president of the United States, b. Braintree, Mass., 11 July, 1767. Son of the preceding. Received the greater part of his education while with his father in Europe, and entered the senior class at Harvard, graduating with it in 1788. Practised law at Boston until 1794, when he was appointed minister to Holland by Washington. In 1797 he was appointed minister to Prussia by his father, with the advice of Washington, serving until 1801. Was U. S. senator from Massachusetts, 1802–8, resigning on account of political difference with his state's legislature. Lectured at Harvard as professor of rhetoric, 1806–9. Was appointed minister to Russia by Madison in 1809, remaining at St. Petersburg until 1814, when he formed one of the commission at Ghent to complete the treaty of peace with Great Britain. Was minister to England, 1815–17, and secretary of state under Monroe, 1817–25. Succeeded the latter as president in 1825. Failing of a reëlection, he represented a Massachusetts district in congress from 1831 until his death. During this period he constantly advocated the anti-slavery cause in congress and gained the title of "the old man eloquent." There have been published, besides his orations and political papers, "Letters on Silesia" (1804), "Lectures on Rhetoric" (1810), "Dermot Mac Morrogh" (1832), "Poems" (1848), and "Memoirs of John Quincy Adams" (1874-7). Died, Washington, D. C., 23 Feb., 1848.

ADAMS, Samuel, statesman, b. Boston, Mass., 27 Sept., 1722. Distantly related to President John Adams. Graduated at Harvard. Entered business as a young man and was unsuccessful. Succeeding to the ownership of his father's brewery on the latter's death in 1748, he soon after became tax-collector of Boston and entered vigorously into politics. Draughted the instructions given by the town of Boston in 1764 to its representatives in regard to the stamp-act. Served as a member of the Massachusetts legislature from 1765 to 1774. Was chiefly instrumental in compelling Governor Hutchinson to withdraw the British troops from Boston after the "Boston massacre." Organized the "committees of correspondence" in Massachusetts in 1772, and the "Boston tea-party" of the following year. Was elected a delegate to the Continental congress, 1774–81. President of the Massachusetts senate in 1781. Urged and carried the adoption of the federal constitution by Massachusetts in 1788. Was lieutenant-governor of that state from 1789 to 1794, and governor from 1794 to 1797. Selections from his political writings are given in "The Life and Public Services of Samuel Adams" (1865), by W. V. Wells. Died, Boston, Mass., 2 Oct., 1803.

ALBEE, John, b. Bellingham, Mass., 3 April, 1833. Obtained his education at Phillips academy, Andover, and at Cambridge, Mass. In 1865 Mr. Albee purchased the ancient Jaffrey estate at New Castle, N. H., and made it his permanent residence, carrying on the farm in summer and devoting his winters to writing. He has lectured before the Concord school of philosophy and elsewhere. Author of "Literary Art" (1881), "Poems" (1883), and a "History of New Castle, N. H." (1884).

ALCOTT, Amos Bronson, educator, b. Wolcott, Conn., 29 Nov., 1799. Was the son of a farmer of that place, and began the teaching of children there in 1823. Removed to Boston in 1828 and pursued the same occupation with great success, but his school having been denounced by the newspapers on account of the teacher's advanced ideas, he abandoned it and interested himself in the study of philosophy and in various reforms. Visited England in 1842, returning with several friends, with whom he purchased a farm called "Fruitlands" at Harvard, Mass., and attempted to establish a new community. The experiment failing, Mr. Alcott returned to Boston. There, and later at Concord, Mass., he followed the life of a peripatetic philosopher, conversing on philosophical and practical questions, in villages and cities, whenever invited. He attached great importance to diet and government of the body and still more to race and complexion. Was a founder of the Concord school of philosophy and one of its leading spirits. Besides contributing to "The Dial" (1839–42) and other periodicals, he published "Tablets" (1868), "Concord Days" (1872), "Table Talk" (1877), "Sonnets and Canzonets" (1882), and an "Essay" presented to Emerson on his birthday (1865). Died, Boston, Mass., 4 Mar., 1888.

ALCOTT, Louisa May, b. Germantown, Penn., 29 Nov., 1832. Daughter of Amos Bronson Alcott, by whom, and by Henry D. Thoreau, she was educated. In 1840 her family removed to Concord, Mass., which was her principal place of residence thereafter. For some years she was occupied with teaching. Her first literary work consisted of stories, for which she received no compensation. In 1862 and 1863 she served as a hospital nurse in Washington, and her experiences at this time are told in "Hospital

Sketches" (1863, revised edition 1869). She wrote chiefly for young people, some of her books reaching large sales. Among them are "Flower Fables" (1855), "Little Women" (1868), "Little Men" (1871), "Eight Cousins" (1874), and "Lulu's Library" (1885). Died, Boston, Mass., 6 Mar., 1888.

ALDEN, Henry Mills, b. Mt. Tabor, Vt., 11 Nov., 1836. Graduated at Williams college, and at the Andover theological seminary. Came to New York city in 1861 and engaged in teaching, contributing occasional articles to the "Atlantic Monthly," and doing editorial work for newspapers, until 1863. In 1863–4 he delivered a series of twelve Lowell lectures at Boston on "The Structure of Paganism." United with Dr. A. H. Guernsey in preparing "Harper's Pictorial History of the Rebellion" (1863–5). Became managing editor of "Harper's Weekly" in 1864, and four years later editor of "Harper's Magazine."

ALDRICH, James, b. Mattituck, L. I., N. Y., 14 July, 1810. Began life as a business man, but in 1836 devoted himself to literary pursuits. Edited several popular periodicals at New York, and in 1840 established the "Literary Gazette," in which many of his best poems first appeared. A collection of "Poems" (1884) has been privately printed by his daughter, Mrs. Elizabeth A. Ely. Died, New York, N. Y., 9 Sept., 1856.

ALDRICH, Thomas Bailey, b. Portsmouth, N. H., 11 Nov., 1836. He was taken as a child to Louisiana, where he remained for a number of years. While preparing for college at Portsmouth the death of his father caused a change in his plans, and he took a position in the counting-room of an uncle in New York city. Soon began writing for periodicals and, meeting with success, resigned his business desk after three years' service, and became "reader" for a New York publishing-house. He formed successive editorial connections with the "New York Evening Mirror," the "Home Journal," and the "Saturday Press," in the same city. Later, was editor of "Every Saturday," in Boston, 1865–74. Had been for some years a regular staff contributor to the "Atlantic Monthly" when in 1881 he succeeded William Dean Howells as editor of that magazine. Mr. Aldrich had published one volume of verse, "The Bells" (1854), when "The Ballad of Babie Bell, and Other Poems" appeared in 1856 and established his reputation as a poet. Other volumes of poetry are "Pampinea, and Other Poems" (1861), "Cloth of Gold, and Other Poems" (1874), "Flower and Thorn" (1876), "Friar Jerome's Beautiful Book" (1881), "Mercedes, and Later Lyrics" (1884), "Wyndham Towers" (1889), besides several collective editions of his poetical works. Some of his prose volumes are "Out of his Head, a

Romance" (1862), "The Story of a Bad Boy" (1870), "Marjorie Daw, and Other People" (1873), "Prudence Palfrey" (1874), "The Queen of Sheba" (1877), and "The Stillwater Tragedy" (1880).

ALEXANDER, Archibald, divine, b. Rockbridge Co., Va., 17 April, 1772. The son of a Virginia farmer. He was ordained a Presbyterian minister, 1794, and was president of Hampden Sydney college 1796–1807. Preached at Philadelphia from 1807 to 1812, when he became principal professor in the theological school then started at Princeton, N. J., filling the position until his death. Of his many theological works the best known is the first, "Outlines of the Evidences of Christianity" (1823). Died, Princeton, N. J., 22 Oct., 1851.

ALGER, William Rounseville, clergyman, b. Freetown, Mass., 30 Dec., 1822. Graduated at the Harvard theological school, and became pastor of Unitarian churches in New York, Boston, and other cities. Among his published works are "The Poetry of the East" (1856), "A Critical History of the Doctrine of a Future Life" (1861), "The Solitudes of Nature and of Man" (1866), and "A Symbolic History of the Cross of Christ" (1881).

ALLEN, Benjamin, author of "Urania, or the True Use of Poesy," published at New York city in 1814. No other facts concerning this writer have been obtained.

ALLEN, Ethan, soldier, b. Litchfield, Conn., 10 Jan., 1737 (Du Puy). Removed in 1766 to that part of Vermont known as the "New Hampshire grants," then claimed by New York state. Allen raised and headed a company of men called the "Green Mountain Boys," who successfully resisted the New York authorities. With this force he also effected the surprise and capture of Fort Ticonderoga, 10 May, 1775. Was for three years a prisoner in the hands of the British. Obtained from congress the recognition of Vermont as a separate state. Besides his "Narrative of Captivity" (1779), he brought out a book directed against the Christian religion. Died, Burlington, Vt., 12 Feb., 1789.

Allen, William [*Noted Saying:* Vol. XI., page 451], b. Edenton, N. C., 27 Dec., 1806. U. S. representative from Ohio, 1833–5, and U. S. senator, 1837–49. Died, near Chillicothe, O., 11 July, 1879.

ALLSTON, Washington, artist, b. Waccamaw, near Georgetown, S. C., 5 Nov., 1779. Received his preparation for college at Newport, R. I., where he became acquainted with Malbone, and first developed an interest in art. Graduated at Harvard, delivering a poem at commencement. Disposing of his estate in South Carolina, he entered on a course of art-studies at the Royal Academy of London, England, remaining there, and at Paris and Rome, from 1801 until 1809. While in America, 1809–11, he married the sister of Dr. William Ellery Channing. She died in 1813, and later in life he married a sister of Richard Henry Dana. Returning to England in 1811, Allston resided there until 1818, painting during this period many of his best pictures, and publishing a volume of poems, "The Sylphs of the Seasons" (1813). Returned to America in 1818, and lived at Boston and Cambridge, Mass., for the remainder of his life. Among his most noted pictures are portraits of Benjamin West, Coleridge, and himself, "Saul and the Witch of Endor," "The Angel Uriel in the Sun," "Spaletro's Vision of the Bloody Hand," and the noted "Belshazzar's Feast"—the plan of which was changed shortly before his death and the painting left unfinished. Wrote "Monaldi: a Tale" (1841). His "Lectures on Art, and Poems" (1850) were edited and published after his death by Richard H. Dana, Jr. Died, Cambridge, Mass., 9 July, 1843.

ALSOP, George, colonist, b. England, 1638. Emigrated to Maryland, 1658, and completed a term of four years' service in Baltimore county of that colony. Had returned to England by 1666, where he published "A Character of the Province of Maryland" (1666). Of his subsequent life nothing is known.

ALSOP, Richard, b. Middletown, Conn., 23 Jan., 1761. Studied, but did not graduate, at Yale. From 1791 to 1805, in conjunction with the other so-called "Hartford Wits," he was principal contributor to the series of satirical papers afterward collected in "The Echo" (1807). Also wrote "A Poem; Sacred to the Memory of George Washington" (1800), "The Enchanted Lake, or the Fairy Morgana" (1808), and several translations. Died, Flatbush, L. I., N. Y., 20 Aug., 1815.

AMES, Fisher, statesman, b. Dedham, Mass., 9 April, 1758. Son of Nathaniel Ames. Graduated at Harvard. Began practising law at Dedham, 1781, after several years of teaching. His political contributions to the periodicals, signed "Lucius Junius Brutus" and "Camillus," earliest brought him into notice. In 1788 he was elected to the first U. S. congress, serving eight years. He was chosen to deliver the address of that body to Washington on the latter's retirement from the presidency, and delivered the eulogy on Washington before the Massachusetts legislature in February, 1800. One of Ames's most important speeches in congress was that supporting the terms of Jay's treaty with Great Britain in 1796. Shortly after this, failing health obliged him to retire from public life. A collection of his speeches and writings was published in 1809, and there have appeared since, "Works of Fisher Ames" (1854) and

"Speeches of Fisher Ames in Congress" (1871). Died, Dedham, Mass., 4 July, 1808.

AMES, Nathaniel, physician, b. Bridgewater, Mass., 1708. Was interested in astronomy and brought out annually from 1725 until his death a popular almanac known as the "Astronomical Diary." Resided at Dedham, Mass. Married Mary Fisher, their son being Fisher Ames, the orator. Died, Dedham, Mass., 11 July, 1764.

ANDERSON, Joseph, clergyman, b. Ross-shire, Scotland, 16 Dec., 1836. Came to America, 1842. Graduated at the college of New York. Became pastor of a Congregational church in Waterbury, Conn., 12 Feb., 1865. For several years a member of the corporation of Yale university. Has contributed poetry to the magazines, and written a number of works on archæological, ethnological, and historical subjects.

ANDREW, John Albion, statesman, b. Windham, Me., 31 May, 1818. Graduated at Bowdoin. Was admitted to the bar of Boston in 1840. Soon connected himself with the anti-slavery movement, and was counsel in several noted fugitive-slave trials. Was elected a member of the Massachusetts legislature, 1858, and was governor of the same state, 1861–6, sending the first troops to Washington in the civil war. Died, Boston, Mass., 30 Oct., 1867.

ANDREWS, Stephen Pearl, b. Templeton, Mass., 22 Mar., 1812. Studied at Amherst college, and practised law in Louisiana and Texas. Afterward removed to Boston and became active in the anti-slavery movement. His "Basic Outline of Universology" (1872) is an exposition of his theory of the unity of law in the universe, which theory extends to a universal language, named by him "Alwato." Published numerous works explaining and defending his ideas. Died, New York, N. Y., 21 May, 1886.

ANTHONY, Susan Brownell, reformer, b. South Adams, Mass., 15 Feb., 1820, of Quaker parentage. Taught school in New York state from 1835 to 1850. In 1852 she organized the Woman's New York state temperance society, and became a leader in temperance and woman's rights movements. She was also active as an anti-slavery agitator before and during the civil war. Joint author with two others of "The History of Woman Suffrage" (1881).

ANTROBUS, John, artist, b. Walsall, Staffordshire, England, 1831. Came to America in 1849. Has resided chiefly in Detroit, Mich., though he has spent some time in study at London and Paris. Has gained reputation as a portrait-painter. His poems have been published in the periodicals. One of them, "The Cowboy," was inspired by his noted picture bearing the same title.

APPLETON, Thomas Gold, b. Boston, Mass., 31 Mar., 1812. Graduated at Harvard, and was a classmate of Wendell Phillips and John Lothrop Motley. Travelled extensively in Europe and the East. Was the founder of the Boston literary club, and was noted for his witty conversation. Published "Nile Journal" (1876), "Syrian Sunshine" (1877), and a volume of poems. Died, New York, N. Y., 17 April, 1884.

ARISTOCRACY, The Author of.—The editors are not at liberty to give any information respecting this writer, beyond the fact that their selections from "Aristocracy," etc., appear legitimately in "A Library of American Literature."

ARNOLD, Benedict, soldier, b. Norwich, Conn., 14 Jan., 1741. Was a successful merchant at New Haven, Conn., and captain of the governor's guards when he led them to Cambridge, Mass., on receipt of the news of the battle of Lexington. Assisted at the capture of Ticonderoga. Was promoted to be a major-general in the Continental army for gallant services. The exposure of his subsequent treason by the capture of Major André occurred on 23 Sept., 1780. Arnold escaped to the British army. Died, London, England, 14 June, 1801.

ARNOLD, George, b. New York, N. Y., 24 June, 1834. In early life resided at Alton, Ill., where his parents remained until 1849, when they removed to the settlement of Fourierites at Strawberry Farms, in Monmouth county, N. J. Began the study of painting when eighteen years old, but soon after devoted himself to literature. Contributed articles of every description to the magazines and newspapers, and wrote a popular series of sketches called "McArone Papers," which appeared in "Vanity Fair" and other journals from 1860 until his death. Served in the Union army during the civil war, and was stationed for a period at one of the forts on Staten Island. "Drift: a Sea-shore Idyl: and Other Poems" (1866) and "Poems, Grave and Gay" (1866) were edited by William Winter. Died, Strawberry Farms, N. J., 3 Nov., 1865.

ASTOR, William Waldorf, diplomatist, b. New York, N. Y., 31 Mar., 1848. Received his education in that city from Professor Hinkel of Marburg university, Germany. Studied art for several years. Graduated at the Columbia law school, practised law in New York, and was a member of the state senate at Albany for three years. Was appointed U. S. minister to Italy by President Arthur, 1882, resigning in 1885. Has chiefly been occupied with the study of books. Succeeded to the estate of his father, John Jacob Astor, Feb., 1890. Author of "Valentino," an Italian romance (1885) and of "Sforza: a Story of Milan" (1889).

ATKINSON, Edward, economist, b. Brookline, Mass., 10 Feb., 1827. Early devoted himself to the study of economic questions. Has delivered numerous addresses, and published many pamphlets and articles, on these subjects. Some of them are "Cheap Cotton by Free Labor" (1861), "Our National Domain" (1879), "Labor and Capital" (1880), "Addresses at Atlanta, Ga., on the Cotton Exposition of 1881," "The Railway and the Farmer" (1881), and "The Distribution of Products" (1885).

AUDUBON, John James, naturalist, b. near New Orleans, La., 4 May, 1780. Was sent to France for his education, where he studied art in the studio of the painter David. His father, a Frenchman by birth, encouraged the son's interest in natural history, and placed him at the age of seventeen on a farm at Mill Grove, near Philadelphia, Penn., to facilitate his studies. In 1808, having made some unsuccessful attempts in business at New York, Audubon sold this farm and removed to Louisville, Ky. There, and in many sections of the country, he occupied himself with excursions into the woods and fields in search of specimens. The plates for his great work, "The Birds of America" (1830–8), were made in England, where he went in 1826, and he was enabled to carry the enterprise through financially by the efforts of European naturalists. "Ornithological Biography" (1831–9) comprises the text descriptive of the birds portrayed in the former work. Audubon returned to America in 1840, and purchased an estate on the Hudson, now known as Audubon park, New York city, remaining there until his death. "Quadrupeds of America" (1846–54) was prepared with the assistance of his sons. Died, "Minnie's Land," New York, N. Y., 27 Jan., 1851.

AURINGER, Obadiah Cyrus, b. Glens Falls, N. Y., 4 June, 1849. Served for some years in the U. S. navy, and since 1875 has followed the occupation of a farmer in his native place. Has brought out two volumes of poetry, "The Voice of a Shell" (1877) and "Scythe and Sword" (1887).

AUSTIN, Jane [Goodwin], b. Worcester, Mass., 25 Feb., 1831. The daughter of Isaac Goodwin of Worcester. She received her education in Boston schools, and in 1850 was married to Loring H. Austin of the latter city, where she has since resided. Some of her books are "Fairy Dreams" (1859), "Dora Darling" (1864), "A Nameless Nobleman" (1881), "The Desmond Hundred" (1882), and "Nantucket Scraps" (1883).

AUSTIN, William, lawyer, b. Charlestown, Mass., 2 Mar., 1778. Graduated at Harvard. Is first noticed as delivering an oration at Charlestown, Mass., in 1801, on the anniversary of the battle of Bunker Hill. This was published at the time. The two following years he spent in England, and his stay abroad resulted in a volume of "Letters from London" (1804), wherein many distinguished residents of the city are described. About 1805 Austin fought a duel with James H. Elliott,—the result of a newspaper controversy,—and was slightly wounded. His remarkable story, "Peter Rugg, the Missing Man," was contributed to the "New England Galaxy" (1824–6), of which he was then editor. He gained eminence as a lawyer in Suffolk and Middlesex counties, Mass. In 1807 appeared "An Essay on the Human Character of Jesus Christ," a volume of Unitarian views. Died, Charlestown, Mass., 27 June, 1841.

BACON, Delia, b. Tallmadge, Ohio, 2 Feb., 1811. Sister of Leonard Bacon. Pursued the occupation of a teacher, and lived chiefly at Boston. Inaugurated the Shakespeare-Bacon controversy in the "Atlantic Monthly" for 1856. Followed this article with "Philosophy of the Plays of Shakespeare Unfolded" (1857). Died, Hartford, Conn., 2 Sept., 1859.

BACON, Leonard, divine, b. Detroit, Mich., 19 Feb., 1802. Graduated at Yale. Became pastor of a Congregational church in New Haven, Conn., 1825, and was elected professor of theology at Yale in 1866. A brave and able controversialist, both in sectarian and religious matters. Author of "Thirteen Historical Discourses" (1839), "Slavery Discussed in Occasional Essays" (1846), "Christian Self-Culture" (1863), and many addresses and pamphlets. Died, New Haven, Conn., 24 Dec., 1881.

BACON, Nathaniel, colonist, b. Suffolk, England, 1647 (Edw. Eggleston). Came to Virginia, 1673, and established a plantation at the head of tide-water, James River. Soon became a member of Sir William Berkeley's council. In 1675, an Indian war being in progress, and the colonists being displeased with Governor Berkeley's inaction, they chose Bacon as their general, but the governor refused to commission him. He marched against the Indians, and was declared a rebel early in 1676. He then invaded Jamestown and obtained his commission by force from the governor, and the so-called "Bacon's rebellion" ensued. Accounts of this affair are found in the "Aspinwall" and "Burwell" papers, published by the Mass. Hist. Soc., and in the manuscript relation by "T. M." given in "Force's Historical Tracts." Died, probably near Gloucester C. H., Va., 1 Oct., 1676.

BACON, Theodore, lawyer, b. New Haven, Conn., 6 May, 1834. Son of Leonard Bacon. Graduated at Yale. Has practised law at Rochester, N. Y., since 1856, with the exception of three years' service in the Union army during the civil war. Has contributed to the periodicals, and has written "Delia Bacon, a Biographical Sketch" (1888).

BAGBY, George William, "Moses Adams," b. Buckingham Co., Va., 13 Aug.,

1828. Graduated at the medical school of the university of Pennsylvania. Became a journalist and edited several Virginia newspapers. Was editor of the "Southern Literary Messenger," 1859–65. Gained reputation as a humorous lecturer and writer. Was state librarian of Virginia, 1870–8. In 1884 there appeared posthumously "Miscellaneous Writings of Dr. George W. Bagby." Died, Richmond, Va., 29 Nov., 1883.

BAIRD, Henry Martyn, educator, b. Philadelphia, Penn., 17 Jan., 1832. Graduated at the university of New York, where he became professor of Greek in 1859. Author of "Modern Greece" (1856), and of a history of the Huguenots in France. Two parts of the latter comprise "The Rise of the Huguenots" (1879) and "The Huguenots and Henry of Navarre" (1886). The third part will complete the work with the revocation of the Edict of Nantes.

BAKER, George Augustus, lawyer, b. New York, N. Y., Aug., 1849. Graduated at the college of New York. Has practised his profession chiefly in that city. Author of a volume of poems, "Point-Lace and Diamonds" (1875), and of "Mrs. Hephaestus, and Other Short Stories" (1887).

BAKER, William Mumford, clergyman, b. Washington, D. C., 27 June, 1825. Graduated at Princeton. Was pastor of Presbyterian churches in Texas, Ohio, and Massachusetts. During the civil war, while residing at Austin, he retained his Union principles and wrote in the form of a novel an account of his experiences, published as "Inside: a Chronicle of Secession" (1866). Other books were "The New Timothy" (1870) and "His Majesty Myself" (1879). Died, South Boston, Mass., 20 Aug., 1883.

BALDWIN, Joseph G., jurist, b. Sumter, Ala., 18—. Was judge of the supreme court of California from 1857 to 1863, and chief justice, 1863–4. Author of "The Flush Times of Alabama and Mississippi" (1853) and "Party Leaders" (1854). Died, San Francisco, Cal., 30 Sept., 1864.

BALLOU, Hosea, clergyman, b. Richmond, N. H., 30 April, 1771. The son of a Baptist clergyman, he educated himself, and became pastor of a Universalist church in 1794. After several changes, he was permanently settled over the second Universalist society of Boston in 1817. He founded the "Universalist Magazine" and the "Universalist Expositor." Chief among his works are "Notes on the Parables" (1804) and "A Treatise on the Atonement" (1804). Died, Boston, Mass., 7 June, 1852.

BANCROFT, George, b. Worcester, Mass., 3 Oct., 1800. Graduated at Harvard. Continued his studies in Germany, graduating in 1820 at the university of Göttingen. Enjoyed intimacy with Goethe and with other eminent German writers. Decided upon writing history as the main work of his life. Was tutor of Greek at Harvard, 1822–3, and in 1823 established a collegiate school at Northampton, Mass. Was elected to the Massachusetts legislature in 1830, but declined to serve. Issued the first volume of his "History of the United States" in 1834. Was collector of the port of Boston from 1838 to 1841, and in 1845 received from President Polk the appointment of secretary of the navy. As secretary he planned and established the naval academy at Annapolis, and issued the orders by which California was annexed to the United States. Was U. S. minister to Great Britain, 1846–9, to Russia in 1867, to the North German confederation in 1868, and to the German empire, 1871–4. He was given the degree of D. C. L. by Oxford in 1849, and was enrolled as member of many European learned societies. The final edition of "The History of the United States of America" was published, 1884–5. Other works are an oration on Andrew Jackson (1845), "The Necessity, the Reality, and the Promise of the Progress of the Human Race" (1854), "Literary and Historical Miscellanies" (1855), "Memorial Address before both Houses of Congress on Abraham Lincoln" (1866), and "A Plea for the Constitution of the United States of America, Wounded in the House of its Guardians" (1886).

BANCROFT, Hubert Howe, b. Granville, O., 5 May, 1832. Removed from Buffalo, N. Y., where he had been employed in his brother's book-store, to California in 1852, and four years later established a bookselling and publishing house at San Francisco. About the same time he began to search for and collect books and manuscripts relating to the history of that portion of North America which is west of the Rocky mountains. The collection numbers about fifty thousand volumes, and has been placed in a fire-proof building. Many of the manuscripts are narratives taken down from the lips of early residents of California. In 1869 Mr. Bancroft began the task of indexing his library and of selecting and setting in order the materials for his "History of the Pacific States." This work is complete in thirty-nine volumes, most of which had been published before 1890. In the preparation of the text, the preliminary labors were performed by assistants, Mr. Bancroft revising and editing the whole, and himself writing the portions of greatest significance.

BARLOW, Joel, diplomatist, b. Redding, Conn., 24 Mar., 1754. (Todd's Biog.) Son of a farmer. Graduated at Yale. Served in the Continental army while an undergraduate. Delivered at the commencement exercises of his class a poem entitled "The Prospect of Peace" (1778). Was a chaplain in the army, 1780–3. Afterward studied law, and was admitted to the bar at Hartford, Conn., in 1786. While in that city he founded a weekly newspaper, "The American Mercury," and was associated with the "Hartford Wits" in the production of "The Anarchiad." The publication of his epic poem, "The Vision of Columbus" (1787), brought him reputation, and obtained for him the agency in Europe of the Scioto land company for the sale of its rights in American government lands. The company proving a swindle, Barlow resigned his agency and interested himself in the French Girondist movement. He also busied himself in English politics, and his "Advice to the Privileged Orders" (1791) was proscribed by the British government. In 1793 he was defeated as a candidate for deputy from Savoy, France, and the same year composed his well-known poem, "The Hasty Pudding." Was U. S. consul at Algiers, 1795–7, and performed valuable services in the liberation of American prisoners and in negotiating treaties with the Barbary powers. From 1797 until 1805 he lived at Paris. Returned to America in 1805, and built himself a handsome house at Washington, residing there until his appointment as U. S. minister to France in 1811. Invited to a conference with Napoleon at Wilna, he became involved in the latter's retreat from Moscow, and died of exhaustion at an obscure village in Poland. His early poem, "The Vision of Columbus," was amended and published with extensive additions as "The Columbiad" in 1807. Died, near Cracow, Poland, 24 Dec., 1812.

BARNARD, Charles, dramatist, b. Boston, Mass., 13 Feb., 1838. Engaged in business in that city and afterward became a journalist. More recently devoted himself to dramatic writing. A resident of Stamford, Conn. Author of "The County Fair" (1888), besides several plays written in collaboration with others. Has written a number of books on gardening; also, "The Tone Masters" (1871) and "Knights of To-day" (1881).

BARNARD, Frederick Augustus Porter, educator, b. Sheffield, Mass., 5 May, 1809. Graduated at Yale. Was a professor in the university of Alabama, 1837–54. Took orders in the Protestant Episcopal church, 1854. Became president of Columbia college in 1864, resigning in 1888. Published "Letters on Collegiate Government" (1855), "History of the United States Coast Survey" (1857), "Recent Progress in Science" (1869), and "The Metric System" (1871). Died, New York, N. Y., 27 April, 1889.

BARR, Amelia Edith [Huddleston], b. Ulverton, Lancashire, England, 29 Mar., 1831. Received her education at the Glasgow high school. Was married to Robert Barr, the son of a Scotch clergyman, in 1850, and came to America with him in 1854, residing at Austin and Galveston, Tex., until the death of her husband and sons by yellow fever in 1867. In 1869 she removed to New York city, and has since lived there and at Cornwall-on-the-Hudson. In 1871 she began contributing to magazines and periodicals. Author of many novels, among others "Romance and Reality" (1872), "Jan Vedder's Wife" (1885), "A Bow of Orange Ribbon" (1886), and "Remember the Alamo" (1888).

BARRON, Elwyn Alfred, journalist, b. Nashville, Tenn., 6 Mar., 1855. Graduated at Robert college, then at Lookout Mountain. Has been editorial writer and dramatic critic on the Chicago "Inter-Ocean" since 1879. Author of "The Viking," a blank-verse drama (1888). Several of his plays have been acted, among them "A Moral Crime" (1885).

BARTOL, Cyrus Augustus, clergyman, b. Freeport, Me., 30 April, 1813. Graduated at Bowdoin. Studied at the Harvard divinity school. Became colleague pastor of the West church (Unitarian) of Boston, 1837, and pastor in 1861. Has been prominent in social reforms and as a philanthropist. Two of his books are "Discourses on the Christian Spirit and Life" (1850) and "Radical Problems" (1872).

BARTRAM, William, botanist, b. Kingsessing, Philadelphia Co., Penn., 9 Feb., 1739. Son of John Bartram, founder of the first botanical garden in the United States. As a young man he established himself in business in North Carolina, but soon abandoned it to accompany his father in the latter's travels through Florida. The son remained in that state and resided for some time on the St. John's river, engaged in the cultivation of indigo. Returning to Philadelphia in 1771, he devoted himself entirely to the study of botany. During 1773–8 he was occupied with botanical explorations in the Southern states. He was a member of several scientific societies, and made many discoveries in the botany of North America. He published "Travels through North and South Carolina, Georgia, East and West Florida" (1791). Died, Kingsessing, Penn., 22 July, 1823.

BASCOM, John, educator, b. Genoa, N. Y., 1 May, 1827. Graduated at Williams. Became professor of rhetoric there, 1855. Was elected president of the university of Michigan in 1874, serving until 1887. Among his books are "Political Economy" (1859), "Science, Philosophy, and Religion" (1871), "Philosophy of English Literature" (1874), "Natural Theology" (1880), and "Problems in Philosophy" (1885).

BATES, Arlo, journalist, b. East Machias, Me., 16 Dec., 1850. Graduated at Bowdoin. A resident of Boston, Mass., since

1876. Edited, 1878–9, "The Broadside," a civil-service reform paper, and in 1880 became editor of the Boston "Sunday Courier." His first book, "Patty's Perversities" (1881), appeared in the "Round Robin Series." It was followed by "The Pagans" (1884), "A Wheel of Fire" (1885), "Berries of the Brier," poems (1886), "Sonnets in Shadow" (1887), "A Lad's Love" (1887), and "The Philistines" (1889).

BATES, Charlotte Fiske, b. New York, N. Y., 30 Nov., 1838. After the death in 1847 of her father, Hervey Bates, resided at Cambridge, Mass., until 1888, when she removed to New York city. Assisted Longfellow in compiling his "Poems of Places," making several translations for the work. Author of "Risk, and Other Poems" (1879), and editor of the "Cambridge Book of Poetry" (1882).

Bates, Edward [*Noted Saying:* Vol. VII., page 191], lawyer, b. Goochland Co., Va., 4 Sept., 1793. Attorney-general of the United States, 1861–4. Died, St. Louis, Mo., 25 Mar., 1869.

BATES, Elizabeth [Sears], educator, b. North San Juan, Cal., 18—. A resident of San Francisco, and a teacher in the public schools of that city. Has contributed poetry and fiction to the periodicals.

BATES, Harriet Leonora [Vose], "Eleanor Putnam," b. Quincy, Ill., 30 July, 1856. She was the wife of Arlo Bates, who has edited and published a volume of her articles, contributed to the "Atlantic Monthly," as "Old Salem" (1886), and more recently a novel left in manuscript, "A Woodland Wooing" (1889). Died, Boston, Mass., 18 Mar., 1886.

BATES, Katharine Lee, educator, b. Falmouth, Mass., 18—. Graduated at Wellesley college, where she became associate professor of English literature. Author of "The College Beautiful, and Other Poems" (1887), and "Rose and Thorn," a story (1889).

BATES, Margret Holmes [Ernsperger], b. Fremont, O., 6 Oct., 1844. After teaching for several years in Ohio and Indiana, was married, 1865, to Charles A. Bates, and became a resident of Indianapolis, Ind. Has written "Manitou" (1881) and "The Chamber over the Gate" (1886), besides shorter works of fiction in periodicals.

BAXTER, James Phinney, merchant, b. Gorham, Me., 23 Mar., 1831. A son of Elihu Baxter, M. D., of that place. A successful merchant and manufacturer, having his home at Portland, Me., to the public library of which city he presented a handsome building. Author of "Idyls of the Year" (1884), and a contributor to colonial historical research.

BAYARD, James Asheton, statesman, b. Philadelphia, Penn., 28 July, 1767. Graduated at the college of New Jersey. Began the practice of law at Wilmington, Del. A

member of the U. S. house of representatives, 1797–1803, and of the U. S. senate, 1804–13. He served upon the commission which completed the treaty of peace with Great Britain at Ghent in 1814. He was distinguished as a lawyer and political orator, and was a leader in the Federalist party. Died, Wilmington, Del., 6 Aug., 1815.

BAYLOR, Frances Courtenay, b. Fayetteville, Ark., 20 Jan., 1848. The daughter of an army officer, and descended from an old Virginia family. Visited Europe after the civil war and again in 1873. Resided near Winchester, Va., after 1876. Author of "On Both Sides," an international novel (1886), and "Behind the Blue Ridge : a Homely Narrative" (1887).

Bee, Bernard E. [*Noted Saying:* Vol. VII., page 193], b. Charleston, S. C., about 1823. Served as brigadier-general in the Confederate army, and was killed at the battle of Bull Run, 21 July, 1861.

BEECHER, Henry Ward, clergyman, b. Litchfield, Conn., 24 June, 1813. Son of Lyman Beecher. Graduated at Amherst. Studied divinity at the Lane theological seminary, Cincinnati, of which his father was president. Preached first at Lawrenceburg, Ind., and afterward at Indianapolis until 1847, when he was called to the pastorate of the newly-formed Plymouth Congregational church at Brooklyn, N. Y. This position he filled for the remainder of his life, and his oratorical powers gained him such reputation that his congregation became and continued to be one of the largest in the country. In 1863 he visited England and delivered a series of effective addresses in behalf of the Union cause. These were published at the time and have since been collected in a volume, with other speeches and sermons on the war, as "Patriotic Addresses" (1887). His sermons were stenographically reported after 1859 and printed weekly as "Plymouth Pulpit." Was one of the first contributors to the "Independent" and its editor for a time. In 1870 became editor of the "Christian Union." He was in constant demand as a lecturer and platform speaker. Some of his numerous books are "Lectures to Young Men" (1844), "Star Papers" (1855–8), "Eyes and Ears" (1864), "Norwood," a novel (1867), "Life of Jesus the Christ : Earlier Scenes" (1871), "Yale Lectures on Preaching" (1872–4), and "Evolution and Religion" (1885). Died, Brooklyn, N. Y., 8 Mar., 1887.

BEECHER, Lyman, clergyman, b. New Haven, Conn., 12 Oct., 1775. Graduated at Yale, where he also studied theology under Timothy Dwight. Preached at East Hampton, L. I., from 1798 until 1810, when he became pastor of the Congregational church at Litchfield, Conn. While at Litchfield he was prominent in the organization of the

Bible, educational, and missionary societies. In 1826 he was called to the pastorate of the Hanover street church in Boston. Six years later he assumed the presidency of the Lane theological seminary at Cincinnati, holding this position until 1852. The remainder of his life was passed in retirement at Brooklyn, N.Y. Of his numerous theological writings the best known are collections of sermons on "Temperance" and "Political Atheism." He supervised the publication of his "Works" (1852–3), and his "Autobiography and Correspondence" (1864) was edited by Charles Beecher. Died, Brooklyn, N.Y., 10 Jan., 1863.

BEERS, Ethelinda [Elliott], "Ethel Lynn Beers," b. Goshen, N.Y., 13 Jan., 1827. The authorship of her most noted poem, "All Quiet along the Potomac," which appeared in "Harper's Weekly" for 1861, was falsely claimed by several persons. "All Quiet along the Potomac, and Other Poems" was published in 1879. Died, Orange, N.J., 10 Oct., 1879.

BEERS, Henry Augustin, educator, b. Buffalo, N.Y., 2 July, 1847. Graduated at Yale, where, after several years' service as tutor, he became assistant professor of English in 1875, and full professor in 1880. Author of two books of poems—"Odds and Ends" (1878) and "The Thankless Muse" (1885)—and of "A Century of American Literature" (1878), "Life of N. P. Willis" (1885), and "Outline Sketches of English and American Literature" (1886–7).

BELKNAP, Jeremy, clergyman, b. Boston, Mass., 4 June, 1744. Graduated at Harvard. Entered the ministry, and preached at Dover, N.H., 1767–87. He then became pastor of the Federal street church in Boston, retaining the connection until his death. Began his historical studies soon after his settlement in New Hampshire, making special studies of matters relating to that state. His "History of New Hampshire" (1784–91) is much valued as an authority. Founded the Massachusetts historical society in 1790, and on 23 Oct., 1792, delivered a discourse before it commemorative of the three hundredth anniversary of the discovery of America. Author of "The Foresters, an American Tale" (1792), "American Biographies" (1794–8), and several sermons and theological works. Died, Boston, Mass., 20 June, 1798.

BELLAMY, Edward, b. Chicopee Falls, Mass., 26 Mar., 1850. Studied at Union college and in Germany. Was admitted to the bar, 1871. Engaged in journalistic work on the New York "Evening Post," and from 1872 to 1876 was assistant editor of the Springfield, Mass., "Union." Subsequently resided at his birthplace, mainly occupied with literary work. His novels are "Six to One, a Nantucket Idyl"

(1877), "Dr. Heidenhoff's Process" (1879), "Miss Ludington's Sister" (1884), and "Looking Backward" (1888). "Looking Backward," a study in socialism, gained an enormous sale at home and abroad, and caused the founding of "Nationalist" clubs throughout the United States.

BELLAMY, Joseph, clergyman, b. Cheshire, Conn., 1719. Graduated at Yale. Preached at Bethlehem, Conn., from 1740 until his death. Established there a divinity school, and became noted as an instructor of theological students. His numerous published writings were collected into three volumes of "Works" in 1811. Died, Bethlehem, Conn., 6 Mar., 1790.

BELLAW, Americus Wellington, b. Troy, O., 17 Mar., 1842. Began his permanent residence at Sidney, O., 1867. Contributed humorous work, under the pseudonyms "Washington Whitehorn" and "Joe Jot," to the New York "Saturday Journal" for many years. A writer of verse for the leading magazines and newspapers.

BELLOWS, Henry Whitney, clergyman, b. Boston, Mass., 11 June, 1814. Graduated at Harvard. Pastor of a Unitarian church in New York city from 1839 until his death. Was a founder of the "Christian Inquirer." During the civil war was president of the U. S. sanitary commission. The most notable of his lectures and addresses was "The Relation of Public Amusements to Public Morality" (1857). Died, New York, N.Y., 30 Jan., 1882.

BENEDICT, Frank Lee, b. Alexander, Genesee Co., N.Y., 6 July, 1834. Received his education from private tutors, and devoted himself almost entirely to literary work. Passed much of his life in Europe. More recently resided in New York city and in Philadelphia. Some of his many novels are "My Daughter Elinor" (1869), "Miss Van Kortland" (1870), "St. Simon's Niece" (1876), and "The Price She Paid" (1881).

BENEZET, Anthony, philanthropist, b. St. Quentin's, France, 31 Jan., 1713. His family were Huguenots, and, settling in Philadelphia, became Quakers. Benezet took a position as teacher in that city and remained in similar employment for the rest of his life. Devoted much of his time to charitable pursuits, and gained prominence as an opponent of slavery. Author of several anti-slavery pamphlets, one of which was "A Caution and Warning to Great Britain and her Colonies" (1766 ; London, 1767). Died, Philadelphia, Penn., 3 May, 1784.

BENJAMIN, Park, journalist, b. Demarara, British Guiana, 14 Aug., 1809. Graduated at Trinity. Edited the "New England Magazine," 1835–7, and in 1837 transferred it to New York city as the "American Monthly Magazine." Assisted

Greeley in the "New Yorker." In 1840 established the "New World," and was connected with other journalistic ventures in various states. Wrote many poems and delivered lectures, but they were not published collectively. Died, New York, N. Y., 12 Sept., 1864.

BENJAMIN, Samuel Greene Wheeler, b. Argos, Greece, 13 Feb., 1837. Graduated at Williams. Was for some years assistant librarian at the Albany state library. An extensive writer on art, being himself an artist as well as an author. Has travelled widely in Europe and the East. Was appointed U. S. minister to Persia, 1883, resigning in 1885. Some of his many published works are "Constantinople, Isle of Pearls, and Other Poems" (1860), "The Choice of Paris, a Romance of the Troad" (1870), "What is Art?" (1877), "Contemporary Art in Europe" (1877), and "Persia and the Persians" (1886).

BENSEL, James Berry, b. New York, N. Y., 2 Aug., 1856. Resided chiefly at Lynn, Mass. His life was a painful struggle with poverty and disease. Author of "King Cophetua's Wife," a novel (1883), and "In the King's Garden, and Other Poems" (1885). Died, New York, N. Y., 3 Feb., 1886.

BENTON, Joel, b. Amenia, Dutchess Co., N. Y., 29 May, 1832. Attended school in his native place, and for a while edited the Amenia "Times." His life has been devoted to literary and philosophical studies, which have resulted in numerous contributions to magazines, etc. In 1883 he published "Emerson as a Poet."

BENTON, Thomas Hart, statesman, b. near Hillsborough, N. C., 14 Mar., 1782. Studied for a time at the university of North Carolina. In 1810 removed to the vicinity of Nashville, Tenn., at which place he was admitted to the bar. Was aide to General Jackson in the war of 1812. Established a newspaper at St. Louis, Mo., 1815, and for his efforts in behalf of the admission of that state to the Union was made U. S. senator in 1821, holding office for thirty years. He became noted as an advocate of measures looking toward the opening of the West, and as an opponent of Calhoun and nullification. His exertions in behalf of gold and silver coinage gained him the name of "Old Bullion." Opposition to advanced slavery legislation and the Missouri compromise finally lost him his seat in the senate. He afterward served one term as U. S. representative. Published "Thirty Years' View" (1854–6), a record of events during his stay in the senate, and prepared an abridgment of the debates of congress. Died, Washington, D. C., 10 April, 1858.

BERKELEY, George, bishop of Cloyne, b. Kilkenny, Ireland, 12 Mar., 1684. Graduated at Trinity college, Dublin. Became a clergyman of the Church of England, and was made dean of Derry in 1724. Soon after, he issued proposals for founding a college at the Bermuda islands, to educate clergymen for the American colonies. He obtained the promise of a grant of £20,000 for this project from the English government, and sailed for Newport, R. I., arriving, Jan., 1729. There he purchased a farm, and settled down to carry out his plans, but learning that the promised money would not be given, he returned to England, 1731. Was appointed bishop of Cloyne two years later. During his stay in America he wrote what is perhaps his most noted contribution to theological and philosophical literature, "Alciphron, or the Minute Philosopher" (1732). An edition of his "Life and Works" (1871) has been published in England. Bishop Berkeley made valuable presents of books and land to Yale and other American colleges. From 1752 until his death he lived in retirement at Oxford. Died, Oxford, England, 14 Jan., 1753.

BERKELEY, Sir William, b. near London, England, about 1610. Graduated at Oxford. After some experience in colonial matters he was appointed governor of Virginia by Charles I. in 1641, and came to America, 1642. He held his position for the royalist party until the puritan parliament sent a fleet against him in 1651, when he was compelled to resign. Was reappointed at the restoration, and governed the colony with success until the so-called "Bacon's rebellion" in 1675–6. Having finally succeeded in crushing this, and having executed a number of its leaders, he returned to England. Accounts of this affair, with Berkeley's proclamation, are found in the "Aspinwall" and "Burwell" papers, published by the Mass. Hist. Soc., and in the manuscript relation by "T. M.," given in "Force's Historical Tracts." Died, Twickenham, England, 13 July, 1677.

BETHUNE, George Washington, clergyman, b. New York, N. Y., Mar., 1805. Graduated at Dickinson college, Carlisle, Penn. Entered the Dutch Reformed ministry, ultimately settling in Brooklyn, N. Y. Resigned on account of ill health in 1859. Published "Lays of Love and Faith" (1848), "Orations and Discourses" (1850), and "The Fruit of the Spirit," besides miscellaneous contributions in the religious press. Died, Florence, Italy, 27 Apr., 1862.

BEVERLY, Robert, b. Virginia, about 1670. A son of Major Robert Beverly, who emigrated to Virginia from Yorkshire, England, about 1660, settled in Middlesex county, and became clerk of the Virginia house of burgesses. The son received his education in England. He resided at "Beverly Park," in King and Queen county, and was clerk of the Virginia council in 1697, and a member of the house of burgesses 1699–1700. "The History and Present State of Virginia," the first authoritative history of the colony, was published at London in 1805. Died, Virginia, about 1735 (R. A. Brock).

BIDDLE, Nicholas, financier, b. Philadelphia, Penn., 8 Jan., 1786. Graduated at the college of New Jersey. After holding several minor diplomatic positions in Europe, was a member of the Pennsylvania legislature for two terms. Became a director of the U. S. bank, 1819, and was its president, 1823–36. Besides his financial and legal publications, he edited the Philadelphia "Port Folio," 1806–23. Died, Philadelphia, Penn., 27 Feb., 1844.

BIGELOW, John, journalist, b. Malden-on-the-Hudson, N. Y., 25 Nov., 1817. Graduated at Union college. Practised law at New York city for ten years, and after several journalistic connections became in 1849 joint owner of the New York "Evening Post" with William Cullen Bryant, and was its managing editor until 1861. In the latter year he was made U. S. consul at Paris. Was U. S. minister to France, 1865–7, and secretary of state for New York, 1867–8. Having found the original manuscript of Franklin's autobiography while in France, he edited it for publication in 1868. Afterward edited "The Complete Works of Benjamin Franklin" (1888); also, "The Writings and Speeches of Samuel J. Tilden" (1885). Among his original works are "Les Etats-Unis d'Amérique en 1863" and "Life of William Cullen Bryant" (1890).

BIGELOW, Poultney, lawyer, b. New York, N. Y., 10 Sept., 1855. Son of John Bigelow. Graduated at Yale and studied in Germany. Was for some time editor of "Outing." A writer for the magazines, and author of "The German Emperor" (1889).

BIGLOW, William, educator, b. Natick, Mass., 22 Sept., 1773. Graduated at Harvard. Taught school at Salem, Mass., and was afterward head master of the Boston Latin school. Contributed freely to the periodicals of the day, particularly metrical compositions. Published a "History of Natick" (1830) and several other books. Died, Boston, Mass., 12 Jan., 1844.

BIRD, Robert Montgomery, b. New Castle, Del., 5 Feb., 1805 (F. M. Bird). Wrote three tragedies, of which "The Gladiator" was frequently played by Forrest and continues to hold the stage. Published "Calavar" (1834), "The Infidel" (1835), "Sheppard Lee" (1836), "Nick of the Woods" (1837), "Robin Day" (1839), and other novels. Was editor and part owner of the Philadelphia "North American Gazette." Died, Philadelphia, Penn., 22 Jan., 1854.

BISHOP, Mary Catherine, b. Carrollton, Ill., 18—. Early removed to California,

and made her home at Belmont. A contributor of poetry and fiction to the periodicals.

BISHOP, William Henry, b. Hartford, Conn., 7 Jan., 1847. Graduated at Yale. Studied architecture at New York city and passed some time in the government architect's office at Washington. Afterward edited a paper at Milwaukee, Wis., returning to New York city in 1877, where he resided until 1888. In the latter year visited Europe for an extended stay. His first story, "One of the Thirty Pieces," appeared in the "Atlantic Monthly" for 1876. His books are "Detmold, a Romance" (1879), "The House of a Merchant Prince" (1883), "Choy Susan, and Other Stories" (1884), "Old Mexico and her Lost Provinces" (1884), "The Golden Justice" (1886), and "The Brown Stone Boy" (1888).

Black Hawk, or *Makataemishkiakiak* [*Noted Saying:* Vol. XI., page 450], b. Kaskaskia, Ill., 1767. A leading chief of the Sac and Fox tribes of Indians. Served with the British army in the war of 1812, and carried on a campaign against the U. S. forces in 1831–2. Died on the Des Moines river, 3 Oct., 1838.

BLAINE, James Gillespie, statesman, b. West Brownsville, Penn., 31 Jan., 1830. Graduated at Washington college, Penn., and taught in institutions at Blue Lick Springs, Ky., and Philadelphia. Subsequently edited papers at Kennebec and Portland, Me., until his election to the Maine legislature in 1858. Was U. S. representative from Maine, 1862–76, and was in 1876 appointed by the governor of that state to fill an unexpired term in the U. S. senate, being elected his own successor shortly after. Was appointed secretary of state by President Garfield in 1881, and by President Harrison in 1889. Was the unsuccessful candidate of the Republican party for the presidency in 1884. Author of "Twenty Years of Congress" (1884–6).

BLEDSOE, Albert Taylor, educator, b. Frankfort, Ky., 9 Nov., 1809. Graduated at the U. S. Military academy. Was professor of mathematics at several Southern colleges, and chief of the war bureau in the Confederate government. Author of "Was Secession a Constitutional Right previous to the War of 1861?" (1866), and a contributor to David Christy's "Cotton is King" (1860). Died, Alexandria, Va., 8 Dec., 1877.

BLEECKER, Ann Eliza [Schuyler], b. New York, N. Y., Oct., 1752. Daughter of Brandt Schuyler of that city. Was married in 1769 to John J. Bleecker, and resided at Tomhannock (sometimes written Tomhanick), near Albany, N. Y., with a few interruptions until her death. Some of her poems were published in the early numbers of the "New York Magazine." In 1793 appeared "The Posthumous Works of Ann Eliza

Bleecker," edited by her daughter. Died, Tomhannock, N. Y., 23 Nov., 1783.

BLOEDE, Gertrude, "Stuart Sterne," b. Dresden, Germany, 10 Aug., 1845. Daughter of Dr. Gustavus Bloëde, with whom she came to the United States in 1850. Has resided at Brooklyn, N. Y., since 1861, where she has given instruction in German. Has written for the magazines, and is the author of "Poems" (1874), "Giorgio, and Other Poems" (1881), and "Beyond the Shadow" (1888).

BLOOD, Henry Ames, b. Temple, N. H., 7 June, 1838. Graduated at Dartmouth. After teaching for a few years, accepted a permanent situation in the department of state at Washington. A contributor of verse to the periodicals, and author of several unpublished dramas.

BOKER, George Henry, diplomatist, b. Philadelphia, Penn., 6 Oct., 1823. Graduated at Princeton, and studied for the law, but did not enter the profession. Travelled in Europe and on his return published "The Lesson of Life, and Other Poems" (1847). In 1848 appeared "Calaynos," a tragedy, which was acted with success in March, 1849, at Sadlers's Wells Theatre in London. Subsequent dramas, both tragedies and comedies, that have been published and produced on the stage are "Anne Boleyn," "The Betrothal," "Leonor de Guzman," "All the World a Mask," and "Francesca da Rimini." These were collected in "Plays and Poems" (1856). "Poems of the War" (1864) contained some of the most noted lyrical efforts of the civil war, and augmented the effect of Mr. Boker's work at that time as secretary of the Philadelphia Union League. He afterward became president of this organization. Other books are "Konigsmark, the Legend of the Hounds, and Other Poems" (1869), "The Book of the Dead" (1882), and "Sonnets" (1886). In 1871 he was appointed by President Grant minister to Constantinople, and in 1875 minister to Russia, resigning in 1879. Died, Philadelphia, Penn., 2 Jan., 1890.

BONER, John Henry, b. Salem, N. C., 31 Jan., 1845. Received an academic education, and, learning the printer's trade, edited papers in Salem and Asheville, N. C. Was chief clerk of the N. C. house of representatives, 1869–70. In 1871 entered the civil service at Washington. Removed to New York city in 1887, and became a member of the staffs of "The Century Dictionary" and "A Library of American Literature." Besides contributing to the magazines, is the author of "Whispering Pines," poems (1883).

BOOTH, Mary Louise, journalist, b. Millville, now Yaphank, N. Y., 19 April, 1831. Resided mainly in New York city. Began writing at an early age, and devoted much time to the translation of French standard literature. During the civil war she rendered valuable services to the Union cause by her translations of French writings favoring the North. In 1859 she published a "History of the City of New York" (revised and enlarged, 1867 and 1880). She was editor of "Harper's Bazar" from its establishment in 1867 until her death. Died, New York, N. Y., 4 Mar., 1889.

BOTTA, Anne Charlotte [Lynch], b. Bennington, Vt., 1820. Received her education at Albany, N. Y. About 1842 made her permanent residence in New York city, where her receptions always have been attended by people noted in art and letters. Was married to Prof. Vincenzo Botta in 1855. Besides contributions to periodicals, has published "Poems" (1848 and 1884) and "Handbook of Universal Literature" (1860 and 1887).

BOTTA, Vincenzo, educator, b. Cavaller Maggiore, Piedmont, Italy, 11 Nov., 1818. Was educated at the university of Turin, in which he became professor of philosophy. Came to America in 1853, and was made professor of the Italian language and literature at the university of New York. Author of Italian state reports on the German universities and schools, of a "Discourse on the Life, Character, and Policy of Cavour" (1862), and of "Dante as Philosopher, Patriot, and Poet" (1865).

BOUDINOT, Elias, philanthropist, b. Philadelphia, Penn., 2 May, 1740. Studied law under Richard Stockton and practised in New Jersey. Was president of the Continental congress, 1782–4. Member of the U. S. house of representatives, 1789–95. Appointed director of the mint in 1795, he resigned ten years later, and retired to Burlington, N. J., where he was largely occupied in charitable pursuits. Published, among other works, "A Star in the West" (1816), an attempt to identify the lost tribes of Israel with the American Indians. Died, Burlington, N. J., 24 Oct., 1821.

BOVEE, Christian Nestell, lawyer, b. New York, N. Y., 22 Feb., 1820. Was for several years engaged in mercantile pursuits in that city, where he was subsequently admitted to the bar, and where he afterward practised his profession. Author of "Thoughts, Feelings, and Fancies" (1857) and "Intuitions and Summaries of Thought" (1862).

Bowen, Henry Chandler [*Noted Saying:* Vol. XI., page 453], b. Woodstock, Conn., 11 Sept., 1813. From 1839 to 1859 was with Theodore McNamee a member of the New York mercantile firm of Bowen & McNamee. Founded the N. Y. "Independent" in 1848.

BOWKER, Richard Rogers, journalist, b. Salem, Mass., 4 Sept., 1848. Graduated at the college of New York. Was for several years the literary editor of the N. Y. "Evening Mail." From 1870 to 1890 was connected with "The Publishers' Weekly," latterly as editor and proprietor. Also an editor of "The Library Journal" and of "The American Catalogue." Has been deeply interested in economics and in political and copyright reforms. Some of his publications on these subjects are "Of Work and Wealth" (1883), "Copyright : its Law and its Literature" (1886), and "Economics for the People" (1886).

BOWLES, Samuel, journalist, b. Springfield, Mass., 9 Feb., 1826. Entered the office of his father's paper, the "Springfield Republican," at an early age. In 1844 he brought about the change of the paper from a weekly to a daily journal, and in 1851 succeeded to its full control. Soon made it the most influential provincial newspaper in New England, a distinction it has since maintained. Mr. Bowles published several volumes of letters of travel. In 1885 appeared "The Life and Times of Samuel Bowles, by George S. Merriam." Died, Springfield, Mass., 16 Jan., 1878.

BOWNE, Eliza [Southgate], b. Scarboro, Me., 24 Sept., 1783. Daughter of Dr. Robert Southgate of that place, and niece of Rufus King. Was married in 1803 to Walter Bowne, afterward mayor of New York. Her letters, which are full of entertaining accounts of country and city life early in this century, have been preserved. Died, Charleston, S. C., Jan., 1809.

BOYESEN, Hjalmar Hjorth, educator, b. Fredericksvaern, Norway, 23 Sept., 1848. Studied at Leipsic, Germany, and graduated at the university of Norway. Removed to America in 1868, and edited at Chicago, Ill., a Scandinavian paper, entitled "Fremad." Assumed the professorship of German at Cornell, 1874, and six years later was appointed to the same position at Columbia college. While in New York city he has lectured before societies and in public on literary topics. His story, "Ilka on the Hill-Top," was dramatized as "Alpine Roses" and successfully produced in 1884. Has written, among other books, "Gunnar, a Norse Romance" (1874), "Falconberg" (1878), "Goethe and Schiller, their Lives and Works" (1878), "Ilka on the Hill-Top, and Other Stories" (1881), "A Daughter of the Philistines" (1883), and "Vagabond Tales" (1889).

BRACKENRIDGE, Henry Marie, jurist, b. Pittsburgh, Penn., 11 May, 1786. Son of the succeeding. Was admitted to the bar, 1806. Six years after was appointed a district judge in Louisiana. Was U. S. judge for the western district of Florida, 1821–32, and served on diplomatic commissions to South America and Mexico. Pub-

lished "History of the Late War between the United States and Great Britain" (about 1816), and "Recollections of Persons and Places in the West" (1834). Died, Pittsburgh, Penn., 18 Jan., 1871.

BRACKENRIDGE, Hugh Henry, jurist, b. near Campbelton, Scotland, 1748. Was brought to America in 1753 by his father, who established himself as a farmer in York county, Penn. The son taught school to obtain the means of completing his education and graduated at Princeton. Remained there as a tutor while studying for the ministry, though he did not follow that profession regularly. After conducting an academy in Maryland for several years, he removed to Philadelphia in 1776, and edited the "United States Magazine." Subsequently settled at Pittsburgh, practised law, and rose to be judge of the state supreme court from 1799 until his death. His chief work, "Modern Chivalry, or the Adventures of Captain Farrago" (1796–1806), is a satire on the political follies of a new country. Besides numerous contributions to periodicals, he composed with Philip Freneau a poetical dialogue, "The Rising Glory of America" (1772), also "The Battle of Bunker's Hill, a Dramatic Piece in Five Acts" (1776), and "Incidents of the Insurrection in the Western Parts of Pennsylvania" (1794). Died, Carlisle, Penn., 25 June, 1816.

BRADFORD, William, colonist, baptized at Austerfield, Yorkshire, England, 19 Mar., 1590, and probably born there not long before. Early became a Puritan of the Pilgrim type, and, with Robinson, W. Brewster, and others, removed to Holland at the age of eighteen to avoid religious persecution, remaining there twelve years. Sailed from Delft Haven, the port of Leyden, in the *Mayflower*, about the first of Aug., 1620, reaching Cape Cod 11 Nov., and landing at Plymouth 11 Dec. following. At the death of John Carver succeeded as governor of Plymouth colony, 1621, being annually reelected (with the exception of four years when he declined serving) for the rest of his life. His "History of Plymouth Plantation," left in manuscript, was used by Nathaniel Morton in his "Memorial," which is largely an abridgment of it, and by Thomas Prince and Governor Hutchinson in their histories of New England. Prince deposited Bradford's manuscript in the tower of the Old South church in Boston, whence it was probably removed during the British occupation of Boston in the Revolution. Supposed to have been lost, it was discovered in the Fulham library near London, England, in 1855 and published the next year. It is the most valuable record of Plymouth colony for the period it covers. In connection with Edward Winslow, Governor Bradford wrote the "Relation or Journal" of the first year at Plymouth, published at London in 1622, and long incorrectly styled "Mourt's Relation." A portion of his letter-book was found at Halifax and published in 1794. He left also verses on various subjects and some theological papers which have been printed. Was familiar with several languages, and a hard student, his historical work being characterized by vigorous simplicity of style combined with unusual discrimination. Died, Plymouth, Mass., 9 May, 1657.

BRADLEY, Mary Emily [Neely], b. Easton, Md., 29 Nov., 1835. Resided as a girl in Accomac county, Va. Published her first story in "Neal's Saturday Gazette," 1848. Was married to George T. Bradley in 1853, and subsequently lived chiefly in New York city. Author of a number of books for children and of a volume of poems, "Hidden Sweetness" (1886), besides much fugitive verse.

BRADSTREET, Anne [Dudley], "the Tenth Muse," b. probably at Northampton, England, 1612–13. Daughter of Gov. Thomas Dudley of Massachusetts. Was married at sixteen to Simon Bradstreet, son of a non-conformist clergyman, and then steward to the Countess of Warwick. With her husband, sailed for New England, probably in Winthrop's company, April, 1630. Resided at Charlestown and other places in the colony, but was a permanent resident of Andover by 1644. Her husband became governor of Massachusetts. A volume of her poems was published at London in 1650, entitled "The Tenth Muse Lately sprung up in America," with introductory verses by Nathaniel Ward and others. It was considered remarkable at the time, but it is now chiefly interesting as the first formal exhibition of poetical effort in New England. Much of the verse is a metrical transcript of her readings. A second edition, with additions, appeared after her death under the title, "Several Poems Compiled with great variety of Wit and Learning, full of Delight" (1678). In 1867 appeared "The Works of Anne Bradstreet in Prose and Verse. Edited by John H. Ellis." Died, Andover, Mass., 16 Sept., 1672.

Bragg, Edward Stuyvesant [*Noted Saying:* Vol. XI., page 460], b. Unadilla, N. Y., 20 Feb., 1827. Brigadier-general in the Union army during the civil war. Chairman of the Democratic national convention, 1884.

BRAINARD, John Gardiner Calkins, journalist, b. New London, Conn., 21 Oct., 1796. Graduated at Yale. Edited the Hartford "Connecticut Mirror" from 1822 until shortly before his death. An enlarged edition of his "Poems" (1825) was published as "Literary Remains" (1832) with an introduction by Whittier. Died, New London, Conn., 26 Sept., 1828.

BRAINERD, David, missionary, b. Haddam, Conn., 20 April, 1718. Studied at Yale, but did not graduate. Began his work among the Indians at Kent, Conn., 1741. Afterward accepted an appointment from the Scottish society for promoting Christian knowledge, as their missionary to the Indians. Pursued this vocation until his death, which was induced by exposure. Selections from his journals were published in 1746, and in 1749 appeared "Memoirs of the Rev. David Brainerd, chiefly taken from his own Diary. By Rev. Jonathan Edwards." Died, Northampton, Mass., 9 Oct., 1747.

BRIDGE, Thomas, clergyman, b. near London, England, 1657. Came to New England, and graduated at Harvard. After visiting Europe as a merchant, entered the ministry. Preached at Jamaica and Bermuda, and in 1705 became colleague pastor with Benjamin Wadsworth of the First church at Boston. Published several sermons. Died, Boston, Mass., 26 Sept., 1715.

BRIGGS, Charles Frederick, b. Nantucket, Mass., 1804. Established the "Broadway Journal," 1844, of which Poe afterward became editor. Associate editor of "Putnam's Magazine," 1853–6. In 1874 joined the staff of the N. Y. "Independent." Author of "Harry Franco, a Tale of the Great Panic" (1839), and "Working a Passage, or Life on a Liner" (1844). Died, Brooklyn, N. Y., 20 June, 1877.

BRISTED, Charles Astor, b. New York, N. Y., 1820. Graduated at Yale and at Cambridge university. Much of his life was passed in Europe. His last years were spent at Washington, D. C. Contributed largely to newspapers and magazines, and was the author of "The Upper Ten Thousand" (1852) and "Five Years in an English University" (1852). Died, Washington, D. C., 15 Jan., 1874.

BROMLEY, Isaac Hill, journalist, b. Norwich, Conn., 6 Mar., 1833. Graduated at Yale. Studied law and practised at New Haven, Conn., until 1858, when he founded the Norwich "Morning Bulletin." Served in the U. S. army, 1862–4. Was editor of the Hartford "Evening Post," 1868–72, and a member of the N. Y. "Tribune" editorial staff, 1873–83. In 1885 he accepted a position in the Union Pacific railroad management.

BROOKS, Charles Timothy, clergyman, b. Salem, Mass., 20 June, 1813. Graduated at Harvard. Pastor of the Unitarian church in Newport, R. I., from 1837 until 1873. Besides many translations from the German, several volumes of his poems have appeared, including "Songs of Field and Forest" (1854) and "Poems, Original and Translated" (1885). Died, Newport, R. I., 14 June, 1883.

BROOKS, Maria [Gowen], "Maria del Occidente," b. Medford, Mass., about 1795. She was the daughter of a man of culture, among whose friends were several Harvard professors. On his death she became engaged at an early age to Mr. Brooks, a merchant of Boston, who took charge of her education and subsequently married her. She soon began the writing of verse, and in 1820 published her first volume, "Judith, Esther, and Other Poems." Her husband dying in 1823, she removed to Cuba and there resided with an uncle. Becoming in a few years the inheritor of his property, she returned to the United States and settled down at Hanover, N. H. There she occupied herself with the revision of her poem, "Zophiël, or the Bride of Seven," which had been written in Cuba, and the first canto of which had appeared in 1825. "Zophiël" was published in complete form at London in 1833, under the supervision of Robert Southey, whom Mrs. Brooks had visited in 1831. He greatly admired her work, and styled her "Maria del Occidente." After her return to America, she published a partly autobiographical romance, "Idomen, or the Vale of Yamuri" (1843). Died, Matanzas, Cuba, 11 Nov., 1845.

BROOKS, Noah, journalist, b. Castine, Me., 30 Oct., 1830. Was engaged in journalistic work in Boston from 1850 to 1854. After some experience in western states as a merchant and farmer, he for several years edited a paper in Marysville, Cal., removing thence to Washington, D. C., in 1862, and serving as correspondent of the Sacramento "Union" during the civil war. Was a member of the editorial staff of the N. Y. "Tribune" from 1871 to 1875, and of the N. Y. "Times" from the latter date until 1884, when he accepted the editorship of the Newark, N. J., "Daily Advertiser." He has contributed to the magazines, and has published several books for young people, the titles of which are "The Boy Emigrants" (1876), "The Fairport Nine" (1881), "Our Base-Ball Club" (1883), and "Abraham Lincoln, a Biography" (1888), the last of these a model short history of its subject by one close to the President.

BROOKS, Phillips, clergyman, b. Boston, Mass., 13 Dec., 1835. Graduated at Harvard. Entered the Episcopal ministry. Was rector of churches at Philadelphia, and in 1869 became rector of Trinity church at Boston. Author of "Lectures on Preaching" (1877), "The Influence of Jesus" (1879), and several volumes of sermons.

BROTHERTON, Alice [Williams], b. Cambridge, Ind., 18—. Has resided chiefly in or near Cincinnati, O., where she was educated in the high schools. Was married to William E. Brotherton in 1876. A writer for the magazines, and the author of "Beyond the Veil," poems (1886), and "The Sailing of King Olaf, and Other Poems" (1887).

BROWN, Charles Brockden, b. Philadelphia, Penn., 17 Jan., 1771. Of Quaker descent. Early manifested an interest in literature. Received his education at the school of Robert Proud, author of a history of Pennsylvania. Began the study of law at Philadelphia, but instead, finding himself becoming more and more absorbed in literary work. At the time of his first visit to New York city in 1796, he had contributed various articles to Philadelphia periodicals, particularly a series of essays entitled "The Rhapsodist" in the "Columbus Magazine." His visits to New York became frequent, until that city was practically his residence. He published in 1797 a work on marriage and divorce, entitled "The Dialogue of Alcuin," which met with small success. The following year his earliest written novel, "Sky Walk, or the Man Unknown to Himself," failed of publication through the death of the printer. Portions of this work were subsequently embodied in "Edgar Huntley." Soon after this he published "Wieland, or the Transformation" (1798), which became an immediate success and gained the author permanent reputation. This was followed in rapid succession by "Ormund" (1799), "Edgar Huntley" (1799), "Arthur Mervyn" (1799–1800), "Jane Talbot" (1801), and "Clara Howard" (1801), and these novels form the first significant body of fiction produced by an American author. In 1799 Brown began the issue of the "Monthly Magazine and American Review," a periodical which lasted but a few months. From 1803 to 1808 he edited "The Literary Magazine and American Register." He was also the author of several political essays which appeared from 1803 to 1809. Died, probably in Philadelphia, Penn., 22 Feb., 1810.

BROWN, John, "of Osawatomie," emancipator, b. Torrington, Conn., 9 May, 1800. Descended from Peter Brown, of the *Mayflower*. Chiefly engaged as a farmer and currier in early life. Became intensely interested in the suppression of slavery, devoting his energies and time to the practical work of assisting slaves to escape. Resided in Pennsylvania, Ohio, and Massachusetts, 1834–46, and settled in 1846 at North Elba, N. Y. Joined his five sons in 1855 on their settlement at Osawatomie, Kan. The Kansas struggle caused much conflict and frequent outrages. In 1858 he, with twenty-two armed followers, took forcible possession of the U. S. arsenal at Harper's Ferry, Va. The citizens joined the military in subduing the little band, Brown's two sons being killed in the fight. Declined to countenance plans for his escape. Was tried, sentenced, and, with four of his men, was executed at Charlestown, Va., 2 Dec., 1859. He predicted that a war would precede the suppression of slavery.

BROWN, Joseph Brownlee, b. Charleston, S. C., 4 Oct., 1824. Graduated at Dartmouth. Studied law and afterward took up teaching as a profession, but became a confirmed invalid in 1865. Up to that time he had been one of the most promising of the group of young transcendentalists influenced by Emerson's writings. Contributed to the "Atlantic Monthly." Died, Brooklyn, N. Y., 21 Oct., 1888.

BROWN, Phœbe [Hinsdale], b. Canaan, N. Y., 1783. Was married to Timothy H. Brown. Author of several hymns, among them that entitled, "I Love to steal Awhile Away." Died, Henry, Ill., 10 Oct., 1861.

BROWNE, Charles Farrar, "Artemus Ward," b. Waterford, Me., 23 April, 1834. Learned the trade of a printer, and worked as a compositor on papers in Skowhegan, Me., and Boston. Published his first humorous writings in the "Carpet-Bag," a comic paper of the latter city. Removed to Ohio, and about 1858 became local reporter on the Cleveland "Plaindealer." For the latter he began writing under his well-known pseudonym, assuming the character of a showman. His reputation increasing, he was invited to New York to edit "Vanity Fair," a humorous weekly started just before the civil war. On the failure of this venture, he visited California and Utah. Returning, he delivered a series of comic lectures on Mormonism, which were widely popular. His health had begun to fail when he sailed for England in June, 1866, but in the following autumn he was able to lecture for a few months, repeating his American successes. Increasing illness prevented his return to the United States. Author of "Artemus Ward, His Book" (1862), "Artemus Ward, His Travels" (1865), and "Artemus Ward in London" (1867), collected and edited by Melville D. Landon as "Artemus Ward, His Works Complete" (1875). Died, Southampton, England, 6 Mar., 1867.

BROWNE, Francis Fisher, journalist, b. South Halifax, Vt., 1 Dec., 1843. Learned the printer's trade in his father's newspaper office at Chicopee, Mass. Served in the U. S. army during the civil war. Resided at Chicago, Ill., after 1867, engaged in literary and editorial work, and founded there, in 1880, "The Dial," a monthly literary journal. Published "The Every-Day Life of Abraham Lincoln" (1886), and edited several valuable anthologies of poetry.

BROWNE, John Ross, traveller, b. Ireland, 1817. Besides making several journeys through Europe and the East, he was at different times U. S. inspector of customs for the Pacific coast and U. S. minister to China. Some of his works are "Etchings of a Whaling-Cruise" (1846), "Yusef, or the Journey of the Fragi" (1853), and "Resources of the Pacific Slope" (1869). Died, Oakland, Cal., 9 Dec., 1875.

BROWNE, Junius Henri, journalist, b. Seneca Falls, N. Y., 13 Oct., 1833. Graduated at St. Xavier college, Cincinnati. A staff correspondent of many leading American papers, particularly of the N. Y. "Tribune." While war correspondent of the latter, was captured at Vicksburg and spent two years in seven Southern prisons. Resided at New York city after 1867. Author of "Four Years in Secessia" (1865), "The Great Metropolis" (1870), and "Lights and Sensations in Europe" (1872).

BROWNELL, Henry Howard, b. Providence, R. I., 6 Feb., 1820. Graduated at Trinity college. Taught school for a time at Mobile, Ala., and, returning to Hartford, was there admitted to the bar in 1844. Abandoned law for literary work in 1849. He had already published a volume of "Poems" (1847), and he continued his poetical contributions to the magazines through the remainder of his life. Was chiefly occupied up to the time of the civil war with the writing of popular histories. Some of these are "The People's Book of Ancient and Modern History" (1851), "The Discoverers, Pioneers, and Settlers of North and South America" (1853), and a history of the war of 1812. A poetical version, early in the civil war, of Farragut's "general orders" to his fleet attracted that commander's attention, and led to Brownell's appointment as acting ensign on board the *Hartford*. In this capacity he witnessed the battle of Mobile bay, afterward making it the subject of his long war poem, "The Bay Fight." At the close of the war he accompanied Farragut on his cruise to the ports of Europe, resigning and returning to Hartford in 1868. His "Lyrics of a Day" appeared in 1864, and "War Lyrics, and Other Poems" in 1866. Died, Hartford, Conn., 31 Oct., 1872.

BROWNELL, William Crary, b. New York, N. Y., 30 Aug., 1851. Graduated at Amherst. Was a member of the N. Y. "World" staff, 1871–9, and subsequently wrote for "The Nation." After several years of travel abroad, he entered a N. Y. publishing-house in an editorial capacity. A contributor to the magazines, and author of "French Traits : an Essay in Comparative Criticism" (1889).

BROWNSON, Orestes Augustus, b. Stockbridge, Vt., 16 Sept., 1803. Gave up Presbyterianism to become a Universalist minister, 1825, and edited the "Gospel Advocate" and the "Philanthropist." In 1832 adopted Unitarian views, and held a pastorate in Boston until his resignation in 1843. Wielded a large influence in politics as an independent thinker. Founded the Boston "Quarterly Review" in 1838. In 1844 entered the Roman Catholic church, his individualism involving him in controversies with his ecclesiastical superiors. Advocated what would now be classed as Christian socialism. Besides his writings in what from 1844 he entitled "Brownson's Quarterly Review" (finally given up in 1875), he published "New Views of Christian Society and the Church" (1836), "The Convert, or Leaves from my Experience" (1857), "The American Republic, its Constitutional Tendencies and Destiny" (1865), and "Conversation on Liberalism and the Church" (1870). Died, Detroit, Mich., 17 April, 1876.

BRYANT, William Cullen, journalist, b. Cummington, Mass., 3 Nov., 1794. The son of Dr. Peter Bryant, a physician of that place, who was a member of the Massachusetts legislature for several terms. William Cullen early developed the faculty of composing in verse, and his first published poem appeared in the "Hampshire Gazette" for 1807. The following year he published "The Embargo, or Sketches of the Times," a satirical poem. Studied for a year at Williams college, which he left to devote himself to law. Was admitted to the bar at Plymouth, Mass., 1815, and practised at Plainfield for one year, and at Great Barrington for nine. During this period his "Thanatopsis," written in his eighteenth year, appeared in the "North American Review" (1817), besides several subsequent contributions, and he was invited to deliver a poem before the $\Phi B K$ society at Harvard. He responded with "The Ages," issued the same year (1821) in a volume with other poems. Removed to New York city in 1825. After acting as assistant editor of a review, he became in the following year a member of the editorial staff of the "Evening Post," of which he was made editor-in-chief, 1828. This position he held until his death, a period of fifty years. Several trips to Europe and the East were described in letters to that paper. These were afterward collected in book form as "Letters of a Traveller" (1852), "Letters from Spain and Other Countries" (1859), and "Letters from the East" (1869). Some of his numerous addresses and commemorative discourses were gathered in a volume entitled "Orations and Addresses" (1873). Perhaps the most notable of these was that delivered at the N. Y. Academy of Music on "The Life, Character, and Genius of Washington Irving" (1860). The same year he acted as chairman at the Cooper Institute meeting addressed by Abraham Lincoln. Collective editions of his "Poems" were published in 1832, 1846, 1855, and 1876. Single volumes of verse were "The Foun-

tain, and Other Poems" (1842), "The White-Footed Deer, and Other Poems" (1844), and "Thirty Poems" (1864). His translations of the "Iliad" and "Odyssey" into English blank verse appeared, 1870–2. In 1883 and 1884 a final edition of "The Poetical Works and Prose Works of William Cullen Bryant" was published, edited by his son-in-law, Parke Godwin. Died, New York, N. Y., 12 June, 1878.

BUCKINGHAM, Joseph Tinker, journalist, b. Windham, Conn., 21 Dec., 1779. Began work as a printer at Walpole, N. H. After several failures in starting periodicals, he edited with Samuel L. Knapp "The New England Galaxy," 1817–28. Founded in 1824 the Boston daily "Courier," and was its editor until 1848. In 1831 he established "The New England Magazine." His books are "Specimens of Newspaper Literature" (1850) and "Personal Memoirs" (1852). Died, Cambridge, Mass., 11 April, 1861.

BUCKMINSTER, Joseph Stevens, clergyman, b. Portsmouth, N. H., 26 May, 1784. Graduated at Harvard. Taught at the Exeter, N. H., academy, while following his theological studies. Was ordained pastor of the Brattle street church at Boston in 1805, preaching a doctrine then known as Liberal Christian, closely resembling that of the later Unitarians. Gained reputation as a pulpit orator and as an advanced religious thinker. Two volumes of his "Sermons" (1814–29) were brought out posthumously. Died, Boston, Mass., 9 June, 1812.

BUEL, Clarence Clough, journalist, b. Laona, Chautauqua Co., N. Y., 29 July, 1850. Studied at the university of Minnesota and at German universities. Was a member of the N. Y. "Tribune" staff from 1875 to 1881, and in the latter year became assistant editor of "The Century Magazine." A contributor to the magazines, and associated with Robert Underwood Johnson in editing "Battles and Leaders of the Civil War" (1889).

BULKLEY, Peter, clergyman, b. Odell, Bedfordshire, England, 31 Jan., 1583. Graduated at Cambridge university. Preached at his birthplace for twenty years, was silenced for non-conformity, and emigrated to Cambridge, Mass., in 1635. Founded Concord, Mass., the next year; was its first minister, and remained there until his death. "The Gospel-Covenant," a sermon, was published in 1646. Died, Concord, Mass., 9 Mar., 1659.

BUNCE, Oliver Bell, b. New York, N. Y., 8 Feb., 1828. Was for some years the head of a publishing and bookselling firm bearing his name, but subsequently became editor of "Appletons' Journal" in New York, and literary adviser of the publishing house of D. Appleton & Co. In addition to contributions to the magazines, his books are "A Bachelor's Story" (1859), "Life Before Him" (1860), "Bensley" (1863), "Bachelor Bluff, His Opinions, Sentiments, and Disputations" (1882), "My House, an Ideal" (1885), and "Timias Terrystone" (1885). "Don't" (1884), a small book on manners, reached a sale of one hundred thousand copies in America alone. Died, New York, N. Y., 15 May, 1890.

BUNNER, Henry Cuyler, journalist, b. Oswego, N. Y., 3 Aug., 1855. Received his education at a French school in New York city. Entered a Portuguese business firm in that city for a short time, and afterward worked as a reporter. Was made assistant editor of the N. Y. "Puck," at its commencement in 1877, and soon after became editor of the same paper. Author of "A Woman of Honor" (1883), "Airs from Arcady and Elsewhere," poems (1884), "The Midge" (1886), "The Story of a New York House" (1887), and "In Partnership" (1884), a collection of stories by H. C. Bunner and Brander Matthews. "The Tower of Babel," a drama by H. C. Bunner and Julian Magnus, was produced at Philadelphia in 1883.

Burchard, Samuel Dickinson [*Noted Saying:* Vol. XI., page 460], b. Steuben, N. Y., 6 Sept., 1812. Became pastor of a Presbyterian church in New York city, 1839.

BURDETTE, Robert Jones, journalist, b. Greensborough, Penn., 30 July, 1844. Served in the Union army during the civil war. Edited several papers at Peoria, Ill., and in 1874 joined the staff of the Burlington, Iowa, "Hawkeye." Well-known as a writer and lecturer on humorous subjects.

BURGES, Tristam, statesman, b. Rochester, Mass., 26 Feb., 1770. Graduated at Brown. Began to practise law at Providence, R. I., 1799. Was chief-justice of the R. I. supreme court, 1815–25, and a member of the U. S. house of representatives, 1825–35. From 1815 to 1828 he was professor of oratory and belles-lettres at Brown. A leader in the Federalist party. Selections from his speeches and writings are given in "Memoirs of Tristam Burges" (1835). Died, Providence, R. I., 13 Oct., 1853.

BURLEIGH, George Shepard, journalist, b. Plainfield, Conn., 26 Mar., 1821. Was engaged until the age of twenty-five in farming, varied by a brief experience as assistant editor of the "Charter Oak," of Hartford, the earliest Liberty party paper in Connecticut. Married and removed to Little Compton, R. I., in 1849, where he afterward mainly resided. Contributed extensively to the press, particularly to anti-slavery, reform, and literary journals, and published poems and articles in the magazines. His books are "The Maniac, and Other Poems" (1849), "Signal Fires on the Trail of the Path-Finder" (1856), and an unpublished translation of Victor Hugo's "Légende des Siècles," of which the first volume has been printed.

BURLEIGH, William Henry, journalist, b. Woodstock, Conn., 2 Feb., 1812. Brother of the preceding. Was editor of various anti-slavery papers in New York state and Pennsylvania, and of the Hartford "Charter Oak" from 1843 to 1850. Subsequently became harbor-master of New York city. Editions of his "Poems" were issued in 1841 and 1871. Died, Brooklyn, N. Y., 18 Mar., 1871.

BURNETT, Frances Eliza [Hodgson], b. Manchester, England, 24 Nov., 1849. Her parents emigrated to the United States at the close of the civil war, and settled at Newmarket, Tenn., removing a year later to Knoxville in the same state. Her first printed story was contributed to "Godey's Lady's Book," when she was sixteen years old. She continued to write for this periodical, and also for "Peterson's Magazine," in which her first novel, "Dorothea" (1873), appeared. It was afterward published in book form with the title "Vagabondia" (1889). Meanwhile, in 1872, a story in English dialect, "Surly Tim's Trouble," was sent to the "Century Magazine" (then "Scribner's Monthly") and accepted with a request for further manuscripts. She was married, 1873, to Dr. Luan M. Burnett, of Knoxville, and thereafter resided chiefly at Washington, D. C., making extended visits to England and the Continent. "That Lass o' Lowrie's" (1877) was extremely popular in both America and England, and gained her a wide reputation. It was dramatized by Joseph Hatton and A. Mathison and by Charles Reade in England, and by Julian Magnus, the latter's play being produced at Booth's theatre, New York city. Other novels and collections of stories are "Surly Tim, and Other Stories" (1877), "Haworth's" (1879), "Earlier Stories" (1879), "Louisiana" (1880), "A Fair Barbarian" (1881), "Through One Administration" (1883), "Little Lord Fauntleroy" (1886), "Sara Crewe" (1888), "Editha's Burglar" (1888), "The Pretty Sister of José" (1889), and "Little Saint Elizabeth" (1890). Several of these have been dramatized by Mrs. Burnett and others, and produced, among them "A Fair Barbarian" and "Little Lord Fauntleroy," the latter with Elsie Leslie Lyde in the leading part.

Burr, Aaron [*Noted Sayings:* Vol. XI., page 449], b. Newark, N. J., 6 Feb., 1756. Served in the Continental army. Vice-president of the United States, 1801–5. Died, Staten Island, N. Y., 14 Sept., 1836.

BURRITT, Elihu, reformer, b. New Britain, Conn., 8 Dec., 1810. Supported himself at the forge while pursuing his education, and thus gained the name of "the learned blacksmith." Was noted as a linguist, and as an advocate on the lecture-platform and in papers edited by himself of anti-slavery, peace, temperance, and other reforms. Among his numerous books are "Sparks from the Anvil" (1848) and "Lectures and Addresses" (1870). Died, New Britain, Conn., 9 Mar., 1879.

BURROUGHS, John, b. Roxbury, N. Y., 3 April, 1837. His father was a farmer of English descent. The son grew up on the farm and received a common-school education. At the age of seventeen he removed to Olive, in Ulster county, where he taught school for several years. In 1863 received an appointment in the treasury department at Washington, and afterward became chief of the organization division in the bureau of national banks. Leaving Washington in 1872, he was made receiver of a bank at Middletown, N. Y., and the following year settled permanently at West Park on the Hudson. Until 1884 he occasionally acted as U. S. national-bank examiner, but otherwise was mainly occupied with literature and with the supervision of his fruit-farm at West Park. His first article was published in the "Atlantic Monthly" for 1860. To this magazine and to the "Century" he contributed numerous papers afterward gathered in his books. His first published volume related to Walt Whitman, of whom he became an enthusiastic admirer, and bore the title "Notes on Walt Whitman, as Poet and Person" (1867). This was followed by "Wake Robin" (1871), "Winter Sunshine" (1875), "Birds and Poets" (1877), "Locusts and Wild Honey" (1879), "Pepacton" (1881), "Fresh Fields" (1884), "Signs and Seasons" (1886), and "Indoor Studies" (1889).

BUSHNELL, Frances Louisa, b. Hartford, Conn., 18—. Daughter of Horace Bushnell. She received her education at Hartford, which city became her permanent residence. A contributor of poetry to the "Atlantic Monthly" and other leading magazines.

BUSHNELL, Horace, divine, b. New Preston, Conn., 14 April, 1802. Graduated at Yale. Entered the Congregational ministry, having a pastorate at Hartford, Conn., from 1833 until his resignation in 1859. Author of "God in Christ" (1849), "Christ in Theology" (1851), "Work and Play," a collection of addresses (1864), and "Woman Suffrage, the Reform against Nature" (1869). Died, Hartford, Conn., 17 Feb., 1876.

Butler, Benjamin Franklin [*Noted Saying:* Vol. VII., page 193], lawyer, b. Deerfield, N. H., 5 Nov., 1818. Served as major-general in the Union army. Subsequently U. S. representative from Massachusetts and governor of the same state.

BUTLER, William Allen, lawyer, b. Albany, N. Y., 20 Feb., 1825. Graduated at the university of New York, and attained reputation in his profession. A resident of New York and vicinity. "Nothing to Wear," a metrical satire on society, was published anonymously in "Harper's Weekly," 1857, and afterward as a volume, gaining a wide circulation. Some of his more serious work appeared in a collection of "Poems" (1871). Also published two novels and several legal and biographical works.

BUTTERWORTH, Hezekiah, journalist, b. Warren, R. I., 22 Dec., 1839. Was educated at the common schools, and spent some years travelling in Europe. Became assistant editor of the Boston "Youth's Companion" in 1871. Besides the popular "Zig-Zag Journeys" (1876–90) for children, is the author of "Poems for Christmas, Easter, and New Year's" (1883), and of several cantatas.

BYFIELD, Nathaniel, jurist, b., it is said, Long Ditten, Surrey, England. Emigrated to Boston, 1674, and was one of the first settlers of Bristol, R. I., where he became a leading merchant and served as judge of the court of common pleas for thirty-eight years. He removed to Boston in 1724 and held similar office in that city. His "Account of the Late Revolution in New England" was published at London in 1689. It describes the deposition of Gov. Edmund Andros. Died, Boston, Mass., 6 June, 1733.

BYLES, Mather, clergyman, b. Boston, Mass., 26 Mar., 1706. A descendant of Richard Mather and John Cotton. Graduated at Harvard. Became pastor of the Hollis street church at Boston in 1733. Retained his pastorate until 1776, when the connection was dissolved by his congregation on account of his outspoken loyalty to the king, although he had avoided the subject of politics in his pulpit. The following year he was arrested and sentenced to banishment as an enemy of the country, but was finally released, and spent the remainder of his life in retirement at Boston. While noted as a pulpit orator, he is chiefly remembered for his poetry and wit. Many of his quips and humorous sayings are still preserved. "Poems on Several Occasions" appeared in 1736, and was preceded and followed by a number of separately printed poems. Several of his sermons were also published. Died, Boston, Mass., 5 July, 1788.

BYNNER, Edwin Lassetter, lawyer, b. Brooklyn, N. Y., 5 Aug., 1842. Graduated at the Harvard law school. Was admitted to the bar at Worcester, Mass., and practised at St. Louis, New York city, and Boston, where in 1886 he gave up his profession for literature. Some of his novels are "Nimport" (1877), "Penelope's Suitors" (1884), "Agnes Surriage" (1886), and "The Begum's Daughter" (1890).

BYRD, Col. William, founder of Richmond and Petersburg, Va., b. Westover, Va., 16 Mar., 1674. Was educated in England under the care of Sir Robert Southwell, and also studied in the Low Countries. Was called to the bar in the Middle temple. Returning to Virginia, he succeeded to his father's large estate and to the latter's position as receiver-general of the colony. Served as a member of the colony's council for thirty-seven years, and finally became its president. Was noted for his wit and learning, and gathered at the family seat of "Westover" the largest library in Virginia. A manuscript volume of his writings, known as the "Byrd Manuscripts," has been twice printed; once partially in 1841, and again in 1866 completely under the title "History of the Dividing Line, and Other Tracts, from the Papers of William Byrd." The title piece is a lively and entertaining account of the experiences of the commission appointed to survey the dividing line between the colonies of Virginia and North Carolina, of which commission Colonel Byrd was a member. The colonel, as his epitaph indicates, was "the constant enemy of all exorbitant power and a hearty friend to the liberties of his country." He encouraged emigration to the colonies in every way, and took much pains to develop their mining interests. Died, Westover, Va., 26 Aug., 1744.

CABLE, George Washington, b. New Orleans, La., 12 Oct., 1844. Of Virginia descent on his father's side. The failure and death of his father necessitated the son's leaving school when fourteen, and taking a position as clerk, which he held for several years. In 1863 he joined the Confederate army, and served in the 4th Mississippi cavalry. Returned to New Orleans at the close of the war and, after engaging in various occupations, studied civil-engineering and joined a state surveying expedition for restoring the levees of the Atchafalaya river. Having contracted malarial fever, he applied himself during a long convalescence to studies of Louisiana life and character, which were afterward utilized in his writings. Occasional contributions to the New Orleans "Picayune," over the signature "Drop-Shot," led to an editorial connection with that paper, which was brought to a close by his refusal, on religious grounds, to attend and criticise a theatrical performance. He then became accountant for a large firm of cotton factors at New Orleans, holding the position until the death of the head of the house in 1879. Meanwhile his stories of Creole life in the magazines had brought him reputation, and he now adopted literature as a profession. Removed to Simsbury, Conn., in 1885, and the following year to Northampton, Mass. Reforms of contract-labor in Southern prisons and plans

for the amelioration of the colored race received much attention from him. Author of "Old Creole Days" (1879–83), "The Grandissimes" (1880), "Madame Delphine" (1881), "Dr. Sevier" (1883), "The Creoles of Louisiana" (1884), "The Silent South" (1885), "Bonaventure" (1888), "Strange True Stories of Louisiana" (1889), "The Negro Question" (1890), and "Life of William Gilmore Simms" (1890).

CABOT, James Elliot, b. Boston, Mass., 18 June, 1821. Graduated at Harvard. A resident of Boston and vicinity, and was, with Emerson and others, a member of the Saturday and Adirondac clubs in old "Dial" days. Was requested by relatives of Mr. Emerson to assist him in examining his correspondence and papers with a view to the preparation of an authorized memoir. This was written by Mr. Cabot and published in 1887 as "A Memoir of Ralph Waldo Emerson." Has also contributed papers to the "Atlantic Monthly" and other magazines.

CALEF, Robert, merchant, b. probably in England, about 1648. Recent investigations by the Hon. Arthur B. Calef, of Middletown, Conn., have confirmed earlier statements that the author of "More Wonders of the Invisible World" (1700) was Robert Calef the elder, and not his son Robert who died in 1722. The father is first heard of in Boston, Mass., where his seventh child was born in 1688. From papers of Calef on record it is certain that some of his older children were born in Great Britain. He was a constable at Boston in New England as early as 1792, being recorded as a taxpayer the year previous. He filled the positions of surveyor of highways in 1697, of clerk of the market in 1698, of overseer of the poor in 1702–4, and of assessor in 1706–7, declining a reëlection in the latter case. In 1707 he purchased land in Roxbury, now a part of Boston, and resided there until his death, at which time he was a selectman of the former place. It is believed that his business was that of a "clothier" or manufacturer of and dealer in cloth. His book was the final blow to the witchcraft delusion in New England, and although the Mathers and their friends published a refutation of it and disparaged the author in every way, he seems to have gained his point. In the words of Judge Calef, "I think it the impartial judgment of all who have carefully read what Robert Calef has written that he was a man of fair education and of considerably wide reading for his time, that he possessed a logical mind, and that he arranged his facts and conclusions so compactly that it was difficult to assault them." Died, Roxbury, Mass., 13 April, 1719.

CALHOUN, John Caldwell, statesman, b. Abbeville district, S. C., 18 Mar., 1782.

He was of Irish descent. Graduated at Yale. Studied law at Litchfield, Conn., and began practice in South Carolina, 1807. A member of his state legislature, 1808–10, and of the U. S. house of representatives from 1811 to 1817. In 1817 he was appointed secretary of war by President Monroe, holding the office until his election (1824) as vice-president under J. Q. Adams. Was reëlected to the vice-presidency, but resigned this office in 1831 to serve in the U. S. senate. Retired from that body in 1843, and was secretary of state under President Tyler, 1844–5. Reëntered the senate, 1845, remaining until his death. He advocated the war of 1812, and supported the establishment of the United States bank and the tariff of 1816, while in congress. As secretary of war he instituted many reforms in his department, and favored the Missouri compromise. While vice-president, having become an advocate of free-trade, he brought forward the doctrine of nullification in opposition to the tariff of 1828. The exposition of this doctrine by Robert Y. Hayne led to the famous debate with Webster. As senator, Calhoun was the acknowledged champion of state-rights and slavery. His collected "Works" were published, 1851–4. Died, Washington, D. C., 31 Mar., 1850.

CALLENDER, John, clergyman, b. Boston, Mass., 1706. Graduated at Harvard. Presided over the first Baptist church of Rhode Island at Newport from 1731 until his death. Published "A Centennial Discourse on the Civil and Religious Affairs of the Colony of Rhode Island" (1739) and several sermons, besides making a valuable collection of papers relating to the history of the Baptists in America. Died (interred at Newport, R. I.), 26 Jan., 1748.

CALVERT, George Henry, b. Baltimore, Md., 2 Jan., 1803. Great-grandson of Lord Baltimore. Graduated at Harvard. Edited the Baltimore "American" for a few years. Settled at Newport, R. I., 1843. Besides translations from the German, he published "Scenes and Thoughts in Europe" (1846–52), "Joan of Arc" (1860), "The Gentleman" (1863), "Anyta, and Other Poems" (1863), "Goethe, his Life and Works" (1872), and "Essays Æsthetical" (1875). Died, Newport, R. I., 29 May, 1889.

CAREY, Henry Charles, political economist, b. Philadelphia, Penn., 15 Dec., 1793. Succeeded his father, Mathew Carey, as publisher, 1821, retiring in 1838. Was chiefly occupied thereafter with writing works on political economy. Some of his books are "The Principles of Political Economy" (1837–40), "Letters on International Copyright" (1853), "Principles of Social Science" (1859), and a volume of "Miscellaneous Works" (1869). Died, Philadelphia, Penn., 13 Oct., 1879.

CAREY, Mathew, publisher, b. Dublin, Ireland, 28 Jan., 1760. Having been imprisoned by parliament for agitating the Irish cause in his paper, the "Volunteer's Journal," he emigrated to Philadelphia in 1784. Entered the publishing business in 1791. Of his many political and economical writings, the best known was his "Olive Branch" (1814), an attempt to harmonize existing parties during the war of 1812. Died, Philadelphia, Penn., 16 Sept., 1839.

CARLETON, Henry Guy, b. Fort Union, New Mexico, 21 June, 1855. Educated by the Jesuits of Santa Clara college, Cal. Served as 2d lieutenant in the 8th U. S. cavalry, 1873–6, being assigned to Indian service in New Mexico and Texas. Afterward held editorial positions on journals in New Orleans and New York city. Author of several plays, among them "Memnon, a Tragedy" (1884), purchased by John McCullough, who died before its production, "Victor Durand" (produced 1884), and "The Pembertons" (produced 1890).

CARLETON, Will, b. Hudson, Lenawee Co., Mich., 21 Oct., 1845. Graduated at Hillsdale college. Engaged in journalism at Chicago and Hillsdale, and subsequently gave lectures and readings throughout the United States, making his home at Brooklyn, N. Y. His poems of domestic life have been widely popular. Author of "Farm Ballads" (1873), "Farm Legends" (1875), "City Ballads" (1885), and "City Legends" (1889).

CARNEGIE, Andrew, iron-master, b. Dunfermline, Scotland, 25 Nov., 1835. His family came to America in 1845, and settled at Pittsburgh, Penn. When twelve years old he began work as a telegraph-messenger, becoming an operator, and later manager of the telegraph lines in the Pennsylvania railroad office at Pittsburgh. He was soon promoted to be superintendent of the Pittsburgh division of the Pennsylvania railroad, and successful ventures with Woodruff, inventor of the sleeping-car, and in the oil-fields, were followed by the establishment of a rolling-mill. Mr. Carnegie's interest in steel and iron industries expanded until he controlled a system including nine establishments and representing a capital of $20,000,000. Privately printed accounts of his travels were rewritten and published as "An American Four-in-Hand in Britain" (1883) and "Round the World" (1884). The popular "Triumphant Democracy, or Fifty Years' March of the Republic," appeared in 1886. Mr. Carnegie has given large sums for the founding of free libraries in the United States and Scotland.

CARPENTER, Amelia Walstien [Jolls], b. Stephentown, Rensselaer Co., N. Y., 23 Feb., 1840. Graduated at Columbia institute, Old Chatham, N. Y. Was married to Cromwell A. Carpenter, and removed to Kalamazoo, Mich. After her husband's death resided in her native town. A contributor of verse and fiction to the magazines.

CARPENTER, Esther Bernon, b. Wakefield, R. I., 18—. Studied at St. Mary's hall, Burlington, N. J. Chiefly a resident of Wakefield. Besides writing for the magazines, published "The Huguenot Influence in Rhode Island" and "South-County Neighbors" (1887).

CARPENTER, Henry Bernard, clergyman, b. Dublin, Ireland, 22 April, 1840. Graduated at Oxford. Taught at Enniskillen, Ireland, and subsequently was ordained and appointed chaplain to the Earl of Belmore. Came to the United States in 1874. Was pastor of the Hollis street church at Boston, Mass., from 1878 to 1887, when he resigned, and left the ministry, on the sale of the church property. Author of "Liber Amoris, an Epic Romaunt" (1886), and of uncollected poems in the magazines.

CARRYL, Charles Edward, broker, b. New York, N. Y., 30 Dec., 1841. Was an officer and director in various railway companies from 1863 to 1872, and became a member of the New York stock exchange in 1874. Published "Davy and the Goblin" (1885).

CARTER, Robert, journalist, b. Albany, N. Y., 5 Feb., 1819. Removed to Boston, Mass., in 1841, and with J. R. Lowell began the publication of a magazine, which soon failed. Joined the Free-soil party in 1848, and in 1854 called together the first Republican convention at Worcester, Mass. Was at different times editor of the Rochester, N. Y., "Democrat" and of "Appletons' Journal." Besides much work on the "American Cyclopædia," he wrote "A Summer Cruise on the Coast of New England" (1864). Died, Cambridge, Mass., 15 Feb., 1879.

CARY, Alice, b. Miami Valley, near Cincinnati, O., 20 April, 1820. Studied at home with her sister Phœbe, and when eighteen years old began writing poems and sketches for the press. The Cary sisters removed to New York city in 1852, where they afterward chiefly resided, returning occasionally to their early farm-home. For some years they held weekly receptions in New York which were attended by many leading artistic and literary people. In 1850 they published a volume of "Poems by Alice and Phœbe Cary." This was followed on Alice's part by two series of prose sketches, "Clovernook, or Recollections of our Neighborhood in the West" (1851–3), and by "Hagar, a Story of To-day" (1852), "Lyra, and Other Poems" (1853), "Married, not Mated" (1856), "Pictures of Country Life" (1859), "Ballads, Lyrics and

Hymns" (1866), "The Bishop's Son" (1867), and "The Lover's Diary," poems (1867). Died, New York, N. Y., 12 Feb., 1871.

CASS, Lewis, statesman, b. Exeter, N. H., 9 Oct., 1782. Began to practise law at Zanesville, Ohio, in 1803. Was elected to the Ohio legislature, served in the war of 1812, and was governor of Michigan, 1813–31. Resigned the office to become secretary of war under President Jackson. Was U. S. minister to France, 1836–42, and filled three terms as U. S. senator from Michigan. A supporter of the compromise of 1850, but favored the Union cause in the civil war. Published "France, its King, Court, and Government" (1840). Died, Detroit, Mich., 17 June, 1866.

CATHERWOOD, Mary [Hartwell], b. Luray, O., 16 Dec., 1847. Graduated at the Granville, O., female college. Was married, 1877, to James S. Catherwood, and subsequently lived at Hoopeston, Ill. Author of "Craque-o'-doom" (1881), "The Romance of Dollard" (1889), and "The Story of Tonty" (1890).

CATLIN, George, painter, b. Wilkesbarre, Penn., 1796. After practising law in Connecticut, removed to Philadelphia and became a painter. From 1832 to 1839 he travelled among the American Indians, of whom he made nearly five hundred portraits. The rest of his life was chiefly spent in Europe. Published "Illustrations of the Manners, etc., of the North American Indians" (1841). Died, Jersey City, N. J., 23 Dec., 1872.

CAVAZZA, Elisabeth [Jones], b. Portland, Me., 18—. Daughter of Charles Jones, a merchant of that city. Was married, 1885, to Nino Cavazza, son of Professor Cavazza of the Royal academy at Modena, Italy, and member of a noble family. A resident of Portland, and after her husband's death a constant writer of verse, fiction, and criticism for the magazines and newspapers.

CAWEIN, Madison Julius, b. Louisville, Ky., 23 Mar., 1865. Graduated at the Louisville high school, and became accountant in a business office of the same city. Author of several volumes of verse, including "Blooms of the Berry" (1887), "The Triumph of Music" (1888), "Accolon of Gaul, with Other Poems" (1889), "Lyrics and Idyls" (1890).

CHADWICK, John White, clergyman, b. Marblehead, Mass., 19 Oct., 1840. Graduated at the Harvard divinity school, and became pastor of a Unitarian church in Brooklyn, N. Y., in 1864. His sermons, of a broadly liberal type, have gained him reputation as a preacher. Author of "A Book of Poems" (1876), "The Faith of Reason" (1879), "The Man Jesus" (1881), and "In Nazareth Town," poems (1883).

CHALKLEY, Thomas, Quaker preacher, b. London, England, 3 Mar., 1675. First visited America in 1698, where he spent a year in travelling and preaching. Afterward settled his family in Philadelphia, and made many journeys and voyages thence in the pursuit of his vocation. "A Journal of the Life, Labours, Travels, etc., of Thomas Chalkley" (1749) contains also several of his tracts. Died, Tortola, Friendly Islands, 4 Sept., 174–.

CHANLER, Amélie [Rives], b. Richmond, Va., 23 Aug., 1863. Grand-daughter of Senator William C. Rives of Virginia. Was married, 1888, to John Armstrong Chanler, of New York city. Author of "A Brother to Dragons, and Other Old-Time Tales" (1888), "The Quick or the Dead?" (1888), "Virginia of Virginia" (1888), "Herod and Mariamne" (1889), and other novels and poems.

CHANNING, Edward Tyrrel, educator, b. Newport, R. I., 12 Dec., 1790. Brother of the succeeding. Studied at Harvard. Edited the "North American Review," to which he contributed freely, 1818–19, and was Boylston professor of rhetoric at Harvard from 1819 to 1851. His "Lectures read to the Seniors of Harvard College" (1856) were brought out posthumously. Died, Cambridge, Mass., 8 Feb., 1856.

CHANNING, William Ellery, divine, b. Newport, R. I., 7 April, 1780. His father was for many years attorney-general of Rhode Island, and his maternal grandfather was William Ellery, a signer of the Declaration of Independence. As a child he was brought under the influence of Dr. Samuel Hopkins and Ezra Stiles, both at that time clergymen in Newport. Graduated at Harvard with the highest honors; then became private tutor in a family at Richmond, Va., where he remained for two years. Returned to Newport in 1800 with impaired health, which followed him through life, and devoted himself to theology. His studies were continued at Cambridge, and in 1803 he was ordained pastor of the Federal street Congregational church in Boston. His pastorate continued until his retirement in 1840, although an associate was provided in 1824. His reputation as a preacher soon increased his congregation, necessitating the building of a larger church in 1809. Six years later he was active in the liberal Congregational movement which developed into Unitarianism, and became its acknowledged leader. His sermon on the Unitarian belief, preached at the ordination of Jared Sparks in Baltimore, 1819, attracted wide attention and elicited many replies from Trinitarian writers. Dr. Channing was deeply interested in all social reforms. He preached several notable sermons against war, and labored to promote the cause of temperance. His address on self-culture at Boston, 1838, and his course of lectures on the elevation of the laboring classes, in 1840, among many other discourses on the subject of education, were not without effect. Slavery received his early attention, and he was led to more earnest opposition by a sojourn at the island of Santa Cruz in 1830. He addressed a meeting of abolitionists at Faneuil hall in 1837. Of several works on the subject, that entitled "Slavery" (1841) gained the widest circulation. A member of the Boston Anthology club, he contributed to several of the periodicals edited by his fellow members, particularly the "North American Review" and "Christian Examiner." In the latter were published (1826–9) his "Remarks on the Character and Writings of John Milton," his articles on Bonaparte, and that on Fenélon. The first collective edition of his works was made, 1841, and in 1848 appeared "Memoir of William Ellery Channing," edited by his nephew and containing selections from his correspondence. Died, Bennington, Vt., 2 Oct., 1842.

CHANNING, William Ellery, 2d, b. Boston, Mass., 10 June, 1818. A nephew of William Ellery Channing. Studied at Harvard, not remaining to graduate. After 1842 resided in Concord, Mass., with brief intervals of editorial work at New York city and New Bedford, Mass. He married a sister of Margaret Fuller Ossoli. Author of "Poems" (1843 and 1847), "The Woodman" (1849), "Near Home" (1858), "The Wanderer" (1872), all in verse, and of "Conversations in Rome" (1847) and "Thoreau : the Poet-Naturalist" (1873).

CHANNING, William Henry, clergyman, b. Boston, Mass., 25 May, 1810. A nephew of William Ellery Channing, and cousin of W. E. C., 2d. Graduated at Harvard. Was pastor of several Unitarian churches in America and subsequently of Hope street chapel in Liverpool, England. Was chaplain of the U. S. senate for two years during the civil war. Edited "Memoir of William Ellery Channing" (1848), and was associated with Emerson and James Freeman Clarke in preparing the "Memoirs of Margaret Fuller Ossoli" (1852). Died, London, England, 23 Dec., 1884.

CHASE, Philander, divine, b. Cornish, N. H., 14 Dec., 1775. Graduated at Dartmouth. Was ordained in 1799, and after missionary labors in western New York and Louisiana settled at Hartford, Conn. In 1817 began missionary work in Ohio. Was made bishop of Ohio, 1819. Resigning in 1831, he was four years later made bishop of Illinois. Founded two colleges and a theological seminary with funds raised by himself. Published his "Reminiscences" (1848). Died, Peoria, Ill., 20 Sept., 1852.

CHASE, Salmon Portland, statesman, b. Cornish, N. H., 13 Jan., 1808. Nephew of Philander Chase. Graduated at Dartmouth, entered the bar and practised at Cincinnati, defending many notable cases against fugitive slaves and those who aided them. Was elected to the U. S. senate as an abolitionist by a coalition vote of Democrats and Free-soilers, 1849. Elected governor of Ohio, 1855. Was appointed secretary of the treasury by President Lincoln, 1861, resigning the office in 1864, and being appointed chief justice of the United States the same year. In the latter capacity he afterward presided at the impeachment of President Johnson, 1868. Did notable service to the government and the Union by his vigorous financial policy during the war, in the issue of "greenbacks" and by other measures to sustain the struggle. Compiled a summary of the laws of Ohio, with a historical sketch of the state (3 vols., 1832). Died, New York, N. Y., 7 May, 1873.

CHAUNCY, Charles, clergyman, b. Boston, Mass., 1 Jan., 1705. Great-grandson of Charles Chauncy, the second president of Harvard. Graduated there, and became pastor of the first church of Boston in 1727, retaining the connection until his death, a period of sixty years. Was noted as an opponent of the methods of Whitefield and other revivalists, and published several works directed against them, chief of which is "Seasonable Thoughts on the State of Religion in New-England" (1743). While preparing this volume, he travelled more than three hundred miles for the purpose of consulting the ministers and principal men of numerous New England towns. Besides some sixty sermons he published, amongst others, the following books: "A Complete View of Episcopacy" (1771), "The Mystery Hid from the Ages, or the Salvation of All Men" (1784), and "The Fall of Man, and its Consequences" (1785). He was a firm adherent to the American cause in the Revolution. Died, Boston, 10 Feb., 1787.

CHEEVER, George Barrell, clergyman, b. Hallowell, Me., 17 April, 1807. Graduated at Bowdoin. Pastor of Congregational churches at Salem, Mass., and New York city until 1870. In 1835 received a month's imprisonment for libel, and resigned his first pastorate, on account of his temperance sketch, "Deacon Giles's Distillery," published in a Salem paper. Edited the "Evangelist" for some years after 1845. Author of "The Hill Difficulty, with Other Miscellanies" (1849), "Guilt of Slavery, and Crime of Slaveholding" (1860) and many other books.

CHENEY, John Vance, b. Groveland, Livingston Co., N. Y., 29 Dec., 1848. Graduated at Temple Hill academy, Geneseo, N. Y. After several years of teaching, was admitted to the bar of Massachusetts and practised law at New York city. Removed to San Francisco, Cal., 1876, where he became librarian of the Free Public library, 1887. Author of "The Old Doctor" (1885), "Thistle-Drift," poems (1887), "Wood-Blooms," poems (1888), and a volume of essays.

CHILD, Francis James, educator, b. Boston, Mass., 1 Feb., 1825. Graduated at Harvard ; connected with that institution as instructor and professor since his graduation, having held the chairs of rhetoric and English literature. Supervised the publication of an American edition of the British poets, for which he edited the works of Spenser and made his collection of "English and Scottish Ballads" (1857–8). A revised edition of the "Ballads" appeared in 1886–90, with many changes and additions.

CHILD, Lydia Maria [Francis], b. Medford, Mass., 11 Feb., 1802. Commenced to write stories early in life, her first novel, "Hobomok," appearing in 1821. Established and edited the "Juvenile Miscellany," 1826–34. Was married, 1828, to David L. Child. Published the first anti-slavery book in America, "An Appeal for that Class of Americans called Africans" (1833). Edited at New York city, in association with her husband, the "National Anti-Slavery Standard" from 1840 to 1844. Afterward removed to Wayland, Mass., which became her permanent residence. She was a prolific writer in the periodical press, and among her many publications are "The Rebels, or Boston Before the Revolution" (1822), "The American Frugal Housewife" (1829), "Philothea," a classical romance (1835), "The Power of Kindness" (1851), "Autumnal Leaves" (1856), "Looking Toward Sunset" (1864), "The Freedman's Book" (1865), "Miria, a Romance of the Republic" (1867), and "Aspirations of the World" (1878). Died at Wayland, Mass., 20 Oct., 1880.

CHOATE, Rufus, lawyer, b. Essex, Mass., 1 Oct., 1799. Graduated at Dartmouth. Began the practice of law at Danvers, Mass., 1823. Removed to Salem, 1828, and was elected U. S. representative for two terms. Made his permanent residence at Boston after 1832. Succeeded Daniel Webster as U. S. senator, 1841–5. On the death of the latter became the leading lawyer of Massachusetts. His eulogy on Webster, delivered at Dartmouth, 1853, is the most noted of his orations. Made a number of brilliant speeches as representative and senator. A collection of his "Writings" has been published (1862), also, "Addresses and Orations" (1878). Died, Halifax, N. S., 13 July, 1859.

Christy, David [*Noted Saying* : Vol. VII., page 192], b. Ohio, 1802. Author of

"Cotton is King; or, Slavery in the Light of Political Economy" (1855). This work was republished, 1860, in a volume with pro-slavery writings by other men. No other facts concerning this writer have been obtained.

CHURCH, Benjamin, soldier, b. Plymouth, Mass., 1639. Bred to the trade of a carpenter. Resided chiefly in Plymouth and Duxbury, Mass., and in Little Compton, R. I., of which latter place he was the first settler. While he was laying out his farm there in June, 1675, the Indian war with King Philip broke out, in which he at once took an active and soon a leading part. His campaigns against the Indians were almost invariably successful, and the war was ended by the killing of Philip and the capture of the latter's chief captain, Annawon, in August and September, 1676. Church afterward headed several expeditions against the French and Indians in eastern New England, the last of which, in 1704, was so vigorously conducted as to insure peace in that district for a number of years. He reached the grade of colonel in the colonial forces. His "Entertaining Passages Relating to Philip's War" was dictated to his son in 1715 and published the following year. Died, Little Compton, R. I., 17 Jan., 1718.

CHURCH, Benjamin, physician, b. Newport, R. I., 24 Aug., 1734. Graduated at Harvard. Early became identified with the Revolutionary movement. Extravagant habits induced him to accept British money, and while physician-general to the American army he was convicted of treason, in 1775, and sentenced to solitary confinement. His health failing, he was permitted to leave Boston, and he sailed in a vessel that was never afterward heard from. "The Times: a Poem, by an American" (1765) appeared as a pamphlet of sixteen pages. Lost at sea, 1776.

CLAP, Roger, colonist, b. Salcomb Regis, Devonshire, England, 6 April, 1609. Emigrated to Nantasket, Mass., 30 May, 1630, and settled at Dorchester. Captain of Boston Castle, in Boston harbor, from 1665 to 1686. Left in manuscript "Memoirs of Capt. Roger Clap," edited and published by Thomas Prince in 1731. Died, Boston, Mass., 2 Feb., 1692.

Clapp, Henry [Noted Saying: Vol. VII., page 192], b. Nantucket, Mass., 11 Nov., 1814 (Wm. Winter). Founder and editor of the N. Y. "Saturday Press," 1858-60. Died, New York, N. Y., 2 April, 1875.

CLARK, James Gowdy, composer, b. Constantia, N. Y., 28 June, 1830. Resided in central and western New York until 1877, when he removed to Minneapolis, Minn., and more recently to San Francisco. Known as a composer of both the words and the music of many popular songs, which he himself sung before audiences in most of the

states of the Union. Author of "Poetry and Song" (1886).

CLARK, Kate [Upson], b. Camden, Ala., 22 Feb., 1851. Was married to Edward P. Clark, of the N. Y. "Evening Post" in 1874. Latterly a resident of Brooklyn, N. Y. Has contributed much prose and verse to the magazines and periodicals.

CLARK, Willis Gaylord, journalist, b. Otisco, N. Y., 5 Mar., 1810. Entered journalism in 1830 at Philadelphia, and owned and edited the "Gazette" of that city. Contributed to the "Knickerbocker" and other magazines. His twin brother, Lewis Gaylord Clark, published his "Literary Remains" (1844), and the only collection of Willis Gaylord's poems made during his life was reissued in 1847. Died, Philadelphia, Penn., 12 June, 1841.

CLARKE, Isaac Edwards, lawyer, b. Deerfield, Mass., 1 July, 1830. His family home was at Northampton. Graduated at Yale. After several years' residence in Europe was admitted to the bar at Frankfort, Ky. Removing to New York in 1860, he was, with the exception of a period of service during the war as U. S. provisional marshal for Louisiana, chiefly occupied with his profession in that city until 1871, after which he held a confidential position in the Bureau of Education at Washington. His important report, "Industrial and High Art Education in the United States" (Part I., 1885) will be complete in four volumes.

CLARKE, James Freeman, clergyman, b. Hanover, N. H., 4 April, 1810. Graduated at Harvard. Was pastor of a Unitarian church at Louisville, Ky., until 1841, when he established the Church of the Disciples at Boston, Mass., where he preached for the remainder of his life. The most important of his many theological works were "Orthodoxy: its Truth and Errors" (1866) and "Ten Great Religions" (1871-83). Was associated with Emerson and W. H. Channing in the preparation of the "Memoirs of Margaret Fuller Ossoli" (1852). Died, Jamaica Plain, Mass., 8 June, 1888.

CLAY, Cassius Marcellus, politician, b. Madison Co., Ky., 19 Oct., 1810. Graduated at Yale. Was a member of the Kentucky legislature for several terms. Early became interested in the anti-slavery movement, and in 1845 started an anti-slavery paper at Lexington, Ky. Served in the Mexican war. Was U. S. minister to Russia, 1861-9, with the exception of two years. His "Memoirs, Writings, and Speeches" were published in 1886.

CLAY, Henry, statesman, b. "The Slashes," Hanover Co., Va., 12 April, 1777. His father was a Baptist clergyman. He was educated at a country school, and when fourteen years old secured a clerical position in the court of chancery at Richmond. Studied law, was admitted to the bar in 1797, and removed to Lexington, Ky., to practise. Was a member of the Kentucky legislature, 1803–6 and 1807–8, and in 1806 and 1809 filled unexpired terms in the U. S. senate. Elected to the U. S. house of representatives from 1811 to 1825, he was its speaker for the entire period of his service, with the exception of one term. Was secretary of state under President J. Q. Adams, 1825–9, and was U. S. senator from Kentucky, 1831–42 and 1849–52. In 1814 he served on the commission which signed the Ghent treaty with Great Britain. Nominated for the presidency against Jackson in 1832 and by the Whig party in 1844, he was both times defeated, but was long the most popular leader in the United States. In congress he headed the agitation for the war of 1812, favored the tariff of 1816, urged the Grecian cause and the recognition of South American republics, and supported the Missouri compromise of 1821. He originated the "American system" of protection and internal improvements. The compromise of 1850 was also carried through by his efforts. Several collections of his speeches and letters have been published. Died, Washington, D. C., 29 June, 1852.

CLEMENS, Samuel Langhorne, "Mark Twain," b. Florida, Mo., 1835. Received his education at a district school in Hannibal, Mo., and was apprenticed to a printer of that place when thirteen years old. In 1851, having worked at his trade in various cities of the Union, he became a pilot on the Mississippi river. Ten years later he removed to Nevada as private secretary to his brother, then secretary of that territory. Engaged in mining adventures there and in California, and was occupied with journalism for several years in Virginia city, Nev., and in San Francisco. Visited the Sandwich Islands, 1866, and on his return delivered a series of humorous lectures in the West. Much of his newspaper work had been published over the signature "Mark Twain" (a phrase used in soundings on the Mississippi river). Mr. Clemens came to the Eastern states in 1867 and brought out his first volume, "The Jumping Frog, and Other Sketches," retaining his pseudonym, which he adopted permanently. A visit to Europe and the East with a party of tourists was humorously described in his "Innocents Abroad" (1869), which reached an enormous sale. This was followed by "Roughing It," sketches of life in the West (1872), by "The Gilded Age" (1873), written in conjunction with Charles Dudley Warner and successfully produced as a drama (with John T. Raymond as "Col. Mulberry Sellers") the following year at New York city, and by "Adventures of Tom Sawyer" (1876), "A Tramp Abroad" (1880), "The Prince and the Pauper" (1882), "Life on the Mississippi" (1883), "Adventures of Huckleberry

Finn" (1885), and "A Connecticut Yankee at King Arthur's Court" (1889). Of these "The Prince and the Pauper" has also been dramatized and produced. Founded the New York publishing firm of Charles L. Webster & Co., in 1884.

CLEVELAND, Aaron, clergyman, b. Haddam, Conn., 3 Feb., 1744. Was for a number of years engaged in mercantile pursuits at Norwich and Guilford, Conn. Elected to the Connecticut legislature in 1779. Subsequently entered the Congregational ministry, and was pastor of a church near Hartford. Published a poem on "Slavery" (1775), a few sermons, and a number of fugitive poems. Was noted as a wit and preacher. Died, New Haven, Conn., 21 Sept., 1815.

CLEVELAND, Grover, twenty-second president of the United States, b. Caldwell, Essex Co., N. J., 18 Mar., 1837. Greatgrandson of Aaron Cleveland. Received an academic education at Clinton, N. Y., and was admitted to the bar at Buffalo in 1859. Was mayor of Buffalo, 1882, and governor of New York state, 1883–5. From 1885 to 1889 was president of the United States. At the expiration of his term he resumed the practice of the law in New York city.

CLEVELAND, Rose Elizabeth, b. Fayetteville, N. Y., 1846. Sister of President Cleveland. Early removed to Holland Patent, N. Y., where she chiefly resided when not occupied as an educator and lecturer at young ladies' seminaries. She was mistress of the executive mansion at Washington, D. C., from her brother's inauguration as president until his marriage in 1886. Author of "George Eliot's Poetry, and Other Studies" (1885), and "The Long Run," a novel (1886).

CLIFFTON, William, b. Philadelphia, Penn., 1772. Of Quaker parentage. He supported Washington's administration with satirical poems directed against the opponents of Jay's treaty. In 1800 appeared "Poems, chiefly Occasional, by the late Mr. Cliffton." Died, Philadelphia, Penn., Dec., 1799.

CLINTON, De Witt, statesman, b. Little Britain, Orange Co., N. Y., 2 Mar., 1769. Graduated at Columbia. Was admitted to the bar in 1788, but devoted his attention chiefly to politics. Served a number of terms in the New York legislature and as mayor of New York city. Was U. S. senator, 1802–3, lieutenant-governor of New York, 1811–13, and governor, 1817–22 and 1825–8. Was the unsuccessful Peace candidate for president in 1812. Instituted many reforms in his city and state, and effected the construction of the Erie canal. His "Life and Writings" was published in 1849. Died, Albany, N. Y., 11 Feb., 1828.

CLYMER, Ella [Dietz], actress, b. New York, N. Y., 18—. Made her début at New

York city in 1872. Acted in England with success from 1874 to 1881, when she returned to America and abandoned the stage on account of ill-health. A founder of the "Sorosis" society, of which she became president in 1889. Author of three volumes of poems, "The Triumph of Love" (1878), "The Triumph of Time" (1884), and "The Triumph of Life" (1885).

COAN, Titus Munson, physician, b. Hilo, Hawaiian Islands, 1841. Graduated at Williams college. Studied medicine in New York city, where he returned to practise after serving in the U. S. navy during 1863–5. Contributed essays to the "Galaxy," 1869–77, to "Harper's," and to other leading magazines. Author of numerous articles on hygiene, the mineral springs of Europe, etc., and of "Ounces of Prevention" (1885). Established at New York the "Bureau of Revision" for the criticism, editing, and placing of authors' manuscripts.

COFFIN, Charles Carleton, b. Boscawen, N. H., 26 July, 1823. Studied civil-engineering, but finally entered journalism. Served as field-correspondent ("Carleton") for the Boston "Journal" in the civil war, and became a popular lecturer. Author of "Days and Nights on the Battle-Field" (1864), "Four Years of Fighting" (1866), "Building the Nation" (1883), and several other works on similar themes.

COGSWELL, Mason Fitch, physician, b. Canterbury, Conn., 28 Sept., 1761. Graduated at Yale. Became a physician of distinction in Hartford, Conn. With others of the so-called "Hartford Wits" he contributed to "The Echo" (1791–6). Died, Hartford, Conn., 10 Dec., 1830.

COLDEN, Cadwallader, colonial governor, b. Ireland, 17 Feb., 1688. His family resided at Dunse, Scotland. Graduated at the university of Edinburgh. Emigrated to Philadelphia, Penn., in 1708, and practised medicine there for ten years, when he removed to New York at the suggestion of Governor Hunter, and was appointed to numerous offices, serving as lieutenant-governor of New York from 1761 until his death, and several times as acting governor. Gained reputation for scientific investigations and was an active royalist. "The History of the Five Indian Nations" (1727, enlarged ed. 1747) was written to correct false impressions of the English government concerning the Indians. Colden also published several scientific works. Died, Spring Hill, near Flushing, L. I., N. Y., 21 Sept., 1776.

COLEMAN, Benjamin, clergyman, b. Boston, Mass., 19 Oct., 1673. Graduated at Harvard. After preaching a few years in England, became in 1699 pastor of the Brattle street church in Boston, Mass., organized at that time in opposition to the Cambridge Platform. Gained reputation as a preacher, and was active in public affairs. Author of numerous sermons and several poems. Some of the latter are found in his "Life and Character" (1749) by E. Turell, his son-in-law. Died, Boston, Mass., 29 Aug., 1747.

COLES, Abraham, physician, b. Scotch Plains, N. J., 26 Dec., 1813. Graduated at Jefferson medical college, Philadelphia. Resided at Newark, N. J., after 1836, and subsequently at Scotch Plains. Author of "Dies Iræ, in Thirteen Original Versions" (1859), published with other translations as "Latin Hymns" (1868), and of "The Evangel in Verse" (1874) and "The Light of the World" (1884).

COLLIER, Thomas Stephens, sailor, b. New York, N. Y., 4 Nov., 1842. Entered the U. S. navy as apprentice boy, 1857. Served through the civil war, becoming boatswain in 1866. Was placed on the retired list of navy officers, 1883, and afterward resided at New London, Conn. A writer for the magazines, and author of "Song Spray," poems (1890).

COLLYER, Robert, clergyman, b. Keighley, Yorkshire, England, 8 Dec., 1823 Was early apprenticed to the blacksmith's trade. Came to America in 1850, and served as a Methodist preacher while following his trade. His views changing, he founded and became pastor of a Unitarian church at Chicago in 1859, and twenty years later removed to New York to fill a similar position. Besides fugitive verse he published several prose volumes, including "Nature and Life" (1866), "The Simple Truth" (1877), and "Lectures to Young Men and Women" (1886).

COLTON, Walter, clergyman, b. Rutland, Vt., 9 May, 1797. Graduated at Yale, and became a Congregational clergyman. Was appointed chaplain in the U. S. navy, 1830. After several voyages was made alcalde of Monterey, Cal., 1846, and established there the first California newspaper. The best-known of his books of travel is "Three Years in California" (1850, new ed. 1859). Died, Philadelphia, Penn., 22 Jan., 1851.

CONE, Helen Gray, educator, b. New York, N. Y., 8 Mar., 1859. Graduated from the Normal college of New York city, at which institution she became instructor in English literature. A contributor to the magazines, and author of "Oberon and Puck: Verses Grave and Gay" (1885).

CONGDON, Charles Taber, journalist, b. New Bedford, Mass., 7 April, 1821. Studied at Brown university. Was a member of the N. Y. "Tribune" editorial staff, 1857–62, and, besides contributions to the magazines and newspapers, published "Tribune Essays" (1869) and "Reminiscences of a Journalist" (1880).

CONRAD, Robert Taylor, lawyer, b. Philadelphia, Penn., 10 June, 1810. In 1838 became a judge of the court of criminal sessions of that city, and was afterward elected mayor. Was editor of "Graham's Magazine" for several years. Is best known as the author of "Aylmere, or the Bondman of Kent," a tragedy produced by Forrest in 1841. "Aylmere . . . and Other Poems" appeared in 1852. Died, Philadelphia, Penn., 27 June, 1858.

CONWAY, Katherine Eleanor, b. Rochester, N. Y., 18—. Began journalistic and literary work in 1873, and in 1883 joined the editorial staff of the Boston "Pilot." Author of "On the Sunrise Slope," poems (1881), and co-editor with Mrs. Clara Erskine Clement of "Christian Symbols and Stories of the Saints" (1886).

CONWAY, Moncure Daniel, b. "Middleton," Stafford Co., Va., 17 Mar., 1832. Graduated at Dickinson college, Carlisle, Penn. Began the study of law, but soon entered the Methodist ministry, preaching in various circuits of Virginia. As a law student he had held extreme Southern opinions, and had expressed them in articles in the Richmond "Examiner." But his political and religious beliefs underwent a change; he came under the influence of Emerson and the radical group, and shortly entered the divinity school at Cambridge, Mass. On graduating in 1854, he intended to preach in Virginia, but was driven away by his former neighbors on account of his anti-slavery proclivities. The latter also led to his dismissal from a Unitarian church at Washington, D. C. He became pastor of one at Cincinnati, O., in 1857, and in 1863 visited England for the purpose of writing and lecturing in behalf of the anti-slavery party. The same year formed a pastoral connection with the (ultra-liberal)South Place chapel at London, which lasted until 1884, when he returned to the United States. Chief among his books are "Tracts for To-day" (1858), "Testimonies concerning Slavery" (1865), "Idols and Ideals" (1877), "Demonology and Devil-Lore" (1879), "The Wandering Jew"(1881), and "The Sacred Anthology," selections from the sacred writings of all ages (1873).

COOK, Ebenezer. Nothing is known of this author. It is not certain whether he signed his real name to "The Sot-Weed Factor," published at London, in 1708, or whether the signature "Eben. Cook, Gent.," is a mere pseudonym. The work itself is a satirical poem, purporting to give an account of the trials of a merchant-adventurer to Virginia, "sot-weed" being an early name for tobacco.

COOKE, George Willis, clergyman, b. Comstock, Mich., 23 April, 1848. Entered the Unitarian ministry, 1872. Pastor at Dedham, Mass., 1880-7, and non-resident pastor of the First church at Sharon, Mass., after 1887. Lectured at the Concord school of philosophy, and in various cities of the Union. Author of "Ralph Waldo Emerson" (1881) and "George Eliot" (1883)—critical studies of their subjects' lives, writings, and philosophies—and of "Poets and Problems" (1886).

COOKE, John Esten, b. Winchester, Va., 3 Nov., 1830. Received a private education and practised law for a few years, abandoning the profession for literary work. Was in active service with the Confederate army during the whole of the civil war. His books chiefly consist of romances founded on early life in Virginia and on the events of the rebellion. He was the author of a number of fugitive poems. Some of his works are "Leather Stocking and Silk, a Story of the Valley of Virginia" (1854), "Henry St. John, Gentleman, a Tale of 1774-5" (1859), "Surrey of Eagle's Nest" (1866), "Hilt to Hilt" (1869), "The Virginia Bohemians" (1880), and "The Maurice Mystery" (1885). He also published lives of Stonewall Jackson and Robert E. Lee. Died, near Boyce, Clarke Co., Va., 27 Sept., 1886.

COOKE, Philip Pendleton, lawyer, b. Martinsburg, Va., 26 Oct., 1816. Brother of John Esten Cooke. Graduated at the college of New Jersey. Literature and field-sports received his chief attention. "Florence Vane" is his best-known lyric. Author of "Froissart Ballads, and Other Poems" (1847). Died, near Boyce. Va., 21 Jan., 1850.

COOKE, Rose [Terry], b. West Hartford, Conn., 17 Feb., 1827. Received her education at the Hartford female seminary. Married and removed to Winsted, Conn., in 1873, where she afterward resided. Contributed many stories and poems to periodicals. The following books have been published: "Poems by Rose Terry" (1860), "Happy Dodd"(1875), "Somebody's Neighbors" (1881), "Root-Bound" (1886), "The Sphinx's Children and Other People's" (1886), and "Poems, Collective Edition" (1888).

COOLBRITH, Ina D., b. near Springfield, Ill., 18- . Early removed to California, residing at Los Angeles, and more recently at San Francisco. In 1872 became librarian of the Oakland free library. A constant writer for the "Overland Monthly," "Harper's," and other leading magazines. Published in 1881 "A Perfect Day, and Other Poems."

COOMBS, Anne [Sheldon], b. Albany, N. Y., 18—. Was taken as a child to Brooklyn, N.Y., where, and in New York city, she afterward lived. Was married, 1882, to Charles A. Coombs. Author of the novels, "As Common Mortals" (1886), "A Game of Chance" (1887), and "The Garden of Armida" (1889).

COOPER, George, b. New York, N. Y., 14 May, 1840. Was educated at the public schools of that city. A resident of West Hoboken, N. J., where he engaged in songwriting and in contributing to children's and other magazines.

COOPER, James Fenimore, b. Burlington, N. J., 15 Sept., 1789. Of Quaker descent. His father, William Cooper, owned extensive tracts of land in New York state, and founded the village of Cooperstown at Otsego lake. He removed his family from New Jersey to this place in 1790, nine years after erected the family mansion known as Otsego Hall, and was U. S. representative from the district for several years. The novelist received his early education here and at Albany, where he was fitted for college. Entered Yale, 1803, and was expelled in his junior year for a breach of discipline. Deciding to enter the U. S. navy, he shipped as a sailor before the mast on a merchant-vessel, by way of preparation. After a voyage to England and Spain was appointed midshipman in the navy, 1808, and was detailed to service on Lakes Ontario and Champlain, thus gaining familiarity with scenes subsequently portrayed in his novels. On marrying into the De Lancey family of Westchester county, N. Y., he made his residence there, having resigned his commission in 1811. From 1814 to 1817 lived at Cooperstown, then returned to Westchester county. Was chiefly occupied with farming until led by the success of his second novel, "The Spy" (1821), to remove to New York city and devote himself entirely to literary work. His first book, "Precaution" (1820), had been written partly as an experiment because of his dissatisfaction on reading a novel treating of English society, and his belief that he could write a better one. In 1823 appeared "The Pioneers," the earliest written of the "Leather-Stocking" tales. Their order in narration is as follows : "The Deerslayer" (1841), "The Last of the Mohicans" (1826), "The Pathfinder" (1840), "The Pioneers" (1823), and "The Prairie" (1827). Continued success and increased fame followed the publication of "The Pilot" (1823–4), the writing of which was suggested by a lack of genuine sea element in Scott's "The Pirate." Other sea tales of Cooper's are "The Red Rover" (1828), "The Water-Witch" (1830), "Homeward Bound" (1838), "The Wing-and-Wing" (1842), "Afloat and Ashore" (1844), etc. In 1826 he sailed for Europe, remaining abroad until 1833. For a portion of this period he was nominally U. S. consul at Lyons. In 1836–8 he published ten volumes of travels, covering his stay in Europe, with the titles "Sketches of Switzerland" and "Gleanings in Europe." A defender of republican institutions in general, notably in "The Bravo" (1831), and of his country in particular while away from home, he felt himself at liberty on his return to criticise severely the ways of his fellow countrymen. This action on his part, together with an unfortunate meddling in political questions and a bitter local dispute with the citizens of Cooperstown, brought upon him much abuse from the press, to which he responded with suits for libel. These he conducted himself, and they were usually successful, but made him unpopular. The most important of the suits related to the fairness of his "History of the Navy of the United States" (1839), which was established. A few years after his return from Europe, Cooperstown became his permanent home. Died, Cooperstown, N. Y., 14 Sept., 1851.

COPWAY, George, or *Kagegagahbowk*, b. on Rice lake, Ontario Co., Canada, N. W., 1818. A chief of the Ojibway tribe of Indians. Was converted to Christianity in 1830, and was afterward a missionary to the Indians. Lectured in the United States and Europe, and was a journalist in New York city. Published several books, among which are "Recollections of a Forest Life" (1847) and "Traditional History and Characteristic Sketches of the Ojibway Nation" (1850). He succumbed to an inclination for strong drink, and died in reduced circumstances at Pontiac, Mich., about 1869.

CORSON, Hiram, educator, b. Philadelphia, Penn., 6 Nov., 1828. After several years' employment in the Congressional and Smithsonian libraries at Washington, became a private instructor in English literature at Philadelphia. Professor of English literature at St. John's college, Annapolis, 1865–70, and at Cornell university after 1870. In addition to annotated texts of early English writers, published a "Hand-Book of Anglo-Saxon and Early English" (1871) and "An Introduction to the Study of Robert Browning" (1886).

CORWIN, Thomas, statesman, b. Bourbon Co., Ky., 29 July, 1794. Was admitted to the bar of Kentucky, 1818, and gained reputation for his oratorical powers. U. S. representative for seven terms, and U. S. senator, 1845–50, resigning to become secretary of the treasury under President Fillmore. A leader of the Whig party for many years. His "Life and Speeches" was published in 1859. Died, Washington, D. C., 18 Dec., 1865.

COTTON, John, clergyman, b. Derby, England, 4 Dec., 1585. Graduated at Cambridge. Preached for twenty years at Boston in Lincolnshire. Summoned before the church tribunal for non-conformity, he escaped to America, sailing with Thomas Hooker and arriving at Boston in New England, 4 Sept., 1633. Became "teacher" of the First church of Boston, holding the position for life. Was declared an advocate of their principles by Mrs. Anne Hutchinson and the other so-called Antinomians in 1637, but he stated that they had concealed their extreme views from him. Engaged in a controversy with Roger Williams on the subject of religious toleration, and published "The Bloudy Tenent, washed, and made white in the bloud of the Lambe" (1647). Nearly fifty of his books were published, among which were "Milk for Babes," a popular catechism for children, and "Meat for Strong Men," an exposition of civil government founded with religious motives. His elaborate discussion of the "Singing of Psalms" (1650) is characteristic of the man and the time. Cotton considered twelve hours of study a day's work. To his opinion and example was probably due the observance in New England of Saturday evening as a part of the sabbath. Died, Boston, Mass., 23 Dec., 1652.

COX, Samuel Sullivan, statesman, b. Zanesville, O., 30 Sept., 1824. Graduated at Brown university. Edited a newspaper at Columbus, O., 1853–5. Was elected to congress from that state in 1857, and served four terms. Removed to New York city in 1866, and was reëlected to congress almost continuously from 1868 until his death. In 1885 he was appointed U. S. minister to Turkey, resigning in 1886. Gained reputation as a humorous lecturer and writer, as well as for being a ready debater. His most important legislative effort was in behalf of the creation of the four new states, the Dakotas, Washington, and Montana. Author of "The Buckeye Abroad" (1851), "Puritanism in Politics" (1863), "Why We Laugh" (1876), "Three Decades of Federal Legislation" (1885), and "Diversions of a Diplomat in Turkey" (1887). Died, New York, N. Y., 10 Sept., 1889.

COXE, Arthur Cleveland, divine, b. Mendham, N. J., 10 May, 1818. Grandson of Aaron Cleveland. Graduated at the university of New York. Was rector of Protestant-Episcopal churches at Hartford, Conn., and Baltimore, Md., 1843–63, and in 1864 became bishop of western New York. "Advent, a Mystery" (1837), and "Christian Ballads" (1840) are two of his volumes of poems, the latter still having a popular sale. Author of several theological works.

COZZENS, Frederick Swartwout, merchant, b. New York, N.Y., 5 Mar., 1818. A leading vintner in that city for many years. "The Sparrowgrass Papers" (1856) originally appeared in the "Knickerbocker," and gained the author reputation as a humorist. He also published "Sayings of Dr. Bushwhacker" (1867). Died, Brooklyn, N. Y., 23 Dec., 1869.

CRANCH, Christopher Pearse, painter, b. Alexandria, Va., 8 Mar., 1813. A leading contributor to "The Dial," 1840–3.

Studied art in Europe, where he resided, 1846–63. Subsequently lived at Cambridge, Mass., and New York city. Author of "Poems" (1844), "The Æneid of Virgil Translated into English Verse" (1872), "The Bird and the Bell" (1875), and "Ariel and Caliban, with Other Poems" (1887).

CRANDALL, Charles Henry, b. Greenwich, Washington Co., N. Y., 19 June, 1858. Was educated in his native town. A resident of Springdale, Conn., and there occupied with journalism and literary work.

Crapo, William Wallace [*Noted Saying:* Vol. XI., p. 458], b. Dartmouth, Mass., 16 May, 1830. Graduated at Yale. Was admitted to the bar, and was city solicitor of New Bedford, Mass., for fifteen years. U. S. representative from Massachusetts, 1875–83.

CRAWFORD, Francis Marion, b. Baths of Lucca, Italy, 2 Aug., 1854. Son of Thomas Crawford, the American sculptor, and nephew of Julia Ward Howe. Was sent as a boy to St. Paul's school, Concord, N. H. Returning to Europe, he was at Cambridge university from 1870 to 1874, and for several years studied philosophy and the languages at Heidelberg, the Polytechnicum (Carlsruhe), and the university of Rome. Visited India with the purpose of perfecting his knowledge of Oriental languages and mysteries, and assumed the editorship of a newly-established newspaper at Allahabad, capital of the northwest provinces. This venture proving unsuccessful, he came to America once more, and passed the academic year of 1880–1 at Harvard in a course of Sanscrit and Zend with Prof. C. R. Lanman, receiving a diploma from the university. At this period he contributed to periodicals a number of reviews dealing with political, social, and economic philosophy. His attention was turned to fiction by his uncle, Mr. Samuel Ward of New York city, to whom he related some of his experiences in the Orient and who advised him to make them the basis of a novel. "Mr. Isaacs" appeared in 1882, and was immediately successful. Mr. Crawford resided in New York city and Boston until 1884, after which he made his home at Sorrento, Italy, and devoted himself entirely to literature. His other works are "Dr. Claudius" (1883), "To Leeward" (1883), "A Roman Singer" (1884), "An American Politician" (1884), "Zoroaster" (1885), "A Tale of a Lonely Parish" (1886), "Saracinesca" (1887), "Marzio's Crucifix" (1887). "Paul Patoff" (1887), "With the Immortals" (1888), "Sant' Ilario," sequel to "Saracinesca" (1889), and "Greifenstein" (1889). Contributed "A National Hymn" to the Constitutional centennial at Philadelphia, 1887.

CREVECŒUR, J. Hector St. John de, agriculturist, b. Caën, Normandy, 1731.

Emigrated to America in 1754, and established himself on a farm near New York city. Visited Europe in 1780, and while in London published his "Letters from an American Farmer" (1782). This volume was translated into French, and its glowing descriptions of farm-life in America caused the emigration of some five hundred French families to the Ohio region, where most of them perished. Crevecœur was French consul at New York from 1783 to 1793, when he returned to France. Died, Sarcelles, France, Nov., 1813.

Crittenden, Thomas Leonidas [*Noted Saying;* Vol. XI., page 452], b. Russellville, Ky., 15 May, 1815. Rose to the rank of lieutenant-colonel in the Mexican war, and to that of major-general in the Union army during the civil war.

CROCKETT, David, pioneer, b. Limestone, Greene Co., Tenn., 17 Aug., 1786. Received his first schooling at the age of eighteen. Removing to a wild part of Tennessee in 1809, he gained reputation as a hunter, and served in the Creek war of 1813. Was twice a member of the Tennessee legislature, and twice U. S. representative from Tennessee. Took service with Texas in its war for independence. Published "A Narrative of David Crockett. . . . Written by Himself" (1834). Fell in defence of the Alamo, Texas, 6 Mar., 1836.

CROLY, Jane [Cunningham], "Jennie June," b. Market Harborough, England, 19 Dec., 1831. Was brought to America in 1841, and became a resident of New York city. Was married, 1857, to David G. Croly, a New York journalist. In 1860 she assumed the editorship of "Demorest's Mirror of Fashion," afterward "Demorest's Illustrated Monthly," and held that position for many years. Invented the system of manifold newspaper correspondence. Was the founder of "Sorosis," and its president for fourteen years. Among her books are "Talks on Women's Topics" (1863), "For Better or Worse" (1875), and "Three Manuals for Work" (1885–9).

CROSBY, Frederick K., b. Newton, Mass., 9 Oct., 1845. Graduated at the Philadelphia dental college. Settled at St. John, N. B., 1871. Contributed poetry to leading American magazines. "Into Light, and Other Poems" (1876) was published after his death. Died, San Diego, Cal., 3 Dec., 1874.

CROSSWELL, William, clergyman, b. Hudson, N. Y., 7 Nov., 1804. Graduated at Yale. Took holy orders in 1828, and was rector of an Episcopal church in Boston, Mass., until his death. Some of his hymns and religious poems appeared in "Poems, Sacred and Secular," edited by Arthur Cleveland Coxe (1859). Died, Boston, Mass., 9 Nov., 1851.

CUDWORTH, James, colonist, b. England. Emigrated to Plymouth colony, and had settled at Scituate by 1634. Representative from that place to the Plymouth general court, 1649–56. Served as magistrate for the next two years, but became unpopular with the authorities because of his leniency to the Quakers. Was subsequently commander of the Plymouth forces in the early part of King Philip's war. Elected deputy-governor in 1681, and sent to England as the colony's agent the year after. Died, London, England, 1682.

CURTIS, George Ticknor, lawyer, b. Watertown, Mass., 28 Nov., 1812. Graduated at Harvard. Practised law at Boston until 1862, and after that at New York city and Washington, D. C. Besides a number of legal works, has written "History of the Origin, Formation, and Adoption of the Constitution of the United States" (1855–8) and "Creation or Evolution?" (1887).

CURTIS, George William, b. Providence, R. I., 24 Feb., 1824. After a year's experience in business in New York, at the age of eighteen joined the Brook Farm association at West Roxbury, Mass., remaining a year and a half. Thence removed to Concord, where he lived on familiar terms with the resident literary and philosophical circle. From 1846 to 1850 travelled extensively in Europe and the East, completing his education, and gathering material for subsequent volumes. The first of these appeared soon after his return as "Nile Notes of an Howadji" (1851), followed by "The Howadji in Syria" (1852). Letters to the N. Y. "Tribune" from various watering-places appeared as "Lotus-Eating" (1852). In the same year Mr. Curtis began his connection with "Putnam's Magazine." He eventually became editor and part proprietor, and at the time of its failure in 1857 gave up his entire fortune to protect its creditors, finally clearing away the debts in 1873. Of his contributions to this magazine there have been collected "The Potiphar Papers" (1853) and "Prue and I" (1856). In 1862 was published "Trumps, a Novel," from the columns of "Harper's Weekly." He began lecturing in the winter of 1853, an occupation in which he met with success. Inaugurated in 1853 the editorial department of "Harper's Magazine" known as the "Editor's Easy Chair," which he has continuously written, and was a regular editorial contributor to "Harper's Weekly" after 1857. In constant demand as an orator for state occasions, and gained a high reputation for his addresses and orations. At various times declined to serve in high diplomatic positions.

CURWEN, Samuel, loyalist, b. Salem, Mass., 17 Dec., 1715. Graduated at Harvard. Studied for the ministry, but failing health led him to engage in commercial pursuits. Served in the expedition against Louisburg in 1745, was impost officer for Essex county, Mass., from 1759 to 1764, and in 1775, when obliged to sail for England on account of his loyalist views, was a judge of admiralty. Returned to Salem in 1784. "The Journal and Letters of the late Samuel Curwen" (1842, revised ed. 1864) relate his experiences while in exile. Died, Salem, Mass., 9 April, 1802.

CUSHING, Caleb, jurist, publicist, etc., b. Salisbury, Essex Co., Mass., 17 Jan., 1800. Graduated at Harvard and studied for the law. Was elected to congress as a Whig in 1835, but united with President Tyler and the Democratic party in 1841. Shortly after, was appointed commissioner to China, and negotiated the first treaty of the United States with that country. Left the bench of the supreme court of Massachusetts to become attorney-general of the United States, 1853-7. In 1866 was one of three commissioners appointed by President Johnson to revise and codify the laws of the United States, and in 1872 was a member of the counsel for the settlement of the *Alabama* claims. His purely literary work was not important. Died, Newburyport, Mass., 2 Jan., 1879.

CUSTER, Elizabeth [Bacon], b. Monroe, Mich., 18—. Was married to Major-General, then Major, George A. Custer, 9 Feb., 1864. Accompanied him to the seat of war during the succeeding year, and afterward on his service in the West. Author of "'Boots and Saddles,' or Life in Dakota with General Custer" (1885), and "Tenting on the Plains, or General Custer in Kansas and Texas" (1887).

CUTLER, Elbridge Jefferson, educator, b. Holliston, Mass., 28 Dec., 1831. Was professor of modern languages at Harvard from 1865 until his death. Contributed to the "Atlantic Monthly" and other periodicals, and published "War Poems" (1867) and "Stella" (1868). Died, Cambridge, Mass., 27 Dec., 1870.

DABNEY, Richard, b. Louisa Co., Va., about 1787. Received a fair classical education, and was assistant teacher at a school in Richmond. He was afterward employed by Mathew Carey, the Philadelphia publisher. His last years were spent in retirement at his native place. Published "Poems, Original and Translated" (1812, revised ed. 1815). Died, Louisa Co., Va., Nov. 1825.

DAGGETT, Rollin Mallory, b. Richville, N. Y., 22 Feb., 1831. For several years U. S. minister to the Hawaiian Islands. Chiefly a resident of Virginia city, Nev., occupied with journalistic work.

DANA, Charles Anderson, journalist, b. Hinsdale, N. H., 8 Aug., 1819. Studied at Harvard, which he left on account of trouble with his eyes, afterward receiving his degree. Joined the Brook Farm association at Roxbury, Mass., in 1842. After some journalistic experience in Boston, he became managing editor of the N. Y. "Tribune" in 1847, retaining the connection until 1862, and resigning on account of a difference of opinion with Mr. Greeley as to the military policy of the government. From 1863 until the close of the civil war he was assistant secretary of war under Secretary Stanton, frequently visiting the front. Reorganized the N. Y. "Sun" in 1868, and was its editor thereafter. Edited with George Ripley "The American Cyclopædia" (1857–63), of which a revised edition was published, 1873–6. Also edited "The Household Book of Poetry" (1857), which passed through many editions.

DANA, Richard Henry, b. Cambridge, Mass., 15 Aug., 1787. Entered Harvard, but did not graduate, being involved in the students' rebellion of 1807. Studied law with his cousin, Francis Dana Channing, and was admitted to the bar of Boston, 1811. Became active in politics as a Federalist, and was elected to the Massachusetts legislature. Having joined the Boston Anthology club in 1814, he became a contributor to the "North American Review," founded by that organization the following year, and was associate editor of the "Review" with Edward Tyrrel Channing, 1818–20. He next began the publication at New York of a literary periodical entitled "The Idle Man," which received articles and poems from Bryant, Allston, and others, but reached only six numbers. Dana's first volume of "Poems," containing "The Buccaneer," appeared in 1827, and six years later he brought out at Boston a collective edition of his "Poems and Prose Writings" (enlarged ed. 1850). In 1849 and succeeding years he delivered a course of lectures on Shakespeare in several Eastern cities of the United States. The remainder of his life was passed in retirement at Boston and at his country seat on Cape Ann. Died, Boston, Mass., 2 Feb., 1879.

DANA, Richard Henry, Jr., lawyer, b. Cambridge, Mass., 1 Aug., 1815. Son of the preceding. Graduated at Harvard. His course at Harvard was interrupted by trouble with his eyes, and he made a two years' voyage to the Pacific coast, returning in 1836 and graduating the following year. He had shipped as a common sailor, and his experiences are told in his popular book, "Two Years before the Mast" (1840). This passed through many editions in America and Europe, and was adopted by the British admiralty for distribution in the navy. Mr. Dana was admitted to the Massachusetts bar in 1840 and practised with success, being much sought after in maritime cases. In 1841 he published "The Seaman's Friend," a manual of laws bearing on the relations of masters and sailors. He edited a new edition of Wheaton's "International Law" (1866) with original annotations, and delivered lectures on the same subject before the Harvard law school, 1866–7. Was nominated as U. S. minister to England by President Grant in 1876, but was not confirmed by the senate. Died, Rome, Italy, 7 Jan., 1882.

DANDRIDGE, Danske [Bedinger], b. Copenhagen, Denmark, 186–. Great-grand-daughter of Eliza Southgate Bowne. At the time of her birth, her father, Henry Bedinger, was U. S. minister to Denmark. She was married, 1877, to Stephen Dandridge of Shepherdstown, W. Va., which place became her home. Author of "Joy, and Other Poems" (1888).

DAVENPORT, John, clergyman, b. Coventry, England, 1597. Studied at Oxford. After varying experiences as a nonconformist clergyman in England and Holland, at the suggestion of John Cotton emigrated to Boston in New England, 1637. In March, 1638, sailed thence to Quinnipiac, now New Haven, Conn., with a company, and founded the colony, 14 April, 1638. While at New Haven he concealed the regicides Whalley and Goffe in his house for a month in 1661, and preached sermons in their behalf. Called to Boston in 1668 as pastor of the First church, his views on infant baptism caused a split in the congregation, and led to the formation of the Old South church. Author of "The Knowledge of Christ" (1653), "A Discourse about Civil Government in a New Plantation" (1663), and a volume of sermons, "The Saints Anchor-Hold" (1701). Died, Boston, Mass., 15 Mar., 1670.

DAVIES, Samuel, clergyman, b. Newcastle Co., Del., 3 Nov., 1724 (Albert Barnes). Was fitted for the ministry at the school of the Rev. Samuel Blair. As a dissenting minister, came into collision with the Virginia authorities, but was victorious on an appeal to the king, who decided that the colony was included in the "act of toleration." Was chiefly instrumental in establishing the first Virginia presbytery. Succeeded Jonathan Edwards as president of the college of New Jersey in 1759. His collected "Sermons" appeared in 1797. Died, Princeton, N. J., 4 Feb., 1761.

DAVIS, Jefferson, statesman, b. Christian Co., Ky., 3 June, 1808. Graduated at West Point. Served in the Black Hawk war, 1831–2, retiring from the army in 1835. Was U. S. representative from Mississippi, 1845–6. Rejoined the army, 1846, and fought at Monterey. Was U. S. senator, 1847–51, and was President Pierce's secretary of war, 1853–7. His advocacy of state-rights culmi-

nated in his speech in the senate, 1861, on his withdrawal because of the secession of Mississippi. Was appointed president of the Confederate states, 9 Feb., 1861. In April the war opened. In Nov., 1861, he was elected president for six years, his term of office ending when he, his wife, and a small escort were captured near Irwinsville, Ga., 10 May, 1865. He was confined as a prisoner of state in Fortress Monroe for two years. In April, 1866, was indicted for high treason, but was admitted to bail a year later, his first bondsman being Horace Greeley. Was never brought to trial, being included in the general amnesty of 1868. A lady bequeathed to him her estate at Beauvoir, Miss., where he spent the remainder of his life, unreconciled to the Union to the last. Wrote "The Rise and Fall of the Confederate Government" (1881), which contains a number of his speeches. In 1890 a "Memoir" was issued by his wife. Died, New Orleans, La., 6 Dec., 1889.

DAVIS, Mary Evelyn [Moore], b. Talladega, Ala. Was married, 1874, to Thomas E. Davis, editor of the New Orleans "Picayune," and thereafter resided in that city. Author of "Minding the Gap, and Other Poems" (1870), and "In War Times at La Rose Blanche" (1887).

DAVIS, Rebecca [Harding], b. Washington, Penn., 24 June, 1831. Resided in Wheeling, W. Va. until her marriage in 1863 to L. Clark Davis, editor of the "Inquirer" of Philadelphia, which latter city was afterward her home. She contributed many short stories and sketches to the "Atlantic Monthly" and other magazines, and published "Margaret Howth" (1861), "Dallas Galbraith" (1868), "A Law unto Herself" (1878), and several other novels.

DAY, Richard Edwin, b. West Granby, Oswego Co., N. Y., 27 April, 1852. Graduated at Syracuse university. Became associate editor of the Syracuse "Standard" in 1882. Author of "Lyrics and Satires" (1883) and "Poems" (1888).

Decatur, Stephen [*Noted Saying:* Vol. IV., page 490], b. Sinnepuxent, Md., 5 Jan., 1779. Captain and commodore in the U. S. navy, 1804–15. Navy commissioner from 1815 until his death, in a duel, near Bladensburg, Md., 22 Mar., 1820.

De FOREST, John William, soldier, b. Humphreysville, now Seymour, Conn., 31 Mar., 1826. Travelled extensively in Europe while a young man, completing his education mainly in foreign countries. Served as captain and major in the Union forces during the civil war, and retained his connection with the army for a few years after. He contributed to "Harper's Magazine" a number of articles descriptive of battles in which he had participated. Author of "A History of the Indians of Connecticut" (1853), several books of travel, and eleven novels, including "Miss Ravenel's Conversion" (1867), "Kate Beaumont" (1872), and "Honest John Vane" (1875).

De KAY, Charles, journalist, b. Washington, D. C., 25 July, 1848. A grandson of Joseph Rodman Drake. Graduated at Yale. Became a member of the staff of the N. Y. "Times" in 1877. A writer for the magazines, and author of "The Bohemian" (1878), "Hesperus, and Other Poems" (1880), "The Vision of Nimrod" (1881), "The Vision of Esther" (1882), "The Love Poems of Louis Barnaval" (1883), and "Barye: Life and Works" (1889).

DELAND, Margaretta Wade [Campbell] (Margaret Deland), b. Alleghany, Penn., 23 Feb., 1857. She was brought up in the family of her father's brother, the Hon. Benjamin Campbell. Studied at Pelham priory, New Rochelle, N. Y., and at the Cooper Union in New York city. Taught industrial design in the N. Y. Normal college, 1878-9. Was married, 1880, to Lorin F. Deland, of Boston, Mass., which city became her residence. Author of "The Old Garden, and Other Verses" (1886), "John Ward, Preacher," a popular novel dealing with theological questions (1888), "Florida Days" (1889), and "Sidney" (1890).

DEMING, Philander, b. Carlisle, Schoharie Co., N. Y., 6 Feb., 1829. His father was a Presbyterian minister, and at one time special missionary at various places in central and northern New York state. The son taught school in the winter time and with his brothers built and operated successfully during the summer an old-fashioned sawmill on the northern edge of the Adirondack forest. He attended and graduated at Vermont university and the Albany law school. Was chiefly occupied as a writer for the press and as stenographic reporter of the supreme court, third judicial district, N. Y. He resigned his official position in 1882. Afterward resided in Albany, spending the summer months at his northern home. In addition to his contributions to the "Atlantic Monthly" and other magazines, published "Adirondack Stories" (1880) and "Tompkins and Other Folks" (1885).

DEMOCRACY, The Author of.—The editors are not at liberty to give any information respecting this writer, beyond the fact that their selection from "Democracy" (1880) appears legitimately in "A Library of American Literature."

DENNETT, John Richard, journalist, b. Chatham, N. B., 1837. Graduated at Harvard. Settled at Beaufort, S. C., remaining there until after the civil war. An extended tour through the Southern states, and a notable series of letters to the N. Y. "Nation" describing the Southern situation, led to an editorial position on that paper. Was also for several years assistant professor of rhetoric at Harvard. Died, Westborough, Mass., 26 Nov., 1874.

DENNIE, Joseph, journalist, b. Boston, Mass., 10 Aug., 1768. Graduated at Harvard. Studied law, but soon entered journalism. Edited "The Farmer's Weekly Museum" at Walpole, N. H., from 1796 until 1798. The following year removed to Philadelphia, where he established "The Port Folio" in 1800, of which he was editor until his death. His contributions to these journals under the signature "The Lay Preacher" gained him reputation. Died, Philadelphia, Penn., 7 Jan., 1812.

DENTON, Daniel, colonist. Thought to have been a son of Rev. Richard Denton, a non-conformist emigrant clergyman of Hempstead, L. I. A resident of Jamaica, L. I., and justice there in 1666. Published "A Brief Description of New York: Formerly Called New Netherlands" (1670), the first printed account, in the English language, of New York and New Jersey. Still at Jamaica in 1686, but not heard of thereafter.

DEPEW, Chauncey Mitchell, lawyer, b. Peekskill, N. Y., 23 April, 1834. Graduated at Yale. Was admitted to the bar, and was a member of the N. Y. assembly, 1861-2. Elected secretary of state of New York, 1863, and subsequently appointed U. S. minister to Japan. Became counsel of the N. Y. and Harlem railroad, 1866, and of the N. Y. Central and Hudson River road, 1869. Was made president of the latter, 1885. Was one of the prominent candidates for the Republican presidential nomination at the Chicago convention of 1888. Noted as an orator and after-dinner speaker. Author of "Orations and After-Dinner Speeches" (1890).

DERBY, George Horatio, "John Phœnix," b. Dedham, Mass., 3 April, 1823. Graduated at West Point, and entered the U. S. army. Served as a lieutenant in the Mexican war and was promoted for meritorious conduct. Remained in the government service until his death. His humorous writings were collected in "Phœnixiana" (1855) and "The Squibob Papers" (1859). Died, New York, N. Y., 15 May, 1861.

De VERE, Mary Ainge, "Madeline Bridges," b. Brooklyn, N. Y., 18—. A constant resident of that city. Contributed to the "Galaxy," "Littell's Living Age," "Century," "Independent," and other periodicals, 1870-90. Author of "Love Songs, and Other Poems" (1870), and of "Poems" (1890).

DEWEY, George W., b. Baltimore, Md., 1818. Was taken in youth to Philadelphia, Penn., and afterward lived there. Author of fugitive poems, among which is that entitled "Blind Louise." No other information concerning this writer has been obtained.

DEWEY, Orville, clergyman, b. Sheffield, Mass., 28 Mar., 1794. Graduated at Williams. At first a Congregational minister, he soon joined the Unitarians, becoming assistant to Dr. Channing. Was Unitarian minister at New Bedford, Mass., for several years, and at New York, 1835–48. Subsequently held charges at Albany and Boston. An edition of his "Works" appeared, 1847, and in 1884 his "Autobiography and Letters." Died, Sheffield, Mass., 21 Mar., 1882.

DICKINSON, Anna Elizabeth, orator, b. Philadelphia, Penn., 28 Oct., 1842. Her father's death two years later caused her to be educated in the Friends' free schools of that city. Made her first speech, Jan., 1860, at a meeting of Progressive Friends, held to consider "Woman's Rights and Wrongs," and at once gained reputation as a speaker. Spoke frequently thereafter on the same subject, and on temperance and slavery. Delivered an effective address at Music hall, Boston, Mass., in the spring of 1862, on the "National Crisis," and the following winter was engaged by the Republican committee of New Hampshire to assist in their campaign. Her success as an orator led to similar engagements in Connecticut, New York, and Pennsylvania. After the war, continued as a lecturer until 1876, when she made her début as an actress in a drama of her own writing, entitled "A Crown of Thorns." Met with little success in this and in Shakespearian parts. "An American Girl" was successfully produced by Miss Fanny Davenport in 1880. Author of "What Answer?" a novel (1868), and "A Paying Investment" (1876).

DICKINSON, Charles Monroe, journalist, b. Lowville, Lewis Co., N. Y., 15 Nov., 1842. Educated at the Fairfield, N. Y., seminary. Was admitted to the bar at Binghamton, N. Y., 1865. Practised law in that city and in New York city until 1878, when he became editor and proprietor of the Binghamton "Republican." Author of "The Children, and Other Verses" (1889).

DICKINSON, John, statesman, b. Maryland, 13 Nov., 1732. Studied law at Philadelphia and at the Temple in London, and practised with success in the former city. Was a member of the first Colonial congress in 1765. "The Farmer's Letters to the Inhabitants of the British Colonies" (1767) and a number of public papers denouncing British oppression were written by him, but he was not prepared to sign the Declaration of Independence in 1776. He served in the Continental army, however, and was president of Delaware, 1781–2, and of Pennsylvania, 1782–5. "Letters of Fabius on the Federal Constitution" (1788) were in support of that instrument. He also issued "The Political Writings of John Dickinson" (1801). Died, Wilmington, Del., 14 Feb., 1808.

DICKINSON, Jonathan, merchant, b. possibly in England. A member of the society of Friends. First heard of at Elizabeth parish, near Black river, Jamaica, in Mar., 1696. Was wrecked on the coast of Florida, 23 Sept. of the same year, while voyaging with his family from Jamaica to Philadelphia. The party was taken captive by Indians, but finally reached St. Augustine, arriving at Philadelphia, Feb., 1797. Dickinson became prominent as a politician and merchant in the latter city. He published an account of his shipwreck and captivity, entitled "God's Protecting Providence Man's Surest Help and Defence" (1699). Died, Philadelphia, Penn., 18 June, 1722.

DINSMOOR, Robert, b. Windham, N. H., 7 Oct., 1757. Of Scottish descent. Served, as a young man, in the Continental army, and subsequently followed the occupation of a farmer in his native town. His poems are largely imitative of Burns. He styled himself the "Rustic Bard." Published "Incidental Poems" (1828). Died, Windham, N. H., 16 Mar., 1836.

DIX, John Adams, b. Boscawen, N. H., 24 July, 1798. Served in the war of 1812 as lieutenant. Settling at Albany in 1830, he entered public life, becoming U. S. senator and secretary of the treasury under Buchanan. At the outbreak of the civil war he was appointed major-general of volunteers. Was afterward U. S. minister to France and governor of New York. His "Speeches" (1864) and "Memoirs" (1883) have been published. Died, New York, N. Y., 21 April, 1879.

DOANE, George Washington, clergyman, b. Trenton, N. J., 27 May, 1799. Graduated at Union college. Took orders in the Episcopal church, 1821. Was a professor at Trinity college, 1824–8, and afterward officiated at Trinity church, Boston, until his election as bishop of New Jersey in 1832. His "Life and Writings" (1860) were edited by his son. Died, Burlington, N. J., 27 April, 1859.

DODD, Anna Bowman [Blake], b. Brooklyn, N. Y., 18—. Daughter of Stephen M. Blake of Brooklyn. Her family removed to New York city in 1854, where she was married, 1883, to Edward W. Dodd of that city. A critical writer for the London "Art Journal," "Harper's Magazine," and other periodicals, and author of "Cathedral Days" (1886), "The Republic of the Future," a satire on socialism (1887), and "Glorinda: a Story" (1888).

DODGE, Mary Barker [Carter], b. Bridgewater, Bucks Co., Penn., 18—. Her father, William S. Carter, was English by birth. Mrs. Dodge received her education in Philadelphia. She was married, 1850, to Mr. Charles F. Dodge, of Dodgeville, Mass., and resided for some years at Williamsport, Mass. After 1877 she frequently changed her residence. Author of "Belfry Voices" (1870) and "The Gray Masque, and Other Poems" (1885).

DODGE, Mary [Mapes], b. New York, N. Y., 1838. Daughter of Prof. James J. Mapes, a scientist of that city. Was married to William Dodge, a New York lawyer of repute. After his early death she developed an inclination for literature inherited from her father. She was, with Donald G. Mitchell and Harriet Beecher Stowe, one of the earliest contributors to the N.Y. "Hearth and Home." A volume of "Irvington Stories" (1864) for children met with success, and was soon followed by "Hans Brinker, or the Silver Skates" (1865), a juvenile story of life in Holland. This became a little classic, and was translated into French, German, Dutch, Russian, and other languages. At the commencement of the "St. Nicholas" magazine for young folks in 1873, Mrs. Dodge assumed the editorship, a position she still held in 1890. During her early widowhood, she made her home at the Mapes farm, near Waverly, N. J., subsequently returning to New York city, where she became a leader in literary and artistic circles. Other books, besides those already mentioned, are "A Few Friends, and How They Amused Themselves" (1869), "Rhymes and Jingles" (1874), "Theophilus and Others" (1876), "Along the Way," poems (1879), and "Donald and Dorothy" (1883).

DORGAN, John Aylmer, lawyer, b. Philadelphia, Penn., 12 Jan., 1836. Graduated at the Philadelphia central high school. Was occupied in a law office of that city until his early death by consumption. Contributed poetry to the "Atlantic Monthly" and other magazines, and published "Studies," poems (1862, revised eds., 1864 and 1866). Died, Philadelphia, Penn., 1 Jan., 1867.

DORR, Julia Caroline [Ripley], b. Charleston, S. C., 13 Feb., 1825. Resided in New York until her marriage, in 1847, to Seneca R. Dorr, when she removed to Rutland, Vt., where she subsequently lived. Became a contributor to the magazines shortly after her marriage, and published four novels, a book descriptive of "Bermuda" (1884), and the following volumes of verse: "Poems" (1871), "Friar Anselmo, and Other Poems" (1879) "Daybreak, an Easter Poem" (1882), and "Afternoon Songs" (1885).

DOUGLAS, Stephen Arnold, statesman, b. Brandon, Vt., 23 April, 1813. Began to practise law at Jacksonville, Ill., in 1834, and rose through various state offices to be U. S. representative, 1843–7, and U. S. senator, 1847–61. As the Democratic candidate for president, was defeated by Lincoln in 1860. He advocated the theory of leaving the question of slavery to the citizens of states and territories, which was known as "popular sovereignty," but loyally supported the Union at the outbreak of the civil war. Died, Chicago, Ill., 3 June, 1861.

DOUGLASS, Frederick, emancipator, b. Tuckahoe, Talbot Co., Md., Feb., 1817. Escaped from slavery at Baltimore in 1838, and after lecturing as agent of the Massachusetts anti-slavery society for several years, edited "The North Star" at Rochester, N. Y., from 1847 until the abolition of slavery. Was afterward U. S. marshal for the District of Columbia, and U. S. minister to Hayti. Author of "Life and Times of Frederick Douglass" (1882).

DOWNING, Andrew Jackson, landscape-gardener, b. Newburgh, N.Y., 20 Oct., 1815. Conducted a nursery with his brother at that place and studied landscape-gardening. His first book, "Landscape Gardening and Rural Architecture" (1841), at once became a standard on its subject. It was followed by "Cottage Residences" (1842), "Fruits and Fruit Trees of America" (1845), and, after his death, by "Rural Essays" (1853). Drowned in the Hudson, at the burning of the steamboat *Henry Clay*, near Yonkers, N. Y., 28 July, 1852.

DRAKE, Joseph Rodman, b. New York, N. Y., 17 Aug., 1795. Was made an orphan while quite young, and underwent a hard experience with poverty. In 1813 he entered upon the study of medicine, receiving his degree three years later. Soon married the daughter of Henry Eckford, a wealthy shipbuilder, and was thereby placed in comfortable circumstances. Visited Europe with his wife in 1818. He passed the winter of 1819–20 at New Orleans, on account of failing health, and returned to New York in the spring with an attack of consumption that soon proved fatal. Drake composed verses as a child. The earliest poem which has been preserved, "The Mocking Bird," was written at the age of fourteen. His acquaintance with Fitz-Greene Halleck began in 1812, and seven years later they contributed to the N. Y. "Evening Post" the series of humorous poems known as the "Croaker" papers. These verses were lively sallies at local public characters, and created much amusement. They were published in a volume by the Bradford club of New York, 1860. "The Culprit Fay," written in 1819, or, according to one account, in 1816, grew out of a conversation with some of Drake's fellow authors, in which it was asserted by them that American rivers were not a suitable theme for romantic treatment. This poem, the "American Flag," and a selection from his other metrical writings, were published by his daughter as "The Culprit Fay, and Other Poems" (1836). New editions appeared in 1847 and 1865. Died, New York, N. Y., 21 Sept., 1820.

DRAKE, Samuel Gardner, antiquarian, b. Pittsfield, N. H., 11 Oct., 1798. Established an antiquarian bookstore at Boston, 1830, and edited and reprinted many valuable works relating to colonial history. A founder of the N. E. Historic-genealogical society and of the Boston Prince society. Author of "The History and Antiquities of Boston" (1856) and "History of the French and Indian War" (1870). Died, Boston, Mass., 14 June, 1875.

DRAPER, John William, scientist, b. St. Helen's, near Liverpool, England, 5 May, 1811. Studied for a while at the university of London. Came to America in 1832, and graduated as a physician at the university of Pennsylvania. Was connected with the medical department of the university of New York as professor and president from 1839 until 1873. His discoveries in photography and other departments of physics gave him a national and foreign reputation. Besides his technical writings, he was the author of "History of the Intellectual Development of Europe" (1862), "Thoughts on the Future Civil Policy of America" (1865), and "History of the Conflict between Religion and Science" (1874). Died, Hastings-on-Hudson, N. Y., 4 Jan., 1882.

DRAYTON, William Henry, statesman and jurist, b. "Drayton Hall," Ashley River, S. C., Sept., 1742. Graduated at Oxford. Opposed the early patriotic movements preceding the Revolution, and was appointed privy councillor and assistant judge of the province, but soon adopted the American cause and lost his judgeship by publishing a pamphlet containing an American "bill of rights." In March, 1776, was again made privy councillor and also chief justice by the South Carolina government, and in the latter capacity delivered several important charges to the Charleston grand jury expounding American principles. He left materials for a history of the Revolution, afterward edited by his son. Died, Philadelphia, Penn., 3 Sept., 1779.

DRISLER, Henry, educator, b. Staten Island, N. Y., 27 Dec., 1813. Graduated at Columbia, where he was adjunct-professor and professor of Latin from 1845 to 1867, becoming professor of Greek in the latter year. Acting president of Columbia, 1888–9. Editor of numerous classical text-books, and of new editions of Liddell and Scott's Greek Lexicon (1851–83).

DUDLEY, Thomas, colonist, b. Northampton, England, 1576 (Savage). Was steward for the Earl of Lincoln, and rehabilitated his estates. Became a non-conformist, and sailed with Winthrop's company as deputy-governor of the Massachusetts colony, in the summer of 1630. Served as governor four years and as deputy-governor thirteen years. Was the principal founder of Cambridge, Mass. Died, Roxbury, Mass., 31 July, 1653.

DUFFIELD, Samuel Willoughby, clergyman, b. Brooklyn, N. Y., 24 Sept., 1843. Graduated at Yale. Was for many years pastor of a Presbyterian church in Bloomfield, N. J. A writer for the religious press over the signature "Anselmus," and author of "Warp and Woof" (1870) and "English Hymns, their Authors and History" (1886). Died, Bloomfield, N. J., 12 May, 1887.

DUGANNE, Augustine Joseph Hickey, b. Boston, Mass., 1823. Served as a colonel in the N. Y. volunteers during the civil war. Some of his war poems were favorites with the soldiers. Was afterward employed on the N. Y. "Tribune." Published several books, among which are "Hand Poems" (1844), "Poetical Works" (1856), and "Camps and Prisons" (1865). Died, New York, N. Y., 20 Oct., 1884.

DUNLAP, William, painter and dramatist, b. Perth Amboy, N. J., 19 Feb., 1766. His father was an Irish officer, who settled at that place after taking part in the attack on Quebec. The family removed to New York city early in the Revolution, where the son lost the sight of his right eye by an accident. On his recovery, he devoted himself to the study of drawing and painting. Visited England in 1784, and received instruction from Benjamin West, the artist, for three years. On his return to America, began writing for the stage. His first play was accepted, but not produced. His five-act comedy, "The Father," was brought out with success at New York, 7 Sept., 1789. This was followed by other plays, particularly "Leicester" (1794), the first American tragedy regularly produced. In 1796 Dunlap joined the management of the John street theatre in New York, and two years later became manager of the old Park street theatre. There he put on the stage a number of his own dramas, among others his blank-verse tragedy of "André" (1798). His course as a manager was brought to an end by bankruptcy in 1805, and the remainder of his life was chiefly devoted to art and literature. His paintings were mostly portraits, but in the latter part of his life he completed a series of pictures on Scriptural subjects, which were exhibited through the country. He was a founder and vice-president of the National Academy of Design. Some of his books are "The Life of George Fred. Cooke" (1812), "Life of Charles Brockden Brown" (1815), "A History of the American Theatre" (1832), and "History of the Rise and Progress of the Art of Design in the United States" (1834). The Dunlap society of New York city takes its name from this author, and has issued scholarly reprints of some of his plays, etc. Died, New York, N. Y., 28 Sept., 1839.

DURIVAGE, Francis Alexander, b. Boston, Mass., 1814. A nephew of Edward Everett. Engaged in journalistic work at Boston as a young man, and afterward contributed verse, fiction, and humorous sketches to the magazines. Author of "Life Scenes from the World around Us" (1853). Died, New York, N. Y., 1 Feb., 1881.

DUYCKINCK, Evert Augustus, b. New York, N. Y., 23 Nov., 1816. Graduated at Columbia. Studied law, which he gave up for literary pursuits after being admitted to the bar in 1837. Travelled in Europe and on his return edited, at New York, with Cornelius Mathews, a monthly periodical entitled "Arcturus, a Journal of Books and Opinion" (1840-2). Also edited, with his brother, George Long Duyckinck, the N. Y. "Literary World" (1847-53), a weekly review of literature and art. Evert and George Duyckinck were engaged for many years in writing the "Cyclopædia of American Literature," the first edition of which appeared in 1856. Ten years later a new edition was issued, with a supplement by Evert Duyckinck. Other works of the latter were "National Gallery of Eminent Americans" (1866), "History of the World" (1870), and "Biographies of Eminent Men and Women of Europe and America" (1873-4). Died, New York, N. Y., 13 Aug., 1878.

DWIGHT, John Sullivan, musical critic, b. Boston, Mass., 13 May, 1813. Graduated at Harvard. Entered the Unitarian ministry. Shortly after, joined the community at Brook Farm, of which he was a founder. Resided at Boston after 1848, chiefly occupied with musical criticism, and was editor of "Dwight's Journal of Music" (1852-81). Author of original verse and of translations from German poetry.

DWIGHT, Theodore, journalist, b. Northampton, Mass., 15 Dec., 1764. Brother of Timothy Dwight. Editor of newspapers at Hartford, Conn., Albany, N. Y., and New York city, until his retirement in 1836. A principal contributor to "The Echo" (1791-6), and "The Political Green-House" (1799), metrical satires written by the so-called "Hartford Wits." Secretary of the "Hartford Convention," 1814, and author of a "History" (1833) of that assemblage. Died, New York, N. Y., 12 June, 1846.

DWIGHT, Timothy, divine, b. Northampton, Mass., 14 May, 1752. Son of a merchant of that place. His mother was a daughter of Jonathan Edwards, and he received his earliest instruction from her. Graduated with honors at Yale when seventeen years old, and continued there as student and tutor from 1769 to 1777. In the latter year he abandoned the study of the law, which he had taken up, and was appointed a chaplain in the Continental army, serving until his father's death in 1778 necessitated his return to Northampton. During the period of this chaplaincy he wrote his popular war-song, "Columbia." Remained at Northampton for five years, engaged in managing his family's farm and in occasional preaching. From 1783 until 1795 he was pastor of the church at Greenfield, Conn., at the same time conducting an academy for the education of both sexes. In 1795 was chosen president of Yale college, to succeed President Stiles, and continued in the position until his death, holding at the same time the professorship of theology and the college pastorate. President Dwight introduced many reforms into the administration of the college and tripled the number of its students during his presidency. His divinity sermons were published after his death, in five volumes, as "Theology, Explained and Defended" (1818), a work which has passed through numerous editions in America and Europe. Three years later appeared his "Travels in New England and New York" (1821), detailing his observations during a succession of summer journeys through those regions. In addition to these works there were published during his life "The Conquest of Canaan," an epic poem (1785), "The Triumph of Infidelity," a satirical poem (1788), "Greenfield Hill," a poem (1794), and "Remarks on the Review of Inchiquin's Letters" (1815), besides several minor works and many discourses. Died, New Haven, Conn., 11 Jan., 1817.

EASTMAN, Charles Gamage, journalist, b. Fryeburg, Me., 1 June, 1816. Graduated at the university of Vermont. Founded the "Lamoille River Express" at Johnson, Vt., 1838, and the "Spirit of the Age" at Woodstock, Vt., 1840. In 1846 bought the "Vermont Patriot" of Montpelier. Was a member of the state senate, 1851-2. Author of "Poems" (1848, revised ed. 1880). Died, Montpelier, Vt., 1860.

EATON, Arthur Wentworth Hamilton, b. Kentville, N. S., 10 Dec., 1854. Graduated at Harvard. Was for several years rector of an Episcopal church at Boston, Mass. Afterward taught and lectured on English literature. Author of "The Heart of the Creeds" (1888) and "Acadian Legends and Lyrics" (1889).

Eaton, Dorman Bridgman [*Noted Saying:* Vol. XI., page 458], b. Hardwick, Vt., 27 June, 1823. A member of the bar of New York city, and U. S. civil service commissioner under Presidents Grant, Hayes, and Cleveland.

EDWARDS, Harry Stillwell, journalist, b. Macon, Ga., 23 April, 1854. Graduated from the law department of Mercer university, Macon. Began the practice of law. In 1879 joined the editorial staff of the Macon "Telegraph," of which he became part owner two years later. Subsequently was editor of the Macon "Sunday Times" and "Evening News" respectively until 1888. His dialect stories and poems were published chiefly in the "Century" and "Harper's" magazines. Some of them are collected in "Two Runaways, and Other Stories" (1889).

EDWARDS, Jonathan, divine, b. East Windsor, Conn., 5 Oct., 1703. Son of Rev. Timothy Edwards of that place. Became deeply interested in religion while a child, and began the study of metaphysics about the time of his admission to Yale, which took place in his thirteenth year. Gained high honors at college, and remained two years after graduation, while studying for the ministry. Preached at New York for eight months in 1722–3, and subsequently held a tutorship at Yale until 1726, when he became the colleague of his grandfather, the Rev. Solomon Stoddard, in the church at Northampton, Mass. Although his ministry at this place was noted for its revivals of religious interest, notably in 1735, he was finally dismissed in 1750 for insisting on too strict observances by partakers of the communion. From that time until 1757 he was missionary to the Indians and minister at Stockbridge, Mass. In the latter year he was offered and accepted the presidency of the college of New Jersey at Princeton, taking office the following February. He had served but one month when his inoculation for the smallpox was attended with fatal results. Selections from the note-books of Edwards are to be found in the "Memoir" by S. E. Dwight (1830), and they display early and deep insight into natural philosophy and metaphysical mysteries. His famous "Freedom of the Will" (1754) has established his reputation as the equal, if not the superior, of any philosopher of his period. All of his treatises and sermons are imbued with the spirit of Calvinism pure and simple. Of the sermons, the most noted is that entitled "Sinners in the hands of an angry God," preached at Enfield, Conn., in 1741. His power over language and his earnestness were such that, in spite of a slender frame and somewhat weak voice, the effect on his hearers was often extraordinary. Some of his works are "Narrative of Surprising Conversions" (1736), "Treatise on Religious Affections" (1746), and "Original Sin" (1757). Editions of his writings were published in 1809, 1830, and 1852. Died Princeton, N. J., 22 Mar., 1758.

EGAN, Maurice Francis, educator, b. Philadelphia, Penn., 24 May, 1852. Graduated at La Salle college. In 1878 was made professor of English literature at Georgetown college. From 1881 to 1888 was editor of the N. Y. "Freeman's Journal," becoming in the latter year professor of English literature and *belles-lettres* in the university of Notre Dame, Ind. Author of "That Girl of Mine," a novel (1879), "Preludes" (1880), "Songs and Sonnets" (1886), and "Lectures on English Literature" (1889).

EGGLESTON, Edward, b. Vevay, Ind., 10 Dec., 1837. Delicate health prevented him from attending a college. Pursued his studies in the intervals of illness at home, and gained a fair knowledge of Latin and Greek, besides extensive familiarity with English and Continental literature. Became a Methodist preacher at the age of nineteen, riding a four-weeks circuit in Indiana. Six months of this work obliged him to remove to Minnesota for his health, where he became a general agent of the Bible society, and was pastor of several different churches. He was finally compelled to abandon ministerial duties and enter journalism. Removed to Evanston, Ill., in 1866, where he held an editorial position on the "Little Corporal," to which he had already contributed children's stories. The following year became editor of the Chicago "Sunday-School Teacher," the circulation of which increased sevenfold under his management. From 1870 to 1872, having come East in the former year, he was successively literary editor of the N. Y. "Independent" and editor of "Hearth and Home." To the latter of these periodicals was contributed his novel "The Hoosier Schoolmaster" (1871), which reached a large sale in book form. Dr. Eggleston was pastor of a church in Brooklyn, N. Y., 1874–9, and was again obliged to retire by failing health, making his home at Lake George, N. Y. Some of his works are "End of the World" (1872), "The Circuit Rider" (1874), "Christ in Literature" (1875), "Roxy" (1878), "The Graysons" (1888), "History of the United States and its People: for the Use of Schools" (1888), and "A History of Life in the United States," part of which has appeared in the "Century Magazine."

EGGLESTON, George Cary, journalist, b. Vevay, Ind., 26 Nov., 1839. Brother of Edward Eggleston. Graduated at Richmond college, Va. Studied law and began practice, abandoning it to serve through the civil war in the Confederate army. Entered journalism in Brooklyn, N. Y., 1870. Was for a time editor of "Hearth and Home," and was literary editor of the N. Y. "Evening Post," 1875–81. Became editor-in-chief of the N. Y. "Commercial Advertiser," 1886. Author of "A Rebel's Recollections" (1875), "Strange Stories from History" (1885), and several books for boys. Edited "American War Ballads and Lyrics" (1889).

ELIOT, Charles William, educator, b. Boston, Mass., 20 Mar., 1834. Graduated at Harvard, 1853. Became tutor in mathematics at that university, 1854, and was appointed assistant professor of mathematics and chemistry, 1858. Studied chemistry in Europe, 1863–5, and in 1865 accepted the professorship of chemistry at the Massachusetts institute of technology. Was made president of Harvard, 1869. During his administration the system of elective studies superseded that of prescribed courses in the university. Among the most notable of many addresses on public occasions and before learned societies, are those delivered at the inauguration of Daniel C. Gilman as president of Johns Hopkins university and at the Harvard $\Phi B K$ reunion of 1888.

ELIOT, John, "the apostle of the Indians," b. probably in Widford, Hertfordshire, England, where he was baptized on 5 Aug., 1604 (Ellsworth Eliot). Graduated at Cambridge university. Was subsequently an usher at the school kept by Rev. Thomas Hooker, near Chelmsford, Essex. Emigrated to New England to avoid religious persecution, arriving at Boston, 3 Nov., 1631. Preached there for a while in the absence of John Wilson, and on the latter's return was established "teacher" of the church at Roxbury, Thomas Welde being his colleague. Was concerned with Welde and Richard Mather in preparing the "Bay Psalm Book" (see MATHER, RICHARD). In 1646 made first serious efforts toward the conversion of the Indians, in which he took an active interest for the rest of his life, though retaining his position at Roxbury. Converts were collected from different Indian settlements at Natick, Mass., and a town of "praying Indians" established there in 1651. A church was formed in 1660. Eliot had begun the translation of the Bible into one of the Mohegan dialects as early as 1651, and the New Testament in Indian was printed at Cambridge, Mass., 1661. The Old Testament appeared in 1663. These were preceded and followed by numerous other translations. Various tracts describing the progress of Indian regeneration were published, portions of them being written by Eliot. Such were "The Clear Sun-shine of the Gospel Breaking Forth Upon the Indians" (1648), "The Light appearing more and more towards the perfect Day" (1651), etc. Of his own writings in English were published "The Christian Commonwealth" (1654), "The Communion of Churches" (1665), and "The Harmony of the Gospels" (1678). The settlements of converted Indians were much reduced during King Philip's war, and gradually disappeared after Eliot's death. Died, Roxbury, Mass., 20 May, 1690.

ELLIOTT, Maud [Howe], b. Boston, Mass., 9 Nov., 1855. Daughter of Julia Ward Howe. Early began writing for the press. Was married, 1887, to John Elliott, an English artist, their home being at Chicago, Ill. Author of "A Newport Aquarelle" (1883), "The San Rosario Ranch" (1884), "Atalanta in the South" (1886), and "Mammon" (1888).

ELLSWORTH, Erastus Wolcott, inventor, b. East Windsor, Conn., 27 Nov., 1822. Graduated at Amherst. Resided during youth in New York, and subsequently at East Windsor Hill, occupied partly with farming, but chiefly with his inventions, of which he patented a number in drawing-instruments and hydraulic and steam machinery. Author of a volume of "Poems" (1855), and an occasional contributor to the magazines.

ELLSWORTH, Oliver, jurist, b. Windsor, Conn., 29 April, 1745. Graduated at Princeton. Began the practice of law at Hartford, Conn., in 1771. Took an active part in the Revolutionary government of Connecticut, was elected to the Continental congress in 1783, and attended the Philadelphia constitutional convention of 1787. Was successively U. S. senator from Connecticut, 1789–95, and chief justice of the U. S. supreme court, 1796–1800. In 1800 he headed the commission which effected a convention with France. Died, Windsor, Conn., 26 Nov., 1807.

EMERSON, Ralph Waldo, modern Platonist, and chief of the Concord group, b. Boston, Mass., 25 May, 1803. His ancestors on the father's side, with one exception, were clergymen for six generations. He was also a descendant of the Rev. Peter Bulkley. His father was Rev. William Emerson, pastor of the First church at Boston. William Emerson founded the Boston Anthology club, which was organized in 1804 to conduct the "Monthly Anthology." The father dying in 1811, Ralph Waldo's education was supervised by his mother, a very superior woman. He was also much influenced by his father's sister, Miss Mary Moody Emerson, to some of whose writings those of her nephew bear a marked resemblance in style and thought. Emerson entered the Boston Latin school in 1813, and Harvard four years later. While at school he composed a number of pieces in verse, and excelled in his themes. At Harvard he continued his literary work and was chosen poet for class-day. Graduating in 1821, he became instructor at his older brother's school for young ladies in Boston. Afterward studied theology under Dr. Channing and as a special student at the Cambridge divinity school, and was "approbated to preach" by the Middlesex association of ministers in 1826. Was chosen colleague of Henry Ware, Jr., by the Second church of Boston, Mar., 1829, and soon after succeeded to the full pastorate. The connection lasted until 1832, when he resigned on account of scruples against administering the communion, although he continued always to preach at some church on Sundays until 1838, and thereafter occasionally as late as 1847. Visited Europe early in 1833, and became acquainted with Carlyle and other distinguished men of letters. Returning in the autumn, he delivered his first lectures at Boston. He lived in the "Old Manse" at Concord for a year, and in 1835 purchased the house in the same town which became his permanent home. Edited with a preface the first edition of Carlyle's "Sartor Resartus," 1836, and soon after with George Ripley and F. H. Hedge formed the society of Transcendentalists, which started "The Dial" in 1840. Succeeded Margaret Fuller as editor of that periodical two years later and conducted it until 1844, contributing some forty articles and poems. His volume "Nature" had appeared in 1836. His first collection of "Essays" was made in 1841. This and the succeeding prose volumes were chiefly composed of his lectures. They were "Essays" (1841), "Essays, Second Series" (1844), "Miscellanies" (1849), "Representative Men" (1850), "English Traits" (1856), "The Conduct of Life" (1860), "Society and Solitude" (1870), "Letters and Social Aims" (1875), and a posthumous volume, "Lectures and Biographical Sketches." "Poems" (1846) was followed by "May-Day, and Other Pieces" (1867), and collective editions of Mr. Emerson's poetry were published in 1876 and subsequently. He contributed to the "Memoirs of Margaret Fuller Ossoli" (1852), and edited "Parnassus" (1874), an anthology of his poetical favorites. Revisited Europe in 1847 and 1872, lecturing extensively in England during the former trip. In 1883 "The Correspondence of Thomas Carlyle and Ralph Waldo Emerson: 1834–1872" was published, and in 1887 the authoritative "Memoir" by J. E. Cabot. Died, Concord, Mass., 27 April, 1882.

EMMONS, Nathanael, divine, b. East Haddam, Conn., 1 May, 1745. Graduated at Yale. Was pastor of the Second church at Wrentham, Mass., from 1773 until 1827, when he retired from the pulpit. Published many sermons and articles in the religious periodicals. Assisted in founding the Massachusetts missionary society. Gained reputation as an able theologian of the Hopkinsian school. His "Works" (1842) were published in six volumes. Died, Franklin, Mass., 23 Sept., 1840.

ENGLISH, Thomas Dunn, physician, b. Philadelphia, Penn., 29 June, 1819. Graduated in medicine at the university of Pennsylvania, and was admitted to the bar, 1842, but was chiefly occupied with journalism and literature until 1859. He then established himself as a physician in New Jersey, and was a resident of Newark in 1890. Author of the popular ballad "Ben Bolt," of "Poems" (1855), "The Logan Grazier"

(poem), "American Ballads" (1882), and a number of novels and dramas.

EVANS, Nathaniel, clergyman, b. Philadelphia, Penn., 8 June, 1742. Graduated at the college of Philadelphia. Preached in Gloucester county, N. J., as a missionary of the British society for propagating the gospel in foreign parts, having previously been ordained in England by the Bishop of London. "Poems on Several Occasions" (1772) were collected and published by his friends after his death. Died, Gloucester Co., N. J., 29 Oct., 1767.

EVARTS, William Maxwell, statesman and lawyer, b. Boston, Mass., 6 Feb., 1818. Graduated at Yale. Entered the bar, 1841. Held public offices and won distinction in leading cases. Chairman of New York delegation in Republican national convention of 1860, and proposed Seward for president. Leading counsel for President Johnson when impeached, and for Henry Ward Beecher, 1875. Was counsel for the United States before the Geneva court of arbitration on the *Alabama* claims, 1872, and secretary of state in President Hayes's cabinet. Became U. S. senator from New York in 1885. Delivered orations at the Philadelphia Centennial of 1876, and at the unveiling of the Seward, Webster, and Liberty statues in New York city.

EVERETT, Alexander Hill, diplomatist, b. Boston, Mass., 19 Mar., 1792. Brother of Edward Everett. Graduated at Harvard. Soon entered the U. S. diplomatic service as secretary at St. Petersburg. Was afterward U. S. minister to the Netherlands and to Spain, and was appointed U. S. commissioner to China, 1845. Edited the "North American Review," 1829–34, and two volumes of "Critical and Miscellaneous Essays" (1845–6). Died, Macao, China, 28 June, 1847 (Appleton).

EVERETT, David, journalist, b. Princeton, Mass., 29 Mar., 1770 (Drake). Graduated at Dartmouth. Studied law and practised for some years. Contributed to Joseph Dennie's "Farmer's Museum," and in 1809 edited the Boston "Patriot." Published two volumes of selections from his writings and a drama. Died, Marietta, O., 21 Dec., 1813.

EVERETT, Edward, b. Dorchester, Mass., 11 April, 1794. Son of a Boston clergyman. Graduated at Harvard, where he remained as tutor for two years, delivering the $\Phi B K$ poem of 1812. Became pastor of the Brattle street Unitarian church at Boston, 1813. Was appointed professor of Greek at Harvard the following year, and studied four years in Europe to fit himself for the position, which he filled from 1819 to 1824. Edited the "North American Review" during the same period. Was U. S. representative from Massachusetts, 1825–35, and was for four years after governor of the state, being a Whig in politics. From 1841 to 1845 was U. S. minister to England, and succeeded Daniel Webster as secretary of state, 1852–3. In 1853 he became U. S. senator from Massachusetts, retiring in 1854 on account of ill health. Attention was called to his qualities as an orator by his $\Phi B K$ address at Harvard in 1824 on "Literature in America." Thereafter he was in constant demand as a public speaker, and delivered a long succession of orations, addresses, and eulogies. He raised, 1856–9, nearly $60,000 for the purchase of Mt. Vernon, by the repetition of his oration on Washington through the country, and received $10,000 more for the same purpose from the N. Y. "Ledger" for a series of articles. For other charities he obtained about $20,000 from the proceeds of various addresses. The unsuccessful candidate, for the presidency, of the party of compromise in 1860, he exerted himself in behalf of the Union during the civil war, and delivered the oration at the consecration of the national cemetery at Gettysburg, Nov., 1863. Four volumes of his "Orations and Speeches" (1850–68) were published. Died, Boston, Mass., 15 Jan., 1865.

FAUGERES, Margaretta V. [Bleecker], b. Tomhannock (sometimes written Tomhanick), near Albany, N. Y., 1771. Daughter of Ann Eliza Bleecker. Was married to Peter Faugeres, a New York physician, and lived with him in great poverty. After his death supported herself by teaching. Some of her poems are appended to her mother's "Posthumous Works" (1793), which she edited. Died, New York, N. Y., 9 Jan., 1801.

FAUNTLEROY, Virginia Peyton, b. Arcata, Cal., 18—. After 1881 resided at Santa Maria in the same state, where she engaged in teaching. A contributor of poetry to the magazines.

FAWCETT, Edgar, b. New York, N. Y., 26 May, 1847. Graduated at Columbia. With the exception of occasional visits to Europe, a constant resident of New York city, making his summer home at Rye, N. Y. An author by training and profession, and entirely devoted to literary work. The scenes of most of his novels are laid in his native city. Some of his many volumes of fiction are "Purple and Fine Linen" (1873), "A Hopeless Case" (1881), "The Adventures of a Widow" (1884), "Social Silhouettes" (1885), "The House at High Bridge" (1887), "Olivia Delaplaine" (1888), and "Solarion" (1889). Author of several plays, the most successful of which was "The False Friend" (produced, 1880). His volumes of poetry are "Short Poems for Short People" (1871), "Poems of Fantasy and Passion" (1878), "Song and Story" (1884), "The Buntling Ball" (1884), and "Romance and Revery" (1886). He also

brought out "Agnosticism, and Other Essays" (1889).

FAY, Theodore Sedgwick, diplomatist, b. New York, N. Y., 10 Feb., 1807. Studied law, but soon entered journalism. Was secretary of the American legation at Berlin, 1837–53, and U. S. minister to Switzerland until 1861. Afterward resided chiefly at Berlin. Published "Dreams and Reveries of a Quiet Man" (1832), "Norman Leslie" (1835), "Ulric, a Poetic Romance" (1851), and "Great Outlines of Geography" (1867).

FEARING, Lillien Blanche, b. Davenport, Ia., 1864. Graduated at the Iowa college for the blind. A continuous resident of Davenport. Author of "The Sleeping World, and Other Poems" (1887).

FELTON, Cornelius Conway, scholar, b. Newbury, Mass., 6 Nov., 1807. Graduated at Harvard, where he became Eliot professor of Greek literature in 1834, and president of the university in 1860. Contributed many papers to the magazines. Besides several Greek text-books and translations of German and French standard works, he was the author of "Familiar Letters from Europe" (1864) and "Greece, Ancient and Modern" (1867). Died, Chester, Penn., 26 Feb., 1862.

FENNER, Cornelius George, clergyman, b. Providence, R. I., 30 Dec., 1822. Graduated at Brown university, and became a Unitarian clergyman at Cincinnati, O. In 1846 appeared his "Poems of Many Moods." Died, Cincinnati, O., 4 Jan., 1847.

FERGUSON, Elizabeth [Graeme], b. near Philadelphia, Penn., 1739. Daughter of Thomas Graeme, a Philadelphia physician. Was married to a Scotch gentleman named Ferguson, from whom she was separated by the Revolution. Was afterward concerned in the British attempt to purchase Joseph Reed's influence with Washington, and was the recipient of Reed's memorable reply. Some of her verse is included in the "Poems" of Nathaniel Evans, and the manuscript of her metrical translation of Fénelon's "Telemaque" is preserved in Philadelphia. Died, near Philadelphia, Penn., 23 Feb., 1801.

FESSENDEN, Thomas Green, journalist, b. Walpole, N. H., 22 April, 1771. Graduated at Dartmouth. Studied law at Rutland, Vt. While a student, contributed several humorous poems to the Walpole "Farmer's Museum," among which was the popular "Country Lovers." Went to London in 1801 as agent for a hydraulic machine, and lost his property in this and in other investments. While there, published anonymously a poem, "Terrible Tractoration" (1803), satirizing the medical profession. It proved a success financially. Returned to America in 1804, and at New York edited for two years "The Weekly Inspector." He was editor of various journals in Vermont until 1822, when he founded "The New England Farmer" at Boston, and conducted it until his death. Some of his publications were "Original Poems" (1806), "Democracy Unveiled" (1806), and "Pills, Poetical, Political," etc. (1809). Died, Boston, Mass., 11 Nov., 1837.

Fessenden, William Pitt [*Noted Saying:* Vol. XI., page 455], b. Boscawen, N.H., 16 Oct., 1806. U. S. senator from Maine, 1854-69. Died, Portland, Me., 8 Sept., 1869.

FESTETITS, Kate [Neely], b. Warrenton, Va., 13 Mar., 1837. Graduated at a seminary in Washington, D. C. Was afterward engaged in editorial and literary work at New York city. Was married, 1871, to Carl A. Festetits. Removed to Washington in 1885. A writer for the magazines and author of a number of books for children.

FIELD, Eugene, journalist, b. St. Louis, Mo., 2 Sept., 1850. A portion of his early life was passed in Vermont and Massachusetts. Studied at the university of Missouri. From 1873 to 1883 was connected with various newspapers in Missouri and Colorado. Joined the staff of the Chicago "Daily News," 1883. Author of "Denver Tribune Primer" (1882), "Culture's Garland" (1887), "A Little Book of Western Verse" (1889), and "A Little Book of Profitable Tales" (1889).

FIELD, Henry Martyn, clergyman, b. Stockbridge, Mass., 3 April, 1822. Graduated at Williams. Preached at St. Louis, Mo., and West Springfield, Mass., until 1854, when he joined the staff of the N. Y. "Evangelist," of which journal he afterward became editor and proprietor. An extensive traveller. Among other works author of "A History of the Irish Rebellion of 1798" (1851), "Summer Pictures from Copenhagen to Venice" (1859), "From Egypt to Japan" (1878), "On the Desert" (1883), "Old Spain and New Spain" (1888), and "Bright Skies and Dark Shadows" (1890).

FIELD, Kate, journalist, b. St. Louis, Mo., 18—. Daughter of the late Joseph M. Field, the actor and dramatist. Received her early education in Massachusetts, and afterward studied music in Italy. Was for some years a European correspondent of the N. Y. "Tribune" and other newspapers. More recently delivered lectures through the United States on contemporaneous subjects. In 1889 established at Washington, D. C., "Kate Field's Washington," a weekly journal. Among her books are "Planchette's Diary" (1868), "Haphazard" (1873), and "Ten Days in Spain" (1875).

Field, Stephen Johnson [*Noted Saying:* Vol. XI., page 461], b. Haddam, Conn., 4 Nov., 1816. Brother of Henry M. Field. Appointed a justice of the supreme court of the United States by President Lincoln in 1863.

FIELDS, Annie [Adams], b. Boston, Mass., 1834. Daughter of Dr. Z. B. Adams. Educated at the school of George B. Emerson in Boston. Was married to James T. Fields and afterward lived at Boston and Manchester-by-the-Sea, Mass. Author of "Under the Olive," poems (1881), "How to Help the Poor" (1885), and "James T. Fields: Biographical Notes and Personal Sketches" (1882).

FIELDS, James Thomas, publisher, b. Portsmouth, N. H., 31 Dec., 1816. Educated at Portsmouth. While a clerk in a book-store at Boston, 1834, he wrote for the papers, and read his first poem before the Boston Mercantile library association, 1835. Became a partner in the publishing-house of Ticknor, Reed & Fields, 1838, retiring in 1870. Edited the "Atlantic Monthly," 1862-70. Visited Europe four times between 1851 and 1869. Had intimate relations with many eminent authors, which served him well as lecturer and writer. Published "Poems" (1849), "A Few Verses for a Few Friends" (1858), "Yesterdays with Authors" (1871), "Hawthorne" (1876), and "In and Out of Doors with Dickens" (1876). Died, Boston, Mass., 24 April, 1881.

FINCH, Francis Miles, jurist, b. Ithaca, N. Y., 9 June, 1827. Graduated at Yale. Practised law at Ithaca until 1881, when he was elected a member of the court of appeals of the state of New York. Author of a number of fugitive poems, of which "The Blue and the Gray" is the best known. It appeared in the "Atlantic Monthly" for 1867.

FINN, Henry J., actor, b. New York, N. Y., 1782 (Duyckinck). He had acted in minor parts at New York city, when he visited England in 1801. There he made successful appearances at the London Haymarket and elsewhere, returning to America ten years later. The remainder of his life he passed as manager and actor, chiefly at Boston. Published a series of "Comic Annuals." Perished in the burning of the steamboat *Lexington,* L. I. sound, 13 Jan., 1840.

FISHER, George Park, divine, b. Wrentham, Mass., 10 Aug., 1827. Graduated at Yale. Pursued his theological studies at home and in Germany. In 1854 was appointed professor of divinity at Yale, and in 1861 professor of ecclesiastical history. Some of his works are "Essays on the Supernatural Origin of Christianity" (1865), "History of the Reformation" (1873), "The Beginnings of Christianity" (1877), "Faith and Rationalism" (1879), "The Grounds of Theistic and Christian Belief" (1883), "History of the Christian Church" (1888), and "Nature and Method of Revelation" (1890).

FISKE, John, b. Hartford, Conn., 30

Mar., 1842. His name was originally Edmund Fiske Green, but in 1855 he assumed the name of his maternal great-grandfather. Resided at Middletown, Conn., as a boy, where he chiefly educated himself, and was far advanced in the study of languages and philosophy when he entered Harvard. After graduation he studied law and practised for a short time, but soon abandoned the profession. Early formed a decision to devote his life to the study of the origin and progress of the human race, particularly in relation to Christianity, evolution, and general history. His lectures and books were almost entirely along these lines. In 1869 and 1871 he discoursed on philosophy at Harvard, and from 1872 to 1879 was assistant librarian of the university, being elected one of its overseers the latter year. Lectures on American history, delivered at Boston in 1879, were repeated by invitation before university audiences in London and Edinburgh. Those delivered at the Concord school of philosophy, 1884–5, perhaps attracted the most attention, and were at once brought out in volumes with the titles, "The Destiny of Man, Viewed in the Light of his Origin" (1884), and "The Idea of God, as Affected by Modern Knowledge" (1885). His other works are "Tobacco and Alcohol" (1868), "Myths and Myth-Makers" (1872), "Outlines of Cosmic Philosophy, Based on the Doctrine of Evolution" (1874), "The Unseen World" (1876), "Darwinism, and Other Essays" (1879), "Excursions of an Evolutionist" (1883), "American Political Ideas" (1885), "The Critical Period of American History: 1783–1789" (1888), "The Beginnings of New England, or the Puritan Theocracy in its Relations to Civil and Religious Liberty" (1889), "The War of Independence," for young people (1889). "A History of the American People" has long been planned by this author. Joint editor with Gen. James Grant Wilson of Appletons' "Cyclopædia of American Biography" (1886–9).

FITZHUGH, George, lawyer, b. Prince William Co., Va., 2 July, 1807. Practised criminal law in his native state, and wrote for the press. Though connected by marriage with Gerrit Smith, and a friend of Harriet Beecher Stowe, was a vigorous defender of slavery. Wrote "Sociology for the South" (1854), and "Cannibals All! or, Slaves without Masters" (1857). Died, Huntsville, Tex., 30 July, 1881.

FLAGG, Wilson, naturalist, b. Beverly, Mass., 5 Nov., 1805. Gained reputation as a lecturer and a writer in the press on natural science and politics. Was in Boston customhouse, 1844–8, with which exception he adhered to lecturing. Among his books are "Studies in the Field and Forest" (1857), "Birds and Seasons of New England" (1875), and "A Year among the Trees" (1881). Died, Cambridge, Mass., 6 May, 1884.

Flanaghan, Webster [*Noted Saying:* Vol. XI., page 456], b. Cloverport, Ky., 9 Jan., 1832. At one time lieutenant-governor of Texas. A delegate from Texas to the Republican convention of 1880 at Chicago.

FLASH, Henry Lynden, b. Cincinnati, O., 20 Jan., 1835. Graduated at the Western military institute of Kentucky. Served in the Confederate army during the civil war. Was occupied with mercantile pursuits at New Orleans from 1866 to 1886, when he retired and removed to Los Angeles, Cal. Author of "Poems" (1860) and of several popular ballads of the civil war.

FLEMING, Maybury, journalist, b. Boston, Mass., 13 May, 1853. Graduated at the university of New York. Engaged in teaching for a few years, and in 1878 accepted an editorial position on the N. Y. "Mail and Express." A contributor of poetry to the magazines.

FLETCHER, Julia Constance, "George Fleming," b. Rio Janeiro, Brazil, 18–. Daughter of James C. Fletcher, who was U. S. consul at Naples, Italy, 1873–7. Her first novel, "Kismet" (1877), was the outcome of a journey up the Nile, made in 1876 with Thomas Gold Appleton and other friends. On her mother's marriage to Eugene Benson, the artist, Miss Fletcher remained with them at Rome. In 1886 she removed to Venice. She was at one time engaged to be married to the Earl of Lovelace, Lord Byron's grandson, but the engagement was broken off. Her other novels are "Mirage" (1878), "The Head of Medusa" (1880), "Vestigia" (1884), "Andromeda" (1885), and "The Truth about Clement Ker" (1889).

FLINT, Timothy, clergyman, b. North Reading, Mass., 11 July, 1780. Graduated at Harvard. Was pastor of a Congregational church at Lunenburg, 1802–14. From 1815 to 1825 he was a missionary and teacher in Ohio and the Mississippi valley. Edited for a time the Cincinnati "Western Review" and the N. Y. "Knickerbocker," but was afterward chiefly occupied with the writing of novels and of descriptive books relating to the South and West. The best known of these are "Francis Berrian" (1826) and "Recollections . . . of the Valley of the Mississippi" (1826). Died, Salem, Mass., 16 Aug., 1840.

FOLGER, Peter, colonist, b. probably in Norwich, England, about 1618. Emigrated to Watertown, Mass., in 1635. Afterward removed to Martha's Vineyard, where he assisted in teaching the Indians, and from there to Nantucket. Was the maternal grandfather of Benjamin Franklin, who speaks highly in his "Autobiography" of Folger's poem, "A Looking-Glass for the

Times, or the Former Spirit of New England revived in this Generation" (1675). Died, Nantucket, Mass., 1690.

FOLLEN, Charles Theodore Christian,educator,b. Romröd, Hesse Darmstadt, 4 Sept., 1796. Graduated at the university of Giessen. Became professor of civil law at Basle, but was driven away from Europe for revolutionary opinions, and came to America, 1824. Was professor of German at Harvard, 1830-4, and subsequently taught in various towns of Massachusetts. His "Works" (1841) were brought out posthumously. Perished in the burning of the steamboat *Lexington*, L. I. sound, 13 Jan., 1840.

FOOTE, Mary [Hallock], b. Milton, N. Y., 19 Nov., 1847. Was married, 1876, to Arthur D. Foote, a mining engineer, and afterward lived in the mining districts of California and Colorado. More recently removed to Boisé city, Idaho. Made many illustrations in black and white for books and magazines. Her drawings of Western and Mexican life and scenery are particularly successful. Author of the novels "The Led-Horse Claim" (1883), "John Bodewin's Testimony" (1886), and "The Last Assembly Ball" (1888).

FOSTER, Hannah [Webster], b. probably Boston, Mass., about 1759. The daughter of Grant Webster, a merchant of that city. Was married to the Rev. Dr. John Foster, who was minister of Brighton, Mass., from 1784 to 1827. After his death resided at Montreal, Canada. Published "The Coquette, or the History of Eliza Wharton" (1797), the earliest, or one of the earliest, of American novels. Died, Montreal, Canada, 17 April, 1840.

FOSTER, Stephen Collins, composer, b. Pittsburgh, Penn., 4 July, 1826. Began the study of vocal and instrumental music at an early age. Some of his most popular songs were composed before he was twenty years old. "Old Folks at Home" appeared about 1850. This has had a larger sale than any other American song. Foster wrote both the words and the music of his songs and ballads, of which there are about one hundred and twenty-five. His negro melodies formed nearly one-fourth of the whole number. Resided mainly in New York and Pittsburgh. Died, New York, N. Y., 13 Jan., 1864.

FRANCIS, John Wakefield, physician, b. New York, N. Y., 17 Nov., 1789. Graduated at Columbia. Began the practice of medicine at New York city, 1811. Professor of materia medica at the Columbia college of physicians and surgeons, 1813-26. Was a founder and member of various learned societies. Besides numerous professional writings, he published "Old New York" (1857) and "Reminiscences of S. L. Mitch-

ill" (1859). Died, New York, N. Y., 8 Feb., 1861.

FRANKLIN, Benjamin, statesman and philosopher, b. Boston, Mass., 17 Jan., 1706. The son of Josiah Franklin, a tallow-chandler and soap-boiler of that city, who had emigrated to New England in 1682 from Banbury, England. Benjamin's mother was the second wife of his father, and was the daughter of Peter Folger, author of "A Looking-Glass for the Times." Franklin was set at work in his father's establishment, when ten years old, but, proving restless, was soon after apprenticed to his brother James, a printer. He now devoted his spare time to reading and studying, and later on contributed anonymous articles to his brother's paper. In 1723 he decided to break this connection and ran away to Philadelphia, where he followed his trade for a short time and then visited England, returning in 1726. By 1729 he had established himself in the printing business at Philadelphia, and soon became editor and proprietor of the "Pennsylvania Gazette." Was instrumental in founding the Philadelphia library in 1731, and began the publication of "Poor Richard's" almanac the year after. Meanwhile, he became prominent in public affairs, and after filling several minor offices was made deputy postmaster-general for all the American colonies in 1753. The year before this, his discovery that lightning and the electric fluid are identical gained him great honor in Europe. At the Albany congress of 1754, just before the outbreak of the French and Indian war, Franklin proposed the plan of union for defence finally adopted by the congress, but rejected by the colonies. He was the agent of the Pennsylvania assembly in England from 1757 to 1762, and was sent again as the colony's agent to oppose the stamp-act in 1764, afterward undergoing the noted examination before the house of commons. Remained in England as the representative of Pennsylvania and several other colonies until 1775. After signing the Declaration of Independence, was appointed ambassador to France, in 1776, holding this position until 1785. Was principally concerned in procuring the treaty of 1778 with France, and with Jay and Adams conducted the negotiations for the treaty of 1783 with England. Returned to America in 1785, and was president of Pennsylvania from 1785 to 1788, also serving as a delegate to the Federal convention of 1787. His varied writings were collected and published by Jared Sparks as "The Works of Benjamin Franklin" (1840-50), and a subsequent and more complete collection has been edited by John Bigelow (1887-9). Died, Philadelphia, Penn., 17 April, 1790.

FREDERIC, Harold, journalist, b.

Utica, N. Y., 19 Aug., 1856. Joined the staff of the Utica "Herald," 1876, and became its editor in 1880. Was editor of the Albany "Evening Journal," 1882–4, and in 1884 accepted the position of London correspondent of the N. Y. "Times." Author of the novels "Seth's Brother's Wife" (1887), "The Lawton Girl" (1890), and "In the Valley" (1890).

FRÉMONT, John Charles, explorer, b. Savannah, Ga., 21 Jan., 1813. Graduated at Charleston college. Was successively civil engineer in the U. S. topographical survey corps, commander of the U. S. exploring party of 1842 in the Rocky mountains, discoverer of the Great Salt lake, soldier in Mexico, and governor of California, before his thirty-fourth year. Was the first and unsuccessful candidate for president of the Republican party in 1856. Served as major-general in the civil war, but was removed from command by President Lincoln for various reasons, among which was his issuing an unauthorized proclamation emancipating the slaves of belligerents. He was governor of Arizona, 1871–8. Besides reports of his expeditions, author of "Memoirs of my Life" (1886). Restored by President Harrison to the rank of major-general in the regular army, upon the retired list, April, 1890.

FRENCH, Alice, "Octave Thanet," b. Andover, Mass., 18—. Graduated at the Andover academy. Early removed with her father, Judge French, to Davenport, Ia., where she afterward lived, passing her winters at a plantation on the Black river, Arkansas. Author of "Knitters in the Sun," a volume of short stories (1887), "Expiation," a novel (1890), and a history of Arkansas.

FRENEAU, Philip, b. New York, N. Y., 2 Jan., 1752. Of Huguenot descent, and the son of a New York wine-merchant. Graduated at Princeton, and with H. H. Brackenridge delivered at commencement a poetical dialogue on "The Rising Glory of America," composed by both, or perhaps altogether by Freneau. In 1776 and 1780 he made mercantile voyages to the West Indies, was captured by the British during the second of these, and was put on board a prison-ship at New York. His experiences while a prisoner are detailed in "The British Prison-Ship, a Poem, in four Cantos" (1781). He had previously published "Voyage to Boston" (1774) and "General Gage's Confession" (1775). Many of his patriotic and satirical poems written during the Revolution appeared in the Philadelphia "Freeman's Journal." From the end of the Revolution until 1791 Freneau was chiefly engaged in sailing vessels for the West Indian trade. During the latter year he became editor of the "National Gazette"

of Philadelphia. He was occupied with this and with other editorial connections until about 1798, when he resumed a seafaring life, which lasted until the war of 1812. The remainder of his life was passed quietly at his home in New Jersey. He supervised the publication of several editions of his poems, among which are "The Poems of Philip Freneau, written chiefly during the late War" (1786), "Poems Written between the Years 1768 and 1794" (1795), "Poems Written and Published during the American Revolutionary War" (1809), and "A Collection of Poems on American Affairs" (1815). Of these, the edition of 1795 was printed by the author himself at his press in Monmouth, N. J. Died, near Freehold, N. J., 18 Dec., 1832.

FRISBIE, Levi, educator, b. Ipswich, Mass., 15 Sept., 1783 (Drake). Graduated at Harvard, where he was tutor and professor of Latin from 1805 until 1817. In the latter year was made professor of natural religion, moral philosophy, and civil polity. Soon after his early death, appeared "Miscellaneous Writings of Professor Frisbie" (1823). Died, Cambridge, Mass., 9 July, 1822.

FROTHINGHAM, Nathaniel Langdon, clergyman, b. Boston, Mass., 23 July, 1793. Graduated at Harvard. Pastor of the First Congregational (Unitarian) church at Boston from 1815 to 1850. Published "Sermons in the Order of a Twelvemonth" (1852), "Metrical Pieces" (1855), and about fifty separate sermons. Died, Boston, Mass., 3 April, 1870.

FROTHINGHAM, Octavius Brooks, clergyman, b. Boston, Mass., 26 Nov., 1822. Graduated at Harvard. A Unitarian preacher at Salem, Mass., Jersey city, and New York, until 1879, when he resigned his charge for a more strictly literary life. His position in religious matters was of the most advanced radical type. Published, among other works, "Stories from the Lips of the Teacher" (1863), "The Religion of Humanity" (1873), "Life of Theodore Parker" (1874), "Transcendentalism in New England" (1876), "The Cradle of the Christ" (1877), "Life of George Ripley" (1882), and numerous sermons.

FURNESS, Horace Howard, b. Philadelphia, Penn., 2 Nov., 1833. Always a resident of that city. Graduated at Harvard. Studied law and was admitted to the bar in 1859. Early devoted his attention to the study of Shakespeare, and in 1871 issued the first volume of a new Variorum Edition of the plays, containing the best criticisms that have been written and with notes by the editor. Seven volumes have been published, including "Romeo and Juliet" (1871), "Macbeth" (1873), "Hamlet" (1877), "King Lear" (1880), "Othello"

(1886), "The Merchant of Venice" (1888), and "As You Like It" (1890). His article on "Homœopathy" in the American "Encyclopædia Britannica" attracted much attention. Dr. Furness, as a member of the "Seybert commission for investigating modern spiritualism," made important contributions to the "Preliminary Report" (1887) of that body to the university of Pennsylvania.

GALLAGHER, William Davis, journalist, b. Philadelphia, Penn.,21 Aug.,1808. Edited various papers in Ohio, and was associate editor of the Cincinnati "Gazette," 1839–50. Afterward joined the Louisville "Courier." Published "Erato," a three-volume collection of poems (1835–7), and "Miami Woods, A Golden Wedding, and Other Poems" (1881).

GALLATIN, Albert, statesman, b. Geneva, Switzerland, 29 Jan., 1761. Graduated at the university of Geneva. Came to America, 1780, and engaged in trading through New England. Finally settled in Fayette county, Penn., 1784. Was elected to the U. S. senate, 1793, but was declared ineligible. Was U. S. representative from 1795 until 1801, in which year he was appointed secretary of the treasury by Jefferson, holding office until 1813. Signed the Ghent treaty with Great Britain in 1814, and was U.S. minister to France, 1815–23. Resided permanently in New York city after 1827, where he became president of various learned societies. He rose to be leader of the Republican-Democratic party, and as secretary of the treasury he was recognized as one of the leading financiers of his period. His publications, financial and otherwise, are to be found in "The Writings of Albert Gallatin" (1879), edited by Henry Adams. Died, Astoria, L. I., N. Y., 12 Aug., 1849.

GALLOWAY, Joseph, loyalist, b. near West River, Anne Arundel Co., Md., about 1730. Studied law and practised at Philadelphia. Was elected to the Pennsylvania assembly in 1757 and held office until 1774, with brief intervals of retirement. He was a member of the Continental congress in 1774, and attempted, unsuccessfully, to effect a compromise between Great Britain and the colonies. Two years later he joined the British forces, and was made superintendent of police at Philadelphia. Sailed for England in June, 1778, and did not return. His pamphlets and personal influence did much harm to the American cause. Died, Watford, Herts, England, 29 Aug., 1803.

GARDEN, Alexander, soldier, b. Charleston, S. C., 4 Dec., 1757. Studied at the university of Glasgow. After travelling in Europe, returned to America, 1780, and served in the Continental army as aide-de-camp to General Greene, and afterward as a lieutenant in Lee's legion. Published "An-ecdotes of the Revolutionary War in America" (1822). Died, Charleston, S. C., 29 Feb., 1829.

GARDINER, John Sylvester John, clergyman, b. Haverford West, So. Wales, June, 1765. Was pastor of an Episcopal parish near Beaufort, S. C., and was assistant rector and rector of Trinity church at Boston from 1792 until his death. For some years president of the Boston Anthology club and the editor of its "Review." Died, Harrowgate, England, 29 July, 1830.

GARFIELD, James Abram, twentieth president of the United States, b. Orange, O., 19 Nov., 1831. Graduated at Williams. Entered the Ohio state senate in 1859. Was appointed lieutenant-colonel of volunteers at the opening of the civil war, rising to the grade of major-general. At the request of President Lincoln he resigned from the army in December, 1863, to accept a seat in the U. S. house of representatives, to which he was continuously reëlected until 1880. In the latter year he was chosen U. S. senator from Ohio, and was nominated and elected president of the United States by the Republican party. Four months after his inauguration he was fatally shot by a disappointed office-seeker. In addition to his speeches in congress, he delivered numerous orations and addresses on public occasions. In 1882 appeared "The Works of James Abram Garfield, edited by Burke A. Hinsdale." Died, Elberon, N. J., 19 Sept., 1881.

GARRISON, Wendell Phillips, journalist, b. Cambridgeport, Mass., 4 June, 1840. Son of William Lloyd Garrison. Graduated at Harvard. Became literary editor of the N. Y. "Nation" at its commencement, 1865, and after 1866 resided at Orange, N. J. Besides contributing to the leading magazines, author and compiler of books on the management of children and joint author with his brother, F. J. Garrison, of "William Lloyd Garrison : the Story of his Life, told by his Children" (4 vols., 1885–9).

GARRISON, William Lloyd, journalist, b. Newburyport, Mass., 10 Dec., 1805. Learned the trade of a printer, and edited the Newburyport "Free Press," and other papers, until he became associate editor of the Baltimore "Genius of Universal Emancipation." Founded the "Liberator" at Boston in 1831, and conducted it until the close of the civil war. Was a stalwart abolitionist, preferring imprisonment in Maryland to paying fines for his then illegal denunciations of slavery. Was exposed to public odium, and threatened with violence, a reward having been set upon his head in Georgia. His share in founding the American anti-slavery society intensified this hostility, and even in Boston he was led through the streets by a furious mob, with a rope around his body, being finally rescued and put into jail for safety. In his advocacy of abolition he ignored party politics and repudiated the Constitution. At the breaking out of the war he urged its prosecution to the end, as the only way to stamp out slavery. When the victory was gained a sum of $30,000 was raised as an acknowledgment of his national services, and since his death a statue has been erected to his honor at Boston. His writings consisted chiefly of editorials, selections from which, with various notable speeches, are given in "William Lloyd Garrison: the Story of his Life, Told by his Children" (1885-9). Died, New York, N. Y., 24 May, 1879.

GAYARRÉ, Charles **Étienne Arthur**, historian, b. New Orleans, La., 9 Jan.,1805. Educated at the college of New Orleans. Was admitted to the bar in 1829, and was made presiding judge of the city court of New Orleans in 1833. Travelled in Europe from 1835 to 1844, and on returning was secretary of state of Louisiana, 1846–53. Sympathized with the secessionists in the civil war. More recently served as reporter of the Louisiana superior court. Devoted much labor to investigations into the history of his state, and published "Histoire de la Louisiane" (1847), "Romance of the History of Louisiana" (1848), "Louisiana, its Colonial History and Romance" (1851), "Louisiana, its History as a French Colony" (1852), "History of the Spanish Domination in Louisiana" (1854), these being revised and reissued in three volumes as the "History of Louisiana" (1866). Other works are "Fernando de Lemos," a novel (1872), with a sequel, "Albert Dubayet" (1882), two comedies—"The School for Politics" and "Dr. Bluff" (1854)—and addresses delivered on public occasions.

GEORGE, **Henry**, political economist, b. Philadelphia, Penn., 2 Sept., 1839. Began life as a sailor, and after 1858 resided in California, where he was occupied as a journalist for many years. His volume, "Progress and Poverty," setting forth his views as to land and its rent, was published in 1879, and at once drew attention. Successful lecture-tours in England and Scotland were followed by his nomination in 1886 by the United Labor party as candidate for mayor of New York city. Of three candidates he received the second highest number of votes. The same year he established the N. Y. "Standard," a weekly paper devoted to his principles. He has written "The Irish Land Question" (1881), "Social Problems" (1884), and "Protection or Free Trade" (1886).

GIBBONS, **James Sloan**, merchant, b. Wilmington, Del., 1 July, 1810. A member of the Quaker sect. Entered business at New York city in 1835. His song, "We are

Coming, Father Abra'am, Three Hundred Thousand More," was published in the N.Y. "Evening Post" of 16 July, 1862. At the time of the draft-riots of 1863 in New York, his house was sacked on account of his anti-slavery views. He was for a time one of the editors of the "Anti-Slavery Standard," and published two works on finance, "The Banks of New York" (1858) and "The Public Debt of the United States" (1867).

GIBSON, **William Hamilton**, painter, b. Sandy Hook, Conn., 5 Oct., 1850. Educated in Washington, Conn., and at the Brooklyn, N. Y., Polytechnic institute. Resided in New York city and Brooklyn after 1870. His art-studies were chiefly in the direction of landscape painting and botanical drawing. Was made a member of the N. Y. Water-color society in 1885, to whose exhibitions he began contributing in 1872. About the year 1879 turned his attention to descriptive writing, and afterward contributed to the magazines many articles on nature and out-door life, illustrated by his own drawings. These were collected in volumes as "Camp-Life in the Woods" (1876), "Tricks of Trapping and Trap-Making" (1876), "Pastoral Days, or Memories of a New England Year" (1881), "Highways and Byways" (1883), and "Happy Hunting-Grounds" (1887).

GIDDINGS, **Joshua Reed**, statesman, b. Athens, Penn., 6 Oct., 1795. Early removed to Ohio, and served in the war of 1812. Was U. S. representative from that state, 1838–59. On his first election, as a Whig, began his opposition to slavery, being an active supporter of John Quincy Adams. Opposed the compromise of 1850. Author of "Speeches" (1853) and "The Rebellion: its Authors and Causes" (1864). Died, Montreal, Canada, 27 May, 1864.

GILDER, **Richard Watson**, b. Bordentown, N. J., 8 Feb., 1844. Received his education chiefly at Bellevue seminary, Bordentown, a college established by his father, Rev. William H. Gilder. Served in Landis's Philadelphia battery through the emergency campaign of 1863, on the occasion of the Confederate invasion of Pennsylvania. Began the study of law at Philadelphia. This being interrupted by the death of his father, in 1864, he joined the staff of the Newark, N. J., "Daily Advertiser." Resigning in 1868, he founded the Newark "Morning Register," with Newton Crane as joint editor, and the following year became editor of "Hours at Home," a New York monthly journal. Upon the establishment of the "Century Magazine" (then "Scribner's Monthly") in 1870, "Hours at Home" was purchased by the former's proprietors, and Mr. Gilder was chosen associate editor of the magazine by its editor, Dr. J. G. Holland. On the death of the latter he succeeded to the editorship. His first volume of poems, "The New Day," appeared in 1875, and was followed by "The Celestial Passion" (1878) and "Lyrics" (1878). A collective edition of "Lyrics and Other Poems" was published in 1885.

GILES, Henry, clergyman, b. Co. Wexford, Ireland, 1 Nov., 1809. Was brought up a Catholic, but entered the Unitarian ministry, filling pastorates in England and Scotland. In 1840 came to the United States as a lecturer, and subsequently resided there. Author of "Illustrations of Genius" (1854) and "Lectures and Essays on Irish and Other Subjects" (1869). Died, Hyde Park, Mass., 10 July, 1882.

GILMAN, Arthur, b. Alton, Ill., 22 June, 1837. Established himself as a banker in New York city, 1857. From 1862 to 1871 was occupied as an educator in Lenox, Mass. Planned the educational institution known as "The Harvard Annex" in 1876, and was its executive officer from the beginning. Author of "First Steps in English Literature" (1870), "History of the American People" (1883), and editor of "The Story of the Nations Series," several volumes of which he wrote.

GILMAN, Caroline [Howard], b. Boston, Mass., 8 Oct., 1794. Daughter of Samuel Howard, a shipwright of that city. Was married, 1819, to Rev. Samuel Gilman, who was pastor of the Unitarian church at Charleston, S. C., from 1819 until his death in 1858. Mrs. Gilman remained at Charleston until 1870, when she removed to Cambridge, Mass. During the latter portion of her life she lived in the family of a daughter at Washington. She began to write poetry at the age of sixteen. The best known of her many works are "Recollections of a New England Housekeeper" (1835) and "Recollections of a Southern Matron" (1836). New editions were published in 1867. The contents of these volumes were taken from "The Rose," a magazine edited by her from 1830 to 1839. Died, Washington, D. C., 15 Sept., 1888.

GILMAN, Daniel Coit, educator, b. Norwich, Conn., 6 July, 1831. Graduated at Yale, continuing his studies in Germany. Was professor of physical geography at Yale from 1856 to 1870, accepting the presidency of the university of California, 1872. In 1875 he became first president of Johns Hopkins university. Delivered numerous addresses and orations before learned societies and at universities. These and articles contributed to magazines and reviews mainly dealt with his views on educational matters. Also published "Life of James Monroe" (1883).

GILMAN, Nicholas Paine, clergyman, b. Quincy, Ill., 21 Dec., 1849. Graduated at the Harvard divinity school. Was pastor of several Unitarian churches in eastern Massachusetts, 1872–84, and from 1875 to 1878 a professor in Antioch college. In 1888 assumed the editorship of the Boston "Literary World." A contributor to the magazines and author of "Profit-Sharing between Employer and Employee" (1889).

GILMORE, James Roberts, "Edmund Kirke," b. Boston, Mass., 10 Sept., 1823. Became a merchant in New York, but had retired at the beginning of the civil war, during the course of which he wrote a number of tales and sketches of Southern life, founded on its events and dealing with the race question. Engaged in business a second time until 1883, when he finally adopted a literary career, making his residence at Lake George, N. Y. His works include "Among the Pines" (1862), "Adrift in Dixie" (1863), "The Rear-Guard of the Revolution" (1886), and "John Sevier as a Commonwealth-Builder" (1887).

GILMORE, Patrick Sarsfield, musician, b. near Dublin, Ireland, 28 Dec., 1829. Devoted himself at an early age to the study of bands and band-music. Emigrating to Canada, he finally settled in Boston. In 1861 accompanied a Massachusetts regiment to the war as band-master. After the war resided at Boston and New York, in the former of which cities he managed the "Peace Jubilees" of 1869 and 1872. The composer of various songs and marches. "When Johnny Comes Marching Home" was published in 1863 under the pseudonym "Louis Lambert."

GODFREY, Thomas, b. Philadelphia, Penn., 4 Dec., 1736. Son of Thomas Godfrey, inventor of the quadrant. Received a common-school education and was apprenticed to the trade of a watchmaker. Abandoning his trade, he took the position of a factor or purchasing agent in North Carolina, where he resided for most of his brief remaining life. His poetical contributions to Philadelphia periodicals had gained him some reputation, and he published one long poem, "The Court of Fancy" (1762). Is chiefly remembered as the author of what was probably the first drama written in America, "The Prince of Parthia." It was offered to a dramatic company, but was not produced. "Juvenile Poems on Various Subjects, and Prince of Parthia" (1765) was issued posthumously. Died, near Wilmington, N. C., 3 Aug., 1763.

GODKIN, Edwin Lawrence, journalist, b. Moyne, Co. Wicklow, Ireland, 2 Oct., 1831. Graduated at Queen's college, Belfast. Was correspondent of the London "Daily News" in the Crimean war from 1854 to 1856. Came to America in the latter year, and was admitted to the bar in New York city, 1859, practising law for a few years until his health failed. He was American correspondent of the "Daily News," and a member of the N.Y. "Times" editorial staff from 1862 to 1865, when he assumed the editorship, and the year after became part proprietor, of the N. Y. "Nation." In 1881 the "Nation" was made the weekly edition of the N. Y. "Evening Post," and Mr. Godkin became joint editor and proprietor of the combined journals. Author of "History of Hungary" (1856) and "Government" (1871), besides contributions to the reviews and magazines.

GODWIN, Parke, editor, b. Paterson, N. J., 25 Feb., 1816. Graduated at Princeton. A member of the staff of the N. Y. "Evening Post" from 1837 to 1853. Married a daughter of William Cullen Bryant. Was editor of "Putnam's Monthly" for some years, and in 1865 again became Mr. Bryant's associate on the "Evening Post." Author of "Popular View of the Doctrines of Fourier" (1844), "Out of the Past," essays (1870), and "Cyclopædia of Biography" (1871). Edited with a memoir the final edition of Bryant's works, 1883-4.

GOODALE, Dora Read, b. Mount Washington, Berkshire Co., Mass., 29 Oct., 1866. (See GOODALE, ELAINE.)

GOODALE, Elaine, b. Mount Washington, Berkshire Co., Mass., 9 Oct., 1863. The Goodale sisters, daughters of Henry S. Goodale, received their education mainly from their mother, while residing at "Sky Farm," their father's estate at Mount Washington. They began the composition of verses while very young, and their poems were published in the magazines as early as 1877. Elaine Goodale, after some years' experience as teacher in Hampton institute, Va., became a government teacher at White river camp, lower Brulé agency, Dakota. Her services in this capacity and a number of able articles on Indians and their instruction led to her appointment in 1890 as superintendent of all Indian schools in South Dakota. Dora Read Goodale became a resident of Northampton, Mass., where she engaged in the study of art. The poems of the sisters have been published together in volumes as "Apple Blossoms : Verses of Two Children" (1878), "In Berkshire with the Wildflowers" (1879), "Verses from Sky Farm" (1880), and "All Round the Year" (1881).

Goodloe, William Cassius [*Noted Saying:* Vol. XI., page 460], b. Madison Co., Ky., 1841. At one time U. S. minister to Belgium. Was in 1888 the Kentucky member of the Republican national committee. Died, Lexington, Ky., 10 Nov., 1889.

GOODRICH, Samuel Griswold, "Peter Parley," publisher, b. Ridgefield, Conn., 19 Aug., 1793. Began as a publisher at Hartford, Conn. Travelled in Europe during 1824, and on his return removed his business to Boston. Issued there, 1828-42, "The Token," one of the "annuals" of that period. It embraced contributions from a number of young writers, whom Goodrich was fond of encouraging. Among other works the "Twice-told Tales" of Nathaniel Hawthorne first appeared in "The Token." Goodrich was the author or editor of about one hundred and seventy volumes, most of them edited under his pseudonym. They were largely compilations. Some of his original works were "The Outcast, and Other Poems" (1836), "Sketches from a Student's Window" (1841), and "Recollections of a Lifetime" (1857). Was at one time a member of the Massachusetts senate, and was U. S. consul to Paris during President Fillmore's administration. His last years were passed in New York city. Died, New York, N. Y., 9 May, 1860.

GOOKIN, Daniel, colonist, b. Kent, England, about 1612. Emigrated to Virginia in 1621, and removed to Boston, New England, in 1644, finally settling at Cambridge. Served as magistrate from 1652 to 1686, except in 1676. Was chosen in 1656 superintendent of all Indians subject to the colony of Massachusetts, and in 1681 was appointed major-general of the colony. Resisted, though unsuccessfully, the measures that ended in the loss of the Massachusetts charter in 1686. Was appointed one of the licensers of the printing press in Cambridge, 1662. "Historical Collections of the Indians in New England," written in 1674, was first published in the Massachusetts historical society's collections for 1792. Died, Cambridge, Mass., 19 Mar., 1687.

GORDON, Armistead Churchill, lawyer, b. Albemarle Co., Va., 20 Dec., 1855. Educated at the university of Virginia. Studied law and entered on the practice of his profession at Staunton, Va. Joint author with T. N. Page of "Befo' de War : Echoes in Negro Dialect" (1888), and a contributor of verse and fiction to the magazines.

GOTTHEIL, Gustav, clergyman, b. Pinne, Prussia, 28 May, 1827. Studied at the university of Berlin. Was rabbi of Reform Jewish churches at Berlin and at Manchester, England, and was called to the Temple Emmanuel in New York city, 1873. A contributor of numerous articles to the periodicals. "Hymns and Authors" appeared in 1887.

GOULD, Hannah Flagg, b. Lancaster, Mass., 3 Sept., 1789. The daughter of a Revolutionary soldier, with whom she early removed to Newburyport, Mass., remaining there until her death. Several editions of her "Poems" were published, one in three volumes in 1836. Died, Newburyport, Mass., 5 Sept., 1865.

GRADY, Henry Woodfen, journalist,

b. Athens, Ga., 17 May, 1851. Graduated at the university of Georgia. Edited several local papers in Georgia and was for a few years a member of the N.Y. "Herald" staff. In 1880 purchased an interest in the Atlanta, Ga., "Constitution," and became a leading writer for that paper. Gained reputation as an orator by his speech on "The New South" at the New England society's dinner in New York city, 1886, and thereafter until his death spoke and wrote much on the same topic. "Life of Henry W. Grady" appeared in 1890, and contains a number of his speeches. Died, Atlanta, Ga., 23 Dec., 1889.

GRANT, Robert, lawyer, b. Boston, Mass., 24 Jan., 1852. Graduated at Harvard. Studied for the law and entered practice at Boston. Some of his books are " The Little Tin Gods on Wheels " (1879), " The Confessions of a Frivolous Girl " (1880), and " The Knave of Hearts " (1886).

GRANT, Ulysses S., soldier, and eighteenth president of the United States, b. Point Pleasant, Clermont Co., O., 27 April, 1822. Appointed to a West Point cadetship, 1839. Graduated, 1843. A second lieutenant in 1845, he joined the army in Texas, where he had several commands, distinguishing himself in the Mexican war. Was a captain in 1853, after hard service in California and Panama. Resigned, 1854, and took a farm near St. Louis until 1860, then became clerk in his father's hardware store, Galena, Ill. Was appointed colonel of an Illinois regiment, 1861, and later major-general of volunteers. Made a gallant capture of guns and prisoners at Columbus, on the Mississippi, afterward winning most substantial victories by taking Forts Henry and Donelson. For over-zeal was relieved of command from February to March, 1862, when he was reinstated, and met the enemy at Shiloh. After this was second in command under Halleck. Captured Vicksburg, 4 July, 1863, receiving a gold medal from congress and the rank of major-general in the regular army. Was given the supreme command, Mar., 1864. Received Lee's surrender at Appomattox, 9 April, 1865. Was elected president of the United States, 1868, and again in 1872. Made a tour of the world in 1877, being received with enthusiasm by sovereigns and peoples everywhere. In 1884 lost his fortune through the fraudulent management of a banking firm in which he was partner. To provide for his family he wrote his "Memoirs" during the fatal and rapid progress of a cancer at the root of his tongue. The book brought nearly half a million of dollars to his widow—the greatest success a single work has ever had. Died, Mt. McGregor, near Saratoga, N. Y., 23 July, 1885.

GRAY, David, journalist, b. Edin-

burgh, Scotland, 8 Nov., 1836. Came to America, 1849. In 1856 joined the staff of the Buffalo, N. Y., "Courier," of which he was editor, 1876–82, resigning on account of ill-health. "Letters, Poems, and Selected Prose Writings of David Gray" (1888) was edited posthumously by J. N. Larned. Died, Binghamton, N. Y., 17 Mar., 1888.

GRAYDON, Alexander, b. Bristol, Penn., 10 April, 1752. Received his education in Philadelphia. Was appointed a captain in the Revolutionary army in 1775, was soon taken prisoner, and remained in confinement or at liberty on parole until 1778, when he was exchanged. He did not return to the army, but resided subsequently at and near Harrisburg, Penn., having being appointed prothonotary of Dauphin county. Contributed to the periodicals of his time and published "Memoirs of a Life Chiefly Passed in Pennsylvania" (1811). Died, Philadelphia, Penn., 2 May, 1818.

GREELEY, Horace, journalist, b. Amherst, N. H., 3 Feb., 1811. Third son of a poor farmer. At fourteen was apprenticed to the publisher of the "Northern Spectator," Poultney, Vt., receiving board, lodging, and $40 per annum. The paper failing in 1830, he worked for a while at Erie, Penn., and then made his way to New York city, arriving with all his worldly goods in a handkerchief-bundle, Aug., 1831. After working in newspaper offices, he tried, 1833, to own a printing-office, and with Jonas Winchester started "The New Yorker," in 1834, which lasted several years, a literary success but a pecuniary failure. James G. Bennett offered him a share in starting the N. Y. "Herald," which was declined. Edited "The Jeffersonian" at Albany for W. H. Seward and Thurlow Weed as a campaign paper, 1838–9 ; also, on his own account, "The Log Cabin," which was a success, and gave him position. Established "The Tribune" on General Harrison's election, beginning 10 April, 1841. Henry J. Raymond was chief assistant until 1843. In 1847 Charles A. Dana became managing editor. George William Curtis, Margaret Fuller, and Bayard Taylor were also on the staff. Gained much popularity as a lecturer, and was a life-long apostle of various reforms. Was elected to the U. S. house of representatives in 1848, and exposed the abuses of mileage allowances by which members profited dishonestly. Was delegate-at-large to the convention for revising the state constitution, 1867. Advocated the abolition of slavery before and during the civil war. At the close of the war boldly urged a general amnesty, and civil rights for the negro. Signed the bond as one of Jefferson Davis's bail, at loss of considerable popularity, and injured the large sale of

"The American Conflict" (1864–6). Was nominated for the presidency by Republicans dissatisfied with Grant's renomination. The action of the Democrats in also formally nominating Greeley chilled much of the sentiment in his favor. Went on a tour through the country speaking in his own behalf, but lost the election, and, ill with over-effort, and with the strain of his wife's illness and death, broke down, and soon followed her to the grave. Published several books and essays between "Hints toward Reforms" (1850) and "Recollections of a Busy Life" (1868), but is mainly eminent as the founder of the N. Y. "Tribune" and its chief for thirty-one years. Died, Pleasantville, Westchester Co., N. Y., 29 Nov., 1872.

GREELY, Adolphus Washington, explorer, b. Newburyport, Mass., 27 Mar., 1844. Joined the 19th Massachusetts regiment at the outbreak of the civil war, and in Mar., 1865, was made brevet major of volunteers. Became a 1st lieutenant in the regular army, 1873. Headed the *Proteus* Arctic expedition of 1881, remaining in the polar regions until June, 1884, when the seven survivors of that party were finally rescued. In 1887 succeeded to the command of the signal-service with the rank of brigadier-general. Author of "Three Years of Arctic Service" (1886).

GREEN, Joseph, merchant, b. Boston, Mass., 1706. Graduated at Harvard. Commenced business as a distiller in his native place, and gained a large competence later in life. Was noted as a wit and poet, particularly in connection with Mather Byles, whose rival he was. His parody of Byles's "Hymn written during a voyage" is very neatly done, Byles's reply being vulgar and unfit to print. Originally a member of the American party, he satirized the addresses of Governor Belcher and lampooned the British government in various ways. In 1776, however, he was proscribed and exiled for adherence to the crown. "Poems and Satires" appeared in 1780. Died, London, England, 11 Dec., 1780.

GREENE, Albert Gorton, lawyer, b. Providence, R. I., 10 Feb., 1802. Graduated at Brown. Practised law at Providence. Was clerk of the municipal court for twenty-five years, and its judge, 1858–67. Began the Harris collection of American poetry, now in Brown university. Among his fugitive poems the best-known are "The Baron's Last Banquet," "Old Grimes," and "The Militia Muster." Died, Cleveland, O., 4 Jan., 1868.

GREENE, George Washington, b. East Greenwich, R. I., 8 April, 1811. Studied at Brown university. Was U. S. consul at Rome, 1837–45, and professor of modern languages at Brown, 1848–52. Elected to the R. I. legislature, 1865. Became professor of American history at Cornell, 1872. Author of "Biographical Studies" (1860), "Historical View of the American Revolution" (1865), and "Life of Gen. Nathanael Greene," his grandfather (1867–71). Died, East Greenwich, R. I., 2 Feb., 1883.

GREENE, Homer, b. Ariel, Penn., 10 Jan., 1853. Graduated at Union college. A resident of Honesdale, Penn., and there occupied with law and civil engineering. Author of "The Blind Brother" (1887) and "Burnham Breaker" (1887), novels, and of numerous poems. Among the latter is "What my Lover Said."

GREENE, Sarah Pratt [McLean], b. Simsbury, Conn., 3 July, 1858. Studied at South Hadley seminary. Her experiences while teaching a country school near Plymouth, Mass., are related in "Cape Cod Folks" (1881), which involved her in lawsuits with some of the characters described. Was married, 1887, to Franklin Lynde Greene of Frémont, O. Other books are "Towhead : the Story of a Girl" (1884) and "Lastchance Junction, Far, Far West : a Novel" (1889).

GREEY, Edward, merchant, b. Sandwich, Kent, England, 1 Dec., 1835. Received a military education and was made captain in the English army, 1860. Saw service in China, and was for several years attaché of the British legation in Japan. Established himself as a merchant at New York city, 1868. Author of several plays and of books dealing with Japanese life and history. Among the latter are "The Wonderful City of Tokio" (1882) and "The Golden Lotus" (1883). Also a translator of Japanese novels. Died, New York, N. Y., 1 Oct., 1888.

GRISWOLD, Rufus Wilmot, b. Benson, Vt., 15 Feb., 1815. Before he was twenty had managed to see much of his own land and of Europe. Entered the Baptist ministry and received the degree of D.D. After a short pulpit career gave it up for journalism. Assisted Horace Greeley in "The New Yorker," and was editor of "Graham's Magazine," 1842–3. Edited the "International Magazine," 1852, these connections bringing him into personal relations with a number of rising authors. Published his first book, "Poems," in 1841, and the better known "Poets and Poetry of America" in 1842. In 1849 he became Edgar Allan Poe's literary executor, at the poet's own request, and brought out a collection in three volumes of Poe's tales, essays, and poems (1850). It was prefaced by a striking obituary article on Poe, originally written off-hand for the N. Y. "Tribune," and by a memoir which excited so much controversy that it has been omitted from recent editions. Griswold's other productions include "Christian Ballads"

(1844), "Prose Writers of America" (1846), "Female Poets of America" (1848), "Poets and Poetry of England" (1845), and "Sacred Poets of England and America" (1849). Died, New York, N. Y., 27 Aug., 1857.

GUERNSEY, Clara Florida, b. Pittsford, Monroe Co., N. Y., 1 Oct., 1839. Studied at the Troy, N. Y., female seminary. A resident of Rochester from childhood. Took an active interest in missions and in the affairs of the Seneca nation of Indians. Author of numerous books for children, and a contributor to the leading magazines.

GUINEY, Louise Imogen, b. Boston, Mass., 7 Jan., 1861. Daughter of Gen. Patrick R. Guiney, killed during the civil war while serving in the Union army. She graduated at Elmhurst academy, Providence, R. I., and afterward lived in Boston and vicinity, occasionally visiting Europe. Author of "Songs at the Start" (1884), "Goose-Quill Papers" (1885), "The White Sail, and Other Poems" (1887), and "Brownies and Bogies" (1888).

GYLES, John, soldier. Was taken captive by the Indians at Pemaquid, Me., in August, 1689, when about twelve years old. Remained among the French and Indians until 1698, when he was returned to New England and entered the military service of Massachusetts. Was still in service when he brought out his "Memoirs of Odd Adventures, Strange Deliverances, etc., in the Captivity of John Gyles, Esq., Commander of the Garrison on St. George's River" (1736).

HADLEY, James, philologist, b. Fairfield, Herkimer Co., N. Y., 30 March, 1821. Educated at Fairfield academy. Graduated at Yale. Was professor of Greek at Yale from 1851 until his death, and also lecturer on civil law. One of the American committee of revisers of the New Testament, and a member of various learned bodies. Author of a "Greek Grammar for Schools and Colleges" (1860), "Brief History of the English Language" for Webster's Dictionary (1864), "Elements of the Greek Language" (1869), and there were brought out posthumously "Twelve Lectures on Roman Law" (1873) and "Essays Philological and Critical" (1873). Died, New Haven, Conn., 14 Nov., 1872.

HALE, Edward Everett, clergyman, b. Boston, Mass., 3 April, 1822. Graduated at Harvard. Entered the ministry and was successively pastor of Unitarian churches in Worcester and Boston, Mass. Began literary work at an early age in the office of the Boston "Advertiser." Founded in 1869 "Old and New," which was subsequently merged into "Scribner's Monthly." Always identified with humanitarian projects, and created through the medium of his book, "Ten Times One is Ten" (1870), clubs devoted to charitable objects, comprising a membership of

fifty thousand in all parts of the world. A prominent figure in the "Chautauqua" literary society, and an extensive writer for its publications. Published in the "Atlantic Monthly" for Dec., 1863, "The Man Without a Country," a story which purported to be written by an officer of the navy, and which gained wide popularity, giving a strong impulse to national feeling at the North. Some of Dr. Hale's books are "The Rosary" (1848), "Kansas and Nebraska" (1854), "If, Yes, and Perhaps" (1868), "Puritan Politics in England and New England" (1869), "His Level Best, and Other Stories" (1870), "In His Name" (1874), "Workingmen's Homes, Essays and Stories" (1874), "Philip Nolan's Friends" (1876), "The Bible and its Revision" (1879), "Franklin in France" (1887), and a "Life of Washington" (1887), besides important contributions to Justin Winsor's "Memorial History of Boston" and "Narrative and Critical History of America." A journal with the title "Lend a Hand; a Record of Progress and Journal of Organized Charity" was founded by Dr. Hale in 1886.

Hale, Nathan [*Noted Saying :* Vol. XI., page 447], b. Coventry, Conn., 6 June, 1755. Served as a captain in the Continental army. Was hung as a spy by the British, New York, N. Y., 22 Sept., 1776.

HALE, Sarah Josepha [Buell], b. Newport, N. H., 24 Oct., 1788 (Horatio Hale). Was married, 1813, to David Hale, a lawyer. On his death in 1822, devoted herself to literature, and edited at Boston the "Ladies' Magazine," 1828–37. This was combined with "Godey's Lady's Book," which she edited until 1877. Resided at Philadelphia after 1841. Was an early advocate of higher education for women. Besides several novels and volumes of poems, published "Woman's Record" (1853). Died, Philadelphia, Penn., 30 April, 1879.

HALL, James, b. Philadelphia, Penn., 19 Aug., 1793. Served in the war of 1812, and afterward practised law at Shawneetown, Ill., where he became judge of the circuit court. Removing to Cincinnati in 1833, he engaged in banking until his death. Edited the "Western Monthly Magazine," and published several books on Western history, among them "Sketches of the West" (1835) and "The Romance of Western History" (1857). Died, near Cincinnati, O., 5 July, 1868.

HALLECK, Fitz-Greene, accountant, b. Guilford, Conn., 8 July, 1790. A descendant of John Eliot. Received his education at the schools of his native place, and from 1805 to 1811 was clerk in the shop of a relative. Removed to New York city, 1811, and obtained a clerical position in the banking-house of Jacob Barker, by whom he was employed for twenty years. In 1832 entered the service of John Jacob Astor as book-keeper, remaining with him until the latter's death in 1849. The rest of his life was passed quietly at Guilford. His reputation as a poet dated from the publication of the "Croaker" papers, a series of poetical satires on public characters of the period, contributed by Rodman Drake and himself to the N. Y. "Evening Post " in 1819. Their well-known friendship had begun seven years before. In the autumn of the same year Halleck's poem "Fanny" appeared, and met with success. "Marco Bozzaris" was first published, 1825, in the N. Y. "Review," edited by William Cullen Bryant. The first volume of Halleck's poems was brought out in 1827 with the title "Alnwick Castle, with Other Poems." After that year he wrote but little. His "Poetical Writings " (1869) were edited by Gen. James Grant Wilson, who is also the author of "The Life and Letters of Fitz-Greene Halleck" (1869). Died, Guilford, Conn., 19 Nov., 1867.

HALPINE, Charles Graham, "Miles O'Reilly," b. Oldcastle, County Meath, Ireland, 20 Nov., 1829. Graduated at the university of Dublin. Emigrated to America, and formed editorial connections with newspapers in Boston and New York. Entered the U. S. army at the opening of the civil war, and rose to the rank of brigadier-general of volunteers, resigning in 1864, and devoting himself again to journalism. Humorous sketches of army life, and satirical poems purporting to be written by an Irish private, were contributed by Halpine to the N. Y. "Herald " and other papers, and were afterward published as "Life and Adventures, Songs, etc., of Private Miles O'Reilly" (1864) and "Baked Meats of the Funeral " (1866). In 1869 appeared "The Poetical Works of Charles G. Halpine." Died, New York, N. Y., 3 Aug., 1868.

HALSTEAD, Murat, journalist, b. Paddy's Run, Butler Co., O., 2 Sept., 1829. Graduated at Farmer's college, Ohio. Was connected with various newspapers in Cincinnati until he joined the "Commercial," now the "Commercial-Gazette," of that city in 1853, of which he became proprietor and editor-in-chief in 1867. Delivered several addresses on public occasions.

HAMILTON, Alexander, statesman, b. Island of Nevis, West Indies, 11 Jan., 1757. Supposed to have been the son of a Scottish merchant of Nevis. This gentleman having become a bankrupt, the youth entered the West India office of Nicholas Cruger, a N.Y. merchant. Hamilton had already received some schooling, and, his abilities being recognized, he was in 1772 sent to Boston for education. Studied at Elizabeth, N. J., and entered Kings, now Columbia, college, 1773. During 1774-5, a speech at a public meeting, and several pamphlets advocating

the cause of the colonies, brought him while yet a student into public notice. Was appointed captain of artillery, Mar., 1776, and a year later became aide-de-camp to Washington. This position he resigned early in 1781. Later in the year he received a command in the army, and performed valuable services at the capture of Yorktown. After that event he returned to New York, and was chiefly occupied with the study and practice of law, until the agitation for a constitution commenced. Was a delegate to the convention at Annapolis in 1786, and to the Philadelphia convention of 1787. Contributed more than half the papers which compose "The Federalist " and in other ways was instrumental in obtaining the consent of New York state to the Constitution. Was first secretary of the treasury under Washington from 1789 to 1795, during which period he planned and carried out the organization of the U. S. financial system. At the same time took an active interest in other public affairs, contributing political articles to the press. In 1798, on the threatened outbreak of war with France, was appointed second in command of the U. S. army under Washington, succeeding to the chief command on the latter's death. Was fatally wounded in a duel with Aaron Burr, the result of a political quarrel. His "Works" were edited by his son in 1850. A more complete edition was brought out by H. C. Lodge in 1875. Died, New York, N. Y., 12 July, 1804.

HAMMOND, James Henry, statesman, b. Newberry, S. C., 15 Nov., 1807. Graduated at South Carolina college. Was U. S. representative from South Carolina, 1835-6, governor, 1842-4, and U. S. senator from 1857 until his state seceded in 1860. Published pamphlets and articles in the Southern interest, and to promote practical progress. Died, Beech Island, Aiken Co., S. C., 13 Nov., 1864.

HAMMOND, John, colonist. It is only known of him that he emigrated to Virginia from England in 1635, residing there nineteen years and in Maryland two years. He was then obliged by local disturbances to leave the colonies and return to England, where he published "Leah and Rachel, or the Two Fruitfull Sisters Virginia and Mary-land : Their Present Condition, Impartially stated and related " (1656).

HARBAUGH, Thomas Chalmers, b. Middletown, Md., 13 Jan., 1849. Was brought as a child to Casstown, O., where he afterward resided. Followed the occupation of a literary journalist, contributing both prose and verse to the periodicals. Often recited poems on occasions. Author of "Maple Leaves," poems (1883).

HARDY, Arthur Sherburne, educator, b. Andover, Mass., 13 Aug., 1847. Passed one year at Amherst college, going thence to West Point, where he graduated. Was 2d lieutenant in the 3d artillery regiment, U. S. A., 1869–70, resigning to become professor of civil engineering and applied mathematics at Iowa college. During 1873–4 he was a student at the Paris École des ponts et chaussées, and in 1874 accepted the professorship of civil engineering at the Chandler scientific school of Dartmouth college. Four years later he was made professor of mathematics at Dartmouth. Author of "Francesca of Rimini," a poem (1878), "Elements of Quaternions" (1881), "But yet a Woman," novel (1883), "New Methods in Topographical Surveying" (1884), "The Wind of Destiny," novel (1886), and "Passe Rose," novel (1889). Also translated from the French, with notes, Argand's "Imaginary Quantities" (1881).

HARLAND, Henry, "Sidney Luska," b. New York, N. Y., 1 Mar., 1861. Studied at the college of New York and at Harvard. Resided at Rome and London for some time, and wrote letters of travel from both places to American journals. From 1883 to 1886 held a position in the surrogate's office at New York city, resigning in the latter year to devote himself to literature. Author of "As it was Written" (1885), "Mrs. Peixada" (1886), "The Yoke of the Thorah" (1887), "My Uncle Florimond" (1888), "Grandison Mather" (1889), "A Latin-Quarter Courtship, and Other Stories" (1889), "Two Voices" (1890), and "Two Women or One" (1890).

HARNEY, William Wallace, journalist, b. Bloomington, Ind., 20 June, 1831. Studied at Louisville college, Ky. Was professor of English and the classics at the Kentucky normal school for several years. Joined the staff of the Louisville "Democrat," 1859, and succeeded his father as editor-in-chief, 1869. The same year removed to Florida, where he engaged in orange-culture. His numerous poems and articles appeared chiefly in periodicals.

HARPER, Robert Goodloe, lawyer, b. near Fredericksburg, Va., 1765. Graduated at the college of New Jersey. Studied law at Charleston, S.C. Practised until 1794, when he became U. S. representative from South Carolina, serving until 1801. Was U. S. senator from Maryland, 1815–16. While in congress, as a leading Federalist, supported the administration of Washington. His "Select Works" appeared in 1814. Died, Baltimore, Md., 15 Jan., 1825.

HARRIS, Joel Chandler, journalist, b. Eatonton, Ga., 9 Dec., 1848. Was apprenticed at the age of fourteen to the publisher of the "Countryman," a small weekly paper of central Georgia. There he learned the trade of a printer, and contributed to the "Countryman" his first literary efforts. After the war went to New Orleans as private secretary of the editor of the "Crescent Monthly," and subsequently was editor of the Forsyth, Ga., "Advertiser." From 1871 to 1876 he was a member of the staff of the Savannah "Daily News," accepting an editorial position on the Atlanta "Constitution" in the latter year. For this paper he wrote the material contained in his volume of negro folk-lore entitled "Uncle Remus: his Songs and his Sayings" (1880). This book met with immediate success, and was followed by "Mingo, and Other Sketches" (1883), "Nights with Uncle Remus" (1884), "Free Joe, and Other Georgian Sketches" (1888), "Daddy Jake the Runaway, and Short Stories told after Dark" (1889). In 1890 Mr. Harris succeeded to Henry W. Grady's editorial chair on the "Constitution." Much of that paper's reputation as a champion of the "New South" was due to the former's contributions.

HARRIS, Miriam [Coles], b. Dosoris Island, L. I. Sound, N. Y., 7 July, 1834. Studied at St. Mary's hall, Burlington, N. J. Was married, 1864, to Sidney Harris, and afterward lived at New York city. Some of her novels are "Rutledge" (1860), "Louie's Last Term at St. Mary's" (1863), "Frank Warrington" (1871), and "A Perfect Adonis" (1875).

HARRIS, Thaddeus Mason, clergyman, b. Charlestown, Mass., 17 July, 1768. Graduated at Harvard. After being librarian of Harvard for two years, was made pastor of the first Unitarian church [at Dorchester, Mass., retaining the connection until his death. The author of several published sermons and discourses. Died, Boston, Mass., 3 April, 1842.

HARRIS, William Torrey, educator, b. North Killingly, Conn., 10 Sept., 1835. Studied at Phillips academy, Andover, Mass., and at Yale, afterward receiving the degree of M.A. from the latter institution. Removing to St. Louis, Mo., he was a teacher in that city from 1858 to 1867, when he became its superintendent of schools. His thirteen annual school reports, 1868–80, gained him wide reputation as an educator, and brought him the honorary titles of "Officer of the Academy" and "Officer of Public Instruction" from the French government. He founded "The Journal of Speculative Philosophy," 1867, of which in 1890 he had edited, with numerous contributions of his own, twenty-one volumes. Was assistant editor of "Johnson's Encyclopædia," writing forty articles in the department of philosophy and psychology. In 1880 Dr. Harris resigned his position as superintendent and removed to Concord, Mass., where with Mr. Amos Bronson Alcott he was active in founding the Concord school of philosophy, and was one of the most frequent lecturers at its sessions. Was connected with the American social science association for fifteen years, writing many papers for the annual meetings. A constant contributor of articles on philosophy, education, and art to " The North American Review," " The Forum," " Journal of Social Science," " The Western," and other leading reviews. He was the representative of the U. S. bureau of education at the Brussels international congress of educators, 1880, and in 1889 was appointed by President Harrison U. S. commissioner of education. Author of " Introduction to the Study of Philosophy" (1889) and " The Spiritual Sense of Dante's ' Divina Commedia ' " (1890).

HARRISON, Benjamin, twenty-third president of the United States, b. North Bend, O., 20 Aug., 1833. A grandson of President William Henry Harrison. Graduated at Miami university. Studied for the law, beginning practice at Indianapolis, Ind., 1854, and afterward making that city his home. Served through the civil war in the Union army, becoming brevet brigadier-general of volunteers. Was elected U. S. senator from Indiana, 1880, and nine years later was inaugurated president of the United States.

HARTE, Francis Bret, b. Albany, N. Y., 25 Aug., 1839. The son of a professor in the Albany female academy. The latter dying during his son's childhood, Bret Harte received only a common-school education, and at the age of seventeen removed to California with his mother. He taught school at Sonora in that state, and this venture failing, successively worked as a miner, a printer's apprentice, and as an express messenger and agent in various mountain towns, gaining the impressions of Western life afterward made use of in his literary work. Settled at San Francisco in 1857, soon obtaining an editorial position on " The Golden Era." In 1864 he succeeded Charles Henry Webb in the editorship of " The Californian," then a weekly literary journal, in which his " Condensed Novels " originally appeared. Previous to his connection with this paper Mr. Harte filled various small offices until his appointment, 1864, as secretary of the U. S. branch mint at San Francisco. On the establishment of "The Overland Monthly" in 1868 Mr. Harte became its editor, and published in the second number his first notable study of California life, " The Luck of Roaring Camp." This was followed by several other overland sketches and by some of his most popular poems, that commonly known as " The Heathen Chinee" appearing in the issue for Sept., 1870. The same year he resigned his office as secretary of the mint, and in 1871 removed to New York city, his growing reputation having brought him many offers of literary work from the East. He was appointed U. S. consul at Crefeld, Germany, 1878, and in 1880 U. S. consul at Glasgow,

Scotland, retaining his office at the latter place until 1885. Subsequently lived in and near London, England. His first book, "Condensed Novels " (1867), was followed by " Poems " (1870), " The Luck of Roaring Camp, and Other Sketches " (1871), " East and West Poems" (1871), " Poetical Works" (1873), " Mrs. Skaggs's Husbands " (1873), " Echoes of the Foot Hills " (1874), " Tales of the Argonauts " (1875), " Two Men of Sandy Bar " (1876), " Thankful Blossom " (1876), " The Story of a Mine" (1877), " Drift from Two Shores" (1878), " The Twins of Table Mountain, and Other Stories " (1879), " Flip, and Found at Blazing Star " (1882), " In the Carquinez Woods" (1883), " On the Frontier " (1884), " By Shore and Sedge " (1885), " Maruja, a Novel " (1885), " Snow-Bound at Eagle's" (1886), " A Millionnaire of Rough and Ready " (1887), " The Queen of the Pirate Isle," for children (1887), " The Argonauts of North Liberty " (1888), " A Phyllis of the Sierras " (1888), " Cressy " (1889), " The Heritage of Dedlow Marsh " (1889), and " A Waif of the Plains " (1890).

HASSARD, John Rose Greene, journalist, b. New York, N. Y., 4 Sept., 1836. Graduated at St. John's college, Fordham, N. Y. He was assistant editor of the "American Cyclopædia," 1857–64, and in 1866 joined the editorial staff of the N. Y. " Tribune," becoming its musical critic the following year. Succeeded George Ripley as literary editor of that journal, 1880. Author of "Life of Archbishop Hughes" (1866), "The Ring of the Nibelungs" (1877), and " A Pickwickian Pilgrimage " (1881). Died, New York, N. Y., 18 April, 1888.

HAWKINS, Willis Brooks, journalist, b. Aurora, Ill., 15 Aug., 1852. Began editorial work on the Minneapolis " Tribune," 1874. Was editor and part proprietor of a paper in his native city, 1876–83, and afterward special editorial writer for the Chicago "News" and Washington, D. C., " Post." In 1890 became editor of the Washington "Evening Critic."

HAWKS, Francis Lister, clergyman, b. New Berne, N. C., 10 June, 1798. Graduated at the university of North Carolina. Entered the Episcopal ministry, 1827. Was rector of churches at New York, New Orleans, and Baltimore. Declined three elections as bishop. Was first president of the university of Louisiana. Author of "Contributions to the Ecclesiastical History of the United States " (1836–9) and " History of North Carolina" (1857–8). Died, New York, N. Y., 27 Sept., 1866.

HAWTHORNE, Julian, b. Boston, Mass., 22 June, 1846. Son of Nathaniel Hawthorne. Resided with his father at Liverpool and on the Continent, 1853–60, entering Harvard in 1863. Took a course of civil engineering at the same institution in 1868, and studied at Dresden, Germany, 1868–70. Was employed as a hydrographic engineer in the New York city dock department for the two following years. He then returned to Dresden and devoted himself entirely to literary work. Resided at that city and in Great Britain until 1882, after which he made his home in New York city, and more recently at Sag Harbor, Long Island. He was for some time connected with the London "Spectator," and contributed to the "Contemporary Review" in 1875 a series of articles entitled "Saxon Studies," afterward published as a volume. Among his novels and collections of short stories are "Bressant" (1873), "Idolatry" (1874), "Garth" (1875), "Archibald Malmaison" (1878), "Ellice Quentin," "Prince Saroni's Wife," "Sebastian Strome" (1880), "Fortune's Fool" (1883), "Dust" (1884), "Beatrix Randolph" (1884), "Noble Blood" (1884), "Love—or a Name" (1885), "The Trial of Gideon" (1886), "A Dream and a Forgetting" (1888), "The Professor's Sister" (1888), and "Constance" (1889). He has also issued "Confessions and Criticisms" (1887) and "Nathaniel Hawthorne and his Wife: a Biography" (1885).

HAWTHORNE, Nathaniel, b. Salem, Mass., 4 July, 1804. A descendant of William Hathorne, who emigrated from England with John Winthrop in the *Arbella*. William's son John was one of the judges in the witchcraft trials at Salem, and the latter's grandson was Capt. Daniel Hathorne, of Revolutionary fame. The romancer was a grandson of Captain Hathorne, and was responsible for the changed spelling of the family name. His father, who was master of a merchant-vessel, died when Nathaniel was four years old. The son received a portion of his early education at Salem from Joseph E. Worcester, the lexicographer. He was fitted for college at Salem, also, and entered Bowdoin in 1821, counting among his classmates Henry W. Longfellow, George B. Cheever, and John S. C. Abbott. His lifelong friend, President Franklin Pierce, was a member of the preceding class. From the year of his graduation until 1839 he lived chiefly at Salem in great retirement, having but few friends and devoting himself to perfecting his literary talents. His first novel, "Fanshawe," was brought out anonymously in 1826, and meeting with little success was suppressed. The manuscript of a collection of stories which he afterward put into a publisher's hands was withdrawn and destroyed. Received his first practical encouragement from Samuel G. Goodrich, who published four of Hawthorne's stories in "The Token" for 1831, one of the "annuals" of that time. The same publisher engaged him as editor of the "American Magazine of Useful and Entertaining Knowledge," which con-

nection lasted from 1836 to 1838. At this period he contributed some of his best stories to the "New England Magazine," "The Knickerbocker," and the "Democratic Review." The first volume of "Twice-Told Tales" appeared in 1837. Two years later he was appointed a weigher and gauger by George Bancroft, then collector of customs at Boston. Losing the position with a change of government in 1841, he joined the Brook Farm association, remaining but a few months. His marriage and removal to the "Old Manse" in Concord, Mass., followed in 1842. While there the second volume of "Twice-Told Tales" (1845) and the two volumes of "Mosses from an Old Manse" (1846) were collected from his published writings. An appointment as surveyor in the custom-house of Salem, 1846, was brought to an end in 1849 by trumped-up charges. The following year he issued "The Scarlet Letter." Removed to Lenox, Mass., and at that place wrote "The House of the Seven Gables" (1851) and "The Wonder Book" (1851). The succeeding two years were marked by brief residences at West Newton and Concord, and by the publication of "The Blithedale Romance" (1852), a campaign life of Franklin Pierce (1852), and "Tanglewood Tales" (1853). In 1853 he accepted from President Pierce an appointment as U. S. consul at Liverpool, England, remaining there four years, and afterward travelling on the Continent. Returning to England he brought out "The Marble Faun" (1860), and the same year sailed for America, passing the remainder of his life at "The Wayside," the house purchased by him at Concord in 1852. During this period he wrote for the "Atlantic Monthly" the papers which were collected in a volume as "Our Old Home" (1863) and the uncompleted works published after his death as "The Dolliver Romance," "Septimius Felton," and "Dr. Grimshawe's Secret." "American and English Note-Books" and "French and Italian Note-Books" were edited posthumously by Mrs. Hawthorne, and in 1885 appeared "Nathaniel Hawthorne and his Wife: a Biography," by his son, Julian Hawthorne. Died, Plymouth, N. H., 18 May, 1864.

HAY, John, b. Salem, Ind., 8 Oct., 1838. Graduated at Brown university. Studied law at Springfield, Ill., and entered the bar in 1861. Soon after was made a private secretary of President Lincoln and filled this position until the latter's death. Also acted in the capacity of adjutant and aide-de-camp, and saw service under Generals Hunter and Gillmore as major and assistant adjutant-general. Received the brevets of lieutenant-colonel and colonel. After the civil war was U. S. secretary of legation at Paris, 1865–7, and chargé d'affaires at Vienna, 1867–8. He was also secretary of legation at Madrid from 1868 to 1870. Returning to the United States in the latter year, he accepted an editorial position on the N. Y. "Tribune," resigning and removing to Cleveland, O., in 1875. From 1879 to 1881 he was assistant secretary of state under President Hayes, and subsequently made his home at Washington. Author of "Pike County Ballads, and Other Pieces" (1871), "Castilian Days" (1871), "Poems" (1890), and joint author with John G. Nicolay of "Abraham Lincoln : a History," the authoritative biography of its subject, first published in the "Century Magazine" for 1887–9.

HAYES, Isaac Israel, explorer, b. Chester Co., Penn., 5 Mar., 1832. Graduated at the medical school, university of Pennsylvania. In 1853 sailed with Dr. Kane on his expedition in search of Sir John Franklin. Headed an expedition fitted out by public subscription, 1860, in search of the open polar sea. Returning in 1862, he entered the Union army as surgeon, rising to the rank of brevet lieutenant-colonel. Published "An Arctic Boat-Journey" (1860), "The Open Polar Sea" (1867), and "The Land of Desolation" (1871). Died, New York, N. Y., 17 Dec., 1881.

HAYES, Rutherford Birchard, nineteenth president of the United States, b. Delaware, O., 4 Oct., 1822. Graduated at Kenyon college. Studied law and practised at Cincinnati. Served with distinction in the Union army during the civil war, gaining the rank of brevet major-general of volunteers. Was U. S. representative from Ohio, 1865–7, and governor of that state, 1867–73. A subsequent election as governor in 1875 was followed the next year by his election to the presidency, his term expiring in 1881. Afterward lived in retirement at Frémont, O.

HAYNE, Paul Hamilton, b. Charleston, S. C., 1 Jan., 1830. A nephew of Robert Young Hayne. His early education was superintended by his uncle, his father having died shortly after Paul's birth. Graduated at the university of South Carolina. Began to practise law, but soon abandoned the profession for literary pursuits. Was successively editor of "Russell's Magazine" and the Charleston "Literary Gazette," besides contributing to the "Southern Literary Messenger" and other periodicals. Entered the Southern army at the outbreak of the civil war and served until obliged to resign by failing health. His house and all his personal property having been destroyed at the bombardment of Charleston, he removed his family to a farm in the pine woods near Augusta, Ga., and again resumed journalistic work. During the war he wrote a number of popular war lyrics. The remainder of his life was overshadowed by a hard struggle to support his family under an increasing burden of ill health. Author of "Poems" (1855), "Sonnets and Other Poems" (1857), "Avolio, a Legend of the Island of Cos" (1859), "Legends and Lyrics" (1872), "The Mountain of the Lovers, and Other Poems" (1873), "Life of Robert Y. Hayne" (1878), "Life of Hugh S. Legaré" (1878), and "Poems, Complete Edition" (1882). Died, Copse Hill, Forest Station, Ga., 6 July, 1886.

HAYNE, Robert Young, statesman, b. St. Paul's Parish, Colleton District, S. C., 10 Nov., 1791. Studied law at Charleston, and was admitted to the bar in 1812. Served in the war of 1812. A member of the South Carolina legislature from 1814 to 1818, and attorney-general of the state, 1818–22. In 1822 he became U. S. senator from South Carolina, holding office until 1832. As senator he was an opponent of the protective system, and in the debate on the tariff of 1824 first advanced the theory that congress has no constitutional right to impose duties on imports for the protection of home industries. In Jan., 1830, the theory of nullification having already been expounded by Calhoun, Hayne introduced it into the senate in connection with his speeches on Foote's resolution, eliciting the famous "reply" of Daniel Webster. Resigned his position as senator, Dec., 1832, to become governor of South Carolina and take part in the nullification proceedings of that month. Issued his counter-proclamation to that of President Jackson at this time, but, a compromise having been effected, presided over the state convention which repealed the ordinance of nullification. Served as governor until 1834. The remainder of his life was chiefly occupied with state improvements. The "Life and Speeches of Robert Y. Hayne" appeared in 1845. Died, Asheville, N. C., 24 Sept., 1839.

HAZELTINE, Mayo Williamson, journalist, b. Boston, Mass., 24 April, 1841. Graduated at Harvard, and afterward studied at Oxford. Practised law until 1878, when he became literary editor of the N. Y. "Sun" and editorial writer on the same paper. In 1889 he assumed in addition the managing editorship of the N. Y. "Ledger." Author of "Chats about Books, Poets, and Novelists" (1883) and several pamphlets.

HEADLEY, Joel Tyler, b. Walton, Delaware Co., N. Y., 30 Dec., 1813. Graduated at Union. Assistant editor of the N. Y. "Tribune," 1846. Published as articles, afterward collected, "The Adirondack, or Life in the Woods" (1849). Was secretary of state of New York state, 1855. Issued "Napoleon and his Marshals" (1846), "Washington and his Generals" (1847), lives of Cromwell, Havelock, and Washington, "Grant and Sherman, their Campaigns and Generals" (1865), and "The Great Rebellion" (1864).

HEARN, Lafcadio, b. Leucadia, Santa Maura, Ionian Islands, 27 June, 1850. His father was an Englishman and his mother a native Greek. Received his education in Great Britain and France, and removed to America on his father's death, following the occupation of a journalist in Cincinnati and New Orleans. Author of "Stray Leaves from Strange Literature" (1885), "Some Chinese Ghosts" (1887), "Chita : a Memory of Last Island" (1889), "Two Years in the French West Indies" (1890), and "Youma" (1890).

HEDGE, Frederic Henry, b. Cambridge, Mass., 12 Dec., 1805. Graduated at Harvard, and entered the Unitarian ministry. Became professor of ecclesiastical history at Harvard, 1857, and of German in 1872. Assumed the editorship of the "Christian Examiner," 1858. Author of "The Prose Writers of Germany" (1848), "Reason in Religion" (1865), "Primeval World of Hebrew Tradition" (1870), and "Ways of the Spirit, and Other Essays" (1877).

HEILPRIN, Michael, scholar, b. Piotrkow, Poland, 1823. Held an official literary position under Kossuth during the latter's supremacy in Poland. Emigrated to America, 1856, became a member of the "American Cyclopædia" staff, and wrote for the N. Y. "Evening Post" and "Nation." Author of "The Historical Poetry of the Ancient Hebrews" (1879–80). Died, Summit, N. J., 10 May, 1888.

HELPER, Hinton Rowan, projector, b. near Mocksville, N. C., 27 Dec., 1829. While a young man, spent many years in travelling in North, South, and Central America. Projector of a proposed railway from the straits of Magellan to Behring sea. Was consul at Buenos Ayres from 1861 to 1867. His book, "The Impending Crisis of the South" (1857), an anti-slavery argument from an economic point of view, was adopted as a campaign document by the Republican party in 1860. Other books are "The Land of Gold" (1855), "Nojoque" (1867), "The Negroes" (1868), and "The Three Americas Railway" (1881).

HENDERSON, Isaac, b. Brooklyn, N. Y., 13 Feb., 1850. Graduated at Williams. Connected with the N. Y. "Evening Post" as part owner and publisher from 1872 to 1881, and in the latter year relinquished his interest to devote himself entirely to literature. Resided at Rome, Italy, 1882–6, and after that at London, England. Author of "The Prelate" (1886) and "Agatha Page" (1888).

HENRY, Patrick, statesman, b. Studley, Hanover Co., Va., 29 May, 1736. After unsuccessful attempts at business, began the practice of law in 1760. His first case of importance was the so-called "Parson's cause," which he won against the united influence of the clergy of Virginia, establishing his reputation as an orator by his address to the court. In May, 1765, he was elected to the Virginia house of burgesses and shortly after introduced and carried through in an eloquent speech his famous resolutions against the Stamp Act. Eight years later he was associated with Jefferson and the Lees in establishing the "committees of correspondence" between the colonies. He was the first member of the Continental congress of 1774 to address that body. As governor of Virginia, 1776–9, he took an active part in forwarding American interests. At the Virginia convention to ratify the Federal constitution in 1788 he opposed that instrument and proffered amendments of which some were subsequently adopted. Resumed his law practice at the close of the Revolution, finally retiring in 1794. Died, Red Hill, Charlotte Co., Va., 6 June, 1799.

HERBERT, Henry William, "Frank Forester," b. London, England, 7 April, 1807. Graduated at Oxford. His father was Dean of Manchester and cousin to the Earl of Carnarvon. Came to America, 1830, and after teaching school and writing for the journals edited the "American Monthly," 1833–6. Found his most profitable work in novel-writing, and was the first to introduce field-sports into American fiction. Among his novels are "Cromwell" (1837), "Marmaduke Wyvil" (1843), "The Puritans of New England" (1853), and "Sherwood Forest" (1855). Besides various histories he wrote "My Shooting Box" (1846), "Frank Forester and his Friends" (1849), "American Game in its Season" (1853), and "The Horse and Horsemanship in North America" (1857). There were issued posthumously "Fugitive Sporting Sketches" (1879) and "Poems, a Memorial Volume" (1887). Died, by his own hand, New York, N. Y., 17 May, 1858.

HEWITT, Abram Stevens, statesman, b. Haverstraw, N. Y., 31 July, 1822. Graduated at Columbia, and studied for the law, but, his eyesight failing, entered the iron business as the partner of Peter Cooper. U. S. representative from New York, 1874–86. Was elected mayor of New York city in 1886, serving one term. Several of his speeches on important occasions have been published.

HIGGINSON, Francis, clergyman, b. Claybrooke, Leicestershire, England, 1587. Graduated at Cambridge university. Became minister at his native place, but was obliged to retire on account of non-conformity. Accepted an offer from the Massachusetts Company, and sailed for Salem, Mass., with their second supply, arriving there 29 June, 1629. Was ordained "teacher" of the church at Salem, with Samuel Skelton as "pastor," but soon contracted a hectic fever. His last sermon was preached on the occasion of John Winthrop's arrival with the colony's third supply. His "True Relation of the Last Voyage to New England" was written in 1629 and printed in Governor Hutchinson's "Collection" (1769). "New England's Plantation" was published at London in 1630. Died, Salem, Mass., 6 Aug., 1630.

HIGGINSON, John, clergyman, b. Claybrooke, England, 6 Aug., 1616. Son of Francis Higginson, with whom he emigrated to America, 1629. He was chaplain of the fort at Saybrook, 1637–41, and afterward resided at Guilford as assistant to the Rev. Henry Whitefield. Was pastor of the church in Salem, Mass., from 1660 until his death. Author of several published sermons. Died, Salem, Mass., 9 Dec., 1708.

HIGGINSON, Thomas Wentworth, b. Cambridge, Mass., 22 Dec., 1823. A descendant of Francis Higginson. Was a younger schoolmate of James Russell Lowell. Graduated at Harvard. Entered the ministry and became pastor of non-denominational churches in Newburyport and Worcester, Mass. Was an ardent anti-slavery agitator, and was indicted with Wendell Phillips and Theodore Parker at the time of the "Anthony Burns riot" in 1853. Took an active part in the colonization of Kansas in 1856, and was cognizant of John Brown's plans for freeing the slaves. Raised two companies for the war in Aug., 1862, and in November was appointed colonel of the first regiment recruited from contraband slaves. Served with distinction until October, 1864, when he was obliged to resign from the effects of a wound. His experiences during this period are told in "Army Life in a Black Regiment" (1870). Was subsequently occupied with literary pursuits, to which he had devoted himself on retiring from the pulpit in 1858. Much of his best work was done for the "Atlantic Monthly," to which he was one of the earliest contributors. Many of these papers have been collected in volumes. Among his numerous works are "Out-Door Papers" (1863), "Malbone, an Oldport Romance" (1869), "Atlantic Essays" (1871), "The Sympathy of Religions" (1871), "Young Folks' History of the United States" (1875), "Common Sense about Women" (1882), "Life of Margaret Fuller Ossoli" (1884), "The Monarch of Dreams" (1887), "Hints on Writing and Speechmaking" (1887), "Travellers and Outlaws: Episodes in American History" (1888), and "The Afternoon Landscape: Poems and Translations" (1889). Prominently connected with the woman-suffrage movement, and an extensive writer for the

Boston "Woman's Journal" and other reform publications. Held several public offices in Massachusetts, and in 1889 was appointed state historian of the soldiers and sailors of Massachusetts in the civil war.

HILDRETH, Charles Lotin, b. New York, N. Y., 28 Aug., 1856. Educated at the college of New York. An editorial writer for the N. Y. "World," 1883–8, and afterward a member of the staff of "Belford's Magazine." Author of "Judith," a novel (1876), "The New Symphony, and Other Stories" (1878), and "The Masque of Death, and Other Poems" (1889).

HILDRETH, Richard, b. Deerfield, Mass., 22 June, 1807. Graduated at Harvard. Was associate editor of the Boston "Atlas," 1832–40. On account of ill-health went to Demerara, British Guiana, and edited "The Guiana Chronicle" and "The Royal Gazette" in support of the anti-slavery movement initiated by the British government. Was appointed U. S. consul at Trieste, 1861, but resigned through failing health. He had previously been a member of the N. Y. "Tribune" staff for some years. Author of the first American anti-slavery novel, "The Slave" (1836), better known by its later title, "The White Slave" (revised ed. 1852), "Theory of Morals" (1844), "Theory of Politics" (1853), "Despotism in America" (1854), "Japan as It Was and Is" (1855), "History of Banks" (1857), and his principal work, "History of the United States" (1849–52), of which a revised edition appeared in 1880. Died, Florence, Italy, 11 July, 1865.

HILL, Adams Sherman, educator, b. Boston, Mass., 30 Jan., 1833. Graduated at Harvard. Studied law, but did not practise. A member of the N. Y. "Tribune" staff, 1856–9, and correspondent of that and other papers at Washington, D. C., 1861–4. In 1872 was appointed assistant professor, and in 1876 Boylston professor of rhetoric at Harvard. Author of "Principles of Rhetoric" (1879) and "Our English" (1889).

HILL, George, b. Guilford, Conn., 29 Jan., 1796. Graduated at Yale. Held positions in the U. S. navy and in the state department at Washington, and was for a time U. S. consul to Asia Minor. Author of "The Ruins of Athens, and Other Poems" (1834, enlarged ed. 1839). Died, New York, N. Y., 15 Dec., 1871.

HILL, Thomas, educator, b. New Brunswick, N. J., 7 Jan., 1818. Graduated at Harvard. Became pastor of a Unitarian church at Waltham, Mass. Was appointed president of Antioch college, O., 1859, and of Harvard, 1862. Resigned in 1868 from ill-health. More recently was pastor of a church in Portland, Me. Author of "Christmas, and Poems on Slavery" (1843), "Geometry and Faith" (1849), "Jesus, the Interpreter of

Nature" (1859), and " Practical Arithmetic" (1881).

HILLARD, George Stillman, lawyer, b. Machias, Me., 22 Sept., 1808. Graduated at Harvard and entered the bar. Elected to the Massachusetts senate, 1850. Was solicitor of the city of Boston, 1854–6, and U. S. district-attorney for Massachusetts, 1866–70. Was associate editor of the "Christian Register" for a time, and of "The Jurist" with Charles Sumner. A member of the editorial staff of the Boston "Courier" from 1856 to 1861. Delivered many occasional addresses and lectures, and wrote various memoirs. Among his published writings are " Memorial of Daniel Webster" (1852), " Six Months in Italy" (1853), " Life and Campaigns of George B. McClellan" (1864), " Political Duties of the Educated Classes" (1866), and "Life of George Ticknor" (1873). Died, Boston, Mass., 21 Jan., 1879.

HILLHOUSE, James Abraham, b. New Haven, Conn., 26 Sept., 1789. Graduated at Yale. Was engaged in mercantile pursuits for a few years at New York city, but retired in 1822, and spent the remainder of his life at his country seat near New Haven. Besides several separate dramas and poems, issued "Dramas, Discourses, and Other Pieces" (1839). Died, New Haven, Conn., 5 Jan., 1841.

HINSDALE, Burke Aaron, educator. b. Wadsworth, O., 31 Mar., 1837. Studied at Hiram college. Was pastor of Christian churches in Ohio until 1869, when he became a professor, and the following year president, of Hiram college. He was superintendent of public schools at Cincinnati, 1882–6. Among his books are "Genuineness and Authenticity of the Gospels" (1870), " The Life and Works of James A. Garfield" (1882–5), and " The Old Northwest" (1888).

HITCHCOCK, Edward, geologist, b. Deerfield, Mass., 24 May, 1793. Entered the ministry, and was pastor of a Congregational church at Conway, Mass., 1821–5. Professor of chemistry and natural history at Amherst college from 1825 to 1845. In the latter year became president and professor of geology, resigning the presidency in 1854. Author of numerous geological works and state reports, one of which was "The Religion of Geology" (1852). Died, Amherst, Mass., 27 Feb., 1864.

HITCHCOCK, Roswell Dwight, scholar, b. East Machias, Me., 15 Aug., 1817. Graduated at Amherst. Pastor of Congregational churches until appointed professor of natural and revealed religion at Bowdoin, 1852. Was afterward professor of church history in the Union theological seminary at New York, 1855, becoming its president in 1880. Visited Palestine, 1869, and was elected president of the American Palestine exploration society, 1871. Author

of several books and papers, among them " Complete Analysis of the Bible" (1869) and " Socialism" (1879). Was joint editor of several hymn-books, and of a volume showing the various readings of the American and English New Testament revisers. Died, Somerset, Mass., 16 June, 1887.

HOBART, John Henry, divine, b. Philadelphia, Penn., 14 Sept., 1775. Graduated at the college of New Jersey. Took orders in the Episcopal church, 1798. Became assistant rector of Trinity church, New York city, 1800. Elected assistant bishop of New York, 1811, and bishop, 1816. Was instrumental in founding the General theological seminary. Of his numerous publications, the "Apology for Apostolic Order" (1807) brought him into prominent notice, and his sermon comparing America and England (1825) was widely discussed. Died, Auburn, N. Y., 12 Sept., 1830.

HOFFMAN, Charles Fenno, b. New York, N. Y., in 1806. Studied at Columbia college. Entered the bar, but left it to become associate editor of the N. Y. "American." Founded the "Knickerbocker Magazine," 1833, and shortly after became editor and owner of the "American Monthly." Edited the N. Y. "Mirror" and "Literary World" for a time. Was a versatile and voluminous writer until his brain became affected, in 1849, this causing his retirement to the Harrisburg insane asylum for the rest of his life. Among his books are "A Winter in the West" (1835), "Wild Scenes in Forest and Prairie" (1837), "Vanderlyn," a novel (1837), "Greyslaer, a Romance of the Mohawk" (1840), "The Vigil of Faith, a Legend of the Adirondacks," poems (1842), "Lays of the Hudson, and Other Poems" (1846), "Love's Calendar, and Other Poems" (1848), and "Poems," complete (1873). Died, Harrisburg, Penn., 7 June, 1884.

HOLLAND, Josiah Gilbert, b. Belchertown, Mass., 24 July, 1819. Graduated at the Berkshire medical college, Pittsfield, Mass. Wrote for the "Knickerbocker," and became superintendent of public schools at Vicksburg, Miss. In 1849 became associate editor of the Springfield, Mass., "Republican," increasing its influence and winning a name. Reprinted from its columns articles forming a "History of Western Massachusetts" (1855). Wrote a series of "Timothy Titcomb's Letters to Young People, Married and Single," of which nine editions in book-form were quickly sold (1858). In the same year issued "Bitter Sweet," a dramatic poem of New England life. His first novel appeared in 1860, "Miss Gilbert's Career." Of his "Life of Abraham Lincoln" (1865) over a hundred thousand sold. In 1866 disposed of his share in the "Springfield Republican" for fourteen times what it had cost him. Travelled in

Europe for some time, where he planned a monthly magazine on new lines, in which he was financially backed by Scribner, Armstrong & Company and Roswell Smith, he having a one-third proprietorship as editor. This later became the "Century Magazine," which he conducted until his death. Was a popular lecturer on social topics. Appointed on the board of education for New York city in 1872, and was afterward its president. Also chairman of the trustees of the college of New York. Published various works in addition to the aforenamed: "Lessons in Life"(1861), "Letters to the Joneses" (1863), "Plain Talks on Familiar Subjects" (1865), "Kathrina," a poem (1867), "The Marble Prophecy, and Other Poems" (1872), "The Mistress of the Manse," a poem (1874), "Arthur Bonnicastle" (1873), "The Story of Sevenoaks" (1875), and "Nicholas Minturn" (1876), the last three being novels. Died, New York, N. Y., 12 Oct., 1881.

HOLLEY, Marietta, "Josiah Allen's Wife," b. Ellisburg, Jefferson Co., N. Y., 1844. Always a resident of that village. A well-known humorous writer for the periodicals, and author of "Josiah Allen's Wife" (1878), "My Opinions and Betsey Bobbet's" (1872), "Sweet Cicely" (1885), "Samantha at Saratoga" (1887), and "Poems" (1888).

HOLMES, Abiel, clergyman, b. Woodstock, Conn., 24 Dec., 1763. Graduated at Yale. Pastor of Congregational churches at Midway, Ga., 1785–91, and at Cambridge, Mass., 1792–1832. Published "The Annals of America" (1805, enlarged ed. 1829) and "The Life of Ezra Stiles" (1798), besides several sermons. Died, Cambridge, Mass., 4 June, 1837.

HOLMES, Oliver Wendell, b. Cambridge, Mass., 29 Aug., 1809. Son of Abiel Holmes. Attended the Phillips academy in Andover for a year and was graduated at Harvard in the celebrated class of 1829, which included James F. Clarke, B. R. Curtis, Chandler Robbins, S. F. Smith (author of "America"), Wm. H. Channing, and Benjamin Peirce. Contributed largely to "The Collegian," but his first published poem appeared in the Boston "Advertiser," 1830. It was a spirited protest against the intended breaking-up of the worn-out frigate "Constitution." The verses were widely reprinted, the ship was saved, and early laurels were won. Disliking law he gave it up after a year's study and turned to medicine, to which he devoted two and a half years at home, and three in hospital work at Edinburgh and Paris. Took his degree in 1836, and his first volume of "Poems" appeared a few months later. Was appointed professor of anatomy and physiology at Dartmouth, 1839, and established a practice in Boston, 1840. In 1847 became Parkman professor of anatomy at the medical school of Harvard, resigning in 1882. A complete list of his professional publications would fill a large space; they include lectures, addresses, and special papers in medical journals, a selection of which was published under the title "Currents and Counter-Currents in Medical Science, with Other Addresses and Essays" (1861). "Medical Essays" appeared in 1883. In 1852 his literary success was equalled by that of his lectures in the lyceums on "The English Poets of the Nineteenth Century." When the "Atlantic Monthly" was founded in 1857, Dr. Holmes contributed the famous series of papers and poems afterward published as "The Autocrat of the Breakfast Table" (1859). This was followed by "The Professor at the Breakfast Table" (1860), "The Poet at the Breakfast Table" (1873), "The New Portfolio" (1886), and "Over the Teacups" (1890). The novels "Elsie Venner" and "The Guardian Angel" appeared in 1861 and 1868. Besides a multitude of fugitive pieces and poems for occasions, he issued in book-form "Urania," poem (1846), "Astrea," poem (1850), "Songs in Many Keys" (1861), "Soundings from the Atlantic," essays (1863), "Mechanism in Thought and Morals" (1871), "Songs of Many Seasons" (1874), "The School-boy" (1878), "John Lothrop Motley, a Memoir" (1878), "The Iron Gate, and Other Poems" (1880), "Pages from an Old Volume of Life" (1883), "Life of Ralph Waldo Emerson" (1884), "A Mortal Antipathy" (1885), and an account of a holiday taken in his seventy-eighth year, "Our Hundred Days in Europe" (1887). Another volume followed in 1888, "Before the Curfew, and Other Poems." Throughout his long career Dr. Holmes occupied a unique position as the writer and reciter of brilliant "occasional" and memorial poems.

HOLYOKE, Edward, colonist. Emigrated from Staffordshire, England, to Lynn, Mass., about 1636. Represented that town at the general court many years, but lived most of his days at Rumney Marsh, now Chelsea, Mass. Great-grandfather of Edward Holyoke, president of Harvard. Wrote "The Doctrine of Life, or of Man's Redemption" (1658), a copy of which he left to each of his sons-in-law "as their best legacy." Died, Rumney Marsh, now Chelsea, Mass., 4 May, 1660.

HONEYWOOD, St. John, lawyer, b. Leicester, Mass., 7 Feb., 1763 (Drake). Graduated at Yale. Studied law at Albany, N. Y., and practised at Salem in the same state for the remainder of his life. A volume of his "Poems" (1801) was issued posthumously. Died, Salem, Washington Co., N. Y., 1 Sept., 1798.

HOOKE, William, clergyman, b. Southampton, England, 1601. Graduated at Oxford university. Took orders, but was obliged to emigrate about 1636, on account of non-conformity. Minister at Taunton, Mass., and at New Haven, Conn., until 1656, when he returned to England and was appointed private chaplain to Oliver Cromwell, his wife's cousin. Was silenced at the restoration. Author of several sermons. Died, in or near London, England, 21 Mar., 1678.

Hooker, Joseph [*Noted Saying:* Vol. XI., page 454), b. Hadley, Mass., 13 Nov., 1814. Served in the Mexican war, and in the civil war gained the rank of major-general in the Union army. Died, Garden City, N. Y., 31 Oct., 1879.

HOOKER, Thomas, clergyman, b. near Leicester, England, about 1586. Graduated at Cambridge university. Stationed at Chelmsford, Essex, until silenced for non-conformity. Removed to Holland, where he preached three years, sailing for Boston in New England with John Cotton, 1633. Became pastor at Newtown, now Cambridge, Mass., but, differing with the Boston leaders in church matters, went through the woods to the Connecticut river in May, 1636, with most of his congregation, and founded the town of Hartford. His published writings number twenty-three titles, many being large treatises. A series of sermons on "The Soul" contains some of his best work. "The Poor Doubting Christian drawn to Christ" had reached a seventh edition in 1743. He mollified expositions of the sternest Puritan theology with descriptions of God's mercy to pardoned sinners. His fame as a pulpit orator was widely spread. Died, Hartford, Conn., 7 July, 1647.

HOOPER, Johnson J., lawyer, b. North Carolina, about 1815. Was solicitor of the ninth circuit of Alabama from 1849 to 1853. Secretary of the provisional Confederate congress, 1861. Author of "Adventures of Captain Simon Suggs" (1845) and "Widow Rugby's Husband, and Other Tales of Alabama" (1851). Died, Alabama, 1863.

HOPKINS, Lemuel, physician, b. Waterbury, Conn., 19 June, 1750. Began the practice of medicine at Litchfield, Conn., in 1776, and removed to Hartford about 1784. With others of the so-called "Hartford Wits" he contributed to "The Anarchiad" and "The Echo." Specimens of his poetry are also to be found in Smith's "American Poems" (1793), and in other early collections. Died, Hartford, Conn., 14 April, 1801.

HOPKINS, Mark, scholar, b. Stockbridge, Mass., 4 Feb., 1802. Graduated at Williams and at the Berkshire school of medicine. Was appointed professor of moral philosophy and rhetoric at Williams, 1830.

Took a preacher's license in 1832. Was president of Williams from 1836 to 1872, resigning in the latter year, but continuing his professorship of moral philosophy and theology, and occupying the college pulpit from 1836 to 1883. Was made president of the American board of foreign missions in 1857. Among his published works are "Lectures on the Evidences of Christianity" (1846), "Essays and Discourses" (1847), "Lectures on Moral Science" (1862), "Baccalaureate Sermons" (1863), "The Law of Love and Love as a Law, or Christian Ethics" (1869), "An Outline Study of Man" (1873), "Strength and Beauty" (1874, new ed. 1884, entitled "Teachings and Counsels"), and "The Scriptural Idea of Man" (1883). Died, Williamstown, Mass., 17 June, 1887.

HOPKINS, Samuel, divine, b. Waterbury, Conn., 17 Sept., 1721. Graduated at Yale. Studied theology under Jonathan Edwards. Preached at Housatonnoc, now Great Barrington, Mass., 1743–69, and at Newport, R. I., from 1770 until its occupation by the British in 1776. Returned to Newport in 1780 and remained there until his death. He originated anti-slavery legislation in Rhode Island, and in "A System of Doctrines Contained in Divine Revelation" (1793) expounded the theological system since known as "Hopkinsianism." In 1805 appeared "The Works of Samuel Hopkins." Died, Newport, R. I., 20 Dec., 1803.

HOPKINSON, Francis, b. Philadelphia, Penn., 21 Sept., 1737. The son of Thomas Hopkinson, who emigrated to Philadelphia from London in 1731. Graduated at the college of Philadelphia. Studied law and was admitted to the bar in 1761. The same year he served as secretary at a conference between the government of Pennsylvania and the Indians, and composed his poem "The Treaty" on that event. Visited England in 1766, remaining two years, and on returning to Philadelphia resumed his law practice. Obtained an official appointment from the royal government in 1772, which he afterward lost on account of his republican principles. Having resided for several years at Bordentown, N. J., he was made one of New Jersey's representatives in the congress of 1776, and signed the Declaration of Independence. He had already published "The Pretty Story" (1774), and this, "The Prophecy" (1776), and "The Political Catechism" (1777), were of much benefit to the American cause. Held several offices under the Continental government, and was judge of admiralty for Pennsylvania, 1779–89. In 1790 he was appointed U. S. district judge for the same state. Hopkinson's "Battle of the Kegs," written Jan., 1778, was one of the most popular ballads of the Revolution. His pen was constantly at work for the American side and was particularly directed against American loyalists. He prepared a collection of his writings for the press, which was brought out posthumously as "The Miscellaneous Essays and Occasional Writings of Francis Hopkinson, Esq." (1792). Died, Philadelphia, Penn., 9 May, 1791.

HOPKINSON, Joseph, lawyer, b. Philadelphia, Penn., 12 Nov., 1770. Son of Francis Hopkinson. Graduated at the university of Pennsylvania. Began practice in 1791 at Easton, Penn., soon removing to Philadelphia, where he rose to eminence in his profession. Was U. S. representative from Pennsylvania, 1815–19. He was appointed judge of the U. S. district court for the eastern district of that state in 1828, holding the office until his death. Was an officer in several learned societies, before which he delivered various addresses. Is best known for his national song, "Hail, Columbia," written in 1798, to the air of the "President's March," for the benefit performance of a Philadelphia actor. It was composed with the intention of reconciling the political parties of the time—bitterly divided with respect to the war with France—on the common ground of devotion to country. Died, Philadelphia, Penn., 15 Jan., 1842.

HOUGHTON, George Washington Wright, journalist, b. Cambridge, Mass., 12 Aug., 1850. Graduated at the Cambridge high school, and afterward became editor of "The Hub," a trade-paper of New York city. Author of "Songs from Over the Sea" (1874), "The Legend of St. Olaf's Kirk" (1880), and "Niagara, and Other Poems" (1882).

HOUSE, Edward Howard, b. Boston, Mass., 5 Sept., 1836. Educated himself, and studied music for a few years, entering journalism in 1854. Was connected with the N. Y. "Tribune" as associate editor, critic, and correspondent, 1859–73. Professor of the English language and literature at the university of Tokio, Japan, 1871–3. Edited "The Tokio Times," a weekly journal written by himself, from 1877 to 1880. More recently resided in New York city. Noted as a traveller, and for his efforts to protect Japan from foreign impositions. Among his works are "The Simonoseki Affair" (1874), "The Japanese Expedition to Formosa" (1875), "Japanese Episodes" (1882), and "Yone Santo: a Child of Japan" (1888).

HOWARD, Blanche Willis, b. Bangor, Me., 16 July, 1847. Descended from an old New England family. Studied at a young ladies' school in New York city, after leaving which she spent a year in Chicago, Ill., with a married sister. In 1875 she settled at Stuttgart, Germany, chiefly engaged in literary work, at the same time directing the education of young ladies studying in that city. Made her first success in literature with the popular story "One Summer" (1875). It was followed by "One Year Abroad" (1877), "Aunt Serena" (1880), "Guenn: a Wave on the Breton Coast" (1883), "Aulnay Tower" (1886), "Tony, the Maid" (1887), and "The Open Door" (1889).

HOWARD, Bronson, dramatist, b. Detroit, Mich., 7 Oct., 1842. His father, Charles Howard, was mayor of that city. Though the latter was deeply engrossed in business, it was only through his encouragement, in every possible way, that the son adopted and pursued a literary calling. Bronson was prepared for Yale at New Haven, but the failure of his eyes prevented him from pursuing his studies, except in the way of listening to the class lectures. He was a journalist in New York city from 1867 to 1872, connected successively with the "Evening Gazette," "Evening Mail," "Tribune," and "Evening Post," and afterward with the London "Pall Mall Gazette." His chief plays have been produced in New York city, and are as follows: "Saratoga" (1870, London 1874, as "Brighton"), "The Banker's Daughter" (1878, London 1879, as "The Old Love and the New"), "Old Love Letters" (1878), "Young Mrs. Winthrop" (1882, London 1885), "One of our Girls" (1885), "The Henrietta" (1887), and "Shenandoah" (1889). Other plays are "Diamonds," "Hurricanes," "Wives," "Green Room Fun," "Met by Chance," "Moorcroft," and "Baron Rudolph."

HOWARTH, Ellen Clementine [Doran], b. Cooperstown, N. Y., 17 May, 1827. The daughter of a calico-printer, and employed in factory-work at the age of seven. Was married to Joseph Howarth, in the same occupation. Lived at Trenton, N. J., in extremely reduced circumstances until friends secured her a comfortable subsistence. Author of "Poems" (1867), edited by Richard Watson Gilder, and also of the song "'Tis but a Little Faded Flower."

HOWE, Edgar Watson, journalist, b. in the present town of Treaty, Wabash Co., Ind., 3 May, 1854. Received a brief common-school education, and worked as a printer for some years. In 1878 became editor of the Atchison, Kan., "Daily Globe." Among his novels are "The Story of a Country Town" (1882), "A Moonlight Boy" (1887), and "A Man Story" (1888).

HOWE, Julia [Ward], b. New York, N. Y., 27 May, 1819. She was highly educated under private tutors and wrote verse at an early age. Also showed a talent for dramatic writing, which developed later. Was married, 1843, to Dr. Samuel Gridley Howe, distinguished as a philanthropist, sympathizer with the Greeks and Poles, and benefactor of the blind, whose education he greatly promoted. Soon afterward visited Europe, where she devoted herself to the study of philosophy and social questions. Spoke Italian, French and modern Greek fluently. Published a volume of poems, "Passion Flowers" (1854), and another, "Words for the Hour" (1856). These were followed by two tragedies in blank verse, "The World's Own" (produced 1855) and "Hippolytus" (written 1858). With Dr. Howe edited "The Commonwealth" in Boston in the interest of the anti-slavery movement, for several years before the war. When hostilities broke out she composed the impressive "Battle Hymn of the Republic." Accomplished a large amount of platform work, lecturing throughout the country in behalf of various movements for the good of the people. In 1869 joined the crusade for the political equality of women. Delivered many addresses for the cause, contributed liberally of her means and by her pen, and was made president of the New England women's club in 1872. Was privileged to address the Massachusetts legislature several times in furtherance of social reforms. Her other books are "A Trip to Cuba" (1860), "Later Lyrics" (1866), "From the Oak to the Olive" (1868), "Modern Society" (1881), and "Life of Margaret Fuller" (1883). Mrs. Howe also preached in various Unitarian pulpits.

HOWELL, Elizabeth [Lloyd], b. Philadelphia, Penn., 18—. Was married, 1853, to Robert Howell of that city, where she continued to reside after his death in 1857. Author of several poems, some of which appeared in "The Wheatsheaf" for 1852, besides the well-known piece entitled "Milton's Prayer for Patience."

HOWELLS, William Dean, b. Martin's Ferry, Belmont Co., O., 1 Mar., 1837. His father soon after became the editor of a weekly newspaper at Hamilton, O., in the office of which the son learned to set type. The family removed to Dayton in 1849, and subsequently to Jefferson, where Mr. Howells began writing for his father's journal. In 1858 he joined the editorial staff of the "Ohio State Journal" at Columbus. Two years later he issued with John J. Piatt "Poems of Two Friends." The writing of a campaign life of President Lincoln followed in 1860, and the next year he was appointed U. S. consul at Venice, remaining until 1865, his stay resulting in the volumes of sketches entitled "Venetian Life" (1866) and "Italian Journeys" (1867). After a short period of work on the N. Y. "Tribune" and "Nation," he became in 1866 assistant editor of the "Atlantic Monthly." Succeeded James T. Fields as editor, 1871, retaining the position until 1881. Visited Europe, 1882, and afterward divided his time between Boston, Mass., and New York city. In 1886 he formed

a connection with the publishing firm of Harper & Brothers, arranging to write for them exclusively, and also commenced and continued to contribute "The Editor's Study" of their magazine. In addition to the works already mentioned, is the author of "Suburban Sketches" (1868), "No Love Lost, a Poem of Travel" (1868), "Their Wedding Journey" (1871), "A Chance Acquaintance" (1873), "A Foregone Conclusion" (1874), "Out of the Question" (1876), "A Counterfeit Presentment" (1877), "The Lady of the Aroostook" (1878), "The Undiscovered Country" (1880), "A Fearful Responsibility" (1882), "Dr. Breen's Practice" (1883), "A Modern Instance" (1883), "A Woman's Reason" (1884), "Three Villages" (1885), "The Rise of Silas Lapham" (1885), "Tuscan Cities" (1885), "The Minister's Charge" (1886), "Indian Summer" (1886), "Modern Italian Poets" (1887), "April Hopes" (1887), "Annie Kilburn" (1888), "A Hazard of New Fortunes" (1889), and a series of farce dramas, of which the first, "The Parlor Car," was published in 1876.

HOYT, Ralph, clergyman, b. New York, N. Y., 18 April, 1806. After a term as journalist entered the Protestant Episcopal ministry, 1842, and devoted his life to promoting the welfare of the poor of New York city. Issued "Echoes of Memory and Emotion," poems (1859), and "Sketches of Life and Landscape," poems (1852, new ed. 1873). Died, New York, N. Y., 11 Oct., 1878.

HUBBARD, William, clergyman, b. Tendring, Essex, England, 1621. Came to New England with his father's family, 1635, and settled in Ipswich, Mass. Graduated at Harvard. Was assistant pastor and pastor of the church at Ipswich from 1656 until his death. He gained considerable reputation as a scholar, and was influential in the colony's church affairs. His most important book was "A Narrative of the Troubles with the Indians in New-England" (1677). It describes the wars with the Indians from the settlement of the colony until the end of King Philip's war, and is a valuable record in spite of many errors. Another work, "History of New England," which was left in manuscript and first published by the Mass. Hist. Soc. in 1815, is largely a compilation from other colonial writers. Hubbard also issued several sermons. Died, Ipswich, Mass., 14 Sept., 1704.

HUDSON, Henry Norman, clergyman, b. Cornwall, Vt., 28 Jan., 1814. Graduated at Middlebury. Became a Protestant Episcopal minister, 1849. Lectured on Shakespeare, afterward publishing an edition of the poet's works, with "Life and Notes," 11 vols. (1851-6). Edited the N. Y. "Churchman" and "American Church Monthly." Was a chaplain during the war, and wrote

"A Chaplain's Campaigns with General Butler" (1865). Author of "Lectures on Shakespeare" (1848) and "Shakespeare, His Life, Art, and Characters" (1872). Died, Cambridge, Mass., 16'Jan., 1886.

HUDSON, Mary [Clemmer], b. Utica, N. Y., 1839. Contributed to the Springfield, Mass., "Republican" at an early age. Was long the Washington correspondent of the N. Y. "Independent." Among her books are "Victoria" (1864), "Ten Years in Washington" (1871), and "Poems" (1882). Was twice married, first to Rev. Daniel Ames, and after a divorce to Edmund Hudson, editor of the "Army and Navy Register." Died, Washington, D. C., 18 Aug., 1884.

HUGHES, John, Catholic archbishop, b. Annalogham, Co. Tyrone, Ireland, 24 June, 1797. Emigrated to America, 1817. Studied theology at Mt. St. Mary's college, Md., and was ordained a Catholic priest, 1826. After twelve years' service at Philadelphia he was consecrated, in 1838, coadjutor bishop at New York city. Succeeded to the bishopric four years later, and was made archbishop in 1850. Engaged in numerous religious controversies with Protestant clergymen. Early in the civil war was commissioned by the U. S. government to support the national cause in Europe with his personal influence, and remained abroad for several months. His "Complete Works" appeared in 1866. Died, New York, N. Y., 3 Jan., 1864.

HUMPHREYS, David, diplomatist, b. Derby, Conn., July, 1753. Graduated at Yale. Entered the Continental army as captain on the outbreak of the Revolution, and was aide-de-camp to Washington from 1780 until its close. Afterward resided with Washington for long periods. Served as secretary of legation under Franklin and others, and was appointed first U. S. minister to Portugal in 1790, and subsequently minister to Spain, returning to America in 1802. Held the rank of brigadier-general in the war of 1812. His "Miscellaneous Works" appeared in 1804. Died, New Haven, Conn., 21 Feb., 1818.

HUNT, Theodore Whitefield, educator, b. Metuchen, N. J., 19 Feb., 1844. Graduated at the college of New Jersey, where he subsequently became professor of rhetoric and English literature, after studying for two years at the university of Berlin. Among his books are "Principles of Written Discourse" (1884), "English Prose and Prose Writers" (1887), and "Studies in Literature and Style" (1890).

HUNT, William Morris, artist, b. Brattleboro', Vt., 31 Mar., 1824. Pursued his art-studies in Europe, returning in 1855, and establishing himself at Boston. His best-known works were the two allegorical paintings in the capitol at Albany, N. Y., and various masterly portraits. "Talks on Art, Jotted down and Edited by Helen M. Knowlton" (1875–83) comprise selections from his studio-advice to his pupils. Died, Appledore, Isles of Shoals, N. H., 8 Sept., 1879.

HUTCHESON, Helen [Thayer], b. near Quasquetion, Ia., 22 April, 1860. Her family early removed to Washington, D. C., where she afterward resided. Her poems came out posthumously in the "St. Nicholas" magazine. Died, Washington, D. C., 29 April, 1886.

HUTCHINSON, Margaret, b. Massachusetts, about 1753. Fifth child and second daughter of Gov. Thomas Hutchinson. Sailed for England with her father in the summer of 1774, and was presented at the English court. Some of her letters are given in "Diary and Letters of Thomas Hutchinson" (1884–6). Died, Chelsea, England, 21 Sept., 1777.

HUTCHINSON, Thomas, governor of Massachusetts, b. Boston, Mass., 9 Sept., 1711. Son of a Boston merchant of the same name, and a descendant of Mrs. Anne Hutchinson, the religious agitator. Graduated at Harvard. Entered his father's establishment, but abandoned business for law and politics. Was a representative of Boston in the general court from 1737 to 1748, and in the latter year carried through his bill to substitute silver for the then greatly depreciated paper currency of Massachusetts. Was a member of the colony's council, 1749–66, and was appointed a judge of probate, 1752, and chief-justice of the colony, 1760. He had already been made lieutenant-governor, and held the position until commissioned governor in 1771. His house was sacked, and his large collection of papers relating to American history destroyed, at the time of the Stamp Act excitement. After a long struggle with the Revolutionary party, he was finally removed from the governorship, and sailed for England in June, 1774, being succeeded by General Gage. The first two volumes of his valuable "History of the Colony of Massachusetts Bay" were issued, 1764–7, and the third was brought out posthumously, in 1828. His "Diary and Letters," edited by Peter O. Hutchinson, appeared, 1884–6. Died, Brompton, England, 3 June, 1780.

HUTTON, Laurence, b. New York, N. Y., 8 Aug., 1843. Was a merchant in his native city for some years. Began writing for the press about 1870, and was for a time dramatic critic of the N. Y. "Evening Mail." In 1886 became conductor of the "Literary Notes" department in "Harper's Magazine." Edited the "American Actor Series" (1881–2) and several other works relating to the stage, and wrote "Plays and Players" (1875), "Literary Landmarks of

London" (1885), and "Literary Landmarks of Edinburgh" (1890).

INGERSOLL, Charles Jared, lawyer, b. Philadelphia, Penn., 3 Oct., 1782. Was U. S. representative from Pennsylvania, 1813-15 and 1841-7, and U. S. district attorney for the same state from 1815 until 1829. Author of "Edwy and Elgiva," a tragedy (1801), "Inchiquin, the Jesuit's Letters on American Literature and Politics" (1810), and a history of the war of 1812. Died, Philadelphia, Penn., 14 May, 1862.

INGERSOLL, Robert Green, lawyer, b. Dresden, N. Y., 11 Aug., 1833. Early removed to Illinois. Studied law and practised at Shawneetown and Peoria until the civil war, when he was made colonel of an Illinois regiment. Became attorney-general of Illinois, 1866. Gained national prominence as an orator by his speech nominating James G. Blaine for the presidency at the Republican national convention of 1876. Noted as a writer and speaker against the church theologies. Some of his writings are "The Gods" (1878), "Ghosts" (1879), "Some Mistakes of Moses" (1879), "Lectures Complete" (1883), and "Prose Poems and Selections" (1884).

IRVING, Washington, b. New York, N. Y., 3 April, 1783. His father emigrated from Scotland and entered trade in New York city. There the son received his education at sundry small schools, taking up the study of law at the age of sixteen. His brother, Peter Irving, having assumed the editorship of the N. Y. "Morning Chronicle" in 1802, Washington contributed his first literary work to this journal over the pseudonym, "Jonathan Oldstyle." In 1804 failing health compelled him to abandon his legal studies, and he spent the succeeding two years in European travel. During 1807 he issued, with his brother, William Irving, and James K. Paulding, the fortnightly numbers of "Salmagundi, or the Whim-Whams and Opinions of Launcelot Langstaff, Esq." The next year was occupied with the writing of "A History of New York, . . . by Diedrich Knickerbocker" (1809), which had been projected by Peter Irving and himself, but which is the work of Washington Irving. This book brought him reputation and money. He had again taken up law on returning to America, but finally abandoned it, and entered the business firm of his brothers as a silent partner in 1810. During the war of 1812 he held an editorial connection with the Philadelphia "Analectic Magazine," for which he wrote a number of articles. Sailed for England in 1815, remaining abroad until 1832. The failure of his brothers' firm in 1818 turned his entire attention to literature. "The Sketch-Book of Geoffrey Crayon, Gent.," was sent to New York city and issued in parts

during 1819, and the next year it was published at London by Murray, who gave the author over £400 for the copyright. "Bracebridge Hall, or the Humorists" (1822) and "Tales of a Traveller" (1824) followed. From 1826 to 1829 passed much of his time in Spain, and gathered the materials used in "The Life and Voyages of Christopher Columbus" (1828), "Chronicle of the Conquest of Granada" (1829), and "The Alhambra, or the New Sketch-Book" (1832). He was secretary of the U. S. legation at London, 1829-31, and in 1832 returned to America, being received with public honors. Built for himself the villa called "Sunnyside," at Irvington, N. Y., and thereafter resided in that place, with the exception of the years from 1842 to 1846, when he represented the United States at the court of Madrid. During this period he brought out "Tour on the Prairies" (1835), "Astoria" (1836), "Adventures of Captain Bonneville" (1837), a new and successful edition of his complete works (1848-50), "Mahomet and his Successors" (1849-50), "Oliver Goldsmith, a Biography" (1849), "Wolfert's Roost, and Other Papers" (1855), and "Life of George Washington" (1855-9). In 1866 appeared "Spanish Papers, and Other Miscellanies," edited posthumously by his nephew, P. M. Irving, who also prepared "The Life and Letters of Washington Irving" (1862-3). Died, Irvington, N. Y., 28 Nov., 1859.

IRVING, William, merchant, b. New York, N. Y., 15 Aug., 1766. Brother of Washington Irving. From 1787 to 1791 traded with the Indians on the Mohawk river. In 1793 married a sister of James K. Paulding, and settled permanently in New York city. Was U. S. representative from New York, 1813-19. He wrote the greater portion of the verses contained in "Salmagundi" (1807). Died, New York, N. Y., 9 Nov., 1821.

Jackson, Andrew [*Noted Saying:* Vol. IV., page 490], b. in the Waxhaw settlement, N. C., 15 Mar., 1767. U. S. senator from Tennessee, 1797-8. Major-general in the U. S. army in the war of 1812. Seventh president of the United States, 1829-37. Died, near Nashville, Tenn., 8 June, 1845.

JACKSON, Helen Maria [Fiske], "H. H.," b. Amherst, Mass., 18 Oct., 1831. The daughter of Prof. Nathan W. Fiske of Amherst college. Studied at the Ipswich, Mass., female seminary. Was married at the age of twenty-one to Capt. Edward B. Hunt, of the U. S. army. Resided at various military posts until his death in Oct., 1863. In 1866 Mrs. Hunt removed to Newport, R.I., which was her home until 1872. Beyond some early verses in a Boston paper, she had shown no evidences of literary development until 1865, when she began to contribute poems to the

N. Y. "Nation." These were followed by poems and prose articles in the "Independent" and "Hearth and Home," and she soon became a productive writer. A winter's residence in Colorado in 1873–4, for the benefit of her health, resulted in her marriage, 1875, to Mr. William S. Jackson, a merchant of Colorado Springs. This was her home until she died, though she visited New Mexico and California, and spent one winter in New York city, gathering facts at the Astor library for her book in behalf of the Indians, "A Century of Dishonor" (1881). The latter was followed by "Ramona" (1884), a novel dealing with the same subject. Her other books include "Verses by H. H." (1870, enlarged ed. 1874), "Bits of Travel" (1873), "Bits of Talk about Home Matters" (1873), "Sonnets and Lyrics" (1876), several books for children, and two novels in the "No Name" series, "Mercy Philbrick's Choice" (1876) and "Hetty's Strange History" (1877). She is commonly supposed to have written most of the stories published under the name of "Saxe Holm." Died, San Francisco, Cal., 12 Aug., 1885.

JAMES, Henry, theologian, b. Albany, N. Y., 3 June, 1811. Graduated at Union college. Joined the religious sect founded by Sandeman, and later tended toward Swedenborgianism. Resided at Cambridge, Mass., after 1866. Lectured and wrote much, and issued "What is the State?" (1846), "Moralism and Christianity" (1850), "Personal Recollections of Carlyle" and other "Tribune" letters, "The Church of Christ not an Ecclesiasticism" (1854), and "The Secret of Swedenborg" (1869). Died, Cambridge, Mass., 18 Dec., 1882.

JAMES, Henry, Jr., b. New York, N. Y., 15 April, 1843. Son of Henry James, who directed his education in New York city and during a residence in Europe. Studied at the Harvard law school for two years, and in 1865 began writing for the magazines. Returned to England in 1869, where, and in Italy, he afterward lived, with the exception of a brief visit to the United States in 1874–5, when he was editorially connected with the "Atlantic Monthly." Originated the class of fiction known as "transatlantic," and has been denominated a leader in the neorealistic school of novelists. Also gained reputation as a critical writer. His published works are "Poor Richard" ("Atlantic Monthly," 1867), "Watch and Ward" (1871), "Roderick Hudson" (1875), "Transatlantic Sketches" (1875), "A Passionate Pilgrim" (1875), "The American" (1877), "Daisy Miller: a Study" (1878), "An International Episode" (1878), "The Europeans" (1878), "French Poets and Novelists" essays (1878), "Confidence" (1879), "Hawthorne" in "English Men of Letters Series" (1880), "Washington Square" (1880), "A

Bundle of Letters" (1880), "Diary of a Man of Fifty" (1880), "The Portrait of a Lady" (1881), "The Siege of London" (1883), "Portraits of Places" (1884), "A Little Tour in France" (1884), "Tales of Three Cities" (1884), "The Author of Beltraffio" (1885), "The Bostonians" (1886), "Princess Casamassima" (1886), "The Aspern Papers" (1888), "Partial Portraits" (1888), "The Reverberator" (1888), "A London Life" (1889), and "The Tragic Muse" (1890).

JAMES, T. C. Accredited in Elihu H. Smith's collection of "American Poems" (1793) with the authorship of a poem entitled "The Country Meeting."

JANVIER, Margaret Thomson, "Margaret Vandegrift," b. New Orleans, La., 18—. Sister of Thomas A. Janvier, and a resident of Philadelphia. Author of a number of books for children, among them "Clover Beach" (1880), "The Absent-Minded Fairy, and Other Verses" (1883), and "The Dead Doll, and Other Verses" (1888).

JANVIER, Thomas Allibone, "Ivory Black," b. Philadelphia, Penn., 16 July, 1849. Son of a merchant of that city, near which he resided in youth, receiving his education chiefly at country schools. Was engaged for some time at Philadelphia in the silk-importing business, and afterward as a journalist for twelve years. Visited Mexico, 1881–2, and during the summers of 1885–7, removing to New York city in 1887. A writer for the magazines, and author of "The Mexican Guide" (1886), "Color Studies," stories (1885), and "The Aztec Treasure House, a Romance" (1890).

JARVES, James Jackson, art connoisseur, b. Boston, Mass., 20 Aug., 1820. Settled in Hawaii, and founded "The Polynesian," 1838. Appointed director of the government press and special commissioner of the kingdom to negotiate treaties with the United States and France. Collected works of art there and in Europe, giving old paintings to Yale and to the art gallery of Cleveland, O., and Venetian glass to the art museum of New York. Published several books on the history, scenery, and art of Polynesia, and two on the "Sights and Principles" of Paris and Italy (1853–5); also, "Art Studies" (1861), "The Art Idea in America" (1866), "Art Thoughts" (1869), "The Art of Japan" (1876), and "Italian Rambles" (1884).

JAY, John, statesman, b. New York, N. Y., 12 Dec., 1745. Of Huguenot descent. Graduated at Kings, now Columbia, college. Was admitted to the New York bar in 1768, and was a delegate to the first Continental congress in 1774. He drew up for this body its "Address to the People of Great Britain," and for the congress of 1775 its "Address to the People of Canada." Absence in connection with the New York convention of 1776 prevented his signing the Declaration of Independence. He, however, secured the approval of that instrument by the New York convention, of which he was a leading member. Was successively chief-justice of New York, president of the Continental congress, and minister to Spain, sailing for the latter country in Oct., 1779. Three years later with Adams and Franklin he conducted the negotiations for the treaty of 1783 with Great Britain. Was secretary of foreign affairs from 1784 to 1789, and after the adoption of the Federal constitution, to which he had contributed his influence by writing for "The Federalist" (1788), was offered by Washington any office at the latter's disposal, choosing that of chief-justice of the United States. In 1794 he was appointed special envoy to Great Britain, and completed the agreement with that country known as "Jay's treaty." Was governor of New York from 1795 to 1801, and, declining a reappointment as chief-justice of the United States, spent the remainder of his life in retirement. "The Life of John Jay, by his Son" (1833) contains many of his state papers. Died, Bedford, Westchester Co., N. Y., 17 May, 1829.

JAY, John, 2d, diplomatist, b. New York, N. Y., 23 June, 1817. Grandson of John Jay. Graduated at Columbia. Studied for the law. A champion of the colored race, and conducted several leading cases involving the liberties of fugitive slaves. U. S. minister to Vienna, 1869–75. Was appointed by President Cleveland Republican member of the civil service commission, over which he presided. A member of various learned societies. Among his addresses are "Caste and Slavery in the American Church" (1843), "The Great Conspiracy and England's Neutrality" (1861), and "The Memories of the Past" (1867).

JEFFERSON, Joseph, actor, b. Philadelphia, Penn., 20 Feb., 1829. Third of the name, in direct descent of a family of actors. Made his earliest appearance on the stage as a child of three years. Gained his first reputation at New York city as Asa Trenchard in "Our American Cousin," 1858. In collaboration with Dion Boucicault constructed the play of "Rip Van Winkle," producing it at London, England, 1865. "The Autobiography of Joseph Jefferson" appeared in the "Century Magazine" for 1890.

JEFFERSON, Thomas, third president of the United States, b. "Shadwell," Albemarle Co., Va., 2 April, 1743. Graduated at William and Mary college, and was admitted to the bar of Virginia, 1767. Two years later he was elected a member of the Virginia house of burgesses, to which body he presented his draught of instructions for the Virginia delegates to the Continental congress of 1774. They were not adopted, but were soon after published in pamphlet form with the title "A Summary View of the Rights of British America." In June, 1775, he became a member of the Continental congress, and on 10 June, 1776, was appointed chairman of the committee to prepare the Declaration of Independence, which he drafted. For the ensuing three years he chose to serve in the Virginia legislature, which was then largely occupied in revising the laws and statutes of the state. He was governor of Virginia, 1779–81, and in 1784 was sent to join Franklin and Adams in the completion of treaties with European powers. The following year he was made minister to France, returning to America, 1789, and serving as secretary of state under Washington until 1794. While in Paris he published his "Notes on the State of Virginia" (1784). In 1796 was elected vice-president of the United States. Four years later, as the candidate of the Republican-Democratic party, he defeated John Adams for the presidency, and was reëlected for a second term in 1804. At the end of his second term he retired from public life and devoted himself largely to the furtherance of education in Virginia, founding the university of Virginia in 1819. "The Writings of Thomas Jefferson" were published by order of congress in 1854. Died (on the same day with John Adams), Monticello, Va., 4 July, 1826.

JENNISON, Lucy White, "Owen Innsly," b. Newton, Mass., 18—. Daughter of Samuel Jennison, a member of the Boston bar. Educated at private schools in the latter city. Much of her life has been passed in Europe, particularly in Italy, which became her adopted home. At one time a correspondent of the Springfield, Mass., "Republican." Some of her poems were collected in "Love Poems and Sonnets" (1882).

JEWETT, Sarah Orne, "Alice Eliot," b. South Berwick, Me., 3 Sept., 1849. Daughter of Dr. Theodore H. Jewett, a physician of reputation. Received her education at Berwick academy, and contributed a story to the "Atlantic Monthly" as early as 1869. Her stories and novels chiefly are concerned with New England life and character. Travelled extensively in Europe and Canada, making her home at South Berwick and at Boston, Mass. Some of her books are "Deephaven" (1877), "Play-Days" (1878), "Old Friends and New" (1880), "Country By-Ways" (1881), "The Mate of the Daylight" (1883), "A Country Doctor" (1884), "A Marsh Island" (1885), "A White Heron" (1886), "The Story of the Normans" (1887), "The King of Folly Island, and Other People" (1888), and "Betty Leicester" (1889).

Johnson, Andrew [*Noted Saying*: Vol. XI., page 455], b. Raleigh, N. C., 29 Dec.,

1808. Seventeenth president of the United States, 1865–9. Died, near Carter's Station, Tenn., 31 July, 1875.

JOHNSON, Captain Edward, colonist, b. England, 1599 (W. F. Poole). A resident of Herne Hill, near Canterbury, Kent, at the time of his sailing with John Winthrop's fleet in 1630. Returned to England, and again emigrated to Massachusetts, settling at Charlestown in 1636. One of the founders of Woburn, Mass., 1642, and its representative in the general court for many years. Experience in military matters gave him place on all committees charged with those affairs. "A History of New England," or, "Wonder-working Providence of Sions Saviour in New England" (1654), was written to correct false reports of the colony spread by disappointed adventurers. It treats of events from 1628 to 1652. Died, Woburn, Mass., 23 April, 1672.

JOHNSON, Helen [Kendrick], b. Hamilton, Madison Co., N. Y., 4 Jan., 1843. Daughter of Prof. Asahel C. Kendrick. Was married, 1869, to Rossiter Johnson. Author of a number of books for children and of "Our Familiar Songs, and Those who made Them" (1881) and "Raleigh Westgate, a Romance" (1889).

JOHNSON, Oliver, emancipator, b. Peacham, Vt., 27 Dec., 1809. Began life as a printer; then edited the "Christian Soldier," 1831–3. Was one of the founders of the New England anti-slavery society in 1832, and wrote and lectured as its agent. From 1865 to 1870 was managing editor of the N. Y. "Independent," and afterward of the "Weekly Tribune" until 1872, when he became editor of the "Christian Union." Author of "William Lloyd Garrison and his Times, or Sketches of the Anti-Slavery Movement in America," 1880. Died, Brooklyn, N. Y., 10 Dec., 1889.

JOHNSON, Robert Underwood, b. Washington, D. C., 12 Jan., 1853. Graduated at Earlham college, Richmond, Ind. Resided at New York city after 1873, connected with the editorial department of the "Century Magazine," of which he became associate editor in 1881. A contributor to the magazines, and associated with Clarence C. Buel in editing "Battles and Leaders of the Civil War" (1889). As secretary of the joint committee of the authors' and publishers' copyright leagues, Mr. Johnson has been an indefatigable advocate of international copyright.

JOHNSON, Rossiter, b. Rochester, N. Y., 27 Jan., 1840. Graduated at the University of Rochester. Was associated with Robert Carter in editing the Rochester, N. Y., "Democrat" (Republican paper), 1864–8, and was assistant editor of the "American Cyclopædia," 1873–7. Edited a number of important compilations, and

wrote "Phaeton Rogers, a novel of Boy Life" (1881), "Idler and Poet," poems (1883), and "A Short History of the Secession" (1888), and other historical works.

JOHNSON, Samuel, clergyman, b. Salem, Mass., 10 Oct., 1822. Graduated at Harvard. Became a Unitarian preacher of the free religious type. Attained prominence as an anti-slavery lecturer. Several of his hymns are in general use. Compiled with Samuel Longfellow "Hymns for Public and Private Devotion" (1846), revised as "Hymns of the Spirit" (1864). Published also "India" (1872), "China" (1877), and "Persia" (1885), a series of works on Oriental religions. Died, North Andover, Mass., 19 Feb., 1882.

JOHNSON, Virginia Wales, b. Brooklyn, N. Y., 28 Dec., 1849. Lived in that city and New York until 1875, after which she resided in Europe, chiefly at Florence. Among her numerous novels are "Joseph, the Jew" (1873), "The Calderwood Secret" (1875), "The Neptune Vase" (1881), and "The House of the Musician" (1887).

JOHNSON, William Martin, physician, b. about 1771. Adopted as a child by Ebenezer Albee, a retired sea-captain of Wrentham, Mass. Studied medicine at Easthampton, L. I., and practised for a while at Georgetown, S. C., where he contracted a fever that was ultimately fatal. Specimens of his poetry have been preserved by John Howard Payne, in articles contributed to the "Democratic Review" (1838). Died, Jamaica, L. I., N. Y., 21 Sept., 1797.

JOHNSTON, Richard Malcolm, educator, b. Hancock Co., Ga., 8 Mar., 1822. Graduated at Mercer university, Ga. Studied for the law, but in 1857 assumed the professorship of literature at the university of Georgia. Resigned this position in 1861, and established a boarding-school for boys at Sparta, Ga., and afterward near Baltimore, Md. A volume of character studies with the title "Dukesborough Tales" appeared in 1883, collected from the files of the "Southern Magazine," and gained for him a late but substantial reputation which was sustained by subsequent work in the magazines. There have also been published a "Biography of Alexander H. Stephens" (1883), "Old Mark Langston" (1884), "Two Gray Tourists" (1885), "Mr. Absalom Billingslea and other Georgia Folk" (1887), and "Ogeechee Cross-Firings" (1889).

JOHNSTON, William Preston, educator, b. Louisville, Ky., 5 Jan., 1831. Graduated at Yale. Served in the Confederate army during the civil war, and rose to the grade of colonel. Afterward was a professor at Washington and Lee university until 1880, when he accepted the presidency of the Louisiana state university. In 1884 became the first president of Tulane university, New Orleans. He published, 1878, "The Life of General Albert Sidney Johnston," who was his father.

JONES, Amanda Theodosia, b. Bloomfield, Ontario Co., N. Y., 19 Oct., 1835. Engaged in teaching for some years, and from 1854 to 1873 was connected editorially with various journals. More recently made her home at Chicago, Ill., where she was occupied as an inventor. Author of "Ulah, and Other Poems" (1860), "Atlantis, and Other Poems" (1866), and "A Prairie Idyl, and Other Poems" (1882).

JONES, Charles Colcock, Jr., lawyer, b. Savannah, Ga., 28 Oct., 1831. Graduated at Princeton. Practised law in Savannah until the outbreak of the civil war, when he entered the Confederate army, rising to the grade of colonel. Subsequently followed his profession in New York city and Augusta, Ga. A voluminous writer on historical subjects relating to the South. Some of his books are "Historical Sketch of Tomo-Chi-Chi, Mico of the Yamacraws" (1868), "The Siege of Savannah in 1779" (1874), and "The History of Georgia" (1883).

JONES, Hugh, clergyman; b. England, 1669 (Appleton). Came to America in 1696, and served as a Church of England rector in Virginia and Maryland until his death. Was at one time chaplain to the Virginia assembly and professor of mathematics in William and Mary college. Published "The Present State of Virginia" (1724) and several text-books. Died, Cecil Co., Md., 8 Sept., 1760.

JONES, John Paul, naval commander, b. Kirkbean, Scotland, 6 July, 1747. He was the son of John Paul, a farmer, and assumed the name of Jones in 1773. Was appointed a first lieutenant in the American navy, Dec., 1775, and soon after distinguished himself by capturing sixteen English prizes in a period of six weeks. He was the victor in several desperate encounters with British ships of the line, of which the most noted was that with the *Serapis* in the *Bon Homme Richard*, 23 Sept., 1779. For this he received the thanks of congress. Served against the Turks in the Russian navy 1787-8. Died, Paris, France, 18 July, 1792.

JONES, Thomas, jurist, b. Fort Neck, Queens Co., N. Y., 30 April, 1731. Graduated at Yale. Admitted to the bar of New York, 1755. In 1773 succeeded his father as judge of the N. Y. supreme court. Was imprisoned as a loyalist several times during the Revolution, and removed to England permanently in 1781. His manuscript "History of New York during the Revolution" was published by the N. Y. Hist. Soc. in 1879. Died, Hoddesdon, Hertfordshire, England, 25 July, 1792.

JOSSELYN, John, colonist, b. England.

Came to Boston in New England, July, 1638. Visited his brother at Scarborough, Me., and returned to England late in 1639. Again sailed for Boston, 1663, and remained with his brother eight years, when he returned and brought out "New England's Rarities Discovered" (1672) and "An Account of Two Voyages to New England" (1674). Of his subsequent life nothing is known.

JUDD, Sylvester, clergyman, b. Westhampton, Mass., 23 July, 1813. Graduated at Yale. Of markedly religious temperament, he felt impelled to give up the more rigid tenets of the Puritanism in which he had been reared. Entered the divinity school of Harvard and took his degree, 1840, accepting the pastorate of the Unitarian church at Augusta, Me. In his last year at Harvard issued "A Young Man's Account of his Conversion from Calvinism." His first literary production was a work of fiction, "Margaret, a Tale of the Real and Ideal, including Sketches of a Place not before described, called Mons Christi." This he commenced in 1843 and brought out in 1845 (revised ed. 1851). It was an attempt "to fill up a gap long left open in Unitarian literature—that of imaginative writings." The book is mainly valuable for its faithful portrayal of life and character in New England under the strict orthodoxy of that period, and for its exquisite descriptions of nature. In 1850 was issued "Philo, an Evangeliad," a poetic "attempt" at a Unitarian epic, to parallel the Calvinistic "Course of Time," by Pollok, then in the height of its popularity. In the same year appeared his second novel, "Richard Edney and the Governor's Family, a Rus-Urban Tale." Was a frequent and favorite platform-speaker, advocating the abolition of slavery, temperance, and other reforms. A volume of discourses entitled "The Church" was published the year following his death. Died, Augusta, Me., 26 Jan., 1853.

JUDSON, Emily [Chubbuck], "Fanny Forester," b. Eaton, N. Y., 22 Aug., 1817. Wrote for the N. Y. "Mirror," 1844-6. Some of her stories were published with the title "Alderbrook" in 1846. Became the third wife of Adoniram Judson, 1846, and went with him to Bengal, remaining until his death in 1850. Returned to New York city, and issued "An Olio of Domestic Verses" (1852) and "Kathayan Slave" (1853). Died, Hamilton, N. Y., 1 June, 1854.

KANE, Elisha Kent, explorer, b. Philadelphia, Penn., 20 Feb., 1820. Studied at the university of Virginia. Graduated head of his class in medicine at the university of Pennsylvania, 1842. Entered the U. S. navy, 1843, and served as surgeon of the *Advance* in the first Grinnell Arctic expedition to search for Franklin, 1850. At request of Lady Franklin assumed command of the second expedition, 1853, suffering severely, and being forced to abandon his ship, 1855. Received the medal of the Royal geographical society, 1856, and the gold medal of the French société de géographie, 1858. Issued "The United States Grinnell Expedition" (1854) and "Arctic Explorations; the Second Grinnell Expedition" (1856). Died, Havana, Cuba, 16 Feb., 1857.

Kearny, Philip [*Noted Saying:* Vol. VII., page 193], b. New York, N. Y., 2 June, 1815. Served in the Mexican war, and also as brigadier-general in the Union army during the civil war. Killed, near Chantilly, Va., 1 Sept., 1862.

KEENAN, Henry Francis, b. Rochester, N. Y., 4 May, 1849. Served in the Union army during the civil war. Joined the staff of the Rochester "Chronicle," 1868, and followed journalism in that city and New York until 1883. Some of his novels are "Trajan" (1884), "The Aliens" (1886), and "One of a Thousand" (1887).

KEMBLE, Frances Ann, actress, b. London, England, 27 Nov., 1809. First appeared in Covent Garden, 1829, as Juliet. Came to America, 1832, playing with great success until 1834, when she was married to Pierce Butler, from whom she was separated in 1846. Gave Shakespearian readings, 1849–68. Wrote "Francis the First," a drama (produced 1832), "Poems" (1844 and 1859), "Records of a Girlhood" (1879), "Records of Later Life" (1882), and "Notes on Some of Shakespeare's Plays" (1882).

KENNAN, George, traveller, b. Norwalk, Huron Co., O., 16 Feb., 1845. Visited Kamtchatka in 1865, and was engaged for three years in exploring and laying out routes for the proposed Russo-American telegraph line. In 1870 and 1871 travelled extensively in Russia, Daghestan, and Chechina. His most important journey was that made in 1885–6 through Siberia with the purpose of observing the Russian exile system, which he did very thoroughly. His experiences were described in a series of articles in the "Century Magazine," 1889–90. He also wrote "Tent Life in Siberia" (1870).

KENNEDY, John Pendleton, lawyer and politician, b. Baltimore, Md., 25 Oct., 1795. Graduated at Baltimore college. Served as a volunteer at the battles of Bladensburg and North Point in the war of 1812. Was admitted to the bar, and practised law at Baltimore until 1838, meanwhile filling two terms in the Maryland legislature. U. S. representative from the same state, with the exception of one term, from 1837 to 1845. He became a leader in the Whig party in congress, and wrote and spoke against slavery and in behalf of protection. Was secretary of the navy under President Fillmore, 1852–3, and furthered

the expedition of Commodore Perry to Japan and Dr. Kane's second expedition in search of Sir John Franklin. Subsequently visited Europe thrice, the last time as U. S. commissioner to the Paris exposition of 1867. Author of "A Defence of the Whigs" (1844), "The Red Book," a fortnightly periodical of a satirical character (1818–19), "Swallow Barn" (1832), "Horse-Shoe Robinson" (1835), "Rob of the Bowl" (1838), and "Memoirs of the Life of William Wirt" (1849). Died, Newport, R. I., 18 Aug., 1870.

KENT, James, jurist, b. Putnam Co., N. Y., 31 July, 1763. Graduated at Yale. Studied law, and was admitted to the bar at Poughkeepsie, N. Y., 1785, where he practised for several years. A member of the state legislature in 1790, 1792, and 1796. Was professor of law at Columbia college, 1793–8, having meanwhile removed to New York city. Appointed by Governor Jay a justice of the supreme court in 1798, he changed his residence to Albany, where he lived until 1823. In 1814 he was made chancellor of New York, being retired at the age of sixty by the terms of the existing state law. He again became professor of law at Columbia in 1824, and his lectures at that college are the foundation of "Commentaries on American Law" (1826–30, revised ed. 1832). His decisions as justice and chancellor are to be found in the reports of the various courts. Died, New York, N. Y., 12 Dec., 1847.

KENYON, James Benjamin, clergyman, b. Frankfort, Herkimer Co., N. Y., 26 April, 1858. Graduated at the Adams, N. Y., collegiate institute. Entered the Methodist Episcopal ministry, 1878, and became pastor of a church at Watertown, N. Y. Author of "The Fallen, and Other Poems" (1876), and "In Realms of Gold," poems (1887).

KETCHUM, Annie [Chambers], educator, b. Scott Co., Ky., 8 Nov., 1824. She was principal of advanced schools in Memphis, Tenn., and Georgetown, Ky., before her marriage and after her husband's death. More recently she became an instructor in elocution. Author of a volume of poems, "Lotos-Flowers" (1877), besides several prose volumes.

KEY, Francis Scott, lawyer, b. Frederick Co., Md., 1 Aug., 1779. Graduated at St. John's college, Annapolis. Studied law with his uncle, Philip Barton Key, and began practice at Frederick, Md., in 1801. Afterward removed to Washington, where he was made district attorney of the District of Columbia. Just previous to the bombardment of Fort McHenry, near Baltimore, by the British fleet in 1814, he had visited the latter in a flag-of-truce vessel, and was detained until after the engagement, which he witnessed. His experiences resulted in the composition of his song, "The Star-Spangled Banner," on the following morning. It was at once printed, and was sung, to the air "Anacreon in Heaven," throughout the country. An edition of his "Poems" was issued posthumously in 1857. Died, Washington, D. C., 11 Jan., 1843.

KIMBALL, Harriet McEwen, b. Portsmouth, N. H., 2 Nov., 1834. Daughter of Dr. David Kimball. Received her education mainly at home. Always resided in Portsmouth, where she was chiefly instrumental in establishing that city's cottage hospital. Her books are "Hymns" (1867), "Swallow-Flights of Song" (1874), "The Blessed Company of all Faithful People" (1879), and "Poems," complete (1889).

KIMBALL, Richard Burleigh, lawyer, b. Plainfield, N. H., 11 Oct., 1816. Graduated at Dartmouth. Entered the bar, and, after a sojourn in Paris, practised first in Waterford, N. Y., and afterward in New York city. Went to Texas, founded the town of Kimball, and built the railroad from Galveston to Houston, of which he was president, 1854–60. Contributed variously to magazines, and is the author of "Letters from England" (1842), "St. Leger, or the Threads of Life" (1850), "Romance of Student Life Abroad" (1852), "Undercurrents of Wall Street" (1861), "Was He Successful?" (1863), and "To-Day in New York," (1870).

KING, Charles, soldier, b. Albany, N. Y., 12 Oct., 1844. Great-grandson of Rufus King. Graduated at West Point. Served in the U. S. army from 1866 to 1879, when he was retired from active service, in consequence of a wound received in the Apache campaign of 1874. Was promoted captain, 1879, and the following year became professor of military science in the university of Wisconsin. Some of his novels are "The Colonel's Daughter" (1882), "Marion's Faith" (1886), "Dunraven Ranch" (1887), and "Between the Lines" (1889).

KING, Clarence, geologist, b. Newport, R. I., 6 Jan., 1843. Graduated at the Yale Sheffield scientific school. Was a member of the California geological survey, 1863–6, making valuable discoveries in palæontology. Headed the government survey of the fortieth parallel for the Union and Central Pacific railroads, 1867–73, his reports being published, 1870–8. One of these volumes, "Systematic Geology" (1878), is wholly by Mr. King. From 1878 to 1881, as director of the U. S. geological survey, organized that bureau from the various branches then in existence, retiring by previous agreement when his work was completed. A writer for the magazines, and author of "Mountaineering in the Sierra Nevada" (1871).

KING, Edward, b. Middlefield, Mass.,

31 July, 1848. Began contributing verse and prose to the periodicals at an early age. Resided at Paris, France, after 1868, engaged as foreign correspondent of American papers. Among his books are "My Paris, or French Character Sketches" (1868), "Echoes from the Orient," poems (1880), "The Gentle Savage," novel (1883), and "A Venetian Lover," poem (1887).

KING, Grace Elizabeth, b. New Orleans, La., 18—. Daughter of William W. King, a leading lawyer of that city for thirty years. Miss King was educated at home and in the French schools of New Orleans. Always a resident there or on her father's plantation. Her sketches of Creole life, contributed to the "New Princeton Review," 1886–8, gained her reputation and form the novel "Monsieur Motte" (1888). Other works are "Bonne Maman" (1886) and "Earthlings" (1889).

KING, Thomas Starr, clergyman, b. New York, N. Y., 17 Dec., 1824. Was pastor of Universalist and Unitarian churches in Boston, Mass., and San Francisco, Cal. Gained a wide reputation as a lecturer, and was largely instrumental in preserving California to the Union in the presidential campaign of 1860, when it was proposed to create a Pacific republic. Published "The White Hills, their Legends, Landscape, and Poetry" (1859), a volume descriptive of the White mountains, which he spent much time in exploring. Posthumous collections of review-articles and sermons were "Patriotism, and Other Papers" (1865), "Christianity and Humanity" (1877), and "Substance and Show, and Other Lectures," (1877). Died, San Francisco, Cal., 4 Mar., 1864.

KINNEY, Coates, b. Penn Yan, N. Y. 24 Nov., 1826. Was bred to the law, and occupied himself at times with journalism and politics. Was elected a member of the Ohio state senate in 1882. His poems have been collected as "Ke-u-ka, and Other Poems" (1855) and "Lyrics of the Ideal and Real" (1887).

KINNEY, Elizabeth Clementine, [Dodge], b. New York, N. Y., 18 Dec., 1810. Grand-daughter of Aaron Cleveland. Was married, 1830, to Edmund Burke Stedman, of Hartford, Conn. After his death in 1836, resided at Plainfield, N. J., and became a contributor of verse to the leading magazines of the day. Was married, 1841, to William B. Kinney, founder of the Newark, N. J., "Advertiser." On the latter's appointment to the court of Turin, 1851, she accompanied him to Europe, remaining abroad until 1865. Author of "Felicita, a Metrical Romance" (1855), "Poems" (1867), and "Bianca Capello, a Tragedy" (1873). Died, Summit, N. J., 19 Nov., 1889.

KIP, Leonard, lawyer, b. New York,

N. Y., 13 Sept., 1826. Graduated at Trinity college, Hartford. Subsequently practised his profession at Albany, N. Y., where he afterward resided. A brother of Bishop W. I. Kip. His books are "California Sketches" (1850), "Volcano Diggings" (1851), "Ænone, a Roman Tale" (1866), "The Dead Marquise" (1873), "Hannibal's Man, and Other Christmas Stories" (1878), "Under the Bells" (1879), and "Nestlenook" (1880).

KIP, William Ingraham, divine, b. New York, N.Y., 3 Oct., 1811. Of Huguenot descent. Graduated at Yale. Gave up the study of law for divinity, graduating at the N. Y. general theological seminary, 1835. Soon entered the Protestant Episcopal church as assistant minister of Grace church, New York city. Rector of St. Paul's, Albany, from 1838 until his appointment as missionary bishop of California in 1853, where he won success as a worker and writer. He became bishop in 1857. His principal books are "The Double Witness of the Church" (1844), "The Christmas Holidays in Rome" (1845), "The Catacombs of Rome" (1854), "The Unnoticed Things of Scripture" (1868), and "The Church of the Apostles" (1877).

KIRK, Ellen Warner [Olney], "Henry Hayes," b. Southington, Conn., 6 Nov., 1842. Wife of John Foster Kirk, and daughter of the geographer Jesse Olney. The latter's death in 1872 led her to develop an early inclination for writing. Her first novel, "Love in Idleness," appeared in 1876. Others are "A Midsummer Madness" (1884), "The Story of Margaret Kent" (1886), and "Sons and Daughters" (1887).

KIRK, John Foster, b. Fredericton, N. B., 22 Mar., 1824. Removed to the United States in 1842. Was secretary to William H. Prescott for eleven years before the historian's death. A frequent contributor to periodicals, and editor of "Lippincott's Magazine" from 1870 to 1886. Edited a revised edition of Prescott's writings with corrections and additions left by the author in manuscript, and himself issued an important work, the "History of Charles the Bold, Duke of Burgundy" (1863–8). In 1886 was appointed lecturer on European history at the university of Pennsylvania.

KIRKLAND, Caroline Matilda [Stansbury], b. New York, N. Y., 12 Jan., 1801. Was married to Prof. William Kirkland of Hamilton college and with him removed to Michigan about 1839. During a residence of three years in a sparsely settled region, she published lively descriptions of frontier life. The first of these was "A New Home: Who'll Follow?" (1839). "Forest Life" (1842) and "Western Clearings" (1846) succeeded. She was stricken with paralysis while actively engaged in promoting the great sanitary fair held in New York city during the civil war. Died, New York, N. Y., 6 April, 1864.

KIRKLAND, Joseph, lawyer, b. Geneva, N. Y., 7 Jan., 1830. The son of Prof. William Kirkland and Caroline Matilda Stansbury Kirkland. His early life was passed in the backwoods of central Michigan, where he received a common-school education and occasional instruction at home. He came with his parents to New York, 1842, and remained with them in that city until 1856. In the latter year he removed to Chicago and subsequently to the prairies of central Illinois. At the opening of the civil war he joined the 12th Illinois volunteers as a private, and was afterward promoted through the successive grades to be major. Subsequently resided in central Illinois and more recently in Chicago, where he followed his profession and at the same time occupied himself with literary work. The studies for his three novels of Western life were made during long residence on the prairies. The titles of these volumes are "Zury" (1887), "The McVeys" (1889), and "The Captain of Company K" (1889). In 1889 Major Kirkland accepted the position of regular literary reviewer of the Chicago "Tribune."

KNAPP, Gilbert Peter, b. New York, N. Y., 3 Nov., 1855. Chiefly a resident of that city, and engaged in mercantile pursuits. A contributor to the magazines.

KNIGHT, Sarah [Kemble], b. Boston, Mass., 19 April, 1666. Daughter of Thomas Kemble, a merchant of that city. Her husband was Richard Knight, also of Boston. Became a resident of Norwich, Conn., about 1715, at which time she was a widow, and carried on extensive real estate transactions in that place. Is remembered for her account of her horseback journey from Boston to New York in 1704, first published in "The Journals of Madam Knight, etc., from the Original Manuscripts" (1825). Died, New London, Conn., 25 Sept., 1727.

KNOX, Thomas Wallace, traveller, b. Pembroke, N. H., 26 June, 1835. Served as volunteer aid in the U. S. army during the civil war, and afterward followed journalism in New York city. Made tours of the world in 1866 and 1877 as correspondent for newspapers. Was a member of the international jury at the Paris exposition of 1878. Among his works are "Camp-Fires and Cotton-Field," war-letters (1865), "Overland through Asia" (1870), and "The Boy Travellers" series (1879–90).

LADD, Joseph Brown, physician, b. Newport, R. I., 1764. Studied medicine in his native town, and in 1784 removed to Charleston, S. C., where he entered on the successful practice of his profession. He was soon after fatally wounded in a duel arising from a newspaper controversy. Published "Poems of Arouet" (1786). Died, Charleston, S. C., 2 Nov., 1786.

LAMAR, Mirabeau Bonaparte, b. Louisville, Ga., 16 Aug., 1798. Engaged in business in early life. Removed to Texas, 1835, and served in the Texan war for independence and later in the Mexican war. Was president of Texas, 1838–41. Author of "Verse Memorials" (1857). Died, Richmond, Tex., 19 Dec., 1859.

LAMB, Martha Joanna Reade [Nash], b. Plainfield, Mass., 13 Aug., 1829. Received a private education. She resided in Chicago for several years, and in 1866 removed to New York city. Gained reputation as a historical writer, and is the author of numerous articles in reviews and magazines dealing with kindred subjects. In 1877–81 she published the "History of the City of New York," her most important work. Other books are "The Homes of America" (1879), "Wall Street in History" (1883), and "Historical Sketch of New York for the Tenth Census" (1888). In 1883 Mrs. Lamb assumed the editorship of "The Magazine of American History."

Lamont, Daniel Scott [*Noted Saying:* Vol. XI., page 458]. b. Cortlandville, Cortland Co., N.Y., 9 Feb., 1851. Private secretary to President Cleveland, 1885–9.

LANIER, Clifford, b. Griffin, Ga., 24 April, 1844. Brother of Sidney Lanier. Served through the last three years of the civil war in the Confederate army. Variously occupied at Montgomery, Ala., where he was at one time superintendent of city schools. Author of "Thorn-Fruit," (novel (1867), and of poems contributed to the periodicals.

LANIER, Sidney, b. Macon, Ga., 3 Feb., 1842. Son of Robert S. Lanier, a member of the Macon bar. Graduated at Oglethorpe college, Midway, Ga., 1860. At the outbreak of the civil war enlisted in the 2d Georgia battalion, Confederate volunteers. Served in Virginia with the army, and finally was captured near the close of the war, while attempting to run the blockade with a vessel, and was a prisoner at Point Lookout for five months. About this time contracted the affection of the lungs which followed him through life, and of which he died. After the war filled a clerkship and taught school in Alabama towns. Studied and practised law at Macon with his father from 1868 to 1872, and in 1873 removed to Baltimore, Md. where he afterward chiefly resided, with the exception of repeated trips in search of health. Obtained an engagement as first flute for the Peabody symphony concerts in that city, having been a fine musician from early years, and devoted himself to the study of literature and music. He had already written a novel, "Tiger-Lilies" (1867), descriptive of his experiences in the war. His poem "Corn," in "Lippincott's Magazine" for 1874, attracted attention, and led to his appointment to write the words of the cantata for the opening of the Centennial exhibition of 1876. Other poems and prose articles followed, and in 1879 he was made lecturer on English literature at Johns Hopkins university, advancing there the theories as to the relation between music and poetry contained in "The Science of English Verse" (1880). His second and last course of university lectures was delivered in the winter of 1880–1. His remaining books are, "Florida: its Scenery, Climate, and History" (1876), "Poems" (1877), "The Boy's Froissart" (1878), "The Boy's King Arthur" (1880), "The Boy's Mabinogion" (1881), "The Boy's Percy" (1882), and "The English Novel and the Principles of its Development" (1883). "Poems by Sidney Lanier, Edited by his Wife, with a Memorial by William Hayes Ward" appeared in 1884. Died, Lynn, N. C., 7 Sept., 1881.

LANIGAN, George Thomas, journalist, b. St. Charles, P. Q., Canada, 10 Dec., 1845. Early became a writer for the press, and, after holding editorial positions in Montreal and Chicago, served on the staff of the N. Y. "World," 1874–83. Gained reputation as a humorist, and issued "Canadian Ballads" (1864) and "Fables, by G. Washington Æsop" (1878). Died, Philadelphia, Penn., 5 Feb., 1886.

LARCOM, Lucy, b. Beverly, Mass., 1826. Worked, as a young girl, in the mills of Lowell, Mass., and subsequently studied at Monticello female seminary, in Illinois. During her residence at Lowell, contributed to John G. Whittier's paper in that place. Was editor of "Our Young Folks" from 1866 to 1874. Afterward resided in her native town. Author of "Ships in the Mist, and Other Stories" (1859), "An Idyl of Work, a Story in Verse" (1875), "Wild Roses of Cape Ann, and Other Poems" (1880), and "Poetical Works" (1885).

LARNED, Augusta, b. Rutland, Jefferson Co., N. Y., 16 April, 1835. Studied at the Spingler institute in New York city. Entered journalism in that city, corresponding for newspapers and contributing verse, fiction, and sketches to the magazines. Some of her books are "Home Stories" (1872–3), "Talks with Girls" (1873), and "Village Photographs" (1887).

LATHROP, George Parsons, b. Oahu, Hawaiian Islands, 25 Aug., 1851. Studied in New York city and at Dresden, Germany, from 1867 to 1870. Soon after took up literature as a profession. Was assistant editor of the "Atlantic Monthly," 1875–7. Edited the Boston, Mass., "Courier" until 1879, when he purchased Hawthorne's former home, "The Wayside," at Concord,

Mass., remaining there for four years, engaged in literary work. Afterward resided in New York city and New London, Conn. His dramatic adaptation, in blank verse, of Tennyson's "Elaine" was produced at the former city in 1877. Author of "Rose and Rooftree," poems (1875), "A Study of Hawthorne" (1876), "Afterglow," novel (1876), "An Echo of Passion" (1882), "In the Distance" (1882), "Spanish Vistas" (1883), "History of the Union League in Philadelphia" (1883), "Newport" (1884), "True" (1884), "Behind Time" (1888), and "Would You Kill Him?" (1889).

LATHROP, Rose [Hawthorne], b. Lenox, Mass., 20 May, 1851. Daughter of Nathaniel Hawthorne. Lived as a child in Europe, where she afterward studied art. Was married, 1871, to George Parsons Lathrop. Wrote many short stories for the magazines, besides a volume of poems entitled "Along the Shore" (1888).

LAURENS, Henry, statesman, b. Charleston, S. C., 1724. At the outbreak of the Revolution he had retired from a successful business life. Served in the South Carolina provincial congress, and was president of the Continental congress from Nov., 1777, to Dec., 1778. Was appointed minister to Holland, 1779, but was captured on his way thither and imprisoned in the Tower of London for more than a year. Subsequently signed with Jay and Franklin the preliminaries of the treaty of peace with Great Britain. Died, Charleston, S. C., 8 Dec., 1792.

Lawrence, James [*Noted Saying :* Vol. XI., page 448], b. Burlington, N. J., 1 Oct., 1781. Captain in the U. S. navy during the war of 1812. Fatally wounded in action, 1 June, 1813. Died at sea, 6 June, 1813.

LAWSON, Deodat, clergyman. The dates and places of his birth and death are not known, though it is probable that he was born and died in England. He was the son of Thomas Lawson, minister of Denton, in the county of Norfolk. First heard of at Martha's Vineyard in 1671, and took the freeman's oath at Boston in 1680. He was called to the ministry at Salem village late in 1683, but the Salem church being divided by disputes, his ordination could not be agreed on, and he returned to Boston. Was minister of the Second church at Scituate by 1693, and remained there until 1696, when he sailed for England, being formally dismissed in 1698. Was invited to Salem in 1692 to assist at the witchcraft proceedings, and preached a sermon advocating the trials, on lecture-day, 24 Mar., 1692. This sermon, which undoubtedly influenced the popular mind against the accused, was published the following year with the title "Christ's Fidelity the only Shield against Satan's Malignity." It was republished at London in 1704, with an appendix describing the witchcraft trials, which latter had already appeared in a briefer form in 1693.

LAWSON, John, b. Scotland. Sailed to America from Cowes, England, arriving at Charleston, S. C. After extensive travels among the Indians of North and South Carolina, he became surveyor-general of the former colony, in 1700, serving twelve years. Issued at London "A New Voyage to Carolina" (1700), afterward republished as "The History of Carolina" (1714), an account of his experiences in the colonies. Killed by Indians on the Neuse river, N. C., 1712.

LAWTON, William Cranston, b. New Bedford, Mass., 22 May, 1853. Graduated at Harvard. Was classical master at the New Bedford high school for several years. Resided mainly in Europe during 1880–3, engaged in foreign travel and study. Afterward taught classics at Boston, Mass. An extensive writer on classical subjects for the "Atlantic Monthly" and other periodicals. "Three Dramas of Euripides," translations with an essay and notes, appeared in 1889.

LAZARUS, Emma, b. New York, N. Y., 22 July, 1849. Of Jewish parentage. Received her education at home under private instruction. Verses written between the ages of fourteen and seventeen appeared as "Poems and Translations" (1867). "Admetus, and Other Poems" (1871) first attracted public attention, and was followed by "Alide," a romance (1874). She thereafter contributed frequently to "Lippincott's" and the "Century" magazines. In 1881 her translation of "Poems and Ballads of Heine" was issued, and the next year "Songs of a Semite." The persecutions of her race in Russia during 1881–2 aroused her sympathies, and she accomplished much in alleviating the sufferings of refugees from that country to America. Her writings after this period were chiefly concerned with Jewish subjects. A collective edition of her "Poems, Narrative, Dramatic, and Lyric" was brought out posthumously in 1888. Died, New York, N. Y., 19 Nov., 1887.

LEA, Henry Charles, publisher, b. Philadelphia, Penn., 19 Sept., 1825. Entered his father's publishing-house in Philadelphia at the age of eighteen, and in 1865 became proprietor of the business. Made a life-long study of mediæval European history. Was active in furthering the system of bounties by which the city of Philadelphia raised its quota of troops during the civil war, at which time he also wrote numerous political pamphlets. In addition to magazine and review articles, published "Superstition and Force : Essays on the Wager of Law, the Wager of Battle, the Ordeal, and Torture" (1866), "Sacerdotal

Celibacy in the Christian Church" (1867), "Studies in Church History" (1869), and "A History of the Inquisition of the Middle Ages" (1888).

LEARNED, Walter, b. New London, Conn., 22 June, 1847. Received his education in that city, where he became assistant treasurer of the savings bank of New London. A contributor to the magazines, and author of "Between Times," poems (1889).

LEDYARD, John, traveller, b. Groton, Conn., 1751. Studied, but did not graduate, at Dartmouth. Pursued a course of preparation for the ministry, and, being rejected as a candidate for ordination, adopted a seafaring life. Sailed with Captain Cook on his third voyage. Subsequently travelled extensively in northern Europe and Russia. Published "Journal of Capt. Cook's Last Voyage" (1783). Died, Cairo, Egypt, 17 Jan., 1789.

Lee, Arthur [*Noted Saying:* Vol. XI., page 447], b. Stratford, Va., 20 Dec., 1740. Brother of Richard Henry Lee. Was U. S. commissioner to France, and a member of the Continental congress. Died, Urbana, Va., 12 Dec., 1792.

LEE, Henry, soldier, b. Westmoreland Co., Va., 29 Jan., 1756. Graduated at the college of New Jersey. Was appointed captain of one of the six companies of cavalry raised by Virginia in 1776. Promoted to be major two years later, he was given an independent command which he soon raised to a high point of military efficiency. It became known as "Lee's Legion," and he himself was named "Light-horse Harry," in recognition of his daring exploits. In 1780, having become lieutenant-colonel, he joined General Greene's army in South Carolina. Was a member of the Continental congress in 1786, and of the Virginia constitutional convention of 1788. Was afterward sent to the South Carolina legislature, and was governor, 1792–5. Elected a U. S. representative in 1799, he was called upon by congress to deliver his oration on the death of Washington. Author of "Memoirs of the War in the Southern Department of the United States" (1812). Died, Cumberland Island, Ga., 25 Mar., 1818.

LEE, Richard Henry, statesman, b. Stratford, Va., 20 Jan., 1732. After completing a course of law studies, served in the Virginia house of burgesses from 1761 to 1788. He was a delegate to the first Continental congress in 1774, and in the congress of 1775 drafted the address to the people of Great Britain adopted by that body. On 7 June, 1776, he made the original motion in congress that the colonies were "free and independent states," and was a signer of the Declaration of Independence. U. S. senator from Virginia, 1789–92. Died, Chantilly, Va., 19 June, 1794.

LEGARÉ, Hugh Swinton, lawyer, b. Charleston, S. C., 2 Jan., 1797. Graduated at the university of South Carolina. Practised law at Charleston. A member of the South Carolina legislature for several years, and U. S. representative for one term. Was chargé d'affaires at Brussels, 1832–6, and attorney-general of the United States, 1841–3. His "Writings" (1846) were collected posthumously. Died, Boston, Mass., 20 June, 1843.

LEGARÉ, James Mathews, inventor, b. Charleston, S.C., 26 Nov., 1823. Patented several inventions which failing health prevented him from fully developing. Published "Orta-Undis, and Other Poems" (1847), and contributed from time to time poems and prose articles to several magazines. Died, Aiken, S. C., 30 Mar., 1859.

LEGGETT, William, journalist, b. New York, N. Y., 1802. Studied at Georgetown college, D. C., and served in the U. S. navy, 1822–6. A member of the staff of the N. Y. "Evening Post," 1829–36. Was appointed diplomatic agent to Guatemala, but died before sailing. Author of "Leisure Hours at Sea" (1825), "Tales of a Country Schoolmaster" (1835), "Naval Stories" (1834), and "Political Writings" (issued posthumously, 1840). Died, New Rochelle, N. Y., 29 May, 1839.

LEIGHTON, William, b. Cambridge, Mass., 22 June, 1833. Graduated at Harvard. Entered the business of manufacturing glass, and after 1868 resided at Wheeling, W. Va. Among his books are "The Sons of Godwin," a tragedy (1876), "At the Court of King Edwin: a Drama" (1878), "Shakespeare's Dream, and Other Poems" (1881), and "The Subjection of Hamlet" (1882).

LELAND, Charles Godfrey, "Hans Breitmann," b. Philadelphia, Penn., 15 Aug., 1824. Graduated at Princeton, and completed his education at European universities. Early became a contributor to the magazines, and edited periodicals in New York city and Philadelphia. Became a student of the life and language of the gypsies, in this country as well as in England, where he lived for long periods. To him belongs the credit for the introduction of classes in the industrial arts in the public schools of Philadelphia, and he is the inventor of the method pursued in these classes. Devoted many years to the extension of this system. His most important book on the subject is "Practical Education" (1888), a work on the art of learning, to be followed by "Home Arts and Industries : a Series of Manuals for Schools or Self Instruction." Among his earlier writings "Meister Karl's Sketch-Book" (1856) and "Hans Breitmann's Ballads" (1871), the latter a series of studies in German-American dialect, gained him popularity. Other works are "The Music Lesson of Confucius, and Other Poems" (1872), "The Gypsies" (1882), "The Algonkin Legends of New England" (1884), and a "Dictionary of Jargons."

LESLIE, Eliza, b. Philadelphia, Penn., 15 Nov., 1787. A sister of the artist, Charles Robert Leslie. Resided chiefly in Philadelphia. Her first volume was a cookery book, and she was encouraged by its success to write fiction. Besides a number of books for children, she wrote "Pencil Sketches" (1833–7), chiefly stories contributed to the magazines, and "The Behavior Book" (1853). Died, Gloucester, N. J., 2 Jan., 1858.

LESTER, Charles Edwards, b. Griswold, Conn., 15 July, 1815. A descendant of Jonathan Edwards. Was U. S. consul at Genoa, 1840–6. Subsequently resided chiefly in New York city, occupied with literary pursuits. Author of "The Glory and the Shame of England" (1841), "Life and Public Services of Charles Sumner" (1874), "Our First Hundred Years" (1874), and "History of the United States" (1883). Died, Detroit, Mich., 29 Jan., 1890.

LEWIS, Charles Bertrand, "M. Quad," journalist, b. Liverpool, O., 15 Feb., 1842. Educated at the Michigan agricultural college. Served for two years in the U. S. army during the civil war. Became a member of the Detroit, Mich., "Free Press" staff in 1869, and gained reputation as a writer of humorous and pathetic sketches. Much of his work was published as the proceedings of "Brother Gardner's Lime-Kiln Club" (1883–8).

LEWIS, Charlton Thomas, lawyer, b. West Chester, Penn., 25 Feb., 1834. Graduated at Yale. Entered the Methodist Episcopal ministry, and was pastor of several churches, subsequently filling positions as professor at Bloomington, Ill., and Troy universities. Practised law in New York city after 1864. Author of "A History of the German People" (1870), and prepared almost all of "Harper's Latin Dictionary" (1880).

LEWIS, Tayler, scholar, b. Northumberland, N. Y., 1802. Graduated at Union college. Became professor of Greek in the university of New York, 1838, and from 1849 until his death was professor of Greek, biblical, and Oriental literature at Union. Some of his numerous works are "The Six Days of Creation" (1855), "The Bible and Science" (1856), and "Heroic Periods in a Nation's History" (1866). Died, Schenectady, N. Y., 11 May, 1877.

LIEBER, Francis, publicist, b. Berlin, Germany, 18 Mar.,1800. Joined the Prussian army in 1815 and fought at Waterloo. Was imprisoned for Liberalism in Berlin and forbidden the Prussian universities. Graduated at Jena. Took refuge in England, 1825,

coming to America in 1827, where he settled down to literary work and lecturing. Was engaged, 1832, to form a plan of education by the trustees of Girard college, and in 1835 was appointed professor of history and political economy at the university of South Carolina, retaining the position until 1856. He then accepted the same chair at Columbia college, adding, in 1860, the professorship of political science in its law school. In 1863 he started the Loyal publication society, which issued papers upholding the Union cause. He was intrusted, 1865, with the superintendence of the collection and arranging of the Confederate government records. Was appointed, 1870, final arbitrator of the disputes between the United States and Mexico. Among his many publications are a "Manual of Political Ethics" (1838), "Essays on Property and Labor" (1842), "The West, and Other Poems" (1848), and "Civil Liberty and Self-Government" (1853, revised ed. 1874). Died, New York, N. Y., 2 Oct., 1872.

LINCOLN, Abraham, sixteenth president of the United States, b. Hardin, now Larue Co., Ky., 12 Feb., 1809. Descended from Samuel Lincoln of Norwich, England, who settled in Massachusetts. His family removed to Indiana in 1816, and to Illinois in 1830. Received a backwoods education, supplemented by untiring self-culture. Was captain of a company in the Indian war of 1832 for a few weeks. After hard experience in farming and kindred occupations, took up the study of law. Was postmaster at New Salem, Ill., 1833–6. Elected to the state legislature, 1834–42. Settled in the practice of law at Springfield, and was elected U. S. representative, 1846. Became a prominent Whig leader, and, later, head of the Republican party in Illinois. The famous debate with Senator Douglas in 1858 gave him a wider reputation as a leader of originality, talents, and force, which was broadened into national fame by his memorable address at Cooper Institute, New York city, Feb., 1860. Three months later he was nominated for the presidency at the Chicago convention, and was elected in November. The war opened in April, 1861. The final proclamation of freedom was issued, 1 Jan., 1863. He was reëlected for a second term in 1864, and on 9 April, 1865, Lee surrendered at Appomattox. On 14 April Lincoln was assassinated. A collection of his writings, speeches, and letters is to be edited by John G. Nicolay and John Hay, whose "Abraham Lincoln : a History" appeared in the "Century Magazine" for 1887–9. Died, Washington, D. C., 15 April, 1865.

LINN, John Blair, clergyman, b. Shippensburg, Penn., 14 Mar., 1777. Graduated at Columbia college. Studied law under

Alexander Hamilton, but subsequently entered the Presbyterian ministry. While a student, had produced an unsuccessful play in New York. Was assistant pastor of a church in Philadelphia from 1799 until his death. Author of poems entitled "The Death of Washington" (1800) and "The Power of Genius" (1801). Died, Philadelphia, Penn., 30 Aug., 1804.

LIPPINCOTT, Sarah Jane [Clarke], "Grace Greenwood," b. Pompey, N. Y., 23 Sept., 1823. Chiefly a resident of Philadelphia and New York city, though she spent much time in Europe. Well-known as a writer for children and a lecturer. Some of her books are "Greenwood Leaves" (1850), "Poetical Works" (1851), "Haps and Mishaps of a Tour in Europe" (1854), and "New Life in New Lands" (1873).

LITCHFIELD, Grace Denio, b. New York, N. Y., 19 Nov., 1849. Daughter of Edwin C. Litchfield. Resided for a number of years in Europe, returning to America and settling permanently at Washington, D. C., in 1888. Among her novels are "The Knight of the Black Forest" (1885) and "A Hard-Won Victory" (1888).

LIVINGSTON, Robert R., statesman, b. New York, N. Y., 27 Nov., 1746. A descendant of the first owner of Livingston manor. Graduated at Kings, now Columbia, college. Was admitted to the New York bar in 1773. Appointed recorder of New York city the same year, but soon lost this position through his republicanism. Was a member of the Continental congress, 1775–7 and 1779–81, and was appointed on the committee to draft the Declaration of Independence, though unable to be present when it was signed. Was chancellor of New York state from 1777 to 1801, and administered the presidential oath to Washington. Minister to France, 1801–5, obtaining the Louisiana cession from Napoleon in 1803. Died, Clermont, N. Y., 26 Feb., 1813.

LIVINGSTON, William, statesman, b. Albany, N. Y., 30 Nov., 1723. Grandson of Robert, the first owner of Livingston manor. Graduated at Yale. Studied law with William Smith, father of the chief-justice of the same name, and prepared in conjunction with the first "Digest of the Colony Laws" (1752-62). Purchased land at Elizabethtown, N. J., and built the house called "Liberty Hall," removing his residence there in 1772. Was a delegate to the first Continental congress in 1774; was assigned to the command of the New Jersey militia the following year, and was elected governor of New Jersey continuously from 1776 until his death. He furnished valuable aid to the American cause during the whole of the Revolution. Had previously written extensively for periodicals and published several pamphlets on the popular side. In 1787 he was a delegate to the Constitutional convention. Died, Elizabethtown, N. J., 25 July, 1790.

LLOYD, David Demarest, journalist, b. New York, N. Y., 1 Sept., 1851. Graduated at the college of New York. Soon after became a reporter for the N. Y. "Tribune." Resigned in 1871 to become private secretary to Chief-Justice Chase, returning, on the latter's death, to the "Tribune," where he was promoted to the editorial staff. As correspondent at Albany in 1875, was active in exposing the canal ring. Besides contributing to the magazines, was the author of four successful plays, "For Congress" (produced 1883), "The Woman Hater" (1885), "The Dominie's Daughter" (1887), and "The Senator" (1889). Died, Weehawken, N. J., 4 Sept., 1889.

LOCKE, David Ross, "Petroleum V. Nasby," journalist, b. Vestal, Broome Co., N. Y., 20 Sept., 1833. Learned the trade of a printer in the office of the Cortland "Democrat." Was a journeyman printer and afterward reporter on several Western papers, and in 1852 became editor of the Plymouth, O., "Advertiser." Issued the first of the political satires known as the "Nasby" letters in the Findlay "Jeffersonian," of which he was then editor, 21 April, 1861. These letters were highly valued by President Lincoln, Chief-Justice Chase, and other administration leaders as factors in preserving Union sentiment at the North. Mr. Locke assumed editorial charge of the Toledo, O., "Blade" in 1865, finally becoming proprietor. The first volume of "Nasby" letters was brought out as "Divers Views, Opinions, and Prophecies of Yours Trooly, Petroleum V. Nasby" (1865). This and several succeeding volumes were collected as "The Struggles—Social, Financial, and Political—of Petroleum V. Nasby" (1872). Also wrote "The Moral History of America's Life-Struggle" (1872) and "A Paper City," novel (1878). Died, Toledo, O., 15 Feb., 1888.

LOCKE, Richard Adams, journalist, b. New York, N. Y., 1800. At different times editor of the N. Y. "Sun" and "The New Era." Chiefly remembered as the perpetrator of the "moon hoax," which appeared in the "Sun," 1835, with the title "Great Astronomical Discoveries Lately Made by Sir John Herschel, LL.D., F.R.S., etc." It was reprinted as a pamphlet, 1859. Died, Staten Island, N. Y., 16 Feb., 1871.

LODGE, Henry Cabot, legislator, b. Boston, Mass., 12 May, 1850. Graduated at Harvard, where he lectured on American history, 1876–9, and was made overseer in 1884. Was editor of the "North American Review," 1873–6. A member of the Massachusetts legislature in 1880–1, and was elected U. S. representative from the same state, 1886. Author of "Life and Letters of George Cabot" (1877), "Short History of English Colonies in America" (1881), "Studies in History" (1884), and several volumes of the "American statesmen series," among which is "George Washington" (1889). Also edited an edition of Alexander Hamilton's works, 1885, with introduction and notes.

LONG, John Davis, legislator, b. Buckfield, Me., 27 Oct., 1838. Graduated at Harvard. Studied law and established a practice at Boston, Mass., 1862. Speaker of the Massachusetts house, 1876–8, and governor of the state, 1880–2. Was elected U.S. representative in 1883 and for succeeding terms. Issued a translation of Virgil's "Æneid" (1879), and wrote fugitive verse.

LONGFELLOW, Henry Wadsworth, b. Portland, Me., 27 Feb., 1807. Son of Stephen Longfellow, at one time U. S. representative from Maine, whose ancestors had emigrated from Yorkshire, England, about 1675. Henry Wadsworth passed his youth at Portland and was there fitted for college, entering the sophomore class at Bowdoin in 1822, and numbering Nathaniel Hawthorne, George B. Cheever, and J. S. C. Abbott among his classmates. While at college he contributed a number of poems to the Boston "United States Literary Gazette" and other periodicals. Graduating in 1825, he sailed for Europe the following year to prepare himself by study in foreign countries for appointment to the chair of modern languages at Bowdoin. He resided in France, Spain, Italy, and Germany until 1829, when he returned and entered upon the duties of his professorship. He soon began writing for the "North American Review" and "New England Magazine," publishing in the latter a portion of the papers afterward collected as "Outre Mer; a Pilgrimage beyond the Sea" (1835). He was married in 1831 to a young lady of Portland. Receiving the offer of the professorship of modern languages at Harvard, he resigned his position at Bowdoin, and in 1835 again visited Europe for a course of preliminary study. The illness and death of his wife late in that year interfered somewhat with his plans, but he remained at Heidelberg through the winter, visiting Switzerland in the summer. He filled the professorship at Harvard from 1836 to his retirement in 1854. The beginning of this period was marked by a return to poetical composition. Some of his best-known poems were written at this time, and his first volume of verse, "Voices of the Night" (1839), was an immediate success. It had been preceded by "Hyperion; a Romance" (1839), in which some of his experiences during his last trip to Europe are shadowed forth. The character of the heroine is thought to resemble that of Miss Frances Appleton, whom he met at that time, and who became his wife in 1843. He purchased the old "Craigie house" at Cambridge soon after his marriage, and it became his permanent home. Volumes of poetry followed in quick succession, and his fame broadened rapidly. They were "Ballads and Other Poems" (1841), "Poems on Slavery" (1842), "The Spanish Student" (1843), "The Belfry of Bruges, and Other Poems" (1846), "Evangeline, a Tale of Acadie" (1847), "The Seaside and the Fireside" (1850), "The Golden Legend" (1851), "The Song of Hiawatha" (1855), and "The Courtship of Miles Standish" (1858). His translation of Dante's "Divine Comedy" was taken up as a relief from the melancholy induced by the death of his wife by fire in 1861. It appeared in 1867. His remaining books of verse were "Tales of a Wayside Inn" (1863), "Flower de Luce" (1867), "The Divine Tragedy," including the title piece, "The Golden Legend," and "The New England Tragedies" (1871), "Three Books of Song" (1872), "Aftermath" (1874), "The Masque of Pandora" (1875), "Keramos" (1878), "Ultima Thule" (1880), and "In the Harbor" (1882). A voyage to England in 1868 was the occasion of his receiving the degrees of LL.D. from Cambridge and D.C.L. from Oxford. A marble bust of the poet was placed in the Poets' Corner of Westminster Abbey, Mar., 1884. "Life of Henry Wadsworth Longfellow" and "Final Memorials," chiefly compiled from his letters and diaries by his brother, Samuel Longfellow, appeared in 1886–7. Died, Cambridge, Mass., 24 Mar., 1882.

LONGFELLOW, Samuel, clergyman, b. Portland, Me., 18 June, 1819. Brother of H. W. Longfellow. Graduated at Harvard. Pastor of Unitarian churches at Brooklyn, N. Y., and Germantown, Penn., until 1882, when he settled at Cambridge, Mass. Author of several popular hymns, and joint compiler of "Hymns of the Spirit" (1864) and "Thalatta, a Book for the Seaside" (1853). Published "Life of Henry Wadsworth Longfellow" (1886) and "Final Memorials of H. W. L.," 1887.

LONGSTREET, Augustus Baldwin, lawyer and educator, b. Augusta, Ga., 22 Sept., 1790. Graduated at Yale. Admitted to the bar in Georgia, 1815. Was made judge of the superior court of Ocmulgee circuit, 1822, and declining a reëlection continued his law practice. In 1838 entered the Methodist Episcopal ministry, and the following year became president of Emory college, Ga. Ten years later he was made president of the university of Mississippi. Was a frequent contributor to the newspapers and magazines, and founded the "Augusta Sentinel." Some of his sketches were gathered in a volume as "Georgia Scenes"

(1840), and gained a permanent reputation. Died, Oxford, Miss., 9 Sept., 1870.

LORD, William Wilberforce, clergyman, b. Madison Co., N. Y., 28 Oct., 1819. Tutor at Amherst, 1847. Accepted orders in the Protestant Episcopal church, officiating for several years at Vicksburg, Miss. Served as chaplain in the Confederate army. More recently, rector of a church in Cooperstown, N. Y. Author of "Poems" (1845), "Christ in Hades" (1851), and "André, a Tragedy" (1856).

LORING, Frederick Wadsworth, journalist, b. Boston, Mass., 12 Dec., 1848. Graduated at Harvard, 1870, and the following year was variously employed in writing for periodicals. Accompanied the U. S. exploring expedition of 1871 to Arizona, as correspondent of "Appletons' Journal." Best known by his poem "In the Old Churchyard at Fredericksburg." Killed by Indians, near Wickenburg, Arizona, 5 Nov., 1871.

LOSSING, Benson John, artist-author, b. Beekman, Dutchess Co., N. Y., 12 Feb., 1813. Owned and edited the "Poughkeepsie Telegraph," and in 1838 illustrated with wood-cuts and edited the "Family Magazine." One of the pioneer wood-engravers of the country. Settled permanently at New York city in 1839. Among the great number of his publications, mostly illustrated by himself, are "Pictorial Field-book of the Revolution" (1850–2), "The Hudson, from the Wilderness to the Sea" (1866), "Pictorial Field-book of the Civil War" (1866–9), "Life and Times of Peter Schuyler" (1870), "Cyclopædia of United States History" (1881), "Mary and Martha Washington" (1886), and "The Empire State, a Compendious History of the Commonwealth of New York" (1887).

LOUGHEAD, Flora [Haines], b. Milwaukee, Wis., 12 July, 1855. Daughter of John P. Haines. Graduated at Lincoln university, Ill. Was married, 1886, to John Loughead. Had previously been occupied as an independent journalist in Denver, Col., and in San Francisco, which latter city became her permanent home. Besides many stories contributed to the periodicals, wrote "The Libraries of California" (1878), "The Man who was Guilty," novel (1886), and "Quick Cooking" (1888).

LOUNSBURY, Thomas Raynesford, educator, b. Ovid, N. Y., 1 Jan., 1838. Graduated at Yale. Shortly after graduating in 1859, became a writer, chiefly in the department of biography, for Appletons' "American Cyclopædia," and continued in that employment until he was commissioned, Aug., 1862, first lieutenant in the 126th regiment N. Y. S. volunteers. Was made prisoner at Harper's Ferry in September, and exchanged in November, remaining in

the field until after Gettysburg, when he was detailed as adjutant-general of the draft rendezvous at Elmira, N. Y. Was mustered out of service at the close of the civil war, and was for three years teacher and private instructor in and near New York city. During this period he devoted much time to the study of Anglo-Saxon and Early English. In 1870 was appointed instructor, and the following year professor of English, at the Yale Sheffield scientific school. Edited the department of Middle English (Chaucer) in "The Century Dictionary," and prepared students' editions of Chaucer's "House of Fame" and "Parlament of Foules." Author of "James Fenimore Cooper," a biography (1883) and "History of the English Language" (1879).

LOW, Samuel, b. 12 Dec., 1765. This fact, obtained from a statement in a stanza contained in his "Poems" (1800), is all that is known of him. The collection was published by T. & J. Swords, of New York city.

LOWELL, James Russell, b. Cambridge, Mass., 22 Feb., 1819. Youngest son of the Rev. Charles Lowell, and descended from English settlers of 1639. Entered Harvard at sixteen, graduating in 1838. His first important literary effort was a class-poem, satirizing the abolitionists and the Concord transcendental school. Admitted to the bar, 1840. Issued his first volume of poems, "A Year's Life," 1841. Married, 1844, Maria White, whose anti-slavery convictions influenced his after career. Both wrote in "The Liberty Bell" and "Anti-Slavery Standard." In these and the Boston "Courier" most of his earlier poems appeared. "The Pioneer," 1843, a serial in which Poe, Hawthorne, Elizabeth Barrett (Browning), and others were to have written, did not survive its third number. In the "Courier" (1846–8) the "Biglow Papers" appeared, with instant success. Of a slightly earlier date were "A Legend of Brittany" (1844), "Conversations with Some of the Old Poets," critical essays (1845), and "The Vision of Sir Launfal" (1845). His satire, "A Fable for Critics," came out anonymously, 1848. A collective edition of "Poems" was issued in 1849, and various contributions found a welcome in the magazines. Visited Europe in 1851. Two years later his wife died. Succeeded Longfellow in the chair of modern languages and belles-lettres at Harvard, 1855. From 1857 to 1862 wrote essays for the "Atlantic Monthly," and from 1863 to 1872 acted as joint editor with Prof. C. E. Norton of the "North American Review." A second series of the "Biglow Papers" came out in the "Atlantic Monthly" during the civil war, and was reissued in book-form, 1866. It was preceded by the volume of "Fireside Travels" (1864). "Under the Willows" followed in 1869, and the essays "Among my Books" (1870) and "My Study Windows" (1871). During the Centennial celebrations he delivered three odes—at Concord, 19 April, 1875, at Cambridge, Mass., under the Washington elm, 3 July, 1875, and at Boston, 4 July, 1876. Was appointed to the Spanish mission by President Hayes, 1877, and thence transferred to London in 1880, resigning in 1885. Delivered at London a memorable address on the unveiling of the bust of Coleridge in Westminster Abbey, and the volume "Democracy, and other Addresses" (1887) includes this and other notable speeches in England, where his services were in great request. Resumed his lectures at Harvard on his return to America. "Heartsease and Rue," poems, and "Political Essays" appeared in 1888. Was made D.C.L. by Oxford, 1873, LL.D. by Cambridge, 1874, and was rector of St. Andrew's university during a portion of his mission to England.

LOWELL, Maria [White], b. Watertown, Mass., 8 July, 1821. Was married, 1844, to James Russell Lowell. Beloved for her graces of person and character. Wrote much in behalf of the abolition of slavery. A privately printed volume of her poems was issued in 1855. Died, Cambridge, Mass., 27 Oct., 1853.

LOWELL, Robert Traill Spence, clergyman, b. Boston, Mass., 8 Oct., 1816. Elder brother of James Russell Lowell. Graduated at Harvard. Gave up medicine for divinity, and became deacon in the Protestant Episcopal church at Bermuda, 1842, of which colony he was also made an inspector of public schools. Was stationed at Newfoundland, 1843–6. After occupying several livings settled as head master of St. Mark's school, Southborough, Mass., 1869, until appointed professor of Latin in Union college, Schenectady, N. Y. Published in 1858 his best-known work, a clerical novel, "The New Priest in Conception Bay" (new ed., 1889). "Fresh Hearts that Failed Three Thousand Years Ago, and Other Poems" appeared in 1860. His miscellaneous writings include "A Story or Two from a Dutch Town" (1878).

LUCAS, Eliza, b. about 1721. The daughter of Lieutenant-colonel Lucas, governor of Antigua. Removed to South Carolina in 1739, and was married to Charles Pinckney, afterward chief-justice of the province. The "Journal and Letters of Eliza Lucas" was privately printed in 1850. Died 1792.

LÜDERS, Charles Henry, b. Philadelphia, Penn., 25 June, 1858. Studied at the university of Pennsylvania. A continuous resident of Philadelphia after 1872. A writer of verse and prose for the magazines and joint author with S. D. Smith, Jr., of "Hallo, My Fancy!" poems (1887).

LUDLOW, Fitz Hugh, b. New York, N. Y., 11 Sept., 1836. Graduated at Union college. Edited the N. Y. "Vanity Fair," 1858–60, and was at times connected with the N. Y. "World" and "Evening Post." Contributed numerous articles, stories, and poems to the magazines, and wrote "The Hasheesh Eater" (1857), "The Opium Habit" (1868), and "The Heart of the Continent" (1870). Died, Geneva, Switzerland, 12 Sept., 1870.

LUNT, George, lawyer, b. Newburyport, Mass., 31 Dec., 1803. Graduated at Harvard, and practised law. Was U. S. district attorney during President Taylor's administration. Associate editor of the Boston "Courier" during the civil war. Author of "Poems" (1839), "Three Eras of New England" (1857), "Radicalism in Religion, Philosophy, and Social Life" (1858), and "Miscellanies, Poems, etc." (1884). Died, Boston, Mass., 17 May, 1885.

LYTLE, William Haines, soldier, b. Cincinnati, O., 2 Nov., 1826. Graduated at Cincinnati college, and studied for the law. Served as captain in the Mexican war, and in the civil war as colonel, and was promoted brigadier-general of volunteers for gallant conduct, having been twice wounded in action. His poems were published in the periodicals, some of them being collected in Coggeshall's "Poets and Poetry of the West" (1860). Fell, while leading a charge, at the battle of Chickamauga, Tenn., 20 Sept., 1863.

MABIE, Hamilton Wright, journalist, b. Cold Spring, N. Y., 13 Dec., 1845. Graduated at Williams. Entered journalism, and became associate editor of the N. Y. "Christian Union" in 1884. A contributor to the reviews and magazines, and author of "Norse Stories, Retold from the Eddas" (1882) and "My Study Fire," literary studies (1890).

MACDONOUGH, Augustus Rodney, lawyer, b. Middletown, Conn., 20 Nov., 1820. Was taken to sea in 1824 by his father, Commodore Macdonough, U. S. N., then commanding the Mediterranean squadron. Graduated at Yale. Studied law and practised in St. Louis, Mo., and New York city, until 1873, when he became secretary of the Erie railroad company. An early member of the N. Y. Century club, and its secretary for thirty years. A contributor of articles and criticisms to the magazines, and translator of "Nature and Life," papers by Papillon, (1875), and "Aucassin and Nicolette" (1880).

MacKELLAR, Thomas, printer, b. New York, N. Y., 12 Aug., 1812. In 1860 became the head of a large type-foundry at Philadelphia, Penn. Author of "Hymns and Metrical Psalms" (1883).

MACON, John Alfred, journalist, b. Demopolis, Ala., 15 Nov., 1851. Educated at the university of Virginia. Removed to St. Louis, Mo., 1882, and became a member of the "Post-Dispatch" editorial staff. Afterward joined the staff of the N.Y. "World." Contributed verse to the magazines, and issued "Uncle Gabe Tucker," in dialect (1881).

MADISON, James, fourth president of the United States, b. Port Conway, King George Co., Va., 16 Mar., 1751. Graduated at Princeton. Studied law, and in 1776 was a delegate to the state convention which formed the first Virginia constitution. After serving in the state legislature, he became a member of the Continental congress in 1780, returning to the legislature four years later. In both bodies he advocated measures looking to the strengthening of the Federal government, and in 1787 was chosen a delegate to the Constitutional convention at Philadelphia. He was one of its leading spirits, and afterward supported the proposed Constitution by powerful arguments in his contributions to "The Federalist" (1788), and by active service in the Virginia convention called to ratify that instrument. His reports of the debates of the Philadelphia convention, with selections from his correspondence, were published by order of congress in 1840. From 1789 until 1797 he was a member of the U. S. house of representatives, and was secretary of state under Jefferson from 1801 to 1809. He succeeded the latter as president, and was re-elected for a second term. The chief event of his administration was the war of 1812. Died, Montpellier, Va., 28 June, 1836.

MANN, Horace, educator, b. Franklin, Mass., 4 May, 1796. Graduated at Brown. Admitted to the bar, 1823. Was a member of the Massachusetts legislature, and was elected U. S. representative from the same state, as an anti-slavery candidate. Secretary of the Massachusetts board of education, 1837–48, and published a valuable series of school reports. President of Antioch college from 1852 until his death. His "Life and Complete Works" were brought out in 1869. Died, Yellow Springs, O., 2 Aug., 1859.

MANN, Samuel Eleazer, b. Lawrence, Mass., 10 April, 1853. Graduated at the Worcester Polytechnic institute. Engaged for some years in teaching in Connecticut. Latterly a resident of Apopka, Fla., occupied with study and literary work.

MANSFIELD, Lewis William, b. Kent, Conn., 16 May, 1816. A resident of Cohoes, N. Y. Author of "The Morning Watch," poems (1850), "Up-Country Letters" (1852), "Country Margins" (1855), besides numerous fugitive poems in later years.

Maroy, William Learned [*Noted Say-*

ing: Vol. VII., page 191], b. Southbridge, Mass., 12 Dec., 1786. U. S. senator from New York, 1831–3. Subsequently governor of that state for three terms. Died, Ballston Spa, N. Y., 4 July, 1857.

MARKHAM, Charles Edwin, b. Oregon, 23 April, 1852. Graduated at the California State normal school, and subsequently became a member of the faculty of Christian college at Santa Rosa. Author of "In Earth's Shadow," poems (1890), and "Songs of a Dream-Builder" (1890).

MARSH, George Perkins, philologist and diplomat, b. Woodstock, Vt., 15 Mar., 1801. Graduated at Dartmouth. Was U. S. representative from Vermont, 1842–9, when he was appointed U. S. minister to Turkey. Returning in 1853, he was appointed in 1861 to the Italian mission, which position he held until his death. His principal works are "Compendious Grammar of the Old Northern or Icelandic Language" (1838), "The Origin and History of the English Language" (1862), and "Man and Nature" (1864), the latter afterward revised and republished in 1874 as "The Earth as Modified by Human Action." Died, Vallombrosa, Italy, 24 July, 1882.

MARSHALL, John, jurist, b. Fauquier Co., Va., 24 Sept., 1755. Received his early education from a local clergyman. Served in the Continental army, becoming captain in 1779. Was admitted to the bar, 1780, and resigned from the army to practise his profession, Jan., 1781. Elected to the Virginia house of burgesses, 1782, of which body he was a member, at intervals, until 1796. Removed his residence to Richmond, 1783. Chosen to the Virginia Constitutional convention of 1788, he advocated the instrument under consideration and assisted to secure its ratification. Was one of the U. S. commission sent to negotiate with France in 1797. Elected U. S. representative from Virginia in 1799, he served the administration of Adams with powerful effect during one session, being appointed secretary of state in May, 1800. Received the appointment of chief justice of the United States, Jan., 1801, holding office until his death. A volume of his historic decisions as chief justice was published in 1839 as "The Writings of John Marshall on the Federal Constitution." Author of "The Life of George Washington" (1805, revised ed. 1832). Died, Philadelphia, Penn., 6 July, 1835.

MARSHALL, Thomas Francis, lawyer and politician, b. Frankfort, Ky., 7 June, 1801. A nephew of John Marshall, and justly famed as a wit and orator. After serving as judge of a Louisville circuit court, he was U. S. representative, 1841–3. During his later years he lectured on historical and geological subjects, and in the cause of temperance. A volume of his "Speeches and

Writings" was issued in 1858. Died, near Versailles, Ky., 22 Sept., 1864.

MARTIN, Edward Sanford, b. "Willowbrook," Owasco Lake, N. Y., 2 Jan., 1856. Graduated at Harvard. Edited the N. Y. "Life" at its start in 1883, and in 1884 became associate editor of the Rochester, N.Y., "Union and Advertiser." Author of "A Little Brother of the Rich, and Other Poems" (1888).

MARTIN, Luther, lawyer, b. New Brunswick, N. J., 9 Feb., 1748 (Appleton). Graduated at Princeton. Admitted to the bar, 1771. Was attorney-general of Maryland from 1778 to 1805. A delegate from that state to the Constitutional convention of 1787, he opposed the Constitution, being an advocate of state-rights. Acted as counsel for Aaron Burr in the latter's trial for treason. Was chief judge of the court of oyer and terminer at Baltimore, 1814–6. Died, New York, N. Y., 10 July, 1826.

MASON, Caroline Atherton [Briggs], b. Marblehead, Mass., 27 July, 1823. A resident of Fitchburg, Mass. A volume of poems was brought out in 1852 with the title "Utterance, a Collection of Home Poems." Her subsequent writings appeared in periodicals, to which she was a frequent contributor.

MASON, Major John, colonist, b. England, about 1600. Settled at Dorchester, Mass., about 1630. Had seen service in the Netherlands and elsewhere. Removed to Windsor, Conn., in 1635, and in 1637 led the combined colonial forces against the Pequot Indians at Mystic. Soon after was appointed major-general of the Connecticut colony, and continued in that position for life. Removed to Norwich in 1659, where he wrote "A Brief History of the Pequot War," at the government's request, first printed in Increase Mather's "Relation of Troubles by the Indians" (1677). Died, Norwich, Conn., about 1672.

MATHER, Cotton, clergyman, b. Boston, Mass., 12 Feb., 1663. Son of Increase Mather. His mother was a daughter of the Rev. John Cotton. Graduated at Harvard when only sixteen years old, and was ordained minister of the North church in Boston, as his father's colleague, 1685, retaining the connection through life. He had, before graduation, attained wide reputation as a student and reader, and he habitually devoted the greater part of the day to his books and writing. The list of his published volumes numbers nearly four hundred, and they bristle with quotations from and references to his vast stores of information. Mather was the last of his family, and in fact of New England ministers generally, to wield great influence in civil matters, and his power was undoubtedly weakened by his participation in the witch-craft delusion of 1692. Of this movement he was one of the leading spirits. It began with the trial and execution of an Irish washerwoman named Glover, at Boston, in 1688. This affair was described by Mather in a book with the title "Late Memorable Providences, relating to Witchcraft and Possession." When the manifestations at Salem commenced, he composed a letter urging the magistrates to proceed with the trials, which was signed by himself and eleven other clergymen. He was present at the execution of Rev. George Burroughs, and addressed the crowd on that occasion. When the reaction began to set in, he was called upon by the acting governor to justify the proceedings, and wrote and published in Oct., 1692, "The Wonders of the Invisible World." He never retracted his opinions or expressed any regret for his course, and as late as 1724, in his life of Increase Mather, repeated earlier statements. It should be said, in extenuation of his conduct, that witchcraft was commonly believed in at the time, and that his abnormal conceit and credulity were more to blame than any intentional bigotry. In many other respects, Mather was a public benefactor. He advocated the introduction of inoculation for smallpox, established a school for colored children at his own expense, wrote and spoke in behalf of temperance, and labored to raise the condition of seafaring men, besides exercising a careful supervision over public morals. He corresponded with eminent men in England and Europe, and was the recipient of honors from those countries. Is said to have gathered the largest private library in the colonies. His most important book was that entitled "Magnalia Christi Americana; or, The Ecclesiastical History of New-England" (1702). It contains a vast amount of information concerning the early history of New England, largely set forth in biographies of the leading divines and civil officers, but while indispensable to the student of those times, its value is impaired by Mather's frequent inaccuracy and verbose style. He became an overseer of Harvard and aspired to be president of the college, but was disappointed in this ambition. Died, Boston, Mass., 13 Feb., 1728.

MATHER, Increase, clergyman, b. Dorchester, Mass., 21 June, 1639. Son of Richard. Graduated at Harvard and at Trinity college, Dublin. After preaching in various parts of England and in the island of Guernsey, he returned to America in 1661 on account of the Restoration, being unwilling to conform. He divided his time between the North church at Boston and his father's church at Dorchester until 1664, when he was regularly ordained pastor of the former, holding the position until his death. He was elected president of Harvard in 1681, but did not accept. Was elected acting president, 1685, became president in 1692 and served until 1701. By his own statement, he concurred in the opinion of the twelve clergymen who advised Gov. William Phips to proceed with the witchcraft trials in June, 1692, but having become convinced of the unreliability of the so-called "spectre-evidence," he published a book called "Cases of Conscience concerning Witchcrafts and Evil Spirits personating Men" (1693), deprecating convictions for this alone. In this book, however, he expresses his approval of his son Cotton's "Wonders of the Invisible World." He had meanwhile rendered the colony valuable services in England. Originally a leader in the opposition to the surrender of the colony's charter, demanded by Governor Andros in 1687, he was sent to England the year after to plead the colony's cause. He obtained a new and fairly satisfactory charter from William and Mary, and returned with it in 1692. This instrument united the colonies of Massachusetts and Plymouth under one jurisdiction, and remained in force up to the Revolution. The list of his published volumes numbers one hundred and thirty-six, some of which are "The Life and Death of Rev. Richard Mather" (1670), "Heavens Alarm to the World" (1681), and "An Essay for the Recording of Illustrious Providences" (1684), also known as "Remarkable Providences." Died, Boston, Mass., 23 Aug., 1723.

MATHER, Richard, clergyman, b. Lowton, Lancashire, England, 1596. Graduated at Oxford. Preached at Toxteth, near Liverpool, until 1634, when he was silenced for non-conformity. Sailed from Bristol in the *James*, arriving at Boston, 17 Aug., 1635. Became "teacher" of the church at Dorchester, a position he held for life. Mather was the first of the family of Congregational ministers who formed what is known as the "Mather dynasty." He was selected to answer the thirty-two questions in regard to church-government, propounded to the New England ministers by the magistrates in 1639, and was the chief designer of the "Cambridge Platform," adopted by the New England synod of 1648. With John Eliot and Thomas Welde he made the metrical version of the Psalms, known as the "Bay Psalm Book" and used by the churches of New England for many years. His "Journal" was first printed in 1846. Author of a "Discourse on the Church Covenant" (1639), a "Treatise on Justification" (1652), etc. Died, Dorchester, Mass., 22 April, 1669.

MATHER, Samuel, clergyman, b. Boston, Mass., 30 Oct., 1706. Son of Cotton, and grandson of Increase. The last of the family to attain prominence. Graduated at Har-

vard. Four years after his father's death became associate pastor of the former's church in Boston, and ten years later separated from it with a portion of the congregation, establishing a new church, where he preached until his death. Published "The Life of the Very Reverend and Learned Cotton Mather" (1729) and several sermons and miscellaneous essays. Died, Boston, Mass., 27 June, 1785.

MATHEWS, Albert, "Paul Siegvolk," lawyer, b. New York, N. Y., 8 Sept., 1820. Cousin of Cornelius Mathews. Graduated at Yale. In 1845 was admitted to the bar of New York city, where he afterward practised. Issued "Walter Ashwood; a Love Story" (1860) and "A Bundle of Papers" (1879), besides various contributions to the periodicals.

MATHEWS, Cornelius, b. Portchester, N. Y., 28 Oct., 1817. Graduated at the university of New York, and entered the bar. With Evert A. Duyckinck edited "Arcturus" (1840), a monthly magazine, and was one of the founders of the international copyright club. Wrote poems, novels, essays, critiques, satires, and dramas. Author of "Behemoth; a Legend of the Mound-Builders" (1839), "The Politicians, a Comedy" (1840), "Puffer Hopkins" (1841), "Poems on Man" (1843), "Indian Fairy Tales" (1868), besides "Witchcraft, a Tragedy" (1846), and other dramas which were performed. Died, New York, N. Y., 24 Mar., 1889.

MATTHEWS, Brander, "Arthur Penn," b. New Orleans, La., 21 Feb., 1852. Graduated at Columbia. Studied for the law, but devoted himself to literature and the drama. A resident of New York city, though often visiting England. Besides editing numerous theatrical works, is the author of "The Theatres of Paris" (1880), "French Dramatists of the Nineteenth Century" (1881), "The Home Library, by Arthur Penn" (1883), "The Last Meeting," novel (1885), "A Secret of the Sea, and Other Stories" (1886), "Pen and Ink; Papers on Subjects of More or Less Importance" (1888), and "A Family Tree, and Other Stories" (1889). Some of his plays are "Margery's Lovers," comedy (produced at London, 1884), "A Gold Mine," comedy (with George H. Jessop, 1887), "This Picture and That," comedy (1887), and "On Probation," comedy (with George H. Jessop, 1889).

MAURY, Matthew Fontaine, scientist, b. Spottsylvania Co., Va., 14 Jan., 1806. Entered the U. S. navy, and while in service issued "Maury's Navigation" (1834). In 1839 was incapacitated for active duty by lameness, and wrote valuable papers suggesting reforms in the navy. Was appointed in 1842 superintendent of the U. S. hydrographical office, with which the U. S. observatory was shortly after combined. Entered the Confederate navy in 1861, serving as its agent in Europe. Was appointed minister in the cabinet of Emperor Maximilian, in Mexico. Ultimately became professor of physics in the military institute of Virginia. His "Physical Geography of the Sea" (1855, revised ed. 1860), brought him many honors from the learned societies of Europe. Was author of a number of treatises on geography, astronomy, and meteorology. Died, Lexington, Va., 1 Feb., 1873.

MAXWELL, William, lawyer, b. Norfolk, Va., 27 Feb., 1784. Graduated at Yale. Admitted to the bar, 1808. Was a member of the Virginia legislature, and was president of Hampden Sidney college, 1838–44. Edited the "Virginia Historical Register" for several years, and issued "Poems" (1816). Died, Richmond, Va., 9 Jan., 1857.

MAY, Samuel Joseph, clergyman, b. Boston, Mass., 12 Sept., 1797. Graduated at Harvard. Was pastor of a Unitarian church at Brooklyn, N. Y., for several years. Soon espoused the anti-slavery cause, and became general agent of the Massachusetts anti-slavery society, 1835. From 1845 to 1868 was pastor of a church at Syracuse, N. Y. Published "Some Recollections of our Anti-Slavery Conflict" (1869). Died, Syracuse, N. Y., 1 July, 1871.

MAYER, Brantz, b. Baltimore, Md., 27 Sept., 1809. Was appointed secretary of legation at Mexico, 1843. Founded the Maryland historical society, 1844. Was made paymaster in the U. S. army, 1863. Some of his works are "Mexico ; Aztec, Spanish, and Republican" (1851), "Captain Canot ; or Twenty Years of an African Slaver" (1854), and "Baltimore as It Was and Is" (1871). Died, Baltimore, Md., 21 Mar., 1879.

MAYHEW, Jonathan, clergyman, b. Martha's Vineyard, Mass., 8 Oct., 1720. Graduated at Harvard. Pastor of the West church in Boston, Mass., from 1747 until his death, becoming noted for his advanced theological views. An early advocate of civil and religious freedom, he sympathized with the opponents of the Stamp Act and preached a vigorous sermon on its repeal. Collections of his sermons were published in 1749 and 1767. Died, Boston, Mass., 9 July, 1766.

MAYO, William Starbuck, physician, b. Ogdensburg, N. Y., 20 April, 1812. Graduated at the N. Y. college of physicians and surgeons. Travelled in Barbary and Spain, and after his return resided at New York city. Author of "Flood and Field" (1844), "Kaloolah" (1849), "The Berber, or the Mountaineer of the Atlas" (1850), and "Never Again," novel (1873).

McCABE, William Gordon, educator, b. near Richmond, Va., 4 Aug., 1841. Graduated at the university of Virginia. Served through the civil war in the Confederate army, becoming captain of artillery. Afterward head-master of the university school at Petersburg, Va. Besides editing several classical text-books, is the author of popular war poems, and of "The Defence of Petersburg, Campaign of 1864–5" (1876).

McCARTHY, Harry, actor. A Scotsman by birth, and said to be author of the popular Southern war ballad, "The Bonnie Blue Flag," sung by his sister at the New Orleans Variety theatre early in the civil war.

McCLELLAN, George Brinton, soldier, b. Philadelphia, Penn., 3 Dec., 1826. Graduated at West Point. Served in the Mexican war as lieutenant, and was promoted for gallant conduct. Resigned from the army in 1857, and became president of a railroad. On the outbreak of the civil war was appointed major-general of Ohio volunteers. Successful operations in West Virginia gained him a promotion as major-general of the regular army, and he was placed in command of the Army of the Potomac shortly after the first battle of Bull Run. Soon becoming commander-in-chief of the Union armies, he brought them to a high point of organization, but his campaigns in the East were unsuccessful in their results, and ended in dissatisfaction on the part of the government. He was permanently suspended from command, 7 Nov., 1862. Was the Democratic candidate for president in 1864. He afterward travelled in Europe. Published a "Report on the Organization and Campaigns of the Army of the Potomac" (1864). "McClellan's Own Story" (1887) was brought out after his death. Died, Orange, N. J., 29 Oct., 1885.

McCLELLAND, Mary Greenway, b. Norwood, Nelson Co., Va., 18—. Received a home education, and always resided at her native place. Besides stories and poems in the magazines, wrote "Oblivion," novel (1885), "Princess" (1886), "Jean Monteith" (1887), "Madame Silva" (1888), and "Burkett's Lock" (1889).

McCORD, Louisa Susannah [Cheves], b. Columbia, S. C., 3 Dec., 1810 (Appleton). Was married, 1840, to David J. McCord, and settled on her husband's plantation on the Congaree river. Wrote a translation of Bastiat's "Sophisms of the Protective Policy" (1848), "My Dreams," poems, (1848), "Caius Gracchus," a tragedy (1851), and contributed articles on public questions to the "Southern Quarterly Review." Died, Charleston, S. C., 27 Nov., 1880.

McDOWELL, Katharine Sherwood [Bonner], "Sherwood Bonner," b. Holly Springs, Miss., 26 Feb., 1849. Was married, 1870, to Edward McDowell. Was for a time private secretary of Henry W. Longfellow, returning to her native place in 1878. Author of "Like unto Like" (1881) and "Suwanee River Tales " (1884). Died, Holly Springs, 22 July, 1883.

McELROY, William Henry, "Richard Scudder," journalist, b. Albany, N. Y., 13 Sept., 1838. Graduated at Union college. For several years associate editor of the Albany, N. Y., "Journal." In 1882 joined the editorial staff of the N. Y. "Tribune." Wrote, over his own name and his pseudonym, articles and sketches for these journals and for the "Atlantic Monthly" and other magazines. Delivered several poems on occasions, among others that at the bicentennial celebration of Albany.

McGAFFEY, Ernest, lawyer, b. London, O., 30 Aug., 1861. Removed to Chicago, Ill., 1881, and became a member of the bar of that city. At one time Eastern correspondent for the Chicago "Inter-Ocean." Contributor of numerous poems and sketches to the periodicals.

McKAY, James Thomson, b. New York, N. Y., 2 Jan., 1843. Was chiefly educated at Huntington, L. I., where he afterward resided, engaged in writing verse and fiction for the magazines. Died, Huntington, L. I., N. Y., 19 May, 1890.

McMASTER, Guy Humphreys, jurist, b. Clyde, N. Y., 31 Jan., 1829. Graduated at Hamilton college. Practised law in Steuben county, N. Y., until elected county judge in 1864. In 1884 he was chosen as surrogate of the same county. His notable war-lyric, "Carmen Bellicosum," was contributed to the "Knickerbocker Magazine" in 1849. The same year he published "The History of Steuben County, N. Y." His subsequent literary work was limited to occasional poems and a series of letters from abroad to the "Steuben Courier." Died, Bath, N. Y., 13 Sept., 1887.

McMASTER, John Bach, educator, b. Brooklyn, N. Y., 29 June, 1852. Graduated at the college of New York, where he became instructor in grammar. Having made a study of civil engineering, was appointed instructor in that study at the college of New Jersey, 1877. In 1883 he was made professor of American history in the university of Pennsylvania. Author of a "History of the People of the United States " (1883–5) and "Life of Benjamin Franklin " (1887); also a frequent contributor to the magazines.

McNamee, Theodore [*Noted Saying :* Vol. XI., page 452], b. Cooperstown, N. Y., 11 Oct., 1813. From 1839 to 1859 was with Henry C. Bowen a member of the N. Y. firm of Bowen & McNamee, silk merchants. Died, New York, N. Y., 11 Jan., 1871.

MELLEN, Grenville, lawyer, b. Biddeford, Me., 19 June, 1799. Graduated at Harvard. Practised law at Portland and North Yarmouth, Me., until 1828. Afterward resided in Boston and New York. Published "The Martyr's Triumph, Buried Valley, and Other Poems " (1833). Died, New York, N. Y., 5 Sept., 1841.

MELVILLE, Herman, b. New York, N. Y., 1 Aug., 1819. Grandson of a member of the Boston "tea-party." At eighteen went to sea as a common sailor, landed at Liverpool, saw London, and shipped again for home. In 1841 joined a whaler for the sperm-fishery in the Pacific. After eighteen months' cruising the ship put into the Marquesas islands, whereupon Melville ran away, on account of the captain's severity, and with a shipmate lost his way in a forest on the island of Nukuhiva, where the Typee cannibals lived. Was captured by them, his mate escaping, and kept for four months in virtual but friendly captivity. On the arrival of an Australian ship a fight took place ; he was rescued and joined the crew. After two more years afloat came home, and published "Typee " (1846) in New York and London simultaneously. It proved a success, and was succeeded by "Omoo " (1847), a continuation of his adventures, and a novel, "Redburn " (1848). In 1849 issued a philosophical romance, "Mardi, and a Voyage Thither," followed by "White Jacket, or the World in a Man of War " (1850), "Moby Dick " (1851), "Pierre, or the Ambiguities" (1852), "Israel Potter, his Fifty Years of Exile " (1855), "The Piazza Tales " (1856), "The Confidence Man " (1857), "Battle-Pieces, and Aspects of the War," poems (1866), and "Clarel, a Pilgrimage in the Holy Land," poem (1876). Mr. Melville voyaged around the world in 1860, and on his return held for some time a position in the custom-house of New York, in which city he afterward led a retired life.

MEREDITH, William Tuckey, b. Philadelphia, Penn., 16 June, 1839. Served as an officer of the U. S. navy with Farragut at the battle of Mobile bay, and was afterward his secretary. Subsequently became a banker in New York city. Author of the poem, "Farragut."

MESSINGER, Robert Hinckley, b. Boston, Mass., 1811. Studied at the Boston Latin school. Afterward engaged in business at New York city. Some of his poems appeared in the "American," 1827–38. Among them is "A Winter Wish," or "Give me the Old." Died, Stamford, Conn., 1 Oct., 1874.

MILLER, Cincinnatus Hiner (Joaquin), b. Wabash District, Ind., 10 Nov., 1841. In 1854 was taken by his family to Willamette valley, Oreg., and soon after tried gold-mining in California without success. Returned to Oreg., 1860, studied law for a few months, and was admitted to the bar of Lane county. Edited the Eugene "Democratic Register," 1863, and then practised law at Canyon city, being judge of Grant county, Oreg., from 1866 to 1870.

Visited England and the Continent in the latter year, and issued his first volume of verse with the title "Songs of the Sierras" (1871). Subsequently became a journalist at Washington, D. C., removing to Oakland, Cal., in 1887. Author of "Songs of the Sunlands" (1873), "Songs of the Desert" (1875), "The Baroness of New York," novel (1877), "Songs of Italy" (1878), "The Danites in the Sierras," novel (1881), "Memorie and Rime" (1884), "'49, or the Gold-Seekers of the Sierras" (1884), and "Songs of the Mexican Seas" (1887). Of these "The Danites" was successfully produced as a drama.

MILLER, Harriet [Mann], "Olive Thorne Miller," b. Auburn, N. Y., 25 June, 1831. Studied at private schools. When eleven years old, she went with her family to Ohio. Was married, 1849, to Watts S. Miller of Lewis county, N. Y., and lived in Chicago for twenty years. Subsequently resided in Brooklyn, N. Y. An extensive writer for children, but gained her chief reputation by books and articles descriptive of birds and their habits. Besides her books for children, wrote "Bird Ways" (1885) and "In Nesting Time" (1888).

MILLER, John, clergyman. Little is known of him beyond the facts that he was a graduate of an English university, was appointed chaplain to two companies of grenadiers at New York city, 1692, reached the colony the next year and remained until 1695. His "Description of the Province and City of New York" was first printed from the manuscript at London, 1843.

MINOT, George Richards, jurist, b. Boston, Mass., 22 Dec., 1758. Graduated at Harvard. Admitted to the bar, 1781. Appointed judge of probate for Suffolk county, 1792, and in 1800 municipal judge at Boston. A founder of the Massachusetts historical society. Published "The History of the Insurrections in Massachusetts in the Year 1786" (1786) and a continuation of Hutchinson's "History." Died, Boston, Mass., 2 Jan., 1802.

MITCHEL, Ormsby MacKnight, astronomer, b. Morganfield, Union Co., Ky., 28 July, 1809. Graduated at West Point. Was professor of mathematics and astronomy in Cincinnati college from 1836 to 1844, when he became director of the Cincinnati observatory, founded by himself. Served in the Union army during the civil war, and was made major-general of volunteers in 1862. Author of "The Planetary and Stellar Worlds" (1848), "The Orbs of Heaven" (1851), and "The Astronomy of the Bible" (1863). Died, Beaufort, S. C., 30 Oct., 1862.

MITCHELL, Mrs. Agnes E.—An American woman, sometime resident in Michigan. "When the Cows come Home" has been a familiar poem for many years.

MITCHELL, Donald Grant, "Ik Marvel," b. Norwich, Conn., 12 April, 1822. Graduated at Yale. A subsequent residence on his grandfather's farm, for the benefit of his health, excited the interest in agricultural matters afterward exemplified in his books on rural life. While there he was a contributor to the Albany "Cultivator," to which paper he also sent letters from Europe during a trip made in 1844-5. On his return he published "Fresh Gleanings, or a New Sheaf from the Old Field of Continental Europe" (1847). The study of law, upon which he now entered, proved too confining, and he again visited Europe, and was an observer of the events described in "The Battle Summer, being Transcriptions from Personal Observations in Paris during the Year 1848" (1849). "The Lorgnette, or Studies of the Town, by an Opera-Goer" (1850) was first issued as a weekly periodical in the style of Irving's "Salmagundi" and afterward in book form. "Reveries of a Bachelor" (1850) next appeared, and is perhaps the most popular of his works. This was followed by "Dream Life" (1851), in the same shadowy vein. Appointed U. S. consul at Venice in 1853, he resigned after a few months and collected material for a proposed history of Venice, never published. Returning to America in 1855, he purchased an estate in the neighborhood of New Haven, Conn., where he afterward resided. His works on country life consist of "My Farm of Edgewood" (1863), "Wet Days at Edgewood" (1865), and "Rural Studies, with Hints for Country Places" (1867). Also, the author of "English Lands, Letters, and Kings" (1889-90). He delivered lectures on literature at Yale, was a member of the council of the Yale art school from its foundation, and was one of the judges of industrial art at the Centennial exhibition of 1876.

MITCHELL, Edward Page, journalist, b. Bath, Me., 24 Mar., 1852. Graduated at Bowdoin college. Entered journalism on the Boston, Mass., "Advertiser," 1871-2, and in 1874 became a member of the editorial staff of the N. Y. "Sun." Contributed stories and sketches to the magazines.

MITCHELL, Jonathan, clergyman, b. Halifax, Yorkshire, England, about 1625. Brought to America, 1635. Graduated at Harvard. Served as pastor of the church at Cambridge, Mass., from 1650 until his death, and was a fellow of Harvard for the same period. Among his published sermons are "An Election Sermon" (1667) and "A Discourse of the Glory to which God hath called Believers by Jesus Christ" (1677). Died, Cambridge, Mass., 9 July, 1668.

MITCHELL, Langdon Elwyn, "John Philip Varley," b. Philadelphia, Penn., 17 Feb., 1862. Son of S. Weir Mitchell. Studied at the Harvard law school, was admitted to the bar at New York city, and afterward travelled in Europe. A contributor to the magazines, and author of "Sylvian, and Other Poems" (1885).

MITCHELL, Silas Weir, physician, b. Philadelphia, Penn., 15 Feb., 1829. Studied at the university of Pennsylvania. Attained prominence in his profession, having made important researches in physiology and nervous affections. These were described in numerous articles. Also the author of a number of volumes of fiction and poetry, including "Hephzibah Guinness" (1880), "The Hill of Stones, and Other Poems" (1882), "In War Time" (1884), "Roland Blake" (1886), "A Masque, and Other Poems" (1887), and "The Cup of Youth, and Other Poems" (1889). "Doctor and Patient" (1888) is one of several popular medical works.

MITCHELL, Walter, clergyman, b. Nantucket, Mass., 22 Jan., 1826. Graduated at Harvard. Admitted to the bar of Massachusetts in 1849, but entered the Episcopal ministry in 1859. Was rector of churches in Stamford and Middletown, Conn., in Philadelphia, Mt. Kisko, N. Y., and other places, and was a member of the staff of "The Churchman." In addition to poems and articles in the magazines, the author of "Bryan Maurice," a novel (1866, republished 1888) and a volume of "Poems."

MITCHILL, Samuel Latham, scientist, b. North Hempstead, Queens Co., N. Y., 20 Aug. 1764. Studied medicine in New York city and at the university of Edinburgh. Subsequently studied law, but devoted the greater portion of his life to scientific pursuits. Became professor of chemistry at Columbia college, 1792, and was professor of natural history at the N. Y. college of physicians and surgeons from 1808 until 1820. Was U. S. representative for four terms, and U. S. senator from 1804 to 1809. A founder of the Society for the promotion of agriculture, and of the N. Y. Literary and philosophical society. Was founder and editor of the N. Y. "Medical Repository," which he conducted for sixteen years. Equally distinguished as a wit, scholar, and citizen. He contributed many papers on scientific subjects to the publications of learned societies, and delivered numerous addresses, the most noted of which was that on the completion of the Erie canal. Was also the author of fugitive poems. Died, New York, N. Y., 7 Sept., 1831.

MONROE, James, fifth president of the United States, b. Westmoreland Co., Va., 28 April, 1758. Served in the Revolutionary war, gaining the rank of captain. Rose through minor offices to be U. S. senator from Virginia and governor of that state, and was at different times U. S. minister to France and England. Was secretary of

state and of war under President Madison, whom he succeeded as president in 1817, being reëlected for a second term. Originated the "Monroe Doctrine," which deprecates interference by European powers in American affairs. Died, New York, N. Y., 4 July, 1831.

MONTGOMERY, George Edgar, journalist, b. New York, N. Y., 6 Feb., 1856. Studied at the college of New York and in Paris. For some years dramatic editor of the N. Y. "Times." Correspondent at New York city for many leading American journals. A contributor of verse and prose to the magazines.

MOODY, James, loyalist, b. about 1744. He was a farmer in New Jersey at the outbreak of the Revolution, and, being harassed for his loyalist views, joined the British forces in 1777. Was afterward captured and imprisoned at West Point, but managed to escape. He performed valuable services as a spy and partisan fighter on the British side. He published at London "Lieut. Moody's Narrative of his Exertions and Sufferings" (1783). Died, Sissibou, N. S., 3 April, 1809.

MOORE, Clement Clarke, educator, b. New York, N. Y., 15 July, 1779. Graduated at Columbia. Devoted himself to the study of Hebrew. Was a professor at the N. Y. General theological seminary from 1821 until his death. He gave to this institution the plot of ground on which it stands. Besides compiling the earliest Hebrew and Greek lexicon published in America, he was the author of "Poems" (1844), the most noted of which was "A Visit from St. Nicholas." Died, Newport, R. I., 10 July, 1863.

MORGAN, Appleton, b. Portland, Me., 2 Oct., 1846. Graduated at Racine college, Wis., and was admitted to the bar at New York city. Founded there, 1885, the Shakespeare society, of which he became first president. Advanced new theories as to the composite authorship of Shakespeare's plays, and published "The Shakespearian Myth" (1881, revised ed. 1888) and "Shakespeare in Fact and in Criticism" (1888).

MORGAN, Bessie. Was in 1884 a contributor to the "Century Magazine" of New York city.

MORRELL, William, clergyman. Came to Plymouth colony with Capt. Robert Gorges in Sept., 1623. Settled at Wessaguscus (now Weymouth), but returned to England, probably in the spring of 1625, a year after the dispersion of Gorges's colony. The same year he brought out in London "Nova Anglia," a Latin poem descriptive of New England, with a free translation in English verse, both composed during his stay in America. Bradford says that he brought with him an order giving him superintendency over all the New England churches, but thought best not to produce it.

MORRIS, George Pope, journalist, b. Philadelphia, Penn., 10 Oct., 1802. Founded, with Samuel Woodworth, the N. Y. "Mirror" in 1823; and in 1846, the "Home Journal," in conjunction with N. P. Willis. Is best known as the writer of several popular songs. He was the author of a drama, "Briercliff," successfully produced in 1837. A complete edition of his "Poems" appeared in 1860. Died, New York, N. Y., 6 July, 1864.

MORRIS, Gouverneur, statesman, b. Morrisania, N. Y., 31 Jan., 1752. Graduated at Kings, now Columbia, college. Began the practice of law at New York city in 1771. Was a member of the provincial congress of New York from 1775 to 1777, and of the Continental congress from the latter year until 1780, and took a prominent part in the financial legislation of the time. From 1791 to 1794 he was engaged in diplomatic service for the United States in England and France. Was U. S. senator from New York, 1800–3, and on the appointment of the N. Y. canal commission in 1810 was made chairman of that body, holding the position until his death. "The Life of Gouverneur Morris," with selections from his papers and correspondence, was issued by Jared Sparks in 1832. Died, Morrisania, N. Y., 6 Nov., 1816.

MORRIS, Harrison Smith, b. Philadelphia, Penn., 4 Oct., 1856. Received his education in that city, which became his permanent residence. A contributor to the magazines, and joint author with John A. Henry of "A Duet in Lyrics" (1883).

MORRIS, Ramsay, actor, b. New York, N. Y., 22 Mar., 1858. Studied at the Jesuit colleges. Made his début as an actor in New York, 1879, and was subsequently connected with theatres in that city as actor and manager. Besides fugitive verse, is the author of a novel, "Crucify Her" (1889), which he dramatized and produced as "The Tigress."

MORSE, James Herbert, educator, b. Hubbardston, Mass., 8 Oct., 1841. Graduated at Harvard. Soon after removed to New York city, where he established a university school. A frequent contributor of verse and prose to the magazines and reviews, and author of "Summer-Haven Songs" (1886).

MORSE, John Torrey, Jr., b. Boston, Mass., 9 Jan., 1840. Graduated at Harvard, of which he became an overseer in 1876. A member of the Massachusetts legislature for one term, and much occupied with historical studies. Author of "Famous Trials" (1874), "Life of Alexander Hamilton" (1876), and edited the "American statesmen series," several volumes of which he wrote.

MORSE, Samuel Finley Breese, inventor, b. Charlestown, Mass., 27 April, 1791. Graduated at Yale. Studied art at London and devoted himself to painting until his discovery of the American system of telegraphy in 1832. Was a founder of the National Academy of Design, and its first president from 1826 to 1842. His working model of the telegraph was completed in 1835, and the first line from Washington to Baltimore put in operation in 1844. Wrote a number of controversial pamphlets concerning the telegraph. His "Life" (1875) was written by S. I. Prime. Died, New York, N. Y., 2 April, 1872.

MORTON, Nathaniel, colonist, b. probably in Leyden, Holland, 1613. Emigrated to New England with his father's family, arriving at Plymouth in July, 1623. His mother is believed to have been a sister of Governor Bradford. Was elected secretary of Plymouth colony in 1647, and held that position until his death. His "New England's Memorial" (1669), down to the year 1647, is largely an abridgment of Bradford's "History," to which he had access in manuscript. Several of his poems, of which the early Pilgrims are the subjects, are extant. Died, Plymouth, Mass., 29 June, 1685.

MORTON, Sarah Wentworth [Apthorpe], b. Braintree, Mass., 29 Aug., 1759. Was married, 1778, to Perez Morton, afterward attorney-general of Massachusetts. Contributed verses to the "Massachusetts Magazine" under the name "Philenia." Author of "Ouabi," an Indian tale in four cantos (1790), and "My Mind and its Thoughts" (1823). Died, Quincy, Mass., 14 May, 1846.

MORTON, Thomas, colonist. "Of Clifford's Inn, Gent.," as he calls himself, first came to New England in June, 1622, perhaps with Thomas Weston's company. Morton is next heard of as one of Captain Wollaston's party, which settled at Mount Wollaston in the present town of Quincy, Mass., some time in 1625. In Wollaston's absence, he gained control of the company, and greatly scandalized the Plymouth people by erecting a Maypole and indulging with his companions in wild revelries, and particularly by supplying the Indians with firearms. After several warnings, an expedition headed by Capt. Miles Standish captured him in 1628, and he was returned to England a prisoner. Soon after Morton's arrest the Maypole was cut down, and the revellers at "Merry Mount" were admonished, by John Endicott. Mount Wollaston had been renamed "Merry Mount" by Morton, and Hawthorne's story of the same name is based on this affair. Morton escaped punishment in England and astonished the Pilgrim fathers by returning to Plymouth in 1629 with Isaac Allerton, the colony's agent in England, and as the latter's secretary. He was ejected from the town, and, returning to Mount Wollaston, soon gave further offence by injuries to the Indians. Was again arrested and sent, Dec., 1630, to England, where he also was under suspicion of murder. After a term of imprisonment in Exeter jail, he wrote and published his "New English Canaan" (1637), which combines, with more or less valuable descriptions of New England's inhabitants and natural features, satirical accounts of his troubles with the Massachusetts colonists and of their life in general. It is thought that by his information he enabled Archbishop Laud to imprison Edward Winslow in the Fleet for seventeen weeks in 1635, and he certainly effected other injuries to the New Englanders. Returning to Plymouth still a third time, 1643, he was apprehended and locked up for a year, at the end of which period, "being old and crazy," he was fined and released, nominally to secure his fine, but really to enable him to leave the place. This he did, removing to Agamenticus, in Maine, and dying there in poverty and neglect before the end of 1646.

MOTLEY, John Lothrop, b. Dorchester, Mass., 15 April, 1814. Graduated at Harvard, 1831, and finished his studies at Berlin and Göttingen. At the latter place began his lifelong friendship with Bismarck. His first book was a novel, "Morton's Hope" (1839). He was appointed secretary of the American legation at St. Petersburg in 1841, but soon resigned the position. His earliest venture in the historical field was an essay on Peter the Great in the "North American Review" (1845), which commanded special attention. "Merry Mount, a Romance of the Massachusetts Colony" (1849) was his last effort in fiction. At the time of its publication he had for some time been preparing for an extensive work on Holland, which occupied him for ten years before it was completed in 1855. It appeared in three volumes as "The Rise of the Dutch Republic," and was shortly after translated into French under Guizot's supervision, who wrote an introduction. Dutch and German translations were also made. In 1858 Motley returned to England, where he received the honor of D. C. L. of Oxford. Continuing his scheme of Dutch history, the first part of "The History of the United Netherlands" was published, 1860, and had an equally flattering reception with the former volumes. In 1861 Mr. Motley was appointed U. S. minister to Austria, by President Lincoln, holding office until 1867. During the civil war he contributed a powerful essay to the London "Times" on "The Causes of the American Civil War," which did good service to the Union cause. In 1868 he issued the concluding part of "The History of the United Netherlands." Settled in Boston the same year and devoted himself to literary work. When the presidential campaign of 1868 was started he delivered two addresses which attracted widespread attention and influenced the public mind : "Four Questions for the People at the Presidential Election" and "Historic Progress and American Democracy." Soon after the election, President Grant appointed him minister to England. This was in April, 1869, but he was recalled in November, 1870. The Queen of Holland offered the use of her villa at the Hague to Mr. Motley, which he accepted, and there wrote his other standard historical work, "The Life and Death of John of Barneveld, Advocate of Holland, with a View of the Primary Causes and Movements of the Thirty Years' War" (1874). The death of his wife in 1874 increased the disheartenment caused by his recall from the English mission, and by the shock of a paralytic seizure in 1873. He undertook no important literary task thenceforth. "The Correspondence of John Lothrop Motley, D. C. L." (1889) was edited by George William Curtis. Died, "Kingston-Russell House," Dorsetshire, England, 29 May, 1877.

MOULTON, Louise [Chandler], b. Pomfret, Conn., 5 April, 1835. Received her education at the seminary of Mrs. Emma Hart Willard, in Troy, N. Y. As a young girl she wrote for publication over the signature "Ellen Louise." Was married, 1855, to William A. Moulton, a publisher of Boston, Mass. Subsequently resided there, with the exception of frequent visits to England and France. Wrote letters of travel from those countries to American journals. Mrs. Moulton was literary executor of Philip Bourke Marston, the English poet, and edited collections of his verse. Some of her books are "This, That, and the Other," stories, essays, and poems (1854), "Juno Clifford," novel (1855), "Bed-Time Stories," for children (1873), "Poems" (1877), "Swallow-Flights, and Other Poems" (1878), "Random Rambles" (1881), "Ourselves and Our Neighbors" (1887), "Some Women's Hearts" (1888), and "In the Garden of Dreams, Lyrics and Sonnets" (1890).

MUHLENBERG, William Augustus, clergyman, b. Philadelphia, Penn., 16 Sept., 1796. Graduated at the university of Pennsylvania. Entered the Episcopal ministry, and was rector of churches at Lancaster, Penn., and New York city. Was prominent in denominational school and hospital organization. Author of several popular hymns and of "Evangelical Catholic Papers" (1875-7). Died, New York, N. Y., 8 April, 1877.

MULFORD, Elisha, divine, b. Montrose, Penn., 19 Nov., 1833. Graduated at Yale, and studied theology in New York city and at German universities. Was rector of Protestant Episcopal churches in Connecticut and New Jersey, 1861–4. In 1864 returned to Montrose, Penn., where he lived until 1877, unattached to any congregation. Was rector at Friendsville, Penn., from 1877 to 1881, when he became lecturer on apologetics at the Cambridge, Mass., Episcopal theological school. His residence at Montrose was marked by the writing of his great political treatise, "The Nation: the Foundations of Civil Order and Political Life in the United States" (1870). "The Republic of God, an Institute of Theology," appeared in 1881. Died, Cambridge, Mass., 9 Dec., 1885.

MULLANY, Patrick Francis, (Brother Azarias,) educator, b. Co. Tipperary, Ireland, 29 June, 1847. Came to America as a youth and joined the Brothers of the Christian schools. Professor of mathematics and English literature at Rock Hill college, Md., from 1866 to 1878, when he became its president. In 1889 removed to New York city. Some of his works are "Philosophy of Literature" (1874), "Development of English Literature" (1880), "Address on Thinking" (1881), and "Dante" and "Aristotle," papers read at the Concord school of philosophy, 1886–7.

MUNFORD, William, lawyer, b. Mecklenburg Co., Va., 15 Aug., 1775. Educated at William and Mary college. Studied law, and in 1797 became a member of the Virginia legislature. Subsequently was appointed to the state council, and in 1811 was made clerk of the house of delegates. Author of "Poems," etc. (1798), and "Homer's Iliad: Translated by William Munford" (1846). Died, Richmond, Va., 21 June, 1825.

MUNKITTRICK, Richard Kendall, b. Manchester, England, 5 Mar., 1853. Resided for some years at Summit, N. J., engaged in journalistic work in New York city. A contributor of verse to the magazines.

MURFREE, Mary Noailles, "Charles Egbert Craddock," b. Grantlands, near Murfreesboro', Tenn., 18—. A descendant of Col. Hardy Murfree, of the Continental army, from whom her native town was named. Lameness debarred her from entering into the amusements of other children, and she became a constant student and reader of books. Her father was a resident of Nashville, Tenn., but his means having become diminished through the civil war, the family returned to the home at Grantlands, spending their summers near Beersheba, a village in the Tennessee mountains. During this period Miss Murfree made the studies subsequently utilized in her works of fiction. The family residence was afterward changed to St. Louis, Mo. It was not until her reputation had been gained over her masculine pseudonym that Miss Murfree revealed her identity. She then made her home in the Eastern states for a few years, returning to the West in 1890. Her books are "In the Tennessee Mountains," stories (1884), "Where the Battle was Fought" (1884), "Down the Ravine" (1885), "The Prophet of the Great Smoky Mountains" (1885), "In the Clouds" (1886), "The Story of Keedon Bluffs" (1887), and "The Despot of Broomsedge Cove" (1888).

MURRAY, Lindley, grammarian, b. Swetara, or Swatara, Penn., 22 April, 1745. His father was a member of the Society of Friends, and established himself as a merchant in New York city, 1753. Lindley Murray was admitted to the bar at that city in 1766. He subsequently abandoned his profession for mercantile pursuits, and retired from business with a competency at the close of the Revolution. In 1784 he removed to England and purchased an estate not far from York, where he resided until his death, engaged chiefly in literary pursuits. The first edition of his "English Grammar" (1795) was prepared for the use of a young ladies' school in York. Other publications were "The Power of Religion on the Mind" (1787), "Biographical Sketch of Henry Tuke" (1815), and "Memoirs of the Life and Writings of Lindley Murray" (1826). Died, near York, England, 16 Feb., 1826.

NADAL, Ehrman Syme, b. Lewisburg, W. Va., 13 Feb., 1843. Graduated at Yale. Second secretary of the U. S. legation at London, 1870–1 and 1877–84. For some years a member of the N. Y. "Nation" staff. Contributed a number of articles to reviews and magazines, among them one on the U. S. diplomatic service, and delivered several lectures. Author of "Impressions of London Social Life" (1875) and "Essays at Home and Elsewhere" (1882).

NEAL, John, b. Portland, Me., 25 Aug., 1793. Educated himself, and after a few years in business at Baltimore, was admitted to the bar of that city, 1819. The success of his early novels in England led him to visit that country in 1823, and he is said to have been the first American who wrote on American topics in the British quarterly magazines. He enjoyed the intimate friendship of Jeremy Bentham. On his return he established "The Yankee," 1828, and continued to be an active and versatile journalist for half a century. It is also claimed that he was the originator of the woman's suffrage movement, the first to establish a gymnasium in this country, and one of the earliest to encourage Poe's talents. Some of his novels are "Keep Cool" (1817), "Niagara" (1819), "Logan" (1821), "Randolph" (1823), "Seventy-six" (1823), "Brother Jonathan" (1825), and "Rachel Dyer" (1828). Other books are "The Battle of Niagara, with Other Poems" (1818), "Authorship, by a New Englander over the Sea" (1830), "The Down-Easters" (1833), "Wandering Recollections of a Somewhat Busy Life" (1869). Died, Portland, Me., 21 June, 1876.

NEWELL, Robert Henry, "Orpheus C. Kerr," b. New York, N. Y., 13 Dec., 1836. Literary editor of the N. Y. "Mercury," 1858–62, and a member of the staff of the N. Y. "World" from 1869 to 1874. Subsequently was editor of "Hearth and Home." Besides a collective edition of his writings over his pseudonym during the civil war, issued "The Palace Beautiful, and Other Poems" (1865) and several novels.

NICHOLS, Starr Hoyt, b. Danbury, Conn., 16 Nov., 1834. A Congregational clergyman at Chicago and Cincinnati, 1860–8. Subsequently a business man in Philadelphia and New York city. An occasional contributor of prose and verse to the magazines, and author of "Monte Rosa ; the Epic of an Alp" (1883, revised ed. 1886).

NICOLAY, John George, b. Essingen, Bavaria, 26 Feb., 1832. Brought to America in 1838. After some journalistic experience, was private secretary of Abraham Lincoln from the latter's nomination in 1860 until his assassination. U. S. consul at Paris, 1865–9, and marshal of the U. S. supreme court, 1872–87. Issued "Campaigns of the Civil War" (1881), and is joint author with Col. John Hay of "Abraham Lincoln : a History," first published in the "Century Magazine," 1887–9.

NILES, Nathaniel, clergyman and politician, b. South Kingston, R. I., 3 April, 1741. Graduated at Princeton. Studied law and medicine, and finally theology, the latter under Dr. Joseph Bellamy, preaching in several towns in New England. Removing to Vermont after the Revolution, he became successively speaker of the legislature, judge of the supreme court, and U. S. representative. His most noted literary production was "The American Hero," a Sapphic ode, written in 1775. Died, West Fairlee, Vt., 31 Oct., 1828.

NILES, Samuel, clergyman, b. Block Island, R. I., 1 May, 1674. Graduated at Harvard. Preached at Kingston, R. I., from 1702 until 1710, and afterward at Braintree, Mass. Author of several theological and historical works, and left in manuscript "A Summary Historical Narrative of the Wars in New-England," subsequently printed in the Mass. historical society's "Collections." Died, Braintree, Mass., 1 May, 1762.

NOAH, Mordecai Manuel, journalist, b. Philadelphia, Penn., 19 July, 1785. Devoted his early years to law and politics. Accepted a consulate in Tunis, 1813. Returned to New York city, 1815, and started several unsuccessful newspapers. In 1843 estab-

lished the "Sunday Times and Messenger," which he edited until his death. Author of "Travels in England, France, Spain, and Barbary" (1819), a volume of addresses and essays, "Gleanings from a Gathered Harvest" (1845), and several dramas. Died, New York, N. Y., 22 May, 1851.

NOBLE, Lucretia Gray, b. Lowell, Mass., 18—. Early removed to Wilbraham, in the same state, where her father, a retired clergyman, brought his children to be educated. Afterward resided there. A contributor of essays and poems to the magazines, and author of "A Reverend Idol," novel (1882).

NORDHOFF, Charles, journalist, b. Erwitte, Prussia, 31 Aug., 1830. Brought to America in 1835. Entered the U. S. navy at the age of fourteen and remained there and in the merchant marine nine years. Was a member of the N. Y. "Evening Post" editorial staff from 1861 to 1871. In 1874 joined the staff of the N. Y. "Herald," becoming its Washington correspondent. Some of his numerous books are "Man-of-War Life" (1855), "Nine Years a Sailor" (1857), "Secession is Rebellion" (1860), "Northern California, Oregon, and the Sandwich Islands" (1874), and "God and the Future Life" (1881).

NORTON, Andrews, clergyman, b. Hingham, Mass., 31 Dec., 1786. Graduated at Harvard, where he was librarian, 1813–21, and professor of sacred literature, 1819–30. Wrote extensively on biblical subjects in the "Christian Examiner" and other periodicals. Issued "Reasons for Not Believing the Doctrines of Trinitarians," etc. (1833), "Historical Evidences of the Genuineness of the Gospels" (1837–44), "Tracts Concerning Christianity" (1852), besides various poems. Died, Newport, R. I., 18 Sept., 1853.

NORTON, Charles Eliot, b. Cambridge, Mass., 16 Nov., 1827. Son of Andrews Norton. Graduated at Harvard. Subsequently travelled in Europe and India. Edited, during the civil war, the pamphlets issued by the Loyal publication society, and was editor of the "North American Review" from 1863 to 1868. Was elected professor of the history of art at Harvard university in 1875. Some of his books are "Notes of Travel and Study in Italy" (1860), "The New Life of Dante Alighieri, Translated, with Essays and Notes" (1867), and "Historical Studies of Church-Building in the Middle Ages" (1880).

NORTON, John, clergyman, b. Bishop's Stortford, Hertfordshire, England, 6 May, 1606. Graduated at Cambridge university. Became a non-conformist and, at the solicitation of Edward Winslow, emigrated to Plymouth in New England, Oct., 1635. Settled as minister at Ipswich, Mass., the following year. Assisted in forming the "Cambridge Platform" in 1648. At the death of John Cotton, succeeded him as "teacher" of the First church at Boston, 23 July, 1656. Was sent with Simon Bradstreet to England in 1662 to obtain confirmation of the charter from Charles II. In this they were successful, but the king imposed conditions of civil and church government extremely distasteful to the colonists, and their agents suffered in popularity. Norton advocated stern measures against the Quakers. His chief books were "Responsio ad totem questionem syllogen" (1649), much thought of for its "elegant Latinity," and "Abel being Dead yet Speaketh, or, Life of Mr. John Cotton" (1658). Died, Boston, Mass., 5 April, 1663.

NORTON, John, clergyman, b. 1651. Nephew of the preceding. Graduated at Harvard. Served as pastor of the church at Hingham, Mass., from 1678 until his death. Besides an "Election Sermon" (1708), he published an elegiac poem appended to the posthumous edition of Mrs. Anne Bradstreet's "Poems." Died, Hingham, Mass., 1716.

NORWOOD, Colonel, adventurer. Styles himself a near relative of Sir William Berkeley, governor of Virginia. Made a remarkable voyage to America in 1649, described in his "Voyage to Virginia," reprinted in "Force's Historical Tracts." The original date of publication is unknown, and nothing is known of the author save his statements in the book. A Major Henry Norwood was treasurer of Virginia in 1661, but there is no direct evidence that the men were identical.

NOTT, Eliphalet, clergyman, b. Ashford, Conn., 25 June, 1773. Graduated at Brown university. After missionary service in western New York, was pastor of the Presbyterian church at Albany from 1798 to 1804. In the latter year he became president of Union college, holding this office until his death. Besides a noted "Discourse on the Death of Hamilton" (1804), the author of "Lectures on Temperance" (1847) and "Counsels to Young Men." Died, Schenectady, N. Y., 29 Jan., 1866.

NOYES, James, clergyman, b. Wiltshire, England, 1608. Graduated at Oxford university. Came to New England on account of non-conformity in 1634. Preached for more than twenty years at Newbury, Mass. Published "The Temple Measured" (1637) and "Moses and Aaron, or the Rights of Church and State" (1661). Died, Newbury, Mass., 22 Oct., 1656.

NOYES, Nicholas, clergyman, b. Newbury, Mass., 22 Dec., 1647. Graduated at Harvard. Preached at Haddam, Conn., for thirteen years, and at Salem, Mass., from 1683 until his death. Was active in the prosecution of the witchcraft trials at Salem

Village in 1692, and is thought never to have changed his views in regard to them. Published an election sermon, "New England's Duty and Interest" (1698), and a number of poems, chiefly obituary in character. Died, Salem, Mass., 13 Dec., 1717.

NYE, Edgar Wilson, "Bill Nye," b. Shirley, Me., 25 Aug., 1850. Settled in Wyoming as a young man, studied law, and was admitted to the bar. Afterward removed to New York city. Gained reputation as a writer and lecturer on humorous subjects. Among his books are "Bill Nye and the Boomerang" (1881), "The Forty Liars" (1883), and "Remarks" (1886).

OAKES, Urian, clergyman, b. England, 1631–2. Brought to New England, 1634. Graduated at Harvard. Preached temporarily at Roxbury, Mass., but was finally settled at Titchfield, Hampshire, England, where he served until 1662, being silenced after the Restoration. He preached privately in England until 1671, when he returned to America and became pastor of the church at Cambridge, Mass., holding the position for the remainder of his life. In 1675 he became temporary president, and in 1680 president, of Harvard. His most important literary work is "An Elegie upon The Death of the Reverend Mr. Thomas Shepard" (1677). Author of several sermons, among them "Sincerity and Delight in the Service of God" (1682). Died, Cambridge, Mass., 25 July, 1681.

O'BRIEN, Fitz-James, journalist, b. Limerick, Ireland, 1828. Studied at the university of Dublin. Came to America about 1852, and settled in New York city, where he became an active contributor to daily, weekly, and monthly journals. The list of his articles in "Harper's Magazine" numbers sixty-six. His most notable story, "The Diamond Lens," appeared in the first volume of the "Atlantic Monthly." He was a leader among the gatherings of young wits and journalists in New York city before the civil war. Entered the U. S. army at the beginning of hostilities and was fatally wounded, Feb., 1862, although he lingered for nearly two months. In 1881 was published "The Poems and Stories of Fitz-James O'Brien; Edited, with a Sketch of the Author, by William Winter." Died, Cumberland, Md., 6 April, 1862.

O'CONNOR, Michael, soldier, b. about 1837. Sergeant in the 140th regiment of N. Y. volunteers. The author of a war ballad, "Réveille." Died, Potomac Station, Va., 28 Dec., 1862.

O'CONNOR, William Douglas, b. Boston, Mass., 2 Jan., 1832. Was associate editor of the Boston "Commonwealth," a Free-Soil paper, before he was twenty. Edited the Philadelphia "Saturday Evening Post," 1854–60, and in 1861 was made corresponding clerk of the U. S. light-house board at Washington, becoming chief clerk in 1873. Was afterward assistant general superintendent of the life-saving service, the annual reports of which he wrote for a number of years. Early contributed stories and poems to the magazines. In 1866 appeared "The Good Gray Poet," a spirited defence of Walt Whitman, and twenty-one years later Mr. O'Connor wrote a notable series of letters to the N. Y. "Tribune," scoring the public authorities of Boston for suppressing a volume of Whitman's poems. He became identified with the defenders of the Baconian theory of the authorship of Shakespeare's plays, and issued "Hamlet's Note-Book" (1886) on this subject. Some of his works are "Harrington ; a Story of True Love" (1860), "The Ghost" (1856 and 1875), "To Fanny," poem ("Atlantic Monthly," 1871), and "The Carpenter ; a Christmas Story" ("Putnam's Magazine," 1868). Died, Washington, D. C., 9 May, 1889.

ODELL, Jonathan, clergyman, b. Newark, N. J., 25 Sept., 1737. Graduated at the college of New Jersey. After serving as surgeon in the British army, took orders, and in 1767 became rector of a church at Burlington, N. J. Was noted as a loyalist in the Revolution, and left America at its close. His poems are in "The Loyalist Poetry of the Revolution" (1857) and "The Loyal Verses of Joseph Stansbury," etc. (1860). Died, Fredericton, N. B., 25 Nov., 1818.

O'HARA, Theodore, soldier, b. Danville, Ky., 11 Feb., 1820. Entered the U. S. army, 1846, and was brevetted major for gallantry in the Mexican war. Afterward practised law at Washington, D. C. Was a colonel in the Confederate army. The best-known of his poems is "The Bivouac of the Dead," written in memory of the Kentuckians who fell at Buena Vista. Died, near Guerryton, Ala., 6 June, 1867.

OLMSTED, Frederick Law, landscape-gardener, b. Hartford, Conn., 26 April, 1822. Travelled extensively in Europe for the purpose of observing the systems of landscape-gardening in vogue there, and published on his return "Walks and Talks of an American Farmer" (1852). Several books on the effect of slavery on agriculture, written from personal observation before the civil war, were combined in "The Cotton Kingdom" (1861), a work much quoted in war times. In 1856 he was appointed superintendent of construction of the new Central Park in New York city, for which his own plans were accepted, and became noted for similar work in many of the leading cities of the United States.

O'REILLY, John Boyle, journalist, b. Dowth Castle, Co. Meath, Ireland, 28 June, 1844. Entered journalism on the "Drogheda Argus." Removed to England at the age of eighteen and enlisted in the Tenth Hussars as an agent of the Fenian society. He was detected and sentenced to death for high treason in 1866, his sentence being commuted to twenty years' penal servitude. After a year's imprisonment, escaped from the western coast of Australia in an open boat, was picked up by an American whaling bark, and reached Philadelphia, Penn., in 1869. The following year became editor of the Boston, Mass., "Pilot," of which he was afterward co-proprietor. Author of "Songs of the Southern Seas" (1873), "Songs, Legends, and Ballads" (1878), "Moondyne," novel (1879), "Statues in the Block," poems (1881), "In Bohemia" (1886), "The Ethics of Boxing" (1888), "Stories and Sketches" (1888), and a work on Ireland in preparation in 1890.

ORNE, Caroline Frances, b. Cambridge, Mass., 18—. Always a resident of Cambridge. Issued in 1876 "Morning Songs of American Freedom."

OSBORN, John, physician, b. Sandwich, Mass., 1713. Graduated at Harvard. Educated for the ministry, but finally entered on the practice of medicine at Middletown, Conn. His "Whaling Song" was long popular with sailors. Died, Middletown, Conn., 31 May, 1753.

OSGOOD, Frances Sargent [Locke], b. Boston, Mass., 18 June, 1811. Daughter of John Locke, a merchant. Some of her early verses were noticed by Mrs. Lydia Maria Child, who had them inserted in the "Juvenile Miscellany." Edited the "Ladies' Companion" for a time. Sat to S. S. Osgood, the artist, for her portrait, a friendship resulting which led to their marriage. They went to London, and remained there four years, he painting portraits, she writing for the magazines and bringing out a volume of poems, "A Wreath of Wild Flowers from New England" (1839). The Osgoods returned to Boston in 1840, but soon afterward settled in New York city. Poe, who had favorably reviewed her poems, sent her a copy of "The Raven," asking her opinion of it, and for an introduction to her. She was fascinated by his appearance and genius, and addressed some verses to him, as Israfel, in the "Broadway Journal." To this Poe replied with the stanzas inscribed to her, and the "Valentine" containing her name in cryptogram. She records that though they were friends till his death, they only met during the first year of their acquaintance. Published "The Floral Offering" (1847). A complete collection of her poems was issued after her death. Died, Hingham, Mass., 12 May, 1850.

OSGOOD, Kate Putnam, b. Fryeburg, Me., 1841. A sister of James R. Osgood, the publisher. Chiefly resided in Boston, Mass., and vicinity, visiting France and **Germany**

during 1869–74. Early began contributing verse and stories to the magazines, and wrote the well-known poem of the civil war, "Driving Home the Cows."

OSGOOD, Samuel, clergyman, b. Charlestown, Mass., 30 Aug., 1812. Graduated at Harvard. Was pastor of a Unitarian church at New York city from 1849 until 1869, when he resigned and joined the Protestant Episcopal church. Was associate editor of the "Christian Inquirer" (1850–4), and issued, among other books, "Studies in Christian Biography" (1851), "Milestones in Our Life's Journey" (1855), "Student Life" (1861), and "American Leaves" (1867). Died, New York, N. Y., 14 April, 1880.

OSSOLI, Sarah Margaret [Fuller], b. Cambridgeport, Mass., 23 May, 1810. Exceptionally precocious in her youth, she was a prominent member of the transcendental circle of which Emerson was the centre. She taught pupils for a few years, and wrote for the papers, also contributing translations from the German. Edited "The Dial," 1840–1. Became literary critic of the N. Y. "Tribune" under Greeley, 1844, and wrote many articles upon her investigations into the social condition of the people in the great city. In 1846 went to Europe, where she was well received in literary and aristocratic circles. Was married, 1847, to the Marquis Ossoli, in Italy, and distinguished herself by devotion to the wounded during the revolutionary struggle of 1849 in that country. Was in the confidence of Mazzini. On the capture of Rome by the French, she, her husband, and child removed to Florence, and embarked at Leghorn in the merchantman "Elizabeth" for America, May, 1850. After a perilous voyage the ship was wrecked off Fire Island, and the family perished. Of her writings there were published in her lifetime "Summer on the Lakes" (1843), "Woman in the Nineteenth Century" (1844), and "Papers on Literature and Art" (1846); these and other of her works were collectively brought out by her brother, 1855. "Memoirs of Margaret Fuller Ossoli" (1852) was written by Emerson, Freeman Clarke, and W. H. Channing, and lives have been issued by T. W. Higginson and Julia Ward Howe. Died, by shipwreck, Fire Island beach, N. Y., 16 July, 1850.

OTIS, Harrison Gray, statesman, b. Boston, Mass., 8 Oct., 1765. Graduated at Harvard. Admitted to the bar, 1786. Served a number of terms in the Massachusetts legislature, was U. S. representative, 1797–1801, and U. S. senator, 1817–22. A Federalist in politics, he took part in the Hartford convention of 1814. Gained reputation as an orator. The most important of his speeches was his eulogy on Hamilton, delivered at Boston, 1804. Died, Boston, Mass., 28 Oct., 1848.

OTIS, James, statesman, b. West Barnstable, Mass., 5 Feb., 1725. Graduated at Harvard. Began the practice of law at Plymouth, Mass., 1748. Settled permanently at Boston two years later, where he met with success in his profession. Opposed the granting of "writs of assistance" to search private houses and shops in Massachusetts for smuggled goods in his famous speech before Chief-Justice Hutchinson, 1761. Became a leader in the patriotic party, and on 6 June, 1765, proposed the assembling of the congress of delegates from American colonies, which presented a petition to parliament against the Stamp Act. In 1769 became involved in a quarrel with some commissioners of customs, and was attacked by them, receiving injuries in the head which developed a previous tendency to mental derangement. Nevertheless, he took part in the battle of Bunker Hill, and attempted to resume his law practice, but finally retired to Andover, Mass. He was killed by a stroke of lightning while standing at an open doorway. His political pamphlets are "A Vindication of the Conduct of the House of Representatives" (1762), "Rights of the British Colonies Asserted and Proved" (1764), and "Considerations on behalf of the Colonists" (1765). Died, Andover, Mass., 23 May, 1783.

OWEN, Robert Dale, b. Glasgow, Scotland, 7 Nov., 1801. His father was Robert Owen, the English social reformer. After spending three years at the college of Hofwyl in Switzerland, Robert Dale came to the United States in 1825. He served two terms as U. S. representative from Indiana, and was chargé d'affaires and U. S. minister at Naples, 1853–8. A controversy on divorce with Horace Greeley, and various pamphlets in behalf of the Union and advocating emancipation, published during the civil war, attained enormous circulation. His most important works related to spiritualism, in which he was a life-long believer. They were "Footfalls on the Boundary of Another World" (1860) and "The Debatable Land between this World and the Next" (1872). Besides these appeared a novel, "Beyond the Breakers" (1870), and an autobiography, "Threading my Way" (1874). Died, Lake George, N. Y., 24 June, 1877.

PAGE, Thomas Nelson, lawyer, b. "Oakland," Hanover Co., Va., 23 April, 1853. Studied at Washington and Lee university, and graduated in law at the university of Virginia. Entered the bar and practised at Richmond, Va. His first story of Virginia life, "Marse Chan," was printed in the "Century Magazine" for 1884. He had previously written dialect poetry. A volume of stories was brought out in 1887 with the title, "In Ole Virginia," and was followed by "Two Little Confederates" (1888) and "Befo' de War ; Echoes in Negro Dialect," by A. C. Gordon and T. N. Page (1888).

PAINE, Robert Treat, Jr., b. Taunton, Mass., 9 Dec., 1773. Graduated at Harvard. After unsuccessful attempts at business, edited the "Federal Orrery," 1794–7. Was admitted to the Boston bar in 1802, but soon abandoned his practice for a desultory career. Gained reputation for his poetical writings, which sold extensively and brought him large sums of money. Among these were "The Invention of Letters" (1795), "The Ruling Passion" (1797), and his songs "Rise, Columbia" and "Adams and Liberty." In 1812 his "Works, in Verse and Prose" were brought out posthumously. Died, Boston, Mass., 13 Nov., 1811.

PAINE, Thomas, publicist, b. Thetford, Norfolk Co., England, 29 Jan., 1737. The son of a stay-maker of his native town, he followed his father's trade until 1759, when he became an exciseman. Was engaged in this occupation and in teaching at London until 1774. Being dismissed from the excise service, he emigrated to America by the advice of Franklin, who had discovered his literary ability. Shortly after became editor of the "Pennsylvania Magazine" at Philadelphia. His pamphlet, "Common Sense" (1776), a summary of the reasons for American independence, was effective in preparing the popular mind for the Declaration. He was voted five hundred pounds by the Pennsylvania legislature for writing it, and received other honors. In December, 1776, the first number of "The Crisis" appeared, a series of popular papers on the war, designed to keep up public enthusiasm. The last number was issued at the close of hostilities in 1783. Paine served for a short time in the Continental army, and was secretary of the congressional committee on foreign affairs, 1777–9. Was clerk of the Pennsylvania assembly in 1780, and the next year accompanied Henry Laurens on a successful mission to France for effecting a loan to the American government. In 1785 received large grants of land and money from congress and the states for his services in the war. Two years later sailed for England, whence he was outlawed for publishing his "Rights of Man" (1791–2), a spirited defence of the French revolution. Became a French citizen and was elected to the French national convention. Expelled from this body as a foreigner, he was thrown into prison, and narrowly escaped being guillotined. Wrote a portion of "The Age of Reason" (1794–6) during this imprisonment. Returned to America, 1802, and lived in retirement at New York for the rest of his life. Died, New York, N. Y., 8 June, 1809.

PALFREY, John Gorham, b. Boston, Mass., 2 May, 1796. Graduated at Harvard. Pastor of the Brattle street Unitarian church at Boston, from 1818 to 1831, and professor of sacred literature in Harvard, 1831–9. Entered the state legislature, 1842, was secretary of state, 1844–8, U. S. representative, 1847–9, and postmaster of Boston, 1861-7. Supported the abolition movement ardently, liberated and made provision for a number of slaves bequeathed to him, and was present as a representative of the United States at the anti-slavery congress in Paris, 1867. Contributed largely to the press on abolition topics. Edited the "North American Review" from 1835 to 1843. Author of a collection of "Academical Lectures on the Jewish Scriptures and Antiquities" (1833–52), "Elements of Chaldee, Syriac, Samaritan, and Rabbinical Grammar" (1835), "The Relation between Judaism and Christianity" (1854), and "A Compendious History of New England" (1866–90). Died, Cambridge, Mass., 26 April, 1881.

PALMER, John Williamson, b. Baltimore, Md., 4 April, 1825. Graduated at the university of Maryland. Studied medicine, and was the first city physician of San Francisco, Cal., in 1849. Was Confederate war correspondent for the N. Y. "Tribune," 1863–4. Settled permanently in New York city in 1870. Afterward became a member of the staff of "The Century Dictionary." His poem, "Stonewall Jackson's Way," was one of the most popular ballads of the civil war. His writings include "The Golden Dagon, or Up and Down the Irrawaddi" (1853), "The New and the Old, or California and India in Romantic Aspects" (1859), "After His Kind, by John Coventry," a novel (1886), and a number of uncollected poems.

PALMER, Ray, clergyman, b. Little Compton, R. I., 12 Nov., 1808. Graduated at Yale. Pastor of Congregational churches at Bath, Me., and Albany, N. Y., 1835-66. From 1866 until 1878 was secretary of the American Congregational union. Author of a number of favorite hymns. His books include "Spiritual Improvement" (1839), "Hymns and Sacred Pieces" (1865), "Hymns of my Holy Hours" (1866), and "Complete Poetical Works" (1876). Died, Newark, N. J., 29 March, 1887.

PARKER, Theodore, clergyman, b. Lexington, Mass., 24 Aug., 1810. Virtually educated himself until 1830, when he entered Harvard, working on a farm while studying. Received an honorary degree in 1840. Was tutor in a private school at Waterton, 1832–42, and was ordained to the Unitarian ministry in 1837, at West Roxbury, where he preached until 1845. His gifts becoming more widely known, a new society was organized in Boston, of which he accepted the pastorate in 1846, resigning on account of impaired health in 1859. Was an ardent advocate of abolition, and of all social reform movements, on the platform, in the pulpit and the press, and in constant acts of practical philanthropy. He established and edited the "Massachusetts Quarterly Review," 1849–52. Among his publications are the widely-known "Discourse on Matters Pertaining to Religion" (1842), of which there have been many editions, "Sermons on Theism, Atheism, and Popular Theology" (1852) and "Ten Sermons of Religion" (1853). An English edition of his works was issued posthumously by Frances Power Cobbe (12 vols., 1863–65), and a Boston edition appeared in 1870; also, "Historic Americans," including studies of Washington, Franklin, Adams, and Jefferson (1870). Biographies of Theodore Parker have been written by John Weiss, O. B. Frothingham, and others. Died, Florence, Italy, 10 May, 1860.

PARKMAN, Francis, b. Boston, Mass., 16 Sept., 1823. Graduated at Harvard. Began the study of the law, but soon gave this up and travelled for a year in Europe. In pursuance of a plan to write the history of the contest that ended French domination in North America, and with the purpose of gaining from the Indians and frontiersmen whatever recollections and traditions of early times might remain with them, as well as to make a personal study of Indian character and customs, he made an expedition to the Rocky mountains in 1846, and lived among the Dakotas and other tribes of the Northwest for several months, undergoing hardships that permanently injured his health. His experiences at this time were related in a series of articles contributed to the "Knickerbocker Magazine," which were collected and published as "The Oregon Trail" (1849). The scope of his historical plan was afterward enlarged to embrace an account of French American history from the beginning, under the general title "France and England in North America." His first historical work, "The Conspiracy of Pontiac" (1851), is practically a supplement to this series. Of the series proper the following volumes have appeared : "Pioneers of France in the New World" (1865), "Jesuits in North America" (1867), "Discovery of the Great West" (1869), "The Old Régime in Canada" (1874), "Count Frontenac and New France under Louis XIV." (1877), and "Montcalm and Wolfe" (1884). With the completion of a volume to precede the last, and to cover the period from 1700 to 1748, the series will be ended. In his investigations for this work, the historian, besides many trips to Europe for the purpose of consulting state papers and other similar sources of information, has made it a point to visit the scenes of the events he describes, and has thus been able to give

a local atmosphere to his recitals not otherwise obtainable. Mr. Parkman also published a novel, "Vassall Morton" (1856). His writings attained for him a leading position among scholars and historians, and proved popular with the masses. They were completed under the disadvantage of partial blindness. Mr. Parkman resided for the most part in the neighborhood of Boston, and was for some years an overseer of Harvard.

PARSONS, George Frederic, journalist, b. Brighton, Eng., 15 June, 1840. Followed the sea for a few years, and in 1863 began newspaper work at Vancouver Island. Afterward became editor of the Sacramento, Cal., "Record-Union." In 1883 joined the editorial staff of the N. Y. "Tribune." Wrote introductions to several of Miss K. P. Wormeley's translations of Balzac, besides "Life of James W. Marshall," discoverer of gold in California (1871), and "Middle Ground," novel (1874).

PARSONS, Thomas William, b. Boston, Mass., 18 Aug., 1819. Educated at the Boston Latin school. After a course of private studies, went to Europe, 1836, finding special pleasure in mastering Italian during his stay in Italy. Here he made a translation of Dante's "Inferno," which was published in Boston on his return in 1843, and was very favorably received by the reviewers. Resolving to devote himself to the healing art, he studied dental surgery, in which he took his degree at Boston, and soon formed a lucrative practice. A few years later removed to England, where he combined the practice of his profession with literary studies and writing. Issued the first volume of his collected poems under the title "Ghetto di Roma" (1854), in which were several pieces that had attracted attention in the London periodicals. In 1867 a quarto illustrated edition of the "Inferno" was published. Another volume was privately printed in 1867, entitled "The Magnolia, and Other Poems" ; this was followed by "The Old House at Sudbury" (1870), and by "The Shadow of the Obelisk, and other Poems" (1872). After 1872 the author resided at Boston, Mass., a frequent contributor of poems, essays, and miscellaneous pieces to the periodicals. His lines "On a Bust of Dante" have gained permanent reputation.

PARTON, James, b. Canterbury, England, 9 Feb., 1822. Was brought to America when five years old. Educated in New York city and vicinity, he became a teacher, and subsequently assistant editor of the "Home Journal." Published "The Life of Horace Greeley, Editor of the New York Tribune" (1855), gathering many of his facts from Greeley's early neighbors and associates in Vermont and New Hampshire. This work was very successful, and Mr. Parton took up literature as a profession. In 1875 he removed from New York to Newburyport, Mass., which became his permanent residence. Author of "Life and Times of Aaron Burr" (1857) "Life of Andrew Jackson" (1859–60), "Life and Times of Benjamin Franklin" (1864), "Life of Thomas Jefferson" (1874), and "Life of Voltaire" (1881), for the last of which he made long and special studies.

PAULDING, James Kirke, b. Pleasant Valley, Dutchess Co., N. Y., 22 Aug., 1779. His family's residence in that place was temporary, and after the Revolution they returned to their old home in Westchester county. His sister married William Irving, brother of Washington Irving, and on Paulding's removal to New York city as a young man, he became associated with the brothers in literary composition. The result of this partnership was the publication of "Salmagundi: or the Whim-Whams and Opinions of Launcelot Langstaff and Others." This humorous discussion of local affairs was brought out in twenty numbers during 1807 and 1808. A pamphlet on "The United States and England" (1814), in reply to an attack on the former country by the London "Quarterly," attracted the notice of President Madison, and led to Paulding's appointment as secretary to the board of navy commissioners at Washington. He became navy agent at New York city in 1825, resigning this position twelve years later, when made secretary of the navy by President Van Buren. At the close of the latter's administration, Paulding retired to a country home in Dutchess county, where he afterward resided. The success of "Salmagundi" had given him confidence in his abilities, and from 1812 to 1849 he was actively engaged in literary production, chiefly of fiction. Among his books are "The Diverting History of John Bull and Brother Jonathan" (1812), "The Backwoodsman," a poem (1818), "Konigsmarke" (1823), "Tales of the Good Woman" (1829), "The Dutchman's Fireside" (1831), "Westward Ho!" (1832), "Life of George Washington" (1835), "The Book of St. Nicholas" (1837), and "The Puritan and his Daughter" (1849). Died, Hyde Park, Dutchess Co., N. Y., 6 April, 1860.

PAYNE, John Howard, dramatist, b. New York, N. Y., 9 June, 1791. As a boy of fourteen edited the "Thespian Mirror." Studied at Union college, where he edited "The Pastime." Made his *début* as an actor at the Park theatre, New York city, 24 Feb., 1809, as Norval. Played with great success in England afterward, where he enjoyed intimacy with Washington Irving, Coleridge, Lamb, and other literary notables. Besides his original dramas, translated and adapted a number of plays from the French. His version of "Brutus" (produced 1818) was made with the help of

seven older plays on the same subject. Charles Kemble bought a batch of his pieces for Covent Garden theatre, among them "Clari, the Maid of Milan," which was sold for $150. In it occurs the song "Home, sweet home," which was sung by Miss M. Tree, sister of Charles Kean's wife. This song made the fortune of the opera and of the publishers, 100,000 copies having been rapidly sold, but the author reaped no reward. He returned to New York in 1832, issued the prospectus of a paper which never appeared, and varied his professional work with that of journalism. Several benefits were given to him, and in 1841 he accepted an appointment as U. S. consul at Tunis, where he passed the remaining eleven years of his life. He was buried there, but his remains were reinterred, at the charge of the late W. W. Corcoran, at Washington, in 1883. A volume of his collected works, edited by Gabriel Harrison, with a memoir, was issued in 1875. Died, Tunis, Africa, 9 April, 1852.

PAYNE, William Morton, educator, b. Newburyport, Mass., 14 Feb., 1858. Early removed to Chicago, Ill., where in 1876 he became professor of physical science at the Chicago high school. Was also literary editor of the Chicago "News," 1884–8, and of the "Evening Journal" after 1888. Besides frequent contributions to "The Dial," 1883–90, issued "Our New Education" (1884) and "Sigurd Slembe, by Björnstjerne Björnson, translated from the Norwegian" (1888).

PEABODY, Andrew Preston, clergyman, b. Beverly, Mass., 19 Mar., 1811. Graduated at Harvard. Was pastor of a Unitarian church at Portsmouth, N. H., 1826–60. Became professor of Christian morals at Harvard, 1860, resigning in 1881. Edited the "North American Review," 1852–61. Besides many sermons and articles in the periodicals, issued "Lectures on Christian Doctrine" (1844), "Christianity and Science" (1874), "Christian Belief and Life" (1875), "Harvard Reminiscences" (1888).

PEABODY, Oliver William Bourne, b. Exeter, N. H., 9 July, 1799. Twin brother of W. B. O. Peabody. Graduated at Harvard. Entered the bar, and practised at Exeter, 1819–30. In 1830 settled in Boston, and became assistant editor of the "North American Review." Pastor of a Unitarian church at Burlington, Vt., from 1845 until his death. Besides contributing to the magazines, issued several biographies, and edited an edition of Shakespeare. Died, Burlington, Vt., 5 July, 1848.

PEABODY, William Bourne Oliver, clergyman, b. Exeter, N. H., 9 July, 1799. Graduated at Harvard. Was pastor of the Unitarian church at Springfield, Mass., from 1820 until his death. Edited the "Springfield Collection of Hymns" (1835), wrote the report of the Massachusetts survey commissioners on "The Birds of the Commonwealth" (1839), and contributed articles and poems to the reviews and magazines. His "Literary Remains" (1850) were edited by his brother. Died, Springfield, Mass., 28 May, 1847.

PEALE, Rembrandt, artist, b. Bucks Co., Penn., 22 Feb., 1778. Early developed a taste for art, and painted a portrait of Washington when seventeen years old. Studied under Benjamin West in London, and was chiefly occupied during life with portrait-painting in the eastern cities of the United States, having many distinguished sitters. Published several works on art, and "Portfolio of an Artist" (1839). Died, Philadelphia, Penn., 3 Oct., 1860.

PECK, Harry Thurston, educator, b. Stamford, Conn., 24 Nov., 1856. Graduated at Columbia, where he afterward became professor of Latin. Besides contributions to the magazines, issued "The Semitic Theory of Creation" (1886) and "Suetonius" (1889).

PECK, Samuel Minturn, b. Tuskaloosa, Ala., 4 Nov., 1854. Graduated at the university of Alabama, and in medicine at New York city. A resident of his native place, occupied with literary work and farming. "Cap and Bells," a collection of his verse, published in the magazines, appeared in 1886.

PEIRCE, Benjamin, mathematician, b. Salem, Mass., 4 April, 1809. Graduated at Harvard, where he was professor of mathematics, 1833–42, and of astronomy and mathematics from 1842 until his decease. Was superintendent of the U. S. coast survey, 1867–74. Made many valuable original contributions to the science of astronomy. Author of a series of elementary mathematical works, and of "Analytic Mechanics" (1855), "Linear Associative Algebra" (1870), and "Ideality in the Physical Sciences" (1881). Died, Cambridge, Mass., 6 Oct., 1880.

PENHALLOW, Samuel, jurist, b. St. Mabon, Cornwall, England, 2 July, 1665. Emigrated to New England, with the purpose of becoming a Congregational minister, July, 1686. Settled at Portsmouth, in the New Hampshire colony, where he entered trade and married a wealthy wife, gaining great influence in the town and being successively appointed a member of the council, treasurer of the colony, and justice and chief-justice of the superior court. Published "A History of the Wars of New-England with the Eastern Indians" (1726). Died, Portsmouth, N. H., 2 Dec., 1726.

PENN, William, founder of Pennsylvania, b. London, England, 14 Oct., 1644. Son of Admiral Penn. While at Oxford

university, he came under the influence of Thomas Roe, a Quaker preacher, and heading a students' rebellion against ceremonies, was expelled. Received harsh treatment for his religious beliefs from his father, who, however, finally relented and supported him in his course. Was imprisoned at various times for holding Quaker meetings and publishing controversial tracts. His most famous work, "No Cross, No Crown," was written in prison in 1668. At his father's death, he inherited the latter's fortune and, becoming interested in American colonization, obtained from the king, 24 Feb., 1681, the grant of Pennsylvania, in payment of a debt. As sole proprietor of the province, he drafted a constitution establishing liberty of conscience and a representative government. Came to America, Sept., 1682, and negotiated his famous treaty with the Indians the following month. An imprisonment for debt in the Fleet through the faithlessness of his steward, and many troubles in his family, brought on attacks of palsy in 1712, which left him with a weakened mind, although he lingered for several years after. Died, Ruscombe, Berkshire, England, 30 July, 1718.

PENNYPACKER, Isaac Rusling, b. Phœnixville, Penn., 11 Dec., 1852. Received his education at private schools. Literary editor of the Philadelphia "Inquirer," and a resident of that city. Author of "Gettysburg, and Other Poems" (1890).

PERCIVAL, James Gates, geologist, b. Berlin, Conn., 15 Sept., 1795. Graduated at Yale, and wrote a tragedy, "Zamor," which was included in the commencement exercises of his year, 1815. Studied medicine and began practice at Charleston, S. C., issuing there his first volume of poems, "Prometheus," in 1820. Was appointed surgeon in the U. S. recruiting service at Boston, 1824, at the same time continuing his literary work. Returned to New Haven, Conn., 1827, and, taking up the study of geology, was in 1835 appointed with Prof. C. U. Shepard to make a survey of the mineralogy and geology of Connecticut. His "Report on the Geology of the State of Connecticut" was published in 1842. In 1853 he was appointed geologist of Wisconsin. Is said to have been familiar with ten languages, being a philologist, geologist, botanist, musician, and poet. Wrote several tragedies, collected in his "Poetical Works" (1859). "Life and Letters," edited by Julius H. Ward, appeared in 1866. Died, Hazel Green, Wis., 2 May, 1856.

PERCY, George, colonist, b. Syon House, Northumberland Co., England, 4 Sept., 1586 (R. A. Brock). Eighth son of the eighth Earl of Northumberland. Served as a soldier in the Netherlands, and afterward joined the Virginia company, sailing with

Capt. Christopher Newport and Capt. John Smith, 19 Dec., 1606. Succeeded Smith as president and governor at Jamestown in the fall of 1609. Was superseded in office by Sir Thomas Gates on his arrival in May, 1610, and was appointed captain under Lord Delawarr the month after. A portion of his manuscript, "A Discourse of the Plantation of the Southern Colonie in Virginia by the English," was published in Purchas's "Pilgrimes," 1625. The remainder has been lost. Died, England, Mar., 1632.

PERRY, George, journalist, b. Richmond, Mass., 1828. Graduated at Williams college, and spent several years in Monmouth county, N. J., as a member of the "North American Phalanx," a Fourierite community there established. Removing to New York and engaging in journalistic work, he became associated with N. P. Willis as assistant editor of the N. Y. "Home Journal," succeeding to the editorship on the latter's death in 1867. Mr. Perry's poem "Siva, Destroyer" was found among his papers after his death. Died, New York, N. Y., 15 Nov., 1888.

PERRY, Nora, journalist, b. Dudley, Mass., 1841. Her family soon after removed to Providence, R.I. Her first serial story was printed in "Harper's Magazine" for 1859–60. She was for some time Boston correspondent of the Chicago "Tribune," and afterward of the Providence "Journal." Author of "After the Ball, and Other Poems" (1875), "Book of Love Stories" (1881), "For a Woman," novel (1885), and "New Songs and Ballads" (1886).

Perry, Oliver Hazard [*Noted Saying:* Vol. IV., page 490], b. South Kingston, R. I., 23 Aug., 1785. Served in the U. S. navy from 1799 until his death. Died, Port Spain, Island of Trinidad, 23 Aug., 1819.

PERRY, Thomas Sergeant, b. Newport, R. I., 23 Jan., 1845. Grandson of Oliver H. Perry. Graduated at Harvard, and studied at French and German universities. At different times instructor in German and English at Harvard. Edited the "North American Review," 1872–4. Some of his books are "Life and Letters of Francis Lieber" (1882), "English Literature in the Eighteenth Century" (1883), and "The Evolution of the Snob" (1887).

PETERS, Phillis [Wheatley], b. Africa, about 1754. Brought to America in 1761, and purchased at the Boston slave-market by John Wheatley of that place. Within sixteen months after her arrival she had learned to read the English language, and being encouraged in her studies, soon developed a talent for metrical composition. Visited England in 1774, and received attentions from various prominent people. After the breaking up of her master's family, was married, 1778, to John Peters, one of her own

race, with whom she resided in great poverty until her death. Besides several single poems, she brought out "Poems on Various Subjects, Religious and Moral, by Phillis Wheatley, Negro Servant to Mr. John Wheatley, of Boston, in New England" (1773). Died, Boston, Mass., 5 Dec., 1784.

PETERS, Samuel, clergyman, b. Hebron, Conn., 12 Dec., 1735. Graduated at Yale. Travelled in Europe, and entered the ministry as a Church of England clergyman in 1759, although of Puritan descent. Three years later became rector of churches at Hebron and Hartford, Conn., residing at the former place. His activity in the loyalist cause involved him in difficulties with the Revolutionary party, whose unwelcome visits to his house induced him to sail for England, 1774. His property was afterward confiscated, and he received remuneration for this from the British government. Returned to America, 1805, residing chiefly in New York city. In 1781 he published "A General History of Connecticut," satirizing the country and its people and full of preposterous exaggerations. He also wrote "A History of the Rev. Hugh Peters" (1807), his great-uncle. Died, New York, N. Y., 19 April, 1826.

PETERSON, Henry, publisher, b. Philadelphia, Penn., 7 Dec., 1818. Entered the publishing business in 1839. Was for twenty years assistant editor of the Philadelphia, Penn., "Saturday Evening Post." Author of "Poems" (1863 and 1883), "Universal Suffrage" (1867), "The Modern Job," poem (1869), "Faire-Mount," poem (1874), "Confessions of a Minister" (1874), "Bessie's Lovers" 1877, "Cæsar, a Dramatic Study" (1879), and a drama, "Helen; or, 100 Years Ago" (produced, 1876).

Petigru, James Lewis [*Noted Saying:* Vol. XI., page 453], b. Abbeville District, S. C., 10 Mar., 1789. Attorney-general of his state, 1822–30, and afterward an opponent of secession. Died, Charleston, S. C., 3 Mar., 1863.

PHELPS, Charles Henry, lawyer, b. Stockton, Cal., 1 Jan., 1853. Studied at the university of California, and graduated at the Harvard law school. Practised law in San Francisco, 1874–80, and edited "The Californian" (now "Overland Monthly") from 1880 to 1882. In the latter year removed to New York city, where he resumed his law practice. A contributor to the magazines, and author of "Californian Verses" (1882).

Phelps, Edward John [*Noted Saying:* Vol. XI., page 461], b. Middlebury, Vt., 11 July, 1822. Became professor of law at Yale university in 1881, and was U. S. minister to Great Britain, 1885–9.

PHELPS, William Walter, diplomatist, b. New York, N. Y., 24 Aug., 1839. Graduated at Yale. Studied law and began a successful practice in New York city. The death of his father, John J. Phelps, necessitating the care of a large estate, obliged him to relinquish his profession. Was elected U. S. representative from New Jersey, 1872, as a Republican, his independent attitude in regard to the civil rights bill, since declared unconstitutional, costing him his reëlection for the succeeding term. Appointed U. S. minister to Austria by President Garfield in 1881, he resigned the position on the latter's death. Was again U. S. representative from New Jersey in 1883 and following terms, until he declined to be a candidate. In 1889 he was appointed U. S. minister to Germany by President Harrison. Always a leader in matters relating to Yale university, he was foremost in the agitation which resulted in the representation of graduates on its board of trustees, being himself regularly elected as member of that body. Besides a number of notable speeches in congress, he delivered numerous addresses before societies, etc.

PHILLIPS, Wendell, orator, b. Boston, Mass., 29 Nov., 1811. Graduated at Harvard. Admitted to the bar, 1834. Joined the abolition movement in 1835. An unpremeditated speech in Faneuil Hall, 1837, began his renown as an orator. His fine presence, polished language, grasp of subject, and religious earnestness made him a doughty champion of reforms. While willing to earn an income by literary lectures, he freely gave his services to the anti-slavery movement. In 1840 represented the Massachusetts Abolitionists at the world's anti-slavery conference in London, and urged the policy of admitting women to membership. From 1843 he denounced the "compromise laws," insisting that slavery must be crushed at any cost. Differed from Garrison, who wished to dissolve the anti-slavery society at the close of the civil war. Phillips held that their work would be incomplete until the negro obtained the suffrage. This attitude caused his election to the presidency of the society, which office he held until 1870. Was nominated for governor of Massachusetts by the Labor Reform party, but not elected. Gave active support to most reforms, including prohibition and woman suffrage. Issued several controversial pamphlets and lectures, and "Speeches, Lectures, and Letters" (1863). Died, Boston, Mass., 2 Feb., 1884.

PIATT, John James, b. James Mill, now Milton, Ind., 1 Mar., 1835. Studied at Kenyon college. Removed to Illinois in 1856. Soon after began contributing poems to the Louisville "Journal," and became confidential secretary to George D. Prentice and a writer for the paper. In 1860, issued with W. D. Howells, then at Columbus, O., "Poems of Two Friends." The following year received an appointment as clerk in the U. S. treasury department at Washington, D. C. "The Nests at Washington, and Other Poems," by Mrs. Piatt and himself, appeared in 1864. Became enrolling clerk of the U. S. house of representatives, 1870, and in 1871 its librarian, having resigned his treasury clerkship in 1867, and passed three years in journalistic work at Cincinnati, O. Was appointed U. S. consul at Cork, Ireland, 1882, remaining through two changes of administration. Besides the volumes already mentioned, wrote "Poems in Sunshine and Firelight" (1866), "Western Windows, and Other Poems" (1869), "Landmarks, and Other Poems" (1871), "Poems of House and Home" (1879), "Idyls and Lyrics of the Ohio Valley" (1884 and 1888), "At the Holy Well" (1887), and edited "The Union of American Poetry and Art" (1880-1).

PIATT, Sarah Morgan [Bryan], b. Lexington, Ky., 11 Aug., 1836. A granddaughter of Morgan Bryan, one of the settlers of Kentucky. Attended the Henry female college at Newcastle, Ky. Received early encouragement in her literary efforts from George D. Prentice and Fitz-Greene Halleck. Her first poems were published in the Louisville "Journal." Was married, 1861, to John J. Piatt. Besides collective volumes of her own and her husband's verse, is the author of "A Woman's Poems" (1871), "A Voyage to the Fortunate Isles" (1874), "That New World, and Other Poems" (1876), "Poems in Company with Children" (1877), "Dramatic Persons and Moods" (1880), "An Irish Garland" (1884), and "The Witch in the Glass, and Other Poems" (1889).

PICKERING, Timothy, statesman, b. Salem, Mass., 17 July, 1745. Graduated at Harvard. Admitted to the bar, 1768. Served through the Revolution in the Continental army, of which he became quartermaster-general. Was U. S. secretary of war, 1794-5, and secretary of state, 1795-1800. U. S. senator from Massachusetts, 1803-11, he was identified with the Federalists during this period and during his following two terms as U. S. representative. Many of his letters and an account of his political writings are to be found in "The Life of Timothy Pickering" (1863-73). Died, Salem, Mass., 29 Jan., 1829.

PIERPONT, John, clergyman, b. Litchfield, Conn., 6 April, 1785. Graduated at Yale. Admitted to the Massachusetts bar, 1812. Gave up law for the Unitarian ministry in 1819, when he assumed the pastorate of the Hollis street church at Boston, Mass., retaining it until 1845. Differences arising between his congregation and himself respecting his advocacy of the abolition and temperance movements, he resigned his charge and accepted a pulpit in Troy, N. Y. Preached there and at Medford, Mass., until 1856. Was the candidate of the Liberty party for governor, and in 1850 of the Free-Soil party for U. S. representative. In his old age volunteered and served as army chaplain early in the civil war, but infirmity induced him to accept the offer of a clerkship in the treasury department at Washington, D. C., which he retained until his death. Issued a collection of verse, "Airs of Palestine, and Other Poems" (1816, new edition 1840) and "Poems" (1854). Died, Medford, Mass., 27 Aug., 1866.

PIKE, Albert, lawyer, b. Boston, Mass., 29 Dec., 1809. Did not complete his Harvard course. Went on a tour of exploration through the West, 1831, ending at Fort Smith, Ark., having walked five hundred miles of the way. In 1833 was associate editor of the "Arkansas Advocate." Commanded a squadron in the Arkansas regiment during the Mexican war, and was a Confederate commissioner in negotiating treaties with the Indians at the opening of the civil war, a detachment of whom he led, as brigadier-general, into action. Settled in the practice of law at Memphis, Tenn., 1866, and edited the Memphis "Appeal." Removed his practice to Washington in 1868, retiring in 1880. Held a high position in Freemasonry. Author of "Hymns to the Gods" in "Blackwood's Magazine" (1839), afterward included in "Nugæ" (1854). Privately printed collections of his poems were issued in 1873 and 1881.

PILCH, Frederick Henry, lawyer, b. Newark, N. J., 5 Mar., 1842. Served during the civil war in the Union army until honorably discharged for disability incurred therein. Studied law, and began practice at Newark, 1874, where he became a leading member of the bar. A contributor of verse to the periodicals, and author of "Homespun Verses" (1882). Died, Bloomfield, N. J., 3 Dec., 1889.

Pinckney, Charles Cotesworth [Noted Saying: Vol. IV., page 490], b. Charleston, S. C., 25 Feb., 1746. Served in the Continental army. Appointed U. S. minister to France in 1796. Died, Charleston, S. C., 16 Aug., 1825.

PINKNEY, Edward Coate, b. London, England, 1 Oct., 1802. Son of William Pinkney. Served in the U. S. navy, 1816–24. Admitted to the Maryland bar, 1824. Was appointed professor of rhetoric and belles-lettres at the university of Maryland, in recognition of his poetic gifts. Edited the "Marylander" in 1827. Author of "Poems" (1825, new eds. 1838 and 1844). Died, Baltimore, Md., 11 April, 1828.

PINKNEY, Ninian, soldier, b. Baltimore, Md., 1776 (Appleton). Brother of William Pinkney. Took service in the U. S.

army as lieutenant in 1799, and distinguished himself in the war of 1812. Was made colonel in 1820. Published "Travels in the South of France" (1809), a book much praised by Leigh Hunt. Died, Baltimore, Md., 16 Dec., 1825.

PINKNEY, William, statesman, b. Annapolis, Md., 17 Mar., 1764. Was admitted to the Baltimore bar in 1786. Soon gained reputation in his profession and as an orator. A member of the Maryland legislature, 1788–92, and afterward of the state council. He was U.S. commissioner at London, 1796–1804, and U. S. minister to England, 1807–11, and was subsequently U. S. representative and senator. Selections from his oratory are to be found in "Life, Writings, and Speeches of William Pinkney" (1826). Died, Washington, D. C., 25 Feb., 1822.

PLIMPTON, Florus Beardsley, journalist, b. Palmyra, Portage Co., O., 4 Sept., 1830. Entered journalism at the age of twenty-one and served in an editorial capacity on various newspapers in Ohio, New York, and Pennsylvania, until 1860, when he joined the staff of the Cincinnati "Commercial." With this paper he remained for the rest of his life, becoming associate editor. Shortly after his death appeared a volume of "Poems" (1886). Died, Cincinnati, O., 23 April, 1886.

POE, Edgar Allan, b. Boston, Mass., 19 Jan., 1809. His grandfather, David Poe, was a resident of Baltimore, Md., and was there stationed as assistant quartermaster-general in the Continental army during the Revolution. General Poe's son, also named David, early adopted the stage as a profession, but is said to have been inferior as an actor to his wife, Elizabeth Arnold, the mother of Edgar Allan Poe. The latter was born while his parents were members of a stock company at Boston. Both of them having died, he was adopted in Dec., 1811, by the wife of Mr. John Allan, a merchant of Richmond, Va. At the age of six Poe had begun to show unusual talents. From 1815 to 1820 the Allans resided in England, and during this period he attended the Manor House school in the suburbs of London. Returning to Richmond, he entered the university of Virginia, Feb., 1826. Nine months later, Mr. Allan removed him from the university on account of debts incurred, although Poe headed his class in certain studies. A brief stay in Mr. Allan's counting-room was followed by Poe's desertion of the family in the spring of 1827. He went to Boston, and soon issued there his first volume, "Tamerlane, and Other Poems." In May, 1827, he entered the U. S. army as a private, enlisting as Edgar A. Perry. He was assigned to Battery H, of the 1st Artillery, and saw service at Boston, Charleston, S. C., and Fortress Monroe. By Jan., 1829,

Poe had been promoted sergeant-major, undoubtedly for merit, and soon after endeavored to secure an appointment to West Point. This he received in 1830, meanwhile bringing out at Baltimore his second volume, "Al Aaraaf, Tamerlane, and Minor Poems" (1829). Stood in his studies at West Point, but, determining to leave, purposely neglected his duties and was dismissed Mar., 1831. Shortly after this he published at New York city, with money obtained by subscriptions from his classmates, his third book, "Poems" (1831). He lived at Baltimore during the following years in straitened circumstances until he obtained, 1833, a $100 prize for his story, "A Manuscript Found in a Bottle." This led to an appointment as editor of the "Southern Literary Messenger," at Richmond, and he made that journal a success by his criticisms and stories. He is supposed to have privately married his cousin Virginia Clemm, in 1835. The public ceremony took place in 1836. The following year he left the "Messenger" and went to New York city, finishing there "The Narrative of Arthur Gordon Pym" (1838) already begun, and variously engaged in literary work. Removing to Philadelphia he assumed the editorship of Burton's "Gentleman's Magazine," July, 1839. This connection was broken off a year later. Meanwhile, "Tales of the Grotesque and Arabesque" (1840) had appeared at Philadelphia. The first of several efforts to start a magazine of his own came to an end with his engagement, April, 1841, as editor of "Graham's Magazine," which he conducted successfully, and of which, as in the previous case, his editorship ended in about a year. After further unsuccessful attempts at founding a magazine, Poe and his family returned to New York in 1844, and he afterward resided there. The appearance of his poem "The Raven," in 1845 brought him new reputation, and soon after he filled short engagements on the N. Y. "Evening Mirror" and "Broadway Journal." Overwork, the use of stimulants, poverty, the prolonged illness of his wife, and her death in Jan., 1847, undermined his constitution, and he finally died, under circumstances that are not quite clear, at a hospital in Baltimore. "The Conchologist's First Book" (1839), "Tales" (1845), "The Raven, and Other Poems" (1845), and "Eureka, a Prose Poem" (1848), appeared during his life, and a collection of his works was issued, 1850, by his literary executor, Dr. R. W. Griswold (q. v.). Died, Baltimore, Md., 7 Oct., 1849.

POLLOCK, Edward, lawyer, b. Philadelphia, Penn., 2 Sept., 1823. Received no schooling, but educated himself at home. Was placed in a cotton-factory by his father when ten years old, and at fourteen apprenticed himself to a sign-painter. In 1852 he went to California, and having already written for the press in Philadelphia, became a regular contributor to the San Francisco "Pioneer." Studied law and was admitted to the bar in 1856. A volume of "Poems" was brought out posthumously in 1876. Died, San Francisco, Cal., 13 Dec., 1858.

POOL, Maria Louise, b. Rockland, Mass., 20 Aug., 1845. Daughter of Elias Pool, a manufacturer of that place. Removed to Brooklyn, N. Y., 1870, and subsequently to Wrentham, Mass. A contributor to the magazines, and author of "A Vacation in a Buggy" (1887) and "Tenting at Stony Beach" (1888).

PORTER, Horace, soldier, b. Huntingdon, Penn., 15 April, 1837. Graduated at West Point. Served through the civil war, becoming aide-de-camp to General Grant and receiving the brevet of brigadier-general in the regular army. Was private secretary to Grant during the latter's first presidential term. Resigned from the army, 1873, and engaged in railroad affairs. Author of "West Point Life" (1866), and a writer for the magazines.

PORTER, Noah, educator, b. Farmington, Conn., 14 Dec., 1811. Graduated at Yale, where he was a tutor, 1833–5. Entered the Congregational ministry, and was pastor of the church in New Milford, Conn., from 1836 to 1843, and then at Springfield, Mass., from 1843 to 1846. His first book was "The Educational Systems of the Puritans and Jesuits Compared" (1851). In 1846 was appointed professor of moral philosophy and metaphysics at Yale, and was made president in succession to Dr. Theodore D. Woolsey, 1871, resigning the station in 1886. Was chief editor of Webster's Dictionary on its revision in 1864 and 1880. His best-known work is "The Human Intellect, with an Introduction upon Psychology and the Human Soul" (1868), an accepted text-book that has run through many editions. Other volumes are "Books and Reading" (1870), "American Colleges and the American Public" (1871), "The Sciences of Nature versus the Science of Man" (1871), "Evangeline ; the Place, the Story, and the Poem" (1882), "Science and Sentiment" (1882), "Elements of Moral Science" (1885), "Life of Bishop Berkeley" (1885), "Kant's Ethics, a Critical Exposition" (1886), and "Fifteen Years in the Chapel of Yale College" (1888).

PORY, John, colonist, b. about 1570. Graduating at Cambridge university, he engaged in historical studies under Hakluyt. After some experience as a diplomat, was chosen secretary of the Virginia colony, Feb., 1619. On his arrival was appointed speaker of the house of burgesses which met 30 July, 1619, the first representative body elected in the colony. Returned in 1622 by way of New England, where he met William Bradford. Was sent by the king in 1623 to report on the condition of Virginia. His account of three excursions of discovery in Virginia during 1621–2 is given in Smith's "Generall Historie." Died before or during 1636.

POTTER, Henry Codman, clergyman, b. Schenectady, N. Y., 25 May, 1835. Graduated at the theological seminary of Virginia. Rector of Protestant-Episcopal churches at Troy, N. Y., and Boston, Mass., until 1868, when he was called to Grace church in New York city. Was elected assistant-bishop to his uncle, Horatio Potter, 1883, succeeding the latter as bishop of New York in 1887. Author of "Sisterhoods and Deaconesses" (1872), "The Gates of the East" (1876), and "Sermons of the City" (1877).

POWERS, Horatio Nelson, clergyman, b. Amenia, Dutchess Co., N. Y., 30 April, 1826. Graduated at Union college. Became rector of Episcopal churches in Chicago, Ill., Bridgeport, Conn., and Piermont, N. Y. Was president of Griswold college from 1864 to 1867. A poet and literary critic, and the author of "Through the Year" (1875), "Poems, Early and Late" (1876), and "Ten Years of Song" (1887).

PRENTICE, George Denison, journalist, b. Preston, Conn., 18 Dec., 1802. Graduated at Brown. Edited various papers in New England until 1831, when he became editor of the Louisville, Ky., "Journal." Author of "Life of Henry Clay" (1831) and "Prenticeana, or Wit and Humor" (1860). His "Poems" were issued posthumously in 1876. Died, Louisville, Ky., 22 Jan., 1870.

PRENTISS, Seargent Smith, orator, b. Portland, Me., 30 Sept., 1808. Graduated at Bowdoin. Admitted to the bar, 1829. Was elected to the legislature of Mississippi, 1835, and to the U. S. house of representatives, 1837. Made a number of famous speeches and addresses. His "Memoirs" (1855) were edited by his brother, the Rev. G. L. Prentiss. Died, Longwood, near Natchez, Miss., 1 July, 1850.

PRESCOTT, Mary Newmarch, b. Calais, Me., 2 Aug., 1849. Sister of Harriet Prescott Spofford. Early removed to Newburyport, Mass., where she afterward resided. Wrote many stories and poems for the magazines. Issued but one volume, "Matt's Follies," for children (1873). Died, Deer Island, Amesbury, Mass., 14 June, 1888.

PRESCOTT, William Hickling, b. Salem, Mass., 4 May, 1796. Graduated at Harvard. An accident by which one of his eyes was blinded and the sight of the other permanently impaired caused him to abandon an intention to study law, and he devoted himself to historical research. He made use of a writing apparatus invented for the blind, and employed readers when engaged in his studies. These extended over a period of forty years. Having determined upon Spanish history as his field, he accumulated large stores of hitherto unused material, employing his many influential friends to procure copies of manuscripts and purchase books when on their travels in Europe. He had trained his memory so highly that he was able safely to remember the material for a chapter of from forty to fifty pages during the reading of the records until ready to write it out. The first work published was "The History of the Reign of Ferdinand and Isabella the Catholic" (1838). This was at once successful, and was translated into five European languages. It was followed by the "History of the Conquest of Mexico" (1843) and the "History of the Conquest of Peru" (1847), a volume of "Miscellanies" appearing in 1845. Mr. Prescott visited Europe in 1850, where many honors were conferred upon him by learned societies. The next work issued was "The History of the Reign of Philip II., King of Spain" (1855), of which the concluding volume was unfinished at his death. He also wrote a supplementary volume to Robertson's "History of Charles V.," entitled "Life of Charles V. after his Abdication" (1857). Died, Boston, Mass., 28 Jan., 1859.

PRESTON, Harriet Waters, b. Danvers, Mass., 18—. Her first literary work consisted of translations from the French. Passed much of her life in Great Britain and France. Author of "Aspendale" (1872), "Love in the Nineteenth Century" (1874), "Georgics of Virgil," translated (1881), several novels, and a number of critical papers in the magazines.

PRESTON, Margaret [Junkin], b. Philadelphia, Penn., 18—. Daughter of Rev. Dr. Junkin, the founder of Lafayette college, who in 1848 became president of Washington and Lee university at Lexington, Va., where Mrs. Preston afterward resided. Her first book, "Silverwood," a novel, appeared anonymously, 1856. In 1857 she was married to Col. John T. L. Preston, a professor at the Virginia military institute. "Beechenbrook, a Rhyme of the War," was published, 1866, and was followed by "Old Songs and New" (1870). Later volumes are "Cartoons" (1875), "For Love's Sake" (1887), and "Colonial Ballads," etc. (1887). Mrs. Preston, though a Northerner by birth, always was identified as a writer with the South.

PRIME, Samuel Irenæus, editor, b. Ballston, N. Y., 6 Nov., 1812. Graduated at Williams. Resigned from the Presbyterian ministry on account of bronchial trouble, and became editor of the N. Y.

"Observer" in 1840. Some of his books are "Travels in Europe and the East" (1855), "The Power of Prayer" (1858), "Letters from Switzerland" (1860), "Songs of the Soul" (1874), and "Irenæus Letters" (1880 and 1885). Died, Manchester, Vt., 18 July, 1885.

PRIME, William Cowper, journalist, b. Cambridge, N. Y., 31 Oct., 1825. Graduated at the college of New Jersey. Practised law in New York until 1861, when he acquired an interest in the N. Y. "Journal of Commerce" and was for several years its editor. Made several trips to Egypt and Palestine. Was appointed professor of the history of art at his own college in 1884. Some of his books are "The Owl-Creek Letters" (1848), "Tent Life in the Holy Land" (1857), "I Go A-Fishing" (1873), and "Holy Cross" (1877).

PRINCE, Thomas, clergyman, b. Sandwich, Mass., 15 May, 1687. Graduated at Harvard. After preaching for some years in Suffolk, England, he became in 1718 pastor of the Old South church at Boston, Mass., serving in that capacity until his death. In 1703 he began collecting manuscripts relating to the history of New England, which with books by early New England writers he stored in the tower of the Old South church. This valuable collection was looted by British soldiers during the Revolution, but part of it is still preserved at Boston. Besides numerous sermons, Prince wrote and edited several historical works. The most noted of these is "The Chronological History of New England" (1736), of which, however, but one volume was published, chiefly occupied with annals of the world down to the settlement of New England. Two parts of a second volume appeared in 1755, but they do not bring the history beyond 1633. Died, Boston, Mass., 22 Oct., 1758.

PROCTOR, Edna Dean, b. Henniker, N. H., 10 Oct., 1838. Early removed to Concord, N. H., and subsequently made her residence in Brooklyn, N. Y. An extensive traveller in Europe. Besides articles and verse in the magazines, is the author of "Poems" (1866) and "A Russian Journey" (1872).

PROUDFIT, David Law, "Peleg Arkwright," b. Newburgh, N. Y., 27 Oct., 1842. Served in the Union army during the civil war, gaining the rank of major. Afterward entered business in New York city. His poems have been collected as "Love among the Gamins" (1877) and "Mask and Domino" (1888).

PRYOR, Roger Atkinson, lawyer, b. Dinwiddie Co., Va., 19 July, 1828. Graduated at Hampden-Sidney college. Studied law, but before the civil war engaged in journalism, and founded at Richmond a newspaper called "The South," for the fur-

therance of state-rights. Was U. S. representative for part of one term and refrained from taking his seat on being reëlected at the opening of the war. Joined the Confederate army and became a brigadier-general. At the close of the war removed to New York and thereafter practised law in that city. Delivered a number of addresses and orations on public occasions.

PUTNAM, George Haven, publisher, b. London, England, 2 April, 1844. Studied at Göttingen. Served in the Union army during the civil war. With his father and brothers founded the publishing firm of G. P. Putnam & Sons at New York city in 1866. Connected with various reform movements and a leader in the movement for international copyright. Author of "International Copyright" (1879) and of articles in the magazines.

PUTNAM, Mary Traill Spence [Lowell], b. Boston, Mass., 3 Dec., 1810. Sister of James Russell Lowell. Was married, 1832, to Samuel R. Putnam of Boston, and chiefly resided there. Noted as a linguist, and wrote a number of articles on Polish and Hungarian literature, besides "Record of an Obscure Man" (1861), "Tragedy of Errors, and Tragedy of Success," a dramatic poem (1862), and "Memoir of Charles Lowell," her father (1885).

PYLE, Howard, artist, b. Wilmington, Del., 5 Mar., 1853. Studied art in Philadelphia, and, after a brief residence in New York city, returned to Wilmington. Chiefly occupied as an artist with book and magazine illustration, most of his own writings being illustrated by himself. Some of his books are "The Merry Adventures of Robin Hood" (1883), "The Rose of Paradise" (1887), and "Otto of the Silver Hand" (1888).

QUAKERS, The Massachusetts, some of whose letters and protests are given in Vol. I., were subjected to grievous punishments and outlawry by the Puritan authorities of the Boston colony, 1656–62. Fines, scourging, and imprisonment were inflicted upon men and women alike. "Three victims had their right ears cut off, and four suffered the death penalty," according to Hallowell's book, "The Quaker Invasion of Massachusetts" (1883), wherein may be found a spirited defence of the "invaders," and many facts relating to Leddra, the Southwicks, and other persecuted disciples of the Inward Light. Governor Endicott was their most powerful and relentless foe. Some of Whittier's finest ballads were suggested by the records and incidents of the colonial "reign of terror."

QUINCY, Edmund, b. Boston, Mass., 1 Feb., 1808. Second son of Josiah Quincy, 3d. Graduated at Harvard. An active contributor to anti-slavery literature. Author of a memoir of his father (1867) and of "Wensley," novel (1854), and "The Haunted Adjutant, and Other Stories" (issued posthumously, 1885). Died, Dedham, Mass., 17 May, 1877.

QUINCY, Josiah, Jun., lawyer, b. Boston, Mass., 23 Feb., 1744. Graduated at Harvard. Studied law at Boston and became a leading advocate. Began the publication of articles, supporting the patriotic cause, in the Boston "Gazette," 1767. With John Adams was called upon by Captain Preston to defend the latter and his soldiers for the "Boston massacre," 1770, and secured the acquittal of Preston and five of the soldiers. Published, May, 1774, his "Observations on the Act of Parliament commonly called the Boston Port Bill." Sailed for England, September of the same year, partly to improve his health, and partly to serve the interests of the colonies in that country. Returning in Mar., 1775, with important verbal messages from the American leaders at London, he died within sight of land. In 1825 appeared "Memoir of the Life of Josiah Quincy, Jun., by his Son." Died, off Gloucester, Mass., 26 April, 1775.

QUINCY, Josiah, 3d., statesman and educator, b. Boston, Mass., 4 Feb., 1772. Son of Josiah Quincy, Jun. Graduated at Harvard. Entered the bar at Boston, 1793. Was a member of the state legislature for a number of terms, and U. S. representative from 1805 to 1813. As mayor of Boston, 1823–8, he introduced many reforms in the municipal government. Was president of Harvard, 1829–45, and managed that institution with success. In politics was an extreme Federalist. His chief work was "The History of Harvard University" (1840). A volume of his speeches was published in 1874. Died, Quincy, Mass., 1 July, 1864.

QUINCY, Josiah, 4th, b. Boston, Mass., 17 Jan., 1802. Eldest son of Josiah Quincy, 3d. Graduated at Harvard, and entered the legal profession. Held various municipal appointments in Boston, of which he was mayor, 1845–49. "Figures of the Past" appeared in 1883. Died, Quincy, Mass., 2 Nov., 1882.

RALPH, James, b. probably in Philadelphia, Penn., about 1695. Was an intimate friend of Benjamin Franklin and accompanied him to England in 1724. After unsuccessful attempts as an actor and journalist he became a political pamphleteer and was employed by both the English parties of the time. Was satirized by Pope in the "Dunciad" for his poetical efforts, one of which was "Zeuma, or the Love of Liberty" (1729). Among his prose works were a "History of England" (1744) and "The Case of Authors by Profession or Trade Stated"

(1758). Died, Chiswick, England, 24 Jan., 1762.

RAMSAY, David, physician, b. Lancaster Co., Penn., 2 April, 1749. Graduated at the college of New Jersey. Studied medicine at the college of Philadelphia, and practised with success at Charleston, S. C. Served in the South Carolina legislature, 1776–83, and also as a surgeon in the Continental army. Was taken prisoner at the capture of Charleston, 1780, and confined for eleven months at St. Augustine. A delegate to the Continental congress from 1782 until 1786, he was afterward a member of the senate of South Carolina for many years. Besides numerous medical works, he brought out "History of the Revolution in South Carolina" (1785), "The History of the American Revolution" (1789), "Life of George Washington" (1801), and "History of South Carolina" (1808). Died, Charleston, S. C., 8 May, 1815.

RANDALL, James Ryder, journalist, b. Baltimore, Md., 1 Jan., 1839. Studied at Georgetown college, D. C. Early removed to Louisiana, where he obtained a position on the New Orleans "Sunday Delta." His popular Southern war song, "Maryland, My Maryland," was written at Poydras college, La., in 1861. It was one of a number of similar songs written by Mr. Randall, who is also the author of much fugitive verse. In 1866 he became editor-in-chief of the Augusta, Ga., "Constitutionalist," and subsequently held other editorial positions in the South.

RANDOLPH, Anson Davies Fitz, publisher, b. Woodbridge, N. J., 18 Oct., 1820. Educated in one of the public schools of New York city. At a very early age he entered the N. Y. book house of the American Sunday school union. Established himself as a bookseller and publisher in the same city, 1851. Was for many years a contributor to the periodical press, and in 1867 at the request of his friend, Charles Scribner, collected his poems in a volume as "Hopefully Waiting, and Other Verses" (enlarged ed. 1885).

RANDOLPH, John, "of Roanoke," statesman, b. Cawsons, Chesterfield Co., Va., 2 June, 1773. A descendant of Pocahontas. Received an irregular schooling in Virginia, and studied for brief periods at the college of New Jersey and at Columbia. Studied law with his uncle, Edmund Randolph, at Philadelphia. Was elected U. S. representative from Virginia in 1799, and was reëlected, with the exception of three terms, until his retirement in 1829. During two of these, 1825–7, he was a member of the U. S. senate. Appointed minister to Russia in 1830, he returned to America the following year on account of illness. Was for some years a leader of the Republican-

Democratic party in congress, but became estranged from Jefferson and opposed many of the measures of his former party associates. He was opposed to the Missouri compromise of 1820, and styled its Northern advocates "doughfaces." A constant partisan of state-rights, and a defender of the South Carolina nullification proceedings, he nevertheless manumitted by will all his slaves, to the number of three hundred. A master of sarcasm, his unsparing use of invective involved him in a duel with Henry Clay, in which Randolph threw away his fire, but escaped injury. Died, Philadelphia, Penn., 24 May, 1833.

RANDOLPH, Sir John, lawyer, b. Turkey Island, Va., 1693 (M. D. Conway). Graduated at William and Mary college. Studied law in England, and early became attorney-general of Virginia. Was knighted while in England on business for his college, and was in 1736 speaker of the Virginia house of burgesses. Selections from his "Breviate Book" are given in the "Virginia Historical Register" for 1848. Randolph collected materials for a history of Virginia, which were utilized by his nephew, William Stith. Died, Williamsburg, Va., 9 Mar., 1737.

RAY, William, b. Salisbury, Conn., 9 Dec., 1771. Early removed to New York state, where he was engaged in trade during most of his life. Shipped as a sailor on the frigate *Philadelphia* in 1803, and was soon after made prisoner at Tripoli. Published "Poems . . . with a brief sketch of the Author's Captivity and Sufferings" (1821). Died, Auburn, N. Y., 1827.

RAYMOND, Henry Jarvis, journalist, b. Lima, N. Y., 24 Jan., 1820. Graduated at the university of Vermont. After contributing to Greeley's "New Yorker," was made assistant editor of the "Tribune," 1841. From 1843 to 1851 was connected editorially with the N. Y. "Courier and Enquirer." Became a member of the state legislature, 1849, and speaker of the assembly, 1851. Established the N. Y. "Times" in the latter year. Was lieutenant-governor of New York, 1854. Helped to organize the Republican party, and worked hard in Frémont's interest. Speaker of the assembly for the second time, 1861. Was elected U. S. representative, 1864, and supported President Johnson's reconstruction policy. Declined the Austrian mission, 1867. Issued "Political Lessons of the Revolution" (1854), "Letters to Hon. W. L. Yancey" (1860), and "Life and Services of President Lincoln; with his State Papers, etc." (1865). Died, New York, N. Y., 18 June, 1869.

RAYMOND, Rossiter Worthington, b. Cincinnati, O., 27 April, 1840. Studied at several German universities. Served in the U. S. army during the civil war. Was

U. S. commissioner of mining statistics, 1868–76, and editor of the "Engineering and Mining Journal" after 1868. Author of several books for children and contributed poetry to the magazines, in addition to his works on engineering.

READ, Thomas Buchanan, artist and poet, b. Chester Co., Penn., 12 Mar., 1822. Educated himself as an artist at an early age, leaving his home and residing for brief periods at Cincinnati, New York, and Boston. Published a number of poems in the Boston "Courier," 1843–4, and, removing to Philadelphia in 1846, brought out there his first volume of verse, "Poems" (1847). Studied art at Florence and Rome from 1853 to 1858, and spent much of his later years at the latter place. Of his paintings the best-known are the one illustrating his poem "Sheridan's Ride," the group of Longfellow's daughters, and the portrait of Mrs. Browning. Some of his books are "Female Poets of America" (1848), a compilation illustrated with portraits drawn by himself, "The New Pastoral" (1855), "The Wagoner of the Alleghanies" (1862), and "A Summer Story, Sheridan's Ride, and Other Poems" (1865). Died, New York, N. Y., 11 May, 1872.

REALF, Richard, b. Framfield, near Lewes, Sussex, England, 14 June, 1834. Emigrated to America, 1854, and settling in Kansas, entered into the plans of John Brown, though in Texas at the time of the Harper's Ferry raid. Served through the civil war in the Union army. Afterward lectured and wrote for the newspapers in Pittsburgh, Penn. Author of "Guesses at the Beautiful," poems (London, 1852), and much fugitive verse. Died, Oakland, Cal., 28 Oct., 1878.

RED JACKET, or *Sagoyewatha,* Indian chief, b. "Old Castle," Seneca Lake, N. Y., about 1752. A leading chief of the Senecas, and greatest in authority among the Six Nations. Fought on the side of the English in the Revolution and on that of the Americans in the war of 1812. Became noted as an orator. His "Life" was written by W. L. Stone (1841). Died, Seneca Village, N. Y., 20 Jan., 1830.

REED, Henry, educator, b. Philadelphia, Penn., 11 July, 1808. Graduated at the university of Pennsylvania, where he was professor of rhetoric and English literature, 1835–54. Visited Europe in 1854. "Lectures on English Literature, Chaucer to Tennyson" (1855), "Lectures on English History and Tragic Poetry, as Illustrated by Shakespeare" (1856), and "Lectures on the British Poets" (1857) were issued posthumously. Perished in the foundered ship *Arctic,* 27 Sept., 1854.

REESE, Lizette Woodworth, b. Waverly, Md., 186–. Early removed to Baltimore, which became her permanent residence. A writer of verse for the magazines, and author of "A Branch of May," poems (1887).

REID, Whitelaw, journalist, b. near Xenia, O., 27 Oct., 1837. Graduated at Miami university. Entered journalism as the editor of the Xenia "News." Was soon called to the staff of the Cincinnati "Gazette," and became correspondent of that journal at the outbreak of the civil war. He performed volunteer staff duty in several engagements, and was present at Fort Donelson, Shiloh, and Gettysburg. His letters from Washington and the seat of war over the signature "Agate" attracted general attention. From 1863 to 1865 was librarian of the U. S. house of representatives. Engaged in the culture of cotton in Louisiana for a year, and on his return to the North issued "After the War," a book on the Southern situation (1866). Two years later appeared "Ohio in the War : her Statesmen, her Generals, and Soldiers." Joined the editorial staff of the N. Y. "Tribune," 1868, and succeeded Mr. Greeley as its editor, 1872. After twice declining similar appointments from former presidents, accepted in 1889 the U. S. mission to France from President Harrison. Author of "Schools of Journalism" (1871), "The Scholar in Politics" (1873), and "Some Newspaper Tendencies" (1879).

RICH, Hiram, banker, b. Gloucester, Mass., 28 Oct., 1832. Received his education at the schools of his native town, which was his permanent home, with the exception of a few years' residence in Boston and New York. Entered the banking business, 1857, and became cashier of the Cape Ann national bank at Gloucester in 1865. A contributor of poetry to the "Atlantic Monthly," "The Century," and other leading magazines.

RICH, R. Nothing is known of him beyond his statements in the preface to "Newes from Virginia" (1610), that he was a "soldier" and made the Virginian voyage, returning before his book was published.

RICHARDSON, Albert Deane, journalist, b. Franklin, Mass., 6 Oct., 1833. Became field correspondent for the N. Y. "Tribune" at the opening of the civil war. Was captured at Vicksburg, and passed nearly two years in seven Southern prisons. After the war devoted himself to writing and lecturing. Among his writings are "The Field, the Dungeon, and the Escape" (1865), and "Garnered Sheaves" (issued posthumously, 1871). Died, New York, N. Y., 2 Dec., 1869.

RICHARDSON, Charles Francis, educator, b. Hallowell, Me., 29 May, 1851. Graduated at Dartmouth. A member of the N. Y. "Independent" editorial staff, 1872-8. In 1882 became professor of the Anglo-Saxon and English language and literature at Dartmouth. Author of "A Primer of American Literature" (1876), "The Cross," poems (1879), "The Choice of Books" (1881), and a history of "American Literature : 1607-1885" (1887-9).

RIDEING, William Henry, journalist, b. Liverpool, England, 17 Feb., 1853. His father was an officer of a Cunard steamship. Held various editorial positions in the United States and England until 1883, when he settled permanently in Boston, Mass. His works include "Pacific Railways Illustrated" (1878), "Stray Moments with Thackeray" (1880), and "A Little Upstart," novel (1885).

RIDPATH, John Clark, educator, b. Putnam Co., Ind., 26 April, 1840. Graduated at Asbury (now De Pauw) university, where he became a professor in 1869. Ten years later he was elected vice-president of the university. Author of "A Popular History of the United States" (1876), "Life and Work of Garfield" (1881-2), "Life of James G. Blaine" (1884), and "A Cyclopædia of Universal History" (1880-5).

RILEY, James Whitcomb, "Benj. F. Johnson, of Boone," b. Greenfield, Ind., 1853. His father was a leading attorney of that place. The son first adopted the occupation of a sign-painter, and tiring of this, next became a member of a strolling company of actors, for whom he was accustomed to remodel plays, compose songs, etc. Afterward joined the staff of the Indianapolis "Journal," and more recently delivered poetical lectures, or recitations of his own poems. He began contributing verse to the periodicals in 1875, his poems in the Hoosier or Indiana dialect being most successful and gaining him wide reputation. His published works are "The Old Swimmin-Hole, and 'Leven More Poems, by Benj. F. Johnson, of Boone" (1883), "The Boss Girl, and Other Sketches," poems and stories (1886), "Character Sketches and Poems" (1887), "Afterwhiles" (1888), and "Pipes o' Pan at Zekesbury" (1889).

RIORDAN, Roger, b. Cappoquin, Co. Waterford, Ireland, 21 May, 1847. Received his education at Albert institute, Dublin. For some years a journalist in New York city. Also a writer for the magazines.

RIPLEY, George, journalist, b. Greenfield, Mass., 3 Oct., 1802. Graduated at Harvard, where he was afterward instructor in mathematics and natural philosophy while studying in the Harvard divinity school. Became minister of a Unitarian society in Boston, 1826, resigning the pastorate in 1841. In 1836, with Emerson and F. H. Hedge, organized the society of Transcendentalists, which started "The Dial" in 1840, and was resident editor of that journal at Boston for a short time. Dr. Ripley was a founder and the leading member of "The

Brook Farm Institute of Agriculture and Education" at West Roxbury, Mass., which lasted from 1841 to 1847. While there he began, in 1845, the publication of "The Harbinger," a periodical devoted to Fourierism, which system had recently been adopted by the Brook Farm association. After his removal, in 1847, from West Roxbury to the neighborhood of New York city, he continued to edit this paper until 1849. Debts falling to his share from the Brook Farm experiment were laboriously paid off in the succeeding years. His connection with the N. Y. "Tribune" began in 1849 and lasted until his death, and he brought its literary department to a high standard of excellence. In association with Charles A. Dana, edited the "New American Cyclopædia," 1857–63, of which a new edition, revised by the original editors, appeared in 1873–76. His "Life" was written, 1882, by Octavius B. Frothingham. His writings have not been collected. Died, New York, N. Y., 4 July, 1880.

RIPLEY, Roswell Sabine, soldier, b. Worthington, Franklin Co., O., 14 Mar., 1823. Graduated at West Point. Served in the U. S. army during the Mexican war. Entered the Confederate army at the opening of the civil war, reaching the rank of brigadier-general. Author of "The War with Mexico," a history (1849). Died, New York, N. Y., 26 Mar., 1887.

RIVINGTON, James, royalist printer and journalist, b. London, England, about 1724. Came to America, 1760. Established himself as a printer at Philadelphia, and afterward at New York city. Started "The New York Gazetteer," 1773. His office was mobbed in 1775 on account of his support of the British government, and he sailed for England. Returning to New York on its occupation by the British, he published "The Royal Gazette," 1777–83. Having supplied Washington with secret information toward the close of the Revolution, he was allowed to remain in New York after the war. Died, New York, N. Y., July, 1802.

ROBERTS, Sarah, b. Portsmouth, N. H., 26 July, 1812. Daughter of Edmund Q. Roberts, the first diplomatic representative of the United States in Asia. Was married, 1858, to Dr. James Boyle, and afterward resided in New York city. (At the time of her representation in Vol. VII., the facts of her marriage, etc., were not in possession of the editors, and consequently she appears under her maiden and best-known name.) Wrote "My Childhood" (1852), "My Stepmother" (1857), and "Poems." Her most familiar piece is "The Voice of the Grass." Died, New York, N. Y., 16 Mar., 1869.

ROBINSON, Annie Douglas [Green], "Marian Douglas," b. Plymouth, N. H.,

12 Jan., 1842. Early removed to Bristol, N. H., and afterward resided there. Was married, 1877, to Frank W. Robinson. A contributor of verse and prose to the magazines, and author of "Picture Poems," for children (1872), and "Peter and Polly," story (1876).

ROBINSON, Edward, scholar, b. Southington, Conn., 10 April, 1794. Graduated at Hamilton college. After study in Europe, was appointed professor of sacred literature at Andover, 1830, and edited the "Biblical Repository." Appointed professor of biblical literature in Union theological seminary, New York, 1837. In 1838 and 1852 explored Palestine with the Rev. Eli Smith. Published a number of translations and editions of theological and other works, and wrote "Biblical Researches in Palestine" (1841) and "Later Researches" (1856). "Physical Geography of the Holy Land" was brought out posthumously in 1865. Died, New York, N. Y., 27 Jan., 1863.

ROBINSON, Tracy, b. Clarendon, Orleans Co., N. Y., 22 Dec., 1833. Studied at Rochester university. Was superintendent and general agent of railroads in Tennessee and Louisiana until 1861, when he entered the employ of the Panama railroad at the isthmus of Panama, and was its fiscal and shipping agent until 1874. Subsequently engaged in private business at Colon and New York city. A writer for the magazines, and author of "Song of the Palm, and Other Poems" (1888).

ROCHE, James Jeffrey, journalist, b. Queens Co., Ireland, 31 May, 1847. Was soon after brought to Prince Edward Island. Studied at St. Dunstan's college. Removed to Boston, Mass., 1866, where he engaged in commercial pursuits. In 1883 became assistant editor of the Boston "Pilot." Besides writing for the magazines, issued "Songs and Satires" (1887).

ROE, Edward Payson, clergyman, b. Moodna, New Windsor, Orange Co., N. Y., 7 Mar., 1838. Studied at Williams, not graduating on account of trouble with his eyes. Took a theological course at the Union theological seminary, and served as chaplain in the U. S. volunteers from 1862 to 1865. In the latter year accepted the pastorate of a Presbyterian church at Highland Falls, N. Y. His first novel, "Barriers Burned Away" (1872), was the outcome of a visit to Chicago just after the great fire. It originally appeared as a serial in the N. Y. "Evangelist." The success of this and following books, and failing health, induced him to resign his pastorate, and he purchased a farm at Cornwall, N. Y., where his leisure time was occupied with the cultivation of small fruits. Some of his numerous works are "Opening a Chestnut Burr" (1874), "A Knight of the Nineteenth Century" (1877), "Success with Small Fruits" (1880), "A Young Girl's Wooing" (1884), "Nature's Serial Story" (1885), and "Miss Lou" (1888). Died, Cornwall, N. Y., 19 July, 1888.

ROGERS, John, clergyman, b. Coggeshall, Essex, England, about 1630. Brought to New England, 1636. Graduated at Harvard. Preached at Ipswich, Mass., and afterward practised medicine there. Was elected president of Harvard, April, 1682, and was installed, Aug., 1683. The only one of his literary productions which has survived is a complimentary poem prefixed to Mrs. Anne Bradstreet's "Poems." Died, Cambridge, Mass., 2 July, 1684.

ROHLFS, Anna Katharine [Green], b. Brooklyn, N. Y., 11 Nov., 1846. Studied at Ripley female college, Poultney, Vt. Made an immediate success with her first novel, "The Leavenworth Case" (1878). Was married, 1884, to Charles Rohlfs and subsequently removed to Buffalo, N. Y. Some of her works are "The Defence of the Bride, and Other Poems" (1882), "Hand and Ring" (1883), "The Mill Mystery" (1886), and "Risifi's Daughter," drama (1887).

ROLFE, John, colonist. Sailed for Virginia in the *Sea Venture* with Sir Thomas Gates, from Plymouth, England, 1 June, 1609. Stranded on the Bermudas, reaching Jamestown, May, 1610. Was the first colonist to plant tobacco, in 1612. Married Pocahontas, who was his second wife, 5 April, 1614. Visited England with her in 1616, was appointed secretary and recorder-general of Virginia, and returned to the colony in May, 1617, Pocahontas having died in Gravesend harbor on the return voyage. Many prominent Southern families trace their descent from her daughter. His letter to Sir Thomas Dale was printed in Ralph Hamor's "True Discourse," published in 1615. He married a third wife, who survived him. Died, Virginia, 1622.

ROLLINS, Alice [Wellington], b. Boston, Mass., 12 June, 1847. Was educated by her father, Ambrose Wellington. After spending some time in Europe, she was married, 1876, to Daniel M. Rollins of New York city, where she afterward resided. Some of her books are "The Ring of Amethyst," poems (1878), "The Story of a Ranch" (1885), "The Three Tetons" (1887), and "Uncle Tom's Tenement" (1888).

ROOSEVELT, Theodore, legislator, b. New York, N. Y., 27 Oct., 1858. Graduated at Harvard. Soon after entered the N. Y. legislature, where he distinguished himself by effecting state and municipal reforms. Was appointed U. S. civil-service commissioner by President Harrison in 1889. Author of "History of the Naval War of 1812" (1882), "Hunting Trips of a Ranchman" (1886), "Essays on Practical Politics" (1888), and "The Winning of the West" (1889).

ROOT, George Frederick, composer, b. Sheffield, Mass., 30 Aug., 1820. Received a common-school education, and studied music while working on a farm. Became an instructor in music at Boston. Removed to New York, 1844, and to Chicago, 1860, where he founded the music-publishing firm of Root & Cady. This firm, which owed much of its success to Root's own songs, was brought to an end by the great Chicago fire. His first song, "Hazel Dell," appeared in 1853, and "The Battle Cry of Freedom" was first sung by the Hutchinson family at a mass-meeting in New York city. Other popular songs are "Tramp, Tramp, Tramp," and "Just Before the Battle, Mother."

ROSE, Aquila, b. England, about 1695. Emigrated to America when he reached manhood. Is favorably spoken of by Franklin in the latter's "Autobiography." Was clerk of the Pennsylvania assembly at the time of his death. His "Poems on Several Occasions" (1740) were issued posthumously by his son, Joseph Rose. Died, Philadelphia, Penn., 22 Aug., 1723.

ROWLANDSON, Mary [White]. The dates and places of her birth and death are not known. She was the wife of Rev. Joseph Rowlandson, first pastor of Lancaster, Mass., and was taken captive by Indians at the destruction of that town, 10 Feb., 1676. Her sufferings while a prisoner are related in her book, "A Narrative of the Captivity and Restoration of Mrs. Mary Rowlandson" (1682), which passed through many editions.

ROWSON, Susanna [Haswell], b. Portsmouth, England, 1762. Came to America in 1767 with her father, who was a British revenue officer, and who resided at Nantucket, Mass., until banished for his political views during the Revolution. The daughter married in London William Rowson, bandmaster of the Royal guards, and with him returned to America in 1793, where she followed the profession of an actress for four years. Subsequently conducted a school for girls until 1822, for most of the time at Boston, Mass. Besides her novels, one of which, "Charlotte Temple : or, a Tale of Truth" (1790), gained great popularity, she wrote several plays, in some of which she acted. Author of "Miscellaneous Poems" (1804). Died, Boston, Mass., 2 Mar., 1824.

RUSH, Benjamin, physician, b. Byberry, near Philadelphia, Penn., 24 Dec., 1745. Graduated at the college of New Jersey, and studied medicine at Edinburgh. Began practice in Philadelphia, 1769. Was medical professor at the university of Pennsylvania for forty-four years. Delegate to the

Continental congress, and signed the Declaration of Independence. Surgeon-general in the American army, 1777–8. Treasurer of the U. S. mint, 1799–1813. He wrote many medical works, and a volume of "Essays" (1798). Died, Philadelphia, Penn., 19 April, 1813.

RUSSELL, Irwin, b. Port Gibson, Miss., 3 June, 1853. One of the earliest Southern writers to make a literary use of negro character. Led an unsettled life, and involved himself in much suffering. His dialect and other verse was collected after his death and published as "Poems" (1888). Died, New Orleans, La., 23 Dec., 1879.

RYAN, Abram Joseph, Father Ryan, b. Norfolk, Va., 15 Aug., 1839. Entered the Roman Catholic priesthood, and served through the civil war as chaplain in the Confederate army, writing a number of popular war poems during and after that struggle. Edited various religious journals, and held a pastorate for some years at Mobile, Ala. A volume of "Poems" appeared in 1880. Died, Louisville, Ky., 22 April, 1886.

SAGE, Adoniram Judson, clergyman and educator, b. Massillon, O., 29 Mar., 1836. Graduated at Rochester university. Pastor of a church at Hartford, Conn., 1872–84. Previously filled the chair of Latin in Rochester university, and was professor in Morgan Park theological seminary, Chicago, from 1884 to 1888. Contributed poems and articles to the periodicals.

SALTUS, Edgar Evertson, b. New York, N. Y., 8 June, 1858. Was educated at European universities, and graduated at the Columbia law school. Gave much time to the study of pessimistic philosophy. Author of "Balzac," a biography (1884), "The Philosophy of Disenchantment" (1885), "The Anatomy of Negation" (1886), and of "Mr. Incoul's Misadventure" (1887) and several other novels.

SALTUS, Francis Saltus, b. New York, N. Y., 23 Nov., 1849. Brother of E. E. Saltus. Passed much of his life in Europe. Contributed largely in prose and verse to the periodicals, and issued "Honey and Gall," poems (1873). Left several volumes of poetry and a "Life of Donizetti" in manuscript at his death. "Shadows and Ideals, Poems," appeared in 1890. Died, Tarrytown, N. Y., 25 June, 1889.

SANBORN, Franklin Benjamin, journalist, b. Hampton Falls, N. H., 15 Dec., 1831. Graduated at Harvard. Was elected secretary of the Massachusetts state Kansas committee in 1856. He was after 1863 frequently a member of the Massachusetts state board of charities, in which he held important offices and inaugurated numerous reforms. One of the founders of the American social science association, and of the

Concord school of philosophy, in both of which organizations he held the position of secretary for long periods. Became a member of the Springfield, Mass., "Republican" staff in 1868. Besides many reports as secretary of associations, he contributed to the periodicals, and brought out a "Life of Thoreau" (1882) and "Life and Letters of John Brown" (1885).

SANDERSON, John, b. near Carlisle, Penn., 1783. Professor of Latin and Greek in the Philadelphia high school, 1836–44. Issued "Sketches of Paris" (1838, republished as "The American in Paris") and "The American in London," the latter in the "Knickerbocker Magazine." Died, Philadelphia, Penn., 5 April, 1844.

SANDS, Robert Charles, journalist, b. Flatbush, L. I., 11 May, 1799. Graduated at Columbia. Edited in college "The Moralist" and "Academic Recreations." Was admitted to the bar in 1820. Contributed verse and prose to the papers, and started the "St. Tammany Magazine." In 1824 established the "Atlantic Magazine," which became the "New York Review," of which he was co-editor with William Cullen Bryant, 1825–7. An editor of the N. Y. "Commercial Advertiser," 1827–32. With Bryant and Verplanck issued the "Talisman" annual, 1828–30. In addition to contributions to periodicals he wrote a "Life of Paul Jones" (1831). His collected "Writings" were issued, with a memoir, by Gulian C. Verplanck in 1834. Died, Hoboken, N. J., 17 Dec., 1832.

SANGSTER, Margaret Elizabeth [Munson], b. New Rochelle, N. Y., 22 Feb., 1838. Was married, 1858, to George Sangster. Became successively associate editor of the N. Y. "Hearth and Home," "Christian at Work," and "Christian Intelligencer." Editor of "Harper's Young People," 1882–9, and in 1889 succeeded Mary L. Booth as editor of "Harper's Bazar." Author of "Poems of the Household" (1882) and "Home Fairies and Heart Flowers" (1887).

SARGENT, Epes, b. Gloucester, Mass., 27 Sept., 1813. Studied at Harvard. Became assistant editor of the N. Y. "Mirror," 1839, and editor of the Boston "Evening Transcript," 1846. Subsequently devoted himself entirely to literary work. His "Bride of Genoa" (1836) and other of his plays were successfully produced. Edited numerous reprints of English works, and wrote "Life of Henry Clay" (1843), "Songs of the Sea" (1847), "Arctic Adventures" (1857), and several novels. Died, Boston, Mass., 31 Dec., 1880.

SAVAGE, Minot Judson, clergyman, b. Norridgewock, Me., 10 June, 1841. Studied at Bowdoin college, and graduated at the Bangor, Me., theological seminary. In 1874 became pastor of the "Church of the Unity"

at Boston, Mass. Author of "Bluffton," novel (1878), "Poems" (1882), and numerous religious works.

SAWYER, Charles Carroll, composer, b. Mystic, Conn., 22 April, 1839. His family removed to Brooklyn, N. Y., in 1848, and he afterward resided there. His song "When this Cruel War is Over" was written in the autumn of 1861, and over one million copies were sold. Some of his other popular songs are "Swinging in the Lane" (1866), "Peeping Through the Bars" (1887), and "At those Lovely Gates of Pearl" (1890).

SAXE, John Godfrey, b. Highgate, Vt., 2 June, 1816. Graduated at Middlebury college. Entered the bar, 1843. In 1850 bought the Burlington, Vt., "Sentinel," and conducted it for six years. Attorney-general of Vermont and deputy collector of customs, 1856. Twice nominated as Democratic candidate for governor of Vermont, but failed of election. Wrote and lectured considerably ; then edited the Albany, N. Y., "Evening Journal." His humorous verses appeared frequently in the "Knickerbocker" and in "Harper's Magazine," and he occasionally read poems before college and other societies. Issued "Progress, a Satirical Poem" (1846), "Humorous and Satirical Poems" (1850), "The Money King, and Other Poems" (1859), "The Masquerade, and Other Poems" (1866), "Poems" (1868), "Fables and Legends of Many Countries" (1872), and "Leisure-Day Rhymes" (1875). Died, Albany, N. Y., 31 Mar., 1887.

SAXTON, Andrew Bice, b. Middlefield, N. Y., 5 April, 1856. Engaged in teaching, and subsequently accepted an editorial position on the Oneonta, N. Y., "Herald." A contributor of poetry to the magazines.

SCHAFF, Philip, divine, b. Coire, Switzerland, 1 Jan., 1810. Educated at the universities of Tübingen, Halle, and Berlin. Theological lecturer in Berlin university, 1842-4. Became professor of church history and exegesis in the theological seminary at Mercersburg, Penn., 1844. In 1854 visited Europe as the representative of the German churches of America in the conventions held at Frankfort and Basle. In 1862 was appointed lecturer on ecclesiastical history at Andover, and in 1870 professor of apologetics and symbolics in the Union theological seminary of New York city, where he resided after 1863. Was president of the American Bible revision committee of 1871. Edited several important works, including the English translation of Lange's "Critical Commentary on the Bible," in 24 volumes. Some of his many books are "History of the Christian Church" (1858–88), "Revision of the English Version of the New Testament" (1874), "History and Collection of the Creeds of Christendom" (1876),

"Dictionary of the Bible" (1880), "Church and State in the United States" (1888), and "Literature and Poetry" (1890).

SCHOOLCRAFT, Henry Rowe, ethnologist, b. Watervliet, N. Y., 29 Mar., 1793. Graduated at Union. Was appointed Indian agent at Sault Ste. Marie, 1822, where he married the granddaughter of an Ojibway chief, who had been educated in Europe. Issued "Notes on the Iroquois" (1846–8), "Personal Memoirs of a Thirty Years' Residence with the Indian Tribes" (1851), "Historical and Statistical Information Respecting the History, Condition, and Prospects of the Indian Tribes of the United States" (1851–5), and "The Myth of Hiawatha, and Other Oral Legends" (1856). Died, Washington, D. C., 10 Dec., 1864.

SCHOULER, James, lawyer, b. West Cambridge, now Arlington, Mass., 20 Mar., 1839. Graduated at Harvard. Entered the bar at Boston, Mass., where he afterward practised. In 1884 became lecturer at the Boston university law school. Besides several legal works, wrote "History of the United States under the Constitution" (1880–90).

SCHURZ, Carl, journalist, b. Liblar, near Cologne, Germany, 2 Mar., 1829. Studied at the university of Bonn, which he left to join the revolution of 1849. Came to America in 1852, and took an active part in politics among the Western German Americans, as a Republican. Was appointed U. S. minister to Spain by President Lincoln, but resigned and entered the Union army, becoming major-general of volunteers. Was U. S. senator from Missouri, 1869–75, and secretary of the interior under President Hayes. After the war edited newspapers in Detroit, St. Louis, and New York city. Author of "Speeches" (1865) and "Life of Henry Clay" (1888).

SCHUYLER, Eugene, diplomatist, b. Ithaca, N. Y., 26 Feb., 1840. Graduated at Yale, and entered the bar. Was U. S. consul, consul-general, and secretary of legation in various European countries from 1866 to 1882, when he received the mission to Greece, Servia, and Roumania. Returned to the United States in 1884. Author of "Turkestan" (1876), "Peter the Great" (1884), and "American Diplomacy and the Furtherance of Commerce" (1886).

SCOLLARD, Clinton, educator, b. Clinton, Oneida Co., N. Y., 18 Sept., 1860. Graduated at Hamilton college, and pursued graduate studies at Harvard. In 1888 became assistant professor of rhetoric at Hamilton. Author of "Pictures in Song" (1884), "With Reed and Lyre" (1886), and "Old and New World Lyrics" (1888).

Scott, Winfield [*Noted Saying*: Vol. XI., p. 454], b. near Petersburg, Va., 13 June, 1786. Commander-in-chief of the U.

S. army, 1841–61. Died, West Point, N. Y., 29 May, 1866.

SCOTTOW, Joshua, merchant, b. England, about 1615. He was admitted to membership in the Old church at Boston, Mass., 19 May, 1639, and was a resident of Boston for the remainder of his life. Author of "Old Men's Fears for their own Declensions" (1691) and "A Narrative of the Planting of the Massachusetts Colony" (1694). Died, Boston, Mass., 20 Jan., 1698.

SCUDDER, Horace Elisha, b. Boston, Mass., 16 Oct., 1838. Graduated at Williams. Taught school in New York city for three years, and then removed to Boston, devoting himself exclusively to literary work. He had written considerably for children, including "Seven Little People" stories (1862) and "Dream Children" (1863), when in 1867 he assumed the editorship of the "Riverside Magazine for Young People." Continued in this position for four years and was afterward associated with the firm of Houghton, Mifflin & Co. Succeeded Mr. Aldrich as editor of the "Atlantic Monthly," 1890. Issued "Stories from My Attic" (1869), "The Bodley Books" for children (1875–87), "The Dwellers in Five-Sisters Court" (1876), "Men and Manners in America" (1876), "Stories and Romances" (1880), "The Children's Book" (1881), "Boston Town" (1881), "Life of Noah Webster" (1882), "History of the United States" (1884), "Men and Letters" (1888), and joint author with Mrs. Bayard Taylor of "Life and Letters of Bayard Taylor" (1884).

SCULL, Nicholas, surveyor, b. near Philadelphia, Penn., 1687. Was a friend of Franklin, who mentions him in his "Autobiography" as a member of the "Junto," formerly called the "Leather Apron Club." He afterward became surveyor-general of Pennsylvania. Published "Kawanio Che Keeteru," a metrical satire, in 1756. Died, Philadelphia, Penn., 1762.

SEARING, Laura Catherine [Redden], "Howard Glyndon," b. Somerset Co., Md., 9 Feb., 1840. Became deaf at the age of ten, and lost the power of speech, though she afterward regained the latter. Wrote much for the newspapers as correspondent and editor. Was married, 1876, to Edward W. Searing of New York city, removing to California in 1886. Issued "Idyls of Battle" (1864) and "Sounds from Secret Chambers" (1873).

SEARS, Edmund Hamilton, clergyman, b. Sandisfield, Mass., 1810. Graduated at Union college. Entered the Unitarian ministry and was pastor of several churches in Massachusetts. Edited the "Monthly Religious Magazine" for some years. Author of "Regeneration" (1853), "Pictures of the Olden Time" (1857),

"Christian Lyrics" (1860), and "Sermons and Songs of the Christian Life" (1875). Died, Weston, Mass., 14 Jan., 1876.

SECCOMB, John, clergyman, b. Medford, Mass., 25 April, 1708. Graduated at Harvard. Preached in the town of Harvard, Mass., from 1733 to 1757, and at Chester, Nova Scotia, from 1763 until his death. His "Father Abbey's Will" was written in 1730, and it was published in the "Gentleman's Magazine" for 1732 as a specimen of American humorous poetry. Two of his sermons were subsequently issued. Died, Chester, Nova Scotia, 1792.

SEDGWICK, Catherine Maria, b. Stockbridge, Mass., 28 Dec., 1789. Daughter of Judge Theodore Sedgwick. Was principal of a ladies' school at Stockbridge for half a century. Her first two novels, anonymously published, "A New England Tale" (1822) and "Redwood" (1824), were so successful that she continued to write. In addition to magazine matter she brought out "The Traveller" (1825), "Hope Leslie, or Early Times in Massachusetts" (1827), "Clarence, a Tale of Our Own Times" (1830), "Le Bossu" (1832), "The Linwoods, or Sixty Years Since in America" (1835), "Tales and Sketches" (1835, new ed. 1858), "The Poor Rich Man and the Rich Poor Man" (1836), "Live and Let Live" (1837), "A Love-Token for Children" (1837), "Means and Ends, or Self-Training" (1837), "Letters From Abroad" (1841), "Historical Sketches of the Old Painters" (1841), "Wilton Harvey, and Other Tales" (1845), "Morals of Manners" (1846), "Facts and Fancies" (1848), and "Married or Single?" (1857). Died, near Roxbury, Mass., 31 July, 1867.

SEWALL, Harriet [Winslow], b. Portland, Me., 30 June, 1819. Of Quaker descent. Was married, 1848, to Charles List, of Philadelphia; and in 1857 to Samuel E. Sewall, of Boston, Mass., where she subsequently resided. Author of the poem "Why thus Longing?" "Poems, with a Memoir by Ednah D. Cheney," appeared in 1889. Died, Wellesley, Mass., Feb., 1889.

SEWALL, Jonathan Mitchel, lawyer, b. Salem, Mass., 1748. Graduated at Harvard. Entered a business life, which he abandoned for the law. Was register of probate for Grafton county, N. H., in 1774, and subsequently removed to Portsmouth in the same state. Is remembered for a popular Revolutionary ballad, and for his couplet containing the words "no pent-up Utica." Author of "Miscellaneous Poems" (1801). Died, Portsmouth, N. H., 29 Mar., 1808.

SEWALL, Samuel, jurist, b. Bishop-Stoke, or Basingstoke, England, 28 Mar., 1652. Was brought to America by his mother, arriving at Boston, July, 1661. Graduated at Harvard. Studied for the ministry, but his marriage with the daughter of John Hull, mint-master of the Massachusetts colony, turned him to secular pursuits. He had charge of the Boston printing-press for some three years, became an assistant in 1684, and was annually chosen a member of the governor's council from 1692 to 1725. Was elected judge of the Massachusetts superior court in 1692, and chief-justice, 1718, holding office until 1728, and was probate judge of Suffolk county from 1715 to the same year. He was a member of the special court of oyer and terminer, appointed to conduct the witchcraft trials at Salem, 1692. Five years later, having become convinced of his error, he stood up in church while his written confession and request for forgiveness was read. In 1699 Sewall was appointed a commissioner of the society for propagating the gospel among the Indians. He published an anti-slavery tract, "The Selling of Joseph" (1700), "Prospects touching the Accomplishment of Prophecies" (1713), "A Memorial Relating to the Kennebec Indians" (1721), and "A Description of the New Heaven" (1727). His diary, covering a period of fifty-five years, was issued in three volumes by the Mass. Hist. Soc. (1878–82), which has also published his letter-book, both containing valuable records of and comments on events of the period covered. Died, Boston, Mass., 1 Jan., 1730.

SEWARD, William Henry, statesman, b. Florida, Orange Co., N. Y., 16 May, 1801. Graduated at Union college. Entered the bar, 1822, and settled in Auburn, N. Y. Was elected to the state senate, 1830, and nominated for governor in 1834, when he was defeated, but was successful in 1838, and again in 1840. Became a U. S. senator in 1849, being already known as a prominent abolitionist leader. Was reëlected to the U. S. senate, 1855, and supported Frémont for the presidency in 1856. Was a candidate for that office in the convention which nominated Lincoln, by whom he was afterward appointed secretary of state. Refused to accept despatches in which England and France claimed the right of neutrality during the civil war, and rejected the French emperor's suggestion of mediation. While convalescing from an accident, was stabbed at the time of Lincoln's assassination by one of the conspirators, but recovered after severe suffering. As President Johnson's secretary of state, supported the latter's reconstruction policy and negotiated the acquisition of Alaska in 1867. Retired from office in 1868. A journey around the world in 1870 is described in "Travels Around the World" (issued posthumously, 1873). Wrote "Life and Public Services of John Quincy Adams" (1849). An edition of his "Works" was published

in five volumes, 1853–84. Died, Auburn, N. Y., 10 Oct., 1872.

SHANLY, Charles Dawson, journalist, b. Dublin, Ireland, 9 Mar., 1811. Graduated at Trinity college, Dublin. Emigrated to Canada and settled in New York city, where he became a constant contributor to the periodicals. His poem "The Fancy Shot," or "Civil War," appeared in the London "Once a Week" early in the war. Author of several humorous books. Died, Arlington, Fla., 15 Aug., 1875.

SHAW, Henry Wheeler, "Josh Billings," b. Lanesborough, Mass., 21 April, 1818. Began writing humorous articles in phonetic spelling about 1860. His burlesque "Farmers' Allminax" (1870) had a great vogue during ten years. Delivered humorous lectures from 1863 onward. Author of "Josh Billings, His Sayings" (1866), and "Josh Billings, His Works" (1876). Died, Monterey, Cal., 14 Oct., 1885.

SHAW, John, physician, b. Annapolis, Md., 4 May, 1778. Graduated at St. John's college. Studied medicine in Philadelphia and Edinburgh. Was for a time surgeon in the U. S. navy, and afterward practised at Baltimore. His "Poems" (1810) were issued posthumously. Died on a voyage to the Bahamas, 10 Jan., 1809.

SHEA, John Gilmary, b. New York, N. Y., 22 July, 1824. Was bred to the law, but occupied himself chiefly with literary pursuits, having written and edited numerous historical works. Connected in an editorial capacity with several Catholic and secular periodicals. His most important books are "The Discovery and Exploration of the Mississippi Valley" (1853), "History of the Catholic Missions among the Indian Tribes of the United States" (1854), and "Catholic Church in Colonial Days" (1886).

SHEDD, William Greenough Thayer, theologian, b. Acton, Mass., 21 June, 1820. Graduated at the university of Vermont. Held several professorships until 1863, when he became professor of biblical literature in the Union theological seminary, assuming the chair of systematic theology in 1874. Besides translations of German treatises, is the author of a number of theological works, including "A History of Christian Doctrine" (1863) and "Doctrine of Endless Punishment" (1885).

SHEPARD, Thomas, clergyman, b. Towcester, Northamptonshire, England, 5 Nov., 1605. Graduated at Cambridge university. Preached at Earls-Colne, Essex, being silenced for non-conformity in 1630 and 1633. Sailed from Gravesend in the *Defence*, reaching Boston, Oct., 1635. Succeeded Hooker in the pastorate at Cambridge, Mass., Feb., 1636, which position he held until his death. Was instrumental in the location of Harvard college at Cambridge, and rendered the college many services. A collective edition of his numerous treatises, etc., appeared at Boston, 1853. Died, Cambridge, Mass., 25 Aug., 1649.

SHEPHERD, Nathaniel Graham, journalist, b. New York, N. Y., 1835. Entered the insurance business in that city. Was a war correspondent for the N. Y. "Tribune" during a portion of the civil war, and afterward followed journalism. Author of several popular war-poems, including "Roll-Call." Died, New York, N. Y., 23 May, 1869.

SHERIDAN, Philip Henry, soldier, b. Albany, N. Y., 6 Mar., 1831. Graduated at West Point. After several years' service in the U. S. army in Western states, he was appointed captain, May, 1861. He was put in command of the cavalry corps of the army of the Potomac, April, 1864, having then risen to the grade of major-general of volunteers. For his Shenandoah campaign, in which his celebrated ride occurred, he was made major-general in the regular army, Nov., 1864, and received the thanks of congress. Took a prominent part in the closing manœuvres of the war. On the retirement of General Sherman, 1883, he became general-in-chief of the U. S. army, and in 1888 congress restored and bestowed on him the rank of general, to exist during his lifetime. "Personal Memoirs of P. H. Sheridan" appeared, 1888. Died, Nonquitt, Mass., 5 Aug., 1888.

SHERMAN, Frank Dempster, b. Peekskill, N. Y., 6 May, 1860. Received the degree of Ph.B. from Columbia, and afterward studied at Harvard. Became a fellow of Columbia, 1887, and subsequently instructor of the department of architecture in the same college. Author of "Madrigals and Catches" (1887) and a volume of children's poems, and joint author with John Kendrick Bangs of "New Waggings of Old Tales" (1888).

SHERMAN, William Tecumseh, soldier, b. Lancaster, O., 8 Feb., 1820. Graduated at West Point in 1840. Served as second lieutenant, 3d artillery, in Florida, commanding a detachment in Picolata, 1841. Was adjutant-general to Gen. S. W. Kearny in the Mexican war, 1846. Became captain, 1850, but resigned in 1853 to manage a bank in San Francisco. Practised law in Leavenworth, Kan., 1858-9. Superintendent of state military academy at Alexandria, La., 1860. When that state seceded, joined the Union forces. Was commissioned colonel, 1861, and commanded a brigade at Bull Run. Was made brigadier-general of volunteers, Aug., 1861, and was second in command under Gen. R. Anderson in Kentucky. Later was assigned to the 5th division, army of the Tennessee. Wounded in the hand at Shiloh, and mentioned by Grant in despatches for bravery and skill. Promoted brigadier-general in the regular army after the capture of Vicksburg. In Feb., 1864, received the thanks of congress for services in the Chattanooga campaign, and on 16 Nov. began his famous march through Georgia, covering three hundred miles in twenty-four days. Became major-general and afterward general, and otherwise received the highest honors from his countrymen. Retired at his own wish in 1884, that Sheridan might be general. Published his own "Memoirs" (1875).

SHILLABER, Benjamin Penhallow, "Mrs. Partington," b. Portsmouth, N. H., 12 July, 1814. Edited various journals at Boston, Mass., from 1840 to 1866, and afterward resided at Chelsea, Mass. Wrote "Life and Sayings of Mrs. Partington" (1854), "Partingtonian Patchwork" (1873), "Lines in Pleasant Places" (1875), "Ike and his Friends" (1879), and "Wide Swath," a volume of collected verse (1882).

SHINN, Charles Howard, b. Austin, Tex., 29 April, 1852. Brother of Milicent W. Shinn. Graduated at Johns Hopkins university. Connected with periodicals in San Francisco, Cal., and New York city until 1885, when he joined the staff of the "Overland Monthly." A contributor to the magazines and author of "Mining Camps, a Study in American Pioneer Government" (1885) and various historical and economic pamphlets.

SHINN, Milicent Washburn, b. Washington Township, Alameda Co., Cal., 15 April, 1858. Of New England and *Mayflower* descent. Graduated at the university of California. Edited a commercial paper in San Francisco for a short time. Afterward taught school, and in 1882 assumed the editorship of the new "Overland Monthly," which then succeeded "The Californian." A writer of poems, sketches, stories, and critiques for the magazines, besides purely editorial work.

SHURTLEFF, William Steele, jurist, b. Newbury, Vt., 17 Feb., 1830. Graduated at Yale. Studied at the Dane law school in Cambridge. After two years' army service during the civil war, became judge of probate at Springfield, Mass., 1863, a position he held continuously. In addition to numerous contributions to the magazines, delivered a number of poems on occasions, notably the ode at the celebration of the 250th anniversary of the founding of Springfield.

SIGOURNEY, Lydia [Huntley], b. Norwich, Conn., 1 Sept., 1791. A school-teacher until her marriage in 1819 to Charles Sigourney. Brought out her first book, "Moral Pieces in Prose and Verse," in her twenty-fourth year. Her husband's fortune becoming impaired, she adopted literature as a profession, gaining marked success, which enabled her to gratify her instincts of practical beneficence during the whole of her fifty years' residence at Hartford, Conn. Among her numerous publications are a poem on "The Traits of the Aborigines of America" (1822), "A Sketch of Connecticut Forty Years Since" (1824), "Letters to Young Ladies" (1833), "Zinzendorff, and Other Poems" (1836), "Letters to Mothers" (1838), "Pocahontas, and Other Poems" (1841), "Scenes in my Native Land" (1844), "Voice of Flowers" (1845), "The Weeping Willow" (1846), "Water Drops, a Plea for Temperance" (1847), "Whisper to a Bride" (1849), "Letters to my Pupils" (1850), "Olive Leaves" (1851), "Past Meridian" (1854), "Lucy Howard's Journal" (1857), "The Daily Counsellor," poems (1858), "Gleanings," poems (1860), and "The Man of Uz, and Other Poems" (1862). "Letters of Life" (1866) was issued posthumously. Died, Hartford, Conn., 10 June, 1865.

SILL, Edward Rowland, educator, b. Windsor, Conn., 29 April, 1841. Graduated at Yale. Afterward resided chiefly in California, with the exception of a few years as teacher in Ohio. Was professor of English literature at the university of California, 1874–82. Author of "The Hermitage, and Other Poems" (1867) and "Venus of Milo, and Other Poems" (1883). "Poems" (1888) was issued posthumously. Died, Cleveland, O., 27 Feb., 1887.

SIMMS, William Gilmore, b. Charleston, S. C., 17 April, 1806. Published "Lyrical and Other Poems" in his twenty-first year, and became editor and owner of the Charleston "City Gazette" in 1828. Issued two other poetical works before 1831. Versatile and prolific with his pen. Another poem, "Atalantis, a Tale of the Sea," appeared in 1832. Was for several years in the state legislature. Settled down to novel-writing, and was praised by Poe as second among native authors to Cooper. His many works include "The Yemassee" (1835, revised ed. 1853), "The Partisan" (1835), "Palayo" (1838), "The Kinsman" (1841, new ed. 1854, entitled "The Scout"), "Confession, or the Blind Heart" (1842), "Castle Dismal" (1845), "The Wigwam and the Cabin, or Tales of the South" (1845–6), "Areytos, or Songs and Ballads of the South" (1846), "Poems" (1853), "The Maroon, and Other Tales" (1855), "War Poetry of the South" (1867). In addition to these he produced a number of local histories, biographies, several dramas which were performed, and contributed largely to the periodical press. A selection of his best works was issued in 19 volumes, 1859. Died, Charleston, S. C., 11 June, 1870.

SLOSSON, Annie [Trumbull], b. Stonington, Conn., 18—. Studied at the Hartford, Conn., female seminary. Was married, 1867, to Edward Slosson of New York city, where she afterward lived. A contributor of fiction to the magazines, and author of "China Hunters' Club" (1878) and "Fishin' Jimmy" (1889).

SMALLEY, George Washburn, journalist, b. Franklin, Mass., 2 June, 1833. Graduated at Yale. Studied at the Harvard law school, and was admitted to the bar at Boston, Mass. Practised there until the beginning of the civil war, when he became correspondent for the N. Y. "Tribune" in South Carolina, Virginia, and Maryland, distinguishing himself by timely and brilliantly written reports from the seat of war. Joined the editorial staff of that journal late in 1862. Three years later was sent to report the war of 1866 between Prussia and Austria. In 1867 became representative of the "Tribune" at London. His letters on European politics and society attracted wide attention.

SMEDES, Susan [Dabney], b. Raymond, Hinds Co., Miss., 10 Aug., 1840. The daughter of Thomas S. Dabney, a planter. Was married, 1860, to Lyell Smedes, by whom she was soon left a widow. More recently became a resident of Helena, Montana. "Memorials of a Southern Planter" (1887) relates to her father, and is descriptive of life on a Southern plantation.

SMITH, Abigail [Adams], b. Braintree, Mass., 14 July, 1765. Daughter of President John Adams, whom she joined in France, 1784, and afterward accompanied to London. Was married, 1786, to Col. William S. Smith, her father's secretary of legation. In 1841 appeared the "Journal and Correspondence of Miss Adams." Died, Quincy, Mass., 14 Aug., 1813.

SMITH, Belle Eugenia, b. Litchfield, O., 18—. Graduated at Tabor college, Ia. Resided at Percival, Ia., 1850–74. In 1874 became an instructor at Tabor college. Author of the poem "If I should die to-night."

SMITH, Elihu Hubbard, physician, b. Litchfield, Conn., 4 Sept., 1771. Graduated at Yale. Began practice in New York city, 1793. Fell a victim to the yellow-fever epidemic of 1798. Established with Dr. S. L. Mitchill the "Medical Repository," and edited the first collection of "American Poems" (1793). One of "The Hartford Wits." Died, New York, N. Y., 21 Sept., 1798.

SMITH, Elizabeth Oakes [Prince], b. Cumberland, Me., 12 Aug., 1806. Was early married to Seba Smith, whom she assisted in his editorial work. Resided in New York city after 1842. Author of "Riches Without Wings" (1838), "The Sinless Child, and Other Poems" (1841), "Woman and

Her Needs" (1847), "Hints on Dress and Beauty" (1852), "Bald Eagle, the Last of the Ramapaughs" (1867), besides some tragedies and much fugitive verse.

SMITH, Florence, b. New York, N. Y., 11 Mar., 1845. Daughter of Augustus F. Smith, of that city, where she resided, at Fort Washington. "Piero's Painting, and Other Poems" (1872) was published as a memorial volume. Died, Fort Washington, N. Y., 19 July, 1871.

SMITH, Gerrit, philanthropist, b. Utica, N. Y., 6 Mar., 1797. Graduated at Hamilton. Succeeded to a large estate, the income of which he systematically devoted to philanthropic purposes. Was an early advocate of anti-slavery, and assisted the movement in many conspicuous ways. Was elected U. S. representative in 1852. Several volumes of his speeches and writings were published, and his "Life" (1878) was written by O. B. Frothingham. Died, New York, N. Y., 28 Dec., 1874.

SMITH, (Captain) John, traveller and colonist, b. Willoughby, Lincolnshire, England, 1579. According to his own writings, the hero in youth of many chivalrous exploits in eastern Europe, where he claimed to have taken an important part in the wars with the Turks. His first authenticated adventure was in the settlement of Virginia. He sailed from London with Capt. Christopher Newport, 19 Dec., 1606, reaching Cape Henry 26 April, 1607. To him is unquestionably due the preservation of the Jamestown settlement during his stay. Much distrusted at first by the other leaders, his abilities as a manager and in dealing with the Indians were finally recognized, and he was elected president and governor of Virginia, 10 Sept., 1608. He cleared the colony of several unruly spirits, but some of them returning with the advance ships of Sir Thomas Gates's fleet, and Smith being badly wounded by the explosion of a powder-pouch, he was unable to resist adverse influences, and withdrew to England in the autumn of 1609. The colony soon got into difficulties, and was barely saved from destruction by the arrival of Lord Delawarr. Smith's story of his rescue by Pocahontas, which does not appear in his early works on Virginia, was perhaps an after invention, although she may have caused Powhatan to favor him during his captivity. He headed a fishing-adventure to New England in 1614, and while there sailed in an open boat from Penobscot to Cape Cod, gathering data for his map of New England. This was the first to give a clear idea of the topography of that coast. Subsequent voyages were unsuccessful. He wrote many books concerning the new country, and planned many expeditions, but never saw America again. An overbearing and boastful address, together with the disadvantages of lowly birth, prevented him from realizing the benefits of undoubted ability as an organizer and explorer. His books are interesting, in spite of their literary uncouthness, and they preserve much information concerning the early days of the Virginia colony that would otherwise have been lost. There were published "A True Relation," etc. (1608), "A Map of Virginia," etc. (1612), "A Description of New England" (1616), "New England's Trials" (1620), "The Generall Historie of Virginia," etc. (1624), "An Accidence," etc. (1626), "A Sea Grammar" (1627), "The True Travels, Adventures and Observations of Captain John Smith" (1630), and "Advertisements for the Unexperienced Planters of New England" (1631). In some of these Smith's work was partly or wholly editorial, portions of the text being by other hands. Died, London, England, 21 June, 1631.

SMITH, May Louise [Riley], b. Brighton, Monroe Co., N. Y., 27 May, 1842. Was married, 1869, to Albert Smith of Springfield, Ill., and subsequently resided in New York city. "Sometime," "If," and "Tired Mothers" are among her most popular poems. Author of "A Gift of Gentians, and Other Verses" (1882), and "The Inn of Rest" (1888).

SMITH, Samuel Francis, clergyman, b. Boston, Mass., 21 Oct., 1808. Graduated at Harvard. Pastor of Baptist churches in Maine and Massachusetts for many years. Afterward edited the Baptist missionary publications. Author of numerous hymns, including "America" (written 1832). Edited "Lyric Gems" (1843), "The Psalmist" (1843), and "Rock of Ages" (1866).

SMITH, Seba, "Major Jack Downing," b. Buckfield, Me., 14 Sept., 1792. Graduated at Bowdoin. Edited the Portland, Me., "Argus," "Family Recorder," and "Daily Courier." Settled in New York city, 1842. Wrote the humorous letters afterward collected as "The Life and Writings of Major Jack Downing" (1833). Issued "Powhatan," a romance in verse (1841), "New Elements in Geometry" (1850), and "Way Down East" (1855). Died, Patchogue, L. I., N. Y., 29 July, 1868.

SMITH, Stephen Decatur, Jr., b. Philadelphia, Penn., 28 Oct., 1861. A resident of that city. Joint author, with C. H. Lüders, of "Hallo, My Fancy!" (1887), and a contributor of verse to the periodicals.

SMITH, William, jurist, b. New York, N. Y., 25 June, 1728. Son of an eminent lawyer of the same name. Graduated at Yale. Began the practice of law in his native city and attained a high place in his profession. Became chief-justice of the colony, 1763, and a member of the council, 1769. After some hesitation joined the royalist party, about 1778, and was subsequently made chief-justice of Canada. Author of "The History of the Province of New-York" (1757), afterward completed from the author's manuscript and republished by the N. Y. Hist Soc. (1826–9). Died, Quebec, Canada, 3 Nov., 1793.

SNIDER, Denton Jaques, b. Mt. Gilead, O., 9 Jan., 1841. Graduated at Oberlin. For many years a lecturer on literature in St. Louis, Mo., and elsewhere. Also lectured at the Concord school of philosophy. Author of "A System of Shakespeare's Dramas" (1877), "Delphic Days" (1880), "A Walk in Hellas" (1881), "Agamemnon's Daughter" (1885), "Commentary on Goethe's Faust" (1886), and "Commentary on Shakespeare's Tragedies" (1887).

SPARKS, Jared, educator, b. Willington, Conn., 10 May, 1789. Graduated at Harvard. Entered the Unitarian ministry at Baltimore, 1819, and edited the "Unitarian Miscellany" (1821–3). Purchased the "North American Review" in 1824, and was its editor until 1831. Was professor of history at Harvard, 1839–49, and its president, 1849–53. Issued numerous works, original and edited, including "The Diplomatic Correspondence of the American Revolution" (12 vols., 1829–30), "Life of Gouverneur Morris" (1832), "The Writings of George Washington," including his correspondence, addresses, private and official papers, with a "Life" (12 vols., 1834–8), "Remarks on American History" (1837), "The Library of American Biography" (1834–8 and 1844–7), "The Works of Benjamin Franklin, with Notes, and a Life of the Author" (10 vols., 1836–40), and "Correspondence of the American Revolution," letters of eminent men to Washington (4 vols., 1853). Wrote biographies of Ethan Allen, Benedict Arnold, and others. Bequeathed his valuable collection of manuscripts and original data for a history of American diplomacy to Harvard. Died, Cambridge, Mass., 14 Mar., 1866.

SPOFFORD, Harriet Elizabeth [Prescott], b. Calais, Me., 3 April, 1835. The daughter of Joseph N. Prescott. At the age of fourteen she removed to Newburyport, Mass. Graduated at Pinkerton academy, Derry, N. H. Her father becoming incapacitated for work by paralysis, she contributed to her family's support by writing stories for various periodicals. This early work was not afterward acknowledged or collected. A story entitled "In a Cellar," published in the "Atlantic Monthly" for 1859, first attracted attention to her abilities as an author. She was married, 1865, to Richard S. Spofford, formerly a law-partner of Caleb Cushing, and afterward lived at Deer island, in the Merrimack river, and within the boundaries of Amesbury, Mass. Author

of "Sir Rohan's Ghost," romance (1859), "The Amber Gods, and Other Stories" (1863), "Azarian," an episode (1863), "New England Legends" (1871), "The Thief in the Night" (1872), "Art Decoration applied to Furniture" (1881), "Marquis of Carabas" (1882), "Poems" (1882), "Hester Stanley at St. Mark's" (1883), "The Servant Girl Question" (1884), and "Ballads about Authors" (1887).

SPRAGUE, Charles, b. Boston, Mass., 26 Oct., 1791. Was cashier of the Globe bank in Boston, 1824–65. Won prizes for prologues at the opening of theatres in several cities, and delivered poems before various societies. Among his pieces are "The Winged Worshippers," "Curiosity," and "The Family Meeting." A collected edition of "Poetical and Prose Writings" was published in 1841 (revised eds. 1850–76). Died, Boston, Mass., 22 Jan., 1875.

SPRAGUE, William Buell, clergyman, b. Andover, Conn., 16 Oct., 1795. Graduated at Yale. Was pastor of Congregational and Presbyterian churches in West Springfield, Mass., and Albany, N. Y., 1819–69. Best remembered for his "Annals of the American Pulpit" (9 vols., 1857–69). Also wrote "Letters from Europe" (1828), "Lectures on Revivals" (1832), "Letters to Young Men" (1845), and "Visits to European Celebrities" (1855). Died, Flushing, N. Y., 7 May, 1876.

SQUIER, Ephraim George, archæologist, b. Bethlehem, N. Y., 17 June, 1821. Entered journalism in 1843. After investigating and describing the antiquities of the Mississippi valley, was appointed chargé d'affaires to Central America in 1849, where and subsequently in Peru he continued his researches. Issued "Serpent Symbols" (1852), "Nicaragua" (1852), "Waikna" (1855), "The States of Central America" (1857), and "Peru" (1877). Died, Brooklyn, N. Y., 17 April, 1888.

STANLEY, Henry Moreland [Morton, in Appletons' Cyc. Amer. Biog.], explorer, b. near Denbigh, Wales, 1840. His name at first was John Rowlands, and from three to thirteen years of age he was cared for and educated at the St. Asaph poorhouse. Emigrated to New Orleans, La., in 1855, where he was adopted by the gentleman whose name he assumed. Served in the Confederate army, was taken prisoner, and afterward entered the U. S. navy. Was in Spain as correspondent for the N. Y. "Herald," when detailed by its editor in 1869 to find Dr. David Livingstone, at that time in Africa, and from whom no word had been received for over two years. The expedition left Zanzibar in March, 1871, and Dr. Livingstone was found the following November. Was again sent out in 1874 to explore unknown portions of Africa, and identified the river Lualaba with the Congo by descending it to the mouth of the latter, a perilous journey of eight months. During 1879–82 was occupied in founding the Congo free state. In 1887 was sent to rescue Emin Pasha, then cut off in an interior province of Africa, and after traversing the great Congo forest three times, successfully accomplished the mission, reaching the eastern coast in Dec., 1889. His experiences are related in "How I Found Livingstone" (1872), "Through the Dark Continent" (1878), "The Congo and the Founding of its Free State" (1885), and "In Darkest Africa" (1890).

STANSBURY, Joseph, loyalist, b. England, 1750. Arrived in Philadelphia, 1767, where he established himself as a merchant. Was twice imprisoned during the Revolution for his loyalist views and for services to the British government, having been appointed commissioner of the city watch during the occupation of Philadelphia by the English. Resided in New York city after the war. His poems are collected in "The Loyal Verses of Joseph Stansbury," etc. (1860). Died, New York, N. Y., 1809.

STANSBURY, Mary Anna [Phinney], b. Vernon, N. Y., 5 Oct., 1842. Studied at Lawrence university, Wis. Was married, 1861, to E. P. Humphrey, and after his death to Dr. Emory Stansbury, of Appleton, Wis., where she afterward resided. A writer of verse and fiction for the magazines. Author of the poem "How he Saved St. Michael's."

STANTON, Elizabeth [Cady], reformer, b. Johnstown, N. Y., 12 Nov., 1815. A leader in the abolition movement, and present at the anti-slavery conference in London, 1840. With Lucretia Mott convened the first Woman's Rights gathering in 1848. President of the national committee of the woman suffrage movement, 1855–65, and of the association until 1873. Besides lectures and addresses, joint author with two others of "The History of Woman Suffrage" (1881).

STEIN, Orth Harper. The editors have been unable to obtain information concerning this writer.

STEPHENS, Alexander Hamilton, statesman, b. Taliaferro Co., Ga., 11 Feb., 1812. Graduated at Franklin college, and entered the bar, 1834. Elected to the state legislature, 1836. Secured the first charter ever granted to a college for women (Macon, Ga.) for classics and sciences. In 1843 was elected U. S. representative, and successfully championed several important legislative reforms, retiring in 1859. Opposed the secession of Georgia, but accepted the vice-presidency of the Confederacy in 1861. Was held for five months as a prisoner of state in 1865. In 1867 issued the first volume of

"The War between the States," the second following in 1870. Reëlected to congress, 1874, resigning in 1882. The same year became governor of Georgia. Died, Atlanta, Ga., 4 Mar., 1883.

STEPHENS, Anna Sophia [Winterbotham], b. Derby, Conn., 1813. Was married, 1831, to Edward Stephens. Edited the "Portland [Me.] Magazine," 1835–7. Resided in New York city after 1837. Was at different times assistant editor of "Graham's" and "Peterson's" magazines. Among her novels are "Mary Derwent" (185–), "Fashion and Famine" (1854), and "The Old Homestead" (1855). Died, Newport, R. I., 20 Aug., 1886.

STEPHENS, John Lloyd, traveller, b. Shrewsbury, N. J., 28 Nov., 1805. Graduated at Columbia, and practised law in New York city. Explored Central America in 1839, and in 1849 became an officer, and afterward president, of the Panama railroad company. "Incidents of Travel in Yucatan" (1843) is the most important of his numerous books of travel. Died, New York, N. Y., 10 Oct., 1852.

STEPHENS, William, colonial governor, b. Isle of Wight, England, 28 Jan., 1671. Graduated at Cambridge university, and was a member of the British parliament in 1696. Removed to America about 1730, and, after serving in several less important capacities, was governor of Georgia from 1743 to 1750. "A Journal of the Proceedings in Georgia" and "State of the Province" were published, 1742. Died, Georgia, Aug., 1753.

STEVENS, Abel, clergyman, b. Philadelphia, Penn., 19 Jan., 1815. Entered the Methodist Episcopal ministry. Edited several Methodist periodicals, 1840–56, and from 1865 to 1874 was associate editor of the "Methodist." Author of a series of standard historical works on Methodism, including "History of the Religious Movement of the Eighteenth Century, called Methodism" (1858–61), and "History of the Methodist Episcopal Church in the United States of America" (1864–7).

STEVENS, Thaddeus, statesman, b. Danville, Caledonia Co., Vt., 4 April, 1792. Graduated at Dartmouth. Studied law and established a practice at Gettysburg, Penn. Was a member of the state legislature, 1833–8. Became a stalwart abolitionist and champion of free schools. Was elected U. S. representative as a Whig, 1848–53, and again from 1858 to his death as a leading Republican. His vigorous speeches and untiring efforts in behalf of the Union during the civil war gained him the title of "the great commoner." Urged President Lincoln to proclaim emancipation, and did his utmost to gain the suffrage for the negro. Proposed the impeachment of President

Johnson, and was chairman of the House committee appointed to conduct the trial. Bequeathed ground for a cemetery in Lancaster, Penn., for the poor, and endowed an orphan asylum for white and colored children. Died, Washington, D. C., 11 Aug., 1868.

STILES, Ezra, educator, b. North Haven, Conn., 29 Nov., 1727. Graduated at Yale. Remained at New Haven until 1755, engaged in the study of theology and law, and as a tutor in the college. Finally accepted a call to preach at Newport, R. I., where he was pastor from 1756 until the occupation of the town by the British army during the Revolution. In 1777, while residing at Portsmouth, N. H., was elected president of Yale, holding office until his death. Author of a number of sermons and addresses, among which is the sermon preached at the close of the Revolution, and entitled "The United States Elevated to Glory and Honor" (1783). His most important literary work was his "History of Three of the Judges of Charles I." (1794). He left, in manuscript, diaries and writings filling forty-five bound volumes, now preserved at Yale. Died, New Haven, Conn., 12 May, 1795.

STILLMAN, William James, painter and journalist, b. Schenectady, N. Y., 1 June, 1828. Graduated at Union college. Followed the profession of an artist until 1869, when he devoted himself mainly to literature. Was U. S. consul at Rome from 1861 to 1865, and filled the same position in Crete from 1865 to 1869. Was correspondent for the London "Times" in south-eastern Europe from 1875 to 1882, and again at Rome after 1885, having meanwhile been art-critic for the N. Y. "Evening Post." Author of "Cretan Insurrection" (1874), "Herzegovina and the Late Uprising" (1877), and "On the Track of Ulysses" (1887), besides contributions to the magazines.

STIMSON, Frederic Jesup, "J. S. of Dale," lawyer, b. Dedham, Mass., 20 July, 1855. Graduated at Harvard. Entered the bar, and was assistant attorney-general of Massachusetts, 1884–5. Some of his novels are "Guerndale" (1882), "The Crime of Henry Vane" (1884), and "The Residuary Legatee" (1888).

STITH, William, clergyman, b. Virginia, 1689. Was ordained in England as a Church of England clergyman, and was made master of the William and Mary college grammar school in 1731. He was chaplain of the Virginia house of burgesses in 1738, and for the last three years of his life was president of William and Mary college. His "History of the First Discovery and Settlement of Virginia" (1747) is based largely on the writings of Captain John Smith and on more trustworthy records and manuscripts to which Stith had access. The latter have been destroyed by fire. But one volume of the "History" was completed, bringing the record to 1624. Died, Williamsburg, Va., 27 Sept., 1755.

ST. JOHN, Peter. A resident of Norwalk, Conn. Supposed to be the author of the Revolutionary ballad entitled "Taxation of America." By some authorities the authorship is attributed to Samuel St. John, who was born and died in New Canaan, Conn.

STOCKTON, Francis Richard, b. Philadelphia, Penn., 5 April, 1834. Graduated at the Central high school of that city. Devoted a number of years to engraving and designing on wood, and contributed pictures to "Vanity Fair," a comic paper published in New York city before the war, and to other illustrated periodicals. Was at the same time engaged in literary and journalistic work. An editorial connection with the Philadelphia "Post" was followed in 1872 by his abandonment of engraving and by his acceptance of an editorial position on the N. Y. "Hearth and Home." He soon joined the staff of the "Century Magazine" (then "Scribner's Monthly"), and on the establishment of the "St. Nicholas Magazine" for young folks in 1873, became assistant editor of the latter. Resigned this position in 1880 to devote himself to purely literary work. His first volume was a collection of stories for children, originally contributed to the "Riverside Magazine," and published in 1869 as "The Ting-a-Ling Stories." Other books for children are "Roundabout Rambles" (1872), "What might have been Expected" (1874), "Tales out of School" (1875), "A Jolly Fellowship" (1880), "The Floating Prince" (1881), "The Story of Viteau" (1884), and "Personally Conducted" (1889). His novels and volumes of short stories include "Rudder Grange" (1879), "The Lady, or the Tiger? and Other Stories" (1884), "The Late Mrs. Null" (1886), "The Casting away of Mrs. Lecks and Mrs. Aleshine" (1886), "The Hundredth Man" (1887), "The Christmas Wreck, and Other Tales" (1887), "The Bee Man of Orn, and Other Fanciful Tales" (1887), "The Dusantes" (1888), "Amos Kilbright, with Other Stories" (1888), "The Great War Syndicate" (1889), "The Stories of the Three Burglars" (1890), and "The Merry Chanter" (1890).

STODDARD, Charles Warren, b. Rochester, N. Y., 7 Aug., 1843. Visited the Hawaiian islands in 1864, and afterward resided there for long periods. Travelled in all parts of the world during 1873–8, as correspondent of the San Francisco "Chronicle." Professor of English literature at Notre Dame university, Ind., 1885–6.

Author of "Poems" (1867), "South-Sea Idyls" (1873), "Mashallah" (1881), and "The Lepers of Molokai" (1885).

STODDARD, Elizabeth Drew [Barstow], b. Mattapoisett, Mass., 6 May, 1823. The daughter of a captain and ship-owner of that place. Received her education at a young ladies' seminary. Was married, at twenty-eight, to Richard Henry Stoddard, and soon developed a talent which has placed her among the select American poets, although her poems have not been collected in a volume. At the time of the civil war she published three novels, "The Morgesons" (1862), "Two Men" (1865), and "Temple House" (1867), realistic and dramatic studies of coast-life. These were republished in 1888, and were the subject of marked attention from the critical press.

STODDARD, Lavinia [Stone], b. Guilford, Conn., 29 June, 1787. Was taken as a child to Paterson, N. J., and was there married, 1811, to Dr. William Stoddard, with whom she established an academy at Troy, N. Y. Author of fugitive poems, among which is that entitled "The Soul's Defiance." Died, Blakely, Ala., 1820.

STODDARD, Richard Henry, journalist, b. Hingham, Mass., 2 July, 1825. His father was a sea captain of that place, who died in 1835, and the son was brought by his mother to New York city the same year. There he received a common-school education, supplemented by private reading and study during several years' work in an iron-foundry. Early commenced the writing of verse, and in 1849 published a volume of poems entitled "Footprints," of which, however, he suppressed the entire edition. "Poems" (1852) next appeared, and he became a regular contributor to the magazines. He did not depend on literary work alone as a means of support, but held several official and editorial positions. Served in the custom-house and dock department at New York from 1853 to 1873, was literary editor of the N. Y. "World" from 1860 to 1870, and in 1880 became literary editor of the N. Y. "Mail and Express." Edited several anthologies of English verse, the "Bric-à-Brac Series" (1874), and various editions of standard works, with prefaces and introductions by himself. Some of his own books are "Songs of Summer" (1856), "The King's Bell" (1862), "Abraham Lincoln, a Horatian Ode" (1865), "The Book of the East," poems (1871), "The Lion's Cub," poems (1890), and a collective edition of his "Poems" (1880).

STODDARD, William Osborn, b. Homer, Cortland Co., N. Y., 24 Sept., 1835. Graduated at the university of Rochester. Edited various journals until the civil war, and was a private secretary of President Lincoln, 1861-4. Was afterward occupied as an inventor. Author of "Verses of Many Days" (1875), "Dab Kinzer" (1881), "The Volcano under the City" (1887), and "Lives of the Presidents" (1886-90).

STONE, John Augustus, dramatist and actor, b. Concord, Mass., 1801. For his play "Metamora" Edwin Forrest paid him five hundred dollars, and for "The Ancient Briton" one thousand dollars. These plays and "Fauntleroy, the Banker of Rouen" were written specially for Forrest and were produced by him. "Metamora" still holds the stage. Stone wrote several other dramas, and occasionally acted. He drowned himself in the Schuylkill river while suffering mental derangement. Died, near Philadelphia, Penn., 1 June, 1834.

STONE, Samuel, clergyman, b. Hertford, England, 30 July, 1602. Graduated at Cambridge university. Sailed for Boston with Thomas Hooker in 1633, to escape religious persecution, and became the latter's colleague, first at Cambridge, Mass., and afterward at Hartford, Conn., which was named from his birthplace. Printed a sermon, "A Congregational Church," etc. (1652), and left in manuscript a "Body of Divinity," much used by theological students of the time. Died, Hartford, Conn., 20 July, 1663.

STONE, William Leete, journalist, b. New Paltz, N. Y., 20 April, 1792. Editor and part proprietor of the N. Y. "Commercial Advertiser," 1821-44. Collected much information respecting the Indians, which he utilized in his principal works, "Life of Joseph Brant" (1838), "Life of Red Jacket" (1840), "Poetry and History of Wyoming" (1841), and "Uncas and Miantonomoh" (1842). Died, Saratoga, N. Y., 15 Aug., 1844.

STORRS, Richard Salter, clergyman, b. Braintree, Mass., 21 Aug., 1821. Graduated at Amherst. Entered upon his pastorate at the Brooklyn, N.Y., Church of the Pilgrims in 1846. Some of his numerous works are "Early American Spirit and the Genesis of It" (1875), "Recognition of the Supernatural in Letters and Life" (1881), "Manliness in the Scholar" (1883), "Divine Origin of Christianity Indicated by its Historical Effects" (1884), and "Forty Years of Pastoral Life" (1886).

STORY, Joseph, jurist, b. Marblehead, Mass., 18 Sept., 1779. Graduated at Harvard. Studied law at Salem, Mass., where he began practice in 1801. Resided there until his appointment as associate justice of the U. S. supreme court in Nov., 1811, holding the office until his death. He had meanwhile been elected to the Massachusetts legislature and to the U. S. house of representatives as a Republican-Democrat, though he opposed the embargo of 1808. Became the first incumbent of the Dane professorship of law at Harvard, 1829. His legal decisions in his own circuit fill thirteen volumes, and he furnished a large portion of the opinions in the thirty-five volumes of supreme court reports issued during his term as justice. Besides these, he issued thirteen volumes of legal works, including "Commentaries on the Constitution of the United States" (1833) and "Commentaries on the Conflict of Laws" (1834). "Miscellaneous Writings" appeared in 1835, and his "Life and Letters" (1851) was edited by his son, W. W. Story. Died, Cambridge, Mass., 10 Sept., 1845.

STORY, William Wetmore, sculptor, b. Salem, Mass., 12 Feb., 1819. Son of Chief-Justice Joseph Story. Graduated at Harvard. Entered the bar, and edited the U. S. First Circuit Reports (1842–7). Wrote a "Treatise on the Law of Contracts not under Seal" (1844) and another on the "Law of Sales of Personal Property" (1847). Gave up law for sculpture, and settled in Italy in 1848. Among the best-known of his art-productions are the statue of his father in the Mount Auburn cemetery chapel; Edward Everett, in the Boston public garden; the seated statue of George Peabody, near the Royal Exchange, London; and busts of Lowell, Theodore Parker, and Josiah Quincy. The figures of Cleopatra and Semiramis in the N. Y. museum of art are also from his studio. Besides his legal works, is the author of "Poems" (1847 and 1856), "Life and Letters of Joseph Story" (1851), "The American Question" (1862), "Roba di Roma, or Walks and Talks about Rome" (1862), "Proportions of the Human Figure, according to a New Canon for Practical Use" (1866), "Graffiti d'Italia" (1868), "The Roman Lawyer in Jerusalem" (1870), "Nero" (1875), "Castle of St. Angelo" (1877), "He and She, or a Poet's Portfolio" (1883), "Fiammetta" (1885), and "Poems" (1886).

STOWE, Harriet Elizabeth [Beecher], b. Litchfield, Conn., 14 June, 1812. Daughter of Lyman Beecher. At the age of thirteen attended the school kept by her eldest sister, Catherine Esther, at Hartford, Conn. Here she staid until 1832, when her father removed to Cincinnati. Was married to the Rev. Calvin E. Stowe in 1836. Both sympathized strongly with the anti-slavery movement, sheltering many fugitives in their house. They also visited some of the slave-states, and studied the subject on the spot. In 1849 appeared "The Mayflower, or Short Sketches of the Descendants of the Pilgrims." On Mr. Stowe's being appointed to a professorship at Bowdoin, they removed to Brunswick, Me., in 1850. Two years later he accepted a professorship at the Andover, Mass., theological seminary. The story of "Uncle Tom's Cabin, or Life among the Lowly" was written to enable the Northern public to realize the horrors of slavery. It first appeared in the "National Era" of Washington, D.C., running from June, 1851, to April, 1852, and was then brought out in book-form. For the first year it produced no marked effect, and the author became disheartened. But it made its way so effectively that within five years 500,000 copies were sold in the United States, besides an enormous sale in England. The book was translated into many languages. Various dramatic versions of it continue to hold the provincial stage. In answer to many hostile criticisms Mrs. Stowe published "A Key to Uncle Tom's Cabin, Presenting the Original Facts and Documents upon which the Story is Founded, together with Corroborative Statements verifying the Truth of the Work" (1853); also "A Peep into Uncle Tom's Cabin, for Children" (1853). Failing health from the strain of excitement induced her to visit England, where she had a cordial reception from all classes. The account of this journey, which extended over the continent of Europe, was published as "Sunny Memories of Foreign Lands" (1854). Next appeared "Dred, a Tale of the Great Dismal Swamp" (1856). A novel, "The Minister's Wooing," came out in 1859. Mrs. Stowe removed to Hartford in 1864, where she afterward remained. Issued "Old Town Folks," 1869, following that work by a paper in the "Atlantic Monthly" and "Macmillan's Magazine" on "The True Story of Lord Byron's Life." The latter raised a storm of adverse criticism that elicited in reply "Lady Byron Vindicated, a History of the Byron Controversy" (1869). Published "Pink and White Tyranny," a society novel (1871), and among her other productions are "Religious Poems" (1865), "Men of Our Times" (1868), "Footsteps of the Master" (1876), "Poganuc People" (1878), and "A Dog's Mission" (1881).

STRACHEY, William, colonist. First heard of as sailing for the Virginia colony with Sir Thomas Gates and Sir George Somers, 15 May, 1609. Cast away with them on the Bermuda islands, finally reaching Jamestown in May, 1610. The colony was then abandoned, but meeting Lord Delawarr on the way out of James river, all returned to Jamestown, Strachey receiving the appointment of secretary. He had returned to London by 1612, when he brought out "For the Colony in Virginea Britannia; Laws Divine, Morall and Martiall." His description of a storm off the Bermudas in "A True Reportory of the Wracke and Redemption of Sir Thomas Gates," given in the fourth volume of Purchas's "Pilgrimes" (1613), was supposed by some to have suggested the opening scene of Shakespeare's "Tempest." In 1849 the Hakluyt society published his "Historie of Travaile into Virginia Britannia" from a manuscript in the British museum. It was written about 1618. Date of death unknown.

STREET, Alfred Billings, b. Poughkeepsie, **N. Y., 18 Dec., 1811.** Edited the Albany, N. Y., "Northern Light," 1843–4, and was state librarian of New York from 1848 until his death. Wrote largely for periodicals, and issued among other works "The Burning of Schenectady, and Other Poems" (1842), "Fugitive Poems" (1846), "Woods and Waters" (1860), and "Forest Pictures in the Adirondacks," poems (1865). Died, Albany, N. Y., 2 June, 1881.

STRONG, Josiah, clergyman, b. Naperville, Du Page Co., Ill., 19 Jan., 1847. Graduated at Western Reserve college. Entered the Congregational ministry, and after holding several pastorates, became in 1886 general agent of the Evangelical Alliance in the United States. Author of "Our Country; its Possible Future and its Present Crisis" (1885).

STUART, Moses, philologist, b. Wilton, Conn., 26 Mar., 1780. Graduated at Yale, and became a Congregational minister at New Haven, Conn. Was professor of sacred literature at the Andover, Mass., theological seminary, 1810–48. Author of a Hebrew grammar (1813 and 1821), of numerous "Commentaries" on the books of the Bible, and of many other philological and theological works. "Miscellanies" appeared in 1846. Died, Andover, Mass., 4 Jan., 1852.

STURGIS, Russell, architect, b. Baltimore, Md., 16 Oct., 1836. Graduated at the college of New York, where he was for a time professor of architecture. Visited Europe in 1880 and 1884. Otherwise a resident of New York city. A lecturer and writer for the periodicals on art and architecture.

SULLIVAN, Thomas Russell, b. Boston, Mass., 21 Nov., 1849. Engaged in business at London, Paris, and Boston until 1888, when he adopted a purely literary life. Author of a novel, "Roses of Shadow" (1885), and several plays, including "The Catspaw" (1881), "Merely Players!" (1886), and a dramatization of Stevenson's "Dr. Jekyll and Mr. Hyde" (produced 1886). Joint author with W. W. Chamberlin of "Hearts are Trumps!" (produced 1878) and "Midsummer Madness" (produced 1880).

SULLIVAN, William, lawyer, b. Saco, Me., 12 Nov., 1774. Graduated at Harvard. Studied law and practised at Boston, Mass. Was elected for a number of terms to the Massachusetts legislature. Issued political, moral, and historical "Class-Books" (1831–3) and "Familiar Letters on the Public Men of the Revolution" (1834). Died, Boston, Mass., 3 Sept., 1839.

SUMNER, Charles, statesman, b. Boston, Mass., 6 Jan., 1811. Graduated at Harvard. Adopted the legal profession, and

wrote for the "American Jurist." Was reporter of the U. S. circuit court from 1835 to 1837, when he visited Europe, remaining until 1840. Sympathized strongly with the abolition movement. His oration at Boston, 4 July, 1845, on "The True Grandeur of Nations," an eloquent plea against war, made him famous. Published "Orations and Speeches" (1850). Was elected U. S. senator, 1851. The following year his speech, "Freedom National, Slavery Sectional," established his position as a party leader. A controversial rivalry between Sumner and Stephen A. Douglas resulted from this. The fury of partisan feeling culminated in a violent assault on Sumner by Preston A. Brooks, a representative from South Carolina, who dealt a series of blows with a club on Sumner's head in the senate chamber, 1856. The provocation had been Sumner's sharp rebuke of Senator Butler, a relative of Brooks's, in the debate on the admission of Kansas. Sumner was incapacitated for a considerable period. He was reëlected to the senate in 1857, and soon after went to Europe for surgical treatment. Resumed attendance, 1859. Made a powerful speech on "The Barbarism of Slavery," 1860. Was appointed chairman of the committee on foreign affairs, 1861. Stood for emancipation throughout the war, and voted for President Johnson's impeachment as a necessity to the final crushing of slavery. In 1872 introduced a bill giving every legal civil right to the negro, which did not win his party's support. "Works of Charles Sumner," 15 vols., were issued, 1870–83. Died, Washington, D. C., 11 Mar., 1874.

SUMNER, William Graham, educator, b. Paterson, N. J., 30 Oct., 1840. Graduated at Yale. After a few years' service as an Episcopal clergyman in New York city, became professor of political and social science at Yale in 1872. Some of his works are "History of American Currency" (1874), "Andrew Jackson as a Public Man" (1882), "Economic Problems" (1884), "Essays in Political and Social Science" (1885), and "Protectionism" (1885).

SWING, David, clergyman, b. Cincinnati, O., 23 Aug., 1830. Graduated at Miami university. Head master of the university grammar school from 1854 to 1866. In the latter year was called to be pastor of a Presbyterian church in Chicago. He was tried for heresy in 1874 and was acquitted, but shortly afterward he withdrew with his congregation from the Presbyterian church and formed an independent society. In addition to several volumes of sermons he has published "The Motives of Life," "Club Essays," and "Truths for To-day" (1874).

SWINTON, John, journalist, b. Salton, Haddingtonshire, Scotland, 12 Dec., 1830. Came to Canada in 1843, and finally settled at New York city in 1857. Was a member of the N. Y. "Times" editorial staff during the civil war, afterward becoming managing editor of the N. Y. "Sun." From 1883 to 1887 he published "John Swinton's Paper," a weekly journal devoted to the furtherance of labor-reform. His most important publications are "New Issue: the Chinese-American Question" (1870), "A Eulogy on Henry J. Raymond" (1870), "John Swinton's Travels" (1880), and "Oration on John Brown" (1881).

SWINTON, William, b. Salton, Scotland, 23 April, 1833. Brother of John Swinton. Occupied as teacher and professor until 1858, when he joined the staff of the N. Y. "Times" and was its army correspondent during the civil war. Was subsequently professor of belles-lettres at the university of California. After 1874 resided in Brooklyn, N. Y., occupied with the preparation of educational works. Wrote several military histories, including "Campaigns of the Army of the Potomac" (1866) and "The Twelve Decisive Battles of the War" (1867).

SYMMES, Thomas, clergyman, b. Bradford, Mass., 1 Feb., 1678. Graduated at Harvard. Minister at Boxford, Mass., 1702–8, and at Bradford, Mass., from 1708 until his death. Author of "Lovewell Lamented; or a Sermon occasioned by the fall of the brave Capt. John Lovewell" with "Historical Memoirs of the Late Fight at Piggwacket" (1725). Died, 6 Oct., 1725.

Taney, Roger Brooke [*Noted Saying:* Vol. XI., page 453], b. Calvert Co., Md., 17 Mar., 1777. Chief-justice of U. S. supreme court, 1836–64. Died, Washington, D. C., 12 Oct., 1864.

TAPPAN, William Bingham, b. Beverly, Mass., 29 Oct., 1794. For many years a general agent of the American Sunday-school union. Was licensed to preach in 1841. Author of several volumes of poetry, largely religious. Died, West Needham, Mass., 18 June, 1849.

Tattnall, Josiah [*Noted Saying:* Vol. XI., page 453], b. near Savannah, Ga., 9 Nov., 1795. An officer in the U. S. navy until 1861. Served through the civil war in the Confederate navy. Died, Savannah, Ga., 14 June, 1871.

TAYLOR, Bayard, traveller, diplomatist, and journalist, b. Kennett Square, Chester Co., Penn., 11 Jan., 1825. Of Quaker lineage. Received a high-school education. Contributed poems to local newspapers as early as 1841, and in 1844, assisted by the advice of Rufus W. Griswold, brought out his first volume, "Ximena, and Other Poems." The same year made an arrangement with three newspapers, including the N. Y. "Tribune," by which he was to supply them with letters from abroad, and commenced

his famous walk through Europe, which lasted two years. On his return these letters were collected as "Views Afoot, or Europe seen with Knapsack and Staff" (1846). Of his subsequent books of travel eleven titles appeared, covering his journeyings in all parts of the world. The final one of the series was "Egypt and Iceland" (1874). On arriving home from one of his trips in 1853, he commenced a course of popular lectures through the country, an occupation frequently afterward followed with success. His connection with the N. Y. "Tribune" was maintained with longer or shorter intervals until his death. Of his volumes of poems there appeared "Rhymes of Travel" (1848), "A Book of Romances, Lyrics, and Songs" (1851), "Poems of the Orient" (1854), "The Poet's Journal" (1862), "The Picture of St. John" (1869), "The Masque of the Gods" (1872), "Lars, a Pastoral of Norway" (1873), "The Prophet" (1874), "Home Pastorals" (1875), "The National Ode," delivered at the Centennial of Independence (1876), and "Prince Deukalion" (1878). Deep studies in the life and works of Goethe culminated, 1870–1, in a poetical translation of "Faust," preserving the original metres. The completion of an intended life of Goethe, on a scale not hitherto attempted, was prevented by death. Mr. Taylor wrote four novels, among which "The Story of Kennett" (1866) is included. Some of his miscellanies were collected, edited, and issued posthumously by his wife, Marie Hansen-Taylor, who also, with the aid of Horace E. Scudder, completed in 1884 the "Life and Letters of Bayard Taylor." Mr. Taylor was U. S. secretary of legation at St. Petersburg in 1862, and had but recently presented his credentials as U. S. minister to Germany when overtaken by fatal illness. Died, Berlin, Germany, 19 Dec., 1878.

TAYLOR, Benjamin Franklin, b. Lowville, N. Y., 19 July, 1819. Graduated at Madison university. Early entered journalism, and was field-correspondent of the Chicago "Journal" during the civil war. Subsequently became a traveller and lecturer. Was popular as a poet in the West. Among his books are "Pictures in Camp and Field" (1871), "Old-Time Pictures, and Sheaves of Rhyme" (1874), and "Complete Poems" (1887). Died, Cleveland, O., 24 Feb., 1887.

Taylor, Zachary [*Noted Saying:* Vol. XI., p. 452], b. Orange Co., Va., 24 Sept., 1784. Served as major-general in the Mexican war. Twelfth president of the United States, 1849–50. Died, Washington, D. C., 9 July, 1850.

TECUMSEH, Indian chief, b. near the present town of Springfield, O., about 1768. A leading chief of the Shawnees. From 1804 until his death was constantly engaged in inciting the frontier tribes of the

United States to revolt against the whites. Joined forces with the English in the war of 1812. His "Life" was written by Benjamin Drake (1841). Fell at the battle of the Thames, Canada, 5 Oct., 1813.

TENNEY, Tabitha [Gilman], b. Exeter, N. H., 1762. Daughter of Samuel Gilman of that place. Educated by her mother. Was married, 1788, to Samuel Tenney, and, on his election to congress, accompanied him to Washington for several seasons. Author of "Female Quixotism : exhibited in the Romantic Opinions and Extravagant Adventures of Dorcasina Sheldon" (1808). Died, Exeter, N. H., 2 May, 1837.

TERHUNE, Mary Virginia [Hawes], "Marion Harland," b. Amelia Co., Va., 183–. Was married, 1856, to Rev. Edward P. Terhune, pastor of a Presbyterian church at Brooklyn, N. Y. In 1888 she founded the "Home-Maker," a domestic magazine. Her novels include "Alone" (1853), "Miriam" (1860), "Judith" (1883), and many others. Of her several books on domestic economy the most noted is "Common Sense in the Household" (1871).

THACHER, Anthony, colonist, b. England, about 1588. A resident of Salisbury, Wiltshire. Sailed for Boston in the *James*, arriving 3 June, 1635. Wrecked on Thacher's island, Cape Ann, the August following, when all on board were lost, except his wife and himself. His "Narrative" was written as a letter shortly after this event, and was first printed in Increase Mather's "Illustrious Providences" (1684). Died, Yarmouth, Mass., 1668.

THACHER, James, physician, b. Barnstable, Mass., 14 Feb., 1754. Studied medicine there under Dr. Abner Hersey, and served as a surgeon in the American army through the Revolution, being present at many important actions in that struggle. Subsequently practised at Plymouth, Mass. Issued a number of medical works and an "American Medical Biography" (1828). The chief of his more purely literary publications is his "Military Journal of the American Revolutionary War" (1823, revised ed. 1827). It is a trustworthy and interesting record of events witnessed by the author. Died, Plymouth, Mass., 26 May, 1844.

THAXTER, Celia [Laighton], b. Portsmouth, N. H., 29 June, 1836. Her father was Thomas B. Laighton, keeper of the lighthouse on the Isles of Shoals, N. H. Her girlhood and much of her subsequent life were passed on these islands. She was married, 1851, to Levi Lincoln Thaxter, well known as an interpreter of Browning's poetry. A series of papers by Mrs. Thaxter in the "Atlantic Monthly" was collected as "Among the Isles of Shoals" (1873). This was followed by "Poems" (1874), "Drift-

weed" (1878), "Poems for Children" (1884), and "The Cruise of the Mystery, and Other Poems" (1886).

THAYER, Stephen Henry, banker, b. New Ipswich, N. H., 16 Dec., 1839. Studied at Appleton academy, N. H. Removed to Tarrytown, N. Y., in 1868, and afterward resided there, conducting a banking business in New York city. A contributor of poetry and essays to the magazines, and author of "Songs of Sleepy Hollow" (1886).

THAYER, William Roscoe, b. Boston, Mass., 16 Jan., 1859. Graduated at Harvard. Occupied with editorial work in Philadelphia, Penn., from 1882 to 1885. Became instructor in English at Harvard, 1888. Issued "Confessions of Hermes, and Other Poems" (1884), "Hesper; an American Drama" (1888), and "The Best Elizabethan Plays" (1890).

THOMAS, Edith Matilda, b. Chatham, O., 12 Aug., 1854. Educated at the Geneva, O., normal school. She had contributed occasionally to various periodicals when in 1881 she made the acquaintance of Mrs. Helen Jackson. Mrs. Jackson became deeply interested in Miss Thomas's poetical work, and encouraged her to write for the magazines. The latter's poems at once came into popular favor. In 1888 Miss Thomas removed to New York city. Her volumes are "A New Year's Masque, and Other Poems" (1885), "The Round Year" (1886), and "Lyrics and Sonnets" (1887).

THOMAS, Frederick William, b. Providence, R. I., 25 Oct., 1808. Was admitted to the bar and practised law at different periods, but was chiefly occupied with journalism in Ohio and South Carolina. Author of the song "'Tis said that absence conquers love," and issued "The Emigrant," poem (1833), "The Beechen Tree, and Other Poems" (1840), and several novels. Died, Washington, D. C., 30 Sept., 1866.

THOMAS, Gabriel, colonist. The dates and places of his birth and death are not known. A member of William Penn's company of Quakers, sailing from England in one of the first vessels, the *John and Mary*, 1681. He resided in Pennsylvania and New Jersey for fifteen years, and had returned to England by 1698, when he published "An Historical and Geographical Account of the Province and Country of Pensilvania, and of West-New-Jersey."

THOMPSON, Benjamin, Count Rumford, physicist and statesman, b. Woburn, Mass., 26 Mar., 1753. Received a common-school education, which he followed up with mathematical and medical studies. He afterward attended a course of lectures in physics at Harvard. Taught school at Rumford (now Concord), N. H., and received an appointment in the militia, but official jealousy and suspicion of his loyalty to the

American cause deprived him of this office and prevented him from joining the Continental army. Sailed for England in 1775, and became under-secretary in the British colonial office. In 1781 returned to America as an officer in the British army. Entered the service of the elector of Bavaria at the close of the Revolution as aide-de-camp and chamberlain. Reorganized the Bavarian army and instituted many domestic reforms. Became minister of war, and in 1790 was made a count of the Holy Roman Empire, with the title of Rumford, taken from his place of residence in New Hampshire. From 1795 to 1799 lived at intervals in England, and in 1802 removed permanently to Paris. During all his residence in Europe he had been occupied with scientific investigations, which resulted in numerous useful inventions. At Paris he chiefly interested himself with researches in light and heat. Some of his many pamphlets and papers were collected as "Essays, Political, Economical, and Philosophical" (1796), and in 1876 appeared "Rumford's Complete Works," in five volumes. Died, Auteuil, near Paris, France, 21 Aug., 1814.

THOMPSON, Daniel Pierce, b. Charlestown, Mass., 1 Oct., 1793. Graduated at Middlebury college, and entered the bar. Was clerk of the Vermont legislature, 1830–3, and compiled the "Laws of Vermont from 1824 to 1834." Was judge of probate, 1837–40, clerk of the supreme court, 1843–5, and secretary of state, 1853–5. From 1849 to 1856 edited the "Green Mountain Freeman." Among his publications are "The Adventures of Timothy Peacock, Esq., or Freemasonry Practically Illustrated" (1835), "May Martin, or the Money-Diggers" (1835), "The Green Mountain Boys, a Romance of the Revolution" (1840), "Locke Amsden, or the Schoolmaster" (1845), "Lucy Hosmer" (1848), "The Rangers, or the Tory's Daughter" (1851), "Tales of the Green Mountains" (1852), "Gaut Gurley, or the Trappers of Lake Umbagog" (1857), "The Doomed Chief" (1860), "Centeola, and Other Tales" (1864), and "History of Montpelier, 1781–1860." Died, Montpelier, Vt., 6 June, 1868.

THOMPSON, John, clergyman, b. near Belfast, Ireland, about the beginning of the eighteenth century. Ordained deacon in the Church of England at London, 1734. Subsequently became rector of St. Mark's parish, Culpeper county, Va., and married the widow of Governor Spotswood. His amusing letter, presenting arguments why she should marry him, is preserved in Slaughter's "History of St. Mark's Parish."

THOMPSON, John Randolph [Reuben, in Appleton's Cyc. Amer. Biog.], journalist, b. Richmond, Va., 23 Oct., 1823. Graduated at the university of Virginia. Entered the profession of the law at Richmond, but soon abandoned it to assume the editorship of the "Southern Literary Messenger," which he held for twelve years. This magazine under his administration attained a position of much literary importance. He was obliged to resign his office in 1859, on account of failing strength, and for a while edited a paper in Augusta, Ga. Sailed for London in 1863, and gained a temporary improvement in health. While there contributed to various English journals. Returned to America and was literary editor of the N. Y. "Evening Post" until 1872, when his health again failed, and a trip to Denver, Col., proved of no avail. His poems have never been collected. Died, New York, N. Y., 30 April, 1873.

THOMPSON, Maurice, b. Fairfield, Ind., 9 Sept., 1844. Was taken as a child to Kentucky, and subsequently to northern Georgia, where he received his education from private tutors. Entered the Confederate service at the opening of the civil war and served through that struggle. Afterward removed to Indiana, and was occupied with railroad surveying and engineering for some years. Finally studied law and established a practice at Crawfordsville, Ind. From 1885 to 1889 he was state geologist of Indiana, resuming his law business in the latter year. A frequent contributor to the magazines and periodicals. Became in 1890 a staff writer for the N. Y. "Independent." His volumes include "Hoosier Mosaics" (1875), "The Witchery of Archery" (1878), "A Tallahassee Girl" (1882), "His Second Campaign" (1882), "Songs of Fair Weather" (1883), "At Love's Extremes" (1885), "Byways and Bird Notes" (1885), "Sylvan Secrets, in Bird-Songs and Books" (1887), "The Story of Louisiana" (1888), and "A Fortnight of Folly" (1888).

THOMPSON, William Tappan, journalist, b. Ravenna, O., 31 Aug., 1812. After various journalistic adventures, founded in 1850 the Savannah, Ga., "Morning News," for which he wrote until his death. Served in the Confederate army during the civil war. Author of several humorous books, of which "Major Jones's Courtship" (1840) is the most noted. Died, Savannah, Ga., 24 Mar., 1882.

THOREAU, Henry David, b. Concord, Mass., 12 July, 1817. Graduated at Harvard, 1837. His father was a man of small means, and Henry kept himself, working in various ways, teaching school, lecturing, writing, surveying, making pencils, engineering, and carpentering. He had little respect for society, much for simplicity of life; carried his individualism into practice, withdrew from society, and never married. In 1839 he and a brother spent a week in a home-made boat, camping out. Ten years later appeared his account of the trip, "A Week on the Concord and Merrimac Rivers" (1849), a book of unique interest. With a few dollars of capital he bought some lumber, cut and carried more, built himself, 1845, a hut on the edge of Walden pond, on ground owned by Emerson, and lived in it for two and a quarter years. He farmed a little and did odd jobs for neighbors to eke out his sustenance during the winter months. In his account of his life here, "Walden, or Life in the Woods" (1854), he tells how he managed. He was always a resident of Concord. Though a stoic in practice, he had a soaring imagination, and enjoyed to the full companionship with Homer and with the great poets down to the seventeenth century. Went to prison rather than pay taxes to a state that sanctioned slavery. Held strong views upon social questions, and found keen enjoyment in associating with and learning the habits of the birds and animals. In his early manhood he had written some verse, of which fragments only remain. Contributed much to "The Dial," "Democratic Review," "Graham's," "Putnam's," and the "Union" magazines, the "Atlantic Monthly," and the N. Y. "Tribune." He was a close student of nature, and original in his interpretations. Five additional books appeared after his death, "Excursions in Field and Forest," with a memoir by Emerson (1863), "The Maine Woods" (1864), "Cape Cod" (1865), "Letters to Various Persons" (1865), and "A Yankee in Canada" (1866). Died, Concord, Mass., 6 May, 1862.

THORPE, Thomas Bangs, journalist, b. Westfield, Mass., **1** Mar., 1815. Edited various papers in Louisiana, and in 1859 became proprietor of the N. Y. "Spirit of the Times." His sketch entitled "Tom Owen, the Bee-Hunter," first brought him reputation. Among his books are "Mysteries of the Backwoods" (1846), "The Hive of the Bee-Hunter" (1854), and "Scenes in Arkansaw" (1858). Died, New York, N. Y., Oct., 1878.

TICKNOR, Francis Orrery, physician, b. Baldwin Co., Ga., 1822. Studied medicine in New York city and Philadelphia, and practised as a physician near Columbus, Ga. His lyrics of the civil war were favorites in the South. A posthumous volume of "Poems" appeared in 1879, edited by Paul H. Hayne. Died, near Columbus, Ga., 1874.

TICKNOR, George, b. Boston, Mass., 1 Aug., 1791. Graduated at Dartmouth. Admitted to the bar, 1813. Spent four years in study in Europe. Was appointed during his absence professor of modern languages and literature in Harvard. His lectures attracted many scholarly auditors besides the students. Resigned his chair in 1835, after having introduced new and valuable methods based on his observations at European colleges. Spent four years in Europe, 1835–8, and, returning, devoted his whole time to the production of his great work, the "History of Spanish Literature" (1849, new and revised editions in 1854, 1863, and 1871). This was accepted at once as a standard work by European critics. In addition to this he brought out a "Syllabus of a Course of Lectures on the History and Criticism of Spanish Literature" (1823), "Outline of the Principal Events in the Life of General Lafayette" (1825), "Remarks on Changes lately Proposed or Adopted in Harvard University" (1825), "Report of the Board of Visitors on the U. S. Military Academy at West Point" (1826), "Remains of Nathan Appleton Haven, with a Memoir" (1827), and "Life of William Hickling Prescott" (1863). The "Life, Letters and Journals of George Ticknor" appeared in 1876. Died, Boston, Mass., 26 Jan., 1871.

TILDEN, ——, b. 1686. Issued a volume entitled "Tilden's Miscellaneous Poems on Divers Occasions, Chiefly to Animate and Rouse the Soldiers" (1756). It was written at the time of the French and Indian war, and was reprinted in the N. Y. "Historical Magazine" for 1859–60. Tilden died about 1766.

TILTON, Theodore, journalist, b. New York, N. Y., 2 Oct., 1835. Graduated at the college of New York. Joined the editorial staff of the N. Y. "Independent" in 1856, retaining the connection until 1871. Founded and edited the N. Y. "Golden Age," 1872–4. Devoted much time to lecturing. Resided in Europe after 1883. Author of "The Sexton's Tale, and Other Poems" (1867), "Tempest Tossed," romance (1873), and "Thou and I," poems (1880).

TIMROD, Henry, b. Charleston, S. C., 8 Dec., 1829. Studied, without graduating, at the university of Georgia. Began the study of the law, but abandoned it, and followed the occupation of a private tutor until the civil war. He then entered journalism, first as a war correspondent, and afterward as editor of a paper in Columbia, S. C. All his belongings were destroyed by the burning of that city at the time of Sherman's march to the sea, and he succumbed to a burden of ill-health and poverty within two years. Many of his war lyrics were favorites in the South. A volume of his poems was published in 1860, and in 1873 appeared "The Poems of Henry Timrod, Edited, with a Sketch of the Poet's Life, by Paul H. Hayne." Died, Columbia, S. C., 6 Oct., 1867.

TINCKER, Mary Agnes, b. Ellsworth, Me., 18 July, 1833. Studied at the Blue Hill, Me., academy. Became a member of the Roman Catholic church in 1863, and acted as hospital nurse in Washington, D.

C., during the latter part of the civil war. Afterward resided in Boston until 1873, chiefly occupied in writing for the "Catholic World." In that year she went to Italy, returning to Boston in 1887. Her books include "The House of Yorke," novel (1872), "A Wingèd Word," stories (1873), "Grapes and Thorns" (1874), "Six Sunny Months" (1878), "Signor Monaldini's Niece" (1879), "By the Tiber" (1881), "The Jewel in the Lotus" (1884), "Aurora" (1885), and "Two Coronets" (1889).

"T. M." The manuscript relation signed with these initials was purchased by Rufus King at an auction sale in London, and by him forwarded to Thomas Jefferson in 1803. It is dated 13 July, 1705, thirty years after the events it describes, and is in the form of a report to Robert Harley, principal secretary of state of Great Britain, who had asked the writer for an account of the so-called "Bacon's Rebellion." The manuscript was first printed in the Richmond, Va., "Enquirer" for Sept., 1804, and afterward in "Force's Historical Tracts." "T. M." is supposed by Charles Campbell to have been Thomas Matthews, son of Col. Samuel Matthews, sometime governor of Virginia. "T. M.," by his own account, was a member of the Virginia assembly.

TODD, John, clergyman, b. Rutland, Vt., 9 Oct., 1800. Graduated at Yale. Was pastor of the first Congregational church in Pittsfield, Mass., from 1842 to 1872. A founder of the Mount Holyoke female seminary. His writings were voluminous, and some of his books reached a sale of over a hundred thousand copies. Author of "Lectures to Children" (1834–58), "Student's Manual" (1835), and "Woman's Rights" (1867). Died, Pittsfield, Mass., 24 Aug., 1873.

TOMPSON, Benjamin, educator, b. Braintree, Mass., 14 July, 1642. Graduated at Harvard. Became principal of the Harvard preparatory school at Cambridge, 1670. The first native New England poet. Selections from his "New England's Crisis" are given in Kettell's "Specimens of American Poetry." The poem was published about 1675, and dealt with King Philip's war, then in progress. Several short pieces by Tompson are found in Mather's "Magnalia." Died, probably at Roxbury, Mass., 13 April, 1714.

TOOMBS, Robert, legislator, b. Washington, Ga., 2 July, 1810. Graduated at Union college, and entered the bar. Was U. S. representative from Georgia, 1845–53, and U. S. senator, 1853–61. Resigned from the senate at the opening of the civil war, and became a member of the Confederate cabinet. Soon after entered the Confederate army as brigadier-general. Refused to take the oath of allegiance after the war, and never regained his political rights. Died, Washington, Ga., 15 Dec., 1885.

TOURGÉE, Albion Winegar, b. Williamsfield, O., 2 May, 1838. Served in the Union army during the civil war. Subsequently established himself as a lawyer and editor at Greensboro', N. C., meeting with the experiences which form the basis of his reconstruction novels. Was judge of the superior court of North Carolina, 1868–74. Edited "The Continent" at Philadelphia, 1882–5. Author of "A Fool's Errand" (1879), "Bricks without Straw" (1880), and "An Appeal to Cæsar" (1884).

TOWLE, George Makepeace, b. Washington, D. C., 27 Aug., 1841. Graduated at Yale. Was for several years U. S. consul in France and England, returning to America in 1870, and entering journalism at Boston, Mass. Some of his books are "Glimpses of History" (1865), "American Society" (1870), "Beaconsfield" (1878), "Certain Men of Mark" (1880), "England and Russia in Asia" (1885), and "England in Egypt" (1886).

TOWNSEND, George Alfred, "Gath," b. Georgetown, Del., 30 Jan., 1841. Entered journalism in 1860. Was correspondent for the N. Y. "Herald" and "World" during the civil war, and afterward became a lecturer and general writer for periodicals. Author of "Campaigns of a Non-Combatant" (1865), "Poems" (1870), "Washington Outside and Inside" (1871), "Tales of the Chesapeake" (1880), and "The Entailed Hat" (1884).

TOWNSEND, Mary Ashley [Van Voorhis], "Xariffa," b. Lyons, Wayne Co., N. Y., 1832. Was married to Gideon Townsend of New Orleans, La., which city became her permanent home. Was appointed to deliver the poem at the opening of the New Orleans exposition of 1884. Her books are "The Brother Clerks" (1859), "Poems" (1870), "The Captain's Story" (1874), and "Down the Bayou, and Other Poems" (1882).

TROWBRIDGE, John Townsend, b. Ogden, Monroe Co., N. Y., 18 Sept., 1827. The son of a farmer, he gained his education in country schools and by self-instruction. Removed to New York city, 1846, and to Boston, 1848, supporting himself by contributions to periodicals. Subsequently devoted himself entirely to literary work. Gained reputation as a writer of popular books for the young, and as a delineator of New England life. "The Vagabonds" is his best-known poem. Some of his books are "Father Brighthopes" (1853), "Neighbor Jackwood," novel (1857), "The Drummer-Boy," (1863), "The Vagabonds, and Other Poems" (1869), "Coupon Bonds, and Other Stories" (1871), "The Emigrant's Story, and Other Poems" (1875), and "The Lost Earl, and Other Poems" (1888).

TRUMBULL, James Hammond, philologist, b. Stonington, Conn., 20 Dec., 1821. Resided in Hartford, Conn., after 1847, and was secretary of state for Connecticut, 1861-4. Was made president of the Connecticut Hist. Soc. in 1863, and became an officer and member of many other learned societies. Issued numerous works relating to the Indian languages of North America and the history of Connecticut.

TRUMBULL, John, lawyer, b. Westbury, now Watertown, Conn., 24 April, 1750. Cousin of Gov. Jonathan Trumbull. Graduated at Yale, 1767, having passed the entrance-examination when seven years old, though not admitted until the age of thirteen. In 1769 published with Timothy Dwight, in Boston and New Haven periodicals, a series of essays after the manner of the "Spectator." Was tutor at Yale from 1771 to 1773, when he was admitted to the bar at New Haven. Afterward studied in the office of John Adams at Boston, finally returning to New Haven to practise. Published "The Progress of Dulness," 1772-4, a satirical poem on the educational methods of the time. He contributed to the literature of the Revolution an "Elegy on the Times" (1774), relating to the Boston port bill, and his famous "M'Fingal, a Modern Epic Poem" (1774-82). The latter was written in Hudibrastic verse, and satirized the follies of his countrymen as well as those of their enemies. More than thirty pirated editions of this poem were issued. Trumbull removed to Hartford in 1781, and was there associated with the "Hartford Wits" in the production of "The Anarchiad" (1786-7). In 1801 he was made judge of the superior court, serving until 1819. From 1825 until his death he resided at Detroit, Mich. "The Poetical Works of John Trumbull" appeared in 1820. Died, Detroit, Mich., 10 May, 1831.

TRUMBULL, John, artist, b. Lebanon, Conn., 6 June, 1756. Graduated at Harvard. Served as an aide-de-camp of Washington early in the Revolution, but resigned in 1777, and studied art at London under Benjamin West. He remained in Europe for long periods, and when in America resided chiefly in New York city. His best-known paintings are the historical scenes in the rotunda of the capitol at Washington, and his portraits of George Washington. Issued his "Autobiography," 1841. Died, New York, N. Y., 10 Nov., 1843.

TUCKER, Nathaniel Beverley, b. Matoax, Va., 6 Sept., 1784. Son of St. George Tucker. Graduated at William and Mary college. Entered the bar, and was judge in the circuit court of Missouri, 1815-30. Appointed professor of law in William and Mary, 1834, where he continued until his death. The most striking of his books was "The Partisan Leader; by Edward William Sydney" (1836). It purported to be a historical novel, written as in 1856, and it was a singularly accurate forecast of the course of events during the civil war. It was suppressed, reissued in 1861, with the title "A Key to the Disunion Conspiracy," and again suppressed. Also wrote "George Balcombe," novel (1836), and "Principles of Pleading" (1846). Died, Winchester, Va., 26 Aug., 1851.

TUCKER, St. George, jurist, b. Island of Bermuda, 10 July, 1752. Graduated at William and Mary college. His law-practice in Virginia was interrupted by service in the American army during the Revolution. Appointed a judge in the Virginia general court, 1787. Judge of the state court of appeals, 1804-11. Author of several important legal works and a volume of poetical satires, besides fugitive poems. Died, Warminster, Nelson Co., Va., 10 Nov., 1828.

TUCKERMAN, Bayard, b. New York, N. Y., 2 July, 1855. Graduated at Harvard. A resident of his native city, and chiefly occupied with literary work. Issued "A History of English Prose Fiction" (1882) and "Life of General Lafayette" (1889), and edited, with an introduction, "Diary of Philip Hone" (1889).

TUCKERMAN, Henry Theodore, b. Boston, Mass., 20 April, 1813. Visited France and Italy in 1833 and 1837. Settled in New York city, 1845, and from that time pursued an unbroken literary career, chiefly as a critic and essayist. Author of "The Italian Sketch Book" (1835), "Rambles and Reveries" (1841), "Thoughts on the Poets" (1846), "Artist-Life, or Sketches of American Painters" (1847), "Characteristics of Literature" (1851), "Poems" (1851), "A Month in England" (1853), "Leaves from the Diary of a Dreamer" (1853), "Essays, Biographical and Critical" (1857), "America and her Commentators" (1864), "A Sheaf of Verse" (1864), "The Criterion, or the Test of Talk about Familiar Things" (1866), "Maga Papers about Paris" (1867), "Book of the Artists" (1867), and "Life of John Pendleton Kennedy" (1871). Died, New York, N. Y., 17 Dec., 1871.

TUDOR, William, b. Boston, Mass., 28 Jan., 1779. Graduated at Harvard. A founder of, and a frequent contributor to, the Boston "Monthly Anthology" (1803-11). In 1815 began at Boston the publication of the "North American Review," the first four volumes of which were mostly written by him. Was elected to the Massachusetts legislature, and held U. S. diplomatic positions in Peru and Brazil. Originated the Bunker Hill monument. Author of "Letters on the Eastern States" (1820),

"Miscellanies" (1821), etc. Died, Rio Janeiro, Brazil, 9 Mar., 1830.

TURELL, Ebenezer, clergyman, b. Boston, Mass., 5 Feb., 1702. Graduated at Harvard. Minister at Medford, Mass., 1724–78. In addition to one or two sermons, he published "The Life and Character of the Reverend Benjamin Colman" (1749), his father-in-law, and "Memoirs of the Life and Death of the Pious and Ingenious Mrs. Jane Turell" (1735), his wife. Died, Medford, Mass., 8 Dec., 1778.

TURELL, Jane [Colman], b. Boston, Mass., 25 Feb., 1708. Daughter of Benjamin Colman, and educated by him, showing early proficiency. Was married, 1726, to the Rev. Ebenezer Turell. Much of her poetry is preserved in his "Memoirs of the Life and Death of the Pious and Ingenious Mrs. Jane Turell" (1735). Died, Medford, Mass., 26 Mar., 1735.

Tweed, William Marcy [*Noted Saying:* Vol. XI., page 455], b. New York, N. Y., 3 April, 1823. Was appointed commissioner of public works in that city, 1870. Died there, 12 April, 1878.

TYLER, Moses Coit, educator, b. Griswold, Conn., 2 Aug., 1835. Graduated at Yale. Entered the Congregational ministry and was pastor of a church at Poughkeepsie, N. Y., 1860–2. Was appointed professor of the English language and literature at the university of Michigan in 1867, remaining there until 1881, when he became professor of American history at the university of Cornell. In the latter year he was ordained a deacon in the Protestant Episcopal church. At one time literary editor of "The Christian Union." Author of "Brawnville Papers" (1868), "A History of American Literature" (Vols. I., II., 1879), "Manual of English Literature" (1879), and "Life of Patrick Henry" (1888).

TYLER, Royall, jurist, b. Boston, Mass., 18 July, 1758. Graduated at Harvard. Studied law with John Adams. During the Revolution, and afterward at the time of Shays's rebellion, served for short periods as aide-de-camp to Gen. Benjamin Lincoln. While visiting New York city on matters connected with the latter event, he wrote the play entitled "The Contrast, a Comedy in Five Acts," the first American comedy regularly produced by a company of professional actors. It was acted by the "American company" at the John street theatre, 16 April, 1787, and met with considerable success. The following month another play by Tyler, "May-Day in Town, or New York in an Uproar," a comic opera in two acts, was brought out by the same company. In 1797 "A Good Spec, or Land in the Moon," was produced at Boston, and at least one other play from his pen is known to have been acted. "The Contrast" was printed,

1790, and was reissued, 1887, by the Dunlap society of New York city, with an introduction by Thomas J. McKee. Tyler removed to Vermont, 1790, where he continued to practise his profession. In 1794 he was elected a judge, and in 1800 chief-justice, of the supreme court of that state. At the same time he was very active in literary work, writing for a number of periodicals, and producing in book form "The Algerine Captive" (1797), "Moral Tales for American Youths" (1800), and "The Yankey in London" (1809). Some of his lighter work, contributed to the Walpole, N. H., "Farmer's Weekly Museum," is collected with that of Joseph Dennie in "The Spirit of the Farmer's Museum" (1801). "Reports of Cases in the Supreme Court of Vermont" appeared in 1809. Died, Brattleboro', Vt., 16 Aug., 1826.

UNDERHILL, Capt. John, colonist. Came to Massachusetts with John Winthrop in 1630. Had served as a British officer in the Netherlands and elsewhere. Gained distinction in the expedition against the Pequot Indians in 1637, sharing command at the destruction of the Mystic fort. Shortly after, he was removed from office and banished from the Massachusetts colony with other so-called Antinomians. Visited England and issued his "Newes from America" in 1638. Became governor of Dover and Exeter in the New Hampshire settlement, and later removed to Connecticut and Long Island, in which places he held several public offices. Carried on for the Dutch governor at New Amsterdam his war with the Connecticut Indians in 1646. Supposed to have died at Oyster Bay, L. I., about 1672.

UPHAM, Charles Wentworth, b. St. John, N. B., 4 May, 1802. Graduated at Harvard. Entered the Unitarian ministry, resigning from ill health, 1844. Was mayor of Salem, Mass., a member of the Massachusetts legislature, and was U. S. representative, 1853–5. Chiefly remembered for his "Lectures on Witchcraft, a History of the Salem Delusion" (1831), which he enlarged and issued as "Salem Witchcraft" (1867). Also wrote several biographies. Died, Salem, Mass., 14 June, 1875.

UPTON, George Melville, b. Sutter Creek, Amador Co., Cal., 28 Oct., 1861. For some time occupied with literary and journalistic work at San Francisco, and more recently a writer for the Denver, Col., "Times." Contributor of verse to the magazines.

Van Buren, Martin [*Noted Saying:* Vol. XI., page 450], b. Kinderhook, N. Y., 5 Dec., 1782. Eighth president of the United States, 1837–41. Died, Kinderhook, 24 July, 1862.

VAN RENSSELAER, Mariana [Griswold], b. New York, N. Y., 25 Feb., 1851.

Daughter of George Griswold. Was married, 1874, to Schuyler Van Rensselaer, of her native city. A writer on art and architecture for the magazines, and author of "American Etchers" (1886), "Henry Hobson Richardson and his Works" (1888), and "Six Portraits; Della Robbia, Correggio," etc. (1889).

VENABLE, William Henry, educator, b. near Waynesville, Warren Co., O., 29 April, 1836. Graduated at the Lebanon, O., normal school. Was a professor at the Chickering institute, Cincinnati, from 1862 to 1881, when he became its president, retiring in 1886. Issued "June on the Miami, and Other Poems" (1871), "Melodies of the Heart" (1885), and several historical works.

VERPLANCK, Gulian Crommelin, b. New York, N. Y., 6 Aug., 1786. Graduated at Columbia, and entered the bar. Professor of Christian evidences and moral science in the N. Y. Protestant Episcopal General theological seminary, 1821–5. U. S. representative from New York, 1825–33, and a member of the state senate, 1838–41. Delivered many addresses, and published, among other writings, "The Bucktail Bards, a Political Tale," and "The Epistles of Brevet Major Pindar Puff," political satires (1819), "Essays on the Nature and Uses of Various Evidences of Revealed Religion" (1824), and "Shakespeare's Plays; with His Life, a Critical Introduction, and Notes" (1847). Was co-editor with Bryant and R. C. Sands of the "Talisman" annual (1828–30), of which selections were published as "Miscellanies from the Talisman" (1833). Died, New York, N. Y., 18 Mar., 1870.

VERY, Jones, b. Salem, Mass., 28 Aug., 1813. Graduated at Harvard. Entered the Unitarian ministry, and preached occasionally, though never regularly ordained. Author of "Poems and Essays" (1839). Editions of his "Poems" were published in 1883 and 1886, containing memoirs of the author. Died, Salem, Mass., 8 May, 1880.

VINCENT, Marvin Richardson, clergyman, b. Poughkeepsie, N. Y., 11 Sept., 1834. Graduated at Columbia. Pastor of Presbyterian churches in Troy, N. Y., and New York city from 1863 to 1888. In the latter year became a professor in the N. Y. Union theological seminary. Issued a number of religious works, including several volumes of sermons.

WADSWORTH, Benjamin, clergyman, b. Milton, Mass., 1669. Graduated at Harvard. Preached at the First church in Boston from 1693 to 1725. President of Harvard from the latter year until his death. Author of a number of published sermons, among them "King William Lamented in America" (1702). Died, Cambridge, Mass., 16 Mar., 1737.

WALKER, Amasa, political economist, b. Woodstock, Conn., 4 May, 1799. In business until 1840. Professor of political economy at Oberlin college, 1842–8, and lecturer on the same subject at Amherst, 1860–9. U. S. representative from Massachusetts, 1862–3. Among his writings are "The Nature and Uses of Money and a Mixed Currency" (1857) and "The Science of Wealth, a Manual of Political Economy" (1866). Died, North Brookfield, Mass., 29 Oct., 1875.

WALKER, Francis Amasa, statistician, b. Boston, Mass., 2 July, 1840. Son of Amasa Walker. Graduated at Amherst. Served through the civil war in the Union army, receiving the brevet of brigadier-general of volunteers. Superintendent of the censuses of 1870 and 1880. Professor of political economy in the Yale Sheffield scientific school, 1873–81. Became president of the Massachusetts institute of technology in 1881. His works include "The Wages Question" (1876), "Money" (1878), "Land and Its Rent" (1883), and "Political Economy" (1883).

WALKER, Katharine Kent [Child], b. Pittsfield, Vt., 1842. Was married, 1863, to Rev. Edward A. Walker, of Worcester, Mass. After his death in 1866, resided chiefly in New Haven, Conn. Author of the article entitled "The Total Depravity of Inanimate Things," published in the "Atlantic Monthly" for 1864, and of a "Life of Christ" (1869).

WALKER, Robert James [John, in Appletons' Cyc. Amer. Biog.], statesman and financier, b. Northumberland, Penn., 23 July, 1801. Graduated at the university of Pennsylvania. Practised law in Mississippi, and was U. S. senator from that state, 1837–45. Secretary of the treasury under President Polk, 1845–9. As financial agent of the United States, disposed of large quantities of government bonds in Europe during the civil war. His most important publications were four letters on "American Finances and Resources" (London, 1863–4). Died, Washington, D. C., 11 Nov., 1869.

WALLACE, Horace Binney, b. Philadelphia, Penn., 26 Feb., 1817. Graduated at the college of New Jersey. Studied medicine, chemistry, law, and finally philosophy, overstudy in the latter causing insanity, during which he committed suicide. Issued a novel, "Stanley" (1838), and edited several legal works. His "Art, Scenery, and Philosophy in Europe" (1855) and "Literary Criticism and Other Papers" (1856) were brought out posthumously. Died, Paris, France, 16 Dec., 1852.

WALLACE, Lewis, soldier, b. Brookville, Franklin Co., Ind., 10 April, 1827. Was a lieutenant in the Mexican war and afterward practised law in his native state.

Served in the civil war and rose to the rank of major-general of volunteers, receiving special mention from General Grant for meritorious conduct. Afterward followed the legal profession in Crawfordsville, Ind., excepting the interval from 1881 to 1885, when he was U. S. minister to Turkey. Author of "The Fair God" (1873) and "Ben-Hur, a Tale of the Christ" (1880). The latter of these novels reached a sale of nearly three hundred thousand copies. In 1888 appeared "The Boyhood of Christ."

WALLACE, William Ross, lawyer, b. Lexington, Ky., 1819. Practised law in New York city after 1841, contributing occasionally to the magazines. His "Meditations in America, and Other Poems" (1851) contains the piece entitled "Of thine own country sing." Other popular poems were "The sword of Bunker Hill" (1861), "Keep step with the music of the Union" (1861), and "The Liberty Bell" (1862). Died, New York, N. Y., 5 May, 1881.

WALLEY, Thomas, clergyman, b. England, about 1616. Ejected from a rectorship at London for non-conformity, and emigrated to New England, 1663, settling at Barnstable, Cape Cod. Was opposed to harsh treatment of the Quakers and to the abuse of the friendly Indians in King Philip's war. Published "Balm in Gilead to heal Sions Wounds" (1669), an election-sermon. Died, Barnstable, Mass., 24 Mar., 1679.

WALSH, Robert, b. Baltimore, Md., 1784. After a long sojourn in Europe, returned and edited "The American Review of History and Politics," the earliest American quarterly, 1811–13, and again from 1827 to 1837. U. S. consul at Paris, 1845–51. Author of "Essay on the Future State of Europe" (1813), "An Appeal from the Judgments of Great Britain respecting the United States of America" (1819), and "Didactics ; Social, Literary," etc., (1836). Died, Paris, France, 7 Feb., 1859.

WALWORTH, Jeannette Ritchie [Hadermann], b. Philadelphia, Penn., 22 Feb., 1837. Was early taken to Natchez, Miss. Was married to Maj. Douglas Walworth, and removed to Arkansas, subsequently residing in Louisiana and in New York city. Author of numerous works of fiction, including "Forgiven at Last" (1870), "The Bar Sinister" (1885), and "Southern Silhouettes" (1887).

WARD, Elizabeth Stuart [Phelps], b. Andover, Mass., 13 Aug., 1844. Daughter of Prof. Austin Phelps, of the Andover theological seminary, and Elizabeth (Stuart) Phelps, the latter a popular author of her period. Mrs. Ward always resided at Andover, where she became identified with local charitable organizations. She also took a deep interest in temperance and other re-

form movements, including that in behalf of the advancement of women. Was married, 1888, to Rev. Herbert D. Ward, of New York city. Author of "Poetic Studies," poems (1875), "Songs of the Silent World" (1885), "The Struggle for Immortality," essays (1889), and many works of fiction, among which are "Ellen's Idol" (1864), "Mercy Gliddon's Work" (1866), "The Gates Ajar" (1868), "Men, Women, and Ghosts" (1869), "The Silent Partner" (1870), "The Trotty Book" (1870), "The Story of Avis" (1877), "Old Maids' Paradise" (1879), "Beyond the Gates" (1883), "Dr. Zay" (1884), "The Gates Between" (1887), "Come Forth" (1890), and, in collaboration with her husband, "The Master of the Magicians" (1890).

WARD, Nathaniel, lawyer and clergyman, b. probably in Haverhill, Suffolk, England, 1578–80 (John Ward Dean). Son of an eminent divine. Graduated at Cambridge university. Bred to the law, and practised for some years, but had entered the ministry by 1618. Silenced for non-conformity in 1633. Came to New England and settled as minister at Ipswich (formerly Agawam), Mass., in 1634, resigning this position two years later. Ward, John Cotton, and others were appointed by the general court of Massachusetts in March, 1638, to draw up models of a code of laws for the colony. That of Ward's was adopted as the "Body of Liberties" in Oct., 1641, and was the first code adopted in New England. "The Simple Cobler of Aggawam in America," his most noted book, was sent for publication to England late in 1646. Four editions appeared in 1647. It abounds in humorous and sarcastic hits at his religious and political opponents. Other books are "A Religious Retreat Sounded to a Religious Army" (1647), "Sermon before Parliament" (1647), etc. Returned to England in 1647, settled as minister at Shenfield, Essex, in 1648, and probably died there, Oct., 1652.

WARD, Samuel, b. New York, N. Y., 27 Jan., 1813. Brother of Julia Ward Howe. Graduated at Columbia. Specially skilled in European languages and Indian dialects. Was several times employed on diplomatic missions for the United States to Central and South America. After 1862 lived for many years at Washington, D. C. Issued "Lyrical Recreations" (1871). Died, Pegli, Italy, 19 May, 1884.

WARD, William Hayes, b. Abington, Mass., 25 June, 1835. Graduated at Amherst. Pastor of a Congregational church in Kansas, 1860–1, and professor of Latin at Ripon college, Wis., until 1868. In 1870 became superintending editor of the N. Y. "Independent." Headed the Wolfe expedition to Babylonia, 1884, and issued a pamphlet report on his return. An extensive writer on archæological subjects, and a contributor to the magazines.

WARE, Henry, Jr., clergyman, b. Hingham, Mass., 21 April, 1794. Brother of William Ware. Graduated at Harvard. Pastor of the Second Unitarian church, Boston, 1817–30, and Parkman professor in the Harvard divinity school, 1830–42. His works include " On the Formation of Christian Character" (1831), "Life of the Saviour" (1832), and several biographies. Died, Framingham, Mass., 22 Sept., 1843.

WARE, William, clergyman, b. Hingham, Mass., 3 Aug., 1797. Graduated at Harvard. Entered the ministry, and was pastor of the First Congregational church in New York city, 1821–36, after which he officiated for short periods in Waltham and West Cambridge, Mass. He was obliged to forego preaching on account of ill-health. Was editor and proprietor of the "Christian Examiner," 1839–44. After making a tour of Europe in 1848–9, he delivered a course of lectures on European travel. Contributed a series of descriptive papers to the " Knickerbocker Magazine," which were afterward collected into a volume as "Letters from Palmyra" (1837), republished in England under the title, "Zenobia; or the Fall of Palmyra" (1838). This was followed by "Probus" (1838, revised and reissued as " Aurelian," 1848), "Julian, or Scenes in Judea" (1841), "American Unitarian Biography" (1850–1), "Sketches of European Capitals" (1851), and "Lectures on the Works and Genius of George Washington Allston" (1852). Died, Cambridge, Mass., 19 Feb., 1852.

WARING, George E., Jr., sanitary expert, b. Poundridge, Westchester Co., N. Y., 4 July, 1833. Studied agriculture with Prof. James J. Mapes, and was agricultural and drainage engineer of Central park, New York city, 1857–61. Served in the Union army during the civil war, becoming colonel in the Missouri cavalry. Was occupied with agriculture and engineering at Newport, R. I., from 1867 to 1877, when he turned his attention entirely to drainage engineering. Appointed a member of the National board of health in 1882. Some of his technical works are " Elements of Agriculture " (1854), "Draining for Profit and Draining for Health " (1867), " Handy Book of Husbandry" (1870), and "Sewerage and Land Drainage" (1888). His literary works include "Whip and Spur " (1875), "The Bride of the Rhine " (1877), and "Tyrol and the Skirt of the Alps" (1879).

WARNER, Charles Dudley, journalist, b. Plainfield, Mass., 12 Sept., 1829. Graduated at Hamilton college. While there contributed articles to the " Knickerbocker Magazine." Projected a literary monthly at Detroit in 1853, but, the plan failing, joined a surveying party on the Missouri frontier, remaining with them during 1853 and 1854. In 1856 he graduated at the law school of the university of Pennsylvania, and practised law at Chicago until 1860. In that year he became assistant editor, and in 1861 editor, of the Hartford "Press." This paper was in 1867 consolidated with the Hartford "Courant," and Mr. Warner became joint editor of the latter journal, which position he afterward held. Passed long periods in European and Eastern travel, and some of his letters to the " Courant " were gathered in a volume entitled "Saunterings "(1872). Other books of travel are "My Winter on the Nile " (1876) and "In the Levant " (1877). He had previously written a series of sketches for the "Courant," describing in a humorous way his experiences as an amateur gardener. These were collected and published as "My Summer in a Garden" (1870), with an introduction by Henry Ward Beecher, and made a hit. "Backlog Studies' (1872) consists of essays in a similar vein, some of which had appeared in the predecessor of the "Century Magazine." Other books are "Baddeck and That Sort of Thing" (1874), "In the Wilderness" (1878), "Captain John Smith" (1881), "Washington Irving" (1881), "Roundabout Journey" (1883), "Their Pilgrimage" (1886), and "On Horseback" (1888). The last two volumes and several series of articles on the present condition of the United States and Mexico are the outcome of a staff-editorship on "Harper's Magazine," assumed in 1884, and including the supervision of the "Editor's Drawer" of that periodical. Delivered numerous addresses and orations on public occasions, and before learned societies and college alumni.

WARNER, Susan, "Elizabeth Wetherell," b. New York, N. Y., 11 July, 1819 (A. B. Warner). Daughter of Henry Warner, of the N. Y. bar. Her popular novel, "The Wide, Wide World," appeared in 1851, and finally reached a sale of a quarter of a million copies, exclusive of European editions. This book was followed by "Queechy" (1852), "The Law and the Testimony" (1853), "Hills of the Shatemuc" (1856), "The Old Helmet" (1863), "Melbourne House" (1864), "Daisy" (1868), "Stories on the Lord's Supper " (1875), "The Broken Walls of Jerusalem" (1878), and "The Kingdom of Judah" (1878). Died, Highland Falls, N. Y., 17 Mar., 1885.

WARREN, Emily. An early contributor to the San Francisco, Cal., "Overland Monthly."

Warren, Fitz-Henry [*Noted Saying:* Vol. XI., page 454], b. Brimfield, Mass., 11 Jan., 1816. Brigadier-general of volunteers in the Union army during the civil war. At one time connected with the N. Y.

"Tribune." Died, Brimfield, Mass., 21 June, 1878.

WARREN, Joseph, physician and soldier, b. Roxbury, Mass., 11 June, 1741. Great-grandson of Robert Calef. Graduated at Harvard. Began the practice of medicine, 1764. Wrote numerous articles criticising the British government from the passage of the stamp-act in 1765. Was elected president of the Massachusetts congress, 31 May, 1775. Fourteen days later was made a major-general by that body. Delivered the annual commemorative orations on the "Boston Massacre" in 1772 and 1775. Fell at Bunker's Hill, 17 June, 1775.

WARREN, Mercy [Otis], b. Barnstable, Mass., 25 Sept., 1728. A sister of James Otis. Was married, 1754, to James Warren, a Plymouth merchant, afterward president of the Massachusetts provincial congress. Mrs. Warren was an intimate friend of the Massachusetts leaders in the American Revolution, and was in continual correspondence with them during the war, her advice being sought by them and often followed. Author of "The Adulator" (1773) and "The Group" (1775), dramatic satires at the expense of the loyalists; also two tragedies "The Sack of Rome" and "The Ladies of Castile." The latter was included in a volume of "Poems, Dramatic and Miscellaneous" (1790). In 1805 appeared her "History of the American Revolution," a well-written work, valuable from the author's contemporaneous knowledge of events. It involved her in a long correspondence with John Adams, to whose early monarchical tendencies she had referred. These letters were published by the Mass. Hist. Society in 1878, as the "Correspondence of John Adams and Mercy Warren." Died, Plymouth, Mass., 19 Oct., 1814.

WASHINGTON, George, first president of the United States, b. on Pope's Creek, Westmoreland Co., Va., 22 Feb., 1732. The son of Augustine and Mary Ball Washington. Received a common-school education. From sixteen until nineteen years of age was public surveyor of Culpeper county, Va. Served with honor in the French and Indian war, particularly at General Braddock's defeat, where he acted as voluntary aide to the latter, who disregarded his advice. Was a member of the Virginia house of burgesses, 1760–75. A delegate to the first and second Continental congresses, and was chosen by the second commander-in-chief of the Continental army, 15 June, 1775. He compelled the British to evacuate Boston in March, 1776. Was defeated at the battles of Long Island (Aug., 1776), White Plains (Oct., 1776), Brandywine (Sept., 1777), and Germantown (Oct., 1777). Won the battles of Trenton (Dec., 1776) and Princeton (Jan., 1777), and finally captured Cornwallis's army at Yorktown, Va., 19 Oct., 1781, with the aid of the French army under Rochambeau. Resigned his commission as commander-in-chief, 23 Dec., 1783. Was president of the Constitutional convention of 1787. Inaugurated president of the United States, 30 April, 1789, he was reëlected for a second term, and declined a third in his "Farewell Address," issued 19 Sept., 1796. Selections from his papers and letters were published in twelve volumes by Jared Sparks as "The Writings of Washington" (1834–7), and a more complete and corrected collection has been prepared by Worthington C. Ford (1888–90). Died, Mount Vernon, Va., 14 Dec., 1799.

WASSON, David Atwood, clergyman, b. Brooksville, Me., 14 May, 1823. Studied at Bowdoin college. Became a Unitarian clergyman, and in 1865–6 was minister of Theodore Parker's society in Boston. Afterward held a position in the custom-house of that city. His work in prose and verse appeared in the periodicals. A posthumous volume of "Poems" was brought out in 1888. Died, West Medford, Mass., 21 Jan., 1887.

WATSON, Elkanah, agriculturist, b. Plymouth, Mass., 22 Jan., 1758. During the early portion of his life was engaged in business at Providence, R. I. Carried government despatches to Franklin at Paris in 1779, and remained in France for several years. In 1789 removed from Providence to Albany, N. Y., and later to Pittsfield, Mass., where he occupied himself with agricultural pursuits and founded the Berkshire agricultural society. At Albany he had taken a prominent part in furthering state improvements. Issued among other works "History . . . of the Western Canals in the State of New York" (1820) and "History of Agricultural Societies" (1820). "Men and Times of the Revolution" (1856) was edited by his son from his journals and letters. Died, Port Kent, N. Y., 5 Dec., 1842.

WATSON, John Fanning, b. Batsto, Burlington Co., N. J., 13 June, 1779. Engaged in mercantile pursuits at Philadelphia, Penn., for the greater part of his life, and was cashier of the Bank of Germantown for thirty-three years. Published "Annals of Philadelphia" (1830), "Historic Tales of Olden Time" (1832), and "Annals and Occurrences of New York City and State" (1846). Died, Germantown, Penn., 23 Dec., 1860.

WATTERSON, Henry, journalist, b. Washington, D. C., 16 Feb., 1840. Entered journalism at an early age in that city. Served through the civil war in the Confederate army. In 1867 succeeded George D. Prentice as editor of the Louisville, Ky., "Courier," which the following year became the "Courier-Journal." U. S. representative from Kentucky, 1876–7. A contributor to the periodicals, and delivered numerous addresses on occasions.

WAYLAND, Francis, scholar, b. New York, N. Y., 11 Mar., 1796. Graduated at Union college. Pastor of Baptist church at Boston, Mass., 1821–6. President of Brown university, 1827–55. Some of his works are "Occasional Addresses" (1833), "Elements of Moral Science" (1835), "Elements of Political Economy" (1837), and "Elements of Intellectual Philosophy" (1854). Died, Providence, R. I., 30 Sept., 1865.

WEBB, Charles Henry, "John Paul," b. Rouse's Point, N. Y., 24 Jan., 1834. Ran away to sea as a lad, returning after three years and engaging in business at Chicago. A member of the N. Y. "Times" editorial staff from 1860 to 1863, when he removed to California. Founded "The Californian," a weekly journal, in 1864, and edited it at intervals until 1866. Afterward became a banker and broker in New York city. Also patented "Webb's adder" and other inventions. Author of several plays and travesties and of "John Paul's Book" (1874), "Parodies, Prose, and Verse" (1876), and "Vagrom Verse" (1889).

WEBSTER, Daniel, statesman, b. Salisbury (now Franklin), N. H., 18 Jan., 1782. Graduated at Dartmouth. Studied law at Salisbury and with Christopher Gore at Boston, and was admitted to the bar, 1805. Practised at Boscawen, N. H., until 1807, when he removed to Portsmouth, soon establishing a reputation, which in after years became unsurpassed, as a lawyer and orator. Was U. S. representative from New Hampshire, 1813–17, and from Massachusetts, 1823 –7. In 1827 he was made U. S. senator from the same state. He held this office until 1839, and again from 1845 to 1850, having meanwhile been secretary of state for three years under Presidents Harrison and Tyler. He resumed that dignity for the last two years of his life under President Fillmore. As a Federalist he opposed in congress the war of 1812, and generally supported his party during his first two terms. In his second period of service, after advocating free trade at first, he became on election to the U. S. senate a supporter of Henry Clay and the protective system. This involved him in the great debate with Hayne, when the latter expounded the theory of nullification. Three years later, in 1833, Webster and Calhoun debated the same theme. Webster's speech in behalf of the compromise of 1850 alienated many of his Northern adherents. The most famous of his public orations are those on the Bunker Hill monument and on the Pilgrim anniversary, and the eulogium on Jefferson and Adams. A collection of his "Works" was published in 1851, and one of his "Private Correspondence" in 1856. Died, Marshfield, Mass., 24 Oct., 1852.

WEBSTER, Noah, philologist, b. Hartford, Conn., 16 Oct., 1758. Graduated at Yale, serving in the Continental army during a portion of his college course. Studied law and was admitted to the bar, 1781, but soon began teaching at Goshen, N. Y. In 1783 published at Hartford his famous spelling-book, of which over sixty millions have been sold. It appeared as the first part of "A Grammatical Institute of the English Language," of which the remaining two parts, an English grammar and reader, followed in the next two years. "Dissertations on the English Language," a series of lectures, was issued in 1789. At that date he again began to practise law in Hartford, having edited the "American Magazine" at New York city during the previous year. From 1793 to 1798 he edited an administration newspaper at the latter city. Subsequently resided chiefly in New Haven, Conn., where in 1807 he began the preparation of "An American Dictionary of the English Language" (1828). An enlarged edition was published in 1840, since which time the work has been frequently reëdited and extended by various scholarly hands. Other books were "A Collection of Essays and Fugitive Writings" (1790) and "A Collection of Papers on Political, Literary, and Moral Subjects" (1843). From 1812 to 1822 he lived at Amherst, Mass., where he took an active interest in the founding of Amherst college. Died, New Haven, Conn., 28 May, 1843.

WEED, Thurlow, journalist, b. Cairo, N. Y., 15 Nov., 1797. Began life as a printer. After various journalistic experiences, established the Albany, N. Y., "Evening Journal" in 1830, and conducted it until 1865 in the Whig and Republican interests. Visited Europe with Archbishop Hughes in 1861 to secure the non-intervention of the powers in favor of the Confederate government. His "Autobiography" (1883) was issued posthumously. Died, New York, N. Y., 22 Nov., 1882.

WEEKS, Robert Kelley, b. New York, N. Y., 21 Sept., 1840. Graduated at Yale. Studied for the law, but soon abandoned it, and devoted himself to literary work. Author of "Poems" (1866) and "Episodes and Lyric Pieces" (1870). Died, New York, N. Y., 13 April, 1876.

WEEMS, Mason Locke, clergyman, b. Dumfries, Va., about 1760 (Appleton). Studied theology at London, and was at one time rector of Mt. Vernon parish, during Washington's residence there. Afterward a book-agent for Mathew Carey of Philadelphia. Besides temperance tracts which he sold on his travels, he wrote "The Life of

George Washington" (1800), "The Life of Benjamin Franklin" (1817), "The Life of William Penn" (1819), and, from material furnished by Gen. Peter Horry, "The Life of Gen. Francis Marion" (1805). These books are written in a romantic, exaggerated style and contain various apocryphal stories of their subjects. Died, Beaufort, S. C., 23 May, 1825.

WEISS, John, clergyman, b. Boston, Mass., 28 June, 1818. Graduated at Harvard. Pastor of a Unitarian church at Watertown, Mass., 1843–70, excepting a withdrawal of several years on account of his abolitionist and woman's rights views. Lectured on Greek religious ideas and on Shakespearian subjects. Issued "Life and Correspondence of Theodore Parker" (1864), "American Religion" (1871), and "Wit, Humor, and Shakespeare" (1876). Died, Boston, Mass., 9 Mar., 1879.

WELBY, Amelia B. [Coppuck], b. St. Michael's, Md., 3 Feb., 1819 (Drake). Was married, 1838, to George B. Welby, of Louisville, Ky. Wrote a number of poems for the Louisville "Journal," which were published in a volume entitled "Poems by Amelia" (1849). Died, Louisville, Ky., 3 May, 1852.

WELCH, Philip Henry, journalist, b. Angelica, N. Y., 1 Mar., 1849. Followed mercantile pursuits for a number of years. Entered journalism on the Rochester, N. Y., "Post Express" in 1882. Two years later joined the staff of the N. Y. "Sun." He gained wide reputation as a writer of jokes. Author of "The Tailor-Made Girl" (1888) and "Said in Fun" (1889). Died, Brooklyn, N. Y., 24 Feb., 1889.

WELDE, Thomas, clergyman, b. England. Graduated at Cambridge university. Preached for some time at Terling, Essex. Emigrated to Boston in New England, 1632, and was at once ordained the first minister of Roxbury. Was a leader in the trial and banishment of Mrs. Anne Hutchinson and other so-called Antinomians. With Richard Mather and John Eliot published the "Bay Psalm Book" in 1640 (see MATHER, RICHARD). Was sent to England with Hugh Peters in 1641 as the colony's agent, and did not return. Obtained a living at Gateshead, England, from which he was ejected at the restoration. The preface to "A Short Story . . . of the Antinomians" (1644) is undoubtedly his, the authorship of the book itself being in dispute. Died, England, about 1662.

WELLS, David Ames, economist, b. Springfield, Mass., 17 June, 1828. Graduated at Williams. Engaged in scientific studies under Agassiz at Harvard. Edited a number of compilations of writings on the natural sciences, from 1850 to 1866. Issued in 1864 a political tract entitled "Our Burden and Our Strength," which reached an enormous circulation. Was U. S. special commissioner of revenue, 1866–70, commissioner on tax legislation for the state of New York, 1870–3, and was afterward occupied as an arbitrator in railroad matters. At first an advocate of protection, he was led by his studies to embrace free trade, and wrote numerous books and pamphlets advocating the latter system. Besides his reports as government and state commissioner, there have appeared, among other similar writings, "The Creed of the Free-Trade" (1875), "Why We Trade, and How We Trade" (1878), "Our Merchant Marine" (1882), "Practical Economics" (1885), and "Relation of the Tariff to Wages" (1888).

WENDELL, Barrett, educator, b. Boston, Mass., 23 Aug., 1855. Graduated at Harvard, where he became instructor in 1880, and subsequently assistant professor of English. A contributor of fiction and verse to the magazines, and author of "The Duchess Emilia; a Romance" (1885) and "Rankell's Remains" (1887).

WHEATON, Henry, lawyer, b. Providence, R. I., 27 Nov., 1785. Graduated at Brown. Entered the bar, 1805. Edited the N. Y. "National Advocate," 1812–15. Held various judicial appointments until he went to Denmark as U. S. chargé d'affaires in 1827. Was U. S. minister to Prussia, 1835–46. His works include "History of the Northmen, or Danes and Normans" (1831) and "Elements of International Law" (1836). Died, Roxbury, Mass., 11 Mar., 1848.

WHEELER, Capt. Thomas, colonist, b. England. Had emigrated to Concord, Mass., by 1642. A captain in King Philip's war, 1675–6, and in charge of the troops at the siege of Quaboag, now Brookfield, Mass., an account of which is given in "A Thankefull Remembrance of Gods Mercy to several Persons at Quaboag or Brookfield" (1676). Died, Concord, Mass., 16 Dec., 1686.

WHIPPLE, Edwin Percy, b. Gloucester, Mass., 8 Mar., 1819. Educated at the English high school, Salem, Mass. At fourteen began to write for the newspapers. Was appointed superintendent of the news room of the merchants' exchange, Boston, 1837. A critique on Macaulay in the "Boston Miscellany" (1843) gained him a place among the foremost critical writers, and won Macaulay's thanks. Lectured the same year on "The Lives of Authors," and thus began a long and successful platform career. In "Essays and Reviews" (2 vols., 1849) were comprised a series of careful studies of notable poets, statesmen, preachers, novelists, and advocates. A selection of lectures entitled "Literature and Life" appeared in 1849. Gave up his superintendency of the news room to devote himself exclusively to literary work in 1860. Was literary editor of the Boston "Globe," 1872-3. Besides much magazine work there appeared during his life "Character and Characteristic Men" (1866), "The Literature of the Age of Elizabeth" (1869), and "Success and its Conditions" (1871). Edited with James T. Fields the "Family Library of British Poetry" (1878). "Recollections of Eminent Men" (1887), "American Literature, and Other Papers" (1887), and "Outlooks on Society, Literature, and Politics" (1888) were issued posthumously. Died, Boston, Mass., 16 June, 1886.

WHISTLER, James Abbott McNeill, painter, b. Lowell, Mass., 1834. Studied at West Point. Received instruction in art from the painter Gleyre at Paris, and resided in London after 1863. Attracted attention for his daring experiments with colors. Author of "Ten O'Clock," a lecture (1888), and "The Gentle Art of Making Enemies" (1890).

WHITAKER, Alexander, clergyman, b. Cambridge, England, 1585. Graduated at Cambridge university. Was comfortably settled as a Church of England clergyman in one of the northern counties of England, but came to Virginia as a missionary with Sir Thomas Dale in May, 1611, and was settled as minister at Henrico the same year. Removed to Jamestown in 1614, and afterward to Bermuda Nether Hundred. The evidence that he married John Rolfe and Pocahontas is merely inferential. His "Good Newes from Virginia" appeared in London, 1613. Died, by drowning, in Virginia, before July, 1617.

WHITCHER, Frances Miriam [Berry], "Widow Bedott," b. Whitesboro, N. Y., 1 Nov., 1811. Began contributing poems and humorous sketches to the press about 1846. Was married, 1847, to Rev. Benjamin W. Whitcher, of Elmira, N. Y. "The Widow Bedott Papers" (1856) and "Widow Spriggins" (1867) were collected posthumously from her writings. Died, Whitesboro, N. Y., 4 Jan., 1852.

WHITE, Andrew Dickson, educator, b. Homer, N. Y., 7 Nov., 1832. Graduated at Yale, and continued his studies in Europe. Accepted the chair of history and English literature at the university of Michigan, 1857. Entered the New York state senate, 1864, where he effected valuable school legislation and managed the incorporation of Cornell university. In 1865 was elected the first president of that institution, to which he presented a large endowment and a valuable historical library. His health obliged him to resign this position in 1885. From 1879 to 1881 he was U. S. minister to Germany, and he served in other diplomatic positions. In addition to contributions to the magazines and reviews, he issued, among other works, "Outlines of a Course of Lectures on History" (1861), "The Warfare of Science" (1876), and "On Studies in General History," etc. (1885).

WHITE, Horace, journalist, b. Colebrook, N. H., 10 Aug., 1834. Graduated at Beloit college, Wis. Entered journalism, and joined the staff of the Chicago "Tribune," of which he was editor and a chief proprietor from 1864 to 1874. His noted account of the great Chicago fire of 1871 was contributed in the form of a letter to the Cincinnati "Commercial." Joint editor with E. L. Godkin of the N. Y. "Evening Post" after 1883. Edited American editions of Frederic Bastiat's "Sophismes économiques" (1869) and Luigi Cossa's "Scienza della finanze" (1888).

WHITE, Richard Grant, b. New York, N. Y., 22 May, 1821 (Stanford White). Graduated at the university of New York. Intended for the ministry, he first took up medicine and then law, and was admitted to the bar in 1845. Literature, however, soon engrossed his attention. He was a writer of musical, dramatic, and art criticisms for the N. Y. "Courier and Enquirer" from 1845 to 1859, and the last four years its editor. Some of his essays were gathered in a volume entitled "Biographical and Critical Hand-Book of Christian Art" (1853). A series of articles in "Putnam's Magazine" questioning the reliability of Collier's folio-MS. emendations of Shakespeare appeared in 1853, and was published with other studies in Shakespeare as "Shakespeare's Scholar" (1854). This volume gained him the fullest recognition as a scholar and critic. From 1857 to 1865 appeared a twelve-volume edition of Shakespeare's Works, with notes and essays. A fancy for anonymous writing was well illustrated during the civil war, when he wrote the celebrated "New Gospel of Peace; According to St. Benjamin" (1863-6), a satire which had a wide-spread effect in crystallizing the feeling of loyalty at the North. He also contributed a series of letters to the London "Spectator" over the signature of "A Yankee," which were of undoubted service to the Union cause. He became an authority on the English language, and published "Words and Their Uses" (1870) and "Every-Day English" (1881). Other works were "Life and Genius of Shakespeare" (1865), "England Without and Within" (1881), "The Riverside Edition of Shakespeare" (1883), and "The Fate of Mansfield Humphreys" (1884). At the time of his resignation in 1878, Mr. White had been for nearly twenty years chief of the U. S. revenue-marine bureau in the district of New York. Died, New York, N. Y., 8 April, 1885.

WHITE, William, clergyman, b. Philadelphia, Penn., 4 April, 1748. Graduated at the college of Philadelphia. Was rector of various churches at Philadelphia until 1786, when he was elected first Protestant Episcopal bishop of Pennsylvania. His most important literary work was "Memoirs of the Protestant Episcopal Church in the United States" (1820). Selections from his letters appear in the "Memoir" of his life (1839). Died, Philadelphia, Penn., 17 July, 1836.

WHITING, Charles Goodrich, journalist, b. St. Albans, Vt., 30 Jan., 1842. Was taken as a child to Springfield, Mass., where he afterward resided. In 1866 became a reporter for the Springfield "Republican," of which journal he was made literary editor and general editorial writer in 1874. Delivered the ode at the dedication of the soldiers' monument in Springfield, 1885. "The Saunterer" (1886) contains selections from his writings in prose and verse.

WHITMAN, Sarah Helen [Power], b. Providence, R. I., 1803. Best known for her intimate friendship with Poe, with whom, in her widowhood, she made a conditional engagement of marriage. Wrote frequently for the periodicals. Issued "Hours of Life, and Other Poems" (1853), and "Edgar Poe and His Critics" (1860). "Poems" (1879) was brought out posthumously. Died, Providence, R. I., 27 June, 1878.

WHITMAN, Walt(er), b. West Hills, Long Island, N. Y., 31 May, 1819. Educated in public schools. In early manhood followed the callings of printer in summer and school-teacher in winter, and assisted as editor of several country papers. In 1847–8 tramped through various states and part of Canada. Published "Leaves of Grass" (1855), being his own compositor. Another edition followed in 1856. These poems attracted wide notice, being of a new order in motive and rhythm. Much controversy in regard to them has raged from then to now, the author's interest being served thereby, and by the action of the Massachusetts authorities in suppressing on the score of indecency a reissue in 1881. An expurgated edition appeared in England, where a school of admirers grew up and continued to flourish. Whitman volunteered as army nurse during the war, serving in Washington and Virginia, 1862–5. His constitution was impaired by this good work. Received an appointment as clerk in the Interior Department at Washington in 1865, from which he was deposed in 1866 by a superior who did not approve of his poetry. W. D. O'Connor's pamphlet, in denunciation of this absurd act, was entitled "The Good Gray Poet," a sobriquet which permanently attached itself to Whitman. Shortly afterward he was made a clerk in the attorney-general's office, holding his new position for eight

years. A sharp paralytic stroke in 1873 led to his continuous enfeeblement, and he afterward resided at Camden, N. J. His popularity was not that of lucrative sales. From time to time his many friends on both sides the ocean took measures to supply his modest needs. In 1887 he was invited to give a lecture upon Abraham Lincoln at the Madison square theatre, New York city, the ticket-takers and ushers being his fellow authors. Following the "Leaves of Grass" came "Drum Taps" (1865), a reminiscence of the war, and prose "Memoranda during the War" (1867). Later appeared "Democratic Vistas" (1870), of which an English edition was issued in 1888 with a new preface by the author. "Passage to India" was brought out in the same year (1870), and contains his most popular poem, the "Burial Hymn of Lincoln." Among later volumes are "After All, not to Create Only" (1871), "As Strong as a Bird on Pinions Free" (1872), "Specimen Days, and Collect" (1883), "November Boughs" (1888), "Sands at Seventy" (1888), and collective editions of his works entitled "Leaves of Grass and Two Rivulets; Centennial Edition" (1876) and "Complete Poems and Prose" (1889).

WHITNEY, Adeline Dutton [Train], b. Boston, Mass., 15 Sept., 1824. Was married at the age of nineteen and removed to Milton, Mass., where she afterward mainly resided. Author of books for young people, including "A Summer in Leslie Goldthwaite's Life" (1866), and of several novels and volumes of poems, among the latter of which are "Pansies" (1872), "Daffodils" (1887), and "Bird-Talk" (1887).

WHITNEY, Anne, sculptor, b. Watertown, Mass., 2 Sept., 1821 (Appleton). Cultivated an early taste for art and literature during a four years' residence in Europe, whence she returned in 1873 and established a studio in Boston. Two of her best-known works are the statue of Samuel Adams, in Washington, and the Leif Erikson fountain, in Boston. Published a volume of "Poems" (1859.)

WHITNEY, William Dwight, philologist, b. Northampton, Mass., 9 Feb., 1827. Graduated at Williams, and then studied in Germany. Accepted the professorship of Sanskrit at Yale in 1854, to which were added the duties of the chair of comparative philology in 1870. A member and officer of many learned societies in Europe and America. In 1867 was published "Language and the Study of Language," a series of lectures previously delivered before the Smithsonian Institute. Other books are "Compendious German Grammar" (1869), "German Reader in Prose and Verse" (1870), "Oriental and Linguistic Studies," first, second, and third series (1873–5), "Life and Growth of Language" (1876),

"Essentials of English Grammar" (1877), "Sanskrit Grammar" (1879), and "Practical French Grammar" (1886). Much of Professor Whitney's most important work was contributed to literary and philological magazines. He superintended the revision of "Webster's Dictionary," and was chief of the editorial staff of "The Century Dictionary."

WHITON, James Morris, clergyman, b. Boston, Mass., 11 April, 1833. Graduated at Yale. Rector of Hopkins grammar school, New Haven, Conn., 1854–64. Pastor of Congregational churches in Massachusetts and New Jersey until 1886, when he assumed charge of Trinity Congregational church, Tremont, New York city. His religious works include "Is Eternal Punishment Endless?" (1876), "The Gospel of the Resurrection" (1881), and "The Law of Liberty, and Other Discourses" (1889).

WHITTIER, Elizabeth Hussey, b. Haverhill, Mass., 7 Dec., 1815. Sister of John G. Whittier. She wrote a number of graceful poems, selections from which are included by her brother in his "Hazel Blossoms" (1874). Died, Amesbury, Mass., 3 Sept., 1864.

WHITTIER, John Greenleaf, b. Haverhill, Mass., 17 Dec., 1807. His ancestors had been members of the Society of Friends, almost from their first emigration to Massachusetts in 1738, and Mr. Whittier retained their faith. Received a slender schooling as a boy, and was chiefly occupied with farmwork until his twentieth year, when, at the suggestion of William Lloyd Garrison, to whose journal, the Newburyport "Free Press," he had contributed verses, Whittier studied for two terms at the Haverhill academy. The money to pay for his attendance was earned by a winter's work at shoemaking, and by a term of school-teaching. During the winter of 1828–9 he edited at Boston the "American Manufacturer," at the same time contributing poetry to John Neal's magazine, "The Yankee." From 1830 to 1832 he edited successively the Haverhill "Gazette" and the Hartford, Conn., "New England Weekly Review," in the latter of which over forty of his poems first appeared. Returning to Haverhill in 1832 he remained there until 1837, engaged in managing the family farm and in anti-slavery agitation, at the same time writing for the anti-slavery press and for various magazines. He was made secretary of the American anti-slavery society in 1836, and the following year removed to Philadelphia, where he edited the "Pennsylvania Freeman" for two years. In 1840 he took up his permanent residence at Amesbury, Mass., and afterward lived there and at "Oak Knoll" in Danvers. Most of his literary work from 1847 to 1857 was printed in the "National

Era" of Washington, D. C., a leading anti-slavery paper. In the latter year the "Atlantic Monthly" was founded, and thereafter he wrote chiefly for that magazine. His works include "Legends of New England in Prose and Verse" (1831), "Poems, chiefly relating to Slavery" (1838), "Ballads" (1838), "Lays of My Home, and Other Poems" (1843), "Voices of Freedom" (1849), "Songs of Labor, and Other Poems" (1850), "The Chapel of the Hermits, and Other Poems" (1853), "A Sabbath Scene" (1853), "The Panorama, and Other Poems" (1856), "Home Ballads" (1860), "In War Time, and Other Poems" (1863), "Snow Bound" (1866), "The Tent on the Beach, and Other Poems" (1867), "Among the Hills, and Other Poems" (1868), "Miriam, and Other Poems" (1870), "The Pennsylvania Pilgrim" (1872), "Mabel Martin" (1874), "Hazel Blossoms" (1875), "Centennial Hymn" (1876), "The Vision of Echard" (1878), "The King's Missive" (1881), "The Bay of Seven Islands" (1883), "Poems of Nature" (1885), and "St. Gregory's Guest, and Recent Poems" (1886); also the following prose volumes : "The Stranger in Lowell" (1845), "Supernaturalism in New England" (1847), "Leaves from Margaret Smith's Journal" (1849), "Old Portraits and Modern Sketches" (1850), and "Literary Recreations" (1854). A complete edition of "The Writings of John Greenleaf Whittier" appeared in 1888–9.

WIGGLESWORTH, Michael, clergyman, b. England, 18 Oct., 1631. Brought to America, 1638. Graduated at Harvard, where he served as a tutor while studying for the ministry. Was ordained pastor of the church at Malden, Mass., in 1657. He filled this position until his death, with the exception of periods amounting to about twenty years, during which he was prevented from preaching by feeble health. This time he devoted to the study and practice of medicine, and to literary composition. His most important poem, "The Day of Doom, or a Poetical Description of the Great and Last Judgment" (1662), embodied the theological beliefs of the early New England Congregationalists, in their gloomiest aspects. It ran through ten or twelve editions, and was a favorite with this class of religious people in New England up to the end of the eighteenth century. Another poem, "Meat out of the Eater, or Meditations concerning the necessity, end, and usefulness of Afflictions unto God's Children," was published in 1669. Several poems left in manuscript have recently been printed in the issues of historical societies. Died, Malden, Mass., 10 June, 1705.

WILCOX, Ella [Wheeler], b. Johnstown, Wis., 18—. Studied at the university of Wisconsin. Was married, 1884, to Robert

M. Wilcox, of Meriden, Conn., and afterward removed to New York city. Author of "Maurine, and Other Poems" (1882), "Poems of Passion" (1883), "Mal Moulée," novel (1885), and "Poems of Pleasure" (1888).

WILDE, Richard Henry, scholar, b. Dublin, Ireland, 24 Sept., 1789. At different times attorney-general of Georgia and U. S. representative from the same state. Passed much time in studying Italian literature in Italy, where he also discovered Giotto's portrait of Dante. Wrote fugitive poems, including the song "My life is like the summer rose," and "Conjectures and Researches concerning the Love, Madness, and Imprisonment of Torquato Tasso" (1842). Died, New Orleans, La., 10 Sept., 1847.

WILKESON, Samuel, b. Buffalo, N. Y., 9 May, 1817. Graduated at Union college, and entered the bar. Edited various newspapers in Albany, N. Y., joining the staff of the N. Y. "Tribune" before the civil war. Worked for that journal and for the N. Y. "Times" until 1868, when he connected himself with the Northern Pacific railroad, of which he was secretary, 1869–89. Died, New York, N. Y., 2 Dec., 1869.

WILKINS, Mary Eleanor, b. Randolph, Mass., 18—. Daughter of Warren E. Wilkins. Educated at Mt. Holyoke seminary. Early removed to Brattleboro', Vt., returning to Randolph in 1883. A writer for the magazines, and author of " A Humble Romance, and Other Stories " (1887).

WILKINSON, James, soldier, b. near Benedict, Md., 1757. Served during the Revolution in the Continental army. Afterward traded in Kentucky, and was accused of a scheme to found a western republic. Rejoined the American army, 1791, and was its general-in-chief, 1796–1812, excepting two years. Issued "Memoirs of My Own Times" (1816). Died, near Mexico, Mex., 28 Dec., 1825.

WILKINSON, William Cleaver, clergyman, b. Westford, Vt., 19 Oct., 1833. Graduated at Rochester university. Pastor of Baptist churches in New Haven, Conn., and Cincinnati, O., until 1866. Professor in the Rochester theological seminary, 1872–81. Wrote several text-books on Greek and German literature, etc., for the Chautauqua university, and "The Dance of Modern Society" (1869), "The Baptist Principle" (1881), "Poems" (1883), and "Edwin Arnold as Poetizer and Paganizer" (1884).

WILLARD, Emma [Hart], b. New Berlin, Conn., 23 Feb., 1787. Was married, 1809, to Dr. John Willard. Principal of various schools in Vermont and New York until 1821, when she founded the Troy female seminary, conducting it until 1838. Wrote and lectured extensively on educational questions, and published many popular school books. Author of the poem "Rocked in the cradle of the deep" and much other fugitive verse. Died, Troy, N. Y., 15 April, 1870.

WILLARD, Samuel, clergyman, b. Concord, Mass., 31 Jan., 1640. Graduated at Harvard. Became assistant pastor of the old South church in Boston, 1678. In 1701 he accepted the superintendency of Harvard, on the resignation of Increase Mather. Was an opponent of the witchcraft proceedings. Author of several published sermons, and " A Compleat Body of Divinity" (issued posthumously, 1726). Died, Boston, Mass., 12 Sept., 1707.

WILLIAMS, Francis Howard, b. Philadelphia, Penn., 2 Sept., 1844. Always a resident of that city, where he became treasurer of a trust company. A reviewer and writer for the daily press, and issued " The Princess Elizabeth, a Lyric Drama" (1880), "Theodora, a Christmas Pastoral" (1882), " The Higher Education," comedy (1883), "Master and Man, a Play" (1886), and " Boscosel " in " The Septameron " (1888).

WILLIAMS, George Washington, b. Bedford Springs, Penn., 16 Oct., 1849. His father was of Welsh and negro parentage, his mother of German and negro extraction. Served in the Union army during the civil war, then in the Mexican army. Held several political offices in Ohio and elsewhere, and was appointed U. S. minister to Hayti by President Arthur. Author of " History of the Negro Race in America " (1883), "The Negro Troops in the War of the Rebellion " (1887), and " History of the Reconstruction of the Insurgent States " (1889).

WILLIAMS, John, clergyman, b. Roxbury, Mass., 16 Dec., 1664. Graduated at Harvard. Minister at Deerfield, Mass., from 1686 until his death, except for the period of his captivity in Canada from 1704 to 1706. Related his experiences as a prisoner in "The Redeemed Captive Returning to Zion" (1707). Died, Deerfield, Mass., 12 June, 1729.

WILLIAMS, Roger, colonist, b. probably in London, England, about 1600 (H. F. Waters). Sir Edward Coke supervised his education. Graduated at Cambridge university, became a clergyman, and soon after a non-conformist. Sailed in the *Lion* from Bristol, arriving at Nantasket, Mass., 5 Feb., 1631. Declined to join with the Boston congregation because they would not declare themselves separatists from the English church, and because of his opinion that civil magistrates had no jurisdiction in religious matters. Called as "teacher" of the church at Salem, April, 1631, but withdrew to Plymouth during the summer. On the death of Samuel Skelton, was regularly ordained his successor at Salem in August, 1634. The same year was summoned before the Massachusetts general court to explain his expressed opinion that the colonists had no right to their lands save as purchased from the Indians, but professed his loyalty. Persisting in his views concerning this and other questions, particularly as to man's responsibility to God alone in matters of religion not affecting the civil peace, he was banished from the colony by the general court, 3 Nov., 1635. Hearing of his plan to settle at Narragansett bay, they decided to return him to England, but he escaped to Rhode Island in January, 1636. Went first to Seekonk, but in June removed across the bay to Providence, purchasing land of the Indians, and founding the colony on a basis of religious toleration. Conveyed his ownership in the land to his companions in 1638. Started the first Baptist church in America, Mar., 1639, but soon changed his views again and became a "Seeker." Visited England, June, 1643, and obtained a charter for the Rhode Island colony. On the voyage wrote "A Key into the Languages of America" (1643). Governor of Rhode Island from 1654 to 1658. Became an adept in Indian dialects, and rendered to the colony that had banished him great services, by effecting treaties with the Narragansetts in the Pequot war and in 1645. Engaged in a controversy with John Cotton on religious liberty, in the course of which he published "Mr. Cottons Letter Lately Printed, examined" (1644), "The Bloudy Tenent of Persecution" (1644), and "The Bloody Tenent yet more Bloody" (1652). Other books were "The Hireling Minister None of Christ's" (1652), "Experiments of Spiritual Life and Health" (1652), and "George Fox digg'd out of his Burrowes" (1676), the last being an account of a dispute with the Quakers. Died, probably at Providence, R. I., early in 1683.

WILLIS, Nathaniel Parker, b. Portland, Me., 20 Jan., 1806. Graduated at Yale. His father had established various periodicals, including the "Youth's Companion," in which the son's earliest verses appeared. In 1829 the latter founded the "American Monthly Magazine," which two years later was merged in the "New York Mirror," conducted by George P. Morris. In 1831 went on a tour through Europe and the East, writing letters of his journeys to his paper. He was taken to task by English reviewers for reporting private conversations, and a severe rebuke by Captain Marryat in the "Metropolitan Magazine" led to a duel, in which, however, no blood was shed. After a sojourn at home he returned to England in 1839, and again in 1844. Left the "Mirror" in 1839 through a misunderstanding with his partner, Morris, and published the "Corsair," to which Thackeray contributed. Resumed relations with Morris, and in 1846 started with the latter the

"Home Journal," of which he remained associate editor until his death. The same year purchased the estate near Newburgh, N. Y., named by him "Idlewild," and afterward resided there. Some of his volumes are "Scripture Sketches" (1827), "Melanie, and Other Poems" (1835), "Pencillings By The Way" (1835), "Inklings of Adventure" (1836), "Loiterings of Travel" (1839), "Letters from under a Bridge" (1840), "Lady Jane, and Other Poems" (1844), "Dashes at Life with a Free Pencil" (1845), "People I Have Met" (1850), "Hurrygraphs" (1851), "Outdoors at Idlewild" (1854), "Paul Fane," novel (1857), "The Convalescent" (1859), and "Poems, Sacred, Passionate, and Humorous" (1864). Died, Idlewild, near Newburgh, N. Y., 20 Jan., 1867.

WILLSON, Forceythe, b. Little Genesee, N. Y., 10 April, 1837. Studied at Harvard. Was taken as a child to Kentucky, where he afterward formed an editorial connection with the Louisville "Journal." Wrote a number of popular war poems during the civil war. These were collected in "The Old Sergeant, and Other Poems" (1867). Died, Alfred, N. Y., 2 Feb., 1867.

WILSON, Alexander, ornithologist, b. Paisley, Scotland, 6 July, 1766. Followed the trades of a weaver and peddler in his native place for several years, during which period he issued two volumes of verse and his popular poem, "Watty and Meg." Emigrated to America, 1794, and for the next eight years was occupied with his former trades and with school-teaching in New Jersey and Pennsylvania. Becoming acquainted with the naturalist William Bartram, and with an eminent engraver at Philadelphia, he was encouraged by them, about 1804, to begin serious studies for his "American Ornithology" (1808–14). Thereafter, until his death, he was constantly occupied with this work, making numerous excursions through the country in search of new specimens of birds. Eight volumes were completed during his life, and the ninth was afterward finished by a friend. In 1876 appeared a collection of his "Poems and Literary Prose." Died, Philadelphia, Penn., 23 Aug., 1813.

WILSON, Augusta [Evans], b. Columbus, Ga., 8 May, 1835. Was taken as a child to Mobile, Ala., and there wrote her first novel in 1851, published as "Inez, a Tale of the Alamo" (1855). It was followed by "Beulah" (1859), which was immediately successful. Miss Evans was married, 1868, to L. M. Wilson, of Mobile. "St. Elmo" (1866) and "Vashti" (1869) are among her other novels.

WILSON, Epiphanius, b. Liverpool, England, 6 Jan., 1845. Graduated at Kings college, Nova Scotia, where he was professor of classics for some years. Latterly an editor of the N. Y. "Churchman." Contributed to the periodicals for many years.

WILSON, Henry, statesman, b. Farmington, N. H., 16 Feb., 1812. Educated himself under great difficulties. Was elected to the legislature of Massachusetts in 1840. Edited the Boston "Republican" as a Freesoil organ, 1848–50. President of the state senate, 1850, and succeeded Everett as U. S. senator from Massachusetts, 1855. Raised and led the 22d regiment of Massachusetts volunteers to the seat of war in 1861. Was elected vice-president in 1872. Published many addresses, histories of anti-slavery and reconstruction measures in the 37th–40th congresses, a series of articles on Secretary Edwin M. Stanton, 1868, and "History of the Rise and Fall of the Slave Power in America" (1872–5), uncompleted at the time of his death. Died, Washington, D. C., 22 Nov., 1875.

WILSON, James, statesman, b. near St. Andrews, Scotland, 14 Sept., 1742. Studied at several universities in Scotland. Came to America at twenty-one, and practised law at Reading and Carlisle, Penn. Was a delegate to the Continental congress of 1775, and signed the Declaration of Independence. Was a member of the Constitutional convention of 1787, and in 1789 was appointed a judge of the U. S. supreme court. Died, Edenton, N. C., 28 Aug., 1798.

WILSON, Robert Burns, painter, b. Washington Co., Penn., 30 Oct., 1850. Early removed to Frankfort, Ky., and devoted himself to the study of landscape painting. Some of his pictures were exhibited at the New Orleans exposition of 1884, where they attracted attention. A contributor of verse to the magazines, and author of "Life and Love. Poems" (1887).

WINCHELL, Alexander, geologist, b. North East, Dutchess Co., N. Y., 31 Dec., 1824. Graduated at Wesleyan university. Was elected a professor at the university of Michigan in 1853, and afterward served there in positions of increasing importance, excepting a few years at Syracuse university. Author of "Sketches of Creation" (1870), "The Doctrine of Evolution" (1874), "Sparks from a Geologist's Hammer" (1881), and "Walks and Talks in the Geological Field" (1886).

WINSLOW, Edward, colonist, b. Droitwich, Worcestershire, England, 19 Oct., 1595. Of an old English family. While travelling on the Continent, fell in with the Pilgrims at Leyden, and joined their church in 1617. Sailed in the *Mayflower*, Aug., 1620 (see BRADFORD, WILLIAM). By timely treatment of Massasoit when dangerously ill in 1623, he saved that sachem's life and insured his faithfulness to a treaty made with Bradford three years before. This treaty was kept by the Indians until King

Philip's war in 1675. Was assistant governor at Plymouth from 1624 to 1647, excepting the years 1633, 1636, and 1644, when he served as governor. Agent of the colony in England, 1623, 1624, 1635, and 1646, where he rendered valuable services, and wrote two books defending the colonists from the attacks of Samuel Gorton and others. These were "Hypocrisee Unmasked" (1646), to which is appended the "Briefe Narration," and "New England's Salamander" (1647). Works descriptive of the colony's experiences were "Good News from New England" (1624), "The Glorious Progress of the Gospel amongst the Indians in New England" (1649), and Winslow's share in "Bradford's and Winslow's Journal," otherwise known as "Mourt's Relation" (1622). Winslow did not return from England after 1646, but remained there until appointed by Cromwell head commissioner of the expedition, under Admiral Penn, against the Spaniards in the West Indies. This proved unsuccessful, and Winslow, falling ill, died at sea on the voyage from St. Domingo to Jamaica, 8 May, 1655.

WINSOR, Justin, librarian, b. Boston, Mass., 2 Jan., 1831. After a year at Harvard, he continued his studies at Paris and at Heidelberg. Was superintendent of the Boston public library from 1868 until his appointment as librarian of Harvard in 1877. Issued numerous historical and bibliographical works, and edited, with original contributions, "Memorial History of Boston" (1880–1) and "Narrative and Critical History of America" (1884–9).

WINTER, William, journalist, b. Gloucester, Mass., 15 July, 1836. Received his early education at Cambridge, Mass., and graduated at the Harvard law school. Was admitted to the bar at Boston, but did not practise. Was a lecturer for lyceums for a time, and also occupied with literary work. In 1854 and 1858 issued his first volumes of poems, entitled "The Convent, and Other Poems" and "The Queen's Domain." Removed to New York city in 1859, where he became literary critic for the "Saturday Press." Was dramatic critic of the N. Y. "Albion" from 1861 to 1865, when he accepted the same position on the N. Y. "Tribune," still holding it in 1890. Recited a number of poems on public occasions, among them that at the dedication of the actors' monument to Edgar A. Poe in New York city, 1885. Some of his books are "My Witness," poems (1871), "Sketch of the Life of Edwin Booth" (1871), "Thistle-Down," poems (1878), "The Jeffersons" (1881), "Henry Irving" (1885), "The Stage-Life of Mary Anderson" (1886), "English Rambles, and Other Fugitive Pieces" (1884), "Shakespeare's England" (1886), and "Wanderers," poems (1888).

WINTHROP, John, colonist, b. Edwardston, near Groton, Suffolk, England, 12 Jan., 1588. Studied at Cambridge university. Succeeded his father as lord of Groton Manor. Gave up or lost his position as an attorney of the court of wards in London, perhaps through his non-conformist sympathies, and was elected governor of the Massachusetts Company, 20 Oct., 1629. Sailed from Yarmouth in the *Arbella* with the company's second supply, arriving at Salem, 12 June, 1630, and bringing the charter with him. Settled first at Charlestown, but had removed to Boston by November. Was active in the banishment of the so-called Antinomians in 1637, holding that the colony's existence depended on its religious unity. Had previously taken part in Roger Williams's banishment, but continued his private relations with the founder of Rhode Island, and was his life-long correspondent. In 1638 saved the colony's charter, which had been called for from England, by a diplomatic letter excusing the sending of it. In 1643 headed the commissioners of Massachusetts who met with others from the Plymouth, Connecticut, and New Haven colonies and formed the old New England Union and Confederation, of which Winthrop was the originator and first president. Was elected governor of Massachusetts eleven times, and held many other important offices. His "Modell of Christian Charity," written on the voyage from England, was first printed by the Mass. Hist. Society. The "History of New England," a fount of information concerning events in Massachusetts for the period it covers, was written as a daily journal in three manuscript volumes. Of these the first two were copied and printed in 1790. On the discovery of the third in the tower of the old South church in 1816, the whole work was edited and printed by James Savage in 1825–6 (revised ed. 1853). "Life and Letters," by Robert C. Winthrop, appeared in 1866. Winthrop's speech defining civil liberty, made after his acquittal from charges of unduly exercising his power as a magistrate, has become a classic. Died, Boston, Mass., 26 Mar., 1649.

WINTHROP, John, scientist, b. Boston, Mass., 19 Dec., 1714. A descendant of the governor of Massachusetts. Graduated at Harvard, where he was professor of mathematics and natural philosophy, 1733–79. Was a warm supporter of the American cause in the Revolution, and held several important offices in the Massachusetts government. Among other scientific works, wrote " A Lecture on Earthquakes " (1755) and " Cogitata de Cometes " (1766). Died, Cambridge, Mass., 3 May, 1779.

WINTHROP, Margaret, third wife of Gov. John Winthrop of Massachusetts, b. England, about 1591. Daughter of Sir John Tyndal, of Great Maplested, Essex. Was there married to John Winthrop, April, 1618. Followed him to New England in Aug., 1631. Died, Boston, Mass., 14 June, 1647.

WINTHROP, Robert Charles, statesman, b. Boston, Mass., 12 May, 1809. A descendant of Gov. John Winthrop. Graduated at Harvard. Entered the bar, 1831. Elected to the Massachusetts legislature, 1834–40, being speaker of the assembly, 1838–40, U. S. representative from Massachusetts in the Whig interest, 1840–50, being speaker, 1847–49. Succeeded Daniel Webster in the U. S. senate, 1850. Holding independent views he gradually withdrew from party politics and did not seek election after 1851. Acted as president of the Boston Provident association for a quarter of a century, and for nearly a third as president of the Massachusetts Hist. Soc. Was called upon for many of the most important occasional addresses of his time, including those at the laying of the foundation stone of the national monument to Washington in 1848, and at its completion in 1885. He delivered the oration on the 250th anniversary of the landing of the Pilgrims, 1870, the Boston Centennial oration, 1876, and the address on the 100th anniversary of the surrender of Cornwallis at Yorktown, 1881. His collected " Addresses and Speeches " have been published in four vols., 1852–86. Also wrote " Life and Letters of John Winthrop " (1864) and " Washington, Bowdoin, and Franklin " (1876).

WINTHROP, Theodore, b. New Haven, Conn., 22 Sept., 1828. A descendant of Gov. John Winthrop. Graduated at Yale, where he remained for a year, engaged in advanced studies. Visited Europe for his health in 1849, returning in 1851, and taking a position at Panama in the employ of the Pacific Mail steamship company. In 1853 he accompanied the expedition of Lieutenant Strain to survey a canal route across the isthmus of Panama. Made his residence in New York city the following year, and studied law under Charles Tracy. Was admitted to the bar, 1855, but devoted himself almost entirely to literary work, and completed the novels published after his death. Joined the 7th N. Y. regiment at the opening of the civil war, accompanied it to Washington, and became military secretary of Gen. Benjamin F. Butler, with the rank of major. With his commanding officer planned the attack on the Bethels, and was shot through the heart while rallying his men. His article, "The March of the Seventh," in the "Atlantic Monthly," had attracted attention, and the publication of his novels and miscellanies during the succeeding two years established his reputation as a writer. They were "Cecil Dreeme" (1861), "John Brent" (1862), "Edwin Brothertoft" (1862),

"The Canoe and the Saddle" (1862), and "Life in the Open Air, and Other Papers" (1863). Fell at Great Bethel, Va., 10 June, 1861.

WIRT, William, lawyer, b. Bladensburg, Md., 8 Nov., 1772. Of German and Swiss parentage. Was admitted to the bar and began practice at Culpeper Court House, Va., 1792. After 1799 resided chiefly at Richmond, until his appointment as attorney-general of the United States in 1817. This position he held for twelve years. Had previously served one term in the Virginia legislature, and had been for brief periods chancellor of the eastern district of Virginia and U. S. attorney for that state. His best-known legal argument was that against Aaron Burr, in 1807, at the latter's trial for treason. Wirt contributed "The Letters of the British Spy" to the Richmond "Argus" in 1803. These were at once gathered in a volume and passed through many editions. He also wrote for the Richmond "Enquirer" a series of papers in the style of "The Spectator," entitled "The Rainbow" and "The Old Bachelor." In 1817 appeared his "Sketches of the Life and Character of Patrick Henry." His oration on the deaths of Jefferson and Adams, delivered in the U. S. house of representatives, 19 Oct., 1826, was the most notable of his addresses. Many of his letters are contained in John P. Kennedy's "Memoirs of the Life of William Wirt" (1849). After retiring from his attorney-generalship in 1829, he made his residence at Baltimore. In 1832 he was the candidate of the anti-Masonic party for the presidency of the United States. Died, Washington, D. C., 18 Feb., 1834.

WISE, Henry Augustus, "Harry Gringo," naval officer, b. Brooklyn, N. Y., 12 May, 1819. Entered the U. S. navy, 1834, and served in the Mexican war. Was commander in the civil war until appointed, 1862, assistant chief in the bureau of ordnance and hydrography. Author of "Los Gringos, an Interior View of Mexico and California," etc. (1849), "Tales for the Marines" (1855), "Scampavias, by Harry Gringo" (1857), "Story of the Gray African Parrot" (1859), and "Captain Brand of the Schooner *Centipede*" (1864). Died, Naples, Italy, 2 April, 1869.

WISE, Isaac Mayer, clergyman, b. Steingrub, Bohemia, 3 April, 1819. Graduated at the university of Vienna. Rabbi of congregations in New York state until 1854, when he accepted a similar position in Cincinnati, O. Issued "History of the Israelitish Nation" (1854), "Judaism; its Doctrines and Duties" (1862), and "The Cosmic God" (1876).

WISE, John, clergyman, baptized, Roxbury, Mass., 15 Aug., 1652. Graduated at Harvard. Minister at Ipswich, Mass., from 1683 until his death. Was imprisoned and removed from his position by Governor Andros for opposing the tax-laws promulgated in 1688. Restored to his pulpit after the revolution of the following year. An early and powerful advocate of civil liberty and of local jurisdiction in the churches. Opposed and defeated a movement to centralize church government, with his work, "The Churches' Quarrel espoused" (1710). This was republished in 1772, with his other book on the same subject, "A Vindication of the Government of the New England Churches" (1717), by the organizers of the Revolution. Died, Ipswich, Mass., 8 April, 1725.

WITHERSPOON, John, clergyman and statesman, b. Yester, near Edinburgh, Scotland, 5 Feb., 1722. Graduated at Edinburgh university. Was a Presbyterian minister at Beith and Paisley, Scotland, until 1768, when he became president of the college of New Jersey. Was an active member of the Continental congress from 1776 to 1783, and signed the Declaration of Independence. Selections from his numerous writings were published as "Works of the Rev. John Witherspoon" (1800). Died, near Princeton, N. J., 15 Sept., 1794.

WOLCOTT, Roger, statesman and soldier, b. Windsor, Conn., 4 Jan., 1670. Established himself in business at Windsor, and became interested in local and colonial affairs. Gained great influence in Connecticut, and rose through minor offices to be chief-justice and governor of the colony. Was second in command at the capture of Louisburg in 1745. "Poetical Meditations" appeared in 1725. Died, East Windsor, Conn., 17 May, 1767.

WOLLEY, Charles, clergyman, b. Lincolnshire, England, about 1652. Graduated at Cambridge university. Came to New York with Sir Edmund Andros in 1678 and served as chaplain of Fort James until 1680, when he returned to England. Little is known of his after life. He issued at London "A Two Years Journal in New York" (1701).

WOOD, George, b. Newburyport, Mass., 1799. Educated by Samuel L. Knapp, an active writer of the time. From the age of twenty, until his death, he was a government clerk at Washington, but found leisure to compose several works of a satirical character, aimed at current social follies. Of these "Peter Schlemihl in America" (1848) and "Modern Pilgrims" (1855) were the most noted. Another book, "Future Life, or Scenes in Another World" (1858) was republished, after Miss Phelps's "The Gates Ajar," as "The Gates Wide Open," and reached a large sale. Died, Saratoga, N. Y., 24 Aug., 1870.

WOOD, William, colonist. Emigrated

to Massachusetts, 1629, returning to England in 1633. "New England's Prospect," the first printed description of Massachusetts, appeared in 1634. Wood is thought to have again sailed for New England, and to have represented Lynn in the general court of 1636, settling at Sandwich, Mass., the following year, and dying at the latter place in 1639.

WOODBERRY, George Edward, b. Beverly, Mass., 12 May, 1855. Graduated at Harvard. Professor of English literature in the state university of Nebraska, 1877–8 and 1880–2. A member of the editorial staff of the N. Y. "Nation," 1878–9. A regular contributor to the "Atlantic Monthly," and author of a "History of Wood Engraving" (1883), "Life of Edgar Allan Poe" (1885), and "The North Shore Watch, and Other Poems" (1890).

WOODBRIDGE, Benjamin, clergyman, b. Wiltshire, England, 1622 (D. G. Mitchell). Emigrated to New England about 1640. Entered Harvard, and was its first graduate in 1642. Returned to England in 1647, and preached at Newbury, Berkshire, until 1662, when he was ejected for non-conformity. Was at one time the chaplain of Charles II., with whom he was a favorite. Is best known by his verses on the death of John Cotton, given in Mather's "Magnalia." Died, Inglefield, Berkshire, England, 1 Nov., 1684.

WOODBURY, Levi, jurist, b. Francestown, N. H., 22 Dec., 1789. Graduated at Dartmouth, and entered the bar. Judge of the supreme court of Connecticut, 1817–19. Settled in Portsmouth and was governor of New Hampshire, 1823–4, speaker of the U.S. house of representatives, 1825, and U. S. senator, 1825–31. Secretary of the navy, 1831–4, secretary of the treasury, 1834–41, and a justice of the U.S. supreme court from 1845 until his death. "The Writings of Levi Woodbury" were issued posthumously in 1852. Died, Portsmouth, N.H., 4 Sept., 1851.

WOODS, Kate [Tannatt], b. Peekskill, N. Y., 18—. Was married to Col. George H. Woods, of the U. S. army. After his death in 1884 resided at Salem, Mass. Author of numerous books for children, and an editorial writer for the Boston "Globe" and other journals.

WOODWORTH, Samuel, b. Scituate, Mass., 13 Jan., 1785. Edited various papers until his establishment, with George P. Morris, of the N. Y. "Mirror" in 1823. Resigned his editorship the following year, and became a general writer for the press. Author of a number of operettas. Several editions of his poems were issued. Of his poems only that known as "The Old Oaken Bucket" is remembered. Died, New York, N. Y., 9 Dec., 1842.

WOOLF, Benjamin Edward, b. London, England, 16 Feb., 1836. Brought to America, 1839. Studied music, and was employed as a member and leader of orchestras in New York city, Boston, Philadelphia, and New Orleans, from 1856 to 1871. During this period wrote many plays for the theatres with which he was connected, among which is "The Doctor of Alcantara." In 1871 joined the editorial staff of the Boston "Saturday Evening Gazette." Author of about sixty plays. They include "The Earl's Daughter," "Marie," "The Professor," and "The Mighty Dollar." The last of these was produced by W. J. Florence in New York city, 1875. Also a composer of music, and a contributor to the magazines. Some of his farces and an opera, "Pounce and Co.," have been published.

WOOLMAN, John, Quaker preacher, b. Northampton, N. J., Aug., 1720. Until twenty-one years of age he worked on the family farm, but received some schooling. Subsequently taught school and attended the Quaker meetings at Mt. Holly, N. J. Adopted the life of an itinerant preacher in 1746, supporting himself by working as a tailor. Visited the Indians of the Susquehanna river in 1763. As early as 1753 began to speak and write against slavery, publishing in that year a tract entitled "Some Considerations on the Keeping of Negroes." Contracted a fatal illness while on a visit to England in 1772. "The Works of John Woolman" were brought out posthumously in 1774–5. His "Journal" was republished in 1871, with an introduction by John G. Whittier. Died, York, England, 7 Oct., 1772.

WOOLSEY, Sarah Chauncey, "Susan Coolidge," b. Cleveland, O., 18—. Niece of Theodore D. Woolsey. A resident of Newport, R. I. Author of several books for children, including "The New Year's Bargain" (1871) and "What Katy Did" (1872); also "Verses" (1880), "A Guernsey Lily" (1881), and "A Little Country Girl" (1885).

WOOLSEY, Theodore Dwight, scholar, b. New York, N. Y., 31 Oct., 1801. Graduated at Yale. Studied theology at Princeton. Resided in Europe, 1827–30, while pursuing advanced studies in Greek. Was professor of Greek in Yale from 1831 until 1846, and president of the same college, 1846–71. Was chairman of the American committee of New Testament revision, 1871–81. Edited the "New Englander," 1843–4, and wrote much for the magazines. Besides his original works, edited annotated editions of Greek plays for students, 1834–43, and also editions of Lieber's "Civil Liberty" and "Political Ethics." Was considered an authority in all matters relating to international law. Issued "Introduction to the Study of International Law" (1860, fifth edition 1879), "Essays on Divorce Legislation" (1869),

"Religion of the Present and of the Future" (1871), "Political Science, or the State, Theoretically and Practically Considered" (1877), "Communism and Socialism, in their History and Theory" (1880), "Eros, and Other Poems" (1880), and "Helpful Thoughts for Young Men" (1882). Died, New Haven, Conn., 1 July, 1889.

WOOLSON, Constance Fenimore, b. Claremont, N. H., 18—. Grand-niece of James Fenimore Cooper. Was taken as a child to Cleveland, O., and received her education there and at the French school of Madame Chegaray in New York city. Resided at Cleveland until the death of her father, Charles Jarvis Woolson, in 1869, spending her summers during this period on the island of Mackinac, in the straits connecting Lakes Huron and Michigan. From 1873 to her mother's death in 1879 she lived with the latter in Florida and neighboring states. She then visited Europe, and was still residing there in 1890, having made her home chiefly at Rome, Venice, and Florence. Her first contribution to a magazine was a story in "Harper's" for 1870. It was followed by other stories, sketches, and poems, of which the poems were not collected in a volume. Her works of fiction include "Castle Nowhere ; Lake-Country Sketches" (1875), "Rodman the Keeper; Southern Sketches" (1880), "Anne" (1882), "For the Major" (1883), "East Angels" (1886), and "Jupiter Lights" (1889).

WORCESTER, Noah, clergyman, b. Hollis, N. H., 25 Nov., 1758. Taught school for some years, and in 1786 became a Congregational minister, preaching in several towns in New Hampshire and Massachusetts. From 1813 to 1829 he edited various periodicals at Brighton, Mass. Founded the Massachusetts peace society, 1815. Author of a number of theological works. His chief book was "A Solemn Review of the Custom of War" (1814). Died, Brighton, Mass., 31 Oct., 1837.

WORK, Henry Clay, composer, b. Middletown, Conn., 1 Oct., 1832. Removed to Illinois when quite young. Returning to Connecticut in 1845, he became a printer's apprentice in Hartford. Here his first song was written, entitled "We're Coming, Sister Mary." In 1855 he removed to Chicago, and continued his trade as a printer. "The Year of Jubilee" or "Kingdom Coming" was written in 1861 and published in 1862 by Root & Cady, of Chicago, for whom he afterward composed exclusively. His most popular song, "Marching through Georgia," appeared in 1865, after Sherman's successful march to the sea. His songs, of which he composed the words as well as the music, were both grave and gay, and numbered over sixty. Died, Hartford, Conn., 8 June, 1884.

WORMELEY, Katharine Prescott, b. Suffolk, England, 14 July, 1832. Daughter of Admiral Wormeley, of the British navy, who was a Virginian by birth. Served at the headquarters of the U. S. sanitary commission in the Peninsular campaign of the civil war. Her volume, "The Other Side of War" (1889), consists of letters written at that time. Translated fifteen volumes of the works of Honoré de Balzac, 1886-90.

YONGE, Francis. Author of "A Narrative of the Proceedings of the People of South Carolina in 1719" (1726). Yonge styles himself "Surveyor-General of South Carolina," and his narrative is an account of the revolution against the lords-proprietors of the province in 1719, with a description of his previous unsuccessful mission to the latter in London.

YOUMANS, Edward Livingston, scientist, b. Coeymans, N. Y., 3 June, 1821. The loss of eyesight in youth, afterward partially regained, interfered somewhat with his early studies, but perseverance in his profession identified him with the popular science movement which he may be said to have initiated in this country. Founded and edited the "Popular Science Monthly" from 1872 to his death. Originated "The International Scientific Series" in 1871. Issued "Alcohol and the Constitution of Man" (1853), "Handbook of Household Science" (1857), and introductions to several collections of writings by foreign scientists. Died, New York, N. Y., 18 Jan., 1887.

YOUNG, Charles Augustus, astronomer, b. Hanover, N. H., 15 Dec., 1834. Graduated at Dartmouth. Professor at the Western reserve college, O., before and during the civil war, in which, however, he saw some service. Professor of astronomy at Dartmouth from 1865 to 1877, when he assumed the same chair at the college of New Jersey. Noted for his success in solar observations. Author of "The Sun" (1881) and "A Text-Book of General Astronomy" (1888).

YOUNG, William, dramatist, b. Monmouth, Ill., 7 Sept., 1847. Graduated at Monmouth college. Studied law in Chicago, and at the age of twenty was ready for admission to the bar, but went on the stage instead, to fit himself for dramatic writing. After a brief experience as an actor, went abroad, to study stage-art more satisfactorily, residing for long periods in London. Otherwise lived in the New England and Western states. His plays have been produced in New York city and Chicago as follows: "Jonquil" (1871), "The Rogue's March" (1872), "Pendragon," tragedy, in verse (1881), "The House of Mauprat" (with John G. Wilson, 1882), "The Rajah," comedy (1883), and "Ganelon," tragedy, in verse (1889). Contributed numerous poems to the magazines, some of which were collected in "Wishmakers' Town" (1885).

APPOINTED LIBRARIAN OF CONGRESS, 1864.

GENERAL ·INDEX.

DIRECTIONS FOR CONSULTING THE INDEX.

Names of Authors from whose writings Selections have been made are indicated by small capitals, thus:—BANCROFT, GEORGE, **6:** 3–17.

Pseudonyms, etc., are indicated by lower-case letters, thus:—" Downing, Major Jack " (Pseud.).—See *Seba Smith*.

General Topics, such as Anecdote, Biography, Criticism, etc., are indicated by black-letter capitals, thus:—**ANECDOTE.**

Sub-topics and Synonyms are in lower-case black letters, thus:—**Adventure.**

Under the Topical heads, where the Author's name follows a Selection, it is printed in *italics*. But where the Author's name precedes a Selection, it is printed in SMALL CAPITALS.

Volumes are indicated by black-letter numerals, thus:—**10.**

Pages are indicated by numerals in plain type, thus:—448–50.

GENERAL INDEX.

This Personal and Topical Index covers the entire Work.

Names of Authors represented by Selections are in small-capitals ; names of other persons, in lower-case.

General Topics are in black-letter capitals ; sub-Topics and Synonyms, in black-letter lower-case.

Topics are grouped, as far as possible, under a few general heads. Where the alphabetical arrangement, under a topical head, is by authors, their names are in small-capitals,—otherwise, in italics.

Numerals designating the respective Volumes are in black-letter ; page-numerals, in plain type.

HISTORY.—ABBOTT, "The History of Napoleon Bonaparte,"**6** :234 ; ADAMS, C. F., Citizen Genest and Neutrality,**6**: 351; ADAMS, HANNAH, "A Summary History of New England," **4** : 65–67 ; ADAMS, HENRY, "History of the U. S. A. " (Jefferson's Administrations), **11** : 418–424,—Jefferson, 418,—The American of 1800, 420 ; ALSOP, "A Character of the Province of Mary-Land," **1** : 403–410,—Virtues of the Marylanders, 403,—Indian Customs, etc., 405 ; ANONYMOUS, How the English Settled in Maryland, **1** : 44 ; BACON, NAT., His Declaration against Sir W. Berkeley, **1** : 448 ; BACON'S REBELLION, Accounts of, from the Burwell and Aspinwall Papers,**1**: 448–478 ; BACON, L., The Puritans, **6** : 88 ; BAIRD, "History of the Rise of the Huguenots of France," **9** : 19–23 ; BANCROFT, GEORGE, "History of the U. S. of A., from the Discovery of the Continent," **6** : 3–17,—Liberty Enlightening the World, 3,—The Acadian Exiles, 7,—George the Third, 9,—The Battle of Lexington, 10,—Fort Moultrie, 13,—Europe and America at the Time of Washington's Inauguration, 15; BANCROFT, H. H., "Hist. of the Pacific States of No. America," **9** : 27–40,—How they Found the Pacific Gold, 27,—Argonaut Life and Character, 32 ; BENTON, "Thirty Years' View," **5** : 27–36 ; BELKNAP, "The History of New Hampshire," **3** : 313–321,—The Siege of Louisbourg, 313,—The War in New Hampshire, 319 ; BERKELEY, SIR W., Declaration against Nat. Bacon, **1** : 445 ; and see 448–478, *passim ;* BEVERLY, "The History and Present State of Virginia," **2** : 265–272,—The Royalist Governor Nicholson, 265 ; BLAINE, President Johnson and Reconstruction, **8** : 458 ; BOOTH, M. L., New York at the Beginning of the War, **8** : 547 ; BRACKENRIDGE, H. M., "History of the Late War between the U. S. and Great Britain, **5** : 106–111,—The *Constitution* and the *Guerriere*, 106,—Battle of the Thames, 108 ; BRADFORD, His "Dialogue," **1** : 93,—Recollections of Puritan Strictness, 93,—"History of Plymouth Plantation," 95–115,—How the Colony was troubled with a Hypocrite, 98,—The Pestilent Morton and his Merry Mount, 107, —Life and Death of Elder Brewster, 111 ; BRADFORD'S AND WINSLOW'S JOURNAL, Excursion up Cape Cod, **1** : 116,—Story of the First Encounter, 120,—Landing of the Pilgrims, etc., 124 ; BYFIELD, " An Account of

POETRY.

POLITICS, GOVERNMENT, Etc.

THE END.

Complete Index of Portraits and Illustrations.

COMPLETE INDEX OF PORTRAITS AND ILLUSTRATIONS.

ACKNOWLEDGMENTS.

The Editors and the Publishers of this work are under obligations to many Publishing Houses, without whose generous coöperation the LIBRARY OF AMERICAN LITERATURE could not be completed upon its design. Besides our general thanks to authors, editors, etc., whose copyrighted works are represented in the course of this series, special acknowledgment is here made to the following proprietors of matter used in the present volume:

Messrs. D. APPLETON & Co., New York.—*McMaster's History of the People of the United States.*

The ARGONAUT PUBLISHING COMPANY, San Francisco.—*Selections from The Argonaut.*

Messrs. A. C. ARMSTRONG & SON, New York.—*Miss King's Monsieur Motte ; The New Princeton Review.*

BELFORD COMPANY, New York.—*Hildreth's The Masque of Death ; Saltus's A Transient Guest.*

Messrs. ROBERT BONNER'S SONS, New York.—*Grady's The New South (from The New York Ledger).*

The BOWEN-MERRILL COMPANY, Indianapolis.—*Riley's Afterwhiles, — The Boss Girl, — The Old Swimmin'-Hole.*

BRENTANO'S, New York.—*(Varley) Mitchell's Sylvian.*

The CASSELL PUBLISHING COMPANY, New York.—*P. Bigelow's The German Emperor; Miss Cone's Oberon and Puck ; Day's Poems ; Sidney (Harland) Luska's A Latin-Quarter Courtship ; Kenyon's In Realms of Gold.*

The CATHOLIC PUBLICATION SOCIETY COMPANY, New York.—*Miss Conway's On the Sunrise Slope.*

The CENTURY COMPANY, New York.—*Edwards's Two Runaways ; J. Jefferson's Autobiography ; Nicolay's and Hay's Abraham Lincoln : A History; Russell's Poems ; The Century Magazine ; St. Nicholas.*

Messrs. CUSHING & BAILEY, Baltimore.—*Miss Reese's A Branch of May.*

Messrs. DE WOLFE, FISKE & Co., Boston (by transfer from Messrs. CUPPLES & HURD).—*Mrs. Greene's Cape Cod Folks, — Towhead ; Rideing's A Little Upstart.*

Messrs. DODD, MEAD & Co., New York.—*Schouler's History of the United States under the Constitution ; Tuckerman's Life of Lafayette.*

Messrs. E. H. HAMES & Co., Boston.—*Selections from The Literary World.*

Messrs. HARPER & BROTHERS, New York.—*Mrs. Rives Chanler's Virginia of Virginia ; Curtis's The Correspondence of J. L. Motley ; Ripley's The War with Mexico ; Miss Wilkins's A Humble Romance ; Woodberry's History of Wood Engraving ; Harper's New Monthly Magazine ; Harper's Weekly.*

Messrs. HENRY HOLT & Co., New York.—*Miss McClelland's Oblivion.*

ACKNOWLEDGMENTS.

Messrs. HOUGHTON, MIFFLIN & Co., Boston.—*The Atlantic Monthly ; T. Bacon's Biography of Delia Bacon ; Mrs. (Eleanor Putnam) Bates's Old Salem ; Mrs. Deland's John Ward, Preacher ; Gilman's Profit Sharing between Employer and Employee ; Grant's The Knave of Hearts ; Miss Guiney's Songs at the Start,—The White Sail ; Henderson's The Prelate ; Howe's Story of a Country Town ; Mrs. Lathrop's Along the Shore ; Miss (Craddock) Murfree's In the Tennessee Mountains ; Payne's Sigurd Slembe (Björnson); Miss Thomas's A New Year's Masque,—The Round Year,—Lyrics and Sonnets ; Mrs. Van Rensselaer's Six Portraits ; Wendell's The Duchess Emilia ; Woodberry's The North Shore Watch.*

The D. LOTHROP COMPANY, Boston.—*Bensel's In the King's Garden ; Scollard's With Reed and Lyre.*

Messrs. MACMILLAN & Co., London and New York.—*Crawford's Greifenstein.*

Messrs. A. C. McCLURG & Co , Chicago.—*Burron's The Viking ; Mrs. Catherwood's The Story of Tonty ; Miss Fearing's The Sleeping World.*

Mr. DAVID McKAY, Phila.—*Lüders's and Smith's Hallo, My Fancy ! ; Thayer's The Confessions of Hermes.*

Messrs. MITCHELL & MILLER, New York.—*Martin's A Little Brother of the Rich.*

Messrs. JOHN P. NORTON & Co., Louisville.—*Cawein's Accolon of Gaul.*

The OVERLAND MONTHLY COMPANY, San Francisco.—*Selections from The Overland Monthly.*

Messrs. WM. A. POND & Co., New York.—*Mrs. Howarth's Song, 'Tis but a little faded Flower.*

Messrs. PORTER & COATES, Phila.—*MacKellar's Hymns ; Pennypacker's Gettysburg.*

Messrs. G. P. PUTNAM'S SONS, New York.—*Mrs. Dandridge's Poems ; the Misses Goodale's Apple-Blossoms,—All Round the Year ; Richardson's American Literature ; Mrs. Rollins's The Ring of Amethyst ; Roosevelt's Hunting Trips of a Ranchman.*

Messrs. A. D. F. RANDOLPH & Co., New York.—*Mrs. Slosson's Fishin' Jimmy.*

Messrs. ROBERTS BROTHERS, Boston.—*Miss Carpenter's South-County Neighbors ; Mrs. Elliott's The San Rosario Ranch ; Miss Fletcher's Mirage,—Vestigia ; R. T. S. Lowell's The New Priest in Conception Bay ; H. Adams's History of the United States.*

Messrs. CHARLES SCRIBNER'S SONS, New York.—*Brownell's French Traits ; Bunner's Airs from Arcady,—Love in Old Cloathes ; Mrs. Coombs's As Common Mortals ; Frederic's Seth's Brother's Wife ; Gordon's and Page's Befo' de War ; Lathrop's An Echo of Passion ; Matthews's Playing a Part ; Page's In Ole Virginia ; Pyle's Otto of the Silver Hand ; Scribner's Magazine ; Stimson's Mrs. Knollys.*

Messrs. E. STEIGER & Co., New York.—(Brother Azarias) *Mullany's Address On Thinking.*

Messrs. FREDERICK A. STOKES & BROTHER, New York.—*Peck's Cap and Bells ; Scollard's Old and New World Lyrics ; Sherman's Madrigals and Catches.*

Messrs. TICKNOR & Co., Boston.—*Acknowledgment is again due for the original grant of matter contained in certain works, now transferred to Messrs. Houghton, Mifflin & Co., and represented among the publications credited to the last-named firm.*

The UNIVERSITY OF NOTRE DAME, South Bend, Ind.—*Egan's Preludes.*

Messrs. WHITE & ALLEN, New York.—*Eaton's Acadian Legends and Lyrics.*

The fine portraits of Gilder and Harris (Vol. X.), and of Page (Vol. XI.), are from electrotypes supplied by Messrs. Harper & Brothers.

For an acknowledgment of certain other engravings, etc., attention is invited to the recapitulation which follows the Preface in this Volume.